D1546405

Dmitri Shostakovich

A Catalogue, Bibliography, and Discography

THIRD EDITION

DEREK C. HULME

SCARECROW PRESS • 2002

SCARECROW PRESS, INC.

Published in the United States of America
by Scarecrow Press, Inc.
A Member of the Rowman & Littlefield Publishing Group
4720 Boston Way, Lanham, Maryland 20706
www.scarecrowpress.com

PO Box 317
Oxford
OX2 9RU, UK

British Library Cataloguing in Publication Information Available

First edition published by Kyle and Glen Music, Muir of Ord, Ross-shire IV6 7UQ, 1982
ISBN 0-19-816204-9
Second edition published by Oxford University Press, 1991
ISBN 0-19-816204-9

Oxford University Press, Walton Street, Oxford OX2 6DP
Oxford New York Toronto Delhi Bombay Calcutta Madras Karachi Petaling Jaya
Singapore Hong Kong Tokyo Nairobi Dar es Salaam Cape Town Melbourne Auckland
and associated companies in Berlin Ibadan

Oxford is a trademark of Oxford University Press
Published in the United States by Oxford University Press, New York

Library of Congress Cataloging-in-Publication Data

Hulme, Derek C.
    Dmitri Shostakovich : a catalogue, bibliography, and discography /
Derek C. Hulme. -- 3rd ed.
        p. cm.
Includes bibliographical references and indexes.
    ISBN 0-8108-4432-X (hardcover : alk. paper)
 1.   Shostakovich, Dmitriaei Dmitrievich, 1906-1975--Bibliography. 2.
Shostakovich, Dmitriaei Dmitrievich, 1906-1975--Discography. I. Title.
    ML134.S485 H8 2002
    016.78 ' 092--dc21

                                                    2002011012

Third edition typeset by JCGraphics, Vermont

203182

To my wife Helen Killoran

and with a deep debt of gratitude
to surgeon John L. Duncan and his support team
at Raigmore Hospital, Inverness
for performing a life-saving operation
in November 1999

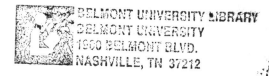

Contents

Foreword to the Second Edition
by Irina Shostakovich

I take particular pleasure in writing a few words to introduce this new edition.

Derek Hulme has invested in this book a colossal amount of work, not from obligation or necessity, but for love of Shostakovich's music—for his own satisfaction, as it were. This feeling is most movingly reflected in the immense and solicitous care he has lavished on every detail: nothing has been allowed to escape. This same feeling caused Mr Hulme to study the Russian language and to make numerous visits to Leningrad and Moscow in the course of his researches.

The book is in the form of a catalogue of Shostakovich's music, greatly expanded for this new edition in comprehensiveness and circumstantial information. I hope that it will be of use, not only to scholars, publishers, and performers, but will also appeal to the ever-increasing circle of lovers of Shostakovich's music, collectors of his recordings, all those who are interested in the personality of the man and who acknowledge a common response to the power of his music.

The book tells one much about Shostakovich's compositions, gives what amounts to a 'biography' of each of them, and outlines the 'path of life' along which they have been destined to travel through succeeding generations.

The author undertook the publication of the first edition at his own expense, and in consequence it could not achieve a wide distribution. The present, second, edition has been realized by Oxford University Press—the University which honoured Shostakovich with an Honorary Doctorate during his lifetime—and will be accessible to far more people. It makes a significant contribution to the study of Shostakovich's art, and I salute it as a tribute to his memory and his heritage.

Irina Shostakovich
Moscow, October 1990

Preface

The compiler became seriously interested in the music of Shostakovich in 1942 when he bought 'on spec.' the six expensive red label HMV 78s of the Fifth Symphony. The symphony so thrilled him from the first hearing he made a point of looking in the *Radio Times* for broadcasts of other works by this composer. Such airings, even after the inauguration of the BBC's Third Programme in 1946, were very infrequent so whenever a new composition was heard he jotted down some impressions and wrote a synopsis noting highlights to listen for in future performances. A collection of press cuttings about Shostakovich was also started.

Work on a suitably epic monograph of Shostakovich, thematically illustrated, with critical assessments of his compositions and detailed information on the lesser-known film and stage productions was begun in the summer of 1973 though this was abandoned four years later. The composer kindly answered letters and gave much useful information, also correcting several opus numberings and dates. A working knowledge of the Russian language was acquired and visits to the USSR and other Eastern Bloc countries were made from February 1975.

With the publication of Grigori Shneyerson's Festschrift for Shostakovich, which for the first time contained a definitive list of opus numbers, it became possible to complete an interim catalogue of straightforward fact from the compiler's copious notes assembled for the monograph.

It is hoped that this guide, though another small step only towards a full and worthy appraisal of Shostakovich's prolific and diverse output, will prove a helpful reference source for

  (i) general music-lovers in the presentation of non-technical background information,
 (ii) musicians by providing details of published scores,
(iii) gramophiles with the comprehensive British and Russian discography, and
 (iv) students wishing to explore deeper into the problems of structure, key distinction, harmonic progressions; the turbulent life and times of the composer, etc., via the extensive bibliography.

The additional entries incorporated in this greatly enlarged and thoroughly revised second edition, together with corrections and modifications to the existing material, are largely due to further research and new information which has come to light subsequent to, and to some extent because of, the publication of the 1982 catalogue. Some older record issues still lack certain details of essential data precluding their entry in this work.

The compact disc was introduced in 1983 and this new medium now features noticeably in the text under many opus numbers, either as digital remastering of analogue recordings or as brand-new issues. While the coverage concentrates on British and Soviet releases, that of continental and New World origin is considerably widened in this edition.

The compiler purposely awaited the issue in 1988 of the remaining scores of the forty-two Soviet *Shostakovich Collected Works* before completing the typescript. Music, books, and recordings issued to the end of the 1980s have been included with limited updating to 1 March 1990 for other material.

Additions and corrections from users of this Catalogue will be gratefully received by the compiler and acted on for any further printing.

Muir of Ord   D.C.H.
1990

Preface to Third Edition

In this third edition there are changes, revisions, and expansions under each opus, especially extensive in the Recordings section. Only 12 pages of the 1991 edition have remained entirely untouched. An important improvement is the substitution of hitherto unknown or approximate performance dates of many analogue recordings by the actual dates or years, disclosed in the liner notes, when transferred to digital compact discs. Special mention must be made of the exceptional contribution from Peter Bromley and his many colleagues in the recording industry over the last ten years for vital information on recordings past and present.

Particular attention has been given to the cross-referencing of material re-used in other compositions; for example in the Ballets Opp. 22, 27, and 39; the Ballet Suites, and film music scores.

The Bibliography and the BBC Broadcasts section have been updated with considerable additions. The Appendices are largely unchanged, though the list of cassettes on pages 388–92 of the second edition has been deleted. A further 1545 performers have been added to the Index of Names, indicative of the flourishing interest in the works of Dmitri Shostakovich.

This must be the compiler's final rewriting of the whole catalogue though he hopes to be spared for periodical supplementary booklets of revisions and additions. All errors, omissions, and indulgences are his own as are the opinions expressed in the Appendices.

Muir of Ord   D.C.H.
2001

Acknowledgements

The compiler is pleased that he was able to thank Dmitri Shostakovich for his inspired compositions before his untimely death and is indebted to his wife, Irina, for considerable encouragement by telephone and letter.

Grateful acknowledgement is made to the authors of the books and articles listed in the bibliography and the reviews of concert and recorded performances for indispensable information on the composer and his works.

The following persons, in various kind ways, helped make possible this study of Shostakovich:

Sadie Alford, Novosti Press Agency; Gwen Bainham, of Newport, Gwent; G. M. Beckett, secretary to Sir Adrian Boult; John R. Bennett, gramophile of Jedburgh, Roxburgh; Frederick A. Booth, of Holmfirth, Yorkshire; Jeremy Caulton, general manager of Sadler's Wells Opera; Nicholas Chadwick, music librarian of the British Library; William Crawford, of New York; Terry Cushion, of Chatham, Kent; Howard Thomas Davis, violist of the Alberni Quartet; Donald Dean, of Pateley Bridge, Yorkshire; James F. Devlin, writer on music of Sheffield; Margaret Doull, of Edinburgh; Tom Duerden, of Barnston, Wirral; Penny Dutson, EMI Records; David J. Fanning, lecturer in music, Manchester University; Lawrence D. Gaugham, of Alexandria, Vancouver, USA; Alan George, violist of the Fitzwilliam Quartet; Sue Harris, BBC Library: Lisbeth Holm, Music Library of Radio Sweden; Frank van Hoof, of Vrouwenpolder, Netherlands; Eric A. Hughes, information officer of the National Sound Archive; Robin Hulme, of Aberdeen; Emanuel Hurwitz, leader of the Aeolian Quartet; George Hutchinson, honorary secretary of South Place Sunday Concerts; Jenny Killick, Riverside Studios producer; Lillian Knapp, Colbert Artists Management, New York; Jacques Lacas, of St-Jérôme, Quebec, Canada; Alan Lawson, band manager of the Fairey Band; Robert Layton, the musicologist; Vic Lewis, the conductor and composer; Dr Clark McAlister, of South Miami, Florida; Don H. MacLeod, of Sydney, Australia; John McLeod, the Scottish composer and conductor; Sheila Malham, Aldeburgh Festival Association; Olivia Maxwell, music and arts researcher; Alan Mercer, DSCH Society; Dr G. Rex Meyer, of Beecroft, New South Wales; Miriam Millar, BBC Music library; O. W. Neighbour, formerly music librarian of the British Library; Geoffrey Norris, the musicologist; Hugh Ottaway, the musicologist; Anthony Phillips, director of International Operations, The Entertainment Corporation; Richard R. Pleak, of New York; Gennadi Nikolayevich Rozhdestvensky, the conductor; John Shirley-Quirk, the baritone; Freda Steel, administrator of the Northern

Dance Theatre; Ronald Stevenson, the Scottish composer; Malcolm Taylor, librarian of the English Folk Dance and Song Society; Philip S. Taylor, Collets; Matthew B. Tepper, of Minneapolis, Minnesota; Robert Threlfall, the musicologist; Emmie Tillett, of Ibbs & Tillett; Emmanuel Utwiller, of Paris; J. F. Weber, gramophile of Utica, New York; David Williams, Decca Record Company; Elizabeth Wilson, the cellist; Manashir Abramovich Yakubov, Russian musicologist; Anatoli Ivanovich Zhelezny, gramophile of Kiev, Ukraine; and the helpful staff of the libraries mentioned in section 13 of the Introduction and the representatives of several music publishing houses listed in Appendix I.

In the later stages the copy-editor, Mrs Mary A. Worthington, did not complain when bombarded with pages of involved amendments and made several friendly suggestions which considerably improved the layout of the text.

Finally, to Helen, sincerest thanks for years of wifely patience and sacrifice during the compilation of this catalogue.

Many of the above and the following individuals have kindly provided information incorporated into the third edition:

> Yuri Alturov, gramophile of Kharkov, Ukraine;
> Kenzo Amoh, gramophile of Tokyo, Japan;
> John Berrie, The Friends of S. Richter;
> Christer Bouij, musicologist of Örebro, Sweden;
> Arthur Brocklebank, musicologist of Dingwall;
> Peter Bromley, gramophile of Bicester;
> Ismene Brown, ballet reviewer for *The Daily Telegraph*;
> Lucinda Ellis, of Brighton Festival;
> Laurel E. Fay, musicologist of New York;
> Allan B. Ho, musicologist of Southern Illinois University;
> Edward Johnson, of the Leopold Stokowski Society;
> Robert Jordan, of Vancouver, Canada;
> Gerard McBurney, the composer;
> Robert Matthew-Walker, musicologist of London;
> Robert Osborne, bass-baritone of New York;
> Ben Pernick, gramophile of Long Island, New York;
> Onno van Rijen, gramophile of Zoeterwoude, The Netherlands;
> John Riley, of the British Film Institute;
> Phil Rubenstein, of Brookline, Massachusetts;
> Malcolm Walker, gramophile of Harrow

Abbreviations

G	*Gramophone* (date of review)
Glinka Museum	State Central Glinka Museum of Musical Culture, Moscow
I	Date of issue of recording (may be listed or advertised for the preceding month's release in music magazines)
P	Date of original recording
CIS Archives of Literature and Art	Central State Archives of Literature and Art of the CIS (formerly USSR), Moscow
VAAP	The Copyright Agency of the CIS (formerly USSR)
WERM	Clough and Cuming, *The World's Encyclopaedia of Recorded Music* (Sidgwick & Jackson, London, rev. ed. 1966).

Dates have been homogenized in the form 25 September 1906 (or abbreviated 25 Sept. 1906)

Introduction

The main section of the catalogue covers the compositions, work by work. As it will be some years before a strictly chronological and complete listing can be attempted, the order and numbering of Grigori Shneyerson's list of 1976 is adopted. Discrepancies in the guise of earlier or incorrect numeration are noted under the 'Music' heading. Dated works without opus numbers are allotted a provisional letter designation (e.g. Sans op. A) and inserted where appropriate. These carry no official endorsement and are used solely to facilitate indexing in this guide. Rather than slotting in certain undated and minor works in somewhat arbitrary positions, these have been assembled, for the time being, under Sans op. X.

Where full information is known about a composition, details are presented under ten or eleven headings: Form, Instrumentation, Composed, Dedication, Première, Arrangements, Music, Duration, Ballets (and Films), and Recordings. Bibliographical references and Notes are added for a number of works.

1. Title

A brief title, sufficient for positive identification, is allocated. Former titles, established subtitles, and nicknames follow where relevant.

2. Form

Under this heading a description of the type of composition is given. Former titles assigned by the composer and also unauthorized, though established, subtitles and nicknames follow where relevant.

3. Instrumentation

The instrument or combination for which a work was originally composed is given. Instruments not conventionally featured in a symphony orchestra are noted. Precise details of the instrumentation of orchestral works are furnished where known. To avoid confusion and to clarify doubling, abbreviations are not used though it should be understood that 'horn' refers to the French horn in F and, unless otherwise stated, 'trumpets' are in B flat.

4. Composed

The period of composition or date of completion is disclosed on very few published scores. Usually the year (or years) of composition from the lists of Nicolas Slonimsky, Grigori Shneyerson, and the compiler's (with the dates kindly checked by the composer) must suffice. The occasion for which the work was written can be added in certain cases.

5. Dedication

The dedicatee's full name is followed by a note of his or her profession or standing.

6. Première

Details of first performances are listed in the order of date, venue, and artist(s). A few noteworthy United Kingdom and United States of America premières are mentioned.

7. Arrangements

The reduction for piano(s) of orchestral compositions, and accompaniments to concertos and vocal works, by the composer and other hands are listed. Known transcriptions and translations of vocal works to languages other than the original Russian are credited. Suites assembled from film and stage productions by the composer and fellow musicians, Lev Atovmyan, Gennadi Rozhdestvensky, Lev Solin, and others are itemized.

8. Music

Former opus numbers designated by the composer and errors in previous numbering are indicated here. Publication of the work is detailed in the order of publishing firm, their edition or plate number, the year of issue, a description of contents when other than a standard score, and the height to the nearest half-centimetre. As a guide, miniature scores are usually trimmed within the range 16.5 to 23 cm., and piano scores and parts are commonly between 29 and 31 cm. in height, though it should be noted that library-bound editions can run a centimetre or so larger.

Some popular works, such as the *Three Fantastic Dances,* the Polka from *The Golden Age,* the *Twenty-four Preludes,* and individual items from *A Child's Exercise Book,* appear in numerous editions and are not fully catalogued.

For collections of Shostakovich's music and addresses of music publishers see Appendix I.

9. Duration

Timings are those specified in the printed score and/or a range taken from recordings and broadcast performances. These are included solely to indicate the approximate duration as a guide in tentatively arranging programme schedules.

10. Ballets and films

Brief credits are given for ballets and films in addition to those based on the original score. For television and theatre productions see Appendix II.

11. Recordings

The following data are given: country of origin (if not Britain or universal); company and manufacturer's disc number(s); size, speed and type of reproduction (if not 12 inch/300 mm., 33⅓ rpm, long-playing stereophonic); performers—soloists, orchestra, conductor *et al.*; couplings; year of performance, publication or issue and the review date in the magazine *Gramophone*. The Soviet Union (USSR), Commonwealth of Independent States (CIS), United States of America (USA), and Czechoslovakia (Czech) are abbreviated—all other countries are named in full. Sizes of 10 inch/250 mm. and 7 inch/175 mm., speeds of 78 and 45 rpm, transfers from 78s to microgroove, artificial stereo transcription of monophonic (or, as some prefer, monaural) recordings, quadraphonic, digital, and compact disc releases are indicated.

The key artist (e.g. the soloist in a sonata or concerto, the singer in an orchestrated song cycle, or the conductor in a purely orchestral work) is capitalized to facilitate locating a particular recording.

For convenience, 'viola player' is shortened to 'violist'. The personnel of piano trios are named in the order of violinist, cellist, and pianist and of string quartets, first and second violinists, violist, and cellist. The vocal register of a character in an opera can be determined by referring to the singer(s) at première or recorded performances in the Index of Names.

Couplings or fill-ups are given in square brackets. With collections of music by Shostakovich, the supporting works are indicated by their opus numbers. When the backing is by another composer his or her name only is given—details of the composition can be found in record catalogues, guides, or journals.

Multiple entries under each work are listed as near as possible to a chronological order of performance date. Reviews may be consulted in *Gramophone* for professional evaluation when the month of issue is stated (e.g. G Oct. 1975).

The date of recording refers to the original recording if known (e.g. P 1963) or the year of first issue (e.g. I 1966). Dates are frequently problematic since there may be a considerable delay between the date of performance and the original issue. The year given on Western record labels is not always reliable and the 'P' often refers to the year of publication and not performance. To exemplify: the label of Shostakovich's Fifth Symphony on RCA Victor SB 6651 gives P 1966, whereas Edward Greenfield in his portrait of André Previn discloses that this was recorded in August 1965. The matrix of Karajan's performance of the Tenth Symphony gives P 1967 while the label states P 1969. The actual date of performance was November 1966 and the record was issued in January 1969. Dates, therefore, are to be taken as approximate and recognized purely as an indication of the age of the recording. Soviet LP recording dates are taken from a confidential chart and dates of issue from *Melodiya* catalogues. The monthly list of releases has been superseded by a quarterly catalogue since the end of 1971. For the more recent years a lowercase letter (*a, b, c,* or *d*) is added to indicate the particular quarterly catalogue issue. To complicate matters it should be noted (though the peculiarity is ignored in this discography) that Soviet records are generally obtainable months in advance of the official release date (e.g. the compiler purchased the recording of Opp. 142 and 143, C10 05137-8, in a Moscow record shop on 6 February 1975, whereas its release was not announced until the third quarter of that year!). In the spring of 1990, owing to a severe paper shortage in the USSR, the detailed quarterly trade promotion catalogue was replaced by a crudely printed cumulative order list. Henceforward, the quarterly letters refer to the *Melodiya* magazine published by Muzyka.

The 'I date' refers to the British date of release and may be helpful in tracing evaluations, lists of new releases, and advertisements in various music magazines, especially when the recording was not reviewed in *Gramophone*.

The information on the recorded performance is as complete as a layman can determine. Regrettably insufficient sleeve-note data were available to meet the admirable standards set by the writers Alan Kelly, John F. Perkins, and John Ward in their article 'Discography: which goals are attainable?', published in *Recorded Sound*, 59: 453–5 (July 1975). All disc and tape labels should give, as an absolute minimum, the actual date and location of recording, and it would be useful if the origin of reissued performances was declared.

For information on the history of recording, four special USSR recordings, and the composer on records, see Appendix III.

12. Notes

Full details of the sources are given or, if taken from a literary work included in the bibliography, the author's name mentioned.

13. Bibliography

The bibliography gives details of the essential literature and the most helpful sources consulted in the preparation of this guide. References are given under opus numbers where the article covers that particular work. Many articles refer to several compositions and readers are referred to the main bibliography where a perusal of the article and book titles, or the brief summaries of contents added in square brackets, will indicate possible profitable sources.

Hundreds of books were examined in the public libraries of Aberdeen, Derby, Dingwall, Dorset County, Inverness, Nottingham County, and Worcester. Rewarding visits were made to the Central Music and Charing Cross Libraries in the City of Westminster, the King's College Library of Music and Fine Arts of the University of Aberdeen, and the Mitchell Library Music Room, Glasgow. The bibliography does not purport to be exhaustive; e.g. a further 113 references in the English language will be found in David Moldon's book and another 123 in Russian in Marina Sabinina's review of Shostakovich's symphonies. It gives details of the essential literature and the most helpful sources consulted in the preparation of this guide. See under Baxandale, Berger, Bernandt and Yampolsky, Fay, Khentova, Olkhovsky, Schwarz, and Yakovlev for further extensive bibliographies. These list important books and articles written by musicologists of the calibre of Boris Asafiev, Leo Mazel, lzrail Nestiev, Ivan Sollertinsky, and the composer himself.

Residing away from the centres of literary and musical activity, the compiler is grateful for the services of the National Library of Scotland, through the Librarian of the Ross and Cromarty District of the Highland Region, in obtaining several important and out-of-print books for study.

Reviews of recorded and live performances appearing in monthly magazines, including *The Gramophone* (*Gramophone* from June 1969), *Records and Recordings, Hi-fi News & Record Review, The Musical Times*[1]; and the initially weekly, and from 30 September 1978 fortnightly, *Classical Music;* and newspapers, *The Daily Telegraph, The Scotsman,* and others, are too numerous for specific mention but their assistance was inestimable. Background information on the composer, contemporary performers, the Russian film industry and the arts was found in *Soviet Weekly* which, sadly, ceased publication on 5 December 1991.

Publications of the Long-Playing Record Library, Blackpool (from *The Stereo Record Guides, Guides to Bargain Records,* and *The Great Records* to *The Penguin Guide to Compact Discs and Cassettes Yearbook 1998*—all edited by Ivan March) provided much useful information. The Tantivy Press yearbook *International Music Guide* (edited up to 1981 by Derek Elley), launched in 1977, gives worldwide reports of concerts and festivals. The coverage extended to the USSR in 1981 with reports by Grigori Shneyerson (1981 and 1982) and Mark Manuilov

---

[1]Six further monthly magazines for record collectors, namely *Classic CD* (issued with a cover compact disc of excerpts from recent releases, running to 130 issues dated May 1990 to November 2000), *Classics* (a *Gramophone* publication covering budget-priced CDs), *BBC Music Magazine* (including a compact disc of complete works mostly from broadcast performances); and *CD Review* and *Classic FM* (both with cover discs) appeared in May 1990, March 1992 (for eleven issues only), September 1992, April 1994 (also short-lived), and March 1995 respectively; and the latest *International Record Review* launched in March 2000.

(1983–5). (The final two years of this guide, retitled *International Music & Opera Guide,* does not include USSR reports.)

Brief notices of a selection of noteworthy broadcasts heard on BBC Radio 3 (launched on 29 September 1946), likewise found helpful, are appended to the Bibliography.

Spellings

Inconsistencies abound in musical literature. Spellings especially of Russian writers, musicians, and composers vary considerably. Here an attempt has been made, at least, to spell each name the same throughout. In most cases the compiler has returned to the Russian source and made his own transliteration so as not to lose the advantage of reversibility—hence 'Kirill' and 'Maksim', though two films of the *Maxim Trilogy* retain this spelling of Maksim as they were billed in the West. Exceptions to this procedure had to be made where after continued general usage incorrect deviations have been universally accepted and to change them would affect alphabetical indexing or seem disturbingly unfamiliar. These include 'Tchaikovsky' (Pyotr, but not Aleksandr, André, or Boris) and 'Tcherepnin' in place of 'Chaikovsky' and 'Cherepnin'. In other cases the Cyrillic letter 'Ч' appears as 'ch', apart from the conductor Markevitch who preferred the form 'tch'. The conductor Koussevitzky signed his name thus and this spelling has been preserved rather than the more phonetically consistent but not instantly recognizable 'Kusevitsky'. 'Musorgsky' is now preferable to 'Mussorgsky' or 'Moussorgsky'. The spelling 'Rakhmaninov' is gaining favour among musicologists, though the composer did sign his letters 'Rachmaninoff'. A few other deviations from the strict transliteration will be noted (e.g. 'Eisenstein' for 'Eizenstein', 'Gnessin' for 'Gnesin'—and similarly, 'Kissin' for 'Kisin', 'Meyerhold' for 'Meierkhold', 'Richter' for 'Rikhter', and 'Schnittke' for 'Shnitke'—the former spelling adopted by the composer out of deference to his Germanic roots). In general the spellings will be found to be considerably closer to those adopted by Boris Schwarz (1983) than to his fellow Russian-born lexicographer, Nicolas Slonimsky (1984, see p. xxxvi).

Transliterations are useful for pronunciation purposes but annoying when one wishes to translate libretti with the aid of a Russian dictionary. For this reason the compiler prefers, where possible, to buy the Russian editions of Shostakovich's songs and choral works. Ideally the libretti supplied with British recordings should provide the Russian text, an English transliteration and a prose translation. With the help of the middle column of the chart THE RUSSIAN ALPHABET (Appendix VII) it is possible to transliterate with fair accuracy to the original Russian. An index of Russian titles of stage works, films, etc., with transliterations, is provided.

Departing from Russian practice in transliterated titles of journals and publishing firms, the second word—when not a place-name—is capitalized (e.g. 'Sovetskaya Muzyka', 'Sovetskii Kompozitor', and 'Molodaya Gvardiya').

Following Boris Schwarz's scholarly example, the English spelling of 'conservatory' is adopted and, likewise, 'bolshoi' and 'malyi' are used for 'large' and 'small' respectively when referring to Soviet concert-halls. 'Jazz Orchestra' has been retained in the titles of two suites of light music, though this is patently misleading. The Soviet people freely use the term 'England' for the United Kingdom, as we Britons tend to apply 'Russia' for the whole of the USSR. Scottish friends of the compiler have objected strongly to Robert Burns being dubbed an English poet so, therefore, the name 'British' has been substituted in the titles of two song cycles. 'Folk song', or in its hyphenated form, appears throughout as 'folksong'.

Index of Names

The names of musicians, arrangers, orchestras, ensembles, librettists, translators, film-directors, producers, and other persons associated with Shostakovich and mentioned in this book are included. The occupation of each individual is given in parentheses, though vocations (e.g. acting, composing, sculpting, etc.) not relevant to their connection with the composer are ignored. Composers of the couplings and fill-ups of recorded works and persons mentioned in passing in this Introduction and in the Appendices are not indexed.

Sovetskii Kompozitor's annual illustrated 100-page calendar *V mire muzyki* ('In the World of Music') provided much helpful biographical information.

The numbers refer to opus number entries and not to page numbers. The adoption of this procedure will be found useful as an indication of the works of Shostakovich associated with each name. Quartets that have recorded the whole cycle of string quartets will list the opus numbers 49, 68, 73, 83, 92, 101, 108, 110, 117, 118, 122, 133, 138, 142, and 144. Orchestras and conductors that have recorded all fifteen symphonies will list the numbers 10, 14, 20, 43, 47, 54, 60, 65, 70, 93, 103, 112, 113, 135, and 141. Capital letters indicate the composition without opus numbers (i.e. Sans opp.). Such works were labelled 'bez op.' in Shostakovich's typed lists and initially the compiler was tempted to adopt this convenient abbreviation.

Index of Compositions

Works are listed alphabetically and also classified under the headings Ballets, Cantatas, Choral Works, Concertos, Films, Instrumental Works, Juvenilia, Marches, Miscellaneous Works, Operas, Overtures, Patriotic Works, Piano Duos, Piano Solos, Sans opp., Sonatas, Song Cycles, Songs, Stage Productions, String Quartets, and Symphonies.

CATALOGUE

Juvenilia

The Soldier

An extended descriptive piano 'poem' composed in his tenth year was subtitled 'Ode to Liberty.'

Hymn to Freedom

A piano piece written in 1915–16.

Funeral March

A piano composition written in 1917 with the dedication 'In memory of the fallen heroes of the October Revolution'.

The Gipsies

An opera after the long dramatic poem written by Aleksandr Pushkin in 1827. A theme from this opera was utilized in *Suite on Verses of Michelangelo,* Opus 145.

Revolutionary Symphony

Rusalochka

A ballet based on Hans Christian Andersen's fairy tale 'The Little Mermaid'.

In the Forest

A trilogy for piano. Fragments, included in the composer's notebook dated 1919, preserved in the Shostakovich family archive.

Fantasy for two pianos

This work was dedicated to the Petrograd Conservatory's principal, Aleksandr Konstantinovich Glazunov.

Notes: The first five juvenilia were stated to have been destroyed after the composer's graduation in 1925, though, according to Bogdanova (1979), three numbers from *The Gipsies* are preserved in the CIS Archives of Literature and Art (namely these are a duet of Zemfira and Aleko, the Old Man's arietta, and a vocal trio) and in 1984 a manuscript of the *Funeral March* was found in the archive of a pianist relative, Nina Kokoulina.

The Soldier, Funeral March, and *In the Forest* together with a Polka and two Mazurkas will be published in Volume 109 and fragments of *The Gipsies* opera will appear in Volumes 54 (full score) and 55 (piano score) of the *New Collected Works.*

Sans op. A   Early Piano Pieces

Minuet, Prelude, and Intermezzo

Form: Three brief pieces for piano:

1. Minuet—Allegretto
2. Prelude—Lento, ma non troppo
3. Intermezzo—Allegretto

Composed: 1919–20, at Petrograd.

Arrangement: Intermezzo completed by Robert Matthew-Walker in 1989.

Music: The three pieces were found among the papers of Professor Aleksandra Rozanova and are now preserved at the Glinka Museum. The autograph of the Intermezzo is incomplete.

Muzyka, No. 10285 (in the supplement to Volume 39 of *Collected Works* with Opp. 5, 12, 13, 34, 61, and 69), 1983, 30 cm.

Duration: 2' 36"–3' 16"; with completion of No. 3—4' 23".

Recordings: USSR: Melodiya C10 26307 004. Viktoria POSTNIKOVA (piano). [Album 6 of 'From Manuscripts of Different Years'—Sans opp. X, J, S, D; Opp. 41 and 128.] P 1983–6, 1 1988*d*.

AVM Classics Compact Disc AVZ 3020. Nos. 1–3 twice with No. 3 completed by R. Matthew-Walker in first set. Martin JONES. ['Piano Music Volume II'—Opp. 13, 34, and 22*a*; Sans opp. S and T.] P London 1–2 June 1989.

Opus 1   Scherzo in F sharp minor

Form: A piece for full orchestra marked '[Allegretto]—Meno mosso—[Tempo I]'.

Instrumentation: piccolo, 2 flutes, 2 oboes, 2 A clarinets, 2 bassoons ~ 4 horns, 2 trumpets, 3 trombones, tuba ~ timpani, triangle, cymbals, bass drum ~ strings.

Composed: Autumn or early winter (not later than December) 1919, at Petrograd.

Dedication: 'Dedicated to my teacher Maksimilian Oseyevich Shteinberg' (composer/music teacher).

Première: UK: 17 February 1996, Royal Festival Hall, London; BBC Symphony Orchestra, Mark Elder. (Broadcast on BBC 3, 16 May 1996).

Arrangement: Originally for piano (Rabinovich).

Music: Autograph score preserved at the CIS Archives of Literature and Art, also a fair copy by the composer stored at the Shteinberg fund, Institute of the Theatre, Music and Cinematography, Leningrad. The first page of the former is reproduced in Volume 10 of *Collected Works*. The first theme later utilized as a basis for the 'Clockwork Doll', Op. 69 No. 6.

Muzyka, No. 11678 (in Volume 10 of *Collected Works* with Opp. 3, 7, 16, 42, and Sans op. E), 1984, full score, 30 cm.

Duration: Approx. 5 minutes in score; 4' 53".

Recordings: USSR; Melodiya C10 19103 004. USSR Ministry of Culture Symphony Orchestra, Gennadi ROZHDESTVENSKY. [Album 2 of 'From Manuscripts of Different Years'—Opp. 3, 7, 26, and 21.] P 22 Mar. 1982, I 1983*d*. *Reissued:* Olympia Compact Disc OCD 194. [Opp. 3, 7, 100, 59, 26, and 37.] I Feb. 1988, G June 1988 ~ Japan: Icone Compact Disc ICN 9415-2. [Opp. 54, 3, and 26.] I Sept. 1994. ~ BMG Melodiya Compact Discs 74321 59058-2 (two-disc set). [Opp. 36, 4, 17, Z, H, C, 16, 3, 7, 26/D, 59, E, 128, 30*a*, and 19.] I and G Mar. 1999.

Opus 2   Eight Preludes

Form: Eight short pieces for piano:

1. G minor
2. G major
3. E flat minor
4. B flat major
5. A minor—Allegro
6. F minor
7. D flat major
8. D flat major

Composed: Autumn 1919—prior to 8 May 1920, at Petrograd.

Dedication: 1. Boris Mikhailovich Kustodiev (artist)

2, 3, 4, and 5. Mariya Dmitrievna Shostakovich (elder sister)

6, 7, and 8. 'N.K.' = Natalya Kube (first girl friend)

Première: 15 July 1926, Kharkov; Dmitri Shostakovich.

Music: Manuscript lost. The beginning of No. 5 is illustrated on a plate, after page 64, in Khentova (1975).

Recordings: —

Note: The key signature of No. 3 is given as E flat minor by Sadovnikov and E minor in Volume 39 of *Collected Works*.

Sans op. B   Five Preludes

Form: Five preludes for piano, selected by the composer from eight contributed to a projected collection of twenty-four written in collaboration with fellow-students Pavel Feldt and Georgi Klements:

1. No. 2 in A minor—Allegro moderato e scherzando (Opus 2 No. 5)
2. No. 3 in G major—Andante (Opus 2 No. 2)

3. No. 4 in E minor—Allegro moderato
4. No. 15 in D flat major—Moderato (Opus 2 No. 7 or 8)
5. No. 18 in F minor—Andantino (Opus 2 No. 6)

Composed: 1919–21, at Petrograd.

Arrangements: Nos. 1 and 2 transcribed for wind orchestra by Alfred Schnittke in 1976.

Music: The original notebook containing the eighteen completed Preludes is in Irina Shostakovich's possession. Autograph copies of Nos. 2 and 18 preserved at both the CIS Archives of Literature and Art and the Glinka Museum, and of the set in the Gavriil Yudin family archive.

Muzgiz, No. 3184 (in *D. Shostakovich: Compositions for fortepiano*, Volume 1, with Opp. 5, 12, 13, 22*a* Polka, 34, and 61), 1966, 29 cm.

Hans Sikorski, No. 2184, 1966, 31.5 cm.

MCA, *c.*1968.

Edition Peters, No. 5717 (plate no. 12524 with Opp. 5 and 13), 1970, 30 cm.

Muzyka, No. 10285 (in the supplement to Volume 39 of *Collected Works* with Opp. 5, 12, 13, 34, 61, and 69), 1983, 30 cm.

Duration: 5' 40"–6' 09".

Recordings: USA: Orion ORS 6915. Vladimir PLESHAKOV (piano). [Opp. 5, 12, and 13; and Prokofiev.] P 1969.

Bulgaria: Balkanton BKA 10294. Nos. 1, 2, and 3. Krasimir GATEV (piano). [Sans op. S and Op. 5; Prokofiev and Kabalevsky.] P early 1980s?

USSR: Melodiya C50 20749 006. Rimma BOBRITSKAYA (piano). ['For Children'—Opp. 69, 97*a*, and 3*a*; Sans opp. P and S.] P 1983, I 1984*d*.

AVM Classics AVM 1003 and Compact Disc AVMCD 1003. Martin JONES (piano). [Opp. 12, 61, and 5; Sans op. S.] P not stated, G Oct. 1988.

France: Accord Compact Disc 202812. Caroline WEICHERT (piano). [Opp. 13 and 34; Sans op. S.] P Sept. 1993, I 1994.

Olympia Compact Disc OCD 574. Colin STONE (piano). [Opp. 34, 12, and 61.] P London Sept. 1995, I Mar. 1996, G June 1996.

Chandos Compact Disc CHAN 9792. Nos. 1 and 2 arr. Schnittke. Russian Symphony Orchestra, Valeri POLYANSKY. ['The Unknown Shostakovich'—Opp. 23 and 125, Sans op. W.] P Mosfilm Studio Jan. 1998, I Jan. 2000.

Reference: Bogdanova (in Kandinsky).

Note: In 1975 Sofya Khentova wrote that the Five Preludes include four from the former Preludes of Opus 2 which were the most popular at the Conservatory: the A minor (No. 2) with its scherzo character, G major (No. 3), F minor (No. 18) which approaches the poetical perfection of the Opus 34 No. 10 Prelude in C sharp minor and, in the same laconic vein, of a mere 19 bars, the D flat major (No. 15)

Sans op. C   I Waited for Thee in the Grotto (Rimsky-Korsakov)

Form: Transcription of the fourth and last song of Rimsky-Korsakov's Opus 40 cycle, to texts of Mikhail Lermontov and Apollon Maikov, composed in 1897. Maikov's poem 'I waited for thee in the grotto at the appointed hour', is scored for full orchestra with harp.

Composed: 1921, at Petrograd.

Arrangement: English translation of the text by Joan Pemberton Smith.

Music: Manuscript.

Duration: 2' 30".

Recordings: USSR: Melodiya C10 14415-6. Alla ABLABERDYEVA (soprano), USSR Symphony Orchestra, Gennadi Rozhdestvensky. [Album 1 of 'From Manuscripts of Different Years'—Opp. 4, 16, 17, 23, and 36; Sans opp. H and Z] P 1980, I 1981*b*. *Reissued:* HMV Melodiya ASD 1650331. [As Russian release.] G July 1983 ~ Germany: Melodia Eurodisc 201974-366. [As Russian release.] ~ BMG Melodiya Compact Discs 74321 59058-2 (two-disc set). [Opp. 36, 4, 17, Z, H, 16, 1, 3, 7, 26/D, 59, E, 128, 30*a*, and 19.] I and G Mar. 1999.

Opus 3   Theme and Variations in B flat minor

Form: Theme, 11 variations and finale for full orchestra:

Theme—Andantino and Variations:
 1. Andantino
 2. Più mosso (Vivace)
 3. Andante
 4. Allegretto
 5. Andante
 6. Allegro
 7. Moderato—Allegro—Moderato
 8. Largo
 9. [Allegro]
 10. Allegro molto
 11. Appassionato
      Finale—Allegro—Maestoso
      Coda—Presto

Instrumentation: piccolo (= flute III), 2 flutes, 2 oboes, 2 B flat clarinets, 2 bassoons ~ 4 horns, 3 trumpets, 3 trombones, tuba ~ timpani, triangle, cymbals, bass drum ~ optional celesta and piano in Variation 5 (a suggestion marked on the manuscript by M. Shteinberg) ~ strings.

Composed: 1921–2, at Petrograd.

Dedication: 'To the bright memory of Nikolai Aleksandrovich Sokolov' (music teacher—counterpoint and fugue).

Arrangement: Opus 3*a*—a reduction for piano by the composer.

Music: Autograph score preserved at the CIS Archives of Literature and Art. Muzyka, No. 11678 (in Volume 10 of *Collected Works* with Opp. 1, 7, 16, 42, and Sans op. E), 1984, full score, 30 cm.

Duration: Approx. 15' 30" in score; 15' 15"–15' 19".

Recordings: USSR: Melodiya C10 19103 004. USSR Ministry of Culture Symphony Orchestra, Gennadi ROZHDESTVENSKY. [Album 2 of 'From Manuscripts of Different Years'—Opp. 1, 7, 26, and 21.] P 22 Mar. 1982, I 1983*d*. *Reissued:* Olympia Compact Disc OCD 194. [Opp. 1, 7, 100, 59, 26, and 37.] I Feb. 1988, G June 1988 ~ Japan: Icone Compact Disc ICN 9415-2. [Opp. 54, 1, and 26.] I Sept. 1994 ~ BMG Melodiya Compact Discs 74321 59058-2 (two-disc set). [Opp. 36, 4, 17, Z, H, C, 16, 1, 7, 26/D, 59, E, 128, 30*a*, and 19.] I and G Mar. 1999.

　　　USSR: Melodiya C50 20749 006. Opus 3*a*. Rimma BOBRITSKAYA (piano). ['For Children'—Opp. 69 and 97*a*; Sans opp. B, P, and S.] P 1983, I 1984*d*.

Opus 4   Two Fables by Krylov

Form: Two songs for mezzo-soprano (or female chorus in No. 2) and orchestra with harp and celesta, to texts by fabulist Ivan Krylov—Nos. 12 and 23 of Book 2 of Fables:

1. The Dragonfly and the Ant—Con moto
2. The Ass and the Nightingale—Moderato

Instrumentation: piccolo (= flute III), 2 flutes, 2 oboes, 2 clarinets (B flat and A), 2 bassoons, contrabassoon ~ 4 horns, 3 trumpets, 3 trombones, tuba ~ timpani, triangle, cymbals ~ celesta, harp ~ strings. The composer states that the mezzo-soprano soloist in No. 2 may be replaced by a choir of preferably fewer than twelve alto voices.

Composed: 1922, at Petrograd.

Dedication: Mikhail Vladimirovich Kvadri (fellow student—one of his circle of friends, 'The Moscow Six').

Premières: 2 February 1977, Estonia Concert Hall, Tallinn; Moscow Conservatory Students' Chorus (female section) and Symphony Orchestra.

　　　UK: 22 June 1944, Almeida Theatre, Islington, London; Helen Lawrence (soprano), Contemporary Chamber Orchestra, Odaline de la Martinez.

Arrangements: Reduction for voice and piano by the composer (tempo indication of both songs given as Allegro: No. 2 differs materially from the orchestral version). English translations of the texts by Joan Pemberton Smith and David Fanning; German translation by Jörg Morgener.

Music: Autograph score of the original orchestral version preserved at the CIS Archives of Literature and Art and that of the reduction, at the Glinka Museum.

Muzyka, in *Musical Legacy,* Volume 2, Part 1, 1966, piano reduction.

Muzyka, No. 10113 (in Volume 31 of *Collected Works* with Opp. 21, 46*a,* 140, 79*a,* 143*a,* and 145*a*), 1982, full score, 30 cm.

Muzyka, No. 10283 (in Volume 32 of *Collected Works* with Opp. 21, 46, 62, 79, 84, 86, 91, 98, 100 *et al.*), 1982, reduction, 30 cm.

Hans Sikorski, No. 2322, 1986, reduction with Russian and German texts—the latter by J. Morgener, 31.5 cm.

Duration: No. 1: 2' 38"–3' 15" and No. 2: 4' 20"–5' 28". [The *Collected Works* scores give an excessive total duration of approx. 15 minutes]

Recordings: USSR: Melodiya C10 14415-6. No. 1—Galina Borisova (mezzo-soprano), USSR Symphony Orchestra; No. 2—Moscow Conservatory Chamber Choir, Moscow Philharmonic Orchestra; both conducted by Gennadi ROZHDESTVENSKY. [Album 1 of 'From Manuscripts of Different Years'—Opp. 16, 17, 23, and 36; Sans opp. C, H, and Z.] P 1980, I 1981*b.* *Reissued:* HMV Melodiya ASD 1650331. [As Russian release.] G July 1983 ~ Germany: Melodia Eurodisc 201974-366. [As Russian release.] ~ BMG Melodiya Compact Discs 74321 59058-2 (two-disc set). [Opp. 36, 17, Z, H, C, 16, 1, 3, 7, 26/D, 59, E, 128, 30*a,* and 19.] I and G Mar. 1999.

Deutsche Grammophon Compact Disc 439 860-2GH. Nos. 1 and 2— Larissa Dyadkova (mezzo-soprano), No. 2—Women's Voices of Gothenburg Opera, Gothenburg Symphony Orchestra, Neeme JÄRVI. ['The Orchestral Songs, Vol. 1'—Opp. 46*a,* 140, and 79*a.*] P Gothenburg Aug. 1993, I June 1994.

Germany: Capriccio Compact Disc 10 780. Tamara Sinyavskaya (mezzo-soprano), Cologne Radio Chorus, Helmuth Froschauer (chorusmaster), Cologne Radio Symphony Orchestra, Mikhail YUROVSKY. [Opp. 119 and 114*a.*] P Cologne 12–14 Feb. 1996, I Oct. 1999, G Dec. 1999.

Reference: Bogdanova (in Kandinsky).

Opus 5   Three Fantastic Dances

Form: Three short pieces for piano:

1. March in C major—Allegretto
2. Waltz in C major—Andantino
3. Polka in C major—Allegretto

Composed: 4 December 1920, at Petrograd (*Sovetskya Rossiya*, 29 July 1984).
Dedication: Iosif Zakharovieb Shvarts (fellow student pianist).
Première: 20 March 1925, Moscow Conservatory Malyi Hall; Dmitri Shostakovich.
Arrangements: Transcriptions for violin and piano by Harry Glickman, trombone and piano by Quinto Maganini, trumpet and piano by Timofei Dokshitser, saxophone and piano by Marc Chisson (duration 5' 50"), and bayan ensemble. No. 2 arranged for organ by Willard Nevins; Nos. 2 and 3 for string quartet by Konstantin Mostras, orchestra by Grzegorz Fitelberg, viola and piano by Georgi Bezrukov, and piano four hands by Geoffrey Carroll.
Music: Originally published as Opus 1. Moisenko (1949) writes that the pieces were not published until 1937 at Shostakovich's request, though Martynov (1947) correctly gives the first publication as 1926. Two autograph copies, both marked Opus 5, are in existence; the earlier version preserved at the Leningrad Institute of the Theatre, Music and Cinematography, and the definitive score at the CIS Archives of Literature and Art.

Muzgiz, No. 7078, 1926, numbered Op. 1, 35.5 cm. (and same plate no., 1935).

International Music, No. 2252, 1941, 30.5 cm.

H. W. Gray / Novello, 1943, No. 2 arr. for organ by W. Nevins.

Leeds Music, 1945, arr. for violin and piano by H. Glickman, 31 cm.

Anglo-Soviet Music Press, No. 23, 1945, 33.5 cm. (and 1954, 31 cm.).

Edition Musicus, No. 707, no date, arr. for trombone and piano by Q. Maganini, 31 cm.

Soyuz Sovetskikh Kompozitorov, 1946, numbered Op. 1, 31 cm.

Russian-American Music, New York, 1946, Nos. 2 and 3 arr. for orchestra by G. Fitelberg, piano-conductor scores and parts, 31 cm.

Muzgiz, 1947, Nos. 2 and 3 for string quartet by K. Mostras.

Edwin F. Kalmus, No. 896 (with Opp. 12 and 87 Nos. 1–12), no date, 18 cm.

Hans Sikorski, No. 2182, *c.*1960, 32 cm.

Muzgiz, No. 29138 (in *Collection of Pieces by Soviet Composers* for viola and piano, 1961, No. 3 arr. G. Bezrukov, 29 cm.

Muzgiz, No. 3184 (in *D. Shostakovich: Compositions for fortepiano*, Volume 1, with Sans op. B, Opp. 12, 13, 22*a* Polka, 34, and 61), 1966, numbered Op. 1, 29 cm.

Edition Peters, No. 5717 (plate no. 12524 with Op. 13 and Sans op. B), 1970, numbered Op. 1, 30 cm.

G. Schirmer, *c.*1976, ed. Joseph Prostakoff, 31 cm.

Muzyka, No. 10695, 1980, 29 cm.

Muzyka, No. 10285 (in Volume 39 of *Collected Works* with Opp. 12, 13, 34, 61, 69, and supplement of unnumbered piano pieces), 1983, 30 cm.

Willis Music, Cincinnati, *c*.1989, No. 2 and 3 for piano four hands by
G. Carroll, separate editions, 31 cm.

Duration: Approx. 3' 30" in score; 2' 44"–4' 14"; 2' 50"–3' 45" (BBC Piano
and Organ Catalogue).

Recordings: Parlophone E 11391 (78 rpm). Labelled 'Trois Danses Fantas-
tiques'. Eileen JOYCE. [d'Albert.] P 1938. *Reissued:* Pearl Compact Disc
GEMM CD 9022. [Bach, Mozart, Chopin *et al.*] I 1995.

USA: MCA Records Compact Disc MCAD 4211 (mono). Nos. 1 and 2
arr. Glickman. Jascha HEIFETZ (violin) and Emanuel Bay (piano). ['The
Legendary Decca/Brunswick masters', Volume 1—Prokofiev, Debussy,
Tchaikovsky *et al.*] P 29 Nov. 1945, I 1988.

USA: Mercury MG 10035 (mono). Dmitrl SHOSTAKOVICH. [Opp. 22*a*, 34,
and 69; 'David Oistrakh plays violin favorites'—Chopin/Saraste,
Prokofiev *et al.*] P Prague 1946.

RCA Victor RB 16243 (mono). Waltz arr. Glickman. Jascha HEIFETZ
(violin) and Emanuel Bay (piano). [Brahms, Khachaturyan, Paganini *et al.*]
P 18 Dec. 1947, G June 1961. *Reissued:* USSR: Melodiya D 17429-30
(10" mono). [Brahms, Khachaturyan, Paganini *et al.*] I 1966 ~ USA: RCA
LM 2382 (mono). [Saint-Saëns, Bennet, Brahms *et al.*] ~ RCA Gold Seal
Compact Disc 09026 61766-2 (mono) in set 09026 61778-2. ['The Heifetz
Collection', Vol. 35 of 65—Mendelssohn, Toch, Bennett *et al.*] G Nov.
1994.

USSR: Melodiya M10 39075-6 (mono). Dmitri SHOSTAKOVICH. [In four-
record set 'D. Shostakovich—Pianist'—Opp. 22*a*, 34, 67, and 69.] P 1947,
I 1977*b*. *Reissued:* USSR: Melodiya M10 48089 004 (mono). [In two-record
set 'Rimsky-Korsakov Conservatory, Leningrad, 125th Anniversary'—
Liszt, Prokofiev, Skryabin *et al.*] I 1988*d* ~ Olympia Compact Disc OCD
208. ['125th Anniversary'] I 1988 ~ Olympia Compact Disc OCD 008.
['The Shostakovich CD'—Op. 46 and seventeen further tracks from
Opp. 7, 10, 19, 32, 35, 37, 58*a*, 59, 70, 93, 100, 109, 113, 135, 141, and Sans
op. E not cross-referenced in this catalogue.] I Oct. 1989 ~ Revelation
Compact Disc RV 70008 (mono). ['Shostakovich plays Shostakovich, Vol.
7'—Opp. 134, 22, and 40.] I Sept. 1998, G Feb. 1999.

HMV C 4071 (78 rpm). Moura LYMPANY. [Prokofiev.] P 12 Dec. 1950,
G Mar. 1951. *Reissued:* Cambridge Imprimatur DIMP 2 (mono). [In double
album 'The Lympany Legend'—Liszt, Schumann, Brahms *et al.*] G Mar.
1982.

Canada: Turnabout TV 34792X (mono). Arr. Glickman. Albert PRATZ
(violin) and Glenn Gould (piano). ['The Young Glenn Gould'—Berg,
Taneyev, and Prokofiev.] P 1951, I 1982.

HMV CLP 1057 (mono). Gina BACHAUER. [Liszt and Chopin.] P 29
Sept. 1954, G Nov. 1955.

USA: Classics Editions 1026 (mono). Eldin BURTON. [In Volume 3 of
'Piano Miniatures'.] P 1950s.

France: Pathé DTX 269. Lívia RÉV. [Bach, Mozart, Beethoven *et al.*] I 1959.

Columbia FCX 769 (mono). Dmitri SHOSTAKOVICH. [Opp. 35 and 102.] P Paris 12 Sept. 1958, G Oct. 1961. *Reissued:* USA: Seraphim 60161 (mono). [Opp. 35 and 102.] I 1971 ~ France: Pathé Marconi 2C 061 12114. [Opp. 35 and 102.] I 1972 ~ World Records Retrospect SH 293 (mono). [Opp. 35 and 102.] G July 1979 ~ Russia: Russian Disc R10 00319-20 (DMM mono). [In double album 'For the 85th Anniversary' with Opp. 35, 102, and 135.] I 1991 ~ EMI Classics Compact Disc CDC7 54606-2 (mono). ['Composers in Person' series—Opp. 35, 102, and 87.] I Jan. 1993, G Apr. 1993 ~ Revelation Compact Disc RV 70003. ['Shostakovich plays Shostakovich, Vol. 3'—Op. 87.] I Nov. 1997, G Feb. 1998. NB. Three slight flaws as on the Paris recording and timings confirm that this was recorded in 1958 not *c.*1956.

USSR: Melodiya D 013489-90 (mono). Viktor MERZHANOV. [Prokofiev and Peiko.] P 1964.

France: Erato EFM 42074 (mono). György SZEBÖK. [Khachaturyan and Prokofiev.] P 1964.

East Germany: Eterna 820 307 (mono). Dieter ZECHLIN. [Bach, Bartók, Mozart *et al.*] P 1965.

USSR: Melodiya D 16213-4 (10" mono). Arr. Glickman. Valeriya VILKER (violin) and Bella Rakova (piano). [Janáček, Tchaikovsky, and Stravinsky.] P 1965.

USSR: Melodiya D 17593-4 (10" mono). Arr. Glickman. Grigori FEIGIN (violin) and Yuliya Gushanskaya (piano). [Mozart, Ravel, Khachaturyan *et al.*] P 1966.

USA: Musical Heritage Society MHS 1147 Y. Hans-Helmut SCHWARZ. [Op. 94; Borodin, Glinka, Rakhmaninov *et al.*] P 1966.

USA: Orion ORS 6915. Vladimir PLESHAKOV. [Opp. 12 and 13, Sans op. B; and Prokofiev.] P 1969.

USSR: Melodiya C 04635-6. Arr. Dokshitser and original piano version. Timofei DOKSHITSER (trumpet) and Abram Zhak (piano). [Ravel, Rimsky-Korsakov, Arensky *et al.*] P and I 1974. *Reissued:* USA: Odyssey Melodiya Y 33825. Labelled 'The Incredible Trumpet Virtuosity of Timofey Dokschutzer'.

HMV ASD 3081. Cristina ORTIZ. [Opp. 35 and 102.] P 4 Jan. 1974, G June 1975. *Reissued:* USA: Angel S 37109. [Opp. 35 and 102.] I 1975 ~ EMI Compact Disc CDS7 47790-8. [In two-disc set with Opp. 54, 103, and 102.] I Nov. 1987, G May 1988 ~ HMV Classics 33 Compact Disc 7 67637-2. [Opp. 47 and 102.] I Dec. 1992 ~ EMI Classics / BBC Music Compact Disc 7 67887-2. [Opp. 47 and 102.] I Oct. 1993.

Hungary: Hungaroton SLPX 11825. Arr. Glickman. Leila RÁSONY (violin) and György Miklos (piano). [Khachaturyan, Stravinsky, Chausson *et al.*] P 1976.

USSR: Melodiya C10 08265-6. Arr. Glickman. Aleksandr MELNIKOV (violin) and Boris Levantovich (piano). [Mozart, Dvořák, Rimsky-Korsakov *et al.*] P 1977, I 1977*d*.

Sweden: Bluebell Bell 126. Inger WIKSTRÖM. [Opp. 19 Nos. 3, 4, and 2; 22*a* No. 3; 31 No. 4; 94; 97*a* No. 7; 105 fragment; and Prokofiev.] P Stockholm 28 Jan. and 1 Feb. 1981. *Reissued:* Sweden: Swedish Society Discofil Compact Disc SCD 1031. [Opp. 34, 61, 94, and 19.] I 1988.

Bulgaria: Balkanton BKA 10294. Krasimir GATEV. [Sans op. B and S; Prokofiev and Kabalevsky.] P early 1980s?

Bulgaria: Balkanton BKA 11338. Nikolai EVROV. [Op. 22*a* Polka; Weber, Shchedrin, Gershwin *et al.*] P 1980?

Norway: Simax PS 1014. Jens Harald BRATLIE. [Opp. 8 and 67.] P near Oslo 17 Nov. and 21 Dec. 1981, and 2 Jan. 1982; G July 1982. *Reissued:* Norway: Simax Compact Disc PSC 1014. [Opp. 8 and 67.] I Sept. 1987, G Oct. 1988.

USSR: Melodiya C20 17171007. Arr. for bayan ensemble. Tembrovoe Bayan Ensemble, Valeri SOMOROV. [Shchedrin, Tsygankov, Kuss *et al.*] I 1982*d*.

Apollo Sound AS 1027. Arr. for violin and piano. Katherine SWEENEY (violin) and Albert Alan (piano). [Debussy, Szymanowski, and Prokofiev.] I 1982.

Sweden: BIS LP 276 (DMM) and Compact Disc 276. Ronald PÖNTINEN [Stravinsky, Skryabin, Prokofiev *et al.*] P Djursholm 18–21 June 1984, G Sept. 1985. *Reissued:* Boots Classical Selection Compact Disc DDD 106. [Skryabin, Khachaturyan, and Prokofiev.] I 1988.

France: Arion ARN33 787. Waltz. Sofia MATKOWSKA. ['La Danse par le Disque' Vol. 15—Lully, Chopin, Dargomyzhsky *et al.*] P 1985.

Germany: Eterna DMM7 25 193. Arr. not named. Christian FUNKE (violin) and Herbert Kaliga (piano). ['Cantabile'—Paganini, Kreisler, Rakhmaninov *et al.*] P Leipzig 1986.

AVM Classics AVM 1003 and Compact Disc AVMCD 1003, Martin JONES. [Opp. 12 and 61; Sans opp. B and S.] P not stated, G Oct. 1988.

USA: Cambria Compact Disc 1029. Arr. Glickman. Mischa LEFKOWITZ (violin) and Brent McMunn (piano). [Bartók, Debussy, Bloch *et al.*] P Los Angeles 19–20 Jan. 1987.

France: Accord Compact Disc 20025-2. Caroline WEICHERT. [Opp. 12 and 61.] P Jan. 1988, I 1988, G June 1990.

France: Le Chant du Monde Compact Disc LDC 278 1012. Elena VARVAROVA. [Opp. 12, 61, and 13.] P Paris Sept. 1989, I Feb. 1990.

USA: MCA Classics Art and Electronics Compact Disc AED 10107. Aleksandr SLOBODYANIK. [Musorgsky, Lyatoshinsky, and Prokofiev.] P Moscow Conservatory, date not stated, I 1990.

Hyperion Compact Disc CDA 66620. Tatyana NIKOLAYEVA. [Opp. 34 and 61.] P Hampstead 17–19 Apr. 1992, I July 1992, G Sept. 1992.

France: Erol Records Compact Disc 7014. Arr. for saxophone. Marc CHISSON (soprano saxophone) and Alain Perez (piano). [Opp. 34 and 27; Villa-Lobos, Ravel, Bartók *et al.*] P Bordeaux 14 June 1992.

Koch International Classics Compact Disc 3 7159-2HI. Israel MAR-GALIT. [Op. 35 and Sans op. S; and Schnittke.] P Moscow Conservatory Sept. 1992, I July 1993, G Sept. 1993.

Italy: Real Sound Compact Disc RS 051 0022. Anna MALIKOVA. [Op. 34 and Sans op. S.] P Wesel, Germany Apr. 1997.

France: Suoni e Colori Compact Disc SC 53009. Mikhail MARKOV. [Op. 34; and Galperine.] P Paris Nov. 1998.

Opus 6   Suite for Two Pianos

Alternative titles: Suite in F sharp minor. Title given as 'Sonata for Two Pianofortes' by Martynov (1947).

Form: Four pieces for two pianos:

1. Prelude in F sharp minor—Andantino
2. Fantastic Dance in A minor—Allegro vivo
3. Nocturne in D major—Andante
4. Finale in F sharp minor—Adagio—Allegro molto

Composed: March 1922, at Petrograd.

Dedication: 'To the memory of Dmitri Boleslavovich Shostakovich' (father).

Première: 20 March 1925, Moscow Conservatory Malyi Hall; Dmitri Shosta-kovich and Lev Oborin.

Music: Given as Opus 7 by Rabinovich (1959). In the autograph, preserved at the CIS Archives of Literature and Art, the titles of Nos. 1, 2, and 4 are given in the French language; No. 3 in Russian. A four-bar extract of No. 3 is shown on page 123 of Khentova (1975). The music scheduled to be published in Volume 39 of *Collected Works* was included as a supplement to Volume 13.

Muzyka, No. 11214 (in Volume 13 of *Collected Works* with Opp. 35, 94, 102, and Sans op. 0), 1983, prepared for first publication by Nikolai Kopchevsky, 30 cm.

Hans Sikorski, No. 2338 (with Sans op. 0), 1984, 31.5 cm.

Duration: 22' 50"–27' 20" .

Recordings: USSR: Melodiya C10 18471-2. Viktoria POSTNIKOVA and Nikolai PETROV. [Op. 94.] P 1982, I 1983c.

Chandos ARBD 1175 (digital). Seta TANYEL and Jeremy BROWN. ['Russian Music for Two Pianos'—Op. 94; Khachaturyan and Arutyunyan/ Babadzhanyan.] P London July 1985, I July 1986, G Nov. 1986. *Reissued:* Chandos Compact Disc CHAN 8466. [As LP release.] I May 1987.

Sweden: Bluebell Compact Disc ABCD 049. Folke GRÄSBECK and Alexander ZELYAKOV. [Op. 93.] P Åbo 22 and 24 Jan. 1992, I Mar. 1993.

USA: Audiofon Compact Disc 72053. Valentina LISITSA and Aleksei KUZNETSOV. [Rakhman and Chopin.] P Miami Aug. 1995.

France: Suoni è Colori Compact Disc SC 13008. Incorrectly labelled Op. 61. Thérèse DUSSAUT and Serge POLUSMIAK (piano duo). ['Hommage à Dmitri Chostakovitch, Vol. 2'—Opp. 134 and 94; Sans op. 0 (i).] P Espace Fazioli, Paris Oct.–Nov. 1997.

Germany: CPO Compact Disc 999 599-2. GENOVA & DIMITROV PIANO DUO. [Opp. 94, 95, Sans opp. 0 (ii) and E; Stravinsky, Prokofiev, and Dinicu.] P Hans Rosbaud Studio 4–5 May 1998, I Apr. 1999.

Reference: Bogdanova (in Kandinsky).

Opus 7 Scherzo in E flat major

Form: A composition for full orchestra (with piano) marked 'Allegro'.

Instrumentation: piccolo, 2 flutes, 2 oboes, 2 B flat clarinets, 2 bassoons ~ 4 horns, 2 trumpets, 3 trombones, tuba ~ timpani, side drum, cymbals ~ piano ~ strings.

Composed: Spring–autumn 1923 and completed on 15 October 1924, at Leningrad.

Dedication: Pyotr Borisovich Ryazanov (professor of composition at Leningrad Conservatory).

Premières: 11 February 1981, Leningrad; Leningrad Philharmonic Orchestra. UK: 17 February 1996, Royal Festival Hall, London; BBC Symphony Orchestra, Mark Elder. (Broadcast on BBC 3, 16 May 1996).

Arrangement: Reduction for piano by the composer.

Music: Autograph score preserved at the CIS Archives of Literature and Art. This composition used later in the film score *New Babylon*, Op. 18.

Muzyka, No. 11678 (in Volume 10 of *Collected Works* with Opp. 1, 3, 16, 42, and Sans op. E), 1984, full score, 30 cm.

Duration: Approx. 3' 30" in score; 3' 26"–3' 28".

Recordings: USSR: Melodiya C10 19103 004. USSR Ministry of Culture Symphony Orchestra, Gennadi ROZHDESTVENSKY. [Album 2 of 'From Manuscripts of Different Years'—Opp. 1, 3, 26, and 21.] P 1982, I 1983*d*. *Reissued:* Olympia Compact Disc OCD 194. [Opp. 1, 3, 100, 59, 26, and 37.] I Feb. 1988, G June 1988 ~ BMG Melodiya Compact Discs 74321 59058-2 (two-disc set). [Opp. 36, 4, 17, Z, H, C, 16, 1, 3, 26/D, 59, E, 128, 30*a*, and 19.] I and G Mar. 1999.

Opus 8   Trio No. 1 in C minor

Original title: Poem for Violin, Violoncello, and Fortepiano.

Form: A single-movement composition for violin, cello, and piano:

Andante—Allegro—Moderato—Allegro

Composed: August to October 1923. Started at Gaspra, near Yalta.

Dedication: Tatyana Ivanovna Glivenka (girl friend), who was told of the dedication in the composer's letter to her dated 11 September 1923.

Premières: [First performance in public given during the screening of a silent film: 25 October 1923, 'Harlequinade' Cinema, Petrograd; Veniamen Sher (violin), Grigori Pekker (cello), and Dmitri Shostakovich (piano).]

13 December 1923, Petrograd Conservatory; the composer at the piano.

20 March 1925, Moscow Conservatory Malyi Hall; N. Fyodorov (violin), A. Yegorov (cello), and Lev Oborin (piano).

UK: 29 June 1984, Almeida Theatre, Islington, London; Haroutune Bedelian (violin), Elizabeth Wilson (cello), and Niel Immelman (piano).

Arrangement: Parts prepared for performance and missing bars 257 to 278 in the piano part supplied by Boris Tishchenko in 1981.

Music: Sketch to bar 130, autograph score and parts preserved at the CIS Archives of Literature and Art.

Muzgiz, 1924 (according to Leonid Sabaneyev).

Muzyka, No. 10794 (in Volume 37 of *Collected Works* with Opp. 11, 57, and 67), 1983, score and parts, 30 cm.

Hans Sikorski, No. 2337, 1984, score and parts, 31.5 cm.

Duration: 9' 40"–14' 18".

Recordings: Norway: Simax PS 1014. OSLO TRIO (Stig Nilsson, Aage Kvalbein, Jens Harald Bratlie). [Opp. 5 and 67.] P near Oslo 17 Nov. and 21 Dec. 1981, and 2 Jan. 1982; G July 1982. *Reissued:* Simax Compact Disc PSC 1014. [Opp. 5 and 67.] I Sept. 1987, G Oct. 1988.

Germany: Signum SIG 013-00 (DMM). SERAPHIN TRIO (Wilhelm F. Walz, Jörg Metzger, Arne Torger). [Roslavets and Babadzhanyan.] P 1986. *Reissued:* Germany: Christophorus entreé Compact Disc CHE 0070-2. [Babadzhanyan and Roslavets.] I Aug. 1995.

Pan 170 012 (digital). VIENNA SCHUBERT TRIO (Boris Kuschnir, Martin Hornstein, Claus-Christian Schuster). [Grieg and Zemlinsky.] I July 1987, G Dec. 1987.

Germany: Largo Compact Disc 5112. CLEMENTI TRIO of Cologne (Daniel Spektor, Manuel Gerstner, Deborah Richards). [Tailleferre, Milhaud, and Roslavets.] P Munich 2 Dec. 1986 and 28–30 Sept. 1987. *Reissued:* Germany: EMI Compact Disc CDC5 56618-2. [As original issue.] I 1998.

Finland: Finlandia Compact Disc FACD 364. TRIO FINNICO (Nachum Erlich, Hanna Kiiski, Risto Lauriala). ['Contemporary Piano Trios'— Englund, Copland, and Kokkonen.] P Järvenpää Aug. 1988, I 1989. *Reissued:* Finlandia Ultima Compact Discs 8573 81969-2 (disc one of two-disc set). [Opp. 107 and 126.] G June 2000.

Germany: Dabringhaus und Grimm Compact Disc MD+GL 3334. MÜNCHNER KLAVIERTRIO (Ilona Then-Bergh, Gerhard Zank, Michael Schäfer). [Opp. 67 and 127.] P not stated, I 1989.

EMI Compact Disc CDC7 49865-2. CHUNG TRIO (Kyung-Wha Chung, Myung-Wha Chung, Myung-Whun Chung). [Tchaikovky.] P New York Dec. 1988, I Nov. 1989, G Mar. 1990.

Denmark: Kontrapunkt Compact Disc 32131. COPENHAGEN TRIO (Søreh Elbaek, Troels Hermansen, Morten Mogensen). [Op. 67.] P Lungbye 1992.

France: Le Chant du Monde Russian Season Compact Disc RUS 288 088. MOSCOW TRIO (Vladimir Ivanov, Mikhail Utkin, Aleksandr Bonduryansky). [Opp. 67 and 127.] P Moscow Conservatory Sept.–Nov. 1993, I Sept. 1994.

Japan: Meldec Compact Disc MECC 28004. Aleksandr Melnikov (violin), Natalya Sabinova (cello), and Viktor YAMPOLISKY (piano). [Opp. 13 and 67.] P Mosfilm Studio, Moscow 1–10 Oct. 1994, I June 1995. *Reissued:* Japan: Triton Compact Disc 17 011. [Opp. 13 and 67.] I Feb. 1997.

Naxos Compact Disc 8.553297. STOCKHOLM ARTS TRIO (Dan Almgren, Torleif Thedéen, Stefan Bojsten). [Opp. 67 and 127.] P Stockholm 13–15 Mar. 1995, I Apr. 1997, G July 1997.

Germany: Ars Musici Compact Disc AMP 5057-2. Christian Ludwig (violin), Johann Ludwig (cello), and Carl WOLF (piano). [Beethoven and Schubert.] P Erlangen 'Jugend musiziert' concert 5 June 1995.

Germany: Crescendi Compact Disc CR 33621. TRIO TRE MONDI (Carlos Johnson, Clemens Krieger, Reiko Yoshizumi). [Tchaikovsky.] P Detmold, Germany Feb. 1996, I 2001.

Italy: Real Sound Compact Disc RS 051-0176. TRIO DI TORINO (Sergio Lamberto, Dario Destefano, Giacomo Fuga). [Opp. 57 and 67.] P Wesel, Germany Apr. 1996, I May 2000.

USA: Arabesque Compact Discs Z 6698 (two-disc set). Jaime Laredo (violin), Sharon Robinson (cello), and Joseph KALICHSTEIN (piano). [Opp. 67, 40, 134, and 147.] P Purchase, New York 17–18 Dec. 1995 or 12–13 Sept. 1996, I and G Jan. 1998.

Hungary: Hungaroton Classics Compact Disc HCD 31780. BARTOS TRIO (Galina Danilova, Csaba Bartos, and Irina Ivanickaia). [Opp. 67 and 127.] P Hungaroton Studio 29 May–2 June 1997.

Nimbus Compact Disc NI 5572. VIENNA PIANO TRIO (Wolfgang Redik, Marcus Trefny, and Stefan Mendl). [Op. 67; and Schnittke.] P Nimbus Foundation Hall 6–9 Apr. 1998, I and G Dec. 1998.

Norway: Simax Compact Disc PSC 1147. GRIEG TRIO (Sølve Sigerland, Ellen Margrete Flesjø, Vebjørn Anvik). [Op. 67; Bloch and Martin.] P Lommedalen 12–18 June 1998, I Oct. 1999.

Germany: Thorofon Compact Disc CTH 2397. TRIO BAMBERG (Yevgeni Schuk, Stephan Gerlinghaus, Robert Benz). [Op. 67; and Schnittke.] P Nuremberg June 1998.

Orfeo Compact Disc C 465 991A. MUNICH TRIO (Rudolf J. Koeckert, Gerhard Zank, Hermann Lechler). [Opp. 67 and 127.] P Bavarian Radio Studio 4–5 May and 4–7 June 1999, I Mar. 2001.

Reference: Bogdanova (in Kandinsky).

Note: The first movement of a Quintet was completed on 9 April 1923. This composition was abandoned and the music incorporated in the Piano Trio No. 1. (Khentova 1985).

Opus 9   Three Pieces

Form: Three short pieces for cello and piano:

1. Fantasia in F sharp minor
2. Prelude in A minor
3. Scherzo in C major

Composed: 30 December 1923 in two hours; 6 January and before 11 January 1924 respectively, at Petrograd. A fourth piece written but destroyed a few days later.

Dedication:

1. Zoya Dmitrievna Shostakovich (younger sister)
2. Valerian Mikhailovich Bogdanov-Berezovsky (critic/composer)
3. Volodya I. Kurchavov (poet friend)

Première: 20 March 1925, Moscow Conservatory Malyi Hall, A. Yegorov (cello) and Dmitri Shostakovich (piano).

Music: Manuscript lost.

Recordings: —

Note: The 1996 German Orfeo recording claims that the opening track 'Romance' is one of the above pieces dedicated to the composer's sister. See Opus 97.

Opus 10   Symphony No. 1 in F minor

Form: Symphony for full orchestra (with piano) in four movements:

1. Allegretto—Allegro non troppo
2. Allegro

3. Lento—Largo *attacca*
4. Lento—Allegro molto—Adagio—Largo—Presto

Instrumentation: piccolo (= flute III), 2 flutes (II = piccolo II), 2 oboes, 2 clarinets (B flat and A), 2 bassoons ~ 4 horns, 3 trumpets (I and II B flat, III F), 3 trombones, tuba ~ timpani, triangle, side drum, cymbals, bass drum, gong ~ glockenspiel, piano ~ strings. Glockenspiel used in four bars of fourth movement and piano employed extensively in second and fourth movements. String ensemble much divided at times and numerous solos required, particularly of the leader and first desk cellist.

Composed: 1 July 1923–1 July 1925, at Petrograd / Leningrad. Began with the second movement. Piano score of the third movement completed in February 1925. Final alterations to the orchestration made in June 1926 after the première.

Dedication: Mikhail Vladimirovich Kvadri (composer). NB. This dedication appeared on Ye. Slavinsky's piano four hands score published in 1928 but is missing from all later publications.

Premières: [7 February 1926, Moscow Conservatory; piano reduction played by the composer at a sitting of the State Scientific Council of the People's Commissariat for Education. Early spring 1926, Leningrad Conservatory; four-handed version played by the composer and Pavel Feldt before Aleksandr Glazunov and board of examiners.]

12 May 1926, Leningrad Philharmonic Bolshoi Hall; Leningrad Philharmonic Orchestra, Nikolai Malko. The second movement encored.

Germany: 6 February 1928, Berlin; Berlin Philharmonic Orchestra, Bruno Walter.

USA: 2 November 1928, Philadelphia; Philadelphia Orchestra, Leopold Stokowski.

UK: 1931–32 Hallé Season; Hallé Orchestra, Sir Hamilton Harty.

Arrangements: Reduction for piano by the composer and for piano four hands by Yevgeni Slavinsky. Also two pianos four hands by Pavel Lamm (not published). See also Note.

Music: The autograph score preserved at the CIS Archives of Literature and Art. A page of the first movement is reproduced in Volume 1 of *Collected Works*.

Muzgiz, No. 7671, 1927, 30.5 cm.; reduced reprints with same plate number issued as miniature scores, 19 cm.; also 1931, 1938, 1956, 1957 (foreword by Ivan Martynov), and 1962.

Universal Edition, No. 9029, 1927, reprint of Muzgiz No. 7671.

Muzgiz, No. 7999, 1928, arr. for piano four hands by Ye. Slavinsky.

Universal Edition, No. 9058, 1928, arr. by Slavinsky, 35.5 cm.

Edwin F. Kalmus, No. 157, 1943, 23 cm.

Boosey & Hawkes Inc., No. 576, 1944, 26 cm.

Boosey & Hawkes, No. 604 (A.S.M.P. No. 31), no date, 19 cm.

Edition Musicus, No. 9029, 1940s, 20 cm.

International Music, No. 679, 1944, arr. by Slavinsky, 30.5 cm.

Muzyka, 1966, arr. by Slavinsky, 29 cm.

MCA, no number, *c*.1967, 24 cm.

Edition Peters, No. 5740 (plate no. 12659), 1972?, 18 cm.

Muzyka, No. 8610, 1975, 30 cm.

Muzyka, No. 10713 (in Volume 1 of *Collected Works* with Op. 14), 1987, full score, 30 cm.

Hans Sikorski, No. 2224, 1987, score, 21 cm.

Duration: Approx. 33 minutes in score (28' in MCA score); 27' 00"–35' 42".

Ballets: *Rouge et Noir (L'Étrange Farandole).* Léonide Massine, Ballet Russe de Monte Carlo, Monte Carlo; designer Henri Matisse, 11 May 1939. Same company, New York, 28 October 1939. The four movements of the one-act ballet represent: Aggression, City and Country, Loneliness, Fate. Tamara Toumanova danced the slow movement.

Symphony. Kenneth MacMillan, Royal Ballet, Covent Garden; designer Yolanda Sonnabend, 15 February 1962.

Remember. Oleg Sokolov, an anti-war ballet in four acts with epilogue, Alma Ata, Kazakhstan, summer 1981.

Recordings: USA: Victor 7884-8S in Set M 192 (9 sides 78 rpm). Philadelphia Orchestra, Leopold STOKOWSKI. P Camdem, New Jersey 18 Nov. 1933. *Reissued:* HMV DB 2203-7 (9 sides 78 rpm) and DB 7687-91 (9 sides 78 rpm automatic couplings). [Tchaikovsky] G Sept. 1934 ~ HMV DB 3847-51S (9 sides 78 rpm, last side blank) and DB 8695S-99 (9 sides 78 rpm automatic couplings, first side blank). G Nov. 1940 ~ USA: Victor 7884-8 in Set M 192. [Op. 34 No. 14 arr. for orchestra.] I 1946 ~ Pearl Compact Disc GEMM CDS 9044 (two-disc set, mono). [Opp. 47, 60, and 34 No. 14.] I Nov. 1993, G Jan. 1994.

USA: Columbia 11622-5D in Set M 472 (8 sides 78 rpm). Cleveland Orchestra, Artur RODZINSKI. P 14 Apr. 1941. *Reissued:* Columbia LOX 558-61 (8 sides 78 rpm.) ~ USA: Columbia ML 4101 (mono). [No coupling.] ~ USA: Columbia ML 4881 (mono). [Sibelius.] I 1954 ~ France: Philips A 01179L (mono). [Sibelius.] ~ USA: Columbia Special Products P 14142 (electronic stereo) [No coupling.] ~ USA: Columbia Special Products P 14191 (electronic stereo). [Sibelius.] I 1977 ~ USA: Cleveland Orchestra 75th Anniversary Compact Disc Edition TC 093-75 (second of ten-disc set). [Rimsky-Korsakov.] I Oct. 1993, G Jan. 1995 ~ France: LYS Compact Disc 139 (mono). ['L'Héritage d'Artur Rodzinski, Vol. 1'—Op. 47.] I Mar. 1997.

USA: RCA LM 6711 (transfer from radio broadcast, 1 side in five-record set, mono). NBC Symphony Orchestra, Arturo TOSCANINI. [Op. 60; Haydn, L. Mozart, Brahms, and Sibelius.] P 12 Mar. 1944, I 1967. *Reissued:* RCA Victrola VICS 6038 1-2 (1 side in double album, electronic stereo). [Op. 60.] G July 1970 ~ USSR: Melodiya D 034359-62 (1 side in double album, mono). [Op. 60.] I 1974 ~ Italy: RCA AT 205 (2), Toscanini Edition 47 (1 side in double album, mono). [Op. 60.] I Sept. 1974 ~ Italy: Memories Compact Disc HR 4183 (mono). [Op. 60.] I 1991 ~ RCA Victor Gold Seal Compact Disc GD 60323, Toscanini Edition 28 (mono). [Prokofiev, Glinka, Lyadov, and Stravinsky.] I July 1992, G Nov. 1992.

USSR: MK HD 2689-90 (10" transfer from 78 rpm, mono). All-Union Radio Symphony Orchestra, Constantin SILVESTRI. P 1951, I 1956. *Reissued:* USSR: MK HD 03808-9 (12" mono) [?] I 1957 ~ USA: Monitor MC 2077 (mono) and MCS 2077 (electronic stereo). [Khrennikov.] I *c.* 1965 ~ USSR: M 10 36697-8 (mono). [Britten.] Restored 1974, I 1975.

USSR: 020617-24 (8 sides 78 rpm). Bolshoi Theatre Orchestra, Kirill KONDRASHIN. P 1951. *Reissued:* USSR: MK HD 0408-9 (mono). I 1952 ~ Monarch MLW 318 (mono.). G Jan. 1955 ~ France: Le Chant du Monde LDA 8044 (mono) ~ USA: Vanguard VRS 6030-1 (1 side in two-record set). [Op. 60.] I 1958 ~ USSR: MK D 11129-30 (10" mono). I 1962.

USA: Urania URLP 7128 (mono). Leipzig Radio Symphony Orchestra, Gerhard PFLÜGER. [Op. 70.] P 1954.

USA: Westminster WL 5319 (mono). National Symphony Orchestra of Washington, Howard MITCHELL. [Op. 22a.] P Dec. 1953. *Reissued:* Nixa WLP 5319 (mono). [Op. 22a.] G Mar. 1955 ~ USA: Decca XWM 18293 (mono). [Op. 22a.] I Dec. 1956 ~ MCA Millennium Classics Compact Disc MCD 80112 (mono). [Op. 47.] G Jan. 1997.

Columbia 33 CX 1440 (mono). French National Radio Orchestra, Igor MARKEVITCH. [Prokofiev.] P *c.*1956, G May 1957. *Reissued:* USA: Angel 35361 (mono). [Prokofiev.] I 1957 ~ Music for Pleasure MFP 2080 (mono). [Prokofiev.] G Nov. 1967 ~ France: Columbia FC 1042 (10" mono) ~ EMI Compact Discs CZS5 69212-2 (four-disc set). ['Les introuvables d'Igor Markevitch'—R. Strauss, Bach, Haydn *et al.*] G Mar. 1996.

USA: Columbia ML 5152 (mono). St Louis Symphony Orchestra, Vladimir GOLSCHMANN. [Kabalevsky.] I 1956. *Reissued:* Philips ABL 3176 (mono). [Kabalevsky.] G July 1957.

Pye CCL 30105 (mono). National Youth Orchestra of Great Britain, Walter SUSSKIND. [Bizet and Elgar.] P Colston Hall, Bristol Jan. 1957, G June 1957.

HMV ALP 1554 (mono). Philharmonia Orchestra, Efrem KURTZ. [Prokofiev.] P 4 Mar. 1957, G Mar. 1958. *Reissued:* USA: Capitol G 7118 (mono). [Prokofiev.] I 1958 ~ HMV ASD 263. [Prokofiev.] G Jan. 1959 ~ Italy: Voce del Padrone QALP 10279 (mono) and ASDQ 5269. [Prokofiev.] ~ World Record Club ST 995. [Prokofiev.] G Sept. 1970 ~ Classics for Pleasure CFP 40004. [Prokofiev.] G Sept 1974 ~ USA: Seraphim S 60330. [Prokofiev.] I 1979 ~ EMI Classics Compact Discs CZS7 67729-2 (two-disc set). ['Kurtz Profile'—Prokofiev, Glinka, Kabalevsky *et al.*] I July 1993, G Sept. 1993.

RCA Red Seal RB 16170 (mono) and SB 2051. London Symphony Orchestra, Jean MARTINON. [Op. 22*a*.] P 9–11 Dec. 1957, G Dec. 1959. *Reissued:* USA: RCA Victor LM 2322 (mono) and LSC 2322. [Op. 22*a*.] I 1959 ~ France: RCA Choc 400 298 (mono). [Op. 22*a*.] ~ RCA Victrola VIC 1184 (mono) and VICS 1184. [Op. 22*a*.] G July 1967 ~ Decca Eclipse ECS 580. [Op. 22*a*.] G Feb. 1971 ~ USA: London STS 15180. [Op. 22*a*.]. ~ Germany: Audiophile/RCA Victor LSC 2322. [Op. 22*a*.] I limited LP reissue on 180g. vinyl 1995.

USA: United Artists UAL 7004 (mono) and UAS 8004. Symphony of the Air, Leopold STOKOWSKI. [Op. 34 No. 14 and Op. 29 Entr'acte.] P New York 15–19 Dec. 1958. *Reissued:* Japan: King Records K18C 9333. [As USA release.] I 1982 ~ USA: EMI Classics Compact Discs ZDMB5 6542723 (in two-disc set). [Op. 34 No. 14 and Op. 29 Entr'acte; Respighi, Khachaturyan, Bloch *et al.*] I Nov. 1994.

Columbia C 90541 (mono). French National Symphony Orchestra; André CLUYTENS. [Prokofiev.] I *c*.Aug. 1959.

USA: Columbia ML 5452 (mono) and MS 6124. Philadelphia Orchestra, Eugene ORMANDY. [Op. 107.] P 8 Nov. 1959. *Reissued:* Philips ABL 3315 (mono) and SABL 165. [Op. 107.] G July 1960 ~ CBS BRC 72081 (mono) and SBRC 72081 (NB. Numbered 75081 on continental issues). [Op. 107.] G Sept. 1960 ~ Sony Classical Compact Disc SBK 62642. [Opp. 22, 96, 97, 105, and Sans op. P.] G June 1997.

East Germany: Eterna 720 188 (10" mono). Leipzig Radio Symphony Orchestra, Herbert KEGEL. P 13–17 Nov. 1962, I 1964. *Reissued:* East Germany: Eterna 8 20 675-6 (1 side in double album, mono). [Op. 103.] I 1965 ~ Germany: Berlin Classics Compact Disc 0031702 BC. [Op. 29.] I 1996 ~ Edel Classics Compact Disc 0001842 CCC. [Op. 35.] I 2001.

USSR: Melodiya M10 47571 008 (mono). Isaak Zhuk (violin), USSR Symphony Orchestra, Igor MARKEVITCH. [Glinka, Tchaikovsky, and Borodin.] P Moscow concert 28 Feb. 1963, I 1987*d*.

Czech: Supraphon SUA 10576 (mono) and SUA ST 50576. Czech Philharmonic Orchestra, Karel ANČERL. [Op. 96.] P Prague 7–10 Apr. 1964, G Nov. 1965. *Reissued:* Czech: Supraphon Crystal Compact Disc SUP 006072. [Musorgsky.] I Sept. 1989 ~ Czech: Supraphon Compact Disc 11 1951-2. [Op. 47.] I May 1994 ~ Japan: Denon Compact Disc COCO 78419. [Op. 47.] I Mar. 1995.

USA: Turnabout TV 34223. Zagreb Philharmonic Orchestra, Milan HORVAT. [Op. 70.] P *c*.1965. *Reissued:* France: Philips 836 943 DSY. [Op. 70.] ~ Netherlands: Philips A 02319 L (mono) and 835 194 AY. [Prokofiev.]

Netherlands: Philips 698 061 CL (mono) and 875 044 FY. Vienna Symphony Orchestra, Witold ROWICKI. [Prokofiev.] P 1965. *Reissued:* Philips Compact Disc 446 571-2PM. [Op. 47.] I Sept. 1996.

USSR: Melodiya C10 12543-4. USSR Symphony Orchestra, Yevgeni SVETLANOV. [Svetlanov.] P Moscow concert 30 Dec. 1968, I 1980*b*. *Re-*

issued: USA: Russian Disc Compact Disc RDCD 11 188. [Op. 47.] I Sept. 1993, G Jan. 1994. NB. P date given incorrectly as 30 Dec. 1966.

USA: Command CCSD 11042 (2 sides). Pittsburgh Symphony Orchestra, William STEINBERG. P 1970.

BBC Radio Classics Compact Disc 15656 91542. Royal Philharmonic Orchestra. Jascha HORENSTEIN. [Op. 47.] P Albert Hall, Nottingham concert 18 July 1970, I Mar. 1996, G May 1996.

USSR: Melodiya CM 02581-2. Moscow Radio Symphony Orchestra, Yuri ARANOVICH. [Op. 115.] P 1971, apparently not issued in USSR. *Reissued:* HMV Melodiya ASD 2765. [Prokofiev.] G Apr. 1972 ~ France: Le Chant du Monde LDX 78515 K. [Op. 115.] ~ USA: Angel Melodiya S 40192. [Op. 115.] I 1972.

Decca SXL 6563. Suisse Romande Orchestra, Walter WELLER. [Op. 70.] P 4–6 Sept. 1971, G Jan. 1973. *Reissued:* USA: London 6787. [Op. 70.]

USA: Columbia M 31307. New York Philharmonic Orchestra, Leonard BERNSTEIN. [Op. 70.] P 14 Dec. 1971. *Reissued:* CBS 73050. [Op. 70.] G Dec. 1974 ~ CBS Masterworks 60284. [Op. 107.] G Jan. 1984 ~ Sony Royal Edition Compact Disc SMK 47614. [Op. 54.] G Nov. 1993 and June 1994 ~ Sony Classical Compact Discs SX4K 64206 (four-disc set). [Op. 54.] I Dec. 1995.

USSR: Melodiya CM 03625-6. Moscow Philharmonic Orchestra, Kirill KONDRASHIN. [Op. 14.] P 1972, I 1973. *Reissued:* USA: Angel Melodiya SR 40236. [Op. 14.] I 1973 ~ Germany: Melodia Eurodisc 87 623 XPK (in thirteen-record box set). I 1974 ~ HMV Melodiya BOX 502501 in Set SLS 5025. [Opp. 14 and 27*a* excerpts.] G Dec. 1975 ~ Germany: Melodia Eurodisc 300 594 in Set 300 597-435. [Op. 14.] ~ USSR: Melodiya CM 03625-6. [In first box of Part 1 of *Collected Works on Records* with Op. 14.] I 1980 ~ USA: Musical Heritage Society MHS 824958 Z. [In two-record set with Opp. 14 and 43.] I 1984 ~ HMV Melodiya EX 2903873 (DMM). [On first record in twelve-record box set with Op. 70.] G Dec. 1985 ~ France: Le Chant du Monde Compact Disc LDC 278 1001-2. [In Box 1 of five two-disc sets with Opp. 14, 20, and 43.] G May 1989 ~ BMG Classics Melodiya Compact Disc 74321 19848-2. [Op. 112.] I July 1994, G Nov. 1994.

Italy: Originals Compact Disc SH 863. Danish Radio Symphony Orchestra, Sergiu CELIBIDACHE. ['The Unpublished Celibidache'—Sibelius.] P concert 1973, I Oct. 1995.

Czech: Panton 11 0604 H. Czech Philharmonic Orchestra, Jiří KOUT. [Op. 145.] P Prague 1976, G Dec. 1977.

Germany: Stadt Gelsenkirchen F 666 494 (two-record box set). Gelsenkirchen Municipal Orchestra, Uwe MUND. [Mozart and Verdi.] P 1977–79.

USA: Vox Cum Laude 9003. Cincinnati Symphony Orchestra, Walter SUSSKIND. [Op. 70.] I 1981. *Reissued:* USA: Voxbox Compact Discs CDX

5139 (two-disc set). [Op. 70; Tchaikovsky, Mendelssohn, and Liszt.] I June 1995.

Decca SXDL 7515 (digital). London Philharmonic Orchestra, Bernard HAITINK. [Op. 70.] P Jan. 1979, G May 1981. *Reissued:* USA: London LDR 71017 (digital). [Op. 70.] I 1981 ~ France: Decca 591058 (digital). [Op. 70.] I 1981 ~ Decca Compact Disc 414 677-2DH. [Op. 70.] G June 1986 and Feb. 1988 ~ Decca Ovation Compact Disc 425 063-2DM. [Op. 20.] I Aug. 1993, G Nov. 1993 ~ London Compact Disc 444 431-2. [On first disc of eleven-disc set with Op. 20.] I June 1995.

USSR: Melodiya C10 30485 002. USSR Symphony Orchestra, Gavriil YUDIN. [Op. 70.] P Moscow concert 1 Feb. 1980, I 1990*d*.

East Germany: Eterna 7 29 221 (DMM). Berlin City Symphony Orchestra, Kurt SANDERLING. [Op. 70.] P 8–10 June 1983. *Reissued:* Germany: Berlin Classics Compact Disc 0021812 BC. [Op. 54.] I Jan. 1995.

USSR: Melodiya A10 00101 005 (digital). USSR Ministry of Culture Symphony Orchestra, Gennadi ROZHDESTVENSKY. P 1984, I 1985*d*. *Reissued:* Japan: Victor Compact Disc JVC 1013. [Op. 70.] I 1985 ~ Olympia Compact Disc OCD 161. [Op. 20.] I Nov. 1988, G May 1989 ~ Germany: Melodia Eurodisc Compact Disc 258483. [Op. 14.] ~ USSR: Melodiya Compact Disc SUCD 10 00103. [Op. 20.] I *c*.1990 ~ Olympia Compact Disc OCD 5005. [In Vol. 1 six-disc set of symphonies with Op. 20.] I Dec. 1990 ~ BMG Melodiya Compact Discs 74321 49611-2 (two-disc set). [Opp. 47, 54, and 70.] I Dec. 1997.

Chandos ABRD 1148 (digital). Scottish National Orchestra, Neeme JÄRVI. [Op. 54.] P Glasgow 1 Aug. 1984, G Apr. 1986. *Simultaneous issue:* Chandos Compact Disc CHAN 8411. [Op. 54.] G June 1986 and Feb. 1988.

USA: Sheffield Labs TDC 26 (digital) and Compact Disc CD 26. Moscow Philharmonic Orchestra, Lawrence Leighton SMITH. ['The Moscow Sessions'—first recording of an American leading a Soviet orchestra—Barber and Piston.] P Moscow 9–18 Aug. 1986, I 1987, G Feb. 1988.

Naxos Compact Disc 8.550623. Czecho-Slovak Radio Symphony Orchestra, Ladislav SLOVÁK. [Op. 20.] P Bratislava 20–5 Nov. 1986, I Jan. 1993, G Nov. 1993 ~ Naxos Compact Discs 8.505017. [In five-disc set with Symphonies Nos. 2, 3, 4, 6, 7, 12, and 15.] I 1993.

BBC Records REN 637X (digital) and Compact Disc CD 637X. BBC Welsh Symphony Orchestra, Mariss JANSONS. [Op. 96.] P Swansea Nov. 1986, G Aug. 1987 and Feb. 1988.

Canada: Canadian Broadcasting Corporation Compact Disc SMCD 5074.Vancouver Symphony Orchestra, Rudolf BARSHAI. [Op. 70.] P not stated, I 1988.

Deutsche Grammophon Compact Disc 427 632-2GH2 (two-disc set). Chicago Symphony Orchestra, Leonard BERNSTEIN. [Op. 60.] P Chicago concert June 1988, I Oct. 1989, G Jan. 1990.

Decca Compact Disc 425 609-2DH. Royal Philharmonic Orchestra, Vladimir ASHKENAZY. [Op. 54.] P Walthamstow Nov. 1988, I Apr. 1990, G June 1990.

USA: Arabesque Compact Disc Z 6610. Kraków Philharmonic Orchestra, Gilbert LEVINE. [Opp. 35 and 22*a*.] P Kraków 26–9 May 1989, G Jan. 1990.

Spain: Cepsa Line Compact Disc CACD 9 00804 P. Orquesta Sinfónica de Tenerife, Victor Pablo PÉREZ. ['Festival de Musica de Canarias'— Prokofiev.] P Tenerife concert 29 Jan. 1990. *Reissued:* Germany: Arte Nova Classics Compact Disc 74321 27806-2. [Prokofiev.] I Feb. 1997.

Collins Classics Compact Disc 1192-2. English Chamber Orchestra, Steuart BEDFORD. [Britten.] P London June–July 1990, I July 1991, G Apr. 1992.

Decca Compact Disc 436 469-2DH. Royal Concertgebouw Orchestra, Georg SOLTI. [Stravinsky.] P Amsterdam concert 18–21 Sept. 1991, I Sept. 1992. *Reissued:* Decca Digital Compact Cassette 436 469-5DH. [Stravinsky.] I Mar. 1993.

Austria: Musica Classica Compact Disc 780003-2. Moscow Radio Symphony Orchestra, Vladimir FEDOSEYEV. [Op. 54.] P Bratislava Jan. 1992, I Jan. 1996.

Decca Compact Disc 436 838-2DH. Montreal Symphony Orchestra, Charles DUTOIT. [Op. 141.] P Montreal 15–22 May 1992, I May 1994, G Oct. 1994.

Denon Compact Disc CO 78948. Vienna Symphony Orchestra, Eliahu INBAL. [Op. 141.] P 12–15 Oct. 1992, I July 1995, G Dec. 1995.

Teldec Compact Disc 4509 90849-2. National Symphony Orchestra of Washington, Mstislav ROSTROPOVICH. [Op. 70.] P Jan. 1993, I Apr. 1994, G Oct. 1994. *Reissued:* Teldec Compact Discs 0630-17046-2. [In twelve-disc set of Symphonies.] G Oct. 1997.

EMI Classics Compact Disc CDC5 55361-2. Berlin Philharmonic Orchestra, Mariss JANSONS. [Op. 35.] P Berlin 15–20 June 1994, I Oct. 1995, G Dec. 1995.

RCA Red Seal Compact Disc 09026 68844-2. St Petersburg Philharmonic Orchestra, Yuri TEMIRKANOV. [Opp. 96 and 54.] P St Petersburg 3–4 Jan. 1996, I July 1999.

Japan: Canyon Classics Compact Disc PCCL 00351. Moscow Radio Symphony Orchestra, Vladimir FEDOSEYEV. [Op. 141.] P 15 Apr. 1996.

Telarc Compact Disc CD 80572. Cincinnati Symphony Orchestra, Jesús LÓPEZ-COBOS. [Op. 141.] P Cincinnati 24–5 Sept. 2000, I Aug. 2001, G Oct. 2001.

References: Hughes, Khubov, Sabinina, and Tigranov.

Notes: André Previn states in his autobiography *No Minor Chords* (Doubleday, 1992) that he made a 'completely bizarre brass band [actually for concert band] transcription' *c.* 1951

The Temirkanov 1996 recording respects Shostakovich's later rejection of the side drum crescendo into the last movement as 'a somewhat vulgar effect'.

Opus 11   Prelude and Scherzo

Form: Two pieces for string octet (double string quartet):

1. Prelude in D minor—Adagio
2. Scherzo in G minor—Allegro molto—Moderato—Allegro

Composed: (1) December 1924, at Leningrad; (2) July 1925, at Oranienbaum Slavyansk (west of Leningrad)—now renamed Lomonosov.

Dedication: To the memory of Volodya I. Kurchavov (poet friend).

Premières: 9 January 1927, Stanislavsky Art Theatre Mozart Hall, Moscow; combined Glière and Stradivari Quartets (Yakov and A. Targonsky, A. Vabich, K. Blok/Boris Simsky, Boris Vitkin, Grigori Gamburg, Viktor Kubatsky).

Scotland: 28 August 1962, Edinburgh Usher Hall; members of the Polish Radio Symphony Orchestra, Jan Krenz.

Arrangements: Parts augmented for string orchestra, including a version with double-basses by Lazar Gozman. The Scherzo transcribed for two pianos eight hands by Ed de Boer in 1981.

Music: Rough and clean autograph copies of the two pieces preserved at the CIS Archives of Literature and Art. The former contains drafts for a third piece—a Fugue.

Muzgiz, No. 7902, 1928, 27.5 cm.

Universal Edition, No. 9055, 1928, 27.5 cm.

Leeds Music, *c.*1946, 22 cm.

Soyuz Sovetskikh Kompozitorov, 1947, 28 cm.

Edition Musicus, *c.* 1947, Prelude arr. for string orchestra by Quinto Maganini, 27 cm.

Boosey & Hawkes, No. 603 (A.S.M.P. No. 29), *c.*1950, 19 cm.

Muzyka, 1967, score and parts.

Muzyka, No. 10794 (in Volume 37 of *Collected Works* with Opp. 8, 57, and 67), 1983, 30 cm.

Hans Sikorski, No. 2269, 1998, score, 29.5 cm.

Hans Sikorski, No. 2270, 1998, parts, 29.5 cm.

Duration: (1) 4' 55"–6' 25" and (2) 3' 45"–4' 45"; approx. 10 minutes in score; 10' 40" (Plaistow).

Recordings: USA: General Timely 1300A (78 rpm). New York String Orchestra, Max GOBERMAN. P prior to 1950.

USA: Columbia ML 2121 (10" mono). Stuyvesant Sinfonietta, Sylvan SHULMAN. ['Modern Music for Strings'—Bartók, Rakhmaninov, Shulman, and Hindemith.] P 1950.

USA: MGM E 3684 (mono). Members of the MGM Studio Orchestra (Max Hollander, Leonard Posner, Paul Gershman, Paul Bellams; Emanual Vardi, Walter Trampler; Charles McCracken, Claus Adam), Arthur WINOGRAD. [Prokofiev, Bartók, and Stravinsky.] I 1959.

Oriole Eurodisc SMG 20097. London Soloists' Ensemble, Nicholas ROTH. [Vivaldi, W. F. Bach, and Salzedo.] G July and Dec. 1964.

USSR: Melodiya D 019519-20 (mono) and C 01459-60. BORODIN and PROKOFIEV QUARTETS (Rostislav Dubinsky, Yaroslav Aleksandrov, Dmitri Shebalin, Valentin Berlinsky/Ella Brakker, Nadezhda Baikova, Galina Odinets, Kira Tsvetkova). [Opp. 117 and 122.] P 1964, I 1967. *Reissued:* USA: Seraphim Melodiya S 6035. [In three-record box set with Quartets Nos. 6–11.] ~ HMV Melodiya ASD 3072. [Op. 57 and Stravinsky.] G May 1975 ~ East Germany: Eterna 8 26 598. [Opp. 117 and 112.] ~ BMG Melodiya Compact Discs 74321 40711-2 (six-disc set). [Opp. 73 and 57.] I June 1997 ~ BMG Melodiya Compact Disc 74321 40713-2. [Opp. 57 and 73.] I Dec. 1997.

Philips Vanguard VSL 11025. Scherzo only, arr. for string orchestra. I Solisti di Zagreb, Antonio JANIGRO. [Hindemith, Kelemen, Roussel, and Webern.] G July 1968. *Reissued:* Imp Classics Compact Disc 30367 0228-2. [Bartók.] I Sept. 1997.

USSR: Melodiya D 025115-6 (mono) and C 01769-70. BEETHOVEN and KOMITAS QUARTETS (Dmitri Tsyganov, Nikolai Zabavnikov, Fyodor Druzhinin, Sergei Shirinsky/Avet Gabrielyan, Rafael Davidyan, Genrikh Talalyan, Armen Georgian). [Opp. 122 and 133.] P 1969, G Oct. 1971. *Reissued:* France: EMI 061 91298. [Opp. 122 and 133.]

USSR: Melodiya C10 05191-2. Arr. for string orchestra. Kiev Chamber Orchestra, Igor BLAZHKOV. [Op. 42 and Britten.] P 1974, I 1975c.

USSR: Melodiya C10 09181-2. BORODIN and GNESSIN INSTITUTE QUARTETS (Mikhail Kopelman, Andrei Abramenkov, Dmitri Shebalin, Valentin Berlinsky/Yevgeniya Alikhanova, Valentina Alykova, Tatyana Kokhanovskaya, Marina Yanushevskaya). [In second box of Part 2 of *Collected Works on Records* with Op. 57.] P 1977, I 1978.

Czech: Panton 8111 0195 G. SUK and DOLEŽAL QUARTETS (Ivan Štraus, Voitěch Jouza, Karel Řehák, Jan Štros/Bohuslav Matoušek, Josef Kekula, Karel Doležal, Vladimir Leiner). [Op. 144.] P Prague 1981.

Germany: ECM New Series 1-25037 (two-record set). HAGEN QUARTET (Lukas Hagen, Annette Bik, Veronika Hagen, Clemens Hagen) with Thomas Zehetmair, Daniel Phillips, Hatto Beyerle, and Markus Stocker. [Sans op. P; Caplet, Franck, Poulenc *et al.*] P Lockenhaus Festival concert 1984. *Reissued:* Germany: ECM New Series Compact Discs 827 024-2 (two-disc set). [As LPs.]

Germany: Schwann Musica Mundi VMS 1046 (DMM). DORNBUSCH and BUCHBERGER QUARTETS (personnel not stated). [Glière.] P 1985.

USA: Musicmasters MMD 20109Z (digital). Arr. Gozman. Soviet Émigré Orchestra. Lazar GOZMAN. [Op. 110; and Tchaikovsky.] P 1986. *Reissued:* Olympia Compact Disc OCD 196. [Op. 110; and Tchaikovsky.] I June 1988, G Aug. 1989.

Nimbus Compact Disc NI 5140. MEDICI and ALBERNI QUARTETS (Paul Robertson, David Matthews, Ivo-Jan van der Werff, Anthony Lewis/Howard Davis, Peter Pople, Roger Best, David Smith). [Sans op. D; Mendelssohn.] P 10 May 1988, I Oct. 1988.

Pickwick IMP Classics Compact Disc PCD 1000. Scherzo only, arr. for string orchestra. I Solisti di Zagreb, Tonko NINIC. [Op. 110*a*; and Bartók.] P Zagreb 22–8 June 1991, G Nov. 1992. *Reissued:* Carlton Classics Compact Disc 30367 02282. [Op. 110*a*; and Bartók.]

RCA Victor Compact Disc 09026 61189-2. Arr. for string orchestra. Moscow Virtuosi, Vladimir SPIVAKOV. [Sans op. D; Schnittke and Shchedrin.] P Munich 10–13 Dec. 1991, I Apr. 1998.

Chandos Compact Disc CHAN 9131. ACADEMY OF ST MARTIN-IN-THE-FIELDS CHAMBER ENSEMBLE (Kenneth Sillito, Malcolm Latchem, Josef Frohlich, Robert Heard; Robert Smissen, Stephen Tees; Stephen Orton, Roger Smith). [Enescu and R. Strauss.] P Snape, Suffolk Mar. 1992, I Jan. 1993, G May 1993.

France: Forlane Compact Disc UCD 16693. Scherzo only, arr. for string orchestra. Moscow Conservatory Orchestra, Yuri BASHMET. [Op. 35; Tchaikovsky; Chopin, Haydn *et al.*] P concert 1992, I 1993.

Germany: Pink Compact Disc 10294. SUDDEUTSCHES STREICHOKTETT. [Gade and Svendsen.] P Winterbach, Germany 1993.

Sweden: Intim Musik Compact Disc IMCD 041. CAMERATA ROMANA. [Elgar and Rangström.] P Småland 24 Jan. 1996.

USA: New Albion Compact Disc NA 08B CD. New Century Chamber Orchestra, Stuart CANIN. ['Written with the Heart's Blood'—Opp. 110*a* and 118*a*.] P Tiburon, California Apr. 1996, I Jan. 1997.

France: Suoni e Colori Collection Compact Disc SC 53006. Ricercata de Paris Ensemble, Alexandre BRUSSILOVSKY. ['DSCH Aphorismes'— Opp. 34, 68, 13, Sans op. D; Schnittke—*Prelude in Memory of Shostakovich,* and Steven Gerber—*Elegy on the name 'Dmitri Shostakovich'.*] P Hautes-Alpes, France concert Aug. 1996, I 1997.

Korea: Sony Classical Compact Disc CCK 7772. Korean Chamber Ensemble, Min KIM. [Britten and Grieg.] P Seoul 7–13 Feb. 1998.

Linn Records Compact Disc CKD 095. BT Scottish Ensemble, Clio GOULD. [Opp. 110*a* and 35.] P Glasgow 4–5 Mar. 1998, I Feb. 2000, G June 2000.

France: Syrius Compact Disc SYR 141345. European Camerata, Laurent QUÉNELLE. [Op. 110; and Honegger.] P Alpes-Maritimes, France Aug. 1998.

Opus 12   Piano Sonata No. 1

Alternative titles: Originally known as 'October' and 'October Symphony' (Ilya Ehrenburg quoting Maksimilian Shteinberg—see Schwarz (1972), pp. 79–80).

Form: Sonata for solo piano in one movement, marked 'Allegro—Lento—Allegro'.

Composed: September–October 1926, at Leningrad.

Premières: 12 December 1926, Leningrad Philharmonic Malyi Hall and 9 January 1927, Stanislavsky Art Theatre Mozart Hall, Moscow; Dmitri Shostakovich.

Music: Autograph score preserved at the USSR Archives of Literature and Art.

Muzgiz, No. 7374, 1927, 38 cm. (and same no. with added metronome marks), 1935, 29 cm.

Edwin F. Kalmus, 1940, 31 cm.

Boosey & Hawkes, A.S.M.P. No. 66, 1947, 31 cm.

Muzgiz, No. 3184 (in *D. Shostakovich: Compositions for fortepiano*, Volume 1, with Sans op. B, Opp. 5, 13, 22a Polka, 34, and 61), 1966, 29 cm.

Edition Peters, No. 5706, 1968, 30 cm.

Edwin F. Kalmus, No. 896 (with Opp. 5 and 87 Nos. 1–12), no date, 18 cm.

Muzyka, No. 7775 (with Op. 61), 1973, 29 cm.

Hans Sikorski, No. 2187, 1975, 31.5 cm.

Muzyka, No. 10285 (in Volume 39 of *Collected Works* with Opp. 5, 13, 34, 61, 69, and supplement of unnumbered piano pieces), 1983, 30 cm.

Duration: Approx. 13 minutes in score; 10' 22"–15' 37".

Recordings: USSR: Melodiya D 025805-6 (mono). Anatoli VEDERNIKOV. [Skryabin, Haydn, and Liszt.] P 1969. *Reissued:* USSR: Melodiya C10 09547-8. [In second box of Part 2 of *Collected Works on Records* with Op. 61.] I 1978.

USA: Orion ORS 6915. Vladimir PLESHAKOV. [Opp. 5 and 13, Sans op. B; and Prokofiev.] P 1969.

Netherlands: BV Haast 025. Geoffrey MADGE. [Lourié, Mosolov, and Roslavets.] P Amsterdam Oct. 1978. *Reissued:* Netherlands; BV Haast Compact Disc CD 9602. [Mosolov and Roslavets.] I Mar. 1997.

USSR: Melodiya C10 17985-6. Viktoria POSTNIKOVA. [Op. 61.] P 1982, I 1983b.

USSR: Melodiya C10 18977 007. Igor KHUDOLEI. [Op. 61.] P 1982, I 1983d.

AVM Classics AVM 1003 and Compact Disc AVMCD 1003. Labelled as 'October Symphony'. Martin JONES. [Opp. 61 and 5; Sans opp. B and S.] P not stated, G Oct. 1988.

Italy: Nuova Era Compact Disc 6757. Lilya ZILBERSTEIN. ['Winner of the 1987 Busoni International Piano Competition'—Brahms, Taneyev, Schubert *et al.*] P concert 1987, I 1989.

USSR: Melodiya C10 30205. Oleg VOLKOV. [Op. 13 and 87; Skryabin.] P 1987, I 1991.

France: Accord Compact Disc 20025-2. Caroline WEICHERT. [Opp. 5 and 61.] P Jan. 1988, I 1988, G June 1990.

Deutsche Grammophon Compact Disc 427 766-2GH. Lilya ZILBER-STEIN. [Rakhmaninov.] P Berlin Nov. 1988, I Oct. 1989, G Dec. 1989.

France: Le Chant du Monde Compact Disc LDC 278 1012. Elena VAR-VAROVA. [Opp. 5, 61, and 13.] P Paris Sept. 1989, I Feb. 1990.

Olympia Compact Disc OCD 574. Colin STONE. [Opp. 34, 61, and Sans op. B.] P London Sept. 1995, I Mar. 1996, G June 1996. *Reissued:* Brilliant Classics Compact Discs 6137 (five-disc set). ['Complete Piano Sonatas' op. 61; Prokofiev and Skryabin.] I May 2000.

Athene-Minerva Compact Disc ATH CD18. Raymond CLARKE. [Opp. 34, 61; and 87.] P Nottingham University 7 Jan. and 7 Sept. 1998, I May 1999, G Oct. 1999.

Australia: ABC Classics Compact Disc 461 651-2 (two-disc set). Ayako UESHARA. ['Sydney International Piano Competition 2000, Vol. 1, Solo Highlights'—Granados, Ravel, Liszt *et al.*] P 29 June–9 July 2000.

Opus 13　Aphorisms

Form:　Ten miniatures for piano:

1.	Recitative	$\quad\downarrow = 104$
2.	Serenade	$\quad\downarrow = 208$ sempre $\downarrow = \downarrow$
3.	Nocturne	$\quad\downarrow = 92$
4.	Elegy	$\quad\downarrow = 44$
5.	Marche Funèbre	$\quad\downarrow = 152$
6.	Étude	$\quad\downarrow = 88$
7.	Dance of Death	$\quad\downarrow. = 132–144$
8.	Canon	$\quad\downarrow = 144$
9.	Legend	$\quad\downarrow = 116$
10.	Lullaby	$\quad\downarrow = 63$

Composed:　25 February–7 April 1927, at Leningrad.

Première:　Autumn 1927, Leningrad; Dmitri Shostakovich.

Arrangements:　Transcription for violin, bassoon, piano, and percussion made in 1971 by Boris Bekhterev and Vladimir Spivakov. Transcription of No. 10 for violin and piano by Sergei Sapozhnikov.

Music:　The autograph score was presented on 6 May 1927 to the composer Boleslav Yavorsky, who had suggested the general title *Aphorisms,* with the inscription 'To dear Boleslav Leopoldovich Yavorsky from Shostakovich with love'. The complete score is preserved at the Glinka

Museum. Another autograph copy of the first four pieces, which is subtitled 'Suite', preserved at the CIS Archives of Literature and Art.

Triton, Leningrad, 1927.

Muzgiz, No. 3184 (in *D. Shostakovich: Compositions for fortepiano*, Volume 1, with Sans op. B, Opp. 5, 12, 22*a* Polka, 34, and 61), 1966, 29 cm.

Hans Sikorski, No. 2183, *c*.1966, 32 cm.

MCA, 1968, 31 cm.

Edition Peters, No. 5717 (plate no. 12524 with Op. 5 and Sans op. B), 1970, 30 cm.

Le Chant du Monde, no number, 1970, 32 cm.

Sovetskii Kompozitor, No. 3087, 1974, No. 10 only in *Russian works for violin and piano,* arr. by S. Sapozhnikov, 28.5 cm.

G. Schirmer, No. 3041, 1976, VAAP authorized edition, ed. Joseph Prostakoff, 30.5 cm.

Sovetskii Kompozitor, No. 3988, 1977, transcription for violin, bassoon, piano, and percussion, score and parts, 29 cm.

Muzyka, No. 10285 (in Volume 39 of *Collected Works* with Opp. 5, 12, 34, 61, 69, and supplement of unnumbered piano pieces), 1983, 30 cm.

Duration: 12' 00"–14' 51"; transcription 13' 30"–14' 44".

Recordings: USA: Orion ORS 6915. Vladimir PLESHAKOV. [Opp. 5 and 12, Sans op. B; and Prokofiev.] P 1969.

USSR: Melodiya CM 03945-6. Transcription. Vladimir SPIVAKOV (violin), Valeri Popov (bassoon), Boris Bekhterev (piano), and Valentin Snegiryov (percussion). [Corelli and Mozart.] P 1971, I 1973.

Bulgaria: Balkanton BKA 1767. Zheni ZAHARIEVA. [Schumann and Brahms.] P early 1980s.

USSR: Melodiya C10 30205. Oleg VOLKOV. [Opp. 12 and 87; Skryabin.] P 1987, I 1991. *Reissued:* Brioso Compact Disc BR 105. ['All Russian'— Op. 87; Borodin *et al.* and Skryabin.] I Feb. 1995.

AVM Classics Compact Disc AVZ 3020. Martin JONES. ['Piano Music Volume II'—Sans opp. A, S, and T; Opp. 34, 69, and 22*a*.] P London 1–2 June 1989.

France: Le Chant du Monde Compact Disc LDC 278 1012. Elena VARVAROVA. [Opp. 5, 12, and 61.] P Paris Sept. 1989, I Feb. 1990.

France: Accord Compact Disc 202812. Caroline WEICHERT. [Op. 34; Sans opp. B and S.] P Sept. 1993, I 1994.

Japan: Meldec Compact Disc MECC 28004. Transcription. Aleksandr MELNIKOV (violin), Valeri Popov (bassoon), Viktor Yampolisky (piano), and Sergei Ampleyev (percussion). [Opp. 8 and 67.] P Mosfilm Studio, Moscow 1–10 Oct. 1994, I June 1995. *Reissued:* Japan: Triton Compact Disc 17 011. [Opp. 8 and 67.] I Feb. 1997.

Italy: Nuova Era Compact Disc NE 7263. Jean-Pierre AMENGAUD. [Lourié, Skryabin, Roslavets *et al.*] P Ivrea, Italy Jan. 1995.

France: Suoni e Colori Collection Compact Disc SC 53006. Transcription. Alexandre BRUSSILOVSKY (violin), Amaury Wallez (bassoon), Paul Godart (piano), and Dominique Probst (percussion). ['DSCH Aphorismes'—Opp. 11, 34, 68, Sans op. D; Schnittke—*Prelude in Memory of Shostakovich,* and Steven Gerber—*Elegy on the name 'Dmitri Shostakovich'.*] P Hautes-Alpes, France concert Aug. 1996, I 1997.

Opus 14   Symphony No. 2 in B major

Subtitle: 'To October—a Symphonic Dedication'.

Form: Symphony in one movement, of five continuous sections, for full orchestra (plus factory siren in F sharp) and S.A.T.B. chorus: Largo, ♩ = 152, Allegro molto, Meno mosso, and choral finale setting of Aleksandr Bezymensky's poem 'To October.'

Instrumentation: piccolo, 2 flutes, 2 oboes, 2 B flat clarinets, 2 bassoons ~ 4 horns, 3 trumpets, 3 trombones, tuba ~ timpani, triangle, side drum, cymbals, bass drum ~ F sharp siren, glockenspiel ~ S.A.T.B. chorus ~ strings. The composer provides a low brass option for the four sustained blasts on the factory hooter.

Composed: April–June 1927, at Leningrad. A state commission received in late March 1927 to celebrate the tenth anniversary of the October Revolution.

Dedication: As subtitle and inscribed 'Proletarians of the World, Unite!'

Premières: 5 and 6 November 1927, Leningrad Philharmonic Bolshoi Hall; Leningrad Philharmonic Orchestra and Academy Capella Choir, Nikolai Malko.

4 December 1927, The House of the Soviets Hall of Columns, Moscow; conducted by Konstantin Saradzhev.

22 October 1969, Festival Hall, London; BBC Symphony Orchestra, Colin Davis.

Arrangements: Reduction of the choral section for voices and piano by Yuri Olenev. Translations of the poem in English by Myron Morris and Andrew Huth and in German by Jörg Morgener.

Not an arrangement though inspired by this work and *Testimony,* a pop song entitled 'My October Symphony' achieved hit status in 1990. It was written by the Pet Shop Boys duo Neil Tennant and Chris Lowe, with acoustic string quartet, electric guitar, and keyboard accompaniment.

Music: The autograph score preserved at the CIS Archives of Literature and Art.

Muzgiz, No. 7971, 1927, full score, 35 cm.

Edwin F. Kalmus, No. 1457, *c.*1970, 31 cm.

Muzyka, No. 8998, 1975, full score, 30 cm.

Hans Sikorski, No. 2225, 1984, score with Russian and German texts—the latter by J. Morgener, 21 cm.

Muzyka, No. 11688 (in Volume 9 of *Collected Works* with reductions of Opp. 113 and 135, and choral section of Op. 20), 1984, vocal score of choral section by Yuri Olenev, 30 cm.

Muzyka, No. 10713 (in Volume 1 of *Collected Works* with Op. 10), 1987, full score, 30 cm.

Duration: Approx. 20 minutes in score; 15' 25"–21' 21".

Ballet: *Second Symphony*. Igor Belsky, one-act ballet performed at the Leningrad Malyi Opera Theatre in the 1970s.

Recordings: USSR: Melodiya D 017953-4(mono). Leningrad Philharmonic Orchestra, Krupskaya Institute Chorus, Ivan Poltavtsev (chorus-master), Igor BLAZHKOV (conductor). [Op. 20.] P Leningrad concert 1 Nov. 1965. *Reissued:* USSR: Melodiya D 023831-2 (mono) and CM 01883-4. [Op. 107.] I 1968 ~ USA: Angel Melodiya SR 40099. [Op. 107.] I 1969 ~ HMV Melodiya ASD 2747. [Op. 27*a*.] G Sept. 1971 ~ Germany: Melodia Eurodisc 80528 KK. [Op. 22*a*.] and 85301 MK. [Op. 20.] ~ Italy: EMI 065 93443. [Op. 107.] I 1973 ~ USA: Russian Disc Compact Disc RDCD 11 195. [Op. 93.] I Oct. 1993, G Jan. 1994.

Czech: Supraphon SUA 10958 (mono) and ST 50958. Slovák Philharmonic Orchestra and Chorus, Ladislav SLOVÁK. [Op. 119.] P June 1967, G July 1969. *Reissued:* Czech: Opus 9110 0382. [Op. 70.]

RCA Victor Red Seal RB 6755 (mono) and SB 6755. Royal Philharmonic Orchestra and Chorus, John McCarthy (chorus-master), Igor Buketoff (chorus-director), Morton GOULD (conductor). [Op. 20.] P 1968, G Oct. 1968. *Reissued:* USA: RCA Victor LSC 3044. [Op. 20.] I 1968.

USSR: Melodiya CM 03625-6. Moscow Philharmonic Orchestra, RSFSR Academic Russian Choir, Aleksandr Yurlov (chorus-master), Kirill KONDRASHIN. [Op. 10.] P 1972, I 1973. *Reissued:* USA: Angel Melodiya SR 40236. [Op. 10.] I 1973 ~ Germany: Melodia Eurodisc 87 623 XPK. [In thirteen-record box set.] I 1974 ~ HMV Melodiya ASD 3060. [Prokofiev.] G May 1975 ~ HMV Melodiya BOX 502501 in Set SLS 5025. [Opp. 10 and 27*a* excerpts.] G Dec. 1975 ~ Germany: Melodia Eurodisc 300 594 in Set 597-435. [Op. 10.] ~ USSR: Melodiya CM 03625-6. [In first box of Part 1 of *Collected Works on Records* with Op. 10.] I 1980 ~ USA: Musical Heritage Society MHS 824958 Z. [In two-record set with Opp. 10 and 43.] I 1984 ~ HMV Melodiya EX 2903873 (DMM). [On sixth record in twelve-record box set with Opp. 60 finale and 112.] G Dec. 1985 ~ France: Le Chant du Monde Compact Disc LDC 278 1001-2. [In Box 1 of five two-disc sets with Opp. 10, 20, and 43.] G May 1989 ~ BMG Classics Melodiya Compact Disc 74321 19844-2. [Op. 135.] I July 1994, G Nov. 1994.

Decca SXDL 7535 (digital). London Philharmonic Orchestra and Choir, John Alldis (chorus-master), Bernard HAITINK. [Op. 20.] P Jan. 1981, G July 1982. *Reissued:* USA: London LDR 71035 (digital). [Op. 20.] ~ Decca Compact Disc 421 131-2DH. [Opp. 20 and 22*a*.] I Mar. 1988, G June

1988 ~ Decca Ovation Compact Disc 425 064-2DM. [Op. 93.] I Aug. 1993, G Nov. 1993 ~ London Compact Disc 444 432-2. [On second disc in eleven-disc set with Op. 93.] I June 1995.

USSR: Melodiya A10 00119 002 (one side in two-record set, digital). USSR Ministry of Culture Symphony Orchestra, Yurlov Republican Russian Choir, Rozaliya Peregudova (chorus-master), Stanislav Gusev (chorus-director), Gennadi ROZHDESTVENSKY. [Op. 65.] P 1984, I 1986*a*. *Reissued:* Olympia Compact Disc OCD 200. [Op. 112.] I Dec. 1987, G Apr. 1988 ~ Olympia Compact Disc OCD 258. [Opp. 141 and 19.] I Oct. 1989 ~ Germany: Melodia Eurodisc Compact Disc 258483. [Op. 10.] ~ Olympia Compact Disc OCD 5006. [In Volume 2 five-disc set of symphonies with Opp. 141 and 19.] I Dec. 1990 ~ BMG Melodiya Compact Discs 74321 63462-2 (two-disc set). [Opp. 20, 32, 43, and 23.] I Mar. 1999.

Decca Compact Disc 436 762-2DH. Royal Philharmonic Orchestra, Brighton Festival Chorus, Laszlo Heltay (chorus-master), Vladimir ASHKENAZY. [Opp. 96, 131, and 81.] P Walthamstow Jan. 1989, I June 1994, G Aug. 1994.

Naxos Compact Disc 8.550624. Czecho-Slovak Radio Symphony Orchestra, Ladislav SLOVÁK . [Op. 141.] P Bratislava 8–10 Jan. 1990, I Jan. 1993, G Nov. 1993. *Reissued:* Naxos Compact Discs 8.505017. [In five-disc set with Symphonies Nos. 1, 3, 4, 6, 7, 12, and 15.] I 1993.

Denon Compact Disc CO 75719. Vienna Symphony Orchestra, Chorus Viennesis—Guido Mancusi (chorus-master) and Damenchor des Wiener Singvereins—Johannes Prinz (chorus-master), Eliahu INBAL. [Op. 47.] P Vienna concert 16–18 Oct. 1992, I Apr. 1994, G Aug. 1994.

Teldec Compact Disc 4509 90853-2. London Symphony Orchestra, London Voices, Mstislav ROSTROPOVICH. [Op. 20.] P London 8–9 Feb. 1993, I Sept. 1994, G Oct. 1994. *Reissued:* Teldec Compact Discs 0630-17-46-2. [In twelve-disc set of Symphonies.] G Oct. 1997.

BBC Music Compact Disc BBC MM50. BBC Symphony Orchestra and Chorus, Geoffrey Mitchell Choir, Stephen Jackson (chorus-master), Mark ELDER. [Prokofiev.] P Royal Festival Hall, London concert 17 Feb. 1996, I Oct. 1996 magazine.

Deutsche Grammophon Compact Disc 469 525-2GH. Gothenburg Symphony Orchestra, Neemi JÄRVI. [Opp. 20 and 27*a*.] P Gothenburg Aug. 2000, I Mar. 2001, G May 2001.

Opus 15   The Nose

Form: A satirical opera in three acts, for chamber orchestra (with 2 harps, piano, flexatone, domras, and balalaikas), S.A.T.B. chorus, and 82 singing/speaking parts. Libretto by Yevgeni Zamyatin, Georgi Ionin, Aleksandr Preis, and the composer, based on the short story *Nose* by Nikolai Gogol. The opera falls into sixteen sections:

ACT 1

---

1. Introduction (Overture)—Allegro *attacca*
Scene 1: 2. The barber Ivan Yakovlevich—Adagio *attacca*
Scene 2: 3. The Embankment—Presto
        4. Entr'acte for percussion instruments—Allegro molto
        attacca
Scene 3: 5. The bedroom of Kovalyov—Adagio *attacca*
        6. Galop—Allegro molto *attacca*
Scene 4: 7. Kazan Cathedral—Largo

ACT 2

---

        8. Introduction—Allegro *attacca*
Scene 5: 9. In the newspaper dispatch office—Allegro non troppo
       10. Entr'acte—Largo *attacca*
Scene 6: 11. In Kovalyov's apartment—Allegretto

ACT 3

Scene 7: 12. On the outskirts of St Petersburg—Allegretto *attacca*
Scene 8: 13. In the apartments of Kovalyov and Podtochina—
        Allegretto *attacca*
       14. Intermezzo—Moderato *attacca*

EPILOGUE

Scene 9: 15. In Kovalyov's apartment—Allegro *attacca*
Scene 10: 16. Nevsky Prospect—Andante

Instrumentation: flute (= piccolo), oboe (= cor anglais), B flat clarinet (= E flat, A, and bass clarinet), bassoon (= contrabassoon) ~ horn, trumpet (= cornet), trombone (tenor and bass) ~ triangle, tambourine, castanets, side drum, tom-tom, rattle, cymbals (2 players—*colla bacchetta* and *ordinario*), bass drum, gong ~ whistle, orchestral bells, glockenspiel, xylophone, flexatone ~ small and alto domras, 2 balalaikas ~ 2 harps, piano ~ reduced string section with five-string double basses specified.

Composed: Between the summers of 1927 and 1928. Act 1 was written within a month and Act 2 within a fortnight in January 1928, mostly at Moscow; Act 3 completed in three weeks at Leningrad.

Premières: Suite: 25 November 1928, Moscow Conservatory Bolshoi Hall; Sovphil Orchestra, Nikolai Malko; Ivan Burlak (soloist in Nos. 2 and 6) and N. Barishev (soloist in No. 5).

     26 May 1929, Leningrad Philharmonic Bolshoi Hall; Leningrad Philharmonic Ochestra.

     19 October 1929, Prague.

     Opera: 16 June 1929, Malyi Opera Theatre, Leningrad; concert version.

     14 January 1930, Moscow-Narva House of Culture, Leningrad; three scenes performed with comments by the composer and musicologists,

Yulian Vainkop and Ivan Sollertinsky. Complete opera on 18 January 1930, Malyi Opera Theatre, Leningrad; décor by Vladimir Dmitriev, produced by Nikolai Smolich, and conducted by Samuil Samosud; principal roles—Pavel Zhuravlenko, (Kovalyov), V. Raikov (Ivan Yakovlevich), Pyotr Zasetsky (Ivan), and Ivan Nechayev (Nose).

UK broadcast: 21 October 1972, BBC Radio 3 presentation in Edward Downes's English translation; BBC Northern Symphony Orchestra and Singers, E. Downes; principal roles—Geoffrey Chard (Kovalyov), Michael Langdon (Ivan Yakovlevich), and Nigel Rogers (Ivan and Nose).

UK: 4 April 1973, Sadler's Wells Theatre, London; New Opera Company, Leon Lovett; principal roles—Alan Opie (Kovalyov), Bryan Drake (Ivan Yakovlevich), Neville Williams (Ivan), and Bernard Dickerson (Nose). Performed in Downes's English translation.

USSR revival: 30 October 1974, Moscow Chamber Opera's Youth Group, produced by Boris Pokrovsky, conducted by Gennadi Rozhdestvensky. Principal roles as on the Melodiya recording.

Arrangements: Reduction of the accompaniment for piano by the composer. English translations of the libretto by Merle and Deena Puffer, B. Vierne, and Edward Downes; German translation by Helmut Wagner and Karl Heinz Füssl; Italian version by Fedele D'Amico and Angelo Maria Ripellino; French, anonymously. Overture arranged for piano by Quinto Maganini. Arias Nos. 2, 5, and 6 from Opus 15*a* in Italian translation.

Opus 15*a*—Suite of seven excerpts for chamber orchestra, tenor and baritone soloists, assembled by the composer in May and June 1928. Instrumentation as opera less bells and domras.

1. Overture—Allegro
2. Kovalyov's aria from Scene 5—Largo con moto
3. Percussion Interlude to Scene 3—Allegro molto
4. Interlude to Scene 6—Adagio *attacca*
5. Ivan's aria from Scene 6—Allegretto *attacca*
6. Kovlayov's monologue from Scene 6—Andante
7. Galop from Scene 3—Allegro

Words of No. 5 traditional: Smerdyakov's song from Fyodor Dostoyevsky's novel *The Brothers Karamazov* of 1880.

Music: The autograph full score is the property of the Universal Edition publishing house, Vienna but the whereabouts of the autograph vocal score is not known. A portion of Scene 1 and fig. 504 with start of Epilogue of the autograph scores are reproduced in Volumes 18 and 19 of *Collected Works* respectively. Autograph score of the Suite Opus 15*a* preserved in the Shostakovich family archive.

Sokol, Leningrad, mimeographed format, 1929.

Universal Edition, English translation by Merle Puffer, vocal score.

Edition Musicus, Overture arr. for piano by Q. Maganini, 1940.

Universal Edition, No. 13439, 1962, vocal score with piano reduction by Karl Götz, and German text by Helmut Wagner and Karl Heinz Füssl, 30.5 cm.

Edition Musicus, No. 228, *c.*1964, Overture arr. by Q. Maganini with additional parts and cross-cueing, though employing the original instrumentation, 31 cm.

Santa Fe Opera, *c.*1965, libretto in English translation by Merle and Deena Puffer, 23 pp., 27 cm.

Muzyka, No. 7544, 1974, vocal score in composer's piano reduction, 30 cm.

G. Schirmer, No. 47700, *c.*1977, percussion interlude No. 3 of Suite for triangle, tambourine, castanets, side drum, tom-tom, 3 cymbals, bass drum, and gong; 3 scores.

Muzyka, No. 8392 (Volume 18 of *Collected Works*), 1981, full score, 30 cm.

Muzyka, No. 10714 (Volume 19 of *Collected Works*), 1981, vocal score, 30 cm.

Muzyka, No. 11935 (in Volume 23 of *Collected Works* with Op. 23 and Sans opp. D and K), 1986, full score of Suite Op. 15*a*, 30 cm.

Duration: Opera: 1 hr 43 mins. and Suite Op. 15*a:* 22' 22"–25' 31".

Film: *The Composer Shostakovich.* A Soviet film, produced by Yuri Belyankin, recorded the final rehearsals of the 1974 Moscow revival. For details see under Appendix II.

Recordings: USA: Aries LP 1601. Suite Opus 15*a*. Arias sung in Italian. Tommaso Frascati (tenor), Paolo Pedani (baritone), Rome RAI Symphony Orchestra, Franco MANNINO. [Op. 126.] P Rome concert 13 Apr. 1963. NB. Record label states 'Massimo Freccia conducting Italian Radio Orchestra'.

Italy: Fonit Centra Doc 83 (mono). Italian version by Fedele D'Amico and Angelo Maria Ripellino. Renato Capecchi (Kovalkov), Italo Tajo (Ivan Yakovlevich), Tommaso Frascati (District Inspector), Dino Formichini (Ivan), Antonio Pirino (Nose), Cesy Broggini (Pelageya Podtochina), Jolanda Meneguzzer (Podtochina's daughter), Donatella Rosa (Barber's wife); singers, actors, and instrumentalists of the Maggio Musicale Fiorentino, Adolfo Fanfani (chorus-master), Bruno BARTOLETTI. P Firenze concert 23 May 1964.

USSR: Melodiya C10 07007-10 (complete on 4 sides). Eduard Akimov (Kovalkov), Valeri Belykh (Ivan Yakovlevich), Boris Tarkhov (District Inspector), Boris Druzhinin (Ivan), Aleksandr Lomonosov (Nose), Lyudmila Sapegina (Pelageya Podtochina), Lyudmila Ukolova (Podtochina's daughter), Nina Zazulova (Barber's wife); singers, actors, and instrumentalists of the Moscow Chamber Music Theatre, Vladimir Agronsky (chorus-master), Gennadi ROZHDESTVENSKY (conductor). P 1974, I 1977*a*.

Reissued: HMV Melodiya ASD 3359-60 in Set SLS 5088 (two-record box set with libretto). G Sept. 1977 ~ Germany: Melodia Eurodisc 89 502 XFR (two-record box set) ~ France: Le Chant du Monde LDX 78609-10 (two-record box set). I 1976 ~ USA: Columbia Melodiya M2 34582. I 1977 ~ USSR: Melodiya C10 07007-10 (4 sides, with libretto). [In joint first and second box of Part 3 of *Collected Works on Records* with Op. 114.] I 1978 ~ France: Le Chant du Monde Compact Discs 278 998-9 (two-disc set, with libretto in French only). I 1990 ~ BMG Melodiya Compact Discs 74321 60319-2 (two-disc set, with plot synopsis but no libretto). [Sans op. K.] I Nov. 1998, G May 1999.

Germany: Thorofon Capella MTH 149. Suite No. 3 only. Percussion Ensemble, Siegfried FINK. ['Drums in Concert' recital—Bach, Scarlatti, Haydn *et al.*] P c.1979.

France: Praga Compact Disc PR 250 003. Suite Opus 15*a*. Luděk Löbl (tenor), Jindřich Jindrák (baritone), Boris Avkensentive (balalaika), Czech Philharmonic Orchestra, Gennadi ROZHDESTVENSKY. [op. 141.] P Prague concert 12 Jan. 1979, I June 1992.

USSR: Melodiya C10 28481 006. Suite No. 3 only. Ritmo Percussion Ensemble, Mark PEKARSKY. [Hovaness, Chávez, Fink *et al.*] P 1989, I 1989*d*.

Japan: Toshiba EMI LaserDisc TOWL 3747-8. Eduard Akimov (Kovalkov), Aleksei Mochalov (Ivan Yakovlevich), Boris Tarkhov (District Inspector), Boris Druzhinin (Ivan), Nikolai Kurpe (Nose), Viktor Borovkov (Newspaper man), Lyudmila Sokolenko (Girl), Ashot Sarkisov (Doctor), Lyudmila Kolmakova (Pelageya Podtochina), Elesna Andreyeva (Podtochina's daughter), Mariya Lemesheva (Barber's wife); singers, actors, and instrumentalists of the Moscow Chamber Music Theatre, Vladimir AGRONSKY. [Stravinsky.] P 9 Aug. 1995, I 1996.

Germany: Capriccio Compact Disc 10 779. Suite Opus 15*a*. Text in German and English. Vladimir Katschuk (tenor), Stanislav Suleimanov (baritone), Cologne Radio Symphony Orchestra, Mikhail YUROVSKY. [Opp. 90 and 81.] P Cologne 3–8 June 1996, I July 1999.

References: Bogdanova, Bretanitskaya, Danko, Drew, Fay, Hakopian, Mazel, G. Norris, Sagayev, and Sokolsky.

Opus 16   Tahiti Trot

Form: Transcription of Vincent Youmans' song 'Tea for Two', from the 1925 operetta *No, No, Nanette,* for orchestra, in A flat major marked 'Moderato'.

Instrumentation: piccolo, flute, 2 oboes, 2 B flat clarinets, bassoon ~ 4 horns, 2 trumpets, trombone ~ timpani, triangle, side drum, cymbals ~ glockenspiel/xylophone (one player), celesta, harp ~ strings.

Composed: 1 October 1927, from memory in 45 minutes, as a wager that he could orchestrate the number in an hour, at Nikolai Malko's home.

Dedication: 'To dear Nikolai Andreyevich Malko as a token of my best feelings'.

Premières: 25 November 1928, Moscow Conservatory Bolshoi Hall; Sovphil Orchestra, Nikolai Malko.

UK: 14 August 190, Royal Albert Hall 'Prom', London; BBC Symphony Orchestra, Gennadi Rozhdestvensky. Also broadcast on BBC Radio 3 simultaneously with BBC2 TV.

Arrangements: The piece was included in the ballet music for *The Golden Age*, Opus 22, at the request of Aleksandr Gauk, with slight changes to the orchestration (including the addition of wood block and saxophone).

Rearrangement of Shostakovich's transcription for brass band (featuring two xylophones plus flexatone and two tuned Minton teacups) by Howard Snell. Performed in the 'Best of Brass '84' final on BBC2 TV, 9 November 1984, by the Desford Colliery Dowty Band, conducted by H. Snell. Another brass band transcription by David Purser.

Reduction for organ by Marlya Makarova.

Music: The first 16 bars from the then unpublished manuscript are reproduced in Malko (1966). Full score reconstructed by Gennadi Rozhdestvensky from orchestral parts in Mrs Malko's possession.

[Chappell, No. 28568, 1924, song 'Tea for Two' by Vincent Youmans with lyrics by Irving Caesar, 31 cm.]

Muzyka, No. 11678 (as a supplement to Volume 10 of *Collected Works* with Opp. 1, 3, 7, 42, and Sans op. E), full score, 30 cm.

Duration: 3' 13"–4' 17". [4' 58" in Bolshoi Ballet production of Opus 22, London, July 1986 and 4' 23" as arranged for organ.]

Recordings: USSR: 13266-7 (10" 78 rpm). All-Union Radio Stage Symphony Orchestra, Leonid YURIEV. [Op. 30*a* No. 2.] P 1945. *Reissued:* USA: Colosseum CRLP 167 (mono). ['Footlight Favorites from behind the Iron Curtain'—concert including Opp. 22*a* No. 3 and 30*a* No. 2.] I 1954.

USSR: Melodiya D 005704-5 (8" mono). Labelled as 'Plyaska' ('Folk Dance'). All-Union Radio Stage Symphony Orchestra, Yuri SILANTIEV. [Yurisaly, Feld, Arabobov *et al.*] P 1959.

USSR: Melodiya C10 10399-400. USSR Symphony Orchestra, Yevgeni SVETLANOV. [Opp. 70, 96, and 97*a* No. 8.] P 1978, I 1978*d*. *Reissued:* France: Le Chant du Monde LDX 78687. [As Russian release.] I Mar. 1981 ~ Germany: Melodia Eurodisc 200 539-366. [As Russian release.]

USSR: Melodiya C10 14415-6. Leningrad Philharmonic Orchestra, Gennadi ROZHDESTVENSKY. [Album 1 of 'From Manuscripts of Different Years'—Opp. 4, 17, 23, and 36; Sans opp. C, H, and Z.] P 1980, I 1981*b*. *Reissued:* HMV Melodiya ASD 1650331. [As Russian release.] G July 1983 ~ Germany: Melodia Eurodisc 201974- 366. [As Russian release.] ~ BMG Melodiya Compact Discs 74321 59058-2 (two-disc set). [Opp. 36, 4, 17, Z, H, C, 1, 3, 7, 26/D, 59, E, 128, 30a, and 19.] I and G Mar. 1999.

BBC Radio Classics Compact Disc DMCD 98 (two-disc set). BBC Symphony Orchestra, Gennadi ROZHDESTVENSKY. ['BBC Proms Centenary, 1895–1995'—Berlioz, Tchaikovsky, Elgar *et al.*] P Proms concert 14 Aug. 1981, G Oct. 1995.

Polyphonic PRL 024D (digital). Arr. H. Snell. Desford Colliery Dowty Band, Howard SNELL. ['Best of Brass—Highlights from the BBC Television Brass Band Contest 1984'.] P Derby July and August 1984, G Aug. 1985.

Chandos ABRD 1279 (digital) and Compact Disc CHAN 8587. Scottish National Orchestra, Neeme JÄRVI. [Opp. 70, 96, and 114a.] P Glasgow 14–17 Apr. 1987, I Mar. 1988, G July 1988. *Reissued:* Chandos Compact Disc CHAN 6598. ['Russian Dances'—Rimsky-Korsakov, Glazunov, Prokofiev *et al.*] I Sept 1993

Teldec Compact Disc 8 44136. Arr. D. Purser. London Brass, David PURSER. [Praetorius, Bartók, Schubert *et al.*] P May 1988, I 1988.

USA: Pro-Arte Fanfare Compact Disc CDD 551. Chicago Sinfonietta, Paul FREEMAN. ['Shostakovich Film Festival'—Opp. 97, 111, 116, and 35.] P Oak Park, Illinois May 1990, I Aug. 1991. *Reissued:* Canada: Mastersound Compact Disc DFCDI-015. ['Orchestral Showpieces from Around the World'—Ginastera, Ibert, Walker, and Tills.] I 1991 ~ Canada: Mastersound Compact Disc DFCDI-02 SAMP. ['The Mastersound Sampler'—Arban, Popper, Piatigorsky *et al.*] I 1991 ~ Conifer Classics Compact Disc CLASS 7086. [As USA release.] I Nov. 1991.

Decca Compact Disc 433 702-2DH. Royal Concertgebouw Orchestra, Riccardo CHAILLY. [Op. 35; Sans opp. E and G.] P Amsterdam 3 May 1991, I Jan. 1993, G Mar. 1993.

Bandleader Compact Disc BNA 5061. Arr. H. Snell. Kneller Hall Band, Colonel Frank RENTON. ['Sugar and Spice'—Tchaikovsky, Torch, Prokofiev *et al.*] P Islington 1–2 May 1991, G Dec. 1992.

Olympia Compact Disc OCD 585. Arr. for organ. Mariya MAKAROVA (organ). ['Music for Organ'—Opp. 27, 29, 39, 81, 97, 105, and Sans op. E.] P Moscow Conservatory Jan. 1995, I Mar. 1997.

EMI Classics Compact Disc CDC5 55601-2. Philadelphia Orchestra, Mariss JANSONS. [Op. 103; Sans opp. E and G.] P Collingswood, New Jersey 8, 9, and 11 Mar. 1996, I May 1997, G Sept. 1997. *Reissued:* HMV Classics Compact Disc 5 73047-2. [Sans opp. E and G; Opp. 22, 97, 35, and 89.] I Oct. 1998.

USA: Pope Music Compact Disc PM 1015-2 (silver) and PMG 2015-2 (gold). Russian Symphony Orchestra, Mark GORENSTEIN. ['Russian Pops'—Op. 97 and Sans op. P; Dunayevsky, Khrennikov, Sviridov *et al.*] P Moscow Conservatory Sept. 1996.

USA: Delos Compact Disc DE 3257. Moscow Chamber Orchestra, Constantine ORBELIAN. ['Waltzes'—see Samplers.] P Moscow Conservatory 12–14 July 1999, G Dec. 1999.

References: Malko and Volkov (1978).

Opus 17   Two Pieces by Scarlatti

Form: Transcription for wind ensemble and timpani of two harpsichord pieces by Domenico Scarlatti:

1. Pastorale (Longo catalogue No. 413)—Allegro non tanto
2. Capriccio (Longo catalogue No. 375)—Presto

Instrumentation: piccolo, 2 flutes, 2 oboes, 2 B flat clarinets, 2 bassoons ~ 2 horns, 2 trumpets, trombone ~ timpani. The brass instruments are not employed in No. 1.

Composed: Autumn 1928.

Premières: 25 November 1928, Moscow Conservatory Bolshoi Hall; Sovphil Orchestra, Nikolai Malko.

UK: 22 June 1984, Almeida Theatre, Islington, London; Contemporary Chamber Orchestra, Odaline de la Martinez.

Music: Autograph score found after the composer's death.

Muzyka, No. 27, 1983, photocopied manuscript score numbered Opus 16, 36 cm.

Duration: No. 1: 3' 35" and No. 2: 3' 30"

Recordings: USSR: Melodiya C10 14415-6. Soviet wind ensemble under Gennadi ROZHDESTVENSKY. [Album 1 of 'From Manuscripts of Different Years'—Opp. 4, 16, 23, and 36; Sans opp. C, H, and Z.] P 1980, I 1981*b*. *Reissued:* HMV Melodiya ASD 1650331. [As Russian release.] G July 1983 ~ Germany: Melodia Eurodisc 201974-366. [As Russian release.] ~ France: Praga Compact Disc PR 250 090. [Op. 43.] I Dec. 1995 ~ BMG Melodiya Compact Discs 74321 59058-2 (two-disc set). [Opp. 36, 4, Z, H, C, 16, 1, 3, 7, 26/D, 59, E, 128, 30*a*, and 19.] I and G Mar. 1999 ~ France: Le Chant du Monde Compact Disc PR 7250 090. [Op. 43.] P given as Czech Radio concert 7 July 1981, G Feb. 2001.

Opus 18   New Babylon

Subtitles: 'The Assault on Heaven' [or 'Storming the Skies'] and 'Episodes of the Paris Commune in 1871'.

Form: Music for small orchestra (including flexatone and piano) for the silent film *New Babylon,* directed by Grigorl Kozintsev and Leonid

Trauberg and produced by the FEKS Group, for the Leningrad Sovkino Studio. Screenplay by Kozintsev and Trauberg based on an idea by Pavel Blyakhin. Art direction by Yevgeni Enei.

Instrumentation: flute, oboe, B flat clarinet, bassoon ~ 2 horns, trumpet, trombone ~ timpani, triangle, tambourine, side drum, cymbals, bass drum, gong, flexatone, xylophone (3 percussionists) ~ piano ~ strings.

Composed: December 1928–19 February 1929, at Leningrad.

Premières: The film was first shown in Leningrad on 18 March 1929 but the score was not used until the film was released in a Moscow cinema, where the pit orchestra was conducted by Ferdinand Krish.

Film revival: 21 November 1975, Paris Film Festival; the film shown with the score played by the Ensemble Ars Nova under the direction of Marius Constant.

UK broadcast: 13 March 1978, BBC Northern Ireland Orchestra, Havelock Nelson; Suite Nos. 1, 5, and 6.

UK film revival: 22 September 1982, Queen Elizabeth Hall, London; the film shown with the original accompanying score played by the London Lyric Orchestra, under conductor Omri Hadari.

Netherlands film revival: 21 November 1982, Eindhoven; Brabant Orchestra, O. Hadari (in the presence of Leonid Trauberg, who was seeing his film for the first time in 50 years).

USA film revival: 3 October 1983, Radio City Music Hall, New York; a Corinth Films Release, presented for the first time with a live symphony orchestra, as a special event at the 21st New York Film Festival; Radio City Music Hall Chamber Orchestra, O. Hadari.

BBC Television: 11 January 1985, the first TV showing introduced by Lindsay Anderson; London Lyric Orchestra, O. Hadari.

Arrangement: Suite restored from orchestral parts by Gennadi Rozhdestvensky:

1. War—Allegro non troppo
2. Paris—Allegro moderato *attacca*
3. The Siege of Paris—Largo
4. Operetta—Moderato—Allegretto
5. Paris has stood for centuries—Allegretto
6. Versailles—Adagio—Allegretto [*attacca*]
[7. Finale—Andante—Allegro (this item, banded separately on the recording, is the coda of No. 6 in the printed score).]

No. 1 includes the main theme of Scherzo in E flat major, Opus 7 and No. 6 quotes the solo piano piece 'Old French Song', No. 16 from Pyotr Tchaikovsky's *Album for Children*, Opus 39. The score introduces several other themes, notably the round dance 'La Carmagnole' and the chant 'Ça Ira!' of the French Revolution; Rouget de l'Isle's 'La Marseillaise'; and the waltz and can-can, respectively, from Jacques Offenbach's operettas *La Belle Hélène* and *Orphée aux Enfers*.

Music: Danilevich states that the manuscript was deposited at the Glinka Museum though the composer thought that the music was lost. On 27 January 1976 *Pravda* reported that the orchestral parts had been discovered in a storeroom at the Lenin Library, Moscow by Gennadi Rozhdestvensky.

Sovkino, Leningrad, 1929, parts numbered Opus 17, 34 cm. [The piano part of the Library of Congress copy of ten parts (strings missing) has film cues marked in English in red ink.]

Sovetskii Kompozitor, No. 4191, 1976, *Suite from Music to the Film,* restored by Rozhdestvensky, full score numbered Opus 17, 30 cm.

Duration: Complete film score: 84' 23". Suite: given as 50 minutes in score; the 1975 recording, which has three cuts in No. 4, timed 41 minutes; 44' 19". Film: 96–106 minutes.

Ballet: *The Overcoat.* For details see under Opus 32.

Recordings: USSR: Melodiya C10 07381-2. Suite. Soloist Ensemble of the Moscow Philharmonic Orchestra, Gennadi ROZHDESTVENSKY. P 1975, I 1977b. *Reissued:* HMV Melodiya ASD 3381. [Op. 32.] G Dec. 1977 ~ USA: Columbia Melodiya 34502. I 1977 ~ USSR: Melodiya C10 07381-2. [In fourth box of Part 1 of *Collected Works on Records*.] I 1978 ~ France: Le Chant du Monde LDX 78618. I June 1981 ~ Germany: Melodia Eurodisc 28665 XHK. [On first record in four-record film music album.] I 1981 ~ Japan: Victor Musical Industries Compact Disc VICC 2090. [Op. 22.] I 1989 ~ USA: Russian Disc Compact Disc RDCD 11 064. [Op. 30a.] I Feb. 1995.

Germany: Capriccio Compact Discs 10 341 / 42 (two-disc set). Complete film score in eight parts. Berlin Radio Symphony Orchestra, James JUDD. [Op. 111.] P Berlin 1–12 Oct. 1989 and 7–8 Feb. 1989 (*sic?*), I Oct. 1990.

Chandos Compact Disc CHAN 9600. Suite. Russian State Symphony Orchestra, Valeri POLYANSKY. [Op. 79a.] P Mosfilm Studio Jan. 1995, I Mar. 1998, G June 1998.

References: Egorova, Hoberman, Mercer (in *DSCH*), Riley (in *DSCH*), and Rozhdestvensky.

Opus 19   The Bedbug

Form: Incidental music to the comedy *The Bedbug* by Vladimir Mayakovsky. The score consists of 23 items numbered as follows:

1–3.   March—Tempo di marcia (No. 1 in the Suite)
4. ⎫
5. ⎬ Galop—Allegro (No. 2 in the Suite)
6. ⎭ Foxtrot—Allegro non troppo (No. 3 in the Suite)
7.   Foxtrot (Wedding ['Intermezzo' is an unknown person's title]— Allegretto* (No. 5 in the Suite)

8. [Wedding Scene]—Allegro
9. Waltz—Andante (No. 4 in the Suite)
10. Dance (Foxtrot)
11. (Symphonic Entr'acte—a combination of Nos. 4 and 7)
12. Fire—[Vivo]* and Fire Signals*
13. Fireman's Chorus [The full score inscribed 'Finale of Part 1' by an unknown person]—[Marciale]*
14–18. Scene in the Public Garden (or Boulevard)—[Allegretto moderato] (No. 6 in the Suite)
19. March of the Pioneers—Allegretto*
20. March of the City Elders—[Tempo di marcia]*
21. Flourish—Allegro*
22. Waltz from Act 2—[Moderato]*
23. [Closing March]—[Giocoso] (No. 7 in the Suite)

Instrumentation: 2 flutes, 2 B flat clarinets, 2 soprano saxophones ~ horn, 2 trumpets, trombone, tuba ~ E flat alto, B flat baritone, and bass sax-horns ~ triangle, tom-tom, side drum, cymbals, bass drum ~ flexatone, balalaika, guitar ~ strings. Nos. 4–6 inscribed 'for two accordions' though played by a trio in the production.

Composed: January–February 1929, in less than a month at Moscow and Leningrad.

Premières: 13 February 1929, Meyerhold Theatre, Moscow; directed by Meyerhold; décor by Kukryniksky and Aleksandr Rodchenko.

UK suite: 10 July 1982, Riverside Studios, Hammersmith, London; Haroutune Bedelian (violin), Elizabeth Wilson (cello), and Kathron Sturrock (piano).

USA suite: 12 January 1987, Merkin Concert Hall, New York; De Capo Chamber Players (Joel Lester, André Emelianoff, and Sarah Rothenberg).

Arrangements: Suite of seven numbers from the score:

1. March—Tempo di marcia
2. Galop—Allegro
3. Foxtrot—Allegro non troppo
4. Waltz—Andante
5. Intermezzo—Allegretto
6. Scene in the Boulevard—[Allegretto moderato]
7. Closing March—[Giocoso]

Nos. 2 and 4 taken from *New Babylon,* Opus 18 ('War' and 'Versailles' respectively).

Reduction for piano of the Suite: Nos. 1–4 arranged by the composer and Nos. 5–7 by Lev Solin; and eight items from the incidental music (marked *) by V. Samarin.

Suite (Nos. 1–7) transcribed for piano trio by Gerard McBurney.

Music: Autograph score, numbered Opus 18, preserved at the Bakhrushin State Central Theatrical Museum. Autograph vocal and piano scores of the March, the Waltz for solo piano, 'March of the Pioneers', and other incomplete items preserved at the CIS Archives of Literature and Art. A page of the autograph full score of 'Wedding Scene' at the first flexatone entry reproduced in Volume 27 of *Collected Works*. A page of the autograph score of 'March of the Pioneers' is reproduced on page 78 of Roseberry (1982).

Sovetskii Kompozitor, No. 4028 (in *Dmitri Shostakovich: Music to Plays*), 1977, seven pieces arr. for piano, 29 cm.

Muzyka, No. 11412 (in Volume 28 of *Collected Works* with Opp. 24, 28, 31, 32, 37, 44, 58*a*, 63, 66, 72, and in the supplement, Sans opp. D and K), 1986, vocal and piano scores of fifteen items, 30 cm.

Muzyka, No. 11413 (in Volume 27 of *Collected Works* with Opp. 24, 28, 32, 37, 44, 58*a*, 63, 66, and 72), 1987, eleven items (Nos. 1–3, 7, 8, 12, 13, 14–18, 19, 20, 21, 22, and 23) in full score, 30 cm.

Ballet: *The Bedbug.* Leonid Yakobson, Leningrad, 20 July 1974. A one-act ballet-buffa performed by the Leningrad Ballet Troupe 'Choreographic Miniatures'.

Recordings: Sweden: Bluebell Bell 126. Suite Nos. 3, 4, and 2. Inger WIKSTRÖM (piano). [Opp. 5; 22*a* No. 3; 31 No. 4; 94; 97*a* No. 7; 105 fragment; and Prokofiev.] P Stockholm 28 Jan. and 1 Feb. 1981. *Reissued:* Sweden: Swedish Society Discofil Compact Disc SCD 1031. [Opp. 34, 61, 94, and 5.] I 1988.

USSR: Melodiya A10 00107 009 (digital). Suite Nos. 1, 5, 6, and 7. USSR Ministry of Culture Symphony Orchestra, Gennadi ROZHDESTVENSKY. [Album 3 of 'From Manuscripts of Different Years'—Opp. 125 and 58*a*.] P 1982, I 1985*d*. *Reissued:* Olympia Compact Disc OCD 258. Suite Nos. 1, 5, 6, and 7. [Opp. 14 and 141.] I Oct. 1989 ~ Olympia Compact Disc OCD 5006. Suite Nos. 1, 5, 6, and 7. [In Volume 2 five-disc set of symphonies with Opp. 14 and 141.] I Dec. 1990 ~ BMG Melodiya Compact Discs 74321 59058-2 (two-disc set). Suite Nos. 1, 5, 6, and 7. [Opp. 36, 4, 17, Z, H, C, 16, 1, 3, 7, 26/D, 59, E, 128, and 30*a*.] I and G Mar. 1999.

Whitetower Records Ensemble ENS 132 (digital real time cassette only). Suite Nos. 1, 2, 4–7 arr. G. McBurney. Alexander BALANESCU (violin), Elizabeth WILSON, (cello), and Andrew BALL (piano). ['Music and Revolution', Volume 1—Opp. 34, 97, and Sans op. E with poems.] I 1985.

USSR: Melodiya C10 28379 002. Suite No. 5 arr. L. Solin. Vladimir VIARDO (piano). [Opp. 34, 37, and 58*a*.] P 1986, I 1990*a*.

Chandos Compact Disc CHAN 9907. Suite. Nos. 5, 6, 4, 1, 3, 2, and 7 arr. composer and L. Solin. Rustem HAYROUDINOFF (piano). ['Theatre Music'—Opp. 37, 31, 32, 44, 58*a*, 66, and 22.] P Potton Hall, Suffolk 7–8 Aug. 2000, I Apr. 2001.

Opus 20   Symphony No. 3 in E flat major

Subtitle: 'The First of May' or 'May Day'. Originally called 'A May Symphony' and this subtitle preserved In the piano reduction.

Form: Symphony in one movement, marked 'Allegretto', with four or five subdivisions, for full orchestra and S.A.T.B. chorus (for the choral hymn finale setting of a poem by Semyon Kirsanov).

Instrumentation: piccolo, 2 flutes, 2 oboes, 2 B flat clarinets, 2 bassoons ~ 4 horns, 2 trumpets, 3 trombones, tuba ~ timpani, triangle, side drum, cymbals, bass drum, gong ~ glockenspiel, xylophone ~ S.A.T.B. chorus ~ strings.

Composed: July onwards 1929, at Leningrad.

Premières: 21 January 1930, Moscow-Narva House of Culture, Leningrad; Leningrad Philharmonic Orchestra and Academy Capella Choir, Aleksandr Gauk. [Official première given in Leningrad on 6 November 1931 under the same conductor.]

USA: 30 December 1932, Philadelphia Orchestra, Leopold Stokowski. [Without the choral finale.]

USSR revival: 12 May 1964, Leningrad; Igor Blazhkov.

Arrangements: Reduction for voices and piano by the composer. English translation of the poem by Valeria Vlazinskaya.

Music: The autograph score preserved at the CIS Archives of Literature and Art.

Muzgiz, No. 13064, 1932, with Russian and German texts (the latter by D. Ussov), 33 cm.

Leeds Music, no number, 1946, with Russian and German texts, 21.5 cm.

Muzyka, No. 9000, 1975, full score, 30 cm.

Muzyka, No. 10778 (in Volume 2 of *Collected Works* with Op. 43), 1982, full score, 30 cm.

Muzyka, No. 11688 (in Volume 9 of *Collected Works* with reductions of Opp. 113 and 135, and choral section of Op. 14), 1984, the composer's vocal score of the choral section, 30 cm.

Hans Sikorski No. 2226, 1993, 21 cm.

Duration: Approx. 30 minutes in score; 26' 12"–33' 20"; 25 minutes (M. MacDonald); 28 minutes (Schirmer).

Recordings: USSR: Melodiya D 017953-4 (mono). Leningrad Philharmonic Orchestra, Krupskaya Institute Chorus, Ivan Poltavtsev (chorus-master), Igor BLAZHKOV. [Op. 14.] P concert 12 May 1964. *Reissued:* Germany: Melodia Eurodisc 85301 MK. [Op. 14.] and 85314 KK. [Op. 70.]

RCA Victor Red Seal RB 6755 (mono) and SB 6755. Royal Philharmonic Orchestra and Chorus, John McCarthy (chorus-master), Igor Buketoff (chorus-director), Morton GOULD (conductor). [Op. 14.] P 1968, G Oct. 1968. *Reissued:* USA: RCA Victor LSC 3044. [Op. 14.] I 1968.

USSR: Melodiya CM 04237-8. Moscow Philharmonic Orchestra, RSFSR Academic Russian Choir, Aleksandr Yurlov (chorus-master), Kirill KONDRASHIN. [Op. 54.] P 1972, I 1974c. *Reissued:* USA: Angel Melodiya SR 40245. [Op. 136.] I 1974 ~ Germany: Melodia Eurodisc 87 623 XPK. [In thirteen-record box set.] I 1974 ~ HMV Melodiya ASD 3045. [Op. 10.] G Feb. 1975 ~ HMV Melodiya BOX 502502 in Set SLS 5025. [Op. 43, first movement.] G Dec. 1975 ~ Germany: Melodia Eurodisc 300 595 in Set 300 597-435. [Op. 119.] ~ France: Le Chant du Monde LDX 78622-3. [Op. 43.] ~ USSR: Melodiya CM 04237-8. [In first box of Part 1 of *Collected Works on Records* with Op. 54.] I 1980 ~ HMV Melodiya EX 2903873 (DMM). [On second record in twelve-record box set with Op. 54.] G Dec. 1985 ~ France: Le Chant du Monde Compact Disc LDC 278 1001-2. [In Box 1 of five two-disc sets with Opp. 10, 14, and 43.] G May 1989 ~ BMG Classics Melodiya Compact Disc 74321 19845-2. [Op. 47.] I July 1994, G Nov. 1994.

France: Praga Compact Disc PR 254 055. Czech (Prague) Radio Symphony Orchestra Vacláv SMETÁČEK. [Opp. 131 and 119.] P Czech Radio 1974, I July 1994.

Decca SXDL 7535 (digital). London Philharmonic Orchestra and Choir, John Alldis (chorus-master), Bernard HAITINK. [Op. 14.] P Jan. 1981, G July 1982. *Reissued:* USA: London LDR 71035 (digital). [Op. 14.] ~ Decca Compact Disc 421 131-2DH. [Opp. 14 and 22a.] I Mar. 1988, G June 1988 ~ Decca Ovation Compact Disc 425 063-2DM. [Op. 10.] I Aug. 1993, G Nov. 1993 ~ London Compact Disc 444 431-2. [On first disc of eleven-disc set with Op. 10.] I June 1995.

USSR: Melodiya A10 00129 006 (digital). USSR Ministry of Culture Symphony Orchestra, Yurlov Republican Russian Choir, Rozaliya Peregudova (chorus-master), Stanislav Gusev (chorus-director), Gennadi ROZHDESTVENSKY. P 1984, I 1986a. *Reissued:* Olympia Compact Disc OCD 161. [Op. 10.] I Nov. 1988, G May 1989 ~ Germany: Melodia Eurodisc Compact Disc 258 484. [Op. 54.] ~ USSR: Melodiya Compact Disc SUCD10 00103. [Op. 10.] I 1990c ~ Olympia Compact Disc OCD 5005. [In Volume 1 six-disc set of symphonies with Op. 10.] I Dec. 1990 ~ BMG Melodiya Compact Discs 74321 63462-2 (two-disc set). [Opp. 14, 32, 43, and 23.] I Mar. 1999.

Naxos Compact Disc 8.550623. Czecho-Slovak Radio Symphony Orchestra, Slovak Philharmonic Chorus, Ladislav SLOVÁK. [Op. 10.] P Bratislava 20–6 Jan. 1990, I Jan. 1993, G Nov. 1993. *Reissued:* Naxos Compact Discs 8.505017. [In five-disc set with Symphonies Nos. 1, 2, 4, 6, 7, 12, and 15.] I 1993.

Decca Compact Disc 436 760-2. Royal Philharmonic Orchestra, Bach Choir, David Willcocks (chorus-master), Vladimir ASHKENAZY. [Op. 112.] P Walthamstow May 1992, I Oct. 1994.

Denon Compact Disc CO 75444. Vienna Symphony Orchestra, Vienna Youth Choir, Günther Theuring (chorus-master), Schola Cantorum,

Eliahu INBAL. [Op. 70.] P Vienna concert 13–15 Oct. 1992, I Nov. 1993, G Feb. 1994.

Teldec Compact Disc 4509 90853-2. London Symphony Orchestra, London Voices, Mstislav ROSTROPOVICH. [Op. 14.] P London 8–9 Feb. 1993, I Sept. 1994, G Oct. 1994. *Reissued:* Teldec Compact Discs 0630-17046-2. [In twelve-disc set of Symphonies.] G Oct. 1997.

BBC Proms Compact Disc BBCP 1005-2. London Symphony Chorus, BBC Scottish Symphony Orchestra, Osmo VÄNSKÄ. [Beethoven.] P Proms concert 19 Aug. 1998, I Aug. 1999, G Nov. 1999.

Deutsche Grammophon Compact Disc 469 525-2GH. Gothenburg Symphony Orchestra, Neemi JÄRVI. [Opp. 14 and 27*a*.] P Gothenburg Dec. 1996, I Mar. 2001, G May 2001.

References: Calvocoressi and Sabinina.

Opus 21   Six Romances on Japanese Poems

Form: Suite of six songs for tenor and full orchestra (with two harps):

1. Love (An Epitaph)—Andante
2. Before Suicide—Adagio
3. Immodest Glance—Allegretto
4. For the First and Last Time—Andante
5. Hopeless Love—Adagio
6. Death—Largo

Texts by Japanese poets: No. 1 of unknown antiquity; No. 2 by the seventh-century poet Prince Ootsu; Nos. 3–6 anonymous though No. 3 known to be eighteenth century. Nos. 1–3 from *Japanese Lyric Poetry* collection published in St Petersburg in 1912 in a translation by A. Brandt.

Instrumentation: 2 flutes (II = piccolo), 2 oboes, E flat clarinet, 2 B flat clarinets, bass clarinet, 2 bassoons, contrabassoon ~ 4 horns, 3 trumpets, 3 trombones, tuba ~ timpani, cymbals, gong ~ glockenspiel, xylophone, 2 harps ~ strings. [The early score lists reduced woodwind with single oboe, B flat clarinet, and bassoon.]

Composed: Nos. 1–3 in 1928 (No. 1 dated 7 October); 4 in late 1931; 5 and 6 in April 1932. Written at Leningrad.

Dedication: Nina Vasilievna Varzar (fiancée).

Premières: 24 April 1966, Concert Hall of the Academic Glinka Choir, Leningrad; Anatoli Manukhov (tenor), Leningrad Philharmonic Orchestra, Igor Blazhkov.

UK broadcast: 28 August 1980, Maldwyn Davies (tenor, singing in Russian), Orchestra of the National Centre for Orchestral Studies, Gennadi Rozhdestvensky.

Opus 21*a*: 30 March 1977, All-Union House of Composers, Moscow; Aleksei Maslennikov (tenor) and Liya Mogilevskaya (piano).

Arrangements: Accompaniment arranged for piano by the composer (Opus 21*a*). German translation by Jörg Morgener.

Music: Autograph full and piano scores preserved at the CIS Archives of Literature and Art (orchestral parts and piano score incomplete).

Russian printed edition of manuscript not in the composer's hand, unnumbered and undated, full score, 35 cm. In BBC Music Libirary.

Muzyka, No. 10113 (in Volume 31 of *Collected Works* with Opp. 4, 46*a*, 140, 79*a*, 143*a*, and 145*a*), 1982, full score, 30 cm.

Muzyka, No. 10283 (in Volume 32 of *Collected Works* with Opp. 4, 46, 62, 79, 84, 86, 91, 98, and 100 *et al.*), 1982, reduction, 30 cm.

Hans Sikorski, No. 2296, 1987, reduction with Russian and German texts—the latter by J. Morgener, 31.5 cm

Duration: Approx. 13 minutes in score; 11' 35'–13' 56".

Recordings: USSR: Melodiya C10 10617-8. Aleksei MASLENNIKOV (tenor) and Liya Mogilevskaya (piano). [In third box of Part 3 of *Collected Works on Records* with Opp. 46 and 91 Nos. 2 and 4.] P and I 1978. *Reissued:* USSR: Melodiya C10 15501-2. [Opp. 109 and 146.] I 1981*d* ~ Czech: Supraphon 1112 3148. [Opp. 109 and 146.] I 1986.

USSR: Melodiya C10 19103 004. Aleksei MASLENNIKOV (tenor), USSR Ministry of Culture Symphony Orchestra, Gennadi Rozhdestvensky. [Album 2 of 'From Manuscripts of Different Years'—Opp. 1, 3, 7, and 26.] P 1982, I 1983*d*. *Reissued:* BMG Melodiya Compact Discs 74321 59057-2 (two-disc set). [Opp. 135, 46/141, 62*a*, and Sans op. M.] I Feb. 1999.

Deutsche Grammophon Compact Disc 447 085-2GH. Ilya LEVINSKY (tenor), Gothenburg Symphony Orchestra, Neeme Järvi. ['The Orchestral Songs, Vol. 2'—Opp. 143*a* and 145*a*.] P Gothenburg May 1994, I Dec. 1995, G Jan. 1996.

Germany: Capriccio Compact Disc 10 777. Opus 21*a*. Vladimir KASATSCHUK (tenor), Cologne Radio Symphony Orchestra, Mikhail Yurovsky. [Opp. 145*a* and 46*a*.] P Cologne 22–7 May 1995, I 1998.

Japan: Meister Music Compact Disc MM 1005. Sung in German. Ernst HAEFLIGER (tenor) and Tomoko Okada (piano). ['Ernst Haefliger sings Waka'—Yamada, Einem, Kubelik *et al.*] P Kusatu Ongaku-no-mori Concert Hall Sept. 1994.

Classic FM Compact Disc 75605 57004-2. Opus 21*a*. Mark TUCKER (tenor), Yomiuri Nippon Symphony Orchestra, Tadaaki Otaka. [Op. 47.] P Kamakura 3–6 June 1996, I Nov. 1997, G Jan. 1998.

Note: The text of No. 2, given as by Oxotsuno Otsi on Russian recordings and Otsuno Odzi in *Collected Works* Volumes 31 and 32, should read Ootsu no ooji (= Ootsu called Prince). Prince Ootsu, son of Emperor Temmu, was famous as the poet who wrote four Japanese short poems in *Man yoo shuu* (the oldest Japanese book of poetry, published in 20 volumes around the 8th century). He was executed in 686 on suspicion of conspiracy.

Opus 22   The Golden Age

Alternative titles: *The Age of Gold.* Original working title 'Fashlandiya' and later, 'Dinamiada' (also spelt 'Dynamiada' in English). Presented in Odesssa in 1931 as 'Dinamiada or The Days of Europe'. Also known under the French title of *L'Age d'Or.*

Form: Ballet in three acts, with libretto by Aleksandr Ivanovsky, choreography by Vladimir Chesnakov, Leonid Yakobson, and Vasili Vainomen, and designs by Valentina Khodasevich. The augmented orchestra includes two saxophones, additional brass, banjo, accordions, harmonium, and flexatone. The complete scenario consists of thirty-seven numbers:

1. Introduction

ACT 1

Scene 1: 'The Golden Age Industrial Exhibition'
2. Procession of Guests of Honour
3. Review of Window Displays
4. Demonstration of Exhibits
5. Prestidigitator-Barker: Hindu Dance
6. Prize fighting for publicity
7. Scandal at the Boxing Match

Scene 2: 'Exhibition Hall'
8. Foxtrot: Dance of the Golden Youths
9. Exhibition Director's appearance with Diva
10. Adagio of Diva and the Fascist
11. Arrival of Soviet Football Team
12. Variation of Diva and the Fascist
13. Soviet Dance
14. Scene: Soviet Worker invites Diva to a dance
15. Dance of Diva and the Fascist
16. Dance of the Negro and two Soviet football players
17. Waltz: Alleged Bomb Plotters—'The Hand of Moscow'
18. Confusion among the Fascists
19. A Rare Case of Mass Hysteria
20. Foxtrot . . . foxtrot . . . foxtrot

ACT 2

Scene 3: 'Street in the City'
21. Pantomime: Sleuthing by an Agent Provocateur and an Arrest

Scene 4: 'Workers' Stadium'
22. Workers' Procession to the Stadium
23. Pioneers' Dance—Dances: Boxing, Discus-throwing, Tennis, English Hockey, and Fencing

24. Reception of the Soviet Football Team
25. The Football Match
26. Interlude: Everybody amuse oneself in one's own way
27. Sportive Dance of Western Komsomol members and four Sportsmen
28. General Sportive Dance
29. 'The Red Front' [pre-war anti-fascist organization]

ACT 3
---

30. Introduction

Scene 5: 'Music Hall (Divertissement)'

31. Tap-dance: Shoe Shine of the Best Quality
32. Tango
33. Polka: Once Upon a Time in Geneva—'Angel Of Peace'
34. Touching Coalition of Classes, slightly fraudulent
35. Can-can

Scene 6: 'Outside the Prison'

36. Liberation of Prisoners. General Exposure
37. Finale: Solidarity Dance of Western Workers and the Soviet Team

NB. For performance the order of the numbers was slightly rearranged and the staging titles altered from the composer's musical score of spring 1930:

ACT 1
---

1. Prelude—Allegro non troppo *attacca*
2. Dance of the Maître d'Hôtel and the Aristocrats—Allegretto
3. Sportsmen's Training Session—Allegro vivace *attacca*
4. Entrance of the Maître d'Hôtel and the Aristocrats—Allegretto *attacca*
5. Dance of the Tennis Players and Training Session—Allegro *attacca*
6. The Maître d'Hôtel reports . . . —Moderato non troppo *attacca*
7. Preparations for the Diva's Visit—Moderato—Andante
8. Dance of the Golden Youths—Allegro
9. Adagio
10. Dance of the Diva and Tanya—Andantino
11. Dance—Allegro
12. Conversation between the Diva and the Hero—Allegretto *attacca*
13. Dance of the Diva and the Hero—Andantino—Allegro
14. Dance of the Negro and the White Man—Allegro
15. General Dance—Andantino *attacca*
16. General Confusion—Adagio
17. The Diva's Despair—Allegretto

18. Conversation between the VIP and . . . —Andante
19. Foxtrot—Allegro non troppo

ACT 2
---

20. Galop—Allegro
21. March—Allegretto
22. Football—Allegro
23. Interlude—Andantino
24. Dance of Tanya and Sportsmen from U-Town—Andantino
25. Sports Contest—Allegro
26. Scene and Exit of the Soviet—Allegro
27. Interlude—Allegretto
28. Tango—Largo
29. Tap-dance—Allegretto
30. Polka—Allegretto
31. Eccentric Dance—Presto—Andante—Presto
32. Andante
33. Allegro vivace

ACT 3
---

34. Adagio
35. Adagio—Allegro—Andantino *attacca*
36. Allegro *attacca*
37. Finale—Allegro con brio

Tahiti Trot included as an Entr'acte, No. 27—see Opus 16. Nos. 20 and 33 were later reorchestrated as the Actors' Pantomime, Opus 32*a* No. 5.

NB. The piano score of the ballet (DSCH, Moscow, 1995) is stated to be the composer's final version of the work though this differs in the nomenclature of several numbers and their sequence. Generally the titles agree with the ballet (first listing) under 'Form' and not the composer's musical score (second listing). Nos. 28 and 29 are transposed on Rozhdestvensky's recording of the complete ballet.

New libretto provided for the 206th Bolshoi Theatre season with choreography by Yuri Grigorovich. Score adapted by several of Shostakovich's pupils, notably Veniamin Basner and Isaak Glikman. In this version *Zolotoi Vek* ('The Golden Age') is the name of a Black Sea coast restaurant, set in the year 1923. The slow movements of Piano Concertos Nos. 1 and 2 are incorporated to provide lyrical Adagio scenes. *Tahiti Trot* appears in the Night Club scene at the start of Act 2. The Opus 22*a* Suite (with the Adagio shortened) is included, along with the following familiar items: Interlude from *The Bolt*, Op. 27; Actors' Pantomime from *Hamlet*, Op. 32; Elegy from *The Human Comedy*, Op. 37 (also Ballet Suite No. 3, No. 4), and Blues from *Suite for Jazz Orchestra No. 1*, Sans op. E.

ACT 1

Scene 1: The Young Workers' Theatre performs led by Boris, a
fisherman
Scene 2: The search for Rita leads Boris to 'The Golden Age'
Scene 3: Yashka, the bandit, plans a robbery
Scene 4: Rita and Boris dance. Yashka fights for Rita
Scene 5: Boris and Rita declare their love for each other

ACT 2

Scene 1: Rita rejects Yashka's advances
Scene 2: Robbery by Yashka and his gang
Scene 3: Rita finds Boris by the sea. Fight between the bandits and
fishermen

ACT 3

Scene 1: Merry-making at the bandit's camp
Scene 2: Rita performs her last dance at 'The Golden Age'
Scene 3: Yashka kills former girl-friend Lyushka
Scene 4: Yashka takes Rita hostage but is captured. Happy ending

Items appear in the following order (NB. Numbers refer to the composer's score): ACT 1—1, 2, 24, 2, 5, 21, 11, 23, 18, 8, 30, 32, Op. 32a No. 5,
35, 15, 16, Op. 35 Lento. ACT 2—27, 13, 27, 28/35, 25, 24, 9, 20, Sans op. P
(i) No. 3 Elegy, 31/36. ACT 3—14/31/14/35, 22, 36, Sans op. E No. 3, 19,
17/35, 33, Op. 102 Andante, and 37. The following nine numbers were
not incorporated: 3, 4, 6, 7, 10, 12, 26, 29, and 34.

Composed: Autumn 1929 to spring 1930, at Leningrad. Composed as a
result of a competition for new ballet librettos.

Premières: Suite: 19 March 1930, Philharmonic Hall, Leningrad; Leningrad
Philharmonic Orchestra, Aleksandr Gauk.

Ballet: 26/27 October 1930, Academic Theatre of Opera and Ballet
(Kirov Theatre), Leningrad; produced by Emmanuil Kaplan and conducted by Aleksandr Gauk. The role of Komsomolka (Komsomol member) was danced initially by Galina Ulanova. Number of performances:
ten in 1930 and eight in 1931.

Ballet revival: 14 October 1982, Bolshoi Theatre, Moscow; resurrected
at the suggestion of Shostakovich's widow; new choreography by Yuri
Grigorovich, artistic direction by Simon Virsaladze, directed by Yuri
Simonov, and conducted by Dmitri Kotov.

UK: 30 July 1986, Royal Opera House, Covent Carden, London; Bolshoi Ballet; Sadler's Wells Royal Ballet Orchestra conducted by Aleksandr Lavrenyuk.

USA: 30 June 1987, Metropolitan Opera House, New York; Bolshoi
Ballet, A. Lavrenyuk.

Arrangements: Opus 22*a*—Suite for full orchestra (with soprano saxophone, B flat baritone saxhorn, and harmonium), assembled by the composer. The first version of the Suite in 1929 consisted of seven items: Introduction, Waltz, Tap-dance, Adagio, Foxtrot, Polka, and Dance. In preparing the Suite for publication in 1932, the composer unified the first two items and discarded the Tap-dance and Foxtrot.

1. Introduction—Allegro non troppo (Nos. 1 and 2 In ballet and score)
2. Adagio—(No. 10 in ballet; No. 9 in score)
3. Polka—Allegretto (No. 33 in ballet; No. 30 in score)
4. Russian Dance—Allegro (No. 13 in ballet; No. 11 in score)

Suite: variety of transcriptions including piano solo, two pianos, violin and piano, string quartet, and wind quintet (the last two by Aaron Henry).

Polka—No. 3: reductions by the composer for piano solo in 1935 and piano four hands in 1962; two versions for piano solo by Frederick Block and György Sándor; two versions for two pianos four hands by Pierre Luboshutz and Phyllis Gunther; two versions for violin and piano by Harry Glickman and D. J. Grunes; violin duet and piano, also mandolin quartet, by Sheppard Lehnhoff; arrangements for string quartet by the composer in 1931 (see *Two Pieces for String Quartet*, Sans op. D), S. Lehnhoff, and David Ogden; viola ensemble by Georgi Bezrukov; marimba solo by Anatoli Lyubimov; marimba and piano by Nebojša Živković; woodwind quintet by Jerry Neil Smith, Roger Smith, and Adam Lesnick; band transcriptions by Quinto Maganini and P. J. Lang; brass quintet by R. San Filippo; saxophone quartet by the Aurelia Quartet (Netherlands concert on 15 November 1993, broadcast five days later). The Polka is one of the three themes quoted in Alfred Schnittke's *Dedication to I. Stravinsky, S. Prokofiev and D. Shostakovich.*

Russian Dance—No. 4: reductions for piano solo by F. Block and G. Sándor; transcribed for band by P. J. Lang.

Instrumentation of Suite Opus 22*a*:   piccolo, flute, oboe, cor anglais, E flat clarinet, B flat clarinet, bass clarinet, soprano saxophone, bassoon, contra-bassoon ~ 4 horns, 3 trumpets, 3 trombones, tuba, B flat baritone saxhorn ~ harmonium ~ timpani, triangle, tambourine, side drum, wood block, gong, cymbals, bass drum, xylophone ~ strings.

Music: A photostat of the 1929 Suite manuscript is in the Shostakovich family archive and the autograph score of the 1932 version preserved at the Glinka Museum. A page of the Adagio autograph full score is reproduced in Volume 26 of *Collected Works.*

Suite: Muzgiz, No. 14457, 1935, 30.5 cm.

J. Fischer, New York, No. 7803, *c.*1941, arr. for two pianos by P. Luboshutz.

Boosey & Hawkes, No. 20 (A.S.M.P. No. 37), *c.*1942, 19 cm.

Edwin F. Kalmus, No. 138, 1942, 22.5 cm.

International Music, No. 1314OL.

Muzyka, No. 11695 (in Volume 26 of *Collected Works* with Opp. 27*a* and 39*a*), 1987, full score, 30 cm.

Polka—No. 3: Triton, Leningrad, 1935, arr. for piano by the composer.

Axelrod Music, Providence, No. 521, *c*.1939, arr. for piano.

Edition Musicus, New York, *c*.1939, arr. from original score by Q. Maganini, piano conductor score and 15 parts, 31 cm.

Clayton F. Summy, Chicago, No. 3395, 1940, arr. for string quartet (with ad lib. bass) or string orchestra by S. Lehnhoff, 31 cm.

Russian American Music, New York, 1941, arr. for violin and piano by D. J. Grunes.

Edition Musicus, New York, No. 30, 1942, arr. for band by Q. Maganini, score, 27.5 cm.

Anglo-Soviet Music Press, No. 45, 1942, concert piano transcription by G. Sándor, 30 cm.

Mills Music, New York, 1943, transcribed for band by P. J. Lang, score and parts.

Leeds Music, 1945, arr. for violin and piano by H. Glickman, 30.5 cm.

Russian American Music, New York, 1945, arr. for orchestra by Richard Mohaupt, *c*.21 cm.

Muzgiz, No. 3184 (in *D. Shostakovich: Compositions for fortepiano*, Volume 1, with Sans op. B, Opp. 5, 12, 13, 34, and 61), 1966, arr. for piano, 29 cm.

Sovetskii Kompozitor, No. 4565 (in *Dmitri Shostakovich: Popular Pieces*), 1967, arr. for piano, 28.5 cm.

Kendor Music, New York, No. 6061B, 1973, transcribed for flute, oboe, B flat clarinet, French horn (or B flat clarinet substitute), and bassoon by J. N. Smith (Grade 4—playing time 2' 10"), score and parts, 30.5 cm.

Aaron Henry arr. for wind quartet [publisher and date not stated], score 28 cm. and parts 31 cm.

Belwin Mills, New York, *c*.1975, arr. for two pianos by P. Gunther, 31 cm.

Dorsey Brothers Music, London, Promenade No. 52, 1978, arr. for piano, 30 cm.

Sovetskii Kompozitor, No. 6680 (in *Works by Soviet Composers for Viola Ensemble*), 1984, arr. for 4 violas and double-bass by G. Bezrukov, 29 cm.

International Opus, Richmond, Virginia, *c*.1995, transcribed for wind quintet (bassoon, clarinet, flute, French horn, and oboe) by A. Lesnick, score and parts, 28 cm.

Russian Dance—No. 4: Mills Music, New York, 1943, transcribed for band by P. J. Lang, score and parts.

Russian American Music, New York, 1946, arr. for orchestra by R. Mohaupt, *c*.21 cm.

Anglo-Soviet Music Press, 1955, concert piano transcription by G. Sándor, 29 cm.

Boosey & Hawkes, 1957, arr. by Cyril Watters, piano conductor score and 21 parts, *c*.32 cm. [Also Anglo-Soviet Music Press, 1958, *c*.21 cm.]

Complete score—DSCH Publishers, Moscow, no number, 1995, complete piano score with article on the history of the ballet by Manashir Yakubov in Russian and English, 232 pp., 29 cm.

Duration: Complete 1930 score: 2 hrs 13 mins. Suite Opus 22*a*: 16 minutes in score; 15' 49"–18' 25"; 18' 30" (Plaistow). Polka: 1' 34"–2' 35"; 2' 30" (Aronowsky). [1' 08" stated on Haitink's recording is incorrect.]

Ballet (new version): 1 hr 53 mins.

Additional Ballets: *Pas de trois.* A divertissement choreographed by Vladimir Dokoudovsky to the Polka from *The Golden Age;* Cuerpo de Baile del Teatro Colón ('Original Ballet Russe', director general Colonel W. de Basil), Buenos Aires, Argentina, 1943.

The Dreamers: score adapted in 1975 for this four-act ballet by the composer and Sergei Sarozhnikov from *The Golden Age* and *The Bolt,* choreographed by Natalya Ryzhenko; Stanislavsky and Nemirovich-Danchenko Musical Theatre, Moscow, 19 January 1976.

Film: USSR National TV, 1986, a film of the revised ballet. The Bolshoi Ballet production (in association with BBC TV) available on videocassette: National Video, Home Vision, 'The World of Dance No. 18'. A television presentation of this performance introduced by Michael Berkeley, shown on BBC2 TV on 21 November 1987. Released June 1989 on Castle Vision video CVI 2046.

Recordings: Columbia LB 16 (10" 78 rpm). Polka and Russian Dance. Orchestra Symphonique, Julius EHRLICH. G Sept. 1934.

USA: Victor 11 8239 (78 rpm). Polka only, arr. Q. Maganini. National Symphony Orchestra of America, Hans KINDLER. [Musorgsky.] P 28–9 Jan. 1941. *Reissued:* HMV C 3346 (78 rpm). [Musorgsky.]

USA: Columbia 17404 D in set M 660 (78 rpm). Polka arr. Grunes. Zino FRANCESCATTI (violin) and Max Lanner (piano). [Kreisler.] P 12 Apr. 1946. *Reissued:* Philips NBL 5010 (mono). [Paganini, Albéniz, Kreisler *et al.*] G June 1955 ~ Pearl Compact Disc GEMM CD 9250 (mono). [Lalo, Franck, Debussy *et al.*] I Apr. 1997 ~ Biddulph Compact Disc BID 80169 (mono). [Tartini, Paganini, Wieniawski *et al.*] I Nov. 2000.

USA: Mercury MG 10035 (mono). Polka only. Dmitri SHOSTAKOVICH (piano). [Opp. 5, 34, and 69; 'David Oistrakh plays violin favorites'—Chopin/Saraste, Prokofiev *et al.*] P Prague 1946. *Reissued:* USA: Colosseum CRLP 167 (mono). Polka only. ['Footlight Favorites from behind the Iron Curtain'—concert including Opp. 16 and 30*a* No. 3.] I 1954.

USSR: Melodiya M10 39075-6 (mono). Polka only. Dmitri SHOSTAKOVICH (piano). [In four-record set 'D. Shostakovich—Pianist'—Opp. 5, 34, 69, and 67.] P 1947, I 1977*b* ~ Revelation Compact Disc RV 70008 (mono) ['Shostakovich plays Shostakovich, Vol. 7'—Opp. 134, 5, and 40.] I Sept. 1998, G Feb. 1999.

USA: Columbia 17335 D (78 rpm). Polka only. Oscar LEVANT (piano). [Op. 34 No. 2.] P pre-1949. *Reissued:* USA: Columbia ML 5324 (mono). Polka. ['Some Pleasant Moments in the 20th Century'—Rakhmaninov, Cyril Scott, Prokofiev *et al.*] I 1950s.

Columbia DX 1860 (78 rpm). Polka. New York Philharmonic Orchestra, Efrem KURTZ. [Rimsky-Korsakov.] P *c.*1949, G Jan. 1953. *Reissued:* USA: Columbia ML 4233 (mono). [Op. 30*a* No. 2; Offenbach, Prokofiev *et al.*] ~ USA, Columbia Special Products P 14153 (electronic stereo). [Op. 30*a* No. 2; Offenbach, Prokofiev *et al.*] I 1977.

USA: Victor 2214 (78 rpm). Polka arr. Luboshutz. Pierre LUBOSHUTZ and Genia NEMENOFF (piano duo). [Falla.] P *c.*1950. *Reissued:* USA: Vanguard VSD 2128 (7" 45 rpm). [Op. 30*a* No. 2.]

USA: Westminster WL 5319 (mono). Suite. National Symphony Orchestra of Washington, Howard MITCHELL. [Op. 10.] I 1954. *Reissued:* Nixa WLP 5319 (mono). [Op. 10.] G Mar. 1955 ~ USA: Decca XWM 18293 (mono). [Op. 10.] I Dec. 1956 ~ USA: Westminster Gold WGS 8286. Polka and Russian Dance. ['The Best from the Russia We Love, Volume 2'— Stravinsky, Tchaikovsky, Musorgsky, and Rakhmaninov.] ~ USA: MCA Compact Disc D2-9823A. Suite. [Op. 102.]

USA: RCA LM 2294 (mono) and LSC 2294. Polka only. Boston Pops Orchestra, Arthur FIEDLER. [Rodgers, Gould, Bernstein *et al.*] P 1954, I Sept. 1959. *Reissued:* RCA LSC 2813. [Gounod, Rimsky-Korsakov, Saint-Saëns *et al.*] I July 1965 ~ RCA Gold Seal Compact Disc 09026 62577-2. ['Fiedler at the Ballet'—Tchaikovsky, Chopin, Delibes *et al.*] I Feb. 1995 ~ RCA Victor Living Stereo Compact Disc 09026 68550-2. ['Slaughter on Tenth Avenue'—Rodgers, Bernstein, Copland *et al.*] I 1997.

USA: RCA Bluebird LBC 1086. Polka arr. S. Lehnhoff. AMERICAN ART QUARTET (Edice Shapiro, Robert Sushel, Virginia Majewski, Victor Gottlieb). [Tchaikovsky, Mendelssohn, Rakhmaninov *et al.*] P 1954, I 1955.

HMV BLP 1080 (10" mono). Suite. Philharmonia Orchestra, Efrem KURTZ. [Barber.] P London 25 Mar. 1955, G Apr. 1956. *Reissued:* USA: Capitol EMI G 714. [Barber.] I 1959 ~ HMV HQM 1026 (12" mono). [Kabalevsky, Prokofiev, and Stravinsky.] G Sept. 1966 ~ USA: Testament Compact Disc SBT 1078 (mono). Suite. [Op. 93.] I Nov. 1996, G Feb. 1997.

USA: Capitol SFP 4 8413 (7" 45 rpm). Polka. Capitol Symphony Orchestra, Carmen DRAGON. [Popular pieces.] G May 1959.

USA: Everest LPBR 6027 (mono) and SDBR 3027. Polka only. Stadium Symphony Orchestra of New York, Raymond PAIGE. [Bizet, Dinicu, Dvořák *et al.*] P New York late 1950s, I July 1959. *Reissued:* Everest Compact Disc EVC 9047. [Rimsky-Korsakov, Bizet, Dinicu *et al.*] I 1997.

RCA Red Seal RB 16170 (mono) and SR 2051. Suite. London Symphony Orchestra, Jean MARTINON. [Op. 10.] P 9–11 Dec. 1957, G Dec. 1959. *Reissued:* USA: RCA Victor LM 2322 (mono) and LSC 2322. [Op. 10.] I 1959 ~ France: RCA Choc 400 298 (mono). [Op. 10.] ~ RCA Victrola VIC 1184 (mono) and VICS 1184. [Op. 10.] G July 1967 ~ Decca Eclipse ECS 580. [Op. 10.] G Feb. 1971 ~ USA: London STS 15180. [Op. 10.] ~ Polygram Compact Disc POCL 9439. [Op. 47.] I Oct. 1992 ~ Germany: Audiophile/RCA Victor LSC 2322. [Op. 10.] I limited LP reissue on 180g. vinyl 1995.

USA: Mercury MMA 11092 (mono) and AMS 16041. Polka. Eastman-Rochester Pops Orchestra, Frederick FENNELL. ['Pop-overs'—Rakhmaninov, Rimsky-Korsakov *et al.*] P 1960. Same performance available on Mercury SEX 15008 (7" 45 rpm). G July 1960. Also on Mercury MG 50222 (mono). ['Pop-overs'.] *Reissued:* Mercury Compact Disc 434 349-2MM. ['Popovers'.] G Jan. 1995.

USA: Capitol P 8576 (mono) and SP 8576. Suite. Philharmonia Orchestra, Robert IRVING. [Bartók.] P 20 June 1961, G Sept. 1962. *Reissued:* HMV Classics Compact Disc 5 73047-2. Suite. [Sans opp. E and G; Opp. 16, 97, 35, and 89.] I Oct. 1998.

USSR: MK D 9501-2 (10" mono). Polka. Viola Ensemble of the Central Home of Art Workers, Georgi BEZRUKOV (violist leader). [Bach, Scarlatti, Brahms *et al.*] P 1962.

USA: Capitol P 8391 (mono). Polka. Leonard PENNARIO (piano). ['Keyboard Fantasias'—Chopin, Mendelssohn, Debussy *et al.*] P 1964. *Reissued:* RCA Victrola VIC 1238 (mono) and VICS 1238. Polka. ['Virtuoso Favourites'—J. Strauss, Mendelssohn, Saint-Saëns *et al.*] G July 1968.

USA: Columbia ML 6267 (mono) and MS 6867. Andre KOSTELANETZ and his Orchestra. [Opp. 105 and 97*a* excerpts, Sans op. P.] P New York 23 and 29 Nov. 1965. *Reissued:* Sony Classical Compact Disc SBK 62642. [Opp. 10, 96, 97, 105, and Sans op. P.] G June 1997.

USSR: Melodiya D 018709-10 (mono) and C 01387-8. Suite. Bolshoi Theatre Orchestra, Maksim SHOSTAKOVICH; soloists in No. 2—Aleksandr Stepanov (soprano saxophone), Ivan Butirsky (clarinet), Pyotr Grigoriev (B flat baritone saxhorn), and Leon Zaks (violin); soloist in No. 3—Vladimir Fedin (xylophone). [Op. 27*a*.] P and I 1966. *Reissued:* USSR: Melodiya D 00018303-4 (7" mono). Polka only. [Op. 97*a* and Sans op. P excerpts.] I 1966 ~ USA: Angel Melodiya SR 40062. Suite. [Op. 27*a*.] ~ HMV Melodiya ASD 2763. Suite. [Prokofiev.] G Apr. 1972—HMV Melodiya ASD 3012 in Set SLS 891. Suite Nos. 1, 3, and 4. ['Ballet from the Bolshoi'.] I Aug. 1974 ~ HMV Melodiya BOX 50213 in Set SLS 5025. Nos. 1, 3, and 4. [Op. 141.] G Dec. 1975 ~ USSR: Melodiya C 01387-8. Suite. [In fourth box of Part 1 of *Collected Works on Records* with Op. 27*a*.] I 1978 ~ Germany: Melodia Eurodisc 300 602-435. [In three-record box set with Opp. 93 and 103.] ~ Germany: Melodia Eurodisc 80528 KK. [Op.

14.] ~ Italy: EMI 065 94484. [Op. 27*a*.] I 1978 ~ Japan: Victor Musical Industries Compact Disc VICC 2090. [Op. 18.] I 1989 ~ RCA Gold Seal Compact Disc 74321 32041-2. Polka. [Opp. 47 and 78.] I Mar. 1996 ~ BMG Melodiya Compact Discs 74321 66981-2 (two-disc set). Suite. [Sans op. P, Opp. 27a, 64*a*, and 76*a*.] I Dec. 1999.

USA: Russian Compact Disc RCD 16238. Polka. Nataliya GAVRILOVA (piano). ['Russian Piano School'—Opp. 27, 34, and 97; Babadzhanyan, Rakhmaninov, J. Strauss *et al*.] P 1976–90, I 1998.

CBS SS 63127. Polka. Philadelphia Orchestra, Eugene ORMANDY. ['Russian Dances'—Khachaturyan, Rimsky-Korsakov, Prokofiev *et al*.] P 1967, G Mar. 1968. *Reissued:* CBS 30058. ['Russia's Greatest Hits'.] ~ Sony Essential Classics Compact Disc SBK 53261. [Op. 47; and Prokofiev.] I Jan. 1994, G July 1994.

USA: RCA Red Seal LSC 3133. Suite. Chicago Symphony Orchestra, Leopold STOKOWSKI. [Op. 54.] P 20–2 Feb. 1968. *Reissued:* RCA Red Seal SB 6839. [Op. 54.] G Oct. 1970 ~ France: RCA Red Seal 644 554. [Op. 54.] ~ USA: Time-Life, 'Great Men of Music' box set STL 568. [Opp. 114, 40, 47, 102, 110, and 135.] I 1979 ~ RCA Gold Seal GL 42916. [Op. 54.] G Oct. 1981 ~ RCA Gold Seal Compact Disc 09026 62516-2. [Op. 54; and Khachaturyan.] I 1997 ~ RCA Compact Discs 74321 70931-2 (two-disc set). ['Stokowski the Magician'—Bach, Beethoven, Liszt *et al*.] G Mar. 2000.

France: EMI 2 C 061-80696. Polka arr. White. Ruth WHITE (electronic keyboard). ['Klassik O'Tilt'—Rimsky-Korsakov, Satie, Debussy *et al*.] P Paris post-1968.

CBS Classics 61781. Polka. New York Philharmonic Orchestra, Leonard BERNSTEIN. [Borodin, Prokofiev, Ippolitov-Ivanov *et al*.] P 22 Oct. 1970, G July 1977.

USA: Turnabout TVS 34644. Suite. Seattle Symphony Orchestra, Milton KATIMS; soloists in No. 2—John Budelman (soprano saxophone), Ronald Phillips (clarinet), Dennis Smith (B flat baritone saxhorn), Henry Siegl (violin), and Scott Goff (flute); soloist in No. 3—Randolph Bauuton (xylophone). [Glière and Rimsky-Korsakov.] P 1976, G Mar. 1980.

USA: Kendor Music (number not stated). Polka arr. J. N. Smith. FREDONIA WOODWIND QUINTET—Donald Hartman (flute), John Maier (oboe), James East (clarinet), William Hoyt (horn), and John Gillette (bassoon). [Beethoven, Bach, Handel *et al*.] P 1970s.

Lyntone (Haydn) DEL 100. Polka arr. D. Ogden. DELMÉ QUARTET (Galina Solodchin, David Ogden, John Underwood, Stephen Orton). [Tchaikovsky, Wolf, Puccini *et al*.] I 1977.

Sweden: BIS LP 149. Polka arr. A. Lyubimov. Rainer KUISMA (marimba). [Milhaud, Fissinger, Lemba, and Sibelius.] P Wik Castle, Sweden 11 Aug. 1979.

Decca D 213D 2 (digital). Suite. London Philharmonic Orchestra, Bernard HAITINK. [Op. 60 in box set.] P Nov. 1979, G Nov. 1980. *Reissued:*

USA: London LDR 10015 (digital). Suite. [op. 60.] I 1980 ~ Decca Compact Disc 421 131-2DH. Suite. [Opp. 14 and 20.] I Mar. 1988, G June 1988 ~ Decca Compact Disc 430 727-2DM. [Janáček.] I Aug. 1991, G Dec. 1991.

Bulgaria: Balkanton BKA 11338. Polka. Nikolai EVROV (piano). [Op. 5; Weber, Shchedrin, Gershwin *et al.*] P 1980?

Sweden: Bluebell Bell 126. Polka only. Inger WIKSTRÖM (piano). [Opp. 5; 19 Nos. 3, 4, and 2; 31 No. 4; 94; 97*a* No. 7; 105 fragment; and Prokofiev.] P Stockholm 28 Jan. and 1 Feb. 1981.

Germany: Live Classics Compact Disc LCL 192. Polka. Oleg KAGAN (violin) and Vladimir Skanavi (piano). ['Oleg Kagan Edition', Vol. XX'— Grieg, Szymanowski, Ravel *et al.*] P Moscow concert 9 Jan. 1982, I 1999.

Decca Compact Disc 433 651-2DH. Polka. Shura CHERKASSKY (piano). ['Shura Cherkassky Live Vol. 4'—Paderewski, Tchaikovsky, Chopin *et al.*] P Wigmore Hall, London concert 20 Feb. 1982, G June 1993.

USA: Russian Disc Compact Discs RDCD 10 009 (two-disc set). Complete score of Grigorovich's 1982 revival. Bolshol Theatre Orchestra, Yuri SIMONOV. P Bolshoi Theatre ballet performances 1982, I Sept. 1996.

Belgium: Pavane ADW 7152 (DMM). Polka arr. J. N. Smith. BELGIAN WOODWIND QUINTET—Jean-Michel Tanquy (flute), Louis Op't Eynde (oboe), Hedwig Swimberghe (clarinet), Herman Lemahieu (horn), and Yves Bomont (bassoon). ['Three Centuries of the Woodwind Quintet'— Sweelinck, Cambini, Zemlinsky *et al.*] P 1983, G Feb. 1985.

Germany: Cadenza Compact Disc CAD D 878-8. Polka arr. N. Živković. Nebojša ŽIVKOVIĆ (marimba) and Iris Kobal (piano). ['Marimba and Percussion Solo'—Op. 27; Tanaka and Miki.] P Stuttgart 1987, I 1989.

USA: Philips Compact Disc 426 247-2. Polka. Boston Pops Orchestra, John WILLIAMS. ['Pops a la Russe'—Borodin, Khachaturyan *et al.*] P Boston 4–7 June 1988, I 1990.

USA: Arabesque Compact Disc Z 6610. Suite Nos. 1, 3, and 4. Kraków Philharmonic Orchestra, Gilbert LEVINE. [Opp. 10 and 35.] P Kraków 26–9 May 1989, G Jan. 1990.

AVM Classics Compact Disc AVZ 3020. Polka arr. composer and Russian Dance arr. G. Sándor. Martin JONES (piano). ['Piano Music Volume II'—Sans opp. A, S, and T; Opp. 13, 34, and 69.] P London 1–2 June 1989.

USA: Windham Hill Records Compact Disc WD-1091. Polka arr. S. Lehnhoff. MODERN MANDOLIN QUARTET (John Imholz, Dana Rath, Paul Binkley, Mike Marshall). ['Intermezzo'—op. 49; Haydn, Ravel, Bernstein *et al.*]

Deutsche Grammophon Compact Disc 431 688-2GH. Suite. Gothenburg Symphony Orchestra, Neeme JÄRVI. [Opp. 112 and 32.] P Gothenburg Dec. 1989, I July 1991, G Sept. 1991. *Reissued:* Deutsche Grammophon Compact Discs 459 415-2GTA2 (two-disc set). [Opp. 103, 112, 131, and 32.] I Jan. 1999.

Germany: Signum Compact Disc SIG X11-00. Polka arr. Filippo. BUDAPESTER-BLECHBLÄSER-QUINTETT. ['Brassissimo'—J. Strauss, Civil, Farkas *et al.*] I 1990.

USA: Newport Classic Compact Disc NPT 85583. Polka. Michael PER-LOWIN (pedal steel guitar) with backing of bass, guitar, drums, and percussion. [Copland, Gershwin, Bartók *et al.*] P home studio of performer 1991, I Feb. 1997.

Chandos Compact Discs 9251/2 (two-disc set). Complete score of 37 numbers in composer's order. Royal Stockholm Philharmonic Orchestra, Gennadi ROZHDESTVENSKY; soloists in No. 9—Karl Ove Mannberg (violin) and Sven Westerholm (soprano saxophone). P Stockholm 4–5 and 7–11 June 1993, I Jan. 1994, G May 1994.

Italy: Phoenix Compact Disc PH 00602. Suite. Byelorussian Symphony Orchestra, Antonello GOTTA. [Opp. 35 and 102.] P Minsk 9–11 Dec. 1993, I Jan. 2001.

Naxos Compact Disc 8.553126. Suite. New Zealand Symphony Orchestra, Christopher LYNDON-GEE. [Opp. 35, 102, and 96.] P Wellington 2–4 Nov. 1994, I Sept. 1995.

Czech: Supraphon Compact Disc SU 3278-2 031. Suite. Prague Symphony Orchestra, Maksim SHOSTAKOVICH. [Op. 107.] P Prague concert 14 Nov. 1996, I May 1997, G Dec. 1997. *Reissued:* Czech: Supraphon Compact Disc SU 3415-2. [Opp. 54 and 114*a*.] I and G Awards (Oct.) 1999.

Finland: Ondine Compact Disc ODE 894-2. Can-Can. Helsinki Philharmonic Orchestra, Leif SEGERSTAM. ['Earquake'—Hanson, Rangstrom, Khachaturyan *et al.* NB. CD issued with ear-plugs.] P Finlandia Hall Jan. 1997, I Nov. 1997.

Switzerland: Dynamic Compact Disc CDS 195. Polka. VENICE QUARTET (Andrea Vio, Alberto Battiston, Luca Morassuti, Angelo Zanin). ['Fun Time with the String Quartet'—Thomas-Mifune, Chaplin, Rakhmaninov *et al.*] P Genoa 15–17 Sept. 1997.

EMI Compact Disc CDC5 56970-2. Polka. Hamburg State Philharmonic Orchestra, Ingo METZMACHER. ['Who is Afraid of 20th Century Music?'—Bernstein, Henze, Hindemith *et al.*] P Hamburg New Year concert 31 Dec. 1999–1 Jan. 2000, G Aug. 2000.

Chandos Compact Disc CHAN 9907. Polka. Rustem HAYROUDINOFF (piano). ['Theatre Music'—Opp. 37, 19, 31, 32, 44, 58*a*, and 66.] P Potton Hall, Suffolk 7–8 Aug. 2000, I Apr. 2001.

References: Bogdanova, Goltsman, Grigorovich and Davlekamova, Katonova, Lushina, and Yakubov in Fanning 1995.

Note: See also *Two Pieces for String Quartet,* Sans op. D (i) No. 1.

Opus 23   Entr'acte and Finale

Form: Two compositions for orchestra (including a flexatone), contributed to
an epilogue entitled 'What is modern America like?' for Erwin Dressel's
opera *Der arme Columbus* (alternatively known as *Armer Columbus*—'The
Poor Columbus'), with libretto by Arthur Zweiniger:

1. Entr'acte in C minor (also known as the 'Overture' although it
   appears before the sixth scene of the opera)—Allegretto poco
   moderato
2. Finale in C major—Moderato—Andantino—Allegro

The main theme from the Finale utilized in *The Golden Age,* Opus 22 No.
19 (Foxtrot), *Conditionally Killed,* Opus 31 No. 34 (The Archangel
Gabriel's Number), and the fourth movement of Piano Concerto No. 1,
Opus 35.

Instrumentation: piccolo, 2 flutes (II = piccolo II), 2 oboes, cor anglais, E flat
clarinet, 2 B flat clarinets, bass clarinet, 3 bassoons, contrabassoon ~ 4
horns, 4 trumpets, 3 trombones, tuba ~ timpani, triangle, tambourine,
tom-tom, castanets, side drum, cymbals, bass drum, gong ~ xylophone
(in No. 1), flexatone ~ S.A.T.B. chorus (in Finale) ~ strings.

Composed: Early 1929 (January or February) at the request of the musical
director Samuil Samosud, at Leningrad.

Premières: Opera: 14 March 1929, Malyi Opera Theatre, Leningrad; Samuil
Samosud.

Overture: 10 February 1977, Moscow Conservatory Bolshoi Hall;
Moscow Conservatory Students' Symphony Orchestra, Gennadi Rozhdestvensky.

UK concert and broadcast: 4 April 1979, Royal Festival Hall, London;
BBC Symphony Orchestra, G. Rozhdestvensky.

Finale: 11 February 1981, Leningrad Conservatory Bolshoi Hall;
Leningrad Philharmonic Orchestra, G. Rozhdestvensky.

Music: The autograph scores of both pieces, long believed lost, were discovered in the music libraries of Leningrad Malyi Opera Theatre (Entr'acte
in late 1970s) and Leningrad Kirov Opera and Ballet Theatre (Finale in
early 1980s).

Muzyka, No. 11935 (in Volume 23 of *Collected Works* with Op. 15*a*, and
Sans opp. D and K), 1986, full scores of both pieces, 30 cm.

Duration: Overture: 3' 16"–3' 41". Finale: 4' 15".

Recordings: USSR: Melodiya C10 12547-50 (fourth side in two-record set).
Overture. Moscow Conservatory Students' Symphony Orchestra, Gennadi ROZHDESTVENSKY. [Auber, Hindemith, Suppé *et al.*] P Moscow concert 10 Feb. 1977, I 1980*b*. *Reissued:* HMV Melodiya ASD 3633. Overture,
labelled as 'Christopher Columbus'. [Janáček, Panufnik, Webern *et al.*] G
Mar. 1979.

USSR: Melodiya C10 14415-6. Overture. Leningrad Philharmonic Orchestra, Gennadi ROZHDESTVENSKY. [Album 1 of 'From Manuscripts of Different Years'—Opp. 4, 16, 17, and 36; Sans opp. C, P, and Z.] P 1980, I 1981*b*. *Reissued:* HMV Melodiya ASD 1650331. [As Russian release.] G July 1983 ~ Germany: Melodia Eurodisc 201974-366. [As Russian release.] ~ BMG Melodiya Compact Discs 74321 63462-2 (two-disc set). [Opp. 23 Finale; 14, 20, and 32.] I Mar. 1999.

USSR: Melodiya C10 23081 001. Finale. USSR Ministry of Culture Symphony Orchestra and Chamber Choir, Gennadi ROZHDESTVENSKY. [Album 5 of 'From Manuscripts of Different Years'—Sans opp. D and E; Op. 59.] P 1984, I 1986*c* ~ BMG Melodiya Compact Discs 74321 63461-2 (two-disc set). [Opp. 103, 93, and 91.] I Mar. 1999.

Chandos Compact Disc CHAN 9792. Overture. Russian Symphony Orchestra, Valeri POLYANSKY. ['The Unknown Shostakovich' (*sic*)—Sans opp. W and B, Op. 125.] P Mosfilm Studio Jan. 1998, I Jan. 2000.

Opus 24   The Shot

Alternative title: *The Gunshot.*

Form: Incidental music to a verse play comedy *The Shot* by Aleksandr Bezymensky, comprising eleven mainly untitled episodes:

1. Dundee's Romance—[Allegro moderato]
2. Choir—[Moderato]
3. Third Episode
4. Fourth Episode—[Con moto]
5. [Entry of the Heads of Departments]—[Marciale]
6. [Exeunt the Heads of Departments]—inscribed 'Same as No. 5'
7. [Entry of the Secretaries]—six-bar introduction *attacca*
8. [Entry of the secretaries]—[Tempo ad libitum]
9. Ninth Episode—Allegro
10. Tenth Episode—Allegro
11. Eleventh Episode—Allegretto

Instrumentation: flute, B flat clarinet, bassoon ~ horn, trumpet, trombone, tuba ~ 2 cornets; E flat alto, B flat tenor, and baritone saxhorns ~ timpani, wood block, rattle, tambourine, side drum, cymbals, bass drum, gong ~ 2 balalaikas, piano ~ violins. In the Ninth Episode a four-part chorus shouts (not sings) revolutionary words.

Composed: 1929, at Leningrad.

Première: 14 December 1929, Leningrad Working Youth Theatre (TRAM); directed by Mikhail Sokolovsky and R. Suslovich.

Arrangements: Piano reductions of Nos. 4, 7, 8, 10, and 11 made from the full score by V. Samarin.

Music: Autograph vocal and full scores, discovered in 1984, preserved at the Glinka Museum. 'Dundee's Romance' song taken from the programme booklet of TRAM's 1930 tour of the USSR.

Muzyka, No. 11412 (in Volume 28 of *Collected Works* with Opp. 19, 28, 31, 32, 37, 44, 58a, 63, 66, 72, and in the supplement, Sans opp. D and K), vocal and piano scores of Nos. 1, 2, 4, 5, and 7–11, 30 cm.

Muzyka, No. 11413 (in Volume 27 of *Collected Works* with Opp. 19, 28, 32, 37, 44, 58a, 63, 66, and 72), 1987, full score of Nos. 4, 5, and 7–11, 30 cm.

Duration: 'Dundee's Romance': 2' 47".

Recording of 'Dundee's Romance':

[BBC tape: Konstantin PLUZHNIKOV (tenor) and Larissa Gergieva (piano). P specially recorded in St Petersburg for BBC Broadcast on 31 May 1995.]

Opus 25   Virgin Land

Form: Incidental music to a stage play drama *Soil* by Arkadi Gorbenko and Nikolai Lvov.

Composed: April 1930, at Leningrad.

Première: 9 May 1930, Leningrad Working Youth Theatre (TRAM); directed by Mikhail Sokolovsky and Nikolai Lebedyev.

Music: Manuscript lost.

Recordings: —

Notes: This production was not based on Mikhail Sholokhov's novel *Virgin Soil Upturned,* the first part of which was published in 1932. The subject-matter—the socialist collectivization of the countryside, however, was similar.

In 1932–33 Shostakovich, in conjunction with Fedodosi Rubtsov, also wrote incidental music for the four-act stage play *Combative Course* by A. Gorbenko, N. Lvov, and Mikhail Sokolovsky staged by TRAM. The original music is lost though a typed text is preserved in the Glinka Museum.

Opus 26   Alone

Alternative title: Also translated as *All Alone.*

Form: Music for the sound film *Alone,* with screenplay and direction by Grigori Kozintsev and Leonid Trauberg, for the Leningrad Soyuzkino Studio. A song 'How beautiful life will be' (also translated as 'Happy Days are Coming') provides a leitmotiv for the film. The sound-track carried music only; no human voices apart from scraps of insignificant phrases and fragments of speech introduced by chance. The orchestra is augmented by a brass band, organ, and theremin.

Also three fragments existing in piano arrangements: 'The Beginning', 'The Dream' (later used as No. 34 in *Hamlet,* Opus 32), and 'March'. The opening numbers depict a day-dreaming sequence ending with a tram taking off into the clouds.

Instrumentation: piccolo, 2 flutes, 2 oboes, cor anglais, E flat clarinet, 2 B flat clarinets, bass clarinet, 2 bassoons, contrabassoon ~ 4 horns, 2 trumpets, 3 trombones, tuba ~ timpani, triangle, wood block, side drum, cymbals, bass drum, gong ~ glockenspiel, xylophone, theremin ~ harp, organ ~ soprano and tenor soloists, S.A.T.B. chorus ~ strings. The eight-piece band is employed in Reels 1, 6, and 7; the organ in Reel 3 No. 3 and the theremin in Reel 6 No. 4.

Composed: 1930–1, at Leningrad.

Premières: Film first shown on 10 October 1931 at the Leningrad 'Splendid Palace' cinema. Score conducted by Nikolai Rabinovich.

   Suite: 11 February 1981, Leningrad; Leningrad Philharmonic Orchestra.

Arrangements: Suite of three untitled movements compiled by Gennadi Rozhdestvensky:

Part I—Reel 1 No. 4 and Reel 3 No. 3.
Part 2—Reel 4 No. 9, Reel 3 No. 6, and Reel 4 No. 9.
Part 3—Reel 4 No. 1 *attacca,* Reel 3 No. 2, Reel 5 No. 2, and Reel 2 March.

   Gerard McBurney has arranged a ten-piece Suite from the score: Reels 1 No. 7; 3 Nos. 2 and 6; 4 Nos. 2, 7, and 9; 5 Nos. 3 and 4; 6 No. 4 and Finale.

   A ten-movement cycle selected from the film score and transcribed in 2000 by Dmitri Smirnov for wind ensemble (flute, 2 oboes, 2 clarinets, alto saxophone, 2 bassoons, 2 French horns, trumpet, trombone, percussion, and double bass).

Music: Autograph score preserved at the Glinka Museum, apart from Nos. 2*a*, 3, and a fragment of 4 from Reel 6 which are preserved at the Leningrad Institute of the Theatre, Music and Cinematography. A page of No. 2 from Reel 5 is reproduced in Volume 41 of *Collected Works.*

   Muzyka, No. 10889 (in Volume 41 of *Collected Works* with Opp. 30, 33, 41, 48, 50, 53, 55, 56, 59, and 64), 1987, 29 items in full score plus a fragment of 'The Storm in the Steppe' and 3 items in piano arrangement, 30 cm.

Duration: Film of seven reels. Complete Score: 70' 41"–74' 13". Suite: 12' 12".

Recordings: USSR: Melodiya C10 19103 004. Suite. Ensemble of soloists from the USSR Symphony Orchestra, Gennadi ROZHDESTVENSKY. [Album 2 of 'From Manuscripts of Different Years'—Opp. 1, 3, 7, and 21.] P 30 Sept. 1982, I 1983*d. Reissued:* Olympia Compact Disc OCD 194. [Opp. 1, 3, 7, 100, 59, and 37.] I Feb. 1988, G June 1988 ~ Japan: Icone Compact Disc ICN 9415-2. [Opp. 54, 1, and 3.] I Sept. 1994 ~ BMG Melodiya Compact Discs 74321 59058-2 (two-disc set). [Opp. 36, 4, 17, Z, H, C, 16, 1, 3, 7/D, 59, E, 128, 30*a*, and 19.] I and G Mar. 1999.

Germany: Capriccio Compact Disc 10 562. Complete score. Svetlana Katchur (soprano), Vladimir Kazatchouk (tenor), Berlin Radio Choir, Sigurd Brauns (chorus-master), Berlin Radio Symphony Orchestra, Mikhail YUROVSKY. P Berlin 19–22 Sept. 1995, I Oct. 1996. NB. This recording comprises all the items in *Collected Works* Volume 41, pp. 4–114, with the following additions: Reel 4—an unaccompanied soprano folksong solo interrupted by the tenor song 'How beautiful life will be' between Nos. 3 and 7; Reel 6—No. 4 (with theremin, pp. 471–4) leading *attacca* into No. 2; Reel 7—No. 3 repeated after No. 4 and Reel 4 No. 1 introduced after No. 6 (played softly with oboes replacing trumpets and entitled 'Nightmare' in the liner note).

USA: Russian Disc RDCD 10 007. Complete score. Minsk Chamber Choir, Igor Matukhov (chorus-master), Byelorussian Radio and TV Symphony Orchestra, Walter MNATSAKANOV. P Minsk Nov. 1995, I 1997. NB. This recording comprises the 29 items in *Collected Works* Volume 41, pp. 4–114, with no additional numbers.

Decca Compact Disc 460 792-2DH11. Reel 1 Nos. 1 and 7 (non-vocal); Reel 3 No. 6; Reel 2 March; Reel 3 Nos. 2 and 3; Reel 5 No. 1; Reel 6 Nos. 4, 2*a*, and 3. Fay Lovsky (theremin in Reel 6 No. 4), Royal Concertgebouw Orchestra, Riccardo CHAILLY. ['The Film Album'—Opp. 33, 56, 116, 55, 132, 76*a*, and 97.] P Amsterdam 6, 19, and 22 May 1998, I Mar. 1999, G Apr. 1999.

Opus 27   The Bolt

Alternative title: The original working title was *At the New Machine*.

Form: Ballet in three acts and seven scenes, with libretto by Vladimir Smirnov, décor by Tatyana Bruni and Georgi Korshikov, and choreography by Fyodor Lopukhov.

Overture

ACT 1

Scene 1: 'In the cloakroom'
1. Gymnastics. Radio announcement 1
2. Drinking bout

Scene 2: 'In the workshop'
1. Checking the installation of the machines
2. The Charwomen. Radio-announcement 2
3. March: Scene of the filling workshop
4. Workshop concert; (*a*) The Wreckers. Interlude, (*b*) The Bureaucrat, (*c*) The Blacksmith, and (*d*) Industrial March. Dance of the Komsomol Members and Pioneers
5. Starting up the workshop

Scene 3: 'In the cloakroom'
1. Drinking bout
2. The indignant workers
Scene 4: 'In the workshop'
1. At work

ACT 2

Scene: 'In the Factory Village'
1. Scene of the Sexton, Lad, Cloaked Women, Priest, Pioneers, and Pilgrims
2. Dance of the Priest
3. The Pilgrims
4. Dance: Komsomol Circle
5. Dance of Kozelkov
6. Dance of the Cloaked Women
7. Dance of the Lad
8. Quadrille of the Komsomol Members and dance of the Sexton
9. Scene: Priest with the Sexton; departure of the Pilgrims and Komsomol Members
10. Dance pantomime: from the beer-house
11. Scene: vodka and sabotage
12. Kozelkov's Dance with Friends
13. Kozelkov's Dance (in his absence); Waltz-scherzo (doll-like dance mocking secretary Olga)

ACT 3

Scene 1: 'At the door of the workshop'
1. Musical action and Scene: departure of the workers
2. Scene with the bolt. Pantomime and Dance
3. Scene: exposure of the provocation
4. Musical Entr'acte
Scene 2: 'The Club'
1. March: Red Army
2. Appearance of the agitator-brigade: (*a*) maritime conference, (*b*) the aesthetic Young Lady, (*c*) The Conciliator, (*d*) Textile Workers, (*e*) The Drayman, and (*f*) the female Colonial Slave
3. Komsomol Dance
4. Red Army. Dance performance; (*a*) infantry and artillery, (*b*) Society of Assistance to Defence, Aviation, and Chemical Protection, (*c*) bicyclists, (*d*) Red Army, Red Navy and sailors, (*e*) aviators, and (*f*) the Budyonny Mounted Army
5. Final Dance and Apotheosis

The order and titles of the items in Acts 1 and 3 of the composer's score, as recorded by Rozhdestvensky, differ slightly from the ballet as detailed above, while Act 2 is identical apart from the transposition of the last two numbers. The musical numbers in the piano score, compiled by Manashir Yakubov on the basis of the première programme booklet and archival material, appear as follows:

   1. Overture—Adagio—Allegro

ACT 1

---

   2. Gymnastics—Moderato
   3. Leaving for work—Allegretto *attacca*
   4. Lyonka Tippler (off to work after a drinking bout)—Adagio *attacca*
   5. Mime of the installation of the machines—Allegro
   6. Mime of the Chief Engineer, technicians, and workers—Allegro non troppo
   7. Entry of Kozelkov—Moderato *attacca*
   8. Mime Dance of the Charwomen (Tidying up the workshop)—Allegro
   9. The workers arrive—Allegretto
 10. The Saboteurs (Intermezzo)—Allegretto
 11. The Bureaucrat—Allegretto—Allegro
 12. The Blacksmith—Allegretto
 13. Entry of the Komsomol Members, and Dance of the Pioneers—Allegro
 14. Commissioning of the workshop (First Dance of the Machines)—Allegro
 15. The Hooligan's Mime Dance (Carousing)—Adagio—Allegro
 16. Mime Dance of the Hooligans and Workers (The workers' indignation)—Adagio—Allegro
 17. The workshop in operation (Second Dance of the Machines)—Allegro

---
ACT 2

---

 18. Introduction. Scene with the Sexton, Lad, Beggar Women, Priest, and Pioneers—Andantino
 19. Mime and Dance of the Priest—Adagio—Allegro vivo *attacca*
 20. Entry of the Pilgrims—Andantino
 21. Dance of the Komsomol Members (a Russian, a Georgian, and an Uzbek)—Allegro
 22. Dance of Kozelkov—Andantino
 23. Dance of the Beggar Women—Andantino
 24. Dance of the Lad—Allegro
 25. Dance of the Komsomol Members, Dance of the Sexton, and Scene with the Pilgrims—Allegro—Andantino
 26. Dance of the Hooligans—Largo—Allegro

27. Mime of the Hooligans and Scene with Lyonka and the Priest—
    Andante—Allegro—Adagio
28. Mime of Kozelkov, Boris, and Olga—Allegretto—Allegro
29. Dance of Kozelkov and his Friends—Allegretto—Andante—
    Allegretto—Allegro

ACT 3

30. Entr'acte—Lento
31. The end of the working day—Allegro
32. Scene with the bolt—Andante—Allegro—Adagio
33. March—Allegretto
34. The Naval Disarmament Conference—Allegretto
35. Dance of the aesthetic Young Lady—Allegro—Andantino
36. The Yes-Man—Andantino
37. Dance of the Mill Girls—Allegro
38. Dance of the Drayman—Moderato non troppo
39. Dance of the Colonial Slave Girl—Andante—Allegro
40. Dance of the Komsomol Members—Allegro
41. The conspiracy exposed (The Tale of the Lad)—Andante—
    Allegretto—Allegro
42. Red Army Dances (infantrymen and artillerymen; Association
    for Defence, Aviation, and Chemical Protection; motorcyclists; a
    Red Army soldier and sailor; airmen; and the Budyonny Cavalry
    Corps)—Allegretto—Allegro
43. Final Dance and Apotheosis—Allegro

The Closing March from *The Bedbug*, Opus 19, utilized for 'The Char-women' of Act 1, Scene 2:2 (or No. 8 in the score). The introductory March from *The Bedbug*, along with Reel 3 No. 3 [Allegro] from *Alone*, Opus 26, appear in 'Scene of the filling workshop' of Act 1, Scene 2:3 (or No. 9 in the score). 'The Wreckers' of Act 1, Scene 2:4a (or No. 10 in the score) is taken from No. 18 of the composer's original score of *The Golden Age*, Opus 22. The 'Komsomol Circle' dance of Act 2 No. 4 (or No. 21 in the score) quotes from the Finale of *New Babylon*, Opus 18.

Several numbers of the ballet score were later reused in *The Limpid Stream* (see table under Opus 39).

Composed: 1930–1, at Leningrad. The commission was received in February 1930.

Premières: Ballet: 8 April 1931, Academic Theatre of Opera and Ballet (Kirov Theatre), Leningrad; Aleksandr Gauk. NB. This was the only staged performance (see Yakubov, p. 269 of the complete piano score) though, apparently, it appeared on theatre posters until mid-June 1931.

USSR revival: Sverdlovsk (now Yekaterinburg) Theatre of Opera and Ballet in April 1976.

Suite: 17 January 1933, Leningrad Philharmonic Bolshoi Hall; Leningrad Philharmonic Orchestra, Aleksandr Gauk.

UK: 28 August 1977, Usher Hall, Edinburgh; Concertgebouw Orchestra, Kirill Kondrashin.

Arrangements: Opus 27*a*—Suite for full orchestra (augmented by a military
band in the final number), also known as Ballet Suite No. 5, assembled
by the composer in 1931:

1. Overture (Introduction)—Adagio—Allegro
2. The Bureaucrat (Polka)—Allegretto (Act 1, Scene 2: 4*b*)
3. The Drayman's Dance (Variations)—Moderato non troppo (Act 3, 2: 2*e*)
4. Tango: Kozelkov's Dance with Friends (Tango)—Allegretto—
   Andante—Allegro (Act 2 No. 12)
5. Intermezzo [also Interlude]—Allegretto (Act 1, 2: 4*a*)
6. The Dance of the Colonial Slave (Act 3, 2: 2*f*)
7. The Conciliator (Act 3, 2: 2*c*)
8. General Dance of Enthusiasm and Apotheosis (Finale)—Presto (Act
   3, 2: 5)

Reduction of Nos. 2 and 5 for piano bv Lev Atovmyan.

No. 2 transcribed for band by Donald Hunsberger; retitled 'Satirical
Dance' (Polka) as a piano solo, for clarinet and piano, small and large
orchestra by Quinto Maganini; for brass ensemble by Alan Raph; for two
pianos four hands by Maxwell Powers; and saxophone and piano by
Marc Chisson.

No. 7 arranged for marimba and piano by Nebojša Živković.

Waltz-scherzo (Ballet Suite No. 1, No. 5, and *Four Waltzes,* Sans op. P
No. 2) variously transcribed, including for accordion by Z. Semyonova,
violin and piano by Gotsdener, balalaika by A. Tikhonov, domra and
piano by Rudolf Belov; and in a piano reduction by Bronislava Rozengauz and as an organ solo by Marlya Makarova from Score No. 28.

Scherzo (Ballet Suite No. 4, No. 3) reworked by Atovmyan from Score
No. 37.

Intermezzo (or Interlude), No. 5 appears in *Moscow, Cheryomushki,*
Opus 105 No. 21. Also arranged for wind band and organ solo from
Score No. 10.

See also *Dances of the Dolls,* Sans op. S.

Instrumentation of Suite Opus 27*a*:   piccolo, 2 flutes (II = piccolo II), 2
oboes, cor anglais, E flat clarinet (= bass clarinet), 2 B flat clarinets, 2 bassoons, contrabassoon ~ 6 horns, 3 trumpets, 3 trombones, tuba ~ timpani, triangle, tambourine, side drum, cymbals, bass drum, gong ~
glockenspiel, xylophone ~ strings. Separate band in Finale: E flat and 2 B
flat cornets, 2 trombones, and 2 each of alto, tenor, baritone, and bass
saxhorns. The xylophone is employed in the 1931 Suite (in No. 7) and
not in the 1934 version.

Music: The whereabouts of the autograph score is not known. A manuscript
score of the original Suite is preserved at the Glinka Museum. In 1934
the composer discarded Nos. 6 and 7 and substituted less explicit titles
as indicated above in parentheses. The manuscript score of this version,
inscribed 'To be regarded as the original. D. Shostakovich', preserved at
the CIS Archives of Literature and Art. The score and instrumental parts
of the Suite, prepared for publication by Muzgiz in 1934, reached the
proof-reading stage but was not published.

Edition Musicus, Satirical Dance arr. by Q. Maganini, 1940, for small
orchestra, 31 cm.; 1940, for piano; *c.*1943, for large orchestra, parts, 31
cm.; *c.*1958, for clarinet and piano; *c.*1946, for two pianos four hands by
M. Powers; for brass ensemble by A. Raph.

Muzyka, 1959, Waltz-scherzo arr. for violin and piano by Gotsdener.

Sovetskii Kompozitor, No. 4565 (in *Dmitri Shostakovich: Popular
Pieces*), 1967, Nos. 2 and 5 arr. for piano by L. Atovmyan, 28.5 cm.

Boston Music, USA, 1971, No. 2 transcribed for band by D. Hunsberger, score and parts, 30 cm.

Sovetskii Kompozitor, No. 2473 (in *Young Pieces*—Pieces, Études &
Ensembles, Class VI–VII), 1975, Waltz-scherzo for piano, 28.5 cm.

Sovetskii Kompozitor, No. 4920 (in *D. Shostakovich: Selection of Children's Piano Pieces*), 1979, Waltz-scherzo arr. by B. Rozengauz, 29 cm.

Muzyka, No. 11695 (in Volume 26 of *Collected Works* with Opp. 22*a*
and 39*a*), 1987, full score of Suite (1934 version), 30 cm.

Complete score—DSCH Publishers, Moscow, no number, 1996, complete piano score with article on the history of the ballet by Manashir
Yakubov in Russian and English, 284 pp., 29 cm.

Duration: Suite (1931 version): 27' 44"–28' 56"; 27 minutes (Sadovnikov).
Suite (1934 version): 21' 01". Complete score: 145' 20".

Additional ballets: *The Young Lady and the Hooligan.* Numbers from *The Bolt*
used, with items from Opp. 27, 39, 40, 50*a*, 95, and 97 in a one-act ballet
of seven episodes created for Valeri Panov by Konstantin Boyarsky, with
libretto by Aleksandr Belinsky (after a film script by Vladimir Mayakovsky, based on the novel *The Workers' Lady-Teacher* by Edmondo De
Amicis) and designs by Valeri Dorrer. Premièred at the Leningrad Malyi
Theatre, 28 December 1962, under the conductor Yevgeni Kornblit. The
score of thirteen numbers (duration: 50' 48"–52' 20") assembled by Lev
Atovmyan:

1. Introduction. Adagio—Opus 50*a* ('Maxim Trilogy' Suite—Death of
   the old worker) and Opus 39 (Ballet Suite No. 1, No. 3—Romance)
2. The Street—Opus 39 (Ballet Suite No. 1, No. 6—Galop)
3. The Hooligan—Opus 27 (*The Bolt*, Act 3—The Drayman)
4. The Young Lady—Opus 39 (Ballet Suite No. 1, No. 3—Romance)

5. The School—Opus 39 (Ballet Suite No. 1, No. 4—Polka)
6. The Prayer—Opus 40 (Cello Sonata, 1st movement, 2nd theme orch. Atovmyan)
7. The Cabaret—Opus 27 (*The Bolt,* Act 2—Kozelkov's Dance with Friends)
8. Visions—Opus 97*a* (*The Gadfly,* No. 8—Romance arr. Atovmyan)
9. Scene—Opp. 27 and 40 (reprise of numbers 7 and 6)
10. In the Park—Opp. 95 and 27 (Ballet Suite No. 4, No. 2 and reprise of number 3)
11. Adagio—Opus 39 (Ballet Suite No. 2, No. 2—Adagio)
12. The Brawl—Opus 39 (Ballet Suite No. 4, No. 1—Prelude)
13. Finale—Opus 50a ('Maxim Trilogy' Suite—Death of the old worker)

NB. A shortened version under the title *The Young Girl and the Hooligan,* televised by the BBC on 26 March 1975, was danced by Valeri and Galina Panov with the orchestra conducted by Ashley Lawrence. As the heroine is a young schoolmistress, the word 'Lady' is more appropriate in the title. The scenario is given in Goltsman.

The Dreamers. Score adapted by the composer and Sergei Sarozhnikov from *The Bolt* and *The Golden Age,* choreographed by Natalya Ryzhenko; Stanislavsky and Nemirovich-Danchenko Musical Theatre, Moscow, 19 January 1976.

Paillettes. Norbert Schmucki, Paris Opera Ballet; danced to 'Kozelkov's Dance with Friends', 1986. Available on View Video Dance Series NTSC 1204 videocassette (orchestra and conductor uncredited).

Brian Orsar, representing Canada, skated to excerpts from this ballet suite (the first six bars of No. 1, followed by Nos. 3 and 4) in the 1988 Winter Olympics, Calgary and his farewell routine at the World Figure Skating Championships, Budapest.

Recordings: USA: V-Disc 776 (78 rpm). Satirical Dance. Norwalk Symphony Orchestra, Quinto MAGANINI. ['V-Disc Pops Concert'—Skryabin and Maganini with spoken introductions.] P NBC Studio, New York 17 May 1947.

Germany: Electrola Odeon 0 80610 (mono). Satirical Dance. Hugo KOLBERG (violin) and Felix Schröder (piano). [Piston, Crowther, Suk, and Kroll.] P Berlin 19 May 1960. *Reissued:* USA: Mace MXX 9089 (stereo). [As German release.] I 1965.

USSR: 0039857-8 (8" 78 rpm). Waltz-scherzo arr. Semyonova. Z. SEMYONOVA (accordion), V. Budkin and V. Parkhomov (guitars). [A. Petrov.] P 1963.

USSR: Melodiya D 018709-10 (mono) and C 01387-8. Suite (1931 version). Bolshoi Theatre Orchestra and Zhukovsky Military Air Academy Band, Maksim SHOSTAKOVICH; soloists in Nos. 2 and 7 respectively— Romuald Vladimirov (bassoon) and Leonid Redkin (xylophone). [Op.

22*a*.] P and I 1966. *Reissued:* USA: Angel Melodiya SR 40062. [Op. 22*a*.] ~ HMV Melodiya ASD 2747. [Op. 14.] G Sept. 1971 ~ HMV Melodiya BOX 50251 in Set SLS 5025. Nos. 2, 7, and 8 only. [Opp. 10 and 14.] G Dec. 1975 ~ USSR: Melodiya C 01387-8. [In fourth box of Part 1 of *Collected Works on Records* with Opp. 22*a*.] I 1978 ~ Italy: EMI 065 94484. [Op. 22*a*.] I 1978 ~ BMG Melodiya Compact Discs 74321 66981-2 (two-disc set). [Sans op. P, Opp. 22*a*, 64*a*, and 76*a*.] I Dec. 1999.

USSR: Melodiya CM 02849-50. Waltz-scherzo arr. Tikhonov. A. TIKHO-NOV (balalaika), Osipov Academic Russian Folk Orchestra, Viktor Dubrovsky. [Rimsky-Korsakov, Glazunov, Brahms *et al.*] P 1971, I 1972. *Reissued:* USSR: Melodiya C10 06417-8. [Op. 97*a* No. 8; Fibich, Lalo, Rakhmaninov *et al.*] I 1976*c*.

USSR: Melodiya C20 06529-30. Waltz-scherzo arr. Belov. Rudolf BELOV (domra) and Eleonora Kirillovskaya (piano). [Gluck, Mozart, Tchaikovsky *et al.*] P 1975, I 1976*c*.

Germany: Colosseum SM 631. Satirical Dance arr. for brass ensemble. MUNICH BRASS SOLOISTS (Willi Bauer, Werner Binder, Karl Hertel—trumpets; Olaf Klamand—French horn; Klaus Renk—trombone; Manfred Hoppert—tuba). ['Virtuoso Wind Music'—Albinoni, Purcell, Bozza *et al.*] P date not stated but after 1975.

USA: Russian Compact Disc RCD 16238. Waltz-scherzo arr. for piano by M. Sagradova. Nataliya GAVRILOVA (piano). ['Russian Piano School'—Opp. 22, 34, and 97; Babadzhanyan, Rakhmaninov, J. Strauss *et al.*] P 1976–90, I 1998.

Sweden: Swedish Society Discofil SLT 33254. Satirical Dance arr. Alan Raph. STOCKHOLM PHILHARMONIC BRASS ENSEMBLE (Claes Strömblad and Gunnar Schmidt—trumpets; John Petersen and Rune Bodin—trombones; Ib Lanzky-Otto—French horn; Michael Lind—tuba). [Bozza, Cheetham, Hahn *et al.*] P Råsunda, Sweden 21–3 Mar. 1977.

USSR: Melodiya C10 13297-300. Suite Nos. 1, 2, 5, 7, and 3 on fourth side of double album). Stockholm Philharmonic Orchestra, Gennadi ROZHDESTVENSKY. [Brahms/Schoenberg, Alfvén, and Sibelius.] P Leningrad concert 9–10 Feb. 1979, I 1980*c*.

Denon Compact Disc 38C37 7238. Satirical Dance arr. A. Raph. ENSEMBLE DE CUIVRES GUY TOUVRON (Guy Touvron and Serge Boisson—trumpets; Michel Molinaro—horn; Philippe Cauchy—trombone; Christian Delange—tuba) [Reynaud, Baron, Albeniz *et al.*] P Japan July 1982.

France: Praga Compact Disc PR 250 053. Suite Nos. 1, 2, 5, and 3. Czech Philharmonic Orchestra, Gennadi ROZHDESTVENSKY. [Op. 93.] P Prague concert broadcast 7 Jan. 1983, I Nov. 1994, G Sept. 1995. *Reissued:* France: Le Chant du Monde Compact Disc PR 7250 083. [Op. 93.] G Feb. 2001.

USA: Orion ORS 83462. Waltz-scherzo. Zoe ERISMAN (piano). [Opp. 34, 94, and 39.] P 1983.

USSR: Melodiya C10 21335 006. Intermezzo arr. for wind band. USSR Ministry of Home Affairs Army Orchestra, Vladimir TARASOV. [Sans op. H (ii); Op. 97a No. 3; Puccini, Suppé *et al.*] I 1985b.

Germany: Cadenza Compact Disc CAD D 878-8. 'The Conciliator' labelled as 'Opportunist', arr. N. Živković. Nebojša ŽIVKOVIĆ (marimba) and Iris Kobal (piano). ['Marimba and Percussion Solo'—Op. 22; Tanaka and Miki.] P Stuttgart 1987, I 1989.

Chandos ARBD 1336 (digital) and Compact Disc CHAN 8650. Suite Nos. 1–8. Scottish National Orchestra, Neeme JÄRVI. [Op. 47.] P Glasgow 14 May 1988, I Feb. 1989, G Apr. 1990. *Reissued:* Conifer Classics Compact Disc Class 7090. [Op. 47.] I Nov. 1991 ~ Chandos Compact Discs 7000/1 (two-disc set). [Opp. 114a, 96, and Sans op. P.] I Sept. 1994, G May 1995.

France: Erol Records Compact Disc 7014. Arr. for saxophone. Marc CHISSON (soprano saxophone) and Alain Perez (piano). [Opp. 5 and 34; Villa-Lobos, Ravel, Bartók *et al.*] P Bordeaux 14 June 1992.

Chandos Compact Discs CHAN 9343-4 (two-disc set). Complete score of 43 numbers. Royal Stockholm Philharmonic Orchestra, Stockholm Transport Band, Gennadi ROZHDESTVENSKY (conductor, narrator in Nos. 1 and 7, and pianist in No. 1). P Stockholm 6–11 June 1994, I Mar. 1994, G June 1995.

France: Le Chant du Monde Russian Season Compact Disc RUS 288 105. *The Young Lady and the Hooligan*—complete ballet. Andrei Kolokolov (trumpet in No. 7), Nikolai Kvitko (trumpet in No. 8), Nazar Dzhurin (cello), Mikhail Spivak (violin), Andrei Skorobogatko (oboe), Mikhail Purizhensky (clarinet); Russian Symphony Orchestra, Mark GORENSTEIN. P Mosfilm Studios, Moscow 28 June–1 July 1994, I May 1995. *Reissued:* CDX Russian Season Compact Disc RUS 788 105. I Dec. 1997 ~ France: Le Chant du Monde Russian Season Compact Disc RUS 788164. Nos. 2–5 and 7–10. [Opp. 97, 69; Sans opp. G and P (i).] I July 1999, G Nov. 1999.

USA: Pope Music Compact Disc PM 1002-2. Suite Nos. 1–8. Russian Symphony Orchestra ('Young Russia'), Mark GORENSTEIN. ['Unlikely Silhouettes'—Shchedrin.] P Moscow Conservatory Sept. 1994, I Nov. 1995.

USA: Russian Disc 'Untrodden Paths' Compact Disc RDCD 10 033. *The Young Lady and the Hooligan*—complete ballet. Minsk Symphony Orchestra, Walter MNATSAKANOV. [Sans op. P (i), Suite No. 2.] P Byelorussian Radio Studio Oct. 1994, I July 1995. NB. 'In the Park' split on two tracks—Nos. 10 and 11.

Olympia Compact Disc OCD 585. Waltz-scherzo and Intermezzo arr. for organ. Mariya MAKAROVA (organ). ['Music for Organ'—Opp. 16, 29, 39, 81, 97, 105, and Sans op. E.] P Moscow Conservatory Jan. 1995, I Mar. 1997.

Japan: Canyon Classics Compact Disc PCCL 00292. Suite Nos. 1–8. Czech Philharmonic Orchestra, Kazushi ONO. [Op. 47.] P Prague 28 Mar. 1995, I Sept. 1995.

Denmark: Classico Compact Disc CLASSCD 129. Suite Nos. 2 and 3. Copenhagen Philharmonic Orchestra, Okko KAMU. [Bentzon and Szymanowski.] P Tivoli concert, Copenhagen 2 July 1995, I July 1996, G Oct. 1996.

Decca Compact Disc 452 597-2DH. Suite (1934) Nos. 1–5 and 8. Philadelphia Orchestra, Riccardo CHAILLY. ['The Dance Album'—Opp. 105 and 97.] P New Jersey Dec. 1995, I Oct. 1996, G Dec. 1996.

France: Le Chant du Monde Compact Disc LDC778 1124. Nos. 10 and 28 arr. for organ. Hervé DÉSARBRE (organ). [Opp. 145, 29, and 39; *Tishchenko Portrait of D. D. Shostakovich*—No. 12 of *Twelve Portraits*, Op. 113.] P Glinka Museum, Moscow concert 24 May 1999, I May 2000, G Aug. 2000.

Deutsche Grammophon Compact Disc 469 525-2GH. Suite Nos. 1–8. Gothenburg Symphony Orchestra, Neemi JÄRVI. [Op. 14 and 20.] P Gothenburg Aug. 1999, I Mar. 2001, G May 2001.

Notes: In the second edition No. 2 (e), 'The Goblin', of Act 3 Scene 2, was translated from the 'Domovoi' listed by Sadovnikov in his 1965 Catalogue. 'Domovoi' is a printer's error which should read 'Lomovoi', Russian for 'The Drayman' or 'The Carter'.

The Budyonny Mounted Army, featured in Act 3 of the ballet, named after the legendary Semyon Budyonny · who began his career as a cavalryman and became a Marshal of the Soviet Army. According to Volkov (1979) he was 'famed for his huge moustache and outstanding stupidity'.

References: Bogdanova, Goltsman, and Lopukhov.

Opus 28   Rule, Britannia!

Form: Incidental music to the stage play *Rule, Britannia!* by Adrian Piotrovsky.

1. The Internationale—Allegro—Meno mosso (choral portion)
2. Infantry March—Allegretto
3. [Along the Soviet Route]—Allegro non troppo (choral words not found)
4. Protest]—Allegro
5. [Raising the Banner]—Allegretto
6. [The Banners are Making a Noise]—Allegro (choral number)

No. 1 concludes with the opening eight bars of Pierre Degeyter's melody with Russian text by Arkadi Kots.

Instrumentation: flute (= piccolo), B flat clarinet, bassoon ~ horn, 2 trumpets, trombone, tuba ~ timpani, triangle, side drum, cymbals, bass drum ~ piano ~ strings.

Composed: April 1931, at Leningrad.

Première: 9 May 1931, Leningrad Working Youth Theatre (TRAM), directed by Mikhail Sokolovsky and R. Suslovich, and conducted by N. Dvorikov.

Arrangements: Piano reduction of Nos. 1–3, 5, and 6 by Yuri Olenev. No. 2 modified and reorchestrated by the composer for use in the 'Night Watch' number of *Hamlet, Opus 32.*

Music: Autograph piano score of [Protest], complete with prose text to be spoken against the musical background, and three fragmentary items from Act 4 in piano reduction ('The Cannon', 'Transition to the Little House', and ['Dynamiada'] preserved at the CIS Archives of Literature and Art. Manuscript copies of Nos. 1–3, 5, and 6 in full score discovered in the mid-1980s in the Shostakovich family archive.

   Muzyka, No. 11412 (in Volume 28 of *Collected Works* with Opp. 19, 24, 31, 32, 37, 44, 58*a*, 63, 66, 72, and in the supplement, Sans opp. D and K), 1986, piano and vocal scores of six items, 30 cm.

   Muzyka, No. 11413 (in Volume 27 of *Collected Works* with Opp. 19, 24, 32, 37, 44, 58*a*, 63, 66, and 72), 1987, full score of Nos. 1–3, 5, and 6, 30 cm.

Recordings: —

Opus 29   Lady Macbeth of Mtsensk District

Alternative title: The opera was introduced in 1934 under the title *Lady Macbeth of Mtsensk District* in Leningrad and as *Katerina Izmailova* in Moscow. NB. This fact is circumvented in this catalogue and the latter title reserved for Opus 114.

Form: Opera in four acts for full orchestra, chorus and 17 principals, with libretto by Aleksandr Preis and the composer, based on the novel-sketch *Lady Macbeth of Mtsensk District* written in 1865 by Nikolai Leskov:

ACT 1

Scene 1: In the Izmailovs' house
Scene 2: The Izmailovs' courtyard
Scene 3: Katerina's bedroom

ACT 2

Scene 4: The Izmailovs' courtyard at night
Scene 5: Katerina's bedroom

ACT 3

Scene 6: The Izmailovs' garden before the wedding
Scene 7: In the police station
Scene 8: The wedding feast in the Izmailovs' garden

ACT 4

Scene 9: Convicts' camp on the road to Siberia

Instrumentation: piccolo, 2 flutes (II = piccolo II and flute in G), 2 oboes, cor anglais, E flat clarinet, 2 clarinets (B flat and A), bass clarinet, 2 bassoons, contrabassoon ~ 4 horns, 3 trumpets, 3 trombones, tuba ~ timpani, triangle, wood block, tambourine, side drum, side drum militare, whip, cymbals, bass drum, gong ~ glockenspiel, xylophone, 2 harps, celesta ~ strings. An optional brass band of 2 B flat cornets, 2 E flat cornets, 2 B flat trumpets, 2 E flat alto saxhorns, 2 B flat tenor saxhorns, 2 E flat baritone saxhorns, and 2 bass horns is specified in the 1932 version. An organ replaces the orchestra for the Passacaglia in the 1935 version. String strength specified at 16–18, 14–16, 12–14, 12–14, and 10–12 with double-basses not to be muted throughout the opera.

Composed: 14 October 1930–17 December 1932. The first part of the opera was begun in Leningrad and continued in the Caucasus in autumn 1931. Act 1 was finished in Tbilisi on 5 November 1931. Act 2 was begun in Leningrad on 19 November 1931 and completed in Moscow on 8 March 1932. Act 3 was started in Leningrad on 5 April 1932 and continued in Gaspra, Crimea, with completion on 15 August 1932. Act 4 written in Leningrad.

Dedication: Nina Vasilievna Varzar (fiancée).

Premières: 22 January 1934, Leningrad Malyi Opera Theatre; produced by Nikolai Smolich and Vladimir Dmitriev, under the direction of the conductor, Samuil Samosud; principal roles—Agrippina Sokolova (Katerina), Pyotr Zasetsky (Sergei), Georgi Orlov (Boris), and Stepan Balashov (Zinovi).

24 January 1934, Nemirovich-Danchenko Theatre, Moscow; produced by Boris Mordvinov and conducted by Grigori Stolyarov; principal roles—A. Tulubeva (Katerina), S. Ostroumov (Sergei), Vladimir Kandelaki (Boris), and Sergei Tsenin (Zinovi).

USA: 31 January 1935, Cleveland Metropolitan Opera House; Art of Musical Russia singers under Artur Rodzinski.

New production: 26 December 1935, Bolshoi Theatre, Moscow; conducted by Aleksandr Melik-Pashayev.

UK: 18 March 1936, Queen's Hall, London; Oda Slobodskaya, Hughes Macklin, and Harold Williams in a concert performance (in Michel Calvocoressi's English translation revised by other hands), conducted by Albert Coates.

USA revival: September 1981, War Memorial Opera House, San Francisco; San Francisco Opera Company, Anya Silja in the title role, produced by Gerald Freedman and conducted by Calvin Simmons.

Australia: 29 February 1984, Festival Theatre, Adelaide; State Opera of South Australia production in Edward Downes's English translation; John Tasker (director), Peter Cooke (designer), Beverley Bergen (Katerina), Ron Stevens (Sergei), Gregory Dempsey (Boris), Adelaide Symphony Orchestra, conducted by Patrick Thomas.

UK: 22 May 1987, London Coliseum; English National Opera production in David Pountney's English translation; Stefanos Lazaridis (designer), Josephine Barstow (Katerina), Jacque Trussel (Sergei), Willard White (Boris), Stuart Kale (Zinovi), Mark Elder (conductor). The conductor accepted the 1987 Lawrence Olivier Award for the most outstanding achievement of the year in opera at London's Victoria Palace on 24 January 1988. This ENO production was revived on 15 June 2001 at the Coliseum with Vivian Tierney (Katerina), Robert Brubaker (Sergei), Pavlo Hunka (Boris), Rhys Meirion (Zinovi), and Mark Wigglesworth (conductor).

East Germany: 7 May 1988, Deutsche Oper, Berlin; produced by Günter Krämer and conducted by Jiří Kout; principal roles—Karan Armstrong (Katerina), Jan Blinkhof (Sergei), Dimiter Petkov (Boris), and William Pell (Zinovi).

Arrangements:　Three fragments—'Burying the corpse in the cellar', 'The ghost disappears', and 'The drunks at the wedding'—arranged for small and full orchestra and piano solo by Quinto Maganini. Three extracts—'Dance', 'Interlude', and 'Grotesque Dance'—arranged for piano by Frederick Block.

English translations of the libretto by L. Soudakova, Vladimir Lakond, Sonia Benderoff, Merle Puffer, Michel Calvocoressi, Edward Downes, and David Pountney. German text jointly by Jörg Morgener and Siegfried Schoenbohm.

The first published editions of 1935 show many changes in the text, mainly elimination of vulgarisms, including Katerina's aria and Sergei's recitative in Scene 3. The 'pornophony' interlude at the end of Scene 3 was considerably shortened, and the orchestral Passacaglia between Scenes 4 and 5 replaced by a version for organ [but see Notes].

The opera was reissued in 1963 in an expurgated version—see Opus 114.

See also *Two Pieces for String Quartet,* Sans op. D (i).

Music:　The autograph full score preserved at the CIS Archives of Literature and Art.

J. & W. Chester, London, no number, 1933, crudely mimeographed copy from USSR rehearsal score in the British Museum, oblong format 29 by 19 cm. (Photocopied missing pages supplied by William Crawford of New York, whose vocal score came from the estate of V. Lakond). Each Act paginated separately: 1–74, 1–97, 1–82, and 1–66.

Muzgiz, No. 14346, 1935, vocal score with Russian and English texts (the latter by L. Soudakova), portrait and plates, 321 pp., 30 cm.

Universal Edition, Vienna, No. 10740, 1935, vocal score with German translation.

Kalmus, New York, 1935, libretto only with authorized English synchronized translation by V. Lakond, 23 cm.

A. S. Gilman, Cleveland, 1935, libretto only in English translation by Sonia Benderoff.

Edition Musicus, 1940, three fragments arr. for piano by Q. Maganini, 31 cm.; also for small and full orchestras, score and parts.

Edition Musicus, No. 144, 1942, 'The Road to Siberia', bass solo with piano accompaniment by Q. Maganini and English text by Walter Lake (pseudonym of V. Lakond), 26.5 cm.

Southern Music, New York, 1964, Katerina's Aria—'Oh, I don't feel like sleep anymore', for voice and piano, with English lyric by John Klein and V. Lakond, 31 cm.

Southern Music, New York, 1965, 'The Road to Siberia', bass solo with S.A.T.B. chorus and piano, with English lyric by J. Klein and V. Lakond, score, *c*.19 cm.

Edition Peters, No. 5750 (in collection *Organ Works by Soviet Composers*), 1976, Passacaglia arr. for organ by Leonid Roizman [with preface dated Moscow 1973 by the arranger—spelt Roisman in German], horizontal format 30 cm. NB. Music gives Op. 29; recording Op. 114.

Hans Sikorski, No. 2313, 1979, vocal score with Russian and German texts—the latter by Jörg Morgener and Siegfried Schoenbohm, 320 pp., 31.5 cm. Full score of this version available only on rental.

Hans Sikorski, No. 2329, 1979, Passacaglia arr. for organ, 31.5 cm.

Duration: Approx. 3 hrs in score; 2 hrs 36 mins–2 hrs 40 mins. Films: 2 hrs 40 mins (Pountney—without excisions); 1 hr 36 mins (Weigl—abridged: 13 cuts, principally at start of Scene 5 and whole of Scenes 6 and 7 to the last part of Scene 8). Three fragments: 10 minutes (Musicus). Passacaglia for organ: 6' 25"–8' 35".

Films: The English National Opera's production, introduced by Michael Berkeley, televised on BBC2 TV on 8 November 1987.

RCA Victor Red Seal Laser Disc 781202 and VHS Video 791202. Entr'actes from Scenes 2–5 and 7–8. Berlin Philharmonic Orchestra, Mstislav Rostropovich. ['Concert in Berlin'—Op. 114; Tchaikovsky and Schnittke.] P Philharmonie, Berlin 31 Dec. 1990, I 1992.

Lady Macbeth von Mzensk. A Czechoslovakian colour film of the opera produced by Petr Weigl in 1992, screened on ZDF (Second German Television), 7 March 1993. The cast mimed to the Russian voices on Rostropovich's 1978 HMV recording and crucial German subtitles were provided. Principal acting roles—Markéta Hrubešová (Katerina), Michal Dlouhý (Sergei), Petr Haničinec (Boris), and Václav Neckář (Zinovi). There are thirteen cuts in Scenes 1–4, only the start of Scene 5 is shown, and the whole of Scenes 6 and 7 to the last part of Scene 8 is omitted. This 100-minute version is available on Carlton Entertainment Digital Versatile Disc ID 5655 CLDVD. Reviews G Nov. 2000 and by John Riley in *DSCH Journal* No. 15, pp. 57–9.

Ballet: *The Overcoat.* For details see under Opus 32.

Recordings: USA: Decca Capitol CK 51004 (78 rpm). Orchestral excerpts: 'Burying the corpse in the cellar', 'The ghost disappears', and 'The drunks at the wedding'. Janssen Symphony Orchestra of Los Angeles, Werner JANSSEN. G Apr. 1951.

USA: United Artists UAL 7004 (mono) and UAS 8004. Entr'acte between Scenes 6 and 7. Symphony of the Air, Leopold STOKOWSKI. [Opp. 10 and 34 No. 14.] P New York 15–19 Dec. 1958. *Reissued:* Japan: King Records K18C 9333. [Opp. 10 and 34 No. 14.] I 1982 ~ USA: EMI Classics Compact Discs ZDMB5 6542723 (in two-disc set). [Opp. 10 and 34 No. 14; Bloch, Cesti, and Gabrieli.] I 1994.

East Germany; Eterna 8 20 476. Excerpts. Philine Fischer (soprano), Dresden Philharmonie, Carl von GARAGULY. [Kodály.] P 23–5 June 1964, I 1965. *Reissued:* Germany: Berlin Classics Compact Disc 0031702 BC. [Op. 10.] I 1996. NB. Listed as 'Lady Macbeth Suite' though may be an early performance of Opus 114*a* Nos. 2, 3, 4, and Katerina's aria from Act 1 between Nos. 2 and 3.

USSR: Melodiya CM 04469-70. Passacaglia arr. for organ. Leonid ROIZMAN (organ of Moscow Conservatory Bolshoi Hall). [Glazunov, Gedike, Kikta, and Butsko.] P 1973, I 1974. NB. Listed as from Op. 114.

HMV ASD 3664-6 in Set SLS 5157 (box set complete on six sides with libretto; sung in Russian). Galina Vishnevskaya (Katerina), Nicolai Gedda (Sergei), Dimiter Petkov (Boris), Werner Krenn (Zinovi), Robert Tear (shabby peasant), Taru Valjakka (Aksinya), Martyn Hill (teacher), Leonard Mróz (priest), Aage Haugland (sergeant), Birgit Finnilä (Sonyetka), Alexander Malta (old convict), Leslie Fyson (mill-hand and officer), Steven Emmerson (porter), John Noble (steward), Colin Appleton (1st foreman and coachman), Alan Byers (2nd foreman), James Lewington (3rd foreman), Oliver Broome (policeman), Edgar Fleet (drunken guest), David Beavan (sentry), Lynda Richardson (woman convict); Ambrosian Opera Chorus, John McCarthy (chorus-master), London Philharmonic Orchestra, Mstislav ROSTROPOVICH. P London 1–22 Apr. 1978, G May 1979. Prix Mondail du Disque de Montreux 1980 and the 1980 International Record Critics Award. *Reissued:* USA: Angel SCLX 3866 (six-record box set). I 1979 ~ France: EMI Pathé Marconi 2C 16703374-6 (six-record box set) ~ EMI Compact Discs CDS7 49955-2 (two-disc set). I Feb. 1990, G May 1990 ~ EMI Classics/BBC Music Compact Discs OPCD 21-22 (two-disc set). Act 4 to fig. 475 + 3 bars. ['A Night at the Opera II'—Mozart, Verdi, Leoncavallo *et al.*] I Dec. 1994.

Czech: Supraphon 1116 2843. Katerina's aria from Act 1. Gabriel BEŇAČKOVÁ (soprano), Czech Philharmonic Orchestra, Václav Neumann. [Smetana, Dvořák, Janáček *et al.*] P 1–3 Sept. 1981, G July 1982.

Czech: Panton 81 0681. Passacaglia. Luksaite MRAZKOVA (organ). [Khachaturyan, Falik, Čiurlionis, and Kutavicius.] P Dvořák House, Prague 1986.

Priory Compact Disc PRCD 370. Passacaglia. Keith JOHN (organ). ['Great European Organs No. 26'—Stanford, Reger, Schmidt, and Ravanello.] P Gloucester 3–4 Apr. 1991, I May 1992, G Nov. 1992.

Switzerland: Arts Compact Disc 47273-2. Passacaglia. Arturo SAC-CHETTI (organ). [Glazunov, Taneyev, Lyapunov *et al.*] P Rome May 1991.

Hyperion Compact Disc CDA 66605. Passacaglia. Christopher HER-RICK (organ). ['Organ Fireworks Vol. 4'—Johnson, Lemare, Buck *et al.*] P St Bartholomew's Church, New York 27–8 Feb. 1992, G Oct. and Dec. 1992.

Deutsche Grammophon Compact Discs 437 511-2CH (two-disc set with libretto, 4D audio; sung in Russian). Maria Ewing (Katerina), Sergei Larin (Sergei), Aage Haugland (Boris), Philip Langridge (Zinovi), Heinz Zednik (shabby peasant), Kristine Ciesinski (Aksinya), Ilya Levinsky (teacher), Romuald Tesarowicz (priest), Anatoli Kotcherga (sergeant), Eléna Zaremba (Sonyetka), Kurt Moll (old convict), Grigory Gritziuk (mill-hand), Carlos Alvarez (officer), Guillaume Petitot (porter), Jean-Pierre Mazaloubaud (steward), Alan Woodrow (coachman), Jean-Claude Costa (1st foreman), Jean Savignol (2nd foreman), José Ochagavia (3rd foreman), Philippe Duminy (policeman), Mario Agnetti (drunken guest), Johann Tilli (sentry), Margaret Jane Wray (woman convict); Chorus and Orchestra of the Opéra-Bastille, Paris; Myung-Whun CHUNG. P Paris Feb. 1992, I and G Dec. 1993.

CIS: A-ram Compact Disc ACD 005. Passacaglia. Aleksei PARSHIN (organ). [Goedike, Butuzova, Boellmann, and Widor.] P Moscow Conservatory *c.* 1994.

Olympia Compact Disc OCD 554. Passacaglia. Valeri RUBACHA (organ). ['Russian and Ukrainian Organ Music'—Glinka, Taneyev, Mushel *et al.*] P 1995, I Sept. 1995.

Olympia Compact Disc OCD 585. Passacaglia. Mariya MAKAROVA (organ). ['Music for Organ'—Opp. 16, 27, 39, 81, 97, 105, and Sans op. E.] P Moscow Conservatory Jan. 1995, I Mar. 1997

Germany: Antes Edition Compact Discs BM-CD 15.9001 (three-disc set with synopsis but no libretto; sung in the Morgener/Schoenbohm German translation). Anna-Katharina Behnke (Katerina), Stephen Ibbotson (Sergei), Oleg Bryjak (Boris), Janson Alexander (Zinovi), Stefan Vinke (shabby peasant), Christine Rösch (Aksinya/woman convict), Günter Nowark (teacher), Markku Tervo (priest), Werner-Heiner Adam (steward/sergeant), Wilja Ernst-Mosuraitis (Sonyetka), Christian Rieger (old convict), Almas Svilpa (mill-hand), Edward Gauntt (officer), Dieter Rell (porter/policeman), Doru Cepreaga (coachman/drunken guest), Lomon de Jager (1st foreman), Johannes Eidloth (2nd foreman), Thomas Krause (3rd foreman), Karl-Heinz Haak (sentry); Baden State Opera Choir, Herwig Saffert (chorus-master), Baden State Orchestra, Wolfgang HEINZEL. P Baden State Theatre performances, June 1996, G Sept. 1997.

Olympia Compact Disc OCD 679. Passacaglia. Friedemann HERZ (organ). ['White Music'—Yekimovsky, Knaifel, Pärt *et al.*] P Rheda, Germany Sept. 1999, G May 2000.

France: Le Chant du Monde Compact Disc LDC778 1124. Passacaglia. Hervé DÉSARBRE (organ). [Opp. 145, 27, and 39; Tishchenko *Portrait of D. D. Shostakovich*—No. 12 of *Twelve Portraits,* Op. 113.] P Glinka Museum, Moscow concert 24 May 1999, I May 2000, G Aug. 2000.

References: Ashman, Baxandale, Fanning (in Kovnatskaya), Fay, Fay (in Fanning 1995), Norris, Radamsky, and Volkov.

Notes: Mtsensk is a city 280 kilometres south of Moscow, on the main railway line to Kursk. The title of the opera is frequently given with one or two unnecessary definite articles—e.g. *The Lady Macbeth of the Mtsensk District* as in Kennedy 1980—though it is quite acceptable to use a shorter *Lady Macbeth of Mtsensk* as is the case with Rostropovich's pioneering recording.

The instrumentation given above refers to the 1935 score which states that the passacaglia was replaced by a moderated version played by the organ and the optional band was deleted. However, Laurel E. Fay (in Fanning 1995) has discovered that the instrumentation of 1932 and 1935 is identical. From her research it appears 'Shostakovich envisaged the organ passacaglia, as a self-contained excerpt. . . . But there is no indication that he ever intended the organ version to replace the orchestral in a staged production. . . .' The organ passacaglia was performed at the Leningrad Philharmonic Bolshoi Hall on 17 January 1933 and entered the repertoire of Mikhail Starokadomsky.

The opera was severely attacked in an unsigned editorial 'Muddle instead of music' in the issue of *Pravda* dated 28 January 1936. The author of the article was probably a political journalist, David Zaslavsky (Wilson 1994).

Opus 30   The Golden Mountains

Subtitle: *Happy Street*

Alternative titles: *Mountains of Gold* and also known under the French title *Les Monts d'Or.*

Form: Music for the film *The Golden Mountains,* with screenplay by A. Mikhailovsky, V. Nedobrovo, Sergei Yutkevich, and Leo Arnshtam, directed by S. Yutkevich for the Leningrad Soyuzkino Studio. A song 'If only I had those mountains of gold' provides a leitmotiv for the score. Another song is based on the urban song 'There Used to be Merry Days' and was later used in *Moscow, Cheryomushki,* Opus 105

Instrumentation: piccolo, 2 flutes, 2 oboes, cor anglais, 2 B flat clarinets, bass clarinet, 3 saxophones (soprano, alto, and tenor), 2 bassoons, contrabassoon ~ 8 horns, 4 trumpets, 4 trombones, 2 tubas ~ timpani, side drum, cymbals, bass drum ~ glockenspiel, xylophone, Hawaiian guitar in Waltz, 2 harps ~ organ in Fugue ~ strings.

Composed: Summer-autumn 1931, at Leningrad.

Premières: Film first shown on 6 November 1931 in the Khudozhestvenny (Artistic) Cinema, Leningrad and, in a revised form, on 14 August 1936. Score conducted by Nikolai Rabinovich; organ soloist—Isai Braudo.

Suite: Autumn 1931, Bolshoi Theatre Orchestra, Aleksandr Melik-Pashayev.

Arrangements: Opus 30a—Suite for large orchestra (with triple woodwind, doubled brass, 3 saxophones, harmonium, 2 harps, Hawaiian guitar, and organ) assembled by the composer.

1. Introduction—Moderato
2. Waltz—Andante
3. Fugue—Largo—Allegro
4. Intermezzo—Andante *attacca*
5. Funeral March—Largo *attacca*
6. Finale—Largo

The closing bars of the Third Symphony, Opus 20, were used for the film's final scene and as a coda to the Finale of the Suite.

The Waltz arranged for wind band by Sergei Gorchakov and V. Udalov; folk instrument orchestra by Yuri Chernov; two pianos; trumpet and piano; piano solo; also several other combinations.

Instrumentation of Udalov's arrangement: flute, 3 B flat clarinets ~ 2 E flat tenor horns, 2 trumpets, 3 trombones ~ glockenspiel and side drum, cymbals and bass drum ~ 2 B flat cornets, 2 E flat alto saxhorns, 2 B flat tenor saxhorns, B flat baritone saxhorn, 2 double-bass trombones in C.

Music: Autograph of the film score preserved at the CIS Archives of Literature and Art (full score) and Glinka Museum (full and vocal scores, along with a copy of the Suite in full score). Autograph score of the Suite items Nos. 1 and 2 preserved in the Leningrad Kirov Opera and Ballet Theatre Music Library.

Suite: Muzgiz, No. 14509, 1935, full score, 29 cm.

Waltz: Leeds Music, 1945. arr. for two pianos by Pierre Luboshutz, 31 cm.

Muzyka, 1958, arr. for wind band by S. Gorchakov, score and parts, 19 cm.

Sovetskii Kompozitor, No. 928 (in *Dmitri Shostakovich: Waltzes from Film Music*), 1959, 29 cm.

Muzgiz, Leningrad, No. 1999, 1960, arr. for piano four hands by Mikhail Nyurnberg, 26 cm.

Sovetskii Kompozitor, No. 4565 (in *Dmitri Shostakovich: Popular Pieces*), 1967, arr. for piano by Lev Atovmyan, 28.5 cm.

Muzyka, Leningrad, No. 2035 (in *Dmitri Shostakovich: Pieces for trumpet and piano*), 1976, arr. by Sergei Bolotin, 28.5 cm.

Muzyka, No. 9249, 1976, arr. for wind band by V. Udalov, score and parts, 21.5 cm.

Muzyka, No. 10899 (in Volume 41 of *Collected Works* with Opp. 26, 33, 41, 48, 50, 53, 55, 56, 59, and 64), full score of the Suite, 30 cm.

Duration: Film: 92 minutes. Suite: 14' 00"–23' 26". Waltz: 3' 40" (film); 4' 23"–5' 30" (recordings). 14' 00"–23' 26". Waltz: 4' 23"–5' 30".

Recordings: USSR: 13266-7 (10" 78 rpm). Waltz. All-Union Radio Stage Symphony Orchestra, Leonid YURIEV. [Op. 16.] P 1945. *Reissued:* USA: Colosseum CRLP 167 (mono). ['Footlight Favorites from behind the Iron Curtain'—concert including Opp. 16 and 22*a* No. 3.] I 1954.

USA: Columbia 12881 D (78 rpm). Waltz. New York Philharmonic Orchestra, Efrem KURTZ. P *c.*1950. *Reissued:* USA: Columbia Records ML 4233 (mono). [Op. 22*a* No. 3; Offenbach, Prokofiev *et al.*] ~ USA: Columbia Special Products P 14153 (electronic stereo). [Op. 22*a* No. 3; Offenbach, Prokofiev *et al.*]

USA: Victor 12-3079 (78 rpm). Waltz arr. for two pianos. Pierre LUBOSHUTZ and Genia NEMENOFF. [R. Strauss.] P *c.*1950. *Reissued:* USA: Vanguard VSD 2128 (7" 45 rpm). [Op. 22*a* No. 3.]

USSR: MK D 1556-7 (10" mono). Funeral March. Moscow Radio Band, Leonid KATS. [Sans op. L.] P 1953.

USSR: Melodiya C12 16719009. Fanfare. Bolshoi Theatre Wind Orchestra, Vladimir ANDROPOV. ['Fanfares by Soviet Composers'—Op. 82 Fanfare; Shebalin, Eshpai, Shchedrin *et al.*] I 1982*c.*

USSR: Melodiya C20 20973 007. Waltz arr. Chernov. Academic Russian Folk Orchestra, Nikolai KALININ. [Rimsky-Korsakov, Glinka, Tchaikovsky *et al.*] I 1985*a.*

USSR: Melodiya C10 31619 002. Complete Suite. Nikolai Stepanov (Hawaiian guitar in No. 2), Lyudmila Golub (organ in No. 3), USSR Ministry of Culture Symphony Orchestra, Gennadi ROZHDESTVENSKY. [Album 7 of 'From Manuscripts of Different Years'—Opp. 62*a* and 124.] P 1985, I 1991*c.* *Reissued:* USA: Russian Disc Compact Disc RDCD 11 064. [Op. 18.] I Feb. 1995 ~ BMG Melodiya Compact Discs 74321 59058-2 (two-disc set). [Opp. 36, 4, 17, Z, H, C, 16, 1, 3, 7, 26/D, 59, E, 128, and 19.] I and G Mar. 1999.

RCA Victor Red Seal Compact Disc RD 60226. Suite Nos. 1, 3, 5, and 6. Karol Goleblowsky (organ in No. 3), Belgian Radio Symphony Orchestra, José SEREBRIER. ['Film Music of Shostakovich, Volume 3'—Opp. 78 and 82.] P *c.*1988, I Aug. 1990, G Mar. 1991.

USSR: Melodiya C20 31183 008. Waltz arr. Chernov. Smolensk Russian Folk Orchestra, Viktor DUBROVSKY. [Stravinsky, Musorgsky, Rakhmaninov *et al.*] P 1990, I 1991*b.*

Switzerland: Claves Compact Disc 50-9623. Waltz arr. Chernov. Osipov Balalaika Orchestra, Nikolai KALININ. [Glinka, Rakhmaninov, Rimsky-Korsakov *et al.*] P Moscow 8–11 Dec. 1992, I Oct. 1996.

Germany: Capriccio Compact Disc 10 561. Complete Suite. (Organist in No. 3 not named), Berlin Radio Symphony Orchestra, Mikhail YUROVSKY. [Opp. 41 (i), 45, and 50.] P 13–14 June 1994, I Oct. 1995, G Jan. 1996.

CIS: Manchester Compact Disc CDMAN 129. Waltz. St Petersburg Philharmonic Academic Symphony Orchestra, Vladimir ALTSHULER.

['Shostakovich Theatre and Cinema Music'—Opp. 58*a*, 32*a*, 45, 78, 76, 99, and 37.] P St Petersburg 1995, I 1998.

USA: Citadel Compact Disc CTD 88129. Complete Suite. Aleksandr Nazaruk (organ in No. 3), Belarus State Cinematographic Symphony Orchestra, Walter MNATSAKANOV. [Opp. 36, 59, and 56.] P Mosfilm Studios, Moscow Apr. 1997, I 1998.

References: Egorova and Yutkevich.

Opus 31   Conditionally Killed

Alternative titles: *Allegedly Murdered*. Also translated as *Conditional Death* though recent research by Gerard McBurney favours a buzz-word of the 1930s, *Hypothetically Murdered*. See 'Note' for further suggested titles.

Form: Incidental music for a three-act stage revue *Conditionally Killed*, by Vsevolod Voevodin and Yevgeni Ryss, containing sequences choreographed by Fyodor Lopukhov. Of the thirty-five numbers composed, eleven or so are missing, twenty-five purely instrumental, four very brief choral items, three vocal, and one, 'Beiburzhuyev's [Mr Beat-the-Bourgeois] Monologue', a long episode spoken to music.

   3. Mashenka's First Song—Andantino
   4. Mashenka's Second Song—'Oh, how pleasant it is in the evening'
   6. Transition to the Field Hospital
   7. [Galop]—Allegro
   8. Transition to the Field—Allegro
   9. The Field [A Landscape]—Andantino
  11. Polka—[Con moto]
  12. March [Camouflage]—Allegretto
  15. River-bed—[Moderato—Piu mosso]
  16. Finale to Act 1 (Dance of the Temporary Conquerors)—Moderato
 16*a*. Introduction to Act 2: Petrushka—Allegro *attacca*
  17. Petrushka (Garmoshka)—Allegro
 17*a*. Chorus: 'Look! Look! How quick and nifty we are!'—Allegretto
 17*b*. The Storm—Allegro
 18*a*. Dance—Andante—Allegro
  19. The Arrival of the Lorry
  21. Transition to the Kitchen: Jugglers and Waitresses—Allegretto
 21*a*. The Waitresses—Allegro
  24. [Beiburzhuyev's Monologue]—[Allegretto]
  26. Paradise: 1. Flight of the Cherubs—[Allegretto]
                 2. Flight of the Angels—[Allegro non troppo]
  28. Adagio—[Adagio]
  29. Bacchanalia of John of Kronstadt and Paraskeva Pyatnitsa—Presto
 29*a*. Waltz—[Allegretto moderato]

30. ⎫
31. ⎬ Chorus: Holy! Holy! (S.A.T.B. choir)
32. ⎭

33. Chorus: 'On the sea and on the land, (S.A.T.B. choir)—[Allegretto]
33a. The Twelve Apostles (including vocal solo of the Devil)—
     [Allegretto]
34. The Archangel Gabriel's Number—[Allegretto]
[35. International Peace!]

The March No. 12 is identical to *Hamlet,* Opus 32 No. 43. 'The Archangel
Gabriel's Number' No. 34, foreshadowed in *The Golden Age,* Opus 22
No. 19 (score) or No. 20 (ballet), is quoted in the Finale of Piano Concerto
No. 1, Opus 35. Bacchanalia No. 29 is a reworking of the sexual harassment of Aksinya episode in *Lady Macbeth,* Opus 29 (NB. John of Kronstadt was a late nineteenth century priest, who did good work among
the very poor of St Petersburg, and Paraskeva Pyatnitsa was a female
Greek saint in the early church, whose Orthodox Church feast-day is cel-
ebrated on 28 October though only when it occurs on a Friday). 'The
Jugglers' No. 21 reappears as 'Balda's Work' No. 12 in *The Tale of a Priest
and His Servant Balda,* Opus 36. The text of No. 4 satirizes Mikhail Lermontov's poem *Borodino* and No. 33a is a brief parody of 'Song of the
Golden Calf' from Gounod's *Faust.* Petrushka No. 17 uses a well-known
chatushka, originally a tune with indecent lyrics (see Gerard McBurney's letter in *Tempo* No. 189, June 1994).

Instrumentation: Not known precisely though the composer made over
twenty marginal lists of instruments on the piano score.

Composed: Summer-autumn 1931, at Leningrad.

Premières: 2 October 1931, Leningrad Music Hall; Klavdia Shulzhenko
(singer), Leonid Utyosov's jazz band; directed by Nikolai Petrov and
conducted by Isaak Dunayevsky.

UK: Suite Opus 31a: Nos. 1, 4, 7, 18, 9/10, 13, 14, 15/16, 17, 8, and 19.
20 November 1991, Symphony Hall, Birmingham; City of Birmingham
Symphony Orchestra, Mark Elder and 27 August 1992, Royal Albert
Hall (Prom); BBC Symphony Orchestra, M. Elder.

Arrangements: Piano reduction of the orchestral score by the composer.

Hypothetically Murdered, Opus 31a: Suite for small orchestra (with two
saxophones, piano, accordion, and large percussion battery), reconstructed, orchestrated, and retitled by Gerard McBurney in 1991:

1. Bacchanalia   (Score No. 29)
2. Polka   (11)
3. Transition to the Field   (8)
4. The Field   (9)
5. Dance   (18a)
6. Transition to the Field Hospital   (6)
7. Galop   (7)

8. The Bottom of the River   (15)
9. Introduction to Act 2: Petrushka *attacca*   (16*a*)
10. Petrushka (Garmoshka)   (17)
11. The Storm   (17*b*)
12. The Jugglers   (21)
13. Adagio   (28)
14. Waitresses   (21*a*)
15. Paradise I: Flight of the Cherubim *attacca*   (26)
16. Paradise II: Flight of the Angels   (27)
17. The Archangel Gabriel's Number   (34)
18. Waltz   (29*a*)
19. Finale to Act I: Dance of the Temporary Victors   (16)

Instrumentation of Opus 31*a*:   piccolo, flute, oboe, B flat clarinet, bass clarinet, 2 bassoons, soprano saxophone, tenor saxophone ~ horn, 2 trumpets, 2 trombones, tuba ~ out-of-tune upright piano, accordion ~ timpani and percussion (5 players—triangle, tambourine, wood block, police whistle, whip, lion's roar, thunder-sheet, siren, klaxon, side drum, tenor drum, bass drum; suspended, ordinary, and large cymbals; gong, glockenspiel, xylophone, flexatone) ~ strings (suggested strength 8, 6, 4, 4, 3).

Music: Autograph piano score preserved at the CIS Archives of Literature and Art. The whereabouts of the full score is not known.

Sovetskii Kompositor, No. 4028 (in *Dmitri Shostakovich: Music to Plays*), 1977, 'The Field', Polka, Dance, and 'The Jugglers' in the composer's reduction, 29 cm.

Muzyka, No. 11412 (in Volume 28 of *Collected Works* with Opp. 19, 24, 28, 32, 37, 44, 58*a*, 63, 66, 72, and, in the supplement, Sans opp. D and K), 1986, piano and vocal scores of 21 items, 30 cm.

DSCH Publishers, Moscow, 1995, full score and parts of G. McBurney's reconstruction available for hire.

Duration of Suite: 23' 26"–26' 46" (11 numbers); 39' 12" (21 numbers).

Film: BBC1 TV, 4 October 1992, a television presentation of the 1992 Proms performance, introduced by James Naughtie, preceded by a fifteen-minute interval film showing the Leningrad Music Hall in course of restoration; an interview with Boris Bychkov who had seen the original revue in 1931; a mealtime discussion on the music by Gennadi Rozhdestvensky, Mark Elder, and Gerard McBurney; and clips of Leonid Utyosov conducting his thirties 'jazz band', dancing in a 1925 film, and reminiscing in 1970.

Recordings: Bluebell Bell 126. 'The Jugglers' only. Inger WIKSTRÖM (piano). [Opp. 5; 19 Nos. 3, 4, and 2; 22*a*, No. 3; 94; 97*a* No. 7; 105 fragment; and Prokofiev.] P 28 Jan. and 1 Feb. 1981.

United Compact Disc 88001. Suite Opus 31*a* arr. G. McBurney; score Nos. 6–9, 16*a*, 17*b*, 19, 18*a*, 21, 21*a*, 26–29*a*, 34, 11, 12, 15, and 16. City of Birmingham Symphony Orchestra, Mark ELDER. [Opp. 46*a*, 42; and Sans op. E.] P Birmingham 16–18 Dec. 1992, I Nov. 1993, G Jan. 1994.

France: Le Chant du Monde Compact Disc RUS 288170. Suite Opus 31*a* Nos. 3, 4, 9–10, 14–16, 13, 1, 18, 17, 8, and 19. Tchaikovsky Symphony Orchestra, Vladimir FEDOSEYEV. [Op. 97.] P Moscow Radio Studio 6–10 June 2000, I 2001.

Chandos Compact Disc CHAN 9907. Score Nos. 9, 11, 16, 12, 18*a*, and 1 arr. composer. Rustem HAYROUDINOFF (piano). ['Theatre Music'—Opp. 37, 19, 32, 44, 58*a*, 66, and 22.] P Potton Hall, Suffolk 7–8 Aug. 2000, I Apr. 2001.

Reference: McBurney.

Notes: Nicolas Slonimsky offers *Technically Killed* as yet another translation. Elizabeth Wilson (1994, page 101) argues that *Declared Dead* would be a more accurate title.

In 1999 two further numbers, an Overture and a dance called 'The Ruination of the City', were discovered. The instrumentation adds an alto saxophone and a banjo.

In March 2002 the compiler was informed that the full score had been found in Russia. It will be interesting to compare the composer's orchestration with that of McBurney's reconstruction from the piano score.

Sans op. D   Unnumbered Works 1930s–40s

(i) *Two Pieces for String Quartet*

Form: Two short transcriptions for string quartet:

1. Elegy—Adagio (Katerina's Aria, 'The foal runs after the filly', from Act 1, Scene 3 of *Lady Macbeth of Mtsensk District*, Opus 29, figs. 140–52
2. Polka—Allegretto (*The Golden Age*, Opus 22*a* No. 3)

Composed: During the night of 31 October/1 November 1931, at Batumi, Georgia. The score and parts were presented the following morning at 06.00 as a surprise gift to the touring Vuillaume Quartet before they departed from the same hotel where Shostakovich, on a two-month 'working holiday', was composing Act 1 of *Lady Macbeth*. See *DSCH VI Newsletter* (Mar./Apr. 1988).

Dedication: To the Jean Vuillaume Quartet of Kharkov.

Performances: Date of première not known but dates of its revival as follows:

20 September 1984, Israel Musical Festival, Tel-Aviv and five days later, Moscow Conservatory Malyi Hall; Borodin Quartet (Mikhail Kopelman, Andrei Abramenkov, Dmitri Shebalin, and Valentin Berlinsky).

UK: 26 February 1986, Queen Elizabeth Hall, London; Borodin Quartet.

UK broadcast: 13 July 1986, Fitzwilliam Quartet (Daniel Zisman, Jonathan Sparey, Alan George, and Ioan Davies).

Arrangements: String orchestra arrangements by Christian Sikorski and Alexandre Brussilovsky (both pieces) and Elegy by Misha Rachlevsky. Both pieces transcribed for saxophone quartet.

Music: The composer's original designation of Opus 36 subsequently used for *The Tale of a Priest and his Servant Balda*. Autograph score preserved in the archive of A. O. Staroselsky (2nd violinist of the Vuillaume Quartet) and transferred to the Shostakovich family archive in the late 1980s.

Russian photocopied scores, no number, *c*.1984, 30 cm.

Hans Sikorski, No. 2349, 1984, score and parts, 31.5 cm.

Duration: (1) 3' 48"–6' 31" and (2) 2' 00"–2' 47".

Recordings: Olympia Compact Disc OCD 531. Labelled as Opus 36. SHOSTAKOVICH QUARTET (Andrei Shislov, Sergei Pishchugin, Aleksandr Galkovsky, Aleksandr Korchagin). ['Complete Quartets, Vol. 1'—Opp. 49, 73, and 83.] P 1985, I Apr. 1994, C Sept. 1994.

Decca 411 940-1DH (digital) and Compact Disc 411 940-2DH. FITZWILLIAM QUARTET (personnel as at première—not stated on label or sleeve). [Opp. 127 and 57.] P London Feb. 1986; G Feb., May, and Oct. 1987.

Germany: IMS Polygram ECM New Series 1347 (two-record set) and Compact Disc 833506-2 (two-disc set). Gidon KREMER and Annette Bik (violins), Veronica Hagen (viola), and Thomas Demenga (cello). [Edition Lockenhaus Volumes 4 and 5—Opp. 142 and 138; and Schulhoff.] P 1986, I Apr. 1988.

Nimbus Compact Disc NI 5140. MEDICI QUARTET (Paul Robertson, David Matthews, Ivo-Jan van der Werff, Anthony Lewis). [Op. 11; Mendelssohn.] P 11 May 1988 (Elegy) and 8 June 1988 (Polka), I Oct. 1988.

Philips 432 252-2. Polka only. BORODIN QUARTET (personnel as at première). [Pärt, Gubaidulina, Kupkovic *et al.*] P Lockenhaus concert 15 July 1989. *Reissued:* Philips Compact Disc 432 252-2 in 456 077-2 (elevendisc set). [Bot, Mozart, Thomas *et al.*] I 1997. NB. Originally issued as a free promotional sampler.

RCA Victor Compact Disc 09026 61189-2. Arr. for string orchestra. Moscow Virtuosi, Vladimir SPIVAKOV. [Op. 11; Schnittke and Shchedrin.] P Munich 10–13 Dec. 1991, I Apr. 1998.

USA: Russian Disc Compact Disc RDCD 11 087. Elegy only. BORODIN QUARTET (personnel as at première). [Op. 110; Beethoven.] P St Petersburg concert 12 Dec. 1991, I June 1993, G Oct. 1993.

Switzerland: Claves Compact Disc CD50 9325. Elegy arr. for string orchestra. Kremlin Chamber Orchestra, Misha RACHLEVSKY. ['Elegy: Masterpieces for String Orchestra'—Tchaikovsky, Fibich, Grieg *et al.*] P Mosfilm Studio May–June 1993, I Sept. 1993.

Netherlands: Etcetera Compact Disc KTC 1182. ELEONORA QUARTET (Eleonora Yakubova, Irina Pavlikhina, Anton Yaroshenko, Mikhail Shumsky). [Opp. 73 and 117.] P Moscow Jan. 1994, I Sept. 1994.

Netherlands: Vanguard Classics Compact Disc 99154. Arr. for saxophone quartet. Johan van der LINDEN, Andre Avendo, Arno Bornkamp, and Willem van Merwijk. [Glazunov, Denisov, and Smirnov.] P Zwolle 10–12 Mar. 1994.

Germany: Arte Nova Classics Compact Disc 74321 27759-2. Arr. for string orchestra. Hamburg Soloists, Emil KLEIN. [Bach, Boccherini, Schubert, and Falla.] P Munich 11–13 Apr. 1994, I 1996.

Teldec Compact Disc 4509 94572-2. BORODIN QUARTET (personnel as at première). ['Russian Miniatures'—Borodin, Stravinsky, Schnittke *et al.*] P Berlin Nov. 1994, I Mar. 1995.

Finland: Ondine Compact Disc ODE 845-2. Arr. for string orchestra by C. Sikorski. Tapiola Sinfonietta, Joseph SWENSEN. [Op. 135.] P Espoo Mar. 1995, I Mar. 1996, G Apr. 1996.

France: Suoni e Colori Collection Compact Disc SC 53006. Labelled Op. 36. Arr. for string orchestra by A. Brussilovsky. Ricercata de Paris Ensemble, Alexandre BRUSSILOVSKY. ['DSCH Aphorismes'—Opp. 11, 34, 68, and 13; Schnittke—*Prelude in Memory of Shostakovich,* and Steven Gerber—*Elegy on the name 'Dmitri Shostakovich'.*] P Hautes-Alpes, France concert Aug. 1996, I 1997.

Discipline Global Mobile Compact Disc 9809. MR MCFALL'S CHAMBER. ['Like the Milk'—Piazzolla, Dowland, Hendrix *et al.*] P producer Rick Bamford's front room, Edinburgh Oct. 1997, I June 1999.

Deutsche Grammophon Compact Disc 463 284-2GH5 (five-disc set). EMERSON QUARTET (Eugene Drucker, Philip Setzer, Lawrence Dutton, David Finkel). ['Complete Quartets, Vol. 4'—Opp. 122, 133, and 138.] P Aspen, Colorado concert July 1998, G June 2000.

Germany: Eigen Art Compact Disc 10230. Arr. for string orchestra by C. Sikorski. Bartholdy-Ensemble Rheinfelden, Christian SIKORSKI. ['Miniatures for Chamber Orchestra'—Albinoni, Mozart, Zbinden *et al.*] P Germany 1 Nov. 1999.

References: Hulme (in DSCH) and Yakubov.

(ii) *Overture for the Green Guild*
Form: Orchestration of the overture to Ivan Dzerzhinsky's spectacle-play *The Green Guild,* commissioned by the Leningrad Working Youth Theatre (TRAM) in 1931. Score not published.

Première: March 1932, Leningrad.

(iii) *From Karl Marx to Our Own Days*
Form: Symphonic Poem, with text by Nikolai Aseyev, for solo voices, chorus, and orchestra.

Composed: The first of the projected five sections was completed in February 1932.
Music: Manuscript.
Recordings: —

(iv) *The Big Lightning*

Form: An operetta *The Big* (or *Great*) *Lightning,* with libretto by Nikolai Aseyev, abandoned after the completion of nine numbers. Score prepared for performance by Gennadi Rozhdestvensky:

1. Overture—Allegro *attacca*
2. Scene—Tommy and the Manager—Allegro
3. Architect's Song—Allegretto
4. Scene—An American—Allegro
5. Maiofel's Song—Andantino
6. Telephone call—Allegretto
7. Semyon's Song—Andantino
8. Duet of Yegor and Semyon—Allegro
9. Models' Procession—Allegro

Instrumentation: piccolo, 2 flutes, 2 oboes, cor anglais, E flat clarinet, 2 B flat clarinets, 2 bassoons, contrabassoon, soprano saxophone ~ 4 horns, 3 trumpets, 3 trombones, tuba ~ timpani, triangle, wood block, side drum, cymbals, bass drum, gong ~ glockenspiel, xylophone, flexatone, harp ~ strings ~ soprano, 4 tenor, baritone, and 3 bass soloists, S.A.T.B. chorus.
Composed: 1932 [*Collected Works* states 1933.]
Première: 11 February 1981, Leningrad Conservatory Bolshoi Hall; concert version under G. Rozhdestvensky.
Music: In 1980 two thick autograph scores, orchestral and vocal, were discovered by Rozhdestvensky in the Leningrad Malyi Opera Theatre Library.
   Muzyka, No. 11935 (in Volume 23 of *Collected Works* with Opp. 15*a* and 23, and Sans op. K), 1986, full score of nine numbers, 30 cm.
   Muzyka, No. 11412 (in the supplement to Volume 28 of *Collected Works* with Sans op. K; Opp. 19, 24, 28, 31, 32, 37, 44, 58*a*, 63, 66, and 72), 1986, piano and vocal score of nine numbers, 30 cm.
Duration: Suite of eight numbers (1–5 and 7–9): 16' 10"; Nos. 1–9: 17' 32".
Recordings: USSR: Melodiya C10 23081 001. Suite with No. 6 omitted. Viktor Gusev (Tommy), Anatoli Obraztsov (Manager), Viktor Rumyantsev (Architect), Nikolai Myasoyedev (Maiofel), Nikolai Konovalov (Semyon), Yuri Frolov (Yegor), USSR Ministry of Culture Symphony Orchestra and Chamber Choir, Gennadi ROZHDESTVENSKY. [Album 5 of 'From Manuscripts of Different Years'—Opp. 23 and 59, and Sans op. E.] P 1984, I 1986*c*. *Reissued:* BMG Melodiya Compact Discs 74321 59058-2

(two-disc set). [Opp. 36, 4, 17, Z, H, C, 16, 1, 3, 7, 26/59, E, 128, 30*a*, and 19.] I and G. Mar. 1999.

Chandos Compact Disc CHAN 9522. Suite Nos. 1–9. Vsevold Grivnov (Yegor/Tommy), Dmitri Fadeyev (Semyon/manager), Oleg Dolgov (Architect), Andrei Baturin (Maiofel), Tatyana Sharova (Old Woman), Anatoli Safiulin (voice), Russian State Cappella, Russian State Symphony Orchestra, Valeri POLYANSKY. [Op. 93.] P Moscow Conservatory Apr. 2000, I Oct. 2000, G Mar. 2001.

Notes: 'Molniya' of the Russian title can also be translated as 'zip-fastener'—or 'express telegram' (hence the erroneous title of 'The Long Telegram' that appeared in DSCH Newsletter XV, p. 6).

On the Melodiya recording the characters Maiofel and Semyon are given as Matofel and Selyan.

(v) *Symphony of Psalms (Stravinsky)*
Form: A four-hand piano transcription of Stravinsky's three-movement work:

Part 1. ♩ = 92. Psalm 38, Verses 13 and 14
Part 2. ♪ = 60. Psalm 39, Verses 2, 3, and 4
Part 3. ♩ = 48. Psalm 150 complete

Composed: In an introductory tribute to *I. F. Stravinsky* (Sovetskii Kompozitor, 1973) Shostakovich disclosed that 'soon after the publication [in 1930] I made a four-hand arrangement for fortepiano of *Symphony of Psalms*'.
Music: Autograph found among the composer's papers after his death.
Duration: 20' 14".
Recording: USSR: Melodiya C10 26307 004. Viktoria POSTNIKOVA and Irina SCHNITTKE (piano). [Album 6 of 'From Manuscripts of Different Years'— Sans opp. X, J, A, S; Opp. 41 and 128.] P 1983–6, I 1988*d*.

(vi) *Moderato for Cello*
Form: A short piece for cello and piano
Composed: In the 1930s.
Première: 24 October 1986, Hamburg, at a chamber music concert marking the eightieth anniversary of Shostakovich's birth; David Geringas (cello) and Yevgeni Korolyov (piano).
Music: The manuscript discovered with that of the Cello Sonata in the CIS Archives of Literature and Art and first published by Manashir Yakubov as a supplement to the journal *Sovetskaya Muzyka*, September 1986.

Hans Sikorski, No. 2283 (with Op. 97*a* No. 3), 1986, parts, 31.5 cm.

Muzyka, No. 14908 (in *D. Shostakovich: Pieces for cello and piano*), 1991, parts, 29 cm.

Duration: 2' 36"–3' 57".

Recordings: Decca Compact Disc 421 774-2DH. Lynn HARRELL (cello) and Vladimir Ashkenazy (piano). [Op. 40; Prokofiev.] P Chicago 6 May 1988, I Oct. 1989.

Germany: FSM Fono Compact Disc FCD 97721. DUO POSTIGLIONE— Wolfgang Schultz (cello) and Ginette Kostenbader (piano). [Op. 39; Faure and Schumann.] P Stuttgart 29 Oct. 1988, I 1990.

New Zealand: Manu Classic Compact Disc 1426. Aleksandr IVASHKIN (cello) and Ingrid Wahlberg (piano). ['Russian Elegy'—Genishta, Tchaikovsky, Rimsky-Korsakov *et al.*] P Auckland 10–11 Sept. 1992.

Germany: Es-Dur/Con Brio Compact Disc 2021. David GERINGAS (cello) and Tatyana Schatz (piano). [Op. 40; Prokofiev and Rakhmaninov.] P Hamburg 1994.

Iceland: SkrEƒ Compact Disc 952776. Sigurdur HALLDÓRSSON (cello) and Daníel Thorsteinsson (piano). [Debussy, Hindemith, Björnsson, and Schnittke.] P Fella- and Hólakirkja Church, Reykjavík June–July 1995.

France: Le Chant du Monde Compact Disc LDC 278112. Gary HOFFMAN (cello) and Philippe Bianconi (piano). [Op. 40; and Prokofiev.] P Grenoble 13 and 16 Dec. 1998.

(vii) *Dubinushka*

Form: Arrangement of folksong, with Vasili Bogdanov's revised revolutionary text of 1865, for bass voice and orchestra. Tempo not marked. The English title given as 'Cudgel'.

Instrumentation: 2 flutes, 2 oboes, 2 B flat clarinets, 2 bassoons ~ 4 horns, 2 trumpets, 3 trombones, tuba ~ timpani ~ strings.

Composed: In the late 1930s.

Music: Autograph found by Manashir Yakubov among the composer's papers after his death.

(viii) *Symphony 'Liturgique'* (Honegger)

Form: A four-hand piano transcription of Arthur Honegger's Symphony No. 3:

1. *Dies irae*—Allegro moderato
2. *De profundis clamavi*—Adagio
3. *Dona nobis pacem*—Andante

Composed: Presumably in the late 1940s.

Music: Shostakovich's arrangement will appear in Volume 115 of *New Collected Works*. [Muzyka, Leningrad published a piano four-hands reduction by B. Berezovsky and N. Khotuntsov in 1976 (No. 1920, 28.5 cm.).]

(ix) *Suite on Finnish Themes*

Form: A suite of seven transcriptions of Finnish folksongs for a chamber group and two singers:

1. Polka—Energico in C minor
2. One Summer Night—Giocoso in E minor
3. The Sky is Blue and White—Lento ma non troppo in F sharp minor
4. The Girls of this Village—Andante in E minor
5. The Strawberry is a Red Berry—(Moderata, tempo gusto) in E minor
6. If I could be Idle—Allegretto in F minor
7. My Sweetheart is Beautiful—Allegretto in B minor

Nos 1 and 3 are instrumental numbers; Nos. 2 and 5 for one singer and Nos. 4, 6, and 7 for vocal duo. Nos. 3 and 7 are from a collection of Finnish songs compiled by Ilmari Krohn in the 1880s.

Instrumentation: flute, oboe, clarinet (B flat and A) ~ trumpet ~ tambourine, triangle, side drum ~ piano ~ string quintet ~ two singers.

Composed: Commissioned by the Political Department of the Leningrad Military District. Completed prior to 5 December 1939.

Première: 1 September 2001, Kaustinen, western Finland; Anu Komsi (soprano), Tom Nyman (tenor), Ostrobothian Chamber Orchestra conducted by Juha Kangas. Recorded on BIS CD-1256, October 2001.

Music: Manuscript of eleven instrumental parts and score lacking lyrics.

Reference: Dvortsov (in DSCH) based on 18-page article by Arkadi Klimovitsky.

Opus 32   Hamlet

Form: Incidental music to a stage production of the tragedy *Hamlet, Prince of Denmark,* by William Shakespeare, for small orchestra. Russian translation by Mikhail Lozinsky, with interpolations from the works of Desiderius Erasmus.

ACT I
---

1. Introduction—Allegro non troppo   ⎤
2. Night Watch—Moderato, Poco allegretto ⎬ (No. 1 in the Suite)
3. Shepherd's Pipe—Moderato
4. Funeral March—Adagio (No. 2 in the Suite)
5. Exeunt King and Queen—Allegro
6. Dinner Music—Allegretto
7. Flourish—Allegro   ⎤
8. Dance Music—Allegretto   ⎬ (No. 3 in the Suite)
9. Finale of First Act—Allegro

ACT II
---

10. Entry of Hamlet with the Urchins—Allegro
11. Galop: Ophelia and Polonius—Allegro
12. Scene: Hamlet and Rosencrantz (2 fragments)—Allegretto

13. Arrival of the Players—Allegro
14. Exeunt Polonius, Rosencrantz, and Guildenstern—Allegretto
15. Dialogue of Rosencrantz and Guildenstern—Allegretto
16. Hunting [The Chase]—Allegro assai (No. 4 in the Suite)
17. Finale of Second Act (repeat of last 11 bars of Hunting)

ACT III

18. [Music for the rehearsal of the Strolling Player's spectacle]
    (8 fragments)
19. Entry of the Guests—Moderato (No. 6 in the Suite)
20. Scene with Recorder—Allegro
21. Episode after the Scene with Recorder—Presto
22. Pantomime—Allegro   (No. 7 in the Suite)
23. Hamlet dragging out the corpse of Polonius—Allegretto
24. Hamlet dragging out the corpse of Polonlus (variant)—Allegretto

ACT IV

25. The King distracts the Queen—Allegro
26. After the word 'Heroic': the Combat—Allegro
27. Removal of the dead Player King—Allegro
28. Monologue of [the King] Claudius—Andante
29. Signals to start the Combat (3 fragments)—Allegro
30. Romance at the Banquet (song)—Allegretto
31. The Banquet—Presto (No. 5 in the Suite)
32. Can-can—Allegro (No. 8 in the Suite)
33. Ophelia's Song (vocal)—Allegro (No. 9 (instrumental) in the Suite)

ACT V

34. Lullaby—Andantino (No. 10 in the Suite)
35. Introduction to the Churchyard Scene—Moderato
36. Song of the Gravedigger (unaccompanied)—[Moderato]
37. Requiem (choral)—Adagio (No. 11 (instrumental) in the Suite)
38. Tournament—Allegro (No. 12 in the Suite)
39. Flourish—[Allegro non troppo]
40. Heavy Combat—Allegro
41. Slack Combat—Allegro
42. End of the Tournament—Allegro
43. The March of Fortinbras—Allegretto (No. 13 in the Suite)
44. The Beggars passing by—Moderato con moto
45. Song of Horatio (unaccompanied vocal line)

The text of No. 30 is the Boy's song ('Take, O take those lips away') from
ACT 4 Scene 1 of Shakespeare's *Measure for Measure*. Two versions of No.
43 'The March of Fortinbras' composed—one rejected. No. 36 appears to
be based on the Scottish air 'Coming thro' the Rye'.

Instrumentation: piccolo, flute, oboe, clarinet (B flat and A), bassoon ~ 2 horns, 2 trumpets, trombone, tuba ~ timpani, triangle, tambourine, side drum, cymbals, bass drum, gong ~ strings.

Composed: December 1931 to spring 1932, at Leningrad and Moscow.

Premières: Play: 19 May 1932, Vakhtangov Theatre, Moscow; produced by Nikolai Akimov.

Suite UK broadcast (Nos. 3–7, 9–11, and 13): 25 October 1975, BBC Northern Ireland Orchestra, Havelock Nelson.

Suite UK concert: 19 January 1981, Queen Elizabeth Hall, London; Young Musicians' Symphony Orchestra, James Blair.

Arrangements: Opus 32a—Suite for small orchestra (instrumentation as above) compiled by the composer in 1932:

1. Introduction and Night Watch—Allegro non troppo—Moderato, Poco allegretto
2. Funeral March—Adagio
3. Flourish and Dance Music—Allegro—Allegretto
4. Hunting—Allegro
5. Actors' Pantomime—Presto
6. Procession—Moderato
7. Musical Pantomime—Allegro
8. The Banquet—Allegro
9. Ophelia's Song—Allegro—Meno mosso—Presto
10. Lullaby—Andantino
11. Requiem—Adagio
12. Tournament—Allegro
13. The March of Fortinbras—Allegretto

'Night Watch' [or 'Night Patrol'] is derived from the 'Infantry March' of Opus 28; 'Actors' Pantomime' is a clarified version of the Galop No. 20 and Allegro vivace No. 33 of the composer's original score of Opus 22; 'Lullaby' is taken from 'The Dream' item of Opus 26, and 'The March of Fortinbras', from No. 12 of Opus 31

Piano reduction of the complete Suite Opus 32a by Lev Atovmyan; and Nos. 1 (without the 'Introduction'), 2, 3 (without the 'Flourish'), 4, 5, 10, and 13 by Lev Solin. No. 13 transcribed under the title 'Marche Sarcastique' by Frederick Block, Robert Cray, and Benjamin Suchoff. Nos. 5 and 10 transcribed for string quartet by Viktor Yekimovsky.

Nos. 18 (i) 'The tuning of the instruments' (strings alone), 24, 30, 35, and 44 orchestrated by Gerard McBurney, 27–30 May 1994. Instrumentation as the composer's plus a flexatone.

Concert scenario: Hamlet. Opus 32a Nos. 3, 5, and 11 appear in Gennadi Rozhdestvensky's suite. See under Opus 116.

Music: Autograph piano scores of twenty items preserved at the CIS Archives of Literature and Art and thirteen items in vocal score, along with a complete manuscript copy of the *Hamlet* vocal score and a conductor's list of all the musical items, preserved at the Vakhtangov Theatre Museum. Five fragments of the autograph piano score are reproduced in Volume 28 of *Collected Works*. The whereabouts of the autograph full score is not known, apart from Nos. 22 and 33 which are preserved at the CIS Archives of Literature and Art.

Edward B. Marks, New York, No. 11881, 1943, No. 13 of the Suite arr. for piano by F. Block, 23 cm.

Edward B. Marks, New York, 1945, No. 13 arr. for full symphonic band by R. Cray, conductor's score, *c*.30 cm.

Muzfond, 1946, Suite arr. for piano by L. Atovmyan.

Sovetskii Kompozitor, No. 1777, 1960, full score of Suite, 29 cm.

MCA, 1967, No. 13 arr. for concert band by B. Suchoff, condensed conductor's score, *c*.19 cm.

Sovetskii Kompozitor, No. 4565 (in *Dmitri Shostakovich: Popular Pieces*), 1967, Nos. 2 and 3 arr. for piano by L. Atovmyan, 28.5 cm.

Sovetskii Kompozitor, No. 4028 (in *Dmitri Shostakovich: Music to Plays*), 1977, seven pieces arr. for piano by L. Solin, 29 cm.

Sovetskii Kompozitor, No. 6638 (in *Pieces by Soviet Composers for String Quartet*), 1983, Nos. 10 and 5 of the Suite arr. by V. Yekimovsky, 29 cm.

Muzyka, No. 11412 (in Volume 28 of *Collected Works* with Opp. 19, 24, 28, 31, 37, 44, 58*a*, 63, 66, 72, and in the supplement, Sans opp. D and K), vocal and piano scores, 30 cm.

Muzyka, No. 11413 (in Volume 27 of *Collected Works* with Opp. 19, 24, 28, 37, 44, 58*a*, 63, 66, and 72), 1987, full score of the Suite and all the other orchestral items except Nos. 30 and 35, 30 cm.

Duration: Suite: 19' 40"–31' 47"; 21 minutes (Schirmer); 25 minutes (Sadovnikov). Complete incidental music: 44' 56".

Ballet: *The Overcoat*. A 90-minute ballet, freely based on Nikolai Gogol's novella, created for Rudolf Nureyev by the Danish choreographer Flemming Flindt. The music by Shostakovich, mainly from stage and film scores, was selected and arranged by Rubens Tedeschi with additional orchestrations by Irwin Kostal. Premières at the Maggio Musicale, Italy, on 8 June 1989; Edinburgh Festival, at the Playhouse, 28–30 August 1990, by the San Jose Cleveland Ballet (a joint company from the two cities); and by the same company at the San Jose Center for the Performing Arts, California, 28–30 September 1990. The musical items derive from *Hamlet*, Op. 32 (Suite No. 10 Lullaby used as the Overture and in three of the twelve scenes, No. 5 'Actors' Pantomime', and No. 11 Requiem); *New Babylon*, Op. 18 (Suite No. 3 'The Siege of Paris'); *Lady Macbeth*, Op. 29 ('Katerina's bedroom', Interlude); *The Human Comedy*, Op. 37 ('The Panorama of Paris'); Suite for Jazz Orchestra No. 1, Sans op. E (Polka and Waltz); *The Adventures of Korzinkina*, Op. 59 (Suite No. 3 'The Chase',

No. 5 Intermezzo, and No. 4 'Music in the Restaurant'); *Pirogov*, Op. 76 (Scherzo and Waltz); *The Fall of Berlin*, Op. 82 (Suite No. 4 'In the garden', No. 5 'Storming of the Seelow Heights', and No. 6 'In the destroyed village'); Ballet Suites, Sans op. P (No. 1/2 Pizzicato Dance, No. 2/4 'Sentimental Romance', No. 2/2 Adagio, No. 3/2 Gavotte, and No. 3/3 Dance); *The Gadfly*, Op. 97 (Suite No. 8 Romance); Chamber Symphony, Op. 110*a* (Allegro molto); *A Year as Long as a Lifetime*, Op. 120 ('Morning' and 'Farewell'); and *King Lear*, Op. 137 (No. 56 'Vocalise').

Recordings: USSR: 14057-8 (10" 78 rpm). Suite Nos. 4 and 13. Bolshoi Theatre Orchestra, Yuri FAIER. P 1946.

USSR: 14087-8 (10" 78 rpm). Suite Nos. 3 and 5. Bolshoi Theatre Orchestra, Yuri FAIER. P 1946.

USSR: MK D 09807-10 (1 side in two-record set, mono) and C 0295-8 [later Melodiya CM 0295-8]. Suite Nos. 1–13. Moscow Philharmonic Orchestra, Gennadi ROZHDESTVENSKY. [Op. 43.] P 1961, I 1962. *Reissued:* France: Le Chant du Monde LDX A 78413-4 (1 side in two- record set). [Op. 43.] ~ HMV Melodiya ASD 3381. [Op. 18.] G Dec. 1977 ~ USSR: Melodiya CM 0298-C10 09508. [In fourth box of Part 1 of *Collected Works on Records* with Op. 116*a*.] I 1978 ~ BMG Melodiya Compact Discs 74321 63462-2 (two-disc set). [Opp. 14, 20, 43, and 23.] I Mar. 1999.

USA: Louisville First Edition Records LOU 683 (mono) and LS 683. Order of the numbers rearranged: Nos. 1, 3, 12, 2, 5, 6, 7, 9, 13, 10, 11, 8, and 4. Louisville Orchestra, Jorge MESTER. [Kirchner.] I 1968.

USA: RCA Red Seal LSC 3130. Suite Nos. 1–13. Boston Pops Orchestra, Arthur FIEDLER. [Glazunov, Gershwin, and Ernest Gold.] P 28–9 May 1968. *Reissued:* RCA Red Seal LSB 4017. [As USA release.] G May 1971 ~ RCA Red Seal 'High Performance' Compact Disc 09026 63308-2. [Shchedrin and Glazunov.] I July 1999.

USSR: Melodiya C10 22365 004. Suite Nos. 1, 3–5, 9–11, and 13. Leningrad Chamber Orchestra of Old and Modern Music, Eduard SEROV. ['Music for Theatre'—Opp. 37 and 58*a*.] P 1984, I 1986*a*. *Reissued:* Olympia Compact Disc OCD 131. Suite Nos. as Russian release. [Op. 93.] I Sept. 1988 ~ CIS: Manchester Compact Disc CDMAN 129. Suite Nos. as Melodiya. ['Shostakovich Theatre and Cinema Music'—Opp. 58*a*, 45, 30, 78, 76, 97, 99, and 37.] I 1998.

Deutsche Grammophon Compact Disc 431 688-2GH. Suite Nos. 1–13. Gothenburg Symphony Orchestra, Neeme JÄRVI. [Opp. 112 and 22*a*.] P Gothenburg Dec. 1989, I July 1991, G Sept. 1991. *Reissued:* Deutsche Grammophon Compact Discs 459 415-2GTA2 (two-disc set). [Opp. 103, 112, 131, and 22*a*.] I Jan. 1999.

United Compact Disc 88050-2. Complete score with order of Acts IV and V slightly rearranged and Nos. 18 (i), 24, 30, 35, and 44 orchestrated by Gerard McBurney. Luba Stuchevskaya (Player Queen), Igor Khokhlovin (Player King), Louise Winter (mezzo-soprano), David

Wilson-Johnson (baritone), City of Birmingham Symphony Orchestra, Mark ELDER. [Op. 58*a*.] P Birmingham Town Hall 13–15 June 1994, I Nov. 1994. *Reissued:* Cala Compact Disc CACD 1021. [Op. 58*a*.1] I Aug. 1995, G Jan. 1996.

   Chandos Compact Disc CHAN 9907. Suite Nos. 1–5, 10, and 13 in piano reduction. Rustem HAYROUDINOFF (piano). ['Theatre Music'—Opp. 37, 19, 31, 44, 58*a*, 66, and 22.] P Potton Hall, Suffolk 7–8 Aug. 2000, I Apr. 2001.

Note: Grigori Kozintsev's 1954 stage production of *Hamlet* used numbers from the score to *King Lear,* Opus 58*a* with two additional numbers 'Jig' and Finale.

Opus 33   Counterplan

Alternative titles: *Passer-by, Encounter,* and *Turbine No. 50,000.* [VAAP 1977 mentions a variant title, *Coming your way.*] See also 'Notes'.

Form: Music for the black-and-white film *Counterplan,* with screenplay by Leo Arnshtam, D. Del, and the two directors—Fridrikh Ermler and Sergei Yutkevich—for the Leningrad Rosfilm Studio. Two songs are featured in the score: 'Song of the Counterplan' for solo voice and, in the finale, for chorus; and 'How Long will my Heart Ache?', with traditional words, for unaccompanied women's chorus. Three orchestral excerpts are known:

1. Presto *attacca*
2. Andante
3. Andante—'Song of the Counterplan' orchestral version

Instrumentation: piccolo, 2 flutes, 2 oboes, 2 B flat clarinets, 2 bassoons, contrabassoon ~ 4 horns, 3 trumpets, 3 trombones, tuba ~ timpani, triangle, side drum, cymbals ~ glockenspiel, 2 xylophones, 2 harps ~ strings.

Composed: Autumn 1932, at Leningrad.

Première: Film first shown on 7 November 1932 in Leningrad. Score conducted by Nikolai Rabinovich. Screened at the National Film Theatre, London, in May 1956.

Arrangements: A popular song from the score, 'Song of the Counterplan', in various arrangements, including for mixed chorus by Isaak Dunayevsky, an adaptation as the 'United Nations' Hymn' [given as Opus 59 by Slonimsky (1942)], and as a piano piece. An overblown concert version 'United Nations on the March', was featured as the closing tableau to MGM's revue *Thousands Cheer,* directed in colour by George Sidney and released in 1943. Kathryn Grayson and multinational choir were accompanied by a massive orchestra conducted by José Iturbi. Harold Rome's English lyric revised by Edgar Yip Harburg.

A symphonic transcription of 'United Nations March', marked 'Alert and Confident', made by Leopold Stokowski in 1943 (the conductor's unpublished manuscript score, 33 cm.). Instrumentation: piccolo, flute, oboe, cor anglais, 2 B flat clarinets, bass clarinet, 2 bassoons ~ 2 or 4 horns, 2 or 4 trumpets, 2 trombones, tuba ~ timpani, triangle, side drum, cymbals, bass drum ~ strings.

Shostakovich included 'Song of the Counterplan' in his Opp. 74, 78, and 105.

Music: Autograph copy of the film score preserved in the Music Department of Lenfilm. The whereabouts of the autograph of 'Song of the Counterplan' not known; that of the song 'How Long will my Heart Ache?' in the Glinka Museum, with a Scherzo in piano score and three sketches for the 'Song of the Counterplan'. Autograph scores of the three excerpts preserved at the Leningrad Institute of the Theatre, Music, and Cinematography.

Muzyka, No. 10839 (in Volume 41 of *Collected Works* with Opp. 26, 30, 41, 48, 50, 53, 55, 56, 59, and 64), 1987, three excerpts in full score, 30 cm.

'Song of the Counterplan' (five stanzas by Boris Kornilov):

Muzgiz, No. 13933, 1933, for voice and piano, 18 cm.

Sovetskii Kompozitor, No. 519 (in *D. Shostakovich: Songs*), 1958, 29 cm.

Muzyka, No. 2983 (in *Russian-English Songs by Soviet Composers*, 2nd ed. paperback compiled by L. Shturman; the first of nineteen songs with English translation by Zelikov, 1966, words and melody, 21.5 cm.

Muzyka, No. 4120, 1967, included in a bound volume of patriotic songs, 22 cm.

Muzichna Ukraina, Kiev, No. 42 (with three other Shostakovich songs), 1976, 26 cm.

Muzyka, No. 10179 (in Volume 34 of *Collected Works* with Opp. 88 and 136, and songs), 1985, 'Song of the Counterplan' for two-part chorus and 'How Long will my Heart Ache?' for S.A. chorus, 30 cm. [Sketches for the former and a Scherzo in piano score are published as a supplement to Volume 41.]

'Song of the Counterplan' arrangements:

Workers' Music Association, London, *c*.1939, entitled 'Salute to Life' with English lyric by Nancy Head, for unison choirs of children and adults, 24 cm. [Priced at two old pence.] Reissued in *Popular Soviet Songs* by Workers' Music Association, 1941, pp. 10–11, 25 cm. [Priced at one shilling.]

Leeds Music, 1942, entitled 'United Nations' Hymn', words by Harold Rome.

Leo Feist Inc., New York, No. 7408-2, 1942, entitled 'United Nations on the March' with English lyric by Harold Rome (from the MGM film *Thousands Cheer*), 31 cm.

Charles Brendler orchestration of 'The United Nations' [publisher not stated, 1940s], piano-conductor score and parts, 32 cm.

Sovetskii Kompozitor, No. 4565, 1967(in *Dmitri Shostakovich: Popular Pieces*), arr. for solo piano by Lev Atovmyan, 29 cm.

Duration: Film: 3170 metres. Nos. 1–3: 8' 10"–8' 51".

Recordings: 'Song of the Counterplan' only:

USA: Hollywood Soundstage 409 (mono). 'United Nations on the March'. Kathryn GRAYSON (soprano), MGM Studio Orchestra and UN Chorus, José Iturbi. [*Thousands Cheer* soundtrack.] P 1943.

USA: Victor Red Seal 11-8250 (10" 78 rpm). Orch. by O'Connell. 'The United Nations'. Igor GORIN (baritone), Victor Symphony Orchestra, Charles O'Connell. [Musorgsky.] P c.1943.

USA: Keynote K 1200 (10" 78 rpm). Sung in English. 'The United Nations' (Rome). Paul ROBESON (bass), Keynote Chorus and Orchestra, Charles Lichter. [Registan.] P 1944. *Reissued:* Pearl Compact Disc GEMM 9264 (mono). ['Songs for Free Men'—folksongs, Dzerzhinsky, Knipper, Musorgsky *et al.*] I 1997.

USSR: 15018-9 (10" 78 rpm). Chorus and Orchestra conducted by Viktor KNUSHEVITSKY. P 1947.

USSR: 21043-22819 (10" 78 rpm). All-Union Radio Song Ensemble. [Traditional folksongs.] P 1952–3.

USSR: MK D 5062-3 (10" mono). All-Union Radio Song Ensemble. [Songs from Opp. 72, 80, 82, 86, 99 *et al.*] Possibly a reissue from 78 rpm. *Reissued:* USSR: Melodiya C60 22119 005 and C60 22121 003. [Khrennikov, Bogoslovsky, Dunayevsky *et al.*] Both I 1985*d* ~ USSR: Melodiya C60 24293 007. ['Songs of Struggle and Solidarity'.] I 1987*b*.

France: Le Chant du Monde 504 (10" 78 rpm). Chorus and Orchestra conducted by Roger DÉSORMIÈRE. [Auric.] P c.1957.

USA: Artistic Enterprises B 109. Translated as 'Morning Light'. Sidor BELARSKY (bass) and unnamed pianist. ['Concert of Russian Music'.] P 1960.

East Germany: Aurora 8 15 109. Sung in German. Ernst BUSCH, Leipzig Radio Symphony Orchestra, Adolf Fritz Guhl. [Op. 80.] P 1966.

Chandos Compact Disc CHAN 9349. 'United Nations March' arr. Stokowski. BBC Philharmonic, Matthias BAMBERT. ['Stokowski Encores'—Handel, Gabrieli, J. Clarke *et al.*] P Manchester 13 Oct. 1994, I Mar. 1995, G June 1995.

Orchestral excerpts:

USA: Russian Disc Compact Disc RDCD 10 018. Nos. 1–3. Byelorussian Radio and TV Symphony Orchestra, Walter MNATSAKANOV. [Opp. 50, 53, 55, and 132.] P Minsk Nov. 1995.

Decca Compact Disc 460 792-2DH11. Nos. 1–3. Alexander Kerr (violin in No. 2), Royal Concertgebouw Orchestra, Riccardo CHAILLY. ['The Film Album'—Opp. 26, 56, 116, 55, 132, 76*a*, and 97.] P Amsterdam 6–22 May (No. 3) and 10–11 Sept. 1998, I Mar. 1999, G Apr. 1999.

References: Khentova (1980), Sokhov, and Yutkevich.

Notes: *Vstrechnyi* in its various translations gives the title to the film's most popular song: 'The Song of the Counterplan', 'Song of the Passer-by', 'Song About the First Comer', and 'Song of the On-Coming' (*sic*). Rabinovich (1959) gives 'Song of the Young Workers' which was followed by Zelikov and other translators. Martynov (1962) has 'We're Met by the Breezes of Morning,'and Malcolm MacDonald lists 'We Meet this Morning', both of which derive from the first line of the lyric in English translation—'The cool of the dawn greets us early'. 'Song of the Meeting', adopted in the 1st and 2nd editions of this catalogue, is a simple amalgam of these sources. (DCH).

In honour of Stalin's birthday, 'Salute to Life' was performed by Sir Henry Wood and the BBC Symphony Orchestra in a Bedford studio concert of Russian and Soviet music on 21 December 1941. The invited audience included Agnes Maisky, wife of the Soviet Ambassador, and Russian soldiers and sailors.

'The United Nations March', arranged by Langendoen, was played by the Boston Symphony Orchestra and The Collegiate Chorale, under Leonard Bernstein, at the first Human Rights Day concert on 10 December 1949, in the Carnegie Hall, New York (recorded privately in USA on 8" acetate disc).

Leopold Stokowski's transcription, with an added choral conclusion, was performed by the Symphony of the Air and the Schola Cantorum conducted by Hugh Ross, at a concert on the first United Nations Day, 24 October 1954, in the newly finished UN Headquarters, New York. The 'United Nations Hymn', published in 1942, refers to the topical theme of nations being united in the fight against Nazi Germany and Japan. The United Nations was founded in 1946 but there was not an official 'hymn' of the organisation until one was commissioned by U Thant, then Secretary-General, from Pablo Casals in 1970 to text by W.H. Auden (Edward Johnson *in litt.*).

The working title of the film was *Greeting the Future* and a further alternative title was *Shame*.

Opus 34   Twenty-four Preludes

Form: A collection of piano pieces round the whole cycle of ascending fifths:

1. C major—Moderato
2. A minor—Allegretto
3. G major—Andante
4. E minor—Moderato
5. D major—Allegro vivace—'Velocity Étude'
6. B minor—Allegretto

7. A major—Andante
8. F sharp minor—Allegretto
9. E major—Presto
10. C sharp minor—Moderato non troppo
11. B major—Allegretto
12. G sharp minor—Allegro non troppo
13. F sharp major—Moderato
14. E flat minor—Adagio—'Zoya Prelude'
15. D flat major—Allegretto
16. B flat minor—Andantino
17. A flat major—Largo
18. F minor—Allegretto
19. E flat major—Andantino
20. C minor—Allegretto furioso
21. B flat major—Allegro poco moderato
22. G minor—Adagio
23. F major—Moderato
24. D minor—Allegretto

Composed: 30 December 1932 to 2 March 1933, in Leningrad apart from No. 8 in Moscow.

Premières: Nos. 1–8: 17 January 1933, Leningrad Philharmonic Bolshoi Hall; Dmitri Shostakovich.

Complete cycle: 24 May 1933, Moscow Conservatory Malyi Hall; D. Shostakovich.

No. 14 transcription: 27 December 1935, Philadelphia; Philadelphia Orchestra, Leopold Stokowski.

Arrangements: Duo transcriptions for violin and piano of Nos. 1–3, 5, 6, 8, 10–13, 15–22, and 24 by Dmitri Tsyganov; and Nos. 10, 15, 16, and 24 by Quinto Maganini. Tsyganov's transcriptions grouped into three suites.

Transcription for viola and piano of Nos. 10, 14–18, and 24 by Ye. Strakov.

For flute and piano: No. 10 by Gleb Nikitin; Nos. 10, 15, 16, and 24 by Q. Maganini.

For saxophone and piano: Nos. 10, 13, and 15–18 by Marc Chisson.

Nos. 10 and 16 for trombone by Mikhail Dubirny.

No. 14 transcribed for full orchestra by Leopold Stokowski (1935) and Lev Atovmyan (1944); and for band by George Donald Mairs, Gene Chenoweth, and H. Robert Reynolds. NB. The name 'Zoya Prelude' may be a dedication to the composer's sister or, more likely, refer to its use in the Opus 64*a* Suite.

Nos. 14, 17, and 20 transcribed for wind orchestra and titled 'Three Symphonic Preludes' by Alfred Reed.

No. 15 in an extended transcription for string orchestra by G. Zaborov.

Nos. 13, 14, and 15 for trombone and organ by Jean Douay / Christian Gouinguené.

No. 17 for clarinet and orchestra by Hershy Kay.

No. 19 for symphonic band by Gene Chenoweth.

Four arranged for two trombones or two bassoons by Allen Ostrander.

Suite of Nos. 7, 10, 22, 8, 14, 24, 17, and 5 orchestrated for small orchestra of single woodwind and brass, piano / celesta, and strings by Milko Kelemen.

Suite of Nos. 1, 10, 8, 16, 19, 6, 22, 13, 14, and 15 orchestrated for symphony orchestra by Ed de Boer.

Suite of Nos. 10, 17, 24, 14, 13, 6, and 5 transcribed for string orchestra by Viktor Poltoratsky.

No. 1 used as a theme for a jazz ensemble arrangement by V. Karminsky.

Nos. 1, 3, 7, 8, and 11 transcribed for wind quintet by Bruce Smeaton.

Nos. 6, 15, 17, and 19 transcribed for string quartet by Michael Thomas.

Tsyganov's second suite—Nos. 2, 6, 12, 13, 17, 18, 19, 21, 22, and 20—transcribed for violin and strings by Ilmar Lapinsch.

Nos. 1. 2, 7, 8, 11, 14, 15, 17, 18, and 23 arranged by accordionist Evan Harlan for jazz / folk group; the pieces given subtitles such as 'Mimi Goes Me(n)tal', 'Fireman's Waltz', and No. 14 'Gulag'.

Suite of Nos. 3, 6, 10, 11, 15, 16, 19, and 24 arranged for tenor and bass trombone duet by Douglas Yeo.

Nos. 6, 7, 10, 13–17, 19–21, and 24 arranged for trombone quartet by Hans Peter Gaiswinkler.

No. 17 arranged for strings and piano by Mikhail Turich.

Instrumentation of Stokowski's version of No. 14: piccolo, 3 flutes, 2 oboes, cor anglais, E flat clarinet, 3 B flat clarinets, 3 bassoons, contrabassoon ~ 4 horns, 4 trumpets, 4 trombones, tuba ~ timpani, bass drum, gong ~ harp ~ strings.

Instrumentation of Ed de Boer's suite: piccolo, 2 flutes, 2 oboes, 2 clarinets (B flat and A; clarinet II = E flat clarinet), 2 bassoons, contrabassoon ~ 2 horns, 2 trumpets (C), 2 trombones, tuba ~ timpani, cymbals, bass drum, side drum, tom-tom ~ xylophone, marimba, celesta ~ strings.

Music: Two autograph copies are in existence: one preserved at the Glinka Museum; the other, with the composer's erroneous date of '1933–1934' on the title-page and the last two Preludes missing, preserved at the CIS Archives of Literature and Art. The first page of Prelude No. 1 of the former copy is reproduced in Volume 39 of *Collected Works*.

Piano: Muzgiz, No. 14215, 1935, 31 cm.

Providence, Axelrod, No. 159, *c.*1939, Nos. 13, 17, 7, and 24, 31 cm.

Boston Music, 1943, 30 cm.

International Music, No. 583, 1943, 30.5 cm.
Soyuz Sovetskikh Kompozitorov, 1945, 30 cm.
Anglo-Soviet Music Press, No. 65, *c*.1945, 30.5 cm.
MCA, *c*.1945, 31 cm.
Leeds Music, 1945, Nos. 14 and 24 only, 31 cm.
Soyuz Sovetskikh Kompozitorov, 1946, in four volumes, 29 cm.
Hans Sikorski, No. 2124, *c*.1955, in two volumes, 31.5 cm.
Edition Peters, Nos. 4773*a* and *b*, 1962, in two volumes, 30 cm.
Muzgiz, No. 3184 (in *D. Shostakovich: Compositions for fortepiano,* Volume 1, with Sans op. B, Opp. 5, 12, 13, 22*a* Polka, and 61), 1966, 29 cm.

G. Schirmer, No. 3047, 1976, VAAP authorized edition, ed. György Sándor, 30.5 cm.

Muzyka, No. 10285 (in Volume 39 of *Collected Works* with Opp. 5, 12, 13, 61, 69, and supplement of unnumbered piano pieces), 1983, 30 cm.

Yorktown Music Press, New York, 1984, No. 17 only in album *The Joy of Russian Music* assembled by Dénes Agay, 30 cm.

Violin and piano: Muzgiz, 1937 and 1953, Nos. 10, 15, 16, and 24 arr. D. Tsyganov, 30 cm.

Edition Musicus, 1939, Nos. 10, 15, 16, and 24 arr. Q. Maganini, 31 cm.

Muzgiz, 1961, Nos. 2, 6, 12, 13, 17, 18, 19, 21, 22, and 20 arr. in that order by D. Tsyganov, 29 cm.

MCA, 1966, Nos. 1, 3, 5, 8, 10, 11, 15, 16, and 24 arr. Tsyganov and ed. Carl Rosenthal, 31 cm.

Muzyka, No. 6365, 1969, the nineteen Preludes arr. Tsyganov grouped into three suites, 29 cm.

Hans Sikorski, No. 2323, 1981, the nineteen Preludes as above, 31.5 cm.

Other transcriptions: Affiliated Music, New York, 1939, Nos. 10, 15, 16, and 24 for flute and piano by Q. Maganini (with violin and piano arrangements of same), 31 cm.

Edition Musicus, No. 290, *c*.1941, No. 14 for symphonic band by G. Chenoweth, 27.5 cm.

G. Schirmer, 1944, No. 14 arr. for band by G. D. Mairs, score and parts.

Broude Bros., New York, 1948, No. B.B. 180, No. 14 orchestrated by Stokowski, score, 31 cm.

Wheeling, USA, no date, Nos. 4 [or No. 6 transposed to E minor] and 24 for wind quintet by A. Henry, 28 and 30 cm. respectively.

Edition Musicus, *c*.1954, four arr. for two trombones (or bassoons) by A. Ostrander, 31 cm.

Edition Peters, No. 8072 (Litolff plate no. 30518), 1971, Nos. 7, 10, 22, 8, 14, 24, 17, and 5 arr. for small orchestra by M. Kelemen, score, 19 cm.

Muzyka, No. 8854, 1975, Nos. 10, 14–18, and 24 for viola and piano by Ye. Strakov, 29 cm.

Muzyka, Leningrad, No. 2169 (in *Pieces by Soviet Composers* for flute and piano), 1977, No. 10 arr. G. Nikitin, 28 cm.

Hans Sikorski, 1981, Ed de Boer and V. Poltoratsky's transcriptions available on hire.

G. Schirmer, No. ED 4019, August 1997, Eight Preludes Nos. 3, 6, 10, 11, 15, 16, 19, and 24 for tenor and bass trombone duet by D. Yeo (duration 12' 25"), 30 cm.

Duration: Approx. 31' 30" in score; 25' 19"–36' 54". No. 14 orchestral version: 2' 16"–3' 11".

Film: *Ever Decreasing Circles.* No. 15 played by Ronnie Price used as a signature tune for this comedy series shown on BBC TV in 1983, 1984, 1986, and 1987, with a final special edition on 24 December 1989.

Recordings: USA: Victor 7888 in Set M 192 (78 rpm). No. 14 orchestrated by Stokowski. Philadelphia Orchestra, Leopold STOKOWSKI. [Stravinsky.] P 30 Dec. 1935. *Reissued:* HMV DB 2884 (78 rpm) and DB 8224 (78 rpm automatic couplings). Labelled as 'Prelude in A flat'. [Stravinsky.] G Feb. 1937 ~ Dutton Laboratories Compact Disc CDAX 8002 (mono). [Stravinsky.] I Apr. 1993, G May 1993 ~ Pearl Compact Disc GEMM CDS 9044 (two-disc set, mono). [Opp. 10, 47, and 60.] I Nov. 1993, G Jan. 1994.

USA: Columbia 11524 D in Set M 446 (78 rpm). No. 14 orch. Stokowski. All-American Orchestra, Leopold STOKOWSKI. [Stravinsky.] P 14 Nov. 1940.

Columbia DX 1066 (78 rpm). No. 14 only. Harriet COHEN (piano). [Kabalevsky.] G Feb. 1942.

USSR: 11992-3 (10" 78 rpm). Nos. 22, 8, 14, and 15. Dmitri SHOSTAKOVICH (piano). P 1944. *Reissued:* USSR: 13170-? (10" 78 rpm). Nos. 22 and 8. [?] I 1945 ~ Revelation Compact Disc RV 70007 (mono). Nos. 8 and 22. ['Shostakovich plays Shostakovich, Vol. 6'—Opp. 79, 69, and 67.] I Sept. 1998, G Feb. 1999.

USA: Victor 11-8824 (78 rpm). Nos. 5, 10, and 24. William KAPELL (piano). [Rakhmaninov.] P 11 Dec. 1944. *Reissued:* Pearl Compact Disc GEMM CD 9277 (mono). Nos. 5, 10, and 24. [Khachaturyan, Beethoven, and Brahms.] I 1997 ~ RCA Victor Red Seal Compact Discs 09026 6844-2 (nine-disc set, mono). Nos. 5, 10, and 24. ['William Kapell Edition'—with alternative takes of Nos. 5 and 10 plus 1944 recording of No. 14; Albeniz to Schumann.] I and G Jan. 1999, G Jan. 2001 ~ Naxos Historical Compact Disc 8.110673. Nos. 24, 10, and 5. [Prokofiev and Khachaturyan.] I 2001.

USA: International Piano Archives at Maryland IPAM 1101 (mono). Nos. 24, 10, and 5. William KAPELL. [Recital.] P Carnegie Hall concert 28 Feb. 1945, I 1983. *Reissued:* Dutton Compact Disc CDBP 9701 (mono). [Beethoven and Khachaturyan.] I Oct. 2000.

USA: Mercury MG 10035 (mono). Nos. 8, 14–19, and 24. Dmitri SHOSTAKOVICH. [Opp. 5, 22*a*, and 69; 'David Oistrakh plays violin favorites'—Chopin/Saraste, Prokofiev *et al.*] P Prague 1946.

USSR: 014616-7 (12" 78 rpm). Nos. 16, 22, and 23. Dmitri SHOSTAKOVICH. P 1947.

USSR: Melodiya M10 39075-6 (mono). Nos. 14, 15, 24, 8, 17–19—not No. 16 as stated on label and sleeve. Dmitri SHOSTAKOVICH. [In four-record box set 'D. Shostakovich—Pianist'—Opp. 5, 22*a*, 69, and 67.] P 1947, I 1977*b*. *Reissued:* Revelation Compact Disc RV 70007 (mono). Nos. 14–19 and 24 with No. 16 included. ['Shostakovich plays Shostakovich, Vol. 6'—Opp. 79, 69, and 67.] I Sept. 1998.

Revelation Compact Disc RV 70007 (mono). Nos. 8, 22, and 23. ['Shostakovich plays Shostakovich, Vol. 6'—Opp. 79, 69, and 67.] NB. Nos. 8 and 22 are separately-tracked extra versions on the CD and, with No. 23, stated to be P July 1950. I Sept. 1998.

USA: Columbia MM 856 17597-17600 D (10" 78 rpm, 1 side in four-record set). No. 17 arr. H. Kay. Artie SHAW (clarinet), orchestra conducted by Walter Hendl. [Poulenc.] P 1948. *Reissued:* USA: Columbia ML 4260 (mono). ['Modern Music for Clarinet'—Ravel, Kabalevsky, Milhaud *et al.*] I 1950s.

USA: Columbia 17335 D (78 rpm). No. 2 only. Oscar LEVANT (piano). [Op. 22*a* No. 3.] P pre-1949.

USA: Vox 16023 in Album 165 (78 rpm, in four-record set). Nos. 10 and 24. Shura CHERKASSKY. [Khachaturyan, Tchaikovsky, Skryabin *et al.*] P *c.*1950. *Reissued:* Pearl Compact Disc GE 0138. [Glinka, Rebikov, Tchaikovsky *et al.*] I 2000. NB. P now thought to be New York or Los Angeles 1946.

USA: MCM E 3070 (mono). Complete cycle. Menahem PRESSLER (piano). P 1953, I 1955.

USA: Decca A 592 (10" 78 rpm). Nos. 10 and 15 arr. for violin and piano. Jascha HEIFETZ (violin) and Emanuel Bay (piano). [Rimsky-Korsakov.] P *c.*1954.

USA: Decca FST 153515 (mono). Complete cycle. Robert CORNMAN (piano). P 1955.

USA: RCA Victor LM 1975 (mono). Nos. 2, 14, and 24. Amparo ITURBI (piano). [Ravel, Chabrier, Schubert *et al.*] P 1955, I 1956. *Reissued:* France: RCA Victor 630 354 (mono). [As USA release.] I 1957.

Philips NBE 11014 (7" 45 rpm mono). Nos. 2, 3, 5, 10, 12, 21, and 24. Daniel BARENBOIM (piano). [Kabalevsky.] G Feb. 1956.

USSR: 24485-6 (10" 78 rpm). Nos. 10, 15, 16, and 24 arr. Tsyganov. Yulian SITKOVETSKY (violin) and Naum Valter (piano). P 1955. *Reissued:* USSR: MK D 6089-90 (10" mono). [Szymanowski, Bartók, Wieniawski *et al.*] I 1960 ~ USSR: Melodiya C10 06831-2 (electronic stereo ?). [Third of five records in album 'The Art of Yulian Sitkovetsky'—Mozart, Tchaikovsky, and Prokofiev.] I 1976.

USSR: 26316-7 (10" 78 rpm). Nos. 10, 15, 16, and 24 arr. Tsyganov. Leonid KOGAN (violin) and Dmitri Shostakovich (piano). P 2 Feb. 1956. *Reissued:* USSR: MK D 3036-7 (10" mono). [Opp. 94 and 49.] I 1956 ~ USSR: MK D 0005156-7 (7" 45 rpm mono). [Prokofiev and Rakhmaninov.] I 1959 ~ HMV Melodiya HLM 7096 in Set RLS 721 (mono). [Op. 87.] G Oct. 1976 ~ USSR: Melodiya M10 39077-8 (mono). [In four-record box set 'D. Shostakovich—Pianist' with Op. 57.] I 1977*b* ~ Czech: Multisonic Compact Disc MU 31 0179-2 (mono). ['Russian Treasure'—Opp. 40 and 57.] I Sept. 1993 ~ Revelation Compact Disc RV 70002 (mono). ['Shostakovich plays Shostakovich, Vol. 2'—Opp. 93 and 97.] 1 Oct. 1997, G Feb. 1998.

USSR: Melodiya M10 48767 000 (in four-record box set, mono). Nos. 1, 2, 3, 7, 8, 11, 13, 14, 16, 18, 19, 22, and 23. Heinrich NEUHAUS (piano). ['The Complete Neuhaus, Volume 2'—on fourth record with Prokofiev.] P 1957, I 1990*a*.

USSR: 27878-9 (10" 78 rpm). Nos. 1, 2, 18, and 19. Heinrich NEUHAUS. P most probably from the above session.

USSR: HD 4292-3 (10" mono). Nos. 10, 15, 16, and 24 arr. Tsyganov. Valentin ZHUK (violin) and Ye. Fuks (piano). [Wieniawski, Saint-Saëns, and Tchaikovsky.] I 1958.

USA: RCA LM 2250(mono). Nos. 10, 15, 16, and 24 arr. Tsyganov. Leonid KOGAN (violin) and Andrei Mytnik (piano). [Bloch, Debussy, Glazunov *et al.*] P New York 1958.

USA: United Artists UAL 7004 (mono) and UAS 8004. No. 14 orch. Stokowski. Symphony of the Air, Leopold STOKOWSKI. [Opp. 10 and 29 Entr'acte.] P New York 15–19 Dec. 1958. *Reissued:* Japan: King Records K18C 9333. [Opp. 10 and 29 Entr'acte.] I 1982 ~ USA: EMI Classics Compact Discs ZDMB5 6542723 (in two-disc set). [Opp. 10 and 29 Entr'acte; Bloch, Cesti, and Gabrielli.] I Nov. 1994.

USSR: 0032522-3 (8" 78 rpm). Nos. 10, 15, 16, and 24 arr. Tsyganov. Valeri KLIMOV (violin) and Inna Kollegorskaya (piano). P 1959. *Reissued:* USSR: MK D 05054-5 (mono). [Taneyev, Dvořák, Schumann *et al.*] I 1959.

France: Vogue Compact Disc VG 672 009. Nos. 10, 15, 16, and 24 arr. Tsyganov. Leonid KOGAN (violin) and Andrei Mytnik (piano). [Prokofiev, R. Strauss, and Falla.] P Paris concert 26 Nov. 1959, I 1988.

Czech: Supraphon SUF 20004 (10" mono). Nos. 1 and 4 arr. for violin and piano. Valeri KLIMOV (violin) and Inna Kollegorskaya (piano). [Prokofiev and Ysaÿe.] G Apr. 1961.

USSR: MK D 010223-4 (mono). Nos. 10, 15, 16, and 24 arr. Tsyganov. Boris GUTNIKOV (violin) and Lydia Pecherskaya (piano). [Bach, Mozart, Tchaikovsky *et al.*] P 1962.

[France: EMI unissued stereo recording. Nos. 2, 6, 12, 13, 17, 18, 19, 21, and 20 arr. Tsyganov. Leonid KOGAN (violin) and Georges Solchany (piano). P Paris studio 24 July 1962.]

USSR: Melodiya D 013383-4 (mono). Nos. 17, 10, 13, 14, and 15. Gleb AKHELROD (piano). [Schubert, Liszt, Medtner, and Bartók.] P 1964.

USSR: Melodiya D 15353-4 (10" mono). Nos. 1, 3, 8, 11, and 5 arr. Tsyganov. Aleksei MIKHLIN (violin) and Yelena Seidel (piano). [K. Khachaturyan, Veracini, and Ysaÿe.] P 1965.

USSR: Melodiya D 016139-40 (mono). Nos. 2, 6, 12, 13, 17, 18, 19, 21, 22, and 20 arr. Tsyganov. Vladimir MALININ (violin) and M. Shteri (piano). [Medtner and Skryabin.] P 1965.

USSR: Melodiya D 16333-4 (10" mono). Nos. 2, 6, 12, 13, 17, 18, 19, 21, 22, and 20 arr. Tsyganov. Boris GUTNIKOV (violin) and Lydia Pecherskaya (piano). [Britten.] P 1965.

USSR: Melodiya D 16681-2 (10" mono). Nos. 13, 8, 11, and 5 arr. Tsyganov. Vladimir LANTSMAN (violin) and A. Levina (piano). [Pascal, Ravel, and Paganini.] P 1965.

Czech: Supraphon SUA 50890 (mono). Complete cycle. Klára HAV-LÍKOVÁ (piano). [Hindemith.] P Apr. 1966, I 1968. *Reissued:* USA: Cross-roads 22 16 0204. [Hindemith.] ~ Czech: Opus 9111 0186. [Hindemith.] I 1972.

USSR: Melodiya D 17527-30 (4 sides 10" mono). Complete cycle discussed and performed by Ye. LIBERMAN. P 1966.

USSR: Melodiya D 18345-6 (10" mono). Nos. 10 and 16 arr. for trombone. Mikhail DUBIRNY (trombone). [Schubert, Bozza, Baudo *et al.*] P 1966.

USSR: Melodiya D 019331-2 (mono). Nos. 10, 15, 16, and 24 arr. Tsyganov. Aleksei MIKHLIN (violin) and Yelena Seidel (piano). [Ysaÿe, Vainberg, and Prokofiev.] P 1967.

USSR: Melodiya D 022047-8 (mono). Nos. 10, 15, 16, 24; 2, 6, 12, 13, 17, 18, 19, 21, 22, 20; 1, 3, 8, 11, and 5 arr. Tsyganov. Rafail SOBOLOVSKY (violin), E. Epstein (piano—first and third groups) and Yelena Livshits (piano—second group). [Tartini/Kreisler and Paganini.] P 1968.

USA: Music & Arts Compact Disc CD 847. No. 14 orch. Stokowski. Royal Philharmonic Orchestra, Leopold STOKOWSKI. [Stokowski conducts Music from Russia, Vol. III'—Musorgsky, Glinka, Stravinsky *et al.*] P 24 June 1969, I Jan. 1995.

Italy: Fratelli Fabbri Editori MM 1092 (10" mono). Complete cycle. Albert COLOMBO (piano). I c.1969.

USSR: Melodiya D 028103-4 (mono). Nos. 10, 15, 16, and 24 arr. Tsyganov. Andrei KORSAKOV (violin) and unnamed pianist. [Concert programme by violinists performing at Fourth International Tchaikovsky Competition—Paganini, Prokofiev, Bartók *et al.*] P and I 1970.

Belgium: Melodiya 562 241. Nos. 10, 15, 16, and 24 arr. Tsyganov. Andrei KORSAKOV (violin) and Elizaveta Ginzburg (piano). [Schumann, Ysaÿe, and Vieuxtemps.] P Brussels 26 May 1971. *Reissued:* USSR: Melodiya CM 03125-6. [As original issue.] I 1972.

Sweden: Swedish Society Discofil SLT 33221. Complete cycle. Inger WIKSTRÖM (piano). P Stockholm 12 Sept. 1973. *Reissued:* RCA Gold Seal

GL 25003. [Op. 61.] G Nov. 1976 ~ Sweden: Swedish Society Discofil Compact Disc SCD 1031. [Opp. 61, 94, 5, and 19.] I 1988.

USSR: Melodiya CM 04263-4. Complete cycle. Vera GORNOSTAYEVA (piano). [Prokofiev.] P 1973, I 1974.

Czech: Panton 11 0488 F. Complete cycle. Dagmar BALOGHOVA (piano). [Prigozhin.] P Prague 1974.

USSR: Melodiya C10 05023-4. Nos. 10, 15, 16, and 24 arr. Tsyganov. Vadim BRODSKY (violin) and unnamed pianist. [Concert programme by violinists performing at the Fifth International Tchaikovsky Competition—Bach, Paganini, Shebalin *et al.*] P Moscow concert 1974, I 1975.

USSR: Melodiya C10 05565-6. Nos. 10, 15, 16, and 24 arr. Tsyganov. Ruben AGARONYAN (violin) and Svetlana Navasardyan (piano). [Beethoven, Schubert, Mendelssohn *et al.*] P 1975, I 1975*d*.

USSR: Melodiya C10 07163-4. No. 17 arr. Tsyganov. Gidon KREMER (violin) and Oleg Maizenberg (piano). ['Romantic miniatures'—Khandoshkin, Tchaikovsky, Musorgsky *et al.*] P 1976, I 1977*a*.

Belgium: Cyprès Compact Discs CYP 9612 (on seventh of twelve-disc set). Nos. 10, 15, 16, and 24 arr. Tsyganov. Mikhail BEZVERKHNY (violin) and Bella Rakova (piano). [Bartók and Brahms.] P Brussels Queen Elisabeth Competition concert 29 May 1976, I 2001.

CBS 73589. No. 14 orch. Stokowski. National Philharmonic Orchestra, Leopold STOKOWSKI. [Chopin, Debussy, Rimsky-Korsakov *et al.*] P 12–13 and 16 July 1976, G June 1977.

USA: Russian Compact Disc RCD 16238. Nos. 9, 10, 15, and 24. Nataliya GAVRILOVA (piano). ['Russian Piano School'—Opp. 22, 27, and 97; Babadzhanyan, Rakhmaninov, J. Strauss *et al.*] P 1976–90, I 1998.

USSR: Melodiya C10 09843-4. Nos. 2, 6, 12, 13, 17, 18, 19, 21, 22, and 20 arr. Tsyganov. Nelli SHKOLNIKOVA (violin) and Yuliya Gushanskaya (piano). [Handel, Bach, and Prokofiev.] P 1977, I 1978*c*.

Polydor 2531 096. Nos. 1, 4, 10, 12, 14–16, 19, 22, and 24. Lazar BERMAN (piano). [Musorgsky.] P Hamburg 1977, G Mar. 1979. Music Trades Association Awards 1979—winner of Solo Instrumental category. *Reissued:* USSR: Melodiya C10 16615-6. [Musorgsky.] I 1982*c*.

USSR: Melodiya C10 10993-4. Nineteen arr. Tsyganov not as listed on label and sleeve but grouped as follows: Nos. 1, 3, 8, 11, 5; 10, 15, 16, 24; 2, 6, 12, 13, 17, 18, 19, 21, 22, and 20. Zarius SHIKHMURZAYEVA (violin) and Mikhail Muntyan (piano). [Fauré, Saint-Saëns, and Shchedrin.] P 1978, I 1979*b*.

USSR: Melodiya C10 11163-4. Nos. 1, 3, 8, 11, and 5 arr. Tsyganov. Irina MEDVEDEVA (violin) and Margarita Kravchenko (piano). [Taneyev, Copland, Tchaikovsky *et al.*] P Moscow concert 1978, I 1979*b*.

France: Corelia CC 78 030. Nos. 13–15 arr. for trombone and organ. Jean DOUAY (trombone) and Christian Gouinguené (organ). [Cesare, Gouinguené, Bach *et al.*] P 1978.

Bulgaria: Balkanton BKA 11216. Complete cycle. Marta DEYANOVA (piano). [Prokofiev.] P 1980?

USSR: Melodiya C10 14323-4. No. 15 arr. for string orchestra by G. Zaborov—not Op. 87 No. 15 as stated on label and sleeve. String Ensemble of Siberia (members of the Tyumen State Philharmonic Orchestra), Tatyana Abramova (piano), Mikhail PARKHOMOVSKY. [Khachaturyan, Khrennikov, Karayev, and Svetlanov.] P 1980, I 1981*b*.

USSR: Melodiya C10 17555003. Nos. 12, 6, and 17 arr. Tsyganov. Vladimir SPIVAKOV (violin) and Boris Bekhterev (piano). [Debussy, Ravel, Messiaen *et al.*] P 1982, I 1983*a*.

USA: Orion ORS 83462. Complete cycle. Zoe ERISMAN (piano). [Opp. 94, 39, and 27.] P 1983.

USSR: Melodiya A10 00043 004 (digital). Nos. 7, 10, 22, 8, 14, 24, 17, and 9 orch. M. Kelemen. USSR Ministry of Culture Symphony Orchestra, Gennadi ROZHDESTVENSKY. [Opp. 46 and 91.] P 1983, I 1984*c* ~ BMG Melodiya Compact Discs 74321 63460-2 (two-disc set). [Opp. 113; 112, and 107.] I Mar. 1999.

USSR: Melodiya C60 22481 008. No. 1 arr. for jazz ensemble. Metronom Ensemble, Mikhail YAKON. [Ninth Moscow Festival of Jazz Music, 3rd record.] P 1984, I 1986*a*.

USSR: Melodiya C10 28379 002. Complete cycle. Vladimir VIARDO (piano). [Opp. 37, 58*a*, and 19.] P 1984, I 1990*a*.

Bulgaria: Balkanton BKA 11424. Nos. 10, 14–18, and 24 arr. Ye. Strakov. Ognyan STANCHEV (viola) and Ivan Evtimov (piano). [Op. 147.] P 1984?

Whitetower Records Ensemble ENS 132 (Digital real time cassette). Nos. 6 and 17 arr. Tsyganov—not Atovmyan as stated. Alexander BALANESCU (violin) and Andrew Ball (piano). ['Music and Revolution', Volume 1—Opp. 19, 97, and Sans op. E with poems.] I 1985.

Nimbus Compact Disc NIM 5026. Complete cycle. Marta DEYANOVA (piano). [Skryabin.] P 8–9 Jan. 1985, I Dec. 1985. *Reissued:* Nimbus Compact Disc NIM 5037. Nos. 9 and 10 only. [Oscar Wilde and Ravel.] I Apr. 1986 ~ Nimbus Compact Disc NI 5026. [Skryabin.] I June 1995.

USSR: Melodiya C10 23079 003. Complete cycle. Anait NERSESYAN (piano). P 1985, I 1986*c*.

USSR: Melodiya A10 20101 000 (digital). Nos. 2, 6, 12, 13, 17, 18, 19, 21, 22, and 20 arr. Tsyganov. Maksim VENGEROV (violin) and Irina Vinogradova (piano). ['Opening of the Eighth International Tchaikovsky Competition'—Mozart, Saint-Saëns, Debussy *et al.*] P 11 June 1986, I 1987*c*. NB. Soloist aged eleven years.

USSR: Melodiya C10 24625 006. Nos. 1, 3, 8, 11, and 5 arr. Tsyganov. Ilya KALER (violin) and Anna Balakerskaya (piano). [Eighth International Tchaikovsky Competition—Tchaikovsky, Paganini, Falik, and Ives.] P 23 June 1986, I 1987*c*. *Reissued:* USSR: Melodiya C10 24743 003. [Prokofiev, Tchaikovsky, and Paganini.] I 1987*c*.

Chandos ARBD 1261 (digital) and Compact Disc CHAN 8555. Nine-teen numbers arr. Tsyganov. Eleonora TUROVSKY (violin) and Peter Pet-tinger (piano). [Glazunov and Prokofiev.] P Aldeburgh 13–14 Nov. 1986, G Apr. 1988.

Belgium: Empire Master Sound Compact Disc SBCD 7400. Nos. 2, 6, 12, 13, 17, 18, 19, 21, 22, and 20 arr. Tsyganov. Michaël GUTTMAN (violin) and Simone Guttman (piano). [Martinu, Falla, and Bloch.] P Sand-hausen, West Germany 21–2 Mar. 1988.

RCA Victor Red Seal Compact Disc RD 87947. Nos. 10, 17, 24, 14, 13, 6, and 5 arr. Poltoratsky. Moscow Virtuosi, Vladimir SPIVAKOV. [Opp. 35 and 110*a*.] P Paris 30 July 1988, I Sept. 1989, G Dec. 1989.

France: Rodolphe Compact Disc RPC 32600. Nos. 2, 6, 10, 16, 17, and 24. Vladimir STOUPEL (piano). [Opp. 61 and 87.] P 3–4 Jan. 1989, G Oct. 1990.

Poland: Polmusic Compact Disc 1-1989-1014. Nos. 2, 6, 12, 13, 17, 18, 19, 21, 22, and 20 arr. Tsyganov. Grigori ZHISLIN (violin) and Frida Bauer (piano). [Prokofiev and Stravinsky.] P Warsaw 1989.

Japan: Kosei Compact Disc KOCD 3010. Nos. 14, 17, and 20 arr. Reed, labelled as 'Three Symphonic Preludes'. Tokyo Kosei Wind Orchestra, Alfred REED. ['Guest Conductor Series 9—Reed'.] P Tokyo 16–17 Mar. 1989, I 1989.

AVM Classics Compact Disc AVZ 3020. Complete cycle. Martin JONES (piano). ['Piano Music Volume II'—Sans opp. A, S, and T; Opp. 13, 69, and 22*a*.] P London 1–2 June 1989.

USA: Elektra Nonesuch/Warner Classics Compact Disc 7559-79234-2ZK. Complete cycle . Vladimir VIARDO (piano). [Op. 61.] P New York June 1989, I 1990, G Oct. 1991.

Netherlands: Partridge Compact Disc 1127-2. Complete cycle (adver-tised as 'First recording of the Opus 34 Preludes by Shostakovich' *sic*). Evgenii SOIFERTIS-LUKJANENKO (piano). [Prokofiev.] P Veenendaal Aug. 1989, I UK June 1991.

France: Le Chant du Monde Compact Disc LDC 278 1011. Complete cycle. Elena VARVAROVA (piano). [Opp. 35 and 102.] P Paris Sept. 1989, I Jan. 1990.

Chandos Compact Disc CHAN 8748. Nos. 10, 15, 16, and 24 arr. Tsyganov. Lydia MORDKOVITCH (violin) and Marina Gusak-Grin (piano). ['Poéme'—Chausson, Dvořák, Kroll *et al.*] P Snape 12–14 Feb. 1990, I June 1990, G Nov. 1990.

Decca Compact Disc 433 055-2DH. Complete cycle. Olli MUSTONEN (piano). [Alkan.] P Blackheath Oct. 1990, I July 1991, G Oct. 1991. *Gramo-phone* Record Awards 1992—winner of Instrumental category.

Teldec Compact Disc 2292 46015-2. Nos. 15, 19, 17, and 6 arr. M. Thomas. BRODSKY QUARTET (Michael Thomas, Ian Belton, Paul Cas-sidy, Jacqueline Thomas). ['Brodsky Unlimited'—Falla, Gershwin, Cop-land *et al.*] P Berlin Oct.–Nov. 1990, I Feb. 1992, G Apr. 1992.

Germany: Sound-Star-Ton Compact Disc SST 31109. Complete cycle. Alexander BRAGINSKY (piano). [Op. 61.] P 1990, I 1991.

RCA Victor Red Seal Compact Disc RD 60861. Nos. 24, 12, and 6 arr. Tsyganov. Vladimir SPIVAKOV (violin) and Sergei Bezrodny (piano). ['It Ain't Necessarily So'—Schnittke *Prelude in Memory of Shostakovich;* Gershwin, Ravel, Bartók *et al.*] P Bristol 11–13 Jan. 1991, I 1992.

EMI Classics Compact Disc CDC7 54352-2. Nos. 10 and 15 arr. Tsyganov. Sarah CHANG (on ¼ size violin) and Sandra Rivers (piano). ['Debut'—Sarasate, Elgar, Khachaturyan *et al.*] P New York 16 Mar.–16 Apr. 1991, G Jan. 1993. NB. Soloist aged 9 years.

Sweden: Bluebell Compact Disc ABCD 039. Complete cycle. Folke GRÄSBECK (piano). [Opp. 35 and 110.] P Stockholm 16 May 1991, I Oct. 1991.

Mezhdunarodnaya Kniga Compact Disc MK 417030. Nos. 10, 15, 16, and 24 arr. Tsyganov. Aleksandr SHIRINSKY (violin) and Natalya Rozova (piano). [Prokofiev, Shchedrin, Marcello *et al.*] P Moscow 1991.

Hyperion Compact Disc CDA 66620. Complete cycle. Tatyana NIKO-LAYEVA (piano). [Opp. 61 and 5.] P Hampstead 17–19 Apr. 1992, I July 1992, G Sept. 1992.

France: Erol Records Compact Disc 7014. Nos. 10, 13, and 15–18 arr. for saxophone. Marc CHISSON (soprano and sopranino saxophones) and Alain Perez (piano). [Opp. 5 and 27; Villa-Lobos, Ravel, Bartók *et al.*] P Bordeaux 14 June 1992.

Sony Classical Compact Disc SK 52568. Nos. 10, 15, 16, and 24 arr. Tsyganov. MIDORI (violin) and Robert McDonald (piano). ['Encore!'—Kreisler, Sarasate, Paganini *et al.*] P 17–24 Aug. 1992, G June 1993.

USA: Cembal D'Amour Compact Disc CD 106. Nos. 10, 15, 16, and 24 arr. Tsyganov. Berl SENOFSKY (violin) and Julian Martin (piano). [Vivaldi, Schubert, Chopin *et al.*] P Peabody Institute, Baltimore 1992.

Denmark: Danacord Compact Disc DACOCD 419. Nos. 10 and 14. Nina KAVTARADZE (piano). ['Rarities of Piano Music'—Rakhmaninov, Schoeck, Prokofiev *et al.*] P Husum Festival concert Aug. 1993, I Sept. 1994.

USA: Russian Disc Compact Disc 10 015. Nos. 1–3, 10, 14, 16, 17, and 24. Vladimir YURIGEN-KLEVKE (piano). [Gubaidulina, Pärt, Shchedrin, and Karayev.] P Moscow Feb.–Mar. 1994, I June 1995.

France: Accord Compact Disc 202812. Complete cycle. Caroline WEICHERT (piano). [Op. 13; Sans op. B and S.] P Sept. 1993, I 1994.

Japan: Camerata Compact Disc 28CM 573. Nos. 15, 19, 20, 24, 14, 16, 17, 7, 13, 21, 10, and 6 arr. Gaiswinkler. VIENNA TROMBONE QUARTET (Hans Strocker, Deitner Kublock, Erik Hainzl, Otmar Gaiswinkler). [Tchaikovsky, Musorgsky, and Borodin.] P Vienna 22–4 Sept. 1994.

USA: Pyramid Compact Disc 13510. Complete cycle. Adrienne KRAUSZ (piano). [Chopin.] P Budapest Oct. 1994, I Feb. 1995.

Sweden: BIS Compact Disc CD 717. Nineteen Preludes (Tsyganov's three suites) adapted for guitar and piano. Franz HALÁSZ (guitar) and

Débora Halász (piano). [Castelnuovo-Tedesco, Santorsola, and Hayg.] P Stockholm 22–5 Jan. 1995.

Italy: Dynamic Compact Disc CDS 137. Nos. 10 and 15 arr. Tsyganov. Salvatore ACCARDO (violin) and Laura Manzini (piano). [Tartini-Francescatti, Milstein, Suk *et al.*] P Genoa Mar. 1995, I Sept. 1995. NB. Played on Paganini's Guarneri del Gesù 1742 instrument under police escort!

USA: Mark Set Go Compact Disc MSG 101. Nos. 1, 2, 7, 8, 11, 14, 15, 17, 18, and 23 arr. Harlan. EXCELSIOR (Evan Harlan—accordion, Mimi Rabson—electric violin, Claudio Ragazzi—electric guitar, James Gray—tuba in No. 15, and Grant Smith—drums). ['Declassified'—Barber, Stravinsky, and Poulenc.] P Apr.–May 1995 and Apr. 1996, I 1997.

Olympia Compact Disc OCD 574. Complete cycle. Colin STONE (piano). [Opp. 12, 61, and Sans op. B.] P London Sept. 1995, I Mar. 1996, G June 1996.

USA: Boston Brass Compact Disc BB 1004. Eight Preludes arr. Yeo. Ronald BARRON (tenor trombone) and Douglas YEO (bass trombone). ['In the Family'—Shapero, Campo, Vaughan-Williams *et al.*] P Boston University 13 Dec. 1995.

Germany: Beaux Compact Disc BEAU 2022. No. 17 arr. Turich. Novosibirsk Chamber Orchestra, Mikhail TURICH. [Opp. 73 and 83.] P 1995, I Sept. 2001.

USA: Klavier Compact Disc KCD 11077. No. 14 arr. Reynolds. North Texas College of Music Wind Symphony, Eugene CORPORON. [Op. 63; Whitacre, Ito, and Hindemith.] P Texas Woman's University, Denton 9–11 Feb. 1996.

Japan: Toshiba EMI Compact Disc TOCE 9079. No. 10 only. MORGAŬA QUARTET (Eiji Arai, Takashi Aoki, Hisashi Ono, Ryoichi Fujimori). [Opp. 68 and 108.] P 25–7 Mar. 1996, I June 1996.

France: Suoni e Colori Collection Compact Disc SC 53006. Ten Preludes (Tsyganov's second suite—Nos. 2, 6, 12, 13, 17, 18, 19, 21, 22, and 20) arr. for violin and strings by Ilmar Lapinsch. Ricercata de Paris Ensemble, Alexandre BRUSSILOVSKY (violin and conductor). ['DSCH Aphorismes'—Opp. 11, 68, 13, Sans op. D; Schnittke—*Prelude in Memory of Shostakovich,* and Steven Gerber—*Elegy on the name 'Dmitri Shostakovich'*.] P Hautes-Alpes, France concert Aug. 1996, I 1997.

Japan: ALM Records Compact Disc ALCD 7041. Complete cycle. Izumi SHIMURA (piano). ['A Forest of Preludes'—Hayashi.] P Mitaka City Hall, Tokyo 9–10 Sept. 1996.

Italy: Real Sound Compact Disc RS 051 0022. Complete cycle. Anna MALIKOVA. [Op. 5 and Sans op. S.] P Wesel, Germany Apr. 1997.

Collins Classics 1496-2. Complete cycle. Artur PIZARRO (piano). [Skryabin.] P Rusthall, Kent 20–3 Mar. 1997, I Oct. 1997, G Nov. 1997.

Belgium: Cyprès Compact Disc CYP 2622. Complete cycle. Johan SCHMIDT. [Op. 61.] P Liège 23–4 Feb. 1998, I 1998.

Athene-Minerva Compact Disc ATH CD18. Complete cycle. Raymond CLARKE. [Opp. 12, 61, and 87.] P Nottingham University 10 July 1998, I May 1999, G Oct. 1999.

France: Suoni e Colori Compact Disc SC 53009. Complete cycle. Mikhail MARKOV. [Op. 5; and Galperine.] P Paris Nov. 1998.

Reference: Alekseyev.

Opus 35   Piano Concerto No. 1 in C minor

Form: Concerto for piano, B flat trumpet, and string orchestra in four linked movements:

1. Allegro moderato [or Allegretto] *attacca*
2. Lento [or Largo] *attacca*
3. Moderato *attacca*
4. Allegro con brio

The fourth movement introduces the street tune 'O, du lieber Augustin' on trumpet and quotes from Haydn's Sonata in D major Hob xvi / 37 and Beethoven's Rondo a capriccio in G major, Opus 129 ('Rage over a lost Penny') in the piano cadenza.

Composed: 6 March–20 July 1933. Begun in Leningrad and completed in Peterhof.

Premières: 15 and 17 October 1933, Leningrad Philharmonic Bolshoi Hall; Dmitri Shostakovich (piano), Aleksandr Shmidt (trumpet), Leningrad Philharmonic Orchestra, Fritz Stiedry.

USA: 15 December 1934, Philadelphia Hall; Eugene List (piano), Philadelphia Orchestra, Leopold Stokowski.

UK: 4 January 1936, Queen's Hall, London, 'Winter Prom'; Eileen Joyce (piano), Herbert Barr (trumpet), BBC Symphony Orchestra, Sir Henry Wood.

Arrangements: A two-piano reduction by the composer. The Lento adapted for string orchestra by Grzegorz Fitelberg.

Music: Autograph scores preserved at the CIS Archives of Literature and Art (full score) and the Glinka Museum (reduction). The first page of the autograph full score is reproduced in Volume 12 of *Collected Works*.

Muzgiz, No. 14332, 1934, score, 30 cm. (and same number, 1963, 21 cm.)

Muzgiz, No. 14333, 1934 (also 1935 and 1969), the composer's reduction for two pianos, 30 cm.

Longmans, Green and Co., New York, Longman's Miniature Arrow Score Series of Romantic and Modern Piano Concertos, Volume 9 (Schumann . . . Shostakovich), 1940, score ed. A. E. Wier, 30 cm.

International Music, No. 2158, 1942, reduction, 30.5 cm.

Broude Bros., New York, No. 184, 1943, score, 28 cm.

Russian-American Music, New York, 1946, *Quasi valse,* adaptation of second movement for string orchestra by Grzegorz Fitelberg, score and parts, 30 cm.

Boosey & Hawkes, No. 644 (A.S.M.P. No. 52), 1948, score ed. Hans Swarsenski, 19 cm.

Anglo-Soviet Music Press, No. 53, 1948, reduction, 31 cm.

G. Schirmer, score ed. Vivian Rivkin, 31 cm.

Muzyka, No. 5947 (in *D. Shostakovich: Compositions for fortepiano,* Volume 3, with Opp. 94 and 102). 1970, reduction, 29 cm.

Hans Sikorski, No. 2126, 1972, reduction, 31.5 cm.

Muzyka, No. 8866, 1975, reduction, 29 cm.

Muzyka, No. 11208 (in Volume 12 of *Collected Works* with Op. 102), 1982, 30 cm.

Muzyka, No. 11214 (in Volume 13 of *Collected Works* with Opp. 6, 94, 102, and Sans op. O), 1983, reduction, 30 cm.

Hans Sikorski, No. 2361, 1989, 21 cm.

Duration: 20 and approx. 21 minutes in scores; 19' 54"–25' 27"; 23' 00"–23' 30" (Plaistow).

Ballets: *The Wise Monkeys.* Norman Morrice, Ballet Rambert, Sadler's Wells, 18 July 1960.

The Catalyst. John Cranko, Stuttgart Ballet, 8 November 1961.

In Concert. Simon Mottram, Northern Dance Theatre, Manchester, 26 March 1974.

The Dance House. David Bintley, San Francisco Ballet. UK première: Edinburgh Festival, Edinburgh Playhouse, Scottish Chamber Orchestra, Emil de Cou (conductor), 20 August 1997. Revived by the Birmingham Royal Ballet. Hippodrome, Birmingham, May 1999. The ballet is a response to the death of a colleague from AIDS.

Mercurial Manoeuvres. Christopher Wheeldon, New York City Ballet, Edinburgh Playhouse, 31 August 2001.

Recordings: Columbia DX 1049-51 (5 sides 78 rpm). Eileen JOYCE (piano), Arthur Lockwood (trumpet), Halle Orchestra, Leslie Heward. [Skryabin.] P Manchester 24 Oct. 1941, G Dec. 1941. *Reissued:* USA: Columbia 71421-3D in Set M 527 (5 sides 78 rpm). [Skryabin.] ~ USA: Columbia ML 4389 (mono). [Prokofiev.] ~ HMV EM 29 0462 3. (DMM mono). [On fourth side in two-record set 'The Art of Leslie Heward'— Moeran, Ireland, Sibelius *et al.*] G Aug. 1985 ~ Dutton Laboratories Compact Disc CDAX 8010 (mono). ['Hallé Russian Festival'—Borodin, Lyadov, and Tchaikovsky.] I Nov. 1994, G Feb. 1995.

USA: Opus MLG 71 (mono). William KAPELL (piano), Samuel Krauss (trumpet), Philadelphia Orchestra, Eugene Ormandy. [Falla.] P private recording 1 Dec. 1945, I 1971. *Reissued:* USA: Arbiter Compact Disc 108 (mono). [Beethoven, Bach, and Musorgsky.] I Dec. 1997, G May 1998.

USA: Concert Hall Society H 4 (mono). Noel MEWTON-WOOD (piano), Harry Sevenstern (trumpet), Netherlands Philharmonic Orchestra, Walter Goehr. [Britten.] P 1953, I 1954.

USA: Capitol L 8229 (10" mono). Victor ALLER (piano), Mannie Klein (trumpet), Concert Arts String Orchestra, Felix Slatkin. P 5 May 1953. *Reissued:* USA: Capitol P 8230 (12" mono). [Hindemith.] I 1954 ~ Capitol CGL 7520 (10" mono). G Feb. 1954.

USA: MGM E 3079 (mono). Menahem PRESSLER (piano), Harry Glantz (trumpet), MGM Studio Orchestra, Theodore Bloomfield. [Op. 61.] P 1954. *Reissued:* Parlophone PMC 1023 (mono). [Op. 61.] G Sept. 1955.

USA: Urania URLP 7119 (mono). Margot PINTER (piano), Kurt Bauer (trumpet), Berlin Radio Symphony Orchestra, Günter Wand. [Khachaturyan.] P 1954.

HMV ALP 1349 (mono). Shura CHERKASSKY (piano), Harold Jackson (trumpet), Philharmonia Orchestra, Herbert Menges. [Prokofiev.] P 16 Nov. 1954, G Apr. 1956. *Reissued:* France: Pathé Marconi FALP 397 (mono). [Prokofiev.] ~ Italy: Voce del Padrone QALP 10148 (mono). [Prokofiev.]

USSR: Melodiya M10 39073-4 (mono). Dmitri SHOSTAKOVICH (piano), Iosif Volovnik (trumpet), Moscow Philharmonic Orchestra, Samuil Samosud. [In four-record box set 'D. Shostakovich—Pianist' with Opp. 102 and 94.] P Moscow concert 27 Nov. 1954 (not 1957 as given in booklet), I 1977*b*. This performance also appears on cine-film. *Reissued:* Germany: Melodia Eurodisc 27 235 XDK. [In four-record set 'Shostakovich plays Shostakovich' with Opp. 102 and 94.] ~ USSR: Melodiya C10 14089-90 (electronic stereo). [In third box of Part 1 of *Collected Works on Records* with Opp. 102 and 94.] I 1980 ~ Japan: Victor Musical Industries Compact Disc VICC 2048. ['Pianist = D. Shostakovich'—Opp. 57, 102, and 94.] I 1990 ~ USA: Russian Disc Compact Disc RDCD 15 005 (mono). ['Great Russian Artists: Shostakovich plays Shostakovich'—Opp. 40 and 102.] I Nov. 1993, G Dec. 1993 ~ Revelation Compact Disc RV 70006 (mono). ['Shostakovich plays Shostakovich, Vol. 5'—Opp. 102, 94, and 67.] P date given as 1955, I May 1998.

Columbia FCX 769 (mono). Dmitri SHOSTAKOVICH (piano), Ludovic Vaillant (trumpet), French National Radio Orchestra, André Cluytens. [Opp. 5 and 102.] P Paris 24–6 May 1958, G Oct. 1961 (available on special order), G Fuly 1964 (general release). *Reissued:* USA: Seraphim 60161 (mono). [Opp. 5 and 102.] I 1971 ~ France: Pathé Marconi 2C 061 12114. [Opp. 5 and 102.] I 1972 ~ World Records Retrospect SH 293 (mono). [Opp. 5 and 102.] G July 1979 ~ Russia: Russian Disc R10 00319-20 (DMM mono). [In double album 'For the 85th Anniversary' with Opp. 102, 5, and 135.] I 1991 ~ EMI Classics Compact Disc CDC7 54606-2 (mono). ['Composers in Person'—Opp. 102, 5, and 87.] I Jan. 1993, G Apr. 1993.

France: Erato STU 70477. Annie d'ARCO (piano), Maurice André (trumpet), Jean-François Paillard Chamber Orchestra, Jean-François Paillard. [Op. 61.] P 1959. *Reissued:* USA: Musical Heritage Society 1151W. [Op. 61.] I 1971 ~ France: Erato Compact Disc WE 839. [Op. 61; and Prokofiev.] I 1996.

Westminster XWN 18960 (mono) and WST 14141. Eugene LIST (piano), Fritz Wesenigk (trumpet), Berlin Opera Orchestra, Georg Ludwig Jochum. [Op. 102.] P Vienna Nov. 1960, G Nov. 1961. *Reissued:* World Record Club T 328 (mono) and ST 328. [Op. 102.] ~ MCA Millennium Classics Compact Disc MCD 80107. [Opp. 102 and 67.] I Feb. 1997.

CBS BRG 72350 (mono) and SBRG 72350. André PREVIN (piano), William Vacchiano (trumpet), New York Philharmonic Orchestra, Leonard Bernstein. [Op. 60, fourth movement.] P 8 Apr. 1962, G Dec. 1965. *Reissued:* CBS 73400. [Op. 102.] G May 1975 ~ CBS S 73441 in Set CBS 77394. [Op. 102.] G Oct. 1975 ~ USA: Columbia MS 6392. [Poulenc.] ~ CBS Masterworks 60504. [Op. 102.] I Sept. 1984, G Dec. 1984 ~ CBS Masterworks Compact Disc MPK 44850. [Opp. 102 and 107.] I July 1989, G Nov. 1989 ~ Sony Royal Edition Compact Disc SMK 47618. [Op. 102 and Poulenc.] G Nov. 1993 and June 1994 ~ Philips Classics Compact Discs 456 934-2PM2 (two-disc set). ['Great Pianists of the 20th Century'—Mozart, Poulenc, and Gershwin.] I Oct. 1998, G Apr. 1999.

USSR: MK D 010713-4 (mono) and C 0387-8 (1 side). Mariya GRINBERG (piano), Sergei Popov (trumpet), Moscow Radio Large Symphony Orchestra, Gennadi Rozhdestvensky. [Bach and Franck.] P 1962. *Reissued:* USSR: MK D 011185-7—D 010714 (mono) and C 0455-7—C 0388 (1 side in two-record set). [Op. 65.] I 1962 ~ USSR: Melodiya CM 0455-7—CM 0388 (1 side in two-record set). [Op. 65] ~ USA: Westminster Gold WGS 8325. [Bach and Franck.] ~ Germany: Melodia Eurodisc MK 86 611. [Op. 102.] ~ France: Le Chant du Monde LDX 78355 K (mono). [Op. 102.] ~ HMV Melodiya ASD 2481. [Khachaturyan.] G July 1969.

Netherlands: Philips A 02448 L (mono) and 835 318 AY. Stepan RADIĆ (piano), Stanko Selak (trumpet), Zagreb Philharmonic Orchestra, Milan Horvat. [Op. 70.] P 1966. *Reissued:* France: Philips 6598 102 in set 6747 252. [Op. 54, in two-record set 'Tribute to Dmitri Shostakovich' with Op. 112.] I post-1975.

East Germany: Eterna 8 26 051. Günter KOOTZ (piano), Willy Krug (trumpet), Berlin Radio Symphony Orchestra, Rolf Kleinert. [Prokofiev.] P 29 Mar. 1966, I 1970. *Reissued:* Germany: Edel Classics Compact Disc 0001842 CCC. [Op. 35.] I 2001.

Argo ZRG 674. John OGDON (piano), John Wilbraham (trumpet), Academy of St Martin-in-the-Fields, Neville Marriner. [Stravinsky.] P The Maltings, Snape 14–16 Dec. 1970, G Feb. 1972. *Reissued:* Germany: Teldec EL 166637. [Stravinsky.] Decca Compact Disc 448 577-2DCS. [Bartók.] I June 1996.

USSR: Melodiya CM 02439-40. Pavel SEREBRYAKOV (piano), Vladimir Vakhtenkov (trumpet), Chamber Orchestra of the Leningrad Philharmonic Orchestra, Yuri Serebryakov. [Ustvolskaya and Golts.] P and I 1971.

HMV ASD 3081. Cristina ORTIZ (piano), Rodney Senior (trumpet), Bournemouth Symphony Orchestra, Paavo Berglund. [Opp. 5 and 102.] P 14 June 1974, G June 1975. *Reissued:* USA: Angel S 37109. [Opp. 5 and 102.] I 1975 ~ HMV Greensleeve ED 29 0210 1. [Opp. 5 and 102.] G Oct. 1984 ~ EMI Compact Disc CDS7 47790-8. [In two-disc set with Opp. 54; 103, 102, and 5.] I Nov. 1987, G May 1988.

France: Club National du Disque P 394. Dominique MERLET (piano), Adolf Scherbaum (trumpet), Orchestre Chambre de Paris, Paul Kuentz. [Bartók and Casterede.] P pre-1975.

Czech: Panton 11 0539 G. Dagmar BALOGHOVÁ (piano), Miroslav Kejmar (trumpet), Czech Philharmonic Orchestra, Jiří Kout. [Boháč.] P 1975, I 1976. *Reissued:* Czech: Panton Compact Disc PAN 811309. [Op. 110*a*; and Schnittke.] I 1998.

Germany: RBM 3024. Fany SOLTER (piano), Friedemann Schnackenberg (trumpet), Orchestra Gelmini, Hortense von Gelmini. [Roussel and Genzmer.] P 1975.

USSR: Melodiya C10 06763-4. Eugene LIST (piano), Aleksandr Korolyov (trumpet), All-Union Radio and Television Symphony Orchestra, Maksim Shostakovich. [Op. 102.] P 1975, I 1976*d*. *Reissued:* USA: Columbia Melodiya M 35116. [Op. 102.] I 1978 ~ CBS Masterworks 76822. [Op. 102.] G July 1979 ~ RCA Navigator (Russian Music No. 73) Compact Disc 74321 29254-2. [Opp. 102 and 107.] I Nov. 1995, G Dec. 1995.

USSR: Melodiya C10 09743-4. Vladimir KRAINEV (piano), Aleksandr Korolyov (trumpet), Central Television and All-Union Radio Symphony Orchestra, Maksim Shostakovich. [Barsukov.] P 1977, I 1978*c*. *Reissued:* HMV Melodiya ASD 3713. [Prokofiev.] G Sept. 1979.

USA: Delos DMS 3008 (digital). Carol ROSENBERGER (piano), Stephen Burns (trumpet), Los Angeles Chamber Orchestra, Gerard Schwarz. [Prokofiev.] P California 10 Dec. 1980. *Reissued:* USA: Delos Compact Disc 3021. [Prokofiev and Stravinsky.] G Oct. 1984.

USSR: Melodiya C10 28215 004. Viktoria POSTNIKOVA (piano), Timofei Dokshitser (trumpet), USSR Ministry of Culture Symphony Orchestra, Gennadi Rozhdestvensky. [Dokshitser trumpet transcriptions.] P Moscow Conservatory concert 10 Apr. 1982, I 1990*a*.

USA: Sonora Compact Disc SO 22590CD. Mikhail PETUKHOV (piano), Timofei Dokshitser (trumpet), Bolshoi Theatre Orchestra, Yuri Simonov. [Prokofiev.] P Duisburg, Germany concert 25 Sept. 1982, I 2000.

Classics for Pleasure 4144161 (digital). Dmitri ALEKSEYEV (piano), Philip Jones (trumpet), English Chamber Orchestra, Jerzy Maksymiuk. [Opp. 102 and 89*a* No. 5.] P London May 1983, G Nov. 1983. *Reissued:* USSR: Melodiya A10 00079 002 (digital). [Op. 102.] I 1985*b* ~ USA: Angel AE 34489 (digital). [Opp. 102 and 89*a* No. 5.] ~ Classics for Pleasure CFP

4547 (digital) and Compact Disc CD-CFP 4547. [Opp. 102 and 89*a* No. 5.] I Sept. 1988, G Jan. 1989 ~ HMV Classics Compact Disc 5 73047-2. [Sans opp. E and G; Opp. 16, 22, 97, and 89.] I Oct. 1998.

USSR: Melodiya C10 20419 003. Yevgeni MALININ (piano), Vladimir Goncharov (trumpet), Central Television and All-Union Radio Symphony Orchestra, Vladimir Fedoseyev. [Galynin.] I 1984*c*.

Chandos ABRD 1120 (digital) and Compact Disc CHAN 8357. Dmitri SHOSTAKOVICH junior (piano), James Thompson (trumpet), I Musici de Montréal, Maksim Shostakovich. [Op. 110*a*.] P Montreal Aug. 1984, G Jan. and Apr. 1985.

USSR: Melodiya C10 22845 004. Vladimir KRAINEV (piano), Vladimir Kafelnikov (trumpet), USSR Ministry of Culture Chamber Orchestra (Moscow Virtuosi), Vladimir Spivakov. [Schnittke.] P concert 1984, I 1986*b*. *Reissued:* France: Le Chant du Monde Compact Disc LDC 278 1011. [Opp. 102 and 34.] I Jan. 1990.

Bulgaria: Balkanton BCA 1012. Anton DIKOV (piano), Sofia Chamber Orchestra, Vassil Kazandzhiev (trumpet/conductor). [Pipkov.] P *c*.1986. *Reissued:* Netherlands: Sound Compact Disc CD 3445. [Op.77.] I 1988.

USSR: Melodiya C10 25067 001. Yevgeni KISSIN (piano), Vladimir Kafelnikov (trumpet), USSR Ministry of Culture Chamber Orchestra (Moscow Virtuosi), Vladimir Spivakov. [Mozart.] P 27 Apr. 1986, I 1987*d*. *Reissued:* Germany: Melodia Eurodisc Compact Disc 258317. [Mozart.] I 1987 ~ Olympia Compact Disc OCD 179. [Op. 141.] I Aug. 1988, G May 1989.

Decca Compact Disc 433 702-2DH. Ronald BRAUTIGAM (piano), Peter Masseurs (trumpet), Royal Concertgebouw Orchestra, Riccardo Chailly. [Op. 16; Sans opp. E and G.] P Amsterdam 11 Mar. 1988, I Jan. 1993, G Mar. 1993.

RCA Victor Red Seal Compact Disc RD 87947. Yevgeni KISSIN (piano), Vasili Kan (trumpet), Moscow Virtuosi, Vladimir Spivakov. [Opp. 34 and 110*a*.] P Vienna 12 Aug. 1988, I Sept. 1989, G Dec. 1989. *Reissued:* RCA Victor Red Seal RD 60567 (two-disc set). ['A Musical Portrait'—Rakhmaninov, Prokofiev, Mozart, and Haydn.]

Czech: Opus Compact Disc 91 2210-2. Alexander CATTARINO (piano), Miroslav Kejmar (trumpet), Slovák Radio Symphony Orchestra, Bohdan Warchal. [Op. 110*a*.] F Opus Studio Mar.–May 1989, I 1991. *Reissued:* Switzerland: Point Classics Compact Disc 267 252-2. [Opp. 107 and 110*a*.] I 1996.

USA: Arabesque Compact Disc Z 6610. Garrick OHLSSON (piano), Maurice Murphy (trumpet), Kraków Philharmonic Orchestra, Gilbert Levine. [Opp. 10 and 22*a*.] P Kraków 26–9 May 1989, G Jan. 1990.

USA: Consonance Compact Disc 81 0009. Mikhail PETUKHOV (piano), unnamed trumpeter, String Group of the USSR Symphony Orchestra, Vladimir Kozhukhar. [Schnittke.] P 1989, I May 1995.

Finland: Finlandia Compact Disc FACD 393. Juhani LAGERSPETZ (piano), Jouko Harjanne (trumpet), Tero Latvala (leader), Tapiola Sinfonietta, Juhani Lamminimäki. ['Piano Concertos with Strings'—Jolivet and Klami.] P Espoo Jan. and June 1990, I July 1991, G Oct. 1991. *Reissued:* Finlandia Ultima Compact Discs 8573 81969-2 (disc two of two-disc set). [Opp. 40 and 73.] G June 2000.

Sweden: Bluebell Compact Disc ABCD 039. Folke GRÄSBECK (piano), Aki Välimäki (trumpet), Minsk Chamber Orchestra, Vitali Katayev. [Opp. 34 and 110.] P Esbo, Finland 23 Feb. 1990, I Oct. 1991.

USA: Pro-Arte Fanfare Compact Disc CDD 551. Derek HAN (piano), John Henes (trumpet), Chicago Sinfonietta, Paul Freeman. ['Shostakovich Film Festival'—Opp. 97, 111, 116, and 16.] P Oak Park, Illinois May 1990, I Aug. 1991. *Reissued:* Conifer Classics Compact Disc Class 7086. [As USA release.] I Nov. 1991.

Collins Classics Compact Disc CD 1276-2. Vladimir OVCHINIKOV (piano), John Wallace (trumpet), Philharmonia Orchestra, Maksim Shostakovich. [Musorgsky.] P London Oct. 1990, I Apr. 1991, G Sept. 1991.

Nimbus Compact Disc NI 5308. Martin JONES (piano), Graham Ashton (trumpet), English Chamber Orchestra, William Boughton. [Opp. 102 and 110.] P Leominster 14–15 Nov. 1990, I Oct. 1991.

Decca Compact Disc 436 239-2DH. Peter JABLONSKI (piano), Raymond Simmons (trumpet), Royal Philharmonic Orchestra, Vladimir Ashkenazy. [Rakhmaninov and Lutoslawski.] P London May 1991, I Oct. 1992, G Dec. 1992.

Teldec Compact Disc 9031 73282-2. Elizaveta LEONSKAYA (piano), Gary Bordner (trumpet), Saint Paul Chamber Orchestra, Hugh Wolff. [Opp. 102 and 61.] P Saint Paul, Minnesota Sept. 1991, I Apr. 1993, G June 1993. *Reissued:* Warner Apex Compact Disc 8573 89092-2. [Opp. 102 and 61.] G Oct. 2001.

Austria: Musica Classica Compact Disc 780013-2. Paul GULDA (piano), Vladimir Goncharov (trumpet), Moscow Radio Symphony Orchestra, Vladimir Fedoseyev. [Op. 102.] P Bratislava Jan. 1952, I Jan. 1996.

France: Forlane Compact Disc UCD 16693. Finale only. Aleksandr KOZRINE (piano), Vladimir Puchetchny (trumpet), Moscow Conservatory Orchestra, Yurl Bashmet. [Op. 11; Tchaikovsky, Chopin, Haydn *et al.*] P concert 1992, I 1993.

Koch International Classics Compact Disc 3 7159-2HI. Israela MARGALIT (piano), Mikhail Khanin (trumpet), Moscow Philharmonic Orchestra, Donald Barra. [Sans op. S and Op. 5; and Schnittke.] P Moscow Conservatory Sept. 1992, I July 1993, G Sept. 1993.

Deutsche Grammophon Compact Disc 439 864-2GH (4D Audio). Martha ARGERICH (piano), Guy Touvron (trumpet), Württemberg Chamber Orchestra, Jörg Faerber. [Haydn.] P Ludwigsburg, Germany Jan. 1993, I Dec. 1994, G Jan. 1995.

Italy: Phoenix Compact Disc PH 00602. Maurizio BARBARO (piano), Vladimir Davidovsky (trumpet), Byelorussian Symphony Orchestra, Antonello Gotta. [Opp. 102 and 22*a*.] P Minsk 9–11 Dec. 1993, I Jan. 2001.

Medici-Whitehall Compact Disc MQCD 4003. Julian GALLANT (piano), Tim Hawes (trumpet), Oxford Orchestra da Camera, Stefan Ashbury. ['Piano Concertos of Our Time'—Górecki, Hindemith, and Williamson.] P Chalk Farm, London May 1994, I Sept. 1994.

EMI Classics Compact Disc CDC5 55361-2. Mikhail RUDY (piano), Ole Edvard Antonsen (trumpet), Berlin Philharmonic Orchestra, Mariss Jansons. [Op. 10.] P Berlin 15–22 June 1994, I Oct. 1995, G Dec. 1995.

Germany: Hänssler Classic Compact Disc 98 917. Eugene MURSKY (piano), Wolfgang Bauer (trumpet), Stuttgart Arcata Chamber Orchestra, Patrick Strub. [Op. 110.] P 31 Oct.–2 Nov. 1994, I May 1995.

Naxos Compact Disc 8.553126. Michael HOUSTOUN (piano), John Taber (trumpet), New Zealand Symphony Orchestra, Christopher Lyndon-Gee. [Opp. 102, 96, and 22.] P Wellington 2–4 Nov. 1994, I Sept. 1995.

USA: Brioso Compact Disc BR 109. Oleg VOLKOV (piano), unnamed trumpeter, Moscow Philharmonic Orchestra, Vassili Sinaisky. [Schnittke.] P Moscow June 1995, I Nov. 1995.

Germany: Capriccio Compact Disc 10 575. Thomas DUIS (piano), Reinhold Friedrich (trumpet), Berlin Radio Symphony Orchestra, Lutz KÖHLER. [Jolivet, Denisov, and Rääts.] P Berlin 21–5 Aug. 1995 or 10–11 June 1996, I Oct. 1997.

USA: Audiofon Compact Disc 72060. Valentina LISITSA (piano), Vyacheslav Chtchennikov (trumpet), Yekaterinburg Philharmonic Orchestra, Sarah Caldwell. [Op. 107.] P Yekaterinburg Jan.–Feb. 1996.

South Korea: Samsung Classics Compact Disc SCC 021 SJS. Hae-Jung KIM (piano), John Wallace (trumpet), London Chamber Orchestra, Christopher Warren-Green. [Mozart.] P London 11–13 Mar. 1997.

Germany: Arte Nova Compact Disc 74321 63649-2. Jitka ČECHOVA (piano), Johannes Sondermann (trumpet), SWR Symphony Orchestra, Oswald Sallaberger. [Op. 112.] P Freiburg 12–13 Mar. 1997, I Aug. 1999, G Nov. 1999.

Japan: Studio Frohla Compact Disc B-9801. Makiko NAKACHI (piano), Karel Mnuk (trumpet), Prague Talich Chamber Orchestra, Hideaki Muto. [Mozart.] P Sept. 1997.

EMI Classics Compact Disc CDC5 56760-2. Leif Ove ANDSNES (piano), Håkan Hardenberger (trumpet), City of Birmingham Symphony Orchestra, Paavo Järvi. [Britten and Enesco.] P Birmingham concert 21–3 Oct. 1997, I Sept. 1999.

Linn Records Compact Disc CKD 095. Sophia RAHMAN (piano), John Wallace (trumpet), BT Scottish Ensemble, Clio Gould. [Opp. 110*a* and 11.] P Glasgow 4–5 Mar. 1998, I Feb. 2000, G June 2000.

Sony Compact Disc SK 60677. Yefim BRONFMAN (piano), Thomas Stevens (trumpet), Los Angeles Philharmonic Orchestra, Esa-Pekka Salonen. [Opp. 57 and 102.] P Los Angeles 28 Mar. 1999, I Nov. 1999.

France: Calliope Compact Disc CAL 9299. Yakov KASMAN (piano), Gennady Nikonov (trumpet), Kaliningrad Philharmonic Chamber Orchestra, Emmanuel Leducq-Barome. [Opp. 110*a;* and Schnittke.] P Kaliningrad 1999, I Sept. 2000.

References: Alekseyev, Calvocoressi, and Lander.

Opus 36   The Tale of a Priest and His Servant Balda

Alternative titles: Translated as *The Tale of the Priest and his Blockhead Servant* on the score of the opera. A selection of other variants: *Story of the Priest and His Worker Balda* (Volkov), *Tale of a Priest and His Dumb Hired Man* (Seroff and Rabinovich), *The Tale of the Priest and His Helper, Dolt* (Grigoriev), *Tale of the Priest and His Hired Man Balda* (Rozhdestvensky), and *A Fairy Tale of the Priest and the Knockhead His Servant* (piano suite).

Form: Music for a full-length animated cartoon after the fairy story by Aleksandr Pushkin. The film, directed by Mikhail Tsekhanovsky, was not completed. Only 165 feet of the film survived the bombing of the Leningrad Film Studio in 1941.

Composed: Prologue commenced on 6 March 1933. The 'Scene in the Bazaar' written on 18 September 1934 in the Crimea and the remainder of the score composed on 5 November 1934. Part of the score of 15 numbers was re-orchestrated in 1935. The composer intended reviving his old score in 1975.

Premières: Film: surviving footage, 'Scene in the Bazaar', shown at the Fifth International Film Festival in Moscow on 9 July 1967.

Suite: spring 1935, Leningrad International Music Festival; conducted by Aleksandr Melik-Pashayev.

Suite revival: 25 September 1979, Leningrad; Leningrad Philharmonic Orchestra, Gennadi Rozhdestvensky.

Opera: 25 (public audition) and 28 September 1980, Leningrad; Malyi Opera and Ballet Theatre Company, Nikolai Boyarchikov (choreography), Andrei Petrov (stage-director), Mikhail Travkin (chorus-master), and Valentin Kozhin (conductor).

Piano suite: February 1983, Kiev 'Shostakovich Unknown Pages' concert.

Arrangements: Suite assembled by the composer:

1. Overture—Allegro non troppo
2. The Procession of the Obscurantists—Allegro moderato
3. Carousel—Moderato
4. Scene in the Bazaar—Allegro
5. The Priest's Daughter's Dream—Andante
6. Finale—Allegro non troppo

No. 5, retitled 'Sentimental Romance', is included in the Ballet Suite No. 2, Sans op. P. This piece transcribed for trumpet and piano by Jack

Holland. No. 4 quotes 'The Rushes Sighed', a sentimental song popularly sung by drunken Russians.

Opera: Sofya Khentova was commissioned by the RSFSR Ministry of Culture in 1980 to write the libretto and restore the music for a two-act comic opera. The opera features mime and dancing as well as singing, and is scored for a large symphony orchestra (including saxophones, saxhorn, vibraphone, harp, accordion, bayan, guitar, and balalaika), solo singers, S.A.T.B. chorus, and narrator. Insufficient volume of original material was compensated by repetition of certain fragments and some additions. 'The Priest's Son Dance' was lost and a dance was taken from *The Limpid Stream*, Opus 39. Shostakovich's arrangement of three folksongs from Sans op. Q utilized for the 'Evening Party of the Peasants'. S. Khentova also assembled a suite for pianoforte.

—.Overture (Nos. 1 and 6 in the Suite)

ACT 1

Scene 1: 'The Bazaar'
1. Description of the Bazaar (No. 4 in the Suite)
2. Balda's entrance
3. The Bear's Dance
4. Merry-go-round (No. 3 in the Suite)
5. The Meeting of the Priest and Balda
6. Dialogue of the Priest and Balda
7. Scene 1 Finale—Closing of the Bazaar
    Interlude:
8. The Devils' Procession (No. 2 in the Suite)
9. The Bellringer and Devils' Dance

Scene 2: 'The Village and the Priest's Household'
10. Description of the Village
11. Balda and the Priest's Son at Dinner
12. Balda's Work
13. Balda's Song
14. The Priest's Son Dance
15. Balda and the Priest's Daughter Lullaby
16. ⎫
17. ⎬ Evening party of the Peasants: 'What a song'
18. ⎭   'Fir-grove, my fir-grove'
                                       'The splinter'
19. The Priest's Daughter's Dream (No. 5 in the Suite)
20. The Priest's Daughter's Romance
21. The Priest's Lament
22. The Metropolitan Priest
23. Balda's Farewell

ACT 2

Scene 3: 'At the Devils'
  24. Introduction
  25. Dialogue of the Old Devil and Balda
  26. First Dialogue of the Little Devil and Balda
  27. Second Dialogue of the Little Devil and Balda
  28. Balda's Galop
  29. The Rent
      Interlude:
  30. Balda's Return
      Epilogue:
  31. Balda's Welcome
  32. Looking for the Priest
  33. Three Flicks
  34. Final Chorus

Instrumentation: 2 piccolos, 2 flutes, 2 oboes, cor anglais, E flat clarinet, 2 B flat clarinets, bass clarinet, 2 soprano saxophones, 2 tenor saxophones, 3 bassoons (III = contrabassoon) ~ 4 horns, 3 trumpets, B flat baritone sax-horn, 3 trombones, tuba ~ timpani, triangle, tambourine, wood block, cog rattle, side drum, cymbals, bass drum, pistol, xylophone, vibraphone, glockenspiel, orchestral bells ~ harp ~ accordion, bayan, guitar, balalaika ~ S.A.T.B. chorus ~ strings.

Music: Autograph score of the Suite, found among the composer's papers after his death, now preserved at the Glinka Museum. Autographs of the Overture, 'Dialogues of the Old Devil and Little Devil', and 'The Bell-ringer and Devils' Dance' stored at the CIS Archives of Literature and Art. Khentova (1980) gives six music examples between pages 79 and 87.

  MCA, *c.*1968, 'Sentimental Romance' arr. for trumpet and piano by J. Holland, score and part, 31 cm.

  Sovetskii Kompozitor, Leningrad, No. 902, 1981, Opera ed. S. Khentova, full score, 29.5 cm.

  Muzichna Ukraina, Kiev, No. 3012, 1991, Suite for pianoforte by S. Khentova (Nos. 2, 4, 8, 9, 5, 12, 22, 28/26, 20, and 31), 29 cm.

Duration: Suite: 9' 30"–12' 51". Opera: 75 minutes in score; recorded version 44 minutes.

Recordings: USSR: Melodiya C10 14415-6. Suite. USSR Symphony Orchestra, Gennadi ROZHDESTVENSKY. [Album 1 of 'From Manuscripts of Different Years'—Opp. 4, 16, 17, and 23; Sans opp. C, H, and Z.] P 1980, I 1981*b*. *Reissued:* HMV Melodiya ASD 1650331. [As Russian release.] G July 1983 ~ Germany: Eurodisc 201974-33. [As Russian release.] ~ BMG Melodiya Compact Discs 74321 59058-2 (two-disc set). [Opp. 4, 17, Z, H, C, 16, 1, 3, 7, 26/D, 59, E, 128, 30*a*, and 19.] I and G. Mar 1999.

  USSR: Melodiya C10 19323 008. Opera—edited and with the addition of narrated text. Overture and Nos. 1–3, 8–9, 4–7, 10; 13, 12, 15, 19, 20, 22,

25–9, 31–4. Vladimir Pankratov (Balda), Sergei Safenin (Priest), Yelena Ustinova (Priest's daughter), Anatoli Manukhov (Bellringer), Mikhail Kalinovsky (Old Devil), Nina Romanova (Devil's wife), German Lyudko (Little Devil), Vladimir Matusov (narrator), Mikhail Senchurov (balalaika), Leningrad Malyi Opera and Ballet Theatre Choir and Orchestra, Mikhail Travkin (chorus-master), Valentin KOZHIN. P 1982, I 1984*a*.

USA: Citadel Compact Disc CTD 88129. Complete Suite plus Score No. 20. Belarus RTV Symphony Orchestra, Walter MNATSAKANOV. [Opp. 30*a*, 59, and 56.] P Minsk Feb. 1997, I 1998.

References: Dalley, Gojowy, and Khentova (1980).

Opus 37   The Human Comedy

Subtitle: *Scenes from Parisian Life.*

Form: Incidental music to a play by Pavel Sukhotin, adapted from *Comédie Humaine* by Honoré de Balzac. The score for small orchestra includes at least 27 items of which 23 appear unnumbered in the following order in Volumes 27 and 28 of *Collected Works*. Known score numbers are added:

> Introduction—Moderato
> Overture— Moderato
> Student's Song—Allegretto
> 3. Waltz (for solo piano)—Allegro bravuro
> 2. Elegy (for solo piano)—Moderato
> March—Allegretto
> Merry Paris—Allegretto
> The Theatre—Allegro con brio
> The Theme of Paris—Andantino
> Cruel Paris—Moderato
> 18. Gavotte—Allegretto
> Addition to Gavotte (Trio)
> Flourish—Allegro molto
> The Panorama of Paris—Andantino
> Panic on the Exchange—Presto
> Barrel Organ—Andantino
> Bank of the Seine—Andantino
> Casket with Diamonds—Allegretto
> Police March—Allegretto
> Fanfare—Allegro
> 7/27. Sarabande—Moderato
> Scandal—Allegro molto
> [Episode]—Allegretto

Instrumentation: flute, oboe, B flat clarinet, bassoon ~ 2 horns, 2 trumpets, trombone, tuba, B flat baritone saxhorn ~ timpani, triangle, tambourine, side drum, cymbals ~ piano ~ strings.

Composed: 1933–4, at Leningrad.

Première: Play: 1 April 1934, Vakhtangov Theatre, Moscow; under the direction of A. Kozlovsky and Boris Shchukin.

Arrangements: Piano reduction of the Overture (written, presumably, at a later time to replace the Introduction) by Yuri Olenev.

No. 3 (Waltz) and No. 18 (Gavotte) transcribed for small stage orchestra (violin, piano, B flat clarinet, trumpet, accordion, and percussion; with optional violin, cello, double-bass, B flat clarinet, trumpet, flute, oboe, and trombone) by the composer. These two numbers appear in Ballet Suite No. 3, Sans op. P.

No. 3 (the first Waltz in Ballet Suite No. 3) in piano reduction by Lev Atovmyan and transcribed for wind band by Samuil Senderei.

No. 7/27 (Sarabande) arranged for cello and piano by Juozas Chelkauskas.

No. 18—Gavotte transcibed for guitar by Boris Okunev; for two trombones and piano by K. Serostanov; and used by composer Grigori Kalinkovich as the theme with variations (duration 10' 32") under the title *Concerto for Wind Orchestra*, subtitled 'Metamorphosis on a theme of D. Shostakovich'. See also *Three Violin Duets*, Sans op. P (iii) No. 2.

The Panorama of Paris (Elegy in Ballet Suite No. 3, No. 4) arranged for cello and piano by Atovmyan; violin and piano by Konstantin Fortunatov; in piano reductions by Bronislava Rozengauz and Zinaida Vitkind.

Six numbers arranged for piano from the composer's score by Lev Solin:

1. March—Allegretto
2. Gavotte—Allegretto
3. The Panorama of Paris—Andantino
4. Police March—Allegretto
5. Sarabande—Moderato
6. Waltz—Allegro bravuro

Music: Autograph score preserved at the CIS Archives of Literature and Art. Incomplete manuscript score, differing in instrumentation and sequence of items, preserved in the Vakhtangov Theatre Museum.

Sovetskii Kompozitor, 1946, Waltz arr. for piano by L. Atovmyan, 25 cm.

Muzgiz, No. 22203 (with 'Youth Dance' by Yuri Sviridov), 1951, Gavotte arr. for small stage orchestra, parts, 28.5 cm.

Muzgiz, No. 22205 (with Polka from Opus 39), 1951, Waltz arr. for small stage orchestra, parts, 28.5 cm.

Sovetskii Kompozitor, No. 928 (in *Dmitri Shostakovich: Waltzes from Film Music*), 1959, Waltz only, full score, 29 cm.

Sovetskii Kompozitor, (with 'Lyrical Waltz' by S. Senderei), 1962, Waltz arr. for wind band by S. Senderei, score and parts, 22 cm.

Sovetskii Kompozitor, No. 2718 (in *D. Shostakovich: Pieces for cello and piano*), 1962, Elegy arr. by L. Atovmyan, 29 cm.

Edition Peters, No. 4794 (plate no. 12389—in *Shostakovich: Album of Easy Pieces*), 1967, Elegy arr. K. Fortunatov, 30.5 cm.

Muzyka, No. 4719 (in *D. Shostakovich: Pieces for violin and piano*), 1975, Elegy arr. K. Fortunatov, 28.5 cm.

Sovetskii Kompozitor, No. 4028 (in *Dmitri Shostakovich: Music to Plays*), 1977, six numbers arr. for piano by L. Solin, 29 cm.

Muzyka, No. 9986 (in *Easy Pieces for Trombone*), 1978, Gavotte arr. for two trombones and piano by K. Serostanov, score and parts, 29 cm.

Muzyka, Leningrad, No. 2629 (in *S. Prokofiev and D. Shostakovich: Selection of Fortepiano Pieces for Children*), 1980, Sarabande arr. L. Solin and Elegy retitled 'Lullaby' by Z. Vitkind, 28.5 cm.

Sovetskii Kompozitor, No. 7625 (in *Album of the Violinist*, Volume 1), 1986, Elegy arr. K. Fortunatov, 29 cm.

Muzyka, No. 11412 (in Volume 28 of *Collected Works* with Opp. 19, 24, 28, 31, 32, 44, 58*a*, 63, 66, 72, and in the supplement, Sans opp. D and K), 1986, piano score, 30 cm.

Muzyka, No. 11413 (in Volume 27 of *Collected Works* with Opp. 19, 24, 28, 31, 32, 44, 58*a*, 63, 66, and 72), 1987, full score, 30 cm.

Muzyka, No. 14908 (in *D. Shostakovich: Pieces for cello and piano*), 1991, Sarabande arr. Yu. Chelkauskas, 29 cm.

Ballet: *The Overcoat*. For details see under Opus 32.

Recordings: USSR: Melodiya C20 07011-2. Gavotte arr. for guitar. Boris OKUNEV (guitar). [Narimanidze, Andreyev, Sazonov *et al*.] P 1976, I 1977*a*.

USSR: Melodiya C10 11391-2. Gavotte arr. G. Kalinkovich. RSFSR State Wind Orchestra, Nikolai SERGEYEV. [Tulikov, Gotlib, Sviridov *et al*.] P 1978, I 1979*c*.

USSR: Melodiya C10 22365 004. 'The Panorama of Paris' (with 'The Theme of Paris'), 'Police March', Gavotte, 'Bank of the Seine', and March. Leningrad Chamber Orchestra of Old and Modern Music, Eduard SEROV. ['Music for Theatre'—Opp. 32 and 58*a*.] P 1984, I 1986*a*. *Reissued*: Olympia Compact Disc OCD 194. [Opp. 1, 3, 7, 100, 59, and 26.] I Feb. 1988, G June 1988.

USSR: Melodiya C10 28379 002. 'Police March' arr. L. Solin. Vladimir VIARDO (piano). [Opp. 34, 58*a*, and 19.] P 1986, I 1990*a*.

CIS: Manchester Compact Disc CDMAN 129. Waltz. St Petersburg Philharmonic Academic Symphony Orchestra, Vladimir ALTSHULER. ['Shostakovich Theatre and Cinema Music'—Opp. 32*a*, 58*a*, 45, 30, 78, 76, 97, and 99.] P St Petersburg 1995, I 1998.

Chandos Compact Disc CHAN 9907. Suite Nos. 1, 3, 4, 6, 5, and 2 arr. L. Solin and Trio of No. 2 arr. composer. Rustem HAYROUDINOFF (piano). ['Theatre Music'—Opp. 19, 31, 32, 44, 58*a*, 66, and 22.] P Potton Hall, Suffolk 7–8 Aug. 2000, I Apr. 2001.

Note: For further recordings see under Sans op. P (Ballet Suite No. 3 and *Three Violin Duets*).

Sans op. E   Suite for Jazz Orchestra No. 1

Form: Three numbers for dance band:

1. Waltz—Moderato
2. Polka—Allegretto
3. Foxtrot (Blues)—Moderato

Instrumentation: 3 saxophones —soprano (= alto II), alto, and tenor ~ 2 trumpets, trombone ~ side drum, wood block, cymbal ~ glockenspiel / xylophone, banjo / Hawaiian guitar, piano ~ violin, double-bass.

Composed: February 1934, at Leningrad.

Premières: 24 March 1934, Leningrad.

Germany: Berlin Festival 1983 (RIAS Berlin). The Foxtrot was taped from a performance by the Bolshoi Theatre Ensemble and subsequently broadcast by Sydney Radio, Australia.

UK: 19 March 1986, Queen Elizabeth Hall, London; Chameleon Ensemble (Nos. 1 and 3).

Arrangements: The Waltz and Polka appear in Ballet Suites Nos. 1 and 2, Sans op. P respectively. Orchestral parts of Foxtrot arranged by Vladimir Derzhanovsky in 1939. Reduction of the three numbers for piano by Lev Atovmyan in 1947 and for accordion by V. Gorokhov. The Suite adapted for small mixed ensemble with single strings by Gerard McBurney. The Waltz and Polka arranged for organ by Mariya Makarova. A piano duo version of the Waltz recorded.

Music: Autograph score numbered Opus 38 preserved at the Glinka Museum. Originally published as Opus 38 by the USSR Music Fund in 1941.

Sovetskii Kompozitor, 1960, Suite arr. by V. Gorokhov in third album of accordion pieces.

Muzyka, No. 11678 (in Volume 10 of *Collected Works* with Opp. 1, 3, 7, 16, and 42), 1984, full score, 30 cm.

Duration: Approx. 7 minutes in score; 7' 56"–9' 14".

Ballet: *The Overcoat*. For details see under Opus 32.

Recordings: Whitetower Records Ensemble ENS 132 (digital real time cassette). Nos. 1 and 3 arr. L. Atovmyan. Andrew BALL (piano). ['Music and Revolution', Volume 1—Opp. 19, 34, and 97 with poems.] I 1985.

USSR: Melodiya C10 23081 001. Soloists' Ensemble of the USSR Ministry of Culture Symphony Orchestra, Gennadi ROZHDESTVENSKY. [Album 5 of 'From Manuscripts of Different Years'—Opp. 23 and 59; Sans op. D.] P 1984, I 1986c. *Reissued:* Olympia Compact Disc OCD 156. [Op. 43.] I Sept. 1988 ~ Olympia Compact Disc OCD 5005. [In Vol. 1 six-disc set of symphonies with Op. 43.] I Dec. 1990 ~ BMG Melodiya Compact Discs 74321 59058-2 (two-disc set). [Opp. 36, 4, 17, Z, H, C, 16, 1, 3, 7, 26 / D, 59, 128, 30a, and 19.] I and G Mar. 1999.

Decca Compact Disc 433 702-2DH. Royal Concertgebouw Orchestra, Riccardo CHAILLY. [Opp. 16 and 35; Sans op. G.] P Amsterdam 12 Feb. 1990, I Jan. 1993, G Mar. 1993.

United Compact Disc 88001. City of Birmingham Symphony Orchestra, Mark ELDER. [Opp. 31*a*, 42, and 46*a*.] P Birmingham 16–18 Jan. 1992, I Nov. 1993, G Jan. 1994.

Olympia Compact Disc OCD 585. Nos. 2 and 1 arr. for organ. Marlya MAKAROVA (organ). ['Music for Organ'—Opp. 16, 27, 29, 39, 81, 97, and 105.] P Moscow Conservatory Jan. 1995, I Mar. 1997.

RCA Victor Red Seal Compact Disc 09026 6804-2. Frankfurt Radio Symphony Orchestra, Dmitri KITAYENKO. [Sans opp. P and G.] P Frankfurt 2–5 Jan. 1996, I Aug. 1997, G Oct. 1997.

EMI Classics Compact Disc CDC5 55601-2. Philadelphia Orchestra, Mariss JANSONS. [Opp. 103 and 16, Sans op. G.] P Collingswood, New Jersey 8, 9, and 11 Mar. 1996, I May 1997, G Sept. 1997. *Reissued:* HMV Classics Compact Disc 5 73047-2. [Sans op. G; Opp. 16, 22, 97, 35, and 89.] I Oct. 1998.

Germany: CPO Compact Disc 999 599-2. No. 2 arr. for piano duo. GENOVA & DIMITROV PIANO DUO. [Opp. 94, 6, 95, Sans op. O (ii); Stravinsky, Prokofiev, and Dinicu.] P Hans Rosbaud Studio 4–5 May 1998, I Apr. 1999. NB. Polka incorrectly labelled as from Op. 22.

Note: For further recordings of the Waltz and Polka see under Sans op. P (Ballet Suites Nos. 1 and 2).

Opus 38 Love and Hate

Alternative translation: *Love and Hatred.*
Form: Music for the film *Love and Hate,* with scenario by Sergei Yermolinsky and directed by Albert Gendelshtein for the Mezhrabpomfilm Studio.
Composed: 1934, at Leningrad.
Première: Film first shown on 3 March 1935.
Music: Autograph score of 15 numbers preserved in the Glinka Museum.
Recording: [Meyer (1980) lists a song from the film, performed by choir and orchestra under Viktor Knushevitsky, on USSR: 15018 (78 rpm).]

Opus 39 The Limpid Stream

Alternative titles: *Clear* or *Lucid Stream.* See 'Notes' for further translations. Original working title 'Caprices' (also translated as 'Whims'). The titles 'Two Sylphs', 'Midday', and 'Kuban' considered.
Form: Comedy Ballet in three acts and four scenes, with libretto by Fyodor Lopukhov and Adrian Piotrovsky, choreography by Lopukhov, and designs by Mikhail Bobyshov (Leningrad) and Vladimir Dmitriev (Moscow):

ACT I—The Collective Farm (named 'The Limpid Stream')

Scene 1: 'The wayside halt in early autumn'
  1. Overture
  2. Arrival of brigade of artists
  3. Scene of the two girl friends (Zina and the Ballerina)
  4. Dance-examination
  5. Beginning of the intrigue (Zina's husband, Pyotr, becomes infatuated with the Ballerina)
  6. Musical Entr'acte
Scene 2: 'The day draws to a close'
  7. Termination of the fieldwork and distribution of presents
  8. Genre Dances: (*a*) Russian Dance, (*b*) Chaconne, (*c*) Weaver's Round Dance, (*d*) Dance of the Milkmaid and the Tractor-driver, (*e*) Waltz of the Classical Dancers, (*f*) Comic Dance, and (*g*) Dance of Gorets and Kubanets
  9. The jealousy of Zina
  10. Zina reveals she was formerly a ballet student
  11. Agreement (between Zina and the Ballerina to change places)

ACT 2—In a Woodland Clearing
---

  12. Picnic and invitation to an evening meeting
  13. Scene of the disguising of Zina (as the Ballerina)
  14. Entrance and Dance of the Accordionist and Galya
  15. Joke over the old summer residents: (*a*) entrance to the meeting, (*b*) Variation of the male classical dancer, (*c*) Variation of the Ballerina, and (*d*) Coda
  16. Adagio of Pyotr and the disguised Zina: (*a*) Dance of the conspirators, (*b*) Variation of Zina, and (*c*) Coda
  17. Dance: staging of the play 'Murder'
  18. Variation 'Murder'
  19. Finale-Coda

ACT 3—Harvest Festival (early morning the next day)
---

  20. Musical interjection and swing
  21. March: 'Harvest Festival'
  22. Waltz
  23. Scene of the disclosure of the ruse
  24. Great Adagio (reconciliation of Pyotr and Zina)
  25. Variation of the male classical dancer
  26. Variation of the Ballerina
  27. Variation of Zina
  28. Coda
  29. Final Dance

The above order and numbering sequence corresponds to the first the-atrical version as listed in Sadovnikov. The continuous numeration sys-tem of the official ballet music, with tempo indications, as it appears in the full and piano scores follows:

ACT I

Scene 1:
1. Overture—Allegro
2. Adagio of Zina and Pyotr—Adagio—Allegro—Allegro vivo
3. March—Allegretto
4. Meeting between Two [Girl] Friends—Allegretto
5. Examination Dance—Allegretto—Tempo di mazurka
6. March—Allegretto
7. Scene and Waltz-Entr'acte—Allegretto

Scene 2:
8. The Celebration—Allegro
9. Russian Dance—Allegro
10. Chaconne—Andantino
11. Young Girls' Dance—Allegro
12. Dance of the Milkmaid and the Tractor Driver—Moderato con moto
13. The Ballerina's Waltz—Tempo di valse
14. Comic Dance (Galya and the Concertina Player)—Allegro
15. Dance of the Mountain Tribesmen and Men of Kuban— Presto
16. Departure—Allegro
17. Zina's Jealousy—Allegretto
18. Revelation of Zina's Profession—Allegretto—[Tempo di mazurka]
19. The Plot—Allegro

ACT 2

Scene 3:
20. Invitation to a Rendezvous—Adagio
21. Dressing-up Scene—[Allegro]
22. Entry of the Concertina Player and Galya—Andantino
23. Tango—Allegro—Andante—Allegro
24. Playing Jokes on the Elderly Couple—Allegretto
25. Adagio. Arrival at the Rendezvous—Adagio
26. Waltz. Variation of the Ballet Dancer in Woman's Dress—Allegretto
27. Variation of the Ballerina in Her Partner's Costume—Allegro
28. The Coda—Allegro
29. Adagio. Pyotr and Zina in the Ballerina's Costume—Adagio

30. The Plotters' Dance—[Moderato]
31. Zina's Variation—Presto
32. The Coda—Allegro
33. Dance. Mise-en-scène 'The Murder'—Allegretto poco moderato
34. Variation of the 'Murdered Lady'—Allegro
35. Finale—Coda—Presto

ACT 3

Scene 4:
36. Musical Entr'acte 'Swings'—Allegro molto
37. March. 'The Harvest Celebration'—[Tempo di marcia]
38. Waltz—Andantino
39. The Revelation Scene—Andantino—[Adagio]—Presto
40. The Ballet Dancer's Variation—Allegro
41. The Ballerina's Variation—Allegretto
42. Zina's Variation—Allegro
43. The Coda—[Presto]
44. The Final Dance—Allegro

Pieces not included in the Stage Version of the Ballet:
1. After Reviewing Those in Disguise—[Vivo]
2. The Weavers' Dance—Moderato non troppo
3. After the March and before the Waltz of the Ballet Dancers—[Tempo di marcia]
4. Zina and Pyotr's Dance—[Moderato con moto]
5. Folk Dance—Allegretto
6. Adagio
7. The Coda—Presto

Table of material recycled from *The Bolt,* Opus 27:
1. Overture = 14. First Dance of the Machines
10. Chaconne = 23. The Dance of the Beggar Woman
11. Young Girls' Dance = 37. The Dance of the Mill Girls
19. The Plot = 13. The Entry of the Komsomol Members
23. Tango = 29. The Dance of Kozelkov and His Friends
24. Playing Jokes on the Elderly Couple and 39. The Revelation Scene = The Saboteurs (Intermezzo) which in turn is developed from *The Golden Age,* Opus 22, No. 18.
43. The Coda = 43. Apotheosis
44. The Final Dance = 21. The Dance of the Komsomol Members.

In addition 7. Waltz-Entr'acte and 38. Waltz = Suite for Jazz Orchestra No. 1, Sans op. E No. 1. Nos. 6, 17, 18, and 26 are repeats of Nos. 3, 4, 5, and 7 respectively; No. 16 is a variation of No. 8 and No. 29 is an extended version of No. 2.

Composed: 1934–5, at Leningrad. Autograph scores and signed copies undated.

Premières: 4 June 1935, Malyi Opera House, Leningrad; décor by Mikhail
Bobyshov and conducted by Pavel Feldt. Pyotr Gusev danced the part of
Pyotr.

30 November 1935, Bolshoi Theatre, Moscow; décor by V. Dmitriev,
produced by Boris Mordvinov, and conducted by Yuri Faier.

Suite: 11 March 1945, at Moscow.

Arrangements: Many of the numbers from the ballet score were later sal-
vaged by the composer, assisted by Lev Atovmyan, and assembled into
the Ballet Suites, Sans op. P.

Score Nos. 4, 9, 12, 13, 28, 29, and 41 arranged for organ by Mariya
Makarova.

Romance (Ballet Suite No. 1, No. 3) arranged for violin and piano by
Konstantin Fortunatov. Score No. 4 a.k.a. Romance in F major.

Polka (Ballet Suite No. 1, No. 4) in piano reductions by L. Atovmyan
and Bronislava Rozengauz; transcribed for small stage orchestra (violin,
piano, B flat clarinet, trumpet, accordion, and percussion; with optional
violin, cello, double-bass, B flat clarinet, trumpet, flute, oboe, and trombone) by the composer; and folk orchestra by Aleksandr Shirokov.

Adagio (Ballet Suite No. 2, No. 2) arranged for piano solo by Atovmyan;
cello and piano by both Atovmyan and David Pereira; double-bass and piano
by Rodion Azarkhin; French horn and piano by V. Buyanovsky; tuba and
piano by Roger Bobo; and cello and string orchestra by Saulius Sondetskis.

Pizzicato Dance (Ballet Suite No. 1, No. 2) and Waltz (Ballet Suite No.
3, No. 5) transcribed for string quartet by I. Sirotin.

Nocturne (Original Ballet Suite No. 2, No. 2), Barrel Organ Polka (Ballet Suite No. 1, No. 4), and Skipping-rope Dance (Ballet Suite No. 3, No.
3) in piano reduction by B. Rosengauz.

Prelude (Ballet Suite No. 4, No. 1) reworked by Atovmyan from Score
No. 33.

See also *Dances of the Dolls*, Sans op. S.

Opus 39*a*—Suite for full orchestra compiled by the composer in 1945
and prepared for publication by Konstantin Titarenko in 1986:

1. Waltz—Andantino (Ballet Suite No. 1, No. 1)
2. [Russian Popular Dance]—Moderato con moto (Ballet Suite No. 1, No. 4)
3. Galop—Allegro (Ballet Suite No. 3, No. 6)
4. Adagio—Adagio (Ballet Suite No. 2, No. 2)
5. Pizzicato—Allegretto (Ballet Suite No. 1, No. 2)

No. 2 is untitled and designated No. 10 in the score; the music of the number in the ballet entitled 'Russian Dance' is different. The five items appear
in differing versions and orchestrations in the Ballet Suites Nos. 1–3.

Instrumentation of Suite Opus 39*a*:   piccolo, 2 flutes, 2 oboes, cor anglais, E
flat clarinet, 2 B flat clarinets, 3 bassoons (III = contrabassoon) ~ 4 horns,
3 trumpets, 3 trombones, tuba ~ timpani, triangle, side drum, cymbals ~
glockenspiel, harp ~ strings.

Music: The composer utilized some excerpts from Sans op. E, Opp. 22 and
27. The whereabouts of the score is not known but the Suite reconstructed from orchestral parts preserved at the Rental Library of the
Music Fund of the USSR.

Muzgiz, No. 22205 (with Waltz from Opus 37), 1951, Polka arr. for
small stage orchestra, parts, 28.5 cm.

Ricordi, No. 129644, 1958 (also Edition Peters, No. 4767, 1962, 30 cm.),
Adagio coupled with the Spring Waltz, Opus 78*a* No. 3; arr. for cello and
piano by L. Atovmyan, 31 cm.

Sovetskii Kompozitor, No. 2718 (in *D. Shostakovich: Pieces for cello and
piano*), 1962, Adagio arr. L. Atovmyan, 29 cm.

Sovetskii Kompozitor, No. 4565 (in *Dmitri Shostakovich: Popular
Pieces*), 1967, Adagio and Polka arr. for piano by L. Atovmyan, 28.5 cm.

Muzyka, No. 4719 (in *D. Shostakovich: Pieces for violin and piano*), 1975,
Romance arr. K. Fortunatov, 28.5 cm.

Belwin Mills, New York, No. 4446 (*Two pieces for cello and piano*—with
Op. 78*a* No. 3) *c*.1977, Adagio arr. L. Atovmyan, score, 27 cm. Also
Boosey & Hawkes, No. 20616, *c*.1982.

Sovetskii Kompozitor, No. 4643 (in *Pieces by Soviet Composers* for string
quartet, Book 3), 1978, Pizzicato Dance and Waltz arr. I. Sirotin, 29 cm.

Sovetskii Kompozitor, No. 4920 (in *D. Shostakovich: Selection of Children's Piano Pieces*), 1979, three numbers arr. B. Rozengauz, 29 cm.

Muzyka, No. 9060 (in *Anthology for Violin*, 5th–6th class children's
musical schools), 1983, Romance arr. K. Fortunatov, 29 cm.

Sovetskii Kompozitor, 1984 (in *Pieces for French horn and piano*, Book 3),
Adagio arr. V. Buyanovsky, 29 cm.

Muzyka, No. 11695 (in Volume 26 of *Collected Works* with Opp. 22*a* and
27*a*), 1987, full score of Suite Opus 39*a* plus additional 'Russian Popular
Dance', 30 cm.

Muzyka, No. 14908 (in *D. Shostakovich: Pieces for cello and piano*), 1991,
Adagio arr. L. Atovmyan, 29 cm.

Complete score—DSCH Publishers, Moscow, no number, 1997, complete
piano score with commentary by Inna Barsova and Manashir Yakubov in
Russian and English, 232 pp., 29 cm.

Additional ballets: *The Young Lady and the Hooligan.* Lev Atovmyan used four
numbers from Opus 39 in a ballet of seven episodes created for Valeri Panov
by Konstantin Boyarsky, with libretto by Aleksandr Belinsky (after a film
script by Vladimir Mayakovsky) and designs by Valeri Dorrer; Leningrad
Malyi Theatre, 28 December 1962. For further details see Opus 27.

Recordings: USSR: MK D 0001217-8 (7" mono). Adagio arr. Azarkhin.
Rodion AZARKHIN (double-bass) and Grigori Zinger (piano). [Aleksan-
drov and Kosenko.] P 1963.

Germany: Kaskade D 32 001. Adagio arr. Atovmyan. Günter LÖSCH
(cello) and Siegfried Schubert-Weber (piano). [Glazunov, Benjamin,
Massenet *et al.*] P 1970s.

USSR: Melodiya C20 10671-2. Polka arr. Shirokov. Russian Folk Orchestra, Aleksandr SHIROKOV. [Khvatov, Gorlov, Katayev *et al.*] I 1979*a*.

USA: Orion ORS 83462. Romance and Pizzicato Dance [Waltz-scherzo refers to Op. 27.] Zoe ERISMAN (piano). [Opp. 34, 94, and 27.] P 1983.

USA: Pro Arte PAD 178. Adagio adapted from the cello version. Eugene LEVINSON (double-bass) and Gina Levinson (piano). [Franck, Tchaikovsky, and Rakhmaninov.] I 1984.

Unicorn Kanchana Compact Disc DKP 9069. Adagio arr. Atovmyan. Alexander BAILLE (cello) and Piers Lane (piano). [Opp. 40 and 78; Proko-fiev.] P London 6 and 7 Aug. 1987, G Oct. 1988. *Reissued:* Unicorn Kanchana Souvenir Compact Disc UKCD 2083. [As original release.] I Mar. 1997.

Germany: FSM Fono Compact Disc FCD 97721. Adagio arr. Atovmyan. DUO POSTIGLIONE—Wolfgang Schultz (cello) and Ginette Kostenbader (piano). [Sans op. D; Fauré and Schumann.] P Stuttgart 29 Oct. 1988, I 1990.

Philips Compact Disc 434 106-2PH. Adagio in composer's original ver-sion. Julian LLOYD WEBBER (cello), London Symphony Orchestra, Maksim Shostakovich. [Myaskovsky and Tchaikovsky.] P London Sept. 1991, G May 1992.

USA: Crystal Compact Disc CD 690. Adagio arr. Bobo. Roger BOBO (tuba) and Marie Condamin (piano). [John and Thomas Stevens, Plog, Penderecki *et al.*] P Jerusalem June 1993, I Nov. 1994.

Olympia Compact Disc OCD 585. Nos. 12, 13, 28, 29, 41, 4, and 9 arr. for organ. Mariya MAKAROVA (organ). ['Music for Organ'—Opp. 16, 27, 29, 81, 97, 105, and Sans op. E.] P Moscow Conservatory Jan. 1995, I Mar. 1997.

Chandos Compact Disc CHAN 9423. Complete ballet, apart from Nos. 6, 10–11, 16–19, 23–4, 26, 30, 34, 38–9, and 43 of the composer's original score, revised by G. Rozhdestvensky. Ib Lanzky-Otto (French horn) and Laura Stephenson (harp) in No. 25, Elemér Lavotha (cello) in No. 29, Royal Stockholm Philharmonic Orchestra, Gennadi ROZHDESTVENSKY. P Stockholm 9–14 June 1995, I Jan. 1996.

Naxos Compact Disc 8.554381. Adagio arr. Saulius Sondetskis. Vytau-tas SONDETSKIS (cello), Lithuanian Chamber Orchestra, David Geringas. ['Romantic Music for Cello and Orchestra'—Rimsky-Korsakov, Dvari-onas, Tchaikovsky *et al.*] P Vilnius 4 Mar. 1999, G Oct. 2000.

France: Le Chant du Monde Compact Disc LDC778 1124. Nos. 4 and 12 arr. for organ. Hervé DÉSARBRE (organ). [Opp. 145, 29, and 27; Tishchenko *Portrait of D. D. Shostakovich*—No. 12 of *Twelve Portraits,* Op. 113.] P Glinka Museum, Moscow concert 24 May 1999, I May 2000, G Aug. 2000.

References: Faier, Goltsman, and Lopukhov.

Notes: The ballet was attacked in an unsigned article 'Falsehood in Ballet' in the issue of *Pravda* dated 6 February 1936.

The Russian name of the ballet is *Svetlyi ruchei.* In Russian-English dictionaries the first word translates as light/bright or lucid/clear, while the second appears as brook/rill/stream. A surprisingly wide-ranging variety of titles are found in the English literature. These include *The*

Limpid Brook in early writings (e.g. Calvocoressi 1944 and Moisenko 1949) and *The Bright Stream* commonly in recent works (e.g. MacDonald 1977, Volkov 1979, Kennedy 1980, and Devlin 1983). Other variants are *Clear Water Springs* (Moisenko 1942), *The Sparkling Brook* (Seroff 1943 and Krebs 1970), *Clear Brooks* (Boelza 1943), *Bright Rivulet* (Martynov/ Guralsky 1947), *The Glittering Stream* (D. and I. Sollertinsky 1980), *The Clear Well* (Khentova, Opus 36 score), *Sparkling Stream* (Vishnevskaya 1985), and *The Enlighted Brook* (Cadenza liner-note).

For further recordings see under Ballet Suites Nos. 1–3, Sans op. P and *Dances of the Dolls,* Sans op. S.

Opus 40   Cello Sonata in D minor

Form: Sonata for cello and piano in four movements:

1. Allegro non troppo or (in 1st edition)   Moderato
2. Allegro   Moderato con moto
3. Largo   Largo
4. Allegro   Allegretto

Composed: 14 August (at Moscow)–19 September 1934(at Leningrad). First movement completed in two days.

Dedication: Viktor Lvovich Kubatsky (cellist).

Première: 25 December 1934, Leningrad Conservatory Malyi Hall; Viktor Kubatsky (cello) and Dmitri Shostakovich (piano).

Arrangements: Cello part arranged for viola by both Viktor Kubatsky and Ye. Strakov, and also adapted for double-bass.

Music: The autograph score is in the possession of Viktor Kubatsky's family. Another manuscript is preserved at the CIS Archives of Literature and Art.

Triton, Leningrad, 1935, 30 cm.

Leeds Music, 1947, cello part ed. Gregor Piatigorsky, 30 cm.

Anglo-Soviet Music Press, No. 50, 1947, cello part ed. G. Piatigorsky, 30 cm.

MCA, No. 05418-022, 1947.

International Music, No. 2087, *c.*1962, ed. Leonard Rose, 30.5 cm.

Edition Peters, No. 4748(plate no. 12065), 1962, 31 cm.

Hans Sikorski, No. 2157, 1969, 31.5 cm.

Muzyka, No. 6366, 1971, with added viola part edited in parallel versions by V. Kubatsky and Ye. Strakov, 29 cm.

Muzyka, No. 10927 (in Volume 38 of *Collected Works* with Opp. 134 and 147), 1982, including separate cello part, 30 cm.

DSCH Publishers, Moscow, no number, 1996, with facsimile first page of autograph score and separate cello part edited by V. Kubatsky (fingering and bowing by M. Rostropovich), 29 cm.

Duration: Approx. 28 minutes in score; 20' 12" (no first movement repeat)–
31' 57"; 28' 00"–29' 40" (Plaistow).

Ballets: *Vestige.* Mark Morris choreographed this work for his Dance Company; Pepisco Summerfare at Purchase, New York in the summer of 1986.
The Young Lady and the Hooligan. The second theme of the first movement of the Cello Sonata (fig. 6 minus 2 bars to fig. 10), orchestrated by
Lev Atovmyan for the 1962 ballet. See under Opus 27.

Film: *Young Musician of the Year 1990.* Steven Isserlis gives a Master Class on
the second movement to Paul Watkins (cello), the string entrant winner
in 1988; screened on BBC TV2 on 19 March 1990.

Recordings: USA: Columbia 71614-6D in Set M551 (6 sides 78 rpm). Gregor
PIATIGORSKY (cello) and Valentin Pavlovsky (piano). P Feb. 1940. *Reissued:*
USA: Columbia RL 3015 (mono). [Cui, Rubinstein *et al.*] ~ Biddulph Com-
pact Disc LAB 117 (mono). [Boccherini, Haydn, Schumann *et al.*] I Sept.
1996 ~ Italy: Arlecchino Compact Disc ARL-A 74. ['Gregor Piatigorsky
Legacy, Vol. 2'—Rakhmaninov, Rubinstein, Rimsky-Korsakov *et al.*]

USSR: Melodiya M10 42045-6 (mono). Daniil SHAFRAN (cello) and
Dmitri Shostakovich (piano). [Op. 134.] P 12 Nov. 1946, I 1980*b*. *Reissued:*
Revelation Compact Disc RV 10017 (mono). [Rakhmaninov.] I and G
Oct. 1996 ~ Revelation Compact Disc RV 70008 (mono). ['Shostakovich
plays Shostakovich, Vol. 7'—Opp. 134, 5, and 22.] I Sept. 1998, G Feb.
1999 ~ France: Dante Compact Discs LYS 369-370 (two-disc set). [Opp.
67, 57, and 73.] I 1998 ~ USA/Canada: Eclectra Compact Disc ECCD
2046 (mono). [Opp. 67 and 134.] I 2000.

USA: Music and Arts/Harmonia Mundi Compact Disc CD 644
(mono). Gregor PIATIGORSKY (cello) and Reginald Stewart (piano).
[Brahms, Chopin, Francoeur *et al.*] P Mar. 1947, G Oct. 1991.

Decca LW 5068 (10" mono). Emanuel BRABEC (cello) and Franz
Holetschek (piano). P June 1953, G Jan. 1954. *Reissued:* Decca Eclipse ECS
706 (electronic stereo). [Rakhmaninov.] G Nov. 1973.

Czech: Supraphon LPM 304 (10" mono). Daniil SHAFRAN (cello) and
Nina Musinian (piano). P 1957, G Sept. 1958.

USSR: MK D 4102-3 (10" mono). Mstislav ROSTROPOVICH (cello) and
Dmitri Shostakovich (piano). P 15 Dec. 1957, *Reissued:* Parlophone Odeon
PMA 1043 (mono). [Schumann.] G Dec. 1958 ~ USA: Monitor Collectors
Series MCS 2021 (electronic stereo). [Prokofiev.] I 1958. NB. Bars 84–7
repeated in 2nd movement ~ USSR: Melodiya D 016677-8 (mono).
[Prokofiev.] I 1965 ~ HMV Melodiya HLM 7095 in Set RLS 721 (mono).
[Op. 57.] G Oct. 1976 ~ France: Le Chant du Monde LDZ 78388. [Prokofiev.]
I Mar. 1981 ~ USA: Monitor Collectors Series Compact Disc MCD 62021.
[Prokofiev.] I 1991 ~ Czech: Multisonic Compact Disc MU 31 0179-2
(mono). ['Russian Treasure'—Opp. 34 and 57.] I Sept. 1993 ~ USA: Russian
Disc Compact Disc RDCD 15 005 (mono). ['Great Russian Artists: Shosta-
kovich plays Shostakovich'—Opp. 35 and 102.] I Nov. 1993, G Dec. 1993
and Feb. 1995 ~ EMI Compact Discs CZS5 72016-2 (on eleventh disc of

thirteen disc set, mono). ['Rostropovich: The Russian Years, 1950–74'—
Kabalevsky and K. Khachaturyan.] G May 1997 ~ Revelation Compact Disc
RV 70005. ['Shostakovich plays Shostakovich, Vol. 4'—Op. 57.] I Mar. 1998,
G Aug. 1998 ~ EMI Classics Compact Discs CZS5 72295-2 (two-disc set,
mono). [Opp. 107 and 126; Kabalevsky and Khachaturyan.] I Oct. 1998.

USA: Westminster XWN 18791 (mono) and W 9077. Antonio JANIGRO
(cello) and Eva Wollmann (piano). [Prokofiev.] I 1959.

USA: RCA Victor LM 2553(mono) and LSC 2553. Danill SHAFRAN (cello)
and Lydia Pecherskaya (piano). [Schubert.] P USA 1961. *Reissued:* USSR:
MK D 012507-8 (mono). [Schubert.] I 1963 ~ RCA Victrola VIC 1298 (mono)
and VICS 1298. [Schubert.] G Nov. 1968 ~ USA: Time-Life 'Great Men of
Music' box set STL 568. [Opp. 22a, 114, 47, 102, 110, and 135.] I 1979.

France: Pathé Marconi ASTX 123. Leslie PARNAS (cello) and Bernard
Ringeissen (piano). [Porpora and Debussy.] P not stated, I post-1957.

USSR: MK D 010325-8 (in two-record set, mono). First movement
only. Leslie PARNAS (cello) and Yevgeni Dyachenko (piano). [Performers
at Second International Tchaikovsky Competition, including John
Ogdon.] P 1962, I 1963.

Decca Compact Disc 466 823-2DM. Mstislav ROSTROPOVICH (cello)
and Benjamin Britten (piano). ['Britten at Aldeburgh, Vol. 6'—Op.
127; Bridge and Janáček.] P Aldeburgh concert 14 June 1964, G Aug. 2000.

USA: Nonesuch H 1050 (mono) and H 71050. Harvey SHAPIRO (cello)
and Jascha Zayde (piano). [R. Strauss.] I 1965.

USSR: Melodiya D 018753-4 (mono). Karine GEORGIAN (cello) and
A. Amintayeva (piano). [Locatelli.] I 1966.

CBS BRG 72613 (mono) and SBRG 72613. Pierre FOURNIER (cello) and
Jean Fonda (piano). [Debussy and Martinů.] P 1967, G Jan. 1968.

USA: Discocorp 'I Grandi Interpreti' IGI 321. Mstislav ROSTROPOVICH
(cello) and Aleksandr Dedyukhin (piano). [Chopin.] P concert 1967, I
1975. *Reissued:* USA: Music & Arts Compact Disc CD 965. [Chopin and
Debussy.] I July 1997.

Canada: CBC Radio Canada RM 181. Helene GAGNE (cello) and John
Newmark (piano). [Gagne.] P 1970?

USSR: Melodiya CM 02501-2. Ko IWASAKI (cello) and Shuku Iwasaki
(piano). [Chopin, Granados, Davydov *et al.*] P 1970, I 1971.

Unicorn UNS 242. Gwyneth GEORGE (cello) and Alberto Portugheis
(piano). [Rakhmaninov.] P 16 Feb. 1971, G Oct. 1971.

Finland: Finnlevy SFX 5. Arto NORAS (cello) and Tapani Valsta (piano).
[Schubert.] P Helsinki 17–19 Sept. 1973. *Reissued:* Unicorn Finlandia FA
303. [Schubert.] I 1979 ~ Finlandia Compact Disc FACD 705. [Schubert.] I
Dec. 1991 ~ Finlandia Ultima Compact Discs 8573 81969-2 (disc two of
two-disc set). [Opp. 35 and 73.] G June 2000.

USA: Piper CE 3395. Arr. for double-bass. Barry GREEN (double-bass) and
James Cook (piano). [Bruch, Schumann, and Rakhmaninov.] P early 1970s.

USSR: Melodiya C10 06069-70. Arr. for viola by Kubatsky. Yuri YUROV (viola) and Mikhail Muntyan (piano). [Schumann.] P 1975, I 1976*b*.

USSR: Melodiya C10 07289-90. Boris PERGAMENSHCHIKOV (cello) and Anatoli Ugorsky (piano). [Stravinsky.] P 1976, I 1977*a*.

USSR: Melodiya C10 09537-07191. Labelled as 'First Edition'. Daniil SHAFRAN (cello) and Anton Ginzburg (piano). [In second box of Part 2 of *Collected Works on Records* with Op. 67.] P 1977, I 1978. *Reissued:* USSR: Melodiya C10 11629-07041. [Prokofiev.] I 1979*d*.

USSR: Melodiya C10 10117-8. Mikhail KHOMITSER (cello) and Aleksandr Chaikovsky (piano). [Webern and Shchedrin.] P Prague Spring Festival concert 29 May 1977, I 1978*d*.

France: Gallo 30 136. Dimitry MARKEVITCH (cello) and Paulette Zanlonghi (piano). [Kodály.] P 1970s.

USA: Musical Heritage Society MHS 3829. Harry CLARK (cello) and Sandra Schuldnann (piano). [Prokofiev.] P 1978.

USSR: Melodiya C10 10789-90. Fourth movement only. Michael ERIKSON (cello) and I. Kulikova (piano). [Cellists at the Sixth International Tchaikovsky Competition.] P 1978, I 1979*a*.

Germany: De Camera Magna SM 93716. Erkki RAUTIO (cello) and Ralf Gothóni (piano). [Prokofiev.] P summer 1978.

Czech: Supraphon 1111 2805G Stanislav APOLIN (cello) and Josef Hála (piano). [Prokofiev.] P 10–13 Sept. 1979.

Austria: FSM Aulos FSM 53554 AUL. Daniel Robert GRAF (cello) and Viviane Graf-Goergen (piano). [Franck.] P May 1981.

Sweden: Hot News Artemis ARTE 7110. Leo WINLAND (cello) and Janos Solyom (piano). [Karen Khachaturyan.] P 1981.

Chandos ABRD 1072 (digital). BORODIN DUO—Yuli Turovsky (cello) and Lyubov Yedlina (piano). [Prokofiev.] P London 11–12 Nov. 1981, G Jan. 1983. *Reissued:* Chandos Compact Disc CHAN 8340. [Prokofiev.] I Sept. 1984, G Apr. 1985.

USSR: Melodiya C10 18087004. First movement only. Antony ROSS (cello). [Cellists at the Seventh International Tchaikovsky Competition.] P 1982, I 1983*b*.

USSR: Melodiya C10 23837 007 (DMM). Yevgeni ALTMAN (cello) and Mikhail Voskresensky (piano). [Prokofiev.] P radio 1982, I 1987*a*.

France: Erato STU 71519. Frédéric LODÉON (cello) and Daria Hovora (piano). [Schubert.] G July 1983.

Germany: EMI Electrola Compact Disc CDM7 69514-2. Heinrich SCHIFF (cello) and Aci Bertoncelj (piano). [Lutoslawski and Martinů.] P Eckenhagen 17–18 Nov. 1983, I 1988.

Czech: Panton 81 0696-1. Michaela FUKAČOVÁ (cello) and Ivan Klánský (piano). [Martinů.] P Prague 6–7 June 1985.

Denon Compact Disc C37-7563. Mari FUJIWARA (cello) and Jacques Rouvier (piano). [Debussy and Stravinsky.] G Sept. 1986.

Sweden: BIS Compact Disc CD 336. Torlief THEDEÉN (cello) and Ronald Pöntinen (piano). ['The Russian Cello'—Stravinsky and Schnittke.] P 1–3 May 1986, I Mar. 1987.

USSR: Melodiya C10 24637 000. First movement only. Kirill RODIN (cello) and Galina Brykina (piano). [Eighth International Tchaikovsky Competition—Barber, Prokofiev, Beethoven *et al.*] P 17–28 June 1986, I 1987*c*.

Unicorn Kanchana Compact Disc DKP 9069. Alexander BAILLIE (cello) and Piers Lane (piano). [Pieces from Opp. 39 and 78; Prokofiev.] P London 6 and 7 Aug. 1987, G Oct. 1988. *Reissued:* Unicorn Kanchana Souvenir Compact Disc UKCD 2083. [As original release.] I Mar. 1997.

CBS Masterworks Compact Disc MK 44664. Yo-Yo MA (cello) and Emanuel Ax (piano). [Op. 67.] P Boston 1987, I Dec. 1988, G June 1989.

Lyrinx Compact Disc LYR 074. Raphael SOMMER (cello) and Daniel Adni (piano). [Rakhmaninov.] I May 1988.

Chandos Compact Disc CHAN 8769. Second movement only. Richard MAY (cello) and Elizabeth Burley (piano). ['Solo'—Young British Virtuoso Musicians from the Thames TV series: Sans op. P; Grandjany, Chopin, Fauré *et al.*] P Clandon Park, Surrey Mar. 1988.

Philips Compact Disc 422 345-2PH. Julian LLOYD WEBBER(cello) and John McCabe (piano). [Britten and Prokofiev.] P Snape Apr. 1988, I June 1988, G Oct. 1989.

USSR: Melodiya A10 00505 006 (digital). Leonid GOROKHOV (cello) and Irina Nikitina (piano). [Tortelier and Kodály.] P 1988, I 1990*b*. *Reissued:* USSR: Melodiya Compact Disc SUCD 11 00304. [Boccherini, Haydn, Tortelier, and Kodály.] I 1991*c*.

USA: Sound-Star-ton SST 0208 and Compact Disc SST 30208. Tanya REMENIKOVA (cello) and Alexander Braginsky (piano). [Britten.] P Minneapolis 1988.

Decca Compact Disc 421 774-2DH. Lynn HARRELL (cello) and Vladimir Ashkenazy (piano). [Sans op. D; and Prokofiev.] P Chicago 6 May 1988, I Oct. 1989, G Mar. 1990. *Reissued:* Decca Compact Discs 466 437-2 (third disc of five-disc set). [Opp. 57 and 122.] I 1999.

Germany: Cadenza Compact Disc C 8812-8. Marek JERIE (cello) and Ivan Klánský (piano). ['Russian Chamber Music'—Sans op. P; and Stravinsky.] P Sept. 1988, I 1989.

Italy: Sipario Compact Disc CS 16C. Anton NICULESCU (cello) and Barbara Lolé (piano). [Stravinsky.] P Milan Sept. 1988, I 1990.

Denmark: Kontra Punkt Compact Disc 32018. Erling Blöndal BENGSTSSON (cello) and Nina Kartardze (piano). [Rakhmaninov.] P Denmark Jan. 1989.

Claudio Compact Disc CR 3911-2. Alfia NAKIPBEKOVA (cello) and Eleonora Nakipbekova (piano). [Rakhmaninov.] P St John's Smith Square, London 1–21 May 1989, I Dec. 1989.

France: Le Chant du Monde Compact Discs LDC 278 1018-19 (two-disc set). Ivan MONIGHETTI (cello) and Vasili Lobanov (piano). [Opp. 134, 147, and 67.] P 1989?, I Feb. 1990, G June 1990.

Koch Compact Disc 3 7064-2. Anthony ELLIOT (cello) and Ruth Tomfohrde (piano). [Kabalevsky and Martinů.] P Houston 16–17 Nov. 1989, I Oct. 1991.

Netherlands: Globe Compact Disc GLO 5041. Dmitri FERSHTMAN (cello) and Mila Baslavskaya (piano). [Myaskovsky and Schnittke.] P Amsterdam Mar. 1990, I 1991.

USSR: Melodiya Compact Disc SUCD 10 00088. Gustav RIVINIUS (cello) and Paul Rivinius (piano). [Performers at the Ninth International Tchaikovsky Competition—Brahms and Schnittke.] P Moscow concert 30 June 1990, I 1991*b*.

Belgium: Discover International Compact Disc DICD 920187. Herre-Jan STEGENGA (cello) and Jacob Bogaart (piano). [Rakhmaninov.] P Brussels concert 1990, I Oct. 1994.

Netherlands: Ars Classicum Compact Disc 1155492. Larissa GROENEVELD (cello) and Frank van de Laar (piano). [Trio Dante programme—Glinka, Franck, and Tajcevic.] P 1990.

Academy Sound and Vision Compact Disc CD DCA 756. Bernard GREGOR-SMITH (cello) and Yolande Wrigley (piano). [Prokofiev, Janáček, and Martinů.] P University of Surrey 28–30 Aug. 1990, I Apr. 1991. *Reissued:* ASV Quicksilva Compact Disc CDQS 6218. [Prokofiev, Janáček, and Martinů.] I Nov. 1997.

Pickwick Compact Disc MCD 49. Tim HUGH (cello) and Kathron Sturrock (piano). [Kabalevsky and Schnittke.] P Highgate, London 25–6 July 1991.

United Compact Disc 88006-2. Paul MARLEYN (cello) and Sarah Morley (piano). [Schnittke and Prokofiev.] P East Woodhay, Hants 6–8 Nov. 1991, I Nov. 1993.

Australia: Tall Poppies Compact Disc TP 018. David PEREIRA (cello) and Lisa Moore (piano). ['The Wild Russians'—Schnittke.] P Canberra July 1992, I Feb. 1993.

Belgium: Cyprès Compact Disc 2613. Vivian SPANOGHE (cello) and André De Groote (piano). [Britten and Brahms.] P Liège 15–17 July 1992, I 1997.

France: Auvidis-Valois Compact Disc V 4666. Sonia WIEDER-ATHERTON (cello) and Laurent Cabasso (piano). [Prokofiev.] P Metz Sept, 1992, I Dec. 1993, G Apr. 1994.

USA: Northeastern Compact Disc NR 245-CD. Ronald THOMAS (cello) and Mihae Lee (piano). [Op. 67.] P Weston, Mass. Jan. 1993, I Dec. 1994.

Canada: CBC Records Compact Disc MVCD 1093. Desmond HOEBIG (cello) and Andrew Tunis (piano). [Rakhmaninov.] P Kitchener, Ontario 8 and 9 Feb. 1993, I Nov. 1996.

Koch Schwann Compact Disc 3-1436-2. Andrzej BAUER (cello) and Ewa Kupiec (piano). [Prokofiev and Stravinsky.] P Lübeck 13–15 Sept. 1993, I May 1996.

Germany: Amp Primavera Compact Disc 5053-2. Jens Peter MAINTZ (cello) and Keiko Tamura (piano). [Bach, Schubert, and Ligeti.] P Hanover 22 Dec. 1993/5 Jan. 1994, I 1995.

Imp Classics Compact Disc PCD 1084. Carlos PRIETO (cello) and Doris Stevenson (piano). [Op. 107; and Saint-Saëns.] P Mexico City 1994, I Aug. 1994.

Germany: Es-Dur/Con Brio Compact Disc 2021. David GERINGAS (cello) and Tatyana Schatz (piano). [Sans op. D (iii); Prokofiev and Rakhmaninov.] P Hamburg 1994.

Norway: Simax PSC 1108. Øystein BIRKELAND (cello) and Ian Brown (piano). [Prokofiev and Schnittke.] P Eidsvoll, Norway 17–18 Sept. or 24–6 Oct. 1994.

Germany: Arte Nova Classics Compact Disc 74321 27805-2. Emil KLEIN (cello) and Cristian Beldi (piano). [Prokofiev.] P Hamburg Apr. 1995.

Germany: Cybele Compact Disc 300 101. DUO HALSDORF-HÄNSCHKE— Jean Halsdorf (cello) and Michael Hänschke (piano). [Hänschke and Beethoven.] P Moers 8–11 Apr. 1995.

Denmark: Kontrapunkt Compact Disc 32216. Michaele FUKAČOVÁ (cello) and Ivan Klánský (piano). [Prokofiev and Stravinsky.] P May 1995, I Feb. 1996, G Aug. 1996.

RCA Victor Red Seal Compact Disc 09026 68437-2. Steven ISSERLIS (cello) and Olli Mustonen (piano). [Janáček and Prokofiev.] P Blackheath, London May 1995, I and G May 1996.

USA: Sonora Compact Disc SO 22572 CD. Dmitri YABLONSKY (cello) and Okhana Yablonskaya (piano). [Prokofiev and Rakhmaninov.] P Boston Nov. 1995, I June 1996.

Czech: Supraphon Compact Disc SU 3243-2 131. Leonid GOROKHOV (cello) and Aleksandr Melnikov (piano). [Prokofiev and Stravinsky.] P Prague 14–17 Nov. 1995, I Sept. 1996.

USA: Arabesque Compact Discs Z 6698 (two-disc set). Sharon ROBINSON (cello) and Joseph Kalichstein (piano). [Opp. 8, 67, 134, and 147.] P Purchase, New York 17–18 Dec. 1995 or 12–13 Sept. 1996, I and G Jan. 1998.

Virgin Classics Compact Disc VC5 45274-2. Truls MØRK (cello) and Lars Vogt (piano). [Prokofiev and Stravinsky.] P Eidsvoll, Norway 6–10 May 1996, I July 1997.

USA: Ongaku Records Compact Disc 024-110. Suren BAGRATUNI (cello) and Adrian Oetiker (piano). [Prokofiev.] P University of Illinois, Champaign-Urbana 23 and 25 Sept. 1996, G Oct. 1998.

Harmonia Mundi Les Noveaux Interpretès Compact Disc HMN91 1628. Xavier PHILLIPS (cello) and Hüseyin Sermet (piano). [Schnittke and Prokofiev.] P Nov. 1996, I Dec. 1997, G Feb. 1998.

Germany: Contempora Compact Disc 96 970203. Guido SCHIEFEN (cello) and Olaf Drebler (piano). [Prokofiev.] P Neumarkt 1996, I 1998.

Carlton Classics Compact Disc 30367 0236-2. Ulrich BOECKHLER (cello) and Susan Starr (piano). [Pärt and Prokofiev.] P Toronto 26–7 Feb. 1997, I Dec. 1997.

Netherlands: AC Classics Compact Disc 1-98038-2. Timora ROSLER (cello) and Klára Würtz (piano). [Schubert and Martinů.] P Kortenhoeve Sept. 1997.

Canada: Disques Pelléas Compact Disc 0109. Yegor DYACHKOV (cello) Jean Saulnier (piano). [Schnittke and Prokofiev.] P St-Irénée, Quebec Nov. 1998, I July 2000.

France: Le Chant du Monde Compact Disc LDC 278112. Gary HOFF-MAN (cello) and Philippe Bianconi (piano). [Sans op. D; and Prokofiev.] P Grenoble 13 and 16 Dec. 1998, G Apr. 2000.

Germany: Berlin Classics Compact Disc 0017062 BC. Jan VOGLER (cello) and Bruno Canino (piano). [Falla and Weill.] P Berlin 27–9 Oct. 1999.

USA: ArtistLed Compact Disc 19901-2. No first movement exposition repeat. David FINKEL (cello) and Wu Han (piano). [Rakhmaninov and Prokofiev.] P New York 3–8 Dec. 1999, I Aug. 2001.

References: Abel-Aziz, Bogdanova, Goltsman, and Lopukhov.

Opus 41 (i)   The Youth of Maxim

Alternative title: *The Bolshevik.* Shown in America under the title 'Varsha-vyanka'.

Form: Music for the first film in the 'Maxim Trilogy', *The Youth of Maxim,* with screenplay and direction by Grigori Kozintsev and Leonid Trauberg for Lenfilm. The film received the First Prize (Silver Goblet) at the International Film Festival, Moscow, 1935. The revolutionary songs 'Warsaw March' ('Varshavyanka') and 'You Fell as Victims' are quoted in the score. Shostakovich wrote a Prologue marked 'Allegro molto' for the opening of the film.

Instrumentation: piccolo, 2 flutes, 2 oboes, E flat and 2 B flat clarinets, 2 bas-soons ~ 4 horns, 3 trumpets, 3 trombones, tuba ~ timpani, side drum, cymbals ~ xylophone, piano ~ soprano soloist ~ strings.

Composed: 1934–5, at Leningrad.

Première: Film first shown on 27 January 1935. Score conducted by Nikolai Rabinovich.

Music: Autograph full score preserved at the Leningrad Archives of Litera-ture and Art, and the autograph vocal score at the Glinka Museum.

Muzyka, No. 10889 (in Volume 41 of *Collected Works* with Opp. 26, 30, 33, 48, 50, 53, 55, 56, 59, and 64), 1987, Prologue in full score, 30 cm.

Duration: Film: 100 minutes. Prologue: 2' 26".

Recording: Germany: Capriccio Compact Disc 10 561. Prologue. Svetlana Katchur (soprano), Berlin Radio Symphony Orchestra, Mikhail
YUROVSKY. [Opp. 30, 45, and 50*a*.] P 28–9 Apr. 1994, I Oct. 1995, G Jan. 1996.
Notes: The remainder of the musical items were not composed by Shostakovich and include songs with bayan and guitar accompaniment, solo
voice, and mixed choir with piano (*'Gaudeamus igitur!'*); the Oira Polka,
Waltzes for bayan, and a Flourish.

The Prologue, describing New Year revelry in St Petersburg, com-
bines three themes: the Oira Polka on woodwind, a Krakowiak (or
Cracovienne—a lively Polish dance) on brass, and the gipsy romance
'Black Eyes' on solo trombone and strings; and also includes a cabaret
song 'I'm a Football-player' and ends with a Can-Can.

Opus 41 (ii)   The Girl Friends

Alternative title: 'Three Women' (American title).
Form: Music for the film *The Girl Friends,* with screenplay by Raya Vasilieva,
directed by Leo Arnshtam for Lenfilm. The pre-revolutionary funeral
anthem 'Tortured by Heavy Bondage' is used in the score which
includes three Preludes for trumpet, string quartet, and piano:

1. Allegro in F major
2. The Forester's Hut—Andante in A minor
3. Prelude in D major

Composed: 1934–5, at Leningrad.
Dedication: Film dedicated to Romain Rolland (writer).
Premières: Film first shown on 19 February 1936. Released in New York,
USA, under the title 'Three Women' on 11 February (the year not given
on the poster).

USSR Preludes: 25 September 1985, Moscow Conservatory Malyi Hall;
I. Skolnik (trumpet), Borodin Quartet (Mikhail Kopelman, Andrei Abra-
menko, Dmitri Shebalin, Valentin Berlinsky), and L. Berlinskaya, (piano).

UK Prelude (*Allegro*): 19 March 1986, Queen Elizabeth Hall, London;
Andrew Crowley (trumpet), Alexander Balanescu and Elisabeth Perry
(violins), Simon Rowland-Jones (viola), Elizabeth Wilson (cello), and
Andrew Ball (piano).
Music: Autograph score preserved at the CIS Archives of Literature and Art.
Three Preludes found by Gennadi Rozhdestvensky at the Glinka
Museum.
Duration: Three Preludes: 7' 35".
Recording: USSR: Melodiya C10 26307 004. Vladimir Pushkarev (trumpet),
Aleksandr Semyannikov and Aleksandr Shanin (violins), Nikolai
Makshantsev (viola), Sergei Mnozhin (cello), and Viktoria POSTNIKOVA
(piano). [Album 6 of 'From Manuscripts of Different Years'—Sans opp.
X, J, A, S, D; and Op. 128.] P 1983–6, I 1988*d*.

Opus 42   Five Fragments

Form: Five short pieces for small orchestra (with harp):

1. Moderato
2. Andante
3. Largo
4. Moderato
5. Allegretto

Instrumentation: piccolo, flute, oboe, cor anglais, E flat clarinet, B flat clarinet, bass clarinet, bassoon, contrabassoon ~ 2 horns, trumpet, trombone, tuba ~ side drum ~ harp in Nos. 2 and 3 ~ strings.

Composed: 9 June 1935, in one sitting, at Leningrad.

Premières: 26 April 1965, Leningrad: Leningrad Philharmonic Orchestra, Igor Blazhkov.

UK: 24 May 1977, St John's Smith Square, London; Kensington Symphony Orchestra, Leslie Head.

Music: Autograph score, numbered Opus 43, preserved at the Glinka Museum.

Moscow, no number, 1974, full score, *c*.30 cm.

Hans Sikorski, No. 2311, 1979, score and 21 parts, 31.5 cm.

Muzyka, No. 11678 (in Volume 10 of *Collected Works* with Opp. 1, 3, 7, 16, and Sans op. E), 1984, full score, 30 cm.

Duration: Approx. 8' 30" in score; 8' 20"–10' 25".

Recordings: USSR: Melodiya C10 05191-2. Kiev Chamber Orchestra, Igor BLAZHKOV. [Op. 11; and Britten.] P 1974, I 1975*c*. *Reissued:* HMV Melodiya ASD 3520. [Op. 112.] G Aug. 1978.

Decca 421 120-1DH (digital) and Compact Disc 421 120-2DH. Royal Philharmonic Orchestra, Vladimir ASHKENAZY. [Op. 47.] P Mar. 1987, G June 1988 and Apr. 1989. *Reissued:* Decca Compact Cassette 421 120-5DH. [Op. 47.] I 1993.

United Compact Disc 88001. City of Birmingham Symphony Orchestra, Mark ELDER. [Opp. 31*a*, 46*a*; and Sans op. E.] P Birmingham 16–18 Dec. 1992, I Nov. 1993, G Jan. 1994.

Opus 43   Symphony No. 4 in C minor

Form: Symphony for large orchestra of *c*.128 performers in three movements:

1. Allegretto poco moderato
2. Moderato con moto
3. Largo—Allegro

Instrumentation: 2 piccolos, 4 flutes, 4 oboes (IV = cor anglais), E flat clarinet, 4 clarinets (B flat and A), bass clarinet, 3 bassoons, contrabassoon ~

8 horns, 4 trumpets, 3 trombones, 2 tubas ~ 6 timpani (2 players), tri-angle, castanets, wood block, side drum, cymbals (2 players—I with drumsticks and II normal mode), bass drum, gong ~ glockenspiel, xylo-phone, celesta, 2 harps ~ strings.

Composed: 13 September 1935–26 Apr. 1936, at Leningrad. The existence of an incomplete first movement mentioned on 5 November 1934. Rehearsals under Fritz Stiedry in autumn 1936 were abandoned on the recommendation of the director of the Leningrad Philharmonic, Isai Renzin.

Premières: 30 December 1961, Moscow Conservatory Bolshoi Hall; Moscow Philharmonic Orchestra, Kirill Kondrashin.

UK: 7 September 1962, Edinburgh; Philharmonia Orchestra, Gennadi Rozhdestvensky.

USA: 15 February 1963, Philadelphia; Philadelphia Orchestra, Eugene Ormandy.

UK concert and broadcast of the original opening pages: 26 February 1998, Barbican Centre, London; London Symphony Orchestra, Mstislav Rostropovich.

Arrangements: Reductions for two pianos by the composer (1936) and Pavel Lamm (not published), and for piano four hands by Lev Atovmyan.

Music: Manuscript lost during the siege of Leningrad. Score reconstructed from parts by Boris Shalman, librarian of the Leningrad Philharmonic. Fragments of the first and third movements preserved at the CIS Archives of Literature and Art. The first page of the autograph full score reproduced in Volume 2 of *Collected Works* is the first 54 bars of the 1934 fragment.

Russian lithographed edition, 1946, composer's reduction for two pianos, 300 copies.

Sovetskii Kompozitor, No. 3184, 1962, 29 cm.

Anglo-Soviet Music Press, No. HS 2218, 1962, miniature score.

Sovetskii Kompozitor, 1969, arr. for piano four hands by L. Atovmyan, 30 cm.

Edwin F. Kalmus, No. 142, no date, 26.5 cm.

Muzyka, No. 9132, 1976, 30 cm.

Muzyka, No. 10778 (in Volume 2 of *Collected Works* with Op. 20), 1982, 30 cm.

Hans Sikorski, No. 2218, 1983, score, 21 cm.

The 1934 fragment marked 'Adagio' will be published in *New Collected Works*, Volume 3 with Symphony No. 3.

Duration: Approx. 60 minutes in score; 58' 22"–67' 17"; 64' 40" (Plaistow). Discarded opening: 6' 20"–6' 40".

Recordings: USSR: MK D 09807-10 (3 sides mono) and MK C 0295-8 (3 sides) [later Melodiya CM 0295-8.] Moscow Philharmonic Orchestra, Kirill KONDRASHIN. [Op. 32.] P and I 1962. *Reissued:* HMV Melodiya ASD 2741

(2 sides). G Oct. 1971 ~ USA: Angel Melodiya SR 40177. I 1971 ~ Germany: Melodia Eurodisc 87 623 XPK. [In thirteen-record box set.] I 1974 ~ Italy: EMI 065 92610. I 1974 ~ HMV Melodiya BOX 502502-3 in Set SLS 5025. [Opp. 20 and 47, first and second movements.] G Dec. 1975 ~ Germany: Melodia Eurodisc 300 596 in Set 300 597-435 ~ France: Le Chant du Monde LDX A 78413-4 (3 sides). [Op. 32.] ~ France: Le Chant du Monde LDX 78622-3 (3 sides). [Op. 20.] ~ USSR: Melodiya CM 0295-6 and C 01109-10 (3 sides). [In first box of Part 1 of *Collected Works on Records* with Op. 70.] I 1980 ~ USA: Musical Heritage Society MHS 824958 Z. [In two-record set with Opp. 14 and 10.] I 1984 ~ HMV Melodiya EX 2903873 (DMM). [Third record in twelve-record box set.] G Dec. 1985 ~ France: Le Chant du Monde Compact Disc LDC 278 1001-2. [In Box 1 of five two-disc sets with Opp. 10, 14, and 20.] G May 1989 ~ BMG Classics Melodiya Compact Disc 74321 19840-2. I July 1994, G Nov. 1994.

USA: Columbia ML 5859 (mono) and MS 6459. Philadelphia Orchestra, Eugene ORMANDY. P 17 Feb. 1963. *Reissued:* CBS BRG 72129 (mono) and SBRG 72129. G Sept. 1963 ~ Italy: CBS CR 135304 (mono) and SCR 135304. I 1963 ~ CBS Classics 61696. G Aug. 1976 ~ Sony Essential Classics Compact Discs SB2K 62409 (two-disc set). [Op. 93.] G Aug. 1996 and Mar. 1997.

USA: Angel S 37284 (quad). Chicago Symphony Orchestra, André PREVIN. P Chicago 1 Feb. 1977. *Reissued:* HMV ASD 3440 (quad). G Mar. 1978 ~ EMI Forte Compact Discs CZS5 72658-2 (two-disc set, stereo). [Op. 47; and Britten.] I June 1998.

Italy: Cin Cin Compact Disc CCCD 1021. Vienna Philharmonic Orchestra, Gennadi ROZHDESTVENSKY. P Vienna concert 16 Apr. 1978, I 1994.

Decca SXL 6927. London Philharmonic Orchestra, Bernard HAITINK. P Jan. 1979, G Nov. 1979. *Reissued:* USA: London 7160 ~ Decca Compact Disc 421 348-2DH. I Dec. 1988, G Mar. 1989 ~ Decca Ovation Compact Disc 425 065-2DM. I Aug. 1993, G Nov. 1993 ~ London Compact Disc 444 433-2. [Third disc in eleven-disc set.] I June 1995.

USA: Russian Disc Compact Disc RDCD 11 190. Bolshoi Theatre Orchestra, Gennadi ROZHDESTVENSKY. P Moscow concert 28 Mar. 1981, I Sept. 1993, G Jan. 1994.

USSR: Melodiya A10 00319 000 (3 sides, digital). USSR Ministry of Culture Symphony Orchestra, Gennadi ROZHDESTVENSKY. ['My work on Symphony No. 4'—talk by Rozhdestvensky, recorded in 1986, with variant passages illustrated on piano and full orchestra, including the opening 6' 20" of the symphony as autograph reproduced in *Collected Works* Volume 2 and the following pages.] P 1985, I 1988*d*. NB. An English translation of Rozhdestvenky's talk, read by Dr John Stratford, is available on a DSCH Society cassette dated Dec. 1990. [Gubaidulina.] *Reissued:* Germany: Melodia Eurodisc 258 485-218 ~ Olympia Compact

Disc OCD 156. [Sans op. E.] I Sept. 1988, C May 1989 ~ Germany: Melodia Eurodisc Compact Disc 258485 ~ Olympia Compact Disc OCD 5005. [In Vol. 1 six-disc set of symphonies with Sans op. E.] I Dec. 1990 ~ France: Praga Compact Disc PR 250 090. [Op. 17.] I Dec. 1995 ~ BMG Melodiya Compact Discs 74321 63462-2 (two-disc set). [Opp. 23; 14, 20, and 23.] I Mar. 1999 ~ France: Le Chant du Monde Compact Disc PR 7250 090. [Op. 17.] P with added audience noise and not Czech Radio concert 28 May 1985, G Feb. 2001.

Japan: Fontec Compact Disc FOCD 3247. New Symphony Orchestra (of Japan), Yasushi AKUTAGAWA. ['Orchestra Works of USSR and China'— Hann-Zhi Li and Zu-Qiang Wu.] P Shinjuku concert 20 July 1986.

Naxos Compact Disc 8.550625. Czecho-Slovak Radio Symphony Orchestra, Ladislav SLOVÁK. P Bratislava 2 May–1 June 1988, I Oct. 1993, G Nov. 1993. *Reissued:* Naxos Compact Discs 8.505017. [In five-disc set with Symphonies Nos. 1, 2, 3, 6, 7, 12, and 15.] I 1993.

Italy: Nuova Era Compact Disc 6734. European Community Youth Orchestra, James JUDD. P Bolzano concert 18 Aug. 1988.

Decca Compact Disc 425 693-2DH. Royal Philharmonic Orchestra, Vladimir ASHKENAZY. P Walthamstow Jan. 1989, I and G Dec. 1989.

Chandos ABRD 1328 (digital) and Compact Disc CHAN 8640. Scottish National Orchestra, Neeme JÄRVI. P Glasgow 5–9 Feb. 1989, I Sept. 1989, G Dec. 1989.

RCA Victor Red Seal Compact Disc RD 60887. Saint Louis Symphony Orchestra, Leonard SLATKIN. P Saint Louis 3 Oct. 1989, I Apr. 1992, G June 1992.

Denon Compact Disc CO 75330. Vienna Symphony Orchestra, Eliahu INBAL. P Vienna 20–4 Jan. 1992, I June 1993, G July 1993.

Teldec Compact Disc 9031 76261-2. National Symphony Orchestra of Washington, Mstislav ROSTROPOVICH. P Washington 8 and 10 Feb. 1992, I Oct. 1992, G Nov. 1992. *Reissued:* Teldec Compact Discs 0630-17046-2. [In twelve-disc set of Symphonies.] G Oct. 1997 ~ Ultima Compact Discs 8573 87799-2 (two-disc set). [Op. 65.] I Apr. 2001, G Sept. 2001.

Germany: Ars Musici Compact Disc AMP 5011-2. German National Youth Orchestra, Rudolf BARSHAI. P Stuttgart concert 15 Aug. 1992, I May 1995.

EMI Classics Compact Disc CDC5 55476. City of Birmingham Symphony Orchestra, Simon RATTLE. [Britten.] P Birmingham 23–4 July 1994, I Sept. 1995, G Nov. 1995.

Belgium: Cyprès Compact Disc CYP 2618. Belgian National Orchestra, Yuri SIMONOV. P Brussels concert 16 Feb. 1996, I June 1997, G Mar. 1998.

Switzerland: Musikszene Schweiz Compact Disc MGB CD 6149. Swiss Philharmonic Orchestra, Mario VENZAGO. P Zürich concert 20 Sept. 1997.

Czech: Supraphon Compact Disc SU 3353-2. Prague Symphony Orchestra, Maksim SHOSTAKOVICH. P Prague concert 3 and 4 Feb. 1998, I and G Jan. 1999.

References: Khubov, Orlov (in Danilevich 1967), Ottaway, Sabinina, and Souster.

Opus 44 Salute to Spain

Form: Incidental music to the play *Salute to Spain* by Aleksandr Afinogenov:

1–3. Fanfares—three flourishes
4. The Song of Rosita (lyric by Afinogenov)—Moderato
5. Funeral March—Andante
6. [Fragment]—Andante
7. March—Allegro non troppo

Instrumentation: 2 flutes, 2 oboes, 2 B flat clarinets, 2 bassoons ~ 4 horns, 4 trumpets, 3 trombones, tuba ~ timpani, side drum, cymbals ~ glocken-spiel ~ strings.

Composed: Commenced on 26 October 1936 and completed in 12 days, at Leningrad.

Première: 23 November 1936, Pushkin Theatre of Drama, Leningrad; designs by A. Akimov, and produced by Sergei Radlov and Nikolai Petrov.

Arrangements: Reduction of the two Marches for piano and reconstruction of 'The Song of Rosita' by Lev Solin. Piano reduction of Three Fanfares and [Fragment] by V. Samarin, and the two Marches by Konstantin Titarenko.

Music: Neither piano nor full scores, apart from 'The Song of Rosita', have been discovered. Score reconstructed from orchestral parts preserved at the Pushkin Theatre's Music Department. A page of an autograph of 'The Song of Rosita' with piano accompaniment, written for the composer's sister Zoya on 24 August 1939, is reproduced on page 166 of Khentova (1980). This is in the key of F sharp minor whereas in the parts it is in B minor.

Sovetskii Kompozitor, No. 4028 (in *Dmitri Shostakovich: Music to Plays*), 1977, March and Funeral March arr. for piano by L. Solin, 29 cm.

Sovetskii Kompozitor, No. 4235 (in *Dmitri Shostakovich: Songs from Plays*), 1977, 'The Song of Rosita' with piano accompaniment, 29 cm.

Muzyka, No. 11412 (in Volume 28 of *Collected Works* with Opp. 19, 24, 28, 31, 32, 37, 58a, 63, 66, 72, and in the supplement, Sans opp. D and K), 1986, piano reductions of seven pieces by V. Samarin, the composer, and K. Titarenko, 30 cm.

Muzyka, No. 11413 (in Volume 27 of *Collected Works* with Opp. 19, 24, 28, 32, 37, 58a, 63, 66, and 72), 1987, seven pieces in full score, 30 cm.

Recording: Chandos Compact Disc CHAN 9907. March and Funeral March arr. L. Solin. Rustem HAYROUDINOFF (piano). ['Theatre Music'—Opp. 37, 19, 31, 32, 58*a*, 66, and 22.] P Potton Hall, Suffolk 7–8 Aug. 2000, I Apr. 2001.

Opus 45   The Return of Maxim

Form: Music for the second film in the 'Maxim Trilogy', *The Return of Maxim*, directed by Grigori Kozintsev and Leonid Trauberg for Lenfilm. The revolutionary songs 'Warsaw March' ('Varshavyanka'), 'Boldly, Comrades, on we March', and 'Renunciation of the Old World' are introduced. The items of the score are numbered from 1 to 17 with extra isolated numbers 20, 30, and 31.

—. Introduction
1. 'A Blue Balloon' (popular song of the 1910s)
2. 'Fourteenth year—running!' (bayan)—Allegro
3. March—Marciale maestoso
4. 'Fascinating Eyes'—Tempo di valse (numbered 31 in autograph score)
5. Allegro con brio
6. Waltz—Allegro molto (numbered 9 in autograph)
7. Polka—Allegro
8. Allegretto
9. Waltz (numbered 30 in autograph)
10. Waltz—Allegro (also numbered 6*a*)
11. Assault—Allegro (con brio)
12.
13. Moderato (bayan)
14.
15. Demonstration—Allegro
16. Funeral March—Maestoso
17. Finale of the film—Allegretto
20. Moderato con moto

Instrumentation: piccolo, 2 flutes, 2 oboes, E flat clarinet, 2 B flat clarinets, 2 bassoons ~ 4 horns, 3 trumpets, 3 trombones, tuba ~ timpani, side drum, cymbals, bass drum ~ xylophone, glockenspiel, harp ~ strings. Certain numbers of the film score call for additional instruments: extra woodwind, celesta, and piano; a separate band of 2 cornets, 2 trumpets and 8 saxhorns (two each of alto, tenor, baritone, and bass); a folk-instrument orchestra of 7 domras, 6 balalaikas, and a bayan; solo voice with bayan (No. 1), guitar (No. 4), and male choir/bayan accompaniment (No. 17).

Composed: December 1936–7.

Première: Film first shown on 23 May 1937. Score conducted by Nikolai Rabinovich.

Arrangements: The Waltz, marked 'Allegro sostenuto', appears as the third item in *Four Waltzes,* Sans op. P; also transcribed for violin duet and piano by Konstantin Fortunatov. Nos. 6 and 11 were later used in *Song of the Great Rivers,* Opus 95.

Music: Thirteen numbers of the autograph full score, including an incomplete 'Fight at the Barricades', are preserved in the Glinka Museum. Full and piano scores, compiled by Vladimir Vasiliev for a restoration of the film in 1965 (with the first page of the former signed by the composer on 6 December 1965), are preserved in the Music Library of the USSR Cinematograph Symphony Orchestra.

    Sovetskii Kompozitor, No. 928 (in *Dmitri Shostakovich: Waltzes from Film Scores*), 1959, the Waltz in full score, 29 cm.

    Boosey & Hawkes, 1960, Waltz [No. 1] arr. Cyril Watters, piano conductor and 23 parts, 30 cm.

    Muzyka, No. 4719 (in *D. Shostakovich: Pieces for violin and piano*), 1975, the Waltz arr. K. Fortunatov, 28.5 cm.

Duration: Film: 95 minutes. Waltz: 3' 10".

Recording: Germany: Capriccio Compact Disc 10 561. Waltz in Suite Op. 50*a.* Berlin Radio Symphony Orchestra, Mikhail YUROVSKY. [Opp. 30, 41 (i), and 50.] P 28–9 Apr. 1994, I Oct. 1995, G Jan. 1996.

    CIS: Manchester Compact Disc CDMAN 129. Waltz. St Petersburg Philharmonic Academic Symphony Orchestra, Vladimir ALTSHULER. ['Shostakovich Theatre and Cinema Music'—Opp. 32*a,* 58*a,* 30, 78, 76, 97, 99, and 37.] P St Petersburg 1995, I 1998.

    USA: Citadel Compact Disc CTD 88135. Waltz in Suite Op. 50*a.* Belarus Radio and TV Symphony Orchestra, Walter MNATSAKANOV. [Opp. 50*a,* 85, and 76.] P Moscow 7 Apr. 1997, I 1999.

Note: See Opus 50*a* for Suite and Sans op. P for the Waltz (No. 3 of both the *Four Waltzes* and *Three Violin Duets*).

Opus 46   Four Romances on Poems by Pushkin

Form: Four songs to verses by Aleksandr Pushkin, of a planned cycle of twelve for bass voice and piano accompaniment:

1. Renaissance—Moderato
2. A jealous maiden, sobbing bitterly—Allegretto
3. Presentiment—Allegro
4. Stanzas—Adagio

Composed: December 1936–2 January 1937 in commemoration of the 100th anniversary of the poet's death. The cycle was begun on 1 August 1936 with the poem 'Devils', set for high voice, though this romance was not included in Opus 46.

Premières: 8 December 1940, Polytechnic Museum Hall, Moscow; Aleksandr Baturin (bass) and Dmitri Shostakovich (piano).

UK: 19 March 1986, Queen Elizabeth Hall, London; John Shirley-Quirk (baritone), David White (clarinet), Frances Kelly (harp), Alexander Balanescu and Elisabeth Perry (violins), Simon Rowland-Jones (viola), Elizabeth Wilson (cello), and Chi-Chi Nwanoku (double-bass).

Arrangements: Opus 46a—accompaniment of Nos. 1, 2, and 3 arranged for harp and string orchestra, with clarinet in No. 3, by the composer in 1937. Cycle orchestrated by Gennadi Rozhdestvensky in 1982 and adapted for single strings, with No. 4 arranged for bass clarinet, harp, and string quintet, by Gerard McBurney. Translations of the poems in English by G. McBurney and Joan Pemberton Smith; and German by Christoph Hellmundt.

Music: Autograph scores of Opp. 46 and 46a preserved at the Glinka Museum. The first page of the autograph of Opus 46 is reproduced in Volume 32 of *Collected Works.*

Music Fund of the USSR, 1943 and 1945.

Sovetskii Kompozitor, No. 1790 (in *Romances on verses of Pushkin*), 1960, 29 cm.

Edition Peters, No. 4793 (with Op. 91), 1967, with German and Russian texts—the former by C. Hellmundt, 27 cm.

Muzyka, No. 4116 (in *Dmitri Shostakovich: Vocal Compositions*), 1967 and 1974, 30 cm.

Muzyka, Leningrad, No. 1996 (in *Romances on verses of Pushkin*), 1976, No. 1 only, 28.5 cm.

Muzyka, No. 10113 (in Volume 31 of *Collected Works* with Opp. 4, 21, 140, 79a, 143a, and 145a), 1982, full score, 30 cm.

Muzyka, No. 10283 (in Volume 32 of *Collected Works* with Opp. 4, 21, 62, 79, 84, 86, 91, 98, 100 *et al.*), 1982, 30 cm.

Duration: Approx. 12 minutes in score; 8' 10"–14' 00".

Recordings: USSR: Melodiya D 022363-4 (mono). Askold BESEDIN (baritone) and Lyubov Yedlina (piano). [Op. 91; Peiko and Baltin.] P 1968.

Czech: Panton 11 0420G. Nos. 1 and 2 only. Jaromír VAVRUŠKA (bass) and Jiří Pokorný (piano). [Opp. 138 and 91 Nos. 2 and 4; and Boris Chaikovsky.] P Prague 1973.

USSR: Melodiya C10 05567-8. Nos. 1, 3, 2, and 4. Sergei YAKOVENKO (baritone) and Mariya Grinberg (piano). [Musorgsky and Sviridov.] P 1975. *Reissued:* USSR: Melodiya C10 10617-8. [In third box of Part 3 of *Collected Works on Records* with Opp. 21 and 91 Nos. 2 and 4.] I 1978.

USSR: Melodiya A10 00043 004 (digital). orchestrated by G. Rozhdestvensky. Anatoli SAFIULIN (bass), USSR Ministry of Culture Symphony Orchestra, Gennadi Rozhdestvensky. [Opp. 91 and 34.] P 1983, I 1984c. *Reissued:* Olympia Compact Disc OCD 008. ['The Shostakovich

CD'—Op. 5 and seventeen further tracks from Opp. 7, 10, 19, 32, 35, 37, 58*a,* 59, 70, 93, 100, 109, 113, 135, 141, and Sans op. E not cross-referenced in this catalogue.] I Oct. 1989 ~ BMG Melodiya Compact Discs 74321 59057-2 (two-disc set). [Op. 135, 21 / 141, 621, and Sans op. M.] I Feb. 1999.

Deutsche Grammophon Compact Disc 439 860-2GH. Opus 46*a* Nos. 1–3. Sergei LEIFERKUS (bass), Gothenburg Symphony Orchestra, Neeme Järvi. ['The Orchestral Songs, Vol. 1'—Opp. 4, 140, and 79*a*.] P Gothenburg May 1993, I June 1994.

United Compact Disc 88001. Opus 46*a* Nos. 1–4 (No. 4 orchestrated by G. McBurney). Dmitri KHARITONOV (bass), City of Birmingham Symphony Orchestra, Mark Elder. [Opp. 31*a,* 42; and Sans op. E.] P Birmingham 16–18 Dec. 1992, I Nov. 1993, G Jan. 1994. *Reissued:* Classic CD 45. No. 1 only. [Ravel, Chopin, Brahms *et al.*] I Jan. 1994.

Germany: Capriccio Compact Disc 10 777. Opus 46*a*. Anatoli BABIKIN (bass), Cologne Radio Symphony Orchestra, Mikhail Yurovsky. [Opp. 145*a* and 21*a*.] P Cologne 17–19 June 1994, I 1998.

France: Le Chant du Monde Russian Season Compact Disc RUS 288089. Nos. 1–4. Pyotr GLUBOKY (bass) and Nataliya Rassudova (piano). [Opp. 62, 91, 121, and 146.] P Moscow Conservatory 21–9 Sept. 1994, I Apr. 1995.

Sweden: Bluebell Compact Disc ABCD 077. No. 2 only. Nicola GEDDA (tenor) and Eva Pataki (piano). [24 Pushkin Songs.] P Stockholm 18–22 Nov. 1987.

Beulah Compact Discs 1-2RF5 (two-disc set) No. 2 only. Helen LAWRENCE (mezzo-soprano) and Julian Rolton (piano). [Op. 91; operatic recital and Pushkin Songs.] P BBC Studio, London 17–18 May 1999, I Dec. 2000.

Reference: Vasina-Grossman (in Daragan).

Note: The title of No. 1 also translated as 'Resurrection', 'Regeneration' and 'Rebirth'; No. 2 appears in some Pushkin anthologies as 'To a youth' or 'Bitterly sobbing', and even 'A youth bitterly sobbing' though it is the maiden who is crying; No. 3, as 'Premonition'; while No. 4 is an untitled verse.

Opus 47   Symphony No. 5 in D minor

Subtitle: 'A Soviet artist's practical creative reply to justified criticism (an unknown musicologist's designation accepted by the composer. *Vechernyaya Moskva* (Moscow evening paper), 25 January 1938). Often dubbed the 'Hamlet Symphony' in Russian monographs (see Notes).

Form: Symphony for full orchestra (with 2 harps and a piano) in four movements:

1. Moderato
2. Allegretto (Scherzo)

3. Largo
4. Allegro non troppo

Instrumentation: piccolo, 2 flutes, 2 oboes, E flat clarinet, 2 clarinets (A and B flat), 2 bassoons, contrabassoon ~ 4 horns, 3 trumpets, 3 trombones, tuba ~ timpani, triangle, side drum, cymbals, bass drum, gong ~ glockenspiel, xylophone, celesta, 2 harps, piano ~ strings. Harps always a2, piano tacet in second movement, all brass tacet and strings divided into 8 parts in third movement.

Composed: 18 April–20 July 1937, at Leningrad. The Largo written in three days.

Premières: Early autumn 1937, Leningrad Union of Composers, Dmitri Shostakovich and Nikita Bogoslovsky (piano duet).

21 November 1937, in celebration of the twentieth anniversary of the October Revolution, Leningrad Philharmonic Bolshoi Hall; Leningrad Philharmonic Orchestra, Yevgeni Mravinsky.

29 January 1938, Moscow Conservatory Bolshoi Hall; USSR State Symphony Orchestra, Aleksandr Gauk.

USA broadcast: 9 April 1938, NBC Symphony Orchestra, Artur Rodzinski.

France: 14 June 1938, Pleyel Hall, Paris; Roger Désormière (conductor).

UK: 13 April 1940, Queen's Hall, London; Alan Bush (conductor).

USA piano reduction of Scherzo: 27 March 1949, Madison Square Gardens, New York; the composer before an audience of 30,000 on the final day of the Cultural and Scientific Congress for World Peace.

Arrangements: Whole symphony arranged for piano four hands by Lev Atovmyan and two pianos four hands by Pavel Lamm (the latter not published). The Scherzo in piano reductions by the composer and Frederick Block, and transcribed for band in two versions by Joseph Paulson and Roger Smith. The fourth movement transcribed for military band by Charles B. Righter and whole symphony for wind orchestra by Yasuhide Ito.

Music: Manuscript lost [by Aleksandr Gauk according to Volkov]. A few pages of sketches in piano score for the third and fourth movements are preserved at the CIS Archives of Literature and Art. A page of the third movement autograph piano score is reproduced in Volume 3 of *Collected Works*.

Muzgiz, No. 16313, 1939, 30 cm.; and with the same plate no., Edition Musicus, New York, no date, 23 cm.

Muzgiz, No. 25550, 1956, foreword by Ivan Martynov; also 1947 and 1961; 1963, parts, 30 cm.

Edward B. Marks, New York, No. 11667, c.1942, Scherzo reduction for piano by the composer, ed. F. Block, 30.5 cm.

Boosey & Hawkes, No. 628 (A.S.M.P. No. 81), c.1942, 19 cm.

Boosey & Hawkes Inc., No. 575, 1944, 26 cm.

Edwin F. Kalmus, No. 165, *c*.1944, 24 cm.

Edwin F. Kalmus, No. A 2427, no date, 30.5 cm.

G. Schirmer, No. 40770, 1944, Scherzo arr. for band by R. Smith, parts, 31 cm.

Leeds Music, New York/Sovetskii Kompozitor, No. 1806, *c*.1945, score reproduced from the Soviet edition, 23 cm.

Weaner-Levant, New York, 1945, Scherzo arr. for band by J. Paulson, score and 37 parts, 30.5 cm.

Boosey & Hawkes, No. 153, 1947, Finale arr. for military band by C. B. Righter, score, conductor's score and 34 parts, 31 cm.

Music Fund of the USSR, 1948, reduction for piano four hands by L. Atovmyan.

Edition Eulenberg, No. 579, 1967, score with foreword by Peter Otto Schneider, 19 cm.

Muzyka, No. 9245 (in Volume 3 of *Collected Works* with Op. 54), 1980, 30 cm.

Hans Sikorski, No. 2227, 1987, score, 21 cm.

Duration: Approx. 45 minutes in score; 40' 15"–53' 40"; 41' 30" (Aronowsky); 45' 50"–47' 25" (Plaistow); [38' 25"—Rodzinski with 37-bar cut, figs. 119–21, in Finale.]

Films: *Rollerball*. This film directed by Norman Jewison and released in 1975, includes excerpts from the Fifth and Eighth Symphonies, along with items by Bach, Albinoni, Tchaikovsky, and Previn. The film score, recorded by the London Symphony Orchestra under André Previn, was issued on United Artists UAS 29865 and reviewed in G Jan. 1976. The 'Theme from Rollerball'—the beginning of the Largo to bar 78 appears as the first item on Trax Classique TRXLP and Compact Disc 131.

A film of *Yevgeni Mravinsky* conducting the Fifth Symphony, performed by the Leningrad Philharmonic Orchestra at a Minsk concert on 20 November 1983, was issued in 1992 on a Japanese LaserDisc—Toshiba TOLW 3667 (colour, mono).

Sounds Magnificent—The Story of the Symphony. A television series written by Herbert Chappell and presented by André Previn with the final programme, shown on BBC2 TV on 17 November 1984, devoted to twentieth-century composers. Excerpts from the symphonies of Vaughan Williams and Roy Harris, and a complete performance of Shostakovich's Fifth performed by the Royal Philharmonic Orchestra. This programme available on videocassette: Nation Video, Home Vision, No. 8339041, and reissued in 1989 on Stylus Video SV 1406.

Rostropovich—Three Friends. A television documentary, produced by Peter Maniura, shown on BBC2 TV on 27 November 1988. Extracts of Rostropovich rehearsing the London Symphony Orchestra in the Largo and Finale of the Fifth Symphony for the 'Music from the Flames' series concert at the Barbican, London, on 15 November 1988. Also archive film of the UK première of the Cello Concerto No. 1 in the presence of the composer. The cellist talks of his personal friendship with Shostakovich, Prokofiev, and Britten.

Rostropovich Returns to Russia. Sony Laser Disc SLV 46387 and VHS Video SHV 46387. The Finale of the Fifth Symphony closing a compilation performed by the National Symphony Orchestra of Washington under Rostropovich in Moscow on 13 February 1990. [Op. 65 third movement; Prokofiev, Tchaikovsky, Dvořák *et al.*]

Recordings: USSR: 06820-33 (14 sides 78 rpm). Leningrad Philharmonic Orchestra, Yevgeni MRAVINSKY. P 27 Mar.–3 Apr. 1938. NB. Mravinsky's first commercial recording. *Reissued:* Japan: BMG Melodiya BOCC3 (bonus disc in four-disc set, mono). I 1998.

Japan: BMG Melodiya BVCX 8020 (in four-disc set, copied from optical soundtrack, mono). Leningrad Philharmonic Orchestra, Yevgeni MRAVINSKY. P Leningrad studio late 1938 to early 1939, I 1998.

USA: Victor 15737-42 in Set M 619 (12 sides 78 rpm). Philadelphia Orchestra, Leopold STOKOWSKI. P 20 Apr. 1939, I Jan 1940. *Reissued:* HMV DB 3991-6 (12 sides 78 rpm) and DB 8933-8 (12 sides 78 rpm automatic couplings). G Sept. 1942 ~ Pearl Compact Discs GEMM CDS 9044 (two-disc set, mono). [Op. 10, 60, and 34 No. 14.] I Nov. 1993, G Jan. 1994 ~ Dutton Laboratories Compact Disc CDAX 8017. [Op. 54.] I May 1996, G Dec. 1996.

USA: Columbia 11861-5D in Set M 520 (10 sides 78 rpm). Cleveland Orchestra, Artur RODZINSKI. P 22 Feb. 1942. NB. Figs. 119–21 cut in Finale. *Reissued:* USA: Columbia Entré RL 6625 (mono). I 1955 ~ USA: Columbia ML 4042 (mono) ~ USA: Columbia Special Products P 14128 (electronic stereo). I 1977 ~ France: LYS Compact Disc 139 (mono). ['L'Heritage d'Artur Rodzinski, Vol. 1'—Op. 10.] I Mar. 1997.

Italy: AS Compact Disc 631. New York Philharmonic Orchestra, Artur RODZINSKI. [Bloch and Schoenberg.] P concert 24 Feb. 1946, I 1991.

Italy: AS Compact Disc 571 (mono). Boston Symphony Orchestra, Serge KOUSSEVITZKY. ['Sergel Koussevitzky Edition'—Op. 70.] P concert 16 Mar. 1948, I 1990.

USA: Urania URLP 7098 (mono). Berlin Radio Symphony Orchestra, Ernest BORSAMSKY. P 1949. *Reissued:* France: Le Chant du Monde LDX-A 8002. ~ France: Dante Compact Discs 429-430 (two-disc set). [Stravinsky, Mahler, and Debussy.] I Mar. 1999.

USA: Pierian Sodality XTV 14450-1 (mono). Harvard-Radcliffe Orchestra, Russell STANGER. P concert 7 Dec. 1950. [Private recording with matrix numbers from the Columbia Records factory. Radcliffe College = women's college affiliated with Harvard University.]

VOX PL 7610 (mono). Vienna Symphony Orchestra, Jascha HORENSTEIN. P Apr. 1952, G May 1953. *Reissued:* VOX Compact Disc 7803 (mono). [Janáček.] I July 2000.

USA: Columbia ML 4739 (mono). New York Philharmonic Orchestra, Dimitri MITROPOULOS. P 1952, I 1953. *Reissued:* USA: Columbia Special

Products P 14185 (electronic stereo). I 1977 ~ Italy: Theorema Compact Disc TH 121.131. I Apr. 1993.

USA: Capitol P 8268 (mono). St Louis Symphony Orchestra, Vladimir GOLSCHMANN. P 15 Dec. 1953. *Reissued:* Capitol CTL 7077 (mono). G Jan. 1955 ~ USA: Pickwick 4016 (stereo) ~ USA: EMI Classics Compact Disc CDM5 66557 (mono). [Franck.] I 1997, G June 1998.

USSR: MK D 02283-4 (mono). Leningrad Philharmonic Orchestra, Yevgeni MRAVINSKY. P 3 Apr. 1954, I 1954. *Reissued:* USA: Vanguard VRS 6025 (mono). I 1956 ~ Japan: VDC Compact Disc 25004 (mono). [Skryabin.] I 1988 ~ BMG Classics Melodiya Compact Disc, Mravinsky Edition Vol. 15, 74321 29404-2 (mono). [Ovsyaniko-Kulikovky = Mikhail Emmanuilovic Goldstein.] P date incorrectly given as 2 Apr. 1954, I Apr. 1996.

Nixa WLP 20004 (mono). Royal Philharmonic Orchestra, Artur RODZINSKI. P 2–4 Oct. 1954, G Dec. 1955. *Reissued:* USA: Westminster XWN 18001 (mono). I 1955 ~ France: Westminster Vega 30 BVG 355-6 (mono) ~ Whitehall WH 20052 (mono). G May 1961 ~ MCA Millennium Classics Compact Disc MCD 80112 (mono). [Op. 10.] I Jan. 1995. NB. Previously the orchestra was given, pseudonymously, as the 'London Philharmonic Symphony Orchestra' as Sir Thomas Beecham would not allow it to record as the RPO.

Italy: Arkadia Compact Disc CDGI 765 1. Turin Symphony Orchestra, Sergiu CELIBIDACHE. [Op. 70.] P Turin 22 Feb. 1955, I 1993.

USA: Everest LPBR 6010 (mono) and SDBR 3010. Stadium Symphony Orchestra of New York, Leopold STOKOWSKI. P 1, 3, and 7–8 Oct. 1958, G June 1959. *Reissued:* World Record Club T 281 (mono) and ST 281 ~ Italy: Classici della Musica Classica SXEG 4093. I 1969 ~ Peerless Classics PC 08. [Issued under the pseudonyms 'Cleveland Festival Orchestra, Leopold Wise'.] I 1974? ~ USA: Philips Legendary Classics Compact Disc 422 306-2PLC. [Skryabin.] I June 1989 USA: Price-Less Compact Disc D 22697. [Prokofiev.] I 1989 ~ Everest Compact Disc EVC 9030. I May 1996. ~ Everest Black Disc LPZ 2016. I Feb. 1998.

Deutsche Grammophon LPM 18566 (mono) and SLPM 138031. Warsaw Philharmonic Orchestra, Witold ROWICKI. P Oct. 1958, G Jan 1960. *Reissued:* Deutsche Grammophon DGM 12020 (mono) and DGS 712020. I 1960 ~ Deutsche Grammophon Galleria Compact Disc 453 988-2GGA. [Tchaikovsky.] I Sept. 1997, G Oct. 1997.

USA: Columbia ML 5445 (mono) and MS 6115. New York Philharmonic Orchestra, Leonard BERNSTEIN. P Boston 20. Oct. 1959. *Reissued:* Philips ABL 3322 (mono) and SABL 164. G Dec. 1960 ~ CBS BRG 72172 (mono) and SBRG 72172. G Dec. 1966 ~ USA: CBS MY 37218. I 1981 ~ USSR: Melodiya C10 18401-2. I 1982 ~ CBS Masterworks Compact Disc CD 44711. [Op. 70.] I Aug. 1988, G Mar. 1989 ~ Sony Royal Edition Compact Disc SMK 47615. [Op. 70.] G Nov. 1993 and June 1994 ~ Sony Classical Compact Discs SX4K 64206 (four-disc set). [Op. 70.] I Dec. 1995 ~ Sony Classical Compact Disc SMK 60694. [Op. 70.] I Sept. 1999.

USA: Victor LM 2261 (mono) and LSC 2261. National Symphony Orchestra of America, Howard MITCHELL. P 1959. *Reissued:* RCA Victrola VIC 1280 (mono) and VICS 1280. G Oct. 1967 ~ France: RCA Choc 400 310 (mono) ~ Camden Classics/Pickwick CCV 5045. I 1976.

Germany: Ode Classics Compact Disc ODCL 1004-2. Hamburg NDR Symphony Orchestra, Takashi ASAHINA. P Hamburg Jan. 1960, I June 1998.

HMV ALP 1886 (mono) and ASD 445. Vienna Philharmonic Orchestra, Constantin SILVESTRI. P 10 and 12–14 Dec. 1960, G Sept. 1972. *Reissued:* USA: Angel 35760 (mono) and S 35760. I 1962 ~ Italy: Voce del Padrone QALP 10349 (mono) and ASDQ 5320. I 1963 ~ World Record Club T 981 (mono) and ST 981. G Aug. 1969.

USA: Mercury SR 90060. Minneapolis Symphony Orchestra, Stanislaw SKROWACZEWSKI. P 25 Mar. 1961, I 1962. *Reissued:* Mercury MMA 11178 (mono) and AMS 16128. G Feb. 1963 ~ France: Philips 6538 019. I 1963 ~ USA: Philips PHC 9081. I 1967 ~ USA: Mercury Living Presence Compact Disc 434 323-2MM. [Khachaturyan.] G Aug. 1993.

Switzerland: Preludio Compact Disc PRL 2156. Czech Philharmonic Orchestra, Leopold STOKOWSKI. [Lutoslawski.] P Prague Spring concert 1961, I 1991.

[Finland: Finnish Radio tape. Leningrad Philharmonic Orchestra, Yevgeni MRAVINSKY. P Helsinki concert 12 June 1961.]

Czech: Supraphon SUA 10423 (mono) and SUA ST 50052 (also ST 50423). Czech Philharmonic Orchestra, Karel ANČERL. P Prague 11–14 Nov. 1961, G Jan. 1965. *Reissued:* Music for Pleasure SMFP 2114. G May 1969 ~ Germany: Eurodisc Supraphon 913160 ~ USA: Vanguard Supraphon SU 1. I 1974 ~ France Ariola 913160 ~ Japan: Supraphon Compact Disc 2 OCO-2816. [Tchaikovsky.] I 1990 ~ Czech: Supraphon Crystal Collection Compact Disc SUP 11 0676-2. [Op. 107.] I Feb. 1993, G Aug. 1993 ~ Czech: Supraphon Compact Disc 11 1951-2. [Op. 10.] I May 1994 ~ Japan: Denon Compact Disc COCO 78419. [Op. 10.] I Mar. 1995.

France: Praga Compact Discs PR 254 002-3 (two-disc set). Czech Philharmonic Orchestra, Karel ANČERL. [Opp. 60 and 70.] P Prague broadcast 1961, I June 1992, G May 1993.

Decca LXT 6018 (mono) and SXL 6018. L'Orchestre de la Suisse Romande, István Kertész. P Geneva 13–14 May 1962, G Dec. 1962. *Reissued:* USA: London CS 6327. I 1962 ~ Decca Ace of Diamonds ADD 179 (mono) and SDD 179. G Sept. 1968 ~ Decca Eclipse ECS 767. G July 1975 ~ Contour CC 7593. I 1983 ~ USA: London STS 15492 ~ Polygram Compact Disc POCL 9439. [Op. 22.] I Oct. 1992.

USSR: Melodiya D 014657-8 (mono) and C 0909-10. Moscow Philharmonic Orchestra, Kirill KONDRASHIN. P 1964. *Reissued:* USA: Angel Melodiya S 40004 ~ Germany: Melodia Eurodisc 73 627 MK ~ Germany: Melodia Eurodisc 87623 XK. [In thirteen-record box set.] I 1974 ~ France: Le Chant du Monde LDX 78624. I 1978 ~ Italy: EMI 065 94481. I 1978 ~ Netherlands: Phonogram Melodia 364 503 ~ USA: Musical Heritage Society MHS 4165.

[In two-record set with Op. 93.] I 1980 ~ USSR: Melodiya C 0909-10. [In first box of Part I of *Collected Works on Records*.] I 1980 ~ HMV Melodiya EX 2903873 (DMM). [Fourth record in twelve-record box set.] G Dec. 1985 ~ France: Le Chant du Monde Compact Disc LDC 278 1003-4. [In Box 2 of five two-disc sets with Opp. 5 and 60.] G May 1989 ~ BMG Classics Melodiya Compact Disc 74321 19845-2. [Op. 20.] I July 1994, G Nov. 1994.

USA: Columbia MS 7279. Philadelphia Orchestra, Eugene ORMANDY. P 1964, I 1969. *Reissued:* CBS SBRG 72811. G June 1970 ~ CBS Classics 61643. G July 1975 ~ Sony Essential Classics Compact Disc SBK 53261. [Op. 22*a*; and Prokofiev.] I Jan. 1994, G July 1994.

Japan: King Record Seven Seas Compact Disc KICC 2076. London Symphony Orchestra, Leopold STOKOWSKI. P Proms concert 17 Sept. 1964, I Sept. 1990. *Reissued:* USA: Music & Arts Compact Disc CD 765. [Musorgsky.] I 1993 ~ BBC Radio Classics Compact Disc 15656 91542. [Op. 10.] I Mar. 1996, G May 1996.

RCA Victor Red Seal RB 6651 (mono) and SB 6651. London Symphony Orchestra, André PREVIN. P 21 and 23 Aug. 1965, G May 1966. *Reissued:* USA: RCA Victor LM 2866 (mono) and LSC 2866. I 1966 ~ RCA Gold Seal GL 42690. G Mar. 1979 ~ USA: Time-Life 'Great Men of Music' box set STL 568. [Opp. 22*a*, 114, 40, 102, 110, and 135.] I 1979 ~ RCA Gold Seal GL 84630 (digital). G Nov. 1986 ~ France: RCA Victor Papillon RC 330 ~ RCA Victor Papillon GL 86801 (digital) and Compact Disc CD 86801. [Rakhmaninov.] I July 1988 ~ RCA Classical Navigator Compact Disc 74321 24212-2. [Op. 116.] I June 1995. NB. The first coupling of the 'Hamlet Symphony' with the *Hamlet* film score ~ RCA Victor 'Basic 100' Compact Disc 09026 68456-2. I Apr. 1996.

USA: Russian Disc Compact Disc RDCD 10 910 (mono). Leningrad Philharmonic Orchestra, Yevgeni MRAVINSKY. [Op. 54.] P Moscow (not Leningrad) concert 24 Nov. 1965, I 1995.

USA: Russian Disc Compact Disc RDCD 11 023. Leningrad Philharmonic Orchestra, Yevgeni MRAVINSKY. [Salmanov.] P Leningrad concert 1966?, I Jan. 1994 ~ Germany: Audiophile Classics Compact Disc APL 101 503. [Myaskovsky.] I Feb. 1995. NB. This reissue is wrongly dated 1983; the duration of all four movements and the timing of audience coughs are identical to the 1965 performance. (K. Amoh).

Philips SAL 3629. London Symphony Orchestra, Witold ROWICKI. P 1967, G Feb. 1968. *Reissued:* France: Philips 6851 138 ~ Philips Compact Disc 446 571-2PM. [Op. 10.] I Sept. 1996.

Italy: Hunt Compact Discs 2 HUNTCD 714 (two-disc set, mono). Leningrad Philharmonic Orchestra, Yevgeni MRAVINSKY. [Mozart, Beethoven, Tchaikovsky, and Glinka.] P Prague Festival concert 26 May 1967 (not 1968), I 1990.

CBS-NEMS 6-64097. Third movement only. Vic Lewis Symphony Orchestra, Vic LEWIS. [Prokofiev, Mahler, and Lewis.] P Nov. 1969, G Oct. 1970.

USSR: Melodiya CM 02353-4. USSR Symphony Orchestra, Maksim SHOSTAKOVICH. P 1970. *Reissued:* HMV Melodiya ASD 2668. G May 1971 ~ USA: Angel Melodiya SR 40163. I 1972 ~ HMV SEOM 20. Second movement only. [Sampler of Russian works.] I Aug. 1975 ~ HMV Melodiya BOX 50253-4 in Set SLS 5025. [Opp 43, second and third movements, and 54.] G Dec. 1975 ~ RCA Gold Seal Compact Disc 74321 32041-2. [Opp. 22*a* and 78.] I Mar. 1996.

Italy: Intaglio Compact Disc INCD 7121. Leningrad Philharmonic Orchestra, Arvid YANSONS. [Tchaikovsky.] P Royal Albert Hall, London concert 13 Sept. 1971.

[Japan: NHK Radio tape broadcast 23 June 1973. Leningrad Philharmonic Orchestra, Yevgeni MRAVINSKY. P Tokyo Bunka-Kaikan Hall concert 26 May 1973 on Mravinsky's first visit to Japan.] Japan: Altus Compact Disc ALT 002. I 2000.

USA: Russian Disc Compact Disc RDCD 11 180 (mono). Leningrad Philharmonic Orchestra, Yevgeni MRAVINSKY. [Prokofiev.] P Leningrad concert 29 June 1973, I Aug. 1994, G July 1995.

Classics for Pleasure 40080. Royal Philharmonic Orchestra, Massimo FRECCIA. P Oct. 1973, G Sept. 1974.

[Japan: Tokyo private archive tape. Leningrad Philharmonic Orchestra, Yevgeni MRAVINSKY. P Tokyo concert 21 May 1975.]

HMV BOX 504401 In Set SLS 5044 (quad). Bournemouth Symphony Orchestra, Paavo BERGLUND. [Op. 93 in two-record box set.] P London 30–1 July 1975, G Mar. 1976. *Reissued:* HMV Greensleeve ESD 7029 (quad). G Feb. 1977 ~ Classics for Pleasure 40330. G June 1980 ~ USA: Angel S 37279 (quad) ~ EMI Eminence/Music for Pleasure EMX 2034. G Aug. 1983 ~ EMI Studio Compact Disc CDM7 63119-2. I Aug. 1989.

USA: RCA Red Seal ARD1 1149 (quad) and ARL1 1149 (stereo). Philadelphia Orchestra, Eugene ORMANDY. P Feb. 1975. *Reissued:* UK: ARL1 1149 (stereo only). G Aug. 1976—USA: RCA Gold Seal AGL1 3886. I 1981.

USSR: Melodiya C10 06515-6. All-Union Radio and Television Large Symphony Orchestra, Vladimir FEDOSEYEV. P 1975, I 1976c. *Reissued:* Deutsche Grammophon 2531 361. I 1975.

Czech: Opus 9110 0523. Slovák Philharmonic Orchestra, Ladislav SLOVÁK. P Sept. 1976, I 1977.

Charisma CAS 1128. Excerpts. London Philharmonic Orchestra, Joseph EGER. [Op. 141 excerpts.] P 1977, I Oct. 1977.

USA: Angel S 37285 (quad). Chicago Symphony Orchestra, André PREVIN. P 25 Jan. 1977. *Reissued:* HMV ASD 3443 (quad). G June 1978 ~ HMV Greensleeve ESD 2900541 (digitally remastered). G June 1984 ~ EMI Eminence Compact Disc CD-EMX 2163. I Aug. 1990, G Mar. 1991 ~ HMV Classics 33 Compact Disc 7 67637-2. [Opp. 102 and 5.] I Dec. 1992 ~ EMI Classics/BBC Music Compact Disc 7 67887-2. [Op. 102.] I

Oct. 1993 ~ EMI Forte Compact Discs CZS5 72658-2 (two-disc set). [Op. 43; and Britten.] I June 1998.

USSR: Melodiya C10 15321-2. Leningrad Philharmonic Orchestra, Yevgeni MRAVINSKY. P Vienna Festival concert 12 (not 13) June 1978, I 1981*d*. *Reissued:* HMV Melodiya ASD 4028 in Set SLS 5212. [Weber, Schubert, Brahms, and Tchaikovsky in four-record box set.] G Apr. 1981 ~ Japan: JVC Compact Disc VDC 1007. I 1985, G Jan. 1988 ~ France: Compact Disc PR 250 085. [Op. 70.] P venue and date given as Prague broadcast 26 May 1967, I Feb. 1995.

USSR: Melodiya C10 10303-4. USSR Symphony Orchestra, Yevgeni SVETLANOV. P 1978, I 1978*d*. *Reissued:* HMV Melodiya ASD 3855. [Op. 96.] G May 1980 ~ Germany: ZYX Russian Art Compact Discs CLA 10011-2 (two-disc set). [Opp. 70 and 60.] I 1998.

USA and UK: CBS Masterworks 35854 (digital). New York Philharmonic Orchestra, Leonard BERNSTEIN. P Tokyo concert 2–3 July 1979, G Dec. 1980. *Reissued:* CBS Compact Disc 35854. G May 1983 ~ CBS Maestro Compact Disc MYK 44770 ~ CBS Masterworks/Sony Classical Compact Disc MDK 44903. [Op. 107.] I Dec. 1989, G Apr. 1990 ~ Fame Music/Sony Compact Disc SBK 64117. [Op. 107.] I 1993 ~ Sony Digital Club Compact Disc SMK 66937. [Op. 107.] I Sept. 1995.

Japan: Victor SJX 9568. Osaka Philharmonic Orchestra, Takashi ASAHINA. P concert 16 Feb. 1981, I July 1982.

USA: Telarc TE 10067 (digital). Cleveland Orchestra, Lorin MAAZEL. P 5 Apr. 1981. *Reissued:* Telarc Compact Disc CD 80067. I Aug. 1983, G Aug. 1985 ~ Telarc Bravo Compact Disc CD 82001. [Stravinsky.] I Aug. 1993, G July 1994.

Decca SXDL 7551 (digital). Concertgebouw Orchestra, Bernard HAITINK. P Amsterdam 25–6 May 1981, G Dec. 1982. *Gramophone* Record Awards 1983—winner of Engineering and Production category, G Oct. 1983. *Reissued:* USA: London 71051 ~ Decca Compact Disc 410 017-2DH. G Sept. 1983 ~ Decca Ovation Compact Disc 425 066-2DM. [Op. 70.] I Aug. 1993, G Nov. 1993 ~ London Compact Disc 444 434-2. [On fourth disc of eleven-disc set with Op. 70.] I June 1995.

Revelation Compact Disc RV 10025. USSR Symphony Orchestra, Yuri TEMIRKANOV. [Prokofiev.] P concert 14 June 1981, I and G Oct. 1996.

France: Forlane UM 3567. Mexico Philharmonic Orchestra, Fernando LOZANO. P Jan. 1982.

Japan: Deutsche Schallplatten ET 5168. Berlin City Symphony Orchestra, Kurt SANDERLING. P East Berlin 19–22 Jan. 1982. *Reissued:* East Germany: Eterna 8 27 793. I 1984 ~ Germany: Berlin Classics Eterna Compact Disc BC 2063-2. I Mar. 1994, G July 1994.

Deutsche Grammophon 2532 076 (digital). National Symphony Orchestra of Washington, Mstislav ROSTROPOVICH. P July 1982, G June and Aug. 1983. *Reissued:* Deutsche Grammophon Compact Disc 410 509-

2GH. G Sept. 1983 ~ Deutsche Grammophon Classikon Compact Disc 439 481-2GCL. [Op. 126.] I June 1995, G Sept. 1995 ~ Deutsche Grammophon Masters Compact Disc 445 577-2GMA. [Prokofiev.] I Apr. 1996. Japan: Victor Musical Industries Compact Disc VDC 25026. Leningrad Philharmonic Orchestra, Yevgeni MRAVINSKY. P Leningrad concert 4 Apr. 1984, I 1989. *Reissued:* France: Erato Compact Disc 2292 45752-2. I Apr. 1992, G June 1992. [NB. Also available in 12-disc set 2292 45763-2.] ~ Japan: Icone Compact Disc ICN 9407-2. I Aug. 1994 ~ Leningrad Masters Compact Disc LM 1311. G Sept. 1996.

USSR: Melodiya AI0 00103 009 (digital). USSR Ministry of Culture Symphony Orchestra, Gennadi ROZHDESTVENSKY. P 1984, I 1985*d*. *Reissued:* Japan: Victor Compact Disc JVC 1012 ~ Olympia Compact Disc OCD 001. Second movement only. ['The Best of Melodiya on Olympia' sampler—Op. 112.] ~ Olympia Compact Disc OCD 113. [Op. 70.] I June 1987, G May 1989 ~ Germany: Melodia Eurodisc Compact Disc 353 118. [In two-disc set with Op. 60.] ~ Olympia Compact Disc OCD 5005. [In Vol. 1 six-disc set of symphonies with Op. 70.] I Dec. 1990 ~ BMG Melodiya Compact Discs 74321 49611-2 (two-disc set). [Opp. 10, 54, and 70.] I Dec. 1997.

RCA Red Seal RL 85608 (digital) and Compact Disc RD 85608. Saint Louis Symphony Orchestra, Leonard SLATKIN. P St Louis 23 Apr. 1986, G May 1987. *Reissued:* USA: RCA Compact Disc 5608-2RC.

Philips 420 069-1PH (digital) and Compact Disc 420 069-2PH. Berlin Philharmonic Orchestra, Semyon BYCHKOV. P 7–8 May 1986, G Mar. 1987 (and article p. 1244) and June 1987.

USSR: Melodiya C10 25185 005. Moscow Conservatory Students' Symphony Orchestra, Dmitri KITAYENKO. P Moscow Conservatory Bolshoi Hall concert 17 Nov. 1986, I 1988*a*. *Reissued:* USA: Russian Disc Compact Disc RDCD 11 188. [Op. 10.] I Sept. 1993, G Jan. 1994. NB. Orchestra given as Moscow Philharmonic and P date, 17 Nov. 1968.

Sweden: BIS Compact Disc CD 357. Stockholm Philharmonic Orchestra, Yuri ARANOVICH. P 27 Nov. 1986, I June 1987, G Jan. 1988.

Naxos Compact Disc 8.550632. Czecho-Slovak Radio Symphony Orchestra, Ladislav SLOVÁK. [Op. 70.] P Bratislava 12–18 Feb. 1987, I Oct. 1993, G Nov. 1993. *Reissued:* Naxos Compact Discs 8.506003. [In six-disc set with Symphonies Nos. 8, 9, 10, 11, 13, and 14.] I 1993 ~ Naxos Compact Discs 8.551172 and 8.556632. Fourth movement. ['Cinema Classics 12—*Rollerball'*—Mozart, Schubert, Beethoven *et al.*] I 1995 and 1998 respectively.

Decca 421 120-1DH (digital) and Compact Disc 421 120-2DH. Royal Philharmonic Orchestra, Vladimir ASHKENAZY. [Op. 42.] P Mar. 1987, G June 1988 and Apr. 1989. *Reissued:* Decca Compact Cassette 421 120-5DH. [Op. 42.] I 1993.

EMI EL 7491811 (digital) and Compact Disc CDC7 49181-2. Oslo Philharmonic Orchestra, Mariss JANSONS. P Oslo 2–5 June 1987, I Nov. 1987,

G Jan. and Mar. 1988. *Reissued:* USA: Angel DS 1-49181 (DMM) and Compact Disc 2-49181.

Chandos ABRD 1336 (digital) and Compact Disc CHAN 8650. Scottish National Orchestra, Neeme JÄRVI. [Op. 27*a*.] P Glasgow 22 Apr. 1988, I Feb. 1989, G Apr. 1990. *Reissued:* Conifer Classics Compact Disc Class 7090. [Op. 27*a*.] I Nov. 1991.

Denon Compact Disc CO 74175. Frankfurt Radio Symphony Orchestra, Eliahu INBAL. P Frankfurt 23–4 Nov. 1988, G Apr. 1990.

USA: MCA Classics Art & Electronics Compact Disc AED 10156. Bolshoi Theatre Orchestra, Mark ERMLER. P Moscow concert 1989, I 1990. *Reissued:* CIS: Russian Compact Disc RCD 13004. I 1995.

USA: Houston Symphony Orchestra Compact Disc—no number. Houston Symphony Orchestra, Christoph ESCHENBACH. P Houston 26–7 Feb. 1989.

France: Ex Libris Compact Disc CD 6101. Swiss Atelier (Workshop) Philharmonic Orchestra, Rudolf BARSHAI. P Zürich concert 16 June 1989. *Reissued:* Switzerland: MCB Musikszene Schweiz Compact Disc CD 6101. I Apr. 1995.

Teldec Compact Disc CD 80215. Atlanta Symphony Orchestra, Yoel LEVI. [Op. 70.] P Atlanta 5 May, 25–6 Sept., and 2 Dec. 1989; G June 1990.

Collins Classics Compact Disc 1108-2. London Symphony Orchestra, Maksim SHOSTAKOVICH. [Op. 96.] P 4–6 Jan. 1990, I May 1990, G Sept. 1990. *Reissued:* Collins Classics Compact Disc 70122. On three-disc set with Opp. 93, 96, 97, and 141.] I Sept. 1991.

Pickwick IMP Classics Compact Disc PCD 940. Hallé Orchestra, Stanislaw SKROWACZEWSKI. P Huddersfield 29–30 Jan. 1990, I Sept. 1990, G Aug. 1991. *Reissued:* Imp Compact Disc PCD 2018. I July 1995.

Academy Sound and Vision Compact Disc CD DCA 707. Royal Philharmonic Orchestra, Enrique BÁTIZ. [Opp. 115 and 131; Sans op. U.] P Morden 1990, I June 1990, G Sept. 1990. *Reissued:* IMG Records Compact Disc IMGCD 1609. [Opp. 115 and 131; Sans op. U.] I June 1994, G Feb. 1995.

Linn Compact Disc CKD 004. Leningrad Symphony Orchestra, Aleksandr DMITRIEV. P Glasgow concert 12 Apr. 1990, 1 Jan. 1992.

Naxos Compact Disc 8.550427. Belgian Radio Philharmonic Orchestra, Alexander RAHBARI. [Op. 70.] P Brussels 26–9 Sept. 1990, I Sept. 1991, G Mar. 1992. NB. Four reviews in *Classics* May 1992.

Denon Compact Disc CO 75719. Vienna Symphony Orchestra, Eliahu INBAL. [Op. 14.] P Vienna concert 26–9 Nov. 1990, I Apr. 1994, G Aug. 1994.

Japan: Victor Musical Industries Compact Disc VICC 74. Moscow Radio Symphony Orchestra, Vladimir FEDOSEYEV. P Moscow concert 18–19 Aug. 1991.

EMI Classics Compact Disc CDC7 54803-2. Philadelphia Orchestra, Riccardo MUTI. [Op. 96.] P Philadelphia 18–20 Apr. 1992, I June 1993, G

Dec. 1993. *Reissued:* USA: EMI Classics Compact Disc CDZ1 79887 (In nine-disc set). ['The Philadelphia Sound'—Op. 96; Berlioz, Prokofiev, Rakhmaninov *et al.*] I Nov. 1994.

Japan: Canyon Classics Compact Disc EC 3672-2. Russian Federation Symphony Orchestra, Yevgeni SVETLANOV. [Op. 96.] P Moscow 15–16 June 1992, I July 1994, G Oct. 1924.

Finland: Ondine Compact Disc ODE 817-2. Helsinki Philharmonic Orchestra, James DE PREIST. [Op. 110*a*.] P Järvenpää Dec. 1992, I May 1994, G Dec. 1994.

Decca Compact Disc 440 476-2DH. Vienna Philharmonic Orchestra, Sir Georg SOLTI. [Mendelssohn.] P Vienna concert 6–7 Feb. 1993, I Sept. 1994, G Oct. 1994.

Japan: Fun House Compact Disc FHCE 2014. Norrköping Symphony Orchestra, Junichi HIROKAMI. [Op. 131.] P Norrköping, Sweden Sept. 1993, I Jan. 1994.

Japan: JVC Victor Compact Disc VICC 163. St Petersburg Symphony Orchestra, Kazuhiko KOMATSU. P St Petersburg concert 12 Apr. 1994, I Mar. 1995.

Decca Compact Disc 448 122-2DH. Montreal Symphony Orchestra, Charles DUTOIT. [Op. 70.] P Montreal May 1994, I Sept. 1995, G Nov. 1995.

Germany: Musicaphon Compact Discs M 56953 (two-disc set). Minsk Philharmonic Orchestra, Pierre-Dominique PONNELLE. [Mahler.] P Minsk 1–7 June 1994, I Sept. 1995.

Germany: Deutsche Schallplatten Compact Disc DS 1035-2. Bohuslav Martinu Philharmonic Orchestra, Elbert Lechtman STEINBERG. [Op. 114*a*.] P Ziln, Czech June 1994, I Nov. 1995

Teldec Compact Disc 4509 94557-2. National Symphony Orchestra of Washington, Mstislav ROSTROPOVICH. P 4–5 June 1994, I Oct. 1995, G Nov. 1995. *Reissued:* Teldec Compact Discs 0630-17046-2. [In twelve-disc set of Symphonies.] G Oct. 1997.

Tring Compact Disc TRP 032. Royal Philharmonic Orchestra, Sir Charles MACKERRAS. [Op. 96.] P London July 1994, I May 1995, G Sept. 1995.

Carlton Classics Compact Disc 30366 0101-2. Boston Philharmonic Orchestra, Benjamin ZANDER. [Op. 107.] P Boston 11 Sept. 1994, I Oct. 1998, G Jan. 1999. *Reissued:* Carlton Classics Compact Discs 30366 01229 (five-disc box set). ['20th Anniversary Edition'—Op. 107; Beethoven, Mahler, Stravinsky, and Ravel.] I June 1999.

Japan: Alfa Music Compact Disc ALCB 3099. Japan Virtuoso Symphony Orchestra, Naoto OHTOMO. [Ravel.] P Tokyo concert 2 Nov. 1994.

Japan: Kosei Shuppan-Sha Compact Disc KOCD 3574. Arr. for wind orchestra by Y. Ito. Tokyo Kosei Wind Orchestra, Frederick FENNELL. [Myaskovsky.] P Tokyo concert 23–4 Mar. 1995, I Oct. 1995.

Japan: Canyon Classics Compact Disc PCCL 00292. Czech Philharmonic Orchestra, Kazushi ONO. [Op. 27.] P Prague 1–2 Apr. 1995, I Sept. 1995.

RCA Victor Red Seal Compact Disc 09026 68548-2. St Petersburg Philharmonic Orchestra, Yuri TEMIRKANOV. [Op. 70.] P 21 Sept. 1995, I Feb. 1997.

USA: Pope Music Compact Disc PM 1009-2 (silver) and PMG 2009-2 (gold). Russian Symphony Orchestra, Mark GORENSTEIN. ['Redemption'—Op. 110*a*.] P Moscow Jan. 1996.

USA: Amadis Compact Disc 7194. National Symphony Orchestra of Ukraine, Theodore KUCHAR. [Op. 77.] P Kiev 28–30 Apr. 1996, I 2000.

Classic FM Compact Disc 75605 57004-2. Yomiuri Nippon Symphony Orchestra, Tadaaki OTAKA. [Op. 21.] P Kamakura 3–6 June 1996, I Nov. 1997, G Jan. 1998.

Japan: Live Notes Compact Disc WWCC 7284. Nagoya Philharmonic Orchestra. Taijiro LIMORI. [Niimi.] P Tokyo 25 July 1996.

Czech: Supraphon Compact Disc SU 3327-2 031. Prague Symphony Orchestra, Maksim SHOSTAKOVICH. P Prague concert 13 Nov. 1996, I Nov. 1997, G Jan. 1998.

Sweden: BIS Compact Discs CD 973-4 (two-disc set). BBC National Orchestra of Wales, Mark WIGGLESWORTH. ['Complete Symphonies, Vol. 2'—Opp. 54 and 93.] P Swansea Dec. 1996, I June 1999, G Aug. 1999. NB. Symphony split between the two discs; the first movement on disc one.

EMI Compact Disc CDC5 56442-2. Vienna Philharmonic Orchestra, Mariss JANSONS. [Op. 110*a*.] P Vienna concert 7–14 Jan. 1997, I Oct. 1997, G Awards (Nov.) 1997.

Japan: Canyon Classics Compact Disc PCCL 00401. Moscow Radio Symphony Orchestra, Vladimir FEDOSEYEV. [Op. 54.] P Moscow Conservatory 3–5 Apr. 1997.

Germany: Antes Edition Compact Disc BM-CD 31.9112. Badische Staatskapelle, Kazushi ONO. [Matsuo.] P Kalsruhe concert 15–16 June 1997, I 1998.

Japan: Brain Compact Disc OSBR 14068. Fourth movement arr. C. B. Righter. Fukuoka Kodai High School Wind Orchestra, Isao YABIKU. ['27th Concert'—Bizet, Loewe, Sibelius *et al.*] P Fukuoka concert 9 Nov. 1997, I 1998.

USA: Delos Compact Disc DE 3246. Dallas Symphony Orchestra, Andrew LITTON. [Opp. 96 and 102.] P Dallas 19–20 May 1998.

USA: Well Tempered Productions Compact Disc WTP 5190. Russian National Orchestra, Vladimir SPIVAKOV. [Op. 70.] P Moscow concert 7 Mar. 2000, I 2001.

References: Barsova (in Bartlett), Boyden, McNaught, Mazel, Ottaway, Sabinina, Shaginyan, Souster, Taruskin (in Fanning 1995), and Tigranov.

Notes: A play, *An Informer's Duty,* by Greg Cullen was broadcast on BBC Radio 3, 4 December 1994. Set in Leningrad 1937, it covers the official attack on Shostakovich and the response to his desperate predicament, culminating in the composition of the Fifth Symphony. With Jonathan

Cullen as Shostakovich, Fiona Shaw as Anna Akhmatova, and John Shrapnel as Stalin.

There are several instances in Russian books and articles of the Fifth Symphony being 'dubbed the Hamlet Symphony'. Rabinovich probably started this, followed by Polyokova, Sabinina, and others so the composer would have known of this nickname. It appears, from Russian sources, in the *Soviet Weekly* obituary of 16 August 1975: 'Shostakovich was spurred on, not disheartened, by criticism [and] wrote his magnificent Fifth ('Hamlet') Symphony'.

Opus 48   Volochayevka Days

Alternative titles: *Intervention in the Far East* and *The Far Fast*. Appears translated as *Volochayev Days* and *Days of Volochayevsk* in some lists.

Form: Music for the film *Volochayevka Days* for Lenfilm with screenplay and direction by Georgi and Sergei Vasiliev (who worked together as 'The Vasiliev Brothers' though, in fact, they were unrelated). A song, 'To the Partisan' (or 'Blue Distances Where the Waves Lap'—words anon.), composed for the film used as a leitmotiv in the Overture, choral numbers, and Finale. The following material is extant:

1. Overture—Allegretto
2.
14. The Japanese Attack—Allegretto
16. [Fragment]—Allegro—Maestoso
    'Thro' the dales and o'er the hills'—The Song of the Far Eastern Partisans (I. Aturov, text by Pyotr Parfenov)—Moderato con moto
    Finale
45. (Variant of No. 14)
46.
    Russian Folksong   No. 1—Moderato
    No. 2—Largo

Instrumentation: piccolo, 2 flutes, 2 oboes, 2 B flat clarinets, 2 bassoons ~ 4 horns, 3 trumpets, 3 trombones, tuba ~ timpani, side drum, cymbals, bass drum ~ male chorus ~ strings

Composed: 1936–7, at Leningrad.

Première: Film first shown on 20 January 1938 and rereleased in March 1968. Score conducted by Nikolai Rabinovich.

Music: Incomplete autograph score preserved at the Glinka Museum.

Muzyka, No. 10179 (in Volume 34 of *Collected Works* with Opp. 88 and 136, and songs), 'To the Partisan' in reduction for male chorus and piano by Aleksandr Pirumov, 30 cm.

Muzyka, No. 10889 (in Volume 41 of *Collected Works* with Opp. 26, 30, 33, 41, 50, 53, 55, 56, 59, and 64), 1987, Nos. 1, 14, 16, and 'The Song of the Far Eastern Partisans' in full score and, in the supplement, two Russian Folksongs in piano arrangements, 30 cm.

Duration: Film: 112 minutes.

Recordings: —

Note: On its first recording the song 'Thro' the dales and o'er the hills' was attributed to Aleksandr V. Aleksandrov as arranger with text by S. Ya. Alymov. Subsequently, the writers were changed to composer I. Aturov and lyricist P. Parfenov. Anatoli Zhelezny (1989, pp. 140–52) argues that Aturov was not involved and Parfenov, composer of four other patriotic songs, probably wrote the melody of this song of the Far Eastern Partisans. See also Opus 74.

Sans op. F   The Internationale

Form: Orchestration for full symphony orchestra, augmented by cornet and 8 saxophones, of Pierre Degeyter's song adopted as the Soviet National Anthem between 1917 and 1944, commissioned in 1937. Text by Eugène Pottier in Russian translation of Arkadi Kots. The Russian lyric was revised by A. Gapov in 1932.

Instrumentation: 3 flutes, 3 oboes, 4 B flat clarinets, 3 bassoons ~ 4 horns, 3 trumpets, 3 trombones, tuba ~ additional band of E flat cornet and 2 each of soprano, tenor, baritone, and bass saxophones ~ timpani, triangle, tambourine, side drum, cymbals, bass drum ~ chimes ~ strings.

Performance: 4 October 1941, Novosibirsk; opening item of inaugural concert after arrival of Leningrad Philharmonic Orchestra and conductor Yevgeni Mravinsky for three-year stay in Siberia.

Music: Muzgiz, No. 693, 1937, 27 cm.

Recordings: —

Opus 49   Quartet No. 1 in C major

Subtitle: Originally entitled 'Springtime'.

Form: String quartet in four movements:

1. Moderato
2. Moderato
3. Allegro molto
4. Allegro

Composed: 30 May–17 July 1938, at Leningrad.

Premières: 10 October 1938, Leningrad; Glazunov Quartet (Ilya Lukashevsky, Aleksandr Pechnikov, Aleksandr Ryvkin, and David Mogilevsky).

16 November 1938, Moscow Conservatory Malyi Hall; Beethoven Quartet (Dmitri Tsyganov, Vasili Shirinsky, Vadim Borisovsky, and Sergei Shirinsky). Encored in its entirety. [Also performed publicly three weeks earlier.]

UK: 13 December 1941, Aeolian Hall, London; Hirsch Quartet (Leonard Hirsch—leader).

Arrangements: Reductions for pianoforte four hands by Yuri Nikolsky (not published) and Anatoli Dmitriev. First movement arranged for mandolin quartet.

Music: Manuscript lost. Autograph piano score, in which the fourth movement comes first and the first movement last, preserved at the CIS Archives of Literature and Art.

Muzgiz, Leningrad, No. 1054, 1939, score, 27 cm. and parts, 32 cm.

International Music, No. 514, 1942, parts, 30.5 cm.

International Music, No. 607, 1942, score, 18 cm.

Edition Musicus, no date, score, 28 cm. and parts, 31 cm.

Hans Sikorski, No. 2242, *c.*1957, parts, 31.5 cm.

Muzyka, 1966, parts, 29 cm.

Muzyka, Leningrad, No. 285 (in Volume I with Quartets 2–4 arr. for piano four hands by A. Dmitriev). 1965. 29.5 cm.

Edition Eulenberg, No. 385, 1968, score, 19 cm.

Edition Peters, No. 5751, 1974, parts, 30 cm.

Muzyka, No. 9816 (in Volume 35 of *Collected Works* Quartets 1–8), 1979, 30 cm.

Hans Sikorski, No. 2265 (with Opp. 68, 73, and 83), 1980, score, 21 cm.

Duration: 14–16 minutes in scores; 12' 48"–15' 06"; 14–15 minutes (Plaistow).

Recordings: USSR: 14736-43 (8 sides 10" 78 rpm). BEETHOVEN QUARTET (personnel as at at première). P 1947. *Reissued:* USSR: MK D 08019-20 (mono). [Opp. 108 and 110.] I 1961 ~ USA: Consonance Blue Label Compact Disc 81.3005 (mono). [Vol. 1—Opp. 68 and 83.] I May 1995.

USA: Columbia 71435-6D in Set X 231 (4 sides 12" 78 rpm). STUYVESANT QUARTET. P pre-1950.

USA: Royale 580-1 in Set 23 (4 sides 12" 78 rpm). YORK QUARTET. P pre-1950.

USA: MGM E 3113 (mono). GUILET QUARTET (Daniel Gullet—leader). [Prokofiev.] P *c.*1954.

Columbia 33 CX 1334 (mono). KOMITAS QUARTET (Avet Gabrielyan, Rafael Davidyan, Genrikh Talayan, Sergei Aslamazyan). [Borodin.] P London Dec. 1954, G Mar. 1956. *Reissued:* USA: Angel 35239 (mono). [Borodin.] I 1955 ~ USSR: MK D 3036-7 (10" mono). [Opp. 34 and 94.] I 1956 ~ USA: Vanguard VRS 6032 (mono). [Op. 57.] I 1958.

Japan: Triton Compact Disc MECC 26018 (mono) BEETHOVEN QUARTET (personnel as at première). [Opp. 92 and 67.] P Moscow Conservatory concert 1960, I 2000.

USSR: MK D 06219-20 (mono). LITHUANIAN STATE QUARTET (Eugeniyus Paulauskas, Korneliya Kalinauskayte, Yuri Fledzhinskas and ? Mikhail Shenderovas). [Haydn.] P 1960.

France: Harmonia Mundi HMO 34 709. BULGARE QUARTET (Dimon Dimov, Aleksandr Thomov, Dmitri Tchikov, Dmitri Kosev). [Borodin.] P St Maxime, Var 1964, I 1967

Leningrad Masters Compact Disc LM 1325. TANEYEV QUARTET (personnel not stated). [Opp. 73 and 83.] P concert 1966, G Sept. 1996.

France: Praga Compact Disc PR 254 042. TÁLICH QUARTET (Petr Messiereur, Jan Kvapil, Jan Tálich, Evžen Rattay). [Opp. 57 and 68.] P Czech Radio broadcast 1966, I May 1994.

USSR: Melodiya D 019277-8 (mono) and C 01447-8. BORODIN QUARTET (Rostislav Dubinsky, Yaroslav Aleksandrov, Dmitri Shebalin, Valentin Berlinsky). [Op. 73.] P and I 1967. *Reissued:* HMV Melodiya ASD 2464. [Tchaikovsky.] G Apr. 1969 ~ USA: Seraphim Melodiya S 6034. [In three-record box set with Quartets 2–5.] ~ HMV Melodiya HQS 1319 in Set SLS 879. [Op. 68.] G June 1974 ~ USSR: Melodiya CM 03059-60. [Op. 73.] I 1972.

Decca Ace of Diamonds SDD 453. GABRIELI QUARTET (Kenneth Sillito, Brendan O'Reilly, Ian Jewel, Keith Harvey). [Op. 73.] P Maltings, Snape Dec. 1973, G Apr. 1975. *Reissued:* USA: London STS 15396. [Op. 73.]

Amon-Ra SARB 01. Scherzo only. DARTINGTON QUARTET (Colin Sauer, Malcolm Latchem, Keith Lovell, Michael Evans). ['Quartet Cameos'— Schubert, Mozart, Tchaikovsky *et al.*] I 1975.

L'Oiseau-Lyre DSLO 31. FITZWILLIAM QUARTET (Christopher Rowland, Jonathan Sparey, Alan George, Ioan Davies). [Op. 68.] P 15–16 Dec. 1977, G Mar. 1979. *Reissued:* Decca 188 D1 in Set D 188 D7. [Op. 68.] G Feb. 1981 ~ Decca Enterprise Compact Discs 433 078-2DM6. [On first disc of six-disc set with Op. 68.] I Apr. 1992, G June 1992 ~ NB. The six-disc set was reissued Feb. 1998 on London Compact Discs 455 776-2LC6 and reviewed G Apr. 1998.

USSR: Melodiya 010 10241-2. TANEYEV QUARTET (Vladimir Ovcharek, Grigori Lasky, Vissarion Soloviev, Iosif Levinzon). [Opp. 108 and 110.] P 1978, I 1978*d. Reissued:* USSR: with same number in first box of Part 2 of *Collected Works on Records.* I 1980 ~ Japan: JVC Victor 5345. [Op. 68.] ~ USSR: Melodiya Compact Disc SUCD 11 00308. [Opp. 83 and 92.] I 1991*c.*

Czech: Supraphon 111 2484. TÁLICH QUARTET (Petr Messieureur, Jan Kyapil, Jan Tálich, Evžen Rattay). [Op. 57.] P Prague 22 Apr. 1978, G Jan. 1981.

USSR: Melodiya C10 11757-8. BORODIN QUARTET (Mikhail Kopelman, Andrei Abramenkov, Dmitri Shebalin, Valentin Berlinsky). [Op. 144.] P 1978, I 1979*d. Reissued:* HMV Melodiya EX 270339-3 (DMM). [In seven-record box set of 15 quartets plus Quintet.] G Mar. 1986 ~ EMI Compact

Disc CDC7 49266-2. [Opp. 117 and 133.] I Nov. 1987 ~ Japan: Victor Musical Industries Compact Disc VICC 40018. [Op. 68.] I 1990 ~ EMI Compact Discs CMS5 65032-2. [In six-disc set of 15 Quartets plus Quintet.] I Mar. 1994 ~ BMG Melodiya Compact Discs 74321 40711-2 (six-disc set). [Opp. 68 and 83.] I June 1997.

USSR: Melodiya C10 14087-8. VILNIUS QUARTET (Audrone Vainiunaite, Petras Kunca, Donatas Katkus, Augustinas Vasiliauskas). [Brahms.] P 1980, I 1981*a*.

Olympia Compact Disc OCD 531. SHOSTAKOVICH QUARTET (Andrei Shislov, Sergei Pishchugin, Aleksandr Galkovsky, Aleksandr Korchagin). ['Complete Quartets, Vol. 1'—Opp. 73 and 83; Sans op. D.] P 1981, I Apr. 1994, G Sept. 1994.

USA: Gasparo GS 223 (DMM). FINE ARTS QUARTET (Ralph Evans, Efim Boico, Jerry Horner, Wolfgang Laufer). [Dvořák and Turina.] P 1985.

Teldec Classics Compact Disc 2292 46009-2. BRODSKY QUARTET (Michael Thomas, Ian Belton, Paul Cassidy, Jacqueline Thomas). [Opp. 73 and 83.] P Berlin July 1989, I Apr. 1990, G June 1990. *Reissued:* Teldec Compact Discs 9031 71702-2. [On first disc of six-disc set with Op. 68.] I Nov. 1990, G June 1992.

USA: Windham Hill Records Compact Disc WD-1091. First movement only, arr. for mandolin quartet. MODERN MANDOLIN QUARTET (John Imholz, Dana Rath, Paul Binkley, Mike Marshall). ['Intermezzo'—Op. 22*a* Polka; Haydn, Ravel, Bernstein *et al*.] P Oct. 1989.

USA: ESS.A.Y. Compact Disc CD 1007. MANHATTAN QUARTET (Eric Lewis, Roy Lewis, John Dexter, Judith Glyde). [Opp. 68 and 73.] P Purchase, New York 27–8 Dec. 1989. *Reissued:* Koch Schwann Musica Mundi Compact Disc 310 128. ['Complete String Quartets, Vol. 1' with Opp. 68 and 73.] I May 1991.

Naxos Compact Disc 8.550973. ÉDER QUARTET (János Selmeczi, Péter Szüts, Sándor Papp, György Éder). ['Complete Quartets, Vol. 2'—Opp. 110 and 117.] P Budapest 14–17 Feb. 1994, I Nov. 1994, G Oct. 1995.

Sony Classical St Petersburg Classics Compact Disc SK 64584. ST PETERSBURG QUARTET (Alla Aranovskaya, Ilya Teplyakov, Andrei Dogadin, Leonid Shukayev). [Opp. 68 and 83.] P Apr. 1994.

Teldec Compact Disc 4509-98417-2. BORODIN QUARTET (personnel as on Melodiya C10 11757-8). [Op. 144.] P Berlin May 1995, I Nov. 1996, G Feb. 1997. *Reissued:* Ultima Compact Discs 8573 87820-2 (two-disc set). [Opp. 57, 67, and 144.] I Apr. 2001, G Aug. 2001.

Netherlands: Globe Compact Disc GLO 5157-0265. RUBIO QUARTET (Dirk Van de Velde, DirkVan den Hauwe, Marc Sonnaert, Peter Devos). ['Complete Quartets, Vol. 1'—Opp. 83 and 110.] P Utrecht Aug. 1996, I Nov. 1996.

Japan: EMI Classics Compact Disc TOCE 9496. MORGAŬA QUARTET (Eiji Arai, Takashi Aoki, Hisashi Ono, Ryoichi Fujimori). [Opp. 101, 122, and 97.] P 11–14 Mar. 1997.

Deutsche Grammophon Compact Disc 463 284-2GH5 (five-disc set). EMERSON QUARTET (Eugene Drucker, Philip Setzer, Lawrence Dutton, David Finkel). ['Complete Quartets, Vol. 1'—Opp. 68 and 73.] P Aspen, Colorado concert June–July 1999, G June 2000.

Sans op. G (i)   Suite for Jazz Orchestra No. 2

Alternative title: The Russian scores give the title *Suite for Variety Stage Orchestra*. See Notes.

Form: Suite of eight numbers for symphony orchestra (plus 4 saxophones, harp, 2 pianos, guitar, and accordion):

1. March—Merrily. Tempo di marcia
2. Dance I—Presto
3. Dance II—Allegretto scherzando
4. Little Polka—Allegretto
5. Lyric Waltz—Allegretto
8. Waltz I—In a restrained manner. Tempo di valse
7. Waltz II—Allegretto poco moderato
8. Finale—Allegro moderato

The March appears in a shortened and simplified form, scored for brass band only, in *The Adventures of Korzinka*, Opus 59; Dance I adapted from *The Gadfly*, Opus 97 No. 3; and Waltz II is a reorchestrated arrangement of *The First Echelon*, Opus 99 No. 8.

Instrumentation: piccolo (= flute II in No. 6), flute, oboe, 2 B flat clarinets (= A in No. 2), 2 E flat alto and 2 B flat tenor saxophones, bassoon ~ 3 horns, 3 trumpets, 3 trombones, tuba ~ timpani, triangle, tambourine, side drum, cymbals, bass drum ~ glockenspiel, xylophone, vibraphone (in No. 6), guitar, accordion, harp, piano (2 in Nos. 2 and 5), celesta (in Nos. 3, 6, and 7) ~ strings.

Première: UK: 1 December 1988, Barbican Hall, London; London Symphony Orchestra, Mstislav Rostropovich. (This performance broadcast three days later).

Arrangements: The Suite arranged for wind band by both Johan de Meij (Nos. 1–8) and Steven Walker (Nos. 1, 2, and 5).

Music: Russian edition, no number or date, 8 photocopied full scores and all parts in copyist's hand, 35.5 cm.

Bronsheim Muziekuitgeverij, Brunssum, Netherlands, no number, 1995, 3 full scores arr. for wind band by Steven Walker, 29.5 cm.

Duration: 24' 01"–25' 43'; 20 minutes (M. MacDonald).

Recordings: Decca Compact Disc 433 702-2DH. Labelled as 'Suite for Promenade Orchestra', arranged in order Nos. 1, 5, 2, 6, 4, 7, 3, and 8. Royal Concertgebouw Orchestra, Riccardo CHAILLY. [Opp. 16 and 35.] P Amsterdam 26 Apr. 1991, I Jan 1993, G Mar. 1993. *Reissued:* Decca Compact Disc 448 185-2DM. Nos. 1, 4, and 7. ['Simply Shostakovich' sampler— Sans op. E; Opp. 16, 22, 47, 70, 93, 97, 102, 110a, 116, and 141 not cross-referenced in this catalogue.] I June 1995 ~ France: Decca Compact Disc Single 443 265-2. Nos. 7, 6, and 4. I 1995.

Netherlands: Mercury/Phonogram Compact Disc Single 8561262. No. 7 titled 'The Second Waltz'. André RIEU Orchestra. I 1994. NB. This 'straight' version reached Position No. 5 In the Dutch Pop-Top 50 chart in December 1994 with gold disc sales of over 50,000.

Netherlands: Philips Compact Disc 314 522 933. No. 7 titled 'The Second Waltz'. Johann Strauss Orchestra, André RIEU. ['From Holland with Love'—Rieu, J. Strauss, Karas *et al.*] P Hilversum 1994, I 1996. NB. This recording released October 1999 in the UK following Rieu's version of 'The Second Waltz' being featured in the film *Eyes Wide Shut.*

Netherlands: Amestel Classics Compact Disc 9501. Suite arr. J. de Meij. Arnhem Symphonic Winds, Johan de MEIJ. [Grieg, Nielsen, Holst *et al.*] P Hilversum Apr.–May 1995, I Aug. 1995.

RCA Victor Red Seal Compact Disc 09026 6830-2. Frankfurt Radio Symphony Orchestra, Dmitri KITAYENKO. [Sans opp. P and E.] P Frankfurt 6–8 Mar. 1995, I Aug. 1997, G Oct. 1997.

EMI Classics Compact Disc CDC5 55601-2. No. 7 only, Philadelphia Orchestra, Mariss JANSONS. [Opp. 103 and 16, Sans op. E.] P Collingswood, New Jersey 8, 9, and 11 Mar. 1996, I May 1997, G Sept. 1997. *Reissued:* HMV Classics Compact Disc 5 73047-2. Waltz No. 2 only. [Sans op. E; Opp. 16, 22, 97, 35, and 89.] I Oct. 1998.

Hertfordshire County Music Service Compact Disc (no number). Nos. 1, 6, 4, 5, and 2. Hertfordshire County Youth Orchestra, Peter STARK. [Britten and Sackman.] P The Barbirolli Hall, St Clement Danes School, Chorleywood Apr. 1997.

France: Le Chant do Monde Russian Season Compact Disc RUS 788164. Nos. 2. 4, 5, 7, and 8. Novosibirsk Philharmonic Orchestra, Arnold KATS. [Opp. 97, 27, 69; and Sans op. P (i).] P Novosibirsk June 1997, I July 1999, G Nov. 1999.

Notes: Volume 10 of *Collected Works* (1984) states that the score of eight numbers is lost. Laurel E. Fay in 1992 wrote 'Contemporary sources indicate that . . . the Jazz Suite No. 2 . . . consisted of only three movements: Scherzo, Lullaby, and Serenade'. However, the Catalogue of the *New Collected Works* (1999) announces that Volume 33 will publish for the first time the 'Sans op. score of Suite for Jazz (Variety) Orchestra No. 2 in eight parts'.

Strictly this work, assembled by person(s) unknown, should be listed as *Suite for Variety Stage Orchestra* but as it has been performed and recorded since 1988 as *Suite for Jazz Orchestra No. 2* this title is here adopted. The original second suite, composed by Shostakovich, is listed below.

(ii) Original Suite for Jazz Orchestra No. 2

Form: Suite of three numbers at first scored as for Jazz Suite No. 1 then augmented at the request of the conductor V. Knusevitsky.

1. Scherzo
2. Lullaby
3. Serenade

The theme of the Scherzo was used five years later in the second movement of Symphony No. 8, Opus 65. Lullaby from the *Choreographic Miniatures* Ballet Suite.

Instrumentation: 2 E flat alto, 2 B flat tenor, and baritone saxophones ~ 4 trumpets, 2 trombones, tuba ~ percussion ~ 'large group' of banjos and guitars, piano ~ 6 violins, 2 basses. NB. The reconstruction percussion comprises a dance band drum kit, xylophone, 3 banjos and 3 guitars.

Composed: 1938, at Leningrad.

Premières: 20 September (Khentova) or 28 November (Slonimsky) 1938, Moscow Radio; State Jazz Band of the USSR, Viktor Knushevitsky.

UK: 9 September 2000, Royal Albert Hall (Proms Last Night); BBC Symphony Orchestra, Andrew Davis. Simultaneously broadcast, televised, and recorded on BBC DVD 8001-9. G Awards (Oct.) 2001.

Arrangement: Reconstructed and orchestrated from five pages of piano sketches by Gerard McBurney in 1999–2000.

Music: Piano score found among the composer's papers in 1990s.

Hans Sikorski, No. 2022, 1973, *Events of a Day* No. 20—Lullaby for piano, 31.5 cm.

Duration: 6' 05".

Reference: McBurney (in DSCH).

Note: A four-movement *Suite for Variety Orchestra No. 2*, discovered in 2000, includes the Lullaby in an altered form.

Opus 50   The Vyborg Side

Form: Music for the final film in the 'Maxim Trilogy', *The Vyborg Side* (or *District*), with screenplay and direction by Grigori Kozintsev and Leonid Trauberg for Lenfilm. The film trilogy awarded a Stalin Prize First Class in 1941. The orchestral parts of a few items, including the Overture, 'The Looting of the Wine Cellars', and Finale, have been located.

Overture—Allegro

Instrumentation: piccolo, 2 flutes, 2 B flat clarinets, 2 bassoons, contrabassoon ~ 4 horns, 4 trumpets, 3 trombones, tuba ~ timpani, side drum, cymbals, bass drum, gong ~ strings.

Composed: Late 1938, at Leningrad.

Premières: Film: 2 February 1939. Score conducted by Nikolai Rabinovich. Suite: UK: 13 December 2001, BBC Radio 3, BBC Philharmonic, Vassili Sinaisky.

Arrangement: Opus 50*a*—Suite for full orchestra (with two harps and optional wind band) and S.A.T.B. chorus, assembled by Lev Atovmyan from Opp. 45 and 89 in 1961:

1. Prelude—'Be bold, Friends . . .'—Moderato—Allegro non troppo—Adagio
2. Attack sequence—Allegro
3. Death of the old worker—Adagio
4. Waltz—Allegro sostenuto
5. Demonstration—'Varshavyanka'—Allegretto
6. Fight at the barricades—Allegro con brio—Presto
7. Funeral March—Tempo de marcia funêbre *attacca*
8. Finale—[no tempo indication]

None of the above numbers relate to Opus 50 though listed as 'Excerpts from Music to the Maxim Trilogy' and numbered Opus 50*a* in Sadovnikov 1965. Nos. 1 and 5 are taken from *The Unforgettable Year 1919*, Opus 89.

Instrumentation of Suite Opus 50*a*:   piccolo, 2 flutes, 3 oboes, E flat clarinet, 3 B flat clarinets, bass clarinet, 2 bassoons, contrabassoon ~ 4 horns, 3 trumpets, 3 trombones, tuba ~ timpani, triangle, side drum, cymbals, bass drum, gong ~ xylophone, glockenspiel, 2 harps ~ strings. Optional band in Nos. 7 and 8 (numbers not specified): cornets, trumpets; alto, tenor, baritone, and bass saxhorns. Chorus in No. 1 (mostly T.B. but S.A.T.B. in the last 13 bars).

Music: The whereabouts of the autograph full score is not known; the autograph vocal score preserved at the Glinka Museum.

Sovetskii Kompozitor, No. 2084, 1951, Opus 50*a* full score [opus no. not stated], 29 cm.

Muzyka, No. 10889 (in Volume 41 of *Collected Works* with Opp. 26, 30, 33, 41, 48, 53, 55, 56, 59, and 64), 1987, Overture in full score, 30 cm.

Duration: Film: 120 minutes. Suite: 28' 02"; 20 minutes (Sadovnikov). Overture: 1' 51"–1' 52".

Recordings: Germany: Capriccio Compact Disc 10 561. Complete Suite Op. 50*a* and Overture Op. 50. Berlin Radio Symphony Orchestra and Chorus, Mikhail YUROVSKY. [Opp. 30, 41 (i), and 45.] P 28–9 Apr. 1994, I Oct. 1995, G Jan. 1996. NB. On this CD the Prologue of the first film of the 'Maxim Trilogy' Op. 41 (i) is followed by the complete Suite Op. 50*a* (with Nos. 7 and 8 not banded separately) and the Overture to *The Vyborg Side* Op. 50.

USA: Russian Disc Compact Disc RDCD 10 018. Overture only. Byelorussian Radio and TV Symphony Orchestra, Walter MNATSAKANOV. [Opp. 53, 55, 33, and 132.] P Minsk Nov. 1995.

USA: Citadel Compact Disc CTD 88135. Complete Suite Op. 50*a*. Belarus Radio and TV Symphony Orchestra and State Chorus, Walter MNATSAKANOV. [Opp. 85 and 76.] P Moscow 7 Apr. 1997, I 1999.

Opus 51   The Friends

Form: Music for the film *The Friends* (or 'The Pals' in VAAP 1977), based on the story by author Betal Kalmykov, directed by Leo Arnshtam for Lenfilm. The score introduces Pierre Degeyter's *Internationale*.
Composed: August 1938, at Leningrad.
Première: Film first shown on 1 October 1938.
Music: Autograph copy of the film score preserved in the Music Department of Lenfilm.
  Muzyka, No. 10179 (in Volume 34 of *Collected Works* with Opp. 88 and 136, and songs), 1985, 'Vocalise' for mixed chorus a cappella reconstructed by Boris Tiles, 30 cm.
Recordings: —

Opus 52   The Great Citizen (Series 1)

Form: Music for part one of the film *The Great Citizen,* based on the story of Sergei Kirov, with script by Mikhail Bleiman and directed by Fridrikh Ermler for Lenfilm. See Opus 55 for part two.
Composed: 1937, at Leningrad.
Première: Film first shown on 13 February 1938.
Music: Autograph copy of the film score preserved in the Music Department of Lenfilm.
Recordings: —
Note: This two-part film presented the official version of the assassination of the popular Party leader of Leningrad, Sergei Kirov (given the fictional name of Pyotr Shakov in this production). Kirov helped to establish Soviet power in the Caucasus after 1917 and was head of the Communist Party in Leningrad from 1926. He supported Stalin against his rivals but is thought to have led the opposition to the leader's personal rule following the 17th Party Congress in 1934. On 1 December 1934 a young Party member named Leonid V. Nikolayev walked into Kirov's Smolny office and shot him. This assassination triggered off the notorious political trials and reign of terror of the thirties, Thousands were arrested, shot, or sent to labour camps and in 1937–8 hundreds of leading Party members in Leningrad were eliminated. Sergei Kirov lives on in the names of numerous places and institutions, among them the Kirov Theatre of Opera and Ballet (formerly the Maryinsky) in Leningrad.

Opus 53   The Man with a Gun

Alternative title: *November.* Title also translated as *Man at Arms.*
Form: Music for the film *The Man with a Gun,* based on the first part of the Lenin trilogy by Nikolai Pogodin, directed by Sergei Yutkevich for Lenfilm. The following items were composed for the film:

1. Overture—Allegretto
2. The October—Allegro moderato—Meno mosso
3. Smolny—Presto
3a. Smolny—Allegretto
4. Finale—Moderato

No. 1 introduces P. Armand's song 'Clouds Hang Heavy o'er the City' which is also sung in its original form in the film.
Instrumentation: piccolo, 2 flutes, 2 oboes, 2 B flat clarinets, 2 bassoons, contrabassoon ~ 4 horns, 3 trumpets, 3 trombones, tuba ~ timpani, triangle, side drum, cymbals, bass drum ~ glockenspiel ~ separate band of 2 cornets, 2 trumpets; 2 E flat alto, 2 B flat tenor, 2 B flat baritone, and 2 bass saxhorns ~ strings.
Composed: September 1938, at Leningrad.
Première: Film first shown on 1 November 1938.
Music: The whereabouts of the film score is not known. Manuscript copies preserved at the Leningrad State Archives of Literature and Art.
     Muzyka, No. 10889 (in Volume 41 of *Collected Works* with Opp. 26, 30, 33, 41, 48, 50, 55, 56, 59, and 64), 1987, full score, 30 cm.
Duration: 10' 20".
Recording: USA: Russian Disc Compact Disc RDCD 10 018. Nos. 1–3*a* and 4; incorrectly labelled Opus 59. Byelorussian Radio and TV Symphony Orchestra, Walter MNATSAKANOV. [Opp. 50, 55, 33, and 132.] P Minsk Nov. 1995.
Reference: Yutkevich.

Sans op. H   J. Strauss II Transcriptions

(i)   *Vienna Blood* (Johann Strauss)
Form: New orchestration and edition of the Johann Strauss II / Adolf Müller operetta of 1899 *Wiener Blut,* with Russian text by V. Tipot.
Composed: 1938, at Leningrad.
Première: 1941, Leningrad Malyi Opera Theatre, produced by Grigori Yaron. Ran for two performances only.

(ii)   *Excursion Train Polka* (Johann Strauss)
Alternative titles: *Pleasure Train Polka.* English title of 'Train of Joy' in composer's hand on Russian score. Tempi not marked.

Form: Reorchestration of the schnell-polka *Vergnügungszug,* Opus 281 of Johann Strauss II, composed for an 1864 concert during Strauss's series of mid-nineteenth-century visits to St Petersburg.

Instrumentation: piccolo, flute, 2 oboes, 2 A clarinets, 2 bassoons ~ 2 horns, 2 trumpets, 3 trombones ~ timpani, triangle/tambourine, cymbal/side drum ~ strings.

Composed: 1940, at Leningrad, as a speciality dance for Galina Isayeva inserted in a production of *Der Zigeunerbaron* ('The Gipsy Baron').

Premières: 1940, Leningrad Malyi Opera Theatre.

UK: 14 August 1981, Royal Albert Hall 'Prom', London; BBC Symphony Orchestra, Gennadi Rozhdestvensky (also broadcast on BBC Radio 3 simultaneously with BBC2 TV). NB. The scheduled British première at a 'Prom' on 23 July 1980 was delayed by a musicians' strike.

Music: USSR, no number or date, mimeographed score inscribed 'To my dear Gennadi on your birthday 4 May 1969, Mama' by Nataliya Pyotrovna Rozhdestvensky (the composer in no way concerned with this dedication).

Duration: 1' 45"–2' 35".

Film: *Rostropovich: Return to Russia.* The video equivalent of the CD performance appears on Sony VHS cassette SHV 46387 and LaserDisc SLV 46387.

Recordings: USSR: Melodiya C10 14415-6. Labelled as 'The Pleasure Train Polka'. Moscow Philharmonic Orchestra, Gennadi ROZHDESTVENSKY. [Album 1 of 'From Manuscripts of Different Years'—Opp. 4, 16, 17, 23, and 36; Sans opp. C and Z.] P 1980, I 1981*b. Reissued:* HMV Melodiya ASD 1650331. [As Russian release.] G July 1983 ~ Germany: Melodia Eurodisc 201974-366. [As Russian release.] ~ BMG Melodiya Compact Discs 74321 59058-2 (two-disc set). [Opp. 36, 4, 17, Z, C, 16, 1, 3, 7, 26/D, 59, E, 128, 30*a,* and 19.] I and G Mar. 1999.

USSR: Melodiya C10 21335 006. USSR Ministry of Home Affairs Army Orchestra, Vladimir TARASOV. [Op. 27*a* No. 5; Op. 97*a* No. 3; Puccini, Suppé *et al.*] I 1985*b.*

USSR: Melodiya C10 21513 003. Bolshoi Theatre Brass Band, Vladimir ANDROPOV. ['Music by the Strauss Family'.] I 1985*c.*

Sony Classical Compact Disc CD 45836. National Symphony Orchestra, Mstislav ROSTROPOVICH. ['Return to Russia'—Tchaikovsky and encores: Gershwin, Grieg, Paganini *et al.*] P Moscow concert 13–14 Feb. 1991, I and G Sept. 1991.

Notes: As no full score of the original Strauss composition was available in Leningrad, Shostakovich was asked to orchestrate the polka from a library copy of the piano score and, as a consequence, omits the representation of the guard's whistle and the tooting of the engine's old-fashioned steam hooter.

The excursion train of the title ran between Vienna and the vine-growing village of Grinzing, a few kilometres to the north-west.

Opus 54   Symphony No. 6 in B minor

Form: Symphony for full orchestra (with harp) in three movements:

1. Largo
2. Allegro
3. Presto

Instrumentation: piccolo, 2 flutes, 2 oboes, cor anglais, E flat clarinet, (= B flat clarinet III), 2 B flat clarinets, bass clarinet, 2 bassoons, contrabassoon (= bassoon III) ~ 4 horns, 3 trumpets, 3 trombones, tuba ~ timpani, triangle, tambourine, side drum, cymbals, bass drum, gong ~ xylophone, celesta, harp ~ strings.

Composed: 15 April–mid-October 1939. First two movements completed in Leningrad before 27 August.

Premières: 21 November 1939, Leningrad Philharmonic Bolshoi Hall; Leningrad Philharmonic Orchestra, Yevgeni Mravinsky. The Finale was encored.

> USA: 29 November 1940, Philadelphia Orchestra, Leopold Stokowski.

> UK: 24 October 1953, Adelphi Theatre, London; London Philharmonic Orchestra, Anatole Fistoulari.

Arrangements: Reductions for piano four hands by Lev Atovmyan (not published) and Boris Tishchenko. Largo arranged for piano eight hands by Pavel Lamm (not published). Reductions for two pianos (Largo only?) and solo piano by the composer.

Music: Published as Opus 53 in some editions. Autograph score lost [by Aleksandr Gauk according to Volkov.] Autograph of the first movement, arranged for two pianos by the composer, preserved at the Glinka Museum.

> Muzgiz, 1941, 21 cm.; No. 29838, 1962, 30 cm. and 1968, 21 cm.

> Leeds Music, no number, 1946, 23 cm.

> Boosey & Hawkes, No. 80 (A.S.M.P. No. 3), 1947, 19 cm.

> Muzyka, Leningrad, No. 1807, 1975, reduction for piano four hands by B. Tishchenko, 28.5 cm.

> Muzyka, No. 9245 (in Volume 3 of *Collected Works* with Op. 47), 1980, 30 cm.

> Hans Sikorski, No. 2228, 1984, 21 cm.

Duration: Approx. 30 minutes in score; 25' 42"–37' 45"; 33 minutes (Schirmer); 29' 10" (Plaistow).

Ballets: *Elegia*. Jiří Kylián, Dutch Dance Company, Circustheatre, Scheveningen (Holland Festival), 15 June 1976; danced by six couples to the music of the Largo, played by the Dutch Ballet Orchestra conducted by Jan Stulen.

> *Solitude*. Simon Mottram, Stockholm Opera, 29 January 1982.

Film: *Bernstein Conducts Shostakovich*. Two concert performances of the Sixth and Ninth Symphonies, filmed at the Musikverein in 1986 with Leonard

Bernstein conducting the Vienna Philharmonic Orchestra. Introduced by Humphrey Burton and screened on BBC2 TV on 19 August 1995. See also Opus 70.

Recordings: USA: Victor 18391-5 (9 sides 78 rpm, last side blank). Philadelphia Orchestra, Leopold STOKOWSKI. P 8 and 28 Dec. 1940. *Reissued:* Victor Set DM 867 (9 sides 78 rpm). [McDonald.] ~ Dell'Arte Compact Disc DA 9023 (mono). [Sibelius.] I Feb. 1992, G June 1992 ~ Dutton Laboratories Compact Disc CDAX 8017. (Op. 47.) I May 1996, G Dec. 1996.

Italy: AS Compact Disc 628 (mono). New York Philharmonic Orchestra, Fritz REINER. [Op. 58; and Copland.] P Carnegie Hall, New York concert 15 Aug. 1943, I 1990 ~ Italy: Legend Compact Disc LGD 122. [Op. 58; and Copland.] I June 1994.

USA: Columbia 12199-203D in Set M 585 (9 sides 78 rpm). Pittsburg Symphony Orchestra, Fritz REINER. [Kabalevsky.] P Pittsburg 26 Mar. 1945. *Reissued:* Columbia LX 998-1002 (9 sides 78 rpm). [Kabalevsky.] G June 1947 ~ USA: Columbia ML 4249(mono) ~ Italy: Arlecchino Compact Disc LYS 093 (mono). [Bartók.] I June 1996 ~ Sony Masterworks Heritage Compact Disc MHK 62343 (mono). [Kodály, Weiner, Bartók *et al.*] I Nov. 1996. ~ France: LYS Compact Disc 093 (mono). [Bartók.] I 1997.

USSR: MK HD 2488-9 (10" mono). Leningrad Philharmonic Orchestra, Yevgeni MRAVINSKY. P 4 Nov. 1946, I 1955. *Reissued:* France: Le Chant du Monde LDXA 8267 (10" mono) ~ USSR: Melodiya D 030615-6 (12"mono). [Haydn.] I 1972 ~ Japan: Victor MK 1023 (12" mono). [Op. 81.] I 1973.

Bulgaria: Balkanton BCA 503 (mono). Sofia State Philharmonic Orchestra, Dobrin PETKOV. [Op. 70.] P mid-1950s.

USSR: MK D 4894-5 (10" mono). Moscow Radio Symphony Orchestra, Aleksandr GAUK. P 1959. *Reissued:* USA: Artia ALP 167 (12" mono). [Galinin.] G Jan. 1961 ~ USA: Bruno BR 14032(mono). [Kabalevsky.] I 1961 ~ USSR: MK D 09618-9928 (mono). [Op. 70.] I 1962 ~ USA: Collana Classica Russa CLAR 4004 (mono). [Kabalevsky.]

World Record Club CM 28 (mono) and SCM 28. London Philharmonic Orchestra, Sir Adrian BOULT. P 1960, G Aug. 1962. *Reissued:* USA: Everest DBR 6007 (mono) and SDBR 3007. G May 1968 ~ Italy: Quadrifoglio VDS 392 ~ USA: Peerless Classics PC 06. [Issued under the pseudonyms 'New York Concert Orchestra, Robert Hornstein'.] I 1974 ~ Vanguard Classics (Everest Collection) Compact Disc EVC 9005. [Op. 70.] I Sept. 1994, G Apr. 1995.

USA: Columbia MS 7221. New York Philharmonic Orchestra, Leonard BERNSTEIN. [Prokofiev.] P 14 Oct. 1963. *Reissued:* CBS SBRG 72730. [Prokofiev.] G Oct. 1969 ~ Sony Royal Edition Compact Disc SMK 47614. [Op. 10.] G Nov. 1993 and June 1994 ~ Sony Classical Compact Discs SX4K 64206 (four-disc set). [Op. 10.] I Dec. 1995.

USSR: Melodiya CM 02657-8. Leningrad Phliharmonic Orchestra, Yevgeni MRAVINSKY. [Honegger.] P Moscow concert 21 Feb. 1965, I 1972. *Reissued:* HMV Melodiya ASD 2805. [Sibelius.] G July 1972 ~ USA: Angel Melodiya SR 40202. [Stravinsky.] I 1972 ~ Italy: EMI 065 94485. [Honegger.] I 1974 ~ USSR: Melodiya C10 12955-6 and C60 12957-8 Second and third movements only. [On first record of 'Leningrad Souvenir'—Glière, Rimsky-Korsakov, Tchaikovsky *et al.*] I 1980*c.* ~ Japan: Icone Compact Disc ICN 9404-2. [Tchaikovsky.] P incorrectly given as Moscow Radio Concert Hall 12 Mar. 1983, I Aug. 1994 ~ Japan: BMG Melodiya BVCX 4028. [Musorgsky, Glazunov, Mozart *et al.*] I 1997.

USSR: Melodiya C 01627-8. Moscow Philharmonic Orchestra, Kirill KONDRASHIN. [Op. 129.] P and I 1967. *Reissued:* USA: Angel Melodiya SR 40064. [Op. 129.] I 1968 ~ France: Le Chant du Monde LDXA 78415. [Op. 129.] I 1968 ~ France: Le Chant du Monde LDX 78595-6. [In two-record set with Op. 60.] ~ HMV Melodiya ASD 2447. [Op. 129.] G Mar. 1969 ~ Germany: Melodia Eurodisc 87623 XK. [In thirteen-record box set.] I 1974 ~ Germany: Melodia Eurodisc 300 699 435. [In three-record box set with Opp. 60 and 65.] ~ USSR: Melodiya CM 04237-8. [Op. 20.] I 1974*c.* ~ HMV Melodiya BOX 502504 in Set SLS 5025. [Op. 47, third and fourth movements.] G Dec. 1975 ~ Italy: EMI 065 94559. [Op. 129.] I 1978 ~ USSR: Melodiya CM 04237-8. [In first box of Part 1 of *Collected Works on Records* with Op. 20.] I 1980 ~ USA: Musical Heritage Society MHS 824389. [In two-record set with Op. 129 and Sans op. P.] I 1981 ~ HMV Melodiya EX 2903873 (DMM). [On second record in twelve-record box set with Op. 20.] G Dec. 1985 ~ France: Le Chant du Monde Compact Disc LDC 278 1003-4. [In Box 2 of five two-disc sets with Opp. 47 and 60.] G May 1989 ~ BMG Classics Melodiya Compact Disc 74321 19847-2. [Op. 93.] I July 1994, G Nov. 1994.

Philips Universo 6580 042. Berlin Radio Symphony Orchestra, Rolf KLEINERT. [Stravinsky.] P 1967, G Dec. 1971. *Reissued:* France: Philips 6598 102 in set 6747 252. [Op. 35 in two-record set 'Tribute to Dmitri Shostakovich' with Op. 112.] I post-1975.

Philips 412 073 1PH. Concertgebouw Orchestra, Kirill KONDRASHIN. [Op. 70.] P Amsterdam concert 21 Jan. 1968, G Aug. 1984. *Reissued:* Philips Collector Series Compact Disc 438 283-2PM. [Nielsen.] I July 1993, G Sept. 1993.

USA: RCA LSC 3133. Chicago Symphony Orchestra, Leopold STOKOWSKI. [Op. 22*a.*] P 20–2 Feb. 1968. *Reissued:* RCA Red Seal SB 6839. [Op. 22*a.*] G Oct. 1970 ~ France: RCA Red Seal 644 554. [Op. 22*a.*] ~ RCA Gold Seal GL 42916. [Op. 22*a.*] G Oct. 1981 ~ RCA Gold Seal Compact Disc 09026 62516-2. [Op. 22*a;* and Khachaturyan.] I 1997 and July 1998, G Aug. 1998.

USA: Philadelphia Orchestra Association Compact Discs POA 100 (third disc in twelve-disc set). Philadelphia Orchestra, Eugene ORMANDY.

[Philadelphia Collection 1917–98—Rakhmaninov, Piston, and Penderecki.] P radio broadcast 15 May 1969, G Feb. 2000.

BMG Melodiya Compact Disc 74321 25198. Leningrad Philharmonic Orchestra, Yevgeni MRAVINSKY. ['Mravinsky Edition, Vol. 9'—Op. 93.] P Moscow concert 27 Jan. 1972, I June 1995. *Reissued:* France: Praga Compact Discs PR 254 017-8 (two-disc set). [Opp. 112 and 103.] P incorrectly given as Prague concert 21 May 1955, I Apr. 1994, G Aug. 1994 ~ USA: Russian Disc Compact Disc RDCD 10 910 (mono). [Op. 47.] P venue incorrectly given as Leningrad, I 1995 ~ France: Le Chant du Monde Compact Disc PR 7254 017 (mono). [Op. 112.] P not Prague 1955, G Feb. 2001.

HMV ASD 3029. London Symphony Orchestra, André PREVIN. [Prokofiev.] P 1 Dec. 1973 and 8 May 1974, G Dec. 1974. *Reissued:* USA: Angel S 37026. [Prokofiev.] I 1974 ~ Germany: EMI Electrola C063 02 520. [Prokofiev.] ~ HMV Master Series EG 2908591 (digital). [Rakhmaninov.] G July 1986 ~ EMI Studio Compact Disc CDM7 695642. [Rakhmaninov.] I 1988, G Dec. 1988.

USSR: Melodiya C10 06881-2. Moscow Conservatory Students' Symphony Orchestra, Leonid NIKOLAYEV. [Weber.] P and I 1976.

USSR: Melodiya C10 09675-6. Leningrad Philharmonic Orchestra, Yuri TEMIRKANOV. [Ravel.] P 1977, I 1978c. *Reissued:* HMV Melodiya ASD 3706. [Op. 70.] G Sept. 1979.

Sweden: BIS LP 332 D. Third movement only. Swedish Radio Symphony Orchestra, Kirill KONDRASHIN. [In five-record box set 'Orchestral Music in the Swedish Radio, 1928–79' with Brahms, Mozart, Falla *et al.*] P concert 13 Oct. 1977.

HMV ASD 3772 in Set SLS 5177. Bournemouth Symphony Orchestra, Paavo BERGLUND. [Op. 103, first and part second movements.] P 5–6 June 1978, G Feb. 1980. *Reissued:* EMI Compact Disc CDS7 47790-8. [In two-disc set with Opp. 103, 35, 102, and 5.] I Nov. 1987, G May 1988.

Bulgaria: Balkanton BCA 10212. Plovdiv State Philharmonic Orchestra, Dobrin PETKOV. [Op. 96.] P 1978? *Reissued:* USA: Monitor MCS 2163. [Op. 96.] I 1981 ~ AVM Classics AVM 1019 and Compact Disc AVMCD 1019. [Op. 112.] I Dec. 1988 and 1994.

East Germany: Eterna 8 27 437. Berlin City Symphony Orchestra, Kurt SANDERLING. P 25–7 Apr. 1979. *Reissued:* Japan: Deutsche Schallplatten ET 5084. I 1980 ~ Germany: Berlin Classics Compact Disc. 0021812 BC. [Op. 10.] G Jan. 1995.

USSR: Melodiya C10 14899-900. Labelled Opus 53. USSR Symphony Orchestra, Yevgeni SVETLANOV. P 1980, I 1981c.

USSR: Melodiya C10 18047-8. USSR Ministry of Culture Symphony Orchestra, Vakhtang ZHORDANIYA. [Op. 70.] P 1981, I 1983b.

USSR: Melodiya. A10 00075 003 (digital). USSR Ministry of Culture Symphony Orchestra, Gennadi ROZHDESTVENSKY. P 1983, I 1985a. *Reissued:*

Japan: JVC/Target Compact Disc VDC 1044. [Op. 112.] G May 1986 Olympia Compact Disc OCD 111. [Op. 112.] I June 1987, G May 1989 ~ Germany: Melodia Eurodisc Compact Disc 258 484. [Op. 20.] ~ Olympia Compact Disc OCD 5005. [In Vol. 1 six-disc set of symphonies with Op. 112.] I Dec. 1990 ~ Japan: Icone Compact Disc ICN 9415-2. [Opp. 3, 1, and 26.] I Sept. 1994 ~ BMG Melodiya Compact Discs 74321 49611-2 (two-disc set). [Opp. 10, 47, and 70.] I Dec. 1997.

Decca 414 125-1DH in Set 411 939-1DH2 (digital). Concertgebouw Orchestra, Bernard HAITINK. [Op. 103, first movement.] P 19 Dec. 1983, G June 1985. *Simultaneous issue:* Decca Compact Disc 411 939-2DH2. [One disc in two-disc set with Opp. 103 and 115.] G Aug. 1985 ~ Decca Ovation Compact Disc 425 067-2DM. [Op. 112.] I Aug. 1993, G Nov. 1993 ~ London Compact Disc 444 435-2. [On fifth disc of eleven-disc set with Op. 112.] I June 1995.

USA: Schwann Musica, Mundi VMS 002 106 (DMM). Rundfunk-Sinfonieorchester Saarbrücken, Myung-Whun CHUNG. [Rimsky-Korsakov.] P June 1985, G June 1987. *Reissued:* Koch Schwann Compact Disc 311 202 G1. [Rimsky-Korsakov.] I Oct. 1991, G Feb. 1992.

Chandos ARBD 1148 (digital). Scottish National Orchestra, Neeme JÄRVI. [Op. 10.] P Glasgow 6 May 1985, G Apr. 1986. *Simultaneous issue:* Chandos Compact Disc CHAN 8411. [Op. 10.] G June 1986 and Feb. 1988.

Deutsche Grammophon 419 771-1GH (digital) and Compact Disc 419 771-2GH. Vienna Philharmonic Orchestra, Leonard BERNSTEIN. [Op. 70.] P Vienna concert Oct. 1986, G Nov. 1987 and Mar. 1988.

Italy: Nuova Era Compact Disc 033 6705. Giovanile Italiana Orchestra, Krzysztof PENDERECKI. [Penderecki.] P concert 8 June 1987, I Apr. 1988, G Nov. 1988.

Decca Compact Disc 425 609-2DH. Royal Philharmonic Orchestra, Vladimir ASHKENAZY. [Op. 10.] P Walthamstow Nov. 1988, I Apr. 1990, G June 1990.

Naxos Compact Disc 8.550626. Czecho-Slovak Radio Symphony Orchestra, Ladislav SLOVÁK. [Op. 112.] P Bratislava 3–12 Dec. 1988, I May 1993, G Nov. 1993. *Reissued:* Naxos Compact Discs 8.505017. [In five-disc set with Symphonies Nos. 1, 2, 3, 4, 7, 12, and 15.] I 1993.

Denon Compact Disc CO 78968. Vienna Symphony Orchestra, Eliahu INBAL. [Op. 112.] P 22–5 Jan. 1991, I Feb. 1996, G Apr. 1996.

EMI Compact Disc CDC7 54339-2. Oslo Symphony Orchestra, Mariss JANSONS. [Op. 70.] P Oslo 25–30 Jan. 1991, I Mar. 1992, G May 1992.

Austria: Musica Classica Compact Disc 780003-2. Moscow Radio Symphony Orchestra, Vladimir FEDOSEYEV. [Op. 10.] P Bratislava Jan. 1992, I Jan. 1996.

Teldec Compact Discs 0630-17046-2 (In twelve-disc set of Symphonies). National Symphony Orchestra of Washington, Mstislav ROS-

TROPOVICH. P 4–5 June 1994, G Oct. 1997. *Reissued:* Teldec Compact Disc 4509 95070-2. [Op. 112.] I Aug. 1999.

RCA Red Seal Compact Disc 09026 68844-2. St Petersburg Philharmonic Orchestra, Yuri TEMIRKANOV. [Opp. 96 and 10.] P St Petersburg 3–4 Jan. 1996, I July 1999.

Japan: Canyon Classics Compact Disc PCCL 00401. Moscow Radio Symphony Orchestra, Vladimir FEDOSEYEV. [Op. 47.] P Moscow Conservatory 3–5 Apr. 1997.

Sweden: BIS Compact Discs CD 973-4 (two-disc set). BBC National Orchestra of Wales, Mark WIGGLESWORTH. ['Complete Symphonies, Vol. 2'—Opp. 47 and 93.] P Swansea Nov. 1997, I June 1999, G Aug. 1999.

Czech: Supraphon Compact Disc SU 3415-2. Prague Symphony Orchestra, Maksim SHOSTAKOVICH. [Opp. 22*a* and 114*a*.] P Prague concert 2 Mar. 1999, I and G Awards (Oct.) 1999.

Delos Compact Discs DE 3283 (two-disc set). Dallas Symphony Orchestra, Andrew LITTON. [Op. 93.] P Dallas concert 1–2 December 2000, I Oct. 2001.

Dunelm Compact Disc DRD 0173. London Shostakovich Orchestra, Christopher LEE. [Barber and Khachaturyan.] P Cyprian's Church, London concert 19 May 2001.

Opus 55   The Great Citizen (Series 2)

Form: Music for part two of the film *The Great Citizen,* based on the story of Sergei Kirov, with script by Mikhail Bleiman and directed by Fridrikh Ermler for Lenfilm. See Opus 52 for part one. The two-part film awarded a Stalin Prize First Class in 1941. The revolutionary anthem 'You Fell as Victims' and the refrain of Degeyter's *Internationale* are featured in the film score, of which three items have been discovered: Overture, Funeral March (marked 'Largo'), and Finale.

Instrumentation of Funeral March: 2 flutes, 2 oboes, 2 B flat clarinets, 2 bassoons ~ 4 horns, 3 trumpets, 3 trombones, tuba ~ timpani, side drum, cymbals ~ harp ~ strings.

Composed: August 1938–9, at Leningrad.

Première: Film first shown on 27 November 1939.

Music: Incomplete orchestral parts of the Overture, Funeral March, and Finale preserved at the Leningrad State Archives of Literature and Art. Autograph score of the Funeral March preserved in the Shostakovich family archive.

Muzyka, No. 10889 (in Volume 41 of *Collected Works* with Opp. 26, 30, 33, 41, 48, 50, 53, 56, 59, and 64), 1987, Funeral March in full score, 30 cm.

Duration: Funeral March: 6' 50"–8' 32".

Recording: USA: Russian Disc Compact Disc RDCD 10 018. Funeral March. Byelorussian Radio and TV Symphony Orchestra, Walter MNATSAKANOV. [Opp. 50, 53, 33, and 132.] P Minsk Nov. 1995.

Decca Compact Disc 460 792-2DG11. Funeral March. Royal Concertgebouw Orchestra, Riccardo CHAILLY. ['The Film Album'—Opp. 33, 26, 56, 116, 132, 76*a*, and 97.] P Amsterdam 10–11 Sept. 1998, I Mar. 1999, G Apr. 1999.

Opus 56   The Silly Little Mouse

Form: Music for a cartoon film, based on the children's fairy story in verse *The Tale of the Stupid Mouse* by Samuil Marshak, directed by Mikhail Tsekhanovsky for Lenfilm. This continuously evolving composition is devoid of separate numbers and could be defined as a children's opera for the screen, with solo singers and orchestra.

Instrumentation: 2 flutes (II = piccolo), 2 oboes (II = cor anglais), 2 B flat clarinets (II = bass clarinet), 2 bassoons (II = contrabassoon) ~ 4 horns, 2 trumpets, 2 trombones ~ timpani, triangle, wood block, tambourine, side drum, cymbals, bass drum ~ glockenspiel, xylophone ~ celesta, harp ~ 3 female and 4 male vocal soloists ~ strings (1 desk of each).

Composed: March 1939, at Leningrad.

Premières: Film first shown on 13 September 1940. Restoration of the concert version first performed in Leningrad, 1979.

Arrangements: English translation of the text by Levon Hakopian. A purely instrumental version by Andrew Cornall.

Music: Shostakovich stated *in litt.* that the film was not completed (momentary confusion with Opus 36?) and he recycled the music for other compositions. The whereabouts of the autograph score is not known. The score has been reconstructed by Boris Tiles from the orchestral parts preserved at the Leningrad State Archives of Literature and Art and the vocal score in the Shostakovich family archive.

Muzyka, No. 10889 (in Volume 41 of *Collected Works* with Opp. 26, 30, 33, 41, 48, 50, 53, 55, 59, and 64), 1987, concert version in full score and, in the supplement, the original vocal score for comparison, 30 cm.

DSCH Publishers, Moscow, 1995, full score and parts available for hire.

Duration: 14' 40"–15' 10". Cornall's arrangement 12' 13".

Recordings: [USSR: Melodiya M52 40441-2 (mono). Marshak's *The Tale of the Stupid Mouse* is read on one side by Z. Bokareva. I 1978*c*.]

USSR: Melodiya C52 16411-2. Complete children's opera. Principal roles—Nina Glinkina (Mouse), Tatyana Sharova, (Cat), and Boris Ulitin (Narrator); Leningrad Conservatory Opera Studio Orchestra, Boris TILES. P 1980, I 1982*b*.

USA: Citadel Compact Disc CTD 88129. Complete children's opera. Libretto in transliterated Russian and English. Yevgeniya Kazantseva (Mouse), Lesliya Liut (Cat), Nina Tishina (Duck), Sergei Schapov (Horse), Oleg Gordinets (Pig), Mikhail Druzhina (Toad and Dog), Yevgeniya Ivanova (Narrator), Belarus RTV Symphony Orchestra, Walter MNATSAKANOVA. [Opp. 30*a*, 36, and 59.] P Minsk Feb. 1997, I 1998.

Decca Compact Disc 460 792-2DH11. Arr. A. Cornall. Royal Concertgebouw Orchestra, Riccardo CHAILLY. ['The Film Album'—Opp. 33, 26, 116, 55, 132, 76*a*, and 97.] P Amsterdam 10–11 Sept. 1998, I Mar. 1999, G Apr. 1999.

Notes: Samuil Marshak wrote a companion story in verse, *The Tale of the Clever Little Mouse,* though this was not filmed.

The lullaby theme is used in the fifth song 'Kreutzer Sonata' of *Satires,* Opus 109.

Opus 57   Piano Quintet in G minor

Form: Quintet for piano, 2 violins, viola, and cello in five movements:

1. Prelude—Lento—Poco più mosso—Lento *attacca*
2. Fugue—Adagio
3. Scherzo—Allegretto
4. Intermezzo—Lento *attacca*
5. Finale—Allegretto

Composed: Summer 1940–14 September 1940, at Moscow. Written at the request of the Beethoven Quartet as a piece to perform with the composer.

Premières: 23 November 1940, Moscow Conservatory Malyi Hall; Dmitri Shostakovich (piano) and the Beethoven Quartet (Dmitri Tsyganov, Vasili Shirinsky, Vadim Borisovsky, and Sergei Shirinsky).

15 December 1940, Leningrad Conservatory Malyi Hall; Dmitri Shostakovich and the Glazunov Quartet (Ilya Lukashevsky, G. Ginzburg, Aleksandr Ryvkin, and David Mogilevsky).

Music: Given as Opus 58 in Russian record catalogues. Autograph score preserved at the Glinka Museum. The autograph score first page of the Finale, marked '*Moderato poco allegretto* $\downarrow$ = 72', reproduced in Volume 37 of *Collected Works.* Awarded a Stalin Prize First Class of 100,000 roubles on 16 March 1941.

Muzgiz (Poligrafkniga), No. C 17Ø 0, 1941, score, 35 cm.

Am-Rus Music Corporation, New York, no number, 1941, score reproduced photographically from the Muzgiz edition in plain red cloth boards with parts, prepared by a copyist, in a rear pocket. [The words 'bass ad lib' on title page cancelled by an over-printed area of black ink.]

Leeds Music, no number, 1948, score and parts, 31 cm.

International Music, No. 2063, *c.*1950, score and parts, 30.5 cm.

Muzgiz, No. 25601, 1962, score and parts, 29 cm.

Edition Peters, No. 4791 (plate no. 25601), 1964, score and parts, 30 cm.

Hans Sikorski, No. 2275, 1964, score and parts, 31.5 cm.

Muzyka, 1968, parts, 29 cm.

Muzyka, No. 10794 (in Volume 37 of *Collected Works* with Opp. 8, 11, and 67), 1983, score and parts, 30 cm.

Duration: Approx. 32 minutes in score; 29 minutes (Sadovnikov); 27' 54"–37' 14"; 31' 30" (Plaistow).

Ballet: *Sacred Circles.* David Drew, Royal Ballet; Royal Shakespeare Theatre, Stratford-upon-Avon, 3 March 1973.

Recordings: Czech: Multisonic Compact Disc MU 31 0179-2 (mono). Dmitri SHOSTAKOVICH and Beethoven Quartet (personnel as at première). ['Russian Treasure'—Opp. 34 and 40.] P 1940, I Sept. 1993.

USA: Columbia 71296-9D in Set M 483 (8 sides 78 rpm). Vivian RIVKIN (piano) and Stuyvesant Quartet.

France: Vogue Archives Soviétiques Compact Disc 651023 (mono). Dmitri SHOSTAKOVICH and Borodin Quartet (Rostislav Dubinsky, Yaroslav Aleksandrov, Dmitri Shebalin, Valentin Berlinsky). [Op. 110.] P 1950.

Decca LXT 2749 (mono). QUINTETTO CHIGIANO (Sergio Lorenzi—piano; Riccardo Brengola, Mario Benvenutti, Giovanni Leone, Lino Filippini). P 24 Oct. 1951, G Dec. 1952. *Reissued:* Decca Eclipse ECS 592 (electronic stereo). [Dvořák.] G May 1971.

USA: American Federation of Musicians CB 158 (mono). Eunice NORTON (piano) and Juilliard Quartet (Robert Mann, Robert Koff, Raphael Hillyer, Arthur Winograd). [Piston.] P Pittsburg 1952, I 1954.

USA: Capitol CTL 7024 (mono). Victor ALLER (piano) and Hollywood Quartet (Felix Slatkin, Paul Shure, Paul Robyn, Eleanor Aller). P Jan. 1952, G Feb. 1953. *Reissued:* USA: Capitol P 8171 (mono) ~ USA: Capitol LAL 9024 (10" mono). Third movement only. [Copland, Beethoven, Delius *et al.*] ~ USA: Testament Compact Disc SBT 1077 (mono). [Franck.] I Jan. 1996, G May 1996.

USSR: MK D 2620-1 (10" mono). Dmitri SHOSTAKOVICH and Beethoven Quartet (personnel as at première). P and I 1955. *Reissued:* France: Le Chant du Monde LDA 8139 (10" mono) ~ Parlophone Odeon PMA 1040 (mono). [Op. 73.] G Aug. 1958 ~ USA: Vanguard VRS 6032 (mono). [Op. 49.] I 1958 ~ HMV Melodiya HLM 7095 in Set RLS 721 (mono). [Op. 40.] G Oct. 1976 ~ USSR: Melodiya M10 39077-8 (mono). [In four-record box set 'D. Shostakovich—Pianist' with Op. 34.] I 1977 ~ France: Le Chant du Monde Compact Disc LDC 278 1000 (mono, double-play). [Opp. 79*a*, 93, and 87.] I Sept. 1989 ~ Japan: Victor Musical Industries Compact Disc VICC 2048. ['Pianist = D. Shostakovich'—Opp. 35, 102, and 94.] I 1990 ~

USA: Vanguard Classics Compact Disc OVC 8077. [Op. 68.] I Sept. 1994 ~ Revelation Compact Disc RV 70005 (mono). ['Shostakovich plays Shostakovich, Vol. 4'—Op. 40.] P date given as 14 July 1950, I Mar. 1998, G Aug. 1998 ~ France: Dante Compact Discs LYS 369-370 (two-disc set). [Opp. 67, 40, and 73.] I 1998.

Japan: Triton Compact Disc MECC 26020 (mono). Lev OBORIN (piano) and Beethoven Quartet (personnel as at première). [Beethoven.] P Moscow Conservatory concert 1960, I 2000.

Czech: Supraphon SUA 10188 (mono) and SUA ST 50045 (also SUA ST 50188). Eva BERNÁTHOVA (piano) and Janáček Quartet (Jiří Travnícek, Adolf Sykora, Jiří Kratochvíl, Karel Krafka). [Op. 83.] P 1960. *Reissued:* USA: Artia ALP 188 (mono) and ALPS 188. [Op. 83.] I 1961, G Mar. 1962.

Italy: Nuova Era Compact Disc 2273 (mono). Movements 1, 2, and 5. Glen GOULD (piano) and Symphonia Quartet. [Prokofiev.] P CBC Television Studios, Toronto 18–19 Sept. 1961, broadcast 14 Jan. 1962, G Dec. 1989. *Reissued:* Sony Compact Disc SMK 52679 (mono). [Gould and Poulenc.]. Also in Sony SX3K 63129 (three-disc set, with J. S. and C. P. E. Bach and Scarlatti). I 1997. NB. This performance available on the seventh mono videocassette Sony SHV 48411 'A Russian Interlude' in *The Glenn Gould Collection*.

L'Oiseau-Lyre OL 267 (mono) and SOL 267. Lamar CROWSON (piano) and the Melos Ensemble (Emanuel Hurwitz, Ivor McMahon, Cecil Aronowitz, Terence Weil). [Prokofiev.] P 1964, G June 1964. *Reissued:* Decca Compact Discs 466 437-2 (third disc of five-disc set). [Opp. 40 and 122.] I 1999.

Poland: Muza XL 0270 (mono). WARSAW QUINTET (Władysław Szpilman—piano; Bronisław Gimpel, Tadeusz Wroński, Stefan Kamasa, Aleksander Ciechański). [Schumann.] I 1965.

USA: Prologue Records DL 15-16. Trilby LUNDBERG (piano), Judith Aller and Alan Stott (violins), Bernard McWilliams (viola), James B. Kreger (cello). I 1966.

Italy: Intaglio Compact Disc INCD 7561. Svyatoslav RICHTER (piano) and Borodin Quartet (Rostislav Dubinsky, Yaroslav Aleksandrov, Dmitri Shebalin, Valentin Berlinsky). [Op. 133.] P Spoleto Festival 17 July 1966, I Aug. 1993.

France: Praga Compact Disc PR 254 042. Miroslav LANGER (piano) and Tálich Quartet (Petr Messieureur, Jan Kvapil, Jan Tálich, Evžen Rattay). [Opp. 49 and 68.] P 1967, I May 1994.

USSR: Melodiya D 022667-8 (mono) and CM 01833-4. Lyubov YEDLINA (piano) and Borodin Quartet (Rostislav Dubinsky, Yaroslav Aleksandrov, Dmitri Shebalin, Valentin Berlinsky). [Stravinsky.] P 1968, I 1969. *Reissued:* HMV Melodiya ASD 3072. [Op. 11; and Stravinsky.] G May 1975 ~ USA: Angel Melodiya SR 40085. [Stravinsky.] ~ Italy: EMI 065 95579 [Stravinsky.] I 1978 ~ USA: Musical Heritage Society MHS 4321. [Stravinsky.] I 1980.

USSR: Melodiya C10 09181-2. Nikolai PETROV (piano) and Borodin Quartet (Mikhail Kopelman, Andrei Abramenkov, Dmitri Shebalin, Valentin Berlinsky). [In second box of Part 2 of *Collected Works on Records* with Op. 11.] P 1977, I 1978.

Czech: Supraphon 111 2484. Miroslav LANGER (piano) and Tálich Quartet (Petr Messieureur, Jan Kvapil, Jan Tálich, Evžen Rattay). [Op. 49.] P Prague 20 Apr. 1978, G Jan. 1981.

Continental Record Distributors CRD 1051. Clifford BENSON (piano) and Alberni Quartet (Howard Davis, Peter Pople, Roger Best, David Smith). [Britten.] P Hampstead 24–7 Oct. 1977, G Nov. 1978. *Reissued:* CRD Compact Disc 3351. [Britten.] G Mar. 1989.

RCA Red Seal RL 25224. Roger WOODWARD (piano) and Edinburgh Quartet (Miles Baster, Peter Markham, Michael Beeston, Christopher Gough). [Op. 67.] P Edinburgh 21–2 Sept. 1978, G Jan. 1980.

France: Solstice MN 01. PRO ARTE QUINTET of Monte-Carlo (Fernande Laurent-Biancheri—piano; Jean Claude Abraham, Renée Charnaix-Anderson, Jean-Pierre Pigerre, Lane Anderson). [Martinů.] P Monaco Apr. and May 1979.

USSR: Melodiya C10 17213-4. Aleksei NASEDKIN (piano) and Shostakovich Quartet (Andrei Shishlov, Sergei Pishchugin, Aleksandr Galkovsky, Aleksandr Korchagin). [Op. 108.] P 1980, I 1982*d*.

Czech: Opus 9111 1273. Marián LAPŠANSKÝ (piano) and Janáček Quartet (Bohumil Smejkal, Adolf Sykora, Jiří Kratochvíl, Karel Krafka). [Janáček.] P 1982.

Academy Sound and Vision ALH 929. MUSIC GROUP OF LONDON (David Parkhouse—piano; Hugh Bean, Penny Hart, Christopher Wellington, Eileen Croxford). [Op. 67.] I Apr. 1983, G July 1983.

Chandos ABRD 1088 (digital). Borodin Trio (Rostislav Dubinsky, Yuli Turovsky, Lyubov YEDLINA) with Mimi Zweig (2nd violin) and Jerry Horner (viola). [Op. 67.] P London June 1983, G Jan. 1984. *Reissued:* Chandos Compact Disc CHAN 8342. [Op. 67.] I Sept. 1984, G Apr. 1985.

USA: Orfeo SO 99 844F. Scherzo only. Vladimir ASHKENAZY (piano), Gidon Kremer, Cho-Liang Lin, Kim Kashkashian, and Misha Maisky. [Ives, Messiaen, Schnittke *et al.*] P July 1983, I 1984.

Decca 411 940-1DH (digital) and Compact Disc 411 940-2DH. Vladimir ASHKENAZY (piano) and Fitzwilliam Quartet (Christopher Rowland, Jonathan Sparey, Alan George, Ioan Davies). [Sans op. D and Op. 127.] P London Sept. 1983; G Feb., May, and Oct. 1987.

HMV Melodiya EL 270338-1 (digital). Svyatoslav RICHTER (piano) and Borodin Quartet (Mikhail Kopelman, Andrei Abramenkov, Dmitri Shebalin, Valentin Berlinsky). [Opp. 108 and 110.] P Moscow concert 5–6 Dec. 1983, G Nov. 1985. *Reissued:* HMV Melodiya EX 270339-3 (DMM). [In seven-record box set of 15 Quartets.] G Mar. 1986 ~ USSR: Melodiya A10 00109 003 (digital). I 1986*a* ~ EMI Melodiya Compact Disc CDC7

47507-2. [Opp. 108 and 110.] I Nov. 1986, G Oct. 1987 ~ EMI Compact
Disc CMS5 65032-2. [In six-disc set of 15 Quartets plus Quintet.] I Mar.
1994 ~ BMG Melodiya Compact Discs 74321 40711-2 (six-disc set). [Opp.
73 and 11.] I June 1997 ~ BMG Melodiya Compact Disc 74321 40713-2.
[Opp. 73 and 11.] I Dec. 1997.

Nimbus Compact Disc NI 5156. John BINGHAM (piano) and Medici
Quartet (Paul Robertson, David Matthews, Ivo-Jan van der Werff,
Anthony Lewis). [Mendelssohn.] P 6–8 June 1988, I Feb. 1989, G May 1989.

Philips Compact Disc 432 079-2PH. Beaux Arts Trio (Isidore Cohen,
Peter Wiley, Menahem PRESSLER) with Eugene Drucker (violin) and
Lawrence Dutton (viola). [Op. 67.] P New York Sept. 1989, I May 1991, G
Aug. 1991.

Finland: Ondine Compact Disc ODE 744-2. KUHMO CHAMBER SOLOISTS
(Konstantin Bogino—piano; Pavel Vernikov, Yoshiko Arai, Vladimir
Mendelssohn, and Anatole Liebermann). [Op. 67.] P Nov. 1989, I June
1990.

Netherlands: Fidelio Compact Disc 8843. REIZEND MUZIEKGEZELSCHAP
(Christian Bor, Paul Rosenthal, Marcus Thompson, Godfried Hoogeveen, Edward Auer). [Op. 67.] P Amsterdam 21 Mar. and 7 Aug. 1990.

Virgin Classics Compact Disc VC7 59312-2. NASH ENSEMBLE (Ian
Brown—piano; Marcia Crayford, Elizabeth Layton, Roger Chase, and
Christopher van Kampen). [Opp. 67 and Sans op. P.] P London Nov.
1990, I Aug. 1993. *Reissued:* Virgin Classics Compact Discs VDB5 61760-2
(two-disc set). [Schoenberg.] I Mar. 2000.

Conifer Classics Compact Disc CDCF 194 (international 75605 51194-
2). Kathryn STOTT (piano) and London Musici Quartet (Lyn Fletcher,
Jackie Hartley, Edward Vanderspar, Martin Loveday). [Ustvolskaya.] P
Bristol 3–4 Dec. 1990, I Jan. 1995.

USA: Russian Disc Compact Disc RDCD 10 031. Constantine ORBELIAN
(piano) and Moscow Quartet (Yevgeniya Alikhanova, Valentina
Alykova, Tatyana Kokhanovskaya, Olga Ogranovich). [Schnittke.] P
Moscow Conservatory May 1991, I June 1994.

France: Auvidis Valois Compact Disc V 4702. PRO ARTE QUINTET of
Monte-Carlo (Fernande Laurent-Biancheri—piano; Bojidar Bratoev,
Daniel Lagard, Jean-Pierre Pigerre, and Shigheki Sakuraba). [Borodin.]
P June 1993, I Apr. 1994, G Oct. 1994.

USA: Greystone Records Compact Disc GS 521. Robert GURALNIK
(piano) and Leontovych Quartet (Yuri Mazurkevich, Yuri Kharenko,
Borys Daviatov, Volodymyr Pantelev). P Purchase, New York May 1994.

Teldec Compact Disc 4509-98414-2. Elizaveta LEONSKAYA (piano) and
Borodin Quartet (Mikhail Kopelman, Andrei Abramenkov, Dmitri She-
balin, Valentin Berlinsky). [Op. 67.] P Berlin Apr. 1995, I Nov. 1996, G
Feb. 1997. *Reissued:* Ultima Compact Discs 8573 87820-2 (two-disc set).
[Opp. 67, 49, and 144.] I Apr. 2001, G Aug. 2001.

Canada: Marquis Classics Compact Disc ERAD 183. Lev NATOCHENNY (piano) and Penderecki Quartet (Piotr Buczek, Jerzy Kaplanek, Dov Scheindlin, Paul Pulford). [Schnittke.] P Toronto 12–13 Oct. 1995, I June 1997.

Italy: Real Sound Compact Disc RS 051-0176. TRIO DI TORINO (Sergio Lamberto, Dario Destefano, Giacomo Fuga) with Marina Bertolo (violin) and Gustavo Fioravanti (viola). [Opp. 8 and 67.] P Wesel, Germany Apr. 1996, I May 2000.

Germany: Edition Abseits Compact Disc EDA 010-2. PIHTIPUDAS QUIN- TET (Jaako Untamala—piano; Götz Bernau, Antti Meurman, Ulla Kekko, and Juhu Malmivaara). [Rubinstein.] P Kuopio, Finland May 1996.

USA: Arabesque Compact Disc Z 6715. BOSTON SYMPHONY CHAMBER PLAYERS (Gilbert Kalish—piano; Malcolm Lowe, Marylou Speaker Curchill, Steven Ansell, Jules Eskin). [Hindemith.] P Tanglewood 'Sum- mers of 1997–1997', I and G Mar. 1999.

Germany: Cybele Compact Disc 350 301. Thomas LEANDER (piano) and Minguet Quartet (Ulrich Isfort, Annette Reisinger, Irene Schwalb, Matthais Diener). [Borodin.] P Viersen 17–19 Dec. 1997.

Linn Compact Disc CKD 065. Ian BROWN (piano) and Schidlof Quartet (Ofer Falk, Rafael Todes, Graham Oppenheimer, Oleg Kogan). [Opp. 108 and 83.] P Horsham 3–5 Oct. 1996, I May 1997, G Oct. 1997.

Denmark: Classico Compact Disc CLASSCD 273. ESBJERG ENSEMBLE (Ulrich Stark—piano; Sakari Tepponen, Niels Christian Øllgaard, Michel Camille, Alexei Kalatchev). [Op. 127.] P Mantziusgården, Den- mark 31 Mar.–2 Apr. 1998.

Sony Compact Disc SK 60677. Yefim BRONFMAN (piano) and Juilliard Quartet (Joel Smirnoff, Ronald Copes, Samuel Rhodes, Joel Krosnick). [Opp. 35 and 102.] P Tanglewood 28–9 June 1999, I Nov. 1999.

References: Beletsky (in Berger), Calvocoressi, Mazel, and Shaginyan.

Opus 58   Boris Godunov (Musorgsky)

Form: Reorchestration of Modest Musorgsky's opera *Boris Godunov* of 1868–72 for stage performance. Opera in four acts with Prologue and ten scenes. Libretto by Musorgsky, based on Aleksandr Pushkin's drama *Boris Godunov* and Nikolai Karamazin's *History of the Russian Empire*.

Instrumentation: piccolo (= flute III), 2 flutes, 2 oboes, cor anglais (= oboe III), E flat clarinet, 2 clarinets (B flat and A), bass clarinet, 2 bassoons, contrabassoon (= bassoon III) ~ 4 horns, 3 trumpets, 3 trombones, tuba ~ separate on-stage band of 2–4 B flat cornets, 4 trumpets, 3–6 French horns, 2–4 B flat baritone saxhorns, and 2–4 bass saxhorns ~ tim- pani, triangle, side drum, cymbals, bass drum, gong ~ glockenspiel, orchestral bells, xylophone, celesta, 2–4 harps, piano ~ strings. Optional balaikas and domras.

Composed: Edited and orchestrated from 24 November 1939 (negotiations with the Kirov Theatre, Leningrad) to 10 May 1940. Acts 1, 2, and 3 completed on 21 January, 4 March, and 1 April respectively, at Leningrad. Act 4 completed at Gaspra, Crimea.

Première: 4 November 1959, Kirov Theatre of Opera and Ballet, Leningrad; designs by G. Moseyev, directed by I. Shlepyanov and conducted by Sergei Yeltsin. Title role sung by Boris Shtokolov. [The 1943 première, with designs by Pavel Williams, was delayed owing to the replacement of Samuil Samosud as principal conductor of the Bolshoi Theatre, Moscow.]

Arrangement: German translation of the libretto by Herkunft.

Music: Sovetskii Kompozitor, No. 2738, 1963, two volumes, full score, 30 cm.

Duration: 3 hrs 22 mins.

Recordings: USA: Unique Opera UORC 337 (mono). Excerpts: Monologue, Clock Scene, and Farewell. Aleksander KIPNIS (bass), New York Philharmonic Orchestra, Fritz Reiner. [Mozart, Tchaikovsky, Rimsky-Korsakov *et al.*] P radio première 23 July 1944. *Reissued:* USA: Discocorp RR 210. [Musorgsky, Mozart, Verdi *et al.*] I 1983 ~ Italy: AS Compact Disc 628. [Op. 54; and Copland.] I 1990 ~ Italy: Legend Compact Disc LGD 122. [Op. 54; and Copland.] I June 1994 ~ USA: Music & Arts Compact Disc 867 (mono). [*Boris Godunov* highlights in Rimsky-Korsakov version.] I 1995 ~ Italy: Arkadia Compact Disc MP 492-3 (mono). Clock Scene only. [Historical bonus disc with 1967 recording.] I May 1995 ~ Italy: Arlecchino Compact Discs ARL 121-3 (three-disc set, mono). Three excerpts on third disc. [Rimsky-Korsakov/Ippolitov-Ivanov version recorded in Moscow, Mar. 1948.] I 1996.

USSR: MK D 9605-6 (10" mono) and C 281-2 (10"). Scenes in the Tsar's chamber from Act 2. Boris Shtokolov (Boris), Konkordiya Slovtsova (Kseniya), Taisiya Kuznetsova (Fyodor), Vladimir Ulyanov (Shuisky); Soloists and Orchestra of the Kirov Opera and Ballet Theatre of Leningrad, Sergei YELTSIN. P 1959, I 1962. *Reissued:* USSR: Melodiya C10 07349-50. [Glinka, Rimsky-Korsakov, Dargomyzhsky *et al.*] I 1977*b* ~ USSR: Melodiya C10 15253-4. [Glinka.] I 1981*d*.

Italy: Arkadia Compact Discs MP 492-3 (three-disc set with comparitive examples from the original version by Musorgsky, revision by Rimsky-Korsakov, and the Kipnis/Reiner recording in Shostakovich's orchestration). Miroslav Čangalović (Boris), Olga Djokić (Kseniya), Milivoj Petrović (Fyodor), Franjo Paulik (Shuisky), Dušan Popović (Pimen); Orchestra, Soloists, and Chorus of the Belgrade National Opera Theatre, Dragomir Radivojević (chorus-master), Dušan MILADINOVIĆ. P Venice concert 3 Jan. 1967, I May 1995.

Germany: Telefunken SAT 22526. Arias and Scenes from Scenes 2, 5, and 7–9, sung in German. Theo Adam (Boris), Roswitha Trexier (Fyodor),

Karl Friedrich Hölzke (Shuisky), Siegfried Vogel (Pimen), Martin Ritz-
mann (False Dmitri), Hanne-Lore Kuhse (Marina), Wifred Schaal (Ran-
goni), Peter Schreier (Yurodivy); Dresden Philharmonic Children' s
Choir—Wolfgang Berger (chorus-master), Leipzig Radio Choir—Horst
Neumann (chorus-master), Dresden Staatskapelle, Herbert KEGEL. P
Dresden studio Mar. 1970, G June 1973. *Reissued:* Germany: Berlin Classics Compact Disc 0120 032.

Philips Compact Disc 442 775-2PH. Coronation Scene—'I am sick at
heart'. Kirov Theatre Chorus and Orchestra, Valeri GERGIEV. ['Russian
Spectacular'—Lyadov and Tchaikovsky.] P Haarlem Apr. 1993, I Feb.
1995, G July 1995.

References: Fay (in M. H. Brown), Levando, and Zaporozhets-Ishlinkskaya.

Op. 58*a*   King Lear

Form: Incidental music to Grigori Kozintsev's stage production of William
Shakespeare's tragedy *King Lear*, in the Russian translation of Mikhail
Kuzmin and A. Radlova:

1. Introduction and Ballad of Cordelia—'Beyond a dark sea on a
   cliff stands a high house'—Moderato (authorship of text not
   established).
2. Return from the Hunt—Allegretto
3–12 The Fool's Songs—ten brief songs, the first to the tune 'Jingle Bells'
   (text by Shakespeare, translated by Samuil Marshak)
13. Finale of Act One—Andante
14. Approach of the Storm (At Regan's castle)—Andante
15. Scene on the Steppe [from Act Three] (At the Hut)—Moderato
16. The Blinding of Gloucester [Earl of Gloster]—Moderato
17. The Military Camp—Andante
18. March—Allegretto poco moderato
19–23. Fanfares—five flourishes—Allegro

Instrumentation: piccolo, flute, oboe, clarinet (A/B flat), 2 bassoons ~ 2
horns, 2 trumpets, trombone, tuba ~ timpani, triangle*, wood block*,
tambourine, side drum*, cymbals, bass drum*, gong* ~ piano* ~ strings.
Instruments marked by an asterisk not used in the two pieces for *Hamlet*
(1954).

Composed: Late 1940, at Leningrad.

Premières: 24 March 1941, Gorky Bolshoi Drama Theatre, Leningrad;
designs by Natan Altman and directed by Grigori Kozintsev.

The Fool's Songs. USA: 10 October 1995, The Sylvia and Danny Kaye
Playhouse, New York; Robert Osborne (bass-baritone) and Norman

Krieger (piano). Osborne's edition of the ten songs using the original Shakespearean texts.

Arrangements: Three orchestral pieces in the composer's piano reduction:

2. Return from the Hunt—Allegretto
15. A Scene from Act Three (At the Hut)—Moderato
18. March—Allegretto poco moderato

Material from Shostakovich's manuscript score restored and arranged for voice and piano by Lev Solin:

3–12. The Fool's Songs
1. Ballad of Cordelia—Moderato

English translation of Nos. 1 and 3–12 by Joan Pemberton Smith and Edition of Nos. 3–12 using the original Shakespearean texts by Robert Osborne.

Hamlet: Music for stage production of William Shakespeare's tragedy *Hamlet, Prince of Denmark,* produced by Grigori Kozintsev in April 1994 at the Leningrad Pushkin Theatre. A large part of Shostakovich's score to *King Lear,* Opus 58a, was utilized with two additional numbers composed in 1954:

'Jig'—Presto
Finale—Moderato

The 'Jig' arranged for cello and piano by Juozas Chelkauskas.

Music: Autograph piano and full scores of *King Lear* preserved in the Shostakovich family archive and manuscript full score only of the two items composed for *Hamlet* (1954) preserved in the Leningrad Pushkin Theatre's Music Department.

Published in the journal *Muzykalnaya Zhizn* ('Musical Life'), 1976, No. 17; 'The Fool's Songs' Nos. 1, 5, 6, and 10 and 'Ballad of Cordelia' for voice and piano.

Sovetskii Kompozitor, No. 4028 (in *Dmitri Shostakovich: Music to Plays*), 1977, three pieces in the composer's piano reduction and 'Jig' for *Hamlet* (1954) arr. for piano by L. Solin, 29 cm.

Sovetskii Kompozitor, No. 4235 (in *Dmitri Shostakovich: Songs from Plays*), 1977, 'The Fool's Songs' and 'Ballad of Cordelia' for voice and piano, 29 cm.

Muzyka, No. 11412 (in Volume 28 of *Collected Works* with Opp. 19, 24, 28, 31, 32, 37, 44, 63, 66, 72, and in the supplement, Sans opp. D and K), 1986, vocal and piano scores of 23 pieces and the two pieces from *Hamlet* (1954), 30 cm.

Muzyka, No. 11413 (in Volume 27 of *Collected Works* with Opp. 19, 24, 28, 32, 37, 44, 63, and 72), 1987, full score of *King Lear* and two pieces from *Hamlet* (1954), 30 cm.

Muzyka, No. 14908 (in *D. Shostakovich: Pieces for cello and piano*), 1991, the *Hamlet* 'Jig' arr. J. Chelkauskas, 29 cm.

Duration: No. 1: 2' 43"–3' 57" and Nos. 3–12: 8' 42"–9' 30". Complete score: 24' 58"–25' 43". *Hamlet* 'Jig': 1' 37" and Finale: 1' 29".

Recordings: USSR: Melodiya C10 09225-6. Nos. 3–12 and 1 (without the 'Introduction'). Yevgeni NESTERENKO (bass) and Yevgeni Shenderovich (piano). [In third box of Part 3 of *Collected Works on Records* with Opp. 123, 121, and 146.] P Jan. 1976, I 1978. *Reissued:* HMV Melodiya ASD 3700. [Opp. 121, 123, and 146; and Musorgsky.] G Sept. 1979 ~ Japan: Victor Musical Industries Compact Disc VICC 40082-83 (two-disc set). ['Shostakovich Songs'—Opp. 121, 123, 127, 140/143*a*, 145*a*, and 146.] I 1991.

USSR: Melodiya A10 00107 009 (digital). Nos. 1 and 3–12. Nataliya BURNASHEVA (mezzo-soprano) in No. 1; Yevgeni NESTERENKO (bass) in Nos. 3–12; USSR Ministry of Culture Symphony Orchestra, Gennadi Rozhdestvensky. [Album 3 of 'From Manuscripts of Different Years'— Opp. 125 and 19.] P 1984, I 1985*d* ~ BMG Melodiya Compact Discs 74321 53457-2 (two-disc set). [Opp. 60 and 65.] I May 1998.

USSR: Melodiya C10 22365 004. Nos. 2, 15, 14, 17–23, and 1. Nina Romanova (mezzo-soprano) in No. 1; Leningrad Chamber Orchestra, Eduard SEROV. ['Music for Theatre'—Opp. 32 and 37.] P 1984, I 1986*a*. *Reissued:* Olympia Compact Disc OCD 182. Nos. 2, 15, 14, 17–23, and 1. [Op. 135.] I Sept. 1988, G Dec. 1988 ~ Olympia Compact Disc OCD 5006. [In Volume 2 five-disc set of symphonies with Op. 135.] I Dec. 1990.

CIS: Manchester Compact Disc CDMAN 129. Nos. as Melodiya. ['Shostakovich Theatre and Cinema Music'—Opp, 32*a*, 45, 30, 78, 76, 97, 99, and 37.] I 1998.

USSR: Melodiya C10 28379 002. 'Scene on the Steppe' only. Vladimir VIARDO (piano). [Opp. 34, 37, and 19.] P 1986, I 1990*a*.

Germany: Capriccio Compact Disc 10 397. Nos. 19, 1, 20, 2, 21, 3–12, 22, 13–17, 23, and 18. Elena Zaremba (mezzo-soprano) in No. 1; Stanislav Suleimanov (bass) in Nos 3–12; Berlin Radio Symphony Orchestra, Mikhail YUROVSKY. [Op. 137.] P Berlin 10–13 December 1990, G Sept. 1992. NB. No. 13 should read 'Finale 1st Act'. *Reissued:* Germany: Capriccio Compact Disc 10 822. No. 1 only. [See 'Movie Madness' under Samplers.] I Oct. 1997.

Koch International Classics Compact Disc 37274-2. Nos. 19, 1, 20, 2, 3–12, 21, 13, 22, 14, 23, and 15–18. KBS Symphony Orchestra, Vakhtang JORDANIA. [Opp. 97*a* and 116*a*.] P Seoul, Korea Feb. 1994, I Sept. 1994, G Dec. 1994. NB. The 'Jester's Songs' Nos. 3–12 'sung' by a bassoon.

United Compact Disc 88050-2. *Hamlet* 'Jig' and Finale and *King Lear* Nos. 1–17, 19–23, and 18. Louise Winter (mezzo-soprano), David Wilson-Johnson (baritone), City of Birmingham Symphony Orchestra, Mark ELDER. [Op. 32.] P Birmingham Town Hall 13–15 June 1994, I Nov. 1994.

Reissued: Cala Compact Disc CACD 1021. [Op. 32.] I Aug. 1995, G Jan. 1996.

Japan: Triton Compact Disc 17 008. Nos. 1 and 3–12. Aleksei MOCHALOV (bass), Moscow Chamber Music Theatre Orchestra, Anatoli Levin. [Opp. 140, 146, 121, and Sans op. X (iii).] P Mosfilm. Studio Nov. 1995, I Nov. 1996.

Chandos Compact Disc CHAN 9907. *Hamlet* 'Jig' and *King Lear* No. 17 arr. composer. Rustem HAYROUDINOFF (piano). ['Theatre Music'—Opp. 37, 19, 31, 32, 44, 66, and 22.] P Potton Hall, Suffolk 7–8 Aug. 2000, I Apr. 2001.

Note: In Shakespeare's play the texts of the Fool's Songs, as arranged in Shostakovich's score, appear in the order 1–4, 7, 5, 10, 8, 9, and 6. *Collected Works* Volume 28 incorrectly states that the Scene from Act Three piece in *Music to Plays* SK 4028 is 'The Military Camp'.

Opus 59 The Adventures of Korzinkina

Alternative title: *Ein Billet V Zone* ('A Ticket to the Fifth Zone').

Form: Music for the film *The Adventures of Korzinkina*, the first of a projected series of comedies, directed by Klementi Mints for Lenfilm. The score said to be saturated with humorous music, including a march, lullaby, and galop; the number 'On the Boulevard'; fragments from Tchaikovsky's *Swan Lake* ballet; Mephistopheles aria from Charles Gounod's *Faust*, and the orchestration of Musorgsky's *Song of the Flea* for bass and symphony orchestra. For the 'Song of Korzinkina' Shostakovich used a melody that the clown Musin played on the concertina in the Leningrad circus. The March is a shortened brass band version of the first number in the *Suite for Jazz Orchestra No. 2*, Sans op. G.

Composed: Autumn 1940, at Leningrad.

Première: Film first shown on 11 November 1940.

Arrangement: Suite of six items assembled by Gennadi Rozhdestvensky:

1. Overture—Allegretto
2. March—Allegretto
3. The Chase (for piano four hands)—Presto
4. Music in the Restaurant—Moderato non troppo
5. Intermezzo
6. Finale—Andantino

Instrumentation of Suite: piccolo, 2 flutes, 2 oboes, E flat clarinet, 2 B flat clarinets, 2 bassoons ~ 4 horns, 2 trumpets, trombone, tuba ~ timpani, triangle, tambourine, side drum, cymbals, bass drum ~ xylophone, harp, piano (2 players) ~ S.A.T.B. chorus~strings.

Music: Film score lost during the Leningrad Blockade. *Song of the Flea* orchestration, along with drafts in piano score, preserved at the CIS Archives of Literature and Art. Ten numbers preserved in the Shostakovich family archive.

Muzyka, No. 10889 (in Volume 41 of *Collected Works* with Opp. 26, 30, 33, 41, 48, 50, 53, 55, 56, and 64), Suite Nos. 1–4 and 6, 30 cm.

Duration: Suite: 9' 10" (Nos. 1–6)–10' 03" (Nos. 1–4 and 6).

Ballet: *The Overcoat*. For details see under Opus 32.

Recordings: USSR: Melodiya C10 23081 001. Suite Nos. 1–6. Nataliya Koridalina and Mikhail Muntyan (piano), USSR Ministry of Culture Symphony Orchestra and Chamber Choir, Gennadi ROZHDESTVENSKY. [Album 5 of 'From Manuscripts of Different Years'—Sans opp. D and E; Op. 23.] P 1984, I 1986c. *Reissued:* Olympia Compact Disc OCD 194. [Opp. 1, 3, 7, 100, 26, and 37.] I Feb. 1988, G June 1988 ~ BMG Melodiya Compact Discs 74321 59058-2 (two-disc set). [Opp. 36, 4, 17, Z, H, C, 16, 1, 3, 7, 26/D, E, 128, 30a, and 19.] I and G. Mar 1999.

USA: Citadel Compact Disc CTD 88129. Suite Nos. 1–4 and 6. Irina Kolesnikova and Nina Kavetskaya (piano), Belarus State Chorus, Belarus RTV Symphony Orchestra, Walter MNATSAKANOV. [Opp. 30a, 36, and 56.] P Minsk Feb. 1997, I 1998.

Sans op. I   Three Pieces for Solo Violin

Form: Music for unaccompanied violin: Prelude, Gavotte, and Waltz.

Composed: 1940, at Leningrad.

Music: Given as Opus 59 by Boelza (1942), Martynov (1947), Slonimsky (1964) *et al.*

Recordings: —

Sans op. J   Wartime Concert Party Pieces

(i) *Oath to the People's Commissar*

Form: A part song for bass soloist, five-part choir, and piano with text by Vissarion Sayanov.

Composed: 12–14 July 1941, at Leningrad.

Arrangements: A second version, 'The Great Day Has Come', with new words also by V. Sayanov. Adaptations for two voices by Lev Atovmyan and for male voice, entitled 'The Song of Liberation' with lyrics by Paula Stone, by D. J. Grunes. Choral arrangement (T.T.B.B.) of the latter by Hugh Ross.

Music: Manuscript lost. Autograph of the second version preserved in the Shostakovich family archive. The original song, along with war songs by seven other Leningrad composers won a prize in August 1941. Published in a collection 'Songs of the Baltic Red Banner', Leningrad on 1 September 1941 and by Muzgiz, 1942. The first 24 bars quoted in Khentova (1979*b*), pp. 26–7.

Russian-American Music, New York, 1944, adaptation 'The Song of Liberation' for voice and piano, 31 cm. Text translated into 15 languages, 43 × 56 cm. Also choral arrangement with piano by H. Ross.

Sovetskii Kompozitor, No. 519 (in *D. Shostakovich: Songs*), 1958, 'The Great Day Has Come' arrangement for two voices by L. Atovmyan, 29 cm.

Muzyka, No. 10179 (in Volume 34 of *Collected Works* with Opp. 88 and songs), 1985, 'The Great Day Has Come' for bass soloist, S.A.T.B. chorus, and piano), 30 cm.

Recording: USA: Eterna 30-28 (78 rpm). 'Oath to Stalin'. [Op. 80 No. 8.], NB. No further details in WERM 3rd Supplement. The title 'Oath to Stalin' heavily scored out by the composer on the compiler's query sheet!

(ii) Twenty-seven Romances and Songs

Form: Arrangements for Leningrad frontline concerts:

1. Ludwig van Beethoven—'Come fill, fill, my good fellow' (Trinklied) from 25 Schottische Lieder, Opus 108 (Russian text by A. Globa).
2. Georges Bizet—'Habanera' from Act 1 of *Carmen*.
3. Zhan Vekerlen—'Pastorale'.
4. Ruggiero Leoncavallo—'Harlequin's Serenade' from Act 2 of *Pagliacci*.
5. Gioacchino Rossini—'Alpine shepherds' song' from *Guillaume Tell*.
6. Aleksei Vertovsky—'Gypsy Song'.
7. Semyon Gulak-Artemovsky—duet of Odarka and Karas, 'From where did you appear?', from Act 1 of the opera *The Zaporozhian Cossack beyond the Danube*.
8. Aleksandr Gurilyov—'Really, I will tell mama' (words by N. Berg).
9. Aleksandr Gurilyov—'The Little Sarafan' (words by A. Polezhayev).
10. Aleksandr Dargomyzhsky—'What it is like in our street' (words by the composer).
11. Aleksandr Dargomyzhsky—comedy song 'The Worm' (words by Vasili Kurochkin after verses by Pierre Béranger).
12. Aleksandr Dargomyzhsky—Bolero 'The Sierra-Nevada [Granada] is clothed in mists' (words by V. Shirkov).
13. Aleksandr Dargomyzhsky—'Feverishness' (words traditional).
14. Modest Musorgsky—'Hopak' (words from 'Haydamaki'—a Ukrainian poem by Taras Shevchenko, in a Russian translation of Lev Mey).

15. Modest Musorgsky—'Parasya's Dumka' from Act 3 of *Sorochintsy Fair*.
16. Modest Musorgsky—'Khivrya's Aria' from *Sorochintsy Fair*.
17. Nikolai Rimsky-Korsakov—'Song of the Varangian (Viking) Merchant' from Scene 4 of *Sadko*.
18. Mikhail Ippolitov-Ivanov—'I am sitting on a little rock'.
19. Matvei Blanter—'Song about Shchors' (words by Mikhail Golodny).
20. Isaak Dunayevsky—'Song of the Sea'.
21. Isaak Dunayevsky—'Anyuta's Song'.
22. Isaak Dunayevsky—'Sing to us, wind' (words by Vasili Lebedev-Kumach).
23. Isaak Dunayevsky 'Oh, good'.
24. Georgi Milyutin—'Do not touch us'.
25. Dmitri and Daniil Pokrass—'Those are not storm clouds' (words by Aleksei Surkov).
26. Daniil Pokrass—'Farewell—He was given an Order to go to the West' (words by Mikhail Isakovsky).
27. David Pritsker—'Song of the Young Girl'.

Composed: 12, 13, and 14 July 1941, at Leningrad.
Music: Autograph score of 111 pages preserved in the archives of Leningrad Conservatory. No. 1 has an accompaniment for cello and piano. The first ten bars of No. 23 are illustrated on page 21 of Khentova (1979*b*). Shostakovich's autograph of 'Oh, good' shows accompaniment for violin and bass clef chords. The original Dunayevsky song is included in *Songs from Soviet Cinema* (see Opus 80).

(iii) *The Fearless Regiments Are on the Move*

Form: Marching song for bass soloists and S.A.T.B. chorus, with lyric by sports journalist L. Rakhmilevich and simple accompaniment for bayan or piano, marked 'Allegro commodo'.
Composed: 15 July 1941, for the music ensemble of the People's Volunteer Corps Theatre, Leningrad.
Music: Manuscript lost. The title changed to 'The Fearless Guards Regiments are Marching On' when the units distinguished themselves in battle on the Leningrad Front and later to 'Song of a Guards Division'.

Sovetskii Kompozitor, No. 3567 (in album 'It is impossible for us to forget all about this journey . . .'), compiled by Aleksandr Tishchenko, 1975, 29.5 cm.

Muzyka, No. 10179 (in Volume 34 of *Collected Works* with Opp. 86 and 136; and songs), 1985, 30 cm.

(iv) *Polka for Harp Duet in F sharp minor* (Balakirev)

Form: A transcription of a piece by Mili Balakirev for two harps, marked 'Allegretto-Scherzando'. May also be played by a large ensemble of harps.

Composed: Late 1941 in Kuibyshev, at the request of harpist Vera Dulova.
Music: Sovetskii Kompozitor, No. 4893 (in *Album of pieces for harp,* Volume 1), 1979, 28.5 cm.
Duration: 2' 43".
Recording: USSR: Melodiya C10 26307 004. Svetlana PARAMONOVA and Irina PASHINSKAYA (harps). [Album 6 of 'From Manuscripts of Different Yeras'—Sans opp. X, A, S, D; Opp. 41 and 128.] P 1983–6, I 1988*d*.

Opus 60   Symphony No. 7 in C major

Subtitle: 'Leningrad Symphony'.
Form: Symphony for large orchestra (with additional brass, 2 harps, and a piano) in four movements:

1. Allegretto—'War'
2. Moderato (poco allegretto)—'Memories'
3. Adagio—'Native Expanses' or 'My Native Fields' *attacca*
4. Allegro non troppo—'Victory'

Instrumentation: piccolo (= flute III), 2 flutes (II = alto flute), 2 oboes, cor anglais, E flat clarinet (= clarinet III B flat and A), 2 clarinets (B flat and A), bass clarinet, 2 bassoons, contrabassoon ~ 8 horns, 6 trumpets, 6 trombones, tuba ~ timpani (5 drums), triangle, tambourine, side drum, cymbals, bass drum, gong ~ xylophone, 2 harps, piano ~ 1st violins (16–20), 2nd violins (16–18), violas (12–16), cellos (10–14), double-basses (8–12). It is desirable to have 2 side drums from fig. 39 and, if possible, 3 side drums from fig. 45 to 11th bar after fig. 51 in first movement. The additional group of brass (3 trumpets, 4 horns, and 3 trombones) is required in first, third, and fourth movements; harps in second and third; piano in first, second, and fourth movements.
Composed: 19 July–27 December 1941. The first three movements composed in besieged Leningrad; first finished on 3 September, second written in 14 days, and third completed in 12 days on 29 September; fourth movement completed at Kuibyshev (reverted to its pre-revolutionary name of Samara in autumn 1991).
Premières: 5 March 1942, Kuibyshev Palace of Culture; Bolshoi Theatre Orchestra, Samuil Samosud. Introductory talk by the composer.

  29 March 1942, The House of the Soviets Hall of Columns, Moscow; combined Bolshoi Theatre and All-Union Radio Symphony Orchestras, Samuil Samosud.

  UK broadcast: 22 June 1942, Maida Vale Studio, London; London Symphony Orchestra, Sir Henry Wood.

  UK concert: 29 June 1942, Royal Albert Hall 'Prom', London; London Symphony Orchestra, Sir Henry Wood.

USA broadcast: 19 July 1942, New York; NBC Symphony Orchestra, Arturo Toscanini.

9 August 1942, Leningrad Philharmonic Bolshoi Hall; Leningrad Radio Orchestra, Karl Eliasberg.

Germany: 21 December 1946, Berlin; Berlin Philharmonic Orchestra, Sergiu Celibidache.

Dedication: 'To the City of Leningrad' (on the autograph score).

Arrangements: Reductions for piano by the composer and Lev Atovmyan; piano four hands by L. Atovmyan, and two pianos four hands by Pavel Lamm (not published). First movement in piano reduction by Anatoli Samonov.

Music: Given as Opus 59 in Slonimsky's list of 1942. Autograph score preserved at the Glinka Museum. The opening bars of the autograph score reproduced in Volume 4 of *Collected Works*. Awarded a Stalin Prize First Class on 11 April 1942.

Muzgiz, No. 17606, 1942, foreword by Lev Danilevich, 30 cm. Reprinted in 1944, 1954, 1958 (23 cm.), 1962, and 1969.

Leeds Music, no number, c.1945, 21.5 cm.

Belwin Mills, Kalmus, New York, No. 1390, no date, miniature score.

Sovetskii Kompozitor, 1968, reduction for piano four hands by L. Atovmyan, 30 cm.

Edition Peters, No. 5727 (plate no. 12626), 1971, 19 cm.

Muzyka, No. 7133 (with compositions by Prokofiev, Khachaturyan, and Kabalevsky), 1975, first movement (with three cuts) in piano reduction by A. Samonov, 29 cm.

Muzyka, No. 9375 (in Volume 4 of *Collected Works* with Op. 65), 1981, 30 cm.

Hans Sikorski, No. 2229, 1982, 21 cm.

Zen-On, Tokyo, 1992, facsimile edition of 'autograph of the fair copy of the full score' with preface in Russian by Manashir Yakubov and translations in English (by Laurel E. Fay), German, and Japanese, 159 pp., 37 cm.

Duration: Approx. 80 minutes in score; 68–86 minutes; 72 minutes (Schirmer); [Aronowsky's average time of 33' 30" is incorrect.]

Ballets: *Leningrad Symphony*. Léonide Massine, Ballet Russe Highlights company, New York; 15 February 1945.

Leningrad Symphony (first movement). Igor Belsky, Academic Theatre of Opera and Ballet (Kirov Theatre), Leningrad; designs by Mikhail Gordon, conducted by Yevgeni Dubovsky, 14 April 1961. This ballet performed the following year at Novosibirsk under the title *Leningrad Poem*.

Leningrad Symphony (first movement). Lyubosh Ogoun, Brno, Czechoslovakia, 1962.

Films: *Leningrad.* Scenes of the composer at work on his symphony in this film directed by Roman Carmen.

A Matter of Survival. Mark Wigglesworth travelled to a snowy St Petersburg for the BBC 2 TV series 'Everything to Play for' to research a thirty-minute programme screened on 26 December 1997. Historic film clips of the city of Leningrad and the composer during the Siege; interviews with 80-year-old oboist Ksenya Matus (who paid for the repair to her instrument for the 9 Aug. 1942 concert with a 'pussy cat'—then preferable to chicken as food), a Siege survivor Leonid Gisen, and 93-year-old conductor Ilya Musin; interspersing a moving commentary by Wigglesworth who rehearsed the San Francisco Symphony Orchestra for their first concert performance of the Leningrad Symphony since 1943.

Recordings: National Sound Archive Tape 11048R. Extract (7 minutes). London Symphony Orchestra, Sir Henry Wood. P London BBC broadcast 22 June 1942.

USA: RCA LM 6711 (transfer from radio broadcast, 3 sides mono in five-record set). NBC Symphony Orchestra, Arturo TOSCANINI. [Op. 10; Haydn, L. Mozart, Brahms, and Sibelius.] P July 1942, I 1967. *Reissued:* RCA Victrola VICS 6038 1-2 (3 sides in double album, electronic stereo). [Op. 10.] G July 1970 ~ USSR: Melodiya D 034359-62 (3 sides mono). [Op. 10.] I 1974 ~ Italy: RCA AT 205 (2), Toscanini Edition 47 (3 sides mono). [Op. 10.] ~ Trax Classique TRXLP 131 and Compact Disc TRXCD 131. First movement excerpt 'The Nazi Invasion'—fig. 19 to end. ['Testimony—Shostakovich's Greatest Hits'—Opp. 47, 97, 102, 110, 67; and Josephs.] I 1988 ~ Italy: Memories Compact Disc HR 4183 (mono). [Op. 10.] I 1991 ~ RCA Victor Gold Seal Compact Disc GD 60293, Toscanini Collection 22 (mono). I Nov. 1991, G Apr. 1992.

Pearl Compact Disc GEMM CDS 9044 (two-disc set, mono). NBC Symphony Orchestra, Leopold STOKOWSKI. [Opp. 10, 47, and 34 No. 14.] P NBC broadcast 13 Dec. 1942, I Nov. 1993, G Jan. 1994.

USA: Urania URLP 601 (4 sides mono). Berlin Philharmonic Orchestra, Sergiu CELIBIDACHE. P Berlin concert 1946. *Reissued:* Italy: Theorema Compact Disc TH 121.122. I Mar. 1993 ~ Italy: Arlecchino Compact Disc ARL 106. ['The Art of Celibadache, Vol. I'.] I Apr. 1995 ~ Italy: Grammofono 2000 Compact Disc AB 78685 (mono). I Feb. 1997 ~ Italy: Magic Talent Compact Disc 48082. I 1998 ~ Italy: Magic Talent Compact Disc 48095. Fourth movement. ['The Great Conductors'—Reiner, Stokowski, Jochum *et al.*] I 1998.

USA: Musicraft 1168-75 in Set 83 (16 sides 78 rpm, in album with notes). Buffalo Philharmonic Orchestra, William STEINBERG. P 4 Dec. 1946. *Reissued:* USA: Allegro ALC 3041 (4 sides mono) ~ France: Dante Compact Disc LYS 186 (mono). [William Steinberg Volume 1—labelled as 'World Première Recording'.] I July 1997.

USSR: MK HD 01380-3 (4 sides mono). Leningrad Philharmonic Orchestra, Yevgeni MRAVINSKY. P 26 Feb. 1953, G Feb. 1965. *Reissued:*

USA: Vanguard VRS 6030-1 (3 sides mono). [Op. 10.] I 1957 ~ USSR: Melodiya D 033449-52—also issued with prefix M10 (3 sides mono). [Op. 77.] I 1972 ~ BMG Classics Melodiya Compact Disc, Mravinsky Edition Vol. 16, 74321 29405-2 (mono). I Apr. 1996.

Czech: Supraphon DV 5444-5 (3 sides mono). Czech Philharmonic Orchestra, Karel ANČERL. [Martinů.] P Prague 20 Sept. 1957. *Reissued:* Czech: Supraphon SUA 10359-60 (3 sides mono). [Martinů.] I 1963, G Feb. 1965 ~ Parliament PLP 127 (4 sides mono). G June 1960 ~ USA: Everest 3404 (2 sides mono). I 1976 ~ Rediffusion Heritage HCH 8003 (2 sides mono). G July 1977 ~ Czech: Supraphon Compact Disc 11 1952-2. I Sept. 1992 ~ Classic CD 37. First movement to fig. 19 + 7 bars. [Mendelssohn, Brahms, Korngold *et al.*] I May 1993 (with magazine article on pp. 28–9) ~ Czech: Supraphon Historical Compact Disc SUP 019522. I Oct. 1993.

USA: Columbia M2L 322 (4 sides mono) and M2S 722 (4 sides). Figs. 25–9 cut in first movement. New York Philharmonic Orchestra, Leonard BERNSTEIN. P 22–3 Oct. 1962. *Reissued:* CBS BRG 72349-50 (3 sides mono) and SBRG 72349-50 (3 sides). [Op. 35.] G Dec. 1965 ~ Sony Royal Edition Compact Disc SMK 47616. G Nov. 1993 and June 1994 ~ Sony Classical Compact Discs SX4K 64206 (four-disc set). I Dec. 1995.

USSR: Melodiya M10 45011 003 (4 sides mono). Leningrad Philharmonic Orchestra, Karl ELIASBERG. P Leningrad concert 27 Jan. 1964, I 1984*a*.

France: Praga Compact Disc PR 254 002-3 (two-disc set). Czech Philharmonic Orchestra, Karel ANČERL. [Opp. 47 and 70.] P Prague broadcast 1967, I June 1992, G May 1993.

USSR: Melodiya D 022141-2 (4 sides mono) and C 01693-6 (4 sides). USSR Symphony Orchestra, Yevgeni SVETLANOV. P and I 1968. *Reissued:* HMV Melodiya ASD 2511-2 in Set SLS 784 (3 sides). [Kabalevsky.] G Dec. 1969 ~ USA: Angel Melodiya SRB 4107 (4 sides). I 1969 ~ Germany: Melodia Eurodisc 87623 XK. [In thirteen-record box set.] I 1974 ~ Netherlands: Phonogram Melodia 058 6005 ~ HMV BOX 502505-6 in Set SLS 5025 (3 sides). [Op. 65, first and second movements]. G Dec. 1975 ~ France: Le Chant du Monde LDX 78611 ~ Germany: ZYX Russian Art Compact Discs CLA 10011-2 (two-disc set). [Opp. 47 and 70.] I 1998.

Revelation Compact Disc RV 10059 (mono). USSR Radio and Television Large Symphony Orchestra, Gennadi ROZHDESTVENSKY. P concert 8 Aug. 1968, I Mar. 1997, G June 1997.

HMV ASD 3021-2 in Set SLS 897 (4 sides). Bournemouth Symphony Orchestra, Paavo BERGLUND. P Southhampton 13–14 Jan. 1974, G Oct. 1974. *Reissued:* HMV Master Series EG 2911351 (DMM). I Feb. 1987, G June 1987 ~ EMI Compact Disc CDC7 47651-2. I Mar. 1987, G Sept. 1987 ~ EMI Classics Compact Discs 5 73839-2 (two-disc set). [Op. 103.] I May 2000.

Czech: Supraphon 1 10 1771-2 (3 sides). Czech Philharmonic Orchestra, Václav NEUMANN. [Op. 70.] P Prague 19–20 Mar. and 16–17 Sept. 1974, G Aug. 1976. *Reissued:* Germany: Musicaphon LC 0522. [Op. 70.] I 1980 ~ Supraphon Compact Disc 11 0723-2. I 1991 ~ France: Atlas Compact Disc CLA-CD 179 ~ Supraphon Compact Discs (two-disc set). SU 0177-2. [Honegger, Martinů, and Schoenberg.] I Nov. 1995.

USSR: Melodiya C10 06435-8 (4 sides). Moscow Philharmonic Orchestra, Kirill KONDRASHIN. P 1975, I 1976c. *Reissued:* HMV Melodiya SLS 5109 (3 sides). [Op. 119.] G Feb. 1978 ~ Germany: Melodia Eurodisc 300 699-435. [In three-record set with Opp. 54 and 65.] ~ France: Le Chant du Monde LDX 78595-6. [In two-record set with Op. 54.] ~ USSR: Melodiya C10 06435-8 (4 sides). [In first box of Part 1 of *Collected Works on Records.*] I 1980 ~ HMV Melodiya EX 2903873 (DMM). [On fifth and sixth (first band) records of twelve-record box set.] G Dec. 1985 ~ France: Le Chant du Monde Compact Disc LDC 278 1003-4. [In Box 2 of five two-disc sets with Opp. 47 and 54.] G May 1989 ~ BMG Classics Melodiya Compact Disc 74321 19839-2. I July 1994, G Nov. 1994.

Decca D 213D 2 (3 sides in box set, digital). London Philharmonic Orchestra, Bernard HAITINK. [Op. 22a.] P Nov. 190, G Nov. 1980. *Reissued:* USA: London LDR 10015 (3 sides digital). [Op. 22a.] I 1980 ~ Decca Compact Disc 417 392-2DH2. [Op. 112 in two-disc set.] I June 1986, G Oct. 1986 ~ Decca Ovation Compact Disc 425 068-2DM. I Aug. 1993, G Nov. 1993 ~ London Compact Disc 444 436-2. [Sixth disc in eleven-disc set.] I June 1995.

USA: Pair Records and Special Music Company Stradivari Classics Compact Disc SCD 6044. Ljubljana Symphony Orchestra, Anton NANUT. P not stated, I 1988.

USSR: Melodiya A10 00257 006 (4 sides digital). USSR Ministry of Culture Symphony Orchestra, Gennadi ROZHDESTVENSKY. P 1984, I 1988b. *Reissued:* Olympia Compact Disc OCD 118. G Aug. 1988 ~ Germany: Melodia Eurodisc Compact Disc 353 118 [In two-disc set with Op. 47.] ~ Olympia Compact Disc OCD 5005. [In Vol. 1 six-disc set of symphonies.] I Dec. 1990 ~ BMG Melodiya Compact Discs 74321 53457-2 (two-disc set). [Opp. 65 and 58a.] I May 1998.

Chandos ABRD 1312 (digital) and Compact Disc CHAN 8623. Scottish National Orchestra, Neeme JÄRVI. P 'dedicated to the memory of Yevgeni Mravinsky' Dundee 22–3 Feb. 1988, G Aug. 1988.

EMI EL7 49494-1 (digital) and Compact Disc CDC7 49494-2. Leningrad Philharmonic Orchestra, Mariss JANSONS. P Oslo Apr. 1988, G Dec. 1988.

Deutsche Grammophon Compact Discs 427 632-2GH2 (two-disc set). Chicago Symphony Orchestra, Leonard BERNSTEIN. [Op. 10.] P Chicago concert June 1988, I Oct. 1989, G Jan. 1990.

Naxos Compact Disc 8.550627. Czecho-Slovak Radio Symphony Orchestra, Ladislav SLOVÁK. P Bratislava 1 Jan.–5 Feb. 1989, I Jan. 1993, G Nov. 1993. *Reissued:* Naxos Compact Discs 8.50517. [In five-disc set with Symphonies Nos. 1, 2, 3, 4, 6, 12, and 15.] I 1993.

France: Erato Compact Disc 2292 45414-2. National Symphony Orchestra of America, Mstislav ROSTROPOVICH. P Washington Jan. 1989, G May 1990. *Reissued:* Teldec Compact Discs 0630-17046-2. [In twelve-disc set of Symphonies.] G Oct. 1997.

Collins Classics Compact Disc 7029-2 (two-disc set). London Symphony Orchestra, Maksim SHOSTAKOVICH. P Watford 1990, I July 1993, G Nov. 1993.

Denon Compact Disc CO 79942. Vienna Symphony Orchestra, Eliahu INBAL. P Vienna 18–22 Mar. 1991, I Nov. 1992, G Apr. 1993.

Dorian Compact Disc DOR 90161. Dallas Symphony Orchestra, Eduardo MATA. P Dallas May 1991, I June 1992, G Sept. 1992.

Sweden: BIS Compact Disc CD 515. Junge Deutsche Philharmonie and members of Moscow Philharmonic Orchestra, Rudolf BARSHAI. P Leipzig concert on War Memorial Day Germany / Soviet Union 22 June 1991, I Dec. 1991, G Apr. 1992.

USA: Vanguard Compact Disc 99043. Swedish Radio Symphony Orchestra, Yevgeni SVETLANOV. P Stockholm 10–11 Sept. 1993, 1 Aug. 1995.

RCA Victor Red Seal Compact Disc 09026 62548-2. St Petersburg Philharmonic Orchestra, Yuri TEMIRKANOV. P St Petersburg 18–19 Jan. 1995, I Mar. 1996, G June 1996.

Japan: Canyon Classics Compact Disc PCCL 00380. The Hague Resident Orchestra, Yevgeni SVETLANOV. P The Hague 19–20 Jan. 1995, I Feb. 1997.

Decca Compact Disc 446 814-2. St Petersburg Philharmonic Orchestra, Vladimir ASHKENAZY. P St Petersburg 5–6 May 1995, I Aug. 1997, G Oct. 1997. NB. Prefaced by the composer's broadcast from besieged Leningrad in 1941.

Chandos Compact Disc CHAN 9621. Russian State Symphony Orchestra, Valeri POLYANSKY. P Moscow Conservatory Oct. 1996, I Apr. 1998.

Sweden: BIS Compact Disc CD 873. BBC National Orchestra of Wales, Mark WIGGLESWORTH. ['Complete Symphonies, Vol. 1'.] P Swansea 2–4 Dec. 1996, I July 1997, G. Aug. 1997.

Teldec Compact Disc 3984 21467-2. New York Philharmonic Orchestra, Kurt MASUR. P three Avery Fisher Hall, New York concerts 21–3 May 1998, I June 2000.

References: Brown, Dolzhansky (in Berger), Dorati, Goltsman, Gow, Grazia, Hughes, Khentova (1979), Lourie, Ottaway, Prokhorova, Sabinina, Shostakovich, Tigranov, and Yarustovsky.

Sans op. K   Wartime Operas

(i) *The Gamblers*

Subtitle: 'Scenes after Gogol' (Rozhdestvensky).

Form: Opera based on the comedy play *The Gamblers* of 1832 by Nikolai Gogol, for six male solo voices and large orchestra (with 2 harps, a piano—mainly in continuo role, and bass balalaika):

1. Overture—Allegretto—to fig. 8
2. Scenes in the hotel—figs. 8 to 104
3. Card gambling scene

Instrumentation: piccolo (= flute III), 2 flutes (II = alto flute), 2 oboes, cor anglais, 4 clarinets (I, II B flat and A; III A = E flat; IV B flat = bass), 3 bassoons (III = contrabassoon) ~ 4 horns, 3 trumpets, 3 trombones, tuba ~ timpani, triangle, tambourine, side drum, castanets, cymbals, bass drum ~ xylophone, bass balalaika, 2 harps, piano ~ strings.

Composed: Begun on 28 December 1941, continued in May and June 1942, but abandoned after composing about 50 minutes of the score. Of the twenty-five scenes, the first seven and most of the eighth completed (or 10 of the 36 pages in one Russian edition). Written at Kuibyshev (Samara).

Premières: 18 September 1978, Leningrad Bolshoi Philharmonic Hall named after Shostakovich; Moscow Chamber Music Theatre Group and Leningrad Philharmonic Orchestra under Gennadi Rozhdestvensky.

Meyer's completed version: 12 June 1983, Wuppertal, West Germany; Wuppertal Sinfonieorchester and nine male voices under the musical direction of Tristan Schick.

UK: 23 and 24 May 1993, Brighton Festival, Roedean Theatre; décor by Nataliya Khrennikova, directed by Boris Pokrovsky and conducted by Anatoli Levin; Vladimir Rybasenko (Aleksei), Boris Tarkhov (Ikharyov), Valeri Belykh (Gavryuska), Nikolai Kurpe and Oleg Gularev (Krugel), and Ashot Sarkisov (Shvokhnev).

Arrangements: Reduction of Overture and commencement of 'Scenes in the hotel' employed for the Scherzo of the Viola Sonata, Opus 147. German translation of the libretto by Georg Schwarz. Completion of the opera by Krzysztof Meyer in German language version by Jörg Morgener.

Music: Incomplete manuscript numbered Opus 63. NB. This work not to be confused (as in *The Phaidon Book of the Opera*, Oxford, 1979) as a setting of Fyodor Dostoyevsky's love story *The Gambler* of 1867. Autograph vocal and full scores preserved in the Shostakovich family archive. The first page of the autograph full score reproduced in Volume 23 of *Collected Works*.

Sovetskii Kompozitor, No. 5564, 1981, full score [numbered Op. 63] ed. G. Rozhdestvensky, 30 cm. In this edition Rozhdestvensky has orchestrated the seven bars after fig. 195, appearing in the composer's piano-vocal score but not in his full score, and provided a fitting three-page termination of the opera.

Sovetskii Kompozitor, No. 5585, 1981, vocal score [numbered Op. 63] ed. G. Rozhdestvensky, 30 cm.

Muzyka, No. 11935 (in Volume 23 of *Collected Works* with Opp. 15*a* and 23, and Sans op. D), 1986, full score with Rozhdestvensky's termination, 30 cm.

Muzyka, No. 11412 (in the supplement to Volume 28 of *Collected Works* with Sans op. D and Opp. 19, 24, 28, 31, 32, 37, 44, 58*a*, 63, 66, and 72), 1986, vocal score, 30 cm.

Duration: Unfinished: recorded portion 46' 35". Meyer's completed version: *c*.1 hr 45 mins.

Film: *Unfinished Masterpieces.* TV film shown on Soviet Television in mid-1980s. The opera performed along with Musorgsky's *The Marriage,* under conductor Gennadi Rozhdestvensky.

Recordings: USSR: Melodiya C10 11599-600. Nos. 1, 2, and 3. Vladimir Rybasenko (Aleksei), Boris Tarkhov (Ikharyov), Valeri Belykh (Gavryushka), Nikolai Kurpe (Krugel), Ashot Sarkisov (Shvokhnev), Yaroslav Radionik (Uteshitelny), Valeri Sudak (balalaika); Leningrad Philharmonic Orchestra, Gennadi ROZHDESTVENSKY. P première 18 Sept. 1978, I 1979*c*. *Reissued:* Germany: Melodia Eurodisc 200 370-405. With German libretto by G. Schwarz. I 1979 ~ HMV Melodiya ASD 3880. G Sept. 1980 ~ BMG Melodiya Compact Discs 74321 60319-2 (two-disc set, with plot synopsis but no libretto). [Op. 15.] I Nov. 1998, G May 1999.

Germany: Capriccio Compact Discs 60 062-2 (two-disc set with Russian, German, and English libretti; Meyer's version sung in Russian). Nikolai Nizinenko (Aleksei), Vladimir Bogachev (Ikharyov), Anatoli Babikin (Gavryushka), Aleksandr Arkhipov (Krugel), Aleksandr Naumenko (Shvokhnev), Stanislav Suleimanov (Uteshitelny), Mikhail Krutikov (Mikhail Glov), Vladislav Verestnikov (Aleksandr Glov), Aleksei Maslennikov (Zamukhrishkin); North-West German Philharmonic Orchestra, Mikhail YUROVSKY. P Herford, Germany 22 Mar.–3 Apr. 1994, I Feb. 1995, G June 1995.

France: Le Chant du Monde Russian Season Compact Disc RUS 288 115. Nos. 1, 2, and 3 with translation of Russian text. Vyatcheslav Pochapski (Aleksei), Nikolai Kurpe (Ikharyov), Pyotr Gluboky (Gavryushka), Aleksandr Arkhipov (Krugel), Mikhail Krutikov (Shvokhnev), Nikolai Rechetniak (Uteshitelny); Bolshoi Theatre Orchestra, Andrei CHISTYAKOV. P Moscow Mar. 1995, I Oct. 1995, G Feb. 1996. *Reissued:* CDM Russian Season Compact Disc RUS 788 115. I Dec. 1997, G Jan. 1998.

References: Bogdanova (in Ziv) and Fay.

Note: Moscow Chamber Opera have solved the problem of staging the incomplete opera by tacking *Rayok,* Sans op. X (ii), on to the end of *The*

Gamblers. At the point where Shostakovich abandoned the opera, offi-
cials arrive to confiscate the music, accusing it of being formalistic. They
replace it with the score of *Rayok* and then perform that work.

(ii) *Rothschild's Violin* (Fleishman)

Alternative title: The story usually translated in English as 'Rothschild's
Fiddle'.

Form: Completion of the one-act opera *Rothschild's Violin* by Shostakovich's
pupil, Veniamin Fleishman, who was killed on active service in September 1941 during the siege of Leningrad. Libretto by Fleishman based on
the story by Anton Chekhov, first published in the Moscow newspaper
Russian News in February 1894. The action takes place in a small provin-
cial town at the end of the nineteenth century.

Instrumentation: piccolo (= flute III), 2 flutes, 2 oboes, cor anglais, E flat clarinet, 2 clarinets (B flat and A), 2 bassoons, contrabassoon ~ 4 horns, 3
trumpets, 3 trombones, tuba ~ timpani, triangle, tambourine, side drum,
cymbals, bass drum ~ glockenspiel, harp ~ strings. Bass, 2 tenors, and
mezzo-soprano soloists and chorus of 6–8 voices.

Composed: Begun by Fleishman in 1939; piano score and part of full score
completed in pencil by the summer of 1941. Shostakovich completed the
'development' and orchestration on 5 February 1944, at Moscow.

Premières: 20 June 1960, Moscow All-Union Home of Composers; Soloists
of the Moscow Philharmonic Society.

April 1968, Leningrad; Experimental Studio of Chamber Opera,
Solomon Volkov (artistic director). Festival concert devoted to works by
Shostakovich's students.

USA: 23 February 1990, Juilliard Opera Center, New York; staged
presentation conducted by Bruno Ferrandis; Valentin Peytchinov
(Yakov), Susan Toth Shafer (Marfa), Charles Workman (Rothschild), and
Matthew Lord (Moisel).

Netherlands: 30 August 1995, Concertgebouw, Amsterdam; concert
performance conducted by Gennadi Rozhdestvensky; Sergei Leiferkus
(Yakov), Marina Shaguch (Marfa), Konstantin Pluzhnikov (Rothschild),
Ilya Levinsky (Moisei); C sharp minor Vocal Ensemble, Rotterdam Philharmonic Orchestra.

Music: Approximately two-thirds of the score orchestrated by Shostakovich, including the beginning up to fig. 17 minus 7 bars and from fig. 92
to the end. Manuscript in Shostakovich's hand preserved at the CIS
Archives of Literature and Art.

Russian edition, no number or date, photocopied copyist's manuscript full score, 26.5 cm.

Muzyka, Moscow, No. 2205, 1965, piano-vocal score ed. Georgi Kirkor
with preface by Aleksandr Livshits, 29 cm.

Duration: 41' 15'–41' 20".
Film: Edgardo Cozarinsky's film in three parts, produced by Serge Lalou. Sergei Makovetsky plays Shostakovich and Dainius Kazlauskas plays Fleishman. The four main characters in the opera are played by actors miming to the voices of Leiferkus, Shaguch, Pluzhnikov, and Levinsky; with the Rotterdam Philharmonic Orchestra conducted by Gennadi Rozhdestvensky. Film completed in November 1995. Premières in UK at the National Film Theatre, London on 18 June 1997 and in USA at Telluride, New Hampshire on 29 Aug. 1997.
Recordings: USSR: Melodiya A10 00019 004 (digital). Complete opera. Anatoli Safiulin (Yakov Matveyevich Ivanov), Nataliya Burnasheva (Marfa), Aleksei Martynov (Rothschild), Aleksandr Naumenko (Moisei Ilyich Shakhkes); Male voices of the USSR Ministry of Culture Chamber Choir, Valeri Polyansky (chorus-master); USSR Ministry of Culture Symphony Orchestra, Gennadi ROZHDESTVENSKY. P 1982, I 1984*a*.

RCA Victor Red Seal Compact Disc 09026 68434-2. Complete opera. Booklet with libretto in Russian, English, German, and French. Sergei Leiferkus (Yakov), Marina Shaguch (Marfa), Konstantin Pluzhnikov (Rothschild), Ilya Levinsky (Molsel), Rotterdam Philharmonic Orchestra, Gennadi ROZHDESTVENSKY. [Op. 79*a*.] P Rotterdam 24–31 Aug. 1995, I Nov. 1996, G Apr. 1997.
References: Fay, Lyachkova (in Bogdanova 1985), Pleak (in *DSCH*), and Rozhdestvensky.

Sans op. L   Solemn March

Form: Ceremonial march for military band, marked 'Allegro non troppo'.
Instrumentation: piccolo, flute, 2 oboes, E flat clarinet, 3 B flat clarinets, 2 bassoons ~ 4 E flat horns, 2 trumpets, 3 trombones ~ side drum, cymbals, bass drum ~ 2 B flat cornets; 2 E flat alto, 3 B flat tenor, baritone, and 2 bass saxhorns.
Composed: 1941, at Kuibyshev (Samara).
Music: Muzyka, No. 17287, 1941, score, 25 cm.

Broadcast Music, New York, No. 811, 1944, piano and violin conductor scores, and 25 parts transcribed by Louis Katzman from original manuscript, 30.5 cm.

Muzyka, No. 8906, 1975, score and parts, 21 cm.
Duration: 5' 42".
Recordings: USSR: MK D 1556-7 (10" mono). Moscow Radio Band, Leonid KATS. [Op. 30.] P 1953.

USSR: Melodiya CM 02303-4. Military Band of the USSR Ministry of Defence, Nikolai SERGEYEV. [Ippolitov-Ivanov, Glière, Myaskovsky *et al.*]

P 1970. *Reissued:* HMV Melodiya CSD 3782. Labelled as 'Festive March'. ['Russian Marches'—Prokofiev, Khachaturyan, Ippolitov-Ivanov *et al.*] G Oct. 1977 ~ France: Le Chant du Monde LDX 78434. ['Soviet Marches'—Ippolitov-Ivanov, Glière, Myaskovsky *et al.*]

Opus 61   Piano Sonata No. 2 in B minor

Form: Sonata for solo piano in three movements:

1. Allegretto
2. Largo
3. Moderato (con moto)—Allegretto con moto—Adagio—Moderato

Composed: January–17 March 1943. First and second movements completed on 18 February and 3 March respectively, at Kuibyshev (Samara); and sonata finished at Arkhangelskoye, near Moscow.

Dedication: To the memory of Leonid Vladimirovich Nikolayev (piano teacher).

Première: 6 June 1943, Moscow Conservatory Malyi Hall; Dmitri Shostakovich.

Music: Autograph score preserved at the Glinka Museum. Originally published up to 1966 as Opus 64.

Muzgiz, No. 17846, 1943, 30 cm.

MCA, *c.*1948, 31 cm.

Anglo-Soviet Music Press, No. 22, 1953, 31 cm.

Edition Peters, No. 4726, 1958, 31 cm.

Muzgiz, 1960, 29 cm.

Muzgiz, No. 3184 (in *D. Shostakovich: Compolitions for fortepiano,* Volume 1, with Sans op. B; Opp. 5, 12, 13, 22*a* Polka, and 34), 1966, 29 cm.

Muzyka, No. 7775 (with Opus 12), 1973, 29 cm.

Hans Sikorski, No. 2321, 1981, 31.5 cm.

Muzyka, No. 10285 (in Volume 39 of *Collected Works* with Opp. 5, 12, 13, 34, 69, and supplement of unnumbered piano works), 1983, 30 cm.

Duration: 18' 45" and approx. 29 minutes in scores; 23' 33"–31' 08"; 25 minutes (Sadovnikov); 28' 30" (Plaistow).

Recordings: USA: MGM E 3079 (mono). Menahem PRESSLER. [Op. 35.] P 1954. *Reissued:* Parlophone PMC 1023 (mono). [Op. 35.] G Sept. 1955.

USSR: MK D 07063-4 (mono). Mariya YUDINA. [Hindemith.] P 1960. *Reissued:* USSR: Melodiya C10 09547-8. [In second box of Part 2 of *Collected Works on Records* with Op. 12.] I 1978 ~ Germany: Melodia Eurodisc 301 982-445. [In four-record Yudina box set.] ~ Italy: Arlecchino Compact Disc ARL 13. ['The Art of Marla Yudina, Vol. 1'—Musorgsky and Prokofiev.]

USA: RCA Red Seal LM 2868 (mono) and LSC 2868. Emil GILELS. [Bach.] P Carnegie Hall, New York 8 Jan. 1965. *Reissued:* RCA Red Seal RB 6678 (mono) and SB 6678. [Liszt.] G Nov. 1966 ~ USSR: Melodiya D 019263-4 (mono). [Schubert.] I 1976 ~ RCA Red Seal LSB 4079. LBach.] G Apr. 1973 ~ USA: RCA AGL1 1337. [Liszt.] ~ USSR: Melodiya M10 39143-4 (mono). [Prokofiev.] I 1976 ~ USA: RCA Compact Disc 09026 63587-2. [Op. 141.] I Feb. 2000.

BMG Melodlya Compact Disc 74321 40120-2. Emil GILELS. ['Gilels Edition' Vol. 4 of five-disc set 74321 40116-2—Schubert, Schumann, and Chopin.] P Moscow concert 13 Mar. 1965, I Jan. 1997.

France; Erato STU 70477. Annie d'ARCO. [Op. 35.] P 1969. *Reissued:* USA: Musical Heritage Society 1151W. [Op. 35.] I 1971 ~ France: Erato Compact Disc WE 839. [Op. 35; and Prokofiev.] I 1996.

Sweden: Swedish Society Discofil SLT 33221. Inger WIKSTRÖM. [Op. 34.] P Stockholm 12 Sept. 1973. *Reissued:* RCA Gold Seal GL 25003. [Op. 34.] G Nov. 1976 ~ Swedish Society Discofil Compact Disc SCD 1031. [Opp. 34, 94, 5, and 19.] I 1988.

Czech: Opus 9111 0342. Lýdia MAJLINGOVÁ. [Denisov, Shchedrin, and Sergei Slonimsky.] P Prague Nov. 1974, G July 1977.

USA: Orion 82429. Sedmara RUTSTEIN. [Skryabin.] P 1982.

USSR: Melodiya C10 17985-6. Viktoria POSTNIKOVA. [Op. 12.] P 1982, I 1983*b*.

USSR: Melodiya C10 18977 007. Igor KHUDOLEI. [Op. 12.] P 1982, I 1983*d*.

Netherlands: Channel Classics Canal Grande Compact Disc 9215. Yuri YEGOROV. [Prokofiev and Babadzhanyan.] P Amsterdam 6 May 1983, I 1992.

Netherlands: Ottavo Compact Disc OTRC 38616. Boris BERMAN. [Op. 87.] P Utrecht Mar. 1986, I Aug. 1989, G Oct. 1989.

AVM Classics AVM 1003 and Compact Disc AVMCD 1003. Martin JONES. [Opp. 12 and 5; Sans opp. B and S.] P date not stated, G Oct. 1988.

Norway: Simax Compact Disc PSC 1036. Wolfgang PLAGGE. [Prokofiev.] P Ski, Oslo Dec. 1987, I June 1989, G Oct. 1989.

France: Accord Compact Disc 20025-2. Caroline WEICHERT. [Opp. 5 and 12.] P Jan. 1988, I 1988, G June 1990.

USA: MCA Classics ART & Electronics Compact Disc ARD 68010. Boris PETRUSHANSKY. [Myaskovsky, Schnittke, and Ustvolskaya.] P date not stated, I 1989.

France: Rodolphe Compact Disc RPC 32600. Vladimir STOUPEL. [Opp. 34 and 84.] P 3–4 Jan. 1989, G Oct. 1990.

France: Le Chant du Monde Compact Disc LDC 278 1012. Elena VAR-VAROVA. [Opp. 5, 12, and 13.] P Paris Sept. 1989, I Feb. 1990.

USA: Elektra Nonesuch/Warner Classics Compact Disc 7559-79234-2ZK. Vladimir VIARDO. [Op. 34.] P New York Nov. 1989, I 1990, G Oct. 1991.

Germany: Sound-Star-Ton Compact Disc. Alexander BRAGINSKY. [Op. 34.] P 1990, I 1991.

Teldec Compact Disc 9031 73282-2. Elizaveta LEONSKAYA. [Opp. 35 and 102.] P Berlin Mar. 1992, I Apr. 1993, G June 1993. *Reissued:* Warner Apex Compact Disc 8573 89092. [Opp. 35 and 102.] G Oct. 2001.

Hyperion Compact Disc CDA 66620. Tatyana NIKOLAYEVA. [Opp. 34 and 5.] P Hampstead 17–19 Apr. 1992, I July 1992, G Sept. 1992.

Olympia Compact Disc OCD 574. Colin STONE. [Opp. 34, 12, and Sans op. B.] P London Sept. 1995, I Mar. 1996, G June 1996. *Reissued:* Brilliant Classics Compact Discs 6137 (five-disc set). ['Complete Piano Sonatas'— Op. 12; Prokofiev and Skryabin.] I May 2000.

Athene-Minerva Compact Disc ATH CD18. Raymond CLARKE. [Opp. 12, 34, and 87.] P Nottingham University 6 Jan. and 9 July 1998, I May 1999, G Oct. 1999.

Belgium: Cyprès Compact Disc CYP 2622. Johan SCHMIDT. [Op. 34.] P Liège 23–4 Feb. 1998, I 1998.

Reference: Alekseyev and Yakubov (in *DSCH*).

Note: In late 1942 the composer abandoned a draft of three pages in C sharp minor headed 'Sonata No. 2 for Piano, Opus 63'.

Opus 62   Six Romances on Verses by British Poets

Original title: The autograph and 1943 published score is titled 'Six Romances for Bass'; later music and lists give 'Six Romances on English Verses' and *Six Romances on Verses by English Poets*. The Soviet musicologist Vera Vasina-Grossman retitled this song cycle 'Six Romances for bass on words of poets of Great Britain' and the title is given as 'Romances on words of W. Raleigh, R. Burns, and W. Shakespeare' in the Muzyka albums.

Form: Six songs for low male voice and piano:

1. The Wood, the Weed, the Wag (To a Son)—Largo
2. O, Wert Thou in the Cauld Blast (In the Fields)—Moderato
3. Macpherson before his Execution (Macpherson's Farewell)— Allegretto
4. Jenny (Coming thro' the Rye)—Moderato
5. Sonnet No. 66 (Tired with all these)—Lento
6. The King's Campaign ('The Grand Old Duke of York' or 'The King of France went up the Hill')—Allegretto

Texts by Sir Walter Raleigh—No. 1; Robert Burns—Nos. 2, 3, and 4; William Shakespeare—No. 5; and traditional nursery rhyme—No. 6 in Russian translations by Boris Pasternak—Nos. 1 and 5; and Samuil Marshak—Nos. 2, 3, 4, and 6.

Composed: 1942, at Kuibyshev (Samara). Nos. 1, 5, and 6 written on 7 May, 24 and 25 October respectively.
Dedications:

  1. Lev Tadevosovich Atovmyan (composer / arranger)
  2. Nina Vasilievna Shostakovich (first wife)
  3. Isaak Davidovich Glikman (musicologist)
  4. Yuri Vasilievich Sviridov (composer)
  5. Ivan Ivanovich Sollertinsky (musicologist)
  6. Vissarion Yakovlevich Shebalin (composer)

Premières: The three Burns' settings, Nos. 2, 3, and 4: 4 November 1942, Kuibyshev; Aleksandr Baturin (bass) and Dmitri Shostakovich (piano).
   6 June 1943, Moscow Conservatory Malyi Hall; Efrem Flaks (baritone) and Dmitri Shostakovich (piano).
   UK: 1 November 1966, Derby Art Gallery; Clive Bemrose (baritone) and Gordon Clarke (piano). Sung in English at a Derby Music Club Meeting.
Arrangements: The accompaniments orchestrated for full symphony orchestra in March 1943 (designated Opus 62*a*) and chamber orchestra in 1971 (see Opus 140). No. 5 transcribed for double-bass and piano by Rodion Azarkhin.
Instrumentation of Opus 62*a*:   piccolo, 2 flutes, 2 oboes, cor anglais, E flat clarinet, 2 B flat clarinets, bass clarinet, 2 bassoons, contrabassoon ~ 4 horns, 3 trumpets, 3 trombones, tuba ~ timpani, triangle, cymbals, bass drum ~ xylophone, celesta ~ harps ('preferably not less than two') ~ strings.
Music: Autograph sketches of Nos. 1, 5, and 6 preserved at the CIS Archives of Literature and Art and score of the whole cycle, at the Glinka Museum. Title page of the 1943 score and first twelve bars of No. 3 reproduced in Glikman (1993).
   Music Fund of the USSR, 1943, Opp. 62 and 62*a*.
   Russian-American Music, 1946, No. 5 only, adaptation by Hugh Ross, 31 cm.
   Leeds Music, 1951 (with two songs from Op. 46).
   Sovetskii Kompozitor, No. 3467, 1963, 29 cm.
   Muzyka, No. 4116 (in *Dmitri Shostakovich: Vocal Compositions*), 1967 and 1974, 30 cm.
   VEB Deutscher Verlag für Musik, No. 9012, 1972, ed. Christoph Hellmundt; with Russian, German, and English texts, 27 cm.
   Sovetskii Kompozitor, No. 4020, 1977, No. 5 arr. for double-bass by R. Azarkhin, 29 cm.
   Muzyka, No. 10283 (in Volume 32 of *Collected Works* with Opp. 4, 21, 46, 79, 84, 86, 91, 98, 100 *et al.*), 1982, 30 cm.
Duration: Approx. 12 minutes in score; 14' 00"–16' 58". Op. 62*a*: 14' 32".

Recordings: USSR: Melodiya C10 05517-8. Nos. 4, 3, and 6. Yevgeni VLADI-
MIROV (bass) and Valentina Strzhizhovskaya (piano). [Koval, Myaskovsky, Terentiev *et al.*] P 1974, I 1975.

USSR: Melodiya C10 08921-2. Nos. 3 and 4 only. Oleg PTUKHA (bass)
and Nadezhda Kushnir (piano). [Opp. 98 and 100 No. 3; and Kabalevsky.] P 1977, I 1978*a*.

USSR: Melodiya C10 11239-40. No. 4 only. Yuri STATNIK (bass) and
Nataliya Rassudova (piano). [Op. 145 No. 4; Rimsky-Korsakov, Verdi,
and recital by Eva Podleshch.] P 1978, I 1979*c*.

USSR: Melodiya C10 31619 002. Complete cycle Op. 62*a*. Anatoli SAFI-
ULIN (bass), USSR Ministry of Culture Symphony Orchestra, Gennadi
Rozhdestvensky. [Album 7 of 'From Manuscripts of Different Years'—
Opp. 30 and 124.] P 1986, I 1991*c*. *Reissued:* BMG Melodiya Compact
Discs 74321 59057-2 (two-disc set). [Opp. 135, 21, 46/141, and Sans op.
M.] I Feb. 1999.

France: Thésis Compact Disc THC 82046. No. 4 only. Nikita STOROJEV
(bass) and Emile Naoumoff (piano). [Op. 98; Titov, Glinka *et al.*] P Paris
Oct. 1990.

France: Le Chant du Monde Russian Season Compact Disc RUS
288089. Complete cycle. Pyotr GLUBOKY (bass) and Nataliya Rassudova
(piano). [Opp. 46, 91, 121, and 146.] P Moscow Conservatory 21–9 Sept.
1994, I Apr. 1995.

Belgium: René Gailly Compact Disc CD92 041. Fyodor KUZNETSOV
(bass) and Yuri Serov (piano). ['Complete Songs, Vol. 1'—Opp. 86, 100,
121, and 127.] P St Petersburg 23 Mar.–4 May 1998.

References: Hulme (in *DSCH*), Spektor, and Vasina-Grossman (in Daragan).

Notes: The first of the three Burns' settings was dedicated to Miss Jessie
Lewars, who nursed the poet during his last illness in 1796; the second
was set in 1788 to the fiddle tune composed by the freebooter, James
Macpherson, on the eve of his execution at Banff on 16 November 1700;
and the third, a revision of an old bawdy song concerning a wanton girl
up to no good in a field of rye. 'Coming thro' the Rye', also in Marshak's
translation, appears in Sans op. M though here Shostakovich orches-
trates its traditional folk melody.

Songs Nos. 2 and 3 are quoted in the Thirteenth Symphony, Opus 113.

Opus 63   Native Leningrad

Form: Incidental music for concert play spectacle *Native Country* (or *Motherland*), scored for tenor and bass soloists, choir, and orchestra. The *Native
Leningrad* Suite comprises four musical items:

1. Overture—'October 1917'—Moderato non troppo
2. Song of the Victorious October (Song of the River Neva)—Allegretto

3. Youth Dance (Dance of the Sailors)—Moderato—Allegro con brio
4. Song of Leningrad—Moderato

Texts of Nos. 1, 2, and 4 by S. Alymov. No. 1 includes choral settings of the Revolutionary songs 'Varshavyanka' (the 'Warsaw March', also known as 'Hostile Whirlwinds') and 'Boldy, friends, on we march!' Dzhambul Dzhabayev's poem 'Leningrad, I'm Proud of Thee' declaimed between Nos. 3 and 4.

Instrumentation: piccolo, flute, 2 oboes, 2 clarinets (B flat and A), 2 bassoons ~ 2 horns, 3 trumpets, 2 trombones, tuba ~ timpani, triangle, tambourine, side drum, cymbals, bass drum ~ balalaika, piano ~ tenor and bass soloists, S.A.T B. chorus ~ strings.

Composed: 20 August 1942, at Kuibyshev (Samara).

Dedication: Written as a tribute to the courage of the citizens of Leningrad.

Premières: 15 October 1942, Moscow Dzerzhinsky Central Club; NKVD Song and Dance Ensemble; scenario by Iosif Dobrovolsky, M. Volpin, and Nikolai Erdman, and directed by Sergei Yutkevich; conducted by Yuri Silantiev.

Suite: 7 November 1942, same venue and forces as above.

Arrangements: Piano reductions of Nos. 1, 2, and 4 by Andrei Sevastyanov. No. 3, titled 'Folk Dance', in a piano reduction by Lev Solin and transcribed for military band by M. Vakhutinsky. Instrumentation of latter: flute, oboe, E flat clarinet, 3 B flat clarinets ~ 2 E flat horns, 2 trumpets, 3 trombones ~ triangle, tambourine, side drum, cymbals, bass drum ~ 2 B flat cornets; 2 E flat alto, 3 B flat tenor, B flat baritone, and 2 bass saxhorns. Parts listed above percussion and 3rd tenor saxhorn not obligatory.

No. 3, titled 'Folk Dances', arranged for standard brass band (with percussion including xylophone, timpani, triangle, side drum, cymbals, and bass drum) by Torgny Hanson. Vakhutinsky's transcription adapted to suit American instruments by H. Robert Reynolds.

Sans op. Y—*My Native Country* [*My Dear Fatherland* on the score.] Yuri Silantiev assembled an omnibus suite from Sans op. N, Opp. 63, 66, and 72 in 1970 and the following four pieces, retitled, derive from Opus 63:

1. Overture—Moderato non troppo
2. On Palace Square (text by Yevgeni Dolmatovsky)—Allegretto
3. Folk Dance—Moderato—Allegro con brio
4. Ode to Leningrad (text by Dolmatovsky)—Moderato

Music: Originally appeared as Opus 61. Autograph vocal and full scores lost; incomplete copies of the vocal score preserved at the Moscow Dzerzhinsky Central Club.

Sovetskii Kompozitor, No. 705, 190, 'Folk Dance' arr. M. Vakhutinsky, score and parts, 21.5 cm.

Sovetskii Kompozitor, No. 2518 (in *My Native Country*), 1972, four pieces arr. Y. Silantiev, 29 cm.

Sovetskii Kompozitor, No. 4028 (in *Dmitri Shostakovich: Music to Plays*), 1977, 'Folk Dance' arr. for piano by L. Solin, 29 cm.

Carl Fischer, New York, *c.*1979, 'Folk Dances for concert band' ed. by H. Robert Reynolds; score, condensed score, and 67 parts, 31 cm.

Muzyka, No. 11412 (in Volume 28 of *Collected Works* with Opp. 19, 24, 28, 31, 32, 37, 44, 58*a*, 66, 72, and in the supplement, Sans opp. D and K), 1986, vocal and piano scores of Nos. 1–4, 30 cm.

Muzyka, No. 11413 (in Volume 27 of *Collected Works* with Opp. 19, 24, 28, 32, 37, 44, 58*a*, 66, and 72), 1987, full score of Nos. 1–4 with S. Alymov's original lyrics, 30 cm.

Salvation Army Brass Band Journal, No. 512 (in Festival Series, Nos. 511–514), Sept. 1994, 'Folk Dance' (titled 'Folk Dances') arr. T. Hanson, full score, oblong format 26.5 × 18.5 cm.

Recording: Saint Petersburg Studio P10 00574. Folk Dance arr. Vakhutinsky. St Petersburg Military District Band, Nikolai USHCHAPOVSKY. ['Contemporary Music for Symphonic Band'—Thorn, Reed, Prokofiev *et al.*] P *c.*1991, I 1992.

Salvationist Publishing Compact Disc. Folk Dance arr. Hanson. The Salvation Army International Staff Band, Lieut-Colonel Robert REDHEAD. ['A Fanfare of Praise'—Silfverberg, Grieg, Tchaikovsky *et al.*] P Air Lyndhurst 1994.

USA: Klavier Compact Disc KCD 11077. Folk Dance arr. Reynolds. North Texas College of Music Wind Symphony, Eugene CORPORON. [Op. 34; Whitacre, Ito, and Hindemith.] P Texas Woman's University, Denton 9–11 Feb. 1996.

Note: See *My Native Country*, Sans op. Y, for recording of Silantiev's suite.

Sans op. M   Eight British and American Folksongs

Original title: *Eight English and American Folksongs*

Form: Eight settings of British and American songs in Russian translation by Sergei Bolotin (Nos. 1, 4, and 8), Tatyana Sikorskaya (Nos. 3, 5, and 7), Bolotin and Sikorskaya (No. 2), and Samuil Marshak (No. 6) for low voice and small orchestra (with harp):

1. The Sailor's Bride—'Blow the wind southerly' (William Julius Mickle)—Allegretto
2. John Anderson, my Jo (Robert Burns)—Lento, espressivo
3. Billy Boy (Northumbrian capstan shanty)—Merrily
4. Oh! the Oak and the Ash (English air)—Moderato

5. Servants of King Arthur (variant of the English folksong 'Three Sons of Rogues')—Merrily
6. Coming thro' the Rye (Robert Burns)—Moderato
7. Spring Round Dance—'Come Lasses and Lads'—Allegro
8. When Johnny Comes Marching Home (Patrick Sarsfield Gilmore)—Allegretto

Instrumentation: 2 flutes, 2 oboes (II = cor anglais), 2 clarinets (A and B flat), 2 bassoons ~ 4 horns, trumpet ~ timpani, triangle, tambourine ~ glockenspiel, harp ~ strings. Harp in Nos. 2 and 6, No. 4 for strings, trumpet in No. 5, and percussion in No. 8 only. Voice part in treble clef for Nos. 1–7 and in bass clef, No. 8.

Composed: 12 May 1943. Inspired by the alliance between the USSR, GB, and USA.

Premières: Nos. 1–7: 25 May 1943, Moscow; Mark Reshetin (bass) and Larissa Yelchaninova (soprano).

Nos. 1–8: 6 March 1944, Moscow; M. Reshetin.

UK broadcast: 29 August 1983, sung in English; Ameral Cunson (mezzo-soprano), BBC Symphony Orchestra, Gennadi Rozhdestvensky.

Belgian broadcast: 29 December 1989 (Russian Winter Festival recording, 17 February 1989), sung In Russian and English; Elena Ivanova (soprano, Nos. 1–8), Sergei Yakovenko (baritone, No. 8), USSR Ministry of Culture Symphony Orchestra, Gennadi Rozhdestvensky.

USA: 10 December 1994, sung in English; Racine, Wisconsin; Robert Osborne (bass-baritone), Racine Symphony Orchestra, Alexander Platt.

Duration: 14' 18"–17' 05'.

Music: Music Fund of the USSR, Nos. 563–570, 1944, mimeographed format, full score edited by Lev Atovmyan, 35 cm.

Recordings: BMG Melodiya Compact Discs 74321 59057-2 (two-disc set). Elena IVANOVA (soprano), Sergei Yakovenko (baritone), USSR Ministry of Culture Symphony Orchestra, Gennadi Rozhdestvensky. [Opp. 135, 21, 46/141, and 62*a*.] P Moscow concert 17 Feb. 1989, I Feb. 1999.

USA Arabesque Compact Disc Z 6708. Nos. 6 and 2 sung in English. Christine ABRAHAM (mezzo-soprano), Vermont University Orchestra, Robert DeCormier. ['Bobby Burns' (*sic*)—Op. 140; Vaughan Williams, Haydn, Beethoven *et al.*] P University of Vermont 1996, I 1998.

Reference: Hulme (in *DSCH*).

Notes: The second song, set to its traditional melody, tells of the wife of a carpenter, John Anderson, recalling happy days with her 'jo' (= darling) husband.

The Scottish song 'Annie Laurie', with music by Lady John Scott and words adapted by her from the poem by William Douglas, arranged for voice and chamber orchestra was probably considered as an item for this cycle. The rough undated draft in the Glinka Museum, in a Russian translation, is marked 'Molto moderato' and scored for 2 flutes, 2 clarinets, 4 horns, and strings.

Opus 64   Zoya

Subtitle: Who is She?

Form: Music for the film *Zoya* directed by B. Chirskov and Leo Arnshtam for Soyuzdetfilm, based on the heroic deeds of the eighteen-year-old partisan girl, Zoya Kosmodemyanskaya, in the early days of the Great Patriotic War. The film awarded a Stalin Prize First Class in 1946. Voluminous score consists of 35 numbers though nothing is known of the nine missing items:

1. Allegretto
2. Moderato
3. Adagio
4. Moderato
5. Moderato
6. Moderato—Allegro—Presto
7. Victory—[Adagio]
8. The Belfry—Allegro
12. Moderato
13. Moderato
16. Allegretto
20. Dneprostoi—Allegretto
21. Adagio
22. The First of May Parade—Allegretto
23. Arrival of the Heroes—Allegro
24. Allegro
25. Recollection—Moderato—Allegro
30. Moscow—Adagio
31. Song about Zoya (lyric by Konstantin Simonov)—Moderato con moto
35. [Con moto]—Allegro

Instrumentation: piccolo, 2 flutes, 3 oboes, E flat clarinet, 3 B flat clarinets, 2 bassoons, contrabassoon ~ 4 horns, 5 trumpets, 5 trombones, 2 tubas ~ timpani, triangle, tambourine, side drum, cymbals, bass drum, gong, xylophone ~ glockenspiel, 2 harps ~ S.A.T.B. chorus ~ strings.

Composed: 1943–4, at Moscow.

Première: Film first shown on 22 November 1944.

Arrangements: Opus 64a—Suite for chorus (in No. 1 only) and large symphony orchestra assembled by Lev Atovmyan:

1. Introduction—'Song about Zoya'—Adagio—Moderato con moto
2. Scene—'Military Problem'—Allegretto—Allegro
3. Prelude—'Tragedy of a Loss'—Adagio
4. March—'Hero's Victory'—Tempo di marcia
5. Finale—'The Heroine's Immortality'—Adagio

No. 1 is based on No. 21 fanfares and No. 7 vocalise of the film score; No. 2 includes Nos. 1, 25, and 24 in their entirety; in No. 3 the orchestration, by Lev Atovmyan, of the piano Prelude Opus 34 No. 14 is sandwiched by an Adagio not published in Volume 41 of *Collected Works;* No. 4 constructed in ABA form from Nos. 23 and 22 (the latter Degeyter's *Internationale*); and No. 5 comprises complete Nos. 3 and 30 ('Moscow' incorporating the 'Slava Chorus'—'Be praised, be praised, may our beloved land be strong forever'—from Mikhail Glinka's *A Life for the Tsar*).

The song, 'Song about Zoya' ('Native Land'), with words by K. Simonov, arranged for S.A.T.B. chorus and piano by L. Atovmyan.

Instrumentation of Suite Opus 61a: As the film score without the glockenspiel and second harp.

Music: Originally known as Opus 68. Listed as Opus 66 in Volkov 1979. Autograph score preserved at the Glinka Museum and a manuscript copy, in the Music Library of the USSR Cinematograph Symphony Orchestra. In both the musical items are numbered 1–17, 20–5, 30, 31, and 35. Atovmyan's Suite preserved at the USSR Radio and Television Music Library.

Russian mimeographed manuscript, no number or date, Suite Opus 64a full score, c.32 cm.

Sovetskii Kompozitor, No. 519 (in *D. Shostakovich: Songs*), 1958, 'Song about Zoya' arr. L. Atovmyan, 29 cm.

Muzyka, No. 10179 (in Volume 34 of *Collected Works* with Opp. 88 and 136, and songs), 1985, 'Song about Zoya' for S.A.T.B. chorus and piano, 30 cm.

Muzyka, No. 10889 (in Volume 41 of *Collected Works* with Opp. 26, 30, 33, 41, 48, 50, 53, 55, 56, and 59), 1987, 20 numbers (as listed under 'Form') in full score, 30 cm.

Duration: Film: 95 minutes. Suite Opus 64a: 30' 27"–31' 41".

Recordings: USSR: Melodiya D 020135-6 (mono) and C 01471-2. Suite Opus 64a. Bolshoi Theatre Orchestra and Chorus, Leon Zaks and Anatoli Levin (violin duo), Maksim SHOSTAKOVICH. [Op. 76a.] P 1966. *Reissued:* USA: Angel Melodiya SR 40160. [Op. 76a.] ~ USSR: Melodiya C 01471-2. [In fourth box of Part 1 of *Collected Works on Records* with Op. 76a.] I 1978 ~ Germany: Melodia Eurodisc 28665 XHK. [On second record in four-record film music album with Op. 76a.] I 1981 ~ BMG Melodiya Compact Discs 74321 66981-2 (two-disc set). [Sans ops P. Opp. 27a, 22a, and 76a.] I Dec. 1999.

Germany: Capriccio Compact Disc 10 405. Suite Opus 64*a*. Berlin Radio Symphony Orchestra and Chorus, Mikhail YUROVSKY. [Op. 82*a*.] P 4–6 Mar. 1991, I Oct. 1995, G Jan. 1996. NB. In No. 1 the chorus sings the vocalise introduction but, after the violin duo, the choral 'Song about Zoya' is played by the orchestra and one of its choruses omitted.

USA: Russian Disc Compact Disc RDCD 10 002. Suite Opus 64*a*. Byelorussian Radio and TV Symphony Orchestra, Minsk Chamber Choir (in No. 1), Igor Matukhov (chorus-master), Walter MNATSAKANOV. [Op. 75.] P Minsk Feb. 1995, I Sept. 1996.

Note: The heroine's childhood is recalled in the opening of the film. During a history lesson at school Zoya tells the class of the heroic action of the patriotic peasant, Ivan Susanin, who accepts a Polish bribe to lead their invading soldiers to the recently-elected Tsar in a Moscow monastery but, craftily, diverts them into a dense forest. When the Poles discover his ruse, they kill him. The chorus from Glinka's opera is heard during this episode and again when Zoya is accompanying her school friend through the deserted Red Square at night. At the end of the film, after her brutal murder by the Nazis, the theme 'Glory' is gradually worked into the score and finally quoted as an exalted hymn of praise.

Sans op. N   National Anthem Contest Entries

(i) *Patriotic Song*

Alternative title: *Glory to our Soviet Motherland.*

Form: Anthem for mixed chorus and piano, with lyric by Yevgeni Dolmatovsky, submitted as an entry for the new Soviet National Anthem contest.

Composed: After the first twelve bars of the Eighth Symphony on 2 July 1943.

Première: Broadcast for the first time on Soviet All-Union Radio in February 1978.

Arrangement: Accompaniment orchestrated by the composer.

Music: Autograph preserved at the CIS Archives of Literature and Art. Words and melody quoted on pages 174–5 of Khentova (1979*b*). Autograph score of the orchestrated version preserved in the Shostakovich family archive.

Muzyka, No. 10179 (in Volume 34 of *Collected Works* with Opp. 88 and 136, and songs), 1985, 30 cm.

Recordings: —

(ii) *Song of the Red Army*

Form: Anthem written in collaboration with Aram Khachaturyan, submitted as a new Soviet National Anthem in 1943, to verses 'Red Army, invincible' by Mikhail Golodny.

Composed: Mid-August 1943. The first eight bars of the melody written by Khachaturyan, the remainder by Shostakovich, who orchestrated the anthem.

Music: Autograph of piano and orchestral scores, in Shostakovich's hand, preserved in the Glinka Museum. Melody quoted on page 177 of Khentova (1979*b*).

Recordings: —

Reference: Volkov (*Testimony*).

(iii) *National Anthem*

Form: Two settings of Sergei Mikhalkov and G. El-Registan's words were composed. The melody of one version, quoted on page 176 of Khentova (1979*b*), was used in *Russian River,* Opus 66 (words by Iosif Dobrovolsky); *Victorious Spring,* Opus 72 (Words by Yevgeni Dolmatovsky); and *My Native Country,* Sans op. Y. *Novorossiisk Chimes,* Sans op. U and the song *Supporters of Peace March,* Sans op. X (i) are based on the first two bars.

The second version was composed jointly with Aram Khachaturyan and orchestrated for full orchestra and two-part chorus by Shostakovich.

Instrumentation (second version):   piccolo, 2 flutes, 2 oboes, 2 clarinets (B flat), 2 bassoons ~ 4 horns, 3 trumpets, 3 trombones, tuba ~ timpani, triangle, side drum, cymbals, bass drum ~ two-part chorus ~ strings.

Music: Autographs of the two versions for two-part chorus and piano preserved in the CIS Archives of Literature and Art. Full score autograph of the second version in F major, signed on behalf of both composers by Shostakovich, preserved in the Glinka Museum.

Notes: The successful entry, an adaptation by Aleksandr Aleksandrov of his 'Hymn of the Bolshevik Party' with new words by Sergei Mikhalkov and G. El-Registan, was adopted as the National Anthem of the USSR from 1 January 1944. Other anthems submitted were composed by Khachaturyan alone and Iona Tuskiya.

The unpopular wordless Mikhail Clinka *Patriotic Song* selected by Boris Yeltsin was replaced by the Aleksandrov anthem for the New Year 2001 with the original lyric rewritten by the 87-year-old Mikhailov.

Opus 65   Symphony No. 8 in C minor

Subtitle: Christened the 'Stalingrad Symphony' after its American première.

Form: Symphony for full orchestra in five movements:

1. Adagio—Allegro non troppo
2. Allegretto

3. Allegro non troppo *attacca*
4. Largo *attacca*
5. Allegretto

The programme note for the Royal Festival Hall performance by the Leningrad Philharmonic Orchestra under Yevgeni Mravinsky, in the presence of the composer, on 23 September 1960—announced as the first UK public performance—listed the movements as '*Adagio*, March Militaire, *Allegro non troppo*, Passacaglia, and *Largo*'.

Instrumentation: 4 flutes (III and IV = piccolo I and II), 2 oboes, cor anglais, E flat clarinet, 2 clarinets (B flat and A), bass clarinet, 3 bassoons (III = contrabassoon) ~ 4 horns, 3 trumpets, 3 trombones, tuba ~ timpani (4 drums), triangle, tambourine, side drum, cymbals (2 players—I with drumsticks and II normal mode), bass drum, gong ~ xylophone ~ 1st violins (16), 2nd violins (14), violas (12), cellos (12), double-basses (10).

Composed: In about 40 days, mainly at the Composer's House at Ivanovo, between 2 July and 9 September 1943. First three movements completed on 3, 18, and 25 August respectively.

Dedication: Yevgeni Aleksandrovich Mravinsky (conductor).

Premières: 3 November 1943, Moscow Conservatory Bolshoi Hall; USSR Symphony Orchestra, Yevgeni Mravinsky.

5 Feb. 1944, Novosibirsk; Leningrad Philharmonic Orchestra, Yevgeni Mravinsky. Introductory talk by Ivan Sollertinsky (who died suddenly six days later. See also Opus 67).

USA: 2 April 1944, Carnegie Hall, New York; New York Philharnonic Orchestra, Artur Rodzinski. A sum of 10,000 dollars was paid by the Columbia Broadcasting System for the privilege of the first broadcast in the West.

UK: 13 July 1944, Bedford Corn Exchange, BBC Symphony Orchestra, Sir Henry Wood. (See Notes).

France: 28 February 1946, Paris; Roger Désormière (conductor).

UK: 23 September 1960, Royal Festival Hall, London; Leningrad Philharmonic Orchestra, Yevgeni Mravinsky. (See under 'Form').

Scotland: 29 August 1962, Usher Hall, Edinburgh; Polish Radio Symphony Orchestra, Jan Krenz. In the presence of the composer.

Arrangements: Reduction for piano four hands ly Lev Atovmyan and two pianos eight hands by Pavel Lamm (the latter not published).

Music: Autograph score inscribed 'Manuscript belongs to N. V. Shostakovich' and preserved at the CIS Archives of Literature and Art.

Muzgiz, 1943; No. 18220, 1946, 30 cm.; and 1963, 22 cm.

Breitkopf & Härtel, No. 3605, 1947, 18.5 cm.

Breitkopf & Härtel, No. 4021 (plate no. 31302), 1947, 33 cm.

Boosey & Hawkes, No. 760, 1965, 19 cm.

Muzyka, 1966, arr. for piano four hands by L. Atovmyan, 29 cm.

Muzyka, No. 9375 (in Volume 4 of *Collected Works* with Op. 60), 1981, 30 cm.

Hans Sikorski, No. 2221, 1991, 21 cm.

Duration: 60 and approx. 62 minutes in scores: 53' 36"–68' 42"; 64 minutes (Plaistow and this is the time allocated for the Prom broadcast on 13 July 1944).

Films: *Rollerball,* directed by Norman Jewison, includes excerpts from the Eighth and Fifth Symphonies. See under Opus 47.

Rostropovich Returns to Russia. The third movement filmed in Leningrad on 16 February 1990. See under Opus 47.

Recordings: Italy: Fonotipia 'Le Grandi Orchestre nel Mondo Volume 12' Compact Disc C015-93 12 (mono). Boston Symphony Orchestra, Serge KOUSSEVITZKY. P concert broadcast 21 Apr. 1944, I 1993 (limited edition of 1000 copies). [NB. Also performances of the 1st movement recorded privately on 22 Apr. 1944, 7 and 24 Apr. 1945.]

USA: BSO-CD2 Compact Disc (mono). First movement only. Boston Symphony Orchestra, Serge KOUSSEVITZKY. [Tchaikovsky, Hanson, Cowell *et al.*] P Boston 25 Apr. 1945, I on fund-raising CD 1988. *Reissued:* Biddulph Compact Disc WHL 045 (mono). [Prokofiev, Rakhmaninov, and Koussevitzky.] I 1996, G Feb. 1997.

Italy: AS Compact Disc 538 (mono). New York Philharmonic Orchestra, Artur RODZINSKI. P concert 15 Oct. 1944, I 1990.

USSR: MK D 03620-1 (2 sides mono). Leningrad Philharmonic Orchestra, Yevgeni MRAVINSKY. P studio 2 June 1947, I 1957. *Reissued:* USSR: Melodiya D 032639-40 (2 sides mono). Restored 1972, I 1973 ~ BMG Classics Melodiya Compact Disc, Mravinsky Edition Vol. 17, 74321 29406-2 (mono). I Apr. 1996.

Revelation Compact Disc RV 10061 (mono). State Radio and Television Large Symphony Orchestra, Aleksandr GAUK. [Op. 96.] P concert 7 Oct. 1959, I Feb. 1997, G Sept. 1997.

BBC Legends Compact Disc BBCL 4002-2. Leningrad Philharmonic Orchestra, Yevgeni MRAVINSKY. P Royal Festival Hall, London concert 23 Sept. 1960, I Nov. 1998 (issued with a bonus CD [Mozart.]), G Dec. 1998.

USSR: MK D 09615-7-D 09799 (3 sides mono). Leningrad Philharmonic Orchestra, Yevgeni MRAVINSKY. [Op. 83.] P Leningrad concert 25 Feb. 1961, I 1962, G July 1966. *Reissued:* UK: MK DO 9615 (3 sides mono) [Op. 83.] ~ USA: Bruno 14064L (2 sides mono). I 1964.

USSR: MK D 011185-7-D 010714 (3 sides mono) and C 0455-7-C 0388 (3 sides). [Later Melodiya CM 0455-7-CM 0388.] Moscow Philharmonic Orchestra, Kirill KONDRASHIN. [Op. 35.] P 1961, I 1962. *Reissued:* HMV Melodiya ASD 2474 (2 sides). G June 1969 ~ USA: Everest SDBR 3250 (2 sides). I 1969 ~ USSR: Melodiya CM 03583-4 (2 sides). I 1973 ~ USA: Angel Melodiya SR 40237 (2 sides). I 1973 ~ Germany: Melodia Eurodisc 87 623 XPK. [In thirteen-record box set.] I 1974 ~ Germany: Melodia

Eurodisc 300 699-435. [In three-record box set with Opp. 54 and 60.] ~ France: Le Chant du Monde LDX 78627 ~ Pye Ember Classics ECL 9003 ~ HMV Melodiya BOX 502506-7 in Set SLS 5025. [Op. 60 conclusion and Op. 70.] G Dec. 1975 ~ HMV Melodiya EX 2903873 (DMM). [Seventh record in twelve-record box set.] G Dec. 1985 ~ France: Le Chant du Monde Compact Disc LDC 278 1005-6. [In Box 3 of five two-disc sets with Opp. 70 and 93.] G May 1989 ~ BMG Classics Melodiya Compact Disc 74321 19841-2. I July 1994, C Nov. 1994.

Czech: Praga Compact Disc PR 250 040 (mono). Moscow Philharmonic Orchestra, Kirill KONDRASHIN. [Op. 115.] P Prague broadcast 29 Sept. 1969, G Sept. 1993.

HMV ASD 2917. London Symphony Orchestra, André PREVIN. P 8–9 Feb. 1973, G Oct. 1973. *Reissued:* USA: Angel S 36980. I 1974 ~ EMI Classics Compact Disc Matrix 18 CDM5 65521-2. I July 1995, G Oct. 1995 ~ HMV Classics Compact Disc HMV5 74370-2. I July 2001.

East Germany: Eterna 8 26 972. Berlin City Symphony Orchestra, Kurt SANDERLING. P East Berlin 9–17 Sept. 1976, I 1977*d*. *Reissued:* East Germany: Deutsches Schallplaten Compact Disc 32 TC 77 ~ Germany: Berlin Classics Eterna Compact Disc BC 2064-2. I May 1994, G July 1994.

Philips Compact Disc 422 442-2PH. Leningrad Philharmonic Orchestra, Yevgeni MRAVINSKY. P Leningrad concert 28 Mar. 1982, G June 1989. *Reissued:* Japan: Icone Compact Disc ICN 9411-2. P incorrectly given as Moscow Radio Concert Hall 15 Mar. 1983, I Sept. 1994. NB. Cor anglais player given as Valeri Sobolev ~ USA: Russian Disc Compact Disc RDCD 10 917. I Aug. 1996, G Feb. 1997 ~ Philips Virtuoso Compact Disc 422 442-2PX. G Sept. 1998. NB. Only the Russian Disc release is remastered at the correct pitch: the Philips and Icone CDs are a semitone sharp.

Decca SXDL 7621 (digital). Concertgebouw Orchestra, Bernard HAITINK. P Amsterdam 20–1 Dec. 1982, G Nov. 1983. *Reissued:* USA: London LDR 71121 (digital) ~ Decca Compact Disc 411 616-2DH. G Apr. 1984 ~ Decca Ovation Compact Disc 425 071-2DM. I Aug. 1993, G Nov. 1993 ~ London Compact Disc 444 437-2. [Seventh disc in eleven-disc set.] I June 1995 ~ Universal Eloquence Compact Disc 467 465-2DEQ. I Apr. 2001.

USSR: Melodiya A10 00119 002 (3 sides in two-record set, digital). USSR Ministry of Culture Symphony Orchestra, Sergei Grishin (cor anglais), Gennadi ROZHDESTVENSKY. [Op. 14.] P 1983, I 1986*a*. *Reissued:* Olympia Compact Disc OCD 143. [Op. 109] I Aug. 1987, G May 1989 ~ Germany: Melodia Eurodisc Compact Disc 258 487 ~ Olympia Compact Disc OCD 5005. [In Vol. 1 six-disc set of symphonies with Op. 109.] I Dec. 1990 ~ BMG Melodiya Compact Discs 74321 53457-2 (two-disc set). [Opp. 60 and 58*a*.] I May 1998.

EMI EL 270290-1 (digital). Bournemouth Symphony Orchestra, Rudolf BARSHAI. P Poole Apr. 1985, G Aug. 1985. *Reissued:* EMI Compact Disc CDC7 47670-2. I Feb. 1989, G June 1989 ~ EMI Compact Disc CDM7 64719-2. Third movement only. ['Bournemouth Symphony Orchestra Centenary'—Auber, Delius, Mendelssohn *et al.*] G Sept. 1993.

USSR: Melodiya Compact Disc SUCD 10 00240. USSR Tele-Radio Large Symphony Orchestra, Vladimir FEDOSEYEV. P Moscow concert 5 May 1985, I 1991*b*.

Australia: ABC Classics Compact Disc 426 510-2. Adelaide Orchestra, Nicholas BRAITHWAITE. P Adelaide Town Hall 1–4 May 1988.

Naxos Compact Disc 8.550628. Czecho-Slovak Radio Symphony Orchestra, Ladislav SLOVÁK. P Bratislava 3–12 Dec. 1988, I Jan. 1993, G Nov. 1993. *Reissued:* Naxos Compact Discs 8.506003. [In six-disc set with Symphonies Nos. 5, 9, 10, 11, 13, and 14.] I 1993.

RCA Victor Red Seal Compact Disc RD 60145. Saint Louis Symphony Orchestra, Leonard SLATKIN. P St Louis 28 Dec. 1988, I Dec. 1989, G Apr. 1990.

Decca 425 675-1DH (digital) and Compact Disc 425 675-2DH. Chicago Symphony Orchestra, Georg SOLTI. P Chicago concert 4–6 Feb. 1989, I July 1989, G Sept. 1989.

Chandos ABRD 1396 (digital) and Compact Disc CHAN 8757. Scottish National Orchestra, Neeme JÄRVI. P Glasgow 7 Feb. 1989, I Feb. 1990, G Apr. 1990.

Philips Compact Disc 432 090-2PH. Berlin Philharmonic Orchestra, Semyon BYCHKOV. P Berlin 21–2 Mar. 1990, I Jan. 1993, G May 1993. *Reissued:* Philips Compact Disc 454 245-2PH. I May 1997.

Denon Compact Disc CO 78910. Vienna Symphony Orchestra, Eliahu INBAL. P Vienna 21–3 Jan. 1991, I Oct. 1994, G Jan. 1995.

Collins Classics Compact Disc 1271-2. London Symphony Orchestra, Maksim SHOSTAKOVICH. P London 8–10 Mar. 1991, I Oct. 1991, G June 1992.

Finland: Ondine Compact Disc ODE 775-2. Helsinki Philharmonic, James DE PREIST. P Järvenpää Apr. 1991, I Apr. 1992, G Oct. 1992.

Telarc Compact Disc CD 80291. Atlanta Symphony Orchestra, Yoel LEVI. P Atlanta, Georgia 14 Apr. 1991, I and G July 1994.

Teldec Compact Disc 9031 74719-2. National Symphony Orchestra of Washington, Mstislav ROSTROPOVICH. P Washington Oct. 1991, I June 1992, G Oct. 1992. *Reissued:* Teldec Compact Discs 0630-17046-2. [In twelve-disc set of Symphonies.] G Oct. 1997 ~ Ultima Compact Discs 8573 87799-2 (two-disc set). [Op. 43.] I Apr. 2001, G Sept. 2001.

Decca Compact Disc 436 763-2DH. Royal Philharmonic Orchestra, Vladimir ASHKENAZY. [Op. 130 and Sans op. U.] P Walthamstow 23–29 Oct 1991, I Feb. 1994, G Apr. 1994.

Deutsche Grammophon Compact Disc 437 819-2GH. London Symphony Orchestra, André PREVIN. P Tooting 9–10 Oct. 1992, I Jan. 1995, G

Mar. 1995. *Reissued:* Deutsche Grammophon Classikon Compact Disc 463, 262-2GCL. I Aug. 1999, G Feb. 2000.

Philips Compact Disc 446 062-2PH. Kirov Orchestra, Valeri GERGIEV. P Haarlem 8–11 Sept. 1994, I June 1995, G Aug. 1995.

Netherlands: Erasmus Compact Disc WVH 143. Byelorussian State Symphony Orchestra, Gerard OSKAMP. P Minsk concert 1995, I 1998.

Delos Compact Disc DE 3204 (Dolby Surround Sound). Dallas Symphony Orchestra, Andrew LITTON. P Dallas 2–3 Jan. 1996, I Mar. 1997, G Sept. 1997.

Germany: BMG RCA Classics Compact Disc 74321 56258-2. Minsk Philharmonic Orchestra, Pierre-Dominique PONNELLE. P 1–4 June 1996, I 1998.

Germany: Arte Nova Compact Disc 74321 51628-2. Novosibirsk Philharmonic Orchestra, Arnold KATS. P Oct. 1996, I Dec. 1997.

Switzerland: Relief Compact Disc CR 991056. Tchaikovsky Symphony Orchestra, Vladimir FEDOSEYEV. P concert 1999, I June 2001.

References: Gow, Gutman, Haas (in Bartlett), Herbage, Hulme (in *DSCH*), Khentova (1979*b* and 1984), Pleak (in *DSCH*), Sabinina, and Yarustovsky.

Notes: The Breitkopf & Härtel scores and parts, used by Western conductors after 1947, incorrectly give E sharp in the Finale coda muted violin solo (at bar 559 before fig. 172), whereas the Muzgiz and Muzyka scores faithfully reproduce the composer's C sharp. This note is wrongly played in the De Preist, Previn, Haitink, Inbal, and Järvi recorded versions but corrected by Slatkin and Solti.

The UK concert and broadcast première was originally scheduled to be performed on 13 July 1944, by the London Philharmonic Orchestra under Sir Adrian Boult, from the Royal Albert Hall as part of Sir Henry Wood's Jubilee Season of Promenade Concerts. However, the concert was cancelled by the authorities as it was realized that the hall's glass dome made it a potential death trap with the onset of Hitler's V-1 flying bomb attacks. The concert and broadcast took place on the same date, transferred to Bedford with substituted orchestra and conductor. (*DSCH Journal 11*).

The second movement quotes the Scherzo theme of the Original Suite for Jazz Orchestra No. 2, Sans op. G (ii).

Opus 66   Russian River

Alternative title: Listed as *The Great River* by Martynov and Rabinovich, with subtitle (*The Volga*) by the latter.

Form: Incidental music for the stage spectacle *Russian River*, scored for choir and orchestra:

1. March—Allegretto
2. Choreographic divertissement 'Football'—Presto

3. Vocal-symphonic picture 'The Battle of Stalingrad'—Moderato—
   Allegro
4. Waltz
5. Final Chorus—Moderato

Lyrics of Nos. 3 and 5 by Iosif Dobrovolsky.

Instrumentation: piccolo, flute, oboe, 2 clarinets (B flat and A), bassoon ~ 2 horns, 3 trumpets, 2 trombones, tuba ~ timpani, side drum, cymbals, bass drum ~ S.A.T.B. chorus in Nos. 3 and 5 ~ strings.

Composed: 17 December 1944, at Moscow.

Première: 17 April 1945, Moscow Dzerzhinsky Central Club; NKVD Song and Dance Ensemble; scenario by Iosif Dobrovolsky, M. Volpin, and Nikolai Erdman; décor by Pyotr Vilyams and produced by Ruben Simonov.

Arrangements: Piano reductions of Nos. 1, 2, and 3 by V. Samarin and of No. 5 by Andrei Sevastyanova. Shostakovich's National Anthem Entry, Sans op. N (iii), is introduced in 'The Battle of Stalingrad', which Yuri Silantiev retitles 'Battle by the Volga' in *My Native Country*, Sans op. Y, and in No. 5—used with a new lyric for 'Song of Victory' in Silantiev's Suite.

Music: Autograph score preserved at the Moscow Dzerzhinsky Central Club and 'The Battle of Stalingrad' autograph in the possession of Karen Khachaturyan. No musical material of the Waltz has been discovered.

Sovetskii Kompozitor, No. 2518 (in *My Native Country*), 1972, 'Battle by the Volga' only, 29 cm.

Muzyka, No. 11412 (in Volume 28 of *Collected Works* with Opp. 19, 24, 28, 31, 32, 37, 44, 58*a*, 63, 72, and in the supplement, Sans opp. D and K), 1986, piano and vocal scores of Nos. 1–3 and 5, 30 cm.

Muzyka, No. 11413 (in Volume 27 of *Collected Works* with Opp. 19, 24, 28, 32, 37, 44, 58*a*, 63, and 72), 1987, full score of Nos. 1–3 and 5 with I. Dobrovolsky's original lyrics, 30 cm.

Recording: Chandos Compact Disc CHAN 9907. 'Football' arr. V. Samarin. Rustem HAYROUDINOFF (piano). ['Theatre Music'—Opp. 37, 19, 31, 32, 44, 58*a*, and 22.] P Potton Hall, Suffolk 7–8 Aug. 2000, I Apr. 2001.

References: Bogdanov-Berezovsky and Khentova (1984).

Note: See *My Native Country*, Sans op. Y, for recording of 'Battle by the Volga'.

Opus 67   Trio No. 2 in E minor

Form: Chamber work for violin, cello, and piano in four movements:

1. Andante—Moderato
2. Allegro con brio or (in earlier editions) Allegro non tropppo
3. Largo *attacca*
4. Allegretto

Composed: In 1944, at the Composers' House at Ivanovo. Begun on 15 February, four days after the death of his friend Ivan Sollertinsky; the second movement finished on 4 August and the whole work completed on
13 August.

Dedication: To the memory of Ivan Ivanovich Sollertinsky (musicologist).

Premières: 14 November 1944, Leningrad Philharmonic Bolshoi Hall and 28
November 1944, Moscow Conservatory Bolshoi Hall; Dmitri Tsyganov
(violin), Sergei Shirinsky (cello), and Dmitri Shostakovich (piano). The
Allegretto repeated as an encore.

   UK: 24 April 1946, Wigmore Hall, London; Boosey & Hawkes ninth
concert; Henry Holst (violin), Anthony Pini (cello), and Peter Stadlen
(piano).

Music: Autograph score preserved at the CIS Archives of Literature and Art.
Awarded a Stalin Prize Second Class in 1946. Not usually designated as
'No. 2' on scores and parts before 1983.

   Muzgiz, No. 18203, 1945, score and parts, 28.5 cm.

   Leeds Music, no number, *c.*1947, with annotations by Harry Sheldon,
parts, 30 cm.

   International Music, No. 2806, *c.*1960, parts, 30.5 cm.

   Edition Peters, No. 4744 (plate no. 12035), 1961, parts, 30 cm.

   Sovetskii Kompozitor, 1962, parts, 29 cm.

   Hans Sikorski, No. 2211, 1962, score and parts, 31.5 cm.

   MCA, 1967, parts, 31 cm.

   Muzyka, No. 2943, 1968, parts, 29 cm.

   Universal Edition, Philharmonia Score No. 181, no date (1968 on back
cover), with detailed analysis in German, English, and French, score,
18.5 cm.

   Muzyka, No. 10794 (in Volume 37 of *Collected Works* with Opp. 8, 11,
and 57), 1983, score and parts, 30 cm.

Duration: 24' 40" in score; 22' 39"–30' 06"; 27' 50"–29' 00" (Plaistow).

Ballets: *About Face.* Alexander Roy, London Dance Theatre; Euston Collegiate Theatre, London, August 1976.

   A Moment of Give. Jeremy James, Spring Loaded company; Linbury
Studio, Royal Opera House, London, 8 April 2000.

Recordings: USSR: 13160-9 (9 sides 10" 78 rpm). Dmitri Tsyganov, Sergel
Shirinsky, and Dmitri SHOSTAKOVICH. [Op. 34 Nos. 22 and 8.] P 1945.
Reissued: USA: Compass Set C 102 (5 sides 10" 78 rpm). [Op. 34 Nos. 22
and 8.] ~ Revelation Compact Disc RV 70007 (mono). ['Shostakovich
plays Shostakovich, Vol. 6'—Opp. 34, 79, and 69.] I Sept. 1998, G Feb.
1999.

   Ultraphon G 14927-9 (6 sides 78 rpm). David Oistrakh, Miloš Sádlo,
and Dmitri SHOSTAKOVICH. P Prague after public performance on 26 May
1947. *Reissued:* USA: Mercury MG 15005 (10" mono). I 1949 ~ USA:
Colosseum CRLPX 011 (mono). [Prokofiev, Rakhmaninov, Glazunov *et
al.*] I 1954 ~ USA: Mercury MG 10045 (mono) ~ USSR: Melodiya M10

39075-6 (mono). [In four-record box set 'D. Shostakovich—Pianist' with Opp. 69, 5, 22*a*, and 34.] I 1977*b* ~ Czech: Supraphon 0 10 2371-2 (mono). [In two-record set 'David Oistrakh in Prague' with Mozart, Brahms, and Beethoven.] I 1978, G Aug. 1979 ~ Canada: Doremi Compact Disc DHR 7701. ['David Oistrakh Collection, Vol. 1'—Tchaikovsky and Schubert.] P date given as 1946, I Mar. 1997 ~ Revelation Compact Disc RV 70006 (mono). ['Shostakovich plays Shostakovich, Vol. 5'—Opp. 35, 102, and 94.] I May 1998 ~ France: Dante Compact Discs LYS 369-370 (two-disc set). [Opp. 40, 57, and 73.] I 1998 ~ USA/Canada: Eclectra Compact Disc ECCD 2046 (mono). [Opp. 40 and 134.] I 2000.

USA: Alco of Hollywood A-3 (6 sides 78 rpm, album). COMPINSKY TRIO (Manuel, Alec, and Sara Compinsky). P *c.*1950.

BBC Legends Compact Disc BRCL 4024-2 (mono). Leonid Kogan, Mstislav Rostropovich, and Emil GILELS. [Op. 107 and Haydn.] P London 28 Feb. 1959, I Sept. 1999, G Nov. 1999.

Czech: Multisonic Compact Disc 31 0105-2 (mono). David Oistrakh, Svyatoslav Knushevitsky, and Lev OBORIN. [Schubert and Haydn.] P Prague radio 1961, I 1993. *Reissued:* France: Praga Compact Disc PR 254 054 (mono). [Opp. 73 and 83.] I July 1994 ~ Japan: Triton Compact Disc MECC 26018 (mono). [Opp. 49 and 92.] P stated Moscow Conservatory concert 1960, I 2000.

USA: Concert-Disc 234. LYRIC TRIO (Arthur Tabachnik, Shirley Evans, Hilde Freund). [Loeillet and Arnold.] P 1963. *Reissued:* Everest SDBR 4234. [Loeillet and Arnold.] G Apr. 1972.

Czech: Supraphon SUA 10019 (mono). CZECH TRIO (Aleksandr Plocek, Saša Večtomov, Josef Páleníček). [Ravel.] P 1963. *Reissued:* Czech: Supraphon Compact Disc CO 4489. [Mozart.] I 1990.

Waverley LLP 1023 (mono) and SLLP 1024. SCOTTISH TRIO (Louis Carus, Joan Dickson, Wight Henderson). [Beethoven.] G Nov. 1964.

USA: Westminster XWN 19063 (mono) and WST 17073. TRIO DI BOLZANO (Giaino Capri, Sante Amadori, Nunzie Montanari). [Ravel.] P 1964. *Reissued:* HMV CLP 1887 (mono) and CSD 1614. [Ravel.] G Aug. 1965 ~ MCA Millennium Classics MCD 80107 (stereo not mono as stated). [Opp. 35 and 102.] I Feb. 1997.

USSR: Melodiya CM 01805-6. Mikhail Vaiman, Mstislav Rostropovich, and Pavel SEREBRYAKOV. [Tishchenko.] P 1966, I 1969. *Reissued:* USA: Angel Melodiya S 40091. [Tishchenko.] I 1969 ~ East Germany: Eterna 8 26 968. [Tishchenko.] ~ HMV Melodiya ASD 2718. [Op. 134.] G Aug. 1971 ~ Italy: EMI 065 95590. [Tishchenko.] ~ Japan: VICC Compact Disc 2152 [Tishchenko.] I 1994.

USSR: Melodiya D 021245-6 (mono) and C 01621-2. Igor Bezrodny, Mikhail Khomitser, and Dmitri BASHKIROV. [Mozart.] I 1969. *Reissued:* France: EMI C063 90278. [Mozart.]

USSR: Melodiya CM 02649-50. Yuri Shvolkovsky, Maris Villerush, and Valdis YANTSIS. [Beethoven.] P and I 1971.

USA: Turnabout TV 34280 S. NEW AMSTERDAM TRIO (John Pintavalle, Heinrich Joachim, Edith Mocsanyi). [Op. 127.] P 1971, G Mar. 1972.

Da Camera Magna SM 92110. Jean-Jacques Kantorow, Philippe Muller, and Jacques ROUVIER. [Martinů.] P 1971, G Jan. 1982.

USSR: Melodiya CM 03723-4. Rostislav Dubinsky, Valentin Berlinsky, and Lyubov YEDLINA. [Ravel.] P 1972, I 1973. *Reissued:* USA: Westminster WGS 8332. [Ravel.]

HMV HQS 1330. Yong-Uck Kim, Ralph Kirshbaum, and André PREVIN. [Ravel.] P 1974, G Sept. 1974.

Sweden: BIS LP 26. Arve Tellefsen, Frans Helmerson, and Hans PÅLS-SON. [Fauré.] P Nacka, Sweden 26–7 Apr. 1975, G Mar. 1977. *Reissued:* HNH 4007. [Fauré.] I 1977 ~ Sweden: BIS Compact Disc CD 26. [Opp. 110 and 127.] I 1991, G Sept. 1992.

Philips 6500 860. BEAUX ARTS TRIO (Isidore Cohen, Bernard Green-house, Menahem Pressler). [Ives.] P 1975, G Jan. 1976. *Reissued:* Philips Musica da camera 412 402-1PC. [Ives.] G June 1985.

USSR: Melodiya C10 06943-4. Mikhail Bezverkhny, Tatyana Prokho-rova, and Aleksandr BONDURYANSKY. [Beethoven.] P 1976, I 1976*d*.

USSR: Melodiya C10 07191-2. Grigori Feigin, Valentin Feigin, and Igor ZHUKHOV. [Haydn.] P 1976, I 1977*a*. *Reissued:* USSR: Melodiya C10 07191-09537. [In second box of Part 3 of *Collected Works on Records* with Op. 40.] I 1978 ~ France: Le Chant du Monde Compact Discs LDC 278 1018-19 (two-disc set). [Opp. 134, 40, and 147.] I Feb. 1990, G June 1990.

RCA Red Seal RL 25224. Miles Baster, Christopher Gough, and Roger WOODWARD. [Op. 57.] P Edinburgh 21–2 Sept. 1978, G Jan. 1980.

USA: Sine Qua Non Superba SAS 2039. APPLE HILL CHAMBER PLAYERS. [Schumann.] P 1978.

Hong Kong: One-Eleven Compact Disc URS 92010. Ruggiero Ricci, Nathaniel Rosen, and Santiago RODRIGUEZ. [Schubert, Spohr, and Wie-niawski.] P concert 1978, I 1992.

USSR: Melodiya C10 14927-8. Vladimir Ivanov, Mikhail Utkin, and Aleksandr BONDURYANSKY. [A. Chaikovsky.] P 1980, I 1981*c*.

New Zealand: Kiwi Records Tartar TRL 016. GAGLIANO TRIO (John Chisholm, Allan Chisholm, Bruce Greenfield). [Ravel.] I 1981.

Phoenix DGS 1006. TRIO ZINGARA (Sophie Langdon, Susan Dorey, Annette Cole). [Ravel.] P London 1–2 Apr. 1981, G Dec. 1982. *Reissued:* Signature KNEW LP 202 and Compact Disc KNEW CD 202. [Ravel.] I 1987 ~ Trax Classique TRXLP 131 and Compact Disc TRXCD 131. Sec-ond and third movements. ['Testimony—Shostakovich's Greatest Hits'—Opp. 47, 97, 102, 60, 110; and Josephs.] I 1988.

Norway: Simax PS 1014. OSLO TRIO (Stig Nilsson, Aage Kvalbein, Jens Harald Bratlie). [Opp. 5 and 8.] P near Oslo 17 Nov. and 21 Dec. 1981, and 2 Jan. 1982; G July 1982. *Reissued:* Simax Compact Disc PSC 1014. [Opp. 5 and 8.] I Sept. 1987, G Oct. 1988.

Academy Sound & Vision ALH 929. MUSIC GROUP OF LONDON (David Parkhouse, Hugh Bean, Eileen Croxford). [Op. 57.] I Apr. 1983, G July 1983.

Chandos ABRD 1088 (digital). BORODIN TRIO (Rostislav Dubinsky, Yuli Turovsky, Lyubov Yedlina). [Op. 57.] P London June 1983, G Jan. 1984. *Reissued:* Chandos Compact Disc CHAN 8342. [Op. 57.] I Sept. 1984, G Apr. 1985 ~ Chandos Compact Discs CHAN 9627 (two-disc set). 3rd and 4th movements. 'In Memory of a great artist—Rostislav Dubinsky'— Op. 127; Tchaikovsky, Mendelssohn, Beethoven *et al.*] I 1998.

Germany: Live Classics Compact Disc LCL 172. Oleg Kagan (violin), Natalia Gutman (cello), and Svyatoslav RICHTER (piano). [Schubert.] P Pushkin Museum, Moscow concert 12 Dec. 1984.

Canada: Fanfare DFL 9021 X (digital). CANADIAN PIANO TRIO (Jaime Weisenblum, Nina Tobias, Stephanie Sebastian). [Gershwin, Davies, and Laloux.] P Toronto June 1985.

France: Harmonia Mundi Ottava LP OTR 58504. GUARNERI TRIO (Mark Lubotsky, Jean Decroos, Danièle Dechenne). [Op. 127.] P 1985, I Apr. 1987.

Czech: Panton 8111 0570. NEW PRAGUE TRIO (Jiří Klika, Jan Zvolánek, Arnošt Střižek). [Beethoven.] P 9–13 Dec. 1985.

Italy: Dynamic FC U23 (digital). TRIO TCHAIKOVSKY (Pavel Vernikov, Anatole Liebermann, Konstantin Bogino). [Rakhmaninov.] P Genoa Feb. 1986. *Reissued:* Dynamic/Essex Records II Canale Compact Disc DC U23. [Rakhmaninov.] G Oct. 1988.

USA: Musicmasters MMD 20152Y-53W (digital, in two-record set). Joseph Swensen, David Finckel, and Yefim BRONFMAN. ['Live from Spoleto Festival USA '86'—Kohly, Dvořák, Mozart, and Vivaldi.] P concert Charleston, S. Carolina May or June 1986, I 1988.

Spain: Harmonia Mundi Iberica HMI 87 001 (digital). TRIO DE BARCELONA (Gerard Claret, Lluis Claret, Albert G. Attenelle). [Ravel.] P Spain 1987.

CBS Masterworks Compact Disc MK 44664. Isaac Stern, Yo-Yo Ma, and Emanuel AX. [Op. 40.] P Purchase, New York 1987, I Dec. 1988, G June 1989.

Sweden: Caprice Compact Disc CAP 21348. GARCIA TRIO (Gustavo Garcia, Göran Holmstrand, Ingemar Edgren). [Turina, Linde, and Ben-Haim.] P 18–19 Apr. 1987, I 1988.

USA: XLNT Music Compact Disc CD-18003. LEONARDO TRIO (Erica Kiesewetter, Jonathan Spitz, Cameron Grant). [Smetana and Martinů.] P New York 28–31 Dec. 1987, I 1988.

Collins Classics 1040-1 (digital) and Compact Disc 1040-2. TRIO ZINGARA (Elizabeth Layton, Felix Schmidt, Annette Cole). [Ravel.] P London 1989, I Oct. 1989, G Mar. 1990.

Switzerland: Relief Compact Disc CR 891 008. TRIO YUVAL (Uri Pianka, Simca Heled, Jonathan Zak). [Tchaikovsky.] P New York 5–7 June 1989, I 1990. *Reissued:* Centaur Compact Disc CRC 2443. [Arensky.] I May 2000.

Germany: Dabringhaus und Grimm Compact Disc MD+GL 3334. MÜNCHER KLAVIERTRIO (Ilona Then-Bergh, Gerhard Zank, Michael Schäfer). [Opp. 8 and 127.] P date not stated, I 1989.

Finland: Ondine Compact Disc ODE 744-2. TRIO TCHAIKOVSKY (Pavel Vernikov, Anatole Liebermann, Konstantin Bogino). [Op. 57.] P July 1989, I June 1990.

Philips Compact Disc 432 079-2PH. BEAUX ARTS TRIO (Isidore Cohen, Peter Wiley, Menahem Pressler). [Op. 57.] P New York Sept. 1989, I May 1991, G Aug. 1991.

Germany: Harmonia Mundi Compact Disc HM 950-2. ALANI TRIO (Annette-Barbara Vogel, Nikolai Schneider, Lars Vogt). [Smetana.] P Heildelberg 2–3 Nov. 1989.

Altarus Compact Disc AIR-CD 9033. FRIEND-SOLOMON-HUGH TRIO (Rodney Friend, Timothy Hugh, Yonty Solomon). [Tchaikovsky.] P not stated, I 1991.

Netherlands: Fidelio Compact Disc 8843. REIZEND MUZIEKGEZELSCHAP (Christian Bor, Nathaniel Rosen, Edward Auer). [Op. 57.] P Amsterdam 21 Mar. and 7 Aug. 1990.

USA: Northeastern Compact Disc NR 245-CD. BOSTON CHAMBER MUSIC SOCIETY (Stephanie Chase, Ronald Thomas, Randall Hodgkinson). [Op. 40.] P Methuen, Mass. Apr. 1990, I Dec. 1994.

Claudio Compact Disc CR 4013-2. BEKOVA SISTERS TRIO (Elvira, Alfia, and Eleonora Nakipbekova). [Arensky.] P 15 July 1990, I July 1991.

Virgin Classics Compact Disc VC7 59312-2. NASH ENSEMBLE (Marcia Crayford, Christopher van Kampen, Ian Brown). [Op. 57 and Sans op. P.] P London Nov. 1990, I Aug. 1993.

Denmark: Kontrapunkt Compact Disc 32131. COPENHAGEN TRIO (Søreh Elbaek, Troels Hermansen, Morton Mogensen). [Op. 8.] P Lungbye 1992.

Koch Discover International Compact Disc DICD 920356. CHO PIANO TRIO (Cho Young Mi, Cho Young Chang, Cho Young Bang). [Mendelssohn.] P Brussels 1992.

Netherlands: Channel Classics Canal Grande Compact Disc CG 9218. OSIRIS TRIO (Peter Blunt, Larissa Groeneveld, Ellen Corver). [Beethoven and Novák.] P Haarlem 10, 11, and 13 Aug. 1992, I May 1993.

France: Le Chant du Monde Russian Season Compact Disc RUS 288 088. MOSCOW TRIO (Vladimir Ivanov, Mikhail Utkin, Aleksandr Bonduryansky). [Opp. 8 and 127.] P Moscow Conservatory Sept.–Nov. 1993, I Sept. 1994.

USA: Mobius Compact Discs 2D 0193 (two-disc set). MOBIUS (Phil Johnson, Mike Fitzpatrick, Xak Bjerken). [Beethoven, Ravel, Brahms, and Mobius.] P 1993.

USA: Gagliano Compact Disc GR 303-CD. FLORESTAN TRIO (Carol Sindell, Hamilton Cheifetz, Harold Gray). [Mendelssohn.] P Portland State University, Oregon 27–9 Dec. 1993.

USA: Arizona Friends of Chamber Music Compact Disc 1994-01. Ani Kavafian (violin), Colin Carr (cello), and James BONN (piano). [Brahms.] P Tucson, Arizona 13 Mar. 1994, I 1996.

Decca Compact Disc 452 899-2DH. Joshua Bell (violin), Steven Isserlis (cello), and Olli MUSTONEN (piano). [Messiaen.] P London 28 Aug. 1994, I July 1997, G Sept. 1997.

Canada: Mastersound Compact Disc MST 33. MCPHERSON TRIO (Pablo Diemecke—violin, Lawrence Skaggs—cello, May-Ling Kwok—piano). [Arensky.] P University of Victoria 29–30 Aug. 1994, 1 Nov. 1995.

Japan: Meldec Compact Disc MECC 28004. Aleksandr Melnikov (violin), Natalya Sabinova (cello), and Viktor YAMPOLISKY (piano). [Opp. 8 and 13.] P Mosfilm Studio, Moscow 1–10 Oct. 1994, I June 1995. *Reissued:* Japan: Triton Compact Disc 17 011. [Opp. 8 and 13.] I Feb. 1997.

Naxos Compact Disc 8.553297. STOCKHOLM ARTS TRIO (Dan Almgren, Torleif Thedéen, Stefan Bojsten). [Opp. 8 and 127.] P Stockholm 13–15 Mar. 1995, I Apr. 1997, G July 1997.

Teldec Compact Disc 4509-98414-2. Mikhail Kopelman, Valentin Berlinsky, and Elizaveta LEONSKAYA. [Op. 57.] P Berlin Apr. 1995, I Nov. 1996, G Feb. 1997. *Reissued:* Ultima Compact Discs 8573 87820-2 (two-disc set). [Opp. 57, 49, and 144.] I Apr. 2001, G Aug. 2001.

Koch Schwann Compact Disc 3-6400-2H1. Lev Atlas (violin), Alexander Volpov (cello), and Phillip SILVER (piano). [Rakhmaninov and Sviridov.] P BBC Scotland May 1995.

USA: Arabesque Compact Discs Z 6698 (two-disc set). Jaime Laredo (violin), Sharon Robinson (cello), and Joseph KALICHSTEIN (piano). [Opp. 8, 40, 134, and 147.] P Purchase, New York 17–18 Dec. 1995 or 12–13 Sept. 1996, I and G Jan. 1998.

Italy: Real Sound Compact Disc RS 051-0176. TRIO DI TORINO (Sergio Lamberto, Dario Destefano, Giacomo Fuga). [Opp. 8 and 57.] P Wesel, Germany Apr. 1996, I May 2000.

Germany: Primavera Compact Disc 5065. TRIO JEAN PAUL (Ulf Schneider, Martin Lôhr, Eckart Heiligers). [Beethoven and Haydn.] P Freiburger Musik Forum June 1996.

Chandos Compact Disc CHAN 9526 (two-disc set). BEKOVA SISTERS (Elvira, Alfia, and Eleonora). [Opp. 127 and 147.] P Highgate, London 19–20 June 1996, I Feb. 1997, G May 1997.

France: Erato Compact Disc 0650-17875-2. Vadim Repin (violin), Dmitri Yablonsky (cello), and Boris BEREZOVSKY (piano). [Tchaikovsky.] P Berlin 23–7 Mar. 1997, I Dec. 1997, G Jan. 1998.

Hungary: Hungaroton Classics Compact Disc HCD 31780. BARTOS TRIO (Galina Danilova, Csaba Bartos, and Irina Ivanickaia). [Opp. 8 and 127.] P Hungaroton Studio 29 May–2 June 1997.

Switzerland: European Mozart Foundation Compact Discs EMF 84 (third disc of four-disc set). Nurit Pacht (violin), Isolde Hayer (cello), and John BLACKLOW (piano). [Armenian songs and Mozart.] P Venice concert 5 July 1997.

Germany: EMI Classics Compact Disc CDC5 56674-2. AHN TRIO (Angella, Maria, and Lucia Ahn). [Dvořák and Suk.] P New York 10–15 July 1997.

France: Lyrinx Compact Disc LYR 182. Régis Pasquier (violin), Roland Pidoux (cello), and Jean-Claude PENNETIER (piano). [Tchaikovsky.] P Marseille 14–16 Nov. 1997.

Germany: EMI Classics Compact Disc CDC5 56673-2. EROICA TRIO (Adela Peña, Sara Sant'Ambrogio, and Erika Nickrenz). [Dvořák and Rakhmaninov.] P Tiburon, California 5–9 Mar. 1998.

USA: Musicians Showcase Compact Disc MS 1046. ARMAN TRIO (Constantin Bogdanas, Dorel Fodoreanu, Deniz Arman Gelenbe). [Dvořák.] P Raleigh, North Carolina concert 6 Apr. 1998.

Nimbus Compact Disc NI 5572. VIENNA PIANO TRIO (Wolfgang Redik, Marcus Trefny, and Stefan Mendl). [Op. 8; and Schnittke.] P Nimbus Foundation Hall 6–9 Apr. 1998, I and G Dec. 1998.

Japan: Deutsche Grammophon Compact Disc POCG 10174. Gidon Kremer (violin), Mischa Maisky (cello), and Martha ARGERICH (piano). [Tchaikovsky and Kiesewetter.] P Tokyo concert May 1998, G Oct. 1999.

Norway: Simax Compact Disc PSC 1147. GRIEG TRIO (Sølve Sigerland, Ellen Margrete Flesjø, Vebjørn Anvik). [Op. 8; Bloch and Martin.] P Lommedalen 12–18 June 1988, I Oct. 1999.

Germany: Thorofon Compact Disc CTH 2397. TRIO BAMBERG (Yevgeni Schuk, Stephan Gerlinghaus, Robert Benz). [Op. 8; and Schnittke.] P Nuremberg June 1998.

Orfeo Compact Disc C 465 991A. MUNICH TRIO (Rudolf J. Koeckert, Gerhard Zank, Hermann Lechler). [Opp. 8 and 127.] P Bavarian Radio Studio 4–5 May and 4–7 June 1999, I Mar. 2001.

USA: MMC Compact Disc 2058. SOLATI TRIO (Sophia Herman, Hrant Tatian, and Ludmilla Lifson). [McKinley, Melloni, and Bullen.] P Cambridge, Mass. I July 1999.

Czech: Vars Compact Disc VA 0106-2. ACADEMIA TRIO (Pavel Šafařík, Jaroslav Matějka, Petr Jiříkovský). [Beethoven.] P Hluboš Castle Sept. 1999.

References: McCreless (in Fanning 1995) and Martynov.

Opus 68   Quartet No. 2 in A major

Form: String quartet in four movements:

1. Overture—Moderato con moto
2. Recitative and Romance—Adagio
3. Valse—Allegro
4. Theme with Variations—Adagio—Allegro non troppo

Composed: 2–20 September 1944, at the Composers' House at Ivanovo. The first movement completed on 5th, second written on the following day, and the third completed on 15 September.

Dedication: Vissarion Yakovlevich Shebalin (composer).

Premières: 14 November 1944, Leningrad Philharmonic Bolshoi Hall and 28 November 1944, Moscow Conservatory Bolshoi Hall; Beethoven Quartet (Dmitri Tsyganov, Vasili Shirinsky, Vadim Borisovsky, and Sergei Shirinsky).

UK: 13 November 1946, London; Boosey & Hawkes concert.

Scotland: 20 August 1962, Edinburgh Freemasons' Hall; Allegri Quartet (Eli Coren, James Barton, Patrick Ireland, and William Pleeth).

Arrangements: Transcription of 'Recitative and Romance' for violin and piano by Dmitri Tsyganov. Reduction for piano four hands by Anatoli Dmitriev.

Music: Originally published as Opus 69 and renumbered in 1965. Autograph score preserved at the Glinka Museum and an autograph piano score, at the CIS Archives of Literature and Art.

Muzgiz, No. 18181, 1945, score 17 cm.

Leeds Music, *c.*1947, parts, 31 cm.

Musica Rara, No. 1078, 1965, score, 18.5 cm.

Musica Rara, No. 1079, 1965, parts, 31 cm.

Muzyka, Leningrad, No. 285 (in Volume 1 with Quartets 1, 3, and 4 arr. for piano four hands by A. Dmitriev), 1965, 29.5 cm.

Sovetskii Kompozitor, 1969, parts, 29 cm.

Edition Eulenberg, No. 386, 1970, score, 19 cm.

Edition Peters, No. 5752 (plate no. 12810), 1975, parts, 30 cm.

Hans Sikorski, No. 2162, 1975, parts, 31.5 cm.

Muzyka, No. 9816 (in Volume 35 of *Collected Works* Quartets 1–8), 1979, 30 cm.

Hans Sikorski, No. 2265 (with Opp. 49, 73, and 83), 1980, score, 21 cm.

Sovetskii Kompozitor, No. 5543, 1981, 2nd movement arr. for violin and piano by D. Tsyganov, score and part, 29 cm.

Duration: Approx. 32 minutes in score; 31' 26"–40' 12"; 34' 50" (Plaistow); Recitative and Romance arr. Tsyganov 10' 15".

Recordings: HMV History of Music in Sound HMS 113 (78 rpm). Valse only. KOECKERT QUARTET (Rudolf Koeckert, Willi Buchner, Oscar Riedi, Josef Merz). [Copland.] *Reissued:* HMV HLP 27 (mono). Valse only. ['Modern Eclecticism'—Stravinsky, Bartók, Janáček *et al.*] G Apr. 1959 ~ USA: RCA Victor LM 6092 (mono). Valse only. ['History of music in sound', Vol. 10.] I 1959.

USA: Urania URLP 7040 (mono). SCHULZ QUARTET (Rudolf Schulz, W. Kirch, H. Wigand, R. Klemm). P Germany, I 1952.

USSR: MK D 3034-5 (10" mono). BEETHOVEN QUARTET (personnel as at première). P 1956. *Reissued:* USA: Vanguard VRS 6033 (mono). [Op. 73.] I

1958 ~ Czech: Supraphon SUF 20039 (10" mono). G July 1960 ~ USSR: Melodiya D 015691-2 (mono). I 1965 ~ Germany: Telefunken TW 30162 (10" mono) ~ USA: Vanguard Classics Compact Disc OVC 8077. [Op. 57.] I Sept. 1994 ~ USA: Consonance Blue Label Compact Disc 81.3005 (mono). [Vol. 1—Opp. 49 and 83.] I May 1995. See Note.

USSR: Melodiya D 019213-4 (mono) and C 01437-8. BORODIN QUARTET (Rostislav Dubinsky, Yaroslav Aleksandrov, Dmitri Shebalin, Valentin Berlinsky). P and I 1967. *Reissued:* USA: Seraphim Melodiya S 6034. [In three-record box set with Quartets 1, 3–5.] ~ HMV Melodiya HQS 1319 in Set SLS 879. [Op. 49.] G June 1974.

Czech: Panton 11 0342-3 H. SUK QUARTET (Antonín Novák, Vojtěch Jouza, Karel Řehák, Jan Štros). [In two-record set with Op. 127; Aristakesyan, Gubaidulina, and Ledenev.] P 1972.

L'Oiseau-Lyre DSLO 31. FITZWILLIAM QUARTET (Christopher Rowland, Jonathan Sparey, Alan George, Ioan Davies). [Op. 49.] P 23–6 May 1977, G Mar. 1979. *Reissued:* Decca 188 D1 in Set D 188 D7. [Op. 49.] G Feb. 1981 ~ Decca Enterprise Compact Discs 433 078-2DM6. [On first disc of six-disc set with Op. 49.] I Apr. 1992, G June 1992.

USSR: Melodiya C10 11609-10. TANEYEV QUARTET (Vladimir Ovcharek, Grigori Lutsky, Vissarion Soloviev, Iosif Levinson). [In first box of Part 2 of *Collected Works on Records.*] P 1978, I 1980. *Reissued:* Japan: JVC Victor 5345. [Op. 49.] ~ USSR: Melodiya Compact Disc SUCD 11 00310. [Op. 118.] I 1991*d.*

Olympia Compact Disc OCD 532. SHOSTAKOVICH QUARTET (Andrei Shislov, Sergei Pishchugin, Aleksandr Galkovsky, Aleksandr Korchagin). ['Complete Quartets, Vol. 2'—Opp. 92 and 108.] P 1981, I May 1994, G Sept. 1994.

France: Praga Compact Disc PR 254 042. STATE QUARTET OF GEORGIA (Konstantin Vardeli, Tamaz Batiashvili, Nodar Zhvaniya, Otar Chubinishvili). [Opp. 49 and 57.] P Czech Radio broadcast June 1981, I May 1994.

USSR: Melodiya C10 19023 001. BORODIN QUARTET (Mikhail Kopelman, Andrei Abramenkov, Dmitri Shebalin, Valentin Berlinsky). P 1982, I 1983*d.* *Reissued:* HMV Melodiya EX 270339-3 (DMM). [In seven-record box set of 15 Quartets plus Quintet.] G Mar. 1986 ~ EMI Compact Disc CDC7 49267-2. [Op. 73.] I Nov. 1987 ~ Japan: Victor Musical Industries Compact Disc VICC 40018. [Op. 49.] I 1990 ~ EMI Compact Discs CMS5 65032-2. [In six-disc set of 15 Quartets plus Quintet.] I Mar. 1994 ~ BMG Melodiya Compact Discs 74321 40711-2 (six-disc set). [Opp. 49 and 83.] I June 1997.

USSR: Melodiya C10 24481 008 (DMM). STATE QUARTET OF GEORGIA (Konstantin Vardeli, Tamaz Batiashvili, Nodar Zhvaniya, Otar Chubinishvili). P 1986, I 1987*c.*

France: REM Compact Disc 311058 XCD. VERLAINE QUARTET (Marie Pascale Meley, Michel Dietz, Jean-Pascal Oswald, Jean Adolphe). [Webern.] P Monte-Carlo 2 May 1987.

Teldec Compact Discs 9031 71702-2. BRODSKY QUARTET (Michael Thomas, Ian Belton, Paul Cassidy, Jacqueline Thomas). [On first disc of six-disc set with Op. 49.] P Berlin July 1989, I Nov. 1990, G June 1992. *Reissued:* Teldec Compact Disc 9031 73110-2. [Op. 92.] I 1991.

USA: ESS.A.Y. Compact Disc CD 1007. MANHATTAN QUARTET (Eric Lewis, Roy Lewis, John Dexter, Judith Glyde). [Opp. 49 and 73.] P Purchase, New York 27–8 Dec. 1989. *Reissued:* Koch Schwann Musica Mundi Compact Disc 310 128. ['Complete string Quartets, Vol. 1' with Opp. 49 and 73.] I May 1991.

Virgin Classics Compact Disc VC7 59281-2. BORODIN QUARTET (Mikhail Kopelman, Andrei Abramenkov, Dmitri Shebalin, Valentin Berlinsky). [Op. 133.] P Snape Nov. 1990, I Feb. 1993, G June 1993. *Reissued:* Virgin Classics Compact Discs VBD5 61630-2 (two-disc set). [Opp. 73, 108, 110, and 133.] I Aug. 1999.

Lydian Compact Disc 18133 (also Donau DCD 8133). MOYZES QUARTET (Stanislav Mucha, František Török, Alexander Lakatoš, Ján Slávik). [Op. 83.] P Bratislava 22–5 Jan. 1992, I 1994. *Reissued:* Dillon Classics Compact Disc 28133. [Op. 83.] I 1996.

Finland: Finlandia Compact Disc 4509 98996-2. SIBELIUS ACADEMY QUARTET (Erkki Kantola, Seppo Tukiainen, Veikko Kosonen, Arto Noras). [Op. 101.] P Järvenpää May 1994, I May 1996.

Sony Classical St Petersburg Classics Compact Disc SK 64584. ST PETERSBURG QUARTET (Alla Aranovskaya, Ilya Teplyakov, Andrei Dogadin, Leonid Shukayev). [Opp. 49 and 83.] P Dec. 1994.

Naxos Compact Disc 8.550975. ÉDER QUARTET (János Selmeczi, Péter Szüts, Sándor Papp, György Éder). ['Complete Quartets, Vol. 4'—Op. 133.] P Budapest 28–31 Mar. 1995, I Apr. 1996, G Apr. 1997.

Denmark: Classico Compact Disc CLASSCD 135. ZAPOLSKI QUARTET (Alexander Zapolski, Jacob Soelberg, Flemming Lave, Vanja Louro). [Op. 110.] P Roskilde, Denmark Aug. and Oct. 1995, I July 1996.

Japan: Toshiba EMI Compact Disc TOCE 9079. MORGAŮA QUARTET (Eiji Arai, Takashi Aoki, Hisashi Ono, Ryoichi Fujimori). [Opp. 108 and 34.] P 25–7 Mar. 1996, I June 1996.

France: Suoni e Colori Collection Compact Disc SC 53006. Recitative and Romance arr. Tsyganov. Alexandre BRUSSILOVSKY (violin) and Pascal Godart (piano). ['DSCH Aphorismes'—Opp. 11, 34, 13, Sans op. D; Schnittke—*Prelude in Memory of Shostakovich,* and Steven Gerber—*Elegy on the name 'Dmitri Shostakovich'.*] P Hautes-Alpes, France concert Aug. 1996, I 1997.

Hyperion Compact Disc CDA 67153. ST PETERSBURG QUARTET (Alla Aranovskaya, Ilya Teplyakov, Konstantin Kats, Leonid Shukayev). [Op. 73.] P St Petersburg Apr. 1999, I Oct. 1999, G Nov. 1999.

Deutsche Grammophon Compact Disc 463 284-2GH5 (five-disc set). EMERSON QUARTET (Eugene Drucker, Philip Setzer, Lawrence Dutton,

David Finkel). ['Complete Quartets, Vol. 1'—Opp. 49 and 73.] P Aspen, Colorado concert June–July 1999, G June 2000.

Reference: Martynov.

Notes: Robert Matthew-Walker reports that the late 1950s Beethoven Quartet Supraphon recording appears not to be the Melodiya performance as the Czech version alone contains 'noises off' in bar 14 of the Finale. The unsigned Supraphon sleeve note states that the first movement forms the prelude to a musical fairy-tale about a man of noble character and his rich emotional life.

Opus 69   A Child's Exercise Book

Alternative title: *Childhood Notebook.*

Form: A suite of seven simple pieces for piano:

1. March—in tempo of March
2. Valse—in tempo of Waltz
3. Sad Tale—Adagio
4. Merry Tale—Allegro
5. The Bear—Allegretto
6. Clockwork Doll—Allegretto
7. Birthday—[no tempo indication]

No. 6 is an adaptation of the first theme of Scherzo in F sharp minor, Opus 1 and No. 7 introduces a miniature fanfare subsequently expanded in the *Festive Overture*, Opus 96.

Composed: Nos. 1–6 on 6 December 1944 and No. 7 on 30 May 1945 (daughter's birthday).

Dedication: Galina Dmitrievna Shostakovich (daughter)

Première: Winter 1944–45, Moscow Union of Soviet Composers Children's Concert; Nos. 1–6, Galina Shostakovich.

Arrangements: Nos. 1 and 6 arranged for violin and piano by Konstantin Fortunatov. Nos. 1, 2, and 4 arranged for guitar solo by Agustín Lara. No. 6 arranged for cello and piano jointly by Roman Sapozhnikov and Georgi Kirkor.

Music: Two autograph copies of Nos. 1–6 preserved at the CIS Archives of Literature and Art and the Glinka Museum. The autograph of No. 7 is missing but there is a copy of it in the former library. Originally issued without an opus number. The pieces are usually published with No. 7 omitted and in the order Nos. 1, 2, 5, 4, 3, and 6. No. 1 included in many Russian albums of children's piano solos.

Music Fund of the USSR, 1945, Nos. 1–6.

Anglo-Soviet Music Press, No. 6 (under the title *Six Children's Pieces*), Nos. 1–6, 1946, 31 cm.

Leeds Music, *c.*1946, Nos. 1–6, 31 cm.

Leeds Music, *c.*1946, Nos. 4 and 6 ed. Joseph Wolman, issued separately, 31 cm.

Hans Sikorski, No. 2122, 1960, 31.5 cm.

Edition Peters, No. 4749 (plate no. 12079), 1961, 31 cm.

Le Chant du Monde, No. 6120, 1960s, 32 cm.

Edition Peters, No. 4794 (plate no. 12389—in *Shostakovich: Album of Easy Pieces*), 1967, Nos. 1 and 6 arr. K. Fortunatov, 30.5 cm.

Ricordi, No. 132260, 1975.

Muzyka, No. 4719 (in *D. Shostakovich: Pieces for violin and piano*), 1975, Nos. 1 and 6 arr. K. Fortunatov, 28.5 cm.

Sovetskii Kompozitor, No. 4920 (in *D. Shostakovich: Selection of Children's Piano Pieces*), 1979, No. 1–6 ed. Bronislava Rozengauz, 29 cm.

G. Ricordi, Buenos Aires, No. 12687, Nos. 2, 4, and 1 (Vals, Un Alegre Cuente de Hadas, and Marcha), arr. for guitar solo by A. Lara.

Muzyka, Leningrad, No. 2629 (in *S. Prokofiev and D. Shostakovich: Selection of Fortepiano Pieces for Children*), 1980, Nos. 1–6 compiled by Zinaida Vitkind, 28.5 cm.

Muzyka, No. 10285 (in Volume 39 of *Collected Works* with Opp. 5, 12, 13, 34, 61, and supplement of unnumbered piano pieces), Nos. 1–7, 1983, 30 cm.

Yorktown Music Press, New York, 1984, No. 6 only in album *The Joy of Russian Music* assembled by Dénes Agay, 30 cm.

Muzyka, No. 14908 (in *D. Shostakovich: Pieces for cello and piano*), 1991, No. 6 arr. R. Sapozhnikov and G. Kirkor, 29 cm.

Duration: 4' 09"–6' 38".

Recordings: USA: Mercury MG 10035 (mono). Seven pieces announced and performed, in the order set out under 'Form', by Dmitri SHOSTAKOVICH. [Opp. 5, 22*a*, and 34; Chopin, Prokofiev *et al.*] P Prague 1946. *Reissued:* USSR Melodiya M10 39075-6 (mono). [In four-record set 'D. Shostakovich—Pianist' with Opp. 5, 22*a*, 34, and 67.] I 1977*b* ~ Revelation Compact Disc RV 70007 (mono). Seven pieces with Nos. 3 and 5 transposed. ['Shostakovich plays Shostakovich, Vol. 6'—Opp. 34, 79, and 67.] I Sept. 1998, G Feb. 1999.

USSR: Melodiya C50 20749 006. Suite of seven pieces performed in the order Nos. 1, 2, 5, 4, 3, 6, and 7. Rimma BOBRITSKAYA. ['For Children'—Opp. 97*a* and 3*a*; Sans opp. P, S, and B.] P 1983, I 1984*d.*

France: Daniel Magne Mag 2015. Nos. 6, 4, and 2. Nadia TRAGINE. [Tchaikovsky, Tcherepnine, Beethoven *et al.*] P Paris 1985.

AVM Classics Compact Disc AVM 3020. Suite of seven pieces performed in the order Nos. 1, 2, 5, 4, 3, 6, and 7. Martin JONES. ['Piano Music Volume II'—Sans opp. A, S, and T; Opp. 13, 34, and 22*a*.] P London 1–2 June 1989.

France: Le Chant du Monde Russian Season Compact Disc LDC 288 034. Suite of seven pieces performed in the order 1, 2, 5, 4, 3, 6, and 7.

Rimma BOBRITSKAYA. ['Russian Miniatures for Piano'—Sans opp. P, S, and Op. 97; Tchaikovsky and Prokofiev.] P Moscow Conservatory Feb. 1991. *Reissued:* France: Le Chant du Monde Russian Season Compact Disc RUS 788034. [As 1991 recording.] I Mar. 1999 ~ France: Le Chant du Monde Russian Season Compact Disc RUS 788164. Nos. 7, 6, and 4. [Opp. 97, 27; Sans opp. G and P (i).] I July 1999, G Nov. 1999.

Germany: Hänssler Classic Compact Disc 98 174. Nos. 1 and 6 arr. Fortunatov. Michael LEMPIK (violin) and Olga Haus (piano). ['Allegro'— Sans op. S; Verdi, Vivaldi, Beethoven *et al.*] P Altensteig 21–3 June 1997.

Opus 70   Symphony No. 9 in E flat major

Form: Symphony for full orchestra in five movements:

1. Allegro
2. Moderato
3. Presto *attacca*
4. Largo *attacca*
5. Allegretto

Instrumentation: piccolo, 2 flutes, 2 oboes, 2 clarinets (B flat and A), 2 bassoons ~ 4 horns, 2 trumpets, 3 trombones, tuba ~ timpani, triangle, tambourine, side drum, cymbals, bass drum ~ 1st violins (16–20), 2nd violins (14–18), violas (12–16), cellos (12–16), double-basses (10–14). String strength not specified in Muzyka (1979) score.

Composed: Mid-July–30 August 1945. Rough sketch of first movement dated 26 July; started at Moscow on 2 August and completed three days later. The remainder composed at the Composers' House at Ivanovo. Movements two to four finished on 12, 20, and 22 August.

Premières: Piano duet version: 4 September 1945, Moscow Philharmonic Hall; Svyatoslav Richter and Dmitri Shostakovich.

Orchestral version: 3 November 1945, Leningrad Philharmonic Bolshoi Hall; Leningrad Philharmonic Orchestra, Yevgeni Mravinsky.

USA: 25 July 1946, Tanglewood; Boston Symphony Orchestra, Serge Koussevitzky.

UK: 27 July 1946, Royal Albert Hall 'Prom', London; London Symphony Orchestra, Basil Cameron.

Arrangements: Reduction for piano and piano four hands by Lev Atovmyan. Transcription for band by William A. Schaefer.

Music: Autograph score and first movement rough sketch preserved at the CIS Archives of Literature and Art.

Music Fund of the USSR, No. 1536-1540, 1945, score, 34 cm.

Muzgiz, No. 18401, 1946, 30 cm.

Leeds Music, no number, *c.*1946, 20 cm.; and *c.*1956, 23 cm.

Boosey & Hawkes, No. 96 (A.S.M.P. No. 18-19), 1946, 20 cm.

Breitkopf & Härtel, No. 3606, c.1947, 18.5 cm.

Edwin F. Kalmus, No. 155, c.1947, 18 cm.

MCA, c.1976, arr. for band by W. Schaefer, score and parts, 30 cm.

Muzyka, No. 9863 (in Volume 5 of *Collected Works* with Op. 93), 1979, 30 cm.

Hans Sikorski, No. 2220, 1991, 21 cm.

Duration: 22 and 24 minutes in scores; 22' 14"–31' 35"; 26' 50"–27' 20" (Plaistow); [36 minutes average time given by Aronowsky is excessive.]

Ballets: *Meeting.* Konstantin Boyarsky, Leningrad Malyi Theatre, 1962. A one-act ballet to music from Symphony No. 9.

Ninth Symphony. Peter van Dÿk, Hamburg, 1964.

The Mad Dictator. Leonid Yakobson (completion by his colleagues), Leningrad, 1985. A miniature ballet performed by the Leningrad Ballet Troupe 'Choreographic Miniatures' to mark the fortieth anniversary of the victory over Fascism, with Valeri Sergeyev in the title role of Hitler. Yakobson commenced work on the dance satire shortly before his death in 1975, basing the scenic design on the wartime cartoons of the Kukryniksy.

Jesus der Menschensohn (Jesus, Son of Man), Iván Markó, Györ Ballet; a seventy-minute ballet to music from Franz Liszt's oratorio *Christus* and the second movement of Shostakovich's Symphony No. 9, produced by Jaszi Dezsö and screened on Austrian ORF 1, 17 April 1987.

Film: *Bernstein Conducts Shostakovich.* A documentary film, directed by Humphrey Burton, screened on BBC2 TV on 19 August 1995. The Musikverein concert performance by the Vienna Philharmonic Orchestra recorded in 1986. Shostakovich's answer to the awesome problem of composing a Ninth Symphony with a movement-by-movement illustrated talk on this 'anti-Ninth' by the conductor. See also Opus 54.

Recordings: USA: V-Disc 716-8 (transfer from ABC radio broadcast, 5 sides 78 rpm). Boston Symphony Orchestra, Serge KOUSSEVITZKY. [Rózsa.] P Tanglewood 25 July 1946.

Italy: AS Compact Disc 571 (mono). Boston Symphony Orchestra, Serge KOUSSEVITZKY. ['Sergei Koussevitzky Edition' with Op. 47.] P concert 10 Aug. 1946 (labelled erroneously as 'First American Performance'), I 1990. *Reissued:* USA: Music & Arts Compact Disc CD 981. [Rimsky-Korsakov and Tchaikovsky.] I Sept. 1997.

USA: Victor 11 9634-6 in Set M 1134 (6 sides 78 rpm). Boston Symphony Orchestra, Serge KOUSSEVITZKY. P 4 Nov. 1946 and second movement on 2 Apr. 1947. *Reissued:* USA: RCA Victor LM 2900 (mono). [Hanson and Foote.] ~ USSR: Melodiya D 031731-4 (1 side in two-record set, mono). [Tchaikovsky, Rakhmaninov, Rimsky-Korsakov *et al.*] I 1972 ~ USA: RCA Victor VCM 6174 (1 side in three-record set, mono). ['Immortal Performances'—Brahms, Tchaikovsky, Rakhmaninov *et al.*] ~ RCA Victrola LVM2 751OC-D (1 side in two-record set, mono).

[Tchaikovsky and Hanson.] G July 1974. NB. The first movement exposition repeat is not observed in this performance.

France: Tahra Compact Disc TAH 290. Berlin Philharmonic Orchestra, Sergiu CELIBIDACHE. [Berlioz and Debussy.] I Berlin concert 31 Aug. 1947. *Reissued:* Holland: Audiophile Classics Compact Disc APL 101 525. [Haydn and Glière.] I 1999.

USA: Columbia 12595-8D in Set 658 (8 sides 78 rpm). New York Philharmonic Orchestra, Efrem KURTZ. P 1950. *Reissued:* USA: Philips A 01607 R (10" mono). I 1950 ~ USA: Columbia ML 4137 (mono) ~ France: Philips L 01 338 L (mono). [Sans op. P.] ~ Philips ABL 3117 (mono). [Prokofiev.] G July 1956 ~ USA: Columbia Special Products P 14147 (electronic stereo). I 1977 ~ CBS Masterworks Portrait Compact Disc MPK 45698 (mono). [Op. 93.] I Dec. 1989, G Feb. 1990.

USA: Urania URLP 7128 (mono). Berlin Radio Symphony Orchestra, Rolf KLEINERT. [Op. 10.] P 1954.

Bulgaria: Balkanton BCA 503 (mono). Sofia State Philharmonic Orchestra, Dobrin PETKOV. [Op. 54.] P mid-1950s.

Italy: Fonit-Cetra Archive Rai LAR 37 (1 side in three-record set). Orchestra Sinfonica di Torino della Radiotelevision Italina, Otto KLEMPERER. [Haydn, Beethoven, Schubert, Wagner, and Stravinsky.] P 21 Dec. 1955, I 1983.

USSR: MK D 03402-3 (mono). Moscow Radio Symphony Orchestra, Aleksandr GAUK. [Op. 89*a*.] P 21 Dec. 1956. *Reissued:* USA: Monitor MC 2015 (mono). [Opp. 89*a* and 96.] I 1958 ~ France: Le Chant du Monde LDXA 8219 (mono). [Op. 79.] ~ USSR: MK D 09618-9928 (mono). [Op. 54.] I 1962.

USA: Everest LPBR 6054 (mono) and SDBR 3054. London Symphony Orchestra, Sir Malcolm SARGENT. [Prokofiev.] P Walthamstow Aug. 1960. *Reissued:* World Record Club T 130 (mono) and ST 130. [Prokofiev.] G Aug. 1962 ~ Italy: TANK STG 7021. [Prokofiev.] I 1969 ~ USA: Peerless Classics PC 26. [Issued under the pseudonyms 'New York Concert Orchestra, Robert Hornstein'.] I 1974? ~ Vanguard Classics (Everest Collection) Compact Disc EVC 9005. [Op. 54.] I Sept. 1994, G Apr. 1995.

Poland: Muza XL 0067 (mono). Polish Radio Symphony Orchestra, Jan KRENZ. [Op. 110.] P 1961. *Reissued:* East Germany: Eterna A33 8 20 305 (mono). [Op. 110.]

USSR: Melodiya D 016471-2 (mono) and C 01109-10. Moscow Philharmonic Orchestra, Y. Neklyudov (bassoon), Kirill KONDRASHIN. [Op. 119.] P 1965, I 1966. *Reissued:* Germany: Melodia Eurodisc 85314 KK. [Op. 20.] ~ HMV Melodiya ASD 2409. [Op. 119.] G Jan. 1969 ~ France: Le Chant du Monde LDX A 78376. [Op. 119.] ~ USA: Angel Melodiya SR 40000. [Op. 119.] ~ Netherlands: MEL 406. [Op. 119.] ~ Italy: EMI 065 93441. [Op. 70.] ~ Germany: Melodia Burodisc 87623 XK. [In thirteen-record box set.] I 1974 ~ HMV Melodiya BOX 502507 in Set SLS 5025.

[Op. 65, third–fifth movements.] G Dec. 1975 ~ USSR: Melodiya C 01109-10. [In first box of Part 2 of *Collected Works on Records* with Op. 43, third movement.] I 1980 ~ HMV Melodiya EX 2903873 (DMM). [First record in twelve-record box set with Op. 10.] G Dec. 1985 ~ France: Le Chant du Monde Compact Disc LDC 278 1005-6. [In Box 3 of five two-disc sets with Opp. 65 and 93.] G May 1989 ~ BMG Classics Melodiya Compact Disc 74321 19846-2. [Op. 141.] I July 1994, G Nov. 1994.

USA: Turnabout TV 34223. Zagreb Philharmonic Orchestra, Milan HORVAT. [Op. 10.] P c.1965. *Reissued:* France: Philips 836 943 DSY. [Op. 10.] ~ Netherlands: Philips 02448 L (mono) and 835 318 AY. [Op. 35.]

USA: Columbia M 31307. New York Philharmonic Orchestra, Leonard BERNSTEIN. [Op. 10.] P New York 19 Oct. 1965. *Reissued:* CBS 73050. [Op. 10.] G Dec. 1974 ~ CBS Masterworks Compact Disc CD 44711. [Op. 47.] I Aug. 1988, G Mar. 1989 ~ Sony Royal Edition Compact Disc SMK 47615. [Op. 47.] G Nov. 1993 and June 1994 ~ Sony Classical Compact Discs SX4K 64206 (four-disc set). [Op. 47.] I Dec. 1995 ~ Sony Classical Compact Disc SMK 60694. [Op. 47.] I Sept. 1999.

France: Praga Compact Disc PR 254 002-3 (two-disc set). Czech Philharmonic Orchestra, Karel ANČERL. [Opp. 47 and 60.] P Prague broadcast 1966, I June 1992, G May 1993.

Italy: Arkadia Compact Disc CDGI 7651. Milan Radio Symphony Orchestra, Sergiu CELIBIDACHE. [Op. 47.] P Milan 17 Feb. 1967, I 1993.

USA: Russian Disc Compact Disc RDCD 11 192. USSR Symphony Orchestra, David OISTRAKH. [Op. 135.] P Moscow concert 6 Oct. 1969, I Oct. 1993, G Jan. 1994.

USSR: Melodiya C10 05203-4. Moscow Symphony Orchestra, David OISTRAKH. [R. Strauss.] P 1970, I 1975c.

Deutsche Grammophon Compact Discs 469 069-2GH4 (four-disc set). Swedish Radio Symphony Orchestra, Sergui CELIBIDACHE. [Dvořák, Franck, Hindemith *et al.*] P Hjalmar, Sweden Mar. 1971, G Feb. 2001.

Decca SXL 6563. Suisse Romande Orchestra, Walter WELLER. [Op. 10.] P 4–6 Sept. 1971, G Jan. 1973. *Reissued:* USA: London 6787. [Op. 10.]

USSR: Melodiya C 04557-8. Moscow Conservatory Students' Symphony Orchestra, Aleksandr LAZAREV. [Glinka and Brahms.] P 1973, I 1974.

Czech: Supraphon 1 10 1771-2 (1 side in two-record set). Czech Philharmonic Orchestra, Václav NEUMANN. [Op. 60.] P Prague Mar.–Sept. 1974, G Aug. 1976. *Reissued:* Germany: Musicaphon LC 0522. [Op. 60.] I 1980.

Czech: Opus 9110 0382. Czech Philharmonic Orchestra, Ladislav SLOVÁK. [Op. 20.] P Feb. 1975.

USSR: Melodiya C10 10399-400. USSR Symphony Orchestra, Yevgeni SVETLANOV. [Opp. 96, 97a No. 8, and 16.] P 1978, I 1978d. *Reissued:* HMV Melodiya ASD 3706. [Op. 54.] G Sept. 1979 ~ France: Le Chant du Monde LDX 78687. [Opp. 96, 97a No. 8, and 16.] I Mar. 1981 ~ Germany: Melodia Eurodisc 200 539-366. [Opp. 96, 97a No. 8, and 16.] ~ Germany:

ZYX Russian Art Compact Discs CLA 10011-2 (two-disc set). [Opp. 47 and 60.] I 1998.

Decca SXDL 7515 (digital). London Philharmonic Orchestra, Bernard HAITINK. [Op. 10.] P Jan. 1979, G May 1981. *Reissued:* USA: London LDR 71017 (digital). [Op. 10.] I 1981 ~ France: Decca 591058 (digital). [Op. 10.] I 1981 ~ Decca Compact Disc 414 677-2DH. [Op. 10.] G June 1986 and Feb. 1988 ~ Decca Ovation Compact Disc 425 066-2DM. [Op. 47.] I Aug. 1993, G Nov. 1993 ~ London Compact Disc 444 434-2. [On fourth disc of eleven-disc set with Op. 47.] I June 1995.

Philips 412 073-1PH. Concertgebouw Orchestra, Kirill KONDRASHIN. [Op.54.] P Amsterdam concert 6 Mar. 1980, G Aug. 1984. *Reissued:* Philips Compact Disc 438 284-2PM. [Prokofiev.] I July 1993, G Sept. 1993.

France: Praga Compact Disc PR 250 085. Czech Philharmonic Orchestra, Zdeněk KOŠLER. [Op. 47.] P Prague broadcast 13 Mar. 1981, 1 Feb. 1995. *Reissued:* France: Le Chant du Monde Compact Disc PR 7250 085. [Op. 47.] G Feb. 2001.

USA: Vox Cum Laude VCL 9003. Cincinnati Symphony Orchestra, Walter SUSSKIND. [Op. 10.] I 1981. *Reissued:* USA: Voxbox Compact Discs CDX 5139 (two-disc set). [Op. 10; Tchaikovsky, Mendelssohn, and Liszt.] I June 1995.

USSR: Melodiya C10 18047-8. USSR Ministry of Culture Symphony Orchestra, Vakhtang ZHORDANIYA. [Op. 54.] P 1981, I 1983*b*.

USA: BRS RTS-3 (digital). National Youth Orchestra of Great Britain, Kirill KONDRASHIN. [Ravel.] P 1982.

USSR: Melodiya A10 00029 000 (1 side in two-record set, digital). USSR Ministry of Culture Symphony Orchestra, Gennadi ROZHDESTVEN-SKY. [Op. 103.] P 1983, I 1984*b*. *Reissued:* Japan: Victor Compact Disc JVC 1013. [Op. 10.] I 1985 ~ Olympia Compact Disc OCD 113. [Op. 47.] I June 1987, G May 1989 ~ Germany: Melodia Eurodisc Compact Disc 258 488. [Op. 112.] ~ Olympia Compact Disc OCD 5005. [In Vol. 1 six-disc set of symphonies with Op. 47.] I Dec. 1990 ~ BMG Melodiya Compact Discs 74321 49611-2 (two-disc set). [Opp. 10, 47, and 54.] I Dec. 1997.

USSR: Melodiya C10 30485 002. USSR Symphony Orchestra, Gavriil YUDIN. [Op. 10.] P Moscow concert 12 Nov. 1985, I 1990*d*.

Deutsche Grammophon 419 771-1GH (digital) and Compact Disc 419 771-2GH. Vienna Philharmonic Orchestra, Leonard BERNSTEIN. [Op. 54.] P Vienna concert Oct. 1985, G Nov. 1987 and Mar. 1988.

Chandos ABRD 1279 (digital) and Compact Disc CHAN 8587. Scottish National Orchestra, Neeme JÄRVI. [Opp. 96, 114*a*, and 16.] P Glasgow 14–17 Apr. 1987, I Mar. 1988, G July 1988.

East Germany: Eterna 7 29 221 (DMM). Berlin City Symphony Orchestra, Claus Peter FLOR. [Op. 10.] P Berlin 23–5 Sept. 1987. *Reissued:* Germany: Berlin Classics Compact Disc 0021722BC. [Kochan.] I Aug. 2000.

Canada: Canadian Broadcasting Corporation Compact Disc SMCD 5074. Vancouver Symphony Orchestra, Rudolf BARSHAI. [Op. 10.] P not stated, I 1988.

Naxos Compact Disc 8.550632. Czecho-Slovak Radio Symphony Orchestra, Ladislav SLOVÁK. [Op. 47.] P Bratislava 7–11 Jan. 1988, I Oct. 1993, G Nov. 1993. *Reissued:* Naxos Compact Discs 8.506003. [In six-disc set with Symphonies Nos. 5, 8, 10, 11, 13, and 14.] I 1993.

Decca Compact Disc 430 227-2DH. Royal Philharmonic Orchestra, Vladimir ASHKENAZY. [Op. 141.] P Walthamstow Jan. 1989, I Sept. 1992, G Oct. 1992.

Telarc Compact Disc CD 80215. Atlanta Symphony Orchestra, Yoel LEVI. [Op. 47.] P Atlanta 5 May, 25–6 Sept., and 2 Dec. 1989; G June 1990.

Decca Compact Disc 430 505-2DH. Vienna Philharmonic Orchestra, Georg SOLTI. [Beethoven.] P Vienna concert 5 and 6 May 1990, I May 1991, G July 1991.

Naxos Compact Disc 8.550427. Belgian Radio Philharmonic Orchestra, Alexander RAHBARI. [Op. 47.] P Brussels 26–9 Sept. 1990, I Sept. 1991, G Mar. 1992. NB. Four reviews in *Classics* May 1992.

Denon Compact Disc CO 75444. Vienna Symphony Orchestra, Eliahu INBAL. [Op. 20.] P Vienna concert 28–30 Nov. 1990, I Nov. 1993, G Feb. 1994.

EMI Compact Disc CDC7 54339-2. Oslo Symphony Orchestra, Mariss JANSONS. [Op. 54.] P Oslo 25–30 Jan. 1991, I Mar. 1992, G May 1992. *Reissued:* HMV Classics Compact Disc 5 73858-2. [Op. 93.] I Apr. 2000, G Sept. 2000.

Dorian Compact Disc DOR 90169. Dallas Symphony Orchestra, Eduardo MATA. [Prokofiev.] P Dallas Jan. and Apr. 1992, I Apr. 1993.

Decca Compact Disc 448 122-2DH. Montreal Symphony Orchestra, Charles DUTOIT. [Op. 47.] P Montreal May 1992, I Sept. 1995, G Nov. 1995.

Teldec Compact Disc 4509 90849-2. National Symphony Orchestra of Washington, Mstislav ROSTROPOVICH. [Op. 10.] P Jan. 1993, I Apr. 1994, G Oct. 1994. *Reissued:* Teldec Compact Discs 0630-17046-2. [In twelve-disc set of Symphonies.] G Oct. 1997.

Finland: Ondine Compact Disc ODE 846-2. Helsinki Philharmonic Orchestra, James DE PREIST. [Op. 112.] P Oct. 1993, I May 1996, G Feb. 1997.

Decca Compact Disc 444 458-2DH. The Solti Orchestral Project Symphony Orchestra, Georg SOLTI. ['Carnegie Hall Project'—Wagner, Brahms, R. Strauss, Smetana.] P New York concert 13 June 1994, I Aug. 1995, G Dec. 1995.

Germany: Undine Compact Discs 40249726 (two-disc set). Movements 3–5. Sinfonieorchester Folkwang Hochschule, David de VILLIERS. [Handel, Monteverdi, Mozart *et al.*] P concert Essen 20 May 1995, I 1997.

RCA Victor Red Seal Compact Disc 09026 68548-2. St Petersburg Philharmonic Orchestra, Yuri TEMIRKANOV. [Op. 47.] P 22 Sept. 1995, I Feb. 1997.

Japan: Canyon Classics Compact Disc PCCL 00356. Moscow Radio Symphony Orchestra, Vladimir FEDOSEYEV. [Op. 114*c*.] P Moscow 18 and 19 Apr. 1996.

Athene-Minerva Compact Disc ATH CD 16. Freiburg Philharmonic Orchestra, Johannes FRITZSCH. [Tchaikovsky.] P Freiburg concert broadcasts 13–14 Jan. 1997, I Mar. 1998.

USA: Well Tempered Productions Compact Disc WTP 5190. Russian National Orchestra, Vladimir SPIVAKOV. [op. 47.] P Moscow concert 7 Sept. 2000, I 2001.

References: Gow, Hulme and Pleak (in *DSCH*), and Sabinina.

Opus 71   Simple Folk

Alternative title: Also translated as 'Plain People'.

Form: Music for the film *Simple Folk,* directed by Grigori Kozintsev and Leonid Trauberg (their last collaboration), for Lenfilm. Five musical numbers composed for the film: 1. Overture, 2. Procession, 3. Departure, 4. Dream, and 5. Finale.

Instrumentation: piccolo, 2 flutes, 3 oboes, E flat clarinet, 2 clarinets, 2 bassoons ~ 4 horns, 3 trumpets, 3 trombones, tuba ~ timpani ~ strings.

Composed: 1945, at Moscow.

Première: Banned in 1946 and not released until 25 August 1956.

Music: Autograph of the film score preserved in the Music Department of Lenfilm.

Duration: Film: 78 minutes.

Recordings: —

Opus 72   Victorious Spring

Form: Incidental music for the concert spectacle *Victorious Spring,* scored for soprano and tenor soloists, choir, and orchestra:

1. Song of the Lantern ('The Torches')—Allegretto
2. Lullaby ('Go to sleep, go to sleep')—Andante
3. Song of Victory—Moderato

The first two songs, for tenor and soprano (with wordless female choir) respectively, are settings of lyrics by Mikhail Svetlov and the third, a National Anthem Contest Entry for choir and orchestra with new verses by Yevgeni Dolmatovsky (the music and instrumentation identical to the 'Final Chorus' of Opus 66).

Instrumentation: No. 1—piccolo, flute, 2 oboes, 2 B flat clarinets, 2 bassoons ~ 4 horns, 3 trumpets, 3 trombones, tuba ~ glockenspiel ~ strings. No. 2—2 B flat clarinets ~ horn ~ glockenspiel ~ strings. No. 3—see Opus 66.

Composed: 1945, at Moscow.

Première: 8 May 1946, Moscow Dzerzhinsky Central Club; NKVD Song and Dance Ensemble; scenario by Iosif Dobrovolsky, M. Volpin, and Nikolai Erdman; directed by Sergei Yutkevich

Arrangements: Piano reductions of the accompaniments to Nos. 1 and 2 by the composer. No. 2 arranged for piano four hands by Edison Denisov. The first part of No. 2 arranged for cello and piano by S. Kalyanov.

Music: Autograph vocal score of songs Nos. 1 and 2 lost; the autograph full score of 'Song of the Lantern' is in the possession of Karen Khachaturyan.

Music Fund of the USSR, 1946, Nos. 1 and 2 for voices and piano.

Sovetskii Kompozitor, No. 519 (in *D. Shostakovich: Songs*), 1958, Nos. 1 and 2 with piano accompaniment, 29 cm.

Muzgiz, 1961, No. 2 arr. E. Denisov in album of easy pieces.

Sovetskii Kompozitor, No. 2518 (in *My Native Country*), 1972, Nos. 1–3, 29 cm.

Sovetskii Kompozitor, No. 4235 (in *Dmitri Shostakovich: Songs from Plays*), 1977, Nos. 1 and 2 for voices and piano, 29 cm.

Muzyka, No. 11412 (in Volume 28 of *Collected Works* with Opp. 19, 24, 28, 31, 32, 37, 44, 58*a*, 63, 66, and in the supplement, Sans opp. D and K), vocal score of Nos. 1 and 2, 30 cm.

Muzyka, No. 11413 (in Volume 27 of *Collected Works* with Opp. 19, 24, 28, 32, 37, 44, 58*a*, 63, and 66), 1987, full score of Nos. 1 and 2, 30 cm.

Muzyka, No. 14908 (in *D. Shostakovich: Pieces for cello and piano*), 1991, No. 2 arr. S. Kalyanov, 29 cm.

Duration: Three songs: 9' 30".

Recordings: USSR: 13843-4 (10" 78 rpm). No. 1 only. Vladimir BUNCHIKOV (tenor) and orchestra conducted by Viktor Knushevitsky. [Mokrousov.] P 1946. NB. The record number in WERM incorrect. *Reissued:* USSR: Melodiya D 15329-30 (mono). ['Songs of the Great Patriotic War'—Aleksandrov, Soloviev-Sedoi, Khrennikov *et al.*] I 1965 ~ USSR: Melodiya D 28835-6 (mono). [Khrennikov, Blanter, Dunayevsky *et al.*] I 1970 ~ USSR: Melodiya C60 22815 004. Translated as 'Song about a Flashlight'. [Anthology of Soviet Songs, Record 5.] I 1986*b*.

USSR: MK D 5062-3 (10" mono). No. 1 only. All-Union Radio Song Ensemble. [Songs from Opp. 33, 80, 82, 86, 99 *et al.*] I 1959. *Reissued:* USSR: 34537-8 (10" 78 rpm). [? Sans op. X—'Native Land' (words traditional).] I 1960.

Reference: Mazel.

Note: See *My Native Country*, Sans op. Y, for recording of Nos. 1–3.

Opus 73   Quartet No. 3 in F major

Form: String quartet in five movements:

1. Allegretto—'Calm unawareness of the future cataclysm'
2. Moderato con moto—'Rumblings of unrest and anticipation'
3. Allegro non troppo—'The forces of war unleashed'
4. Adagio—'Homage to the dead' *attacca*
5. Moderato—'The eternal question—Why? And for what?'

The composer's programmatic titles do not appear on the published scores but confirmed by Borodin Quartet cellist, Valentin Berlinsky.

Composed: 26 January–2 August 1946. The composer began work with the second movement which is dated 26 January. The first, third, fourth, and fifth movements were completed on 9 May, 17 June, 13 July, and 2 August respectively. The first three movements were composed at Moscow, the fourth at Leningrad, and the fifth at Komarovo, Gulf of Finland.

Dedication: To the Beethoven Quartet (Dmitri Tsyganov, Vasili Shirinsky, Vadim Borisovsky, and Sergei Shirinsky).

Premières: 16 December 1946, Moscow Conservatory Malyi Hall; Beethoven Quartet (personnel as the dedication).

8 April 1947, Leningrad; Glazunov Quartet (Ilya Lukashevsky, G. Ginzburg, Aleksandr Ryvkin, and David Mogilevsky).

Opus 73*a*: 10 January 1991, Rotterdam; New Amsterdam Sinfonietta, Lev Markiz.

Arrangements: Reductions for two pianos by the composer written in August 1946 and for piano four hands by Yuri Nikolsky and Anatoli Dmitriev.

First movement transcribed for brass quintet (French horn, trombone, 2 trumpets, and tuba) by Howard Hyde.

Opus 73*a*—Symphony for Strings and Woodwind by Rudolf Barshai in 1990 (Instrumentation: flute, oboe, cor anglais, clarinet (B flat and A), bassoon ~ strings); also transcriptions for string orchestra by Dmitri Sitkovetsky (broadcast on BBC 3, 13 March 1995) and Vladimir Milman ('Chamber Symphony No. 2'); also for strings and piano by Mikhail Turich.

Music: Autograph score of the quartet, the Nikolsky two-piano arrangement, and the piano score preserved at the CIS Archives of Literature and Art.

Music Fund of the USSR, No. 11–15, 1947, score and parts, 33 cm.

Muzgiz, No. 18865, 1947, 16.5 cm. (a number of the original 1000 copies, marked with logo of VOKS—USSR Society for Cultural Relations with Foreign Countries—have the cover titles in Russian and English); and with the same plate no., 1960, 20 cm.

Muzyka, No. 27965, 1961, parts, 29 cm.

Edition Eulenberg, No. 387, no date, score, 19 cm.

Muzyka, Leningrad, No. 285 (in Volume 1 with Quartets 1, 2, and 4 arr. for piano four hands by A. Dmitriev), 1965, 29.5 cm.

Edition Peters, No. 5753, c.1976, parts, 29 cm.

Muzyka, No. 9816 (in Volume 35 of *Collected Works* Quartets 1–8), 1979, 30 cm.

Hans Sikorski, No. 2265 (with Opp. 49, 68, and 83), 1980, score, 21 cm.

Hans Sikorski, No. 2243, 1981, parts, 31.5 cm.

H. Alan Music, Mission Hills, California, c.1991, arr. for brass quintet by H. Hyde, score, 25 cm.

DSCH Publishers, Moscow, 1995, full score and parts of R. Barshai's instrumentation available for hire.

Duration: Approx. 30 minutes in score; 28' 05" (no first movement exposition repeat) and 28' 06" (with repeat)—33' 74"; 33 minutes (Sadovnikov). Opus 73*a*: 32' 33"—33' 15" (with first movement repeat) and 34' 15' (with no repeat).

Ballet: *Tremor.* Richard Alston, Cambridge Arts Theatre, 16 October 2000. Alston's company performed to amplified live string quartet calling themselves 'stringfactory'.

Recordings: USSR: 014612-5 (9 sides 78 rpm). BEETHOVEN QUARTET (personnel as above). [Op. 34 Nos. 16, 22, and 23.] P 1947. *Reissued:* USSR: Melodiya D 015665-9799 (mono). [Op. 83.] I 1965 ~ USA: Consonance Blue Label Compact Disc 81.3007 (mono). [Vol. 3—Op. 101.] I May 1995.

USA: Mercury DM 3 (78 rpm box set). FINE ARTS QUARTET (Leonard Sorkin, Abram Loft, Bernard Zaslav, George Sopkin). P pre-1950. *Reissued:* USA: Mercury MG 10049 (mono). [No coupling.] ~ USA: Gasparo GS 203 and Musicaphon BM 305L 4108 (mono). [Prokofiev on both.]

USSR: MK HD 2534-5 (10" mono). TCHAIKOVSKY QUARTET (Julian Sitkovetsky, Anton Sharoyev, Rudolf Barshai, Yakov Slobodkin). P 9 Aug. 1954 in the presence of the composer, I 1955. *Reissued:* Parlophone Odeon PMA 1040 (mono). [Op. 57.] G Aug. 1958 ~ USA: Vanguard VRS 6033 (mono). [Op. 68.] I 1958 ~ USSR: Melodiya D 028031-2 (mono). [Op. 83.] I 1970 ~ Revelation Compact Disc RV 10016. [Brahms and Grieg.] I Oct. 1996. NB. Though no P date quoted and cellist given as Sitkovetsky this is most probably the Tchaikovsky Quartet ~ France; Dante Compact Discs LYS 369-370 (two-disc set). [Opp. 67, 40, and 57.] NB. P given as Moscow 1946, I 1998.

Czech: Supraphon SUA 10420 (mono) and SUA 50420. SMETANA QUARTET (Jiří Novák, Lubomír Kostecký, Milan Škampa, Antonín Kohout). [Prokofiev.] G Nov. 1964. *Reissued:* USA: Crossroads 22 16 0017 (mono) and 22 16 0018. [Prokofiev.] I 1966.

Leningrad Masters Compact Disc LM 1325. TANEYEV QUARTET (personnel not stated). [Opp. 49 and 83.] P concert 1966, G Sept. 1996.

USSR: Melodiya D 019277-8 (mono) and C 01447-8. BORODIN QUARTET (Rostislav Dubinsky, Yaroslav Aleksandrov, Dmitri Shebalin, Valentin Berlinsky). [Op. 49.] P and I 1967. *Reissued:* USSR: Melodiya CM 03059-60. [Op. 49.] I 1972 ~ USA: Seraphim Melodiya S 6034. [In three-record box set with Quartets 1, 2, 4, and 5.] ~ HMV Melodiya HQS 1320 in Set SLS 879. [Op. 138.] G June 1974 ~ HMV SEOM 20. Second movement only. ['Forward with HMV Melodiya' sampler—Rakhmaninov, Tchaikovsky, Glazunov *et al*.] I Aug. 1975.

USSR: Melodiya C10 11617-8. TANEYEV QUARTET (Vladimir Ovcharek, Grigori Lutsky, Vissarion Soloviev, Iosif Levinson). [In first box of Part 2 of *Collected Works on Records* with Op. 122.] P 1968, I 1980. *Reissued:* Japan: JVC Victor 5346. [Op. 83.] ~ USSR: Melodiya Compact Disc SUCD 11 00311. [Op. 117.] I 1991*d*.

Decca Ace of Diamonds SDD 453. GABRIELI QUARTET (Kenneth Sillito, Brendan O'Reilly, Ian Jewel, Keith Harvey). [Op. 49.] P Maltings, Snape Dec. 1973, G Apr. 1975. *Reissued:* USA: London STS 15396. [Op. 49.]

L'Oiseau-Lyre DSLO 28. FITZWILLIAM QUARTET (Christopher Rowland, Jonathan Sparey, Alan George, Ioan Davies). [Op. 122.] P 23–6 May 1977, G June 1978. *Reissued:* Decca 188 D2 in Set D 188 D7. [Op. 122.] G Feb. 1981 ~ Decca Compact Disc 421 475-2DH. [Opp. 110 and 138.] I Dec. 1988, G Apr. 1989 ~ Decca Enterprise Compact Discs 433 078-2DM6. [On second disc of six-disc set with Op. 83.] I Apr. 1992, G June 1992.

France: Praga Compact Disc PR 254 054. GLINKA QUARTET (Aleksandr Arenkov, Sergei Pishchugin, Misha Geller, Dmitri Ferschtman). [Opp. 67 and 83.] P Czech radio 1977, I July 1994.

Olympia Compact Disc OCD 531. SHOSTAKOVICH QUARTET (Andrei Shislov, Sergei Pishchugin, Aleksandr Galkovsky, Aleksandr Korchagin). ['Complete Quartets, Vol. 1'—Opp. 49 and 83; Sans op. D.] P 1980, I Apr. 1994, G Sept. 1994.

USSR: Melodiya C10 19503 006. BORODIN QUARTET (Mikhail Kopelman. Andrei Abramenkov, Dmitri Shebalin, Valentin Derlinsky). [Op. 110.] P 1983, I 1984*a*. *Reissued:* HMV Melodiya EX 270339-3 (DMM). (In seven-record box set of 15 Quartets plus Quintet.] G Mar. 1986 ~ EMI Compact Disc CDC7 49267-2. [Op. 68.] I Nov. 1987 ~ Japan: Victor Musical Industries Compact Disc VICC 40019. [Op. 83.] I 1990 ~ EMI Compact Discs CMS5 65032-2. In six-disc set of 15 Quartets plus Quintet.] I Mar. 1994 ~ BMG Melodiya Compact Discs 74321 40711-2 (six-disc set). [Opp. 11 and 57.] I June 1997 ~ BMG Melodiya Compact Disc 74321 40713-2. [Opp. 57 and 11.] I Dec. 1997.

USA: Centaur Compact Disc CRC 2020. MANHATTAN QUARTET (Eric Lewis, Roy Lewis, John Dexter, Judith Clyde). [Op. 110.] P Rye, New York Jan. 1984, I 1986.

USSR: Melodiya C10 23563 000 (DMM). ČIURLIONIS QUARTET (Rimantas Suigždinis, Saulius Kiškis, Aloyzas Grižas, Saulius Lipčius). [Op. 122.] P 1985, I 1986*d*.

Czech: Opus Compact Disc 9351 2025. MOYZES QUARTET (Stanislav Mucha, František Török, Alexander Lakatoš, Ján Slávik). [Op. 110.] P Mitice June 1986, I Oct. 1990.

Jecklin-Disco JD 620-1 (digital) and Compact Disc JD 620-2. AMATI QUARTET (Willi Zimmerman, Barbara Suter, Nicolas Corti, Johannes Degen). [Op. 108.] P 1987.

Deutsche Grammophon Compact Disc 435 386-2GH. Symphony for Strings Op. 73*a* arr. Barshai. Chamber Orchestra of Europe, Rudolf BAR-SHAI. [Op. 83*a*.] P Berlin Mar. 1989, I July 1992, G Aug. 1992.

Teldec Classics Compact Disc 2292 46009-2. BRODSKY QUARTET (Michael Thomas, Ian Belton, Paul Cassidy, Jacqueline Thomas). [Opp. 49 and 83.] P Berlin July 1989, I Apr. 1990, G June 1990. *Reissued:* Teldec Compact Discs 9031 71702-2. [On second disc of six-disc set with Op. 83.] I Nov. 1990, G June 1992.

France: Adès Compact Disc 14 161-1. FINE ARTS QUARTET (Ralph Evans, Efim Boico, Jerry Horner, Wolfgang Laufer). [Opp. 108 and 122.] P Paris July 1989, I July 1990, G Oct. 1990.

USA: ESS.A.Y. Compact Disc CD 1007. MANHATTAN QUARTET (personnel as above). [Opp. 49 and 68.] P Jersey City 15–18 Jan. 1990. *Reissued:* Koch Schwann Musica Mundi Compact Disc 310 128. ['Complete String Quartets, Vol. 1' with Opp. 49 and 68.] I May 1991.

Virgin Classics Compact Disc VC7 91437-2. BORODIN QUARTET (personnel as on 1983 recording). [Opp. 108 and 110.] P London Feb.–July 1990, I Sept. 1991, G Dec. 1991. *Reissued:* Virgin Classics Compact Discs VBD5 61630-2 (two-disc set). [Opp. 68, 108, 110, and 133.] I Aug. 1999.

USSR: Melodiya C10 30589 007. GEORGIA STATE RADIO QUARTET (Levan Chkheidze, Georgi Khintibidze, Archil Kharadze, Revaz Machabeli) P Tbilisi 1990, I 1990*d*.

France: Le Chant du Monde Compact Disc LDC 278 1047. ANTON QUARTET (Anton Matalayev, Elena Yakovleva, Dmitri Khlebtsevich, I. Kiritchenko) [Bartók.] P Paris Sept. 1990, I 1991.

Canada: Marquis Classics Compact Disc ERAD 173. PENDERECKI QUARTET (Piotr Buczek, Jerzy Kaplanek, Yariv Aloni, Paul Pulford). [Britten.] P Toronto 2–3 Dec. 1991, I July 1997.

Netherlands: Globe Compact Disc GLO 5093. Symphony for Strings, Op. 73*a* arr. Barshai. New Amsterdam Sinfonietta, Lev MARKIZ. [Op. 147*a*.] P Utrecht Oct.–Dec. 1992, I 1993.

Germany: Thorofon Compact Disc CTH 2264. PHILHARMONIA QUARTET OF BERLIN (Daniel Stabrawa, Christian Stadelmann, Neithard Resa, Jan Diesselhorst). [Mozart.] P Yale University, New Haven Nov. 1992, I Mar. 1995.

RCA Victor Red Seal Compact Disc 09026 68061-2. Chamber Symphony No. 2, Op. 73*a* arr. V. Milman. Moscow Virtuosi, Vladimir SPIVAKOV. ['Stalin Cocktail'—Pärt, Denisov, and Shchedrin.] P Blackheath 4–5 May 1993, I Aug. 1995, G Dec. 1995.

Netherlands: Etcetera Compact Disc KTC 1182. ELEONORA QUARTET (Eleonora Yakubova, Irina Pavlikhina, Anton Yaroshenko, Mikhail Shumsky). [Sans op. D and Op. 117.] P Moscow Jan. 1994, I Sept. 1994.

Dorian Compact Disc DOR 90203. LAFAYETTE QUARTET (Ann Elliott-Goldschmid, Sharon Stanis, Joanna Hood, Pamela Highbaugh). [Borodin and Stravinsky.] P Troy, New York Feb. 1994, I May 1995, G Sept. 1995.

Finland: Finlandia Compact Disc 4509 98997-2. SIBELIUS ACADEMY QUARTET (Erkki Kantola, Seppo Tukiainen, Veikko Kosonen, Arto Noras). [Op. 83.] P Järvenpää May 1994, I May 1996. *Reissued:* Finlandia Ultima Compact Discs 8573 81969-2 (disc two of two-disc set). [Opp. 35 and 40.] G June 2000.

Netherlands: Emergo Classics Compact Disc EC 3956-2. ORLANDO QUARTET (Arvid Engegard, Heinz Oberdorfer, Ferdinand Erblich, Stefan Metz). [Op. 101.] P Renswoude, Netherlands 6–10 June 1994, I Jan. 1995.

Germany: Thorofon Compact Disc CTH 2238. PHILHARMONIA QUARTET OF BERLIN (Daniel Stabrawa, Christian Stadelmann, Neithard Resa, Jan Disselhorst). [Opp. 108 and 133.] P Berlin 1994, I 1998.

Naxos Compact Disc 8.550974. ÉDER QUARTET (János Selmeczi, Péter Szüts, Sandor Papp, György Éder). ['Complete Quartets, Vol. 3'—Op. 92.] P Budapest 6–9 Mar. 1995, I Jan. 1996, G Apr. 1997.

Switzerland: New Classical Adventure Compact Disc 95 08 812. GEWANDHAUS QUARTET (Frank-Michael Erben, Conrad Suske, Volker Metz, Jürnjakob Timm). [Stravinsky and Prokofiev.] P Leipzig Apr. 1995, I Mar. 1996.

Germany: Beaux Compact Disc BEAU 2022. Arr. for strings and piano. Novosibirsk Chamber Orchestra, Mikhail TURICH. [Opp. 83 and 34.] P 1995, I Sept. 2001.

Naim Audio Compact Disc NAIMCD 016. ALLEGRI QUARTET (Peter Carter, David Roth, Jonathan Barritt, Bruno Schrecker). [Haydn and Schumann.] P Oxford 28–30 Jan. 1997, I Jan. 1998, G Apr. 1998.

Netherlands: Globe Compact Disc GLO 5171. RUBIO QUARTET (Dirk Van de Velde, Dirk Van den Hauwe, Marc Sonnaert, Peter Devos). ['Complete Quartets, Vol. 2'—Op. 144.] P Utrecht Sept. 1997, I May 1998.

Sweden: BIS Compact Disc CD 913. YGGDRASIL QUARTET (Henrik Peterson, Per Öman, Robert Westlund, Per Nyström). [Opp. 108 and 110.] P Länna, Sweden Sept. 1997, I Nov. 1998, G Jan. 1999.

Chandos Compact Disc CHAN 9769. SORREL QUARTET (Gina McCormack, Catherine Yates, Vicci Wardman, Helen Thatcher). ['Complete Quartets, Vol. 2'—Opp. 83 and 122.] P Westleton, Suffolk 29 Sept.–1 Oct. 1998, I Jan 2000.

Denmark: Classico Compact Disc CLASSCD 265. CAILIN QUARTET (Clara Baek, Sophia Baek, Stine Hasbirk, Therese Astrand). [Beethoven.] P 1998.

Hyperion Compact Disc CDA 67153. ST PETERSBURG QUARTET (Alla Aranovskaya, Ilya Teplyakov, Konstantin Kats, Leonid Shukayev). [Op. 68.] P St Petersburg Apr. 1999, I Oct. 1999, G Nov. 1999.

Deutsche Grammophon Compact Disc 463 284-2GH5 (five-disc set). EMERSON QUARTET (Eugene Drucker, Philip Setzer, Lawrence Dutton, David Finkel). ['Complete Quartets, Vol. 1'—Opp. 49 and 68.] P Aspen, Colorado concert June–July 1999, G June 2000.

France: Arion Compact Disc ARN 68506. DEBUSSY QUARTET (Christophe Colletts, Dominique Lonca, Vincent Deprecq, Yannick Cailier). ['Complete Quartets, Vol. 2'—Opp. 108 and 118.] P Lyon Nov. 1999, I Dec. 2000.

EMI Debut Compact Disc CDZ5 7439-2. JERUSALEM QUARTET (Aleksandr Pavlovsky, Sergei Bressler, Amichai Gross, Kyril Zlotnikov). [Tchaikovsky.] P Potton Hall, Suffolk Nov. 2000, I June 2001.

Opus 74   Poem of the Motherland

Form: Patriotic cantata for mezzo-soprano, tenor, two baritones, and bass soloists, chorus, and orchestra (with additional brass and a harp). The work includes several Revolutionary and popular songs:

'Boldly, friends, on we march!' (text by Leonid Radin)
'Sacred War, (Aleksandr Aleksandrov, text by Vasili Lebedev-Kumach)
'Thro' the dales and o'er the hills'—The Song of the Far Eastern Partisans (I. Aturov, text by Pyotr Parfenov)
'Song of the Motherland' (Isaak Dunayevsky, text by V. Lebedev-Kumach)
'On Heroic Business' (Vano Muradeli)
'Song of the Counterplan' (from Shostakovich's Opus 33, text by Boris Kornilov)

Instrumentation: 3 flutes (III = piccolo), 3 oboes (III = cor anglais), 3 clarinets, 2 bassoons ~ 4 horns, 2 trumpets, 3 trombones, tuba ~ timpani, side drum, cymbals, triangle, bass drum ~ glockenspiel, harp, metallophone ~ strings. The metallophone is employed solely for a three-bar phrase played four times between figs. 39 and 42 as an introduction to 'Song of the Motherland'. The brass ensemble is augmented by a separate band of 3 trumpets and 3 trombones.

Composed: Completed in early October 1947, at Moscow, for the thirtieth anniversary of the October Revolution. [Not performed at the celebrations for which it was written.]

Première: 19 May 1956.

Arrangement: Reduction for voices and piano by Lev Atovmyan.

Music: Music Fund of the USSR, No. 1592-1597, 1947, full score edited by L. Atovmyan, mimeographed format, 33 cm.

Duration: 16 minutes (Meskhishvili).

Recording: USSR: 015264-7 (4 sides 78 rpm). Mariya Maksakova (soprano), Sergei Lemeshev (tenor), Andrei Ivanov and David Gamrekeli (baritones), Maksim Mikhailov (bass), Bolshoi Theatre Chorus and Orchestra, Konstantin IVANOV. P 1947.

Opus 75   The Young Guard

Form: Music for Parts 1 and 2 of the film, after Aleksandr Fadeyev's novel *The Young Guard,* directed by Sergei Gerasimov for the Gorky Film Studios. The story first appeared in the magazine *Znamya* ('The Banner') in 1945, but was revised in 1947 and 1951. The film was based on the 1947 version and awarded a Stalin Prize First Class in 1949. The score incorporates Pierre Degeyter's *Internationale.*

Instrumentation of the Overture (Moderato non troppo):   2 oboes, 2 B flat clarinets, 2 bassoons ~ 4 horns ~ timpani ~ harp ~ strings.

Composed: Thematic material outlined on 25 April 1947. Score written in summer and autumn of 1948, at Moscow.

Premières: Film: Part 1 first shown on 11 October 1948 and Part 2, on 25 October 1948. Score performed by the USSR Symphony Orchestra and Choir under Aleksandr Sveshnikov.

Suite: 1953, Moscow; Moscow Radio Symphony Orchestra, Aleksandr Gauk.

UK broadcast: 15 November 1986, BBC Symphony Orchestra, Lionel Friend.

Arrangements: Opus 75*a*—Suite for orchestra assembled by Lev Atovmyan in 1951:

1. Prelude—Moderato non troppo
2. By the River—Moderato
3. Scherzo—Presto
4. Uneasy Night—Moderato
5. Song of the Young Guards—Moderato sostenuto
6. Death of the Heroes—Adagio *attacca*
7. Apotheosis—Adagio

Instrumentation of Suite Opus 75*a*:   piccolo, 2 flutes, 2 oboes, cor anglais, E flat clarinet, 2 A clarinets, 2 bassoons, 2 contrabassoons ~ 4 horns, 3 trumpets, 3 trombones, tuba ~ timpani, side drum, cymbals, triangle,

tambourine, bass drum ~ strings. Brass augmented by separate band of 3 trumpets and 3 trombones in No. 3, and two of each in Nos. 1 and 7.
Suite transcribed for wind orchestra by Ye. Dubinsky.

Music: Shostakovich gave this work as Opus 76 in his typed list. Autograph of the film score preserved at the Glinka Museum and a manuscript score, with notes in the composer's hand, in the Music Library of the USSR Cinematograph Symphony Orchestra.

Muzgiz, No. 23653, 1950, Suite Opus 75a in full score, 29 cm.

Muzyka, 1975, Suite arr. for wind orchestra by Ye. Dubinsky, 22 cm.

Muzyka, No. 10890 (in Volume 42 of *Collected Works* with Opp. 78, 80, 82, 95, 97, 111, 116, 132, and 137), 1987, Overture, 30 cm.

A piece from the film score entitled 'Farewell', arranged for string quartet,is scheduled to appear in Volume 101 of *New Collected Works*.

Duration: Film: 101 and 86 minutes. Suite Opus 75a: 25' 51"–30' 14"; 22 minutes (Sadovnikov).

Recordings: Olympia Compact Disc OCD 201. Suite Opus 75a. USSR Cinematograph Symphony Orchestra, Grigori GAMBURG. [Op. 131; Prokofiev and Eshpai.] P 1956, I Dec. 1987.

USA: Russian Disc Compact Disc RDCD 10 002. Suite Opus 75a. Byelorussian Radio and TV Symphony Orchestra, Walter MNATSAKANOV. [Op. 64.] P Minsk Feb. 1995, I Sept. 1996.

Note: The English title of the film frequently appears in the plural. Fadeyev's novel *The Young Guard* is about Oleg Koshevoi, the commissar of the youth resistance organization, who, along with two other male and two female Young Guards, was tortured and murdered by the Nazis in 1943. This book was an instant success on its publication in 1945 but was pronounced to be ideologically harmful and officially condemned in 1948. The author had allegedly failed to point out the role of the Communist Party in organizing underground activities. Fadeyev was hurt by this accusation—Stalin was his idol—but acknowledged his 'errors' and spent almost four years 'correcting' the novel. By 1956 he had become an alcoholic and, after Stalin's denouncement, he shot himself.

Opus 76   Pirogov

Form: Music for the biographical film, based on the life of the surgeon Nikolai Pirogov, with scenario by Yuri German and directed by Grigori Kozintsev for Lenfilm. The film awarded a Stalin Prize Second Class in 1948.

Composed: 1947.

Premières: Film first shown on 16 December 1947.

UK broadcast: 15 November 1986, BBC Symphony Orchestra, Lionel Friend.

Arrangements: Opus 76*a*—Suite for orchestra assembled by Lev Atovmyan in 1951:

1. Introduction
2. Scene
3. Waltz—Allegretto
4. Scherzo
5. Finale

Piano reduction of No. 3 by L. Atovmyan.

Waltz transcribed for percussion ensemble by Vladimena Snamenskov. A recording of a concert performance by I Percussionisti della Scala broadcast on BBC Radio 3 on 7 July 2001.

Instrumentation of Suite Opus 76*a*:   piccolo, 2 flutes, 2 oboes, 2 B flat clarinets, 2 bassoons ~ 4 horns, 3 trumpets, 3 trombones, tuba ~ timpani, triangle, side drum, cymbals, bass drum ~ xylophone, glockenspiel, harp ~ violin solo, strings.

Music: Autograph score of the Suite Opus 76*a* preserved in the Bureau of the Music Fund of the USSR.

Sovetskii Kompozitor, 1948, Waltz arr. for piano by L. Atovmyan, 27 cm.

Muzgiz, 1950, Waltz arr. for small orchestra (with 'Tuva Dance' by Aleksei Aksenov), 14 parts, *c.*29 cm.

Sovetskii Kompozitor, No. 928 (in *Dmitri Shostakovich: Waltzes from Film Music*), 1959, Waltz in full score, 29 cm.

Duration: Film: 10 reels. Suite Opus 76*a*: 16' 22"–17' 56"; 25 minutes (Sadovnikov).

Ballet: *The Overcoat.* For details see under Opus 32.

Recordings: USSR: 16719-17096 (10" 78 rpm). Waltz only. All-Union Radio Stage Symphony Orchestra, Viktor KNUSHEVITSKY. [Dunayevsky.] P 1949.

Poland: Muza 2017 (10" 78 rpm). Waltz only. Polish Radio Symphony Orchestra, Stefan RACHÓN.

USSR: Melodiya D 020135-6 (mono) and C 01471-2. Suite Opus 76*a*. Bolshoi Theatre Orchestra, Maksim SHOSTAKOVICH. [Op. 64*a*.] P 1966. *Reissued:* USA: Angel Melodiya SR 40160. [Op. 64*a*.] ~ USSR: Melodiya C 01471-2. [In fourth box of Part 1 of *Collected· Works on Records* with op. 64*a*.] I 1978 ~ Germany: Melodia Eurodisc 28665 XHK. [On second record of four-record film music album with Op. 64*a*.] I 1981 ~ BMG Melodiya Compact Discs 74321 66981-2 (two-disc set). [Sans op. P, Opp. 27*a*, 22*a*, and 64*a*.] I Dec. 1999.

RCA Victor Red Seal Compact Disc RD 86603. Suite Opus 76*a*. Belgian Radio Symphony Orchestra, José SEREBRIER. [Op. 97*a*.] P Brussels 1987, I Feb. 1988, G May 1988.

Austria: Musica Classic Compact Disc 780005-2. Waltz only. Moscow Radio Symphony Orchestra, Vladimir FEDOSEYEV. ['Symphonic Waltzes from Russia'—Khachaturyan, Glazunov, Tchaikovsky *et al.*] P Bratislava Sept. 1992, I 1992.

CIS: Manchester Compact Disc CDMAN 129. Waltz. St Petersburg Philharmonic Academic Symphony Orchestra, Vladimir ALTSHULER. ['Shostakovich Theatre and Cinema Music'—Opp. 32*a*, 58*a*, 45, 30, 78, 97, 99, and 37.] P St Petersburg 1995, I 1998.

USA: Citadel Compact Disc CTD 88135. Suite Op. 76*a*. Belarus Radio and TV Symphony Orchestra, Walter MNATSAKANOV. [Opp. 50*a* and 85.] P Moscow 7 Apr. 1997, I 1999.

Decca Compact Disc 460 792-2DH11. Suite Nos. 4 and 5. Royal Concertgebouw Orchestra, Riccardo CHAILLY. ['The Film Album'—Opp. 33, 26, 56, 116, 55, 132, and 97.] P Amsterdam 10–11 Sept. 1998, I Mar. 1999, G Apr. 1999.

Monte Carlo: Bel Air Music Compact Disc BAM 2000. Waltz. Russian Philharmonic Orchestra, Konstantin KRIMETS. [Opp. 116 and 97; Sviridov, Dashkevich, Prokofiev *et al.*] P Moscow Radio Studio Jan. 2000.

Note: The Russian surgeon, Nikolai Ivanovich Pirogov (1810–81), although politically opposed to Romanov rule, became famous for his part in the defence of Sevastopol during the Crimean War. An amputation through the ankle joint was subsequently named after him.

Opus 77   Violin Concerto No. 1 in A minor

Form: Concerto for violin and orchestra (with 2 harps and reduced brass) in four movements:

1. Nocturne—Moderato
2. Scherzo—Allegro
3. Passacaglia—Andante *attacca* Cadenza *attacca*
4. Burlesque—Allegro con brio

Instrumentation: piccolo (= flute III), 2 flutes, 2 oboes, cor anglais (= oboe III), 2 B flat clarinets, bass clarinet (= B flat clarinet III), 2 bassoons, contrabassoon (= bassoon III) ~ 4 horns, tuba ~ timpani, tambourine, gong ~ xylophone, celesta, 2 harps ~ strings.

Composed: 21 July 1947—24 March 1948, though not released until 1955. The first, second, and third movements completed on 12 November, 6 December 1947, and 19 January 1948 respectively. Written at Moscow.

Dedication: David Fyodorovich Oistrakh (violinist).

Premières: 29 October 1955, Leningrad Philharmonic Hall; David Oistrakh, Leningrad Philharmonic Orchestra, Yevgeni Mravinsky.

USA: 29 December 1955, Carnegie Hall, New York; D. Oistrakh, New York Philharmonic Orchestra, Dimitri Mitropoulos.

4 February 1956, Moscow; D. Oistrakh, USSR Symphony Orchestra, Ye. Mravinsky.

Arrangements: Reduction for violin and piano by the composer, with the violin part edited by David Oistrakh. Passacaglia arranged for double-bass and piano by Rodion Azarkhin. Burlesque transcribed for domra and balalaika ensemble by Yuri Chernov.

Music: Originally issued as Opus 99 (Opus 77 was then allocated to *Three Pieces for Orchestra*). Incorrectly given as Opus 78 by S. D. Krebs (1970) *et al.* Autograph scores preserved at the Glinka Museum (full score) and the CIS Archives of Literature and Art (reduction). The opening of the Nocturne in both autograph scores is reproduced in Volumes 14 and 15 of *Collected Works*.

> Muzgiz, No. 25755, 1956, score, 29 cm.
>
> Muzgiz, No. 25842, 1956, arr. for violin and piano, 29 cm.
>
> Leeds Music, no number, 1956, reduction, 31 cm.
>
> Muzgiz, 1957, revised score, 29 cm.
>
> Boosey & Hawkes, No. 694, 1957, 19 cm.
>
> Hans Sikorski, No. 2101, *c.*1957, reduction, 31.5 cm.
>
> Edition Peters, No. 4728 (plate no. 11844), 1958, reduction, 31 cm.
>
> Muzgiz, 1960, score, 20 cm.
>
> Muzyka, No. 5913, 1975, reduction, 31 cm.
>
> Sovietskii Kompozitor, No. 4292, 1978, Passacaglia arr. for double-bass and piano by A. Azarkhin, 29 cm.
>
> Muzyka, No. 10712 (in Volume 14 of *Collected Works* with Op. 129), 1981, full score, 30 cm.
>
> Muzyka, No. 10793 (in Volume 15 of *Collected Works* with Op. 129), 1981, reduction for violin and piano, including a separate violin part ed. D. Oistrakh, 30 cm.

Duration: 35 and approx. 40 minutes in scores; 27' 47"–41' 07"; 38' 10"–39' 15" (Plaistow).

Recordings: USA: Columbia ML 5077 (mono). David OISTRAKH (violin), New York Philharmonic Orchestra, Dimitri Mitropoulos. P Dec. 1955, I 1956. *Reissued:* Philips ABL 3101 (mono). G July 1956 ~ USA: Columbia MG 33328 (two-record set). [Mendelssohn, Vivaldi, Mozart, and Bach.] I May 1975 ~ CBS S 73442 in Set CBS 77394 (electronic stereo). G Oct. 1975 ~ CBS Masterworks MP 39771. [Prokofiev.] I Mar. 1986, G Apr. 1987.

Italy: Fonit Cetra DOC 6 (mono). David OISTRAKH accompanied as above. P Carnegie Hall concert 1 Jan. 1956, I 1981. *Reissued:* USA: NYP Compact Disc 9707 (mono) in NYP 9701 (ten-disc set). ['The Historic Broadcasts 1923 to 1987'—on Disc 6 with Wagner and Poulenc.] I 1997 ~ NYP Compact Disc 9712. Burlesque. [Sampler—Ravel, Tchaikovsky, Chopin *et al.*] I with G Nov. 1997 ~ Sony Masterworks Heritage Compact Disc MHK 63327 (mono). [Op. 107.] I June 1998.

Symposium Compact Discs 1142-3 (two-disc set, mono). Max ROSTAL (violin), BBC Symphony Orchestra, Sir Malcolm Sargent. ['Max Rostal in Memoriam'—Bartók, Borg, and Stevens.] P 22 Aug. 1956, I Apr. 1993.

Hong Kong: One-Eleven Compact Disc EPR 95030 (mono). Ruggiero RICCI (violin), USSR Symphony Orchestra, Yevgeni Mravinsky. [Stravinsky and Respighi.] P a genuine concert recording according to the artist who 'Vaguely remembers doing it in the dim and distant past', I 1998. NB. Kenzo Amoh, on checking concert lists in St Petersburg, considers this performance was not conducted by Mravinsky.

USSR: MK D 03658-9 (Mono). David OISTRAKH (violin), Leningrad Philharmonic Orchestra, Yevgeni Mravinsky. P 30 Nov. 1956, I 1957. *Reissued:* France: Le Chant du Monde LDS 8186 (10" mono) ~ USSR: MK D 5540-1 (10" mono). I 1959 ~ USA: Bruno BR 14017 (mono). [Rakov.] I 1958 ~ USA. Monitor MCS 2014 (electronic stereo). I 1958 ~ Parlophone Odeon PM5 1014 (10" mono). G Jan. 1959 ~ USA: Period Everest SHO-ST 2342 (electronic stereo). [Barber.] I 1965 ~ USSR: Melodiya D 033449-52 (1 side in two-record set, mono). [Op. 60.] I 1972 ~ HMV Melodiya ASD 3234-5 in Set SLS 5058 (electronic stereo). [Op. 129 and Khachaturyan.] G Oct. 1976 ~ Germany: Melodia Eurodisc 88 665 XPK. [In thirteen-record Oistrakh box set with Op. 129.] I 1977 ~ France: Le Chant du Monde Compact Disc LDC 278 882. ['The David Oistrakh Edition'—with Op. 129 on 2nd of five discs available singly.] I 1987, G Apr. 1988 ~ Germany: Melodia Eurodisc Compact Disc CD 69084. [Op. 129.] I 1990 ~ USA: Monitor Collectors Series Compact Disc MCD 62014. [Prokofiev.] I 1991 ~ Japan: JVC Melodiya VICC 2132 (mono). [Ravel.] I July 1993 ~ RCA Compact Discs 74321 72914-2 (two-disc set, mono). [Mozart, Brahms, and Beethoven.] I Apr. 2000.

Russia: Syd Records Compact Disc SYD 005. Yulian SITKOVETSKY (violin), USSR State Radio Orchestra, Aleksandr Gauk. ['The Art of Yulian Sitkovetsky, Vol. 5'—Khachaturyan.] P Moscow concert 1956, I 1995.

France: Praga Compact Disc PR 250 052 (mono). David OISTRAKH (violin), Czech Philharmonic Orchestra, Yevgeni Mravinsky. [Op. 129.] P Czech radio concert bay 1957, I 1994, G July 1995. *Reissued:* France: Praga Compact Discs PR 256 007-12 (six-disc set). ['David Oistrakh in Prague'—on sixth disc with Khachaturyan.] I 1998.

[France: EMI unissued stereo recording. Leonid KOGAN (violin), Colonne Orchestra, Pierre Dervaux. P Paris studio 28 (Nocturne) and 29 June 1961.]

[USA: Hall of Fame HOF 512 (mono) and HOFS 512 (electronic stereo). Leonid KOGAN (violin), Leningrad Philharmonic Orchestra, conductor not Yevgeni Mravinsky as stated. P radio broadcast concert 1960s.]

BBC Radio Classics Compact Disc 15656 9170-2. David OISTRAKH (violin), Philharmonia Orchestra, Gennadi Rozhdestvensky, [Opp. 107 and

102.] P Usher Hall, Edinburgh concert 7 Sept. 1962, I May 1996. *Reissued:* BBC Legends Compact Disc BBCL 4060-2. [Op. 129; and Ysaÿe.] I Feb. 2001, G May 2001.

USSR: Melodiya D 8451-2 (10" mono) and C 201-2 (10"), Leonid KOGAN (violin), Moscow Philharmonic Orchestra, Kirill Kondrashin. P Moscow concert 1962, I 1962, G Feb. 1970. *Reissued:* HMV Melodiya ASD 2585. [Op. 107.] G July 1970 ~ USSR: Melodiya C90 06613-4. Second movement only. [Glinka, Kabalevsky, Khachaturyan *et al.*] I 1976 ~ Netherlands: Phonogram Melodia 691 419. [Op. 107.] ~ USA: Russian Disc Compact Disc RDCD 11 025 (mono). [Op. 129.] I Feb. 1994 ~ Italy: Arlecchino Compact Disc ARL 87. ['The Leonid Kogan Legacy, Vol. XVI'—Vainberg.] I 1994 ~ Czech: Supraphon Compact Disc SU 3005-2001. ['Giants of the Violin'—Sibelius and Beethoven.] I 1995. NB. P date given as Prague concert 1964.

Belgium: Cyprès Compact Discs CYP 9612 (on fourth of twelve-disc set, mono). Aleksei MIKHLIN (violin), Belgian National Orchestra, André Cluytens. [Ravel, Schumann, and Rossum.] P Brussels Queen Elisabeth Competition concert 13 June 1963, I 2001.

Revelation Compact Disc RV 10084 (mono). Leonid KOGAN (violin), Moscow Philharmonic Orchestra, Kirill Kondrashin. [Op. 114*a* and 96.] P concert 3 Oct. 1966, I Aug. 1997.

USA: Radiothon CSO CD95-10/20 (two-disc set). Leonid KOGAN (violin), Chicago Symphony Orchestra, Irwin Hoffman. ['Chicago Symphony Orchestra: From the Archives, Vol. 10: Great Soloists'—J. Strauss, Ravel, Castelnuova-Tedesco *et al.*] P Chicago concert 27 and 28 Oct. 1966, I Sept. 1995.

East Germany: Sterna 8 25 874. Gustav SCHMAHL (violin), Dresden Philharmonie, Kurt Masur. P Dresden Aug. 1969. *Reissued:* Germany: Berlin Classics Compact Disc 0091 532BC. [Prokofiev.] I 1995 ~ Germany: Berlin Classics Compact Discs 009150-2 (nine-disc set). ['The Kurt Masur Edition'—Schumann, Tchaikovsky, Grieg *et al.*] I Oct. 1995.

Belgium: René Gailly International Productions Compact Disc CD 86 003. Edith VOLCKAERT (violin), Belgian Radio Symphony Orchestra, René Defossez. [Huybrechts.] P Brussels Queen Elisabeth Competition concert 24 May 1971, I 1993.

USSR: Melodiya CM 04385-6. Burlesque arr. Y. Chernov. A. TSYGANOV (domra), Osipov Academic Russian Folk Orchestra, Viktor Dubrovsky. [Peiko, Shishakov, Gorodovskaya *et al.*] P 1972, I 1974. *Reissued:* HMV Melodiya Classics HQS 1410. [Glinka, Musorgsky, Tchaikovsky *et al.*] G Jan. 1978.

Italy: Intaglio Compact Disc INCD 7241. David OISTRAKH (violin), New Philharmonia Orchestra, Maksim Shostakovich. [Op. 129.] P Royal Festival Hall concert 20 Nov. 1972, I July 1992.

HMV ASD 2936. David OISTRAKH (violin), New Philharmonia Orchestra, Maksim Shostakovich. P 25 Nov. 1972, G Jan. 1974. *Reissued:* USA: Angel S 36964. I 1973 ~ USSR: Melodiya CM 04291-2. I 1974*c*. ~ France: EMI Pathé Marconi C 069 02400 ~ USSR: Melodiya CM 04291-2. [In third box of Part 1 of *Collected Works on Records.*] I 1980 ~ HMV ASD 4046. [Op. 107.] G June 1981 ~ Japan: Toshiba EMI Compact Disc TOCE 3276. [Oistrakh/Yampolsky recital.] I 1997.

USSR: Melodiya CM 03941-2. Igor OISTRAKH (violin), All-Union Radio and Television Symphony Orchestra, Maksim Shostakovich. P 1973, I 1974*a*. *Reissued:* France: Le Chant du Monde LDX 78 576 K.

Sweden: BASF 25 21640-3. Arve TELLEFSEN (violin), Swedish Radio Symphony Orchestra, Gary Bertini. P 1973, I Sept. 1979.

USSR: Melodiya C10 30915 005 (two-record set). Leonid KOGAN (violin), USSR Symphony Orchestra, Yevgeni Svetlanov. [Volume 10 of 'Leonid Kogan's Complete Recordings' with Mendelssohn and Waxman.] P Moscow concert 25 Sept. 1976, I 1991*a*. *Reissued:* Italy: Arlecchino Compact Disc ARL 6. ['The Leonid Kogan Legacy, Vol. I'—Berg.] I 1994. NB. The date of 29 Apr. 1960 is incorrect.

Venezuela: Fundacicu Rito Juan Pro-Musica Volume 11. Jose Francisco Del CASTILLO (violin), Venezuela Symphony Orchestra, Georg W. Schmoehe. P June 1979.

USA: Vox Cum Laude D-VCL 9008 (digital). Fredell LACK (violin), Berlin City Symphony Orchestra, Seigfried Köhler. P Feb. 1980, I Mar. 1982.

Revelation Compact Disc RV 10108. Viktor TRETYAKOV (violin), USSR Symphony Orchestra, Yuri Temirkanov. [Op. 129.] P 16 June 1981, I May 1998.

Germany: Live Classics Compact Disc LCL 105. Oleg KAGAN (violin), USSR Symphony Orchestra, Aleksandr Lazarev. [Tchaikovsky.] P Moscow concert 26 Sept. 1981, I 2000.

USA: WQXR Radiothon Special Edition 88 1/2. Glenn DICTEROW (violin), New York Philharmonic Orchestra, Maksim Shostakovich. [C. P. E. Bach, Haydn, Vivaldi *et al.*] P 9 Jan. 1982, I 1988.

Japan: Icone Compact Disc ICN 9416-2. Sergei STADLER (violin), Leningrad Philharmonic Orchestra, Ravil Martynov. [Arensky.] P Leningrad concert 1983, I Sept. 1994. *Reissued:* Leningrad Masters Compact Disc LM 1320. [Arensky.] G Sept. 1996.

Bulgaria: Balkanton BCA 11385. Stoika MILANOVA (violin), Bulgarian Radio and Television Symphony Orchestra, Vassil Stefanov. P Feb. 1984. *Reissued:* Netherlands: Sound Compact Disc CD 3445. [Op. 35.]

Canada: Canadian Broadcasting Corporation SM 5037. Steven STARYK (violin), Toronto Symphony Orchestra, Andrew Davis. P Toronto 12–13 Jan. 1985. *Reissued:* Canada: CBC Compact Disc SMCD 5037. I 1986 ~ Canada: CBC Compact Disc PSCD 2023. [Prokofiev and Kreisler.] I 2001.

USA: Pyramid Compact Disc 13493. Nell GOTKOVSKY (violin), Bulgarian National Radio Symphony Orchestra, Vassil Kazandzhiev. [Op. 129.] P Sofia Oct. 1987, I 1988, G Oct. 1991.

Philips Digital Classics Compact Disc 422 364-2PH. Viktoria MULLOVA (violin), Royal Philharmonic Orchestra, André Previn. [Prokofiev.] P London 16–21 June 1988, G June 1989.

EMI Compact Disc CDC7 49814-2. Itzak PERLMAN (violin), Israel Philharmonic Orchestra, Zubin Mehta. [Glazunov.] P Tel Aviv concert 27 and 31 July 1988, I Oct. 1989, G Jan. 1990. American Grammy Award 1991—winner of Instrumental Soloist with Orchestra category.

Decca Compact Disc 425 793-2DH. Boris BELKIN (violin), Royal Philharmonic Orchestra, Vladimir Ashkenazy. [Op. 102.] P Walthamstow Nov. 1988, I June 1990, G Aug. 1990.

Chandos Compact Disc CHAN 8820. Lydia MORDKOVITCH (violin), Scottish National Orchestra, Neeme Järvi. [Op. 129.] P Glasgow 16–17 Oct. 1989, I Feb. 1990, G Apr. 1990. The *Gramophone* Awards 1990—winner of Concerto category, G Oct. 1990. *Reissued:* Chandos Compact Disc CHAN 9007. Burlesque. ['The Chandos Sound Experience'—Barber, Janáček, Prokofiev *et al.*] I Feb. 1992.

Virgin Classics Compact Disc VC7 91143-2. Dmitri SITKOVETSKY (violin), BBC Symphony Orchestra, Andrew Davis. [Op. 129.] P London Dec. 1989, I Aug. 1990, G Sept. 1990. Preis der Deutschen Schallplattenkritik award 1990. *Reissued:* Virgin Classics Compact Disc VC7 59601-2. [Op. 129.] I June 1993 ~ Virgin Classics Compact Discs VBD5 61633-2 (two-disc set). [Op. 129 and Prokofiev.] I Aug. 1999.

Germany: Berlin Classics Compact Disc BC 1049-2. Michael ERXLEBEN (violin), Berlin City Symphony Orchestra, Claus Peter Flor. [Hartmann.] P Berlin May 1990, I 1993.

EMI Classics Compact Disc CDC7 54314-2. Nadja SALERNO-SONNENBERG (violin), London Symphony Orchestra, Maksim Shostakovich. [Barber.] P London 8–10 Mar. 1991, I Sept. 1992, G Dec. 1992.

Norway: Grappa Compact Disc CRCD 4050. Arve TELLEFSEN (violin), Royal Philharmonic Orchestra, Paavo Berglund. [Bach.] P London 27–8 Dec. 1991, I 1994.

France: Le Chant du Monde Compact Disc LDC 278-1099. Ivan MONIGHETTI (violin), Prague Radio Symphony Orchestra, Jiří Válek. [Op. 129.] P Czech radio Nov. 1992, I Aug. 1993.

Belgium: René Gailly International Productions Compact Disc CD 87 515 in three-disc set CD 90 006. Keng-Yuen TSENG (violin), National Orchestra of Belgium, Ronald Zollman. [Tchaikovsky.] P Brussels concert 5 June 1993.

Netherlands: BMG RCA Compact Disc 74321 447832. Jaap van ZWEDEN (violin), Netherlands Radio Philharmonic Orchestra, Edo de Waart. [Rihm.] P Utrecht 16–19 Apr. 1994, I 1996.

Teldec Compact Disc 4509-98143-2- Maksim VENGEROV (violin), London Symphony Orchestra, Mstislav Rostropovich. [Prokofiev.] P London May 1994, I Sept. 1994, G Feb. 1995. *Gramophone* Record Awards 1995—winner of Concerto catergory and voted 'Record of the year'.

USA: Amadis Compact Disc 7194. Oleg KRYSA (violin), National Symphony Orchestra of Ukraine, Theodore Kuchar. [Op. 47.] P Kiev 6 May 1994, I 2000.

Sony Classical Compact Disc SK 68338. MIDORI (violin), Berlin Philharmonic Orchestra, Claudio Abbado. [Tchaikovsky.] P Berlin concert 7–11 Mar, 1995, I Oct. 1998, G Dec. 1998.

France: Erato Compact Disc 0630 10696-2. Vadim REPIN (violin), Hallé Orchestra, Kent Nagano. [Prokofiev.] P BBC North Studio, Manchester Mar. 1995, I Nov. 1995, G Jan. 1996.

Japan: Denon Compact Disc COCO 80762. Boris BELKIN (violin), Royal Philharmonic Orchestra, Junichi Hirokami. [Glazunov.] P 25–8 May 1995.

France: Arion Compact Disc ARN 68326. Marie SCHEUBLÉ (violin), Monte-Carlo Philharmonic, James De Priest. [Op. 129.] P Monte-Carlo July 1995, I Mar. 1996.

Japan: Triton Compact Disc 17 006. Maksim FEDOTOV (violin), Russian State Symphony Orchestra, Aleksandr Vedernikov. [Op. 129.] P Moscow Conservatory Dec. 1995, I Nov. 1996.

Naxos Compact Disc 8-550814. Ilya KALER (violin), Polish National Radio Symphony Orchestra, Antoni Wit. [Op. 129.] P Katowice 15–18 Jan. 1996, I Aug. 1997, G Oct. 1997.

Germany: Arte Nova Classics Compact Disc 74321 77066-2. Latica HONDA-ROSENBERG (violin), Slovenian Radio Symphony Orchestra, Lior Shambadal. [Tchaikovsky.] P 16–22 May 2000.

References: Brown, Ottaway, and Shirinsky.

Notes: Many of the above recordings, from early LP days—even a number of Melodiya issues—to the latest CD releases, are labelled as Opus 99.

In the original version the solo violin immediately launches into the Burlesque. At rehearsals, a week before the première, David Oistrakh requested a short break after the physical effort required by the Cadenza in order to restore circulation in his right arm. Shostakovich rewrote a new beginning of the finale which he made an orchestral *tutti*. The original autograph was not destroyed as the composer hoped that one day it would be possible for the soloist to perform his first version.

Opus 78   Michurin

Alternative title: Originally conceived by Aleksandr Dovzhenko as a play entitled *Life in Bloom* and released as a film for the home market under this title.

Form: Music for the biographical colour film based on the life of the horticulturist Ivan Michurin, directed by Aleksandr Dovzhenko for the Dovzhenko Studios, Kiev. The music, scored for chorus and orchestra, includes a folksong 'Beyond the mountains, beyond the valleys'. The film awarded a Stalin Prize Second Class in 1949.

Composed: 1948, at Moscow.

Premières: Film first shown on 1 January 1949.

   UK: 13 and 14 October 1998 (BBC3 broadcast on 12 November 1998), Barbican Centre, London; London Symphony Orchestra, Mstislav Rostropovich; Reminiscence and Winter Garden.

Arrangements: Opus 78*a*—Suite for chorus and orchestra assembled by Lev Atovmyan in 1964:

1. Overture
2. Winter Garden—Adagio (No. 5 in the film score)
3. Spring Waltz—Allegro scherzando
4. Reminiscence—Moderato molto—Allegro—Adagio (No. 3 in the film score)
5. Demonstration in the Town Square
6. Michurin's Monologue
7. Finale

Spring Waltz No. 3 (Ballet Suite No. 2, No. 5 and *Four Waltzes*, No. 1: Sans op. P) variously transcribed, including for cello and piano by L. Atovmyan, violin and piano by Konstantin Fortunatov, and solo piano by Bronislava Rozengauz.

   Suite No. 5 includes the Revolutionary song 'Boldly, friends, on we march!'

   Suite No. 6 includes a choral setting of 'Song of the Counterplan' from Opus 33, marked 'Allegro' (No. 10 in the film score).

   English translation of the choruses in Suite Nos. 1 and 6 by Valeria Vlayinskaya.

Instrumentation of Suite Opus 78*a*:   piccolo, 2 flutes, 2 oboes, 2 clarinets (B flat and A), 2 bassoons ~ 4 horns, 3 trumpets, 3 trombones, tuba ~ timpani, triangle, side drum, cymbals, bass drum ~ glockenspiel, 2 harps ~ S.A.T.B. chorus in Nos. 1, 6, and (wordless) 7 ~ strings. Separate band of 3 trumpets and 3 trombones.

Music: Autograph of the film score preserved at the Glinka Museum and a manuscript copy in the Music Library of the USSR Cinematograph Symphony Orchestra. Autograph of the Suite preserved in the Bureau of the Music Fund of the USSR.

Boosey & Hawkes, No. 20616 (*Two Pieces from Ballet Suite No. 2:* Spring Waltz and Op. 39 Adagio), 1958, arr. L. Atovmyan, score, 31.5 cm.

Sovetskii Kompozitor, No. 928 (in *Dmitri Shostakovich: Waltzes from Film Music*), 1959, Suite No. 3 only, full score, 29 cm.

Sovetskii Kompozitor, No. 2718 (in *D. Shostakovich: Pieces for cello and piano*), 1962, No. 3 only, arr. L. Atovmyan, 29 cm.

Edition Peters, No. 4767 (in *Two Pieces for cello and piano*), 1962, No. 3 arr. L. Atovmyan, 30 cm.

Edition Peters, No. 4794 (plate no. 12389—in *Shostakovich: Album of Easy Pieces*), 1967, No. 3 arr. K. Fortunatov, 30.5 cm.

Muzyka, No . 4719 (in *D. Shostakovich: Pieces for violin and piano*), 1975, No. 3 arr. K. Fortunatov, 28.5 cm.

Belwin Mills, New York, No. 4446 (*Two pieces for cello and piano*—with Op. 39 Adagio), *c.*1977, No. 3 arr. L. Atovmyan, score, 27 cm.

Sovetskii Kompozitor, No. 4920 (in *D. Shostakovich: Selection of Children's Piano Pieces*), 1979, No. 3 arr. B. Rozengauz, 29 cm.

Sovetskii Kompozitor, No. 7625 (in *Album for the Violinist,* Volume 1), 1986, No. 3 arr. K. Fortunatov, 29 cm.

Muzyka, No. 10889 (in supplement to Volume 41 of *Collected Works*), 1987, 'Song of the Counterplan' in full score, 30 cm.

Muzyka, No. 10890 (in Volume 42 of *Collected Works* with Opp. 75, 80, 82, 95, 97, 111, 116, 132, and 137), 1987, 'Reminiscence, and 'Winter Garden' in full score, 30 cm.

Muzyka, No. 14908 (in *D. Shostakovich: Pieces for cello and piano*), 1991, No. 3 arr. L. Atovmyan, 29 cm.

Duration: Film: 101 minutes. Suite Opus 78*a:* 29' 52"; 34 minutes (Sadovnikov).

Recordings: USA: Angel Melodiya SR 40181. Suite Nos. 1, 2, 4, 6, and 7. Moscow Radio Symphony Orchestra and Chorus, Maksim SHOSTAKOVICH. [Op. 120.] P 1966. *Reissued:* Germany: Melodia Eurodisc 28665 XHK. [On third record of four-record film music album with Op. 97*a*.] I 1981 ~ RCA Gold Seal Compact Disc 74321 32041-2. [Opp. 47 and 22*a*.] I Mar. 1996.

Unicorn Kanchana. Compact Disc DKP 9069. Spring Waltz arr. Atovmyan. Alexander BAILLIE (cello) and Piers Lane (piano). [Opp. 40 and 39; Prokofiev.] P London 6 and 7 Aug. 1987, G Dec. 1988. *Reissued:* Unicorn Kanchana Souvenir Compact Disc UKCD 2083. [As original release.] I Mar. 1997.

RCA Victor Red Seal Compact Disc RD 60226. Complete Suite Nos. 1–7 (chorus in No. 7 only). Belgian Radio Symphony Orchestra and Chorus, José SEREBRIER ['Film Music of Shostakovich, Volume 3'—Opp. 82 and 30.] P 1988?, I Aug. 1990, G Mar. 1991.

CIS: Manchester Compact Disc CDMAN 129. Spring Waltz. St Petersburg Philharmonic Academic Symphony Orchestra, Vladimir ALTSHULER. ['Shostakovich Theatre and Cinema Music'—Opp. 32*a*, 58*a*, 45, 30, 76, 97, 99, and 37.] P St Petersburg 1995, I 1998.

Reference: Sobolev.
Notes: For further recordings of the Spring Waltz see Ballet Suite No. 2, Sans op. P (i).

Originally Gavriil Popov was commissioned to write this film score but was severely criticized and dismissed for excessive complication of the musical language and distorting Russian folksongs.

Ivan Vladimirovich Michurin (1855–1935) developed over 300 new types of fruit trees and berry bushes by hybridisation. He founded a horticultural institute in Kozlov and the town was renamed Michurinsk in his honour.

Opus 79   From Jewish Folk Poetry

Form: Song cycle for soprano (S), contralto (C), and tenor (T) with piano accompaniment, to traditional Yiddish and Hebrew texts (apart from No. 7 by B. Shafir), selected from a collection, compiled by I. M. Dobrushkin and A. D. Yunitsky under the editorship of Yuri Sokolov, published by Goslitizdat, Moscow, 1947:

1. Lament for a dead infant—Moderato (S and C)
2. The solicitous mother and aunt—Allegretto (S and C)
3. Lullaby ('Little son, my fairest')—Andante (C)
4. Before a long separation—Adagio (S and T)
5. Warning—Allegretto (S)
6. The abandoned father—Moderato (C and T)
7. Song of want—Allegro (T)
8. Winter—Adagio (T, S, and C)
9. The good life—Allegretto (T)
10. Song of the young girl—Allegretto (S)
11. Happiness—Allegretto (C, S, and T)

Verses translated into Russian by T. Spendiarova (No. 1), A. Globa (Nos. 2 and 4), V. Zvyagintseva (No. 3), N. Ushakov (No. 5), S. Mar (No. 6), B. Semyonov (Nos. 7 and 8), S. Olender (Nos. 9 and 10), and L. Dligach (No. 11).

Composed: 1 August–24 October 1948, at Moscow. Autograph score of the orchestral version Opus 79*a* dated 1 October 1948, though date usually given as 1963.

Premières: 15 January 1955, Leningrad Glinka Concert Hall; Nina Dorliak (soprano), Zara Dolukhanova (mezzo-soprano), Aleksei Maslennikov (tenor), and Dmitri Shostakovich (piano). Nos. 3, 8, and 11 encored three times.

Scotland: 8 Sept. 1962, Leith Town Hall; Elisabeth Söderström (soprano), Janet Baker (mezzo-soprano), Peter Pears (tenor), and Geoffrey Parsons (piano).

Opus 79*a:* 19 February 1964, Gorky (now Nizhni Novgorod); Galina Pisarenko (soprano), Larissa Avdeyeva (mezzo-soprano), Aleksei Maslennikov (tenor), Gorky Philharmonic Orchestra, Gennadi Rozhdestvensky.

USA: 23 and 24 November 1985, Theresa L. Kaufmann Concert Hall, New York; Nadia Pelle (soprano), Gretchen Greenfield (contralto), David Gordon (tenor), Y Chamber Orchestra, Maksim Shostakovich.

Arrangements: Opus 79*a*—accompaniment orchestrated by the composer.

Nos. 3 and 7 transcribed for trumpet and piano, and No. 4 for trumpet duet and piano by Sergei Bolotin.

German translations of the song cycle made separately by Marianne Graefe and Alfred Kurella; English translation by Zofia Weaver.

Instrumentation of Opus 79*a*: 2 flutes (II = piccolo), 2 oboes (II = cor anglais), 2 clarinets (B flat and A), bass clarinet, 2 bassoons, contrabassoon ~ 4 horns ~ timpani, tambourine, cymbals, bass drum, gong ~ xylophone, 2 or 3 harps ~ 1st violins (16–20), 2nd violins (14–18), violas (12–16), cellos (12–16), double-basses (10–14).

Music: Autograph piano and full scores preserved at the CIS Archives of Literature and Art.

Muzgiz, No. 576, 1955, for voices and piano, 30 cm.

Edition Peters, No. 4727 (plate no. 11857), 1958, for voices and piano in M. Graefe's German translation, 27 cm.

Sovetskii Kompozitor, No. 2081, 1961, for voices and piano, 29 cm.

Muzyka, No. 4116 (in *Dmitri Shostakovich: Vocal Compositions*), 1967 and 1974, 34 cm.

Muzyka, Leningrad, No. 2035 (in *Dmitri Shostakovich: Pieces for trumpet and piano*), 1976, Nos. 3, 4 (duet), and 7 arr. S. Bolotin, 28.5 cm.

Muzyka, No. 10113 (in Volume 31 of *Collected Works* with Opp. 4, 21, 46*a*, 140, 143*a*, and 145*a*), 1982, Opus 79*a* full score, 30 cm.

Muzyka, No. 10283 (in Volume 32 of *Collected Works* with Opp. 4, 21, 46, 62, 84, 86, 91, 98, 100 *et al.*), 1982, piano score, 30 cm.

Duration: Approx. 23 and 24 minutes in scores; 23' 00"–27' 40".

Recordings: USSR: 25826-7 (10" 78 rpm). Nos. 6 and 11 only ~ 26830-1 (10" 78 rpm). Nos. 1 and 2 only ~ MK HD 03216-7 (mono). Complete cycle. [Op. 98.]. Nina Dorliak (soprano), Zara Dolukhanova (mezzo-soprano), Aleksei Maslennikov (tenor), and Dmitri SHOSTAKOVICH (piano). P 1955, I 1956. *Reissued:* USA: Artia MK 5006 (mono). [Op. 98.] ~ USA: Monitor MC 2020 (mono). [Kabalevsky and Musorgsky.] I 1961 ~ France: Le Chant du Monde LDXA 8219 (mono). [Op. 70.] ~ HMV Melodiya HLM 7094 in Set RLS 721 (mono). [Opp. 102 and 94.] G Oct. 1976 ~ USSR: Melodiya C10 10521-2 (electronic stereo). [In third box of Part 3 of *Collected Works on Records* with Op. 98.] I 1978 ~ France: Le Chant du Monde Compact Disc LDC 278 1000 (mono, double-play). [Opp. 93, 57, and 87.] I Sept. 1989 ~ USA: Russian Disc Compact Disc RDCD 15 015.

[Ippolitov-Ivanov and Kabalevsky.] I Aug. 1994 ~ Revelation Compact Disc RV 70007 (mono). ['Shostakovich plays Shostakovich, Vol. 6'— Opp. 34, 69, and 67.] I Sept. 1998, G Feb. 1999.

Germany: Wergo 60 023 and UK: Helidor Wergo 2549 007. Opus 79*a*, with German text by A. Kurella. Maria Croonen (soprano), Anneliese Burmeister (contralto), Peter Schreier (tenor), Berlin City Symphony Orchestra, Kurt SANDERLING. [Jewish Chronicle—omnibus composition.] P Berlin Oct. 1963. G July 1970. *Reissued:* France: Berlin Classics Compact Disc 009162 BC. [Jewish Chronicle.] I Nov. 2000.

USA: Bridge Compact Disc BCD 904Q. Benita Valente (soprano), Jan DeGaetani (mezzo-soprano), Jon Humphrey (tenor), and Samuel LIPMAN (piano). ['Jan DeGaetani in Concert, Vol. 3'—Kurtág and Welcher.] P Aspen Music Festival concert summer 1980, I Aug. 1995.

USSR: Melodiya C10 16328-30. Opus 79*a*. Raisa Bobrineva (soprano), Galina Borisova (mezzo-soprano), Aleksei Maslennikov (tenor), USSR Symphony Orchestra, Yevgeni SVETLANOV. [In two-record set 'Yevgeni Svetlanov conducts' with Respighi.] P 1980, I 1982*b*. *Reissued:* France: Le Chant du Monde LDX 78 808 and Compact Disc LDC 278 808. [Prokofiev and S. Slonimsky.] I 1986.

Decca 414 410-1DH2 (in two-record box set, digital). Opus 79*a*. Elisabeth Söderström (soprano), Ortrun Wenkel (contralto), Ryszard Karcykowski (tenor), Concertgebouw Orchestra. Bernard HAITINK. [Opp. 143*a* and 113.] P Amsterdam 12 Dec. 1983, G May 1986. *Reissued:* Decca Compact Disc 417 561-2DH. [Op. 141.] G Apr. 1987 ~ Decca Ovation Compact Disc 425 069-2DM. [Op. 141.] I Aug. 1993, G Nov. 1993 ~ London Compact Disc 444 441-2. [On eleventh disc of eleven-disc set with Op. 141.] I June 1995.

Germany: Thorofon Capella MTH 267 (DMM). Sung in M. Graefe's German translation. Eva Csapó (soprano), Anke Eggers (contralto), Günter Binge (tenor), and Horst GÖBEL (piano). [Op. 127.] P Feb. and June 1984.

B'nai B'nith BB 001 (cassette only). Helen Lawrence (soprano), Carole Rosen (mezzo-soprano), Louis Garb (tenor), and Antony SAUNDERS (piano). [Alman.] P London July 1984, G Sept. 1985.

USA: Jerusalem Records Stradivari Performance Compact Disc SCD 8005. Opus 79*a* Nos. 1–8 sung in Yiddish. Lily Tuneh (soprano), Mira Zahai (alto), Neil Jenkins (tenor), Jerusalem Symphony Orchestra, Yuri ARANOVICH. [Vainberg.] P Israel Festival concert 2 June 1985, I 1988.

USA: Pro-Arte Fanfare Compact Disc CDD 411. No. 3 sung in German. Maureen FORRESTER (contralto) and John Arpin (piano). [Ives, Loesser, Gershwin *et al.*] P Toronto 23 and 24 May 1988.

Chandos Compact Disc CHAN 8800. Opus 79*a*. Nadia Pelle (soprano), Mary Ann Hart (mezzo-soprano), Rodney Nolan (tenor), I Musici de Montreál, Yuri TUROVSKY. [Bloch and Prokofiev.] P Quebec 31

May–1 June 1989, G July 1990. *Reissued:* Chandos Enchant Compact Disc CHAN 7061. [Opp. 110*a* and 118*a*.] I July 1997 ~ Chandos Collect Compact Disc CHAN 6617. [Opp. 110*a* and 118*a*.] I July 2000, G Feb. 2001.

Deutsche Grammophon Compact Disc 439 860-2GH. Opus 79*a*. Luba Orgonasova (soprano), Nathalie Stutzmann (contralto), Philip Langridge (tenor), Gothenburg Symphony Qrchestra, Neeme JÄRVI. ['The Orchestral Songs, Vol. 1'—Opp. 4, 46*a*, and 140.] P Gothenburg Aug. 1993, I June 1994.

Germany: Capriccio Compact Disc 10 778. Op. 79*a*. Nina Fomina (soprano), Tamara Sinyavskaya (alto), Arkadi Mishenkin (tenor), Cologne Radio Symphony Orchestra, Mikhail YUROVSKY. [Opp. 143*a* and 140.] P Cologne 22–7 May 1995, I and G Awards (Oct.) 1998.

RCA Victor Red Seal Compact Disc 09026 68434-2. Opus 79*a*. Booklet with lyrics in Russian, English, German, and French. Marina Shaguch (soprano), Larissa Dyadkova (mezzo-soprano), Konstantin Pluzhnikov (tenor), Rotterdam Philharmonic Orchestra, Gennadi ROZHDESTVENSKY. [Sans op. K.] P Rotterdam 24–31 Aug. 1995, I Nov. 1996, G Apr. 1997.

Chandos Compact Disc CHAN 9600. Opus 79*a*. Tatyana Sharova (soprano), Lyudmila Kuznetsova (mezzo-soprano), Aleksei Martynov (tenor), Russian State Symphony Orchestra, Valeri POLYANSKY. [Op. 18.] P Moscow Conservatory Oct. 1996, I Mar. 1998, G June 1998.

USA: Music Masters Compact Disc 01612 67189-2. Opus 79*a*. Marina Zhukova (soprano), Elena Svechnikova (contralto), Nikolai Kurpe (tenor), Moscow Virtuosi, Vladimir SPIVAKOV. [Op. 94 and Sans op. X (ii).] P Dec. 1996.

France: Le Chant du Monde Russian Season Compact Disc RUS 288 166. Op. 79*a* complete Yiddish version; full text in Yiddish. Eva Ben-Zvi (soprano), Yelena Gubina (alto), Nikolai Kurpe (tenor), Bolshoi Theatre Orchestra, Andre CHISTYAKOV. ['Jewish Music from Russia'—Slonimsky and Prokofiev.] P May 1998, I Mar. 2000.

References: Braun, Ian MacDonald, Polyakova, Sokhor (in Danilevich 1967), and Vasina-Grossman (in Daragan).

Note: Daniel Zhitomirsky states that the première arranged for 20 October 1948 was prohibited 'from above'. (*Daugava*, 1990, No. 3—translated by Tatyana Norbury in DSCH Newsletter No. 18).

Opus 80   The Meeting on the Elbe

Form: Music for the black-and-white film *The Meeting on the Elbe*, directed by Grigori Aleksandrov for Mosfilm. The score includes three orchestrally-accompanied songs with lyrics by Yevgeni Dolmatovsky: 'Longing for the Native Country' in two versions (male chorus and woman's solo with piano trio), 'Song of Peace' (musically identical to 'Hymn to Moscow', Sans op. X), and 'Daybreak' for female chorus; also soldiers' song with words by Vasili Lebedev-Kumach. The film awarded a Czechoslovakian Peace Prize in 1949 and a Stalin Prize First Class in 1950.

The film score comprises 34 numbers though Nos. 12 and 15–17 are lost.

  2. Tommy's Song—'Things are very good with the Yankees'
10. [Jazz piece]—Moderato non troppo
13. Longing for the Native Country—Andante
22. Moderato
23. Moderato
24. Allegretto
25. Moderato con moto
28. Tommy's Song (orchestral version)—Allegretto
34. Song of Peace (orchestral version)—Moderato con moto

Instrumentation: piccolo, 2 flutes, 3 oboes, 3 clarinets (A and B flat), 2 bassoons ~ 4 horns, 3 trumpets, 3 trombones, tuba ~ timpani, triangle, side drum, cymbals, gong ~ celesta, piano ~ tenor soloist, S.A.T.B. chorus ~ strings.

Composed: 1948, at Moscow.

Première: Film first shown on 16 March 1949. 'Longing for the Native Country' sung in the film by Nadezhda Obukhova (mezzo-soprano).

Arrangements: Opus 80*a*—Suite for orchestra and voices assembled by the composer:

1. Prelude
2. Longing for the Native Country
3. Dietrich's departure
4. In the American Zone
5. In the old town
6. Marching Song
7. Conclusion
8. Song of Peace

Volume 42 of *Collected Works* states that the Suite was orchestrated by Lev Atovmyan and consists of three items only: Nos. 1, 2, and 8 of the above list. Nos. 2 and 8, arranged for voice and piano by the composer, have enjoyed independent lives as popular songs. Both transcribed for trumpet and piano by Sergei Bolotin and No. 8 recorded in German translation. The popular song 'Longing for the Native Country' is also known under the titles 'Homesickness', 'Nostalgia', and 'Song about the Motherland'.

The song from the film score 'Daybreak' ('Sunrise Is Near' or 'Dawn is Coming') arranged for voices and piano by Lev Atovmyan.

Music: Autograph of the film score and songs in vocal score preserved at the Glinka Museum.

Muzgiz, 1949, Suite Opus 80*a* songs Nos. 2 and 8.

Muzgiz, No. 20695 (in *Songs of the Soviet Cinema* with Op. 82*a* No. 1 and sixteen other songs), 1950, No. 8, 28.5 cm.

Sovetskii Kompozitor, No. 519 (in *D. Shostakovich: Songs*), 1958, Nos. 2 and 8 (the latter incorrectly given as from *The Fall of Berlin*, Opus 82), and 'Daybreak' for solo voices and piano, 29 cm.

Muzichna Ukraina, Kiev, No. 42 (with two other Shostakovich songs), 1976, Nos. 2 and 8 arr. for tenor and baritone with piano accompaniment (Russian text, and also Ukrainian words by B. Chin for No. 2 and K. Drok for No. 8), 26 cm.

Muzyka, Leningrad, No. 2035 (in *Dmitri Shostakovich: Pieces for trumpet and piano*), 1976, Nos. 2 and 8 arr. S. Bolotin, 28.5 cm.

Muzyka, No. 10179 (in Volume 34 of *Collected Works* with Opp. 88 and 136, and songs), 1985, three Dolmatovsky songs in vocal score (chorus and piano), 30 cm.

Muzyka, No. 10890 (in Volume 42 of *Collected Works* with Opp. 75, 78, 87, 95, 97, 111, 116, 132, and 137), 1987, Score Nos. 10, 13, 22–5, 28, and 34, 30 cm.

Sovetskii Kompozitor, No. 7815 (in *Romances and Songs to verses of Yevgeni Dolmatovsky* with Opp. 86, 98, and Sans op. X), Suite No. 2 arr. for tenor, baritone, and male voice choir and No. 8 for male voice choir, 1987, 29 cm.

Duration: Film: 110 minutes.

Recordings: USSR: 17079-19557 (10" 78 rpm). Song No. 8 sung in Russian. Paul ROBESON (bass) and A. Erokhsin (piano). [Dunayevsky.] P 1949. *Reissued:* USSR: MK HD 2864-5 (10" mono). [Smetana and folksongs.] I 1956 ~ USSR: MK D 04478-9 (mono). [Folksongs.] I 1958 ~ USSR: Melodiya C60 24293 007. ['Songs of Struggle and Solidarity'.] I 1987*b*.

USSR: 17137-8 (10" 78 rpm). Songs Nos. 8 and 2. Georgi VINOGRADOV (tenor), Red Banner Ensemble, Boris Aleksandrov. P 1949.

USSR: 019200 (12" 78 rpm). Songs Nos. 8 and 2. Red Banner Ensemble, Boris ALEKSANDROV. [Tenth side fill-up for Op. 81.] P 1950, I 1951. *Reissued:* USSR: MK HD 3506-7 (10" mono). Songs Nos. 2 and 8. Soloist in No. 2 given as Yevgeni Belyaev (tenor). ['Songs by Soviet Composers'—Soloviev-Sedoi, Shainsky, Novikov *et al.*] I 1956 ~ USSR: MK D 5062-3 (10" mono). Songs Nos. 8 and 2. [Songs from Opp. 33, 72, 82, 86, 99 *et al.*] I 1959 ~ USSR: MK D 6161-2 (10" mono). Song No. 8. [Novikov, A. Aleksandrov, Blanter *et al.*] I 1960 ~ USSR: Melodiya D 020515-6 (mono). No. 8 only. ['Dmitri Shostakovich Monograph'.] I 1967 ~ USSR: Melodiya C60 08163-6 (in two-record set). No. 8 only. [B. Aleksandrov, Shainsky, Tulikov *et al.*] I 1978.

USSR: Melodiya D 020517-8 (mono). Song No. 2. Nadezhda OBUKHOVA (mezzo-soprano) and unnamed piano trio. [Blanter, Listov, Dunayevsky *et al.*] I 1951.

East Germany: Eterna B 5031 (78 rpm). No. 8 sung in German. Ernst BUSCH, Berlin Opera Chorus. [?] P 1953. *Reissued:* USSR: Melodiya C60 13187-8. [Eisler, Palasio, Shneyerson *et al.*] I 1980c.

USA: Eterna 30-28 (78 rpm). No. 8 sung in German. BERLIN OPERA CHORUS. [Sans op. J.] P 1954.

East Germany: Aurora 8 15 109. Song No. 2 sung in German. Ernst BUSCH, Leipzig Radio Symphony Orchestra, Adolf Fritz Guhl. [Op. 33.] P 1966.

USSR: Melodiya C60 23927 001. Song No. 2. Lyudmila ZYKINA (popular singer). ['Songs on Ye. Dolmatovsky's lyrics'.] I 1987a.

USSR: Melodiya C10 26613 008. Song No. 8. Leningrad Electrotechnical Institute Students' Choir, Aleksei Kutuzov (chorus-master), Aleksandr KRYLOV. [Guadeamus, Mozart, Tchaikovsky *et al.*] P 17 May 1987, I 1989a.

Note: Ernst Busch's and the Red Banner Ensemble's 78 rpm recordings of Songs Nos. 8 and 2 broadcast by East Germany Radio on 13 February 1991, in a programme in memory of the destruction of Dresden.

Sans op. O   Piano Duets for Children

(i) *Merry March*
Form: A piece for two pianos four hands for children, marked 'Allegretto'.
Composed: May 1949, at Moscow.
Dedication: Maksim Dmitrievich Shostakovich (son).
Music: Autograph score numbered Opus 81 preserved at the CIS Archives of Literature and Art.
> Muzyka, No. 10285 (in the supplement to Volume 39 of *Collected Works* with Opp. 5, 12, 13, 34, 61, and 69), 1983, 30 cm.
> Hans Sikorski, No. 2338 (with Op. 6), 1984, 31.5 cm.
Duration: 1' 53"; 3 minutes (M. MacDonald).
Recording: France: Suoni e Colori Compact Disc SC 53008. Thérèse DUSSAUT and Serge POLUSMIAK (piano duo). ['Hommage à Dmitri Chostakovitch, Vol. 2'—Opp. 134, 6, and 94.] P Espace Fazioli, Paris Oct.–Nov. 1997.

(ii) *Tarantella and Prelude*
Form: Two pieces for two pianos four hands written for children. The first, piece is a shortened reduction of the Scherzo from *The Unforgettable Year 1919*, Opus 89 composed in 1951 and the second, an arrangement of the Prelude Opus 87 No. 15 by Elena Khoven.

1. Tarantella in G major—Presto
2. Prelude in D flat major—Allegretto

Composed: The original version of the Prelude composed on 30 December 1950 at Moscow and the Tarantella arranged, presumably, in 1954.
Première: 8 November 1954, Moscow Conservatory Malyi Hall.
Music: The whereabouts of the autograph of the Tarantella is not known.
  Muzgiz, 1963, edited by E. Khoven, 29 cm.
  Hans Sikorski, *c*.1964, 32 cm.
  Muzyka, No. 5947 (in *D. Shostakovich: Compositions for fortepiano*, Volume 3, with Opp. 35, 94, and 102), 1970, 29 cm.
  Muzyka, No. 11214 (in Volume 13 of *Collected Works* with Opp. 6, 35, 94, and 102), 1983, Tarantella only, 30 cm.
Duration: Tarantella—1' 24".
Recording:
  Gernany: CPO Compact Disc 999 599-2. Tarantella. GENOVA & DIMITROV PIANO DUO. [Opp. 94, 6, 95, Sans op. E; Stravinsky, Prokofiev, and Dinicu.] P Hans Rosbaud Studio 4–5 May 1998, I Apr. 1999. NB. Tarantella incorrectly labelled as from Op. 97.

Opus 81   The Song of the Forests

Form: Oratorio for tenor (T) and bass (B) soloists, boys' choir of trebles and altos (boys), chorus (S.A.T.B.), and large orchestra (with 2 harps and additional brass) to the text by Yevgeni Dolmatovsky:

1. When the war was over—Andante (B and A.T.B.)
2. Clothe the homeland in forests (The call is heard throughout the land)—Allegro (S.A.T.B.)
3. Recollection of the past—Adagio (B and S.A.T.B.) *attacca*
4. Pioneers plant the forests—Allegretto (boys) *attacca*
5. Young Communists go forward—Allegro con brio (S.A.T.B.)
6. A walk into the future—Adagio (T and S.A.T.B.)
7. Glory—Allegro non troppo (T, B, boys, and S.A.T.B.)

Instrumentation: 3 flutes (III = piccolo), 2 oboes, cor anglais, 3 clarinets (B flat and A), 2 bassoons ~ 4 horns, 3 trumpets, 3 trombones, tuba ~ additional 6 trumpets and 6 trombones in No. 7 ~ timpani, triangle, side drum, cymbals ~ glockenspiel, 2 harps ~ tenor and bass soloists, boys' choir, S.A.T.B. chorus ~ strings.
Composed: Summer 1949 and completed on 15 August 1949, at Komarova village, Gulf of Finland.
Premières: 15 November 1949, Leningrad Philharmonic Bolshoi Hall; Vladimir Ivanovsky (tenor), Ivan Titov (bass), Leningrad Philharmonic

Orchestra and Academy Choir, Yevgeni Mravinsky. The date frequently given as 15 December 1949 as in Sadovnikov (1965), Khentova (1982), Glikman (1993) *et al.*

USA: 4 November 1951, San Francisco; English adaptation by Leo E. Christiansen.

Germany: No. 2 arr. Achim Gorenflo. 5 November 1988, Mundelfingen Festive Hall; Musikkapelle Mundelfingen, Reinhard Mäder.

Arrangements: Reduction of No. 6 for voice and piano and No. 7 for children's chorus and mixed choir by the composer. Piano score by Lev Atovmyan. English translations of the text by Leo E. Christiansen, Myron Morris, and Pat Bayley; and German translation by Erwin Job. Text revised by Ye. Dolmatovsky for the 1962 Muzgiz edition. No. 6 arranged as an organ solo by Isai Braudo in 1965.

No. 2 transcribed for wind band by Achim Gorenflo, in 1988. Instrumentation: 3 flutes (III = piccolo), E flat and 3 B flat clarinets; 2 alto, 2 tenor, and 1 baritone saxophones ~ 3 trumpets, 3 flügel horns, 4 French horns, 2 B flat baritone and I bass saxhorns, 3 trombones, tuba ~ glockenspiel, timpani (2 players), cymbals, triangle.

Music: A piece for two pianofortes, *Merry March*, originally designated Opus 81. The composer's and Lev Atovmyan's autograph scores of *The Song of the Forests* preserved at the CIS Archives of Literature and Art, along with proof sheets marked with the composer's corrections. Awarded a Stalin Prize First Class in 1950.

Muzgiz, No. 20801, 1950 and 1960, piano reduction by L. Atovmyan, 29 cm.

L. E. Christiansen, San Francisco, *c.*1951, lyric adaptation, text only, 22 cm.

Edition Peters, No. 4607, *c.*1952, vocal score, German translation by Erwin Job, 30 cm.

Leeds Music, 1959, vocal score, English translation, 30 cm.

Muzgiz, No. 20914, 1962, full score with revised text, 34.5 cm.

Muzyka, No. 11680 (in Volume 29 of *Collected Works* with Opp. 90 and 119), 1983, full score, 30 cm.

Muzyka, No. 11786 (in Volume 30 of *Collected Works* with Opp. 90 and 119), 1983, vocal score, 30 cm.

Duration: Approx. 33 minutes in score; 36' 20"–37' 59"; 36' 40" (Plaistow); 40 minutes (Schirmer).

Recordings: USSR: 019191-200 (9 sides 78 rpm). Vitali Kilichevsky (tenor), Ivan Petrov (bass), USSR Symphony Orchestra, RSFSR Academic Russian Chorus, Moscow State Choral School Boys' Choir, Aleksandr MRAVINSKY. [Op. 80.] P 12 Dec. 1949. *Reissued:* USSR: MK D 0486-7 (mono). I 1952 ~ USA: Vanguard VRS 422 (mono). I 1952 ~ France: Le Chant du Monde LDXA 8000. (mono). I 1952 and LDX 8387 (mono) ~ Japan: Victor MK 1023 (mono). [Op. 54.] I 1973 ~ Japan: JVC Melodiya

Compact Disc VDC 25005 (mono). [Prokofiev.] I 1988 ~ Japan: BMG Melodiya Compact Disc BVCX 4026 (mono). [Op. 112.] I 1997.

Czech: Ultraphon 5149 C (mono). Soloists, Choir, and Orchestra of the BOLSHOI THEATRE. P Moscow 1954. _Reissued:_ Czech: Supraphon SLPV 177 (mono) ~ Australia: Diaphon DCM-1 (mono) ~ USA: Colosseum CRLP 118 (mono).

USSR: MK D 2879-80 (10" mono). No. 4 only. Moscow State Choral School Boys' Chorus, Aleksandr SVESHNIKOV. [Raukhverger, Milman, Blanter _et al._] P 1956.

USSR: Melodiya D 023225-6 (mono). Vladimir Ivanovsky (tenor), Ivan Petrov (bass); Moscow State Choral School Boys' Choir, Yuli Ulanov (chorus-master); RSFSR Academic Russian Choir, Moscow Philharmonic Orchestra, Aleksandr YURLOV (conductor). P 1968. _Reissued:_ USSR: Melodiya CM 02699-700. I 1972 ~ HMV Melodiya ASD 2875. [Sviridov.] G May 1973 ~ USA: Angel Melodiya SR 40214. I 1974 ~ France: Le Chant du Monde LDX 78602. I UK Apr. 1980 by The Other Labels ~ USA: Russian Disc Compact Disc RD CD 11 048. [0p. 90.] I Oct. 1994.

USSR: Melodiya C10 12415-6. Aleksei Maslennikov (tenor), Aleksandr Vedernikov (bass); Moscow State Choral School Boys' Choir, Aleksandr Sveshnikov (chorus-master); Large Choir of Central Television and All-Union Radio, Klavdi Ptitsa (chorus-master); USSR Symphony Orchestra, Yevgeni SVETLANOV. P Moscow memorial concert 25 Sept. 1978, I 1980a. _Reissued:_ USSR: with same number in third box of Part 1 of _Collected Works on Records._ I 1980.

Japan: Victor Musical Industries Compact Disc VICC 83. Aleksei Martynov (tenor), Aleksandr Vedernikov (bass), 'Spring' Studio Children's Choral School, Yurlov Republican Russian Choir, Moscow Radio Symphony Orchestra, Vladimir FEDOSEYEV. P Moscow 16–17 Aug. 1991, I 1997.

Decca Compact Disc 436 762-2DH. Mikhail Kotlyarov (tenor), Nikita Storojev (bass); Brighton Festival Chorus, Laszlo Heltay (chorus-master); New London Children's Choir, Ronald Corp (chorus-master); Royal Philharmonic Orchestra, Vladimir ASHKENAZY. [Opp. 96, 131, and 14.] P Walthamstow Oct. 1991, I June 1994, G Aug. 1994.

Olympia Compact Disc OCD 585. No. 6 arr. for organ by I. Braudo. Mariya MAKAROVA (organ). ['Music for Organ'—Opp. 16, 27, 29, 39, 97, 105, and Sans op. E.] P Moscow conservatory Jan. 1995, I Mar. 1997.

Germany: Capriccio Compact Disc 10 779. Text in German and English. Vladimir Kasatschuk (tenor), Stanislav Suleimanov (bass), Cologne Radio Chorus, Godfried Ritter (chorus-master), Berlin Children's Radio Chorus, Manfred Roost (chorus-master), Cologne Radio Symphony Orchestra, Mikhail YUROVSKY. [Opp. 90 and 15a.] P Cologne 3–8 June 1996, I July 1999.

RCA Red Seal Compact Disc 09026 68877-2. Sergei Kisseliev (tenor), Gennadi Bezzubenkov (baritone), Glinka College Boys' Choir, Vladimir

Begletsov (chorus-master), St Petersburg Chorus, Valeri Ouspensky (chorus-master), St Petersburg Philharmonic Orchestra, Yuri TEMIRKA-NOV. [Prokofiev.] P St Petersburg 15 and 16 Apr. 1997, I Feb. 1999, G Sept. 1999.

Opus 82   The Fall of Berlin

Form: Music for Parts 1 and 2 of the colour film *The Fall of Berlin,* directed by Mikhail Chiaureli for Mosfilm, scored for chorus and orchestra. The film awarded a Stalin Prize First Class in 1950. The musical material comprises 18 items. The following pieces are not included in the Suite:

  5. 'Beautiful Day'—Allegretto
  8. Allegro
  9. Allegretto
  15. Overture to Part One—Allegro moderato—Maestoso
  17. Concentration Camp—[Con moto]—Allegro

Instrumentation: piccolo, 2 flutes, 3 oboes, 3 clarinets (B flat and A), 2 bassoons ~ 4 horns, 3 trumpets, 3 trombones, tuba ~ timpani, triangle, tambourine, side drum, cymbals, bass drum ~ xylophone, celesta, 2 harps ~ S.A.T.B. chorus, two-part children's choir ~ strings.
Composed: 1949, at Moscow.
Premières: Film first shown on 21 January 1950.
      Suite Opus 82*a:* 10 June 1950; Moscow Radio Orchestra and Choir, Ivan Kuvykin (chorus-master), Aleksandr Gauk (conductor).
Arrangements: Opus 82*a*—Suite for chorus and orchestra assembled by Lev Atovmyan in 1949:

  1. Prelude—Moderato non troppo—Allegro
  2. Scene at the river—Adagio
  3. Attack—Allegro molto
  4. In the garden ('Vocalise')—Andante
  5. Storming of the Seelow Heights—Moderato con moto—Maestoso
  6. In the destroyed village—Andante
  7. Scene in the metro—Allegro
  8. Finale—Moderato non troppo—Allegro

Lyrics of Nos. 1 ('Glory to Stalin') and 8 by Yevgeni Dolmatovsky; No. 4 wordless S.A.T.B. chorus.
      A song from the film score 'Beautiful Day', with lyric by Ye. Dolmatovsky, arranged for two-part children's choir and piano by the composer.
      Prelude, 'March to the Treasurer', and Finale transcribed for military band by Ivan Petrov.

The complete score of 18 items was edited into 16 numbers in the order they appeared in the two parts of the film by conductor Adriano in 1996.

Instrumentation of Suite Opus 82a: as for the film score less 2 horns, 1 harp, and children's choir. S.A.T.B. chorus in Nos. 1, 4, and 8.

Music: Autograph of the film score preserved at the Glinka Museum.

Muzgiz, No. 20695 (in *Songs of the Soviet Cinema* with Op. 80a No. 8 and sixteen other songs), 1950, Suite Opus 82a No. 1, 28.5 cm.

Muzgiz, 1950, song 'Beautiful Day'.

Muzgiz, No. 21760, 1952, Suite Opus 82a full score, 34.5 cm.

Sovetskii Kompozitor, No. 519 (in *D. Shostakovich: Songs*), 1958, song 'Beautiful Day' with piano accompaniment, 29 cm.

Muzyka, No. 10497 (in album *We sing, play and dance,* Issue 2), 1979, song 'Beautiful Day' arr. for voice and piano, 29 cm.

Muzyka, No. 10179 (in Volume 34 of *Collected Works* with Opp. 88 and 136, and songs), 1985, 'Beautiful Day' and 'Vocalise', 30 cm.

Muzyka, No. 10890 (in Volume 42 of *Collected Works* with Opp. 75, 78, 80, 95, 97, 111, 116, 132, and 137), 1987, five items listed under 'Form', 30 cm.

Duration: Film: 2308 and 2273 metres. Suite Opus 82a: 23' 14"–30' 20"; 20 minutes (Sadovnikov).

Recordings: USSR: 18361-2 (10" 78 rpm). Finale only. USSR Radio Symphony Orchestra and Chorus, Aleksandr GAUK. P 1950.

USSR: 19564-19335 (10" 78 rpm). Song 'Beautiful Day'. Kaliningrad Children's Choir of Moscow. A. CHMYREV (chorus-master). [Khachaturyan.] P 1951. *Reissued:* USSR: MK D 5062-3 (10" mono). [Songs from Opp. 33, 72, 80, 86, and 99.] I 1959.

USA: Classics Edition CEC 3009 B (mono). Suite Nos. 1, 4, 5, 6, and 8. USSR Radio Symphony Orchestra and Chorus, Aleksandr GAUK. [Khachaturyan.] P c.1952.

USSR: Melodiya C12 16719009. Fanfare. Bolshoi Theatre Wind Orchestra, Vladimir ANDROPOV. ['Fanfares by Soviet Composers'—Op. 30 Fanfare; Shebalin, Eshpai, Shchedrin *et al.*] I 1982c.

RCA Victor Red Seal Compact Disc RD 60226. Complete Suite Nos. 1–8. Belgian Radio Symphony Orchestra and Chorus, José SEREBRIER. ['Film Music of Shostakovich, Volume 3'—Opp. 78 and 30.] P 1988?, I Aug. 1990, G Mar. 1991.

Germany: Capriccio Compact Disc 10 405. Complete Suite Nos. 1–8. Berlin Radio Symphony Orchestra and Chorus, Mikhail YUROVSKY. [Op. 64a.] P 4–6 Mar. 1991, I Oct. 1995. NB. The choral parts are played by the orchestra in Nos. 1 and 8 though No. 4 includes the S.A.T.B. chorus as in the full score.

Note: Suite Not 5, 'Shturm Zeyelovskikh Vysot', has been translated as 'The storming of Zeyelov Heights', 'Attack on Zeyelovsky Heights', and

'Attack on Zeeloubky Height'. Seelow is 30 miles due east of Berlin and was the scene of a ferocious battle. Before dawn on 16 April 1945 General Zhukov directed batteries of searchlights to blind the Germans and to light their positions but the attack foundered in the smoke and glare. On the next day six armies, including two of tanks, failed to advance. Two inroads were made on the 18th but with no breakthrough. Stalin then ordered Zhukov to reach Berlin by the north of the Heights. A monument commemorates the battle.

Sans op. P   Collections of Light Pieces

(i) *Ballet Suites Nos. 1, 2, 3, and 4*

Form: Four suites of light orchestral music assembled from Shostakovich's ballet, stage, and film scores by the composer then prepared for publication by Lev Atovmyan in 1949 (No. 1—published 1950), 1951 (No. 2), 1952 (No. 3), and 1953 (No. 4):

As published	*Composer's original order and titles where different*
Suite No. 1:	
1. Lyric Waltz—Sans op. E	1/1. Waltz in G minor
2. Dance (Pizzicato)—Opus 39	1/4. Polka Pizzicato
3. Romance—Opus 39	1/6.
4. Polka—Opus 39	1/2. Dance
5. Waltz-scherzo—Opus 27	1/7. Petite Ballerina
6. Galop—Opus 39	1/8.
Suite No. 2:	
1. Waltz—Opus 39	2/1.
2. Adagio—Opus 39	1/3.
3. Polka—Sans op. E	2/3.
4. Sentimental Romance—Opus 36	—
5. Spring Waltz—Opus 78	3/1.
6. Finale (Galop)—Opus 39	2/4.
—	2/2. Nocturne—Opus 39
Suite No. 3:	
1. Waltz—Opus 37	3/5. Waltz in A major
2. Gavotte—Opus 37	3/4.
3. Dance—Opus 39	3/2. Dance in C major
4. Elegy—Opus 37	3/3. Elegy (Romance)
5. Waltz—Opus 39	1/5. Lyric Waltz
6. Galop—Opus 39	3/6. Finale (Galop in F major)

The second item of the four-piece Original Suite No. 2 is the Nocturne from Opus 39 which does not appear in the Published Suites Nos. 1–3.

Suite No. 4:
1. Prelude (Variations)—Andante (quasi Largo)—Opus 39
2. Waltz—Allegretto quasi Allegro—Opus 95
3. Scherzo—Allegro vivo—Opus 27

Instrumentation for all four suites: 3 flutes (III = piccolo), 3 oboes (III = cor anglais), E flat clarinet, 2 B flat clarinets, 2 bassoons, contrabassoon ~ 4 horns, 3 trumpets, 3 trombones, tuba ~ timpani, triangle, tambourine, side drum, cymbals ~ xylophone, celesta, harp (in Suites Nos. 3 and 4), piano (in Suites Nos. 1 and 2) ~ strings.

Composed: 1930–53.

Première: UK broadcast: 16 November 1974, Suite No. 1, BBC Northern Ireland Orchestra, Proinnsias O'Duinn.

Arrangements: Individual items from the suites variously transcribed—see under the original opus numbers.

   Ballet Russe. A selection from the Published Suites Nos. 1 and 2 by G. Schirmer, Inc.: Galop In (Suite No. 1/6), Pizzicato (No. 1/2), Petite Ballerina (No. 1/5), Serenade for Cello (No. 2/2), Playful Polka (No. 2/3), Romance for Trumpet (No. 2/4), Waltz (No. 2/1), Polka (No. 1/4), Grand Waltz (No. 1/1), and Galop (No. 2/6).

Music: Suite No. 1 originally published as Opus 84.

   Muzgiz, No. 20977, 1950, Suite No. 1, full score, 30 cm.

   Muzgiz, No. 21430, 1951, Suite No. 2, full score, 30 cm.

   Muzgiz, No. 22252, 1952, Suite No. 3, full score, 30 cm.

   Muzgiz, No. 23220, 1953, Suite No. 4, full score, 29.5 cm.

   G. Schirmer, *c.*1953, *Ballet Russe*, score and parts.

Duration: Published Suites—No. 1: 11' 45"–14' 06"; 12' 45"–12' 50" (Plaistow); 20 minutes (Sadovnikov).

   No. 2: 17' 45"–20' 10"; 12 minutes (Sadovnikov).

   No. 3: 15' 35"–17' 32"; 16 minutes (Sadovnikov).

   No. 4: 12' 40"; 16 minutes (Sadovnikov).

Ballets: *Dance Suite.* Eight numbers (Introduction, Spring Waltz, Polka, Elegy, Gavotte, Waltz, Galop, and Coda) selected from the Ballet Suites by Aleksei Varlamov, performed at the Bolshoi Theatre, Moscow, in 1959.

   Ballet School or *Leçon de Danse.* A ballet to choreography of Asaf Messerer and music of Glazunov, Lyadov, Lyapunov, Rubenstein, and Shostakovich arranged by Aleksandr Tseitlin. First version performed on 6 May 1961 in Brussels by the Ballet of the 20th Century under the French title. Given in a revised form on 17 September 1962 at the Metropolitan Opera House, New York, by the Bolshoi Ballet. Later danced entirely to the music of Shostakovich adapted from the Ballet Suites.

Just for Fun. Ray Powell, Australian Ballet; Sydney, Her Majesty's Theatre, December 1962 and UK: Birmingham, *c.*1966. Revival: Northern
Dance Ballet, Manchester, 27 December 1975.

Epode. Gerald Arpino, Joffrey Ballet; San Antonio, Texas, 25 May 1979;
danced to the Adagio from Suite No. 2 with Aaron Shapinsky (cello) and
conducted by Terence Kern.

Switch Bitch. Trevor Wood, Festival Ballet; Coliseum, London, May
1982; based on a short story by Roald Dahl and danced to a selection of
pieces from the Ballet Suites.

The Overcoat. For details see under Opus 32.

Recordings: USSR: MK HD 00803-4 (8" mono). Original Suite No. 1. All-
Union Radio Symphony Orchestra, Aleksandr GAUK. P 1952. *Reissued:*
France: Le Chant du Monde LDXA 8046 (mono). [Prokofiev and
Kabalevsky.] I 1952 ~ USA: Vanguard VRS 6004. [Prokofiev.] ~ USSR:
27028-31 (4 sides 10" 78 rpm). I 1956 (after LP issue).

USSR: MK D 01474-5 (mono). Original Suite No. 3. Moscow Radio
Symphony Orchestra, Abram STASEVICH. [Khachaturyan.] P 1953. *Re-
issued:* USA: Classics Edition CE 3012 (mono). Original Suites Nos. 1,
2, and 3. All-Union Radio Symphony Orchestra, Aleksandr GAUK
(Nos. 1 and 2); Moscow Radio Symphony Orchestra, Abram STASEVICH
(No. 3).

USA: Columbia ML 4671 (mono). *Ballet Russe*—a selection from the
Published Ballet Suites Nos. 1 and 2 as listed under 'Arrangements'.
Bernard Greenhouse (cello), Robert Nagel (trumpet), Columbia Sym-
phony Orchestra, Efrem KURTZ. [Tchaikovsky.] P *c.*1953. *Reissued:* France:
Philips L 01 338 L (mono). [Op. 70.]

Poland: Muza 2386 (7" mono). Published/Original Suite No. 3, No. 6
only. Polish Radio Symphony Orchestra, Stefan RACHÓN. [Godard.] P
1954.

USA: Urania URLP 7146 (mono). Published Suite No. 1, labelled Op.
84. Berlin Radio Symphony Orchestra, Adolf Fritz GUHL. [Kabalevsky,
Prokofiev, and Borodin.] P 1955.

USA: Columbia Ml 6267 (mono) and MS 6867. Published Suites No. 1,
Nos. 5, 2, and 6; No. 2, Nos. 3 and 6. André KOSTELANETZ and his Orchestra. [Opp. 22*a*, 97*a*, and 105 excerpts.] P New York 23 and 29 Nov. 1965.
Reissued: CBS BRG 72504 (mono) and SBRG 72504. [Opp. 97*a* and 105
excerpts.] G Feb. 1967 ~ CBS Classics 61220. [Opp. 97*a* and 105 excerpts.]
G May 1971 ~ Sony Classical Compact Disc SBK 62642. [Opp. 10, 22, 96,
97, and 105.] G June 1997.

Netherlands: Audiophile Classics APL 101.527. Published Suites Nos.
1 and 2. Moscow Symphony Orchestra, Emin KHACHATURYAN. [Stravin-
sky.] P 1960s?, I 2000.

USSR: Melodiya D 023999-024000 (mono) and C 01427-8. Published
Suites Nos. 1, 2, and 3. Viktor Elston (oboe), Ivan Pavlov (trumpet), Lev

Vainrot (cello), Bolshoi Theatre Orchestra, Maksim SHOSTAKOVICH. P 1966, I 1967. *Reissued:* USA: Angel Melodiya SR 40115. I 1959 ~ HMV Melodiya ASD 2781. [Op. 115.] G May 1972 ~ USSR: Melodiya C 01427-8. [In fourth box of Part 1 of *Collected Works on Records*.] I 1978 ~ USA: Musical Heritage Society MHS 824389. [In two-record set with Opp. 54 and 129.] I 1981 ~ Italy: EMI Italiana 3C165 95546-8 (fourth side in three-record Russian Ballet set). Suite No. 1, Nos. 2–6; Suite No. 2, No. 1; and Suite No. 3, 3–6. Labelled as all from *The Limpid Stream*, Op. 39, though tracks 4 and 8 derive from Opp. 27 and 37 respectively. [Glière.] ~ BMG Melodiya Compact Discs 74321 66981-2 (two-disc set). Suites Nos. 1, 2, and 3. [Opp. 27*a*, 22*a*, 64*a*, and 76*a*.] I Dec. 1999.

USSR: Melodiya C10 09559-60. Published Suite No. 3, Nos. 2 and 3. Central Television and All-Union Radio Symphony Orchestra, Konstantin IVANOV. ['Symphonic Miniatures'—Boccherini, Grieg, Dvořák *et al.*] P 1978, I 1978*c*.

USSR: Melodiya C50 20749 006. Suite No. 3, No. 4 only. labelled 'Lullaby', arr. for piano. Rimma BOBRITSKAYA (piano). ['For Children'—Opp. 69, 97*a*, and 3*a;* Sans opp. S and B.] P 1983, I 1984*c*.

Chandos ABRD 1370 (digital) and Compact Disc CHAN 8730. Suites Nos. 1, 2, and 3. Timothy Waldon (cello), John Gracie (trumpet), Scottish National Orchestra, Neeme JÄRVI. P Glasgow 22–6 Apr. 1988, I June 1988, G Sept. 1989. *Reissued:* Chandos Collect Series Compact Disc CHAN 6512. Suite No. 1, Nos. 1 and 6; Suite No. 2, No. 3; and Suite No. 3, No. 3. ['Russian Ballet Masterpieces'—Tchaikovsky, Glazunov, Prokofiev, and Stravinsky.] I Oct. 1990 ~ Chandos Compact Discs CHAN 7000/1 (two-disc set). [Opp. 27*a*, 114*a*, 96, and Sans op. P (i) No. 4.] I Sept. 1994, G May 1995.

Chandos ABRD 1319 (digital) and Compact Disc CHAN 8630. Suite No. 4. Scottish National Orchestra, Neeme JÄRVI. [Op. 93.] P Dundee 12 May 1988, I Dec. 1988, C Mar. 1989. *Reissued:* Conifer Classics Compact Disc Class 7006. [Op. 93.] I Nov. 1991 ~ Chandos Compact Discs 7000/1 (two-disc set). [Opp. 27*a*, 114*a*, 96, and Sans op. P (i) Nos. 1–3.] I Sept. 1994, G May 1995.

Germany: Cadenza Compact Disc C 8812-8. Suite No. 2, No. 2 Adagio (wrongly labelled 'Allegro') arr. Atovmyan. Marek JERIE (cello) and Ivan Klánský (piano). ['Russian Chamber Music'—Op. 40; and Stravinsky.] P Sept. 1988, I 1989.

France: Le Chant du Monde Russian Season Compact Disc LDC 288 034. Suite No. 3, No. 4 labelled 'Berceuse' arr. for piano. Rimma BOBRITSKAYA (piano). ['Russian Miniatures for Piano'—Sans op. S, Opp. 97 and 69; Tchaikovsky and Prokofiev.] P Moscow Conservatory Feb. 1991. *Reissued:* Le Chant du Monde Russian Season Compact Disc RUS 788034. [As 1991 recording.] I Mar. 1999.

USA: Sonora Compact Disc SO 22566CD. Suite No. 1, No. 5 arr. for piano duo. Natalia ZUSMAN and Inna HEIFETZ. ['The Revisionist's

Tale'—Op. 94; Schnittke, Glière, and Borodin.] P Boston, Mass. 1994, I Nov. 1995.

Australia: Tall Poppies Compact Disc TP 78. Suite No. 2, Nos. 2 and 5 arr. Pereira. David PEREIRA (cello) and David Bollard (piano). [Schumann, Brahms, Falla *et al.*] P Sydney June 1994.

RCA Victor Red Seal Compact Disc 09026 68304-2. Ballet Suites Nos. 1 and 3. Frankfurt Radio Symphony Orchestra, Dmitri KITAYENKO. [Sans Opp. E and G.] P Frankfurt 2–5 Jan. 1996, I Aug; 1997, G Oct. 1997.

USA: Pope Music Compact Disc PM 1015-2 (silver) and PMG 2015-2 (gold). Suite No. 1, No. 6 labelled as 'The Street'. Russian Symphony Orchestra, Mark GORENSTEIN. ['Russian Pops'—Opp. 97 and 16; Dunayevsky, Khrennikov, Sviridov *et al.*] P Moscow Conservatory Sept. 1996. NB. From Op. 39 not Op. 27 as stated and the ballets 'The Prayer' and 'The Apparition', mentioned in the liner note, refer to Nos. 6 and 8 of *The Young Lady and the Hooligan.*

France: Saison Russe Compact Disc 288149. Ballet Suite No. 1. Russian Symphony Orchestra, Mark GORENSTEIN. [Glinka, Musorgsky, Tchaikovsky *et al.*] P Mosfilm Studios, Moscow Dec. 1996. *Reissued:* France: Le Chant du Monde Russian Season Compact Disc RUS 288164. Ballet Suite No. 1. [Opp. 97, 27, and 69.] I July 1999, G Nov. 1999.

Germany: Obligat Classics Compact Disc ob.01.230. Ballet Suite No. 1. Russian Symphony Orchestra, Mark GORENSTEIN. [Tchaikovsky and Glazunov.] P Munich 29 Sept. and I Oct. 1998.

USA: Delos Compact Disc DE 3257. Suite No. 1, Nos. 1, 2, 4, 5, and 6; Suite No. 2, Nos. 1 and 5*; Suite No. 3, Nos. 1*, 3, 5, and 6; and Suite No. 4, No. 2*. Moscow Chamber Orchestra, Constantine ORBELIAN. ['Waltzes'—see Samplers.] P Moscow Conservatory 12–14 July 1999, G Dec. 1999. NB. In the liner note the waltzes marked * are listed under their opus numbers 78, 37, and 95 respectively.

(ii) *Four Waltzes*

Form: Four light pieces arranged and transcribed by Lev Atovmyan for flute/piccolo, B flat clarinet, and piano:

1. Spring Waltz—Allegretto—for clarinet and piano
   From *Michurin,* Opus 78*a* No. 3.
2. Waltz-scherzo—Allegretto scherzando—for flute and piano
   From *The Bolt,* Opus 27.
3. Waltz—*Tempo di valse*—for flute, clarinet, and piano
   From *The Return of Maxim,* Opus 45 (also Opus 50*a* No. 4).
4. Barrel Organ Waltz—Allegretto—for piccolo, clarinet, and piano
   From *The Gadfly,* Opus 97*a* No. 5. [The English title 'Waltz Charmaine' is an erroneous translation of 'Sharmanka'—the Russian word for barrel organ.]

Music: Sovetskii Kompozitor, No. 536, 1958, 29 cm.

Musica Rara, No. 1093, 1966, parts, 30 cm.

Hans Sikorski, No. 2333, 1983, parts, 31.5 cm.

Duration: 9' 14"–9' 37"; 9' 30"–9' 35" (Plaistow).

Recordings: Germany: ECM New Series 1-25037 (two-record set). Nos. 1 and 2. Eduard BRUNNER (clarinet), Irene Grafenhaver (flute), and Oleg Maizenberg (piano). [Op. 11; Caplet, Franck, Poulenc *et al.*] P Lockenhaus Festival concert 1981. *Reissued:* Germany: ECM New Series Compact Discs 827 024-2 (two-disc set). [As LPs.]

Chandos Compact Disc CHAN 8769. No. 1 only. Duncan PRESCOTT (clarinet) and Scott Mitchell (piano). ['Solo'—Young British Virtuoso Musicians from the Thames TV series: Op. 40; Grandjany, Chopin, Fauré *et al.*] P Clandon Park, Surrey Mar. 1988.

France: Adda Compact Disc 581185. Nos. 1, 2, and 3. Loïc POULAIN (flute), Philippe CUPER (clarinet), and Jacques DELANNOY (piano). ['Russian Music for the Clarinet'—Prokofiev, Khachaturyan, Glazunov, and Stravinsky.] P Paris 1988–89, I 1990.

Switzerland: Tudor Compact Disc 727. Nos. 1–4. András ADORJÁN (flute and piccolo), Eduard BRUNNER (clarinet), and Robert LEVIN (piano). [Prokofiev and Lobanov.] P Munich 20 Feb. 1989, I 1990.

Virgin Classics Compact Disc VC7 59312-2. Nos. 1–4. NASH ENSEMBLE (Phillipa Davies—flute and piccolo, Michael Collins—clarinet, and Ian Brown—piano). [Opp. 57 and 67.] P London Nov. 1990, I Aug. 1993.

(iii) Three Violin Duets

Form: Three light pieces arranged by Konstantin Fortunatov for two violins with piano accompaniment:

1. Prelude—Molto moderato
   From *The Gadfly*, Opus 97*a*—a truncated version of No. 7.
2. Gavotte—Tranquillo, molto leggerio
   From *The Human Comedy*, Opus 37 No. 18.
3. Waltz—*Tempo di valse*
   From *The Return of Maxim*, Opus 45 (also Opus 50*a* No. 4).

Music: Sovetskii Kompozitor, No. 4179 (in *D. Shostakovich: Pieces for violin and piano*), 1975, 28.5 cm.

Kalmus, Melville, New York, No. 4639, 1970s, score and 2 parts, 30 cm.

Duration: 6' 35"–7' 20".

Recordings: HMV ASD 3861. Labelled 'Praeludium', 'Gavotte', and 'Waltzes'. Itzhak PERLMAN and Pinchas ZUKERMAN (violins) and Samuel Sanders (piano). [Moszkowski and Prokofiev.] P New York 1–2 June 1978, G July 1980. American Grammy Award 1980—winner of Chamber Music category. *Reissued:* USA: Angel SZ 37668. [Moszkowski and Prokofiev.] ~ Germany: Elec 065-003 787. [Moszkowski and Prokofiev.] ~

France: EMI 069 03787 [Moszkowski and Prokofiev.] ~ EMI Matrix Compact Disc CDM5 65994-2. [Bartók and Prokofiev.] I Sept. 1996.
Belgium: Arcobaleno/Start Classics Compact Disc AAOC 93262. André and Yaga SIWY (violins) and Daniel Blümenthal (piano). [Martinů, Milhaud, and Moszkowski.] P Brussels 18–19 May 1992, I Dec. 1994.
Austria: ORF Compact Disc CD 205. MARTHA & VAHID KHADEM-MISSAGH (violins) and Meinhard Prinz (piano). [Sarasate, Bériot, Paganini *et al.*] P Vienna Sept.–Oct. 1998, I 1999.
Black Box Compact Disc BBM 1042. Nos. 1 and 2. AMIR and Marat BISENGALIEV (violin duo) and John Leneham (piano). [Four other Shostakovich violin duets not cross-referenced (Polka Ballet Suite No. 1, 4; 'Waltz of Remembrance' No. 5 in *Roundabout of Dances*; Elegy Ballet Suite No. 3, 4; and 'Spanish Dance' Opus 97*a* No. 3)—Wieniawski, Tchaikovsky, Vieuxtemps *et al.*] P Potton Hall, Suffolk 29 Feb. 2000, I Nov. 2000.

Opus 83   Quartet No. 4 in D major

Form: String quartet in four movements:

1. Allegretto
2. Andantino
3. Allegretto *attacca*
4. Allegretto

Composed: April–27 December 1949, mainly at Moscow. First three movements completed on 4 May, 1 June, and 28 August; fourth movement commenced at Sochi in November.
Dedication: In memory of Pyotr Vladimirovich Vilyams (designer). [Not noted on the published score.]
Premières: 3 December 1953, Moscow Conservatory Malyi Hall; Beethoven Quartet (Dmitri Tsyganov, Vasili Shirinsky, Vadim Borisovsky, and Sergei Shirinsky).
   Opus 83*a*: 20 July 1990, BBC Radio 3; BBC Welsh Symphony Orchestra, Rudolf Barshai.
   10 January 1991, Free Trade Hall, Manchester; Hallé Orchestra, R. Barshai. (Broadcast on BBC Radio 3, 26 June 1992).
Arrangements: Arranged for two pianos four hands by the composer and Anatoli Dmitriev. Andantino transcribed for violin and piano by Dmitri Tsyganov. Quartet arranged for strings and piano by Mikhail Turich.
   Opus 83*a*—Chamber Symphony: for small orchestra by Rudolf Barshai in 1990 (Instrumentation: flute, oboe, cor anglais, clarinet (B flat and bass), bassoon ~ 2 horns, trumpet (C and B flat) ~ side drum/whip/gong ~ xylophone/marimba/celesta ~ strings).

Music: Autograph score preserved at the Glinka Museum.
Muzgiz, No. 24262, 1954, score, 20 cm.
Musica Rara, No. 1035, 1961, score, 18.5 cm.
Musica Rara, No. 1035*a*, 1961, parts, 31 cm.
Muzgiz, No. 30662, 1963, parts, 29 cm.
Muzyka, Leningrad, No. 285 (in Volume 1 with Quartets 1–3 arr. for piano four hands by A. Dmitriev), 1965, 29.5 cm.
Edition Eulenberg, No. 388, 1970, score, 19 cm.
Edition Peters, No. 5754, 1973, parts, 30 cm.
Edition Peters, No. 12903, 1977, parts, 29 cm.
Kalmus, Melville, New York, No. 9682, 1970s, parts.
Muzyka, No. 9816 (in Volume 35 of *Collected Works* Quartets 1–8), 1979, 30 cm.
Hans Sikorski, No. 2265 (with Opp. 49, 68, and 73), 1980, score, 21 cm.
Hans Sikorski, No. 2244, 1981, parts, 31.5 cm.
DSCH Publishers, Moscow, 1995, full score and parts of R. Barshai's instrumentation available for hire.

Duration: Approx. 22 minutes in score; 20' 46"–26' 25"; 26' 30" (Plaistow). Opus 83*a*—26' 37"–26' 58".

Recordings: USSR: MK D 2291-2 (10" mono). TCHAIKOVSKY QUARTET (Yulian Sitkovetsky, Anton Sharoyev, Rudolf Barshai, Yakov Slobodkin). P 1954. *Reissued:* USA: Vanguard VRS 6021 (mono). [Op. 92.] I 1955 ~ USSR: MK D 028031-2 (mono). [Op. 73.] I 1970.

Czech: Supraphon SUA 10188 (mono) and SUA ST 50045 (also SUA ST 50188). JANÁČEK QUARTET (Jiří Trávnícek, Adolf Sykora, Jiří Kratochvíl, Karel Krafka). [Op. 57.] P 1960. *Reissued:* USA: Artia ALP 188 (mono) and ALPS 188. [Op. 57.] I 1961, G Mar. 1962.

USSR: MK D 09615-7 and D 09799 (1 side in two-record set, mono). BEETHOVEN QUARTET (personnel as at première). [Op. 65.] P 1962, G July 1966. *Reissued:* USSR: Melodiya D 015665-09799 (mono). [Op. 73.] I 1965 ~ USA: Consonance Blue Label Compact Disc 81.3005 (mono). [Vol. 1—Opp. 49 and 68.] I May 1995.

USA: Mercury MG 50309 (mono) and SR 90309. BORODIN QUARTET (Rostislav Dubinsky, Yaroslav Aleksandrov, Dmitri Shebalin, Valentin Berlinsky). [Op. 110.] P Moscow 1962. *Reissued:* USSR: Melodiya D 019271-2 (mono) and C 01435-6. [Op. 101.] I 1967 ~ USA: Seraphim Melodiya S 6034. [In three-record box set with Quartets 1–3 and 5.] ~ HMV Melodiya HQS 1321 in Set SLS 879. [Op. 92.] G June 1974.

Leningrad Masters Compact Disc LM 1325. TANEYEV QUARTET (personnel not stated). [Op. 49 and 73.] P concert 1963, G Sept. 1996.

USSR: Melodiya D 17635-6 (10" mono). *Andantino* arr. D. Tsyganov. Viktor DANCHENKO (violin) and Mikhail Muntyan (piano). P 1966.

USSR: Melodiya D 026389-90 (mono). *Andantino* arr. D. Tsyganov. Vladimir MALININ (violin) and M. Stern (piano). [Mozart, Schubert, Sarasate *et al.*] P 1969.

USSR: Melodiya D 027229-30 (mono). LITHUANIAN STATE QUARTET (Eugeniyus Paulauskas, Korneliya Kalinauskayte, Yuri Fledzhinskas, R. Kulikauskas). [Bartók.] P 1970.

Sweden: Caprice RIKS LP 24. SAULESCO QUARTET (Mircea Saulesco, Claes Nilsson, Holger Hanson, Åke Olofsson). [Welin and Wirén.] P Stockholm 26–7 May 1971, G Dec. 1974.

USSR: Melodiya CM 03707-8. TANEYEV QUARTET (Vladimir Ovcharek, Grigori Lutsky, Vissarion Soloviev, Iosif Levinzon). [Bartók.] P Leningrad Nov. 1971, I 1973. *Reissued:* USSR: Melodiya C10 11613-4. [In first box of Part 2 of *Collected Works on Records* with Op. 133.] I 1980 ~ Japan: JVC Victor 5346. [Op. 73.] ~ USSR: Melodiya Compact Disc SUCD11 00308. [Opp. 49 and 92.] I 1991c ~ France: Praga Compact Disc PR 245 054. [Opp. 73 and 67.] P given as Czech Radio 1976, I July 1994.

Saydisc Amon Ra SAR 1. DARTINGTON QUARTET (Colin Sauer, Malcolm Latchem, Keith Lovell, Michael Evans). [Op. 117.] P 1973, G May 1973.

L'Oiseau-Lyre DSLO 23. FITZWILLIAM QUARTET (Christopher Rowland, Jonathan Sparey, Alan George, Ioan Davies). [Op. 133.] P Sept. 1976, G Nov. 1977. *Gramophone* Record Awards 1977—winner of Chamber Music category, G Mar. 1978. *Reissued:* Decca 188 D3 in Set D 188 D7. [Op. 92.] G Feb. 1981 ~ Decca Enterprise Compact Discs 433 078-2DM6. [On second disc of six-disc set with Op. 73.] I Apr. 1992, G June 1992.

USSR: Melodiya C10 28377 008. SHOSTAKOVICH QUARTET (Andrei Shishlov, Sergei Pishchugin, Aleksandr Galkovsky, Aleksandr Korchagin). [Op. 101.] P 1981, I 1990a. *Reissued:* Olympia Compact Disc OCD 531. ['Complete Quartets, Vol. 1'—Opp. 49 and 73; Sans op. D.] I Apr. 1994, G Sept. 1994.

USSR: Melodiya C10 19535 003. BORODIN QUARTET (Mikhail Kopelman, Andrei Abramenkov, Dmitri Shebalin, Valentin Berlinsky). [Op. 101.] P 1982, I 1984a. *Reissued:* HMV Melodiya EX 270339-3 (DMM). [In seven-record box set of 15 Quartets plus Quintet.] G Mar. 1986 ~ EMI Compact Disc CDC7 49268-2. [Opp. 101 and 122.] I Nov. 1987, G Sept. 1988 ~ Japan: Victor Musical Industries Compact Disc VICC 40019. [Op. 73.] I 1990 ~ EMI Compact Discs CMS5 65032-2. [In six-disc set of 15 Quartets plus Quintet.] I Mar. 1994 ~ BMG Melodiya Compact Discs 74321 40711-2 (six-disc set). [Opp. 49 and 68.] I June 1997.

Academy Sound and Vision DCA 631 (DMM) and Compact Disc CD DCA 631. COULL QUARTET (Roger Coull, Philip Gallaway, David Curtis, John Todd). [Opp. 101 and 122.] P London Mar. 1988, I and G Apr. 1989.

Teldec Classics Compact Disc 2292 46009-2. BRODSKY QUARTET (Michael Thomas, Ian Belton, Paul Cassidy, Jacqueline Thomas). [Opp. 49 and 73.] P Berlin July 1989, I Apr. 1990, G June 1990. *Reissued:* Teldec Compact Discs 9031 71702-2. [On second disc of six-disc set with Op. 73.] I Nov. 1990, G June 1992.

USA: ESS.A.Y. Compact Disc CD 1008. MANHATTAN QUARTET (Eric Lewis, Roy Lewis, John Dexter, Judith Glyde). [Op. 92.] P Jersey City

15–18 Jan. 1990. *Reissued:* Koch Schwann Musica Mundi Compact Disc 310 129. ['Complete String Quartets, Vol. 2' with Op. 92.] I Aug. 1991.

Deutsche Grammophon Compact Disc 435 386-2GH. Chamber Symphony Op. 83*a* arr. Barshai. Chamber Orchestra of Europe, Rudolf BARSHAI. [Op. 73*a*.] P Berlin Feb. 1991, I July 1992, G Aug. 1992.

Lydian Compact Disc 18133 (also Donau DCD 8133). MOYZES QUARTET (Stanislav Mucha, František Török, Alexander Lakatoš, Ján Slávik). [Op. 68.] P Bratislava 22–5 Jan. 1992, I 1994. *Reissued:* Dillon Classics Compact Disc 28133. [Op. 68.] I 1996.

Naxos Compact Disc 8.550972. ÉDER QUARTET (György Selmeczi, Péter Szüts, Sándor Papp, György Éder). ['Complete Quartets, Vol. 1'—Opp. 101 and 108.] P Budapest 1–4 Dec. 1993, I July 1994.

Deutsche Grammophon Compact Disc 445 864-2CH. HAGEN QUARTET (Lukas Hagen, Rainer Schmidt, Veronika and Clemens Hagen). [Opp. 122 and 142.] P Polling Dec. 1993, I July 1995, G Sept. 1995.

Sony Classical St Petersburg Classics Compact Disc SK 64584. ST PETERSBURG QUARTET (Alla Aranovskaya, Ilya Teplyakov, Andrei Dogadin, Leonid Shukayev). [Opp. 49 and 68.] P Apr. 1994.

Finland: Finlandia Compact Disc 4509 98997-2. SIBELIUS ACADEMY QUARTET (Eikki Kantola, Seppo Tukiainen, Veikko Kosonen, Arto Noras). [Op. 73.] P Järvenpää May 1994, I May 1996.

Germany: Beaux Compact Disc BEAU 2022. Arr. for strings and piano. Novosibirsk Chamber Orchestra, Mikhail TURICH. [Opp. 73 and 34.] P 1995, I Sept. 2001.

Carlton Classics Compact Disc 30366 0062-2. KREUTZER QUARTET (Peter Sheppard, Gordon MacKay, Bridget Carey, Neil Hyde). [Opp. 108 and 110.] P Loughton Jan. 1996, I July 1997, G Awards (Nov.) 1997.

Netherlands: Globe Compact Disc GLO 5157-0265. RUBIO QUARTET (Dirk Van de Velde, Dirk Van den Hauwe, Marc Sonnaert, Peter Devos). ['Complete Quartets, Vol. 1'—Opp. 49 and 110.] P Utrecht Aug. 1996, I Nov. 1996.

Linn Compact Disc CKD 065. SCHIDLOF QUARTET (Ofer Falk, Rafael Todes, Graham Oppenheimer, Oleg Kogan). [Opp. 108 and 57.] P Horsham 3–5 Oct. 1996, I May 1997, G Oct. 1997.

USA: Arabesque Compact Disc Z 6711. Chamber Symphony. Israel Sinfonietta, Uri MAYER. [Op. 110*a*.] P Meneham July 1997.

France: Arion Compact Disc ARN 68461. DEBUSSY QUARTET (Christophe Collette. Dominique Lonca, Vincent Deprecq, Yannick Callier). ['Complete Quartets, Vol. 1'—Opp. 110 and 138.] P Lyon July 1998, I July 1999.

Chandos Compact Disc CHAN 9769. SORREL QUARTET (Gina McCormack, Catherine Yates, Vicci Wardman, Helen Thatcher). ['Complete Quartets, Vol. 2'—Opp. 73 and 122.] P Westleton, Suffolk 29 Sept.–1 Oct. 1998, I Jan. 2000.

Hyperion Compact Disc CDA 67154. ST PETERSBURG QUARTET (Alla Aranovskaya, Ilya Teplyakov, Konstantin Kats, Leonid Shukayev). [Opp. 101 and 110.] P St Petersburg, Apr. 1999, I Dec. 1999, G Mar. 2000.

Deutsche Grammophon Compact Disc 463 284-2GH5 (five-disc set). EMERSON QUARTET (Eugene Drucker, Philip Setzer, Lawrence Dutton, David Finkel). ['Complete Quartets, Vol. 2'—Opp. 92 and 101.] P Aspen, Colorado concert June–July 1999, G June 2000.

Opus 84   Two Romances on Verses by Lermontov

Form: Two song settings on verses by Mikhail Lermontov, for male voice and piano:

1. Ballad ('A beautiful maiden sits by the sea')—Moderato
2. Morning in the Caucasus—Moderato con moto

Composed: 24 (Muzyka score gives 25–6) June 1950, at Komarovo village, Gulf of Finland.

Première: 2 October 1984, Duisberg, Germany, International Shostakovich Festival radio concert; Irina Bogacheva (mezzo-soprano) and Igor Lebedev (piano).

Music: Autograph score preserved at the CIS Archives of Literature and Art. Muzyka, No. 10283 (in Volume 32 of *Collected Works* with Opp. 4, 21, 46, 62, 79, 86, 91, 98, 100 *et al.*), 1982, 30 cm.

Duration: (1) 5' 22" and (2) 2' 46".

Recordings: —

Note: Sadovnikov and other catalogues state that this work is for male voice though the world première was performed by a mezzo-soprano. The *Collected Works* Volume 32 mentions simply 'for voice and piano'.

Opus 85   Belinsky

Form: Music for the biographical film *Belinsky,* based on the life of the literary critic Vissarion Belinsky, with scre.enplay by Yuri German and Galina Serebrovskaya, and directed by Grigori Kozintsev for Lenfilm. The fabric of the film score, for orchestra and chorus, makes use of Fyodosi Rubtsov's collection of Russian folksongs of the mid-nineteenth century. The film opens with a pedlar singing such a song, 'In the Blue Sea', and others are No. 6—'If young lady-mistresses', No. 11—'Girl's Song' (or 'My Talk') and No. 13 'Oh, Little Rowan-tree' (included in the Suite Opus 85a), and No. 18—'Ah! My Love is not alone in the field'.

Composed: 1950.

Première: Film first shown on 4 June 1953. Danilevich (1980) states that the film was not released.

Arrangements: Opus 85*a*—Suite assembled by Lev Atovmyan in 1960:

1. Overture—Allegro
2. Sorrowful Ditty ('Girl's Song'—words traditional—combined with 'Oh, Little Rowan-tree'—words traditional)—Adagio
3. The Strength of the People (lyric by Viktor Nekrasov)—Allegro molto
4. Interlude—Moderato, Pesante *attacca*
5. Song without words ('Vocalise')—Moderato
6. Scene—Moderato con moto *attacca*
7. Finale—Allegro molto

No. 2 for female chorus, clarinet obbligato, and orchestral interludes, in simplified reduction by Aleksandr Pirumov.

No. 3 arranged for male chorus and piano by the composer.

'Oh, Little Rowan-tree' reconstructed from the autograph choral parts, as a separate song for unaccompanied male chorus, by Boris Tiles.

Instrumentation of Suite Opus 85*a*:   piccolo, 2 flutes, 3 oboes, 3 B flat clarinets, 2 bassoons, contrabassoon ~ 4 horns, 3 trumpets, 3 trombones, tuba ~ timpani, triangle, side drum, cymbals, bass drum, gong ~ glockenspiel, xylophone, orchestral bells, harp ~ S.A.T.B. chorus ~ strings.

Music: Autograph of the film score preserved at the Glinka Museum.

Sovetskii Kompozitor, No. 519 (in *D. Shostakovich: Songs*), 1958, 'Girl's Song' combined with 'Oh, Little Rowan-tree', and Nos. 3 and 5 of the Suite, with piano accompaniment, 29 cm.

Sovetskii Kompozitor, No. 1512, 1960, Suite Opus 85*a*, full score, 29 cm.

Muzyka, No. 10179 (in Volume 34 of *Collected Works* with Opp. 88 and 136, and songs), 1985, four choruses—'The Strength of the People', 'My Talk', 'Oh, Little Rowan-tree', and 'Vocalise'—with piano accompaniment, 30 cm.

Recording: USA: Citadel Compact Disc CTD 88135. Suite Op. 85*a*. Belarus Radio and TV Symphony Orchestra and State Chorus, Walter MNAT-SAKANOV. [Opp. 50*a* and 76.] P Moscow 7 Apr. 1997, I 1999.

Note: Vissarion Grigorievich Belinsky (1811–48) was a Russian literary critic and journalist, famous for his analyses of the works of Dostoyevsky, Gogol, Lermontov, and Pushkin.

Opus 86   Four Songs to Words by Dolmatovsky

Form: Four popular songs for voice and wordless chorus a cappella (No. 1) and piano (Nos. 2, 3, and 4), to lyrics by Yevgeni Dolmatovsky:

1. The Homeland Hears (alternatively 'The Motherland Hears' or 'My Country Hearkens')—Allegretto poco moderato [Solemnly in arrangement]

2. Rescue me—Moderato
3. He loves me, he loves me not (or 'We have many girls in the city')—
   Allegretto
4. Sleep, my darling boy (Lullaby)—Moderato

Composed: 1950-1, at Moscow.

Space première: 12 April 1961, 'The Homeland Hears' sung by Yuri Gagarin in orbit of the earth—the first song to be sung in space. [Following Gagarin's example, astronaut Buzz Aldrin reported that a tape recording of 'Fly Me to the Moon', sung by Frank Sinatra, was played on the Moon's Sea of Tranquility on 20 July 1969.]

Arrangements: No. 1 arranged for voice and piano by the composer; also for choir; and the theme used as the signature tune for the USSR Radio news broadcasts.

Music: Autographs of Nos. 1, 3, and 4 preserved at the Glinka Museum. No. 2 is missing and No. 4 appears in two versions with differing words and key signatures (E minor and E major). The autograph of the voice and piano arrangement of No. 1 is in the Shostakovich family archive. A handwritten copy of No. 2 is stored at the CIS Archives of Literature and Art.

    Muzgiz, 1951, Nos. 1, 3, and 4.

    Sovetskii Kompozitor, No. 519 (in *D. Shostakovich: Songs*), 1958, Nos. 1, 2, and 4, 29 cm.

    Edition Peters, No. 4733, 1958, 'Wiegenlied' No. 4 only, German text by B. Tutenberg, 27 cm.

    Muzichna Ukraina, No. 42 (with three other Shostakovich songs), 1976, No. 1 for tenor and S.A.T.B. chorus (Russian text and also Ukrainian lyric by K. Drok), 26 cm.

    Muzyka, No. 10283 (in Volume 32 of *Collected Works* with Opp. 4, 21, 46, 62, 79, 84, 91, 98, 100 *et al.*), 1982, Nos. 1-4 for voice and piano (No. 4 in E major), 30 cm.

    Muzyka, No. 10179 (in Volume 34 of *Collected Works* with Opp. 88 and 136, and songs), 1985, No. 1 for voice and chorus a cappella, 30 cm.

    Sovetskii Kompozitor, No. 7815 (in *Romances and Songs to verses of Yevgeni Dolmatovsky* with Opp. 80, 98, and Sans op. X), 1987, No. 1 melody and three verses, 29 cm.

Duration: 9' 22"; No. 1: 2' 30"–3' 52".

Recordings: USSR: 19120 (10" 78 rpm). No. 1 only. Nina POSTAVNICHEVA and chorus. P 1951.

    USSR: 21348-21717 (10" 78 rpm). No. 1 only. Zhenya TALANOV and RSFSR Academic Russian Choir. [Kompaneyets.] P 1952. *Reissued:* USSR MK D 5062-3 (10" mono). [Songs from Opp. 33, 72, 80, 82, 99 *et al.*] I 1959 ~ USSR: Melodiya CM 03397-400. ['Moscow Souvenir', second record of double album—Kholminov, Pokrass, Fradkin *et al.*] I 1973 ~ USSR: Melodiya C60 09369-70. ['Moscow Souvenir', second

record of double album—Kholminov, Kolmanovsky, Soloviev-Sedoi *et al.*] I 1978c.
    USSR: 34339-40 (10" 78 rpm). No. 1 only. Lithuanian State Choir, Konradas KAVYATSKAS (chorus-master). [Kavyatskas.] P 1960.
    Chapter One CHS 810. No. 3 only. Anya HOLDEN, Alexeyev Balalaika Ensemble, Karl Holden. [Tchaikovsky and folksongs.] G June 1972.
    USSR: C50 16401000. No. 1 only. Moscow State Choral School Boys' Choir, Viktor POPOV. ['Awake Happy People!'—Pakhmutova, Flyarkovsky, Taktakishvili *et al.*] I 1982b.
    Belgium: René Gailly Compact Disc CD92 041. Nos. 1–4. Viktoria YEVTODIEVA (soprano) and Yuri Serov (piano). ['Complete Songs, Vol. 1'—Opp. 62, 100, 121, and 127.] P St Petersburg 23 Mar.–4 May 1998.

Opus 87   Twenty-four Preludes and Fugues

Form: A collection of piano pieces round the whole cycle of ascending fifths:

	PRELUDE	FUGUE	VOICES
1. C major	Moderato	Moderato	4
2. A minor	Allegro	Allegretto	3
3. G major	Moderato con moto	Allegro molto	3
4. E minor	Andante	Adagio	4
5. D major	Allegretto	Allegretto	3
6. B minor	Allegretto	Moderato	4
7. A major	Allegro poco moderato	Allegretto	3
8. F sharp minor	Allegretto	Andante	3
9. E major	Moderato non troppo	Allegro	2
10. C sharp minor	Allegro	Moderato	4
11. B major	Allegro	Allegro	3
12. G sharp minor	Andante	Allegro	4
13. F sharp major	Moderato con moto	Adagio	5
14. E flat minor	Adagio	Allegro non troppo	3
15. D flat major	Allegretto	Allegro molto	4
16. B flat minor	Andante	Adagio	3
17. A flat major	Allegretto	Allegretto	4
18. F minor	Moderato	Moderato con moto	4
19. E flat major	Allegretto	Moderato con moto	3
20. C minor	Adagio	Moderato	4
21. B flat major	Allegro	Allegro non troppo	3
22. G minor	Moderato non troppo	Moderato	4
23. F major	Adagio	Moderato con moto	3
24. D minor	Andante	Moderato	4

Composed: 10 October 1950 to 25 February 1951, following a visit to Leipzig on the occasion of the bicentenary of Johann Sebastian Bach's death. Written in strict numerical order (Volume 40 of *Collected Works* gives the exact date of composition for all the Preludes and Fugues). All were 'played over' by Tatyana Nikolayeva on the day following their composition. The only item to be partly composed then rewritten was the Prelude for No. 16.

Premières: 18 November 1951, Leningrad Glinka Hall; Dmitri Shostakovich (four items).

23 and 28 December 1952, Leningrad Glinka Hall; Tatyana Niko-layeva (the whole cycle in two sessions).

USA: 17 April 1994, Burton Memorial Tower, University of Michigan; Brandon Blazo and Margo Halsted (No. 8 played by carillon duo).

Arrangements: Prelude of No. 15 arranged for piano duet by Elena Khoven—see Sans op. O.

Nos. 1 and 15 (transposed to E flat) transcribed for string quartet by Rostislav Dubinsky.

Nos. 1, 4, 7, and 8 transcribed for reed ensemble by Eduard Wesly.

Preludes of Nos. 3, 5, 6, 9, 10, 17, and 22 transcribed for double-bass and piano by Rodion Azarkhin, with editorial assistance from the composer.

No. 4 arranged for accordion by Yuri Dranga.

No. 8 arraxiged for two carillons by Brandon Blazo and Margo Halsted.

Nos. 4, 13, 20, and 24 arranged for organ by Vera Bakeyeva.

No. 17 transcribed for violin ensemble by Georgi Bezrukov.

No. 24 transcribed for chamber orchestra by Josef Stanek and Jordan Dafor; and arranged for bayan by Anatoli Senin.

Music: Numbered Opus 89 in early publications and on some recordings. Autograph score preserved at the Glinka Museum. The first page of the autograph of Prelude No. 1 is reproduced in Volume 40 of *Collected Works*. *Sovetskaya Muzyka* magazine, 1952, No. 10, two Preludes and Fugues (Nos. 7 and 24) in a supplement.

Muzgiz, Nos. 23149-50, 1952 (and reprinted 1956) in two volumes, 29 cm.

Boosey & Hawkes and Leeds Music, no numbers, 1955, preface and ed. by Irwin Freundlich, in two volumes, 31 cm.

Edition Peters, Nos. 4761*a* (plate no. 11736. Nos. 1–12) and 4716*b* (plate no. 11737. Nos. 13-24), 1956, 30 cm.

Hans Sikorski, No. 2124 (Volume 1: Nos. 1–12), 1957, 31.5 cm.

Edwin F. Kalmus, *c.* 1960, in three volumes, 32 cm.

Edwin F. Kalmus, Nos. 896 (Nos. 1–12, with Opp. 5 and 12) and 897 (Nos. 13–24), *c.* 1968, 18 cm.

Muzyka, No. 4950 (*D. Shostakovich: Compositions for fortepiano,* Volume 2), 1968, 29 cm.

Muzyka, No. 5947 (in *D. Shostakovich: Compositions for fortepiano,* Volume 3), 1970, Prelude of No. 15 arr. for piano duet, 29 cm.

Muzyka, 1972, 30 cm.

Hans Sikorski, No. 2188 (Volume 2: Nos. 13–24), 1972, 31.5 cm.

MCA Music, New York, 1973, single volume ed. by Jullen Musafia, 31 cm.

Sovetskii Kompozitor, No. 4020, 1977, Preludes of Nos. 10 and 17 arr. for double-bass and piano by R. Azarkhin, 29 cm.

Edition Peters, No. 7221, 1978, No. 1 only, 30.5 cm.

Edition Peters, No. 7231, 1979, No. 18 only, 30.5 cm.

Muzyka, No. 10286 (Volume 40 of *Collected Works*), 1980, Nos. 1–24, 30 cm.

Duration: Approx. 2 hrs 32 mins in score; 123' 10"–166' 20". Chamber Orchestra arr. of No. 24; 10' 27"–11' 45".

Ballet: *Three Russian Preludes* . A ballet created by Mark Morris in 1995, to the Preludes of Nos. 17, 22, and 15, as a solo vehicle for Mikhail Baryshnikov. Included in a White Oak Dance Project programme at the London Coliseum, 20-4 August 1996.

Film: *Nikolayeva Plays Shostakovich.* The complete cycle. played by Tatyana Nikolayeva, shown in six instalments between 21 and 30 December 1992, on BBC2 TV.

Recordings: USSR: 21388-9 (10" 78 rpm). No. 23 only. Dmitri SHOSTAKOVICH. P 6 Dec. 1951, I 1952.

USSR: MK D 873-4, (10" mono). Nos. 1, 5, 6, 7, and 8. Dmitri SHOSTAKOVICH. P 6 Dec. 1951 (Nos. 1 and 5), 5 Feb. 1952 (No. 7), 14 Feb. 1952 (No. 6), and 19 Feb. 1952 (No. 8). I 1952. *Reissued:* Revelation Compact Disc RV 70001. Nos. 1–8 and 12–14. ['Shostakovich plays Shostakovich, vol. 1'.] P 5 Feb. 1952 (No. 14) and 19 Feb. 1952 (Nos. 12 and 13), 1 June 1997, G July 1997.

USA: Concert Hall Society CHS 1314 (mono). (Nos. 4, 5, 14, 2; 12, 3, and 16. Dmitri SHOSTAKOVICH. P 1951–52. [Labelled 'Rarities Collection 122'.] *Reissued:* USA. Concert Hall Society H 1509 (mono). I 1957.

Revelation Compact Disc RV 70003. Nos. 16-18, 20, and 22-4. Dmitri SHOSTAKOVICH. ['Shostakovich plays Shostakovich, Vol. 3'.] P 6 Dec. 1951 (Nos. 16 and 23), 5 Feb. 1952 (Nos. 20, 22, and 24), and *c*.1956 (Nos. 17 and 18), I Nov. 1997, G Feb. 1998. NB. Sofia Moshevich in *DSCH Journal* No. 12 argues that the No. 18 is a forgery.

USSR: MK D 02828-9 (mono). Nos. 1, 5, and 24. Emil GILELS. [Scarlatti.] P Moscow 1955, I 1956. *Reissued:* Germany: Melodia Eurodisc 88 802 XK in Set 88 803 XCK (1 side, mono). [Glazunov.] I 1975 ~ Germany: Melodia Eurodisc Compact Disc CD 69098. Nos. 1, 24, and 5. ['Emil Gilels Collection, Vol. 4'—Prokofiev.] I 1991.

USA: Angel 35308 (mono). Nos. 24, 1, and 5. Emil GILELS. [Chopin.] P New York 19–20 Oct. 1955. *Reissued:* Columbia 33 CX 1364 (mono). G Sept. 1956 ~ USA: Seraphim M 60010 (mono). [Chopin.] ~ HMV SLS 290113 (in three-record set, mono). [Rakhmaninov, Chopin, Schubert *et al.*] G June 1984 ~ Testament Compact Disc SBT 1029 (mono). No. 5 only. [Rakhmaninov and Saint-Saëns.] G Feb. 1994. *Reissued:* USA: Testament Compact Disc SBT 1089 (mono). Nos. 1, 5, and 24. [Mozart and Chopin.] I Mar. 1997, G May 1997.

NB. Further pressings of the above two recordings are listed on page

46 of *An Emil Gilels Discography* by Falk Schwarz (The British Institute of Recorded Sound, London, 1980).

Czech: Supraphon FLPM 288 (10" mono). Nos. 3, 6, 7, 2, 18, and 4. Svyatoslav RICHTER. P Prague studio 26-9 Nov. 1956. *Reissued:* USA: Artia ALP 173 (mono). Nos. 3, 6, 7, 2, and 18. [Op. 102.] G May 1961 ~ Dell'Arte DA 9015 (mono). Nos. 2, 3, 4, 6, 7, and 18. [Prokofiev.] G Mar. 1986 ~ Czech: Ultraphon Compact Disc 11 1421-2. Nos. 3, 6, 7, 2, and 18. [Schumann.] I Jan. 1994.

USSR: MK D 4276-7 (10" mono). No. 24 only. Roger BOUTRY. [Balakirev, Debussy, and Boutry.] P 1958.

USSR: MK D 04306-7 (mono). No. 15 only. Eduard MIANSAROV. [Beethoven, Prokofiev, Paganini, and Rakhmaninov.] P 1958.

USSR: MK D 04820-1 (mono). No. 24 only. Lev VLASENKO. [Brahms, Scarlatti, and Chopin.] P 1958.

Parlophone PMC 1056 (mono). Nos. 24, 7, 8, 6, 22, and 20. Dmitri SHOSTAKOVICH. G July 1958. *Reissued:* USA: Seraphim M 60024 (mono). I 1966 ~ USA: Capitol P 18013 (mono).

France: Columbia FCX 771 (mono). Nos. 1, 4, 5, 6, 13, 14, 18, and 23. Dmitri SHOSTAKOVICH. P Paris May 1958. *Reissued:* USSR: Melodiya D 034479-80 (mono). I 1974*c* ~ EMI Classics Compact Disc CDC7 54606-2 (mono). Nos. 1, 4, 5, 23, and 24. ['Composers in Person' series—Opp. 35, 102, and 5.] I Jan. 1993, G Apr. 1993. NB. No. 24 recorded at the session issued on Parlophone PMC 1056.

USSR: Melodiya D 019641-2 (mono). Nos. 3 and 9. Vladimir SOFRONITSKY. [In three-record set 'Sofronitsky plays in the Skryabin Museum'— Skryabin and Prokofiev.] P *c*.1959, I 1967.

USSR: MK D 06459-60 (mono). Nos. 5, 23, 3, 16, 6, 7, 20, and 2. Dmitri SHOSTAKOVICH. I 1960. *Reissued:* USA: Artia MK 1565 (mono). I 1961 ~ HMV Melodiya HLM 7096 in Set RLS 721 (mono). [Op. 34 Nos. 10, 15, 16, and 24.] G Oct. 1976 ~ France: Le Chant du Monde Compact Disc LDC 278 1000 (mono, double-play). [Opp. 79*a*, 93, and 57.] I Sept. 1989 ~ Argentina: Opus RS 018 (mono). A compilation from four or five sessions?: Nos. 16 [not 21 as stated], 14, 22, 8, 12, 4, and 7.

USSR: Melodiya CM 02545-6 (?stereo). Nos. 1, 23, and 24. Dmitri SHOSTAKOVICH. P *c*.1960, I May 1971.

USSR: MK D 09477-84 (8 sides, mono). Complete Cycle. Tatyana NIKOLAYEVA. P 1962. *Reissued:* USSR: Melodiya CM 02377-84 (8 sides). I 1970 ~ USSR: Melodiya CM 02377-84 (8 sides). [The third box of Part 2 of *Collected Works on Records*.] I 1978 ~ Germany: Melodia Eurodisc 86 199 XGK (6 sides, stereo). I 1970s.

USSR: MK D 09919-20 (mono). Nos. 1, 7, 8, and 15. Mariya GRINBERG. [Bach.] P 1962.

USSR: MK D 13053-4 (10" mono) and C 785-6 (10"). No. 17 arr. for string orchestra by G. Bezrukov. Bolshoi Theatre Violinists' Ensemble, Yuli REYENTOVICH. [Bach, Lully, Grieg *et al.*.] P 1963. *Reissued:* USSR: CM

02753-4. [Lully, Grieg, J. F. C. Bach *et al.*.] I 1971 ~ HMV Melodiya SXLP 30259. ['Stringtime in Moscow', Volume 2—Tchaikovsky, Lyadov, Glazunov *et al.*.] G Nov. 1977.
Philips AL 3458 (mono) and SAL 3458. Nos. 14, 17, 15, 4, 12, and 23. Svyatoslav RICHTER. P Paris July 1963, G Nov. 1964. *Reissued:* USSR: Melodiya D 013541-2 (mono). I 1964 ~ USA: Philips PHM 500 048 (mono) and PHS 900 048. I 1964 ~ France: Le Chant du Monde LDX 8324 (mono) ~ Philips Universo 6580 084. G Dec. 1974 ~ Philips Sequenza Special 6527 224. G Mar. 1984 ~ Philips Legendary Classics Compact Disc 462 101-2 PLC. [Bartók.] I Jan. 1990 ~ Philips 438 627-2PH2 (two-disc set and also in 21-disc set 'Richter—The Authorized Edition'). [Prokofiev and Skryabin.] I Mar. 1993, G Aug. 1994.
Italy: Fonit Cetra Compact Disc CDE 1029 (mono). Nos. 1-6. Sergio PERTICAROLI. [Prokofiev.] P 14 Nov. 1964, I 1988.
USSR: Melodiya C10 23321 001 (DMM). Labelled as 'Suite'—Preludes of Nos. 9, 3, 5, 6, 10, and 22 arr. R. Azarkhin. Rodion AZARKHIN (double-bass) and Gennadi Provatorov (piano). [Hindemith, Dvarionas, and Petrov.] P 1965, I 1986*c.* NB. Bars 5–8 of No. 9 in the composer's hand reproduced on the sleeve.
USSR: Melodiya D 020335-6 (mono). No. 1 discussed and performed. Mariya GRINBERG. [Beethoven.] P 1967.
USSR: Melodiya D 23613-4 (10" mono). Nos. 4, 13, 20, and 24 arr. for organ. Vera BAKEYEVA (organ). P 1967.
USSR: Melodiya D 028091-2 (mono). No. 7 only. Yuri SLESAREV. [Pianists at the Fourth International Tchaikovsky Competition.] P and I 1970.
USA: Pyramid Compact Disc 13503. Nos. 19, 21, and 22. Svyatoslav RICHTER. [Myaskovsky and Prokofiev.] P Fêtes Musicales de Touraine concert June 1973, I 1991, G Oct. 1992.
USSR: Melodiya C10 05021-2. No. 7 only [not No. 2 as stated on label and sleeve.] Nataliya GAVRILOVA. [Concert programme by piano performers at the Fifth International Tchaikovsky Competition—Tchaikovsky, Haydn, Chopin *et al.*] P Moscow concert 1974, I 1975.
USSR: Melodiya C10 05481-2. No. 18 only. Myung-Whun CHUNG. [Pianists at the Fifth International Tchaikovsky Competition.] P 1974, I 1975*c.*
RCA Red Seal LRL 2 5100 (two-record box set issued as a Memorial Edition). Complete cycle. Roger WOODWARD. P May-June 1975, G Dec. 1975. *Reissued:* USA: RCA CRL 2 5100 (two-record box set). I 1975.
Czech: Panton 11 0533 G. Nos. 7 and 24. Dagmar BALOGHOVÁ. [Martinů.] P 1976.
USSR: Melodiya C20 07001-2. No. 4 arr. for accordion. Yuri DRANGA (accordion). [Bach, Breme, O. Schmidt *et al.*] P 1976, I 1977*a.*
Czech: Panton 11 0611 G. No. 7 only. Jindra KRAMPEROVÁ. [Debussy, Fiala, and Flosman.] P Prague 1976.

USSR: Melodiya C10 10595-6. No. 24 arr. for organ. Leopoldas DIGRIS (organ of Vilnius Picture Gallery). [Makachinas, Arro, and Kutavichyus.] P 1978, I 1979*a*.

USSR: Melodiya C10 10781-2. No. 7 only. Genichiro MURAKAMI. [Concert programme by piano performers at the Sixth International Tchaikovsky Competition—Chopin, Balakirev, Liszt *et al.*] P Moscow concert 1978, I 1979*a*.

BMG Melodiya Compact Disc 74321 52959-2. No. 21 only. Mikhai PLETNEV. ['International Tchaikovsky Competition, Vol. 2'—Stravinsky, Musorgsky, Liszt, and Shchedrin.] P Moscow concert 1978, I Nov. 1998.

USSR: Melodiya C10 11159-60. Nos. 3 and 5. Dmitri ALEYKSEYEV. [Skryabin and Prokofiev.] P 1978. I 1979*b*.

USSR: Melodiya C20 13077-8. No. 24 arr. for bayan. Anatoli SENIN (bayan). [Mozart and Liszt.] P 1978, I 1980*c*.

USSR: Melodiya C10 14493-4. No. 15 only. Terence JUDD. ['Terence Judd in Moscow'—Tchaikovsky, Balakirev, Skryabin, Rakhmaninov, and Kazhayeva.] P Moscow concert 10 July 1978, I 1981*b*. *Reissued:* Chandos ABR 1090. ['Terence Judd in Moscow'—Liszt, Skryabin, Rakhmaninov *et al.*] I Oct. 1983, G Feb. 1984 ~ Chandos Compact Disc CHAN 9914. ['In Memory of Terence Judd'—Liszt, Ginastera, Barber *et al.*] G Nov. 2001.

USSR: Melodiya C10 15037-8. Nos. 1, 15, and 24. Iloanta MIROSHNIKOVA. [Prokofiev.] P 1980. I 1981*c*.

Czech: Panton 8111 0231. No. 24 arr. J. Stanek. Ostrava Conservatory Chamber Orchestra, Josef STANEK. [Handel, Mozart, and Krejci.] P Ostrava 1981, I 1982.

Bulgaria: Balkanton BKA 11376. Nos. 3, 17, and 24. Krasimir GATEV. [Prokofiev.] P early 1980s.

USSR: Melodiya C10 18099005. Nos. 7 and 2. Mariya Rovena arrieta and Kalle RANDALU respectively. [Pianists at the Seventh International Tchaikovsky Competition.] P 1982. I 1983*b*.

USSR: Melodiya A10 00501 007 (digital). Nos. 21 and 22. Mikhail PLETNEV. [Mozart.] P Moscow concert 28 Feb. 1986, I 1990.

Netherlands: Harmonia Mundi Ottavo Compact Disc MRC 38616. Nos. 19, 1, 2, 4, and 15. Boris BERMAN. [Op. 61.] P Utrecht Mar. 1986, I Aug. 1989, G Oct. 1989.

USSR: Melodiya C10 25787 002. No. 2 only. Nikolal LUGANSKY (14 years old). [Bach, Skryabin, and Rakhmaninov.] P Moscow concert 7 May 1986, I 1988*b*.

USSR: Melodiya A10 00469 007-00476 005 (four-record box set, digital). Complete cycle. Tatyana NIKOLAYEVA. P 1987, I 1990*a*. *Reissued:* Melodiya Compact Discs SUCD 10 00073 (Nos. 1–10), /4 (Nos. 11-16), and /5 (Nos. 17-24). I 1990*b* ~ BMG Classics Melodiya Compact Discs 74321 19849-2 (three-disc set). I July 1994, G Feb. 1995.

USSR: Melodiya C10 30205. No. 15 only. Oleg VOLKOV. [Opp. 12 and 13; Skryabin.] P 1987, I 1991. *Reissued:* USA: Brioso Compact Disc BR 105. ['All Russian'—Op. 13; Borodin *et. al.* and Skryabin.] I Feb. 1995.

Stradivari Compact Disc SCD 6069. No. 24 only. Carah LANDES. [Liszt and Prokofiev.] P New York 6-8 Oct. 1987, I 1992.

Bulgaria: Balkanton BKA 12305-6. No. 24 arr. Dafov. Tolbuhin Chamber Orchestra, Jordan DAFOV. [In double album with Opp. 101, 110, and 108.] P Tolbuhin, Bulgaria Mar. 1988.

France: Rodolphe Compact Disc RPC 32600. Nos. 2, 15, and 24. Vladimir STOUPEL. [Opp. 61 and 34.] P 3-4 Jan. 1989, G Oct. 1990.

Decca Compact Disc 436 451-2 (two-disc set). Nos. 19 and 20. Svyatoslav RICHTER. [Bartók, Hindemith. Prokofiev *et al.*] P Vienna concert 20 Feb. 1989. I Mar. 1993.

Kingdom Compact Disc KCLCD 2023. Nos. 1 to 12. Marios PAPADO-POULOS. P London 30-1 May and 15 Sept. 1990, I Nov. 1990, G Mar. 1991.

Kingdom Compact Discs KCLCD 2024-5 (two-disc set). Nos. 13 to 24. Marios PAPADOPOULOS. P London 15-16 Sept. 1990, I Feb. 1991, G Mar. 1991.

Hyperion Compact Discs CDA 66441-3 (three-disc set). Complete cycle. Tatyana NIKOLAYEVA. P Hampstead 23-6 Sept. 1990, I Feb. 1991. G Mar. 1991 (with article by David Fanning). *Gramophone* Record Awards 1991—winner of Instrumental category and No. 5 included on *Gramophone* Awards CD sampler with the December magazine. Awarded French Prix Maurice Fleuret 1991.

Dorian Compact Disc DOR 90163. Nos. 1 and 15 arr. R. Dubinsky. LAFAYETTE QUARTET (Ann Elliott-Goldschmid, Sharon Stanis, Joanna Hood, Pamela Highbaugh). [Op. 110; and Tchaikovsky.] P Troy, New York May 1991, I June 1992, G July 1992.

Germany: ECM New Series Compact Discs 1469-70 (two-disc set). Complete cycle. Keith JARRETT. P La Chaux-de-Fonds, Switzerland July 1991, I June 1992, G Sept. 1992.

France: Accord Compact Discs 202032 (two-disc set). Complete cycle. Caroline WEICHERT. P Thun, Switzerland 1991-92.

Netherlands: Channel Classics Canal Grande Compact Disc CG 9321. Nos. 1, 4, 7, and 8 arr. E. Wesly. CALEFAX REED ENSEMBLE (Eduard Wesly—oboe and cor anglais, Ivar Berix—clarinet, Raaf Hekkema—alto saxophone, Lucas van Helsdingen—alto/soprano saxophone and bass clarinet, Alban Wesly—bassoon). [Doest, Brumel, and Ockeghem.] P Renswoude, Netherlands 16-19 June 1992, I 1993.

Dynamic Compact Discs CDS 117/1–3 (three-disc set). Complete cycle. Boris PETRUSHANSKY. P Moscow Conservatory Jan. 1992 (Nos. 1–11) and Moscow Radio Studio Jan. 1993 (Nos. 12–24), I Nov. 1994.

Decca Compact Discs 466 066-2DH2 (two-disc set). Complete cycle. Vladimir ASHKENAZY. P Berlin, London, and Watford May 1996-Apr.

1998. I and G June 1999. *Reissued:* Gramophone Compact Disc GCD 0699. No. 7 only. [Sampler.] I June 1999 ~ Gramophone Compact Disc GCD 0202. No. 1 only. [Sampler.] I Feb. 2002 (to accompany article by D. Fanning).

RCA Red Seal Compact Discs 74321 61446-2 (two-disc set). Nos. 20, 15, 10, 14, 9, 4, 8, 3, 22, 2, 21, and 16. Olli MUSTONEN. [Twelve Preludes and Fugues arranged in rising semitones with Bach.] P Henry Wood Hall, London 5–8 June 1997, G Mar. 1999.

Athene-Minerva Compact Disc ATH CD18. No. 24 only. Raymond CLARKE. [Opp. 12, 34, and 61.] P Nottingham University 10 July 1998, I May 1999, G Oct. 1999.

Naxos Compact Discs 8.55475-6 (two-disc set). Complete cycle. Konstantin SCHERBAKOV. P East Woodhay, Berkshire 15–18 June 1999, I Nov. 2000.

References: Dolzhansky, Elder, Fanning, Freundlich, Mnatsakanova/ Nikolayeva (in Danilevich 1967), and Prokhorova.

Opus 88   Ten Poems on Texts by Revolutionary Poets

Form   A cycle of choral settings of poems by Revolutionary poets taken from the collection *The Revolutionary Poetry of 1870–1917,* published in Leningrad in 1950, for mixed chorus a cappella and, in Nos. 9 and 10, boys' choir:

1. Boldly, friends, on we march! (poem by Leonid Radin)—Moderato con moto
2. One of many (Yevgeni Tarasov)—Andantino
3. Onto the streets! (words anon.)—Allegro molto
4. The meeting in transit to exile (Aleksei Gmyrev)—Andante
5. To those condemned to death (Aleksei Gmyrev)—Adagio
6. The Ninth of January (Arkadi Kots)—Moderato
7. The volleys have become silent (Yevgeni Tarasov)—Andante
8. They were victorious (Aleksei Gmyrev)—Allegro
9. May Day Song (Arkadi Kots)—Moderato
10. Song (Vladimir Tan-Bogoraz, after Walt Whitman) ['Democratic Vistas']—Andante con moto

Nos. 1, 3, 4, 5, 7, and 8 translated as 'Have Courage, Friends', 'The Time is Now', 'Face to Face', 'Sentence of Death', 'Silent Guns', and 'Invincible Victors' in the G. Schirmer edition.

No. 6 is used as a leitmotiv in Symphony No. 11, Opus 103.

Composed: Early spring 1951, at Moscow. The score was presented to Aleksandr Sveshnikov on 28 March 1951.

Première: 10 October 1951, Moscow Conservatory Bolshoi Hall; RSFSR Academic Russian Choir and Children's Choir, Aleksandr Sveshnikov.
Arrangements: Adaptation by M. Fremiot, G. Martin, and F. Robert to suit the French translation by F. Hirsch. English translation of the cycle by Jane May.
Music: Autograph score preserved at the Glinka Museum. The opening of the fourth poem is reproduced in Volume 34 of *Collected Works.* Awarded a Stalin Prize Second Class in 1951.

Muzgiz, No. 22595, 1952, 26 cm, and same number, 1962, 27 cm.

Le Chant du Monde, Nos. 420–9, 1952, adaptation by M. Fremlot, G. Martin, and F. Robert with French text by F. Hirsch, parts.

Muzyka, No. 4098, 1967, 29 cm.

G. Schirmer, Nos. 12118–12127, 1977, the ten songs on separate sheets in English translation by Jane May, 26.5 cm.

Joseph Boonin, New Jersey, Nos. 1, 4, and 8.

Muzyka, No. 10179 (in Volume 34 of *Collected Works* with Op. 136 and songs), 1985, 30 cm.
Duration: Approx. 40 minutes in score; 29' 55"–35' 05".
Recordings: USSR: MK D 05642-3 (mono). RSFSR Academic Russian Choir, Aleksandr SVESHNIKOV. P 1959.

USSR: Melodiya D 15571-2 (10" mono). No. 5 only. Byelorussian State Academic Choir. G. SHIRMA. [Wagner, Turenkov, Muradeli *et al.*] I 1965.

USSR: Melodiya D 025505-6 (mono). No. 5 only. Leningrad State University Students' Choir, Grigori SANDLER. [Glière, Glinka, Taneyev *et al.*] P 1969.

USSR: Melodiya C10 04937-8. Leningrad Radio and Television Choir, Grigori SANDLER. P 1974, I 1975*b. Reissued:* USSR: with same number in third box of Part 1 of *Collected Works on Records.* I 1980 ~ Japan: Victor VIC 5359. I 1982.

Czech: Opus 9112 0787. Slovák Philharmonic Chorus, Valentin ILJIN. P Bratislava 1979.

USSR: Melodiya C10 20301 003. Moscow and Novosibirsk Chamber Choirs, 'Spring' Studio Children's Choral School (chorus-masters—Vladimir Minin, B. Pevzner, and Aleksandr Ponomarev), Vladimir MININ. P Moscow concert 29 Sept. 1981, I 1984*c.*

USSR: Melodiya C10 26309 009. No. 7 only, sung in Moldavian. Doina Academic Choral Kapella, Veronica Garshtya (chorus-director), Anatoli ZHAR. [Rakhmaninov, Shebalin, folksongs *et al.*] I 1988*d.*

USA: MCA Classics Art & Electronics Compact Disc AED 10211. No. 6 only. Moscow Conservatory Students' Choir, Boris TEVLIN. [Rakhmaninov, Rimsky-Korsakov, Taneyev *et al.*] P Moscow concert July 1989, I 1990.

France: Le Chant du Monde Russian Season Compact Disc RUS 288160. Moscow Academy of Choral Singing, Viktor POPOV (chorus-master). [Sans op. Q.] P Moscow Conservatory Jan.–Apr. 1998, I July 1999, G Oct. 1999.

Sans op. Q   Ten Russian Folksongs

Form: Arrangements of ten folksongs from the collections of Ivan Prach (Nos. 7-9 from *Russian Folksongs*, published in St Petersburg, 1896), Yevgeniya Lineva (Nos. 5 and 6 from *Great Russian Songs with Traditional Harmony*, Volume 1, St Petersburg, 1904), and Yevgeni Gippius (Nos. 1–4 and 10 from *Russian Folk Songs*, Leningrad, 1943) for soprano (S), alto (A), tenor (T), and bass (B) soloists, chorus (S.A.T.B.), and piano:

1. All of a sudden there was a clap of thunder over Moscow (B and T.B.)
2. Beyond the mountains, beyond the valleys (T and S.A.T.B.)
3. Out of the forest of spears and swords (B and S.A.T.B.)
4. Nights are dark, the clouds are menacing (B and S.A.T.B.)
5. A little cuckoo cuckoos (A and S.A.T.B.)
6. The splinter (A and S.A.T.B.)
7. Fir-grove, my fir-grove (S and S.A.)
8. In my dear father's green garden (S.A.T.B.)
9. I told my sweetheart (S and S.A.T.B.)
10. What a song (B and S.A.T.B.)

Nos. 1-4 and 10 are male soldiers' songs. with words associated with the 1812 war against Napoleon revised with more topical texts during the Great Patriotic War; the remaining songs are women's lyrical songs and a roundelay (No. 7).

Composed: July 1951, immediately after Opus 88, at Moscow.

Premières: 18 October 1971, Magnitogorsk and 3 December 1971, Moscow Conservatory Bolshoi Hall; both performances by the Magnitogorsk State Academic Choir.

Arrangements: *Fourteen Russian Folksongs,* including a selection from the ten above, transcribed for flute and piano by the composer in the 1950s. Accompaniment of Nos. 6, 7, and 10 arranged for bayan by Sofya Khentova in 1978.

Music: Originally designated on the composer's manuscript as Opus 89. Autograph score of the flute arrangements preserved at the CIS Archives of Literature and Art.

Muzgiz, 1952, Nos. 5, 6, and 7, parts for two soloists and choir with piano accompaniment, 30 cm.

Sovetskii Kompozitor, Leningrad, No. 902, 1981. Nos. 10, 7, and 6 with bayan accompaniment included in S. Khentovals comic opera *The Tale of a Priest and His Servant Balda* (see Opus 36), 29.5 cm.

Muzyka, No. 10179 (in Volume 34 of *Collected Works* with Opp. 88 and 136, and songs), 1985, Nos. 1–10, 30 cm.

Duration: Approx. 27 minutes in score; 27' 26".

Recording: USSR: Melodiya C10 16967001. Folksongs Nos. 1-10. Soloists— Yuliya Antonova (No. 9), Gennadi Bezzubenkov (Nos. 1 and 3), Yevgeni

Bortnikov (No. 4), Kira Gerasimova (No. 6), Nina Kuznetsova (No. 7), Zhanna Polevtsova (No. 5), Yevgeni Popov (No. 2), and Aleksandr Seleznev (No. 10); Lyudmila Bogomolova (piano); Glinka State Academic Cappella of Leningrad, Vladimir CHERNUSHENKO (chorus-master). [Op. 104 No. 2; and three Russian folksongs arr. by other hands.] P 1981, I 1982c. *Reissued:* USSR: Melodiya Compact Disc SUCD11 00320. [Op. 104 No. 2; and six Russian folksongs arr. by other hands.] I 1991d.

[USSR: Melodiya C10 19323 008. Folksongs Nos. 10, 7, and 6 in Khentova's edition of *The Tale of a Priest and His Servant Balda*, Opus 36. Vladimir Pankratov (bass), Yelena Ustinova (soprano), Leningrad Malyi Opera and Ballet Theatre Choir and Orchestra, Mikhail Travlin (chorus-master), Valentin KOZHIN. P 1982, I 1984a.]

France: Le Chant du Monde Russian Season Compact Disc RUS 288160. Folksongs Nos. 1–10. Soloists and mixed chorus of the Moscow Academy of Choral Singing, Tamara Kravtchenko (piano), Viktor POPOV (chorus-master). [Op. 88.] P Moscow Conservatory Jan.–Apr. 1998, I July 1999, G Oct. 1999.

Opus 89   The Unforgettable Year 1919

Alternative title: Also translated as *The Memorable Year 1919.*

Form: Music for the film *The Unforgettable Year 1919,* based on the play *Unforgettable 1919* by Vsevolod Vishnevsky, directed by Mikhail Chlaureli for Mosfilm. The music scored for full orchestra (with harp, piano, and additional brass) contains a miniature 'Piano Concerto' (40 pages of full score and appearing as No. 5 in the Suite Opus 89a).

Composed: 1951, at Moscow.

Premières: Film first shown on 3 May 1952.

UK complete suite: 20 May 1984, Barbican Centre, London; Young Musicians' Symphony Orchestra and Brass Ensemble, Tony Gray (pianist in No. 5), James Blair.

Arrangements: Opus 89a—Suite assembled by Lev Atovmyan in 1954:

1. Introduction—Moderato *attacca*
2. Romance: the meeting of Shibayev with Katya—Moderato con moto *attacca*
3. Scene from the Sea Battle—Moderato molto
4. Scherzo—Presto
5. The Assault on Beautiful Gorky—Allegro
6. Intermezzo—Andante
7. Finale—Allegro

Nos. 1 (Prelude) and 5 (Demonstration) of the *Maxim Trilogy* Suite, Opus 50a, relate to this film score and quote the Russian revolutionary marches 'Be bold, Friends . . .' and 'Varshavyanka'.

Instrumentation of Suite Opus 89a: 3 flutes (III = Piccolo), 3 oboes, 3 B flat clarinets. 2 bassoons, contrabassoon ~ 4 horns, 3 trumpets, 3 trombones, tuba ~ additional band of 3 trumpets and 3 trombones in Nos. 4, 5, and 6 ~ timpani (2 players in No. 3), triangle, tambourine. side drum, cymbals, bass drum, gong ~ glockenspiel, xylophone, celesta ~ harp (in film score only), piano (solo in No. 5) ~ strings.

Music: Autograph of the film score preserved in the Music Library of the USSR Cinematograph Symphony Orchestra.

Muzgiz, No. 25026, 1955, Suite Opus 89a, full score, 35 cm.

Duration: Suite—Nos. 1–4 and 7: 16' 30" and No. 5: 7' 30".

Recordings: USSR: MK D 03402-3 (mono). Suite Op. 89a. Moscow Radio Symphony Orchestra. Aleksandr GAUK. [Op. 70.] P 1956. *Reissued:* USA: Monitor MC 2015 (mono). Suite Nos. 1-4 and 7. [Opp. 70 and 96.] I 1958.

Classics for Pleasure 4144161 (digital). No. 5 only. Dmitri ALEKSEYEV (piano), English Chamber Orchestra, Jerzy Maksymiuk. [Opp. 35 and 102.] P London May 1983, G Nov. 1983. *Reissued:* USA: Angel AE 34489 (digital). [Opp. 35 and 102.] ~ Classics for Pleasure CFP 4547 (digital) and Compact Disc CD-CFP 4547. [Opp. 35 and 102.] I Sept. 1988, G Jan. 1989 ~ HMV Classics Compact Disc 5 73047-2. [Sans opp. E and G; Opp. 16, 22, 97, and 35.] I Oct. 1998.

Germany: Capriccio Compact Disc 10 561. Nos. 1 (Prelude) and 5 (Demonstration) in the *Maxim Trilogy* Suite, Opus 50a. Berlin Radio Symphony Orchestra and Chorus, Mikhail YUROVSKY. [Opp. 30, 41 (i), 45, and 50a.] P 28-9 Apr. 1994, I Oct. 1995, G Jan. 1996.

USA: Citadel Compact Disc CTD 88135. Nos. 1 and 5 in the *Maxim Trilogy* Suite, Op. 50a. Belarus Radio and TV Symphony Orchestra and State Chorus, Walter MNATSAKANOV. [Opp. 85 and 76.] P Moscow 7 Apr. 1997, I 1999.

Reference: Belza (1952).

Note: The Scherzo (No. 4 in the Suite) was later arranged for piano duo and appears as the first piece of *Tarantella and Prelude*, Sans op. O (ii).

Opus 90   The Sun Shines over our Motherland

Original title: 'Cantata about the Party'. Earlier working sketches to different texts by Yevgeni Dolmatovsky were titled 'The Standard-bearers of the Twentieth Century' (for men's chorus) and 'Won in Persistent Struggles' (for mixed chorus).

Form: Patriotic cantata for boys' choir, mixed chorus, and orchestra (with 2 harps and additional brass) to a text by Yevgeni Dolmatovsky, marked 'Moderato con moto'.

Instrumentation: piccolo, 2 flutes, 3 oboes, 3 B flat clarinets, 2 bassoons ~ 4 horns, 3 trumpets, 3 trombones, tuba ~ additional band of 3 trumpets and 3 trombones ~ timpani, triangle, side drum, cymbals, gong ~ glockenspiel, 2 harps ~ boys' choir, S.A.T.B. chorus ~ strings.

Composed: Completed on 29 October 1952.

Première: 6 November 1952, Moscow Conservatory Bolshoi Hall; Moscow State Choral Boys' Choir, USSR Symphony Orchestra and Choir, Konstantin Ivanov.

Arrangement: Reduction of the accompaniment for piano by the composer.

Music: Autograph full score preserved at the Glinka Museum. A manuscript copy with the composer's inscription 'Consider this the original. D. Shostakovich. 2 / XII 1952' and proof sheets with his corrections are preserved at the CIS Archives of Literature and Art along with the autograph vocal score.

> Muzgiz, No. 23384, 1953, full score, 28 cm.
>
> Muzyka, No. 6019, 1969, vocal score, 28.5 cm.
>
> Muzyka, No. 11680 (in Volume 29 of *Collected Works* with Opp. 81 and 119), 1983, full score, 30 cm.
>
> Muzyka, No. 11786 (in Volume 30 of *Collected Works* with Opp. 81 and 119), 1983, vocal score, 30 cm.

Duration: Approx. 14 minutes in scores; 12' 15"–13' 50".

Recordings: USSR: MK D 8459-60 (10" mono). Moscow State Choral School Boys' Choir, USSR Symphony Orchestra and Choir, Aleksandr Sveshnikov (chorus-master), Konstantin IVANOV. [Sans op. U; and Kabalevsky.] P concert 1961, I 1962. *Reissued:* USA: Russian Disc Compact Disc RD CD 11 048. [Op. 81.] I Oct. 1994.

> USSR: Melodiya D 019893-4 (mono) and C 01505-6. Moscow State Choral School Boys' Choir, RSFSR Academic Russian Choir, Aleksandr Yurlov (chorus-master), Moscow Philharmonic Orchestra, Kirill KONDRASHIN. [Prokofiev.] P and I 1967. *Reissued:* USA: Angel Melodiya SR 40129. [Prokofiev.] ~ HMV Melodiya ASD 2598. [Op. 112.] G Sept. 1970 ~ HMV Melodiya BOX 50510 in Set SLS 5025. [Op. 112.] G Dec. 1975 ~ USSR: Melodiya C10 14093-4. [In third box of Part 1 of *Collected Works on Records* with Op. 119.] I 1980.

> Germany: Capriccio Compact Disc 10 779. Text in German and English. Cologne Radio Chorus, Godfried Ritter (chorus-master), Berlin Children's Radio Chorus, Manfred Roost (chorus-master), Cologne Radio Symphony Orchestra, Mikhail YUROVSKY. [Opp. 81 and 15a.] P Cologne 3–8 June 1996, I July 1999.

Opus 91   Four Monologues on Verses by Pushkin

Form: Four song settings of Aleksandr Pushkin's verses for bass voice with piano accompaniment:

> 1. Fragment [In a Jewish hut]—Andante
> 2. What does my name mean to you?—Allegro

3. In the depths of the Siberian mines—Adagio
4. Farewell—Allegretto

Composed: Songs written on consecutive days, 5-8 October 1952, at Moscow.
Arrangements: Cycle orchestrated by Gennadi Rozhdestvensky. German translation by Christoph Hellmundt.
Music: Autograph of the songs preserved at the Glinka Museum.
Sovetskii Kompozitor, No. 1790 (in *Romances on verses of Pushkin*), 1960, 29 cm.
Edition Peters, No. 4793 (with Op. 46), 1967, with German and Russian texts—the former by C. Hellmundt, 27 cm.
Muzyka, No. 4116 (in *Dmitri Shostakovich: Vocal Compositions*), 1967 and 1974, 30 cm.
Muzyka, Leningrad, No. 1996 (in *Romances on verses of Pushkin*), 1976, No. 3 only, 28.5 cm.
Muzyka, No. 10283 (in Volume 32 of *Collected Works* with Opp. 4, 21, 46, 62, 79, 84, 86, 98, 100 *et al.*), 1982, 30 cm.
Duration: 12' 25"–14' 30".
Recordings: USSR: Melodiya D 022363-4 (mono). Askold BESEDIN (baritone) and Lyubov Yedlina (piano). [Op. 46; Peiko and Baltin.] P 1968.
Czech: Panton 11 0420 G. Nos. 2 and 4 only. Jaromír VAVRUŠKA (bass) and Jiří Pokorný (piano). [Opp. 138 and 46 Nos. 1 and 2; and Boris Chaikovsky.] P Prague 1973.
USSR: Melodiya C10 10617-8. Nos. 2 and 4 only. Viktor SELIVANOV (baritone) and Lyubov Popova (piano). [In third box of Part 3 of *Collected Works on Records* with Opp. 21 and 46.] I 1978.
USSR: Melodiya A10 00043 004 (digital). Orchestrated G. Rozhdestvensky. Anatoli SAFIULIN (bass), USSR Ministry of Culture Symphony Orchestra, Gennadi Rozhdestvensky. [Opp. 46 and 34.] P 1983, I 1984c ~ BMG Melodiya Compact Discs 74321 63461-2 (two-disc set). [Opp. 93; 103, and 23.] I Mar. 1999.
France: Le Chant du Monde Russian Season Compact Disc RUS 288089. Pyotr GLUBOKY (bass) and Nataliya Rassudova (piano). [Opp. 46, 62, 121, and 146.] P Moscow conservatory 21-9 Sept. 1994, I Apr. 1995.
Beulah Compact Discs 1-2RF5 (two-disc set). Nos. 3 and 4. Helen LAWRENCE (mezzo-soprano) and Julian Rolton (piano). [Op. 46; operatic recital and Pushkin Songs.] P BBC Studio, London 17–18 May 1999, I Dec. 2000.

Opus 92 Quartet No. 5 in B flat major

Form: String quartet in three linked movements:

1. Allegro non troppo *attacca*
2. Andante / Andantino *attacca*
3. Moderato—Allegretto

Composed: The autograph score states that the three movements were completed on 7 September, 19 October, and 1 November 1952. Khentova
mentions that 26 pages of the lst movement were written on 1 January
1952.

Dedication: To the members of the Beethoven Quartet: Dmitri Tsyganov,
Vasili Shirinsky, Vadim Borisovsky, and Sergei Shirinsky.

Première: 13 November 1953, Moscow Conservatory Malyi Hall; Beethoven
Quartet (personnel as the dedication).

Arrangement: Reduction for piano four hands by Anatoli Dmitriev.

Music: The quartet listed as Opus 91 in Corbett (1963). Autograph score preserved in Dmitri Tsyganov's personal collection.

> Music Fund of the USSR, No. 593, 1953, parts in copyist's hand, 29 cm.
>
> Muzgiz, No. 24331, 1954, score, 20 cm.
>
> Musica Rara, No. 1036, 1961, score, 18.5 cm.
>
> Musica Rara, No. 1036*a*, 1961, parts, 31 cm.
>
> Muzgiz, 1963, parts, 29 cm.
>
> Muzyka, Leningrad. No. 530 (in Volume 2 with Quartets 6–8 arr. for
> piano four hands by A. Dmitriev), 1966, 29.5 cm.
>
> Edition Eulenberg, No. 389, 1970, 19 cm.
>
> Belwin Mills, New York, Kalmus chamber music series No. 9681,
> 1970s, parts.
>
> Edition Peters, No. 5755, 1979, parts, 30 cm.
>
> Muzyka, No. 9816 (in Volume 35 of *Collected Works* Quartets 1–8),
> 1979, 30 cm.
>
> Hans Sikorski, No. 2253, 1980, parts, 31.5 cm.
>
> Hans Sikorski, No. 2266 (with Op. 101, 108, and 110), 1980, score,
> 21 cm.

Duration: Approx. 30 minutes in score; 29' 40"–31' 53"; [30' 19"—Berlin
State Opera Quartet with exposition repeat in first movement not
observed.]

Recordings: USSR: MK D 2400-1 (10" mono). BEETHOVEN QUARTET (personnel
as above). I 1954. *Reissued:* France: Le Chant du Monde LDA 8130 (10"
mono) ~ USA: Vanguard VRS 6021 (mono). [Op. 83.] I 1955 ~ USSR:
Melodiya D 015785-6 (mono). [Op. 101.] I 1965.

> Germany: Deutsche Grammophon LPE, 17 211 (10" mono). BERLIN
> STATE OPERA QUARTET (Egon Morbitzer, Wilhelm Martens, Werner Buch-
> holz, Bernard Günther). P *c.*1959, I 1960.
>
> Japan: Triton Compact Disc MECC 26018 (mono). BEETHOVEN QUARTET
> (personnel as above). [Opp. 49 and 67.] P Moscow Conservatory concert
> 1960, I 2000.
>
> USSR: Melodiya 019219-20 (mono) and C 01433-4. BORODIN QUARTET
> (Rostislav Dubinsky, Yaroslav Aleksandrov, Dmitri Shebalin, Valentin
> Berlinsky). [Op. 108.] P and I 1967. *Reissued:* USA: Seraphim Melodiya S
> 6034. [In three-record box set with Quartets 1-4.] ~ HMV Melodiya HQS
> 1321 in Set SLS 879. [Op. 83.] G June 1974.

L'Oiseau-Lyre DSLO 29. FITZWILLIAM QUARTET (Christopher Rowland, Jonathan Sparey, Alan George, Ioan Davies). [Op. 101.] P 20-2 July 1977, G Dec. 1978. *Reissued:* Decca 188 D3 in Set D 188 D7. [Op. 83.] G Feb. 1981 ~ Decca Enterprise Compact Discs 433 078-2DM6. [On third disc of six-disc set with Opp. 101 and 108.] I Apr. 1992, G June 1992.

USSR: Melodiya C10 11611-2 TANEYEV QUARTET (personnel as on the 1979 coupling). [In first box of Part 2 of *Collected Works on Records* with Op. 138.] P Leningrad Mar. 1978, I 1980. *Reissued:* Japan: JVC Victor 5347. [Op. 101.] ~ USSR: Melodiya Compact Disc SUCD11 00308. [Opp. 49 and 83.] I 1991*c* ~ France: Praga Compact Disc PR 250 077. [Opp. 101 and 108.] P given as Czech Radio Sept. 1978, I Mar. 1996.

USSR: Melodiya C10 21943 000. BORODIN QUARTET (Mikhail Kopelman, Andrei Abramenkov, Dmitri Shebalin, Valentin Berlinsky). [Op. 117.] P 1983, I 1985*d*. *Reissued:* HMV Melodiya EX 270339-3 (DMM). [In seven-record box set of 15 Quartets plus Quintet.] G Mar. 1986 ~ EMI Compact Disc CDC7 49270-2. [Op. 144.] I Nov. 1987, G Sept. 1988 ~ Japan: Victor Musical Industries Compact Disc VICC 40020. [Opp. 101 and 108.] I 1990 ~ EMI Compact Discs CMS5 65032-2. [In six-disc set of 15 Quartets plus Quintet.] I Mar. 1994 ~ BMG Melodiya Compact Discs 74321 40711-2 (six-disc set). [Opp. 101 and 108.] I June 1997.

USSR: Melodiya C10 28483 000. SHOSTAKOVICH QUARTET (Andrei Shishlov, Sergei Pishchugin, Aleksandr Galkovsky, Aleksandr Korchagin). [Op. 117.] P 1984, I 1989*d*. *Reissued:* Olympia Compact Disc OCD 532. ['Complete Quartets, Vol. 2'—Opp. 68 and 108.] I May 1994, G Sept. 1994.

Teldec Compact Discs 9031 71702-2. BRODSKY QUARTET (Michael Thomas, Ian Belton, Paul Cassidy, Jacqueline Thomas). [On third disc of six-disc set with Opp. 101 and 108.] P Berlin July 1989, I Nov. 1990, G June 1992. *Reissued:* Teldee Compact Disc 9031 73110-2. [Op. 68.] I 1991.

USA: ESS.A.Y. Compact Disc CD 1008. MANHATTAN QUARTET (Eric Lewis, Roy Lewis, John Dexter, Judith Glyde). [Op. 83.] P Jersey City 15–18 Jan. 1990. *Reissued:* Koch Schwann Musica Mundi Compact Disc 310 129. ['Complete String Quartets, Vol. 2' with Op. 83.] I Aug. 1991.

Naxos Compact Disc 8.550974 ÉDER QUARTET (János Selmeczi, Péter Szüts, Sandor Papp, György Éder). ['Complete Quartets, Vol. 3'—Op. 73.] P Budapest 6-9 Mar. 1995, I Jan. 1996, G Apr. 1997.

Japan: Toshiba EMI Compact Disc TOCE 9306. MORGAŬA QUARTET (Eiji Arai, Takashi Aoki, Hisashi Ono, Ryoichi Fujimori). [Opp. 117 and 100.] P 23-5 Oct. 1996, I Jan. 1997.

Deutsche Grammophon Compact Disc 463 284-2GH5 (five-disc set). EMERSON QUARTET (Eugene Drucker, Philip Setzer, Lawrence Dutton, David Finkel). ['Complete Quartets, Vol. 2'—Opp. 83 and 101.] P Aspen, Colorado concert June-July 1999, G June 2000.

Hyperion Compact Disc CDA 67155. ST PETERSBURG QUARTET (Alia Aranovskaya, Ilya Teplyakov, Aleksei Koptev, Leonid Shukayev). [Opp. 108 and 117.] P St Petersburg Studio Dec. 2000, I Apr. 2001, G July 2001.

Sans op. R   Greek Songs

Form: Four songs arranged for middle voice and piano. The melodies, recorded from Maria Beiku, a member of the Greek Resistance Movement, were handed over to Shostakovich by the Soviet folklorist Lev Kulakovsky:

1. Forward! (subtitled 'Song of the Greek Resistance') ♩= 102) Melody by A. Xenos, words by K. Palamas, translated by Sergei Bolotin and Tatyana Sikorskaya
2. Pentozalis (♩= 96)
   Cretan folksong, translated by S. Bolotin
3. [Mount] Zolongo (♩= 58)
   Greek folksong, translated by T. Sikorskaya
4. Hymn of the ELAS (Ellenikas Laïkos Apeletherotikos Stratos) (♩= 112)
   Melody by A. Tzakonas; words by S. Mavroidi-Papadaki, translated by S. Bolotin

Composed: 1952-3.
Première: France: 17 March 1991, Dimanche; Aleksandr Naumenko (tenor) and Nell Beardmoer (piano).
Music: Autograph of the four songs preserved at the CIS Archives of Literature and Art. No. 1 first published as a supplement to the journal *Sovetskaya Muzyka*, 1954, No. 5 and also in *Pesni naradov mira* (Songs of the Peoples of the World). compiled by Grigori Schneyerson and published by Muzgiz in 1955.

Muzyka, No. 10283 (in Volume 32 of *Collected Works* with Opp. 4, 21, 46, 62, 79, 84, 86, 91, 98, 100 *et al.*), 1982, four songs, 30 cm.
Recordings: —

Sans op. S   Piano Pieces for Children

(i) *Dances of the Dolls*
Form: A suite of seven piano solos for children arranged from orchestral material of earlier ballet and stage works:

1. Lyrical Waltz—Moderato (from Ballet Suite No. 3, No. 5)
2. Gavotte—Tranquillo, semplice (from Ballet Suite No. 3, No. 2)
3. Romance—Moderato, expressivo (from Ballet Suite No. 1, No. 3)
4. Polka—Scherzando, non troppo presto (from Ballet Suite No. 1, No. 2—the Pizzicato Dance)
5. Waltz-scherzo ('The Petite Ballerina')—Animato, ma non troppo presto (from Ballet Suite No. 1, No. 5)

6. Hurdy-gurdy—Allegro non troppo (from Ballet Suite No. 1, No. 4
the Polka)
7. Dance—Scherzando, ma non troppo presto

Composed: Assembled in 1952 from material composed 1930-5.
Arrangements: See Ballet Suites Nos. 1 and 3, Sans op. P, and the original
opus numbers for expanded orchestral versions.
No. 1 transcribed for harp; No. 3 for viola ensemble by Georgi
Bezrukov; No. 5 for bayan by N. Rizolya; No. 6 for harp quartet, also
cello and piano; Nos. 2, 3, 6, and 7 for violin (No. 2 for violin duet) and
piano by Konstantin Fortunatov; Nos. 1-7 for string orchestra; Nos. 1, 2,
3, and 6 for cello and guitar by Bryan Johanson.
Music: Muzgiz, No. 122639, 1952, 29 cm.
MCA Music, New York, *c.*1953, ed. Michael Fredericks, 31 cm.
Hans Sikorski, No. 2123, 1960, under the title 'Tanz der Puppen',
31.5 cm.
Edition Peters, No. 4711 (plate no. 11772), under the title 'Puppen-
tanze', 1962, ed. Walter Frickert, 31 cm.
Boosey & Hawkes, No. 19356, 1965, ed. Martin Hall, 31 cm.
Edition Peters. No. 4794 (plate no. 12389—in *Shostakovich: Album of
Easy Pieces* with Nos. 1 and 3 of Op. 69. Elegy from Ballet Suite No. 3,
Spring Waltz from Sans op. P (ii), and Romance from Op. 97), 1967, Nos.
2, 4, and 7 arr. K. Fortunatov, 30.5 cm.
Muzyka, No. 4719 (in *D. Shostakovich: Pieces for violin and piano*), 1975,
Nos. 2, 3, 6, and 7 arr. K. Fortunatov, 28.5 cm.
Sovetskii Kompozitor, No. 4920 (in *D. Shostakovich: Selection of Chil-
dren's Piano Pieces*), 1979, Nos. 1-3 and 5-7 ed. Bronislava Rozengauz, 29
cm.
Muzyka, Leningrad, No. 2629 (in *S. Prokofiev and D. Shostakovich:
Selection of Fortepiano Pieces for Children*), 1980, Nos. 2 and 5 ed. Zinaida
Vitkind, 28.5 cm.
Sovetskii Kompozitor, No. 6680 (in *Works by Soviet Composers for Viola
Ensemble*), 1984, No. 3 arr. for 3 violas and double-bass by G. Bezrukov,
29 cm.
Muzyka, No. 14908 (in *D. Shostakovich: Pieces for cello and piano*), 1991,
No. 6 only, 29 cm.
Duration: 9' 00"—10' 46".
Recordings: USSR: MK D 5466-7 (10" mono). Nos. 1, 2, 4, 3, and 5. Natan
PERELMAN. [Boccherini, Schubert, and Prokofiev.] P 1959.
USSR: Melodiya D 00015659-60 (7" mono). No. 6 arr. for harp quartet.
E. KUZMICHEVA, A. Buzkova, M. Smirnova, and N. Kochurina. [Glazunov,
Debussy, and Ravel.] P 1965.
USSR: Melodiya G 04697-8. Complete Suite. Lyubov TIMOFEYEVA.
[Prokofiev and S. Slonimsky.] P Nov. 1973, I 1975. *Reissued:* Germany:

Deutsche Grammophon Junior 2546 301. Complete Suite. [Slonimsky and Bartók.] I 1977 ~ Japan: JVC VIC 9554. Complete Suite. [Prokofiev and Slonimsky.] I 1985.

USSR: Melodiya C 04705-6. No. 1 only. Olga ERDELI (harp). [Scarlatti, Schumann, Lyadov *et al*.] P 1974, I 1975.

Poland: Pronil SX 1556. Nos. 1-7 arr. for string orchestra. Capella Arcis Varsoviensis, Marek SEWEN. [Janáček.] P 1975.

USSR: Melodiya C20 12575-6. No. 5 arr. N. Rizolya. Aleksandr DMITRIEV (bayan). [Bach, Franck, Liszt *et al*.] P 1979, I 1980*b*.

Bulgaria: Balkanton BKA 10294. Nos. 4, 5, and 6. Krasimir GATEV. [Sans op. B and Op. 5; Prokofiev and Kabalevsky.] P early 1980s?

USSR: Melodiya C50 20749 006. No. 7 only. Rimma BOBRITSKAYA. ['For Children'—Opp. 69, 97*a*, and 3*a*; Sans opp. B and P.] P 1983, I 1984*d*.

AVM Classics AVM 1003 and Compact Disc AVMCD 1003. Complete Suite. Martin JONES. [Opp. 12, 61, and 5; Sans op. B.] P date not stated, G Oct. 1988.

Greece: Kalyke Compact Disc KNI CDI. Complete Suite. Cilia PETRI-DOU. ['A Child, A Piano & Foreign Lands'—Khachaturyan, Kalomiris, and Petridou.] P 1990.

France: Le Chant du Monde Russian Season Compact Disc LDC 288 034. No. 7 only. Rimma BOBRITSKAYA. ['Russian Miniatures for Piano'— Sans op. P, Opp. 97 and 69; Tchaikovsky and Prokofiev.] P Moscow Conservatory Feb. 1991. *Reissued:* France: Le Chant du Monde Russian Season Compact Disc RUS 788034. [As 1991 recording.] I Mar. 1999.

Netherlands: Globe Compact Disc GLO 5082. Complete Suite. Mila BASLAVSKAYA. ['Russian Piano Music for Children'—Maykapar, Prokofiev, and Tchaikovsky.] P Utrecht Apr. 1992.

Koch International Classics Compact Disc 3 7159-2HI. Complete Suite. Israela MARGALIT. [Opp. 35 and 5; and Schnittke.] P Moscow Conservatory Sept. 1992, I July 1993, G Sept. 1993.

France: Accord Compact Disc 202812. Complete Suite. Caroline WEICHERT. [Opp. 13 and 34; Sans op. B.] P Sept. 1993, I 1994.

USA: Sonora Compact Disc SO 22563CD. Complete Suite. Inna HEIFETZ. [Tchaikovsky and Prokofiev.] P Boston 1993, I Jan. 1998.

USA: Gagliano Compact Disc GR 604-CD. Nos. 1, 2, 3, and 6 arr. Johanson. Hamilton CHEIFETZ (cello) and Bryan Johanson (guitar). [Wm Schuman, Ravel, Falla *et al*.] P Portland State University, Oregon 29 and 30 Mar. 1997.

Italy: Real Sound Compact Disc RS 051 0022. Complete Suite. Anna MALIKOVA. [Opp. 5 and 34.] P Wesel, Germany Apr. 1997.

Germany: Hänssler Classic Compact Disc 98 174. Nos. 6and 7 arr. Fortunatov. Michael LEMPIK (violin) and Olga Haus (piano). ['Allegro'—Op. 69; Verdi, Vivaldi, Beethoven *et al*.] P Altensteig 21-3 June 1997.

(ii) *Murzilka*

Form: A brief undated piece for piano.

Composed: Probably between 1944 and 1952 judging by the style and technique, for his own children.

Duration: 0' 32"—0' 35".

Recordings: USSR: Melodiya C10 26307 004. Viktoria POSTNIKOVA (piano). [Album 6 of 'From Manuscripts of Different Years'—Sans opp. X, T, A, and D; Opp. 41 and 128.] P 1983-6, I 1988*d*.

AVM Classics Compact Disc AVZ 3020. Martin JONES. ['Piano Music Volume II'—Sans opp. A and T; Opp. 13, 34, 69, and 22*a*.] P London 1-2 June 1989.

Opus 93   Symphony No. 10 in E minor

Form: Symphony for full orchestra in four movements:

1. Moderato
2. Allegro
3. Allegretto
4. Andante—Allegro

Instrumentation: piccolo, 2 flutes (II = piccolo II), 2 oboes, cor anglais (= oboe III), E flat clarinet (= clarinet III A and B flat), 2 clarinets (A and B flat), 2 bassoons, contrabassoon (= bassoon III) ~ 4 horns, 3 trumpets, 3 trombones, tuba ~ timpani, triangle, tambourine, side drum, cymbals, bass drum, gong ~ xylophone ~ strings.

Composed: Summer—25 October 1953. The first, second, and third movements completed on 5 and 27 August and 8 September respectively; at Komarovo village, Gulf of Finland. See Note.

Premières: 22 November 1953, Leningrad Philharmonic Bolshoi Hall; Leningrad Philharmonic Orchestra, Yevgeni Mravinsky (who also conducted the Moscow première on 29 December 1953).

USA: 14 October 1954, New York Philharmonic Symphony Society, Dimitri Mitropoulos.

UK: 10 April 1955, Royal Festival Hall, London; London Philharmonic Orchestra, Sir Adrian Boult.

Arrangement: Reduction for piano four hands by the composer.

Music: Autograph score preserved at the Glinka Museum. The opening of the first movement of the autograph score is reproduced in Volume 5 of *Collected Works*.

Muzgiz, No. 24447, 1954, full score, 30 cm.

Muzgiz, No. 24455, 1955, reduction for piano four hands, 28.5 cm.

Le Chant du Monde, No. 429, 1955, 19 cm.

Leeds Music, no number, 1955, 22 cm.
Boosey & Hawkes, No. 687. *c.*1955, 22.5 cm.
Edwin F. Kalmus, No. 158, no date, 26.5 cm.
Muzgiz, 1960, 21 cm.
Muzyka, No. 9863 (in Volume 5 of *Collected Works* with Op. 70), 1979, 30 cm.
Hans Sikorski, No. 2219, 1981, 21 cm.
Duration: 50 minutes in score: 45' 38"–59' 12"; 45' 00" (Aronowsky); 53' 00"–54' 20" (Plaistow).
Ballets: *Tenth Symphony.* Alan Carter, Wuppertal, West Germany, 1967. [*Tenth Symphony.* Konstantin Boyarsky, with libretto by Isaak Glikman. Not performed?]
Film: *La Ley del Deseo* (The Law of Desire). Sections of the symphony used in the score of the Spanish erotic and surreal film of 1986, directed by Pedro Almodóvar.
Recordings: USSR: Melodiya M10 39079-80 (mono). Arr. for piano four hands. Dmitri SHOSTAKOVICH and Moisei VAINBERG (piano). [In four-record set 'D. Shostakovich—Pianist'.] P 15 Feb. 1954, I 1977*b*. *Reissued:* Germany: Melodia Eurodisc 27 235 XDK. [In two-record set 'Shostakovich plays Shostakovich'.] ~ France: Le Chant du Monde Compact Disc LDC 278 1000 (mono, double-play). [Opp. 79*a*, 57, and 87.] I Sept. 1989 ~ Revelation Compact Disc RV 70002 (mono). ['Shostakovich plays Shostakovich, Vol. 2'—Opp. 34 and 97.] I Oct. 1997, G Feb. 1998.

USSR: MK HD 02243-4 (mono). Leningrad Philharmonic Orchestra, Yevgeni MRAVINSKY. P 24 Apr. 1954, I 1954. *Reissued:* USA: Colosseum CRLP 173 (mono). Labelled erroneously as 'National Philharmonic Orchestra conducted by Dmitri Shostakovich'. [Kabalevsky.] I 1954 ~ France: Le Chant du Monde LDXA 8113 (mono). I 1954 ~ Saga XID 5228 (mono). I 1964, Dec. 1984, and May 1985; G July 1985 ~ USA: Concert Hall CHS 1313 (mono). I 1954 ~ Classics Club X 1018 (mono). Issued under the pseudonyms 'Classics Club Philharmonic Orchestra conducted by Feodor Stepanov' ~ Saga Classics Compact Disc SCD 9017 (digitally remastered mono). I Nov. 1991, G June 1992 ~ Saga Classics Compact Disc EC 3366-2. I Apr. 1994.

East Germany: Eterna 72 0006-7 (4 sides, 10" mono). Gewandhaus Orchestra of Leipzig, Franz KONWITSCHNY. P 10 June 1954. *Reissued:* East Germany: LPM 1031-2 (4 sides, 10" mono) ~ Czech: Supraphon MN 799-802 (4 sides, 10" mono) ~ Germany: Berlin Classics Compact Disc 0090 422 BC (two-disc set, mono). [Op. 103.] I Oct. 1995.

USA: Columbia ML 4959 (mono). New York Philharmonic Orchestra, Dimitri MITROPOULOS. P 18 Oct. 1954. *Reissued:* Philips ABL 3052 (mono). G July 1955 ~ France: Philips A 01 175 L (mono) ~ USA: Columbia-Odyssey 3216 0123 (mono). I 1967 ~ CBS Classics 61457 (mono). G Feb. 1981 ~ CBS Masterworks Portrait Compact Disc MPK, 45698 (mono). [Op. 70.] I Dec. 1989, G Feb. 1990.

Italy: Stradivarius STR Compact Disc 10035 (mono). Roma RAI Symphony Orchestra, Artur RODZINSKI. [Prokofiev.] P 18 Mar. 1955, I 1990.
HMV ALP 1322 (mono). Philharmonia Orchestra, Efrem KURTZ. P London 22–3 Mar. 1955, G Feb. 1956. *Reissued:* USA: RCA Victor LM 2081 (mono). I 1957 ~ HMV HQM 1034 (mono). G Nov. 1966 ~ USA: Testament Compact Disc SBT 1078 (mono) [Op. 22.] I Nov. 1996, G Feb. 1997.
France: Praga Compact Disc PR 250 053 (mono). Leningrad Philharmonic Orchestra, Yevgeni MRAVINSKY. [Op. 27.] P Prague concert broadcast 3 June 1955, I Nov. 1994, G Sept. 1995. *Reissued:* France: Le Chant du Monde Compact Disc PR 7250 053 (mono). [Op. 27.] G Feb. 2001.
Deutsche Grammophon DGM 18300 (mono). Czech Philharmonic Orchestra, Karel ANČERL. P Munich 28-9 Oct. 1955, G Sept. 1956. *Reissued:* Decca Gold label DL 9822 (mono) ~ Helidor 478412 (mono) ~ France: Deutsche Grammophon 'Les Grandes Années' Compact Disc 457 080-2. [Ravel and Kodály.] I 1997.
Bulgaria: Balkanton 0150 (mono). Bulgarian State Radio Orchestra, Vassil STEFANOV. P c.1960.
Romania: Electrecord ECE 033 (mono). Rumanian [now Romanian] Radio Symphony Orchestra, Constantin SILVESTRI. P c.1960. *Reissued:* Romania: Electrecord ECE 0633 (mono) and ST-ECE 0634. I 1971.
Poland: Muza XL 0004 (mono). Warsaw Philharmonic Orchestra, Bohdan WODICZKO. P 1961. *Reissued:* East Germany: Eterna A33 8 20 127 (mono) and 8 25 127.
USSR: Melodiya D 018131-2 (mono) and C 01721-2. USSR Symphony Orchestra, Yevgeni SVETLANOV. P 1966, I 1966 (mono) and 1969 (stereo). *Reissued:* HMV Melodiya ASD 2420. G Oct. 1968 ~ USA: Angel Melodiya S 40025. I 1976 ~ HMV SEOM 9. Second movement only. ['Introducing HMV Melodiya' sampler—Tchaikovsky, Schumann, Lyadov *et al.*] G Dec. 1971 ~ Germany: Melodia Eurodisc 87 623 XPK. [In thirteen-record box set.] I 1974 ~ Germany: Melodia Eurodisc 300 602-435. [In three-record box set with Opp. 103 and 22*a*.] ~ HMV Melodiya BOX 502508 in Set SLS 5025. G Dec. 1975 ~ Italy: EMI 065 95569. I 1978 ~ USA: Musical Heritage Society MHS 4166. [In two-record set with Op. 47.] I 1980.
Japan: Japanese Stokowski Society JLSS 0021. Chicago Symphony Orchestra, Leopold STOKOWSKI. P Chicago concert 24 Mar. 1966. *Reissued:* USA: Chicago Symphony Orchestra Compact Disc CSO 90/12.
Deutsche Grammophon SLPM 139 020. Berlin Philharmonic Orchestra, Herbert von KARAJAN. P 28-30 Nov. 1966, G Jan. 1969. *Reissued:* Deutsche Grammophon Galleria Compact Disc 429 716-2GGA. I June 1990, G Aug. 1990 and Nov. 1992. NB. A nine-bar cut from fig. 54 minus 5 bars restored on copies issued from early 1993.
USSR: Melodiya C10 21227 009. Berlin Philharmonic Orchestra, Herbert von KARAJAN. P Moscow concert 29 May 1969, I 1985*b*.
USA: Columbia M 30295. Philadelphia Orchestra, Eugene ORMANDY. P 10–18 Apr. 1968. *Reissued:* CBS SBRG 72886. G June 1971 ~ Sony Essential

Classics Compact Discs SB2K 62409 (two-disc set). [Op. 43.] G Aug. 1996 and Mar. 1997.

USA: Russian Disc Compact Disc RDCD 11 195. Leningrad Philharmonic Orchestra, Yuri TEMIRKANOV. [Op. 14.] P Moscow concert 26 Jan. 1973, I Oct. 1993, G Jan. 1994.

USSR: Melodiya C 04505-6. Moscow Philharmonic Orchestra, Kirill KONDRASHIN. P 20 Oct. 1973, I 1974*d*. *Reissued:* France: Le Chant du Monde LDX 78629. I 1976 ~ USSR: Melodiya C 04505-6. [In second box of Part 1 of *Collected Works on Records.*] I 1980 ~ HMV Melodiya EX 2903873 (DMM). [Eighth record in twelve-record box set.] G Dec. 1985 ~ France: Le Chant du Monde Compact Disc LDC 278 1005-6. [In Box 3 of five two-disc sets with Opp. 65 and 70.] G May 1989 ~ BMG Classics Melodiya Compact Disc 74321 19847-2. [Op. 54.] I July 1994, G Nov. 1994 ~ Japan: Icone Compact Disc INC 9426-2. I Oct. 1994.

Classics for Pleasure CFP 40216. London Philharmonic Orchestra, Andrew DAVIS. P Barking 30 Apr.–1 May 1974, G May 1975 and June 1986. *Reissued:* USA: Seraphim S 60255 ~ Classics for Pleasure CFP 41 4472-1. G Sept. 1985 ~ Classics for Pleasure Compact Disc CD-CFP 6041. I Mar. 1998, G May 1998.

HMV BOX 504402 in Set SLS 5044 (quad). Bournemouth Symphony Orchestra, Paavo BERGLUND. [Op. 47 in two-record box set.] P Southampton 16–17 Mar. 1975, G Mar. 1976. *Reissued:* USA: Angel S 37280 (quad) ~ HMV Greensleeve ESD 7049 (quad). G Oct. 1977 ~ EMI Studio Compact Disc CDM7 63096-2. I Aug. 1989 ~ HMV Classics Compact Disc 5-73858-2. [Op. 70.] I Apr. 2000, G Sept. 2000.

Japan: Victor Musical Industries Compact Disc VDC 25027. Leningrad Philharmonic Orchestra, Yevgeni MRAVINSKY. P Leningrad rehearsal ? 3 Mar. 1976, I 1990. *Reissued:* France: Erato Compact Disc 2292 45753-2. I Apr. 1992, G June 1992. [NB. Also available in twelve-disc set 2292 45763-2.]

USSR: Melodiya M10 44371003 (mono). Leningrad Philharmonic Orchestra, Yevgeni MRAVINSKY. P Leningrad concert 31 Mar. 1976, I 1983*b*. *Reissued:* Japan: Victor VIC 4513, I 1982 ~ USSR: Melodiya C10 28341 005 (two-record set). Second movement only. ['Petersburg-Petrograd-Leningrad' with Glinka, Musorgsky, Rimsky-Korsakov *et al.*] Version not positively identified ~ BMG Melodiya Compact Disc 74321 25198-2. ['Mravinsky Edition, Vol. 9'—Op. 54.] I June 1995 ~ Leningrad Masters Compact Disc LM 1322 (mono). G Sept. 1996.

Decca SXL 6838. London Philharmonic Orchestra, Bernard HAITINK. P Jan. 1977, G Oct. 1977. *Reissued:* USA: London CS 7061. I 1977 ~ Decca Compact Disc 421 353-2DH. I Dec. 1988, G Mar. 1989 ~ Decca Ovation Compact Disc 425 064-2DM. [Op. 14.] I Aug. 1993, G Nov. 1993 ~ London Compact Disc 444 432-2. [On second disc in eleven-disc set with Op. 14.] I June 1995.

East Germany: Eterna 8 27 093. Berlin City Symphony Orchestra, Kurt SANDERLING. P 9-11 and 14 Feb. 1977, I 1986. *Reissued:* Japan: Deutsche Schallplatten ET 5021. I July 1988 ~ Germany: Berlin Classics Compact Disc 0090182 BC. I Nov. 1995.

USA: Classical Excellence CE 11038-9 (4 sides, stereo). Austrian Radio Symphony Orchestra, Milan HORVAT. P 1977. *Reissued:* Switzerland: Point Classics Compact Disc 2671642. I 1994.

RCA Red Seal RL 25049. National Philharmonic Orchestra. Loris TJEKNAVORIAN. P 1977, G July 1978.

USSR: Melodiya C10 09851-2. Moscow Philharmonic Orchestra, Dmitri KITAYENKO. P1977. I 1978c.

Czech: Opus 9110 0846. Slovák Philharmonic Orchestra, Ladislav SLOVÁK. P Bratislava Oct. 1979, I 1980. *Reissued:* Switzerland: Bonton Classics Compact Disc 71 0154-2 0110. I 1994.

Deutsche Grammophon 2532 030 (digital). Berlin Philharmonic Orchestra, Herbert von KARAJAN. P Berlin 20, 23, and 27 Feb. 1981, G Mar. 1982. *Reissued:* Deutsche Grammophon Compact Disc 413 361-2GH, G Aug. 1984 ~ Deutsche Grammophon New Gold Edition Compact Disc 439 036-2GHS. I Jan. 1996, G May 1996.

USSR: Melodiya C10 18617-8. USSR Ministry of Culture Symphony Orchestra, Gennadi ROZHDESTVENSKY. P 1982, I 1983c.

Czech: Supraphon 1110 3190 ZA. Czech Philharmonic Orchestra, František VAJNAR. P 3-5 Mar. 1982, I 1983.

HMV ASD 4405 (digital). London Symphony Orchestra, André PREVIN. P July 1982, G Apr., and Aug. 1983. *Reissued:* USA: Angel DS 37955 (digital). I 1983 ~ EMI Classics Compact Disc CDD7 64105-2. [Prokofiev.] I Nov. 1991. G Jan. 1992 ~ EMI Classics Double Forte Compact Discs CZS5 73369-2 (two-disc set). [Op. 113.] I May 1999, G Aug. 1999.

HMV EL 270315-1 (digital) and Compact Disc CDC7 47350-2. Philharmonia Orchestra, Simon RATTLE. P 3-4 Apr. 1985, G Sept. 1986. *Reissued:* USA: Angel DS 38285 (digital). I 1986 ~ EMI Compact Disc CDZ7 62803-2. Second movement only. ['Simon Rattle sampler'—Janáček, Nielsen, Sibellus *et al.*] I 1989 ~ EMI Classics Studio Plus Compact Disc CDM7 64870-2. [Britten.] I Nov. 1993, G Mar. 1994.

Netherlands: Q Disc Compact Discs 97014 (fourteen-disc set). Concertgebouw Orchestra, Bernard HAITINK. ['The Radio Recordings'—on disc 14.] P Netherlands Radio 8 Dec. 1985, I 1999.

USSR: Melodiya A10 00307 000 (digital). USSR Ministry of Culture Symphony Orchestra, Gennadi ROZHDESTVENSKY. P Jan. 1986, I 1988d. *Reissued:* Olympia Compact Disc OCD 131. [Op. 32.] I Sept. 1988, G May 1989 ~ Germany: Melodia Eurodisc Compact Disc 258 489 ~ Olympia Compact Disc OCD 5006. [In Vol. 2 five-disc set of symphonies with Op. 32.] I Dec. 1990 ~ BMG Melodiya Compact Discs 74321 63461-2 (two-disc set). [Opp. 91; 103, and 23.] I Mar. 1999.

USA: RCA Gold Seal Compact Disc 5608-2 RC. Saint Louis Symphony Orchestra, Leonard SLATKIN. P St Louis 8 and 10 Feb. 1987. *Reissued:* RCA Victor Red Seal Compact Disc RD 86597. G July 1988.

Chandos ABRD 1319 (digital) and Compact Disc CHAN 8630. Scottish National Orchestra, Neeme JÄRVI. [Sans op. P.] P Dundee 12 May 1988, I Dec. 1988, G Mar. 1989. *Reissued:* Conifer Classics Compact Disc Class 7006. [Sans op. P.] I Nov. 1991.

Virgin Classics VC 790784-1 (digital) and Compact Disc VC 790784-2. London Philharmonic Orchestra, Nicholas Busch (French horn), Andrew LITTON. [Op. 96.] P London Sept. 1988, I and G Apr. 1989. *Reissued:* Virgin Classics Ultraviolet Compact Disc 7243 5 611342-2. [Op. 96.] I Aug. 1994, G Aug, and Nov. 1994.

Singapore: Philips Compact Disc 426 228-2. Singapore Symphony Orchestra, Choo HOEY. [Pin.] P and I 1989.

Naxos Compact Disc 8.550633. Czecho-Slovak Radio Symphony Orchestra, Ladislav SLOVÁK. P Bratislava 20-6 June 1989, I Oct. 1993, G Nov. 1993. *Reissued:* Naxos Compact Discs 8.506003, [In six-disc set with Symphonies Nos. 5, 8, 9, 11, 13, and 14.] I 1993.

Teldec Compact Disc 9031 74529-2. London Symphony Orchestra, Mstislav ROSTROPOVICH. P London July 1989, I Oct. 1991, G Mar. 1992. *Reissued:* Teldec Compact Discs 0630-17046-2. [In twelve-disc set of Symphonies.] G Oct. 1997.

Naxos Compact Disc 8.550326. Belgian Radio and Television Philharmonic Orchestra, Alexander RAHBARI. P Brussels 6-8 Sept. 1989, I Feb. 1990.

Telarc Compact Disc CD-80241. Atlanta Symphony Orchestra. Yoel LEVI. P Atlanta 25-6 Sept. 1989, I Oct. 1990, G Jan. 1991.

Denon Compact Disc CO 79474. Vienna Symphony Orchestra, Eliahu INBAL. P Vienna 30 Jan.–2 Feb. 1990, I June 1992, G Sept. 1992.

Collins Classics Compact Disc 1106-2. London Symphony Orchestra, Maksim SHOSTAKOVICH. P London Jan. 1990, I Oct. 1990, G Jan. 1991. *Reissued:* Collins Classics Compact Disc 70122. [In three-disc set with Opp. 47, 96, 97, and 141.] I Sept. 1991.

Decca Compact Disc 430 844-2DH. Cleveland Orchestra, Christoph von DOHNÁNYI. [Lutoslawski.] P Cleveland 12 Feb. 1990, I July 1992, G Sept. 1992.

Delos Compact Disc DE 3089. Helsinki Philharmonic Orchestra, James DE PRIEST. [Op. 96.] P Hyvinkää, Finland 19-20 Apr. 1990, I Oct. 1990, G. Jan. 1991.

RCA Victor Red Seal Compact Disc RD 60448. Royal Concertgebouw Orchestra, Claus Peter FLOR. P Amsterdam 17-18 Aug. 1990, I Feb. 1992, G June 1992.

Decca Compact Disc 433 028-2DH. Royal Philharmonic Orchestra. Vladimir ASHKENAZY. [Op. 110a.] P Watford Sept. 1990, I Nov. 1991. G Jan. 1992.

Decca Compact Disc 433 073-2DH. Chicago Symphony Orchestra, Georg SOLTI. P Chicago concert Oct. 1990, I Mar. 1992, G June 1992.

Pickwick IMP Classica Compact Disc PCD 955. Hallé Orchestra. Stanislaw SKROWACZEWSKI. P Bolton 23-4 Nov. 1990, I July 1991, G Oct. 1991. *Reissued:* IMP Classics 2000 Compact Disc PCD 2043. I Oct. 1997.

Sweden: Bluebell Compact Disc ABCD 049. Arr. for piano four hands. Folke GRÄSBECK and Alexander ZELYAKOV (piano). [Op. 6.] P Åbo 22 and 29 Jan. 1992, I Mar. 1993.

Chandos Compact Disc CHAN 9522. Russian State Symphony Orchestra, Valeri POLYANSKY. [Sans op. D (iv).] P Moscow Conservatory June 1995, I Oct. 2000, G Mar. 2001.

EMI Compact Disc CDC5 55232-2. Philadelphia Orchestra, Mariss JANSONS. [Sans op. V.] P Philadelphia 5-7 Mar. 1994, I Mar. 1995, G June and Aug. 1995.

Tring Compact Disc TRP 080. Royal Philharmonic Orchestra, Frank SHIPWAY. [Op. 97.] P London May 1995, I Sept. 1996.

Sweden: BIS Compact Discs CD 973-4 (two-disc set). BBC National Orchestra of Wales. Mark WIGGLESWORTH. ['Complete Symphonies, Vol. 2'—Opp. 47 and 54.] P Swansea Nov. 1997, I June 1999, G Sept. 1999.

Switzerland: Relief Compact Disc CR 991047. Tchaikovsky Symphony Orchestra, Vladimir FEDOSEYEV. [Op. 97.] P 1998.

Delos Compact Discs DE 3283 (two-disc set). Dallas Symphony Orchestra, Andrew LITTON. [Op. 54.] P Dallas concert 21-4 Sept, and 30 Nov. 2000, I Oct. 2001.

References: *DSCH Journal* No. 1, Fanning, Kravets (in Kovatskaya), Ottaway, Sabinina, Sokolsky, and Tigranov.

Notes: Elizabeth Wilson (1994, pp. 256-7 and 261-2) relates Tatyana Nikolayeva's conviction that the symphony was composed in 1951 'parallel to the creation of the Preludes and Fugues', Opus 87.

The origin of the enigmatic feature of the third movement—the horn call that occurs twelve times—was revealed in *DSCH Journal* No. 1, pp. 24-5. The motif is the encoded name of Elmira Nazirova, at the time of the writing of the symphony, a 25-year-old composer from Azerdaidzhan and an object of his affection. The first and last letters of Elmira are the notes E and A and the middle letters in Tonic Sol-fa notation are 'l' (= note A). 'mi' (= note E), and 'r' (= note D) giving the horn motif EAEDA. See also Nazirova (in Bartlett).

Opus 94   Concertino

Form: A small-scale concerto in A minor for two pianos four hands in one movement: Adagio—Allegretto—Allegro.

Composed: 1953.

Première: 8 November 1954, Moscow Conservatory Malyi Hall; Maksim Shostakovich and Alla Maloletkova (pianoforte duo).

Arrangements: Transcribed for accordion duet by Tamara Murzina and Alla Gatsenko. Orchestral arrangement by Elliot Kaplan for the ballet *Celebration*. Arrangement for twelve-piece brass band by Kenneth Singleton. Transcription for piano and chamber orchestra by Julia Zilberquit in 1996.

Music: Autograph score preserved at the Glinka Museum.

Music Fund of the USSR, No. 461, 1955, 29 cm.

MCA/Leeds Music, No. 2093, 1956, 30 cm.

Muzyka, 1966, revised version.

International Music, No. 2373, 1966, 30.5 cm.

Muzyka, No. 5947 (in *D. Shostakovich: Compositions for fortepiano*, Volume 3, with Opp. 35 and 102), 1970, 29 cm.

Muzyka, No. 2904, 1975, 29 cm.

Hans Sikorski, No. 2185, 1975, 31.5 cm.

Muzyka, No. 11214 (in Volume 13 of *Collected Works* with Opp. 6, 35, 102, and Sans op. O), 1983, 30 cm.

Duration: Approx 9 minutes in score; 7' 48"—11' 22"; 8 minutes (Sadovnikov); 10 minutes (Plaistow). Chamber Orchestra version: 15' 39".

Ballet: *Celebration*. Gerald Arpino, Joffrey Ballet, Chicago Auditorium Theater, 15 May 1980; danced to an orchestrated arrangement by Elliot Kaplan; conducted by Allan Lewis.

Recordings: USSR: MK D 3036-7 (10" mono). Maksim and Dmitri SHOSTAKOVICH. [Op. 34 Nos. 10, 15, 16, and 24; and Op. 49]. P and I 1956. *Reissued:* USA: Monitor MC 2040 (mono). [Prokofiev.] I 1959 ~ USSR: Melodiya M10 39073-4 (mono). [In four-record set 'D. Shostakovich— Pianist' with Opp. 102 and 35.] I 1977*b* ~ HMV Melodiya HLM 7094 in Set RLS 721 (mono). [Opp. 102 and 79.] G Oct. 1976 ~ Germany: Melodia Eurodisc 27 235 XDK. [In two-record set 'Shostakovich plays Shostakovich' with Opp. 35 and 102.] ~ USSR: Melodiya C10 14089-90 (electronic stereo). [In third box of Part 1 of *Collected Works on Records* with Opp. 102 and 35.] I 1980 ~ Japan: Victor Musical Industries Compact Disc VICC 2048. ['Pianist = D. Shostakovich' with Opp. 57, 35, and 102.] 1 1990 ~ Revelation Compact Disc RV 70006 (mono). ['Shostakovich plays Shostakovich, Vol. 5'—Opp. 35, 102, and 67.] I May 1998.

USSR: MK D 5480-1 (10" mono). Anna KLAS and Bruno LUKK. [Milhaud, Kapp, Auster, and Pärt.] P 1959.

USSR: Melodiya C10 15055-6. Galina and Yuliya TURKNY. [Shchedrin, Arutyunyan, and Yevseyev.] P 1962, I 1981*c*.

Italy: Angelicum LPA 5940 (mono) and STA 8940. Gino GORNI and Sergio LORENZI. [Brahms, Dvořák, and Debussy.] P early 1960s, I 1960s and stereo in 1970s.

USSR: MK D 27221-2 (10" mono). Lyubov BRUK and Mark TAIMANOV. [Milhaud, Okunev *et al.*] P 1970.

USA: Kapell SKR 5101. Allison NELSON and Harry Lee NEAL. [Chopin and Ravel.] P 1970.

Classics for Pleasure CFPD 4144383. John OGDON and Brenda LUCAS. [In double album 'Rachmaninov—Music for Four Hands'—Rakhmaninov, Arensky, and Khachaturyan.] P June 1975, G Apr. 1984. *Reissued:* EMI Classics Compact Discs CZS 5 69386-2 (two-disc set). [Rakhmaninov, Arensky, Khachaturyan *et al.*] I May 1996.

USSR: Melodiya C30 08631-2. Arr. for accordion duet. Tamara MURZINA and Alla GATSENKO (accordions). [Dvořák, Rossini, Yutsevich *et al.*] P 1977, I 1978*a*.

USA: Musical Heritage Society MHS 1147Y. DUO DE HEIDELBERG (Hans-Helmut Schwarz and Edith Henrici). [Op. 5; Borodin, Glinka, Rakhmaninov *et al.*] P 1977.

France: Elyon EL 35013. Bernard and Geneviève PICAVET. [Poulenc and Milhaud.] P *c.*1979.

Sweden: Bluebell Bell 126. Inger WIKSTRÖM (piano—both parts). [Opp. 5; 19 Nos. 3, 4, and 2; 22*a* No. 3; 31 No. 4; 97*a* No. 7; 105 fragment; and Prokofiev.] P Stockholm 28 Jan, and I Feb. 1981. *Reissued:* Sweden: Swedish Society Discofil Compact Disc SCD 1031. [Opp. 34, 61, 5, and 19.] I 1988.

USSR: Melodiya C10 18471-2. Viktoria POSTNIKOVA and Nikolai PETROV. [Op. 6.] P 1982, I 1983*c*.

USA: Orion ORS 83462. Zoe ERISMAN (piano—both parts). [Opp. 34, 39, and 27.] P 1983.

Belgium: Terpsichore 1982 029. Levente KENDE and Heidi HENDRICKX. [Ravel, Constant, and Corijn.] P 1984.

Chandos ARBD 1175 (digital). Seta TANYEL and Jeremy BROWN. ['Russian Music for Two Pianos' with Op. 6; Khachaturyan and Arutyunyan/Babdzhanyan.] P London July 1985, I July 1986, G Nov. 1986. *Reissued:* Chandos Compact Disc CHAN 8466. I May 1987.

Pianissimo Compact Disc PP 21192. Claire and Antoinette CANN. ['Gemini Duo Series Volume Three'—Lutoslawski, Horowitz, Poulenc *et al.*] P Hampstead 7-8 Sept. 1987, I Oct. 1993.

USA: Centaur Compact Disc CRC 2261. Arr. K. Singleton. Denver Brass. Kenneth SINGLETON. [Rossini, Grainger, Schmeltzer *et al.*] P Englewood, Colorado 17-19 June 1991, I 1996.

Belgium: Discover International Compact Disc DICD 920150. DUO 'REINE ELISABETH' (Rolf Plagge and Wolfgang Manz). [Stravinsky, Skryabin, and Rakhmaninov.] P Brussels 1992, I and G Nov. 1994.

USA: Sonora Compact Disc SO 22566CD. Natalia ZUSMAN and Inna HEIFETZ (piano duo). ['The Revisionist's Tale'—Sans op. P; Schnittke, Glière, and Borodin.] P Boston, Mass. 1994, I Nov. 1995.

USA: Summit Compact Disc DCD 171. Arr. K. Singleton. Summit Brass, Carl TOPILOW. ['Paving the Way'—Holst, Ewazen, Tomasi *et al.*] P Danville, Kentucky June 1995.

Denmark: Classico Compact Disc CLASSCD 141. ELVIRA PIANO DUO (Mimi Birkelund and Anne Mette Staehr). [Brahms, Mozart, Lutoslawski *et al.*] P Birkerød, Denmark Aug. 1995.

Germany: Amati Compact Disc AMI SRR 9402. MENDELSSOHN DUO (Noriko Ishikawa and Manfred Kratzer). [Clementi, Mendelssohn, Rakhmaninov *et al.*] P Karlsruhe 12-13 Sept. 1995, I 1996.

USA: Music Masters Compact Disc 01612 67189-2. Arr. for piano and chamber Orchestra by J. Zilberquit. Julia ZILBERQUIT (piano), Moscow Virtuosi, Vladimir Spivakov. [Op. 79*a* and Sans op. X (ii).] P Dec. 1996.

France: Suoni e Colori Compact Disc SC 53008. Incorrectly labelled Op. 84. Thérèse DUSSAUT and Serge POLUSMIAK (piano duo). ['Hommage à Dmitri Chostakovitch. Vol. 2'—Opp. 134 and 6; Sans op. O (i).] P Espace Fazioli, Paris Oct.–Nov. 1997.

Germany: CPO Compact Disc 999 599-2. GENOVA & DIMITROV PIANO DUO. [Opp. 6, 95, Sans'op'p. O (ii) and E; Stravinsky, Prokofiev, and Dinicu.] P Hans Rosbaud Studio 4-5 May 1998, I Apr. 1999.

Opus 95   Song of the Great Rivers

Alternative titles: *Unity* and *Seven Rivers*.

Form: Music for the documentary film *Song of the Great Rivers*, directed by the Dutch director Joris Ivens, for the then East German DEFA Studios. The score includes a Waltz and two songs: 'Peaceful Labour' (or 'Poem about Work'), with words by Semyon Kirsanov, for S.A.A.T.B.B. chorus and orchestra; and 'Song of Unity' (also known as 'Song of the Great Rivers' or 'Song of the Working People'), with the German verses of Bertolt Brecht translated by S. Kirsanov, for solo bass, S.A.T.B. chorus, and orchestra. The incomplete manuscript score, orchestral and choral parts stored at the Music Library of the USSR Cinematography Symphony Orchestra consists of three orchestral items depicting the Atom Bomb (using material from the Eighth Symphony, Opus 65) and the following numbers:

Cover [Introduction]—Allegro

1. Song of the Great Rivers ('The great Nile—our benefactor)—Allegro non troppo
2. Prologue (Poem about Work)
3. The Indictment Episode—Adagio
4. 'K.K.K.' [= Klu Klux Klan]—Allegro

6. South Africa—Allegro
7. Children (viola and cello duet)—Moderato. Salt
8. Hard Labour—Moderato

Instrumentation: piccolo, 2 flutes, 3 oboes, E flat clarinet, 2 clarinets (B flat and A), 2 bassoons, contrabassoon ~ 4 horns, 3 trumpets, 3 trombones, tuba ~ timpani, triangle, side drum, cymbals, bass drum, gong ~ glockenspiel, xylophone, celesta ~ harp ~ bass soloist, S.A.T.B. chorus ~ strings.

Composed: 1954, at Moscow. The Waltz dates from 1953 or earlier.

Premières: Film first shown in November 1954. In the film 'Song of Unity' is sung in English by Paul Robeson. Film released in Britain with the English commentary by Alex McCrindle (featured on a BBC2 TV documentary on Joris Ivens, *Too Much Reality*, on 21 January 1982).

Arrangements: Vocal scores of the two songs by the composer. The Waltz appears in Ballet Suite No. 4, Sans op. P; and transcribed for wind orchestra by M. Marantslikht. A version of the Waltz for piano duo recorded. The Cover [Introduction] and No. 6 South Africa utilises material from the film score *The Return of Maxim*, Opus 45.

Music: Autograph of the film score believed to be preserved at the DEFA Studios, formerly in the German Democratic Republic.

Music Fund of the USSR, 1956, 'Peaceful Labour', full orchestral and six-part choral score, 29 cm.

Sovetskii Kompozitor, No. 519 (in *D. Shostakovich: Songs*), 1958, 'Peaceful Labour' and 'Song of Unity' with piano accompaniment, 29 cm.

Sovetskaya Muzyka magazine, 1958, No. 11, 'Song of Unity'.

Sovetskii Kompozitor, No. 928 (in *Dmitri Shostakovich: Waltzes from Film Music*), 1959, Waltz in full score, 29 cm.

Muzgiz, 1961, Waltz arr. for wind orchestra by M. Marantslikht, score and parts.

Muzyka, No. 10179 (in Volume 34 of *Collected Works* with Opp. 88 and 136, and songs), 1985, 'Peaceful Labour' and 'Song of Unity' with piano accompaniment, 30 cm.

Muzyka, No. 10890 (in Volume 42 of *Collected Works* with Opp. 75, 78, 80, 82, 97, 111, 116, 132, and 137), 1987, five items, 30 cm.

Ballet: *The Young Lady and the Hooligan*. The first half of the Waltz used by Lev Atovmyan in the 1962 ballet. See under Opus 27.

Recordings: 'Song of Unity' sung in German by Ernst Busch, recorded in 1967.

Germany: CPO Compact Disc 999 599-2. Waltz arr. for piano duo. GENOVA & DIMITROV PIANO DUO. [Opp. 94, 6, Sans opp. O (ii) and E; Stravinsky, Prokofiev, and Dinicu.] P Hans Rosbaud Studio 4-5 May 1998, I Apr. 1999. NB. Waltz incorrectly labelled as from Op. 22.

USA: Delos Compact Disc DE 3257. Waltz. Moscow Chamber Orchestra, Constantine ORBELIAN. ['Waltzes'—see Samplers. P Moscow Conservatory 12-14 July 1999, G Dec. 1999.

Opus 96   Festive Overture

Alternative titles: *Festival Overture* and *Holiday Overture.*

Form: An occasional overture in A major, marked 'Allegretto', for large orchestra (with optional brass band). The fanfare is based on 'Birthday', No. 7 of Opus 69.

Instrumentation: piccolo, 2 flutes, 3 oboes, 3 A clarinets, 2 bassoons, contrabassoon ~ 4 horns, 3 trumpets, 3 trombones, tuba ~ timpani, triangle, side drum, cymbals, bass drum ~ strings. Optional separate band of 4 horns, 3 trumpets, and 3 trombones for the coda.

Composed: Autumn 1954, at Moscow, for the thirty-seventh anniversary of the October Revolution. [The date is given as 1954 on scores but dated earlier as autumn 1947, for the thirtieth anniversary, in Volume 11 of *Collected Works.*]

Premières: 6 November 1954, Moscow Bolshoi Theatre; Bolshoi Theatre Orchestra, Aleksandr Melik-Pashayev.

USA: 16 November 1955, Utah Symphony Orchestra, Maurice Abravanel and New York; 16 February 1956, New York Philharmonic Orchestra, Dimitri Mitropoulos.

UK: 27 August 1962, Royal Albert Hall 'Prom', London; BBC Northern Orchestra, George Hurst.

Arrangements: Transcribed for military band or wind orchestra by Valeri Petrov, Donald Hunsberger, M. Vakhutinsky, and others; and for brass band by Harry Cornthwaite and Michael Antrobus. Reductions for piano four hands by Emin Khachaturyan and for two pianos four hands by A. Bubelnikov. Arranged for bayan trio by A. Khizhnyak.

The fanfare frequently played at outdoor ceremonies such as at the Bulgarian 9 September celebrations and the 22nd and 23rd Olympic Games. Adopted as the musical emblem for the 22nd Olympic Games, held in Moscow in 1980.

[*The Shot Heard Around the World* by Katherine Kennicott Davis, for S.A.T.B. chorus, organ, and optional 1st and 2nd B flat trumpets—a setting of the Concord Hymn by Ralph Waldo Emerson—stated to be based on an undisclosed Shostakovich theme, entered here on account of the similar trumpet fanfares. Duration: *c.*2' 55". Warner Bros., New York, No. CHO 750 (plate no. TMK-519-9), 1974, score and trumpet parts, 26.5 cm.]

Instrumentation of Vakhutinsky's arrangement: flute (= piccolo), 2 oboes, 3 B flat clarinets, 2 bassoons ~ 2 E flat alto saxhorns, 3 trumpets, 3 trombones ~ timpani, triangle/side drum, cymbals/bass drum ~ 3 B flat cornets, additional 8 saxhorns (2 E flat, 3 B flat tenor, B flat baritone, and bass). Parts for oboes, bassoons, and timpani not obligatory.

Music: Autograph score preserved at the Glinka Museum and its rough copy at the CIS Archives of Literature and Art. The first page of the autograph score is reproduced in Volume 11 of *Collected Works*.

Music Fund of the USSR, 1955 and 1959, score and parts.

Leeds Music and DICA, no number, *c.*1957, 23 cm.

Muzgiz, No. 26026, 1958, arr. for wind orchestra by V. Petrov, score, 29 cm.

Edwin F. Kalmus, No. 526, no date, 26 cm.

Edwin F. Kalmus, No. 2039, no date, conductor's full score, 33.5 cm.

Sovetskii Kompozitor, 1960, reduction for piano four hands by E. Khachaturyan.

Muzyka, No. 2109, 1961, reduction for two pianos four hands by A. Bubelnikov.

Edwin F. Kalmus, No. 3867, no date, above reduction though arranger not credited, 31 cm.

MCA, 1965, arr. for band by D. Hunsberger, score and parts, 31 cm.

Muzyka, No. 6197, 1970, full score, 28.5 cm.

Muzyka, No. 9706, 1977, arr. for military band by M. Vakhutinsky, score, 29 cm.

Midland Music, London, 1979, arr. for brass band by H. Cornthwaite.

Chandos Music, Colchester, No. 490, 1980, arr. for brass band and percussion (timpani, triangle, side drum, cymbals, bass drum) by M. Antrobus, score and parts, 29.5 cm.

Muzyka, No. 11687 (in Volume 11 of *Collected Works* with Sans op. U, Opp. 115, 130, and 131), 1984, 30 cm.

Duration: Approx. 6 minutes in score; 5' 07"–6' 47"; 6' 50" (Plaistow).

Recordings: [USSR: recorded on cine-film. Moscow Philharmonic Orchestra. Samuil SAMOSUD. P 1954.]

USSR: 25529-30 (10" 78 rpm). Bolshoi Theatre Orchestra, Aleksandr MELIK-PASHAYEV. P 1955. *Reissued:* USSR: Melodiya M10 42777-8 (mono). ['Melik-Pashayev Conducts'—Tchaikovsky, Bizet, and Beethoven.] I 1981*b*.

USSR: MK D 00010871-2 (7" mono). Moscow Radio Symphony Orchestra, Aleksandr GAUK. [Glière.] P 1950s, I 1962. *Reissued:* USA: Monitor MC 2015 (mono). [Opp. 70 and 89*a*.] I 1958 ~ Le Chant du Monde LD-S 8218 (10" mono). [Prokofiev.] I 1958 ~ USA: Bruno BR 14050 (mono). [Prokofiev.] I 1961.

USA: Russian Disc Compact Disc RDCD 10 902 (mono). Leningrad Philharmonic Orchestra, Yevgeni MRAVINSKY. [Lyadov and Lyatoshinsky.] P Leningrad concert 23 Feb. 1955 (not 21 Apr. 1955 as stated), I 1994.

Revelation Compact Disc RV 10061 (mono). State Radio and Television Large Symphony Orchestra, Aleksandr GAUK. [Op. 65.] P concert 24 Sept. 1955, I Feb. 1997, G Sept. 1997.

Waverley YLP 055 (mono) and SYLP 5056 (7" 45 rpm). Scottish National Orchestra, Alexander GIBSON. [Kabalevsky.] P May 1962, G Dec. 1962. *Reissued:* Waverley SLLP 1010. [Hamilton, Arnold, Prokofiev, and Kabalevsky.] ~ HMV SXLP 20099. [Prokofiev and Kabalevsky.] G Aug. 1967.

HMV ALP 2009 (mono) and ASD 559. Philharmonia Orchestra, Georges PRÊTRE. [Op. 112.] P 21–2 Mar. 1963, G Nov. 1963. *Reissued:* France: EMI FALP 794. [Op. 112.] ~ Classics for Pleasure CFP 141. [Op. 112.] G Oct. 1970.

USSR: Melodiya D 13213-4 (10" mono). Arr. A. Khizhnyak. URALS BAYAN TRIO (I. Shepelsky, A. Khizhnyak, N. Khudyakov). [Bach, Grieg, Khudyakov *et al.*] P 1964.

Czech: Supraphon SUA 10576 (mono) and SUA ST 50576. Czech Philharmonic Orchestra, Karel ANČERL. [Op. 10.] G Nov. 1965.

USA: Polydor 245006. Boston Pops Orchestra, Arthur FIEDLER. [Copland, Goldmark, and Sullivan.] P 1971. *Reissued:* Polydor 2391 005. [Copland, Goldmark, and Sullivan.] G June 1971.

USA: 2-Mark 40400. Arr. for wind band. Univdrsity of Minnesota Concert Band Ensemble, BENCRISCUTTO. [?] P 1971.

Decca SB 304. Arr. H. Cornthwaite. The Fairey Band, Kenneth DENNISON (conductor), Harry Mortimer (musical adviser). [Grieg, Verdi, Confrey *et al.*] P 1973, G May 1973.

Music for Pleasure MFPA 57009. National Youth Orchestra of Wales, Arthur DAVISON. [Musorgsky.] P 1973, G July 1973. *Reissued:* France: EMI Music for Pleasure 2M 045-05423. [Musorgsky.]

Decca SB 702. Arr. for military band. Band of the Grenadier Guards, Major Peter PARKES. [Riddle, Purcell, Coates *et al.*] P 1973, G Sept. 1973.

Virtuosi VR 7506. Arr. H. Cornthwaite. The Virtuosi Brass Band, Harry MORTIMER. [Binge, Bliss, Verdi *et al.* G Jan. 1976.

USA: Columbia M 35114. Cuts figs. 3 to 4 minus 3 bars and 26 to 33. Columbia Symphony Orchestra, André KOSTELANETZ. ['Festive Overtures'] P New York 17 and 18 Jan. 1977. *Reissued:* Sony Classical Compact Disc SBK 62642. [Opp. 10, 22, 97, 105, and Sans op. P.] G June 1997.

USSR: Melodiya C10 10399-400. USSR Symphony Orchestra, Yevgeni SVETLANOV. [Opp. 70; 97*a* No. 8; and 16.] P 1978, I 1978*d*. *Reissued:* HMV Melodiya ASD 3855. [Op. 47.] G May 1980 ~ USSR: Melodiya C10 13327-8 (in double album with C60 13329-30). ['Moscow Souvenir'—Rimsky-Korsakov, Tchaikovsky, Kabalevsky *et al.*] I 1980*d* ~ USSR: Melodiya C60 14423-4. Fanfare only. ['The Olympic Fanfares Resound in Moscow'— Samaras, Boiko, Pakhmutova *et al.*] I 1981*b* ~ USSR: Melodiya C10 14469-70. Fanfare only. ['Olympic Souvenir'—Glinka, Rakhmaninov, Prokofiev *et al.*] I 1981*b* ~ France: Le Chant du Monde LDX 78687. [As USSR release.] I Mar. 1981 ~ Germany: Melodia Eurodisc 200 539-366. [As USSR release.] ~ USSR: Melodiya C10 21717 004. ['Soviet Overtures'— Glière, Prokofiev, Budashkin *et al.*] I 1985*c*.

Unicorn Chalfont SDG 301 (digital). London Symphony Orchestra, Morton GOULD. [Ginastera, Ravel, and Weinberger.] P Sept. 1978, I Nov. 1979, G Feb. 1980. *Reissued:* Academy Sound and Vision ABM 763 R (digital). [Ginastera, Ravel, and Weinberger.] G Sept. 1984 ~ USA: Varèse/Sarabande VCD Compact Disc 47209. [Ginastera, Granados, Ravel *et al.*]

Bulgaria: Balkanton BCA 10212. Plovdiv State Philharmonic Orchestra, Dobrin PETKOV. [Op. 54.] P c.1978. *Reissued:* USA: Monitor MCS 2163. [Op. 54.] I 1981 ~ Cirrus Classics Compact Discs CRS CD212 (two-disc set). [Prokofiev, Rimsky-Korsakov, Rakhmaninov *et al.*] I 1993.

Chandos BBR 1011. Arr. M. Antrobus. Black Dyke Mills Band, Michael ANTROBUS. ['A Russian Festival'—Rakhmaninov, Musorgsky, Prokofiev *et al.*] P Manchester 24 Feb. 1980, G Aug. 1981. *Reissued:* Chandos CBRD 1009. ['The Chandos Sound of Brass'—German, Langford, Khachaturyan *et al.*] ~ Chandos Compact Disc CHAN 4519. ['A Russian Festival'—Rakhmaninov, Musorgsky, Rimsky-Korsakov *et al.*] I 1992.

Unicorn-Kanchana DKM 6001 (digital). Arr. for military band. Band of the Grenadier Guards, Major D. R. KIMBERLEY. [Parry, Handel, Verdi *et al.*] P Royal Albert Hall, London concert 15 Nov. 1980, G Feb. 1982.

Northern Music Services NMS 401 (mono) and MN 601. Massed Bands, Captain C. R. C. GARRITY. [Grainger, Rimsky-Korsakov, Holst *et al.*] P York concert 1984.

Polyphonic PRM 104 D (digital). Arr. for military band. Massed Bands of the Royal Air Force, Wing Commander Erie BANKS. [Bliss, Sullivan, Ellington *et al.*] P Barbican, London concert May 1985.

Bandleader BND 1021 (digital). Arr. for military band. Royal Artillery Band, Major Frank RENTON. ['Call for the Guns'—Verdi, Sousa *et al.*] P London Oct. 1985, G May 1986.

HMV EL 2705901 (DMM) and Compact Disc CDC7 47885-2. Arr. D. Hunsberger. Central Band of the Royal Air Force, Wing Commander Eric BANKS. ['Strike up the Band'—Gershwin, R. Strauss, Rimsky-Korsakov, *et al.*] P Watford Aug. 1986, G Apr. 1987.

USA: Sheffield Labs TDC 27 (digital) and Compact Disc CD 27. Moscow Philharmonic Orchestra, Lawrence Leighton SMITH. ['The Moscow Sessions'—Glazunov, Copland, Gershwin *et al.*] P Moscow 9–18 Aug. 1986, I 1987, G Feb. 1988.

BBC Records REN 637X (digital) and Compact Disc CD 637X. BBC Welsh Symphony Orchestra, Mariss JANSONS. [Op. 10.] P Swansea Nov. 1986, G Aug. 1987 and Feb. 1988.

Canada: CBC Enterprises Compact Disc SMCD 5069. Edmonton Symphony Orchestra, Uri MAYER. ['Canadian and Russian Overtures'— Borodin, Kabalevsky, Glinka *et al.*] P c.1986, I 1989.

Chandos ABRD 1279 (digital) and Compact Disc CHAN 8587. Scottish National Orchestra, Neeme järvi. [Opp. 70, 114*a*, and 16.] P Glasgow 14–17 Apr. 1987, I Mar. 1988, G July 1988. *Reissued:* Chandos Collect Compact Disc CHAN 6511. [Tchaikovsky, Prokofiev, Glazunov *et al.*] I

Oct. 1990 ~ Conifer Aspects Compact Disc ASP 5072. ['Music Festival of Russia'—Prokofiev, Khachaturyan, Rimsky-Korsakov *et al.*] I Oct. 1991 ~ Chandos Compact Discs 7000/1 (two-disc set). [Opp. 27*a*, 114*a*, and Sans op. P.] I Sept. 1994, G May 1995.

Telarc/Conifer Compact Disc 80170. Cincinatti Pops Orchestra, Erich KUNZEL. ['Symphonic Spectacular'—Wagner, Falla, Bizet *et al.*] P Cincinatti 14–15 Sept. 1987, G Oct. 1989.

Virgin Classics VC 790784-1 (digital) and Compact Disc VC 790784-2. London Philharmonic Orchestra, Andrew LITTON. [Op. 93.] P London Apr. 1988, I and G Apr. 1989. *Reissued:* Virgin Classics Compact Disc VC6 790 848-2. ['Sampler 1990'—Ravel, Bach, Vaughan Williams *et al.*] I Nov. 1989 ~ Virgin Classics Ultraviolet Compact Disc 7243 5 611342-2. [Op. 93.] I Aug. 1994, G Aug. and Nov. 1994.

Japan: Brain Compact Disc BOCD 7001. Arr. D. Hunsberger. Toyama Commercial High School Band, Terunobu TSUJISHIMA. ['All Japan Band Competition, Vol. 1'—Respighi, Delibes, Debussy *et al.*] P Tokyo concert 21 Oct. 1989.

Collins Classics Compact Disc 1108-2. London Symphony Orchestra, Maksim SHOSTAKOVICH. [Op. 47.] P 4–6 Jan. 1990, I May 1990, G Sept. 1990. *Reissued:* Collins Classics Compact Disc 90022. ['Sound Sampling'—Satie, Palestrina, Britten *et al.*] I Nov. 1990 ~ Collins Classics Compact Disc 70122. [In three-disc set with Opp. 47, 93, 97, and 141.] I Sept. 1991.

Music Masters Compact Disc MMCD 410. Arr. D. Hunsberger. Royal Marines Band (Flag Officer Scotland and N. Ireland), Lt Peter J. RUTTER-FORD. ['Celebration'—Arnold, Ravel, Copland *et al.*] P Dunfermline 18–19 Jan. 1990, G Nov. 1990.

Delos Compact Disc DF 3089. Helsinki Philharmonic, James DE PRIEST. [Op. 93.] P Hyvinkää, Finland 19–20 Apr. 1990, I Oct. 1990, G Jan. 1991.

Sony Classical Compact Disc SK 47198. Arr. D. Hunsberger. Eastman Wind Ensemble, Donald HUNSBERGER. ['Live in Osaka'—Bach, Holst, Grainger *et al.*] P Osaka concert June 1990, I June 1992.

Decca Compact Disc 436 762-2DH. Royal Philharmonic Orchestra, Vladimir ASHKENAZY. [Opp. 131, 14, and 81.] P Watford Sept. 1990, I June 1994, G Aug. 1994.

Sweden: Marinens Musikkår Compact Disc MMCD 1. Arr. D. Hunsberger. Royal Swedish Navy Band, Sverker HÅLLANDER. [Popular pieces arr. for band.] P Swedish radio Apr.–May 1991.

EMI Classics Compact Disc CDC7 54803-2. Philadelphia Orchestra, Riccardo MUTI. [Op. 47.] P Philadelphia 18–20 Apr. 1992, I June 1993, G Dec. 1993. *Reissued:* USA: EMI Classics Compact Disc CDZ1 79887 (In nine-disc set). ['The Philadelphia Sound'—op. 47; Berlioz, Prokofiev, Rakhmaninov *et al.*] I Nov. 1994.

Sweden: BIS Compact Disc CD 570. Malmö Symphony Orchestra, James DE PRIEST. [Rosenberg, Bizet, Larsson *et al.*] P. Malmö Concert Hall 29 May–2 June 1992, I and G Jan. 1993.

Japan: Canyon Classics Compact Disc EC 3672-2. Russian Federation Symphony Orchestra and Bolshoi Theatre Brass Ensemble, Yevgeni SVETLANOV. [Op. 47.] P Moscow 15–16 June 1992, I July 1994, G Oct. 1994.

USA: Telarc Compact Disc CD 80305. Arr. J. Pilaflan. EMPIRE BRASS (Rolf Smedvig, Jeffrey Curnow, Timothy Morrison—trumpets; Eric Ruske—horn, Scott A. Hartman—trombone, and J. Samuel Pilafian—tuba). ['On the Edge'—Khachaturyan, Glière, Prokofiev *et al.*] P Lennox, Mass. 29–30 Aug. 1992, G Jan. 1994.

Deutsche Grammophon Compact Disc 439 892-2 (4D Audio). Russian National Orchestra, Mikhail PLETNEV. ['Russian Overtures'—Glinka, Borodin, Prokofiev *et al.*] P Moscow concert Nov. 1993, I and G Dec. 1994.

Tring Compact Disc TRP 032. Royal Philharmonic Orchestra, Sir Charles MACKERRAS. [Op. 47.] P London July 1994, I May 1995, G Sept. 1995. *Reissued:* Sunday Times Music Collection Compact Disc 235. ['RPO 50th Anniversary'—Rakhmaninov, Dvorak, Holst *et al.*] I 1996.

Naxos Compact Disc 8.553126. New Zealand Symphony Orchestra, Christopher LYNDON-GEE. [Opp. 35, 102, and 22.] P Wellington 2–4 Nov. 1994, I Sept. 1995.

Chandos Compact Disc CHAN 7025. BBC Philharmonic, Vernon HANDLEY. ['Brian Kay's Sunday Morning on BBC Radio 3'—Mozart, Bach, Delius *et al.*] P Manchester 20–1 Feb. 1995, I Oct. 1995.

Sweden: Imogena Compact Disc IGCD 062. Arr. M. Antrobus. Göteborg Brass Band, Bengt EKLUND. [Roman, Bellini, Byrd *et al.*] P Lundbymnasiet Mar. 1995.

RCA Red Seal Compact Disc 09026 68844-2. St Petersburg Philharmonic Orchestra, Yuri TEMIRKANOV. [Opp. 10 and 54.]. P St Petersburg 3–4 Jan. 1996, I July 1999.

Sony Classical Compact Disc SK 62622 (SK 62592 in USA). Boston Pops Orchestra, John WILLIAMS. ['Summon the Heroes' (Olympic themes)—Williams, Theodorakis, Arnaud *et al.*] P Boston 6–10 Jan. 1996, I July 1996.

USA: Delos Compact Disc DE 3246. Dallas Symphony Orchestra, Andrew LITTON. [Opp. 47 and 102.] P Dallas 19–20 May 1998.

Note: For the circumstances of this work's commission see Wilson (1994, pp. 264–5).

Opus 97 The Gadfly

Form: Orchestral music for the film, with script by Yevgeni Gabrilovich based on the novel *The Gadfly* by Ethel Lilian Voynich, directed by Aleksandr Faintsimmer for Lenfilm. The score consists of 24 items (Nos. 4, 6, 11, 21, and 24 contain no new themes):

1. Overture—Moderato con moto
2. The Cliff—Moderato

3. Youth—Allegretto moderato
5. Confession (solo organ)—Andante
7. Box on the ear—Andante con moto
8. Laughter—Andante—Adagio
9. Barrel Organ—Allegretto
10. Divine Service at the Cathedral (solo organ)—Andante
12. Exit from the Cathedral—Moderato
13. Contredanse—Moderato con moto
14. Galop—Presto
15. Guitars—Andantino
16. At the Market Place—Presto
17. The Rout—Adagio
18. The Passage of Montanelli—Moderato
19. Finale—Moderato con moto
20. The Austrians—Allegro non troppo
22. The River—Allegro
23. Gemma's Room—Moderato con moto

No. 16 is a revised orchestration of Dance I from *Suite for Jazz Orchestra No. 2*, Sans op. G (ii).

Instrumentation: piccolo, 2 flutes, 2 oboes, 3 clarinets (B flat and A), 2 bassoons ~ 4 horns, 3 trumpets, 3 trombones, tuba ~ timpani, triangle, tambourine, side drum, cymbals, bass drum, gong ~ orchestral bells, harp, organ ~ 2 guitars ~ strings.

Composed: Spring 1955, at Moscow.

Premières: Film first shown on 12 April 1955.

Suite in USA: 18 October 1987, Carnegie Hall, New York; American Symphony Orchestra, José Serebrier.

Arrangements: Opus 97a—Suite derived from the film score numbers quoted in parentheses, assembled by Lev Atovmyan in 1955:

1. Overture—Moderato con moto (1)
2. Contredanse—Moderato (13)
3. People's Holiday ('Folk Festival', 'Folk Feast', 'Tarantella', 'Neopolitan Dance', or 'Spanish Dance')—[Allegro vivace] (16)
4. Interlude—Adagio (17) *attacca*
5. Barrel Organ Waltz—Allegretto (9)
6. Galop—Allegro (14)
7. Prelude—Andantino (15 and 5)
8. Romance—Allegro moderato (3 and 7)
9. Intermezzo—Andante (10, 12, and 18)
10. Nocturne—Moderato (23)
11. Scene—Moderato (2)
12. Finale—Allegro non troppo (20)

Individual numbers of the Suite variously transcribed, including the selection listed below:

Nos. 1–3, 5, 6, and 8–11 for viola and piano by Vadim Borisovsky.

Nos. 1–3, 5, and 8 for organ by Mariya Makarova.

No. 2 for balalaika and bayan by Oleg Glukov.

Nos. 2, 3, 8, and 10 for cello and piano by L. Atovmyan.

Nos. 2, 5, and 10 for piano by Bronislava Rozengauz.

No. 3 for two pianos by the composer; two violins and piano titled 'Spanish Dance' by L. Atovmyan; cello and piano by Juozas Chelkauskas, wind band by Donald Hunsberger, and for brass band by Howard Snell.

Nos. 3 titled 'Neopolitan Dance' and 8 for mandolin by Emanuil Shenykman.

No. 5 appears as the fourth item in *Four Waltzes*, Sans op. P.

No. 7 for two trombones and piano by K. Serostanov. The violin duet with piano version by Konstantin Fortunatov appears as the first item of *Three Violin Duets*, Sans op. P. A piano reduction is titled 'Melodic Moment'.

No. 8 for trombone by Viktor Venglovsky; organ and string orchestra by Peteris Sipolniek; double-bass and piano by Rodion Azarkhin; violin and piano versions by K. Fortunatov and Donald Fraser; cello and piano by J. Chelkauskas; B flat clarinet and piano by Eirian Griffiths; string quartet by D. Fraser; ensemble of 48 violins by Julian Milone; and brass band by Derek Broadbent. Piano versions by M. Sagradova and Harry Rabinowitz (the latter abbreviated).

No. 15 of the film score arranged for two guitars from piano notation (following instructions left by the composer) by Yevgeni Larichev.

Instrumentation of Suite Opus 97*a*—piccolo, 2 flutes, 3 oboes. 3 clarinets (B flat and A = 3 alto saxophones in No. 7), 2 bassoons, contrabassoon ~ 4 horns, 3 trumpets, 3 trombones, tuba ~ timpani, triangle, tambourine, side drum, cymbals, bass drum, gong ~ glockenspiel, xylophone, celesta, piano, harp ~ strings.

Music: The autograph of the film score has not been discovered though a manuscript copy collated with the autograph score is preserved at the Music Library of the USSR Cinematograph Symphony Orchestra. The numbers below refer to the Suite Opus 97*a*.

Sovetskii Kompozitor, No. 928 (in *Dmitri Shostakovich: Waltzes from Film Music*), 1959, No. 5 only, full score, 29 cm.

Muzgiz, No. 28122, 1960, Suite Opus 97*a*, full score, 35 cm.

Sovetskii Kompozitor, No. 2718 (in *D. Shostakovich: Pieces for cello and piano*), 1962, Nos. 2, 8, 10, and 3 arr. L. Atovmyan, 29 cm.

Hans Sikorski, No. 2186, 1964, No. 3 'Tarantella' for two pianos, 31.5 cm.

Edition Peters, No. 4794 (plate no. 12389—in *Shostakovich: Album of Easy Pieces*), 1967, No. 8 arr. K. Fortunatov, 30.5 cm.

MCA, 1968, No. 5 only, score and parts, 31 cm.

Boston Music, No. 13781, *c.*1971, No. 3 arr. for wind band by D. Hunsberger, 31 cm.

Muzyka, 1972, No. 8 only arr. for trombone by V. Venglovsky.

Sovetskii Kompozitor, No. 4719 (in *D. Shostakovich: Pieces for violin and piano*), 1975, No. 7 arr. for violin duet and No. 8 for violin, 28.5 cm.

Sovetskii Kompozitor, No. 3672 (in *Pieces by Soviet Composers for cello and piano*, book 5), 1976, No. 3 arr. J. Chelkauskas, 29 cm.

Muzyka, No. 9104, Nos. 11, 9, 3, and 8 arr. for viola and piano by V. Borisovsky, 29 cm. Also editions grouping Nos. 5. 10, and 6; and 1, 8, and 2.

Muzyka, No. 9986 (in *Easy pieces for trombone and piano*). 1978, No. 7 arr. for two trombones and piano by K. Serostanov, parts, 29 cm.

Muzyka, Leningrad, No. 2330 (with Op. 116), 1978, Nos. 7, 2, 8, and 3 abridged for piano by Zinaida Vitkind, 28.5 cm. Originally published in 1967.

Sovetskii Kompozitor, No. 4920 (in *D. Shostakovich: Selection of Children's Piano Pieces*), 1979, Nos. 2, 5, and 10 arr. by B. Rozengauz, 29.cm.

Standard Music, Portland Street, London, 1983, No. 8 arr. for piano by H. Rabinowitz, 30 cm.

Hans Sikorski, No. 2283 (with Sans op. D), 1986, No. 3 arr. by J. Chelkauskas, parts, 31.5 cm.

Muzyka, No. 10890 (in Volume 42 of *Collected Works* with Opp. 75, 78, 80, 82, 95, 111, 116, 132, and 137), 1987, nineteen items of the film score, 30 cm.

Fentone, Corby, Northants., No. F 399, 1986, No. 8 arr. for violin and piano by D. Fraser, score and part, 31 cm.

Fentone, No. F 401, 1987, No. 8 arr. for B flat clarinet and piano by E. Griffiths, score and part, 31 cm.

Fentone, No. F 427, 1988, No. 8 arr. for string quartet by D. Fraser, score and parts, 31 cm.

Muzyka. No. 14908 (in *D. Shostakovich: Pieces for cello and piano*), 1991, Nos. 8 and 10 arr. J. Chelkauskas and L. Atovmyan respectively, 29 cm.

Duration: Suite Opus 97*a*: 41' 08"–44' 51"; 40 minutes (Sadovnikov). Folk Festival (No. 3): 2' 25"–3' 04"; 3' 00" (Plaistow). Romance (No. 8): 5' 50"–6' 15".

Film: *Reilly—Ace of Spies.* Romance (No. 8), arr. by Harry Rabinowitz, used as a signature tune for this Euston Films twelve-part serial for ITV about the extraordinary life of the British Secret Service's first professional agent, Sidney Reilly.

Ballets: *The Young Lady and the Hooligan.* Romance, arr. Atovmyan, used in 1962 ballet. See under Opus 27.

The Overcoat. Includes Romance. See under Opus 32.

Recordings: Revelation Compact Disc RV 70002 (mono). Guitars No. 15 arr. composer. Dmitri SHOSTAKOVICH (piano). ['Shostakovich plays Shostakovich, Vol. 2'—Opp. 93 and 34.] P 28 May 1955, I Oct. 1997, G Feb. 1998.

USSR: MK D 07939-40 (mono) and C 0123-4. Complete Suite. Grigori
Kemlin (violin), Arnold Ferkelman (cello), USSR Cinematograph Symphony Orchestra, Emin KHACHATURYAN. P 1961. *Reissued:* USSR:
Melodiya D 00018303-4 (7" mono). No. 8 only. [Dances from Op. 22*a* and
Sans op. P.] I 1966 ~ HMV Melodiya ASD 3309. Complete Suite. G Feb.
1977 ~ USSR: Melodiya C 0123-4. Complete Suite. [In fourth box of Part
1 of *Collected Works on Records.*] I 1978 ~ Germany: Melodia Eurodisc
28665 XHK. Complete Suite. [On third and fourth records in four-
record film music album with Opp. 78*a* and 120.] I 1981 ~ Classics for
Pleasure CFP 41 4463 1. Complete Suite. G Sept. 1984 ~ USSR: Melodiya
C12 21317 003. No. 8 only. [Shainsky.] I 1985*b* ~ EMI Classics for Pleasure Compact Disc CD-CFP 4463. Complete Suite. I Nov. 1988, G Apr.
1989.

USSR: MK D 9319-20 (10" mono) and C 277-8 (10"). No. 8 only. Irina
Saitseva (piano), Violins of the Bolshoi Theatre, Yuli REYENTOVICH.
[Shchedrin, Paganini, Mendelssohn *et al.*] P 1962. *Reissued:* USSR:
Melodiya D 19391-2 (10" mono). [Handel, Prokofiev, Rimsky-Korsakov
et al.] I 1967 ~ USSR: Melodiya CM 02925-6. [Prokofiev, Rimsky-
Korsakov, Dvořák, *et al.*] I 1972 ~ USSR: Melodiya CM 03397-400 (two-
record set). ['Moscow Souvenir'—Musorgsky, Prokofiev, Rakhmaninov
et al.] I 1973 ~ HMV Melodiya SXLP 30188. ['Stringtime in Moscow', Vol-
ume 1—Paganini, Dvořák, Handel *et al.*] G Jan. 1976 ~ Helidor 2548 270.
['The Flight of the Bumble Bee'—Rimsky-Korsakov, Fibrich, Dvořák *et al.*]

USSR: MK D 12651-2 (10" mono) and C 711-2. No. 8 arr. for organ and
string orchestra. Peteris Sipolniek (organ), Violin Ensemble of Riga Musical School, I. ABRAMISA. [Handel, Saint-Saëns, Kriesler, and Bach.] P 1963.

USA: Columbia ML 6267 (mono) and MS 6867. Nos. 5, 10, 3, 6, and 7.
André KOSTELANETZ and his Orchestra. [Sans op. P, Opp. 22*a* and 105
excerpts.] P New York 23 and 29 Nov. 1965. *Reissued:* CBS BRG 72504
(mono) and SBRG 72504. [Sans op. P and Op. 105 excerpts.] G Feb.
1967 ~ CBS Classics 61220. [Sans op. P and Op. 105 excerpts.] G May
1971 ~ CBS S 73443 in Set CBS 77394. Nos. 7, 5, 10, 3, and 6. [Op. 107.] G
Oct. 1975 ~ Sony Classical Compact Disc SBK 62642. Nos. 5, 10, 3, 6, and
7. [Opp. 10, 22, 96, 105, and Sans op. P.] G June 1997.

USSR: Melodiya D 19071-2 (10" mono). No. 8 only arr. R. Azarkhin.
Rodion AZARKHIN (double-bass) and Elena Aleksandrova (piano). [Lalo,
Fibrich, Koussevitzky *et al.*] P 1967. *Reissued:* USSR: Melodiya C10
06417–8. [Op. 39 Adagio; Handel, Fibrich, Lalo *et al.*] I 1975.

USSR: Melodiya CM 02805-6. No. 8 arr. for organ and string orchestra,
Peteris Sipolniek (organ), Violins of the Bolshoi Theatre, Yuli REYEN-
TOVICH. [Rakhmaninov, Sarasate, Fauré, and soprano recital.] P 1971, I
1972.

USSR: Melodiya C20 08387-8. No. 2 arr. for balalaika and bayan. Oleg
GLUKHOV (balalaika) and Valeri Azov (bayan). [Chopin, Khachaturyan *et
al.*] P 1976, I 1977*d*.

USA: Russian Compact Disc RCD 16238. No. 8 arr. M. Sagradova. Nataliya GAVRILOVA (piano). ['Russian Piano School'—Opp. 22, 27, and 34; Babadzhanyan, Rakhmaninov, J. Strauss *et al.*] P 1976–90, I 1998.

USSR: Melodiya C10 10399-400. No. 8 only. Genrikh Fridgeim (violin), USSR Symphony Orchestra, Yevgeni SVETLANOV. [Opp. 70, 96, and 16.] P 1978, I 1978*d*. *Reissued:* France: Le Chant du Monde LDX 78687. [Opp. 70, 96, and 16.] I Mar. 1981 ~ Germany: Melodia Eurodisc 200 539-366. [Opp. 70, 96, and 16.].

Hungary: Balkanton BCA 10169. No. 8 only. 202 CHILDREN (violin ensemble of musical schools), Emil YANEV. [Handel, Khristoskov, Bach, and Vivaldi.] P mid-1979.

USSR: Melodiya C60 15069-70. Paraphrase on theme from *Ovod* arr. A. Kalvarsky. Leningrad Concert Orchestra, Anatoli BADKHEN. ['Recollections'—Petrov, Karayev, Fradkin *et al.*] P 1980, I 1981*d*.

Marlborough College SM 237. No. 3 only, arr for wind band. Marlborough College Wind Orchestra, Robert PEEL. [Khachaturyan, Rimsky-Korsakov, Josef Strauss, and Sousa.] P London concert 5 Nov. 1980, G June 1981.

Sweden: Bluebell Bell 126. No. 7 only, labelled 'Melodic Moment'. Inger WIKSTRÖM (piano). [Opp. 5; 19 Nos. 3, 4, and 2; 22*a* No. 3; 31 No. 4; 94; 105 fragment, and Prokofiev.] P Stockholm 28 Jan. 1981 and 1 Feb. 1981.

Contour Red Label CC 7557 (digital). No. 3 only, labelled 'Folkfeast'. London Symphony Orchestra, Yuri ARANOVICH. ['Russian Spectacular' Khachaturyan, Prokofiev, Borodin *et al.*] P 1982, I Apr. 1982. *Reissued:* Pickwick IMP Red Label Compact Disc PCD 804. ['Russian Spectacular'.] I May 1985, G Aug. 1985 ~ Carlton Classics Compact Discs 30368 01247 (two-disc set). ['Russian Spectacular'] I 1998.

USSR: Melodiya C10 17233000. No. 8 only. S. Girshenko (violin), Bolshoi Theatre Orchestra, Mark ERMLER. [In two-record set 'Popular Pieces by Soviet Composers'—Khachaturyan, Shchedrin, Sviridov *et al.*] I 1982*d*. *Reissued:* Germany: ZYX Russian Art Compact Discs CLA 10010-2 (two-disc set). [Denisov, Schnittke, Khachaturyan *et al.*] I 1998.

USA: Nonesuch 7 8019. Nos. 3 and 8 arr. Shenykman. Emanuil SHENYKMAN (mandolin). [Stravinsky, Rakhmaninov *et al.*] P June 1982.

Precision Records & Tapes BUSLP 1004. No. 8 only, arr. Harry Rabinowitz for 'Reilly—Ace of Spies'. OLYMPIA ORCHESTRA. ['Reilly Ace of Themes'—a collection of TV series' theme music.] P 1983. *Reissued:* GNP Crescendo GNPS 2166. ['Secret Agent File'] ~ Ronco RON LP 10. [Mancini, Vangelis, Burgon *et al.*] I 1984.

USSR: Melodiya C50 20749 006. Nos. 2, 10, and 3 arr. for piano. Rimma BOBRITSKAYA (piano). ['For Children'—Opp. 69 and 3*a*; Sans opp. B, P, and S.] P 1983, I 1984*d*.

Classics for Pleasure CFP 414474-1 (digital). No. 8 only. Martin Miller (violin), Hallé Orchestra, Owain Arwell HUGHES. ['Owain Arwen

Hughes conducts Much Loved Music' collection.] P Manchester July 1984, G Jan. 1985. *Reissued:* Classics for Pleasure Compact Disc CFP 9009. [Arnold, Vaughan Williams, Verdi *et al.*] G Nov. 1987.

Polyphonic PRL 024D (digital). No. 3 only, arr. for brass band by H. Snell. Desford Colliery Dowty Band, Howard SNELL. [Lecuona, Puccini, Khachaturyan *et al.*] P Derby July and Aug. 1984. *Reissued:* Music for Pleasure MFP 5782 (digital). Showcase'—J. Strauss, Bach, Saint-Saëns *et al.*] I 1988.

Whitetower Records Ensemble ENS 132 (digital real time cassette only). No. 8 arr. L. Atovmyan. Elizabeth WILSON (cello) and Andrew Ball (piano). ['Music and Revolution', Volume 1—Opp. 19, 34, and Sans op. E with poems.] I 1985.

D Sharp DSLP 1001 and Compact Disc SCD 1001. No. 8 only arr. Atovmyan. London Symphony Orchestra, Yan-Pascal TORTELIER. [Ravel, Prokofiev, and Rimsky-Korsakov.] P London 15–16 Jan. 1985, I Sept. 1985, G Feb. 1986.

USSR: Melodiya C10 21335 006. No. 3 arr. for wind band. USSR Ministry of Home Affairs Army Orchestra, Vladimir TARASOV. [Op. 27*a* No. 5; Sans op. H (ii); Puccini, Suppé *et al.*] I 1985*b*.

Polyphonic PRL 031 D and Compact Disc QPRL 031 D. No. 8 arr. D. Broadbent. Brighouse and Rastrick Band, Derek BROADBENT. [Arban, Berlioz, Delibes *et al.*] P Huddersfield 1986, I Sept. 1988, G Oct. 1989.

EMI EL 270617-1 (digital) and Compact Disc CDC7 49043-2. Nos. 5 and 8. Academy of St Martin-in-the-Fields, Sir Neville MARRINER. [Ponchielli, Nicola, Suppé *et al.*] P 29 Oct.–1 Nov. 1986, G Nov. 1987. *Reissued:* USA: EMI Angel DS 49043 (digital). [As UK release.] I 1987 ~ EMI Eminence Compact Disc CD-EMX 2169. ['Overtures and Interludes'—Ponchielli, Nicolai, Suppé *et al.*] I Nov. 1990 ~ Classics for Pleasure Compact Discs CFPSD 4811 (two-disc set). ['The Best of the Academy'—Grieg, Tchaikovsky, Fauré *et al.*] I 1997 ~ HMV Classics Compact Disc 5 73047-2. [Sans opp. E and G; Opp. 16, 22, 35, and 89.] I Oct. 1998.

RCA Victor Red Seal Compact Disc RD 86603. Complete Suite. Belgian Radio Symphony Orchestra, José SEREBRIER. [Op. 76.] P Brussels 1987, I Feb. 1988, G May 1988.

Grasmere Compact Disc GRCD 35. No. 3 arr. Snell. Williams-Fairey Engineering Band, Roy NEWSOME. ['Tournament for Brass'—Arlen, Ball, Relton *et al.*] P Stockport 1987, G May 1991.

Trax Classique TRXLP 131 and Compact Disc TRXCD 131. No. 8 arr. H. Rabinowitz. Martin JONES (piano). ['Testimony—Shostakovich's Greatest Hits'—opp. 45, 102, 60, 110, 67; and Josephs.] I 1988.

Germany: Capriccio Compact Disc 10 298. Complete Suite. Berlin Radio Symphony Orchestra, Leonid GRIN. [Op. 116.] P Berlin Nov. and Dec. 1988, I Feb. 1990.

Polyphonic Compact Disc QPRL 043 D. No. 8 arr. D. Broadbent. Ley-
land DAF Band, Richard EVANS. ['Romance in Brass'—Grieg, Mozart,
Bizet et al.] P Watford June 1989.

France: VDE Compact Disc CD 624. No. 3 arr. Snell. Ensemble de
cuivres Melódia, Pierre-Alain BIDAUD. ['The European'—Dukas, Harry
James, Wagner et al.] P June 1989 and Jan. 1990, I 1990.

USA: Pro-Arte Fanfare Compact Disc CDD 551. Suite Nos. 1, 8, and 6.
Thomas Yang (violin), Chicago Sinfonietta, Paul FREEMAN. ['Shostakovich Film Festival'—Opp. 111, 116, 16, and 35.] P Oak Park, Illinois, May
1990, I Aug. 1991. Reissued: Conifer Classics Compact Disc Class 7086.
[As USA release.] I Nov. 1991.

Collins Classics Compact Disc 1206-2. Suite Nos. 1–3, 5–8, 10, and 12.
London Symphony Orchestra, Maksim SHOSTAKOVICH; soloists in No.
8—Peter Thomas (violin) and No. 10—Douglas Cummings (cello). [Op.
141.] P London Aug. 1990, I and G May 1991. Reissued: Collins Classics
Compact Disc 70122. [In three-disc set with Opp. 47, 93, 96, and 141.] I
Sept. 1991.

France: Le Chant du Monde Russian Season Compact Disc LDC 288
034. Nos. 2, 3, and 10 arr. for piano. Rimma BOBRITSKAYA (piano).
['Russian Miniatures for Piano—Sans opp. P, S, and Op. 69; Tchaikovsky
and Prokofiev.] P Moscow Conservatory Feb. 1991. Reissued: France: Le
Chant du Monde Russian Season Compact Disc RUS 788034. [As 1991
recording.] I Mar. 1999 ~ France: Le Chant du Monde Russian Season
Compact Disc RUS 788164. Nos. 2 and 3. [Opp. 27, 69; Sans opp. G and P
(i).] I July 1999.

Doyen Compact Disc DOY 004. No. 6 Galop arr. H. Snell. Britannia
Building Society Band, Howard SNELL. [Fucik, Bizet, Bach et al.] P Dews-
bury Mar. 1991, G Aug. 1992.

EMI Eminence Compact Disc CD-EMX 2196. No. 8 only. Tasmin LITTLE
(violin) and Piers Lane (piano). ['Virtuoso Violin'—Kreisler, Brahms,
Drigo et al.] P London 30–I July 1991, G Dec. 1992.

Chandos Compact Disc CHAN 9227. No. 8 only. Emmanuelle
Boisvert (violin), Detroit Symphony Orchestra, Neeme JÄRVI. ['Encore!'—
Chabrier, Glinka, Sibelius et al.] P 31 Jan. 1993, I Dec. 1993, G Aug. 1994.

Austria: Musica Classic Compact Disc 780011-2. No. 8 only. Moscow
Radio Symphony Orchestra, Vladimir FEDOSEYEV. ['Encores'—Tchaikovsky, Glazunov, Sviridov et al.] P Bratislava Nov. 1993, I 1994.

Koch International Classics Compact Disc 37274-2. Complete Suite.
KBS Symphony Orchestra, Vakhtang JORDANIA. [Opp. 58a and 116a.] P
Seoul, Korea Feb. 1994, I Sept. 1994, G Dec. 1994.

Cala Compact Disc CACD 0105. No. 8 arr. J. Milone. The 48 First Violins
of London Philharmonic, Royal Philharmonic, and Philharmonia Orchestras, Geoffrey SIMON. ['The London Violin Sound'—Dvořák, Monti, Gershwin et al.] P Gospel Oak, London May 1994, I Sept. 1994, G Sept. 1995.

Olympia Compact Disc OCD 585. Suite Nos. 7, 5, 2, 8, and 3 arr. for organ. Mariya MAKAROVA (organ). ['Music for Organ'—Opp. 169, 271, 29, 39, 81, 105, and Sans op. E.] P Moscow Conservatory Jan. 1995, I Mar. 1997.

Naxos Compact Disc 8.553299. Complete Suite. National Symphony Orchestra of Ukraine, Theodore KUCHAR. [Op. 111.] P Kiev 12–15 Feb. 1995, I Dec. 1996, G May 1997. *Reissued:* Naxos Compact Disc 8.553216. No. 8 only. ['Romance' sampler—Mozart, Beethoven, Stamitz *et al.*]

Tring Compact Disc TRP 080. Suite Nos. 1, 8, and 11. Jonathan Carney (violin). Royal Philharmonic Orchestra, Frank SHIPWAY. [Op. 93.] P London May 1995, I Sept. 1996.

Denon Compact Disc CO 18004. Nos. 3, 13, 14, and 23 arr. for chamber orchestra. I SOLISTI ITALIANI, Giovanni Guglielmo (violin in No. 3), and Eddy de Rossi (harp in Nos. 3 and 23). [Op. 116; Walton, Lavagnino, Rossellini *et al.*] P Piazzola sul Brenta 9–18 Aug. 1995. NB. 'Youth' No. 3 not from Op. 111.

Sony Classical Compact Disc SK 62007. No. 15 arr. Y. Larichev. John WILLIAMS and Timothy KAIN (guitar duo). ['The Mantis and the Moon Music'—Falla, Granados, Soler *et al.*] P Hampstead 17–20 Aug. 1995.

Decca Compact Disc 452 597-2DH. Nos. 1–3, 7, 9, 13, 14, 16–20, and 23 in original orchestration. Erez Ofer (violin in No. 3), Philadelphia Orchestra, Riccardo CHAILLY. ['The Dance Album'—Opp. 105 and 27.] P New Jersey Dec. 1995, I Oct. 1996, G Dec. 1996.

CIS: Manchester Compact Disc CDMAN 129. Barrel Organ Waltz. St Petersburg Philharmonic Academic Symphony Orchestra, Vladimir ALTSHULER. ['Shostakovich Theatre and Cinema Music'—Opp. 32*a*, 58*a*, 45, 30, 78, 76, 99, and 37.] P St Petersburg 1995, I 1998.

ASV White Line Compact Disc WHL 2103. Romance arr. Otty. Bernard GREGOR-SMITH (cello) and Yolande Wrigley (piano). ['Cello Romance'—Borodin, Fauré, Rakhmaninov *et al.*] P London 3–4 Apr. 1996.

Germany: Orfeo Compact Disc C 443 961 A. Romance arr. for cello and piano. Werner THOMAS-MIFUNE (cello) and Carmen Piazzini (piano). ['Salut D'Amour'—Tchaikovsky, Chopin, Bizet *et al.*] P Wörthsee, 26–7 Apr. 1996, I Dec. 1996. NB. The liner note states that this is one of the three original Opus 9 pieces of 1923 dedicated to the composer's sister.

Teldec Compact Disc 0630 17222-2. No. 8 arr. K. Fortunatov. Gidon KREMER (violin) and Oleg Maizenberg (piano). ['Le Cinema'—Chaplin, Rota, Dunayevsky *et al.*] P Berlin May and Nov. 1996, I 1998.

USA: Pope Music Compact Disc PM 1015-2 (silver) and PMG 2015-2 (gold). Romance. Russian Symphony Orchestra, Mark GORENSTEIN. ['Russian Pops'—Sans op. P and Op. 16; Dunayevsky, Khrennikov, Sviridov *et al.*] P Moscow Conservatory Sept. 1996.

Japan: EMI Classics Compact Disc TOCE 9496. Romance arr. Arai. MORGAŬA quartet (Eiji Aral, Takashi Aoki, Hisashi Ono, Ryoichi Fujimori). [Opp. 49, 101, and 122.] P 11–14 Mar. 1997.

EMI Classics Compact Disc CDC5 56591-2. Nos. 8 and 3. London Philharmonic Orchestra, Joakim Svenheden (violin in No. 8), Mariss JANSONS. [Opp. 141 and 102.] P London 14–16 Apr. 1997, I Oct. 1998,
   Classic FM Compact Disc 75005 57007-2. Romance. Royal Liverpool Philharmonic Orchestra, Libor PEŠEK. ['Adagietto'—Satie, Fauré, Gounod *et al.*] P Liverpool 28 and 30 July 1997.
   Switzerland: Relief Compact Disc CR 991047. Romance. Mikhail Shestakov (violin), Tchaikovsky Symphony Orchestra. Vladimir FEDOSEYEV. [Op. 93.] P 1998, I Mar. 2001.
   Decca Compact Disc 460 792-2DH11. Score No. 3. Alexander Kerr (violin), Royal Concertgebouw Orchestra, Riccardo CHAILLY. ['The Film Album'—Opp. 33, 26, 56, 116, 55, 132, and 76*a*.] P Amsterdam 10–11 Sept. 1998, I Mar. 1999, G Apr. 1999.
   Monte Carlo: Bel Air Music Compact Disc BAM 2000. Romance. Russian Philharmonic Orchestra, Konstantin KRIMETS. [Opp. 116 and 76; Sviridov, Dashkevich, Prokofiev *et al.*] P Moscow Radio Studio Jan. 2000.
   France: Le Chant du Monde Compact Disc RUS 288170. Suite Nos. 1–3, 5-8, and 10–12. Tchaikovsky Symphony Orchestra, Vladimir FEDOSEYEV; soloists in No. 8—Mikhail Chesta (violin) and No. 10—Viktor Simon (cello). [Op. 31.] P Moscow Radio Studio 6–10 June 2000, I 2001.
   Warner Classics UK Compact Disc 8573 88655-2. Romance. Chloë HANSLIP (violin), London Symphony Orchestra, Paul Mann. [Glazunov, Musorgsky, Paganini *et al.*] P Hampstead, London 6–8 Apr. 2001, I Sept. 2001, G Nov. 2001.

Opus 98   Five Romances on Verses of Yevgeni Dolmatovsky

Alternative title: *Songs of Our Days.*
Form: A cycle of five romantic songs for bass voice and piano:

1. The Day of our First Meeting—Moderato con moto
2. The Day of Declaration of Love—Allegretto
3. The Day of Tiffs—Adagio
4. The Day of Happiness—Allegro
5. The Day of Reminiscences—Allegretto

Composed: 3 July–September 1954, at Komarovo village, Gulf of Finland.
Premières: 16 May 1956, Kiev Philharmonic Hall; 14 June, Moscow Conservatory Bolshoi Hall and 25 June 1956, Leningrad Philharmonic Bolshoi Hall; Boris Gmyrya (bass) and Lev Ostrin (piano).
   UK broadcast: 18 January 1988, David Wilson-Johnson (bass-baritone) and David Owen-Norris (piano).

Music: Autographs are preserved at the CIS Archives of Literature and Art and the Glinka Museum. The keys of the Romances differ in the two autographs.

Muzgiz, No. 25942, 1956, 29 cm. and reprinted: Muzyka, No. 25942, 1964, 29 cm.

Muzyka, No. 4116 (in *Dmitri Shostakovich: Vocal Compositions*), 1967 and 1974, 30 cm.

Muzyka, No. 10283 (in Volume 32 of *Collected Works* with Opp. 4, 21, 46, 62, 79, 84, 86, 91, 100 *et al.*), 1982, 30 cm.

Sovetskii Kompozitor, No. 7815 (in *Romances and Songs to Verses of Yevgeni Dolmatovsky* with Opp. 80, 86, and Sans op. X), 1987, 29 cm.

Muzichna Ukraina, Kiev, No. 1567, 'From the repertoire of B. Gmyrya' facsimile edition, 1988, 29 cm.

Duration: Approx. 12 minutes in score; 12' 34"–13' 15".

Recordings: USSR: 26294-5 (10" 78 rpm). Nos. 1 and 2 ~ 26296-7 (10" 78 rpm). Nos. 4 and 5. Boris GMYRYA (bass) and Lev Ostrin (piano). P Moscow June 1956. *Reissued:* USSR: Ministry of Culture HD 03216-7 (mono). The above two performances with No. 3 recorded at the same session. [Op. 79.] I 1956 ~ USA: Artia MK 5006 (mono). [Op. 79.] ~ USSR: Melodiya C10 10521-2 (electronic stereo). Nos. 1–5. [In third box of Part 3 of *Collected Works on Records* with Op. 79.] I 1978.

USSR: Melodiya D 013513-4 (10" mono). Nos. 3 and 5. Nicolai GHIAU-ROV (bass) and A. Zybcev (piano). [Handel, Mozart, Verdi *et al.*] P Moscow concert May 1961, I 1964. *Reissued:* Italy: Arkadia Compact Disc GI 807-1. (mono). [Handel, Stradella, Mozart *et al.*] I May 1995.

USSR: Melodiya D 22725-6 (10" mono). No. 4 only. Askold SUKHIN (bass) and unnamed pianist. [Kabalevsky, Tchaikovsky, Glinka *et al.*.] P 1968.

USSR: Melodiya C10 08921-2. Complete cycle. Oleg PTUKHA (bass) and Nadezhda Kushnir (piano). [Op. 62 Nos. 3 and 4; Op. 100 No. 3; and Kabalevsky.] P 1977, I 1978*a*.

USSR: Melodiya C10 11251-2. Nos. 1 and 4. Aleksandr OGNIVTSEV (bass) and Nikolai Korolkov (piano). [Ippolitov-Ivanov, Medtner, Glière *et al.*] P 1978, I 1979*c*. *Reissued:* USSR: Melodiya C10 19219 001. [Ippolitov-Ivanov, Medtner, Glière *et al.*] I 1983*d*.

Bulgaria: Balkanton BKA 11951. No. 3 only, labelled 'Day of Insults'. Nicola GHIUSELEV (bass) and Theodoz Moussev (piano). [Tchaikovsky, Glinka, Rakhmaninov *et al.*] P Jan. 1986.

France: Thésis Compact Disc THC 82046. No. 2 only. Nikita STOROJEV (bass) and Emile Naoumoff (piano). [Op. 62; Titov, Glinka *et al.*] P Paris Oct. 1990.

Opus 99   The First Echelon

Alternative title: *Virgin Lands.*
Form: Music for the colour film *The First Echelon*, with scenario by Nikolai Pogodin and directed by Mikhail Kalatozov for Mosfilm. Scored for full symphony orchestra (with 3 alto saxophones, vibraphone, harp, and piano).
Composed: 1955–6, at Moscow.
Première: Film first shown on 29 April 1956.
Arrangements: Opus 99*a*—Suite assembled by the composer:

1. Overture—Allegretto poco moderato
2. The Train—Allegro molto
3. Children's Song (text by Sergei Vasiliev)—Allegretto
4. The Field—Allegro molto
5. Evening Landscape—Andantino
6. The Quarry—Allegro
7. Intermezzo—Allegretto
8. Waltz—Allegro poco moderato
9. The Tender Maiden (text by Sergel Vasiliev)—Moderato
10. The Fire—Allegro
11. The House-warming—Allegro

No. 8 reorchestrated as the Waltz II in *Suite for Jazz Orchestra No. 2, Sans op. G.* Transcriptions of No. 3 for wind band accompaniment and of No. 9 for guitar duet. Accompaniment of songs Nos. 3 and 9 arranged for piano by the composer. No. 8 transcribed for wind orchestra by M. Marantslikht.

Instrumentation of Suite Opus 99*a*:   piccolo, 2 flutes, 3 oboes, 3 clarinets (A and B flat), 3 alto saxophones (in No. 11), 2 bassoons, contrabassoon ~ 4 horns, 3 trumpets, 3 trombones, tuba ~ timpani, triangle, side drum, cymbals, bass drum, gong (in No. 10) ~ glockenspiel, xylophone, vibraphone (in No. 4), harp, celesta, piano ~ S.A.T.B. chorus in No. 3 and S.A. in No. 9 ~ strings.

Music: Autograph of the film score preserved in the Music Library of the USSR Cinematograph Symphony Orchestra. Autographs of 'Children's Song' preserved in the Shostakovich family archive, CIS Archives of Literature and Art (with a version for solo tenor and piano), and the Glinka Museum.

Sovetskaya Muzyka magazine, 1954, No. 4, 'Children's Song'.

Muzgiz, 1956 (in album *Siberia is Calling*), 'The Tender Maiden' arr. for solo voice, chorus, and bayan.

Sovetskii Kompozitor, No. 519 (in *D. Shostakovich: Songs*), 1958, songs Nos. 3 and 9 with piano accompaniment, 29 cm.

Sovetskii Kompozitor, No. 928 (in *Dmitri Shostakovich: Waltzes from Film Music*), 1959, No. 8 only, full score, 29 cm.
Sovetskii Kompozitor, 1961, No. 8 arr. for wind orchestra by M. Marantslikht, score.
Sovetskii Kompozitor. No. 2748, 1962, Suite Opus 99*a*, full score, 29 cm.
Muzyka, No. 10179 (in Volume 34 of *Collected Works* with Opp. 88 and 136; and songs), 1985, 'Children's Song' and 'The Tender Maiden' with piano accompaniment, 30 cm.

Duration: Film: 114 minutes. Suite: 40 minutes (Sadovnikov).

Recordings: USSR: 26898-9 (10" 78 rpm). No. 9—L. LAZAREVA and R. LOBACHEVA (guitar duet); No. 3—ALL-UNION SONG ENSEMBLE. P 1956. *Reissued:* USSR: MK D 004146-7 (8" mono). ['Songs of the Virgin Lands'—Muradeli, Klokov, Lavrentev *et al.*] I 1958 ~ USSR: MK D 5062-3 (10" mono). [Songs from Opp. 33, 72, 80, 82, 86 *et al.*] I 1959.

CIS: Manchester Compact Disc CDMAN 129. Op. 99*a* No. 8 Waltz. St. Petersburg Philharmonic Academic Symphony Orchestra, Vladimir ALTSHULER. ['Shostakovich Theatre and Cinema Music'—Opp. 32*a*, 58*a*, 45, 30, 78, 76, 97, and 37.] P St Petersburg 1995, I 1998.

Opus 100   Spanish Songs

Form: A cycle of six traditional folksongs for mezzo-soprano and piano, with the anonymous Spanish lyrics translated into Russian by Sergei Bolotin (Nos. 1 and 3) and Tatyana Sikorskaya (Nos. 2, 4, and 5), and jointly (No. 6).

1. Adios, Granada = Farewell, Granada—Largo
2. Mozuca = Little Stars—Allegro
3. En samir = First Meeting—Largo
4. Ronda = Round Dance (A Birth)—Allegretto
5. Morena salada = Black Eyes—Allegretto
6. [No Spanish title] Dream (Barcarolle)—Allegretto

Composed: July–20 August 1956, at Komarovo village, Gulf of Finland.

Arrangements: Nos. 1, 2, 4, and 6 arranged for trumpet and piano by Sergei Bolotin; No. 2 arranged for double-bass and piano by Rodion Azarkhin. Accompaniment for No. 3 arranged for folk orchestra. No. 5 transcribed for string quartet by Eiji Arai.

Music: Autograph of the cycle preserved in the Shostakovich family archive. The cycle first published as a supplement to the journal *Sovetskaya Muzyka*, 1956. No. 9.
Sovetskii Kompozitor, No. 1822, 1960, 30 cm.
Muzyka, 1966, 29 cm.

Muzyka, No. 4116 (in *Dmitri Shostakovich: Vocal Compositions*), 1967 and 1974, Russian texts and, for the first five, in the original Spanish, 30 cm.

Muzyka, Leningrad, No. 2035 (in *Dmitri Shostakovich: Pieces for trumpet and piano*), 1976, Nos. 1, 2, 4, and 6 arr. S. Bolotin, 28.5 cm.

Sovetskii Kompozitor, No. 4751, 1978, No. 2 arr. for double-bass and piano by R. Azarkhin, 29 cm.

Muzyka, No. 10283 (in Volume 32 of *Collected Works* with Opp. 4, 21, 46, 62, 79, 84, 86, 91, 98 *et al.*), 1982, 30 cm.

Muzyka, No. 13340, 1986, 28 cm. Reprinted from Volume 32 above.

Duration: 13' 45"–16' 55"; 13 minutes (Sadovnikov).

Recordings: Decca SEC 5.500 (7" 45 rpm). Complete cycle, with No. 5 introduced in English by the singer. Oda SLOBODSKAYA (soprano) and Ivor Newton (piano). G Sept. 1962.

USSR: Melodiya D 14787-8 (10" mono). Complete cycle. Nina ISAKOVA (mezzo-soprano) and Yevgeniya Bruk (piano). [Molchanov.] P 1964. *Reissued:* USSR: Melodiya C10 10527-06348. Complete cycle. [In third box of Part 3 of *Collected Works on Records* with Op. 127.] I 1978.

USSR: Melodiya CM 03439-40. Complete cycle. Nina ZAZNOBINA (mezzo-soprano) and Yevgeni Lebedev (piano). [Taneyev, Ippolitov-Ivanov, Rimsky-Korsakov *et al.*] P 1972, I 1973.

USSR: Melodiya C20 05673-4. No. 3 only. Aleksandr VEDERNIKOV (bass), All-Union Radio Folk Orchestra, Vladimir Fedoseyev. [Boiko and two English folksongs.] P and I 1975.

USSR: Melodiya C10 07659-60. No. 2 only. Irina ARKHIPOVA (mezzo-soprano) and Nataliya Rassudova (piano). [Prokofiev, Shebalin, Sviridov *et al.*] P 1976, I 1977*c*.

USSR: Melodiya C10 08921-2. No. 3 only. Oleg PTUKHA (bass) and Nadezhda Kushnir (piano). [Op. 62 Nos. 1 and 3; Op. 98; and Kabalevsky.] P 1977, I 1978*a*.

USSR: Melodiya C10 16747008. Complete cycle. Artur EIZEN (bass) and Albertina Bogdanova (piano). [Spanish folksongs.] P 1981, I 1982*c*. *Reissued:* Olympia Compact Disc OCD 194. [Opp. 1, 3, 7, 59, 26, and 37.] I Feb. 1988, G June 1988.

USSR: Melodiya C10 18599002. Complete cycle. Yevgeniya GOROKHOVSKAYA (mezzo-soprano) and Irina Galovneva (piano). [Musorgsky, Schubert, Liszt *et al.*] I 1983*c*.

Germany: Armida AS 158. Complete cycle. R. Alexander ŠUTEY (bass-baritone) and Gerard Wyss (piano). [Borodin and Rakhmaninov.] P date not stated—prior to 1984.

USSR: Melodiya C10 20867 002. Complete cycle. Aleksandr VEDERNIKOV (bass) and Aleksandr Vedernikov junior (piano). [Ledenev.] P 1984, I 1985*a*.

Philips Compact Disc 446 708-2PH. Complete cycle. Olga BORODINA (mezzo-soprano) and Semyon Skigin (piano). ['Bolero'—Glinka, Dargomyzhsky, Rubenstein *et al.*] P London Jan. 1995, G Feb. 1998.

South Africa: Claremont Compact Disc GSE 1541. Complete cycle. Andrea CATZEL (soprano) and Thomas Rajna (piano). ['A Garland of Spanish Songs'—Rodrigo, Granados, Falla *et al.*] P (in Russian) 1995, I June 1996.
Japan: Toshiba EMI Compact Disc TOCE 9306. No. 5 arr. E. Arai. MORGAŬA quartet (Eiji Arai, Takashi Aoki, Hisashi Ono, Ryoichi Fuji-mori). [Opp. 92 and 117.] P 23–5 Oct. 1996, I Jan. 1997.
Switzerland: Dinemec Classics Compact Disc DCCD 016. Complete cycle. Paul PLISHKA (bass) and Thomas Hrynkiw (piano). ['The Russian Soul'—Medtner, Musorgsky, Rakhmaninov, and Tchaikovsky.] P New York Oct. 1996, I Oct. 1997, G Mar. 1998.
Belgium: René Gailly Compact Disc CD92 041. Complete cycle. Mikhail LUKONIN (baritone) and Yuri Serov (piano). ['Complete Songs, Vol. 1—Opp. 62, 86, 121, and 127.] P St Petersburg 23 Mar.–4 May 1998.

Opus 101   Quartet No. 6 in G major

Form: String quartet in four movements:

1. Allegretto
2. Moderato con moto
3. Lento *attacca*
4. Allegretto

Composed: 7–31 August 1956, at Moscow. The second movement completed on 19 August.
Premières: 6/7 October 1956, Glinka Concert Hall, Leningrad and 23 October 1956, Moscow Conservatory; Beethoven Quartet (Dmitri Tsyganov, Vasili Shirinsky, Vadim Borisovsky, and Sergei Shirinsky).
Arrangements: Chamber Symphony—transcribed for chamber orchestra by Jordan Dafov. Reduction for piano four hands by Anatoli Dmitriev.
Music: Autograph score preserved at the CIS Archives of Literature and Art.
Sovetskii Kompozitor, No. 294, 1957, 22 cm.
Musica Rara, No. 1037, 1961, score, 18.5 cm.
Musica Rara, No. 1037*a*, 1961, parts, 31 cm.
Muzyka, Leningrad, No. 530 (in Volume 2 with Quartets 5, 7, and 8 arr. for piano four hands by A. Dmitriev), 1966, 29.5 cm.
Edition Eulenberg, No. 390, 1970, 19 cm.
Muzyka, No. 9816 (in Volume 35 of *Collected Works* Quartets 1–8), 1979, 30 cm.
Hans Sikorski, No. 2266 (with Opp. 92, 108, and 110), 1980, score, 21 cm.
Hans Sikorski, No. 2254, 1981, parts, 31.5 cm.
Duration: Approx. 25 minutes in score; 22' 01"–27' 17".
Recordings: USSR: MK D 3582-3 (10" mono). BEETHOVEN QUARTET (personnel as at première). P 1956. *Reissued:* USSR: Melodiya D 015785-6 (mono).

[Op. 92.] I 1965 ~ USA: Consonance Blue Label Compact Disc 81.3007 (mono). [Vol. 3—Op. 73.] I May 1995 ~ France: Praga Compact Disc PR 250 077. [Opp. 92 and 108.] P given as Czech Radio 22 Aug. 1977, I Mar. 1996.

USSR: Melodiya D 019271-2 (mono) and C 01435-6. BORODIN QUARTET (Rostislav Dubinsky, Yaroslav Aleksandrov, Dmitri Shebalin, Valentin Berlinsky). [Op. 83.] P and I 1967. *Reissued:* USA: Seraphim Melodiya S 6035. [In three-record box set with Op. 11 and Quartets 7–11.] ~ HMV Melodiya HQS 1322 in Set SLS 879. [Opp. 108 and 122.] G June 1974.

USSR: Melodiya C10 07285-6. TANEYEV QUARTET (Vladimir Ovcharek, Grigori Lutsky, Vissarion Soloviev, Iosif Levinzon). [Op. 142.] P 1976, I 1977*a. Reissued:* With the same number in first box of Part 2 of *Collected Works on Records.* I 1980 ~ Japan: JVC Victor 5347. [Op. 92.] ~ Russia: Melodiya Compact Disc SUCD11 00309. [Opp. 108 and 110.] I 1993*a.*

L'Oiseau-Lyre DSLO 29. FITZWILLIAM QUARTET (Christopher Rowland, Jonathan Sparey, Alan George, Ioan Davies). [Op. 92.] P 20–2 July 1977, G Dec. 1978. *Reissued:* Decca 188 D4 in Set D 188 D7. [Opp. 108 and 138.] G Feb. 1981 ~ Decca Enterprise Compact Discs 433 078-2DM6. [On third disc of six-disc set with Opp. 92 and 108.] I Apr. 1992, G June 1992.

USSR: Melodiya C10 19535 003. BORODIN QUARTET (Mikhail Kopelman, Andrei Abramenkov, Dmitri Shebalin, Valentin Berlinsky). [Op. 83.] P Moscow concert 27 Sept. 1981, I 1984*a. Reissued:* HMV Melodiya EX 270339-3 (DMM). [In seven-record box set of 15 Quartets plus Quintet.] ~ Japan: Victor Musical Industries Compact Disc VICC 40020. [Opp. 92 and 108.] I 1990 ~ EMI Compact Discs CMS5 65032-2. [In six-disc set of 15 Quartets plus Quintet.] I Mar. 1994 ~ BMG Melodiya Compact Discs 74321 40711-2 (six-disc set). [Opp. 92 and 108.] I June 1997.

USSR: Melodiya C10 28377 008. SHOSTAKOVICH QUARTET (Andrei Shishlov, Sergei Pishchugin, Aleksandr Galkovsky, Aleksandr Korchagin). [Op. 83.] P 1981, I 1990*a. Reissued:* Olympia Compact Disc OCD 526. [Op. 108.] I 1993 ~ Olympia Compact Disc OCD 533. ['Complete Quartets, Vol. 3'—Opp. 110 and 117.] I May 1994, G Sept. 1994.

USA: Centaur Compact Disc CRC 2034. MANHATTAN QUARTET (Eric Lewis, Roy Lewis, John Dexter, Judith Glyde). [Op. 118.] P 1986, I Nov. 1988, G June 1989.

Bulgaria: Balkanton BKA 12305-6. Chamber Symphony arr. Dafov. Tolbuhin Chamber Orchestra, Jordan DAFOV. [In double album with Opp. 87 No. 24, 110, and 108.] P Tolbuhin, Bulgaria Mar. 1988.

Teldec Compact Discs 9031 71702-2. BRODSKY QUARTET (Michael Thomas, Ian Belton, Paul Cassidy, Jacqueline Thomas). [On third disc of six-disc set with Opp. 92 and 108.] P Berlin July 1989, I Nov. 1990. G June 1992. *Reissued:* Teldec Compact Disc 9031 73108-2. [Opp. 118 and 142.] I June 1991.

USA: ESS.A.Y. Compact Disc CD 1009. MANHATTAN QUARTET (personnel as above). [Opp. 108 and 110.] P Jersey City 18 Jan. 1990. *Reissued:*
Koch Schwann Compact Disc 310 165. ['Complete String Quartets, Vol. 3'
with Opp. 108 and 110.] I Jan. 1993, G June 1993.

Naxos Compact Disc 8.550972. ÉDER QUARTET (György Selmeczi, Péter
Szüts, Sándor Papp, György Éder). ['Complete Quartets, Vol. 1'—Opp.
83 and 108.] P Budapest 1–4 Dec. 1993, I July 1994.

Netherlands: Emergo Classics Compact Disc EC 3956-2. ORLANDO
QUARTET (Arvid Engegard, Heinz Oberdorfer, Ferdinand Erblich, Stefan
Mertz). [Op. 73.] P Renswoude, Netherlands 6–10 June 1994, I Jan. 1995.

Finland: Finlandia Compact Disc 4509 98997-2. SIBELIUS ACADEMY
QUARTET (Erkki Kantola, Seppo Tukiainen, Veikko Kosonen, Arto Noras).
Eop. 68.] P Järvenpää Dec. 1994, I May 1996.

Japan: EMI Classics Compact Disc TOCE 9496. MORGAŬA QUARTET (Eiji
Arai, Takashi Aoki, Hisashi Ono, Ryoichi Fujimori). [Opp. 49, 122, and
97.] P 11–14 Mar. 1997.

Chandos Compact Disc CHAN 9741. SORREL QUARTET (Gina McCormack, Catherine Yates, Vicci Wardman, Helen Thatcher). ['Complete
Quartets, Vol. 1'—Opp. 108 and 118.] P Westleton, Suffolk 23–5 Feb.
1998, I June 1999, G Oct. 1999.

Deutsche Grammophon Compact Disc 463 284-2GH5 (five-disc set).
EMERSON QUARTET (Eugene Drucker, Philip Setzer, Lawrence Dutton,
David Finkel). ['Complete Quartets, Vol. 2'—Opp. 83 and 92.] P Aspen,
Colorado concert July 1998, G June 2000. *Gramophone* Awards 2000—
complete cycle winner of the Chamber category and Quartet No. 6 first
movement included on sampler CD with the October (Awards) magazine.

Hyperion Compact Disc CDA 67154. ST PETERSBURG QUARTET (Alla Aranovskaya, Ilya Teplyakov, Konstantin Kats, Leonid Shukayev). [Opp. 83
and 110.] P St Petersburg Apr. 1999, I Dec. 1999, G Mar. 2000.

Opus 102   Piano Concerto No. 2 in F major

Form: Concerto for piano and orchestra (with brass reduced to 4 horns) in
three movements:

1. Allegro
2. Andante *attacca*
3. Allegro

Instrumentation: piccolo, 2 flutes, 2 oboes, 2 B flat clarinets, 2 bassoons ~
4 horns ~ timpani and side drum (1 player) ~ strings.
Composed: Completed on 5 February 1957.
Dedication: Maksim Dmitrievich Shostakovich (son).

Premières: Reduction: April 1957, USSR Ministry of Culture; Dmitri and Maksim Shostakovich (pianists).

10 May 1957 (dedicatee's nineteenth birthday), Moscow Conservatory Bolshoi Hall; Maksim Shostakovich (piano), USSR Symphony Orchestra, Nikolai Anosov.

USA: 2 January 1958, Leonard Bernstein (piano soloist and conductor), New York Philharmonic Orchestra.

UK: 5 September 1958, Royal Albert Hall 'Prom', London; Eileen Joyce (piano), BBC Symphony Orchestra, Sir Malcolm Sargent.

Arrangement: 1 May 1997, St John's Smith Square, London; Joanna MacGregor (piano), Marple Band, Elgar Howarth.

Arrangements: Reduction for two piano by the composer. Orchestral parts adapted for brass band instruments by E. Howarth.

Music: Frequently appears as Opus 101 on music and recordings and in catalogues. Autograph full score and two-piano reduction preserved at the CIS Archives of Literature and Art. The first page of the autograph reduction is reproduced in Volume 13 of *Collected Works*.

Sovetskii Kompozitor, No. 619, 1957, reduction for two pianos, 29 cm.

Sovetskii Kompozitor, No. 620, 1957, full score, 29 cm.

Anglo-Soviet Music Press, No. 154, 1957, reduction, 31 cm.

Leeds Music, no numbers, 1957, 23 and 32 cm.

Edition Peters, No. 4772, 1963, reduction, 30 cm.

International Music, No. 2194, no date, reduction, 30.5 cm.

Muzyka, No. 5947 (in *D. Shostakovich: Compositions for fortepiano*, Volume 3 with Opp. 35 and 94), 1970, reduction, 29 cm.

Boosey & Hawkes, No. 796, 1974, score, 21.5 cm.

Muzyka, No. 11208 (in Volume 12 of *Collected Works* with Op. 35), 1982, score, 30 cm.

Muzyka, No. 11214 (in Volume 13 of *Collected Works* with Opp. 6, 35, 94, and Sans op. O), 1983, reduction, 30 cm.

Duration: Approx. 16 minutes in score; 15' 50"–21' 29"; 20' 15"–20' 30" (Plaistow).

Film: *Fantasia 2000*. The first movement of the Second Piano Concerto is used for the fourth sequence of the Walt Disney animated film released formally worldwide on 1 January 2000. The music sets Hans Christian Andersen's tale 'The Steadfast Tin Soldier' and is performed by pianist Yefim Bronfman and the Chicago Symphony Orchestra, conducted by James Levine. Soundtrack on Edel Compact Disc 0105582 DNY.

Ballets: *Concerto*. Kenneth MacMillan, Deutsche Oper Ballet, West Berlin 30 November 1966; American Ballet Theatre, Jürgen Rose (designer), New York State Theater, New York, 18 May 1967; and Royal Ballet, Covent Garden, London, 26 May 1967. The slow movement *pas de deux* is often performed on its own.

Fête Noire. Arthur Mitchell, Dance Theatre of Harlem, Craig Sheppard (pianist), Spoleto Festival, Italy, July 1971 and Sadler's Wells Theatre, London, 11 September 1974.

Recordings: USSR: MK D 06295-8 in set MK D 201 (1 side in two-record set, mono). Dmitri SHOSTAKOVICH (piano), Moscow Radio Symphony Orchestra, Alekeandr Gauk. [Op. 103.] Moscow concert 27 Nov. 1957, G May 1961. *Reissued:* Germany: Melodia Eurodisc MK 86 611 (mono). [Op. 35.] ~ France: Le Chant du Monde LDX 78355 K. [Op. 35.] ~ HMV Melodiya HLM 7094 in Set RLS 721 (mono). [Opp. 94 and 79.] G Oct. 1976 ~ USSR: Melodiya M10 39073-4 (mono). [In four-record box set 'D. Shostakovich—Pianist' with Opp. 94 and 35.] I 1977*b* ~ Germany: Melodia Eurodisc 27 235 XDK. [In two-record set 'Shostakovich plays Shostakovich' with Opp. 35 and 94.] ~ USSR: Melodiya C10 14089-90 (electronic stereo). [In third box of Part 1 of *Collected Works on Records* with Opp. 35 and 94.] I 1980 ~ Japan: Victor Musical Industries Compact Disc VICC 2048. ['Pianist = D. Shostakovich'—Opp. 57, 35, and 94.] I 1990 ~ USA: Russian Disc Compact Disc RDCD 15 005 (mono). ['Great Russian Artists: Shostakovich plays Shostakovich'—Opp. 40 and 35.] I Nov. 1993, G Dec. 1993 and Feb. 1995 ~ Revelation Compact Disc RV 70006 (mono). ['Shostakovich plays Shostakovich, Vol. 5'—Opp. 35, 94, and 67.] P date given as 1959, I May 1998.

Columbia FCX 769 (mono). Dmitri SHOSTAKOVICH (piano), French National Orchestra, André Cluytens. [Opp. 35 and 5.] P Paris 30 May 1958, G Oct. 1961 and July 1964. *Reissued:* USA: Seraphim 60161 (mono). [Opp. 35 and 5.] I 1971 ~ France: Pathé Marconi 2C 061 12114. [Opp. 35 and 5.] I 1972 ~ World Records Retrospect SH 293 (mono). [Opp. 35 and 5.] G July 1979 ~ Russia: Russian Disc R10 00319-20 (DMM mono). [In double album 'For the 85th Anniversary' with Opp. 35, 5, and 135.] I 1991 ~ EMI Classics Compact Disc CDC7 54606-2 (mono). ['Composers in Person' series—Opp. 35, 5, and 87.] I Jan 1993, G Apr. 1993 ~ France: EMI Classics Compact Discs 573180-2 (in four-disc set). ['Andre Cluytens Accompagnateur'—Menotti and Nigg.] I 1999.

Czech: Supraphon LPV 481 (mono). Mikhail VOSKRESENSKY (piano), Prague Radio Symphony Orchestra, Václav Jiráček. [Kabalis.] G Dec. 1959. *Reissued:* USA: Artia ALP 173 (mono). [Op. 87 Nos. 3, 6, 7, 2, and 18.] G May 1961 ~ Czech: Supraphon SUA 10171 (mono). [Kabalis.]

USA: Columbia ML 5337 (mono) and MS 6043. Leonard BERNSTEIN (piano and conductor), New York Philharmonic Orchestra. [Ravel.] P 6 Jan. 1958. *Reissued:* France: Philips Réalitiés C 29 (mono). [Op. 107.] ~ Philips ABL 3300 (mono) and SABL 134. [Ravel.] G Feb. and Aug. 1960 ~ Philips A 01420 L (mono) and 835 525 AY (stereo). [Ravel.] ~ CBS BRG 72170 (mono) and SBRG 72170. [Ravel.] G July 1964 ~ CBS 73400. [Op. 35.] G May 1975 ~ CBS 73441 in Set CBS 77394. [Op. 35.] G Oct.

1975 ~ CBS Classics 60338. [Ravel.] G July 1982 ~ CBS Masterworks 60504. [Op. 35.] I Sept. 1984, G Dec. 1984 ~ CBS Masterworks Compact Disc MPK 44850. [Opp. 35 and 107.] I July 1989, G Nov. 1989 ~ Sony Classical Compact Disc SM3K 47166 (three-disc set). ['Leonard Bernstein: A Portrait: Piano works by various composers'—Gershwin and Ravel.] I Dec. 1991, G Mar. 1992 ~ Sony Royal Edition Compact Disc SMK 47618. [Op. 35 and Poulenc.] G Nov. 1993 and June 1994.

Westminster XWN 18960 (mono) and WST 14141. Eugene LIST (piano), Vienna State Opera Orchestra, Victor Desarzens. [Op. 35.] P Vienna Nov. 1960, G Nov. 1961. *Reissued:* World Record Club T 328 (mono) and ST 328. [Op. 35.] ~ Trax Classique TRXLP 131 and Compact Disc TRXCD 131. Second movement only. Performers given as Daniel Petrov (piano), Vienna Symphony Orchestra, Edouard von Lindenberg—timing 5' 55" as List. ['Testimony—Shostakovich's Greatest Hits'—Opp. 47, 97, 60, 110a, 67; and Josephs.] I 1988 ~ Trax TRX 137. Second movement only. ['100 Greatest Classics', Series 2 Part 3—Britten, Gershwin, Walton *et al.*] I 1988 ~ USA: MCA Compact Disc D2-9823A. [Op. 22a.] ~ MCA Millennium Classics Compact Disc MCD 80107. [Opp. 35 and 67.] I Feb. 1997.

HMV ASD 2709. John OGDON (piano), Royal Philharmonic Orchestra, Lawrence Foster. [Ogdon.] P 21–2 Dec. 1970, G July 1971. *Reissued:* USA: Angel S 36805. [Ogdon.] ~ HMV Concert Classics SXLP 30514. [Bartók.] G June 1981.

DJM LPS 437. Andante only. Kenny CLAYTON (piano), Royal Philharmonic Orchestra, Vic Lewis. ['Mine and Theirs'; Lewis (one side); Rodrigo, Bliss, Tchaikovsky, and Rakhmaninov.] P 6 Sept. 1973.

HMV ASD 3081. Cristina ORTIZ (piano), Bournemouth Symphony Orchestra, Paavo Berglund. [Opp. 35 and 5.] P 29 Dec. 1974, G June 1975. *Reissued:* USA: Angel S 37109. [Opp. 35 and 5.] I 1975 ~ USA: Time-Life 'Great Men of Music' box set STL 568. [Opp. 22a, 114, 40, 47, 110, and 135.] I 1979 ~ HMV Greensleeve ED 29 0210 1. [Opp. 35 and 5.] G Oct. 1984 ~ EMI Compact Disc CDS7 47790-8. [In two-disc set with Opp. 54, 103, 35 and 5.] I Nov. 1987, G May 1988 ~ HMV Classics 33 Compact Disc 7 67637-2. [Opp. 47 and 5.] I Dec. 1992 ~ EMI Classics/BBC Music Compact Disc 7 67848-2. Andante only. [Sampler—Grieg, Mozart, Bach *et al.*] I June 1993 ~ EMI Classics/BBC Music Compact Disc 7 67887-2. [Op. 47.] I Oct. 1993 ~ BBC Music Proms 1994 CD2. Andante only. ['100th Season' sampler two-disc set—Schoenberg, Rakhmaninov, Bridge *et al.*] I July 1994 ~ EMI Seraphim Compact Discs CES 568536-2 (two-disc set). [Tchaikovsky and Dohnanyi.] I May 1995.

USSR: Melodiya C10 06763-4. Eugene LIST (piano), All-Union Radio and Television Symphony Orchestra, Maksim Shostakovich. [Op. 35.] P 1975, I 1976d. *Reissued:* USA: Columbia Melodiya M 35116. [Op. 35.] I 1978 ~ Columbia Masterworks 76822. [Op. 35.] G July 1979 ~ CBS Classics 61885. Second movement only (abridged). ['Contrast'—Rakhmaninov, Debussy, Addinsell *et al.*] G Mar. 1980 ~ RCA Navigator (Russian

Music No. 73) Compact Disc 74321 29254-2. [Opp. 35 and 107.] I Nov. 1995, G Dec. 1995 ~ BBC Proms Compact Discs PRCD00 (two-disc set). First movement. [Sibelius, Weill, Prokofiev *et al.*] I July 2000.

BBC Radio Classics Compact Disc 15656 9170-2. Peter DONOHOE (piano), BBC Symphony Orchestra, Maksim Shostakovich. [Opp. 77 and 107.] P Usher Hall. Edinburgh concert 2 Sept. 1982, I May 1996.

Classics for Pleasure 4144161 (digital). Dmitri ALEKSEYEV (piano), English Chamber Orchestra, Jerzy Maksymiuk. [Opp. 35 and 89*a* No. 5.] P London May 1983, G Nov. 1983. *Reissued:* USSR: Melodiya A10 00079 002 (digital). [Op. 35.] I 1985*b* ~ USA: Angel AE 34489 (digital). [Opp. 35 and 89*a* No. 5.] ~ Classics for Pleasure CFP 4547 (digital) and Compact Disc CD-CFP 4547. [Opp. 35 and 89*a* No. 5.] I Sept. 1988, G Jan. 1989.

USSR: Melodiya C10 21159 007. Vladimir KRAINEV (piano), Leningrad Philharmonic Orchestra, Aleksandr Daltriev. [Khrennikov.] P 1983, I 1985*a*. *Reissued:* France: Le Chant du Monde Compact Disc LDC 278 1011. [Opp. 35 and 34.] I Jan. 1990.

Chandos ABRD 1155 (digital) and Compact Disc CHAN 8443. Dmitri SHOSTAKOVICH junior (piano), Montreal Symphony Orchestra, Maksim Shostakovich. [Op. 118*a*.] P Montreal 5–6 Aug. 1985, I Jan. 1986, G May and July 1986. *Reissued:* Chandos ABRD 1268 (digital) and Compact Disc CHAN 8573. Second movement only. ['Tranquility: a compilation of beautiful slow movements'—Bach, Boccherini, Vivaldi *et al.*] I Dec. 1987.

Virgin V 2526. Andante only. Howard SHELLEY (piano), London Philharmonic Orchestra, Rudolf Barshai. ['Testimony Motion Picture Soundtrack'.] P 1987, I 1988.

Decca Compact Disc 425 793-2DH. Cristina ORTIZ (piano), Royal Philharmonic Orchestra, Vladimir Ashkenazy. [Op. 77.] P Walthamstow Jan. 1989, I June 1990, G Aug. 1990. *Reissued:* Decca Eloquence Compact Disc 467 446-2. [Addinsell, Rakhmaninov, Paganini, and Skryabin.] I Nov. 2000.

Phoenix Compact Disc PHCD 117. Joshua PIERCE (piano), Slovenian RTV Symphony Orchestra, Paul Freeman. [Khachaturyan and Prokofiev.] P Ljubljana, Slovenia, 30 Aug. 1990, I July 1993.

Nimbus Compact Disc NI 5308. Martin JONES (piano), English Chamber Orchestra, William Boughton. [Opp. 35 and 110.] P Leominster 14–15 Nov. 1990, I Oct. 1991.

Teldec Compact Disc 9031 73282-2. Elizaveta LEONSKAYA (piano), Saint Paul Chamber Orchestra, Hugh Wolff. [Op. 35 and 61.] P St Paul, Minnesota Sept. 1991, I Apr. 1993, G June 1993. *Reissued:* Warner Apex Compact Disc 8573 89092-2. [Opp. 35 and 61.] G Oct. 2001.

Austria: Musica Classica Compact Disc 780013-2. Paul GULDA (piano), Moscow Radio Symphony Orchestra, Vladimir Fedoseyev. [Op. 35.] P Bratislava Nov. 1993, I Jan. 1996.

Italy: Phoenix Compact Disc PH 00602. Maurizio BARBARO (piano), Byelorussian Symphony Orchestra, Antonello Gotta. [Opp. 35 and 22*a*.] P Minsk 9–11 Dec. 1993, I Jan. 2001.

Naxos Compact Disc 8.553126. Michael HOUSTON (piano), New Zealand Symphony Orchestra, Christopher Lyndon-Gee. [Opp. 35, 96, and 22.] P Wellington 2–4 Nov. 1994, I Sept. 1995. *Reissued:* Naxos Compact Discs 8.505150 (five-disc set). ['Romantic Piano Concertos Vol. 2'— disc one with Rakhmaninov.] I Oct. 1999.

Carlton Classics Compact Disc 30367 01842. John COVELLI (piano / conductor), Moscow Philharmonic Orchestra. [Saint-Saëns.] P Moscow Film Studios June 1995, I Apr. 1997.

EMI Classics Compact Disc CDC5 56591-2. Mikhail RUDY (piano), London Philharmonic Orchestra, Mariss Jansons. [Opp. 141 and 97.] P London 14–16 Apr. 1997, I Oct. 1998.

Sony Compact Disc SK 60677. Yefim BRONFMAN (piano), Los Angeles Philharmonic Orchestra, Esa-Pekka Salonen. [Opp. 35 and 57.] P Los Angeles 30 Mar. 1998, I Nov. 1999.

Decca Compact Disc 460 503-2DH. Second movement only. Jean-Yves THIBAUDET (piano), BBC Symphony Orchestra, Hugh Wolff. ['Warsaw Concerto'—Addinsell, Rakhmaninov, and Gershwin.] P Watford 7 June 1998, I Oct. 1998.

USA: Delos Compact Disc DE 3246. Andrew LITTON (piano and conductor), Dallas Symphony Orchestra. [Opp. 47 and 96.] P Dallas 30 Sept. 1998.

Sans op. T   Variations on a Theme by Glinka

Form: Variations Nos. 8, 9, and 11 from the cycle *Variations on a Theme by Mikhail Glinka* for piano, composed for children by Dmitri Shostakovich, Eugen Kapp (No. 1), Vissarion Shebalin (Nos. 2 and 3), Andrei Eshpai (No. 4), Rodion Shchedrin (No. 5), Georgi Sviridov (No. 6), Yuri Levitin (No. 7), and Dmitri Kabalevsky (No. 10), to commemorate the centenary of Glinka's death. The theme is 'The Song of Vanya' from Act 3 of the opera *Ivan Susanin.*

8. Adagio
9. Allegretto
11. Moderato maestoso

Composed: 1957.

Music: *Sovetskaya Muzyka* magazine, 1957, No. 2, complete cycle in supplement.

Associated Music Publishers, New York, No. 7729, 1976–7, 11 variations in VAAP authorized edition, 30 cm.

Muzyka, Leningrad, No. 2629 (in *S. Prokofiev and D. Shostakovich: Selection of Fortepiano Pieces for Children*), 1980, No. 9 only, ed. Zinaida Vitkind, 28.5 cm.

Duration: Theme and Variations Nos. 8, 9, and 11: 6' 31".
Recording: AMV Classics Compact Disc AVZ 3020. Theme and Nos. 8, 9, and 11. Martin JONES. ['Piano Music Volume II'—Sans opp. A and S; Opp. 13, 34, 69, and 22*a*.] P London 3 Jan. 1990.

Opus 103   Symphony No. 11 in G minor

Subtitle: 'The Year 1905'.
Form: Symphony for full orchestra (with 2–4 harps) in four linked movements:

1. Palace Square—Adagio *attacca*
2. Ninth of January—Allegro—Adagio—Allegro—Adagio *attacca*
3. Eternal Memory—Adagio *attacca*
4. The Toscin—Allegro non troppo—Allegro—Moderato—Adagio—Allegro

The symphony quotes the tunes of revolutionary songs ('Listen!, 'Arestant'; the funeral march 'You Fell as Victims' and 'Welcome the Free Word of Liberty' in the third movement; 'Rage You Tyrants!, 'Boldly, Comrades, on we March', and 'Warsaw March' in the Finale), while also introducing the composer's own 'Ninth of January'—the sixth of his *Ten Poems on Texts by Revolutionary Poets*, Opus 88 as a leitmotiv and a theme from Georgi Sviridov's musical comedy *Ogonki*.

Instrumentation: piccolo (= flute III), 2 flutes, 2 oboes, cor anglais (= oboe III), 2 clarinets (B flat and A), bass clarinet (= B flat clarinet III), 2 bassoons, contrabassoon (= bassoon III) ~ 4 horns, 3 trumpets, 3 trombones, tuba ~ timpani, triangle, side drum, cymbals, bass drum, gong ~ xylophone, celesta, orchestral bells, 2–4 harps ~ 1st violins (16–20), 2nd violins (14–18), violas (12–16), cellos (10–14), double-basses (10–12).

Composed: In the summer of 1957, at Komarovo village, Gulf of Finland, and completed on 4 August 1957. Written to mark the fortieth anniversary of the October Revolution.

Premières: Reduction: 17 September 1957, House of Composers, Leningrad; Dmitri Shostakovich and Mikhail Meyerovich (pianists).

   30 October 1957, Moscow Conservatory Bolshoi Hall; USSR Symphony Orchestra, Natan Rakhlin.

   3 November 1957, Leningrad; Leningrad Philharmonic Orchestra, Yevgeni Mravinsky.

   UK: 22 January 1958, Royal Festival Hall, London; BBC Symphony Orchestra, Sir Malcolm Sargent.

   USA: 7 April 1958, Houston; Houston Symphony Orchestra, Leopold Stokowski.

   USA: 14 December 1958, Carnegie Hall, New York; Symphony of the Air, Leopold Stokowski.

Arrangements: Reduction for piano four hands by the composer. The second movement 'Ninth of January' arranged for brass band (performance by the Sun Life Band under Barry Pope televised on BBC 2, 27 March 1986).

Music: Autograph score preserved in the CIS Archives of Literature and Art. The opening page of the autograph score is reproduced in Volume 6 of *Collected Works*. Awarded a Lenin Prize on 22 April 1958.

Sovetskii Kompozitor and Muzgiz, No. 26985, 1958, 30 cm.

Muzgiz, No. 27011, 1958, reduction for piano four hands, 29 cm.

Leeds Music/Boosey & Hawkes, No. 705 (plate no. 18428), 1958, 19 cm.

Hans Sikorski, No. 2217, 1958, 21 cm.

Muzyka, 1966, 21 cm.

Kalmus, No. 1460, no date, 26 cm.

Muzyka, No. 10178 (in Volume 6 of *Collected Works* with Op. 112), 1980, 30 cm.

Duration: 57 minutes in score; 53' 42"–69' 36"; 60 minutes (M. MacDonald).

Ballets: *Eleventh Symphony*. Igor Belsky, Leningrad Malyi Theatre; décor by M. Smirnov and Mikhail Shcheglov, ballet in 4 scenes, 7 May 1966.

Symphony of Revolution. Created by Natalya Ryzhenko and Viktor Smirnov-Golovanov, with libretto based on Maksim Gorky's novel *Mother*; using music from Symphonies Nos. 11 and 12; performed at the Odessa Theatre of Opera and Ballet in 1977.

Films: *I Sequestrati di Altona* ('The Condemned of Altona'). Vittorio de Sica used the music of the third movement throughout this 113-minute black and white film of 1963, based on the play by Jean-Paul Sartre.

Battleship Potemkin. The American Corinth Films video tape presentation of Sergei Eisenstein's silent film of 1925 added a score from works of Shostakovich, including the Eleventh Symphony [replacing the original pit orchestra music by Edmund Meisel.]

October. See under Symphony No. 12, Opus 112.

Recordings: USSR: MK D 04234-7 (4 sides mono). USSR Symphony Orchestra, Natan RAKHLIN. P 1957, I 1958.

USSR: MK D 4808-11 (4 sides 10" mono). Leningrad Philharmonic Orchestra, Yevgeni MRAVINSKY. P Leningrad concert 3 Nov. 1957, I 1958 and withdrawn shortly afterwards. *Reissued:* USA: Russian Disc Compact Disc RDCD 11 157 (mono). I Sept. 1993, G Jan. 1994.

USA: Capitol PBR 8448 (4 sides mono) and SPBR 8448. Houston Symphony Orchestra, Leopold STOKOWSKI. P 9–12 Apr. 1958. *Reissued:* World Record Club T 776-7 (mono) and ST 776-7 (4 sides). G Sept. 1968 ~ USA: Capitol SPBO 8700. I 1968. Also: Everest 3310 and Seraphim S 60228. (All 4 sides) ~ USA: EMI Angel Compact Disc CDC7 47419-2. I UK Oct. 1986 ~ USSR: Melodiya C10 19543 001. I 1989 ~ EMI Classicis Compact Disc CDM7 65206-2. I June 1994.

France: EMI FCX 758-9 (3 sides mono; last side blank). French National Radio Orchestra, André CLUYTENS. P in the presence of the composer Paris 19 May 1958. *Reissued:* Columbia 33CX 1604 and CXS 1605 (3 sides mono; last side blank). G Jan. 1959 ~ USA: Angel ANG 35694-5 in Set 3586 (3 sides mono) ~ France: Pathé Marconi 2C 061 12167 (electronic stereo). I 1973 ~ USA: Testament Compact Disc SBT 1099 (stereo). G May 1997.

USA: Russian Disc Compact Disc RDCD 15 100. Moscow Radio Symphony Orchestra, Leopold STOKOWSKI. P Moscow concert in the presence of the composer, 7 June 1958, I June 1996.

USSR: MK D 06295-8 (3 sides in two-record set MK D 201, mono). Leningrad Philharmonic Orchestra, Yevgeni MRAVINSKY. [Op. 102.] P Moscow studio 2 Feb. 1959, I 1960, G May 1961. *Reissued:* Japan: Victor Musical Industries Compact Disc VICC 40122 (one disc in six-disc set, mono). I 1992 ~ Japan: BMG Melodiya Compact Disc BVCX 4025 (mono). [Ustvolskaya.] I 1977 ~ France: Praga Compact Discs PR 254 017-8 (two-disc set, mono). [Opp. 54 and 112.] P given incorrectly as Prague Spring 1967 concert and applause added, I Apr. 1994, G Aug. 1994 ~ Revelation Compact Disc RV 10091 (mono). P date given as 2 Nov. 1959 (confusion with 2.II.59?), I Dec. 1997, G Feb, and Mar. 1998 ~ France: Le Chant du Monde Compact Disc PR 7254018. P date given as Czech Radio broadcast 1967, I autumn 2000 in fifteen-disc set, G Feb. 2001.

East Germany: Eterna 7 20 093-4 (4 sides 10" mono). Dresden Staatskapelle, Franz KONWITSCHNY. P 15–16 May 1959. *Reissued:* East Germany: Eterna 8 20 675-6 (3 sides mono). [Op. 10.] ~ Germany: Berlin Classics Compact Disc 0090 422 BC (two-disc set, mono). [Op. 93.] I Oct. 1995.

USSR: Melodiya CM 04273-4 (2 sides). Moscow Philharmonic Orchestra, Kirill KONDRASHIN. P 1973, I 1974c. *Reissued:* HMV Melodiya ASD 3010. G Sept. 1974 ~ USA: Angel Melodiya SR 40244. I 1974 ~ Germany: Melodia Eurodisc 87 623 XPK. [In thirteen-record box set.] I 1974 ~ France: Le Chant du Monde LDX 78577 ~ HMV Melodiya BOX 502509 in Set SLS 5025. G Dec. 1975 ~ USSR: Melodiya CM 04273-4. [In second box of Part 1 of *Collected Works on Records.*] I 1980 ~ HMV Melodiya EX 2903783 (DMM). [Ninth record in twelve-record box set.] G Dec. 1985 ~ France: Le Chant du Monde Compact Disc LDC 278 1007-8. [In Box 4 of five two-disc sets with Opp. 112 and 113.] G May 1989 ~ BMG Classics Melodiya Compact Disc 74321 19843-2. I July 1994, G Nov. 1994.

HMV ASD 3772-3 in Set SLS 5177 (3 sides). Bournemouth Symphony Orchestra, Paavo BERGLUND. [Op. 54.] P Southampton 18–19 Dec. 1978, G Feb. 1980. *Reissued:* EMI Compact Disc CDS7 47790-8. [In two-disc set with Opp. 54, 35, 102, and 5.] I Nov. 1987, G May 1988 ~ EMI Classics Compact Discs 5 73839-2 (two-disc set). [Op. 60.] I May 2000.

USSR: Melodiya A10 00029 000 (3 sides digital). USSR Ministry of Culture Symphony Orchestra, Gennadi ROZHDESTVENSKY. [Op. 70.] P 1983, I 1984*b*. *Reissued:* Japan: Victor Compact Disc JVC VDC 1042. I 1985 ~ Olympia Compact Disc OCD 152. I Aug. 1988, G Nov. 1988 ~ Germany: Melodia Eurodisc Compact Disc 258 490 ~ Olympia Compact Disc OCD 5006. [In Vol. 2 five-disc set of symphonies.] I Dec. 1990 ~ BMG Melodiya Compact Discs 74321 63461-2 (two-disc set). [Opp. 23; 93, and 91.] I Mar. 1999.

Decca 414 126-1DH in Set 411 939-1DH2 (3 sides digital). Concertgebouw Orchestra, Bernard HAITNIK. [Op. 54.] P 2–4 May 1983, G June 1985. *Simultaneous issue:* Decca Compact Disc 411 939-2DH2 (one disc in two-disc set). [Opp. 54 and 115.] G Aug. 1985 ~ Decca Ovation Compact Disc 425 072-2DM. I Aug. 1993, G Nov. 1993.

BBC Radio Classics Compact Disc BBCRD 9142. BBC Symphony Orchestra, John PRITCHARD. P Royal Festival Hall concert 3 Dec. 1986, I Nov. 1995.

Philips 420 935-1PH (digital) and Compact Disc 420 935-2PH. Berl Philharmonic Orchestra, Semyon BYCHKOV. P 20–2 Mar. 1987, G Nov. 1988.

Naxos Compact Disc 8.550629. Czecho-Slovak Radio Symphony Orchestra, Udislav SLOVÁK. P Bratislava 25 Apr.–4 May 1988, I Oct. 1993, G Nov. 1993. *Reissued:* Naxos Compact Discs 8.506003. [In six-disc set with Symphonies Nos. 5, 8, 9, 10, 13, and 14.] I 1993.

Delos D 3080 (digital) and Compact Disc DE 3080. Sven-Erik Paananen (cor anglais), Helsinki Philharmonic, James DE PRIEST. P Hyvinkää, Finland 23–4 May 1988, G May 1989.

Deutsche Grammophon Compact Disc CD 429 405-2GH. Gothenburg Symphony Orchestra, Neeme JÄRVI. P Gothenburg Dec. 1989, I Aug. 1990, G Sept. 1990. *Reissued:* Deutsche Grammophon Compact Discs 459 415-2GTA2 (two-disc set). [Opp. 112, 131, 32, and 22*a*.] I Jan. 1999.

Koch Schwann Compact Disc 31327-2. NHK Symphony Orchestra, Yukio KITAHARA. P Tokyo concert 25 Mar. 1992, I Apr. 1993.

Denon Compact Disc CO 78920. Vienna Symphony Orchestra, Eliahu INBAL. P 23–7 May 1992, I Mar. 1995, G Apr. 1995.

Teldec Compact Disc 9031 76262-2. National Symphony Orchestra of Washington, Mstislav ROSTROPOVICH. P Washington Oct.–Nov. 1992, I June 1993, G Aug. 1993. *Reissued:* Teldec Compact Discs 0630-17046-2. [In twelve-disc set of Symphonies.] G Oct. 1997.

Decca Compact Disc 448 179-2DH. St Petersburg Philharmonic Orchestra, Vladimir ASHKENAZY. P St Petersburg 22–3 Nov. 1994, I Apr. 1996, G May 1996.

Koch Schwann Compact Disc 374 142. Seattle Symphony Orchestra, Gerard SCHWARZ. P Seattle 5–6 June 1995, I Dec. 1997.

Chandos Compact Disc CHAN 9476. Russian State Symphony Orchestra, Valeri POLYANSKY. P Mosfilm Studio Nov. 1995, I Sept. 1996, G July 1997.

EMI Classics Compact Disc CDC5 55601-2. Philadelphia Orchestra, Mariss JANSONS. [Sans opp. E and G, Op. 16.] P Collingswood, New Jersey 8, 9, and 11 Mar. 1996, I May 1997, G Sept. 1997.

Germany: Arte Nova Classics Compact Disc 74321 54452-2. Jena Philharmonic Orchestra, David MONTGOMERY. P Jena, Germany 2 Sept. 1996, I Apr. 1998.

USA: Angelok[1] Compact Disc ANGCD 9903. Royal Philharmonic Orchestra, Vakhtang JORDANIA. P Gospel Oak, London 5 July 1999, I Dec. 2000.

References: Berger, Dolzhansky (in Berger), Hulme, Leie (in Kandinsky), Ian MacDonald, Matthews, Ottaway, Rienäcker/Reising, Sabinina, Shaginyan, and Tigranov.

Opus 104   Cultivation

Form: Two traditional Russian folksongs arranged for S.A.T.B. chorus a cappella:

1. 'Returning Winds' (or 'Winds were Blowing')—In a reserved manner, unhurriedly
2. How my husband cruelly beat me hard (or 'As I was a Young Girl')—Quickly, gaily

Composed: 1957, at Moscow.

Premières: 24 November 1957, Moscow Conservatory Bolshoi Hall; RSFSR Academic Russian Choir, Aleksandr Sveshnikov.

UK: 11 March 1987, Queen Elizabeth Hall, London; Westminster Singers, Richard Hickox. (A recording of this performance broadcast on BBC Radio 3, 26 April 1987 and 12 March 1991).

Music: Autograph score preserved in the State Russian Folk Choir Academy (Sadovnikov); whereabouts unknown (*Collected Works*).

Sovetskii Kompozitor, Leningrad, Nos. 9 and 17 in the collection *Russian Folk Songs* compiled by Nataliya Kotikova, 1957.

Muzyka, No. 10179 (in Volume 34 of *Collected Works* with Opp. 88 and 136, and songs), 1985, 30 cm.

Duration: Approx. 6 minutes in score; 6' 35": (1) 4' 32"–5' 07" and (2) 0' 56"–1' 28".

Recordings: USSR: Melodiya C 01709-10. Omsk Russian Folk Choir, Georgi PANTYUKOV. No. 2 only. [Russian folksongs—mainly West Siberian.] P 1969.

USSR: Melodiya C10 16967001. No. 2 only. Glinka State Academic Cappella of Leningrad, Vladimir CHERNUSHENKO (chorus-master). [Sans op. Q and three Russian folksongs arr. by other hands.] I 1982*c*. *Reissued:* USSR: Melodiya Compact Disc SUCD11 00320. No. 2 only. [Sans op. Q and six Russian folksongs arr. by other hands.] I 1991*d*.

USA: Yale BYR-024. No. 1 only, translated as 'The Winds Blew'. The Yale Russian Chorus, Michael SCHNACK (conductor). ['The Yale Russian Chorus, Volume 9'—Rakhmaninov, Glazunov _et al._] P Yale May and Dec. 1987.

USSR: Melodiya C10 29653 007. Nos. 1 and 2. Moscow Youth and Students' Choir, Elena Nikolayeva (chorus-master), Boris TEVLIN (chorus-director). [Tchaikovsky, Taneyev, Shebalin _et al._] P 1988. I 1990c.

France: Russian Season Compact Disc RUS 288 121. No. 2 only, translated as 'Me, young lass'. Sveshnikov Russian Academic Choir, Yevgeni TYTIANKO. ['Russian folksongs'—traditional, Rimsky-Korsakov, Varlamov _et al._] P Mosfilm studios, Moscow Feb. 1995.

Philips Compact Disc 456 399-2PH. No. 2 only, translated as 'How was I, a tender young maiden?' St Petersburg Chamber Choir, Nikolai KORNIEV. ['Kalinka: Russian folksongs'—arr. Kozlov, Novikov, Kolovsky _et al._] P St Petersburg May 1996, I Dec. 1998, G Feb. 1999.

Opus 105   Moscow, Cheryomushki

Translation of title: 'The Bird-cherry District of Moscow'.
Alternative titles: _Song Over Moscow_ (American title for Opus 105a).
Originally _Cheryomushki_ and then _New Tenants_. English title given as _Cheryomushki, Moscow_ in Volumes 24 and 25 of _Collected Works_. Retitled _Cheryomushki 1958_ for the British stage première and later, _Cheryomushki_.
Form: Musical Comedy (or Operetta) in three acts of five scenes (Overture-Prologue and 39 numbers), for full orchestra (with harp), 19 singing parts and S.A.T.B. chorus, to libretto by Vladimir Mass and Mikhail Chervinsky:

Overture-Prologue—Allegretto

ACT 1

Scene 1:   'Do not touch!'
    1. Bubentsov and choir of excursionists
    2. Duet: Masha and Bubentsov
    3. Pantomime—Allegretto
    4. Aria: Boris
    5. Serenade: Boris
    6. Song: Lidochka
    7. A drive through Moscow
Dialogue Interlude. 'Reckless love'
    8. Duet: Vava and Drebednev
    9. End of drive through Moscow
Scene 2:   'Registering for a new flat'
    10. Assembly of tenants
    11. Song: Glushkov, the chauffeur of Marina Grove
    12. Song: Baburov, the old Muscovite of Tyoplyi (warm) Lane

13. Song of Cheryomushki
14. Scene: Barabashkin with tenants
15. Song: Boris
16. Scene: Drebednev, Barabashkin, and tenants
17. Finale of Act 1

ACT 2

Musical Interlude: 'Here they are, the keys!'—Allegretto
    18. Couplets: Barabashkin
Scene 3:'Aerial descent'
    19. Duet: Lidochka and Boris
    20. Duet: Lyusya and Glushkov
    21. Couplets: Barabashkin and Drebednev
    22. Duet: Lidochka and Boris
    23. Scene
Dialogue Interlude
    24. Song: Lyusya and the builders
Scene 4:'Alarm bell'
    25. Duet: Masha and Bubentsov
    26. Polka with kisses—Allegretto
    27. Song of Cheryomushki
Dialogue Interlude
    28. Ballet—Andantino
    29. Apotheosis—Presto
    30. Finale of Act 2

ACT 3

    31. Entr'acte—Allegretto
    32. Scene
Scene 5:'Magic hours'
    33. Song: Lidochka
    34. Blossom Waltz—Allegretto
    35. Ditty: Barabashkin
    36. Duet: Lidochka and Boris
    37. Ditty: Glushkov
    38. Scene: Barabashkin
    39. Finale

The 'Song of Cheryomushki' that recurs throughout the score (e.g. at the beginning of the Overture-Prologue and in Nos. 13, 17, and 39) is based on the urban song 'There Used to be Merry Days', previously used in *The Golden Mountains*, Opus 30 film score. Nos. 6 and 22 include arrangements of 'Song of the Counterplan' from Opus 33. No. 7 Includes a fragment from the Galop in Ballet Suite No. 1, Sans op. P. No. 19 includes a fragment from 'Moscow Suburb Nights' (better known in the

West as 'Midnight in Moscow') by Vasili Soloviev-Sedol at fig. 170, which also quotes the popular Russian songs 'It Was in the Garden' at fig. 167, 'The Moon Shines' at fig. 168, 'O My New Porch' at fig. 169, and 'Roasted Chicken' at fig. 180. No. 21 includes an arrangement of the Intermezzo from *The Bolt*, Opus 27*a*.

Instrumentation: piccolo (= flute III), 2 flutes, 3 oboes, 3 clarinets (A and B flat), 2 bassoons ~ 4 horns, 3 trumpets, 3 trombones, tuba ~ timpani, triangle, castanets, tambourine, side drum, cymbals, bass drum, gong ~ glockenspiel, harp ~ strings.

Composed: Preliminary work in the autumn of 1957 but mainly September–November 1958, in Moscow hospital and rest home at Bolshevo, near Moscow.

Premières: 24 January 1959, Moscow Operetta Theatre; Grigori Kigel (designer), Galina Shakhovskaya (choreographer), A. Zaks and Vladimir Kandelaki (producers), Grigori Stolyarov (conductor).

UK: 19–29 October 1994, Lyric Theatre, Hammersmith; Pimlico Opera production in David Pountney's English translation and Gerard McBurney's reorchestration; Paul Andrews (designer), Caroline Pope (choreographer), Lucy Bailey (director); principal roles—Nicole Tibbels (Masha), Gareth Lloyd (Glushkov), Roger Bryson (Drebednev), Richard Suart (Barabashkin), Brian Lipson (Baburov), Meurig Davies (Bubentsov), Rebecca Gale (Lyusya), Anna Barkan (Lidochka), Ian Platt (Boris), Janet Fullerlove (Vava); conducted by Wasfi Kani.

UK: 3 May–22 June 2001, Grand Theatre, Leeds (broadcast on BBC Radio 3 on 5 May); Sadler's Wells; The Lowry, Manchester; Theatre Royal, Nottingham and Newcastle; Opera North production retitled *Paradise Moscow* in David Pountney's English translation and Gerard McBurney's reorchestration with additional arrangements by Jim Holmes; Robert Innes Hopkins (designer), Craig Revel Horwood (choreographer), D. Pountney (director); principal roles—Gillian Kirkpatrick (Masha), Alan Oke (Glushkov), Richard Angas (Drebednev), Campbell Morrison (Barabashkin), Steven Beard (Baburov), Daniel Broad (Bubentsov), Rachael Taylor (Lyushka), Janie Dee (Lidochka), Loren Geeting (Boris), Margaret Preece (Vava); conducted by Steven Sloane and Jim Holmes.

Opus 105*a*:   film first shown on 30 December 1962.

USA: 21 November 1964, Cameo Theater, New York; under the title *Song Over Moscow*.

Arrangements: A German version under the title 'My Ancient, My Young City', with libretto edited by the poet Kuba, produced at Rostock, GDR in 1960. English translation by David Pountney for the 1994 version *Cheryomushki 1958* in Gerard McBurney's orchestration of 1993–94.

'Lyusya's Song of Yearning' (from Overture-Prologue, figs. 12–16) arranged for piano by Bronislava Rozengauz, and cello and piano by S. Kalyanov. Also titled 'Waltz in G minor'.

'Blossom Waltz' (from No. 28. figs. 253-8) reductions for piano by Lev Atovmyan and B. Rozengauz, and as organ solo by Mariya Makarova. Galop arranged for 48 violas by Julian Milone. Suite arranged by Andrew Cornall in 1995:

1. A spin through Moscow—No. 7
2. Waltz—Nos. 2 and 3
3. Dances (Polka—Galop)—Nos. 26 and 19
4. Ballet—No. 28

Instrumentation of *Chemushki 1958:* flute/piccolo, clarinet (B flat and E flat), 2 saxophones (soprano/alto and tenor/baritone) ~ 2 trumpets, trombone ~ upright piano ~ guitar/banjo/ukelele ~ percussion (1 player—side, tenor, and bass drums; 2 tambourines, Rototom, 2 wood blocks, 3 bongos, 2 tom-toms, 2 triangles, 3 suspended cymbals, cymbals, car horn, small glockenspiel, vibraphone, metal twang; 5 electric bells—door chime, school, alarm, public transport, telephone; wind machine, 2 thundersheets) ~ 2 violins, cello, double-bass.

Music: The whereabouts of the autograph score is not known. The definitive manuscript vocal score preserved at the USSR Music Fund. Sergei Glushkov's song 'We're Building a House' was not included in the definitive version of the score. It is published as a supplement to Volumes 24 and 25 of *Collected Works*. An incomplete autograph vocal score preserved in the Shostakovich family archive.

Sovetskii Kompozitor, No. 1308, 1959, vocal score, 30 cm.

Sovetskii Kompozitor, No. 4565 (in *D. Shostakovich: Popular Pieces* for piano), 1967, 'Blossom Waltz' arr. L. Atovmyan, 28.5 cm.

Sovetskii Kompozitor, No. 4920 (in *D. Shostakovich: Selection of Children's Piano Pieces*), 1979, 'Lyusya's Song of Yearning' and 'Blossom Waltz' arr. B. Rozengauz, 29 cm.

Muzyka, No. 11933 (Volume 24 of *Collected Works*), 1986, full score, 30 cm.

Muzyka, No. 11934 (Volume 25 of *Collected Works*), 1986, vocal score 30 cm.

Muzyka, No. 14908 (in *D. Shostakovich: Pieces for cello and piano*), 1991, 'Lyusya's Song of Yearning' arr. S. Kalyanov, 29 cm.

Duration: Musical Comedy: *c.* 1 hr 45 mins—2 hrs 22 mins (recordings); 2 hrs 40 mins (staged). Film: 1 hr 32 mins. Suite (1995): 19' 47".

Films: Opus 105a—*Cheryomushki*, a film based on the musical comedy, directed by Gerbert Rappaport for Lenfilm.

Cheryomushki: 'Another Bite of the Cherry'. A 50-minute documentary, produced by Richard Trayler-Smith, screened on BBC2 TV on 20 August 1995 to mark the 20th anniversary of the composer's death. Includes extracts from the original Moscow stage and Lenfilm productions and the Pimlico Opera presentation (rehearsals and a performance

filmed on 22 October 1994). Recorded observations from David Pountney, Gerard McBurney, Wasfi Kani, stars of the Soviet and British versions, Russian commentators, and current residents of the run-down
Cheryomushki estate.
    Master Class: David Pountney—Opera Director. A BBC TV2 documen-
tary, introduced by James Naughtie on 21 December 2000, included a
runthrough of No. 8—Duet of Vava and Drebednev sung by Frank
Church and Catrin Johnsson and accompanied by Elizabeth Rowe.
Recordings: USSR: MK D 11043-4 (10" mono). Eleven excerpts: Overture,
Nos. 6, 22, 19, 7, 5, 25, 18, 14, 26, and 39. Soloists—as below, Chorus and
Orchestra of Moscow Operetta Theatre, Grigori STOLYAROV. P 1959, I 1962.
    USSR: Melodiya D 034379-82 (4 sides in double album, mono). com-
plete apart from Nos. 9, 15–17, 27, 31, 33, 34, 36, and 37. N. Kuralesina
(Masha), A. Steputenko (Glushkov), A. Tkachenko (Drebednev), Vasili
Alchevsky (Barabashkin), V. Chekalov (Bubentsov), A. Kotova (Lyasya),
Tatyana Shmyga (Lidochka), Nikolai Ruban (Boris), N. Krylova (Vava),
Chorus and Orchestra of Moscow Operetta Theatre, Grigori STOLYAROV.
P 1959, I 1974. *Reissued:* Melodiya M60 39919-22 (mono). No. 7 only. [In
two-record set 'Pages from Soviet Operettas'.] I 1978b.
    USA: Columbia ML 6267 (mono) and MS 6867. Orchestral excerpts:
Galop from No. 19, fig. 175 to end; and Medley—Dance from No. 19,
figs. 169–71, Overture Waltz to fig. 5, and Entr'acte No. 31 from Act 3.
André KOSTELANETZ and his Orchestra. [Opp. 22a and 97a; Sans op. P
excerpts.] P New York 23 and 29 Nov. 1965. *Reissued:* CBS BRG 72504
(mono) and SBRG 72504. [Op. 97a and Sans op. P excerpts.] G Feb.
1967 ~ CBS Classics 61220. [Op. 97a and Sans op. P excerpts.] G May
1971 ~ Sony Classical Compact Disc SBK 62642. Galop and Overture
Waltz. [Opp. 10, 22, 96, 97, and Sans op. P.] G June 1997.
    Sweden: Bluebell Bell 126. 'Lyusya's Song of Yearning' labelled as 'Waltz
in G minor'. Inger WIKSTRÖM (piano). [Opp. 5; 19 Nos. 3, 4, and 2; 22a No. 3;
31 No. 4; 94; 97a No. 7, and Prokofiev.] P Stockholm 28 Jan. and 1 Feb. 1981.
    Cala Compact Disc CACD 0106. Galop arr. J. Milone. The 48 Violas of
Academy of St Martin-in-the-Fields; BBC Symphony, London Philharmonic, and English National Opera Orchestras, Geoffrey SIMON. ['The
London Viola Sound'—Gershwin, Weill, Dvořák *et al.*] P Watford 24 Jan.
1995, I Apr. 1995, G Sept. 1995.
    Olympia Compact Disc OCD 585. 'Blossom Waltz' arr. for organ.
Mariya MAKAROVA (organ). ['Music for Organ'—Opp. 16, 27, 29, 39, 81,
97, and Sans op. E.] P Moscow Conservatory Jan. 1995, I Mar. 1997.
    BBC Music Compact Disc BBC MM132. *Cheryomushki*: Pountney /
McBurney version sung in English—Nos. 7, 2, 3, 5, 17, 11, 12, 1, 4, 6, 13, 8,
9, Overture-Prologue, 14, 18, 16, 19–21, 25, 26, 22, 28, 32, 35, 15, 38, and
39. Cast and orchestra of Pimlico Opera; roles as at Hammersmith stage
performances except for Simon Davies (Glushkov) and Phyllida Hancock

(Lyusya); Wasfi KANI. P Abbey Theatre, St Albans Feb. 1995, I Apr. 1995 magazine with synopsis.

Decca Compact Disc 452 597-2DH. Suite arr. Andrew Cornall. Erez Ofer (violin), Philadelphia Orchestra, Riccardo CHAILLY. ['The Dance Album'— Opp. 27 and 97.] P New Jersey Dec. 1995, I Oct. 1996, G Dec. 1996.

Chandos Compact Discs CHAN 9591(2) (two-disc set with synopsis and libretto in Russian, English, French, and German in 264-page booklet). Andrei Baturin (Bubentsov and Drebednev). Irina Gelakhova (Masha), Mikhail Gouzhov (Baburov), Yelena Prokina (Ludochka), Anatoli Loshak (Boris), Germann Apaikin (Sergei Glushkov), Lydiya Chernykh (Lyusya), Aleksandr Kiselev (Barabashkin), Gennadi Rozhdestvensky (taxi driver—spoken), Zino Vinnikov (violin), Gregor Horsch (cello), Russian State Symphonic Cappella, Valeri Polyansky (chorusmaster), Resident Orchestra of The Hague, Gennadi ROZHDESTVENSKY. P The Hague 30 June–3 July 1997, I Dec. 1997, G Apr. 1998.

RLPO Live Compact Disc RLCD 101. Galop. Royal Liverpool Philharmonic Orchestra, Petr ALTRICHTER. [Rimsky-Korsakov, Musorgsky, and Glinka.] P Liverpool concert 17 Oct. 1998, I Feb. 1999, G May 1999.

EMI Classics Compact Disc CDC5 57129-2. 'A drive through Moscow'. Hamburg State Philharmonic Orchestra, Ingo METZMACHER. ['Who is Afraid of 20th Century Music?'—Gershwin, Honegger, Adams *et al.*] P Hamburg concert 31 Dec. 2000, I Feb. 2001.

References: Kukharsky, McBurney, and Shaginyan.

Notes: Act 2 Scene 3: 'Airborne forces' of previous editions is a possible translation of 'Vozdushnyi desant' though Gerard McBurney suggests 'Aerial descent' would be more appropriate for the unauthorised entry of the flats by means of a building-site crane.

The name of the Cheryomushki District was changed to Brezhnev District after the Soviet leader's death in 1982 but restored to its original name in January 1988.

Opus 106 Khovanshchina (Musorgsky)

Form: Reorchestration of Modest Musorgsky's five-act opera *Khovanshchina* of 1886 for a film version, with scenario by A. Abramova, Dmitri Shostakovich, and Vera Stroeva, for Mosfilm. Shostakovich provided two alternative endings to the final scene.

Instrumentation: 3 flutes (III = piccolo), 3 oboes (III = cor anglais), 3 clarinets (A and B flat; III = bass clarinet), 3 bassoons (III = contrabassoon) ~ 4 horns, 3 trumpets, 3 trombones, tuba ~ separate band of French horns, trumpets, and trombones on and off stage (numbers not specified) ~ timpani, triangle, tambourine, side drum, cymbals, bass drum, gong ~ glockenspiel, orchestral bells, celesta ~ 2–4 harps, piano ~ strings.

Composed: Edited and orchestrated March 1958–26 April 1959, at Moscow. Acts 1 and 4 completed on 16 March and 1 August 1958 respectively.
Premières: Film first shown on 23 May 1959 (orchestra conducted by Yevgeni Svetlanov).

Stage version: 25 November 1960, Kirov Theatre of Opera and Ballet, Leningrad; décor by Fyodor Fyodorovsky, directed by Leonid Baratov, and conducted by Sergei Yeltsin.

UK: 27 August 1962, Edinburgh Festival, King's Theatre; Belgrade National Opera Company, Dušan Miladinović (conductor).

USA: 1 March 1981, Carnegie Hall, New York; Opera Orchestra of New York, concert version sung in Russian, conducted by Eve Queler. See Recordings.

London: 21 October 1982, Royal Opera House, Covent Garden; Vlado Habunek's production rehearsed by Jeremy Sutcliffe, décor by Božidar Rašica; Royal Opera Chorus (chorus-master—John McCarthy) and Royal Opera House Orchestra, under the conductor Yevgeni Svetlanov; principal roles—Yevgeni Nesterenko, (Ivan Khovansky), Robin Leggate (Andrei Khovansky), Robert Tear (Vasili Golitsyn), Donald McIntyre (Shaklovity), Gwynne Howell (Dosifei), Yvonne Minton (Marfa), and Paul Crook (Scribe).

UK broadcast: 8 November 1982, BBC Radio 3; a performance as above direct from the Royal Opera House.

USA: 14 November 1985, Metropolitan Opera, New York; conducted by Neeme Järvi; principal roles—Aage Haugland (Ivan Khovansky), Dénes Gulyás (Andrei Khovansky), Weislaw Ochman (Vasili Golitsyn), Norman Mittelmann (Shaklovity), Martti Talvela (Dosifei), and Stefka Mineva (Marfa).
Arrangements: German and Italian translations of the libretto.
Music: Muzgiz, Nos. 30196 and 30196*a*, 1963, full score of Russian/German edition in two volumes, ed. Pavel Lamm with Preface by Vasili Yakovlev, 30 cm.

Muzyka, No. 2058, 1976, vocal score, ed. P. Lamm with commentaries on editions of Rimsky-Korsakov, Shostakovich, and others, 30 cm.
Duration: 3 hrs 14 mins.–3 hrs 22 mins.
Films: Shostakovich's orchestration, with the final scene completed by Igor Stravinsky, used in the BBC2 TV Russian Season presentation, shown on 9 December 1989. Vienna Philharmonic Orchestra, conducted by Claudio Abbado; principal roles—Nicolai Ghiaurov (Ivan Khovansky), Vladimir Atlantov (Andrei Khovansky), Yuri Maruzin (Vasili Golitsyn), Anatoli Kocherga (Shaklovity), Paata Burchuladze (Dosifei), and Lyudmila Semtschuk (Marfa). Alfred Kirchner's production, with décor by Erich Wonder, introduced by the British opera singer Robert Lloyd. Released Feb. 1993 on Pioneer Laser Disc Video PLM CC 00631 and reviewed G Apr. 1993.

Leonid Baratov's Kirov Theatre production in Shostakovich's orchestration, with décor by Fyodor Fedorovsky, filmed in 1992. Performers as in Valeri Gergiev's 1991 recording except for Konstantin Pluzhnikov doubling as Scribe; Vyacheslav Trofimov (Shaklovity), Tatyana Kravtsova (Emma), Valeri Lebed (Pastor), Mikhail Chernozhukov (Varsonofiev), Andrei Khramtsov (Second Strelets); and the visual addition of the Kirov Ballet. Video directed by Brian Large, released in 1995 on Philips Videocassette 070 433-3PHZ and two Laser Discs 070 433-1PHG2, and reviewed G Dec. 1995.

Recordings: USSR: MK D 012965-6 (mono) and C 0771-2. 'Dawn on the Moscow River', orchestrated by Shostakovich. Bolshoi Theatre Orchestra, Yevgeni SVETLANOV. ['Opera Overtures by Russian Composers'— Glinka, Borodin, and Rimsky-Korsakov.] P 1963. *Reissued:* HMV Melodiya ASD 2646. [Rakhmaninov.] G Jan. 1971 ~ USSR: Melodiya CM 03397-400 (two-record set). ['Moscow Souvenir'—Prokofiev, Rakhmaninov, Rimsky-Korsakov *et al.*] I 1973.

USSR: Melodiya Compact Disc SUCD10 00178. 'Dawn on the Moscow River'—in two versions, orchestrated by Shostakovich and Rimsky-Korsakov. USSR Symphony Orchestra, Yevgeni SVETLANOV. [Musorgsky.] P Moscow concert 5 May 1968, I 1991*d*, G Sept. 1993. *Reissued:* BMG Melodiya Compact Discs 74321 34165-2 (two-disc set). Orchestrated by Shostakovich. ['Orchestral Pictures from Russia'—Borodin, Rimsky-Korsakov, Arensky *et al.*] P date given as 1963, G Apr. 1997.

USA pirate?: HRE 367 (8 sides mono). Stated to be the first recording of the Shostakovich orchestration on the sleeve. No sleeve notes or libretto. Sung in Italian. Nicolai Ghiaurov (Ivan Khovansky), Veriano Luchetti (Andrei Khovansky), Ludovico Spiess (Vasili Golitsyn), Siegmund Nimsgern (Shaklovity), Cesare Siept (Dosifel), Fiorento Cossotto, (Marfa), Herbert Handt (Scribe); Rome RAI Symphony Orchestra and Chorus, Bogomir LESKOVIC. P Rome concert 1973. *Reissued:* Italy: Bella Voce Compact Discs BLV 107 402 (three-disc set). I 1995.

USA: BJRS 1581-3 (three-record set, with libretto). Leonard Mróz (Ivan Khovansky), Dénes Gulyás (Andrei Khovansky), Peter Kazaras (Vasili Golitsyn), Allan Monk (Shaklovity), Paul Plishka (bass), Stefania Toczyska (Marfa); Opera Orchestra of New York, Eve QUELER. P New York concert. 1 Mar. 1981.

Sony Classical Compact Discs S3K 45831 (three-disc set). Nicolai Ghiaurov (Ivan Khovansky), Zdravko Gadjev (Andrei Khovansky), Kaludi Kaludov (Vasili Golitsyn), Stoyan Popov (Shaklovity), Nicola Ghiuselev (Dosifei), Alexandrina Miltcheva (Marfa), Marla Petrova Popova (Susanna), Angel Petkov (Scribe), Maria Dimchevska (Emma), Dimiter Stanchev (Pastor, First Strelets), Stoil Georgiev (Varsonofiev, Second Strelets), Roumen Doikov (Kouzka), Assen Selimski (Streshnev); Sofia National Opera Orchestra and Chorus, Emil TCHAKAROV. P Sofia 1986, G Oct. 1990.

Deutsche Grammophon Compact Discs 429 758-2GH3 (three-disc set, with libretto and English, French, and German translations). Essentially Shostakovich's orchestration with Stravinsky's ending. Aage

Haugland (Ivan Khovansky), Vladimir Atlantov (Andrei Khovansky), Vladimir Popov (Vasili Golitsyn), Anatoli Kotscherga (Shakhlovity), Paata Burchuladze (Dosifei), Marjana Lipovšek (Marfa), Brigitte Poschner-Klebel (Susanna), Heinz Zednik (Scribe), Joanna Borowska (Emma), Wilfried Gahmlich (Kouzka); Vienna Boys Choir, Slovák Philharmonic Chorus, Vienna State Opera Chorus and Orchestra, Claudio ABBADO. P Vienna concerts Sept. 1989, I Nov. 1990, G Nov. 1990 and Oct. 1991.

Erato/Warner Classics Compact Disc 2292 45596-2. Prelude, Persian Dance, and Prince Golitsyn's Departure orchestrated by Shostakovich. Rotterdam Philharmonic Orchestra, James CONLON. [Ravel.] P Rotterdam 7–12 Dec. 1989, I and G Aug. 1991.

Bulgaria: Gega Compact Discs GD 113–15 (three-disc set). Nicola Ghiselev (bass), Stefka Mineva (contralto), Sofia National Opera Chorus and Orchestra, Russlan RAYCHEV. P Sofia 1990, I Aug. 1992.

Philips Compact Discs 432 147-2 (three-disc set, with libretto in English, transliterated Russian, German, and French). Bulat Minjelkiev (Ivan Khovansky), Vladimir Galusin (Andrei Khovansky), Aleksei Steblianko (Vasill Golitsyn), Valeri Alekseyev (Shaklovity), Nikolai Okhotnikov (Dosifei), Olga Borodina (Marfa), Yevgeniya Tselovalnik (Susanna), Konstantin Pluzhnikov (Scribe), Yelena Prokina (Emma), Nikolai Gassiev (Kouzka), Vassili Gerelo (Streshnev), Yevgeni Fedotov (First Strelets), Grigorl Karasev (Second Strelets); Kirov Theatre Chorus and Orchestra, Valeri Borisov (chorus-master), Valeri GERGIEV. P Leningrad Jan.–Feb. 1991, I and G June 1992.

BBC Music Compact Disc BBC MM135. 'Dawn on the Moscow River', orch. Shostakovich. BBC National Orchestra of Wales, David ATHERTON. [Walton, Britten, Lyadov, and Stravinsky.] P Prom, concert 22 Aug. 1994, I July 1995 magazine.

France: Saison Russe Compact Disc 288149. Prelude orch. Shostakovich. Russian Symphony Orchestra, Mark GORENSTEIN. [Sans op. P (i) No. 1; Glinka, Tchaikovsky, Prokofiev et al.] P Mosfilm Studios, Moscow Dec. 1996.

References: Downes, Fay (in M. H. Brown), Johnson, Khubov, G. Norris, and Zaporozhets-Ishlinskaya.

Opus 107   Cello Concerto No. 1 in E flat major

Form: Concerto for cello and small orchestra in four movements:

1. Allegretto
2. Moderato *attacca*
3. Cadenza: Moderato—Allegro *attacca*
4. Allegro con moto

Instrumentation: piccolo (= flute II), flute, 2 oboes, 2 clarinets (B flat and A), bassoon, contrabassoon (= bassoon II) ~ French horn ~ timpani, celesta ~ strings.

Composed: 20 July–1 September 1959, at Komarovo village, Gulf of Finland.

Dedication: Mstislav Leopoldovich Rostropovich (cellist).

Premières: 21 September 1959, USSR Composers' Club, Moscow; reduction performed by N. Rostropovich and the composer.

4 October 1959, Leningrad Philharmonic Bolshoi Hall; M. Rostropovich, Leningrad Philharmonic Orchestra, Yevgeni Mravinsky. Moscow première given five days later. A mono recording of the Leningrad première is reported to exist.

USA: 6 November 1959, Rostropovich, Philadelphia Orchestra, Eugene Ormandy.

UK: 21 September 1960, Royal Festival Hall, London; Rostropovich, Leningrad Philharmonic Orchestra, Gennadi Rozhdestvensky.

Viola and piano reduction: 9 February 1967, Moscow Conservatory Malyi Hall; Mikhail Tolpygo (viola).

Arrangements: Reduction for cello and piano by the composer, with the cello part edited by Mstislav Rostropovich. Cello part arranged for viola by Vadim Borisovsky, with the approval of the composer.

Music: The whereabouts of the autograph full score is not stated in the *Collected Works;* that of the reduction is preserved at the Glinka Museum. The 60th page of the reduction is reproduced in Volume 17 of *Collected Works.*

Muzgiz, No. 28523, 1960, score prepared for publication by Lev Atovmyan, 29 cm.

Muzgiz, No. 28522, 1960, reduction for cello and piano, score and part, 29 cm.

Leeds Music/Anglo-Soviet Music Press, No. 138, 1960, reduction, score and part, 31 cm.

Muzgiz, No. 28523, 1961, pocket score from Muzgiz 1960 plates, 21 cm.

Hans Sikorski, No. 2113, 1962, reduction, 31.5 cm.

Edwin F. Kalmus, *c.*1963, reduction, 31 cm.

Edition Peters, No. 4743 (plate no. 12095), 1963, reduction, 30 cm.

International Music, No. 2192, *c.*1963, reduction, 31 cm.

Muzyka, 1964, reduction.

MCA, No. 04922-044, 1966, miniature score edited by Lewis Roth, 23 cm.

Muzyka, No. 8710, 1975, cello and piano, with added viola part ed. by V. Borisovsky, 28.5 cm.

Hans Sikorski, No. 2335, 1983, 21 cm.

Muzyka, No. 11936 (in Volume 16 of *Collected Works* with Op. 126), 1985, full score, 30 cm.

Muzyka, No. 11947 (in Volume 17 of *Collected Works* with Op. 126), 1986, reduction with separate cello part, 30 cm.

Duration: Approx. 28 minutes in score; 25' 55"–29' 58"; 27' 05"–29' 00" (Plaistow).
Recordings: USA: Columbia ML 5452 (mono) and MS 6124. Mstislav ROS-
TROPOVICH (cello), Mason Jones (French horn), Philadelphia Orchestra,
Eugene Ormandy. [Op. 10.] P 8 Nov. 1959. *Reissued:* France: Philips Réal-
ités C 29 (mono). [Op. 102.] ~ Philips ABL 3315 (mono) and SABL 165.
[Op. 10.] G July 1960 ~ CBS BRG 72081 (mono) and SBRG 72081. [Op.
10.] G Sept. 1960. (NB. numbered 75081 on continental pressings) ~ CBS
S 73443 in Set 77394. [Op. 97a excerpts.] G Oct. 1975 ~ CBS Masterworks
60284. [Op. 10.] G Jan. 1984 ~ CBS Masterworks Compact Disc MPK
44850. [Opp. 35 and 102.] I July 1989, G Nov. 1989 ~ Sony Masterworks
Heritage Compact Disc MHK 63327. [Op. 77.] I June 1998.

BBC Legends Compact Disc BBCL 4024-2 (mono). Mikhail Buyanovsky (French horn), Mstislav ROSTROPOVICH (cello), Leningrad Philharmonic Orchestra, Gennadi Rozhdestvensky. [Op. 67 and Haydn.] P
Usher Hall, Edinburgh 9 Sept. 1960, I Sept. 1999, G Nov. 1999.

USA: Period Showcase SHO 337 (mono) and SHO 2337 (electronic
stereo). Mstislav ROSTROPOVICH (cello), Moscow Philharmonic Orchestra,
Kirill Kondrashin. [Tchaikovsky, Handel, and Chopin.] P Moscow con-
cert early 1960s, I *c.*1963. *Reissued:* Italy: Vedette VMC 3014 (mono) and
VSC 4014 (electronic stereo). [As USA release.] I 1967 ~ USA: Everest
SDBR 3342 (electronic stereo). [Dvořák.] I 1973 ~ Italy: Quadrifoglio
VDS 357 (electronic stereo). [Chopin and Tchaikovsky.]

Italy: Intaglio Compact Disc INCD 7251. Mstislav ROSTROPOVICH
(cello), Czech Philharmonic Orchestra, Kirill Kondrashin. [Op. 126.] P
Prague Spring Festival concert 29 May 1960, I July 1992.

EMI Compact Discs CZS5 72016-2 (on fourth disc of thirteen-disc set,
mono). Mstislav ROSTROPOVICH (cello), Moscow Philharmonic Orchestra,
Gennadi Rozhdestvensky. ['Rostropovich: The Russian Years, 1950–74'—
Opp. 126 and, on eleventh disc, 40.] P Moscow concert 10 Nov. 1961, G
May 1997. *Reissued:* EMI Classics Compact Discs CZS5 72295-2 (two-disc
set, mono). [Opp. 40 and 126; Kabalevsky and Khachaturyan.] I Oct. 1998.

Switzerland: Cascavelle OSR Mémoires Compact Disc VEL 2009
(mono). Pierre FOURNIER (cello), Orchestre de la Suisse Romande, Jascha
Horenstein. [Schumann and Martinů.] P Geneva concert 1962, I Apr.
1992, G Nov. 1992.

USA: Russian Disc Compact Disc RDCD 11 106. Mstislav ROSTROPO-
VICH (cello), Moscow Philharmonic Orchestra, David Oistrakh. [Op.
125.] P Moscow concert 24 Jan. 1965, G July 1994. *Reissued:* Revelation
Compact Disc RV 10087. [Opp. 126 and 109.] I Nov. 1997.

BBC Radio Classics Compact Disc 15656 9170-2. Natalya SHAKHOV-
SKAYA (cello), Moscow Radio Symphony Orchestra, Gennadi Rozhdestvensky. [Opp. 77 and 102.] P Royal Albert Hall Prom concert 18 Aug.
1966, I May 1996.

USA: Russian Disc Compact Disc RDCD 11 109. Mstislav ROS-
TROPOVICH (cello), USSR Symphony Orchestra, Yevgeni Svetlanov. [Op.
126.] P Moscow concert 29 Sept. 1966, I Oct. 1993.

USSR: Melodiya D 023831-2 (mono) and CM 01883-4. Mikhail
KHOMITSER (cello), Moscow Radio Symphony Orchestra, Gennadi
Rozhdestvensky. [Op. 14.] P 1968. *Reissued:* HMV Melodiya ASD 2585.
[Op. 77.] G July 1970 ~ USA: Angel Melodiya SR 40099. [Op. 14.] I
1969 ~ Netherlands: Phonogram Melodia 691 419. Soloist named as
Michaël Phomitzer and Pholitzer (*sic*). [Op. 77.] ~ Italy: EMI 065 93443.
[Op. 14.] I 1973 ~ RCA Navigator (Russian Music No. 73) Compact Disc
74321 29254-2. [Opp. 35 and 102.] I Nov. 1995, G Dec. 1995 ~ BMG
Melodiya Compact Discs 74321 63460-2 (two-disc set). [Opp. 112; 113,
and 34.] I Mar. 1999.

Czech: Supraphon 0 10 0604 (mono) and 1 10 0604. Miloš SÁDLO
(cello), Czech Philharmonic Orchestra, Karel Ančerl. [Honegger.] P
Prague 6–8 June 1968, G July 1970 and Mar. 1981. *Reissued:* Czech:
Supraphon Crystal Collection Compact Disc SUP11 0676-2MM. [Op. 47.]
I Feb. 1993, G Aug. 1993 ~ Supraphon Compact Disc SU1950-2.
[Prokofiev.] I Nov. 1995 ~ Japan: Supraphon Compact Disc COCQ 83010.
[Honegger.] I 1998.

Doremi Compact Discs DHR 7711-3 (three-disc set). Vladimir ORLOFF
(cello), Orchestra Philharmonique de l'ORTF (Paris), Jean Perisson.
['The Art of Vladimir Orloff'—Schumann, Vieru, Elgar *et al.*] P concert
broadcast 5 May 1970, I 1998.

Italy: Ermitage Compact Disc ERM 147. Janos STARKER (cello), Swiz-
zera Italiana Radiotelevisione Orchestra, Marc Andreae. [Bach, Haydn,
and Couperin.] P Lugano, Switzerland 17 Feb. 1972, I 1994.

USSR: Melodiya CM 03467-8. First movement only. V. TAMULIS (cello),
Lithuanian State Philharmonic Orchestra, M. Dvarionaite. [Concert
recital of prize-winner soloists.] P 1972, I 1973.

HMV ASD 2924. Paul TORTELIER (cello), Timothy Brown (French horn),
Bournemouth Symphony Orchestra, Paavo Berglund. [Walton.] P 7–8
Jan. 1973, G Dec. 1973. *Reissued:* HMV ASD 4046. [Op. 77.] G June
1981 ~ EMI Studio Compact Disc CDM7 63020-2. [Walton.] I Apr. 1989,
G July 1989.

Germany: Live Classics Compact Disc LCL 202. Natalia GUTMAN
(cello), USSR Radio and TV Symphony Orchestra, Kirill Kondrashin.
[Op. 126; and Schnittke.] P Moscow concert 21 June 1976, I Jan. 2001.

USSR: Melodiya C10 07263-4. Cello Part arr. for viola by V. Borisovsky. Mikhail TOLPYGO (viola), USSR Symphony Orchestra, Dmitri
Kitayenko. [Bartók.] P 1976, I 1977*a*.

USSR: Melodiya C10 14091-2. Valentin FEIGIN (cello), Central Television
and All-Union Radio Symphony Orchestra, Maksim Shostakovich. [In third
box of Part 1 of *Collected Works on Records* with Op. 129.] P 1978, I 1980.

Czech: Opus 91110 1274-75. Robert COHEN (cello), Slovak Philharmonic Orchestra, Bystrík Režucha. [Handel.] P 1981. *Reissued:* Switzerland: Point Classics Compact Disc 267 252-2. [Opp. 35 and 110*a*.] I 1996.

Chandos ABRD 1085 (digital). Raphael WALLFISCH (cello), English Chamber Orchestra, Geoffrey Simon. [Barber.] P 29–30 Oct. 1982, G Dec. 1983. *Reissued:* Chandos Compact Disc CHAN 8322. [Barber.] G Feb. 1985.

CBS Masterworks 37840 (digital). Yo-Yo MA (cello), Nolan Miller (French horn), Philadelphia Orchestra, Eugene Ormandy. [Kabalevsky.] P 3 May 1982 (Ormandy's last recording), G Mar. 1984. *Reissued:* USA and UK: CBS Masterworks Compact Disc MK 37840. [Kabalevsky.] G May 1985 ~ CBS Maestro/Sony Classical Compact Disc MDK 44903. [Op. 47.] G Apr. 1990 ~ Sony Digital Club Compact Disc SMK 66937. [Op. 47.] I Sept. 1995.

Philips 412 526-1PH (digital). Heinrich SCHIFF (cello), Johannes Ritzkowsky (French horn), Bavarian Radio Symphony Orchestra, Maksim Shostakovich. [Op. 126.] P Munich 2–3 Apr. 1984, G Aug. 1984, Aug. 1985, and June 1986. *Simultaneous issue:* Philips Compact Disc 412 526-2PH. [Op. 126.] G Oct. 1985.

Belgium: Classic Talent Compact Disc DOM 2910 11. Viviane SPANOGHE (cello), Sofia Soloists, Emil Tabakov. [Op. 126.] P Sofia Apr. 1984, I Nov. 1991.

Decca 414 162-1DH (digital) and Compact Disc 414 162-2DH. Lynn HARRELL (cello), Julia van Leer-Studebaker (French horn), Concertgebouw Orchestra, Bernard Haitink. [Bloch.] P Amsterdam 2–3 Apr. 1984, G Feb. 1987.

France: Harmonia Mundi Label Bleu LBL 6505 (digital). Pierre STRAUCH (cello), Les Sinfonietta Régional de Picardie, Alexandre Myrat. [Op. 110*a*.] P not stated, 1986. *Reissued:* France: Harmonia Mundi Compact Disc LBLC 6505. [Op. 110*a*.] I 1988.

Erato Compact Disc ECD 75485. Mstislav ROSTROPOVICH (cello), Hugh Seenan (French horn), London Symphony Orchestra, Seiji Ozawa. [Prokofiev.] P London Nov. 1987, I Oct. 1988, G Jan. 1989. *Reissued:* Erato Compact Disc 2292 45332-2. [Prokofiev.] I 1991, G July 1994.

RCA Victor Red Seal Compact Disc RD 87918-2RC. Natalia GUTMAN (cello), Jeffrey Bryant (French horn), Royal Philharmonic Orchestra, Yuri Temirkanov. [Op. 126.] P Watford 25, 28–9 Nov. 1988, I Nov. 1990, G Jan. 1991.

John Marks Records Compact Disc JMR 3. Nathaniel ROSEN (cello), Sofia State Philharmonic Orchestra, Emil Tabakov. [Tchaikovsky.] P Sofia 15–17 May 1990, I Mar. 1994.

Belgium: Pavane Compact Disc ADW 7286. First movement only. Marie HALLYNCK (cello), National Orchestra of Belgium, Roland Zollman. [Brahms, Arnold, Rakhmaninov *et al.*] P Brussels 8–9 June 1992.

France: Le Chant du Monde Compact Disc LDC 278 1099. Ivan MONIGHETTI (cello), Prague Radio Symphony Orchestra, Vladimir Valek. [Op. 126.] P Czech radio Nov. 1992, I Sept. 1993.

Carlton Classics Compact Disc 30366 01012. Alexander BAILLIE (cello), Boston Philharmonic Orchestra, Benjamin Zander. [Op. 47.] P Cambridge, Mass. concert 2 May 1993, I Oct. 1998, G Jan. 1999. *Reissued:* Carlton Classics Compact Discs 30366 01229 (five-disc box set). ['20th Anniversary Edition'—Op. 47; Beethoven, Mahler, Stravinsky, and Ravel.] I June 1999.

Sweden: BIS Compact Disc CD 626. Torleif THEDÉEN (cello), Malmö Symphony Orchestra, James De Preist. [Op. 126.] P Malmö 15–16 June 1993, I May 1994, G July 1994 and Feb. 1995. Winner of Cannes Classical Music Awards 1994—Solo with Orchestra, 19th and 20th century category.

Deutsche Grammophon Comapct Disc 445 821-2GH. Misha MAISKY (cello), London Symphony Orchestra, Tilson Thomas. [Op. 126.] P London 2–4 Aug. 1993, I Mar. 1995, G Apr. 1995.

Imp Classics Compact Disc PCD 1084. Carlo PRIETO (cello), Orquestra Sinfonica de Xalapa, Herrera de la Fuente. [Op. 40; and Saint-Saëns.] P Vera Cruz 1994, I Aug. 1994.

Naxos Compact Disc 8.550813. Maria KLIEGEL (cello), Polish National Radio Symphony Orchestra, Antoni Wit. [Op. 126.] P Katowice 27 Feb.–1 Mar. 1995, I Sept. 1996, G Oct. 1996.

Virgin Classics Compact Disc VC5 45145-2. Truls MØRK (cello), Richard Bissell (French horn), London Philharmonic Orchestra, Mariss Jansons. [Op. 126.] P 10–11 Mar. 1995, I Nov. 1995, G Feb. 1996.

USA: Audiofon Compact Disc 72060. William De ROSA (cello), Yekaterinburg Philharmonic Orchestra, Sarah Caldwell. [Op. 35.] P Yekaterinburg Jan.–Feb. 1996.

Chandos Compact Disc CHAN 9550. Frans HELMERSON (cello), Russian State Symphony Orchestra, Valeri Polyansky. [Op. 141.] P Mosfilm Studio Mar. 1996, I Apr. 1997, G Awards (Oct.) 1998.

Germany: Arte Nova Classics Compact Disc 74321 49688-2. Kirill RODIN (cello), Russian Philharmonic Orchestra, Konstantin Krimets. [Op. 126.] P Moscow 9–10 July 1996, I Oct. 1997.

Czech: Supraphon Compact Disc SU 3278-2 031. Jiří BÁRTA (cello), Prague Symphony Orchestra, Maksim Shostakovich. [Op. 22*a*.] P Prague concert 14 Nov. 1996, I May 1997, G Dec. 1997. *Reissued:* Czech: Supraphon Compact Disc SU 3414-2. [Op. 126.] I Aug. 1999.

Germany: Antes Compact Disc BM-CD 31.9097. Claudio BOHORQUEZ (cello), Kaliningrad State Symphony Orchestra, Arkadi Feldmann. [Weber and Kalinnikov.] P Karlsruhe concert 21 Nov. 1996, G Apr. 1998.

Finland: Finlandia Compact Disc 3984 21441-2. Arto NORAS (cello), Norwegian Radio Orchestra, Ari Rasilainen. [O*p*. 126; and R. Strauss.] P

Oslo Apr. 1997, I July 1998. *Reissued:* Finlandia Ultima Compact Discs 8573 81969-2 (disc one of two-disc set). [Opp. 126 and 8.] G June 2000.

New Zealand: Ode Manu Compact Disc 1542. Aleksandr IVASHKIN (cello), Moscow Symphony Orchestra, Valeri Polyansky. [Op. 126.] P Moscow Conservatory, 7–9 Oct. 1997, G July 1998.

Channel Classics Compact Disc CCS 15398. Pieter WISPELWEY (cello), Darryl Poulsen (French horn), Australian Chamber Orchestra, Richard Tognetti. [Kodály.] P Sydney Aug. 1999, I Mar. 2000, G Apr. 2000.

Opus 108   Quartet No. 7 in F sharp minor

Form: String quartet in three linked movements:

1. Allegretto *attacca*
2. Lento *attacca*
3. Allegro—Allegretto

The titles Scherzo, Pastorale, and Fugue, originally assigned to the movements, were removed before publication.

Composed: Completed in March 1960, at Moscow.

Dedication: To the memory of Nina Vasilievna Shostakovich (first wife).

Premières: 15 May 1960, Leningrad Glinka Concert Hall and 17 September 1960, Moscow Conservatory Malyi Hall; Beethoven Quartet (Dmitri Tsyganov, Vasili Shirinsky, Vadim Borisovsky, and Sergei Shirinsky).

Netherlands: 15 November 1993 (concert broadcast five days later); transcription by the Aurelia Saxophone Quartet.

Arrangements: Transcriptions for brass ensemble by Paul Archibald and saxophone quartet. Chamber Symphony—transcribed for chamber orchestra by Jordan Dafov. Reduction for piano four hands by Anatoli Dmitriev.

Music: Manuscript lost.

Sovetskii Kompozitor, No. 2019, 1960, parts, 31 cm.

Sovetskii Kompozitor, No. 2020, 1960, score, 22 cm.

Musica Rara, No. 1066, 1960, score, 18.5 cm.

Musica Rara, No. 1066*a*, 1960, parts, 31 cm.

Hans Sikorski, No. 2263, 1960, parts, 31.5 cm.

Leeds Music, *c.*1961, parts, 31 cm.

Muzyka, Leningrad, No. 530 (in Volume 2 with Quartets 5, 6, and 8 arr. for piano four hands by A. Dmitriev), 1966, 29.5 cm.

Edition Eulenberg, No. 391, 1970, score, 19 cm.

Edition Peters, No. 5757, 1973, parts, 31 cm.

Muzyka, No. 9816 (in Volume 35 of *Collected Works* Quartets 1–8), 1979, 30 cm.

Hans Sikorski, No. 2266 (with Opp. 92, 101, and 110), 1980, score, 21 cm.

Duration: 11 and 12 minutes in scores; 11' 41"–16' 32".

Recordings: USSR: MK D 08019-20 (mono). BEETHOVEN QUARTET (personnel as at première). [Opp. 49 and 110.] P 17 Sept. 1960. *Reissued:* Everest Baroque SDBR 2864 (electronic stereo). [Op. 110.] G Jan. 1968 ~ USA: Consonance Blue Label Compact Disc 81.3006 (mono). [Vol. 2—Opp. 110 and 144.] I May 1995.

USSR: MK D 011361-2 (mono). BORODIN QUARTET (Rostislav Dubinsky, Yaroslav Aleksandrov, Dmitri Shebalin, Valentin Berlinsky). [Prokofiev and Hindemith.] P 1963. *Reissued:* USSR: Melodiya D 019219-20 (mono) and C 01433-4. [Op. 92.] I 1967 ~ USSR: Melodiya CM 02337-8. [Prokofiev and Hindemith.] I 1970 ~ USA: Seraphim Melodiya S 6035. [In three-record box set with Op. 11 and Quartets 6, 8–11.] ~ HMV Melodiya HQS 1322 in Set SLS 879. [Opp. 101 and 122.] G June 1974.

Czech: Supraphon SUA 10629 (mono) and SUA ST 50629. SLOVÁK QUARTET (Aladár Móži, Alojz Nemec, Milan Telecký, František Tannenberger). [Bartók, Stravinsky, and Webern.] P 1966, G Aug. 1967.

L'Oiseau-Lyre DSLO 9. FITZWILLIAM QUARTET (Christopher Rowland, Jonathan Sparey, Alan George, Ioan Davies). [Opp. 138 and 142.] P Mar. 1975, G Dec. 1975. *Reissued:* Decca 188 D4 in Set D 188 D7. [Opp. 101 and 138.] G Feb. 1981 ~ Decca Enterprise Compact Discs 433 078-2DM6. [On third disc of six-disc set with Opp. 92 and 101.] I Apr. 1992, G June 1992.

USSR: Melodiya C10 10241-2. TANEYEV QUARTET (Vladimir Ovcharek, Grigori Lutsky, Vissarion Soloviev, Iosif Levinzon). [Opp. 49 and 110.] P 1978, I 1978*d*. *Reissued:* USSR: with the same number in first box of Part 2 of *Collected Works on Records.* I 1980 ~ Japan JVC Victor 5348. [Opp. 110, 122, and 138.] ~ Russia: Melodiya Compact Disc SUCD11 00309. [Opp. 101 and 110.] I 1993*a* ~ France: Praga Compact Disc PR 250 077. [Opp. 92 and 101.] P given as Czech Radio 9 Sept. 1976, I Mar. 1996.

USSR: Melodiya C10 17213-4. SHOSTAKOVICH QUARTET (Andrei Shishlov, Sergei Pishchugin, Aleksandr Galkovsky, Aleksandr Korchagin). [Op. 57.] P 1980, I 1982*d*. *Reissued:* Olympia Compact Disc OCD 526. [Op. 101.] I 1993 ~ Olympia Compact Disc OCD 532. ['Complete Quartets, Vol. 2'—Opp. 68 and 92.] I May 1994, G Sept. 1994.

USSR: Melodiya C10 17869005. BORODIN QUARTET (Mikhail Kopelman, Andrei Abramenkov, Dmitri Shebalin, Valentin Berlinsky). [Op. 142.] P 1981, I 1983*a*. *Reissued:* HMV Melodiya EL 270338-1 (digital). [Opp. 57 and 110.] G Nov. 1985 ~ HMV Melodiya EX 270339-3 (DMM). [In seven-record box set of 15 Quartets plus Quintet.] G Mar. 1986 ~ EMI Melodiya Compact Disc CDC7 47507-2. [Opp. 57 and 110.] I Nov. 1986, G Oct. 1987 ~ Japan: Victor Musical Industries Compact Disc VICC 40020. [Opp. 92 and 101.] I 1990 ~ EMI Compact Discs CMS5 65032-2. [In six-disc set of 15 Quartets plus Quintet.] I Mar. 1994 ~ BMG Melodiya Compact Discs 74321 40711-2 (six-disc set). [Opp. 92 and 101.] I June 1997.

Jecklin-Disco JD 620-1 (digital) and Compact Disc JD 620-2. AMATI QUARTET (Willi Zimmerman, Barbara Suter, Nicolas Corti, Johannes Degen). [Op. 73.] P 1987.

USSR: Melodiya C10 27377 003. LENINGRAD CONSERVATORY STUDENTS' QUARTET (Alla Aranovskaya, Alla Goryainova, Andrei Dogadin, Leonid Shukayev). Prizewinners at the First International Competition for String Quartets named after D. D. Shostakovich—Haydn and Tchaikovsky.] P Leningrad concert 25 Sept. 1987, I 1989*c*.

Bulgaria: Balkanton BKA 12305-6. Chamber Symphony arr. Dafov. Tolbuhin Chamber Orchestra, Jordan DAFOV. [In double album with Opp. 87 No. 24, 101, and 110.] P Tolbuhin, Bulgaria Mar. 1988.

Academy Sound and Vision DCA 629 (DMM) and Compact Disc CD DCA 629. Arr. P. Archibald. ENGLISH BRASS ENSEMBLE (Paul Archibald, Richard Martin—trumpets; James Hardy—horn; David Whitson—trombone; James Gourlay—tuba). ['Russian Brass!'—Prokofiev.] P London June 1988.

Teldec Classics Compact Disc 244 919-2. BRODSKY QUARTET (Michael Thomas, Ian Belton, Paul Cassidy, Jacqueline Thomas). [Opp. 110 and 117.] P Berlin Feb. 1989, I Oct. 1989, G May 1990. *Reissued:* Teldec Compact Discs 9031 71702-2. [On third disc of six-disc set with Opp. 92 and 101.] I Nov. 1990, G June 1992.

France: Adès Compact Disc 14 161-2. FINE ARTS QUARTET (Ralph Evans, Efim Boico, Jerry Horner, Wolfgang Laufer). [Opp. 73 and 122.] P Paris July 1989, I July 1990, G Oct. 1990.

USA: ESS.A.Y. Compact Disc CD 1009. MANHATTAN QUARTET (Eric Lewis, Roy Lewis, John Dexter, Judith Glyde). [Opp. 101 and 110.] P Jersey City 17 May 1990. *Reissued:* Koch Schwann Compact Disc 310 165. ['Complete String Quartets, Vol. 3.' with Opp. 101 and 110.] I Jan. 1993, G June 1993.

Virgin Classics Compact Disc VC7 91437-2. BORODIN QUARTET (personnel as on 1981 recording). [Opp. 73 and 110.] P London July–Sept. 1990, I Sept. 1991, G. Dec. 1991. *Reissued:* Virgin Classics Compact Discs VBD5 61639-2 (two-disc set). [Opp. 68, 73, 110, and 133.] I Aug. 1999.

Naxos Compact Disc 8.550972. ÉDER QUARTET (János Selmeczi, Péter Szüts, Sándor Papp, György Éder). ['Complete Quartets, Vol. 1'—Opp. 83 and 101.] P Budapest 1–4 Dec. 1993, I July 1993.

Germany: Thorofon Compact Disc CTH 2238. PHILHARMONIA QUARTET OF BERLIN (Daniel Stabrawa, Christian Stadelmann, Neithard Resa, Jan Disselhorst). [Opp. 73 and 133.] P Berlin 1994, I 1998.

Carlton Classics Compact Disc 30366 0062-2. KREUTZER QUARTET (Peter Sheppard, Gordon MacKay, Bridget Carey, Neil Hyde). [Opp. 83 and 110.] P Loughton Jan. 1996, I July 1997, G Awards (Nov.) 1997.

Japan: Toshiba EMI Compact Disc TOCE 9079. MORGAŬA QUARTET (Eiji Arai, Takashi Aoki, Hisashi Ono, Ryoichi Fujimorl). [Opp. 68 and 34.] P 25–7 Mar. 1996, I June 1996.

Linn Compact Disc UKD 065. SCHIDLOF QUARTET (Ofer Falk, Rafael Todes, Graham Oppenheimer, Oleg Kogan). [Opp. 83 and 57.] P Horsham 3–5 Oct. 1996, I May 1997, G Oct. 1997.

Chandos Compact Disc CHAN 9741. SORREL QUARTET (Gina McCormack, Catherine Yates, Vicci Wardman, Helen Thatcher). ['Complete Quartets, Vol. 1'—Opp. 101 and 118.] P Westleton, Suffolk 23–5 Feb. 1998, I June 1999, G Oct. 1999.

Sweden: BIS Compact Disc CD 913. YGGDRASIL QUARTET (Henrik Peterson, Per Öman, Robert Westlund, Per Nyström). [Opp. 73 and 110.] P Länna, Sweden May 1998, I Nov. 1998, G Jan. 1999.

Deutsche Grammophon Compact Disc 463 284-2GH5 (five-disc set). EMERSON QUARTET (Eugene Drucker, Philip Setzer, Lawrence Dutton, David Finkel). ['Complete Quartets, Vol. 3'—Opp. 110, 117, and 118.] P Aspen, Colorado concert July 1998, G June 2000.

France: Arion Compact Disc ARN 68506. DEBUSSY QUARTET (Christophe Colletts, Dominique Lonca, Vincent Deprecq, Yannick Cailier). ['Complete Quartets, Vol. 2'—Opp. 73 and 118.] P Lyon Nov. 1999, I Dec. 2000.

Hyperion Compact Disc CDA 67155. ST PETERSBURG QUARTET (Alla Aranovskaya, Ilya Teplyakov, Aleksei Koptev, Leonid Shukayev). [Opp. 92 and 117.] P St Petersburg Studio Dec. 2000, I Apr. 2001, G July 2001.

Opus 109   Satires

Subtitle: *Pictures of the Past* (suggested by the dedicatee).
Form: Song cycle of five romances, for soprano and piano, on verses by Sasha Chorny (pseudonym of Aleksandr Glikberg).

1. To a critic—Moderato
2. Spring awakening (or 'Taste of Spring')—Moderato
3. Descendants (or 'Progeny')—Moderato
4. Misunderstanding—Moderato
5. Kreutzer Sonata—Adagio—Allegretto

In the final song there are predictable references to Beethoven's Sonata in A major, Opus 47, and the Allegretto theme is based on the lullaby in *The Silly Little Mouse*, Opus 56.
Composed: Completed on 19 June 1960 (*Collected Works* Vol. 33—Khentova gives the previous day).
Dedication: Galina Pavlovna Vishnevskaya (soprano).
Première: 22 February 1961, Moscow Conservatory Malyi Hall; Galina Vishnevskaya (soprano) and Mstislav Rostropovich (piano). The whole cycle encored.
Arrangements: Orchestral version prepared by Boris Tishchenko in 1980 at the request of Irina Bogacheva. English and German translations of the poems by Myron Morris and Jörg Morgener respectively.

Instrumentation of Tishchenko's orchestration: 2 flutes, 2 oboes, 2 clarinets, 2 bassoons ~ 2 horns, 2 trumpets, 1 trombone ~ timpani, gong, cymbals ~ xylophone, orchestral bells, harp, piano ~ strings.

Music: Autograph score preserved at the CIS Archives of Literature and Art.

Muzyka, No. 4116 (in *Dmitri Shostakovich: Vocal Compositions*), 1967 and 1974, 30 cm.

Hans Sikorski, No. 2317, 1982, with Russian and German texts—the latter by J. Morgener, 31.5 cm.

Muzyka, No. 11785 (in Volume 33 of *Collected Works* with Opp. 121, 123, 127, 128, 143, 145, and 146), 1984, 30 cm.

Hans Sikorski, 1986, B. Tishchenko's orchestration with German text by J. Morgener, rental only.

Duration: Approx. 14 minutes in score; 14' 13"–14' 54"; 12 minutes (Sadovnikov); orchestral version 16' 16".

Recordings: Revelation Compact Disc RV 10087. Galina VISHNEVSKAYA (soprano) and Mstislav Rostropovich (piano). [Opp. 107 and 126.] P Moscow Conservatory concert 23 Oct. 1967, I Nov. 1997. *Reissued:* BMG Melodiya Compact Disc 74321 53237-2. [Sans op. V, Op. 127; and Prokofiev.] I 1998.

HMV ASD 3222 in Set SLS 5055. Galina VISHNEVSKAYA and Mstislav Rostropovich. [Op. 127.] P 1976, G Sept. 1976. *Reissued:* France: Pathé Marconi 2C 167 02726-8. [Op. 127.] ~ EMI Compact Discs CMS5 65716-2 (three-disc set). [Sans op. V and Op. 127; Rimsky-Korsakov, Tchaikovsky, and Prokofiev.] I Nov. 1995, G Sept. 1996.

France: Praga Compact Disc PR 250 009. Brigita ŠULCOVÁ (soprano) and Zorka Zichova (piano). [Opp. 127 and 145*a*.] P Prague 1976, I 1992.

USSR: Melodiya C10 15501-2. Makvala KARASHVILI (soprano) and Liya Mogilevskaya (piano). [Opp. 21 and 146.] P 1979, I 1981*d*. *Reissued:* Czech: Supraphon 1112 3148. [Opp. 21 and 146.] I 1986.

USSR: Melodiya C10 22267 009. Orchestrated by B. Tishchenko. Irina BOGACHEVA (mezzo-soprano), USSR Ministry of Culture Symphony Orchestra, Gennadi Rozhdestvensky. [Album 4 of 'From Manuscripts of Different Years' with Sans op. W.] P 1984, I 1986*a*. *Reissued:* Olympia Compact Disc OCD 143. Nos. 2, 3, and 4. [Op. 65.] I Aug. 1987 ~ Olympia Compact Disc OCD 008. Nos. 1 and 5. ['The Shostakovich CD'—22-track sampler disc.] I Oct. 1989 ~ Olympia Compact Disc OCD 5005. Nos. 2, 3, and 4. [In Vol. 1 of symphonies with Op. 65.] I Dec. 1990.

France: Le Chant du Monde Compact Discs LDC 278 972/73 (two-disc set). Elena VASSILIEVA (soprano) and Jacques Schab (piano). ['Anthologie de la Melodie Russe et Sovietique'—Musorgsky, Glinka, Gurilev *et al.*] P Paris Oct.–Nov. 1989, I 1990.

CIS: Vista Vera Compact Disc VVCD 98020. Nos. 1, 2, and 5. Viktoria YEVTODIEVA (soprano) and Elena Spist (piano). ['Winners of 2nd Rakhmaninov International Competition—Vocals'—Rakhmaninov, Gavrilin, Glinka ET AL.] I June 1999.

Reference: Sokolsky.

Opus 110   Quartet No. 8 in C minor

Subtitles: Sometimes known as the 'Dresden Quartet' or 'Autobiographical Quartet'.

Form: String quartet in five linked movements:

1. Largo *attacca*
2. Allegro molto *attacca*
3. Allegretto *attacca*
4. Largo *attacca*
5. Largo

The entire work is based on Shostakovich's DSCH motto and uses self-quotations from Symphonies Nos. 1, 5, and 8; Cello Concerto No. 1, Second Piano Trio, and the aria 'Seryozha, My Love' from Act 4 of *Lady Macbeth of Mtsensk*. The aria Is heard in the third movement following quotes from *The Young Guard*, Op. 75*a* No. 6 and the Russian revolutionary song 'Tortured by Grievous Bondage'.

Composed: 12–14 July 1960, at Gohrisch, near Dresden.

Dedication: In memory of the victims of fascism and war.

Premières: 2 October 1960, Leningrad Glinka Hall; Beethoven Quartet (Dmitri Tsyganov, Vasili Shirinsky, Vadim Borisovsky, and Sergei Shirinsky).

Sinfonietta: late 1961, Azerbaidzhan Symphony Orchestra, Abram Stasevich.

Smirnov transcription: Netherlands: 21 March 2001, Utrecht, Blazers Ensemble.

Arrangements: Opus 110*a*—Chamber Symphony: for string orchestra by Rudolf Barshai (1960).

'Sinfonietta in C minor': for string orchestra and timpani by Abram Stasevich (1961) and Sinfonietta for strings, including double-basses, by Lazar Gozman. Also transcriptions for string orchestra and timpani by Saulyus Sondetskis and Mats Liljefors. Other Chamber Symphony transcriptions by Yuri Tsiryuk and Jordan Dafov.

'DSCH': arranged for the Luzern Festival Strings by Rudolf Baumgartner.

'Sinfonia' for string orchestra by Lucas Drew.

Reduction for piano four hands by Anatoli Dmitriev.

Transcribed for wind ensemble (two each of oboes, clarinets, bassoons, and French horns with a double bass) by Dmitri Smirnov in 1999.

Music: Autograph score preserved at the CIS Archives of Literaure and Art. The opening of the autograph score is reproduced in Volume 35 of *Collected Works*.

Sovetskii Kompozitor, No. 2322, 1961, score, 21 cm.

Sovetskii Kompozitor, No. 2323, 1961, parts, 29 cm.

Boosey & Hawkes, No. 729, 1961, score, 19 cm.

Boosey & Hawkes, No. A.S.M.P. 139, 1961, parts, 31 cm.

Edition Eulenberg, No. 392, no date, score, 19 cm.

Muzyka, Leningrad, No. 530 (in Volume 2 with Quartets 5–7 arr. for piano four hands by A. Dmitriev), 1966, 29.5 cm.

Edition Peters, No. 4756*a*, 1968, opus 110*a* arr. R. Barshai, 30 cm.

Edition Peters, No. 4792*a*, *c*.1968, score, 19 cm.

Hans Sikorski, 1969, Sinfonietta arr. A. Stasevich, 36 cm.

Muzyka, No. 9816 (in Volume 35 of *Collected Works* Quartets 1–8), 1979, 30 cm.

Hans Sikorski, No. 2266 (with Opp. 92, 101, and 108), 1980, score, 21 cm.

Hans Sikorski, No. 2140, 1981, parts, 31.5 cm.

Hans Sikorski, 1981, arr. for string orchestra by R. Baumgartner and titled 'DSCH', rental only.

Kalmus, Miami, 1984, Sinfonia arr L. Drew, score and 5 parts, 33 cm.

DSCH Publishers, Moscow, 1995, full score and parts of R. Barshai's Chamber Symphony available for hire.

Duration: 18 and 19 minutes in scores; 18' 18"–29' 50"; 19' 40" (Plaistow).

Ballets: *Fourfold.* Yair Vardi, Ballet Rambert Choreographic Workshop, Nadine Baylis (designer); Riverside Studios Hammersmith, London, April 1978.

The Overcoat. For details see under Opus 32.

Dark Horizons. Oliver Hindle, Birmingham Royal Ballet, Peter Farley (designer); Sadler's Wells Theatre, London, 24 March 1992. The theme of the ballet is the tragedy of the North American Indians forced to live on reservations by their white conquerors.

Film: *The Face Behind the Face.* Filmed on 2 and 3 July 1979 under the working title *The Private Voice*, screened on BBC2 TV on 16 March 1980, with research by Olivia Maxwell and directed by Barrie Gavin. The film includes the Eighth Quartet, and also movements from Nos. 1, 3, 4, 7, 11, 12, and 13, performed by the Fitzwilliam Quartet.

Recordings: USSR: MK D 08019-20 (mono). BEETHOVEN QUARTET (personnel as at première). [Opp. 49 and 108.] P 9 Oct. 1960. *Reissued:* Everest Baroque SDBR 2864 (electronic stereo). [Op. 108.] ~ USA: Consonance Blue Label Compact Disc 81.3006 (mono). [Vol. 2—Opp. 108 and 144.] I May 1995.

Poland: Muza XL 0125 (mono). BORODIN QUARTET (Rostislav Dubinsky, Yaroslav Aleksandrov, Dmitri Shebalin, Valentin Berlinsky). [Op. 70.] P 2 Feb. 1961. *Reissued:* East Germany: Eterna A33 8 20 305 (mono). [Op. 70.] ~ France: Vogue Archives Soviétiques Compact Disc 651023 (stereo). [Op. 57.] I 1991.

Decca LXT 6036 (mono) and SXL 6036. BORODIN QUARTET (personnel as on above recording). [Borodin.] P Decca Studios, London 13 Sept. 1962, G Feb. 1963. *Reissued:* USA: Mercury MG 50309 (mono) and SR 90309. [Op. 83.] ~ USA: London STS 15046. [Borodin.] ~ Decca Ace of Diamonds ADD 156 (mono) and SDD 156. [Borodin.] G May 1967 ~ Decca Eclipse ECS 795. [Borodin.] G Mar 1977 ~ Decca Compact

Disc 425 541-2DM. [Tchaikovsky and Borodin.] I Mar. 1990, G May 1990 ~ Japan: King Records KIJC 9162. [Borodin.] I Mar. 1995.

USSR: Melodiya D 014903-4 (mono). Arr. for string orchestra and timpani by Sondetskis. String Orchestra of Vilnius Artistic School, Saulyus SONDETSKIS. [Rääts and Balsis.] P 1964.

USA: International IRC 3312. VAGHY QUARTET (Deszo Vaghy, Ronald Erickson, Tibor Vaghy, Leszek Zawistowski). [Mozart.] P 1966.

USSR: MK D 019211-2 (mono) and C 01443-4. BORODIN QUARTET (personnel as on earlier recordings). [Op. 118.] P and I 1967. *Reissued:* USA: Seraphim Melodiya S 6035. [In three-record box set with Op. 11 and Quartets 6, 7, 9–11.] ~ HMV Melodiya HQS 1323 in Set SLS 879. [Op. 117.] G June 1974.

USA: Turnabout TV-S 34545. Chamber Symphony arr. Barshai. Württemberg Chamber Orchestra, Jörg FAERBER. [A. Tcherepnin and Mouraviev.] P 1973.

Czech: Panton 11 0396 G. Sinfonietta arr. Stasevich. East Bohemian State Chamber Orchestra, Libor PEŠEK. [Mozart.] P 1974. *Reissued:* Czech: Panton Compact Disc PAN 811309. [Op. 35; and Schnittke.] I 1998.

L'Oiseau-Lyre DSLO 11. FITZWILLIAM QUARTET (Christopher Rowland, Jonathan Sparey, Alan George, Ioan Davies). [Op. 144.] P May 1975, G Apr. 1976. *Reissued:* USA: Time-Life 'Great Men of Music' box set STL 568. [Opp. 22*a*, 114, 40, 47, 102, and 135.] I 1979 ~ Decca 188 D7 in Set D 188 D7. [Op. 144.] G Feb. 1981 ~ Decca Compact Disc 421 475-2DH. [Opp. 73 and 138.] I Dec. 1988, G Apr. 1989 ~ Decca Enterprise Compact Discs 433 078-2DM6. [On fourth disc of six-disc set with Opp. 117 and 118.] I Apr. 1992, G June 1992.

Sweden: Caprice CAP 1052. FRESK QUARTET (Lars Fresk, Hans-Erik Westberg, Lars-Gunnar Bodin, Per-Göran Skytt). [Carlstedt.] P 13–15 May 1975, G Sept. 1977.

Sweden: BIS LP 66. VOCES INTIMÆ QUARTET (Jorma Rakhonen, Ari Angervo, Mauri Pietikäinen, Veikko Höylä). [Rautavaara.] P Nacka, Sweden 27–8 June 1976, I June 1978. *Reissued:* Sweden: BIS Compact Disc CD 26. [Opp. 67 and 127.] I 1991, G Sept. 1992.

USSR: Melodiya C10 09729-30. AZERBAIDZHAN QUARTET (Sarvar Ganiev, Bayandur Mekhtiev, Chingiz Mamedov, Rasim Abdullayev). [Schumann.] P 1977, I 1978*c*.

USSR: Melodiya C10 10241-2. TANEYEV QUARTET (Vladimir Ovcharek, Grigori Lutsky, Vissarion Soloviev, Iosif Levinzon). [Opp. 49 and 108.] P 1978, I 1978*d*. *Reissued:* USSR: with same number in 1st box of Part 2 of *Collected Works on Records.* I 1980 ~ Japan: JVC Victor 5348. [Opp. 108, 122, and 138.] ~ Russia: Melodiya Compact Disc SUCD 11 00309. [Opp. 101 and 108.] I 1993*a*.

USSR: Melodiya C10 10627-8. Arr. Sondetskis. String Orchestra of Vilnius Artistic School, Saulyus SONDETSKIS. [Purcell and Manfredini.] P

1978, I 1979*a. Reissued:* USSR: Melodiya C10 24353 008 (DMM). [Purcell, Manfredini, Čuirlionis *et al.*] I 1978*b.*

Olympia Compact Disc OCD 533. SHOSTAKOVICH QUARTET (Andrei Shislov, Sergei Pishchugin, Aleksandr Galkovsky, Aleksandr Korchagin), ['Complete Quartets, Vol. 3'—Opp. 101 and 117.] P 1978, I May 1994, G Sept. 1994.

USSR: Melodiya C10 11643-4. BORODIN QUARTET (Mikhail Kopelman, Andrei Abramenkov, Dmitri Shebalin, Valentin Berlinsky). [V. Shebalin.] P 1978, I 1979*d. Reissued:* USSR: Melodiya C10 19503 006. [Op. 73.] I 1984*a* ~ HMV Melodiya EL 270388-1 (digital). [Opp. 57 and 108.] G Nov. 1985 ~ HMV Melodiya EX 270339-3 (DMM). [In seven-record set of 15 Quartets plus Quintet.] G Mar. 1986 ~ EMI Melodiya Compact Disc CDC7 47507-2. [Opp. 57 and 108.] I Nov. 1986, G Oct. 1987 ~ Japan: Victor Musical Industries Compact Disc VICC 40021. [Opp. 117 and 118.] I 1990 ~ EMI Compact Discs CMS5 65032-2. [In six-disc set of 15 Quartets plus Quintet.] I Mar. 1994 ~ BMG Melodiya Compact Discs 74321 40711-2 (six-disc set). [Opp. 117 and 118.] I June 1997.

Czech: Opus 9111 1026. KOŠICE QUARTET (Ondřej Lewit, Milan Jirant, Jozef Kýška, Juraj Jánošík). [Mozart.] P Bratislava July 1980, I 1981.

Poland: Poljazz PSJ 184. Chamber Symphony arr. Barshai. Orkiestra Kameralna Wojciecha Rajskiego. [Karłowicz.] P date not stated, 1980?

Bulgaria: Balkanton BKA 10657. Chamber Symphony arr. Barshai. Sofia Soloists' Chamber Ensemble, Emil TABAKOV. [Honegger.] P 1981, I Jan. 1982.

Sweden: Caprice CAP 1266. Arr. Liljefors. Lars-Inge Bjärlestom (cello), Bengt Stark (timpani), Royal Swedish Chamber Orchestra, Mats LILJEFORS. [Rosenberg and Lowenstein.] P Stockholm 16–17 July 1981, I 1984.

New Zealand: Kiwi Pacific SLD 65. AUCKLAND QUARTET (Brecon Carter, Rae Carter, Philip Clark, Virginia Hopkins). [Mozart and Turina.] P Government House, Wellington 14 Aug. 1981.

Poland: Muza SX 2161. Chamber Symphony. Warsaw Chamber Orchestra, Mirosław ŁAWRYNOWICZ. [Kabalevsky and Telemann.] P Warsaw 15–16 Dec. 1982, I 1984.

Phoenix DGS 1038 (digital). Chamber Symphony arr. Barshai. Phoenix Chamber Orchestra, Julian BIGG. [Op. 118*a*.] P London Dec. 1983, G Aug. 1984. *Reissued:* Trax Classique Compact Disc TRX-CD 110. [Op. 118*a*.] G Sept. 1987 ~ Trax Classique TRXLP 131 and Compact Disc TRXCD 131. ['Testimony—Shostakovich's Greatest Hits'—Opp. 47, 97, 102, 60, 67; and Josephs.] I 1988.

Netherlands: Attacca Babel 8416-1 (digital). RAFAEL QUARTET (Ronald Hoogeveen, Rami Koch, Zoltan Benyacs, Henk Lambooy). [Op. 138.] P 19–20 Dec. 1983. *Reissued:* Netherlands: Attacca Babel Compact Disc 8948-5DDD. [Op. 138; and Keuris.] I 1988?

USA: Centaur Compact Disc CRC 2020. MANHATTAN QUARTET (Eric Lewis, Roy Lewis, John Dexter, Judith Glyde). [Op. 73.] P Rye, New York Jan. 1984, I 1986.

Chandos ABRD 1120 (digital) and Compact Disc CHAN 8357. Chamber Symphony arr. Barshai. I Musici de Montréal, Yuli TUROVSKY. [Op. 35.] P Aug. 1984, G Apr. 1985. *Reissued:* Chandos Enchant Compact Disc CHAN 7061. [Opp. 118*a* and 79*a*.] I July 1997 ~ Chandos Collect Compact Disc CHAN 6617. [Opp. 118*a* and 79*a*.] I July 2000, G Feb. 2001.

USA: Musicmasters MMD 20109Z (digital). Sinfonietta arr Gozman. Soviet Émigré Orchestra, Lazar GOZMAN. [Op. 11; and Tchaikovsky.] P 1986. *Reissued:* Olympia Compact Disc OCD 196. [Op. 11; and Tchaikovsky.] I June 1988, G Aug. 1989.

Switzerland: Tibor Varga Collection Compact Disc No. 15. Arr. T. Varga. Orchestre du Festival Tibor Varga Sion, Tibor VARGA. [R. Strauss.] P Summer 1986, I 2000.

Germany: Midas Compact Disc CD 5087. Chamber Symphony. Polish Chamber Orchestra, Wojciech RAJSKI. [Karlowicz and Gorecki.] P Warsaw Sept. 1986, I 1992.

Nimbus Compact Disc NI 5077. MEDICI QUARTET (Paul Robertson, David Matthews, Ivo-Jan van der Werff, Anthony Lewis). [Debussy.] P 16–17 Oct. 1986, I Jan. 1988.

USSR: Melodiya C10 28757 007. Chamber Symphony. Yerevan Chamber Orchestra, Zaven VARDANYAN. [Zograbyan.] P 1986, I 1990*a*.

France: Harmonia Mundi Label Bleu LBL 6505 (digital). Chamber Symphony arr. Barshai. Les Sinfonietta Orchestre Régional de Picardie, Alexandre MYRAT. [Op. 107.] P date not stated, 1986. *Reissued:* France: Harmonia Mundi Compact Disc LBLC 6505. [Op.107.] I 1988.

USSR: Melodiya C10 24855 005. Chamber Symphony. Georgian Chamber Orchestra, Liana ISAKADZE. [Nasidze.] I 1987*d*.

Denon Compact Disc CO 1789. Chamber Symphony arr. Barshai. Auvergne Orchestra, Jean-Jacques KANTOROW. [Schubert/Mahler.] P 19–21 Mar. 1987, G Sept. 1988.

Germany: Obligat Classics Compact Disc ob.01.209. Chamber Symphony. New American Chamber Orchestra. Misha RACHLEVSKY. [Tchaikovsky.] P Munich concert 22 Nov. 1987.

Academy Sound and Vision DCA 631 (DMM) and Compact Disc CD DCA 631. COULL QUARTET (Roger Coull, Philip Gallaway, David Curtis, John Todd). [Opp. 83 and 122.] P London Mar. 1988, I and G Apr. 1989.

Bulgaria: Balkanton BKA 12305-6. Chamber Symphony arr. Dafov. Tolbuhin Chamber Orchestra, Jordan DAFOV. [In double album with Opp. 87 No. 24; 101, and 108.] P Tolbuhin, Bulgaria Mar. 1988.

RCA Victor Red Seal Compact Disc RD 87947. Chamber Symphony arr. Barshai. Moscow Virtuosi, Vladimir SPIVAKOV. [Opp. 35 and 34.] P Paris 30 July 1988, I Sept. 1989.

Czech: Opus Compact Disc 9351 2025. MOYZES QUARTET (Stanislav Mucha, František Török, Alexander Lakatoš, Ján Slávik). [Op. 73.] P Bratislava June 1987, I Oct. 1990. NB. Previously released on Rare Records/Opus BHM 11 (cassette). [On 73.] I Feb. 1990.

Factory FACT 246 (DMM) and Compact Disc FACD 246. DUKE QUAR
TET (Louisa Fuller, Martin Smith, John Metcalfe, Ivan McCready) P Buckingham 20–2 Dec. 1988, I Sept. 1989, G Jan. 1990.

Teldec Classics Compact Disc 244 919-2. BRODSKY QUARTET (Michael
Thomas, Ian Belton, Paul Cassidy, Jacqueline Thomas). [Opp. 108 and
117.] P Berlin Feb. 1989, I Dec. 1989, G May 1990. *Reissued:* Teldec Compact Discs 9031 71702-2. [On fourth disc of six-disc set with Opp. 117 and
118.] I Nov. 1990, G June 1992.

Deutsche Grammophon Compact Disc 429 229-2GH. Chamber Symphony arr. Barshai. Chamber Orchestra of Europe, Rudolf BARSHAI. [Op.
118a.] P Berlin Mar. 1989, I Mar. 1990, G May 1990.

Czech: Opus Compact Disc 91 2210-2. Chamber Symphony arr. Barshai. Slovák Chamber Orchestra, Bohdan WARCHAL. [Op. 35.] P Opus
Studio Mar.–May 1989, I 1991. *Reissued:* Switzerland: Point Classics
Compact Disc 267 252-2. [Opp. 35 and 107.] I 1996.

USA: Elektra-Nonesuch / Warner Classics Compact Disc 7559-79242-
2. KRONOS QUARTET (David Harrington, John Sherba, Hank Dutt, Joan
Jeanrenaud). ['Black Angel'—Crumb, Tallis, Marta, and Ives.] P 1989?, I
1990, G Apr. 1991.

Germany: Aurophon Compact Disc AU 31467/LC 7709. Chamber
Symphony arr. Barshai. CONRAD VON DER GOLTZ CHAMBER ORCHESTRA.
[Tchaikovsky and Mozart.] P Staufen concert—date not stated, I 1990.

Germany: Fidelio Compact Disc 8838. Chamber Symphony arr. Barshai. New Amsterdam Sinfonietta, Lev MARKIZ. [Op. 118a.] P Amsterdam
Sept. 1989, I 1990 ~ *Reissued:* Netherlands: Vanguard Classics Compact
Discs 99306 (two-disc set). [Opp. 118a, 134, and 147.] I Aug. 1999.

Decca Compact Disc 433 028-2DH. Chamber Symphony arr. Barshai.
Royal Philharmonic Orchestra, Vladimir ASHKENAZY. [Op. 93.] P
Walthamstow Jan. 1990, I Nov. 1991, G Jan. 1992.

Sweden: Bluebell Compact Disc ABCD 039. Chamber Symphony arr.
Yuri Tsiryuk. Minsk Chamber Orchestra, Vitali KATAYEV. [Opp. 35 and
34.] P Esbo, Finland 23 Feb. 1990, I Oct. 1991.

Virgin Classics Compact Disc VC7 91432-2. Chamber Symphony arr.
Barshai. Orchestre de Chambre de Lausanne, Aleksandr LAZAREV. [Op.
135.] P Lausanne University Apr. 1990, I July 1991, G Oct. 1991.

USA: ESS.A.Y. Compact Disc CD 1009. MANHATTAN QUARTET (Eric
Lewis, Roy Lewis, John Dexter, Judith Glyde). [Opp. 101 and 108.] P Jersey City 18 May 1990. *Reissued:* Koch Schwann Compact Disc 310 165.
['Complete String Quartets, Vol. 3' with Opp. 101 and 108.] I Jan. 1993, G
June 1993.

Virgin Classics Compact Disc VC7 91437-2. BORODIN QUARTET (personnel as on 1978 recording). [Opp. 73 and 108.] P London July–Sept. 1990, I
Sept. 1991, G Dec. 1991. *Reissued:* Classic CD 18. First and second movements. [Mahler, Chopin, Mozart *et al.*] I Oct. 1991 (the first Shostakovich
work to be featured on a *Classic CD* cover disc; with magazine article on

pp. 64–7) ~ Virgin Classics Compact Discs VBD5 61630-2 (two-disc set). [Opp. 68, 73, 108, and 133.] I Aug. 1999.

Nimbus Compact Disc NI 5308. Chamber Symphony arr. Barshai. English Chamber Orchestra, William BOUGHTON. [Opp. 35 and 102.] P Leominster 14–15 Nov. 1990, I Oct. 1991. *Reissued:* Nimbus Compact Disc NI 5354. First and part second movement accompanying poetry readings by Princess Grace of Monaco and Richard Pasco in 1980. ['Birds, Beasts and Flowers'—Gabrieli, Ives, Ravel *et al.*]

USSR: Melodiya Compact Disc SUCD 11 00301. Chamber Symphony arr. Barshai. Hermitage Theatre Chamber Orchestra, Saulius SONDETSKIS. [Tchalkovsky and Arensky.] P 1990, I 1991.

Dolphin Compact Disc CD 0001. Chamber Symphony arr. Barshai. KREISLER STRING ORCHESTRA (without conductor). [Schoenberg.] P London Dec. 1990, I Aug. 1991.

Dorian Compact Disc DOR 90163. LAFAYETTE QUARTET (Ann Elliott-Goldschmid, Sharon Stanis, Joanna Hood, Pamela Highbaugh). [Op. 87 Nos. 1 and 15; and Tchaikovsky.] P Troy, New York May 1991, I June 1992, G July 1992.

Pickwick IMP Classics Compact Disc PCD 1000. Chamber Symphony arr. Barshai. I Solisti di Zagreb, Tonko NINIC. [Op. 11; and Bartók.] P Zagreb 22–8 June 1991, G Nov. 1992. *Reissued:* Carlton Classics Compact Disc 30367 02282. [Op. 11; and Bartók.]

Norway: Victoria Compact Disc VCD 19060. Arr. L. Drew. TRONDHEIM SOLOISTS, Bjarme Fiskum (director). [Johansen and Bjørklund.] P Trondheim July 1991.

Claves Compact Disc 50 9115. Chamber Symphony arr. Barshai. Kremlin Chamber Orchestra, Misha RACHLEVSKY. [Opp. 118*a* and 144*a*.] P Moscow concert Oct.–Nov. 1991, G Mar. 1993.

USA Russian Disc Compact Disc RDCD 11 087. BORODIN QUARTET (personnel as on 1978 recording). [Sans op. D; and Beethoven.] P St Petersburg concert 12 Dec. 1991, I June 1993, G Oct. 1993.

Slovakia: Opus Compact Disc 91 2437-2. Chamber Symphony. The Young Bratislava Soloists, Jindřich PAZDERA. [Suk, Barber, and Bruckner.] P 1991?

USA: Pro Arte Compact Disc 035090. Chamber Symphony arr. Barshai. Zürich String Orchestra, J. BALKANYI. [?] P Zürich 27–9 Jan. 1992.

Germany: EMI Compact Disc CDC7 54 555-2. Chamber Symphony arr. Barshai. Detmold Chamber Orchestra, Christoph POPPEN. [Bose.] P 11–17 Mar. 1992, I 1993.

Poland: Amadeus Musical Foundation Compact Disc AMF ST 104. Chamber Symphony arr. Barshai. Amadeus Chamber Orchestra, Agnieszka DUCZMAL. [Szynanowski, Gorécki, and Bacewicz.] P Adam Micklewicz University May–June 1992, I 1993. *Reissued:* Conifer Classics Compact Disc CDCF 246. [Gorécki, Kilar, Szymanowski *et al.*] I Nov. 1992.

Belgium: Cypres Compact Disc CYP 5606. Chamber Symphony arr. Barshai. Wallonia Royal Chamber Orchestra, Georges OCTORS. [Stravinsky, Bartók, and Ligeti.] P Liège 12 Oct.–6 Nov. 1992, I 1993.

Finland: Ondine Compact Disc ODE 817-2. Chamber Symphony. Helsinki Philharmonic, James DE PREIST. [Op. 47.] P Kanneltalo, Helsinki May 1993, I May 1994, G Dec. 1994.

Sony Classical St Petersburg Classics Compact Disc SMK 48372. Chamber Symphony arr. Sondetskis. St Petersburg Camerata, Saulius SONDETSKIS. ['In Memorian—Music of Death and Suffering'—Haydn and Hindemith.] P St Petersburg July 1993, I Nov. 1994.

Switzerland: Gallo Compact Disc CD 799. Chamber Symphony arr. R. Baumgartner. Lucerne Festival Strings, Rudolf BAUMGARTNER. [Kokkonen, Martin, and Schoeck.] P Radio DRS Aug. 1993, I 1994.

Bulgaria: Gega New Compact Disc GD 168. SOFIA QUARTET (Vassil Valchev, Nikolai Gagov, Valentin Gerov, Kolya Bespalov). [Opp. 118 and 122.] P Sofia Nov. 1993, I Feb. 1994.

Netherlands: Erasmus Compact Disc WVH 131. Chamber Symphony. Utrecht Conservatory String Orchestra, Viktor LIBERMAN. [Op. 135.] P Rotterdam Jan. 1994.

Naxos Compact Disc 8.550953. Chamber Symphony arr. Barshai. Dalgat String Ensemble, Roland MELIA. [Myaskovsky.] P St Petersburg 5–8 Jan. 1994, I Nov. 1998, G Apr. 1999.

Naxos Compact Disc 8.550973, ÉDER QUARTET (János Selmeczl, Péter Szüts, Sandor Papp, György Éder). ['Complete Quartets, Vol. 2'—Opp. 49 and 117.] P Brussels 14–17 Feb. 1994, I Nov. 1994, G Oct. 1995.

Virgin Classics Compact Disc VC5 45110-2. Chamber Symphony. Norwegian Chamber Orchestra, Iona BROWN. [Stravinsky and Tchaikovsky.] P Eidsvoll, near Oslo Apr.–May 1994, I May 1995.

Germany: Hänssler Classic Compact Disc 98 917. Chamber Symphony arr. Barshai. Stefan Bornscheuer (violin), Chihiro Saito (cello), Stuttgart Arcata Chamber Orchestra, Patrick STRUB. [Op. 35.] P 31 Oct.–2 Nov. 1994, I May 1995.

Collins Classics Compact Disc 1450-2. DUKE QUARTET (Louisa Fuller, Rick Koster, John Metcalfe, Ivan McCready). [Schnittke and Tchaikovsky.] P London 19–21 July 1995, I Nov. 1995, G Feb. 1996.

Denmark: Classico Compact Disc CLASSCD 135. ZAPOLSKI QUARTET (Alexander Zapolski, Jacob Soelberg, Flemming Lave, Vanja Louro). [Op. 68.] P Roskilde, Denmark Aug. and Oct. 1995, I July 1996.

Koch Classics Compact Discs 3-6436-2 Y6 (two-disc set). MEDICI QUARTET (Paul Robertson, Cathy Thompson, Ivo-Jan van der Werff, Anthony Lewis). [Ravel, Smetana, Janáček, and Britten.] P Petersham Oct.–Nov. 1995, I Jan. 1996, G May 1997.

USA: Pope Music Compact Disc PM 1009-2 (silver) and PMG 2009-2 (gold). Chamber Symphony. Russian Symphony Orchestra, Mark GORENSTEIN. ['Redemption'—Op. 47.] P Moscow Jan. 1996.

Carlton Classics Compact Disc 30366 0062-2. KREUTZER QUARTET (Peter Sheppard, Gordon MacKay, Bridget Carey, Neil Hyde). [Opp. 83 and 108.] P Loughton Jan. 1996, I July 1997, G Awards (Nov.) 1997.

Italy: Fonit Cetra Compact Disc NFCD 2043. Chamber Symphony (augmented string parts). Orchestra d'Archi Italiana, Mario BRUNELLO. [Gubaidulina.] P Venice 9 Apr. 1996, I Apr. 1997.

France: Opus 111 Compact Disc OPS 30-165. Chamber Symphony. Musicatreize, Roland HAYRABEDIAN. [Op. 135.] P Miramas, France Apr. 1996.

USA: New Albion Compact Disc NA 088 CD. Chamber Symphony arr. Barshai. New Century Chamber Orchestra, Stuart CANIN. ['Written with the Heart's Blood'—Opp. 11 and 118a.] P Tiburon, California Apr. 1996, I Jan. 1997.

South Korea: Samsung Classics Compact Disc SCC 013SJS. Sejong Soloists, Hyo KANG. [Tchaikovsky, Arensky, and Stravinsky.] P Princeton, New Jersey May 1996.

Germany: ECM New Series Compact Disc 453 512-2. Chamber Symphony. Stuttgart Chamber Orchestra, Dennis Russell DAVIES. [Vasks and Schnittke.] P Stuttgart June 1996, G Sept. 1997.

Netherlands: Globe Compact Disc 5157-0265. RUBIO QUARTET (Dirk Van de Velde, Dirk Van den Hauwe, Marc Sonnaert, Peter Devos). ['Complete Quartets, Vol. I'—Opp. 49 and 83.] P Utrecht Aug. 1996, I Nov. 1996.

Germany: Arte Nova Classics Compact Disc 74321 58967-2. Chamber Symphony arr. Barshai. Hamburg Soloists, Emil KLEIN. [Op. 118a.] P Hamburg Nov. 1996, I Oct. 1998.

Germany: ECM New Series Compact Disc 457 067-2. ROSAMUNDE QUARTET (Andreas Reiner, Simon Fordham, Helmut Nicolai, Anja Lechner). [Burian and Webern.] P Eichstätt Dec. 1996, I Nov. 1997, G Feb. 1998.

EMI Compact Disc CDC5 56442-2. Chamber Symphony arr. Barshai. Vienna Symphony Orchestra, Mariss JANSONS. [Op. 47.] P Vienna concert 7–14 Jan. 1997, I Oct. 1997, G Awards (Nov.) 1997.

Italy: Ark Compact Disc 59004. QUARTETTO FONÈ (Paolo Chiavacci, Marco Facchini, Riichi Uemara, Ilaria Maurri). [Borodin and Maderna.] P Siena Apr. 1997, I 1997.

USA: Arabesque Compact Disc Z 6711. Chamber Symphony. Israel Sinfonietta, Uri MAYER. [Op. 83a.] P Meneham, July 1997.

Switzerland: Gallo Compact Disc CD 929. Arr. Barshai. Young Swiss Chamber Orchestra, Emmanuel SIFFERT. [Hartman.] P 1997.

Sweden: BIS Compact Disc CD 913. YGGDRASIL QUARTET (Henrik Peterson, Per Öman, Robert Westlund, Per Nyström). [Opp. 73 and 108.] P Länna, Sweden Sept. 1997, I Nov. 1998, G Jan. 1999.

Classic FM Compact Disc 75605 57027-2. CHILIGIRIAN QUARTET (Levon Chiligirian, Charles Stewart, Asdis Valdimarsdottir, Philipe de Groote). [Borodin and Dvořák.] P East Woodhay, Berkshire 20–2 Oct. 1997, I Feb. 1998, G Aug. 1998.

Linn Records Compact Disc CKD 095. Chamber Symphony arr. Barshai. BT Scottish Ensemble, Clio GOULD. [Opp. 35 and 11.] P Glasgow 4–5 Mar. 1998, I Feb. 2000, G June 2000.

France: Arion Compact Disc ARN 68461. DEBUSSY QUARTET (Christophe Collette, Dominique Lonca, Vincent Deprecq, Yannick Callier). ['Complete Quartets, Vol. 1'—Opp. 83 and 138.] P Lyon July 1998, I July 1999.

Deutsche Grammophon Compact Disc 463 294-2GH5 (five-disc set). EMERSON QUARTET (Eugene Drucker, Philip Setzer, Lawrence Dutton, David Finkel). ['Complete Quartets, Vol. 3'—Opp. 108, 117, and 118.] P Aspen, Colorado concert July 1998, G June 2000.

France: Syrius Compact Disc SYR 141345. Arr. Barshai. European Camerata, Laurent QUÉNELLE. [Op. 11; and Honegger.] P. Alpes-Martimes, France Aug. 1998.

Germany: Arte Nova Classics Compact Disc 74321 77069-2. RUBIN QUARTET (Imgard Zavelberg, Tinta S. von Altenstadt, Sylvie Altenburger, Ulrike Zavelberg). [Bartók, Stravinsky, and Gubaidulina.] P Cologne 10–14 Aug. 1998.

Germany: Col legno Compact Discs WWE 8CD 20041 (eight-disc set). Chamber Symphony. Stuttgart Chamber Orchestra, Dennis Russell DAVIES. [On eighth disc—Schnittke, Ligeti, and Glass.] P Stuttgart concert 28 Nov. 1998.

Hyperion Compact Disc CDA 67154. ST PETERSBURG QUARTET. (Alla Aranovskaya, Ilya Teplyakov, Konstantin Kats, Leonid Shukayev). [Opp. 83 and 101.] P St Petersburg Apr. 1999, I Dec. 1999, G Mar. 2000.

BBC Music Compact Disc BBC MM95. JERUSALEM QUARTET (Aleksandr Pavlovsky, Sergei Bressler, Amichai Gross, Kyril Zlotnikov). [Beethoven and Haydn.] P Kentish Town, London 14 Oct. 1999, I July 2000 magazine.

France: Calliope Compact Disc CAL 9299. Chamber Symphony. Kaliningrad Philharmonic Chamber Orchestra, Emmanuel LEDUCQ-BAROME. [Op. 35; and Schnittke.] P Kaliningrad 1999, I Sept. 2000.

Delos Compact Disc DE 3259. Chamber Symphony. Moscow Chamber Orchestra, Constantine ORBELIAN. [Schnittke.] P Marin County, California 5 and 7 Mar. 2000.

Chandos Compact Disc CHAN 9955. SORREL QUARTET (Gina McCormack, Catherine Yates, Sarah-Jane Bradley, Helen Thatcher). ['Complete Quartets, Vol. 3'—Opp. 117 and 138.] P The Maltings, Snape 26–30 Mar. 2001, I Sept. 2001, G. Awards (Oct.) 2001.

References: Fiske, Keldysh, and Mason.

Notes: The quartet was written down in three days while convalescing in a ministerial guest-house at Gohrisch (not Görlitz as given in some accounts), a spa town in 'Saxon Switzerland' SE of Dresden near the Czech border.

The publishers, Edition Peters, commissioned an orchestration from Rudolf Barshai in 1960 and the composer named the arrangement: Chamber Symphony.

Sans op. U Novorossiisk Chimes

Subtitle: *The Fire of Eternal Glory.*

Form: Patriotic piece for full orchestra, based on the opening phrase of the National Anthem Contest Entry, Sans op. N (iii). No tempo indication.

Instrumentation: piccolo, 2 flutes, 2 oboes, cor anglais, 3 B flat clarinets, 2 bassoons ~ 4 horns, 3 trumpets, 3 trombones, tuba ~ timpani, triangle, side drum, cymbals ~ celesta ~ strings.

Composed: 1960, at Moscow. Commissioned by representatives of the city of Novorossiisk.

Dedication: In memory of the Heroes of the Great Patriotic War.

Première: 27 September 1960, the tune sounded on a tape recording, performed by the All-Union Radio and Television Symphony Orchestra conducted by Arvid Yansons, at the Flame of Eternal Glory, Heroes Square, Novorossiisk.

Arrangements: Reduction for piano duet by the composer in 1960. Patriotic song, with lyric by Kira Alemasova, for chorus and orchestra; and reduction for S.A.T.B. chorus and piano by G. Kovalyov, marked 'Moderato'. Transcription for trumpet and piano by Sergei Bolotin. Also exists as a piano solo.

    Arranged for wind band by Yevgeni Makarov. Instrumentation: flute, oboe, 3 B flat clarinets, bassoon ~ 4 E flat horns, 2 trumpets, 3 trombones ~ percussion (2 players), chimes ~ separate band of 2 cornets and 10 saxhorns.

Music: The autograph score presented by the composer to the Novorossiisk City Committee.

    USSR, no number or date, mimeographed manuscript one-page arrangement for piano solo.

    The piano duet arrangement published as a supplement to the journal *Muzykalnaya Zhizn* ('Musical Life'), 1960, No. 21 (Sadovnikov) or 22 (*Collected Works*).

    Muzyka, *Choral Conductor's Library* No. 20, 1966, arr. for chorus and and piano.

    Sovetskii Kompozitor, No. 1314 (in collection *In Memory of Heroes*), 1970, arr. for wind band by Y. Makarov, 21.5 cm.

    Muzyka, Leningrad, No. 2035 (in *Dmitri Shostakovich: Pieces for trumpet and piano*), 1976, parts, 28.5 cm.

    Muzyka, No. 11687 (in Volume 11 of *Collected Works* with Opp. 96, 115, 130, and 131), 1984, original orchestral score, 30 cm.

    Muzyka, No. 10179 (as a supplement in Volume 34 of *Collected Works* with Opp. 88 and 136, and songs), 1985, arr. G. Kovalyov, 30 cm.

Duration: 2 minutes (composer and Sadovnikov); 2' 24"–3' 20".

Recordings: USSR: MK D 8459-60 (10" mono). USSR Symphony Orchestra, Arvid YANSONS. [Op. 90; and Kabalevsky.] P 1962.

USSR: Melodiya CM 02137-8. Red Banner Ensemble, Boris ALEKSAN-DROV. [A. Aleksandrov, Blanter, Feltsman *et al.*] P 1970. *Reissued:* HMV Melodiya ASD 3200. ['Cavalry Song'—Knipper, Rubinstein, Serov *et al.*] G Oct. 1976 ~ USSR: Melodiya C60 12741-2. [Shainsky, A. Aleksandrov, Blanter *et al.*] I 1980*b* ~ USSR: Melodiya C60 21747 008. ['Songs about Hero-Cities'.] I 1985*c*.

Academy Sound and Vision Compact Disc CD DCA 707. Royal Phil-harmonic Orchestra, Enrique BÁTIZ. [Opp. 47, 115, and 131.] P Mitcham 1990, I June 1990, G Sept. 1990. *Reissued:* IMG Records Compact Disc IMGCD 1609. [Opp. 479 115, and 131.] I June 1994, G Feb. 1995.

Decca Compact Disc 436 763-2DH. Royal Philharmonic Orchestra, Vladimir ASHKENAZY. [Opp. 130 and 65.] P Walthamstow Apr. 1992; I Feb. 1994, G Apr. 1994.

Opus 111   Five Days, Five Nights

Subtitle: *Dresden Art Gallery.* Music score gives the English title as *Five Days and Five Nights.* Robert Matthew-Walker states that the film is also known as *May 5* (sleeve-note for Opp. 110*a* and 118*a* on Phoenix DGS 1038).

Form: Music for the film *Five Days, Five Nights,* directed by Leo Arnshtam for Mosfilm in collaboration with the then East German DEFA Studios, scored for full orchestra (with harp, organ, and piano). The items are numbered 1 to 18 but nothing is known of Nos. 5, 10, and 17. No. 6 (Largo) for organ and string orchestra appears in the Suite Opus 111*a,* Nos. 3 and 1, in an altered and differently orchestrated version.

1. Introduction
3. Meeting with the liberators on the road
4. "It was nearly half an hour ago"
8. Paul's Soliloquy—Moderato
9. Madonna
11. Fight in the loft
12. Meeting of Katrine and Paul—Allegro
13. Night scene—Andante
14. Katrine's dream—Moderato
15. Solitude
16. Frau Rank's parting with the pictures; Alarm [without tempo]
18. Finale
    Nos. 2, 6, and 7 are without titles.

Instrumentation: as Suite Opus 111*a* plus organ.
Composed: July–August 1960, at Dresden.
Premières: Film first shown on 23 November 1961. [Volume 42 of *Collected Works* gives the release date as 27 February 1961.]
    Suite Opus 111*a*: 7 January 1962, Moscow Radio; USSR Cinemato-graph Symphony Orchestra, Emin Khachaturyan.

Arrangements: Opus 111*a*—Suite assembled by Lev Atovmyan in 1961:

1. Introduction—Adagio
2. Dresden in Ruins—Largo
3. Liberated Dresden—Moderato—Largo—Allegro *attacca*
4. Interlude—Andante—Allegro
5. Finale—Moderato—Allegretto—Largo

No. 3 concludes by quoting the 'Ode to Joy' theme from Ludwig van Beethoven's Symphony No. 9.

Instrumentation of Suite Opus 111*a*: piccolo, 2 flutes, 3 oboes, 3 clarinets (A and B flat), 2 bassoons, contrabassoon ~ 4 horns, 3 trumpets, 3 trombones, tuba ~ timpani, triangle, side drum, cymbals, bass drum, gong ~ glockenspiel, harp, piano ~ strings.

Music: Autograph of the incomplete film score preserved at the Glinka Museum and manuscript copy of ten items of the score and orchestral parts, at the Music Library of the USSR Cinematograph Symphony Orchestra.

Muzyka, No. 6419, 1970, Suite Opus 111*a*, full score, 29.5 cm.

Muzyka, No. 10890 (in Volume 42 of *Collected Works* with Opp. 75, 78, 80, 82, 95, 97, 116, 132, and 137), 1987, No. 6 of the film score, 30 cm.

Duration: Suite: 20' 20"–32' 39"; 32 minutes (Sadovnikov).

Recordings: USSR: MK D 11327-8 (10" mono). Suite Nos. 1–5 complete, with spliced-in exposition to fig. 7 before coda of No. 1 and additional chorale prelude inserted before fig. 11 of No. 2). USSR Cinematograph Symphony Orchestra, Emin KHACHATURYAN. I 1963. *Reissued:* Cinema Records LP 8003 (mono). Suite Nos. 1–5 (with No. 4 cut from fig. 12 and No. 5 starting at fig. 2 plus 5 bars). [Op. 116*a*.] NB. Orchestra and conductor not named on record and sleeve.

RCA Victor Red Seal Compact Disc RD 87763. Suite Nos. 2–4 and 5 (fig. 17 to end). Belgian Radio Symphony Orchestra, José SEREBRIER. [Opp. 116 and 137.] P Brussels 1988, I June 1988, G Oct. 1988.

Germany: Capriccio Compact Discs 10 341/42 (two-disc set). Suite Nos. 1–5 (as score). Berlin Radio Symphony Orchestra, James JUDD. [Op. 18.] P Berlin 1–5 and 22–3 Jan. 1990, I Oct. 1990.

USA: Pro-Arte Fanfare Compact Disc CDD 551. Suite Nos. 2 and 3. Chicago Sinfonietta, Paul FREEMAN. ['Shostakovich Film Festival'—Opp. 97, 116, 16, and 35.] P Oak Park, Illinois May 1990, I Aug. 1991. NB. Labelled as 'Liberated Dresden' but actually 'Dresden in Ruins' figs. 4 to 8 and 11 to end *attacca* 'Liberated Dresden' figs. 3 to 5 and 7 to end. *Reissued:* Conifer Classics Compact Disc Class 7086. [As USA release.] I Nov. 1991.

Naxos Compact Disc 8.553299. Suite Nos. 1–5. National Symphony Orchestra of Ukraine, Theodore KUCHAR. [Op. 97.] P Kiev 12–15 Feb. 1995, I Dec. 1996, G May 1997.

Reference: McKee.

Opus 112   Symphony No. 12 in D minor

Subtitles: 'The Year 1917', and often known as 'The Lenin Symphony'.

Form: Symphony for normal full symphony orchestra in four linked movements:

1. Revolutionary Petrograd—Moderato—Allegro *attacca*
2. Razliv—Adagio *attacca*
3. Aurora—Allegro *attacca*
4. The Dawn of Humanity—L'istesso tempo

Instrumentation: piccolo (= flute III), 2 flutes, 3 oboes, 3 clarinets (B flat and A), 3 bassoons (III = contrabassoon) ~ 4 horns, 3 trumpets, 3 trombones, tuba ~ timpani, triangle, side drum, cymbals, bass drum, gong ~ 1st violins (16–20), 2nd violins (14–18), violas (12–16), cellos (12–16), doublebasses (10–14).

Composed: Completed on 22 August 1961, at Moscow, for the twenty-second Soviet Communist Party Moscow Convention held in October 1961.

Dedication: Vladimir Ilyich Ulyanov Lenin (Bolshevik Party founder).

Premières: Piano reduction: 8 September 1961, RSFSR Composers' Union; Moisei Vainberg and Boris Chaikovsky.

Full orchestra: 1 October 1961, Leningrad Philharmonic Bolshoi Hall; Leningrad Philharmonic Orchestra, Yevgeni Mravinsky; and at Kuibyshev (now Samara) under Abram Stasevich.

14 October 1961, Metrostroi Palace of Culture, Moscow; USSR Symphony Orchestra, Konstantin Ivanov.

UK: 4 September 1962, Usher Hall, Edinburgh Festival; Philharmonia Orchestra, Sir Adrian Boult.

Arrangement: Reduction for piano four hands by the composer.

Music: Autograph score preserved in the Shostakovich family archive.

Sovetskii Kompozitor, No. 2802, 1961, 29 cm. (reprinted with the same no., 1976).

Sovetskii Kompozitor, No. 2809, 1962, reduction for piano four hands, 29 cm.

Breitkopf & Härtel, No. 3574, 1962, 21 cm.

Breitkopf & Härtel, No. 3596 (plate no. 31715), *c*.1962, 33 cm.

Edwin F. Kalmus, No. 171, no date, 26.5 cm.

Muzyka, No. 4137, 1964, 21 cm.

Edition Eulenberg, No. 10031, 1972, 27 cm.

Muzyka, No. 10178 (in Volume 6 of *Collected Works* with Op. 103), 1980, 30 cm.

Hans Sikorski, No. 2210, 1981, 21 cm.

Duration: 40 minutes in score; 34' 25"–44' 08"; 36' 00"–40' 35" (Plaistow).

Ballets: *Allumez les étoiles!* Roland Petit, Marseilles, Ballet de Marseilles, 5 May 1972. A ballet of thirteen episodes, with libretto based on Vladimir

Mayakovsky's poem of 1913, 'Listen!—they are lighting up the stars'; using music from Georgian folksongs, Musorgsky's *Pictures at an Exhibition*, Prokofiev's *Chout* and Violin Concerto No. 2. and Shostakovich's Symphony No. 12.

Symphony of Revolution. Created by Natalya Ryzhenko and Victor Smirnov-Golovanov, with libretto based on Maksim Gorky's novel *Mother;* using music from Symphonies Nos. 11 and 12; performed at the Odessa Theatre of Opera and Ballet in 1977.

Film: *October.* In the summer of 1967 Aleksandr Kholodilin helped Shostakovich select some of his music for the sound track of Sergei Eisenstein and Grigori Aleksandrov's silent film, originally released in 1928. English subtitles and sound effects, though not speech, were added to the restored film. All four movements of Symphony No. 12 were utilized; also considerable excerpts from Symphony No. 11, Opus 103 and Cello Concerto No. 2, Opus 126, with 'The Drayman's Dance' from *The Bolt,* Opus 27 included for two episodes in lighter vein. A Hendring videocassette is available on Moskwood, Haarlem catalogue No. 2121.

Recordings: USSR: MK D 09395-6 (mono) and C 0245-6. Leningrad Philharmonic Orchestra, Yevgeni MRAVINSKY. P 1961 (Mravinsky's last studio recording), I 1962. *Reissued:* USA: Bruno BR 14065L (mono). [Kabalevsky.] I 1964 ~ USA: Artia MK 1580 (mono). P not première concert 1 Oct. 1961 as stated, I 1964 ~ HMV Melodiya ASD 2598. [Op. 90.] G Sept. 1970 ~ USA: Angel Melodiya SR 40128. I 1971 ~ Germany: Melodia Eurodisc 203 637 ~ Germany: Melodia Eurodisc 87 623 XPK. [In thirteen-record box set.] I 1974 ~ France: Le Chant du Monde LDX 78465 ~ HMV Melodiya BOX 502510 In Set SLS 5025. [Op. 90.] G Dec. 1975 ~ Italy: EMI 065 94486. I 1978 ~ Netherlands: Phonogram Melodia 409 ~ Japan: JVC VIC 9533. I 1984 ~ France: Praga Compact Discs PR 254 017-8 (two-disc set) [Opp. 54 and 103.] P not Prague concert 6 Jan. 1962 as stated, I Apr. 1994, G Aug. 1994 ~ Japan: BMG Melodiya Compact Disc BVCX 4026. [Op. 81.] I 1997 ~ France: Le Chant du Monde Compact Disc PR 7254 017. [Op. 54.] P not Prague 1962, G Feb. 2001.

BBC Radio Classics Compact Disc 15656 91832. Philharmonia Orchestra, Gennadi ROZHDESTVENSKY. [Op. 114; and Musorgsky.] P Edinburgh concert 4 Sept. 1962, I Oct. 1996.

Italy: The Classical Society Compact Disc CSCD 125. BBC Symphony Orchestra, Sir Adrian Boult. [Brahms.] P not stated; possibly the London première concert 28 Nov. 1962, I 1991. *Reissued:* Italy: Intaglio Compact Disc INCD 7431. [Brahms.] I 1993.

HMV ALP 2009 (mono) and ASD 559. Philharmonia Orchestra, Georges PRÊTRE. [Op. 96.] P 27–8 Nov. 1962 and 21–2 Mar. 1963, G Nov. 1963. *Reissued:* France: EMI FALP 794. [Op. 96.] ~ Classics for Pleasure CFP 141. [Op. 96.] G Oct. 1970.

Philips Universo 6580 012. Gewandhaus Orchestra of Leipzig, Ogan DURYAN. P Oct. 1967, G Aug. 1972. *Reissued:* France: Philips 6598 103 in set 6747 252. [In two-record set 'Tribute to Dmitri Shostakovich' with Opp. 54 and 35.] I post-1975 ~ Philips Classical Collector Compact Disc 434 172-2PM. [Op. 119.] I Sept. 1992, G Mar. 1993.

Australia: ABC A07003. Sydney Symphony Orchestra, Bernard HEINZE. [Elgar.] P Chastwood, Australia Feb. 1968.

USSR: Melodiya D 32591-2 (10" mono). *V. I. Lenin in Razliv.* Author: P. Nikiti. Narrator: V. Davydov. Music from Op. 112. P 1972, I 1973.

USSR: Melodiya C 04713-4. Moscow Philharmonic Orchestra, Kirill KONDRASHIN. P 1972, I 1975*a. Reissued:* HMV Melodiya ASD 3520. [Op. 42.] G Aug. 1978 ~ USSR: Melodiya C 04713-4. [In second box of Part 1 of *Collected Works on Records.*] I 1980 ~ HMV Melodiya EX 2903873 (DMM). [On sixth record in twelve-record box set with Opp. 60 finale and 14.] G Dec. 1985 ~ France: Le Chant du Monde Compact Disc LDC 278 1007-8. [In Box 4 of five two-disc sets with Opp. 103 and 113.] G May 1989 ~ BMG Classics Melodiya Compact Disc 74321 19848-2. [Op. 10.] I July 1994, G Nov. 1994.

USA: Monitor MCS 2148. Bulgarian Radio and Television Symphony Orchestra, Russlan RAYCHEV. P c.1974. *Reissued:* Italy: Fonit-Cetra LEC 105 ~ France: Harmonia Mundi HM 125 ~ France: Harmonia Mundi Black Label HM 31. I 1977 ~ AVM Classics AVM 1019 and Compact Disc AVMCD 1019. [Op. 54.] I Dec. 1988 (CD reissued 1994).

Decca SXDL 7577 (digital). Concertgebouw Orchestra, Bernard HAITINK. [Op. 115.] P Amsterdam 25–6 Jan. 1982, G June and Aug. 1983. Prize-winner in the Dutch record industry's 1983 Classical Edison Awards. *Reissued:* USA: London 71077. [Op. 115.] ~ France: Decca 591331 (digital) ~ Decca Compact Disc 417 392-2DH2. [Op. 60 in two-disc set.] I June 1986, G Oct. 1986 ~ Decca Ovation Compact Disc 425 067-2DM. [Op. 54.] I Aug. 1993, G Nov. 1993 ~ London Compact Disc 444 435-2. [On fifth disc of eleven-disc set with Op. 54.] I June 1995.

USSR: Melodiya A10 00073 009 (digital). USSR Ministry of Culture Symphony Orchestra, Gennadi ROZHDESTVENSKY. P 1983, I 1985*a. Reissued:* JVC / Target Compact Disc VDC 1044. G May 1986 ~ Olympia Compact Disc OCD 111. [Op. 54.] I June 1987, G May 1989 ~ Olympia Compact Disc OCD 001. 4th movement only. ['The Best of Melodiya on Olympia' sampler—Op. 47.] ~ Olympia Compact Disc OCD 200. [Op. 14.] I Dec. 1987, G Apr. 1988 ~ Germany: Melodia Eurodisc Compact Disc 258 488. [Op. 70.] ~ Olympia Compact Disc OCD 5005. [In Vol. 1 six-disc set of symphonies with Op. 54.] I Dec. 1990 ~ BMG Melodiya Compact Discs 74321 63460-2 (two-disc set). [Opp. 107; 113; and 34.] I Mar. 1999.

Japan: Victor Musical Industries Compact Disc VDC 25028. Leningrad Philharmonic Orchestra, Yevgeni MRAVINSKY. P Leningrad concert 29 (not 30) Apr. 1984 (Mravinsky's last recording). *Reissued:* France: Erato Compact Disc 2292 45754-2. I Apr. 1992, G June 1992. [NB. Also available in 12-disc set 2292 45763-2.] ~ USA: Russian Disc Compact Disc RDCD 10 912. [Glinka.] I Nov. 1996.

Naxos Compact Disc 8.550626. Czecho-Slovak Radio Symphony Orchestra, Ladislav SLOVÁK. [Op. 54.] P Bratislava 5–12 Feb. 1989, I May 1993, G Nov. 1993. *Reissued:* Naxos Compact Discs 8.505017. [In five-disc set with Symphonies Nos. 1, 2, 3, 4, 6, 7, and 15.] I 1993.

Deutsche Grammophon Compact Disc 431 688-2GH. Gothenberg Symphony Orchestra, Neeme JÄRVI. [Opp. 32 and 22*a*.] P Gothenberg Oct. 1990, I July 1991, G Sept. 1991. *Reissued:* Deutsche Grammophon Compact Discs 459 415-2GTA2 (two-disc set). [Opp. 103, 131, 32, and 22*a*.] I Jan. 1999.

Decca Compact Disc 436 760-2. Royal Philharmonic Orchestra, Vladimir ASHKENAZY. [Op. 20.] P Walthamstow Apr. 1992, I Oct. 1994.

Finland: Ondine Compact Disc ODE 846-2. Helsinki Philharmonic Orchestra, James DE PREIST. [Op. 70.] P Oct. 1993 (movements 2–4) and May 1994 (1st movement), I May 1996, G Feb. 1997.

Denon Compact Disc CO 78968. Vienna Symphony Orchestra, Eliahu INBAL. [Op. 54.] P 27–30 Apr. 1994, I Feb. 1996, G Apr. 1996.

Germany: Arte Nova Compact Disc 74321 63649-2. SWR Symphony Orchestra, Michel GIELEN. [Op. 35.] P Baden-Baden 12–13 Sept. 1995, I Aug. 1999, G Nov. 1999.

Teldec Compact Discs 0630-17046-2 (In twelve-disc set of Symphonies). London Symphony Orchestra, Mstislav ROSTROPOVICH. P London Jan. 1995, G Oct. 1997. *Reissued:* Teldec Compact Disc 4509 95070-2. [Op. 54.] I Aug. 1999.

Chandos Compact Disc CHAN 9585. Russian State Symphony Orchestra, Valeri POLYANSKY. [Op. 126.] P Mar. 1996, I Feb. 1998.

References: Hitotsuyanagi, Rienäcker / Reising, Sabinina, and Tigranov.

Note: The 1984 Mravinsky recordings are identical although the USA disc is dated 29 April. Mravinsky and his orchestra used to perform the same programme on consecutive days and it is not known whether this concert refers to the 29 or 30 April 1984.

Sans op. V   Songs and Dances of Death (Musorgsky)

Form: Orchestration of Modest Musorgsky's song cycle for voice and piano, written in 1875 (Nos. 1, 2, and 3) and 1877 (No. 4) to poems by Count Arseni Golenishchev-Kutuzov, for symphony orchestra (with harp):

1. Lullaby—Lento doloroso
2. Serenade—Moderato
3. Trepak—Lento assai Tranquillo
4. The Warrior Captain (or 'The Field Marshal')—Vivo-alla guerra

Instrumentation: 2 flutes (II = piccolo), 2 oboes, 2 clarinets (A and B flat; II = bass clarinet), 2 bassoons (II = contrabassoon) ~ 4 horns, 2 trumpets, 3 trombones, tuba ~ timpani, side drum, cymbals, gong ~

harp ~ 1st violins (12–16), 2nd violins (10–14), violas (8–12), cellos (8–12), double-basses (6–10 five-string specified).
Composed: Orchestrated on 31 July 1962, at Solotcho village near Ryazan.
Dedication: Galina Pavlovna Vishnevskaya (soprano).
Première: 12 November 1962, Gorky (now Nizhni Novgorod); Galina Vishnevskaya, Gorky Philharmonic Orchestra, Mstislav Rostropovich.
Arrangement: English translation of the poems by Joan Pemberton Smith.
Music: Muzyka, No. 3362, 1966, full score, 29 cm.
[Muzyka, Leningrad, No. 2441 (in album *M. Musorgsky: Selected Romances and Songs,* 2nd edition), 1979, Nos. 1–4 in original voice and piano version, 30 cm.]
Duration: 18' 29"–22' 59".
Recordings: BMG Melodiya Compact Disc 74321 53237-2. Complete cycle. Galina VISHNEVSKAYA (soprano), Gorky Philharmonic Orchestra, Mstislav Rostropovich. [Opp. 127 and 109; and Prokofiev.] P Gorky concert 9 Feb. 1963, I 1998.

USSR: Melodiya D 021567-8 (mono) Nos. 1, 2, and 3. Aleksandr VEDERNIKOV (bass), Bolshoi Theatre Orchestra, Mark Ermler. [Glinka, Tchaikovsky, Glazunov *et al.*] P 1968.

HMV ASD 3436 (quad). Complete cycle. Galina VISHNEVSKAYA (soprano), London Philharmonic Orchestra, Mstislav Rostropovich. [Rimsky-Korsakov and Tchaikovsky.] P 1977, G Feb. 1978. *Reissued:* EMI Compact Discs CMS5 65716-2 (three-disc set). [Opp. 127 and 109; Rimsky-Korsakov, Tchaikovsky, and Prokofiev.] I Nov. 1995, G Sept. 1996.

France: Auvidis Valois Compact Disc V 4623. Complete cycle. Dmitri PETKOV (bass), Lorraine Philharmonic Orchestra, Jacques Houtmann. [Musorgsky and Denisov.] P Pont-à-Mousson Oct. 1988, I 1990.

USSR: Melodiya Compact Disc SUCD10 00139. Complete cycle. Irina ARKHIPOVA (mezzo-soprano), USSR Symphony Orchestra, Yevgeni Svetlanov. [No. 43 in series 'Anthology of Russian Symphonic Music'— Musorgsky.] P 1989, I 1991*a.*

RCA Victor Red Seal Compact Disc RD 60195. Complete cycle. Sergei LEIFURKUS (baritone), Royal Philharmonic Orchestra, Yuri Temirkanov. [Musorgsky / Ravel.] P Walthamstow 1 Mar. 1990, I Nov. 1990, G Mar. 1992.

Deutsche Grammophon Compact Disc 437 785-2GH. Complete cycle. Brigitte FASSBÄNDER (mezzo-soprano), Gothenburg Symphony Orchestra, Neeme Järvi. [Op. 135.] P Gothenburg May 1992, I Oct. 1993, G Feb. 1994.

Philips Compact Disc 438 872-2PH. Complete cycle. Dmitri HVOROSTOVSKY (baritone), Kirov Orchestra, Valeri Gergiev. [Rimsky-Korsakov, Borodin, Rubinstein *et al.*] P St Petersburg Jan. 1993.

Sony Classical Compact Disc SK 66276. Complete cycle. Anatoli KOCHERGA (bass), Berlin Philharmonic Orchestra, Claudio Abbado. [Tchaikovsky.] P Berlin 7–30 Nov. 1993, I Dec. 1994.

EMI Compact Disc CDC5 55232-2. Complete cycle. Robert LLOYD (bass), Philadelphia Orchestra, Mariss Jansons. [Op. 93.] P Philadelphla Mar. 1994, I Mar. 1995, G June 1995.

Decca Compact Disc 458 919-2DH. Complete cycle. Sergei ALEK-SASHKIN (bass), Chicago Symphony Orchestra, Sir Georg Solti. [Op. 141.] P Chicago 20–9 Mar. 1997, I Oct. 1998, G May 1999.

Reference: Fay (in M. H. Brown).

Opus 113   Symphony No. 13 in B flat minor

Subtitle: *Babi Yar.*

Form: Symphony for bass soloist, bass choir, and full orchestra (with 2–4 harps and piano), to settings of Yevgeni Yevtushenko's poems, in five movements:

1. Babi Yar—Adagio
2. Humour—Allegretto
3. In the Store—Adagio *attacca*
4. Fears—Largo *attacca*
5. A Career—Allegretto

Instrumentation: piccolo, 2 flutes, 3 oboes (III = cor anglais), 3 clarinets (B flat and A; III = E flat and bass), 3 bassoons (III = contrabassoon) ~ 4 horns, 3 trumpets, 3 trombones, tuba ~ timpani, triangle, castanets, wood block, tambourine, side drum, whip, cymbals, bass drum, gong ~ bass soloist, choir of 40–100 bass voices ~ 1st violins (16–20), 2nd violins (14–18), violas (12–16), double-basses (10–14 five-string specified).

Composed: The piano and full scores of *Babi Yar* completed on 27 March and 21 April 1962 respectively. Originally intended as a one-movement symphonic poem. Subsequently four more movements were written and these were dated 5, 9, 16, and 20 July 1962. The poem 'Babi Yar' was published in *Literaturnaya Gazeta,* 19 September 1961. Nos. 2, 3, and 5 were selected by the composer from Yevtushenko's collection *A Wave of the Hand* published in Moscow, early 1962. 'Fears' was specially written at the composer's request and published in *Komsomolskaya Pravda,* 21 November 1962. Revision of the first movement *Babi Yar* (two four-line passages of the original text changed) in January 1963.

Premières: 18 and 20 December 1962, Moscow Conservatory Bolshoi Hall; Vitali Gromadsky (bass), Republican State and Gnessin Institute Choirs (basses only), Moscow Philharmonic Orchestra, Kirill Kondrashin.

Revised version: Spring 1963 at Minsk and 20 September 1965 at Moscow.

USA: 16 January 1970, Philadelphia; Tom Krause (baritone), Philadelphia Orchestra, Eugene Ormandy.

UK: 14 September 1971, Liverpool Philharmonic Hall; John Shirley-Quirk (baritone), Royal Liverpool Philharmonic Orchestra and Chorus, Charles Groves.

Transcription: Netherlands: July 1993, Limburg; Henk Smit (bass), Belgian military band and chorus, Norbert Nozy.

Arrangements: Reduction for two pianos four hands by the composer. Transcription for military band. English translations of the poems by Valeria Vlazinskaya, and Andrew Hugh; and German, by Jörg Morgener.

Music: Autograph full and vocal scores preserved in the Shostakovich family archive. The first page of the autograph full score is reproduced in Volume 7 of *Collected Works*.

Muzyka, 1967. [Date of the edition analysed by A. Dmitriev in Tigranov—printed but suppressed?]

Edwin F. Kalmus, No. 528, no date, Russian text (revised version), 26.5 cm.

Leeds Music (Canada), no number, 1970, Russian words transliterated (original version), 25 cm.

Sovetskii Kompozitor, No. 2253, 1971, Russian text (revised version), 30 cm.

Hans Sikorski, No. 2207, 1981, Russian and German texts—the latter by Jörg Morgener, 21 cm.

Muzyka, No. 10280 (Volume 7 of *Collected Works*), 1984, Russian text (revised version), 30 cm.

Muzyka, No. 11688 (in Volume 9 of *Collected Works* with reductions of Op. 135 and choral sections of Opp. 14 and 20), 1984, vocal score with Russian text (revised version), 30 cm.

Duration: 56 and approx. 60 minutes in scores; 53' 17"–65' 06".

Recordings: USA: Russian Disc Compact Disc RDCD 11 191. Original version. Vitali Gromadsky (bass), Republican State and Gnessin Institute Choirs (basses only), Moscow Philharmonic Orchestra, Kirill KON-DRASHIN. P Moscow second performance concert 20 Dec. 1962, I Aug. 1993, G Mar. 1994. NB. Fifth movement labelled 'Quarry' (*sic*).

USA: Everest SDBR 3181 (electronic stereo). Revised version. Vitali Gromadsky (bass), RSFSR Academic Russian Choir, Aleksandr Yurlov (chorus-master), Moscow Philharmonic Orchestra, Kirill KONDRASHIN. P Moscow concert 20 Nov. 1965, G Nov. 1967. *Reissued:* France: Classic 920 268 (electronic stereo).

Italy: Memories Compact Disc HR 4101 (digitally remastered stereo). Labelled as 'Rhythmic Version by Massimo Binazzi'. Ruggero, Raimondi (bass), Rome RAI Symphony Orchestra and Male Chorus, Gianni Lazzari (chorus-master), Riccardo MUTI. P Rome concert 31 Jan. 1970.

USSR: Melodiya CM 02905-6. Revised version. Artur Eizen (bass), RSFSR Academic Russian Choir, Aleksandr Yurlov (chorus-master), Moscow Philharmonic Orchestra, Kirill KONDRASHIN. P 1971, I 1972.

Reissued: USA: Angel Melodiya SR 40212. I 1972 ~ HMV Melodiya ASD 2893. G Apr. 1973 ~ France: Le Chant du Monde LDX 78500. I 1973 ~ Germany: Melodia Eurodisc 87 623 XPK. [In thirteen-record box set.] I 1974 ~ Italy: EMI 065 94233. I 1974 ~ Germany: Melodia Eurodisc 300 606-435. [In three-record box set with Opp. 135 and 141.] ~ HMV Melodiya BOX 502511 in Set SLS 5025. G Dec. 1975 ~ USSR: Melodiya CM 02905-6. [In second box of Part 1 of *Collected Works on Records.*] I 1980 ~ HMV Melodiya EX 2903873 (DMM). [Tenth record in twelve-record box set.] G Dec. 1985 ~ France: Le Chant du Monde Compact Disc LDC 278 1007-8. [In Box 4 of five two-disc sets with Opp. 103 and 112.] G May 1989 ~ BMG Classics Melodiya Compact Disc 74321 19842-2. I July 1994, G Nov. 1994.

USA: RCA Red Seal LSC 3162. Original version. Tom Krause (baritone), Male Chorus of the Mendelssohn Club, Robert E. Page (chorusmaster), Philadelphia Orchestra, Eugene ORMANDY. P Jan. 1970. *Reissued:* RCA Red Seal SB 6830. G June 1970 ~ RCA Red Seal RL 01284. [In three-record box set with Opp. 135 and 141.] G Nov. 1978 ~ France: RCA Red Seal 644 550.

[CBS 65052. Poem 'Babi Yar' (original version) read in English, in a translation by George Reavey, by Lawrence Ferlinghetti and in Russian by Yevgeni Yevtushenko. San Francisco and New York poetry concerts. P early 1972.]

HMV ASD 3911. Original version. Dimiter Petkov (bass), Male voices of the London Symphony Chorus, Richard Hickox (chorus-master), London Symphony Orchestra, André PREVIN. P 5–6 July 1979, G Apr. 1981. *Reissued:* USA: Angel SZ 37661. I 1980 ~ Germany: Audiophile/ HMV ASD 3911. I limited LP reissue on 180g. vinyl 1995 ~ EMI Classics Double Forte Compact Discs CZS5 73369-2 (two-disc set). [Op. 93.] I May 1999, G Aug. 1999.

Philips LP 6514 120 (digital). Original version. John Shirley-Quirk (baritone), Bavarian Radio Male Chorus and Symphony Orchestra, Kirill KONDRASHIN. P Munich concert Dec. 1980, G Apr. 1982.

Decca 414 410-1DH2 (3 sides in two-record box set, digital). Original version. Marius Rintzler (bass), Male voices of the Concertgebouw Orchestra Choir, Concertgebouw Orchestra, Bernard HAITINK. [Opp. 143*a* and 79*a*.] P Amsterdam 14–15 Oct. 1984, G May and Sept. 1986. *Simultaneous issue:* Decca Compact Disc 417 261-2DH. G May 1986. *Reissued:* Decca Ovation Compact Disc 425 073-2DM. I Aug. 1993, G Nov. 1993 ~ London Compact Disc 444 439-2. [Ninth disc in eleven-disc set.] I June 1995.

USSR: Melodiya A10 00285 000 (3 sides in double album, digital). Original version. Anatoli Safiulin (bass), Basses of the Yurlov Republican Russian Choir, Stanislav Gusev (chorus-director), Veniamin Kapitonov and Vladimir Sorokin (chorus-masters), Aleksandr Suptel (violin), Olga Mnozhina (viola), Vasili Gorbenko (tuba), Ministry of Culture Symphony Orchestra, Gennadi ROZHDESTVENSKY. [22-minute talk

'Yevgeni Yevtushenko narrates his reminiscences' recorded in 1987.] P Moscow Aug. 1985, I 1988c. *Reissued:* Olympia Compact Disc OCD 132. I Nov. 1988, G May 1989 ~ Japan: JVC Compact Disc VCD 1216 ~ Germany: Melodia Eurodisc Compact Disc 258 491 ~ Olympia Compact Disc OCD 5006. [In Vol. 2 five-disc set of symphonies.] I Dec. 1990 ~ BMG Melodiya Compact Discs 74321 63460-2 (two-disc set). [Opp. 34; 112, and 107.] I Mar. 1999.

Chandos ABRD 1248 (digital) and Compact Disc CHAN 8540. Original version. Nikita Storojev (bass); Men of the CBSO Chorus, City of Birmingham Choir, and University of Warwick Chorus; City of Birmingham Orchestra, Okko KAMU. P Birmingham 9–10 Jan. 1987, I Sept. 1987, G Dec. 1987.

Virgin V 2536. Abbreviated original version first movement sung in English. John Shirley-Quirk (baritone), The Golden Age Singers, London Philharmonic Orchestra, Rudolf BARSHAI. ['Testimony Motion Picture Soundtrack'.] P 1987, I 1988.

Erato Nouveau Compact Disc ECD 75529. Original version. Nicola Ghiuselev (bass), Men of the Choral Arts Society of Washington, National Symphony Orchestra, Mstislav ROSTROPOVICH. P Kennedy Center, Washington Jan. 1988, G June 1989. *Reissued:* Teldec Compact Discs 0630-17046-2. [In twelve-disc set of Symphonies.] G Oct. 1997.

Naxos Compact Disc 8.550630. Peter Mikuláš (bass), Slovak Philharmonic Chorus, Czecho-Slovak Radio Symphony Orchestra, Ladislav SLOVÁK. P Bratislava 22–8 Nov. 1990, I Jan. 1993, G Nov. 1993. *Reissued:* Naxos Compact Discs 8.506003. [In six-disc set with Symphonies Nos. 5, 8, 9, 10, 11, and 14.] I 1993.

Koch Schwann Compact Disc 3 1393-2H1. John Shirley Quirk (baritone), Düsseldorf Musikverein Chorus, Hartmut Schmidt (chorus-master), Düsseldorf Symphony Orchestra, David SHALLON. P Düsseldorf concert Feb. 1991, I June 1995, G Aug. 1995

Teldec Compact Disc 4509 90848-2. Sergei Lieferkus (baritone), Men of the New York Choral Artists, Joseph Flummerfelt (chorus-master), New York Philharmonic Orchestra, Kurt MASUR. [Recitations by Yevgeni Yevtushenko of 'Babi Yar' and 'The Loss'.] P New York concert Jan. 1993, I Apr. 1994, G Oct. 1994.

Denon Compact Disc CO 75887. Robert Holl (bass), Chorus Viennensis, Guido Mancusi (chorus-master), Vienna Symphony Orchestra, Eliahu INBAL. P Vienna concert 13–17 May 1993, I Apr. 1994, G Sept. 1994.

Czech: Supraphon Compact Disc SU 0160-2. Peter Mikuláš (bass), Male Choirs of the Prague Philharmonic and Pavel Kühn Mixed Choir, Prague Symphony Orchestra, Maksim SHOSTAKOVICH. P Prague concert 1 Feb. 1995, I Mar. 1996, G Apr. 1996.

Sony Classical St Petersburg Classics Compact Disc SMK 66591. Sergei Baikov (bass), Estonia National Male Voice Choir, St Petersburg

Camerata Orchestra, Lithuanian Chamber Orchestra, Saulius SONDE-
TSKIS. P Vilnius July 1995, I June 1995, G July 1995.

Decca Compact Disc 444 791-2DH. Sergei Aleksashkin (bass), Sir
Anthony Hopkins (narrator), Chicago Symphony Chorus and Orchestra, Sir Georg SOLTI. Poems read in English before each movement. P
Chicago concerts 23–6 Feb. 1995 and narration taped in studio, I June
1995, G Aug. 1995.

Deutsche Grammophon Compact Disc 449 187-2GH. Anatoli
Kotscherga (bass), National Male Chorus of Estonia, Gothenburg Sym-
phony Orchestra, Neeme JÄRVI. P Gothenburg Nov. 1995, I Jan. 1997, G
June 1997.

Chandos Compact Disc CHAN 9690. Ayik Martyrosyan (bass), Russian State Symphonic Cappella, Russian State Symphony Orchestra,
Valeri POLYANSKY. P Moscow Conservatory Nov. 1996, I Nov. 1998.

BBC Proms Compact Disc BBCP 1002-2. Sergei Leiferkus (baritone),
Leeds Festival Chorus, Huddersfield Choral Society, BBC Philharmonic,
Vassili SINAISKY. [Tchaikovsky.] P Proms concert 21 Aug. 1998, I Aug.
1999, G Nov. 1999.

References: Aranovsky, Kondrashin (in *DSCH*), Ordzhonokidze (in Danilevich 1967), Sabinina, Tigranov, Vishnevskaya, and Yevtushenko (in *DSCH*).

Notes: Melodies of two Burns' settings from Opus 62 appear in this symphony. The theme of 'O, Wert Thou in the Cauld Blast' is quoted at fig. 13
in the first movement. For the significance of this quotation in the 'Anne
Frank episode' see *Shostakovich Reconsidered*, pp. 603–4. The music of the
third song, 'Macpherson before his Execution', is used fittingly between
figs 51 and 62 in the second movement, when Humour breaks into a
dashing dance and goes to his execution as a political prisoner.

Opus 114   Katerina Izmailova

Form: Revised version of the four-act opera *Lady Macbeth of Mtsensk District*,
Opus 29. New symphonic interludes between Scenes 1 and 2 and Scenes
7 and 8, changes made in Scene 3, minor revisions to the vocal lines, and
the eradication of the cruder passages of the libretto (undertaken by
Isaak Glikman at the request of the composer in March–April 1955).

Instrumentation: As Opus 29 with side drum militare and whip not specified and one less cornet in the off-stage band.

Composed: March 1955–31 January 1963. Revisions to the four acts completed on 24 December 1962; 9, 24, and 31 January 1963 respectively.
Some changes introduced into the score after the première.

Premières: 8 January 1963, Moscow Stanislavsky and Nemirovich-Danchenko
Theatre; décor by Iosif Sumbatashvili, produced by Lev Mikhailov,
and conducted by Gennadi Provatorov; principal roles—Eleonora

Andreyeva (Katerina), Gennadi Yefimov (Sergei), Eduard Bulavin (Boris), and M. Shchavinsky (Zinovi). [Unofficial première on 26 December 1962.]

   UK: 2 December 1963, Covent Garden, London; Marie Collier (Katerina), Charles Craig (Sergei), Otakar Kraus (Boris), Edward Downes (conductor). Produced by Vlado Habunek with décor by Božidar Rasiča—both invited from Zagreb.

   Scotland: Katerina's Arias from Acts 1 and 4: 26 August 1962, Edinburgh Festival, Usher Hall; Galina Vishnevskaya, London Symphony Orchestra, Igor Markevitch.

   Suite Nos. 1, 2, 5, and 4: 4 September 1962, Edinburgh Festival, Usher Hall; Barry, Ostlere and Shepherd Brass Band, John Faulds (conductor); Philharmonia Orchestra, Gennadi Rozhdestvensky.

Arrangements: Opus 114*a*—Suite of Five Fragments, not compiled by the composer, for large orchestra (with 2 harps and a 14-piece brass ensemble). In some performances a soprano aria replaces the orchestral No. 2.

1. Entr'acte between Ist and 2nd Scenes—Allegretto
2. Entr'acte between 2nd and 3rd Scenes—Allegro con brio
3. Entr'acte between 4th and 5th Scenes (Passacaglia)—Largo
4. Entr'acte between 6th and 7th Scenes—Allegretto
5. Entr'acte between 7th and 8th Scenes—Presto

Opus 114*b*—Suite of Four Orchestral Items arranged by James Conlon:

1. Dangerous Tension
2. Passacaglia
3. Katerina and Serge
4. The Drunkard

Opus 114*c*—Katerina Izmailova Symphonic Suite, based on themes from the opera by Veniamin Basner:

1. Katerina
2. Father-in-law
3. Night; Ghost
4. Arrest
5. Exile (Prison)

Translation of the libretto: English by Edward Downes, H. B. Partridge, and Julius Rudel; German by Enns Fried; Danish by Holger Boland; Norwegian by Bjørn Larssen; and Swedish by Lars Runsten.

Music: Autograph of the full and vocal scores preserved at the CIS Archives of Literature and Art. The first pages of Acts 1 and 4 of the full score and the first page of the vocal score—all of the 1963 editions designated Op. 29/114 by the composer—reproduced in Volumes 20, 21, and 22 respectively of *Collected Works*.

Muzyka, No. 544, 1963, vocal score listed as opus 29 / 114 with Russian text and music in copyist's hand, 520 pp., 29.5 cm.

Friends of Covent Garden, 1963; Shenval Press, London, 2nd edition 1964, libretto in English translation and synopsis by Edward Downes, and article by the composer, without music, 48 pp., 20 cm.

Hans Sikorski, No. 2129, 1964, German translation by Enns Fried, vocal score arr. Friedrich Buck, 35 cm.

Muzyka, No. 964, 1965, vocal score listed as Opus 29 / 114 with Russian and English texts—the latter by E. Downes, and preface by Lev Lebedinsky, 350 pp., 29 cm.

Muzyka, Nos. 2162 and 2162*a*, 1965, full score with Russian and English texts—the latter by E. Downes, and preface by L. Lebedinsky, in two volumes (Acts 1 and 2, 452 pp.; Acts 3 and 4, 260 pp.), 30 cm.

Muzyka, 1966, libretto only, in Russian, 109 pp., 15 cm.

Hans Sikorski, 1973, Danish translation by Holger Boland, vocal score revised by Friedrich Buck, 31.5 cm.

Hans Sikorski, 1975, Norwegian translation by Bjørn Larssen, rental only.

Hans Sikorski, 1979, Swedish translation by Lars Runsten, rental only.

Muzyka, No. 11679 (Volume 22 of *Collected Works*), 1985, vocal score, 30 cm.

Muzyka, Nos. 11693-4 (Volumes 20 and 21 of *Collected Works*), 1985, full score of two Acts in each, 30 cm.

DSCH Publishers, Moscow, 1995, full score and parts of V. Basner's Symphonic Suite available for hire.

Duration: Opera: 2 hrs 41 mins—2 hrs 59 mins. Film: 120 minutes. Five Entr'actes: 16' 30"–17' 59"; 15 minutes (Schirmer).

Opus 114*c*—Katerina Izmailova Symphonic Suite: 46' 27".

Films: *Katerina Izmailova.* Colour film of the opera, directed by Mikhail Shapiro for Lenfilm, 1966. Galina Vishnevskaya in the title role, Chorus and Orchestra of the Shevchenko Opera and Ballet Theatre, Kiev, conducted by Konstantin Simeonov. Shown in 1967 at the Cannes International Film Festival and the Aldeburgh and Edinburgh Festivals.

RCA Victor Red Seal Laser Disc 781202 and VHS Video 791202. Entr'actes from Scenes 1–2. Berlin Philharmonic Orchestra, Mstislav Rostropovich. ['Concert in Berlin'—Op. 29; Tchaikovsky and Schnittke.] P Philharmonie, Berlin 31 Dec. 1990, I 1992.

Recordings: RCA Red Seal RB 16271 (mono) and SB 2141. Katerina's Aria only. Galina VISHNEVSKAYA (soprano) and Aleksandr Dedyukhin (piano). [Rakhmaninov, Prokofiev, Tchaikovsky, and Glinka.] G Mar. 1962. *Reissued:* USA: RCA Victor LSC 2497. [As original release.] ~ USA: Time-Life 'Great Men of Music' box set STL 568. [Opp. 22*a*, 40, 47, 102, 110, and 135.] I 1979.

BBC Radio Classics Compact Disc 15656 91832. Katerina's arias from Act 1 Scene 3 and Act 4. Galina VISHNEVSKAYA (soprano), London

Symphony Orchestra, Igor Markevitch. [Opp. 114 Suite and 112; and Musorgsky.] P Edinburgh concert 26 Aug. 1962, I Oct. 1996.

BBC Radio Classics Compact Disc 15656 91832. Suite Op. 114*a*: Nos. 1, 2 [with added xylophone as Op. 29 score], 5, and 4. Philharmonia Orchestra, Gennadi ROZHDESTVENSKY. [Opp. 114 arias and 112; and Musorgsky.] P Edinburgh concert 4 Sept. 1962, I Oct. 1996.

USSR: Melodiya D 013709-16 (8 sides mono) and C 0871-8 (8 sides). Eleonora Andreyeva (Katerina), Eduard Bulavin (Boris), Vyacheslav Radzievsky (Zinovi), Gennadi Yefimov (Sergei), Dina Potapovskaya (Aksinya), Vyacheslav Fyodorkin (workman), Vasili Shtefutsa (coachman), Ley Yeliseyev (peasant), Vladimir Popov (janitor), Yevgeni Maksimenko (priest), Mikhail Tyuremnov (clerk), Nikolai Kozlov (worker), Vladimir Generalov (police sergeant), Konstantin Mogilevsky (policeman), Matvei Matveyev (teacher), Georgi Dudarev (old convict), Yevgeni Korenev (sentry), Nina Isakova (Sonyetka), Olga Borisova (woman convict); Chorus and Orchestra of the Stanislavsky and Nemirovich-Danchenko Musical Drama Theatre, Moscow; Gennadi PROVATOROV. P 1963, I 1964. *Reissued:* USSR: Melodiya D 14451-2 (10" mono) and C 989-90 (10"). Arias and scenes from Acts 1 and 4. I 1964–5 ~ USA: Angel Melodiya S 4160 (complete, 6 sides) and S 40022 (excerpts, 2 sides) ~ HMV Melodiya ASD 3204-7 in Set SLS 5050 (four-record box set, with libretto). G Aug. 1976 ~ France: Le Chant du Monde LDX 78400-3 (8 sides) ~ Germany: Melodia Eurodisc 89503-6 (8 sides) ~ USSR: Melodiya C 0871-8 (8 sides, with libretto). [In joint first and second box of *Collected Works on Records* with Op. 15.] I 1978.

Revelation Compact Disc RV 10059. Suite Op. 114*a*. USSR Ministry of Culture Symphony Orchestra, Gennadi ROZHDESTVENSKY. [Opp. 96 and 77.] P 10 Aug. 1965, I Aug. 1997.

USSR: Melodiya D 018233-4 (mono) and C 01359-60. Katerina's Aria from Act 4. Evelina STOITSEVA (soprano). [Arias and scenes from operas by Tchaikovsky, Ponchielli, Verdi, and Puccini.] P 1966.

USSR: Melodiya CM 02927-8. Katerina's Arias from Acts 1 and 4. Svetlana KORETSKAYA (soprano), Stanislavsky and Nemirovich-Danchenko Theatre Orchestra, Dmitri Kitayenko. [Borodin, Khrennikov, Puccini *et al.*] P 1971, I 1972.

USSR: Melodiya CM 04285-6. Katrina's aria from Act 4. Nina FOMINA (soprano), Bolshoi Theatre Orchestra, Mark Ermler. [Glinka, Tchaikovsky, Shebalin *et al.*] P 1973, I 1974*b*. *Reissued:* USSR: Melodiya C10 06871-2. ['Bolshoi Theatre Soloists Sing'—Shchedrin, Molchanov, Prokofiev *et al.*] I 1976*d*.

USSR: Melodiya M10 39657-8 (10" mono). Katerina's Aria from Act 4. Nadezhda KRASNAYA (soprano) and Nataliya Rassudova (piano). [Tchaikovsky, Shaporin, Schubert *et al.*] P concert 1973, I 1977*d*.

USSR: Melodiya C10 18239008. Entr'acte arr. for wind orchestra. Bolshoi Theatre Wind Orchestra, Vladimir ANDROPOV. [Glinka, Verdi, Shchedrin *et al.*] I 1983*b*.

USSR: Melodiya C10 21393 004 (five-record box set, synopsis but no libretto). Gizela Tsipola (Katerina), Aleksandr Zagrebelnyi (Boris), Vladimir Gurov (Zinovi), Sergei Dubrovin (Sergei), Oksana Yatsenko (Aksinya), Andrei Ishchenko (workman), Yuri Khomich (coachman), Nikolai Khoruzhy (peasant), Ivan Chornyi (janitor), Georgi Krasulya (priest), Stepan Matveyev (clerk), Vladimir Lositsky (police sergeant), Anatoli Kocherga (old convict), Aleksandr Chulyok-Zagrai (sentry), Galina Tuftina (Sonyetka), Aza Bakanova (woman convict); Chorus and Orchestra of the Kiev Shevchenko Academic Theatre of Opera and Ballet, Lev Venediktov (chorus-master), Irina Molostova (producer), Stepan TURCHAK. P 1983, I 1985*b*. *Reissued:* France: Le Chant du Monde Compact Discs LDC 278 1021-3 (three-disc set, French and English synopses and French libretto). I Oct. 1989, G Jan. 1990.

Chandos ABRD 1279 (digital) and Compact Disc CHAN 8587. Suite Op. 114*a*. Scottish National Orchestra, Neeme JÄRVI. [Opp. 70, 96, and 16.] P Glasgow 14–17 Apr. 1987, I Mar. 1988, G July 1988. *Reissued:* Chandos Compact Discs 7000/1 (two-disc set). [Opp. 27*a*, 96, and Sans op. P.] I Sept. 1994, G May 1995.

Germany: Deutsche Schallplatten Compact Disc DS 1035-2. Suite Op. 114*b* arr. J. Conlon. Bohuslav Martinů Philharmonic Orchestra, Elbert Lechtman STEINBERG. [Op. 47.] P Ziln, Czech June 1994, I Nov. 1995.

Germany: Capriccio Compact Disc 10 780. Suite Opus 114*a*—not the 1934 version as stated. Cologne Radio Symphony Orchestra, Mikhail YUROVSKY. [Opp. 119 and 4.] P Cologne 12–14 Feb. 1996, I Oct. 1999, G Dec. 1999.

Japan: Canyon Classics Compact Disc PCCL 00356. Suite Op. 114*c* arr. V. Basner. Moscow Radio Symphony Orchestra, Vladimir FEDOSEYEV. [Op. 70.] P Moscow 18 and 19 Apr. 1996.

Austria: Calig Compact Disc CAL 50 992. Suite Op. 114*c* arr. V. Basner. Florian Zwiauer (violin), Wilfried Rehm (cello), Vienna Symphony Orchestra, Vladimir FEDOSEYEV. P Vienna concert 25–7 Feb. 1997, I Jan. 1998, G Apr. 1998.

Czech: Supraphon Compact Disc SU 3415-2. Suite Op. 114*a*, Nos. 5, 1–4. Prague Symphony Orchestra, Maksim SHOSTAKOVICH. [Opp. 54 and 22*a*.] P Prague concert 2 Mar. 1999, I and G Awards (Oct.) 1999.

References: Bogdanova, Britten, Fay, Gukovsky *et al.*, Rotbaum, Sabinina (in Danilevich 1967), Sagayev, Sokolsky, and Vishnevskaya.

Note: The score carries the following 'Composer's Note'. 'The director of any opera house intending to produce the opera *Katerina Izmailova* should bear in mind the following: No cuts whatever are permitted. There are in the opera a number of episodes where the soloists, chorus, and the *banda* perform backstage. The volume of sound should be so regulated that they are well heard in the auditorium. Mutes are not applied to the double-basses, so where all the string parts are marked *con sord.,* but the double-bass part has no such markings, this should not be regarded as a misprint.'

Opus 115   Overture on Russian and Kirghiz Folksongs

Form: Occasional overture for orchestra, marked 'Moderato—Allegro non troppo,—Adagio—Allegro—Presto'. The folksongs developed are 'O, You Tramps'—collected by Aleksandr Medvedev in the Omsk region in 1959; 'Tyryldan' (a mythical creature) and 'Op Maida' (thresher's song)— being Nos. 3 and 8 from Viktor Vinogradov's collection, *One Hundred Kirghiz Songs and Tunes,* published in Moscow, 1956.

Instrumentation: piccolo, 2 flutes, 2 oboes, 2 B flat clarinets, 2 bassoons, contrabassoon ~ 4 horns, 2 trumpets, 3 trombones, tuba ~ timpani, triangle, cymbals ~ 1st violins (16), 2nd violins (14), violas (12), cellos (12), double-basses (10). String strength quoted to be regarded as the minimum.

Composed: September 1963, at Repino, in honour of the 100th anniversary of the voluntary incorporation of Kirghizia into the Russian Empire.

Premières: 10 October 1963, Moscow Conservatory Bolshoi Hall; USSR Symphony Orchestra, Konstantin Ivanov.

   2 November 1963, Theatre of Opera and Ballet, Frunze, Kirghizia.

   UK public: 14 December 1972, Glasgow City Hall; Glasgow Orchestral Society, John McLeod.

Music: The autograph score, presented to the Central Committee of the Communist Party of Kirghizia by the composer, preserved at the Frunze Museum.

   Music Fund of the USSR, 1963.

   Muzyka, No. 3729, 1967, 28.5 cm.

   Muzyka, No. 11687 (in Volume 11 of *Collected Works* with Sans op. U, Opp. 96, 130, and 131), 1984, 30 cm.

Duration: Approx. 8 minutes in score; 9' 10"–10' 25"; 9 minutes (Sadovnikov).

Recordings: Czech: Praga Compact Disc PR 250 040 (mono). Moscow Philharmonic Orchestra, Kirill KONDRASHIN. [Op. 65.] P Prague broadcast 14 Oct. 1964, G Sept. 1993.

   USSR: Melodiya CM 02581-2. Moscow Radio Symphony Orchestra, Maksim SHOSTAKOVICH. [Op. 10.] P 1971. *Reissued:* HMV Melodiya ASD 2781. [Ballet Suites, Sans op. P.] G May 1972 ~ USA: Angel Melodiya S 40192. [Op. 10.] I 1972 ~ France: Le Chant du Monde LDX 78515 K. [Op. 10.]

   Decca SXDL 7577 (digital). Concertgebouw Orchestra, Bernard HAITINK. [Op. 112.] P Amsterdam 1 Feb. 1982, G June 1983. *Reissued:* USA: LDR 71077 (digital). [Op. 112.] ~ Decca Compact Disc 411 939-2DH2. [In two-disc set with Opp. 54 and 103.] G Aug. 1985.

   Deutsche Grammophon Compact Disc 427 616-2GH. Gothenberg Symphony Orchestra, Neeme JÄRVI. [Opp. 141 and 131.] P Gothenberg

May 1988, I Aug. 1989, G May 1991. *Reissued:* Deutsche Grammophon Classikon Compact Disc 469 029-2GCL. [Opp. 141 and 131.] G Aug. 2000.
Academy Sound and Vision Compact Disc CD DCA 707. Royal Philharmonic Orchestra, Enrique BÁTIZ. [Opp. 47 and 131; Sans op. U.] P Mitcham 1990, I June 1990, G Sept. 1990. *Reissued:* IMG Records Compact Disc IMGCD 1609. [Opp. 47 and 131; Sans op. U.] I June 1994.
Reference: Krylova (in Daragan).

Opus 116   Hamlet

Form: Music for the black and white film of William Shakespeare's tragedy *Hamlet, Prince of Denmark,* in Boris Pasternak's Russian translation, directed by Grigori Kozintsev for Lenfilm. Scored for large symphony orchestra (with harp, harpsichord, and piano). Items with tempo indication are included in Volume 42 of *Collected Works:*

1. Overture 'Elsinore'—Largo (No. 1 in the Suite Opus 116*a*)
2. [Decree of the King]
3. Military Music—Allegro [Numbered No. 2 in *Collected Works*]
4. [Royal Fanfare] [No. 3 in *Collected Works*—tempo not stated]
5. Ball at the Palace (No. 2 in the Suite)
6. Story of Horatio and the Ghost—Adagio
7. [Dance of Ophelia]
8. The Ball—Allegretto
9. The Ghost (No. 3 in the Suite)
10. Hamlet's parting with Ophelia—Andante
11. [Hamlet in thought or Palace Music]—Moderato
12. Hamlet's monologue: 'What a piece of work is man!'
13. Arrival of the Players (No. 6 in the Suite)
14. Hamlet's soliloquy: 'Fie upon't! foh! About my brain'—Moderato non troppo
15. The Presentation
16. Hamlet's soliloquy: 'To be, or not to be'—Adagio
17. [Preparation for the spectacle]
18. [Royal fanfare]
19. In the Garden (Court procession) (No. 4 in the Suite)
20. Booth fanfare—Allegro
21. Scene of the Poisoning (No. 5 in the Suite)
22. Flutes—Presto
23. Conscience
24. Hamlet and Gertrude (The Ghost in the Queen's presence)
25. Hamlet's soliloquy and scene on board ship
26. Song of Ophelia—Andantino
27. The Madness of Ophelia—Adagio
28. Death of Ophelia (No. 7 in the Suite)

29. [Song of the Gravedigger]—Moderato non troppo
30. [Hamlet's monologue: 'Alas, poor Yorick!']—Largo
31. War March
32. The Duel between Hamlet and Laertes
33. Death of Hamlet ('The rest is silence')   } (No. 8 in the Suite)
34. Funeral of Hamlet

Instrumentation: piccolo, 2 flutes, 2 oboes, 2 clarinets (A and B flat), 2 bassoons ~ 4 horns, 3 trumpets, 3 trombones, tuba ~ timpani, triangle, tambourine, side drum, whip, bass drum, gong ~ xylophone, celesta, harp, harpsichord, piano ~ strings.

Composed: 1963–4, at Moscow, for the occasion of the 400th anniversary celebration of Shakespeare's birth.

Premières: Film first shown on 24 April 1964 in Moscow. Film score performed by the Leningrad Philharmonic Orchestra under Nikolai Rabinovich.

Suite Opus 116a: 10 February 1965, Leningrad; concert version.

Concert scenario: Hamlet: 26 January 1993, broadcast from the Usher Ball, Edinburgh; Royal Scottish Orchestra, Gennadi Rozhdestvensky.

Arrangements: Opus 116a—Suite assembled by Lev Atovmyan in 1964:

1. Introduction—Largo
2. Ball at the Palace—Presto
3. The Ghost—Largo
4. In the Garden—Moderato ma non troppo
5. Scene of the Poisoning—Largo
6. Arrival and Scene of the Players—Allegro
7. Ophelia—Andante
8. The Duel and Death of Hamlet—Allegro

Reduction for piano of Nos. 4–6, each preceded by Hamlet's motto, by Zinaida Vitkind.

Concert scenario: Hamlet A 32-minute suite of sixteen items culled from Shostakovich's film and stage scores, Opp. 116 and 32 respectively, by Gennadi Rozhdestvenaky, interspersed with fanfares from Aleksandr Varlamov's incidental music to *Hamlet* composed in 1837. The numbers arranged in the following order: Opp. 116a Nos. 3 and 2; 116 Nos. 22, 8, 22, 11; 116a No. 6; 116 No. 22; 32a Nos. 3 and 5; 116 No. 16; 116a No. 7; 116, Nos. 10, 26, 27, and 29; 32a No. 11; and 116a No. 8. Side drum and Varlamov trumpet fanfare added to the three sections of the solo flute theme of Op. 116 No. 22.

Music: The autograph film score preserved in the Shostakovich family archive. The first page of the autograph score is reproduced in Volume 42 of *Collected Works*.

Music Fund of the USSR, 1964, full score of the Suite.
Muzyka, No. 5059, 1968, full score of the Suite, 29 cm.
Muzyka, Leningrad, No. 2330 (with Op. 97*a*), 1978, Suite Nos. 4, 6, and 5 arr. for piano by Z. Vitkind, 28.5 cm. [Originally published in 1967.]

    Muzyka, No. 10890 (in Volume 42 of *Collected Works* with Opp. 75, 78, 80, 82, 95, 97, 111, 132, and 137), 1987, fifteen items, 30 cm.

Duration: Film: 150 minutes. Suite Opus 116*a:* 26' 40"–35' 46"; 42 minutes (Sadovnikov).

Film: Moskwood Video, Haarlem, Netherlands, No. 2644, *c.*1993, videocassette with Dutch subtitles, 142 minutes.

Ballets: *Hamlet.* V. Kamkov, Kirov Ballet, Leningrad Kirov Theatre, 1969; filmed for television.

    Hamlet. M. Mnatsakanyan, Petrozavod Musical-Dramatic Theatre, 1971 and Yerevan, 1972.

    Hamlet. L. Monreal, Boston Ballet, 1975.

    The Idiot. Valeri Panov, Deutsche Oper Ballet, West Berlin, 15 June 1979.

    The Storm. André Prokovsky, London Festival Ballet new splinter group, world première at King's Theatre, Southsea, 27 May 1981. The 40-minute ballet based on Aleksandr Ostrovsky's play of 1859 choreographed to Shostakovich's film score. Décor and costumes by Peter Farmer, scenario by John Aitken, with music selected and arranged by John Riley.

Recordings: USSR: Melodiya D 17691-2 (10" mono). Suite Nos. 1–5, 7 and Score No. 34. Moscow Radio Symphony Orchestra, Nikolai RABINOVICH. P 1966. *Reissued:* USA: Cinema Records LP 8003 (mono). Orchestra and conductor uncredited. [Op. 111*a*.] ~ USSR: Melodiya C10 09508-CM 0298 (stereo). (In fourth box of Part 1 of *Collected Works on Records* with Op. 32*a*.] I 1978 ~ Germany: Melodia Eurodisc 28665 XHK. [On fourth record in four-record film music album with Opp. 97*a* and 120.] I 1981.

    Decca Phase 4 PFS 4315. Suite Nos. 1–3, 5, 6, and 8. National Philharmonic Orchestra, Bernard HERRMANN. ['Music from Great Shakespearean Films'—Walton and Rózsa.] P London Mar. 1974, G Aug. 1975. *Reissued:* USA: London 21132 ~ Decca Cinema Gala Compact Disc 421 268-2DA. [Walton and Rózsa.] I 1989 ~ Unicorn-Kanchana Souvenir Compact Disc UKCD 2066. [Myaskovsky and Kabalevsky.] I Apr. 1994, G Feb. 1995 ~ London Compact Disc 455 156-2LPF. [Walton and Rózsa.] I Oct. 1997.

    RCA Victor Red Seal Compact Disc RD 87763. Suite Nos. 1–8. Belgian Radio Symphony Orchestra, José SEREBRIER. [Opp. 137 and 111.] P Brussels 1988, I June 1988, G Oct. 1988 ~ RCA Classical Navigator Compact Disc 74321 24212-2. Suite Nos. 1–8. [Op. 47.] I June 1995.

    Germany: Capriccio Compact Disc 10 298. Suite Nos. 1–8. Berlin Radio Symphony Orchestra, Leonid GRIN. [Op. 97*a*.] P Berlin Nov. and Dec. 1988, I Feb. 1990.

USA: Pro-Arte Fanfare Compact Disc CDD 551. Suite Nos. 1, 2, 4, 5, and 8. Chicago Sinfonietta, Paul FREEMAN. ['Shostakovich Film Festival'—Opp. 97, 111, 16, and 35.] P Oak Park, Illinois May 1990, I Aug. 1991. *Reissued:* Conifer Classic Compact Disc Class 7086. [As USA release.] I Nov. 1991.

Koch International Classics Compact Disc 37274-2. Suite Nos. 1, 2, and 4. KBS Symphony Orchestra, Vakhtang JORDANIA. [Opp. 97*a* and 58*a*.] P Seoul, Korea Feb. 1994, I Sept. 1994, G Dec. 1994.

Varèse Sarabande Compact Disc VSD 5752. Suite Nos. 2 and 8. Royal Scottish National Orchestra, Cliff EIDELMAN. ['Shakespearian classics from stage and screen'—North, Walton, Doyle *et al.*] P Glasgow 5–6 Aug. 1996, G Mar. 1997.

Denon Compact Disc CO 18004. Score Nos. 26, 27, 29, and 30 arr. for chamber orchestra. I SOLISTI ITALIANI, Edoardo Farina (harpsichord/piano in Nos. 26, 27, and 30), Alessandro Zucchi (percussion in No. 29), and Daniele Ruggieri (piccolo in No. 29). [Op. 97; Walton, Lavagnino, Rossellini *et al.*] P Piazzola sul Brenta 9–18 Aug. 1995. NB. 'Cemetry' No. 29 is not from Op. 111.

Decca Compact Disc 460 792-2DH11. Score Nos. 1, 11, 5, 8, 19, 3, and 21. Royal Concertgebouw Orchestra, Riccardo CHAILLY. ['The Film Album'—Opp. 33, 26, 56, 55, 132, 76*a*, and 97.] P Amsterdam 6, 19, and 22 May 1998, I Mar. 1999, G Apr. 1999.

Monte Carlo: Bel Air Music Compact Disc BAM 2000. Ball at the Palace. Russian Philharmonic Orchestra. [Opp. 97 and 76; Sviridov, Dashkevich, Prokofiev *et al.*] P Moscow Radio Studio Jan 2000.

References: Egorova and Nikelberg.

Note: On the film sound-track a harpsichord sounds during The Madness of Ophelia (No. 27) whereas on the screen she dances to a lute.

Opus 117   Quartet No. 9 in E flat major

Form: String quartet in five linked movements:

1. Moderato con moto *attacca*
2. Adagio *attacca*
3. Allegretto *attacca*
4. Adagio *attacca*
5. Allegro

Composed: 2–28 May 1964. Completed at Moscow.
Dedication: Irina Antonovna Shostakovich (third wife).
Premières: 20 November 1964, Moscow Conservatory Malyi Hall and 21 November 1964, Glinka Concert Hall, Leningrad; Beethoven Quartet (Dmitri Tsyganov, Vasili Shirinsky, Vadim Borisovsky, and Sergei Shirinsky).

UK: 14 November 1965, Conway Hall, London; Alberni Quartet (Dennis Simons, Howard Davis, John White, and Gregory Baron).
Arrangement: Reduction for piano four hands by Anatoli Dmitriev.
Music: Autograph score preserved at the CIS Archives of Literature and Art.
Muzyka, No. 1956, 1966, score, 20 cm.
Muzyka, No. 1957, 1966, parts, 29 cm.
Boosey & Hawkes, No. 793 (plate no. 19520), 1966, score, 19 cm.
Boosey & Hawkes, No. 19524, 1966, parts, 29 cm.
Muzyka, Leningrad, No. 766 (in Volume 3 with Quartets 10 and 11 arr. for piano four hands by A. Dmitriev), 1967, 29.5 cm.
Muzyka, No. 10284 (in Volume 36 of *Collected Works* Quartets 9–15), 1980, 30 cm.
Hans Sikorski, No. 2213, 1980, parts, 31.5 cm.
Hans Sikorski, No. 2267 (with Op. 118), 1981, score, 21 cm.
Duration: 26 minutes in score; 24' 27"–28' 35"; 25' 00" (Plaistow).
Recordings: USSR: Melodiya D 015683-4 (mono) and C 01053-4. BEETHOVEN QUARTET (personnel as at première). [Op. 118.] P 20 Nov. 1964. *Reissued:* USA: Consonance Blue Label Compact Disc 81.3009. [Vol. 5—Opp. 118 and 122.] I Mar. 1996.

USSR: Melodiya D 019519-20 (mono) and C 01459-60. BORODIN QUARTET (Rostislav Dubinsky, Yaroslav Aleksandrov, Dmitri Shebalin, Valentin Berlinsky). [Opp. 122 and 11.] P and I 1967. *Reissued:* USA: Seraphim Melodiya S 6035. [In three-record box set with Op. 11 and Quartets 6–8, 10, and 11.] ~ HMV Melodiya HQS 1323 in Set SLS 879. [Op. 110.] G June 1974 ~ East Germany: Eterna 8 26 598. [Opp. 122 and 11.]

Saydisc Amon Ra SAR 1. DARTINGTON QUARTET (Colin Sauer, Malcolm Latchem, Keith Lovell, Michael Evans). [Op. 83.] P 1973, G May 1973.

Finland: HMV 5E 063-35038. VOCES INTIMÆ QUARTET (Jorma Rakhonen, Ari Angervo, Mauri Pietikäinen, Veikko Höylä). [Segerstam.] P 1974.

L'Oiseau-Lyre DSLO 30. FITZWILLIAM QUARTET (Christopher Rowland, Jonathan Sparey, Alan George, Ioan Davies). [Op. 118.] P 15–16 Dec. 1977, G Feb. 1979. *Reissued:* Decca 188 D5 in Set D 188 D7. [Op. 118.] G Feb. 1981 ~ Decca Enterprise Compact Discs 433 078-2DM6. [On fourth disc of six-disc set with Opp. 110 and 118.] I Apr. 1992, G June 1992.

USSR: Melodiya C10 11615-6. TANEYEV QUARTET (Vladimir Ovcharek, Grigori Lutsky, Vissarion Soloviev, Iosif Levinzon). [In first box of Part 2 of *Collected Works on Records* with Op. 118.] P 1978, I 1980. *Reissued:* Japan: JVC Victor 5349. [Op. 118.] ~ USSR: Melodiya Compact Disc SUCD11 00311. [Op. 73.] I 1991*d*.

USSR: Melodiya C10 21943 000. BORODIN QUARTET (Mikhail Kopelman, Andrei Abramenkov, Dmitri Shebalin, Valentin Berlinsky). [Op. 92.] P Moscow concert 27 Sept. 1981, I 1985*d*. *Reissued:* HMV Melodiya EX 270339-3 (DMM). [In seven-record box set of 15 Quartets plus Quintet.] G Mar. 1986 ~ EMI Compact Disc CDC7 49266-2. [Opp. 49 and 133.] I Nov. 1987 ~ Japan: Victor Musical Industries Compact Disc VICC 40021.

[Opp. 110 and 118.] I 1990 ~ EMI Compact Discs CMS5 65032-2. [In six-disc set of 15 Quartets plus Quintet.] I Mar. 1994 ~ BMG Melodiya Compact Discs 74321 40711-2 (six-disc set). [Opp. 110 and 118.] I June 1997. USSR: Melodiya C10 28483 000. SHOSTAKOVICH QUARTET (Andrei Shishlov, Sergei Pishchugin, Aleksandr Galkovsky, Aleksandr Korchagin). [Op. 92.] P 1985, I 1989*d*. *Reissued:* Olympia Compact Disc OCD 533. ['Complete Quartets, Vol. 3'—Opp. 101 and 110.] I May 1994, G Sept. 1994.

Teldec Classics Compact Disc 244 919-2. BRODSKY QUARTET (Michael Thomas, Ian Belton, Paul Cassidy, Jacqueline Thomas). [Opp. 108 and 110.] P Berlin Feb. 1989, I Oct. 1989, G May 1990. *Reissued:* Teldec Compact Discs 9031 71702-2. [On fourth disc of six-disc set with Opp. 110 and 118.] I Nov. 1990, G June 1992.

USA: ESS.A.Y. Compact Disc CD 1010. MANHATTAN QUARTET (Eric Lewis, Roy Lewis, John Dexter, Judith Glyde). [Op. 118.] P Jersey City 14–15 May 1990. *Reissued:* Koch Schwann Compact Disc 310 166. ['Complete String Quartets, Vol. 4' with Op. 118.] I Dec. 1992.

USA: MCA Classics Art & Electronics Compact Disc AED 10212. GEORGIA STATE RADIO QUARTET (Levan Chkheidze, Georgi Khintibidze, Archil Kharadze, Revaz Machabeli). [Tsintsadze.] P Moscow concert 2–3 June 1990, I 1991.

Netherlands: Etcetera Compact Disc KTC 1182. ELEONORA QUARTET (Eleonora Yakubova, Irina Pavlikhina, Anton Yaroshenko, Mikhail Shumsky). [Sans op. D and Op. 73.] P Moscow Jan. 1994, I Sept. 1994.

Naxos Compact Disc 8.550973. ÉDER QUARTET (János Selmeczi, Péter Szüts, Sándor Papp, György Éder). ['Complete Quartets, Vol. 2'—Opp. 49 and 110.] P Brussels 14–17 Feb. 1994, I Nov. 1994, G Oct. 1995.

Japan: Toshiba EMI Compact Disc TOCE 9306. MORGAŬA QUARTET (Eiji Arai, Takashi Aoki, Hisashi Ono, Ryoichi Fujimori). [Opp. 92 and 100.] P 23–5 Oct. 1996, I Jan. 1997.

Deutsche Grammophon Compact Disc 463 284-2GH5 (five-disc set). EMERSON QUARTET (Eugene Drucker, Philip Setzer, Lawrence Dutton, David Finkel). ['Complete Quartets, Vol. 3'—Opp. 108, 110, and 118.] P Aspen, Colorado concert July 1998, G June 2000.

Hyperion Compact Disc CDA 67155. ST PETERSBURG QUARTET (Alla Aranovskaya, Ilya Teplyakov, Aleksei Koptev, Leonid Shukayev). [Opp. 92 and 108.] P St Petersburg Studio Dec. 2000, I Apr. 2001, G July 2001.

Chandos Compact Disc CHAN 9955. SORREL QUARTET (Gina McCormack, Catherine Yates, Sarah-Jane Bradley, Helen Thatcher). ['Complete Quartets, Vol. 3'—Opp. 110 and 138.] P The Maltings, Snape 26–30 Mar. 2001, I Sept. 2001, G Awards (Oct.) 2001.

References: Hopkins and Martynov.

Note: The first version, a 'Children's Quartet', was completed in the autumn of 1961 but in Shostakovich's own words, 'in an attack of healthy self-criticism, I burnt it in the stove'. (Glikman, p. 168).

Opus 118   Quartet No. 10 in A flat major

Form: String quartet in four movements:

1. Andante
2. Allegretto furioso
3. Adagio *attacca*
4. Allegretto—Andante

Composed: 9–20 July 1964, at Dilizhan Composers' Retreat, Armenia.

Dedication: Moisei Samuilovich Vainberg (composer).

Premières: 20 November 1964, Moscow Conservatory Malyi Hall and 21 November 1964, Glinka Concert Hall, Leningrad; Beethoven Quartet (Dmitri Tsyganov, Vasili Shirinsky, Vadim Borisovsky, and Sergei Shirinsky).

'Western World'; 1965, Weller Quartet recording.

UK: 3 April 1966, Conway Hall, London; Alberni Quartet (Dennis Simons, Howard Davis, John White, and Gregory Baron).

Arrangements: Opus 118*a*—'Symphony for Strings'; for string orchestra by Rudolf Barshai. Reduction for piano four hands by Anatoli Dmitriev.

Music: Autograph score preserved at the CIS Archives of Literature and Art.

Muzyka, No. 2264, 1965, parts, 31 cm.

Muzyka, No. 2265, 1965, score, 20 cm.

Muzyka, 1966, parts, 29 cm.

Musica Rara, No. 1089, 1966, parts, 31 cm.

Musica Rara, No. 1094, 1966, score, 18.5 cm.

Muzyka, Leningrad, No. 766 (in Volume 3 with Quartets 9 and 11 arr. for piano four hands by A. Dmitriev), 1967, 29.5 cm.

Hans Sikorski, 1968, 'Symphony for Strings' arr. R. Barshai, parts available for hire, 31.5 cm.

Muzyka, No. 10284 (in Volume 36 of *Collected Works* Quartets 9–15), 1980, 30 cm.

Hans Sikorski, No. 2214, 1981, parts, 31.5 cm.

Hans Sikorski, No. 2267 (with Op. 117), 1981, score, 21 cm.

DSCH Publishers, Moscow, 1995, full score and parts of R. Barshai's instrumentation available for hire.

Duration: 22 minutes in score; 21' 21"–24' 46"; Opus 118*a*—24' 57"–26' 21"

Recordings: USSR: Melodiya D 015683-4 (mono) and C 01053-4. BEETHOVEN QUARTET (personnel as at première). [Op. 117.] P concert 20 Nov. 1964. *Reissued:* Japan: Triton Meldac Compact Disc MECC 26022 (mono). [Hindemith.] I June 1995 ~ USA: Consonance Blue Label Compact Disc 81.3009. [Vol. 5—Opp. 117 and 122.] I Mar. 1996.

Decca LXT 6196 (mono) and SXL 6196. WELLER QUARTET (Walter Weller, Alfred Staar, Helmut Weis, Ludwig Beinl). [Berg.] P 1964, G Nov. 1965. *Reissued:* USA: London STS 15287. [Berg.] I 1976.

USSR: Melodiya D 019211-2 (mono) and C 01443-4. BORODIN QUARTET (Rostilav Dubinsky, Yaroslav Aleksandrov, Dmitri Shebalin, Valentin Berlinsky). [Op. 110.] P and I 1967. *Reissued:* USA: Seraphim Melodiya S 6035. [In three-record box set with Op. 11 and Quartets 6–9 and 11.] ~ HMV Melodiya HQS 1324 in Set SLS 879. [Op. 133.] G June 1974.

Pye GGC 4104 (mono) and GSGC 14104. AMICI QUARTET (Lionel Bentley, Michael Jones, Christopher Wellington, Peter Halling). [Ives.] P 1967, G Mar. 1968. *Reissued:* Precision Records & Tapes GSGC 2608. [Ives.] I 1983.

L'Oiseau-Lyre DSLO 30. FITZWILLIAM QUARTET (Christopher Rowland, Jonathan Sparey, Alan George, Ioan Davies). [Op. 117.] P 15–16 Dec. 1976, G Feb. 1979. *Reissued:* Decca 188 D5 in Set D 188 D7. [Op. 117.] G Feb. 1981 ~ Decca Enterprise Compact Discs 433 078-2DM6. [On fourth disc of six-disc set with Opp. 110 and 117.] I Apr. 1992, G June 1992.

USSR: Melodiya C10 11615-6. TANEYEV QUARTET (Vladimir Ovcharek, Grigori Lutsky, Vissarion Soloviev, Iosif Levinzon). [In first box of Part 2 of *Collected Works on Records* with Op. 117.] P 1978, I 1980. *Reissued:* Japan: JVC Victor 5349. [Op. 117.] ~ USSR: Melodiya Compact Disc SUCD11 00310. [Op. 68.] I 1991*d*.

USSR: Melodiya C10 17579-80. BORODIN QUARTET (Mikhail Kopelman, Andrei Abramenkov, Dmitri Shebalin, Valentin Berlinsky). [Op. 122.] P 1981, I 1983*a*. *Reissued:* HMV Melodiya EX 270339-3 (DMM). [In seven-record box set of 15 Quartets plus Quintet.] G Mar. 1986 ~ EMI Compact Disc CDC7 49269-2. [Opp. 138 and 142.] I Nov. 1987, G Sept. 1988 ~ Japan: Victor Musical Industries Compact Disc VICC 40021. [Opp. 110 and 117.] I 1990 ~ EMI Compact Discs CMS5 65032-2. [In six-disc set of 15 Quartets plus Quintet.] I Mar. 1994 ~ BMG Melodiya Compact Discs 74321 40711-2 (six-disc set). [Opp. 110 and 117.] I June 1997.

Phoenix DGS 1038 (digital). Symphony for Strings arr. R. Barshai. Phoenix Chamber Orchestra, Julian BIGG. [Op. 110*a*.] P London Dec. 1983, G Aug. 1984. *Reissued:* Trax Classique Compact Disc TRX-CD 110. [Opp. 110*a*.] G Sept. 1987.

Chandos ABRD 1155 (digital) and Compact Disc CHAN 8443. Arr. R. Barshai. I Musici de Montréal, Yuli TUROVSKY. [Op. 102.] P Montreal 5–6 Aug. 1985, I Jan. 1986, G May and July 1986. *Reissued:* Chandos Enchant Compact Disc CHAN 7061. [Opp. 110*a* and 79*a*.] I July 1997 ~ Chandos Collect Compact Disc CHAN 6617. [Opp. 110*a* and 79*a*.] I July 2000, G Feb. 2001.

Olympia Compact Disc OCD 534. SHOSTAKOVICH QUARTET (Andrei Shislov, Sergei Pishchugin, Aleksandr Galkovsky, Aleksandr Korchagin). ['Complete Quartets, Vol. 4'—Opp. 122 and 144.] P 1985, I May 1994. *Reissued:* Classic CD 51. First movement. [Stravinsky, Mozart, Arnold *et al.*] I July 1994.

USA: Centaur Compact Disc CRC 2034. MANHATTAN QUARTET (Eric Lewis, Roy Lewis, John Dexter, Judith Glyde). [Op. 101.] P 1986, I Nov. 1988, G June 1989.

Deutsche Grammophon Compact Disc 429 229-2GH. Symphony for Strings arr. Barshai. Chamber Orchestra of Europe, Rudolf BARSHAI. [Op. 110*a*.] P Berlin Mar. 1989, I Mar. 1990, G May 1990.

Teldec Compact Discs 9031 71702-2. BRODSKY QUARTET (Michael Thomas, Ian Belton, Paul Cassidy, Jacqueline Thomas). [On fourth disc of six-disc set with Opp. 110 and 117.] P Berlin July 1989, I Nov. 1990, G June 1992. *Reissued:* Teldec Compact Disc 9031 73108-2. [Opp. 101 and 142.] I June 1991.

Germany: Fidelio Compact Disc 8838. Symphony for Strings arr. Barshai. New Amsterdam Sinfonietta, Lev MARKIZ. [Op. 110*a*.] P Amsterdam Sept. 1989, I 1990. *Reissued:* Netherlands: Vanguard Classics Compact Discs 99306 (two-disc set). [Opp. 110*a*, 134, and 147.] I Aug. 1999.

Koch Schwann Compact Disc 311 149. Arr. Barshai. Camerata Assindia, Robert MAXYM. [Glazunov.] P Essen Oct.–Nov. 1989, I Dec. 1991.

USA: ESS.A.Y. Compact Disc CD 1010. MANHATTAN QUARTET (personnel as above). [Op. 117.] P Jersey City 14–15 May 1990. *Reissued:* Koch Schwann Compact Disc 310 166. ['Complete String Quartets, Vol. 4' with Op. 117.] I Dec. 1992.

Claves Compact Disc 50 9115. Arr. Barshai. Kremlin Chamber Orchestra, Misha RACHLEVSKY. [Opp. 110*a* and 144*a*.] P Moscow concert Oct.–Nov. 1991, G Mar. 1993.

Bulgaria: Gega New Compact Disc GD 168. SOFIA QUARTET (Vassil Valchey, Nikolai Gagov, Valentin Gerov, Kolya Bespalov). [Opp. 110 and 122.] P Sofia Nov. 1993, I Feb. 1994.

USA: New Albion Compact Disc NA 088 CD. Arr. Barshai. New Century Chamber Orchestra, Stuart CANIN. ['Written with the Heart's Blood'—Opp. 11 and 110*a*.] P Tiburon, California Apr. 1996, I Jan. 1997.

Naxos Compact Disc 8.550977. ÉDER QUARTET (János Selmeczi, Péter Szüts, Sándor Papp, György Éder). ['Complete Quartets, Vol. 6'—Opp. 122 and 138.] P Budapest 29 Apr.–4 May 1996, I May 1998.

Germany: Arte Nova Classics Compact Disc 74321 58967-2. Arr. Barshai. Hamburg Soloists, Emil KLEIN. [Op. 110*a*.] P Hamburg Nov. 1996, I Oct. 1998.

Chandos Compact Disc CHAN 9741. SORREL QUARTET (Gina McCormack, Catherine Yates, Vicci Wardman, Helen Thatcher). ['Complete Quartets, Vol. 1'—Opp. 108 and 101.] P Westleton, Suffolk 23–5 Feb. 1998, I June 1999, G Oct. 1999.

Deutsche Grammophon Compact Disc 463 284-2GH5 (five-disc set). EMERSON QUARTET (Eugene Drucker, Philip Setzer, Lawrence Dutton, David Finkel). ['Complete Quartets, Vol. 3'—Opp. 108, 110, and 117.] P Aspen, Colorado concert July 1998, G June 2000.

France: Arion Compact Disc ARN 68506. DEBUSSY QUARTET (Christophe Colletts, Dominique Lonca, Vincent Deprecq, Yannick Cailier). ['Complete Quartets, Vol. 2'—Opp. 73 and 108.] P Lyon Nov. 1999, I Dec. 2000.
Reference: Martynov.

Opus 119   The Execution of Stepan Razin

Form: Cantata for bass soloist, mixed chorus and orchestra (with 2 harps and piano), to the text of a narrative poem by Yevgeni Yevtushenko, taken from the series *The Bratsk Hydro-electric Power Station*. The score marked 'Moderato non troppo—Andante—Adagio—Moderato—Adagio—Moderato'. The music was awarded a Glinka State Prize in 1968.

Instrumentation: piccolo, 2 flutes, 2 oboes, cor anglais, E flat clarinet, 2 clarinets (B flat and A), bass clarinet, 2 bassoons, contrabassoon ~ 4 horns, 3 trumpets, 3 trombones, tuba ~ timpani, triangle, tambourine, side drum, whip, cymbals, bass drum, gong ~ orchestral bells, xylophone, celesta, 2 harps, piano ~ bass soloist, S.A.T.B. chorus ~ 1st violins (20), 2nd violins (18), violas (16), cellos (14), and five-string double-basses (12). The number of harps and the string strength quoted to be regarded as the minimum.

Composed: Begun in early August 1964 at Lake Balaton, Hungary and completed on 14 September 1964 at Moscow.

Premières: 28 December 1964, Moscow Conservatory Bolshoi Hall; Vitali Gromadsky (bass), RSFSR Academic Russian Choir, Moscow Philharmonic Orchestra, Kirill Kondrashin.

UK: 17 August 1966, Royal Albert Hall 'Prom', London; Vitali Gromadsky, BBC Choral Society and Chorus, BBC Symphony Orchestra, Gennadi Rozhdestvensky.

Scotland: 21 March 1971, Perth City Hall; John Graham (bass), Perth Symphony Orchestra and Choral Society, John McLeod. Sung in Russian—coaching by Basil Almond.

USA: 30 and 31 October 1995, Seattle Opera House; Marc Smith (bass-baritone), Seattle Symphony Chorale, Abraham Kaplan (chorus-master), Seattle Symphony Orchestra, Gerald Schwarz.

Arrangements: Reductions for voices and piano by the composer and Carl A. Rosenthal. Translations of the poem in English by Harold Heiberg and German by Lyubomir Romansky. Themes used in a composition for jazz quartet by Mathias Rissi (saxophonist), recorded on Swiss Unit Records Label, 1 December 1986.

Music: Autograph full and vocal scores preserved at the CIS Archives of Literature and Art. The first page of the autograph full score is reproduced in Volume 29 of *Collected Works*.

Muzyka, No. 2675, 1966, full score, 29 cm.

Muzyka, No. 2676, 1966, vocal score, 28.5 cm.

MCA, 1967, vocal score with English adaptation by H. Heiberg and piano reduction by C. A. Rosenthal, 27 cm.

Hans Sikorski, No. 2154, 1968, vocal score with German text by L. Romansky, 31.5 cm.

Muzyka, No. 11680 (in Volume 29 of *Collected Works* with Opp. 81 and 90), 1983, full score, 30 cm.

Muzyka, No. 11786 (in Volume 30 of *Collected Works* with Opp. 81 and 90), 1983, vocal score, 30 cm.

Duration: Approx. 30 minutes in scores; 23' 48"–31' 41"; 27' 50" (Plaistow); 30 minutes (Sadovnikov).

Ballet: *The Execution of Stepan Razin.* Konstantin Rassadin, Leningrad, 1977. A ballet performed by the Leningrad Ballet Troupe 'Choreographic Miniatures' under the artistic direction of Askold Makarov.

Recordings: USSR: Melodiya D 016471-2 (mono) and C 01109-10. Vitali Gromadsky (bass), RSFSR Academic Russian Choir, Aleksandr Yurlov (chorus-master), Moscow Philharmonic Orchestra, Kirill KONDRASHIN. [Op. 70.] P 1965, I 1966. *Reissued:* USA: Arfa ALP 1024. [Yevtushenko songs by Soviet composers.] I 'dedicated to Yevtushenko's American tour, Nov.–Dec. 1966' ~ HMV Melodiya ASD 2409. [Op. 70.] G Jan. 1969 ~ France: Le Chant du Monde LDX A 78376. [Op. 70.] ~ USA: Angel Melodiya SR 40000. [Op. 70.] ~ Netherlands: MEL 406. [Op. 70.] ~ Italy: EMI 065 93441. [Op. 70.] ~ HMV Melodiya SLS 5109 (1 side in two-record set). [Op. 60.] G Feb. 1978 ~ Germany: Melodia Eurodisc 300 595 in Set 300 597-435. [Op. 20.] ~ USSR: Melodiya C10 14093-4. [In third box of Part 1 of *Collected Works on Records* with Op. 90.] I 1980.

Italy: Intaglio Compact Disc INCD 7371. Vitali Gromadsky (bass), BBC Choral Society and Chorus, BBC Symphony Orchestra, Gennadi ROZHDESTVENSKY. [Prokofiev.] P Royal Albert Hall, London concert 17 August 1966, I Jan. 1993. NB. Orchestra not the Moscow Radio Orchestra.

Czech: Supraphon SUA 10958 (mono) and SUA ST 50958. Bohuš Hanák (bass), Slovák Chorus, Slovák Philharmonic Orchestra, Ladislav SLOVÁK. [Op. 14.] P Czech Radio 1967, G July 1969. *Reissued:* France: Praga Compact Disc PR 254 055. [Opp. 20 and 131.] I July 1994.

Philips Universo 6585 012. Siegfried Vogel (bass), Leipzig Radio Choir, Leipzig Radio Symphony Orchestra, Herbert KEGEL. [Khachaturyan.] P Nov. 1967, G Nov. 1973. *Reissued:* Philips Classical Collector Compact Disc 434 172-2PM. [Op. 112.] I Sept. 1992, G Mar. 1993.

Koch International Classics Compact Disc 3-7017-2. Assen Vassilev (bass), Varna Philharmonic Orchestra and Chorus, Andrei ANDREYEV. [Sviridov.] P Varna 20–6 Dec. 1989, I 1990, G Mar. 1991.

Germany: Capriccio Compact Disc 10 780. Stanislav Suleimanov (bass), Cologne Radio Chorus, Godfried Ritter (chorus-master), Cologne

Radio Symphony Orchestra, Mikhail YUROVSKY. [Opp. 4 and 114*a*.] P Cologne 3–8 June 1996, I Oct. 1999, G Dec. 1999.
Reference: Shlifshteyn (in Danilevich 1967).

Opus 120   A Year as Long as a Lifetime

Subtitle: The working title of *Karl Marx* is mentioned in talks by the composer and in articles from September 1963 onwards. Translated as *A Year as a Life* on the score and *A Year is Worth a Lifetime* on the Angel record; also appears as *A Year is Like a Lifetime*.

Form: Music for the biographical film *A Year as Long as a Lifetime*, based on the life of Karl Marx, directed by Grigori Roshal for Mosfilm. Film script from the play by Galina Serebrykova. The score includes an Offenbachian schnell-polka 'Morning' not included in the Suite Opus 120*a*.

Composed: Completed in June 1965, at Moscow.

Arrangement: Opus 120*a*—Suite assembled by Lev Atovmyan in 1969:

1. Overture—Allegro non troppo
2. The Barricades—Moderato non troppo
3. Intermezzo—Allegro
4. Farewell (Monologue)—Andante
5. Scene (Little Waltz)—Allegretto
6. The Battle—Moderato
7. Finale—Adagio

Instrumentation of Suite Opus 120*a*:   piccolo, 2 flutes, 2 oboes, 2 clarinets (B flat and A), 2 bassoons ~ 4 horns, 3 trumpets, 3 trombones, tuba ~ timpani, triangle, whip, side drum, cymbals, bass drum, gong ~ orchestral bells ~ strings.

Music: Sovetskii Kompozitor, No. 1317, 1970, opus no. not stated, full score of the Suite assembled by L. Atovmyan, 28.5 cm.

Duration: Suite as recorded: 27' 30"; 22 minutes (M. MacDonald).

Ballet: *The Overcoat.* For details see under Opus 32.

Recordings: USSR: Melodiya CM 02523-4. Suite Nos. 1, 2, 3, 4 abridged, 6, and 7. Moscow Radio Symphony Orchestra, Maksim SHOSTAKOVICH. [Op. 136.] P 1966, I May 1971. *Reissued:* USA: Angel Melodiya SR 40181. Suite No. 1, 'Morning', 2, 3, 4 abridged, 6, and 7. [Op. 78*a*.] ~ Germany: Melodia, Eurodisc 28665 XHK. No. 1 and 'Morning'. [On fourth record of four-record film music album with Opp. 97*a* and 116*a*.] I 1981.

Opus 121 Five Romances on Texts from 'Krokodil'

Form: Song cycle for bass voice and grand piano to poems by readers from the 'Believe it or not' feature of the satirical magazine *Krokodil* (Issue No. 24 for 30 August 1965):

1. The evidence of one's own manuscript—Moderato
2. A desire too difficult to gratify—Moderato
3. Discretion—Largo
4. Irinka and the Shepherd—Allegro
5. Excessive delight—Moderato

Composed: 4 September 1965.

Premières: 28 May 1966, Glinka Concert Hall, Leningrad; Yevgeni Nesterenko (bass) and Dmitri Shostakovich (piano).

USA: 4 February 1985, Boston University Concert Hall; Robert Osborne (bass) and Howard Lubin (piano). Sung in Russian.

Arrangements: English and German translations of the text by Joan Pemberton Smith and Jörg Morgener respectively.

Music: Autograph score preserved in the Shostakovich family archive. First published in the journal *Sovetskaya Muzyka*, 1966, No. 1.

Hans Sikorski, No. 2277 (with Op. 123), 1981, with Russian and German texts—the latter by J. Morgener, 29.5 cm.

Muzyka, No. 11785 (in Volume 33 of *Collected Works* with Opp. 109, 123, 127, 128, 143, 145, and 146), 1984, 30 cm.

Duration: Approx. 10 minutes in score; 7' 48"–11' 36".

Recordings: USSR: Melodiya C10 09225-6. Performed in the order Nos. 3, 4, 1, 2, and 5. Yevgeni NESTERENKO (bass) and Yevgeni Shenderovich (piano). [In third box of Part 3 of *Collected Works on Records* with Opp. 58*a*, 123, and 146.] P Jan. 1976, I 1978. *Reissued:* HMV Melodiya ASD 3700. [Opp. 58*a*, 123, and 146; and Musorgsky.] G. Sept. 1979 ~ Japan: Victor Musical Industries Compact Disc VTCC 40082-83 (two-disc set). ['Shostakovich Songs'—Opp. 58*a*, 123, 127, 140/143*a*, 145*a*, and 146.] I 1991.

France: Le Chant du Monde Russian Season Compact Disc RUS 288089. Nos. 1–5. Pyotr GLUBOKY (bass) and Nataliya Rassudova (piano). [Opp. 46, 62, 91, and 146.] P Moscow Conservatory 21–9 Sept. 1994, I Apr. 1995.

Japan: Triton Compact Disc 17 008. Nos. 1 and 3. Aleksei MOCHALOV (bass), Moscow Chamber Music Theatre Orchestra, Anatoli Levin. [Opp. 58*a*, 140, 146, and Sans op. X (iii).] P Mosfilm Studio Nov. 1995, I Nov. 1996.

Germany: MGB Musikszene Schweiz Compact Disc MGB 6145. Sung in German. Rudolf MAZZOLA (bass) and Paul Harris (piano). [Op. 123; Meier and Wellesz.] P Vienna 1–2 Mar. 1997, I Dec. 1997.

Belgium: René Gailly Compact Disc CD92 041. Nos. 1–5. Fyodor KUZNETSOV (bass) and Yuri Serov (piano). ['Complete Songs, Vol. 1'— Opp. 62, 86, 100, and 127.] P St Petersburg 23 Mar.–4 May 1998.

Opus 122   Quartet No. 11 in F minor

Form: String quartet in seven linked movements:

1. Introduction—Andantino   *attacca*
2. Scherzo—Allegretto   *attacca*
3. Recitative—Adagio   *attacca*
4. Étude—Allegro   *attacca*
5. Humoresque—Allegro   *attacca*
6. Elegy—Adagio   *attacca*
7. Finale—Moderato

Composed: Completed on 30 January 1966 at Moscow.

Dedication: To the memory of Vasili Pyotrovich Shirinsky (2nd violinist of the Beethoven Quartet).

Premières: 25 March 1966, USSR Composers' Club, Moscow; 28 May 1966, Glinka Concert Hall, Leningrad; and 6 June 1966, Moscow Conservatory Malyi Hall; Beethoven Quartet (Dmitri Tsyganov, Nikolai Zabavnikov, Fyodor Druzhinin, and Sergei Shirinsky).

   UK: 27 April 1967, Bromsgrove Festival; London String Quartet (Carl Pini, John Tunnell, Keith Cummings, and Douglas Cameron).

Arrangement: Reduction for piano four hands by Anatoli Dmitriev.

Music: Autograph score preserved in the Shostakovich family archive.

   Hans Sikorski, No. 6207, 1966, 32 cm.

   Sovetskii Kompozitor, No. 69, 1967, parts, 29 cm.

   Boosey & Hawkes, No. 827, 1967, score, 19 cm.

   Boosey & Hawkes, No. 19586, 1967, parts, 29 cm.

   Leeds Music, no number, 1967, score, 23 cm.

   Muzyka, Leningrad, No. 766 (in Volume 3 with Quartets 9 and 10 arr. for piano four hands by A. Dmitriev), 1967, 29.5 cm.

   Muzyka, No. 10284 (in Volume 36 of *Collected Works* Quartets 9–15), 1980, 30 cm.

   Hans Sikorski, No. 2268 (with Op. 133), 1980, score 21 cm.

   Hans Sikorski, No. 2264, 1981, parts, 31.5 cm.

Duration: 15 minutes in score; 15' 05"–18' 04"; 15' 30" (Plaistow).

Recordings: USSR: Melodiya D 019519-20 (mono) and C 01459-60. BORODIN QUARTET (Rostislav Dubinsky, Yaroslav Aleksandrov, Dmitri Shebalin, Valentin Berlinsky). [Opp. 117 and 11.] P and I 1967. *Reissued:* HMV Melodiya ASD 2857. [Op. 141.] G Nov. 1972 ~ USA: Seraphim Melodiya S 6035. [In three-record box set with Op. 11 and Quartets 6–10.] ~ HMV Melodiya HQS 1322 in Set SLS 879. [Opp. 101 and 108.] G June 1974 ~ East Germany: Eterna 8 26 598. [Opp. 117 and 11.]

   USSR: Melodiya D 025115-6 (mono) and C 01769-70. BEETHOVEN QUARTET (personnel as at première). [Opp. 133 and 11.] P 1969, G Oct. 1971.

Reissued: France: EMI 061 91298. [Opp. 133 and 11.] NB. Performers incorrectly labelled as 'Komitas Quartet' ~ USA: Consonance Blue Label Compact Disc 81.3009. [Vol. 5—Opp. 117 and 118.] I Mar. 1996.

L'Oiseau-Lyre DSLO 28. FITZWILLIAM QUARTET (Christopher Rowland, Jonathan Sparey, Alan George, Ioan Davies). [Op. 73.] P 15–16 Dec. 1976, G June 1978. *Reissued:* Decca 188 D2 in Set D 188 D7. [Op. 73.] G Feb. 1981 ~ Decca Enterprise Compact Discs 433 078-2DM6. [On fifth disc of six-disc set with Opp. 133 and 138.] I Apr. 1992, G June 1992 ~ Decca Compact Discs 466 437-2 (third disc of five-disc set). [Opp. 40 and 57.] I 1999.

USSR: Melodiya C10 11617-8. TANEYEV QUARTET (Vladimir Ovcharek, Grigori Lutsky, Vissarion Soloviev, Iosif Levinson). [In first box of Part 2 of *Collected Works on Records* with Op. 73.] P 1979, I 1980. *Reissued:* Japan: JVC Victor 5348. [Opp. 108, 110, and 138.] ~ USSR: Melodiya Compact Disc SUCD10 00312. [Opp. 133 and 138.] I 1991*d*.

USSR: Melodiya C10 17579-80. BORODIN QUARTET (Mikhail Kopelman, Andrei Abramenkov, Dmitri Shebalin, Valentin Berlinsky). [Op. 118.] P 1981, I 1983*a*. *Reissued:* HMV Melodiya EX 270339-3 (DMM). [In seven-record box set of 15 Quartets plus Quintet.] G Mar. 1986 ~ EMI Compact Disc CDC7 49268-2. [Opp. 83 and 101.] I Nov. 1987, G Sept. 1988 ~ Japan: Victor Musical Industries Compact Disc VICC 40022. [Opp. 133 and 138.] I 1990 ~ EMI Compact Discs CMS5 65032-2. [In six-disc set of 15 Quartets plus Quintet.] I Mar. 1994 ~ BMG Melodiya Compact Discs 74321 40711-2 (six-disc set). [Opp. 133 and 138.] I June 1997.

USSR: Melodiya C10 23563 000 (DMM). ČIURLIONIS QUARTET (Rimantas Suigždinis, Saulius Kiškis, Aloymas Grižas, Saulius Lipčius). [Op. 73.] P 1985, I 1986*d*.

Academy Sound and Vision DCA 631 (DMM) and Compact Disc CD DCA 631. COULL QUARTET (Roger Coull, Philip Gallaway, David Curtis, John Todd). [Op. 83 and 110.] P London Mar. 1988, I and G Apr. 1989.

Olympia Compact Disc OCD 534. SHOSTAKOVICH QUARTET (Andrei Shislov, Sergei Pishchugin, Aleksandr Galkovsky, Aleksandr Korchagin). ['Complete Quartets, Vol. 4'—Opp. 118 and 144.] P 1984, I May 1994, G Sept. 1994.

France: Adès Compact Disc 14 161-2. FINE ARTS QUARTET (Ralph Evans, Efim Boico, Jerry Horner, Wolfgang Laufer). [Opp. 73 and 108.] P Paris July 1989, I July 1990, G Oct. 1990.

Teldec Compact Discs 9031 71702-2. BRODSKY QUARTET (Michael Thomas, Ian Belton, Paul Cassidy, Jacqueline Thomas). [On fifth disc of six-disc set with Opp. 133 and 138.] P Berlin July 1989, I Nov. 1990, G June 1992. *Reissued:* Teldec Compact Disc 9031 73109-2. [Opp. 133 and 138.] I July 1991.

USA: ESS.A.Y. Compact Disc CD 1012. MANHATTAN QUARTET (Eric Lewis, Roy Lewis, John Dexter, Judith Glyde). [Opp. 133 and 138.] P

Jersey City 17 May 1990, I 1991. *Reissued:* Koch Schwann Compact Disc 3 1070-2. ['Complete String Quartets, Vol. 5' with Opp. 133 and 138.] I Sept. 1993.

RCA Victor Red Seal Compact Disc 09026 61816-2. VOGLER QUARTET (Tim Vogler, Frank Reinecke, Stefan Fehlandt, Stephan Forck). [Debussy and Janáček.] P Neumarkt 10–13 May and 21 June 1993, I May 1994, G July and Nov. 1994.

Bulgaria: Gega New Compact Disc GD 168. SOFIA QUARTET (Vassil Valchev, Nikolai Gagov, Valentin Gerov, Kolya Bespalov). [Op. 110 and 122.] P Sofia Nov. 1993, I Feb. 1994.

Deutsche Grammophon Compact Disc 445 864-2GH. HAGEN QUARTET (Lukas Hagen, Rainer Schmidt, Veronika and Clemens Hagen). [Opp. 83 and 142.] P Abersee bei Gilsen Apr. 1994, I July 1995, G Sept. 1995.

Deutsche Grammophon Compact Disc 463 284-2GH5 (five-disc set). EMERSON QUARTET (Eugene Drucker, Philip Setzer, Lawrence Dutton, David Finkel). ['Complete Quartets, Vol. 4'—Sans op. D, Opp. 133 and 138.] P Aspen, Colorado concert July–Aug. 1994, G June 2000.

Naxos Compact Disc 8.550977. ÉDER QUARTET (János Selmeczi, Péter Szüts, Sándor Papp, György Éder). ['Complete Quartets, Vol. 6'—Opp. 118 and 138.] P Budapest 29 Apr.–4 May 1996, I May 1998.

Japan: EMI Classics Compact Disc TOCE 9496. MORGAŬA QUARTET (Eiji Arai, Takashi Aoki, Hisashi Ono, Ryoichi Fujimori). [Opp. 49, 101, and 97.] P 11–14 Mar. 1997.

Chandos Compact Disc CHAN 9769. SORREL QUARTET (Gina McCormack, Catherine Yates, Vicci Wardman, Helen Thatcher). ['Complete Quartets, Vol. 2'—Opp. 73 and 83.] P Westleton, Suffolk 29 Sept.–1 Oct. 1998, I Jan. 2000.

Opus 123   Preface to the Complete Collection of my Works and a Brief Reflection upon this Preface

Form: Setting of a jocular poem by the composer (the first four lines paraphrasing Aleksandr Pushkin's *History of a versifier* of 1817), for bass voice and grand piano, marked 'Allegretto'.

Composed: 2 March 1966, after intimation of the projected publication of the *Collected Works*.

Premières: 28 May 1966, Glinka Concert Hall, Leningrad; Yevgeni Nesterenko (bass) and Dmitri Shostakovich (piano).

UK: 19 March 1986, Queen Elizabeth Hall, London; John Shirley-Quirk (baritone) and Andrew Ball (piano).

Arrangements: English and German translations of the text by Joan Pemberton Smith and Jörg Morgener respectively.

Music: Autograph score preserved in the Shostakovich family archive.

Hans Sikorski, No. 2277 (with Op. 121), 1981, with Russian and German texts—the latter by J. Morgener, 29.5 cm.

Muzyka, No. 11785 (in Volume 33 of *Collected Works* with Opp. 109, 121, 127, 128, 143, 145, and 146), 1984, 30 cm.

Duration: Approx. 2 minutes in score; 2' 09"–2' 13".

Recordings: USSR: Melodiya C10 09225-6. Yevgeni NESTERENKO (bass) and Yevgeni Shenderovich (piano). [In third box of Part 3 of *Collected Works on Records* with Opp. 58*a*, 121, and 146.] P Jan. 1976, I 1978. *Reissued:* HMV Melodiya ASD 3700. [Opp. 58*a*, 121, and 146; and Musorgsky.] G Sept. 1979 ~ Japan: Victor Musical Industries Compact Discs VICC 40082-83 (two-disc set). ['Shostakovich Songs'—Opp. 58*a*, 121, 127, 140/143*a*, 145*a*, and 146.] I 1991.

Germany: MGB Musikszene Schweiz Compact Disc MGB 6145. Sung in German. Rudolf MAZZOLA (bass) and Paul Harris (piano). [Op. 121; Meier and Wellesz.] P Vienna 1–2 Mar. 1997, I Dec. 1997.

Opus 124   Two Choruses by Davidenko

Form: An arrangement for orchestra (with triple woodwind) of two songs by Aleksandr Davidenko, from the oratorio *The Road of October,* for narrator, soloists, chorus, trumpet, piano, button-accordion, percussion ensemble, and stamping feet, composed by the RAPM group of young Moscow Conservatory composers in 1927 to mark the tenth anniversary of the October Revolution:

1. On the Tenth Verst (words by P. Ediet)
2. The Street in Turmoil (words by M. Shorin)

Instrumentation: 3 flutes, 3 oboes (III = cor anglais), 3 clarinets (B flat and A), 2 bassoons, contrabassoon ~ 4 horns, 3 trumpets, 3 trombones, tuba ~ timpani, triangle, side drum, cymbals, gong ~ strings.

Composed: Completed in August 1963.

Premières: 24 February 1964, Moscow Conservatory Bolshoi Hall; RSFSR Academic Russian Choir, Moscow Radio Symphony Orchestra, Aleksandr Yurlov.

6 November 1967, Leningrad Philharmonic Bolshoi Hall; Krupskaya Institute Chorus, Ivan Poltavtsev (chorus-master), Leningrad Philharmonic Orchestra, Igor Blazhkov. To celebrate the 50th anniversary of the October Revolution.

Music: Originally issued without an opus number.

Muzyka, No. 4822, 1968, score, 29 cm.

Duration: 10 minutes (M. MacDonald); [4' 31"]–5' 32" (1) and 4' 32"–[5' 19"] (2).

Recordings: [USSR: Melodiya D 16975-6 (10" mono) and C 1171-2 (10").
Original a cappella version. RSFSR Academic Russian Choir, Aleksandr
YURLOV. [Davidenko choral pieces and songs.] I 1965. *Reissued:* Olympia
Compact Disc OCD 205. Nos. 1 and 2. [Davidenko ('About Lenin') and
Gadzhiev.] I Feb. 1988.]
    USSR: Melodiya C10 31619 002. USSR Ministry of Culture Chamber
Choir and Symphony Orchestra, Valeri Polyansky (chorus-master),
Gennadi ROZHDESTVENSKY. [Album 7 of 'From Manuscripts of Different
Years'—Opp. 30 and 62*a*.] P 1986, I 1991*c*.
Reference: Levando.

Opus 125   Cello Concerto in A minor (Schumann)

Form: Reorchestration of Robert Schumann's Concerto of 1850 for cello and
orchestra, Opus 129, in three linked movements:

1. Nicht zu schell (Allegro non troppo) *attacca*
2. Langsam (Lento) *attacca*
3. Sehr lebhaft (Molto vivace)

Instrumentation: 2 flutes (II = piccolo), 2 oboes, 2 A clarinets, 2 bassoons ~ 4
horns, 2 trumpets ~ timpani ~ harp ~ strings.
Composed: July 1963, at Dilizhan Composers' Retreat, Armenia. [Oddly
both Shostakovich (*in litt.*) and Shneyerson state 1966 as the year of composition; and the Sollertinskys give July 1969.]
Dedication: Mstislav Leopoldovich Rostropovich (cellist).
Premières: 5 October 1963, Moscow Conservatory Bolshoi Hall; M. Rostropovich, USSR Symphony Orchestra, Boris Khaikin.
    UK: 27 August 1964, Edinburgh Festival, Usher Hall; M. Ros-
tropovich, Scottish National Orchestra, Alexander Gibson.
Music: Muzyka, No. 3473, 1966, miniature score with cello part ed. Ros-
tropovich, 21.5 cm.
Duration: 22' 30"–25' 48".
Recordings: USA: Russian Disc Compact Disc RDCD 11 106. Mstislav
ROSTROPOVICH (cello), USSR Symphony Orchestra, David Oistrakh. [Op.
107.] P Moscow concert 10 Oct. 1969, G July 1994.
    Yugoslavia: Jugoton LSY 61139. Valter DEŠPALJ (cello), RTZ Symphony
Orchestra, Josef Daniel. [Boccherini.] P 1974. *Reissued:* Netherlands: Bril-
liant Classics Compact Discs 99386 (two-disc set). ['The Romantic
Cello'—Vivaldi and Dvořák on CD2]. I 2001.
    USSR: Melodiya A10 00107 009 (digital). Fyodor LUZANOV (cello),
USSR Ministry of Culture Symphony Orchestra, Gennadi Rozhdestvensky. [Album 3 of 'From Manuscripts of Different Years'—Opp. 58*a*

and 19.] P 1983, I 1985*d. Reissued:* Olympia Compact Disc OCD 102. [Brahms.] G Aug. 1987.

Deutsche Grammophon Compact Disc 439 890-2GH. Schumann's violin version of his Cello Concerto, orch. Shostakovich. Gidon KREMER (violin), Boston Symphony Orchestra, Seiji Ozawa. [Op. 129.] P Boston concert Apr. 1992, I and G Sept. 1994.

Chandos Compact Disc CHAN 9792. Aleksandr IVASHKIN (cello), Russian Symphony Orchestra, Valeri Polyansky. ['The Unknown Shostakovich' (*sic*)—Op. 23, Sans opp. W and B.] P Mosfilm Studio Jan. 1998, I Jan. 2000.

Reference: Devlin.

Opus 126   Cello Concerto No. 2 in G major

Form: Concerto for cello and orchestra (with 2 harps and brass reduced to 2 horns) in three movements:

1. Largo
2. Allegretto *attacca*
3. Allegretto

Instrumentation: piccolo, flute, 2 oboes, 2 clarinets (B flat and A), 2 bassoons, contrabassoon (= bassoon III) ~ 2 French horns ~ timpani, tambourine, side drum, tom-tom, side drum *di legno,* whip, bass drum ~ xylophone, harp (minimum of 2 specified) ~ 1st violins (16), 2nd violins (14), violas (12), cellos (12), double-basses (10). Tom-tom and side drum *di legno* may be played by one person. String strength specified as a minimum.

Composed: Begun in spring 1966 at Moscow and completed on 27 April 1966 at the Oreanda Sanatorium, Yalta.

Dedication: Mstislav Leopoldovich Rostropovich (cellist).

Premières: 25 September 1966 (marking the composer's sixtieth birthday), Moscow Conservatory Bolshoi Hall; Mstislav Rostropovich, USSR Symphony Orchestra, Yevgeni Svetlanov.

UK: 5 October 1966, Royal Festival Hall, London; Rostropovich, BBC Symphony Orchestra, Colin Davies.

USA: 26 February 1967, Carnegie Hall, New York; Rostropovich, London Symphony Orchestra, Gennadi Rozhdestvensky.

Arrangement: Reduction for cello and piano by the composer.

Music: Autograph score, along with 17 pages of rough sketches, preserved in the Shostakovich family archive; the whereabouts of the autograph reduction is not known. The opening of the second movement of the autograph full score is reproduced in Volume 16 of *Collected Works.*

Hans Sikorski, No. 2139, 1966, reduction for cello and piano, 31.5 cm.
Leeds Music (Canada), 1967, reduction, 30.5 cm.

Boosey & Hawkes, No. 835, 1968, score, 19 cm.

Sovetskii Kompozitor, No. 71, 1969, reduction, 29 cm.

Sovetskii Kompozitor, No. 72, 1970, full score, 29 cm.

Edition Peters, No. 5719, 1971, reduction, 30 cm.

International Music, c.1973, reduction, 31 cm.

Muzyka, No. 9281, 1976, reduction, 29 cm.

Muzyka, No. 11936 (in Volume 16 of *Collected Works* with Op. 107), 1985, full score, 30 cm.

Muzyka, No. 11947 (in Volume 17 of *Collected Works* with Op. 107), 1986, reduction with separate cello part, 30 cm.

Hans Sikorski, No. 2241, 1990, 21 cm.

Duration: Approx. 36 minutes in score; 30' 59"–37' 32".

Recordings: EMI Compact Discs CZS5 72016-2 (on fourth disc of thirteen-disc set, mono). Mstislav ROSTROPOVICH (cello), USSR Symphony Orchestra, Yevgeni Svetlanov. ['Rostropovich: The Russian Years, 1950–74'— Opp. 107 and, on eleventh disc, 40.] P 25 Sept. 1966 première concert (NB. Not 25 Sept. 1967 as stated in liner notes—a different performance to that on RDCD11 109), G May 1997. *Reissued:* EMI Classics Compact Discs CZS5 72295-2 (two-disc set, mono). [Opp. 40 and 107; Kabalevsky and Khachaturyan.] I Oct. 1998.

Italy: Intaglio Compact Disc INCD 7251. Mstislav ROSTROPOVICH (cello), London Symphony Orchestra, Gennadi Rozhdestvensky. [Op. 107.] P New York concert 26 Feb. 1967, I July 1992.

USA: Russian Disc Compact Disc RDCD 11 109. Mstislav ROSTROPOVICH (cello), USSR Symphony Orchestra, Yevgeni Svetlanov. [Op. 107.] P Moscow concert 25 Sept. 1967, I Oct. 1993.

Revelation Compact Disc RV 10087. Mstislav ROSTROPOVICH (cello), Moscow State Philharmonic Orchestra, David Oistrakh. [Opp. 107 and 109.] P Moscow concert 12 Nov. 1967, I Nov. 1997.

USA: Aries LP 1601. Mstislav ROSTROPOVICH (cello), Chicago Symphony Orchestra, Jean Martinon. [Op. 15a.] P concert. NB. Orchestra and conductor not named on the record or sleeve.

Italy: Stradivarius Compact Disc STR 10049. Mstislav ROSTROPOVICH (cello), Radio-televisione Italiana (RAI) Milan Symphony Orchestra, Piero Bellugi. [Britten.] P Milan concert 15 Mar. 1968, I 1993.

Deutsche Grammophon 2530 653. Mstislav ROSTROPOVICH (cello), Boston Symphony Orchestra, Seiji Ozawa. [Glazunov.] P 8 Nov. 1975, G Nov. 1976. *Reissued:* Deutsche Grammophon Galleria Compact Disc 431 475-2GGA. [Tchaikovsky and Glazunov.] I Apr. 1991, G Aug. 1991 ~ Deutsche Grammophon Compact Discs 437 952-2GX2 (on second of two-disc set). ['Masterpieces for Cello'—Vivaldi, Boccherini, Tartini, Tchaikovsky *et al.*] G Oct. 1994 ~ Deutsche Grammophon Classikon Compact Disc 439 481-2GCL. [Op. 47.] I June 1995, G Sept. 1995.

Czech: Supraphon 1 10 2433 G. Miloš SÁDLO (cello), Prague Symphony Orchestra, Václav Smetáček. [Khachaturyan.] P Prague 1978.

USSR: Melodiya C10 13769-70. Valentin FEIGIN (cello), Central Television and All-Union Radio Symphony Orchestra, Maksim Shostakovich.
[In third box of Part 1 of *Collected Works on Records*.] P and I 1980. *Reissued:* USSR: with same number. I 1981*a* ~ Germany: Melodia Eurodisc
201 975-366.

Philips 412 526-1PH (digital). Heinrich SCHIFF (cello), Bavarian Radio
Symphony Orchestra, Maksim Shostakovich. [Op. 107.] P Munich 26
Nov. 1983, G Sept. 1984, Aug. 1985, and June 1986. *Simultaneous issue:*
Philips Compact Disc 412 526-2PH. [Op. 107.] G Oct. 1985.

Belgium: Classic Talent Compact Disc DOM 2910 11. Viviane
SPANOGHE (cello), Sofia Soloists, Emil Tabakov. [Op. 107.] P Sofia Apr.
1984, I Nov. 1991.

Germany: Live Classics Compact Disc LCL 202. Natalia GUTMAN
(cello), Moscow Philharmonic Orchestra, Dmitri Kitayenko. [Op. 107;
and Schnittke.] P Moscow concert 11 Nov. 1986, I Jan. 2001.

RCA Victor Red Seal Compact Disc RD 87918. Natalia GUTMAN (cello),
Royal Philharmonic Orchestra, Yuri Temirkanov. [Op. 107.] P Watford
25, 28–9 Nov. 1988, I Nov. 1990, G Jan. 1991.

East Germany: Eterna 7 28 042. Peter BRUNS (cello), Berlin City Symphony Orchestra, Claus Peter Flor. [Bruch.] P Berlin 1988. *Reissued:* Germany: Berlin Classics Compact Disc 0120 012. [Bruch.]

Sweden: BIS Compact Disc CD 626. Torleif THEDEÉN (cello), Malmö
Symphony Orchestra, James De Priest. [Op. 107.] P Malmö 8–9 Oct.
1992, I May 1994, G July 1994 and Feb. 1995. Winner of Cannes Classical
Music Awards 1994—19th and 20th century category.

France: Le Chant du Monde Compact Disc LDC 278-1099. Ivan
MONIGHETTI (cello), Prague Radio Symphony Orchestra, Vladimir Válek.
[Op. 77.] P Czech Radio Nov. 1992, I Sept. 1993.

Deutsche Grammophon Compact Disc 445 821-2GH. Mischa MAISKY
(cello), London Symphony Orchestra, Tilson Thomas. [Op. 107.] P London Aug. 2–4 1993, I Mar. 1995, G Apr. 1995.

Naxos Compact Disc 8.550813. Maria KLIEGEL (cello), Polish National
Radio Symphony Orchestra, Antoni Wit. [Op. 107.] P Katowice 27 Feb.–1
Mar. 1995, I Sept. 1996, G Oct. 1996.

Virgin Classics Compact Disc VC5 45145-2. Truls MØRK (cello), London Philharmonic Orchestra, Mariss Jansons. [Op. 107.] P 10–11 Mar.
1995, I Nov. 1995, G Feb. 1996.

Chandos Compact Disc CHAN 9585. Frans HELMERSON (cello), Russian State Symphony Orchestra, Valeri Polyansky. [Op. 112.] P Mar. 1996,
I Feb. 1998.

Germany: Arte Nova Compact Disc 74321 49688-2. Kirill RODIN (cello),
Russian Philharmonic Orchestra, Konstantin Krimets. [Op. 107.] P
Moscow 9–10 July 1996, I Oct. 1997.

Finland: Finlandia Compact Disc 3984 21441-2. Arto NORAS (cello),
Norwegian Radio Orchestra, Ari Rasilainen. [Op. 107; and R. Strauss.] P

Oslo Apr. 1997, I July 1998. *Reissued:* Finlandia Ultima Compact Discs
8573 81969-2 (disc one of two-disc set). [Opp. 107 and 8.] G June 2000.
   New Zealand: Ode Manu Compact Disc 1542. Aleksandr IVASHKIN
(cello), Moscow Symphony Orchestra, Valeri Polyansky. [Op. 107.] P
Moscow Conservatory 7–9 Oct. 1997, G July 1998.
   Czech: Supraphon Compact Disc SU 3414-2. Jiří BÁRTA (cello), Prague
Symphony Orchestra, Maksim Shostakovich. [Op. 107.] P Prague con-
cert 2 Mar. 1999, I Aug. 1999.
Reference: Tarakanov.

Opus 127   Seven Romances on Poems of Aleksandr Blok

Form: Vocal-instrumental Suite for soprano voice, violin, cello, and piano;
settings of poems by Aleksandr Blok:

1. Song of Ophelia—Moderato (accompanied by cello)
2. Gamayun, the bird of prophecy—Adagio (piano)
3. We were together (That troubled night)—Allegretto (violin)
4. The city sleeps (Deep in sleep)—Largo (cello and piano)
5. The storm—Allegro (violin and piano) *attacca*
6. Secret signs—Largo (violin and cello) *attacca*
7. Music—Largo (violin, cello, and piano)

The poems were written on 8 and 23 February 1899, 9 March 1898, 23
and 24 August 1899, and the last two in October 1902 and September
1898 respectively. No. 2 was inspired by a painting of Viktor Vasnetsov.
Composed: Written in hospital after a heart attack and completed on 3 February 1967. Composed for the fiftieth anniversary of the October Revolution.
Dedication: Galina Pavlovna Vishnevskaya (soprano).
Premières: 23 October 1967, during a 'Soviet Music Week', Moscow Conser-
vatory Bolshoi Hall and 28 October 1967 (official première), Moscow
Conservatory Malyi Hall; Galina Vishnevskaya, David Oistrakh (violin),
Mstislav Rostropovich (cello), and Moisei Vainberg (piano—deputizing
for the indisposed Svyatoslav Richter). Encored in it entirety on the lat-
ter occasion.
   UK: 24 June 1968, Aldeburgh Festival; G. Vishnevskaya, Emanuel
Hurwitz (violin), M. Rostropovich, and Benjamin Britten (piano).
   UK: 4 September 1968, Royal Festival Hall, London; G. Vishnevskaya,
D. Oistrakh, M. Rostropovich, and Yevgeni Svetlanov (piano).
Arrangements: English translations by Myron Morris, Cynthia Jolly, and Per
Skans; German translation by Manfred Koerth and Czech by Zdeňka
Psůtkova.
Music: Autograph score preserved in the Shostakovich family archive.
Sovetskii Kompozitor, No. 799, 1969, parts, 29 cm.

Deutscher Verlag für Musik, parts, with German text by Manfred Koerth, 30 cm.

Anglo-Soviet Music Press, No. B & H 20157, 1977, parts, with Russian text and English words by Cynthia Jolly, 31 cm.

Muzyka, No. 11785 (in Volume 33 of *Collected Works* with Opp. 109, 121, 123, 128, 143, 145, and 146), 1984, 30 cm.

Duration: 20 and 22 minutes in scores; 23' 22"–26' 52'"; 25' 45" (Plaistow).

Recordings: Revelation Compact Disc RV 10101. Galina VISHNEVSKAYA (soprano), David Oistrakh (violin), Mstislav Rostropovich (cello), and Moisei Vainberg (piano). P première concert 23 [not 27 as given] Oct. 1967, I Apr. 1998, G July 1998. *Reissued:* BMG Melodiya Compact Disc 74321 53237-2. [Sans op. V, Op. 109; and Prokofiev.] I 1998.

Classical Society Compact Disc CSCD 123. Galina VISHNEVSKAYA (soprano), Emanuel Hurwitz (violin), Mstislav Rostropovich (cello), and Benjamin Britten (piano). [Britten and Bridge.] P Snape concert 24 June 1968, I 1992. *Reissued:* Decca Compact Disc 466 823-2DM. ['Britten at Aldeburgh, Vol. 6'—Op. 40; Bridge and Janáček.] G Aug. 2000.

USSR: Melodiya D 025887-8 (mono). Nadezhda YURENEVA (soprano), Boris Gutnikov (violin), A. Nikitin (cello), and M. Karandashova (piano). [Ippolitov-Ivanov, A. Aleksandrov, Sviridov *et al.*] P and I 1969. *Reissued:* USSR: Melodiya C10 16789 008. 'Song of Ophelia' only. ['The Poetry of A. Blok in Music'—Myaskovsky, Rakhmaninov, Vasilenko *et al.*] I 1982c.

France: Praga Compact Disc PR 250 009. Sung in Czech. Brigita ŠULCOVÁ (soprano), Emil Leichner junior (violin), Antonín Duda (cello), and Emil Leichner (piano). [Opp. 109 and 145a.] P Prague 1970, I 1992.

USA: Turnabout TV 34280 S. Mary Ellen PRACHT (soprano) and New Amsterdam Trio (John Pintavalle, Heinrich Joachim, Edith Mocsanyi). [Op. 67.] P 1971, G Mar. 1972.

Czech: Panton 11 0342 H (1 side in two-record set). Sung in Czech. Brigita ŠULCOVÁ (soprano), and Dvořák Piano Trio (František Pospíšil, Jaroslav Chovanec, Radoslav Kvapil). [Op. 68, first three movements.] P 1972.

USSR: Melodiya C10 06347-8. Margarita MIROSHNIKOVA (soprano), Andrei Korsakov (violin), Viktor Simon (cello), and Iolanta Miroshnikova (piano). ['Songs to verses of Soviet Poets'.] P 1975, I 1976b. *Reissued:* USSR: Melodiya C10 10527-06348. [In third box of Part 3 of *Collected Works on Records* with Op. 100.] I 1978.

Sweden: BIS LP 37. Jacqueline DELMAN (soprano), Emil Dekov (violin), Åke Olofsson (cello), and Lucia Negro (piano). [Messiaen, Pergament, Martin, and Head.] P Nacka Aula, Sweden 23–31 Aug. 1975. *Reissued:* Sweden: BIS Compact Disc CD 26. [Opp. 67 and 110.] I 1991, G Sept. 1992.

USSR: Melodiya C10 06875-6. Galina PISARENKO (soprano), Oleg Kagan (violin), Dmitri Fershtman (cello), and Elizaveta Leonskaya (piano). [Op.

134.] P Moscow concert July 1975, I 1976*d*. *Reissued:* Japan: Victor Musical Industries Compact Disc VICC 40082-83 (two-disc set). ['Shostakovich Songs'—Opp. 58*a*, 121, 123, 140/143*a*, 145*a*, and 146.] I 1991.

HMV ASD 3222 in Set SLS 5055. Galina VISHNEVSKAYA (soprano), Ulf Hoelscher (violin), Mstislav Rostropovich (cello), and Vasso Devtzi (piano). [Op. 109.] P 1976, G Sept. 1976. *Reissued:* France: Pathé Marconi 2C 167 02726-8. [Op. 109.] ~ EMI Compact Discs CMS5 65716-2 (three-disc set). [Sans op. V and Op. 109; Rimsky-Korsakov, Tchaikovsky, and Prokofiev.] I Nov. 1995, G Sept. 1996.

USSR: Melodiya C10 09683-4. Mariya MAIDACHEVSKAYA (soprano), Arkadi Vinokurov (violin), Mariya Chaikovskaya (cello), and Yevgeni Rzhanov (piano). [Lyatoshinsky.] P 1977, I 1978*c*.

Decca 411 940-IDH (digital) and Compact Disc 411 940-2DH. Elisabeth Söderström (soprano), Christopher Rowland (violin), Ioan Davies (cello), and Vladimir Ashkenazy (piano). [Sans op. D and Op. 57.] P Amsterdam Dec. 1983; G Feb., May, and Oct. 1987.

Germany: Thorofon Capella MTH 267 (DMM). Sung in M. Koerth's German translation. Eva CSAPÓ (soprano), Hans Maile (violin), René Forest (cello), and Horst Göbel (piano). [Op. 79.] P Feb. and June 1984.

France: Harmonia Mundi Ottava LP OTR 58504. Tannie WILLENSTYN (soprano) and Guarneri Trio (Mark Lubotsky, Jean Decroos, Danièle Dechenne). [Op. 67.] P 1985, I Apr. 1987.

Norway: Aurora Compact Disc ARCD 1915. Anne-Lise BERNTSEN (soprano), Terje Tønnesen (violin), Aage Kvalbein (cello), and Einar Henning Smeybe (piano). [Berg and Kvandal.] P 1987, I Nov. 1987. *Reissued:* Victoria/Gamut Compact Disc VCD 19017. [Berg and Kvandal.] G Nov. 1991.

Germany: Dabringhaus und Grimm Compact Disc MD+GL 3334. Alla ABLABERDYEVA (soprano) and Münchner Klaviertrio (Ilona Then-Bergh, Gerhard Zank, Michael Schäfer). [Opp. 8 and 67.] P date not stated, I 1989.

Chandos Compact Disc CHAN 8924. Nadia PELLE (soprano) and Borodin Trio (Rostislav Dubinsky, Yuli Turovsky, Lyubov Yedlina). [Arensky and Prokofiev.] P Layer Marney, Essex 2–3 Aug. 1990, I Mar. 1991, G Oct. 1991. *Reissued:* Chandos Compact Discs CHAN 9627 (two-disc set). No. 3 only. ['In Memory of a great artist—Rostislav Dubinsky'—Op. 67; Schubert, Debussy, Brahms *et al*.] I 1998.

France: Le Chant du Monde Russian Season Compact Disc RUS 288 088. Natalya GERASIMOVA (soprano) and Moscow Trio (Vladimir Ivanov, Mikhail Utkin, Aleksandr Bonduryansky). [Opp. 8 and 67.] P Moscow Conservatory Sept.–Nov. 1993, I Sept. 1994.

Naxos Compact Disc 8.553297. Anita SOLDH (soprano) and Stockholm Arts Trio (Dan Almgren, Torleif Thedéen, Sefan Bojsten). [Opp. 8 and 67.] P Stockholm 13–15 Mar. 1995, I Apr. 1997, G July 1997.

Chandos Compact Discs CHAN 9526 (two-disc set). Joan RODGERS (soprano) and the Bekova Sisters (Elvira, Alfia, and Eleonora). [Opp. 67 and 147.] P Highgate, London 19–20 June 1996, I Feb. 1997, G May 1997.

USA: Summit Compact Disc DCD 193. Joanne KOLOMYJEC (soprano), Yehonatan Berick (violin), David Hetherington (cello), and Patricia Parr (piano). [Dohnányi and Bartók.] P Toronto Dec. 1996.

Hungary: Hungaroton Classics Compact Disc HCD 31780. Mária ASZÓDI (soprano) and Bartos Trio (Galina Danilova, Csaba Bartos, Irina Ivanickaia). [Opp. 8 and 67.] P Hungaroton Studio 11–14 Sept. 1997.

Italy: Foné Compact Disc 99 F 31. Sung in Russian but texts printed in Italian only. Raina KABAIVANSKA (soprano) and Arnold Bosman (piano). [Massenet, Chausson, Ravel *et al*.] P Cremona 16 Jan. 1998.

Belgium: René Gailly Compact Disc CD92 041. Viktoria YEVTODIEVA (soprano), Lidiya Kovalenko (violin), Irina Molokina (cello), and Yuri Serov (piano). ['Complete Songs, Vol. 1'—Opp. 62, 86, 100, and 121.] P St Petersburg 23 Mar.–4 May 1998.

Denmark: Classico Compact Disc CLASSCD 273. Nina PAVLOVSKY (soprano), Niels Christian Øllgaard (violin), Dorothea Wolff (cello), and Ulrich Stark (piano). [Op. 67.] P Mantziusgården, Denmark 26–8 May 1998.

Orfeo Compact Disc C465 991A. Alla ABLABERDYEVA (soprano) and Munich Trio (Rudolf J. Koeckert, Gerhard Zank, Hermann Lechler). [Opp. 8 and 67.] P Bavarian Radio Studio 4–5 May and 4–7 June 1999, I Mar. 2001.

References: Levaya, Vasina-Grossman (in Daragan), and Walsh.

Opus 128   Spring, Spring

Form: Song for bass voice and grand piano, marked 'Andante', to words by Aleksandr Pushkin, from chapter seven, stanza II of the poetic novel *Eugene Onegin*, written between 1823 and 1831.

Composed: 1967, with the intention of completing his cycle of 12 Pushkin songs planned in 1936 (see Opp. 46 and 91).

Première: November 1979, Leningrad; Yevgeni Nesterenko (bass).

Arrangement: Orchestrated by Gennadi Rozhdestvensky.

Music: Autograph found among the composer's papers after his death and preserved in the Shostakovich family archive.

   Muzyka, No. 11785 (in Volume 33 of *Collected Works* with Opp. 109, 121, 123, 127, 143, 145, and 146), 1984, 30 cm.

Duration: 2' 03".

Recording: USSR: Melodiya C10 26307 004. Orchestrated by Rozhdestvensky. Yevgeni NESTERENKO (bass), USSR Ministry of Culture Symphony Orchestra, Gennadi Rozhdestvensky. [Album 6 of 'From Manuscripts of

Different Years'—Sans opp. X, J, A, S, D; and Op. 41.] P 1983–6, I 1988*d*. *Reissued:* BMG Melodiya Compact Discs 74321 59058-2 (two-disc set). [Opp. 36, 4, 17, Z, H, C, 16, 1, 3, 7, 26/D, 59, E, 30*a*, and 19.] I and G Mar. 1999.

Opus 129   Violin Concerto No. 2 in C sharp minor

Form: Concerto for violin and small orchestra (with no brass other than 4 horns) in three movements:

1. Moderato—Allegretto
2. Adagio   *attacca*
3. Adagio—Allegro

Instrumentation: piccolo, flute, 2 oboes, 2 clarinets (A and B flat), 2 bassoons, contrabassoon ~ 4 French horns ~ timpani, tom-tom ~ 1st violins (16), 2nd violins (14), violas (12), cellos (12), double-basses (10 including five-string). [String numbers halved in Boosey & Hawkes score.]

Composed: May 1967, at Moscow and Repin; completed on 18 May 1967.

Dedication: David Fyodorovich Oistrakh (violinist). Intended as a gift on his sixtieth birthday but the composer miscalculated his age—see Opus 134.

Premières: First performances on 13 September 1967, Palace of Culture, Bolshevo, near Moscow and 26 September 1967, Moscow Conservatory Bolshoi Hall; David Oistrakh, Moscow Philharmonic Orchestra, Kirill Kondrashin. Official première by the same forces on 26 October 1967.

UK: 19 November 1967, Royal Festival Hall, London; D. Oistrakh, London Symphony Orchestra, Eugene Ormandy.

USA: 11 January 1968, New York; D. Oistrakh, New York Philharmonic Orchestra, Leonard Bernstein.

Arrangement: Reduction for violin and piano by the composer, with the violin part edited by David Oistrakh.

Music: The autograph full and piano scores preserved in the Shostakovich family archive.

Hans Sikorski, No. 6447, 1967, score, 30 cm.

Boosey & Hawkes, No. 836, 1968, score, 19 cm.

Sovetskii Kompozitor, No. 895, 1969, reduction for violin and piano, 28.5 cm.

Sovetskii Kompozitor, No. 896, 1970, score, 29 cm.

Edition Peters, No. 5718, 1970, reduction, 30 cm.

Sovetskii Kompozitor, No. 9227, 1976, reduction, 29 cm.

Muzyka, No. 10712 (in Volume 14 of *Collected Works* with Op. 77), 1981, 30 cm.

Muzyka, No. 10793 (in Volume 15 of *Collected Works* with Op. 77 reduction), 1981, reduction including a separate violin part ed. D. Oistrakh, 30 cm.

Duration: 29 and approx. 30 minutes in scores; 24' 57"–34' 05".

Films: The recorded phone conversation between the composer and dedicatee with excerpts from the concerto, accompanied by still photographs, appears on a Netherlands videocassette Kultur 1130.

A videocassette, Warner Vision 3984 23020-3, of the documentary film by Bruno Monsaingeon entitled 'David Oistrakh—Artist of the People?' includes excerpts from both violin concertos, Opp. 77 and 129, and the telephone discussion of the latter. Reviewed G Aug. 1998.

Recordings: USSR: Melodiya D 021405-6 (mono) and C 01627-8. David OISTRAKH (violin), Moscow Philharmonic Orchestra, Kirill Kondrashin. [Op. 54.] P 21 Nov. 1967, I 1967. *Reissued:* USA: Angel Melodiya SR 40064. [Op. 54.] I 1968 ~ France: Le Chant du Monde LDXA 78415. [Op. 54.] I 1968 ~ HMV Melodiya ASD 2447. [Op. 54.] G Mar. 1969 ~ HMV Melodiya ASD 3235 in Set SLS 5058. [Op. 77.] G Oct. 1976 ~ USSR: Melodiya C10 06907-8. [16-minute phone conversation between D. Oistrakh and the composer concerning rehearsal of the work.] I 1976*d* ~ Italy: EMI 065 94559. [Op. 54.] I 1978 ~ Netherlands: Phonogram Melodia 410 ~ USA: Musical Heritage Society MHS 824389 (in two-record set). [Op. 54 and Sans op. P.] I 1981 ~ Germany: Melodia Eurodisc 88 665 XPK. [In thirteen-record Oistrakh box set with Op. 77.] ~ France: Le Chant du Monde Compact Disc LDC 278 882. ['The David Oistrakh Edition'—with Op. 77 on second of 5 discs available singly.] I 1987, G Apr. 1988 ~ Germany: Melodia Eurodisc Compact Disc CD 69084. [Op. 77.] I 1990 ~ USSR: Melodiya Compact Disc SUCD 10 00242. [Prokofiev and Glière.] I 1991*c* ~ USA: Russian Disc RDCD 11 025. [Op. 77.] I Feb. 1994 ~ Japan: Icone Compact Disc ICN 9408-2. [Op. 141.] I Aug. 1994 ~ RCA Compact Discs 74321 72914-2 (two-disc set). [Mozart, Brahms, and Beethoven.] I Apr. 2000.

USSR: Melodiya C10 14091-2. David OISTRAKH (violin), Moscow Philharmonic Orchestra, Gennadi Rozhdestvensky. [In third box of Part 1 of *Collected Works on Records* with Op. 107.] P Moscow concert 27 Apr. 1968, I 1980.

Italy: Intaglio Compact Disc INCD 7241. David OISTRAKH (violin), USSR Symphony Orchestra, Yevgeni Svetlanov. [Op. 77.] P Royal Albert Hall, London concert 28 Aug. 1968, I July 1992. *Reissued:* BBC Legends Compact Disc BBCL 4060-2. [Op. 77; and Ysaÿe.] I Feb. 2001, G May 2001.

Poland: Muza SX 1749. Wanda WIŁKOMIRSKA (violin), Warsaw Philharmonic Orchestra, Wojciech Michniewski. P Warsaw 15–17 May 1979, I 1986.

Revelation Compact Disc RV 10108. Viktor TRETYAKOV (violin), USSR Symphony Orchestra, Mariss Jansons. [Op. 77.] P 28 Dec. 1979, I May 1998.

France: Praga Compact Disc PR 250 052. Jiří TOMÁŠEK (violin), Prague Radio Symphony Orchestra, Charles Mackerras. [Op. 77.] P Czech radio concert Feb. 1982, I 1994, G July 1995.

USA: Pyramid Compact Disc 13493. Nell GOTKOVSKY (violin), Bulgarian National Radio Symphony Orchestra, Vassil Kazandzhiev. [Op. 77.] P Sofia Oct. 1987, I 1988, G Oct. 1991.

Chandos Compact Disc CHAN 8820. Lydia MORDKOVITCH (violin), Scottish National Orchestra, Neeme Järvi. [Op. 77.] P Glasgow 16–17 Oct. 1989, I Feb. 1990, G Apr. 1990. The *Gramophone* Awards 1990—winner of Concerto category, G Oct. 1990.

Virgin Classics Compact Disc VC7 91143-2. Dmitri SITKOVETSKY (violin), BBC Symphony Orchestra, Andrew Davis. [Op. 77.] P London Dec. 1989, I Aug. 1990, G Sept. 1990. Preis der Deutschen Schallplattenkritik award 1990. *Reissued:* Virgin Classics Compact Disc VC7 59601-2. [Op. 77.] I June 1993 ~ Virgin Classics Compact Discs VBD5 61633-2 (two-disc set) [Op. 77 and Prokofiev.] I Aug. 1999.

Deutsche Grammophon Compact Disc 439 890-2GH. Gidon KREMER (violin), Boston Symphony Orchestra, Seiji Ozawa. [Op. 125.] P Boston concert Apr. 1992, I and G Sept. 1994.

France: Arion Compact Disc ARK 68326. Marie SCHEUBLÉ (violin), Monte-Carlo Philharmonic, James De Priest. [Op. 77.] P Monte-Carlo July 1995, I Mar. 1996.

Japan: Triton Compact Disc 17 006. Maksim FEDOTOV (violin), Russian State Symphony Orchestra, Aleksandr Vedernikov. [Op. 77.] P Moscow Conservatory Dec. 1995, I Nov. 1996.

Naxos Compact Disc 8.550814. Ilya KALER (violin), Polish National Radio Symphony Orchestra, Antoni Wit. [Op. 77.] P Katowice 15–18 Jan. 1996, I Aug. 1997, G Oct. 1997.

Czech: Supraphon Compact Disc SU 3178-2 031. Bohumil KOTMEL (violin), Czech Philharmonic Orchestra, Petr Altrichter. [Dvořák.] P Prague 15–16 Feb. 1996, I Sept. 1996.

Teldec Compact Disc 0630-13150-2. Maksim VENGEROV (violin), London Symphony Orchestra, Mstislav Rostropovich. [Prokofiev.] P Sept. 1996, I Oct. 1997, G Awards (Nov.) 1997.

References: Kay and Shirinsky.

Opus 130   Funeral-Triumphal Prelude

Alternative titles: *Poem of Mourning and Triumph* and *Prelude—Stalingrad.*

Form: Short orchestral piece for large symphony orchestra (with triple woodwind and additional brass band of 13 to 26 players), marked 'Adagio'.

Instrumentation: piccolo, 2 flutes, 3 oboes, 3 B flat clarinets, 2 bassoons, contrabassoons ~ 4 horns, 3 trumpets, 3 trombones, tuba ~ timpani (5 play-

ers), side drum, cymbals, bass drum ~ separate band of 2–4 B flat cor-
nets, 3–6 B flat trumpets and 2–4 each of alto, tenor, baritone, and bass
saxhorns ~ strings.
Composed: 1967. Intended for a recording to be used at the inaugural cere-
mony of the Mamayev Hill war memorial, Volgograd. [An arrangement
of Robert Schumann's *Träumerei* was later used for the Flame of Eternal
Glory tape-recording.]
Dedication: In memory of the heroes of the Battle of Stalingrad.
Première: October 1967, Volgograd (Stalingrad).
Music: Autograph score preserved in the Shostakovich family archive.
Numbered Opus 131 in some lists.
 Muzyka, No. 11687 (in Volume 11 of *Collected Works* with Sans op. U,
Opp. 96, 115, and 131), 1984, full score, 30 cm.
Duration: 'A short piece lasting a mere 2 minutes' (the composer); 2' 43".
Recording: Decca Compact Disc 436 762-2DH. Royal Philharmonic Orches-
tra, Vladimir ASHKENAZY. [Op. 65 and Sans op. U.] P Walthamstow 30
Apr. 1992, I Feb. 1994, G Apr. 1994.
Reference: Khentova (1984).

Opus 131   October

Form: Symphonic poem for orchestra (with triple woodwind), marked
'Moderato—Allegro'. The secondary theme is a reworking of the song
'To the Partisan' from *Volochayevka Days*, Opus 48.
Instrumentation: piccolo, 2 flutes, 2 oboes, cor anglais, 3 clarinets (A and B
flat), 2 bassoons, contrabassoon ~ 4 horns, 3 trumpets, 3 trombones,
tuba ~ timpani, side drum, cymbals ~ strings.
Composed: Started in summer 1967, at Moscow, and completed on 10
August 1967, in the Belovezhskaya Forest. Composed for the fiftieth
anniversary of the October Revolution.
Premières: 16 September 1967, Moscow Conservatory Bolshoi Hall; USSR
Symphony Orchestra, Maksim Shostakovich.
 USA: 10 October 1988, New York Avery Fisher Hall; New York Phil-
harmonic Orchestra, Andrew Davis.
Arrangements: Reduction for piano duet by the composer. Transcription for
military band (with optional oboes, bassoons, saxophones, and brass
band) by Daniil Braslavsky, for the sixtieth anniversary of the October
Revolution.
Music: Autograph score and the composer's reduction for piano duet pre-
served in the Shostakovich family archive. Given as Opus 132 on the
first four scores listed here and by McAllister (1975).
 Hans Sikorski, 1967, parts for hire only, 30 cm.
 Muzyka, No. 5789, 1969, score, 29.5 cm.

Edition Peters, No. 5744 (plate no. 12665), 1972, 18.5 cm.
Sovetskii Kompozitor, No. 4194, 1977, arr. for military band by
D. Braslavsky, 29 cm.
Muzyka, No. 11687 (in Volume 11 of *Collected Works* with Sans op. U,
Opp. 96, 115, and 130), 1984, 30 cm.

Duration: Approx. 13 minutes in score; 12' 27"–15' 43'; 20 minutes (M. Mac-
Donald).

Recordings: [Radio GDR recording broadcast on BBC Radio 3, 25 Aug. 1977.
Berlin Radio Symphony Orchestra, Heinz Rögner.]

Czech: Panton 11 0665-7. Czech Radio Symphony Orchestra, Zdeněk
KOŠLER. ['Soviet Music 1917–77'—Khrennikov, Mirzoyan, Prokofiev *et
al.*] P Czech Radio 1977. *Reissued:* France: Praga Compact Disc PR 254
055. [Opp. 20 and 119.] I July 1994.

Olympia Compact Disc OCD 201. Labelled Op. 132. Moscow Symphony Orchestra, Veronica DUDAROVA. [Op. 75a; Prokofiev and Eshpai.]
P 1982, I Dec 1987.

Deutsche Grammophon Compact Disc 427 616-2GH. Gothenburg
Symphony Orchestra, Neeme JÄRVI. [Opp. 141 and 115.] P Gothenburg
May 1988, I Aug. 1989, G May 1991. NB. Bars 45–6 repeated. *Reissued:*
Deutsche Grammophon Compact Discs 459 415-2GTA2 (two-disc
set). [Opp. 103, 112, 32, and 22a.] I Jan. 1999 ~ Deutsche Grammophon
Classikon Compact Disc 469 029-2GCL. [Opp. 141 and 115.] G Aug.
2000.

Academy Sound and Vision Compact Disc CD DCA 707. Royal Philharmonic Orchestra, Enrique BÁTIZ. [Opp. 47 and 115; Sans op. U.] P
Mitcham 1990, I June 1990, G Sept. 1990. *Reissued:* IMG Records Compact Disc IMGCD 1609. [Opp. 47 and 115; Sans op. U.] I June 1994, G Feb.
1995.

Decca Compact Disc 436 762-2DH. Royal Philharmonic Orchestra,
Vladimir ASHKENAZY. [Opp. 96, 14, and 81.] P Walthamstow Apr. 1992, I
June 1994, G Aug. 1994.

Japan: Fun House Compact Disc FHCE 2014. Norrköping Symphony
Orchestra, Junichi HIROKAMI. [Op. 47.] P Norrköping, Sweden Sept. 1993,
I Jan. 1994.

Opus 132   Sofya Perovskaya

Form: Music for the biographical film *Sofya Perovskaya*, written by Yevgeni
Gabrilovich, based on the life and execution of one of the 'Will of
the People' assassins of Tsar Aleksandr II, and directed by Leo Arnshtam for Mosfilm. The film score for orchestra (with separate wind
band and female chorus) comprises 18 items, of which all but two are
known:

March (Leading to the Execution)—Allegretto
The Execution—Allegretto
1. Allegro
3. Allegretto
Waltz—[Tempo di Valse]
4. Moderato
5. The Duel—Moderato
7. [The Village]—Andante
8. Voronezh—Moderato
9. Andante
10. Allegro
11. Allegro
12. Sofya arrives home after the Prosecutors speech—Moderato
13. The Dream—Adagio
14. At Figner (Andrei Zhelyabov captured)—Allegro
15. Sofya arrives at Figner after the assassination of the Tsar—
Adagio

Instrumentation: piccolo, 2 flutes, 2 oboes, 2 clarinets (B flat and A), 2 bassoons ~ 4 horns, 2 trumpets, 3 trombones, tuba ~ timpani, side drum, cymbals, bass drum ~ xylophone, orchestral bells, harp, celesta, piano ~ 2 each of E flat alto, B flat tenor, B flat baritone, and bass saxhorns ~ S.A. female choir in No. 7 ~ strings. March and The Execution for piccolo solo with side drum accompaniment.
Composed: September 1967.
Première: Film first shown in January 1968. [*Collected Works* states 6 May 1968.]
Music: Autograph score preserved in the Shostakovich family archive.
  Muzyka, No. 10890 (in Volume 42 of *Collected Works* with Opp. 75, 78, 80, 82, 95, 97, 111, 116, and 137), 1987, sixteen items, 30 cm.
Duration of sixteen items: 33' 02".
Recording: USA: Russian Disc Compact Disc RDCD 10 018. Sixteen items as listed under Form. Byelorussian Radio and TV Symphony Orchestra, Walter MNATSAKANOV. [Opp. 50, 53, 55, and 33.] P Minsk Nov. 1995.
  Decca Compact Disc 460 792-2DH11. Waltz only. Royal Concertgebouw Orchestra, Riccardo CHAILLY. [Op. 33, 26, 56, 116, 55, 76*a*, and 97.] P Amsterdam 6–22 May 1998, I Mar. 1999, G Apr. 1999.

Opus 133   Quartet No. 12 in D flat major

Form: String quartet in two movements:

1. Moderato
2. Allegretto—Adagio—Allegretto

Composed: Completed on 11 March 1968, at Repino.

Dedication: Dmitri Mikhailovich Tsyganov (1st violinist of the Beethoven Quartet).

Premières: 14 June 1968, USSR Composers' Club, Moscow; 14 September 1968, Moscow Conservatory Malyi Hall; and 5 November 1968, Glinka Concert Hall, Leningrad; Beethoven Quartet (Dmitri Tsyganov, Nikolai Zabavnikov, Fyodor Druzhinin, and Sergei Shirinsky).

UK: 27 June 1970, Aldeburgh Festival; Aeolian Quartet (Sidney Humphreys, Raymond Keenlyside, Margaret Major, and Derek Simpson).

Arrangements: Reduction for piano four hands by Anatoli Dmitriev and for two pianos by Dmitri Tsyganov.

Music: Autograph score preserved in Dmitri Tsyganov's personal archive (presented at the official Moscow première).

Muzyka, No. 6059, 1969, score, 20 cm.

Muzyka, No. 6171, 1969, parts, 29 cm.

Hans Sikorski, No. 2164, 1969, parts, 31.5 cm.

Hans Sikorski, No. 6226, 1969, score, 21 cm.

Boosey & Hawkes, No. 856, 1970, 19 cm.

Boosey & Hawkes, No. 19910, 1970, parts, 31 cm.

Muzyka, 1972, parts, 29 cm.

Muzyka, 1972, arr. for piano duet by D. Tsyganov, 29 cm.

Edition Peters, No. 5762, 1973, parts, 30 cm.

Muzyka, Leningrad, No. 2026 (in Volume 4 with Quartets 13 and 14 arr. for piano four hands by A. Dmitriev), 1976, 29.5 cm.

Muzyka, No. 10284 (in Volume 36 of *Collected Works* Quartets 9–15), 1980, 30 cm.

Hans Sikorski, No. 2268 (new edition with Op. 122), 1980, score, 21 cm.

Duration: Approx. 26 minutes in score; 23' 00"–28' 56"; 29' 15" (Plaistow).

Recordings: USSR: Melodiya CM 03223-4. BORODIN QUARTET (Rostislav Dubinsky, Yaroslav Aleksandrov, Dmitri Shebalin, Valentin Berlinsky). [Op. 138.] P 25 Dec. 1968, I 1972. *Reissued:* France: Le Chant du Monde LDX 78578 K. [Op. 138.] ~ HMV Melodiya HQS 1324 in Set SLS 879. [Op. 118.] G June 1974.

USSR: Melodiya D 025115-6 (mono) and C 01769-70, BEETHOVEN QUARTET (personnel as at premières). [Opp. 122 and 11.] P 1969, G Oct. 1971. *Reissued:* France: EMI 061 91298. [Opp. 122 and 11.] ~ USA: Consonance Blue Label Compact Disc 81.3008. [Vol. 4—Opp. 138 and 142.] I Mar. 1996.

Italy: Intaglio Compact Disc INCD 7561. BORODIN QUARTET (personnel as above). [Op. 57.] P St John's Smith Square, London 13 July 1970, I Aug. 1993.

L'Oiseau-Lyre DSLO 23. FITZWILLIAM QUARTET (Christopher Rowland, Jonathan Sparey, Alan George, Ioan Davies). [Op. 83.] P Sept. 1976, G

Nov. 1977. *Gramophone* Record Awards 1977—winner of Chamber Music category, G Mar. 1978. *Reissued:* Decca 188 D6 in Set D 188 D7. [Op. 142.] G Feb. 1981 ~ Decca Enterprise Compact Discs 433 078-2DM6. [On fifth disc of six-disc set with Opp. 122 and 138.] I Apr. 1992, G June 1992.

USSR: Melodiya C10 11613-4. TANEYEV QUARTET (Vladimir Ovcharek, Grigori Lutsky, Vissarion Soloviev, Iosif Levinzon). [In first box of Part 2 of *Collected Works on Records* with Op. 83.] P 1979, I 1980. *Reissued:* Japan: JVC Victor 5350. [Op. 142.] ~ USSR: Melodiya Compact Disc SUCD 10 00312. [Opp. 122 and 138.] I 1991*d*.

USSR: Melodiya C10 17375-6. BORODIN QUARTET (Mikhail Kopelman, Andrei Abramenkov, Dmitri Shebalin, Valentin Berlinsky). [Op. 138.] P 1981, I 1982*d*. *Reissued:* HMV Melodiya EX 270339-3 (DMM). [In seven-record box set of 15 Quartets plus Quintet.] G Mar. 1986 ~ EMI Compact Disc CDC7 49266-2. [Opp. 49 and 117.] I Nov. 1987 ~ Japan: Victor Musical Industries Compact Disc VICC 40022. [Opp. 122 and 138.] I 1990 ~ EMI Compact Discs CMS5 65032-2. [In six-disc set of 15 Quartets plus Quintet.] I Mar. 1994 ~ BMG Melodiya Compact Discs 74321 40711-2 (six-disc set). [Opp. 122 and 138.] I June 1997.

Olympia Compact Disc OCD 535. SHOSTAKOVICH QUARTET (Andrei Shislov, Sergei Pishchugin, Aleksandr Galkovsky, Aleksandr Korchagin). ['Complete Quartets, Vol. 5'—Opp. 138 and 142.] P 1985, I June 1994, G Sept. 1994.

Teldec Compact Discs 9031 71702-2. BRODSKY QUARTET (Michael Thomas, Ian Belton, Paul Cassidy, Jacqueline Thomas). [On fifth disc of six-disc set with Opp. 122 and 138.] P Berlin July 1989, I Nov. 1990, G June 1992. *Reissued:* Teldec Compact Disc 9031 73109-2. [Opp. 122 and 138.] I July 1991.

USA: ESS.A.Y. Compact Disc CD 1012. MANHATTAN QUARTET (Eric Lewis, Roy Lewis, John Dexter, Judith Glyde). [Opp. 122 and 138.] P Jersey City 12 June 1990, I 1991. *Reissued:* Koch Schwann Compact Disc 3 1070-2. ['Complete String Quartets, Vol. 5' with Opp. 122 and 138.] I Sept. 1993.

Virgin Classics Compact Disc VC7 59281-2. BORODIN QUARTET (Mikhail Kopelman, Andrei Abramenkov, Dmitri Shebalin, Valentin Berlinsky). [Op. 68.] P Snape Nov. 1990, I Feb. 1993, G June 1993. *Reissued:* Virgin Classics Compact Disc VBD5 61630-2 (two-disc set.). [Opp. 68, 73, 108, and 110.] I Aug. 1999.

Germany: Thorofon Compact Disc CTH 2238. PHILHARMONIA QUARTET OF BERLIN (Daniel Stabrawa, Christian Stadelmann, Neithard Resa, Jan Disselhorst). [Opp. 73 and 108.] P Berlin 1994, I 1998.

Deutsche Grammophon Compact Disc 463 284-2GH5 (five-disc set). EMERSON QUARTET (Eugene Drucker, Philip Setzer, Lawrence Dutton, David Finkel). ['Complete Quartets, Vol. 4'—Sans op. D, Opp. 122 and 138.] P Aspen, Colorado concert July–Aug. 1994, G June 2000 (the first movement included on cover CD).

Naxos Compact Disc 8.550975. ÉDER QUARTET (János Selmeczi, Péter Szüts, Sándor Papp, György Éder). ['Complete Quartets, Vol. 4'—Op. 68.] P Budapest 28–31 Mar 1995, I Apr. 1996, G Apr. 1997.
References: Kay and Keller.

Opus 134   Violin Sonata

Form: Sonata for violin and grand piano in three movements:

1. Andante	or originally	Pastorale
2. Allegretto		Allegro furioso
3. Largo—Andante		Variations on a Theme

Composed: 26 August–23 October 1968, at Moscow, for David Oistrakh's sixtieth birthday. [Originally Opus 129 was intended for this occasion but the composer was a year too early. This sonata was composed to make good the error.] Sketch for the first movement written on 26 June 1945.

Dedication: David Fyodorovich Oistrakh (violinist).

Premières: 8 January 1969, Union of Soviet Composers private hearing; David Oistrakh (violin) and Moisei Vainberg (piano).

3 May 1969, Moscow Conservatory Bolshoi Hall; D. Oistrakh and Svyatoslav Richter (piano).

UK: 3 June 1971, London; Raymond Cohen (violin) and Anthya Rael (piano).

Arrangement: Krzysztof Meyer orchestration for violin and chamber orchestra (double woodwind, French horns, and strings with percussion ensemble of timpani, tambourine, gong, 2 tom-toms, side drum, 2 bongos, orchestral bells, xylophone, vibraphone, marimba, celesta, and harp).

Music: Autograph score preserved at the Glinka Museum. The third movement was a set piece in the 1970 International Tchaikovsky Competition.

Anglo-Soviet Music Press / Hans Sikorski, No. 19949, 1969, parts, 30 cm.

Muzyka, No. 6709, 1970 and 1974, violin part ed. D. Oistrakh, 29 cm.

Edition Peters, No. 5739 (plate no. 12630), 1971, 30 cm.

Hans Sikorski, No. 2519, 1971, 31.5 cm.

Muzyka, No. 10927 (in Volume 38 of *Collected Works* with Opp. 40 and 147), 1982, including separate violin part, 30 cm.

Duration: Approx. 31 minutes in score; 23' 38"–34' 21".

Recordings: USSR: Melodiya M10 42045-6 (mono). David OISTRAKH (violin) and Dmitri Shostakovich (piano). [Op. 40.] P in composer's flat Dec. 1968, I 1980*b*. *Reissued:* Revelation Compact Disc RV 70008 (mono).

['Shostakovich plays Shostakovich, Vol, 7'—Opp. 5, 22, and 40.] I Sept. 1998, G Feb. 1999 ~ USA/Canada: Eclectra Compact Disc ECCD 2046 (mono). [Opp. 40 and 67.] I 2000.

USSR: Melodiya CM 02355-6. David OISTRAKH (violin) and Svyatoslav Richter (piano). P Moscow première 3 May 1969, I 1970. *Reissued:* HMV Melodiya ASD 2718. [Op. 67.] G Aug. 1971 ~ USA: Angel Melodiya SR 40189. [Op. 138.] I 1972 ~ Germany: Melodia Eurodisc 80 531 MK ~ Netherlands: Phonogram Melodia 691 426 ~ HMV Melodiya HQS 1369. [Op. 147.] G May 1977 ~ USSR: Melodiya D 027313-4 (mono) and CM 02355-6. [The latter in second box of Part 2 of *Collected Works on Records.*] I 1978 ~ Italy: EMI 065 99149. I 1978 ~ USA: Mobile Fidelity Sound Lab Compact Disc MFCD 909. [Franck.] I Mar. 1989 ~ France: Le Chant du Monde Compact Discs LDC 278 1018-19 (two-disc set). [Opp. 40, 147, and 67.] I Feb. 1990, G June 1990 ~ USA: Voxbox Compact Discs CDX 5120 (two-disc set). [Khachaturyan, Sibelius, and Franck.] I Nov. 1996 ~ BMG Melodiya Compact Discs 74321 34182-2 and 40711-2 (five-disc set, mono). ['David Oistrakh Edition'—Bartók.] I June 1977, G Feb. 1998.

USSR: Melodiya C10 06875-6. Oleg KAGAN (violin) and Elizaveta Leonskaya (piano). [Op. 127.] P 1976, I 1976*d.*

USSR: Melodiya C10 08753-4. Gidon KREMER (violin) and Andrei Gavrilov (piano). [Schnittke.] P Dec. 1976, I 1978*a. Reissued:* HMV Melodiya ASD 3547. [Schnittke and Prokofiev.] G Sept. 1978 ~ USA: Columbia Melodiya M 35109. [Op. 147.] ~ Germany: Melodia Eurodisc 28 752 KK and Eurodisc Club Edition 31 249 6. [Schnittke.]

USA: Advent E 1069 (cassette). Emanuel BOROK (violin) and Tatiana Yampolsky (piano). [Prokofiev.] *Reissued:* USA: Sine Qua Non SA 2045. I 1983.

USSR: Melodiya C10 12267-8. Pavel KOGAN (violin) and Elizaveta Ginzburg (piano). P 1979, I 1980*a.*

USSR: Melodiya C10 17721006. Olga PARKHOMENKO (violin) and Natalya Derenovskaya (piano). [Ishchenko.] P 1980, I 1983*b.*

Philips 6514 102. Mark LUBOTSKY (violin) and Lyubov Yedlina (piano). [Schnittke—*Prelude in Memory of Shostakovich* and Sonata No. 2.] P 1981, G June 1982.

Chandos ABRD 1089 (digital). Rostislav DUBINSKY (violin) and Lyubov Yedlina (piano). [Schnittke.] P London June 1983, G Jan. 1934. *Reissued:* Chandos Compact Disc CHAN 8343. [Schnittke.] I Sept. 1984, G Apr. 1985.

USA: Orion ORS 82441. STOYANOV DUO—Robert Stoyanov (violin) and Artur Stoyanov (piano). [Haydn.] P supervised by Maksim Shostakovich at El Segundo, California 1983.

USSR: Melodiya C10 21151 009. Grigori ZHISLIN (violin) and Frida Bauer (piano). P 1984, I 1985*a.*

Japan: JVC Compact Disc VDC 5015 (in two-disc set 'To the Memory of David Oistrakh'). Oleg KAGAN (violin) and Svyatoslav Richter (piano).

[Haydn and Brahms.] P Freiburg, West Germany concert 6–8 Mar. 1985. *Reissued:* Russia: Mezhdunarodnaya Kniga Compact Disc MK 418014. [Brahms and Haydn.] I 1992 ~ Olympia Compact Disc OCD 579 (also in five-disc set OCD 5013—'The Richter Collection, Vol. 2'). ['Sviatoslav Richter, Vol. 10'—Haydn and Brahms.] I Mar. 1996.

Russia: Melodiya Compact Disc SUCD 10 00095. Oleg KAGAN (violin) and Svyatoslav Richter (piano). [Op. 147.] P Moscow concert 17 May 1985, I 1993*a*. *Reissued:* Germany: Live Classics Compact Disc LCL 183. [Brahms.] P date given as 13 May 1985, I Mar. 2001.

Sweden: BIS Compact Disc CD 364. Christian BERGQVIST (violin) and Ronald Pöntinen (piano). ['The Russian Violin'—Schnittke and Stravinsky.] P Sweden 22–4 May 1987, G Apr. 1988.

Imp Classics Compact Disc MCD 58. Rimma SUSHANSKAYA (violin) and Roger Vignoles (piano). [Prokofiev.] P Monmouth 29–30 Sept. 1988, I Apr. 1993.

Italy: AS Disc Compact Disc As 5007. Gigino MAESTRI (violin) and Leonardo Leonardi (piano). [Franck.] P Genoa July 1989.

Czech: Panton 81 1013-2 131. Jirí HURNÍK (violin) and Jaromír Klepác (piano). [Stravinsky.] P Prague 23–6 Oct. 1989, I 1992.

Germany: Sound-Star-Ton 0211. Josef RISSIN (violin) and Olga Rissin-Morenova (piano). [Ustvolskaya.] P Wörth spring 1989, I 1991. *Reissued:* Germany: Sound-Star-Ton Compact Disc SST 30211. [Ustvolskaya.] I Nov. 1994.

Chandos Compact Disc CHAN 8988. Lydia MORDKOVITCH (violin) and Clifford Benson (piano). [Prokofiev and Schnittke—*Prelude in Memory of Shostakovich*.] P Snape Maltings 11 Dec. 1990, I Aug. 1991, G Dec. 1991.

USA: Koch International Classics Compact Disc 3-7116-2H1. Pavel BERMAN (violin) and Anne Epperson (piano). [Bloch.] P Purchase, New York 2–3 July 1991, I Apr. 1994.

France: Erato Compact Disc 2292 45804-2. Shlomo MINTZ (violin) and Viktoria Postnikova (piano). [Op. 147.] P Metz Sept. 1991, I Oct. 1992, G Nov. 1992.

Germany: Fidelio Compact Disc 9203. Isabelle van KEULEN (violin) and Ronald Brautigam (piano). [Op. 147.] P Utrecht 23–4 Mar. 1992, I July 1993. *Reissued:* Netherlands: Vanguard Classics Compact Discs 99306 (two-disc set). [Opp. 110*a*, 118*a*, and 147.] I Aug. 1999.

France: REM Editions Compact Disc 311 210. Anton KHOLODENKO (violin) and Sergei Milstein (piano). [Op. 147.] P Tassin-la Demi-Lune summer 1993.

France: Suoni e Colori Compact Disc SC 53008. Alexandre BRUSSILOVSKY (violin) and Pascal Godart (piano). ['Hommage à Dmitri Chostakovitch, Vol. 2'—Sans op. O (i), Opp. 6 and 94.] P Espace Fazioli, Paris Oct.–Nov. 1997.

USA: Arabesque Compact Discs Z 6698 (two-disc set). Jamie LAREDO (violin) and Joseph Kalichstein (piano). [Opp. 8, 67, 40, and 147.] P Purchase, New York 17–18 Dec. 1995 or 12–13 Sept. 1996. I and G Jan. 1998.

Nimbus Compact Disc NI 5631. Daniel HOPE (violin) and Simon Mulligan (piano). [Pärt, Penderecki, and Schnittke.] P Wyastone Leys, Monmouth 5–7 Aug. 1999, I Feb. 2000, G Apr. 2000.

Reference: Shirinsky.

Note: A rough draft and a fair copy of the 1945 unfinished first movement, in G minor and marked 'Moderato con moto', preserved at the CIS Archives of Literature and Art.

Sans op. W   Cello Concerto No. 1 (Tishchenko)

Form: New orchestration of former student Boris Tishchenko's Cello Concerto No. 1, Opus 23 (composed in 1963, originally for 17 woodwind instruments, percussion, and harmonium, but not performed until 1968 in Leningrad). Shostakovich's instrumentation employs a reduced woodwind ensemble of nine players, percussion (including wood block, tom-tom, and xylophone), and strings.

Composed: Shostakovich's orchestration prepared in early 1969. The score presented to Tishchenko on 23 March 1969, the composer's thirtieth birthday.

Music: Manuscript in Shostakovich's hand. [Tishchenko's score published by Muzyka, Leningrad, 1968.]

Duration: 26' 03"–29' 27".

Recordings: [USSR: Melodiya CM 01805-6. In Tishchenko's original orchestration. Mstislav Rostropovich (cello), Leningrad Philharmonic Orchestra woodwind and percussion ensemble, Igor Blazhkov. [Op. 67.] P and I 1969.]

USSR: Melodiya C10 22267 009. Sergei MNOZHIN (cello), USSR Ministry of Culture Symphony Orchestra, Gennadi Rozhdestvensky. [Album 4 of 'From Manuscripts of Different Years'—Op. 109.] P 1984, I 1986a.

Chandos Compact Disc CHAN 9792. Aleksandr IVASHKIN (cello), Russian Symphony Orchestra, Valeri Polyansky. ['The Unknown Shostakovich' (sic)—Opp. 23 and 125, Sans op. B.] P Moscow Conservatory Jan. 1998, I Jan. 2000.

Reference: Kats.

Opus 135   Symphony No. 14

Form: Symphonic song cycle for soprano and bass soloists, string orchestra, and percussion, to texts in Russian translations of Federico García Lorca,

Guillaume Apollinaire, and Rainer Maria Rilke, and the original Russian of William Küchelbecker, in eleven sections:

1. De Profundis (García Lorca)—Adagio (for bass soloist)
2. Malagueña (García Lorca)—Allegretto (soprano) *attacca*
3. Lorelei (Apollinaire)—Allegro molto (soprano and bass) *attacca*
4. The Suicide (Apollinaire)—Adagio (soprano)

5. On Watch (Apollinaire)—Allegretto (soprano) *attacca*
6. Madam, look! (Apollinaire)—Adagio (soprano and bass) *attacca*
7. In prison—At the Sante Jail (Apollinaire)—Adagio (bass)

8. The Zaporozhian Cossack's answer to the Sultan of Constantinople (Apollinaire)—Allegro (bass) *attacca*
9. O Delvig, Delvig! (Küchelbecker)—Andante (bass)

10. The death of the poet (Rilke)—Largo (soprano) *attacca*
11. Conclusion (Rilke)—Moderato (soprano and bass)

Russian translations by I. Tynyanova (No. 1), L. Geleskul (No. 2), M. Kudinov (Nos. 3–8), and T. Silman (Nos. 10 and 11).

Instrumentation: castanets, wood block, whip, 3 tom-toms (soprano, alto, and tenor—1 player) ~ orchestral bells, xylophone, vibraphone, celesta ~ soprano and bass soloists ~ 10 violins, 4 violas, 3 cellos, 2 five-string double-basses.

Composed: Piano vocal score completed in a Moscow hospital on 16 February 1969; the full score at his Moscow apartment on 2 March 1969.

Dedication: Benjamin Britten (composer). Personal score inscribed 'To dear Benjamin Britten as a token of profound respect from a cordially devoted D. Shostakovich 1 XII 1969 Moscow'.

Premières: 21 June 1969, Moscow Conservatory Malyi Hall; Margarita Miroshnikova (soprano), Yevgeni Vladimirov (bass), Moscow Chamber Orchestra, Rudolf Barshai. Special concert for a select audience; the performance introduced by the composer.

29 September 1969, Hall of the Academy Cappella, Leningrad; Galina Vishnevskaya (soprano), Y. Vladimirov (bass), Moscow Chamber Orchestra, Rudolf Barshai. The performance introduced by the composer. NB. The concert took place after sixty rehearsals (Vishnevskaya in *Galina*, p. 401).

UK: 14 June 1970, Aldeburgh Festival; G. Vishnevskaya, M. Reshetin, English Chamber Orchestra, Benjamin Britten.

USA: 1 January 1971, Academy of Music, Philadelphia; Phyllis Curtin (soprano), Simon Estes (bass), Philadelphia Orchestra, Eugene Ormandy.

English translation: 13 September 1972, Queen Elizabeth Hall, London; Philomusica of London, David Littáur (conductor).

Arrangements: Translation in English by Martin Cooper, Igor Buketoff, Valeri Vlazinskaya, and Emily Gill; and in German by Waltraut Levine (for the East German première in 1973) and Jörg Morgener. Version prepared by J. Morgener, with poems in their original languages, approved by the composer in 1971. Reduction for voices and piano by the composer.

Music: The autograph full and piano scores preserved in the Shostakovich family archive. The autograph of the tenth movement purchased for the Britten-Pears Library, Aldeburgh, in January 1991. The first page of the autograph vocal score is reproduced in Volume 9 of *Collected Works*.

Music Fund of the USSR, 1969, reduction with libretto of 11 pp. inserted, 29 cm.

Edwin F. Kalmus, No. 325, 1969, Russian text, 26.5 cm.

Hans Sikorski, No. 2174, 1970, Russian and German texts—Nos. 1–9 of the latter by J. Morgener, 21 cm.

Anglo-Soviet Music Press, *c*.1971, vocal score with text translated into English by M. Cooper, 30 cm.

Muzyka, No. 6830, 1971, full score, 29 cm.

Muzyka, No. 9856 (in Volume 8 of *Collected Works* with Op. 141), 1980, full score, 30 cm.

Muzyka, No. 11688 (in Volume 9 of *Collected Works* with reductions of Op. 113 and choral sections of Opp. 14 and 20), vocal score with Russian text, 30 cm.

Duration: Approx. 42 minutes in score; 47' 04"–53' 11"; 50' 30" (Plaistow).

Recordings: USSR: Melodiya CM 01933-4. Margarita Miroshnikova (soprano), Yevgeni Vladimirov (bass), Moscow Chamber Orchestra, Rudolf BARSHAI. P summer 1969, I 1970. *Reissued:* USA: Angel Melodiya SR 40147. I 1970 ~ Netherlands: Phonogram Melodia 691 430 ~ HMV Melodiya ASD 2633. G Mar. 1971 ~ Italy: EMI 065 91847 ~ HMV Melodiya BOX 502512 in Set SLS 5025. G Dec. 1975.

USA: Russian Disc Compact Disc RDCD 11 192. Galina Vishnevskaya (soprano), Mark Reshetin (bass), Moscow Chamber Orchestra, Rudolf BARSHAI. [Op. 70.] P Moscow première concert 29 Dec. 1969, I Oct. 1993, G Jan. 1994.

BBC Legends Compact Disc BBCB 8013-2. Texts not included. Galina Vishnevskaya (soprano), Mark Reshetin (bass), English Chamber Orchestra, Benjamin BRITTEN. [Britten.] P Snape concert 14 June 1970, G Dec. 1999.

USA: RCA Red Seal LSC 3206. Phyllis Curtin (soprano), Simon Estes (bass), Philadelphia Orchestra, Eugene ORMANDY. P 1971. *Reissued:* RCA Red Seal LSB 5002. G July and Aug. 1971 ~ RCA Red Seal RL 01284. [In three-record box set with Opp. 113 and 141.] G Nov. 1978 ~ USA: Time-Life 'Great Man of Music' box set STL 568. [Opp. 22*a*, 114, 40, 47, 102, and 110.] I 1979.

USSR: Melodiya CM 04009-10. Galina Vishnevskaya (soprano), Mark Reshetin (bass), Moscow Philharmonic Orchestra, Mstislav ROS-TROPOVICH. P studio 1972, I 1974. *Reissued:* Germany: Melodia Eurodisc 87 623 XPK (in thirteen-record box set). I 1974 ~ HMV Melodiya ASD 3090. G Dec. 1975 ~ France: Le Chant du Monde LDX 78554 ~ Germany: Melodia Eurodisc Compact Disc 258492 ~ USSR: Melodiya Compact Disc SUCD 10 00241. I 1991*c* ~ Russia: Russian Disc R10 00321-2 (DMM). [In double-album 'For the 85th Anniversary' with Opp. 35, 102, and 5.] I 1991 ~ Teldec Compact Discs 0630-17046-2. [In twelve-disc set of Symphonies.] G Oct. 1997.

Revelation Compact Disc RV 10101. Galina Vishnevskaya (soprano), Mark Reshetin (bass), Moscow Chamber Orchestra, Mstislav ROS-TROPOVICH. [Op. 127.] P concert 12 Feb. 1973, I Apr. 1998, G July 1998.

USSR: Melodiya C10 05477-8. Yevgeniya Tselovalnik (soprano), Yevgeni Nesterenko (bass), Moscow Philharmonic Orchestra, Kirill KON-DRASHIN. P 1974, I 1975*d*. *Reissued:* Germany: Melodia Eurodisc 300 606-435. [In three-record box set with Opp. 113 and 141.] ~ France: Le Chant du Monde LDX 78633 ~ USSR: Melodiya C10 05477-8. [In second box of Part 1 of *Collected Works on Records*.] I 1980 ~ HMV Melodiya EX 2903873 (DMM). [Eleventh record in twelve-record box set.] G Dec. 1985 ~ France: Le Chant du Monde Compact Disc LDC 278 1009-10. [In Box 5 of five two-disc sets with Op. 141.] G May 1989 ~ BMG Classics Melodiya Compact Disc 74321 19844-2. [Op. 14.] I July 1994, G Nov. 1994.

USSR: Melodiya C10 07673-4. Zara Dolukhanova (soprano), Yevgeni Nesterenko, (bass), Leningrad Chamber Orchestra, Lazar GOZMAN. P 1976, I 1977*c*. *Reissued:* HMV Melodiya ASD 3481. G May 1978.

USA: CBS 37270. Teresa Kubiak (soprano), Isser Bushkin (bass), Rodney Friend (violin), Sol Greitzer (viola), Lorna Munroe (cello), John Shaeffer (double-bass), New York Philharmonic Orchestra, Leonard BERNSTEIN. P 8 Dec. 1976. *Reissued:* CBS Masterworks 74084. G Apr. 1983 ~ Sony Royal Edition Compact Disc SMK 47617. G Nov. 1993 and June 1994 ~ Sony Classical Compact Discs SX4K 64206 (four-disc set). I Dec. 1995.

Decca SXDL 7532 (digital). Sung in the original languages of the poems. Julia Varády (soprano), Dietrich Fischer-Dieskau (baritone), Concertgebouw Orchestra, Bernard HAITINK. P Amsterdam 14–15 Nov. 1981, G Jan. 1982. *Reissued:* USA: London LDR 71032 (digital) ~ Decca Compact Disc 417 514-2DH. [Op. 143*a*.] I Dec. 1986, G Mar. 1987 ~ Decca Ovation Compact Disc 425 074-2DM. [Op. 143*a*.] I Aug. 1993, G Nov. 1993 ~ London Compact Disc 444 440-2. [On tenth disc of eleven-disc set with Op. 143*a*.] I June 1995.

USSR: Melodiya A10 00213 001 (digital). Makvala Kasrashvili (soprano), Anatoli Safiulin (bass), USSR Ministry of Culture Symphony Orchestra, Gennadi ROZHDESTVENSKY. P 1985, I 1987*c*. *Reissued:* Japan:

Victor Compact Disc VDC 1093 ~ Olympia Compact Disc OCD 182. [Op. 58*a*.] I Sept. 1988, G Dec. 1988 ~ Olympia Compact Disc OCD 5006. [In Vol. 2 five-disc set of symphonies with Op. 58*a*.] I Dec. 1990 ~ BMG Melodiya Compact Discs 74321 59057-2 (two-disc set). [Opp. 21, 46/141, 62*a*, and Sans op. M.] I Feb. 1999.

USA: Schwann Musica Mundi VMS 002 107 (DMM). Hildegard Harting (soprano), Peter Meven (bass), Rundfunk-Sinfonieorchester Saarbrücken, Myung-Whun CHUNG. P Saarbrücken 16 May 1986, I Jan. 1988. *Reissued:* Koch Schwann Compact Disc 311 033. I 1993.

Chandos ABRD 1232 (digital) and Compact Disc CHAN 8607. Elizabeth Holleque (soprano), Nikita Storojev (bass), I Musici de Montréal, Eleonora Turovsky (leader), Yuli TUROVSKY. P Quebec 1988, I Sept. 1988, G Dec. 1988.

Virgin Classics Compact Disc VC7 91432-2. Makvala Kasrashvili (soprano), Mikhail Krutikov (bass), Orchestre de Chambre de Lausanne, Aleksandr LAZAREV. [Op. 110*a*.] P Lausanne University Apr. 1990, I July 1991, G Oct. 1991.

Naxos Compact Disc 8.550631. Magdaléna Hajóssyová (soprano), Peter Mikuláš (bass), Czecho-Slovak Radio Symphony Orchestra, Ladislav SLOVÁK. P Bratislava 22 Feb.–4 Mar. 1991, I May 1993, G Nov. 1993. *Reissued:* Naxos Compact Discs 8.506003. [In six-disc set with Symphonies Nos. 5, 8, 9, 10, 11, and 13.] I 1993.

Deutsche Grammophon Compact Disc 437 785-2GH. Lyuba Kazarnovskaya (soprano), Sergei Leiferkus (baritone), Gothenburg Symphony Orchestra, Neeme JÄRVI. [Sans op. V.] P Gothenburg May 1992, I Oct. 1993, G Feb. 1994.

Denon Compact Disc CO 78821. Yelena Prokina (soprano), Sergei Aleksashkin (bass), Wilfried Rehm (cello), Vienna Symphony Orchestra, Eliahu INBAL. P Vienna Apr. 1993, I Mar. 1996.

Netherlands: Erasmus Compact Disc WVH 131. Alexandra Nagelkerke (soprano), Nanco de Vries (bass), Utrecht Conservatory Chamber Orchestra, Viktor LIBERMAN. [Op. 110.] P Rotterdam Jan. 1994.

Finland: Ondine Compact Disc ODE 845-2. Sung in the original languages of the poems. Margareta Haverinen (soprano), Petteri Salomaa (bass-baritone), Tapiola Sinfonietta, Joseph SWENSEN. [Sans op. D.] P Espoo Sept. 1994, I Mar. 1996, G Apr. 1996.

France: Opus Ill Compact Disc OPS 30-165. Sung in the original languages of the poems. Marie-Stéphane Bernard (soprano), Lionel Peintre (baritone), Musicatreize, Roland HAYRABÉDIAN. [Op. 110*a*.] P Miramas, France Apr. 1996, I Nov. 1996, G Dec. 1996.

References: Aranovsky, Kay, Layton, Martynov, Sabinina, and Shaginyan.

Sans op. X   Miscellaneous Works

(i) Songs

'A Toast to our Motherland'

Form: A song with lyric by Iosif Utkin for tenor, mixed chorus, and piano, marked 'Presto'.

Composed: 1944, for an album of songs to lyrics by Utkin.

Music: The whereabouts of the autograph is not known.

Sovetskii Kompozitor (in album *We'll Sing of Our Country*), 1975.

Muzyka, No. 10179 (in Volume 34 *Collected Works* with Op. 88 and 136; and songs), 1985, 30 cm.

'The Black Sea'

Form: A song with lyric by S. Alymov and N. Verkhovsky for solo bass, male chorus and piano, marked 'Allegro moderato'.

Composed: 1944.

Arrangement: A version edited by Aleksandr Tishchenko for an album commemorating the thirtieth anniversary of the Victory of the Soviet People in the Great Patriotic War, with alternative bayan accompaniment.

Music: The whereabouts of the autograph is not known.

Music Fund of the USSR (in collection *Songs of the Navy*, 1st edition), 1944.

Sovetskii Kompozitor, No. 3567 (in album *It is impossible for us to forget all about this journey* . . . compiled by Aleksandr Tishchenko), 1975, 29.5 cm.

Muzyka, No. 10179 (in Volume 34 of *Collected Works* with Opp. 88 and 136; and songs), 1985, 30 cm.

Recordings: Europe: Harmonia Mundi WRC S/R 4283. Bulgarian State Choir. [?]

USSR: Melodiya C60 19135 007. Red Banner Song and Dance Ensemble of the Black Sea Fleet, Ivan SAMOFATOV. [Muradeli, Mitkin, Drago *et al.*] I 1983*d*.

'Our Native Russia has Gained Strength from the Storms'

An unpublished song with words by S. Shchipachev, written in 1945, is preserved at the CIS Archives of Literature and Art. This song for mixed choir and orchestra was intended as the National Anthem of the RSFSR.

'Hymn to Moscow'

An unpublished song, with the subtitle 'Stand Fast, our inviolable National Shrine', to words by I. Frenkel, was written in 1948. Autograph version for choir and piano preserved at the Glinka Museum with a variant for soloist, two-part chorus, and piano preserved at the CIS Archives of

Literature and Art. Musically this song is identical with that of 'Song of Peace' used in *The Meeting on the Elbe*, Opus 80.

'Our Song'
Form: A song for chorus and orchestra with words by Konstantin Simonov.
Composed: 1950, at Moscow.
Arrangements: Reduction by the composer for solo bass, mixed chorus and piano, marked 'Moderato maestoso'. Also for bass soloist and piano, marked 'With moderate movement. Solemnly'.
Music: Autograph score preserved at the Glinka Museum.
Muzgiz, 1950, arrangement for soloist, chorus and piano.
Muzykalnaya Zhizn ('Musical Life') journal, 1982, No. 24, arr. for bass and piano, published as a supplement.
Muzyka, No. 10179 (in Volume 34 of *Collected Works* with Opp. 88 and 136; and songs), 1985, 30 cm.

'Supporters of Peace March'
Alternative titles: *March of Peace Champions* and *Song of Fighters for Peace.*
Form: A marching song for solo tenor, chorus and piano, with words by K. Simonov. The tune is based on the first two bars of *Novorossiisk Chimes*, Sans op. U.
Composed: Possibly in 1950.
Arrangement: For male chorus and piano by the composer.
Music: Autograph preserved at the Glinka Museum. First published in the collection *Siberia is Calling*, Moscow, 1956, chorus and piano.
Sovetskii Kompozitor, No. 519 (in *D. Shostakovich: Songs*), 1958, chorus and piano, 29 cm.
Muzyka, No. 10179 (in Volume 34 of *Collected Works* with Opp. 88 and 136; and songs), 1985, chorus and piano, 30 cm.

'Bird of Peace'
Form: A song for voice and piano by the British composer Joan Smith in a Russian translation by L. Ozerov. Marked 'Unhurried, expressively'. Awarded Second Prize at the Fourth International Festival of Youth, Bucharest.
Composed: 28 August 1953.
Music: Autograph preserved at the Glinka Museum. Published in a supplement to the journal *Sovetskaya Muzyka*, 1953, No. 10. ('Songs of a Friend', fourth collection, Muzgiz No. 23892). NB. The supplement and Meskhishvili name the composer J. Skit.

'There Were Kisses'
Form: A romantic song for bass voice and piano, with lyric by Yevgeni Dolmatovsky. No tempo indications.

Composed: Undated. Possibly written originally for the Opus 98 song cycle in 1954.
Music: Autograph preserved at the CIS Archives of Literature and Art.
Muzyka, No. 10283 (in Volume 32 of *Collected Works* with Opp. 4, 21, 46, 62, 79, 84, 86, 91, 98, 100 *et al.*), 1982, 30 cm.
Sovetskii Kompozitor, No. 7815 (in *Romances and Songs to verses of Yevgeni Dolmatovsky* with Opp. 80, 86, and 98), 1987, 29 cm.

'October Dawn'
Form: A song with lyric by Vladimir Kharitonov for soloists and choir, marked 'Grave'.
Composed: 1957, at Moscow, for the fortieth anniversary of the October Revolution.
Music: The whereabouts of the autograph is not known.
Molodaya Gvardiya, Moscow (in collection *Ring Out, Song!*), 1958.
Sovetskii Kompozitor, No. 519 (in *D. Shostakovich: Songs*), 1958, arr. for two voices and piano, 29 cm.
Muzyka, No. 10179 (in Volume 34 of *Collected Works* with Opp. 88 and 136; and songs), 1985, 30 cm.
Recordings: USSR: MK D 004788-9 (8" mono). V. SOROKIN and Boris SHAPENKO (baritone) with choir. ['Songs of Lenin, the Party and Motherland'—Kabalevsky, B. Aleksandrov, Molchanov *et al.*] P 1958. *Reissued:* USSR: MK D 5062-3 (10" mono). [Songs from Opp. 33, 72, 80, 82, 86, and 99.] I 1959.

'We Cherish the October Dawns in Our Hearts' and
'We Sing Glory to Our Country'
Form: Two songs (also translated as 'We keep the October Uprising in our Hearts' and 'We Glorify the Motherland' respectively)—both marked 'Maestoso'—for chorus and piano to words by V. Sidorov.
Composed: 1957, at Moscow, for the fortieth anniversary of the October Revolution.
Music: The whereabouts of the autographs are not known.
Sovetskii Kompozitor, No. 519 (in *D. Shostakovich: Songs*), 1958, chorus and piano, 29 cm.
Muzyka, No. 10179 (in Volume 34 of *Collected Works* with Opp. 88 and 136; and songs), 1985, chorus and piano, 30 cm.

'To France'
Form: A song for voice, mixed choir, and piano.
Composed: In the 1950s.
Music: The whereabouts of the autograph is not known. Published by Sovetskii Kompozitor in 1960 (Meskhishvili).

'Glory to the Shipbuilders'
Form: A song for mixed chorus a cappella.
Composed: Early 1960s.
Music: Autograph lost. Published in *Znamya Kommunizma* ('Banner of Communism'), Odessa, No. 114, 10 June 1964.

'La Serenata' (Braga)
Form: Transcription of a popular song by Gaetano Braga for two female voices, violin, and piano. Russian translation of M. Marcello's lyric by A. Gorchakova.
Composed: In the 1970s.
Music: Autograph found among the composer's papers after his death.
Duration: 5' 19".
Recording: USSR: Melodiya C10 26307 004. Lyudmila SOKOLENKO (soprano), Lyudmila KOLMAKOVA (mezzo-soprano), Aleksandr Suptel (violin), and Viktoria Postnikova (piano). [Album 6 of 'From Manuscripts of Different Years'—Sans opp. J, A, S, D; Opp. 41 and 128.] P 1983–6, I 1988*d*.

(ii) Cantata

Rayok
Alternative titles: *Little Paradise.* An alternative translation of the Russian title *Rayok* is *Little Eden;* also used colloquially to refer to the topmost gallery in a theatre—'the gods' (UK) or 'peanut gallery' (USA). Labelled as 'Learner's Manual' on the world première recording and titled 'The Antiformalistic Gods' in *Soviet Weekly,* No. 2495, 16 December 1989 (the latter modified to *Antiformalist Gallery* for the UK première). This is without doubt *The Zhdanov Decree* mentioned by Solomon Volkov in *Testimony.*
Form: A satirical semi-staged cantata based on the notorious Conference of Musicians at the Central Committee of the All-Union Communist Party in Moscow, January 1948 and its Decree of 10 February 1948. The score, for four bass singers, a small mixed chorus of musical activists (required mainly for laughter and applause) and piano, uses the original text of speeches by Stalin, Andrei Zhdanov, and his successor, Dmitri Shepilov, in the libretto by the composer (not Lev Lebedinsky as claimed in *Tempo* article). The composer states that the cast may be reduced to one versatile artist, taking the part of the chorus and all four roles in appropriate voices. The melodies of the popular songs 'Suliko', 'Kamarinskaya' and 'Kalinka' are introduced. The added finale quotes music from Jean Robert Planquette's operetta *Les cloches de Corneville* (1877).
Composed: The first part before the appearance of Troikin written secretly in May 1948, with a continuation in 1957 after the Second Congress of

Musicians at which Zhdanov's successor, Dmitri Shepilov, presided. Originally the score purposefully remained incomplete at the 24th bar after fig. 33. A finale, composed between 1965 and 1968, was discovered by Veniamin Basner in May 1989.

Premières: USA: 12, 13, 14, and 17 January 1989, Kennedy Center Concert Hall, Washington and 15 January 1989, Carnegie Hall, New York; Julian Rodescu (Master of Ceremonies), Eric Halfvarson (Yedinitsyn = Stalin or No. 1 lowest grade in Soviet schools), Andrew Wentzel (Dvoikin = Zhdanov or No. 2 failing grade), Jonathan Deutsch (Troikin = Shepilov or No. 3 barely passing grade), Members of the Choral Arts Society of Washington, Norman Scribner (chorus-master), Mstislav Rostropovich (piano).

25 September 1989, Moscow Conservatory Bolshoi Hall; USSR Ministry of Culture under the direction of Valeri Polyansky and Mikhail Kozakov (in the role of reciter); Yuri Vishnyakov (Master of Ceremonies), Yevgeni Chepikov (Yedinitsyn), Anatoli Obraztsov (Dvoikin), Nikolai Konovalov (Troikin), and Igor Khudolei (piano).

UK: 23 and 24 May 1993, Brighton Festival, Roedean Theatre; décor by Nataliya Khrennikova, directed by Boris Pokrovsky and conducted by Anatoli Levin; Aleksei Mochalov (Master of Ceremonies), Vladimir Khrulev and Viktor Bornykov (Yedinitsyn), Eduard Akimov (Dvoikin), Vladimir Rybasenko (Troikin), Moscow Chamber Opera Chorus (Guards and Musical Functionaries); Moscow Chamber Opera Orchestra.

Arrangements: English translation of the libretto by Elizabeth Wilson. Orchestrations by Boris Tishchenko and jointly by Vladimir Spivakov and Vladimir Milman.

Music: Manuscript copies. Additional 10 pages of score discovered after the Erato recording.

Anglo-Soviet Music Press, No. 8261, 1991, vocal score with Russian and English texts (the latter by Elizabeth Wilson), 31 cm.

DSCH Publishers, Moscow, no number, 1995, vocal score with text and thirteen-page commentary in Russian by Manashir Yakubov, 30 cm.

DSCH Publishers, Moscow, 1995, full score and parts of B. Tishchenko's orchestration available for hire.

Duration: Approx. 18 minutes in score; 14' 55"–19' 36"; *c*.40 mins (complete score, including introductory speech).

Recordings: France: Erato Compact Disc ECD 75571. Russian version— Romuald Tesarowicz (Master of Ceremonies), Nicola Ghiuselev (Yedinitsyn), Arkadi Volodos (Dvoikin), Nikita Storojev (Troikin), Audite Nova vocal ensemble, Jean Sourisse (chorus-master); English version— as USA première; Mstislav ROSTROPOVICH (conductor and piano). P Paris Feb. 1989 and Washington Jan. 1989 respectively, G Jan. 1990. Booklet provides libretto in French, English, and Russian.

Japan: Triton Compact Disc 17 008. Aleksei MOCHALOV (bass), Moscow Chamber Music Theatre Orchestra and Chorus, Anatoli Levin, [Opp.

58*a*, 140, 146, and 121.] P Mosfilm Studio Nov. 1995, I Nov. 1996. NB. All roles taken by Mochalov. Orchestrator not credited. Booklet provides libretto in transliterated Russian, English, French, and German.

USA: Music Masters Compact Disc 01612 67189-2. Orch. by V. Spivakov and V. Milman. Aleksei MOCHALOV (bass), Moscow Virtuosi, Vladimir Spivakov. [Opp. 79*a* and 94.] P Dec. 1996. NB. All roles taken by Mochalov.

References: *DSCH,* Lebedinsky, M. MacDonald, Volkov (1979), Werth (1949), and Yakubov (in Bartlett).

Note: The Moscow Chamber Opera use this work in Tishchenko's orchestration as a way in staging a completion of *The Gamblers,* Sans op. K (i).

(iii) *Orchestral*

Intervision

Form: Orchestral fragment of 6 bars marked 'Moderato maestoso' ♩ = 96.

Instrumentation: piccolo, 2 flutes, 3 oboes, 3 B flat clarinets, 2 bassoons, contrabassoon ~ 4 horns, 3 trumpets, 3 trombones, tuba ~ timpani, triangle, cymbals ~ strings.

Composed: Early 1971, at Moscow.

Première: March 1971, USSR TV on eve of the Twenty-Fourth Congress of the Communist Party; recording.

Music: Autograph score preserved in the Shostakovich family archive.
Muzyka, No. 10890 (in Volume 42 of *Collected Works* with Opp. 75, 78, 80, 82, 95, 111, 116, 132, and 137), 1987, 30 cm.

Opus 136   Loyalty

Alternative titles: *Fidelity* and *Faithfulness.*

Form: Settings of eight patriotic ballads by Yevgeni Dolmatovsky for unaccompanied male chorus:

1. In some immemorial year—Moderato
2. People believing in a flame—Allegretto
3. A great name—Allegretto
4. Revolution banner—Allegretto
5. A difficult search for beauty—Allegro non troppo
6. I want to learn all about him—Adagio
7. So this is where the people were!—Andante
8. On meetings of the young generation—Allegretto

Composed: Completed at Repino in April 1970, for the centenary celebrations of Lenin's birth.

Dedication: Gustav Ernesaks (composer and chorus-master).

Premières: 5 December 1970, Estonia Concert Hall, Tallinn (featured in the choir's 3000th programme) and 25 February 1971, Moscow Conservatory Bolshoi Hall; Estonian State Academic Male Voice Choir, Gustav Ernesaks.

Music: Autograph score preserved in the Shostakovich family archive.
Muzyka, No. 6935, 1970, 22 cm.
Muzyka, No. 10179 (in Volume 34 of *Collected Works* with Op. 88 and songs), 1985, 30 cm.

Duration: Approx. 20 minutes in score; 19' 25"; 19' 45" (Plaistow); 25 minutes (M. MacDonald).

Recordings: USSR: Melodiya CM 02523-4. Estonian State Academic Male Voice Choir, Gustav ERNESAKS. [Op. 120.] P 1971, I May 1971. *Reissued:* USSR: Melodiya CM 03466-02523. [Ernesaks.] I 1973 ~ USA: Angel Melodiya SR 40245. [Op. 20.] I 1974 ~ BMG Melodiya Compact Disc 74321 40723-2. [Cherubini.] I Aug. 1997.

Sans op. Y   My Native Country

Alternative title: *My Dear Fatherland.*

Form: A patriotic oratorio for narrator, soloists (soprano, two tenors, and bass), S.A.T.B. chorus and full orchestra, assembled from three works of Shostakovich by Yuri Silantiev (without the composer's participation):

1. Overture—'October 1917'—Moderato non troppo
2. On Palace Square—Allegretto
3. Folk Dance—Moderato—Allegro con brio
4. Ode to Leningrad—Moderato
5. Song of the Lantern—Allegretto
6. Lullaby—Andante
7. Battle by the Volga—Moderato
8. Song of Victory—Moderato

Texts by Yevgeni Dolmatovsky (Nos. 2, 4, 7, and 8) and Mikhail Svetlov (Nos. 5 and 6). Nos. 1–4 from Opus 63; Nos. 5, 6, and 8 from Opus 72; and No. 7 from Opus 66. The melody of Nos. 7 and 8 from Sans op. N (iii).

Instrumentation: As Opus 63 with narrator, a third French horn and optional balalaika (in No. 2); soprano soloist in No. 6.

Composed: 1937–45. The omnibus suite assembled in 1970 for a radio programme celebrating the twenty-fifth anniversary of the victorious end of the Great Patriotic War.

Music: Sovetskii Kompozitor, No. 2518, 1972, titled *My Dear Fatherland,* full score, 29 cm.

Duration: 37' 58".

Recording: USSR: Melodiya CM 02493-4. Lyudmila Belobragina (soprano— No. 6), Andrei Sokolov (tenor—No. 2), Denis Korolyov (tenor—No. 5),

Mark Reshetin (bass—Nos. 2 and 4), Yuri Levitan (narrator), Large Choir and Stage Symphony Orchestra of All-Union Radio, Klavdi Ptitsa (chorus-master), Yuri SILANTIEV (conductor). P 1970, I May 1971.

Opus 137   King Lear

Form: Music for the black and white film of William Shakespeare's play *King Lear*, in Boris Pasternak's Russian translation, directed by Grigori Kozintsev for Lenfilm. Many items are brief and lightly scored, such as the alarums, fanfares, and tuckets; only Nos. 53, 55, and 57 being extended and fully orchestrated.

1. Horn of the Leader of the Beggars (muted horn call for 3 seconds)
2. Horn of the Leader of the Beggars (muted horn call)
3. Departure of the King's wagon train (trumpet flourish)—Allegro
4. Edmund commands the advance (trumpet call for 2 seconds)—Allegro
5. Edmund commands the challenge to duel (20-second trumpet flourish) Allegro
6. Answering trumpeter of Edgar (muted horn call)
7. The Fool's Bell—Allegretto
8. The Fool's Piping Dance (E flat clarinet solo)—Moderato
9. Huntsmen's Horns (fanfare)—Allegro
10. Death's Call (11-second brass flourish)—Adagio
50. Introduction (Passage of time)—Adagio
51. The first sighting of Lear's Castle—Adagio
52. (5-bar brass *pesante* statement)—Moderato
53. Beginning of the Catastrophe—Adagio
54. The Voice of Truth (2' 15")—Adagio
55. The Storm (2' 30")—Moderato
56. People's Weeping (Vocalise)—Adagio
57. The Storm (Beginning)—Adagio
58. Dinner with Gonerill (flute duet with harp accompaniment)—Allegretto
70. End of the film *King Lear*. Finale (E flat clarinet solo—variant of No. 8)—Moderato

Instrumentation: piccolo, 2 flutes, 2 oboes, E flat clarinet, 2 clarinets (A and B flat), 2 bassoons ~ 4 horns, 3 trumpets, 3 trombones, tuba ~ timpani, tambourine, side drum, cymbals, gong ~ glockenspiel, xylophone, harp ~ wordless S.A.T.B. chorus in No. 56 ~ strings. Composer's note: the choir is required to be large with each part performed by no fewer than six performers.

Composed: April–July 1970, at Repino, Moscow, and Leningrad.

Première: Film first shown on 4 February 1971. Film score performed by the Leningrad Philharmonic Orchestra conducted by Dzhemal-Eddin Dalgat and Nikolai Rabinovich.

Music: Autograph score preserved in the Shostakovich family archive.

G. Schirmer, No. 47548, 1976, duet for two flutes and piano (or harp), VAAP authorized version, score and two parts of No. 58, 30.5 cm.

G. Schirmer, No. 12086, 1976, Weeping Song ('People's Weeping') No. 56 for S.A.T.B. a cappella, 30.5 cm.

Muzyka, No. 10179 (in Volume 34 of *Collected Works* with Opp. 88 and 136; and songs), 1985, 'People's Weeping' wordless chorus, 30 cm.

Muzyka, No. 10890 (in Volume 42 of *Collected Works* with Opp. 75, 78, 80, 82, 95, 97, 111, 116, and 132), 1987, twenty items, 30 cm.

Duration: Film: 124–162 minutes. Very fragmentary score has a total playing time of *c*.30 minutes. Recording: 27' 40".

Film: Moskwood Video, Haarlem, Netherlands, No. 2645, *c*.1993, videocassette with Dutch subtitles, 140 minutes.

Ballet: *The Overcoat.* For details see under Opus 32.

Recordings: RCA Victor Red Seal Compact Disc RD 87763. Nos. 8, 50, 51, 53–8, and 70. Belgian Radio Symphony Orchestra and Chorus, José SERE-BRIER. [Opp. 116 and 111.] P Brussels 1988, I June 1988, G Oct. 1988. NB. The item labelled 'After the Storm' should read 'The Storm (Beginning)' as No. 57 precedes No. 55 in the film score.

Germany: Capriccio Compact Disc 10 397. Nos. 1–5, 50–3, 6–9, 54–8, 70, and 10. Berlin Radio Chorus and Symphony Orchestra, Mikhail YUROVSKY. [Op. 58*a*.] P Berlin 10–13 Dec. 1990, G Sept. 1992. NB. No. 56 is labelled incorrectly as 'Water'.

Reference: Kozintsev.

Note: In the film the items appear in the following order: Nos. 8, 1, 51, 53, 3 (thrice), 51 to fig. 4, 9 (thrice), 58, 3, 52, 3 (twice), 57, 55 less the first 16 bars (twice), 10, 50 (part), 56 (part), 54 to fig. 5, 8, 4 (twice), 56 (twice), 5, 6, 5, 10, and 70. Only the final notes of the horn calls of the Beggars are sounded and No. 7 'The Fool's Bell' does not appear. Volume 42 of *Collected Works* incorrectly states that the Opus 58*a* 'Ten Fool's Songs' were utilised in the film score.

Opus 138   Quartet No. 13 in B flat minor

Form: String quartet in one continuous movement:

Adagio—Doppio movimento—Tempo primo

Composed: Begun on 10 August 1969 and completed on 10 August 1970, in hospital at Kurgan (east of the Orals).

Dedication: Vadim Vasilievich Borisovsky (violist of the Beethoven Quartet).
Premières: 11 Decemher 1970, USSR Composers' Club, Moscow; 13 Decem-ber 1970, Glinka Concert Hall, Leningrad and 20 December 1970, Moscow Conservatory Malyi Hall; Beethoven Quartet (Dmitri Tsyganov, Nikolai Zabavnikov, Fyodor Druzhinin, and Sergei Shirinsky).
UK: 11 November 1972, St Mark's Church, Harrogate; Fitzwilliam Quartet (Nicholas Dowding, John Phillips, Alan George, and Ioan Davies).
Arrangements: Reduction for piano four hands by Anatoli Dmitriev. Tran-scription entitled Sinfonia (or Adagio) for Viola and Strings by Alek-sandr Chaikovsky, undertaken as a request by Yuri Basmet.
Music: Autograph score preserved by the Borisovsky family.
Hans Sikorski, No. 2170, 1971, parts, 31.5 cm.
Boosey & Hawkes, No. 20166, 1971, parts, 29 cm.
Muzyka, No. 7350, 1972, miniature score, 19 cm.
Muzyka, No. 7353, 1972, parts, 29 cm.
Edition Peters, No. 5763 (plate no. 12795), 1974, parts, 30 cm.
Boosey & Hawkes, No. 888, 1974, score, 19 cm.
Muzyka, Leningrad, No. 2026 (in Volume 4 with Quartets 12 and 14 arr. for piano four hands by A. Dmitriev), 1976, 29.5 cm.
Hans Sikorski, No. 2209 (with Opp. 142 and 144), 1978, score, 21 cm.
Muzyka, No. 10284 (in Volume 36 of *Collected Works* Quartets 9–15), 1980, 30 cm.
Duration: 18 minutes in score; 15' 10"–20' 54"; 19' 00"–22' 20" (Plaistow); 27' 33" (Sinfonia arr. A. Tchaikovsky).
Recordings: USSR: Melodiya CM 02545-6. BEETHOVEN QUARTET (personnel as at première). [Op. 87 Nos. 1, 23, and 24.] P 1971, I May 1971. *Reissued:* Angel Melodiya SR 40189. [Op. 134.] I 1972 ~ USA Consonance Blue Label Compact Disc 81.3008. [Vol. 4—Opp. 133 and 142.] I Mar. 1996.
USSR: Melodiya CM 03223-4. BORODIN QUARTET (Rostislav Dubinsky, Yaroslav Aleksandrov, Dmitri Shebalin, Valentin Berlinsky). [Op. 133.] P and I 1972. *Reissued:* France: Le Chant du Monde LDX 78578 X. [Op. 133.] ~ HMV Melodiya HQS 1320 in Set SLS 879. [Op. 73.] G June 1974.
Czech: Panton 11 0420 G. SUK QUARTET (Antonín Novák, Vojtěch Jouza, Kárél Rehak, Jan Štros). [Opp. 46 Nos. 1 and 2; 91 Nos. 2 and 4; and Boris Chaikovsky.] P Prague 1973.
L'Oiseau-Lyre DSLO 9. FITZWILLIAM QUARTET (Christopher Rowland, Jonathan Sparey, Alan George, Ioan Davies). [Opp. 108 and 142.] P Mar. 1975, G Dec. 1975. *Reissued:* Decca 188 D4 in Set D 188 D7. [Opp. 101 and 108.] G Feb. 1981 ~ Decca Compact Disc 421 475-2DH. [Opp. 73 and 110.] I Dec. 1988, G Apr. 1989 ~ Decca Enterprise Compact Discs 433 078-2DM6. [On fifth disc of six-disc set with Opp. 122 and 133.] I Apr. 1992, G June 1992.

USSR: Melodiya C10 09337-8. Oleg KRYSA, Aleksandr KRAVCHUK, Anatoli VENZHEGA, and Valentin POTAPOV. [Beethoven.] P 1977, I 1978c.

USSR: Melodiya C10 11611-2. TANEYEV QUARTET (Vladimir Ovcharek, Grigori Lutsky, Vissarion Soloviev, Iosif Levinzon). [In first box of Part 2 of *Collected Works on Records* with Op. 92.] P 1979, I 1980. *Reissued:* Japan JVC Victor 5348. [Opp. 110 and 122.] ~ USSR: Melodiya Compact Disc SUCD 10 00312. (Opp. 122 and 133.] I 1991*d*.

Olympia Compact Disc OCD 535. SHOSTAKOVICH QUARTET (Andrei Shislov, Sergei Pishchugin, Aleksandr Galkovsky, Aleksandr Korchagin). ['Complete Quartets, Vol. 5'—Opp. 133 and 142.] P 1980, I June 1994, G Sept. 1994.

USSR: Melodiya C10 17375-6. BORODIN QUARTET (Mikhail Kopelman, Andrei Abramenkov, Dmitri Shebalin, Valentin Berlinsky). [Op. 133.] P 1981, I 1982*d*. *Reissued:* HMV Melodiya EX 270339-3 (DMM). [In seven-record box set of 15 Quartets plus Quintet.] G Mar. 1986 ~ EMI Compact Disc CDC7 49269-2. [Opp. 118 and 142.] I Nov. 1987, G Sept. 1988 ~ Japan: Victor Musical Industries Compact Disc VICC 40022. [Opp. 122 and 133.] I 1990 ~ EMI Compact Discs CMS5 65032-2. [In six-disc set of 15 Quartets plus Quintet.] I Mar. 1994 ~ BMG Melodiya Compact Discs 74321 40711-2 (six-disc set). [Opp. 122 and 133.] I June 1997.

Netherlands: Attacca Babel 8416-1 (digital). RAFAEL QUARTET (Ronald Hoogeveen, Rami Koch, Zoltan Benyacs, Henk Lambooy). [Op. 110.] P 19–20 Dec. 1983. *Reissued:* Netherlands: Attacca Babel Compact Disc 8948-5DDD. [Op. 110; and Keuris.] I 1988?

Germany: IMS Polygram ECM New Series 1347 (two-record set) and Compact Disc 833506-2 (two-disc set). Gidon KREMER and Thomas Zehetmair (violins), Nobuko Imai (viola), and Boris Pergamentshchikov (cello). [Edition Lockenhaus Volumes 4 and 5—Opp. 142 and Sans op. D; and Schulhoff.] P 1985, I Apr. 1988.

Czech: Panton 81 0752. STAMIC QUARTET (Bohuslav Matoušek, Josef Kekula, Jan Pěruška, Vladimir Leixner). [Schnittke.] P Prague 4–5 May 1987.

Teldec Compact Discs 9031 71702-2. BRODSKY QUARTET (Michael Thomas, Ian Belton, Paul Cassidy, Jacqueline Thomas). [On fifth disc of six-disc set with Opp. 122 and 133.] P Berlin July 1989, I Nov. 1990, G June 1992. *Reissued:* Teldec Compact Disc 9031 73109-2. (Opp. 122 and 133.] I July 1991.

USA: ESS.A.Y. Compact Disc CD 1012. MANHATTAN QUARTET (Eric Lewis, Roy Lewis, John Dexter, Judith Glyde). [Opp. 122 and 133.] P Jersey City 16 June 1990, I 1991. *Reissued:* Koch Schwann Compact Disc 3 1070-2. ['Complete String Quartets, Vol. 5' with Opp. 122 and 133.] I Sept. 1993.

Deutsche Grammophon Compact Disc 463 284-2GH5 (five-disc set). EMERSON QUARTET (Eugene Drucker, Philip Setzer, Lawrence Dutton,

David Finkel). ['Complete Quartets, Vol. 4'—Sans op. D, Opp. 122 and 133.] P Aspen, Colorado concert July–Aug. 1994, G June 2000.

Naxos Compact Disc 8.550977. ÉDER QUARTET (János Selmeczi, Péter Szüts, Sándor Papp, György Éder). ['Complete Quartets, Vol. 6—Opp. 118 and 122.] P Budapest 29 Apr.–4 May 1996, I May 1998.

Sony Classical Compact Disc SK 60550. Sinfonia for Viola and Strings arr. A. Chaikovsky. Yuri BASHMET (viola/director), Moscow Soloists. [Brahms.] P Henry Wood Hall, London 21–2 Mar. 1998, I Nov. 1998, G Mar. 1999.

France: Arion Compact Disc ARN 68461. DEBUSSY QUARTET (Christophe Collette, Dominique Lonca, Vincent Deprecq, Yannick Callier). ['Complete Quartets, Vol. 1'—Opp. 83 and 110 .] P Lyon July 1998, I July 1999.

Chandos Compact Disc CHAN 9955. SORREL QUARTET (Gina McCormack, Catherine Yates, Sarah-Jane Bradley, Helen Thatcher). ['Complete Quartets, Vol. 3'—Opp. 110 and 117.] P The Maltings, Snape 26–30 Mar. 2001, I Sept. 2001, G Awards (Oct.) 2001.

Opus 139   Soviet Militia

Form: March for military band, marked 'Allegretto'.

Instrumentation: flute, 3 B flat clarinets ~ 2 B flat cornets, 2 B flat trumpets, 3 French horns, 2 E flat saxhorns, 2 B flat tenor saxhorns, 2 B flat baritone saxhorns, trombone, 2 double-bass trombones in C ~ timpani, triangle, side drum, cymbals, bass drum.

Composed: October 1970.

Dedication: Mikhail Mikhailovich Zoshchenko (playwright).

Première: 9 November 1970, The House of the Soviets Hall of Columns, Moscow.

Music: Awarded First Prize at the All-Union Literature and Arts Contest on 10 November 1970.

Muzyka, No. 10091 (in album *Marches of Soviet Militia*), 1978, miniature score, 21.5 cm.

Sovetskii Kompozitor, No. 2459, 1972, score, 22 cm.

Duration: 1' 30".

Recording: USSR: Melodiya D 031193-4 (mono). Moscow Kremlin Commandant's Orchestra, N. ZOLOTARYOV. ['Soldier's Order'—Muradeli, Ekimyan, Khachaturyan *et al.*] P 1971, I 1972.

Chandos Compact Disc CHAN 9444. Stockholm Concert Band, Gennadi ROZHDESTVENSKY. ['Russian Concert Band Music'—Prokofiev, Rimsky-Korsakov, Stravinsky *et al.*] P Stockholm 11–12 June 1995, I Apr. 1996.

Opus 140   Six Romances on Verses by British Poets

Original title: *Six Romances on Verses by English Poets.* The title is given as *Six Romances on Verses of W. Raleigh, R. Burns, and W. Shakespeare* in some Russian lists and in the *Collected Works* Volume 31. See also Opus 62.

Form: Orchestral version of Opus 62 for bass soloist and small orchestra.

Instrumentation: flute (= piccolo), bassoon ~ 2 French horns ~ timpani, triangle, cymbals, orchestral bells ~ celesta ~ 10 violins, 4 violas, 3 cellos, 2 five-string double-basses.

Composed: 1971.

Premières: 30 November 1973, Moscow Conservatory Bolshoi Hall.

USA: 23 November 1982, Carnegie Hall, New York; James Morris (bass), Soviet Émigré Orchestra, Lazar Gozman.

Arrangement: English translation of the Russian text by Felicity Ashbee.

Music: Autograph score preserved in the Shostakovich family archive.

Muzyka, No. 10113 (in Volume 31 of *Collected Works* with Opp. 4, 21, 46*a*, 79*a*, 143*a*, and 145*a*), 1982, full score, 30 cm.

Duration: Approx. 15 minutes in score; 14' 09"–15' 19".

Recordings: USSR: Melodiya C10 05837-8. Yevgeni NESTERENKO (bass), Moscow Chamber Orchestra, Rudolf Barshai. [Op. 143*a*.] P Moscow concert Jan. 1974, I 1975*d*. *Reissued:* HMV Melodiya ASD 3324 in Set SLS 5078 (with Op. 145*a*). [Op. 143*a*.] G May 1977. *Gramophone* Record Awards 1977—winner of Solo Vocal category, G Mar. 1978 ~ USA: Columbia M2 34594 (in two-record set with Op. 145*a*). [Op. 143*a*.] ~ USSR: Melodiya C10 05837-8. [In third box of Part 3 of *Collected Works on Records* with Op. 143*a*.] I 1978 ~ Japan: Victor Musical Industries Compact Disc VICC 40082-83 (two-disc set). ['Shostakovich Songs'—Opp. 58*a*, 121, 123, 127 / 143*a*, 145*a*, and 146.] I 1991.

Deutsche Grammophon Compact Disc 493 860-2GH. Sergei LEIFERKUS (bass), Gothenburg Symphony Orchestra, Neeme Järvi. ['The Orchestral Songs, Vol. 1'—Opp. 4, 46*a*, and 79*a*.] P Gothenburg May 1992, I June 1994.

Germany: Capriccio Compact Disc 10 778. Stanislav SULEIMANOV (bass), Cologne Radio Symphony Orchestra, Mikhail Yurovsky. [Opp. 143*a* and 79*a*.] P Cologne 17–19 June 1994, I and G Awards (Oct.) 1998.

Japan: Triton Compact Disc 17 008. Aleksei MOCHALOV (bass), Moscow Chamber Music Theatre Orchestra, Anatoli Levin. [Opp. 58*a*, 146, 121, and Sans op. X (iii).] P Mosfilm Studio Nov. 1995, I Nov. 1996.

USA: Arabesque Compact Disc Z 6708. Nos. 4, 2, and 3 sung in English. Robert OSBORNE (bass-baritone), Vermont University Orchestra, Robert DeCormier. ['Bobby Burns' (*sic*)—Sans op. M; Vaughan Williams, Haydn, Beethoven *et al.*] P University of Vermont 1996, I 1998.

Reference: Spektor.

Opus 141 Symphony No. 15 in A major

Form: Symphony for full orchestra in four movements:

1. Allegretto—'Toy Shop'
2. Adagio—Largo—Adagio—Largo *attacca*
3. Allegretto
4. Adagio—Allegretto—Adagio—Allegretto

Gioacchino Rossini's galop from the fourth section of the Overture to *Guillaume Tell* is quoted five times in the first movement and the Finale introduces the 'fate' motif and drum rhythm accompanying Siegfried's Funeral March in Richard Wagner's *Götterdämmerung* and the melody of Mikhail Glinka's song 'Do not tempt me needlessly'.

Instrumentation: piccolo, 2 flutes, 2 oboes, 2 clarinets in A, 2 bassoons ~ 4 horns, 3 trumpets, 3 trombones, tuba ~ timpani, triangle, castanets, wood block, whip, soprano tom-tom, side drum, cymbals, bass drum, gong ~ glockenspiel, xylophone, vibraphone, celesta ~ 1st violins (16), 2nd violins (14), violas (12), cellos (12), double-basses (10). String strength specified by the composer is not mandatory, however the numbers suggested would give the best results.

Composed: A number of sketches made on 2 April 1971. Begun in late June 1971 at the town of Kurgan (east of the Urals) and completed on 29 July 1971 at the Composers' House, Repino. The two-piano reduction followed.

Premières: 8 January 1972, Moscow Conservatory Bolshoi Hall; All-Union Radio and Television Symphony Orchestra, Maksim Shostakovich. Finale encored.

  5 May 1972, Leningrad; Leningrad Philharmonic Orchestra, Yevgeni Mravinsky.

  UK: 20 November 1972, Royal Festival Hall, London; New Philharmonia Orchestra, Maksim Shostakovich.

  Opus 141*a:* 23 September 1972, Gnessin Institute, Moscow; led by Mark Pekarsky.

  30 October 1972, Moscow Music Club (VDK); Valeriya Vilker (violin), M. Drobinsky (cello), Viktor Derevyanko (piano/celesta); A. Mamyko, Valentin Snegirev, and B. Stepanov (percussion).

  Germany: 5 July 1995, Lockenhaus; led by Gidon Kremer.

Arrangements: Reduction for two pianos dated 4 January 1972 by the composer. A theme from the fourth movement is used in *Variations on a Theme by Shostakovich* by Karl Frederich Miller.

  Opus 141*a:* Chamber version, realised with the composer's approval, by Viktor Derevyanko (assisted by Mark Pekarsky) in August 1972, for violin, cello, piano/celesta, and percussion (three players).

Music: Autograph score preserved in the Shostakovich family archive. The first page of the autograph full score is reproduced in Volume 8 of

Collected Works. Title details of autographed reduction reproduced on inlay card of chamber version compact disc.

Sovetskii Kompozitor, No. 2655, 1972, score, 30 cm.

Anglo-Soviet Music Press, no number, 1972, photocopied score, 28.5 cm.

Hans Sikorski, No. 2172, 1972, 21 cm.

Leeds Music (Canada), no number, 1972, 27.5 cm.

Muzyka, Leningrad, No. 2201, 1977, reduction for two pianos by the composer, 28 cm.

Muzyka, No. 9856 (in Volume 8 of *Collected Works* with Op. 135), 1980, 30 cm.

Duration: Approx. 48 minutes in score; 39' 00"–48' 37"; 39 minutes (M. Mac-Donald); 43' 00"–46' 30" (Plaistow). Opus 141a: 41' 52".

Recordings: USSR: Melodiya CM 03245-6. All-Union Radio and Television Symphony Orchestra, Maksim SHOSTAKOVICH. P and I 1972. *Reissued:* HMV Melodiya ASD 2857. [Op. 122.] G Nov. 1972 ~ USA: Angel Melodiya SR 40213. I 1972 ~ Germany: Melodia Eurodise 87 623 XPK (in thirteen-record box set). I 1974 ~ France: Le Chant du Monde LDX 78535 ~ Netherlands: Phonogram Melodia 562 273.

USA and UK: RCA Red Seal ARD1 0014 (quad). Philadelphia Orchestra, Eugene ORMANDY. P 4–5 Oct. 1972, G Feb. 1973. *Reissued:* RCA Red Seal ARL1 0014 (stereo). G May 1975 ~ RCA Red Seal RL 01284. [In three-record box set with Opp. 113 and 135.] G Nov. 1978 ~ USA: RCA Red Seal Compact Disc 09026 63587-2. [Op. 61.] I Feb. 2000.

Japan: Victor VIC 28053 (mono). Leningrad Philharmonic Orchestra, Yevgeni MRAVINSKY. P Leningrad concert 5 or 6 May 1972—not 26 May 1976 as stated, I 1981. *Reissued:* USSR: Melodiya M10 43653-4 (2 sides in two record album, mono). [Tchaikovsky.] I 1982.

USSR: Melodiya C10 05453-4. Moscow Philharmonic Orchestra, Kirill KONDRASHIN. P 27 May 1974, I 1975d. *Reissued:* USA: MCA 67024 ~ Germany: Melodia Eurodisc 300 606-435. [In three-record box set with Opp. 113 and 135.] ~ East Germany: Eterna 8 26 776 ~ USSR: Melodiya C10 05453-4. [In second box of Part I of *Collected Works on Records.*] I 1980 ~ HMV Melodiya EX 2903873 (DMM). [Twelfth record in twelve-record box set.] G Dec. 1985 ~ France: Le Chant du Monde Compact Disc LDC 278 1009-10. [In Box 5 of five two-disc sets with Op. 135.] G May 1989 ~ BMG Classics Melodiya Compact Disc 74321 19846-2. [Op. 70.] I July 1994, G Nov. 1994 ~ Japan: Icone Compact Disc ICN 9408-2. [Op. 129.] I Aug. 1994. NB. This recording declared the Classic CD Gold Choice by Rob Ainsley in the June 1999 *Classic CD* issue 112, pp. 44–7.

USSR: Melodiya C10 19299 000. Leningrad Philharmonic Orchestra, Yevgeni MRAVINSKY. P Leningrad concert 26 May 1976, I 1984a. *Reissued:* Olympia Compact Disc OCD 224. ['The Mravinsky Legacy Volume 5'—

Wagner and Stravinsky.] G Aug. 1988 ~ Olympia Compact Discs OCD 5002 (in six-disc set). ['The Mravinsky Legacy'—Beethoven, Sibelius, Bruckner *et al.*] I Aug. 1990 ~ BMG Melodiya Compact Disc 74321 25192-2. ['Mravinsky Edition, Vol. 3'—Stravinsky.] I June 1995.

Charisma CAS 1128. Excerpts. London Philharmonic Orchestra, Joseph EGER. [Op. 47 excerpts.] P 1977, I Oct. 1977.

USA: Classical Excellence CS 11043. Austrian Radio Symphony Orchestra, Milan HORVAT. P 1977.

Decca SXL 6906. London Philharmonic Orchestra, Bernard HAITINK. P Mar. 1978, G Mar. 1979. *Reissued:* USA: London 7130 ~ Decca Compact Disc 417 581-2DH. [Op. 79*a*.] G Apr. 1987 ~ Decca Ovation Compact Disc 425 069-2DM. [Op. 79*a*.] I Aug. 1993, G Nov. 1993 ~ London Compact Disc 444 441-2. [On eleventh disc in eleven-disc set with Op. 79*a*.] I June 1995.

East Germany: Eterna 8 27 192. Berlin City Symphony Orchestra, Karl-Heinz Deutscher (violin), Günter Sennewald (cello), Gerhard Haas (trombone), Kurt SANDERLING. P 26 May–2 June 1978. *Reissued:* Japan: Deutsche Schallplatten ET 5061. I Sept. 1979 ~ Germany: Berlin Classics Compact Disc 0090432 BC. I Nov. 1995.

France: Praga Compact Disc PR 250 003. Czech Philharmonic Orchestra, Eduard SEROV. [Op. 15*a*.] P Prague concert 29 Nov. 1979, I June 1992.

USSR: Melodiya C10 18841-2. Novosibirsk Philharmonic Orchestra, Arnold KATS. P 1982, I 1983*d*.

USSR: Melodiya A10 0055 000 (digital), USSR Ministry of Culture Symphony Orchestra, Irina Lozben (flute), Vladimir Pushkarev (trumpet), Sergei Mnozhin (cello), Rashid Galayev (trombone), Andrei Lysenko (xylophone), Gennadi ROZHDESTVENSKY. P Jan. 1983, I 1984*d*. *Reissued:* Japan: JVC Melodiya Compact Disc VDC 528 and VDC 1073. G June 1985 ~ Olympia Compact Disc OCD 179. [Op. 35.] I Aug. 1988, G May 1989 ~ Olympia Compact Disc OCD 258. [Opp. 14 and 19.] I Oct. 1989 ~ Germany: Melodia Eurodisc Compact Disc 258 493 ~ Olympia Compact Disc OCD 5006. [In Volume 2 five-disc set of symphonies with Opp. 14 and 19.] I Dec. 1990 ~ BMG Melodiya Compact Discs 74321 59057-2 (two-disc set). [Opp. 135, 21, 46/62*a*, and Sans Op. M.] I Feb. 1999.

Deutsche Grammophon Compact Disc 427 616-2CH. Gothenburg Symphony Orchestra, Neeme JÄRVI. [Opp. 131 and 115.] P Gothenburg Sept. 1988, I Aug. 1989, G May 1991. *Reissued:* Deutsche Grammophon Classikon Compact Disc 469 029-2GCL. [Opp. 131 and 115.] G Aug. 2000.

Naxos Compact Disc 8.550624. Czecho-Slovak Radio Symphony Orchestra, Ladislav SLOVÁK. [Op. 14.] P Bratislava 5–12 Feb. 1989, I Jan. 1993, G Nov. 1993. *Reissued:* Naxos Compact Discs 8.505017. [In five-disc set with Symphonies Nos. 1, 2, 3, 4, 6, 7, and 12.] I 1993.

Teldec Compact Disc 9031 74560-2. London Symphony Orchestra, Mstislav ROSTROPOVICH. P London Nov. 1989, I Oct. 1991, G Mar. 1992. *Reissued:* Teldec Compact Discs 0630-17046-2. [In twelve-disc set of Symphonies.] G Oct. 1997.

Collins Classics Compact Disc 1206-2. London Symphony Orchestra, Maksim SHOSTAKOVICH. [Op. 97.] P London Aug. 1990, I and G May 1991. *Reissued:* Collins Classics Compact Disc 70122. [In three-disc set with Opp. 47, 93, 96, and 97.] I Sept. 1991.

Decca Compact Disc 430 227-2DH. Royal Philharmonic Orchestra, Vladimir ASHKENAZY. [Op. 70.] P Watford Nov. 1990, I Sept. 1992, G Oct. 1992.

France: Erato Compact Disc 2292 45815-2. Cleveland Orchestra, Kurt SANDERLING. P 18–19 Mar. 1991, G Feb. 1993.

Decca Compact Disc 436 838-2DH. Montreal Symphony Orchestra, Charles DUTOIT. [Op. 10.] P Montreal 15–22 May 1992, I May 1994, G Oct. 1994.

Denon Compact Disc CO 78948. Vienna Symphony Orchestra, Eliahu INBAL. [Op. 10.] P 16–19 Oct. 1992, I July 1995, G Dec. 1995.

Deutsche Grammophon Compact Disc 449 966-2GH. Opus 141*a*— chamber version arr. by V. Derevyanko. Gidon KREMER (violin), Clemens Hagen (cello), Vadim Sakharov (piano/celesta); Peter Sadlo, Edgar Guggeis, and Michael Gärtner (percussion). [Schnittke—*Prelude in Memory of Shostakovich.*] P Abersee bei St Gilgen, Germany Aug. 1995, I Apr. 1997, G June 1997.

Chandos Compact Disc CHAN 9550. Russian State Symphony Orchestra, Valeri POLYANSKY. [Op. 107.] P Mosfilm Studio Mar. 1996, I Apr. 1997, G Awards (Oct.) 1998.

Decca Compact Disc 458 919-2DH. Chicago Symphony Orchestra, Sir Georg SOLTI. [Sans op. V.] P Chicago 20–9 Mar. 1997, I Oct. 1998, G May 1999.

Japan: Canyon Classics Compact Disc PCCL 00351. Moscow Radio Symphony Orchestra, Vladimir FEDOSEYEV. [Op. 10.] P 16 Apr. 1996.

EMI Classics Compact Disc CDC5 56591-2. London Philharmonic Orchestra, Robert Truman (cello), Mariss JANSONS. [Opp. 102 and 97.] P London 14–16 Apr. 1997; I Oct. 1998.

Germany: Ars Musici Compact Disc AMP 5074-2. Federal Youth Orchestra of Germany, Jörg-Peter WEIGLE. [Hindemith.] P Solingen 5–8 Apr. 1999, I 2001.

Telarc Compact Disc CD 80572. Cincinnati Symphony Orchestra, Jesús LÓPEZ-COBOS. [Op. 10.] P Cincinnati 24–5 Sept. 2000, I Aug. 2001, G Oct. 2001.

References: Aranovsky, Kay, Paisov, and Tarakanov.

Notes: Shostakovich called the musical images in the first movement 'a kind of toyshop' and the puzzling quotation from Rossini's *William Tell*

Overture, according to the composer's explanation, is of a toy soldier strutting to the strains of the simplest tune he is able to play. Kurt Sanderling in an interview with Robert Maycock said, "He never liked to talk about his works: it was impossible to talk with him about the Fifteenth. But I sat with him at the Berlin première of this symphony and I told him that I thought the first movement was tragic unlike most people. "You are not wrong," he said, "It *is* tragic marionette-like: we are all marionettes."" (*Classical Music Weekly*, 29 Oct. 1977).

Opus 142 Quartet No. 14 in F sharp major

Form: String quartet in three movements:

1. Allegretto
2. Adagio *attacca*
3. Allegretto—Adagio

Composed: 23 March–11 April 1973 at Repino and completed on 23 April 1973 at Moscow.

Dedication: Sergei Pyotrovich Shirinsky (cellist of the Beethoven Quartet).

Premières: 30 October 1973, USSR Composers' Club, Moscow; 12 November 1973, Glinka Concert Hall, Leningrad and 18 November 1973, Moscow Conservatory Malyi Hall; Beethoven Quartet (Dmitri Tsyganov, Nikolai Zabavnikov, Fyodor Druzhinin, and Sergei Shirinsky).

UK: 16 August 1974, St Mark's Church, Harrogate; Fitzwilliam, Quartet (Christopher Rowland, Jonathan Sparey, Alan George, and Ioan Davies).

Arrangement: Reduction for piano four hands by Anatoli Dmitriev.

Music: Autograph score presented to Sergei Shirinsky on 30 June 1973 and preserved by the Shirinsky family. The quartet awarded a Glinka State Prize in November 1974.

Muzyka, No. 8464, 1974, score, 22 cm.

Muzyka, No. 8465, 1974, parts, 29 cm.

Hans Sikorski, No. 2175, 1974, parts, 31.5 cm.

Muzyka, Leningrad, No. 2026 (in Volume 4 with Quartets 12 and 13 arr. for piano four hands by A. Dmitriev), 1976, 29.5 cm.

Hans Sikorski, No. 2209 (with Opp. 138 and 144), 1978, score, 21 cm.

Muzyka, No. 10824 (in Volume 36 of *Collected Works* Quartets 9–15), 1980, 30 cm.

Duration: 24' 45"–26' 58"; 27 minutes (M. MacDonald).

Recordings: USSR: Melodiya C10 05137-8. BEETHOVEN QUARTET (personnel as at première). [Op. 143.] P 1974, I 1975c. *Reissued:* HMV Melodiya HQS 1362. [Op. 144.] G Nov. 1976 ~ France: Le Chant du Monde LDX 78614. [Op. 147.] I Mar. 1981 ~ USA: Consonance Blue Label Compact Disc 81.3008. [Vol. 4—Opp. 133 and 142.] I Mar. 1996.

L'Oiseau-Lyre DSLO 9. FITZWILLIAM QUARTET (personnel as at UK premiere). [Opp. 108 and 138.] P Mar. 1975, G Dec. 1975. *Reissued:* Decca 188 D6 in Set D 188 D7. [Op. 133.] G Feb. 1981 ~ Decca Enterprise Compact Discs 433 078-2DM6. [On sixth disc of six-disc set with Op. 144.] I Apr. 1992, G June 1992.

USSR: Melodiya C10 07285-6. TANEYEV QUARTET (Vladimir Ovcharek, Grigori Lutsky, Vissarion Soloviev, Iosif Levinzon). [Op. 101.] P 1975, I 1977a. *Reissued:* USSR: with same number in first box of Part 2 of *Collected Works on Records.* I 1980 ~ USA: Columbia Melodiya M 34527. [Op. 144.] I 1977 ~ Japan: JVC Victor 5350. [Op. 133.] ~ USSR: Melodiya Compact Disc SUCD 11 00313. [Op. 144.] I 1991.

France: Praga Compact Disc PR 254 043. GLINKA QUARTET (Aleksandr Arenkov, Sergei Pishchugin, Misha Geller, Dmitri Fershtman). [Op. 144.] P Czech broadcast July 1977, I May 1994.

Czech: Panton 11 0603 G. SUK QUARTET (Antonín Novák, Vojtěch Jouza, Karel Řehák, Jan Štros). [Nasidze.] P Prague 1976.

Finland: Finlandia FA 324. SIBELIUS ACADEMY QUARTET (Erkki Kantola, Seppo Tukiainen, Veikko, Kosonen, Arto Noras). [Sibelius.] P 5 and 8 Nov. 1981, I 1982.

USSR: Melodiya C10 17869005. BORODIN QUARTET (Mikhail Kopelman, Andrei Abramenkov, Dmitri Shebalin, Valentin Berlinsky). [Op. 108.] P 1981, I 1983a. *Reissued:* HMV Melodiya EX 270339-3 (DMM). [In seven-record box set of 15 Quartets plus Quintet.] G Mar. 1986 ~ EMI Compact Disc CDC7 49269-2. [Opp. 118 and 138.] I Nov. 1987, G Sept. 1988 ~ Japan: Victor Musical Industries Compact Disc VICC 40023. [Op. 144.] I 1990 ~ EMI Compact Discs CMS5 65032-2. [In six-disc set of 15 Quartets plus Quintet.] I Mar. 1994 ~ BMG Melodiya Compact Discs 74321 40711-2 (six-disc set). [Op. 144.] I June 1997.

Germany: IMS Polygram ECM New Series 1347 (two-record set) and Compact 833506-2 (two-disc set). Gidon KREMER and Yuzuko Horigome (violins), Kim Kashkashian (viola), and David Geringas (cello). [Edition Lockenhaus Volumes 4 and 5—Opp. 138 and Sans op. D; and Schulhoff.] P 1986, I Apr. 1988.

Olympia Compact Disc OCD 535. SHOSTAKOVICH QUARTET (Andrei Shislov, Sergei Pishchugin, Aleksandr Galkovsky, Aleksandr Korchagin). ['Complete Quartets, Vol. 5'—Opp. 133 and 138.] P 1988, I June 1994, G Sept. 1994.

Teldec Compact Discs 9031 71702-2. BRODSKY QUARTET (Michael Thomas, Ian Belton, Paul Cassidy, Jacqueline Thomas). [On sixth disc of six-disc set with Op. 144.] P Berlin July 1989, I Nov. 1990, G June 1992. *Reissued:* Teldec Compact Disc 9031 73108-2. [Opp. 101 and 108.] I June 1991.

USA: ESS.A.Y. Compact Disc CD 1013. MANHATTAN QUARTET (Eric Lewis, Roy Lewis, John Dexter, Judith Glyde). [Op. 144.] P Jersey City 11

June 1990, I 1991. *Reissued:* Koch Schwann Compact Disc 3 1071-2 ['Complete String Quartets, Vol. 6' with Op. 144.] I Dec. 1993.

Deutsche Grammophon Compact Disc 445 864-2GH. HAGEN QUARTET (Lukas Hagen, Rainer Schmidt, Veronika and Clemens Hagen). [Opp. 83 and 122.] P Abersee bei Gilsen Apr. 1994, I July 1995, G Sept. 1995.

Deutsche Grammophon Compact Disc 463 284-2GH5 (five-disc set). EMERSON QUARTET (Eugene Drucker, Philip Setzer, Lawrence Dutton, David Finkel). ['Complete Quartets, Vol. 5'—Op. 144.] P Aspen, Colorado concert July–Aug. 1994, G June 2000.

Naxos Compact Disc 8.550976. ÉDER QUARTET (János Selmeczi, Peter Szüts, Sándor Papp, György Éder). ['Complete Quartets, Vol. 5'—144.] P Budapest 1–4 Sept. 1996, I Apr. 1998.

Opus 143   Six Songs on Poems of Marina Tsvetayeva

Form: Suite for contralto and piano on poems of Marina Tsvetayeva:

1. My poems—Largo
2. Whence such tenderness?—Allegretto
3. Hamlet's dialogue with his conscience—Largo
4. The Poet and the Tsar—Moderato *attacca*
5. Not a drum was heard—Allegretto
6. To Anna Akhmatova—Largo

The first poem was written in May 1913, Nos. 4 and 5 are from the cycle 'Verses to Pushkin' of 1931, and No. 6 dated 19 June 1916.

Composed: 31 July–7 August 1973, in Estonia; Opus 143*a*: 9 January 1974, at Repino.

Dedication: Irina Pyotrovna Bogacheva (mezzo-soprano of the Kirov Opera, Leningrad).

Premières: 12 November 1973, Glinka Concert Hall, Leningrad [score gives 30 October 1973] and 27 December 1973, Moscow Conservatory Malyi Hall; Irina Bogacheva (mezzo-soprano) and Sofya Vakman (piano).

UK: 17 October 1979, Purcell Room, London; Nicola Lanzetter (contralto) and Stuart Hutchinson (piano).

Opus 143*a*: 6 June 1974, Moscow Conservatory Bolshoi Hall.

UK: 4 July 1985, Barbican Hall, London; Patricia Adkins-Chiti (mezzo-soprano), City of London Sinfonia, Michael Bremner.

Arrangements: English translations of the poems by Felicity Ashbee and Jane May. Opus 143*a*—orchestrated version for small orchestra by the composer.

Instrumentation of Opus 143*a*:   2 flutes, 2 bassoons ~ 2 French horns ~ timpani, side drum, orchestral bells ~ xylophone, celesta ~ 10 violins, 4 violas, 3 cellos, 2 double-basses.

Music: Autograph scores of Opp. 143 and 143*a* preserved in the Shostakovich family archive.

Opus 143: Muzyka, No. 4116 (in *Dmitri Shostakovich: Vocal Compositions*), 1974, 29 cm.

Muzyka, No. 8788, 1975, 28.5 cm.

G. Schirmer, 1979, English transaltion by Jane May.

Muzyka, No. 11785 (in Volume 33 of *Collected Works* with Opp. 109, 121, 123, 127, 128, 145, and 146), 1984, 30 cm.

Opus 143*a*: Muzyka, No. 10113 (in Volume 31 of *Collected Works* with Opp. 4, 21, 46*a*, 140, 79*a*, and 145*a*), 1982, full score, 30 cm.

Duration: Approx. 20 minutes in scores; Opus 143: 16' 35"–19' 25"; Opus 143*a*: 17' 48"–21' 43"; 18 minutes (M. MacDonald).

Recordings: USSR: Melodiya C10 05137-8. Irina BOGACHEVA and Sofya Vakman. [Op. 142.] P 1974, I 1975*c*.

USSR: Melodiya C10 05837-8. Opus 143*a*. Irina BOGACHEVA, Moscow Chamber Orchestra, Rudolf Barshai. [Op. 140.] P July 1974, I 1975*d*. *Reissued:* HMV Melodiya ASD 3324 in Set SLS 5078 (with Op. 145*a*). [Op. 140.] G May 1977. Gramophone Record Awards 1977—winner of Solo Vocal category, G Mar. 1978 ~ USA: Columbia M2 34594 (in two-record set with Op. 145*a*). [Op. 140.] ~ USSR: Melodiya C10 05837-8. [In third box of Part 3 of *Collected Works on Records* with Op. 140.] I 1978 ~ Japan: Victor Musical Industries Compact Disc VICC 40082-83 (two-disc set). ['Shostakovich Songs'—Op. 58*a*, 121, 123, 127, 140/145*a* and 146.] I 1991.

USSR: Melodiya C10 07801-2. Yevgeniya GOROKHOVSKAYA (mezzo-soprano) and Irina Golovneva (piano). [Gavrilin, Prigozhin, and Tishchenko.] P 1976, 1 1977*c*.

Decca 414 410-1DH2 (in two-record box set, digital). Opus 143*a*. Ortrun WENKEL (contralto), Concertgebouw Orchestra, Bernard Haitink. [Opp. 113 and 79*a*.] P Amsterdam 1983, G May 1986. *Reissued:* Decca Compact Disc 417 514-2DH. [Op. 135.] I Dec. 1986, G Mar. 1987 ~ Decca Ovation Compact Disc 425 074-2DM. [Op. 135.] I Aug. 1993, G Nov. 1993 ~ London Compact Disc 444 440-2. [On tenth disc in eleven-disc set with Op. 135.] I June 1995.

USSR: Melodiya 010 22987 002. Nataliya ROZANOVA (mezzo-soprano) and Irina Katayeva (piano). [Messiaen.] P 1984, I 1986*b*.

Belgium: Pavane Compact Disc ADW 7204. Opus 143*a*. Patricia ADKINS-CHITI (mezzo-soprano), RTBF New Symphonic Orchestra, Alfred Walter. ['The Forgotten Europe'—Bartók amd Szymanowski.] P Brussels concert 5 Dec. 1985, I Dec. 1989.

Deutsche Grammophon Compact Disc 447 085-2GH. Opus 143*a*. Elena ZAREMBA (contralto), Gothenburg Symphony Orchestra, Neeme Järvi. ['The Orchestral Songs, Vol. 2'—Opp. 21 and 145*a*.] P Gothenburg Mar. 1994, I Dec. 1995, G Jan. 1996.

Germany: Capriccio Compact Disc 10 778. Opus 143*a*. Tamara
SINYAVSKAYA (alto), Cologne Radio Symphony Orchestra, Mikhail
Yurovsky. [Opp. 140 and 79*a*.] P Cologne 17–19 June 1994, I and G
Awards (Oct.) 1998.
    USA: VAI Compact Disc VAIA 2003. Irina MISHURA (soprano) and
Valéry Ryvkin (piano). [Tchaikovsky and Rakhmaninov.] P New York
Mar. 1996.
    Germany: Zenon Compact Disc 197. Claudia RÜGGEBERG (alto) and
Axel Bauni (piano). [Schoeck and Rihm.] P Essen 16–18 July 1997.
References: Emerson (in Bartlett), Levaya, and Vasina-Grossman (in Daragan).

Opus 144   Quartet No. 15 in E flat minor

Form: String quartet in six linked movements:

1. Elegy—Adagio *attacca*
2. Serenade—Adagio *attacca*
3. Intermezzo—Adagio *attacca*
4. Nocturne—Adagio *attacca*
5. Funeral March—Adagio molto *attacca*
6. Epilogue—Adagio

Composed: Completed on 17 May 1974 in a Moscow hospital.
Premières: 25 October 1974, Leningrad Composers' Club and 15 November
    1974, Glinka Concert Hall, Leningrad; Taneyev Quartet (Vladimir
    Ovcharek, Grigori Lutsky, Vissarion Soloviev, and Iosif Levinzon).
        11 January 1975, Moscow Conservatory Malyi Hall; Beethoven Quar-
    tet (Dmitri Tsyganov, Nikolai Zabavnikov, Fyodor Druzhinin, and Yev-
    geni Altman).
        UK: 5 March 1975, Royal Northern College of Music, Manchester;
    Fitzwilliam Quartet (Christopher Rowland, Jonathan Sparey, Alan
    George, and Ioan Davies).
Arrangements: Reduction for piano four hands by Anatoli Dmitriev. Opus
    144*a*—'Requiem' for string orchestra by Misha Rachlevsky.
Music: Autograph score preserved in the Shostakovich family archive. A
    fragment of the Epilogue is illustrated in Volume 36 of *Collected Works.*
    Muzyka, unnumbered copyist's score, 1974, 22 cm.
    Anglo-Soviet Music Press, *c.*1974, score and parts.
    Muzyka, No. 8961, 1975, parts, 29 cm.
    Muzyka, No. 8962, 1975, score, 21 cm.
    Hans Sikorski, No. 2204, 1975, parts, 31.5 cm.
    Hans Sikorski, No. 2209 (with Opp. 138 and 142), 1978, score, 21 cm.
    Muzyka, Leningrad, No. 2391, 1979, arr. for piano four hands by A.
Dmitriev, 28.5 cm.

Muzyka, No. 10284 (in Volume 35 of *Collected Works* Quartets 9–15), 1980, 30 cm.

Duration: Approx. 37 minutes in score; 34' 40"–38' 50"; 34 minutes (M. Mac-Donald).

Ballet: *To Comfort Ghosts.* Choreographed by Dan Wagoner for Dan Wagoner and Dancers, Joyce Theater, Manhattan, 3 May 1988. A hermetic poem concerning a house divided by strife, performed by four male and four female dancers to the Fitzwilliam Quartet's recording. Presented at Sadler's Wells by the London Contemporary Dance Theatre on 28 November 1989 and at the Stanislavsky and Nemirovich-Danchenko Theatre, Moscow, on 5 July 1990.

Films: *The Composer Shostakovich.* For details see under Appendix II.

Toutes peines confondues ('Combined Sentences'). A French 110-minute 'sophisticated thriller' colour film of 1991, directed by Michel Deville, with background music from Borodin Quartet recordings of Shostakovich's Quartets Nos. 1, 5, 7, 8, 11, 12, and 15. The first excerpt is from the Serenade movement of No. 15

Play: *The Noise of Time,* created by Simon McBurney and performed by the Theatre de Complicite, John Jay College Theatre, Lincoln Center, New York, 1–5 March 2000. This fantasy presentation features events from Shostakovich's life, still and moving computer images projected on a screen, interwoven with a live performance of the last quartet by the Emerson Quartet. The UK première performed by the same company and quartet at the Barbican, London 8–15 July 2001.

Recordings: USSR: Melodiya C10 06495-6. BEETHOVEN QUARTET (personnel as at Moscow première). P 1975, I 1976c. *Reissued:* HMV Melodiya HQS 1362. [Op. 142.] G Nov. 1976 ~ France: Praga Compact Disc PR 254 043. [Op. 142.] P given as Czech Radio broadcast Oct. 1976, I May 1994 ~ USA: Consonance Blue Label Compact Disc 81.3006. [Vol. 2.—Opp. 108 and 110.] I May 1995.

USSR: Melodiya C10 06639-40. TANEYEV QUARTET (personnel as at world première). P 1975; I 1976c. *Reissued:* USSR: with same number in first box of Part 2 of *Collected Works on Records.* I 1980 ~ USA: Columbia Melodiya M 34527. [Op. 142.] I 1977 ~ Japan: JVC Victor 5351 ~ USSR: Melodiya Compact Disc SUCD 11 00313. [Op. 142.] I 1991.

L'Oiseau-Lyre DSLO 11. FITZWILLIAM QUARTET (personnel as at UK première). [Op. 110.] P May 1975, G Apr.1976. *Reissued:* Decca 188 D7 in Set D 188 D7. [Op. 110.] G Feb. 1981 ~ Decca Enterprise Compact Discs 433 078-2DM6. [On sixth disc of six-disc set with Op. 142.] I Apr. 1992, G June 1992.

USSR: Melodiya C10 11757-8. BORODIN QUARTET (Mikhail Kopelman, Andrei Abramenkov, Dmitri Shebalin, Valentin Berlinsky). [Op. 49.] P 1978, I 1979d. *Reissued:* HMV Melodiya EX 270339-3 (DMM). [In seven-record box set of 15 Quartets plus Quintet.] G Mar. 1986 ~ EMI Compact Disc CDC7 49270-2. [Op. 92.] I Nov. 1987, G Sept. 1988 ~ Japan: Victor

Musical Industries Compact Disc VICC 40023. [Op. 142.] I 1990 ~ EMI Compact Discs CMS5 65032-2. On six-disc set of 15 Quartets plus Quintet.] I Mar. 1994 ~ BMG Melodiya Compact Discs 74321 40711-2 (six-disc set). [Op. 142.] I June 1997.

Czech: Panton 8111 0195 G. SUK QUARTET (Ivan Štraus, Vojtěch Jouza, Karel Řehák, Jan Štros). [Op. 11.] P Prague 1981.

CBS Masterworks Compact Disc MK 44924. Gidon KREMER, Daniel Phillips, Kim Kashkashian, Yo-Yo Ma. [Gubaidulina.] P New York concert 29–30 Jan. 1985, I Jan. 1990, G Apr. 1990.

Olympia Compact Disc OCD 534. SHOSTAKOVICH QUARTET (Andrei Shislov, Sergei Pishchugin, Aleksandr Galkovsky, Aleksandr Korchagin). ['Complete Quartets, Vol. 4'—Opp. 118 and 122.] P 1988, I May 1994, G Sept. 1994.

Teldec Classics Compact Disc 246 017-2. BRODSKY QUARTET (Michael Thomas, Ian Belton, Paul Cassidy, Jacqueline Thomas). ['End Games'—Beethoven.] P Berlin Feb. 1989, I Oct. 1989, G Apr. 1990. *Reissued:* Teldec Compact Discs 9031 71702-2. [On sixth disc of six-disc set with Op. 142.] I Nov. 1990, G June 1992.

USA: ESS.A.Y Compact Disc CD 1013. MANHATTAN QUARTET (Eric Lewis, Roy Lewis, John Dexter, Judith Glyde). [Op. 142.] P Purchase, New York 27 July 1990, I 1991. *Reissued:* Koch Scwann Compact Disc 3 1017-2. ['Complete String Quartets, Vol. 6' with Op. 142.] I Dec. 1993.

Claves Compact Disc 50 9115. Op. 144*a*—'Requiem' arr. M. Rachlevsky. Kremlin Chamber Orchestra, Misha RACHLEVSKY. [Opp. 110*a* and 118*a*.] P Moscow concert Oct.–Nov. 1991, G Mar. 1993. *Reissued:* Claves Compact Discs 50 9504/5 (two-disc set). [Schnittke, R. Strauss, and Lekeu.] G Mar. 1996.

Netherlands: Attacca Babel Compact Disc BABEL 9786. SCHÖENBERG QUARTET (Janneke van der Meer, Wim de Jong, Henk Guittart, Viola de Hoog). [Van Vlijem.] P Delft 1–2 July 1993, G May 1998.

Deutsche Grammophon Compact Disc 463 284-2GH5 (five-disc set). EMERSON QUARTET (Eugene Drucker, Philip Setzer, Lawrence Dutton, David Finkel). ['Complete Quartets, Vol. 5'—Op. 142.] P Aspen, Colorado concert July–Aug. 1994, G June 2000.

Teldec Compact Disc 4509 98417-2. BORODIN QUARTET (personnel as on Melodiya C10 11757-8). [Op. 49.] P Berlin May 1995, I Nov. 1996, G Feb. 1997. *Reissued:* Ultima Compact Discs 8573 87820-2 (two-disc set). [Opp. 57, 67, and 49.] I Apr. 2001, G Aug. 2001.

Guild Compact Disc GMCD 7123. 'Requiem' arr. M. Rachlevsky. St. Gallen String Orchestra, Rudolf LUTZ. ['Lamentations'—Reger, Gregorian Chants, and Franck.] P St Gallen, Switzerland concert 1990s, I 1996.

Naxos Compact Disc 8-550976. ÉDER QUARTET (János Selmeczi, Peter Szüts, Sándor Papp, György Éder). ['Complete Quartets, Vol. 5'—Op. 142.] P Budapest 1–4 Sept. 1996, I Apr. 1998.

Netherlands: Globe Compact Disc GLO 5171. RUBIO QUARTET (Dirk Van de Velde, Dirk Van den Hauwe, Marc Sonnaert, Peter Devos). ['Complete Quartets, Vol. 2'—Op. 73.] P Utrecht Sept. 1997, I May 1998.

Opus 145   Suite on Verses of Michelangelo

Working title: For a while the composer considered Andrei Voznesensky's suggestion of 'Michelangelo Memorial' as a title.

Form: Song cycle for bass voice and piano. Settings of eleven poems by Michelangelo Buonarroti, the original Italian translated into the Russian language by Abram Efros (see Note). Verses chosen by the composer from a book *Michelangelo—Life and Works*, compiled by V. Grashchenkov and published by Iskusstvo, Moscow, 1964. The titles provided by the composer:

1. Truth (Sonnet 3 to Pope Julius II)—Adagio
2. Morning (Sonnet 20)—Allegretto
3. Love (Sonnet 25)—Allegretto
4. Separation (Madrigal—Com' arò dunque ardire)—Moderato
5. Anger (Sonnet 4 on Rome in the Pontificate of Julius II)—Allegro non troppo [*attacca* not marked in the score]
6. Dante (Sonnet 1 on Dante Alighieri)—Moderato *attacca*
7. To the Exile (Sonnet 2 on Dante Alighieri)—Largo
8. Creativity (Sonnet 61 on the death of Vittoria Colonna)—Moderato
9. Night— a dialogue (Dialogue between Giovanni Strozzi and the Sculptor)—Andante
10. Death (Sonnet 69)—Adagio
11. Immortality (Epitaph for Cecchino Bracci Fiorentio—Epigrams 14 and 12)—Allegretto

Composed: Completed on 31 July 1974, to commemorate the 500th anniversary of the birth of Michelangelo. Opus 145*a*: completed on 5 November 1974, at Moscow.

Dedication: Irina Antonovna Shostakovich (third wife).

Premières: 23 December 1974, Glinka Concert Hall, Leningrad and 31 January 1975, Moscow Conservatory Malyi Hall; Yevgeni Nesterenko (bass) and Yevgeni Shenderovich (piano).

UK: 25 and 27 September 1976, Somerley Park, Ringwood, Hampshire and Queen Elizabeth Hall, London respectively; John Shirley-Quirk (baritone) and Vladimir Ashkenazy (piano).

Opus 145*a*: 12 October 1975, Moscow Conservatory Bolshoi Hall; Yevgeni Nesterenko, All-Union Radio and Television Symphony Orchestra, Maksim Shostakovich.

UK: 16 April 1977, Liverpool; John Shirley-Quirk, Royal Liverpool Philharmonic Orchestra, Sir Charles Groves.

USA: 12 December 1980; John Shirley-Quirk, Cincinnati Symphony Orchestra, John Nelson.

Arrangements: Andrei Voznesensky's revision of Efros's translation commissioned by the composer not used. English translations of the poems by Dr. Sarah and Eric Walter White, and Felicity Ashbee. German translation by Jörg Morgener. Vocal lines modified to suit the original Italian texts. The music of No. 11 is a restoration of a theme from the composer's juvenile opera *The Gipsies*.

Opus 145*a*—orchestrated version for symphony orchestra by the composer.

Suite accompaniment arranged for organ by Hans Eisenmann.

No. 9 Night arranged for double-bass and piano by Michael Cameron.

Instrumentation of Opus 145*a*: 2 flutes (II = piccolo), 2 oboes, 2 clarinets (A and B flat), 2 bassoons (II = contrabassoon) ~ 4 horns, 2 trumpets, 3 trombones, tuba ~ timpani, triangle, side drum, wood block, whip, bass drum, gong ~ glockenspiel, orchestral bells, xylophone, vibraphone, celesta, harp, piano ~ strings (five-string double-basses specified).

Music: Autograph scores of Opuses 145 and 145*a* preserved in the Shostakovich family archive. The first page of the autograph piano and full scores are reproduced in Volumes 33 and 31 of *Collected Works* respectively.

Opus 145: Muzyka, No. 9048, 1975, 30 cm.

Muzyka, No. 11785 (in Volume 33 of *Collected Works* with Opp. 109, 121, 123, 127, 128, 143, and 146), 1984, 30 cm.

G. Schirmer, No. 3426 (plate no. 48521), *c*.1984, score with Russian and English texts, 31 cm.

Opus 145*a*: Muzyka, no number, 1976, photocopied full score, 30 cm.

Muzyka, No. 10113 (in Volume 31 of *Collected Works* with Opp. 4, 21, 46*a*, 140, 79*a*, and 143*a*), 1982, full score, 30 cm.

Hans Sikorski, No. 2278, 1986, score with Russian and German texts— the latter by J. Morgener, 21 cm.

Duration: Approx. 40 minutes in scores; 33' 09"–42' 55".

Films: *The Composer Shostakovich*. For details see under Appendix II.

Recollections of Shostakovich. An hour-long biographical film (scripted by L. Belokurov and directed by B. Goldenblank), made by the Moscow Central Scientific Film Studios in 1977, ends with Nesterenko singing 'Immortality'.

Yevgeni Nesterenko. A documentary television film about the renowned bass singer, screened on Soviet TV in mid-January 1983, contains reminiscences of Nesterenko's close friendship with the composer during the composition of the song cycle.

Recordings: USSR: Melodiya C10 06161-2. Yevgeni NESTERENKO (bass) and Yevgeni Shenderovich (piano). P Mar. 1975, I 1976*b*.
USSR: Melodiya C10 07395-6. Opus 145*a*. Yevgeni NESTERENKO, All-Union Radio and Television Symphony Orchestra, Maksim Shostakovich. P Dec. 1976, I 1977*b*. *Reissued:* HMV Melodiya ASD 3323 in Set SLS 5078 (with Opp. 140 and 143*a*). G May and Oct. 1977. *Gramophone* Record Awards 1977—winner of Solo Vocal category, G Mar. 1978 ~ USA: Columbia Melodiya M2 34594 (in two-record set with Opp. 140 and 143*a*) ~ France: Le Chant du Monde LDX 78613 ~ USSR: Melodiya C10 07395-6. [In third box of Part 3 of *Collected Works on Records.*] I 1978 ~ Japan: Vic. 5358. I 1982 ~ Japan: Victor Musical Industries Compact Disc VICC 40082-83 (two-disc set). ['Shostakovich Songs'—Opp. 58*a*, 121, 123, 127, 140/143*a*, and 146.] I 1991.
   Czech: Panton 11 0604 H. Nos. 1, 4, 5, 10, and 11. Richard NOVÁK (bass) and Cyril Klimeš (piano). [Op. 10.] P Prague 1976, G Dec. 1977.
   Decca SXL 6849. John SHIRLEY-QUIRK (baritone) and Vladimir Ashkenazy (piano). P Oct. 1976 and Apr. 1977, G May 1978.
   USSR: Melodiya C10 11239-40. No. 4 only. Yuri STATNIK (bass) and Nataliya Rassudova (piano). [Op. 62 No. 4; Rimsky-Korsakov, Verdi, and recital by Eva Podleshch.] P 1978, I 1979*c*.
   East Germany: Eterna, 8 27 209. Opus 145*a*. Hermann-Christian POLSTER (bass), Berlin Radio Symphony Orchestra, Thomas Sanderling. P 3–7 Mar. 1978. *Reissued:* Japan: Tokuma Compact Disc TKCC 70414. I Aug. 1994 ~ Germany: Berlin Classics Compact Disc 0091 932BC. I Jan. 1997.
   France: Praga Compact Disc PR 250 009. Opus 145*a* Nos. 1, 4–6, and 8–11. Sergej KOPČÁK (bass), Prague Radio Symphony Orchestra, Frantísek Vajnar. [Opp. 109 and 127.] P Prague concert 1980, I 1992.
   Czech: Opus 9112 1570. Opus 145*a*. Sergej KOPČÁK (bass), Slovak Philharmonic Orchestra, Libor Pešek. P Bratislava Dec. 1983, I 1985.
   Germany: Teldec Compact Disc 243 714-2. Sung in the original Italian. Dietrich FISCHER-DIESKAU (baritone) and Aribert Rlemann (piano). [Riemann.] P May 1987. *Reissued:* Teldec/ASV Compact Disc 8 44138 [Riemann.] I Oct. 1988, G Jan. 1989 ~ Teldec Compact Disc 4509 97460-2. [Riemann.] I June 1995.
   Decca Compact Disc 433 319-2DH. Opus 145*a*, sung in Russian. Dietrich FISCHER-DIESKAU (baritone), Berlin Radio Symphony Orchestra, Vladimir Ashkenazy. [Op. 146.] P Berlin Jan. 1991, I June 1993, G July 1993.
   Deutsche Grammophon Compact Disc 447 085-2GH. Opus 145*a*. Sergei LEIFERKUS (baritone), Gothenburg Symphony Orchestra, Neeme Järvi. ['The Orchestral Songs, Vol. 2'—Opp. 21 and 143*a*.] P Gothenburg Sept. 1994, I Dec. 1994, G Jan. 1996.
   USA: Zuma Compact Disc ZMA 304. 'Night' arr. Cameron. Michael CAMERON (double-bass) and Ian Hobson (piano). ['Progression'—Bach,

Hindemith, Ben Johnston *et al.*] P University of Illinois, Champaign-Urbana Oct. 1995, I Jan. 1997

Germany: Capriccio Compact Disc 10 777. Opus 145*a*. Anatoli KOTSCHERGA (bass), Cologne Radio Symphony Orchestra, Mikhail Yurovsky. [Opp. 46*a* and 21*a*.] P Cologne 21–3 Feb. 1996, I 1998.

France: Le Chant du Monde Compact Disc LDC778 1124. Arr. Eisenmann. Aleksandr NAUMENKO (bass) and Hervé Désarbre (organ). [Opp. 29, 27, and 39; Tishchenko *Portrait of D. D. Shostakovich*—No. 12 of *Twelve Portraits, Op.* 113.] P Glinka Museum, Moscow concert 24 May 1999, I May 1999, G Aug. 2000.

References: Levaya, Nesterenko, and Vasina-Grossman (in Daragan).

Notes: During rehearsals for the orchestral version, Opus 145*a*, in October 1975, Maksim Shostakovich disclosed to Yevgeni Nesterenko that his father considered this composition took the place of the Sixteenth Symphony in his *œuvre*.

Efros referred to Karl Frey's German edition of Michelangelo's poetry when translating the original Italian into the Russian language but this standard work has only the editorial preface and notes in German and not German versions of the poems as stated in the first and second editions of this catalogue.

Sans op. Z   Song of the Flea (Beethoven)

Form: Orchestration of Ludwig van Beethoven's 'Song of Mephistopheles in Auerbach's cellar', Op. 75 No. 3, for voice and piano, to words from Goethe's *Faust* in a translation by Aleksandr Strugovshchikov.

Composed: Early in 1975 at the request of Yevgeni Nesterenko; unaware, as was Shostakovich, that Igor Stravinsky had orchestrated this piece in 1909.

Première: I April 1975, Leningrad Philharmonic Bolshoi Hall; Yevgeni Nesterenko (bass), Leningrad Philharmonic Orchestra, Yuri Kochnev.

Arrangement: English translation of the text by Joan Pemberton Smith.

Music: Autograph score preserved in the Shostakovich family archive.

Duration: 2' 25".

Recordings: USSR: Melodiya C10 14415-6. Yevgeni NESTERENKO (bass), Soviet ensemble of soloists under Gennadi Rozhdestvensky. [Album 1 of 'From Manuscripts of Different Years'—Opp. 4, 16, 17, 23, and 36; Sans opp. C and H.] P 1980, I 1981*b*. *Reissued:* HMV Melodiya ASD 1650331. [As USSR release.] G July 1983 ~ Germany: Eurodisc 201974-366. [As USSR release.] ~ BMG Melodiya Compact Discs 74321 59058-2 (two-disc set). [Opp. 36, 4, 17, H, C, 16, 1, 3, 7, 26/D 59, E, 128, 30*a*, and 19.] I and G Mar. 1999.

Reference: Nesterenko.

Opus 146   Four Verses of Captain Lebyadkin

Form: Four songs for bass and piano to texts of Fyodor Dostoyevsky, from the novel *The Devils* of 1871:

1. The Love of Captain Lebyadkin (Miss Lisa Tushin)—Allegretto
2. The Cockroach—Moderato
3. The Ball for the Benefit of Governesses—Allegretto
4. A Shining Personality (or 'A Pure Soul')—Allegretto

Composed: Completed on 23 August 1974.
Premières: 10 May 1975, Moscow Conservatory Malyi Hall; Yevgeni Nesterenko (bass) and Yevgeni Shenderovich (piano).
USA: 30 October 1983, Boston University Concert Hall; Robert Osborne (bass) and Howard Lubin (piano). Sung in Russian.
Arrangement: English translation of the texts by Joan Pemberton Smith.
Music: Autograph score preserved in the Shostakovich family archive.
Russian printed edition of manuscript not in the composer's hand, no number or date, 29.5 cm.
Muzyka, No. 11785 (in Volume 33 of *Collected Works* with Opp. 109, 121, 123, 127, 128, 143, and 145), 1984, 30 cm.
Duration: 10' 57"–13' 59".
Recordings: USSR: Melodiya C10 09225-6. Yevgeni NESTERENKO (bass) and Yevgeni Shenderovich (piano). [In third box of Part 3 of *Collected Works on Records* with Opp. 58a, 123, and 121.] P Jan. 1976, I 1978. *Reissued:* HMV Melodiya ASD 3700. [Opp. 58a, 121, and 123; and Musorgsky.] G Sept. 1979 ~ USSR: Melodiya C10 15501-2. [Opp. 109 and 21.] I 1981d ~ Czech: Supraphon 1112 3148. [Opp. 109 and 21.] I 1986 ~ Japan: Victor Musical Industries Compact Disc VICC 40082-83 (two-disc set). ['Shostakovich Songs'—Opp. 58a, 121, 123, 127, 140 / 143a, and 145a.] I 1991.
Czech: Supraphon 1111 2000 G. Josef ŠPAČEK (bass) and Josef Hála (piano). [Op. 147.] P Prague 23–4 Oct. 1978.
Decca Compact Disc 433 319-2DH. Dietrich FISCHER-DIESKAU (baritone) and Vladimir Ashkenazy (piano). [Op. 145a.] P Berlin Jan 1991, I June 1993, G July 1993.
France: Le Chant du Monde Russian Season Compact Disc RUS 288089. Pyotr GLUBOKY (bass) and Nataliya Rassudova (piano). [Opp. 46, 62, 91, and 121.] P Moscow Conservatory 21–9 Sept. 1994, I Apr. 1995.
Japan: Triton Compact Disc 17 008. Aleksei MOCHALOV (bass), Moscow Chamber Music Theatre Orchestra, Anatoli Levin. [Opp. 58a, 140, 121, and Sans op. X (iii).] P Mosfilm Studio Nov. 1995, I Nov. 1996.
Reference: Levaya.

Opus 147   Viola Sonata

Form: Sonata for viola and grand piano in three movements:

1. Aria (or Novello)—Moderato
2. Scherzo—Allegretto
3. Adagio—'In memory of the great Beethoven'

The Overture and start of 'Scenes in the Hotel' of the wartime opera *The Gamblers,* Sans op. K (i), utilized in the Scherzo.

Composed: The first two movements written from late April to June 1975 and the Adagio written in two days, being completed on 5 July 1975. The proofs corrected by Shostakovich in a Moscow hospital bed on 4 and 5 August 1975, five and four days before his death.

Dedication: Fyodor Serafimovich Druzhinin (violist of the Beethoven Quartet). The third movement also dedicated to Ludwig van Beethoven though this is not stated in the score.

Premières: 1 October 1975, Glinka Concert Hall, Leningrad; Fyodor Druzhinin (viola) and Mikhail Muntyan (piano).

UK: 14 June 1976, Jubilee Hall, Aldeburgh; Cecil Aronowitz (viola) and Nicola Grunberg (piano).

USA: 12 November 1976, University of New Mexico, Keller Hall, Albuquerque; Herbert Levinson (viola) and George Robert (piano).

USA: 17 December 190, Chamber Music Society of New York, Lincoln Center; Walter Trampler (viola) and Richard Goode (piano).

Opus 147*a*: Netherlands: January 1992, Amsterdam; V. Mendelssohn's arrangement performed by Lev Markiz (violist/director) and New Amsterdam Sinfonietta.

Arrangements: Viola part arranged for cello by both Daniil Shafran and Iosif Feigelson. Opus 147*a*: orchestrated for viola soloist, strings and celesta by Vladimir Mendelssohn.

Music: Autograph score preserved in the Shostakovich family archive. The first page is reproduced in Volume 38 of *Collected Works.*

G. Schirmer, No. 47675, 1975, score and viola part, 30 cm.

Hans Sikorski, No. 2222, 1975, parts, 31.5 cm.

Muzyka, No. 9679, 1977, viola part ed. F. Druzhinin and with added cello part arr. D. Shafran, 29 cm.

Muzyka, No. 10927 (in Volume 38 of *Collected Works* with Opp. 40 and 134), 1982, including separate viola part, 30 cm.

Duration: Approx.30 minutes in score; 26' 15"–38' 06"; 25 minutes (M. MacDonald).

Films: *Sonata for Viola.* A full-length documentary film, including scenes from the first International Chopin Pianoforte Competition in Warsaw, 1927; the composer playing his Piano Quintet, a trip to Paris in 1958 and other newsreels; with his music performed by Fyodor Druzhinin, David

Oistrakh, Svyatoslav Richter, and Leonard Bernstein among others, was made in Leningrad for release on the eve of the 75th anniversary of Shostakovich's birth. The film was compiled by Semyon Aranovich and Aleksandr Sokurov for Lenfilm.

Yuri Bashmet. A portrait of the Ukrainian viola virtuoso presented on TV's 'The South Bank Show' by Melvyn Bragg on 4 March 1990. Includes takes of Irina Shostakovich talking about the Viola Sonata and part of the Adagio played in the composer's flat by Bashmet and Mikhail Muntyan.

Recordings: USSR: Melodiya C10 06637-8. Fyodor DRUZHININ (viola) and Mikhail Muntyan (piano). P Dec. 1975; I 1976c. *Reissued:* HMV Melodiya HQS 1369. [Op. 134.] G May 1977 ~ USSR: Melodiya C10 06637-8. [In second box of Part 2 of *Collected Works on Records*.] I 1978 ~ USA: Columbia Melodiya M 35109. [Op. 134.] ~ France: Le Chant du Monde LDX 78614. [Op. 142.] I Mar. 1981 ~ Japan: Victor Musical Industries Compact Disc VICC 2049. [Cello arr.] I 1989 ~ France: Le Chant du Monde Compact Discs LDC 278 1018-19 (two-disc set). [Opp. 134, 40, and 67.] I Feb. 1990, G June 1990.

Czech: Opus 9111 0492. Milan TELECKÝ (viola) and Lýdia Majlingová (piano). P May 1976. *Reissued:* Rediffusion Aurora AUR 5051. G May 1977.

Czech: Supraphon 1111 2000 G. Josef SUK (viola) and Jan Panenka (piano). [Op. 146.] P Prague 9 June 1976.

USSR: Melodiya C10 09571-2. Arr. for cello D. Shafran. Daniil SHAFRAN (cello) and Anton Ginzburg (piano). P June 1977, I 1978c. *Reissued:* Japan: Victor Musical Industries Compact Disc VICC 2049. [Op. 147 première Druzhinin/Muntyan recording.] I 1989 ~ USSR: Melodiya Compact Disc SUCD 10 0257. [Schumann and Brahms.] I 1991b.

Sweden: BIS LP 81. Zahari TCHAVDAROV (viola) and Albena Zaharieva (piano). [Reger and Hindemith.] P Sweden 15 Jan. 1977, I 1979. *Reissued:* Sweden: BIS Compact Disc CD 81. [Reger and Hindemith.] I June 1993.

New Zealand: Halcyon Records PM 102. Glynne ADAMS (viola) and Bryan Sayer (piano). [Sculthorpe and Ladd.] P 1977.

USSR: Melodiya C10 10789-90. Second movement only arr. D. Shafran. Nathaniel ROSEN (cello) and J. Hemmel (piano). [Cellists at Sixth International Tchaikovsky Competition.] P 1978, I 1979a.

USSR: Melodiya C10 11381-2. Yuri YUROV (viola) and Vladimir Krainev (piano). [Aristakesyan.] P 1978, I 1979c.

USA: Laurel LP 118. Milan THOMAS (viola) and Doris Stevenson (piano). P 1981.

Russia: Melodiya Compact Disc SUCD 10 00095. Yuri BASHMET (viola) and Svyatoslav Richter (piano). [Op. 134.] P Moscow concert 26 Sept. 1982, I 1993a.

Bulgaria: Balkanton BKA 11424. Ognyan STANCHEV (viola) and Ivan Evtimov (piano). [Op. 34.] P 1984?

Canada: Discopaedia MBS 2021-2 (third side in two-record set). Rivka GOLANI (viola) and Samuel Sanders (piano). [Schubert.] P Toronto Dec. 1984 and Feb. 1985.

Japan: JVC Compact Disc VDC 5016 (in two-disc set 'To the Memory of David Oistrakh'). Yuri BASHMET (viola) and Svyatoslav Richter (piano). [Hindemith and Britten.] P Freiburg, West Germany concert 6–8 Mar. 1985. *Reissued:* Russia: Mezhdunarodnaya Kniga Compact Disc MK 418015. [Britten and Hindemith.] I 1992 ~ Olympia Compact Disc OCD 625. [Hindemith and Britten.] I June 1997.

Czech: Panton Debut 81 0665-1. Jan PĚRUŠKA (viola) and František Kůda (piano). [Britten.] P Prague 24–7 Mar. 1986.

Cuba: Egrem LD 4403. Viera BORISOVA (viola) and Ignacio Pacheco (piano). [Marin.] P Havana, Cuba 1986.

Sweden: BIS Compact Disc CD 358. Nobuko IMAI (viola) and Ronald Pöntinen (piano). ['The Russian Viola'—Rubinstein, Glinka, Glazunov, and Stravinsky.] P 28–30 Dec. 1986, I 1987, G Feb. 1988.

Canada: Société Nouvelle D'Enregistrement SNE 535. Robert VEREBES (viola) and Dale Bartlett (piano). [Beethoven.] P 1987.

USA: Composers Recordings Incorporated ACS 6018 (cassette only). John GRAHAM (viola) and Thomas Muraco (piano). ['Music for the Viola: a Twentieth-Century Anthology; Vol. 3.] P Houston Feb. and Apr. 1988.

Koch Schwann Compact Disc 3-1161-2. Raphael HILLYER (viola) and Reinbert de Leeuw (piano). [Barth and Stravinsky.] P Düsseldorf 14 Dec. 1989, I Dec. 1994, G May 1995.

Germany: ECM New Series Compact Disc 847 538-2. Kim KASHKASHIAN (viola) and Robert Levin (piano). [Bouchard and Chihara.] P 1990, I Jan. 1992, G Sept. 1992.

Italy: Dynamic Compact Disc CDS 61. James CREITZ (viola) and Mihail Sarbu (piano). [Enescu, Stravinsky, Kodály *et al.*] P Genoa 1990, I 1994.

EMI Classics Compact Disc CDC7 54394-2. Tabea ZIMMERMANN (viola) and Harmut Höll (piano). [Britten and Stravinsky.] P Sandhausen 1991, I Jan. 1992, G Mar. 1992.

France: Erato Compact Disc 2292 45804-2. Shlomo MINTZ (viola) and Viktoria Postnikova (piano). [Op. 134.] P Metz Sept. 1991, I Oct. 1992, G Nov. 1992.

USA: RCA Victor Red Seal Compact Disc 09026 61273-2. Yuri BASHMET (viola) and Mikhail Muntyan (piano). [Glinka and Roslavets.] P Henry Wood Hall, London concert 18–20 Sept. 1991, G Mar. 1993. *Reissued:* RCA Digital Compact Cassette 09026 61273-5. [Glinka.] I May 1993.

Germany: Fidelio Compact Disc 9203. Isabelle van KEULEN (viola) and Ronald Brautigam (piano). [Op. 134.] P Utrecht 23–4 Mar. 1992, I July 1993. *Reissued:* Netherlands: Vanguard Classics Compact Discs 99306 (two-disc set). [Opp. 110*a*, 118*a*, and 134.] I Aug. 1999.

Gamut Classics Compact Disc CD 537. Philip DUKES (viola) and Sophia Rahman (piano). [Clarke and Maconchy.] P Petersham 14–16 July 1992, I Feb. 1994, G Apr. 1994.

Netherlands: Globe Compact Disc GLO 5093. Opus 147*a* arr. V. Mendelssohn. Vladimir MENDELSSOHN (viola), New Amsterdam Sinfonietta, Lev Markiz. [Op. 73*a*.] P Utrecht Oct.–Dec. 1992, I 1993.

France: REM Editions Compact Disc 311 210. Anton KHOLODENKO (viola) and Sergei Milstein (piano). [Op. 134.] P Tassin-la-Demi-Lune summer 1993.

Koch International Classic Compact Disc 3-7270-2. Paul SILVERTHORNE (viola) and John Constable (piano). [Britten and Hindemith.] P East Finley Dec. 1993, I Mar. 1995.

Japan: Meister Music Compact Disc MM 1002. Nobuko IMAI (viola) and Friedrich Wilhelm Schnurr (piano). ['A Viola Banquet, Vol. II'— Brahms, Bartók, and Bach.] P Casals Hall, Tokyo Mar. 1994, I Oct. 1994.

USA: Arabesque Compact Discs Z 6698 (two-disc set). Jamie LAREDO (viola) and Joseph Kalichstein (piano). [Opp. 8, 67, 40, and 134.] P Purchase, New York 17–18 Dec. 1995 or 12–13 Sept. 1996, I and G Jan. 1998.

Centaur Compact Disc CRC 2450. Victoria CHANG (viola) and Randall Hodgkinson (piano). [Roslavets.] P Weston, Massachusetts 21 Dec. 1995, I May 2000.

Chandos Compact Discs CHAN 9526 (two-disc set). Arr. D. Shafran. Alfia BEKOVA (cello) and Eleonora Bekova (piano). [Opp. 67 and 127.] P Highgate, London 19–20 June 1996, I Feb. 1997, G May 1997.

Koch Discover International Compact Disc DICD 920538. Felix SCHWARTZ (viola) and Wolfgang Kühnl. (piano). [Schubert and Enescu.] P Berlin 26–7 Feb. 1997, I June 1999.

Switzerland: Pan Classics Compact Disc 510 111. Thomas RIEBL (viola) and Cordelia Höfer (piano). [Taneyev, Rubenstein, and Glinka.] P Schloss Mondsee, Festaal Sept. 1998.

USA: Artona Compact Disc no number. Michael ZARETSKY (viola) and Xak Bjerken (piano). ['Black Snow'—Yakubov and Glinka.] P 1998.

Bibliography

Abdel-Aziz, Mahmud, *Form und Gehalt in den Violoncellowerken von Dmitri Schostakowitsch* (Regensburg, 1992), 166 pp. [A study of the Cello Sonata, Op. 40, in German.]

Abraham, Gerald (Ernest Heal), *Eight Soviet Composers* (Oxford University Press, London, 1943), 13–31. [Covers up to Op. 60.]

—— *Music in the Soviet Union.* The New History of Music: Vol. x, *The Modern Age, 1890–1960,* ed. Martin Cooper (Oxford University Press, London, 1974), 639–700. [A scholarly and critical review of the Soviet scene with music examples from *Lady Macbeth* and a photograph of the original production.]

Alekseyev, Aleksandr Dmitrievich, *Sovetskaya fortepiannaya muzyka 1917–1945* (Muzyka, Moscow, 1974), 248 pp. ['Soviet Fortepiano Music 1917–45': information on Opp. 5 (p. 30), 13, (p. 31), 35 (pp. 87–94 with 9 music examples), 34 (pp. 124–33 with 9 music examples), and 61 (pp. 177–84 with 6 music examples and autograph of first page); bibliography (p. 232) and discography (p. 245).]

Alekseyeva, Nataliya. *Vladimir Fedoseyev: sbornik statei i materialov.* (Muzyka, Moscow, 1989), 288 pp. [A collection of essays and material on the conductor Vladimir Fedoseyev, profusely illustrated in colour and monochrome. In Russian with abridged English translation by Romela Kokhanovskaya and Tatyana Sorokina. Repertoire and discography.]

Alphabetical Catalogue of EMI Records (EMI Records, London, 1960), C 117–18. [Recordings available up to 30 June 1960.]

American Society of Composers, Authors and Publishers (ASCAP) Symphonic Catalog. (R. R. Bowker, New York and London, 1977), 3rd edn., 424–5.

Amoh, Kenzo, *Leonid Kogan Discography* (Amoh Publisher, Tokyo, Japan, Apr. 1997), 58–9. [Paperback. Includes list of record labels, artist index, and appendix 'List of Kogan's Recordings on Melodiya'.]

—— with Forman, Frank; and Hashizume, Hiroshi, *Mravinsky Discography.* (The Japanese Mravinsky Society, Kishiwada, Japan, Mar. 1993, 41–53.

—— and Forman, Frank, *Legacy of Yevgeni Mravinsky* (Ota-ku, Tokyo, Dec. 1998). [Printed from Internet Web Site http://plaza13.mbn.or.jp/ -mravinsky/ 4th edition of the Mravinsky discography with added filmography, broadcasts on radio and television, and artists who performed with the conductor on record.]

————, *Yevgeni Mravinsky A Concert Listing 1930–1987* (Japanese Mravinsky Society, Tokyo, Dec. 2000), 66 pp. [A4 paperback, stiff covers. Includes a graph showing the annual number of his 1137 concerts—maximum of 46 in 1943 and top 100 works performed—Shostakovich's Symphony No. 5 second with 119, an increase of 17 over Fomin 1983, and indices; 12 photographs—8 of programmes.]

———— and Forman, Frank, *Yevgeni Mravinsky Legacy A Recording History 1938–1984* (Japanese Mravinsky Society, Tokyo, Dec. 2000), 48 pp. [A4 paperback, stiff covers. Updated edition of 1998 compilation with graph showing the annual number of his 243 recordings—maximum of 19 being all concert performances in 1965; 11 photographs.]

Andronikov, Irakli (author of folder note), collection of 12 monochrome postcards (Planet Publishing House, Moscow, 1977). [Photographs of Shostakovich, musicians and friends, 1940–70.]

Aranovsky, Mark Genrikovich, *Simfonicheskie iskaniya* (Sovetskii Kompozitor, Leningrad, 1979), 68–80, 230–61. ['Symphonic Quest', subtitled 'Problems of the symphony genre in Soviet music, 1960–75'. Includes a review of Symphonies Nos. 15 and 13–14.]

Arndt, Walter, *Pushkin Threefold* (George Allen & Unwin, London, 1976).

Aronowsky, S., *Performing Times of Orchestral Works* (Ernest Benn, London, 1959), 668–9.

Ashman, Mike, 'Rostropovich and Lady Macbeth', *Gramophone*, Vol. 56, No. 672 (May 1979), 1852–3.

Bainton, Helen, *Facing the Music* (Currawong Publishers, Sydney, NSW, 1967).

Barlow, Harold, and Morgenstern, Sam, *A Dictionary of Musical Themes* (Williams & Northgate, London, 1952 and 11th imp. 1974), 535–59.

Bartlett, Rosamund (ed.), *Shostakovich in Context* (Oxford University Press, New York, 2000), 274 pp., 20 Illustrations. [Contains scholarly essays by Richard Taruskin, David Fanning, Svetlana Savenko, Laurel Fay, Lyudmila Mikheyeva-Sollertinsky—daughter of Ivan, Inna Barsova (Opus 47 final movement), Olga Komok, David Haas ('Shostakovich's Eighth—C minor against the grain'), Manashir Yakubov (*Rayok*), Elmira Nazirova (Symphony No. 10), Lyudmila Kovnatskaya, Caryl Emerson ('Shostakovich . . . : Songs and Dances of Death and Survival'—Opus 143), and R. Bartlett (on Chekhov).

Bawden, Liz-Anne (ed.), *The Oxford Companion to Film* (Oxford University Press, London, 1976).

Baxandale, Lee, *Marxisin and Aesthetics* (Humanity Press, New York, 1973), 152–4. [A selective annotated bibliography up to 1968, valuable for contemporary references to the banning of *Lady Macbeth*.]

Beaumont, Cyril W., *Complete Book of Ballets* (Putman, London, 1956).

Belza, Igor Fedorovich, *Handbook of Soviet Musicians* ed. Alan Bush (Pilot Press, London, 1943), 49–51 and 95–7. [Includes list of works Opp. 1 to 60.]

———— 'Zametki o muzyke filma 'Nezabyvayemyi 1919 god'', *Iskusstvo kino* (Moscow), 1952 No. 9, 87–91. [Notes on the music for Op. 89.]

Bennett, John Reginald, *Melodiya: A Soviet Russian L.P. Discography*, Discographies Number 6 (Greenwood Press, Westport, Conn., 1981), 559–70 *et passim*.

Berger, Lyubov Grigorievna, *Odinnadtsataya simfoniya D. D. Shostakovicha '1905 god' (poyasnenie)* (Sovetskii Kompozitor, Moscow, 1961), 38 pp. [Eleventh Symphony.]

—— (ed.), *Cherty stilya D. Shostakovicha* (Sovetskii Kompozitor, Moscow, 1962), 386 pp. ['Features of the style of D. Shostakovich': a collection of theoretical articles by Lev Mazel, Aleksandr Dolzhansky, Igor Beletsky, and others. Dolzhansky's contribution includes a paper on the first movement of the Seventh Symphony and an examination of the Eleventh Symphony. Beletsky's review of the Piano Quintet runs to 23 pages. Many music examples and a classified bibliography of 248 references dated 1923–62.]

Bernandt, Grigori Borisovich, and Dolzhansky, Aleksandr Naumovich. *Sovetskie kompozitory* (Sovetskii Kompozitor, Moscow, 1957), 664–7. ['Soviet composers': includes information on première performances, Opp. 1 to 98.]

—— and Yampolsky, Izrail Markovich, *Kto pisal o muzyke* (Sovetskii Kompozitor, Moscow), Vol. i (A–I), 1971, 356 pp.; Vol. ii (K–P), 1974, 315 pp.; Vol. iii (R–CH), 1979, 206 pp.; Vol. iv (SH–YA) with Tamara Yefimovna Kiseleva, 1989, 121 pp. [A bio-bibliographical dictionary of music critics and list of writers on music in pre-revolutionary Russia and the USSR. On pp. 35–40 of the fourth volume references to 314 articles written by Shostakovich, 1928–85, are listed chronologically.]

—— and Yampolsky, Izrail Markovich, *Sovetskie Kompozitory i Muzykovedy* (Sovetskii Kompozitor, Moscow), Vol. i (A–I), 1978, 270 pp. [The first of three volumes of a dictionary of Soviet composers and musicologists. See Grigoriev for Vols. ii and iii.]

Biancolli, Louis (ed.), *The Analytical Concert Guide* (Greenwood Press, Conn., 1951), 526–40.

Bibliographic Guide to Music (G. K. Hall & Co., New York). Publications catalogued by The Research Libraries of The New York Public Library and the Library of Congress. Shostakovich pages from 1993, p. 626; 1994, pp. 642–43; 1995, pp. 734–35; 1996, p. 584.]

Blokker, Roy, with Dearling, Robert, *The Music of Dmitri Shostakovich: The Symphonies* (Tantivy Press, London, 1979), 192 pp., 13 photographs. [A readable exploration of the 15 symphonies, with 98 music examples, brief bibliography, annotated discography, and comparative chart of contemporary symphonies.]

Blom, Eric, *Grove's Dictionary of Music and Musicians*, Vol. vii, 5th edn. (Macmillan, London, 1966), 765–7 and Vol. x, Supplement, p. 407. [Shostakovich entry: lists works up to Second Quartet.]

Bobrovsky, Viktor Pyotrovich, *Kamernye instrumentalnye ansambli Shostakovicha* (Sovetskii Kompozitor, Moscow, 1961), 259 pp., 9 photographs. [The chamber music considered.]

Boelza, Egor—see Belza, Igor.

Bogdanova, Alla Vladimirovna, *Katerina Izmailova* (Muzyka, Moscow, 1968), 87 pp., 4 plates. [A small paperback guide to the four acts of the 1963 version of the opera, with a 32-page introduction, 41 music examples, and 11 bibliographic references.]

Opery i balety (Sovetskii Kompozitor, Moscow, 1979), 208 pp., 17 photographs. [A paperback including extended analyses of *The Nose*, pp. 53–108, and *Katerina Izmailova*, pp. 145–94, with 104 music examples and pages from manuscripts of Opp. 19, 28, and 31.]

────── *Pamyati pogibshikh—kompozitorov i muzykovedov 1941–45* (Sovetskii Kompozitor, Moscow, 1985), 8, 70–85. [Articles in memory of the composers and musicologists who perished in the Great Patriotic War, including L. Dyachkova's contribution on Fleishman's opera *Rothschild's Violin* with 31 music examples.]

Bogdanov-Berezovsky, Valerian Mikhailovich, *Stati o muzyke* (Sovetskii Kompozitor, Leningrad, 1960), 163–76. [Article on 'The Eighth Symphony by D. Shostakovich as performed under the baton of Ye. Mravinsky' with 8 music examples.]

Bouij, Christer, *Dmitrij Sjostakovitj och den sovjetiska kulturpolitiken* (Uppsala University, 1984), 382 pp. with 3-page addenda, 1991. [A stiff-card bound thesis in Swedish with a 11-page bibliography, numerous music examples, cartoons, and a 12-page register of persons.]

Boyden, David D., *An Introduction to Music* (Faber and Faber, London, 2nd edn. 1971), 469–70. [A Shostakovich review: 'With a very few early exceptions, his music represents a backward glance. . .' . Detailed analysis of Fifth Symphony.]

Braun, Joachim, 'The Double Meaning of Jewish Elements in Dmitri Shostakovich's Music', *The Musical Quarterly*, Vol. lxxi, No. 1 (Jan. 1985), 68–80. [An in-depth study of the Jewish elements in eleven compositions, with particular emphasis on *From Jewish Folk Poetry*, Music examples from Opp. 79, 87, and 107.]

Bretanitskaya, Alla Leonidovna, *'Nos' D. D. Shostakovicha: Putevoditel* (Muzyka, 1983), 96 pp. [A small paperback guide to *The Nose*. History of the opera, detailed synopsis, bibliography of 60 references, and appendix of 27 music examples.]

British Broadcasting Corporation Music Library, *Chamber Music Catalogue* and *Piano and Organ Catalogue* (BBC, London, 1965).

────── *Song Catalogue II* and *Song Catalogue Titles IV* (BBC, London, 1966).

British Catalogue of Music, British Library Bibliographic Services Division (London, Jan. 1957 to 1988).

British Library, The Catalogue of Printed Music in the (K. G. Saur, London), Vol. 52, Shad-Smir, 153–61. [A list of the music collection to 1980.]

Britten, Benjamin (with annotations by Donald Mitchell), 'Britten on "Oedipus rex" and "Lady Macbeth"', *Tempo*, No. 120 (Mar. 1977), 10–12.

Brockhaus, Heinz Alfred, *Dmitri Schostakowitsch* (Breitkopf & Härtel, Leipzig, 1962), 215 pp. [An expanded dissertation on the symphonies, in German.]

Brook, Donald, *Composers' Gallery* (Rockcliff, London, 1945), 190–8. [An early appreciation of Shostakovich's work up to the Eighth Symphony. Full page portrait.]

Brown, David, 'Recent Trends in Soviet Music', *The Listener,* lxv (1961), 329. [Refers to First Violin Concerto.]

———— 'Russia: Shostakovich', *Music in the Modern Age,* Vol. v: A History of Western Music ed. F. W. Sternfeld (Weidenfeld & Nicholson, London, 1973), 39–45.

———— *Encyclopaedia Britannica* (Chicago, 15th edn. 1974). Vol. 16, 717–18. [Shostakovich entry.]

Brown, Malcolm H., 'The Soviet Russian Concepts of "Intonazia" and "Musical Imagery"', *The Musical Quarterly,* Vol. 60 (1974), 557–67. [Refers to the first movement of Seventh Symphony.]

———— (ed.), *Musorgsky: In Memoriam, 1881–1981.* Studies in Russian Music, No. 3 (UMI Research Press, Ann Arbor, Mich., 1982). [See especially the essay 'Musorgsky and Shostakovich', by Laurel E. Fay, pp 215–26.]

Bruce, George, *Festival in the North: the Story of the Edinburgh Festival* (Robert Hale, London, 1975).

Bush, Alan Dudley, 'Shostakovich and his symphonies', *The Listener,* 27 (4 June 1942), 733. [Mentions Nos. 1 to 7.]

Buske, Peter, *Dmitri Schostakowitsch—Leben und Schaffen des Sowjetischen Komponisten* (Heransgeber Zentralvorstand des Gesellschaft für Deutsch-Sowjetisce, Berlin, DDR, 1975). [This study has a discography which includes several East German Eterna recordings not listed here.]

Calvocoressi, Michel Dimitri, 'Shostakovich: [Piano] Concerto No. 1', *The Listener,* 14 (24 Dec. 1935), 1184.

———— 'The First of May', *The Listener,* 15 (19 Feb. 1936), 373. [Third Symphony.]

———— 'A Russian critic on Shostakovich's Quintet', trans. Ivan Martynov, *The Musical Times,* Vol. 82, No. 1185 (Nov. 1941), 395–6.

———— *A Survey of Russian Music* (Pelican Books, London, 1944), 100–2, 111–14.

Cawkwell, Tim, and Smith, John M., *The World Encyclopedia of Film* (Studio Vista, London, 1972).

Chappell, Herbert, *Sounds Magnificent: the Story of the Symphony* (BBC, London, 1984), 172 pp. [Chapter 8: 'Sounds for Tomorrow?']

Chekhov, Anton Pavlovich, *Rothschild's Fiddle,* The Oxford Chekhov, Vol. viii: *Stories 1893–1895,* trans. Ronald Hingley (Oxford University Press, Oxford, 1978), 93–101.

Chernyavskaya, Tatyana Nikolayevna, *Khudozhestvennaya kultura SSSR* (Russkii Yazyk, Moscow, 1984), 356 pp. ['The Artistic Culture of the USSR' dictionary, with illustrations—many in colour—and descriptions of concert-halls, theatres, film companies, folk instruments, and related musical subjects; besides covering non-musical topics such as literature, painting and architecture.]

Chernyi, Osip Yevseyevich, 'Dmitri Shostakovich', *Novyi mir* [New World], No. 10 (Moscow, 1945), 140–7.

Clough, Francis F., and Cuming, G. J., *The World's Encyclopaedia of Recorded Music*, 1925–50 and including First Supplement, *1950–51* (Sidgwick and Jackson, London, rev. edn. 1966), 558–9, 836. [Also same pagination in paperback: Greenwood, Westport, Connecticut, 1970.] Second Supplement, *1951–52* (Sidgwick and Jackson, London, 1953), 204–5. Third Supplement, *1953–55* (Sidgwick and Jackson, London, 1969), 425–7.

Collaer, Paul, *The New Music Lover's Handbook*, ed. Elie Siegmeister (Harvey House, New York, 1973), 411–14.

Creighton, James, *The Discopaedia of the Violin* (University of Toronto Press, Toronto, 1974), 901. [List of violin works and transcriptions recorded.]

Crimp, Bryan, *The Record Year 1* (Duckworth, London, 1979), 196–8, 455–8; *The Record Year 2* (Duckworth, London, 1981), 193–5, 444–7. [Discography and informative reviews of discs and cassettes released in 1978 and 1979 respectively.)

Cross, Milton, and Ewen, David, *Encyclopedia of the Great Composers and Their Music*, Vol. ii (Doubleday, New York, rev. edn. 1962), 725–37.

Dalley, Janet (trans.), *Pushkin's Fairy Tales* (Barrie & Jenkins, London, 1978), 82–6. [An English prose translation of *The Story of a Priest and his Servant Balda*, written in verse form by Aleksandr Pushkin in 1830.]

Danilevich, Lev Vasilievich, *D. D. Shostakovich* (Sovetskii Kompozitor, Moscow, 1958), 196 pp., 9 photographs. [Including music examples, bibliography, and list of works.]

——— *Nash sovremennik: tvorchestvo Shostakovicha* (Muzyka, Moscow, 1965), 330 pp., 24 plates. ['Our Contemporary: the Works of Shostakovich'. A scholarly review in Russian of his compositions up to the end of 1962— Opp. 1 to 114—with 81 music examples, discography, and utilizing material from this author's 1958 study.]

Danilevich, Lev Vasilievich, (ed.), *Dmitri Shostakovich* (Sovetskii Kompozitor, Moscow, 1967), 536 pp., 45 photographs, 195 music examples. [Articles from newspapers and journals 1932–66, and thirteen articles: 'Shakespeare and Shostakovich' by Daniel Zhitomirsky, 'Remarks on the opera *Katerina Izmailova*' by Marina Sabinina, 'The 30th anniversary of the composition of Symphony No. 4' by Genrikh Orlov, 'Symphony No. 13' by Givi Ordzhonikidze (36 pp.), '*The Execution of Stepan Razin* and the traditions of Musorgsky' by Semyon Shlifshteyn, 'The cycle *From Jewish Folk Poetry* and its place in the works of Shostakovich' by Arnold Sokhor, 'Some observations on the style of the 24 Preludes and Fugues' by Elizaveta Mnatsakanova, 'Performing Shostakovich' (mainly about Op. 87) by Tatyana Nikolayeva, 'Remarks on the musical language of Shostakovich' by Leo Mazel, 'On two methods of thematic development in the symphonies and quartets of Shostakovich' by Viktor Bobrovsky, 'The Alexandrian pentachord in the music of Shostakovich' by Aleksandr Dolzhansky, 'On Shostakovich's orchestration' by Edison Denisov, and 'Some peculiarities of orchestral part-writing in Shostakovich's symphonic works' by Alfred Schnittke.]

—— *Bolshaya sovetskaya entsiklopediya* (Sovetskaya Entsiklopediya, Moscow, 1979), Vol. 29, 457–8. [Shostakovich entry.]

—— *Dmitri Shostakovich—zhizn i tvorchestvo* (Sovetskii Kompozitor, Moscow, 1980), 304 pp., 32 photographs. [The life and work of Shostakovich in minute detail. Footnote references supplied but regrettably no bibliography nor index. A near complete year-by-year list of compositions appended.]

Danko, Larisa Georgievna, *Komicheskaya opera v XX veke* (Sovetskii Kompozitor, Leningrad, 2nd edn. 1986), 176 pp. ['Comic Opera in the Twentieth Century'. Bibliography but no music examples, illustrations, or index. *The Nose* discussed on pages 137–48.]

Dansker, Olga Lvovna (compiler), *S. A. Samosud—stati, vospominaniya, pisma* (Sovetskii Kompozitor, Moscow, 1984), 232pp. [A paperback including details of premières of *The Nose* and *Lady Macbeth;* 9 letters from Shostakovich to the conductor (one reproduced in facsimile) and photographs.]

Daragan, Diva Grigorievna (ed.), *Sovetskaya muzykalnaya kultura* (Muzyka, Moscow, 1980). [A 208-page paperback including two pertinent articles: 'Chamber-vocal compositions of Shostakovich' by Vera Andreyevna Vasina-Grossman (pp. 15–42 dealing with Opp. 46, 62, 79, 127, 143, and 145) and 'Towards the problem of stylistic dramaturgy' by L. Krylova (pp. 43–60 analysing the *Overture of Russian and Kirghiz Folksongs*, Op. 115, with 8 music examples).]

Day, Stanley, and latterly, MacDonald, Calum; Walker, Malcolm, *et al.*, *Gramophone* Classical Catalogue (formerly *The Grammophone Long Playing Classical Record Catalogue*) (General Gramophone Publications, Harrow, 1953–89). [The foremost record catalogue.]

Delson, Viktor Yulievich, *Fortepiannoe tvorchestvo D. D. Shostakovicha* (Sovetskii Kompozitor, Moscow 1971), 248 pp. ['The fortepiano works' with music examples.]

Devlin, James F., 'Dmitri Shostakovich—the vocal music', *Music and Musicians*, Vol. 28, No. 7 (Mar. 1980), 20–2.

—— 'Shostakovich's Re-orchestration of the Schumann Cello Concerto', *Anglo-Soviet Journal*, Vol. xl, No. 3 (May 1980), 19–20. [Op. 125.]

—— 'Dmitri Shostakovich—Pianist', *Anglo-Soviet Journal*, Vol. xli, No. 1 (Sept. 1980), 18–20. [A review of the composer's performances on records.]

—— *Shostakovich* (Novello, Sevenoaks, Kent, 1983), 23 pp. [A concise account of the composer's life and achievements in the series of Novello Short Biographies.]

Diamant, A. 'The Shostakovich Symphonies', *The Gramophone* (Feb. 1943), 133.

Dolmatovsky, Yevgeni Aronovich, *Pesni na stikhi Yevgeni Dolamatovskogo* (Muzyka, Moscow, 1986), 224 pp. ['Songs to verses of Yevgeni Dolmatovsky': words and melodies of 101 songs, including five by Shostakovich—'Song of Peace' and 'Longing for the Native Country' from Op. 80; 'Beautiful Day' from Op. 82; and 'The Homeland Hears' and 'He loves me, he loves me not' from Op. 86.]

Dolzhansky, Aleksandr Naumovich, *24 preludii i fugi Shostakovicha* (Leningrad 1963).

Dorati, Antal, *Seven Decades* (Wayne State University Press, Detroit, 1981), 60–2 [Béla Bartók's dislike of Shostakovich and the reason for the parody of the 'Leningrad Symphony' in the Hungarian's *Concerto for Orchestra*.]

Downes, Edward, *Everyman's Guide to Orchestral Music* (Dent, London, 1976), 852–61. [Analyses of Symphonies Nos. 1, 5, 6, and 9.]

———— *Khovanshchina*—libretto, *The Radio Three Magazine* (Nov. 1982), supplement. [English version of Shostakovich's arrangement, Op. 106.]

Drew, David, *The Nose, New Statesman* (12 June 1964), 922–3.

DSCH Society, founded in June 1987 by Alan Mercer of Alexandra Park, London. [The bi-monthly newsletter contains record, book, and concert reviews, postbag, world-wide concert calendar, and members' services. Important contributions include an article on the film *Testimony* by Ben Kingsley (No. 4), an interview with Rudolf Barshai (No. 5), 'Early Works for String Quartet' by Derek Hulme (No. 6), review of *Rayok* première (No. 11) and comments on this work by Irina Shostakovich (No. 12), an English translation of the 1936 Pravda article 'Muddle instead of music' (No. 12), 'Unpublished letters to Koussevitzky' by Richard Pleak (No. 13), 'Moderato, not Adagio'—second movement of the Ninth Symphony by D. Hulme (No. 14), 'Review: *Rothschild's Violin* by the Julliard' by R. Pleak (No. 16), 'Kondrashin on Shostakovich'—on the difficulties experienced prior to the première of the Thirteenth Symphony (No. 18), the Tanya Glivenko love-letters by John Riley, and 'Shostakovich and Poetry' by Sofya Khentova (No. 20).] The DSCH Society ceased functioning in late 1992 after Newsletter No. 21 when the editor Alan Mercer moved to France. He commenced publishing the *DSCH Journal* in summer 1994. ['Revelations: the 10th Symphony'—the EAEDA horn theme in the third movement is a coded musical signature 'E, La͟, Mi, Re͟, A' = Elmira (No. 1), 'Nothing but trouble: *New Babylon*' by A. Mercer (No. 1), 'Myth, Parisity and Found Music in *New Babylon*' by J. Riley (No. 4), 'Shostakovich and the Scottish Connection', op. 62 and Sans op. M (No. 10) and 'Early British Performances of the Eighth Symphony Reviewed' (No. 11) by D. Hulme, 'Shostakovich, Britten, Beethoven and the *Russian Kontakion for the Departed*'—phrases from the Christian funeral lament quoted in many of Shostakovich's compositions, with music examples (No. 11) and 'Shostakovich and Numbers' by Iain Strachan—evidence of numerical patterning in the string quartets and other compositions (No. 12); 'Muradeli on "The one who does not like me"' by Vladimir Zak— a revealing confession from Vano Muradeli whose opera *The Great Friendship* was the excuse for humiliating Shostakovich at the notorious 1948 conference and 'The New Face of the Twelfth Symphony' by Fumiko Hitotsuyanagi—a coded three-note motif on Stalin's initials ('E flat, B flat, C' = 'Es, B, C' in German notation = 'Yos. V. S.') exposed. (No. 13); 'The Lost Jazz Suite No. 2' by Gerard McBurney and 'Inside the Second Piano Sonata', with 31 end notes and 7 music examples, by Manashir Yakubov

(No. 14); 'Rediscovered: a forgotten composition by Shostakovich' by Viktor Dvortsov—the *Suite on Finnish Themes*: 'Babi Yar' by Yevgeni Yevtushenko—twelve pages on 'The Most Dangerous Symphony' (No. 15). For further information visit the DSCH website http://opus147.free.fr/

Dubinsky, Rostislav Davidovich, *Stormy Applause: making music in a worker's state* (Hutchinson, London, 1989), 292 pp. [A moving account of the Borodin Quartet founder's struggle as a Jewish musician in the bureaucratic Soviet state. The 25th chapter, pp. 278–84, headed 'Shostakovich 1975'. No illustrations, no index.]

Egorova, Tatiana (Yegorova, Tatyana), *Soviet Film Music: An Historical Survey*, trans. Tatiana A. Ganf and Natalia A. Egunova (Harwood Academic Publishers, Amsterdam, 1997), xiii plus 311 pp. [Many references to Shostakovich's film scores including *New Babylon, The Golden Mountains*, and *Hamlet* with an eight-page chapter on *Katerina Izmailova*. Music examples from Opp. 30, 33, 82, 97, 116, and 137. Still photographs from *New Babylon* and *Hamlet*. Paperback in English.]

Elder, Dean, 'Lesson on Performance of a Shostakovich Prelude and Fugue (No. 17 of Op. 87)', *Clavier*, No. 13 (Sept. 1974), 25–33.

Engelmann, Ian, 'Thinking slow, writing quick—an interview with Shostakovich', *The Listener* (1974), 2381, pp. 641–2.

Ewen, David, 'Dmitri Shostakovich', *The Musical Times*, Vol, 74, No. 1112 (Oct. 1935), 890–2.

—— *The World of Twentieth-Century Music* (Hale, London, 1968), 721–38. [Information on main works up to Eleventh Quartet.]

—— *Orchestral Music* (Franklin Watts, New York, 1973), 237–43.

—— *Composers Since 1900* (H. W. Wilson, New York, 1969), 524–31 and First Supplement (1981), 265–6.

Faier, Yuri Fyodorovich, *O sebe, o muzyke, o balete* (Sovetskii Kompozitor, Moscow, 2nd ed., 1974), 302–10. [The conductor's notes on performing the Opus 39 ballet. Many photographs of dancers, musicians, and Bolshoi Theatre productions, including Asaf and Sulamif Messerer as the Classical Dancers in *The Limpid Stream*.]

Fanning, David, *The Breath of a Symphonist: Shostakovich's Tenth Symphony*. Royal Musical Association Monographs 4 (Royal Musical Association, London, 1988), 94 pp. [A major study of the epic Tenth with an almost bar-by-bar analysis (illustrated with 60 music examples), three appendices: the composer's own words on this symphony, a list of thematic allusion and a checklist of corrections and errors in *Collected Works* Vol. 5, and an extensive bibliography.]

—— (ed.), *Shostakovich Studies* (Cambridge University Press, 1955), 289 pp. [The eleven scholarly essays—seven with music examples—cover single-work source-studies on *The Golden Age* (Manashir Yakubov), *Lady Macbeth/Katerina Izmailova* (D. J. Fanning and Laurel E. Fay), Fifth Symphony (Richard Taruskin), and Second Piano Trio (Patrick McCreless); papers on the instrumental works (Yuri Kholopov) and song cycles (Dorothea

Redepenning); discussions on Shostakovich's relationship with his contemporaries Britten (Eric Roseberry) and Schnittke (Aleksandr Ivashkin); and
an analysis of Russian theorists on modality in the composer's music (Ellon
D. Carpenter).]

———, and Fay, Laurel E., *The New Grove Dictionary of Music and Musicians,
second edition*, edit. Stanley Sadie and John Tyrrell, Vol. 23, Scott to Sources,
MS (Macmillan, London, 2001), 279–311. [Shostakovich entry: a persuasive
revised review of the composer's life and works divided into periods differing from Schwarz's, taking into account recent research with many illuminating comments (ex. 'Together the fourth to ninth symphonies might be
taken as evidence for the paradox that the greatest music can be written
under the greatest political pressure'). Impressive updated work-list and
bibliography contributed by L. E. Fay. The whole work will be regularly
updated on the electronic database www.grovemusic.com]

——— 'Shostakovich's Eighth String Quartet on Record', *International Record
Review*, Volume 2 Issue 8 (November 2001), 22–8. [An all-embracing review
of 104 mainly compact disc recordings (44 of the original quartet, 51 of Barshai's Chamber Symphony Opus 110*a*, and nine of other transcriptions)
with six photographs of performers and a discography.]

——— 'In Bach's footsteps.' *Gramophone*, Vol. 79, No. 950 (Feb. 2002), 28–31. [A
review of nine complete cycles and four important excerpts of the Opus 87
Preludes and Fugues. Vladimir Ashkenazy named as an all-round first
recommendation on compact disc.]

Farish, Margaret K., *String Music in Print* (R. R. Bowker, New York, 1973).

——— (ed.), *Orchestral Music in Print* (Musicdata Inc., Phil. 1979), 742–3.

Fay, Laurel E.. 'Shostakovich versus Volkov: Whose *Testimony?*' *The Russian
Review* (USA), Vol. 39, No. 4 (Oct. 1980), 484–93.

——— 'The Intimate Shostakovich', *Keynote* (New York, Oct. 1989), 8–12. [A
review of the quartet cycle, prior to the Manhattan Quartet's performance
of all fifteen in chronological order in four concerts at New York Town Hall,
25 September to 23 October 1989. 'A significant contribution to the twentieth-century repertoire, shares little with the other great cycle of the century,
that of Bartók. Instead, the sound world of Shostakovich's quartets, their
psychological scope and emotional force, suggests most immediate comparison with the legacy of Beethoven'. Six photographs.]

——— *The New Grove Dictionary of Opera*, ed. Stanley Sadie, Vol. 4, Roe-Z
(Macmillan, London; 1992), 358–61. [Shostakovich entry. See also entries for
the operas *The Gamblers* (Vol. 2, 342–3), *Katerina Izmailova* (Vol. 2, 961), *Lady
Macbeth of Mtsensk District* (Vol. 2, 1076–9), *The Nose* (Vol. 3, 621–3), and
Rothschild's Violin (Vol. 4, 410–11).]

——— *Shostakovich: A Life* (Oxford University Press, New York, 2000),
xix + 458 pp., 16 photographs. [A reliable and balanced biography, copi-
ously researched, and commendably readable. A 58-page section of sources
for the 15 chapters, a classified list of works, a glossary of names, and an
exhaustive index.]

Feuchtner, Bernd, 'Und Kunst geknebelt von der groben Macht': Dmitri Schostakowitsch, Künstlerische Identität und staatliche Repression (Sendler Verlag, Frankfurt am Main, 1986), 318 pp, 19 illustrations. [A German monograph with detailed list of sources and bibliography; a catalogue of works (separate page of film scores), music examples in the Appendix, and an index of persons.]

Fiske, Roger, *Chamber Music* (BBC, London, 1969), 75–7. [Refers to Quartets Nos. 7 and 8.]

Fomin, Vitali Sergeyevich, *Stareishii russkii simfonicheskii orkestr* (Muzyka, Leningrad, 1982), 192 pp. [A monograph of the Leningrad Philharmonic Orchestra to celebrate the centenary of its formation in 1882, illustrated with 68 monochrome photographs of the orchestra, conductors, and soloists, and 8 colour plates of the Philharmonic Concert Hall. Alphabetical list by composer of the Russian, Soviet, and world-wide repertoire, noting number of performances of each work, and conductors and soloists in the 60 years to 1981; calendar of places visited in the USSR and abroad.]

——— *Yevgeni Aleksandrovich Mravinsky* (Muzyka, Moscow, 1983), 192 pp. [A monograph in the series on Russian and Soviet conductors. Three photographs relating to Shostakovich. The appendices include Mravinsky's repertoire with number of performances of each work in the years 1932–82 (Shostakovich's Fifth Symphony at 102 only surpassed by the 113 of Tchaikovsky's Fifth), and discography.]

Foreman, Lewis, *Systematic Discography* (Clive Bingley, London, 1974). [A helpful guide for all amateur and professional discographers.]

Forman, Frank, and Amoh, Kenzo, 'Evgeni Mravinsky Discography', *ARSC Journal* of USA, Vol. 25 (1) (Spring 1994), 15–44. [A revised and updated list of Mravinsky recordings first published in Japan.]

Freundlich, Irwin, *Twenty-four Preludes and Fugues* (Leeds Music, New York, 5 April 1955). [Preface to the cycle, Op. 87.]

Fyodosova, Eleonara Petrovna, *Diatonicheskie lady v tvorchestve D. Shostakovicha* (Sovetskii Kompozitor, Moscow, 1980),192 pp. ['Diatonic harmonies in the creative work of D. Shostakovich'. A small paperback analysing passages from many compositions in minute detail, with 105 music examples and a bibliography of 85 references.]

Gabrilovich, Yevgeni Iosifovich, *The Fifth Quarter*, trans. Frances Longman (Progress Publishers, Moscow, 1983), 289 pp. [The moving memoirs of the great screen script-writer responsible for the scenarios of two films associated with Shostakovich. Remarkable for his disclosures on the Soviet film industry during the Great Patriotic War. As Sergei Gerasimov points out in his Afterward: 'to portray Man with love demands a rare talent'. A paperback in English.]

Gammond, Peter, and James, Burnett. *Music on Record—A Critical Guide* (Grey Arrow paperback, Anchor Press, Tiptree), Vol. ii (1962), 125–31 and Vol. iii 1963, 168–70, 211. [Valuable for early LP recordings.]

Gaster, Adrian (ed.), *International Who's Who in Music* (Melrose Press, Cambridge, 9th edn., 1980).

George, Alan, 'Shostakovich', *Nouslit*, York University (Spring 1973), 17–19.

——— *Dmitri Shostakovich: The Complete String Quartets* (Decca Records, London, 1981), 20 pp. [A well-produced illustrated booklet, with notes on all fifteen quartets in English, French, and German to accompany the box set Decca D 188 D7.]

Glikman, Isaak, *Pisma k drugu: Dmitri Shostakovich—Isaaku Glikmanu* (DSCH, Moscow and Kompozitor, St Petersburg, 1993), 336 pp., 39 photographs. [A wealth of information on Shostakovich's lifestyle, that of his family and friends; and notes on the progress of many works contained in a 28-page preface and the 288 letters written by the composer between 30 November 1941 and 23 August 1974. Revealing annotations by Glikman. Photographs of the composer and author; their relatives and friends. An index of names and dated list of the letters.]

——— *Dmitri Chostakovitch: Lettres à un ami*—subtitled 'Correspondance avec Isaac Glikman' (Albin Michel, Paris, 1994), 320 pp. [The above book in French, translated from the Russian by Luba Jurgenson. No photographs.]

——— *The Story of a Friendship*—subtitled 'The Letters of Dmitry Shostakovich to Isaak Glikman with a commentary by Isaak Glikman' (Faber, London 2001), 385 pp. 37 illustrations. [Translated from the Russian by Anthony Phillips with a 100-page end-section of his own footnotes.]

Gogol, Nikolai Vasilievich, *Diary of a Madman and Other Stories*, trans. Ronald Wilks (Penguin Books, Harmondsworth, 1972), 42–70. [The original short story *The Nose* in English.]

Gojowy, Detlef. *Dimitri Schostakowitsch mit Selbstzeugnissen und Bilddokumenten* (Rowohlt Taschenbuch Verlag) Reinbek bei Hamburg, 1983), 158 pp., 60 illustrations. [A monograph in German, with list of works, bibliography, and index of persons.]

——— 'Schostakowitschs: "Märchen vom Popen und seinem Knecht Balda" in Ost-Berlin', *Neue Zeitschrift für Musik* (Sept. 1986), 57–8. [An article in German on an East German performance of Khentova's opera.]

Goltsman, Abram Markovich, *Sovetskie balety* (Sovetskii Kornpozitor, Moscow, 1985), 149–60. [Plots of five Shostakovich ballets: *The Bolt, The Golden Age* (1982 production), *The Limpid Stream, The Young Lady and the Hooligan*, and *Leningrad Symphony* in a paperback dealing with 124 ballets by 88 Soviet composers.]

Goodall, Alison, 'First performances in London, 1951–71', *The Music Yearbook, 1973–4*, ed. Arthur Jacobs (Macmillan, London, 1973).

Gordeyeva, Yevgeniya Mikhailovna (ed.), *Muzyka XX veka. Ocherki*, Part 2, Book 4 (Muzyka, Moscow, 1984), 75–114. [Essays on Shostakovich's music by Marina Sabinina.]

Gow, David, 'Shostakovich's "War" Symphonies', *The Musical Times*, Vol. 105, No. 1453 (Mar. 1964), 191–3.

Grazia, Sebastian de, 'Shostakovich's Seventh Symphony: Reactivity-Speed and Adaptiveness in Musical Syrnbols', *Psychiatry: Journal of the Biology and*

Pathology of Interpersonal Relations, Vol. 6 (2) (May 1943), 117–22. [A scientific article in an American journal dealing with the first movement's short symmetrical theme.]

Greenfield, Edward, *André Previn*, Recordmaster 4 (Jan Allan, London, 1973).

Griffiths, Paul, *The String Quartet—A History* (Thames and Hudson, London, 1983), 210–17. [Part 4, Variation 3: 'Shostakovich and the multiple quartet'—a concise commentary on 'the weightiest long sequence in the genre since Beethoven'.]

Grigoriev (alias Ginzburg), Lev Grigorievich and Platek, Yakov Moiseyevich, *Sovremennye dirizhyory* (Sovetskii Kompozitor, Moscow, 1969). ['Contemporary Conductors.']

—— and Platek, Yakov Moiseyevich, *Sovetskie kompozitory i muzykovedy* (Sovetskii Kompozitor, Moscow), Vol. ii (K–R) (1981), 416 pp. and two-part Vol. iii (S–YA), 1989–90, 216 pp. and forthcoming. [The concluding volumes of a dictionary of Soviet composers and musicologists begun by Bernandt and Yampolsky.]

—— and Platek, Yakov Moiseyevich, *Dmitry Shostakovich—About Himself and His Times*, trans. Angus and Neilian Roxburgh (Progress Publishers, Moscow, 1981), 343 pp., 56 photographs. [A very slightly modified version in the English language of Yakovlev's compilation with a differing selection of photographs. 'A few days ago I read the memoirs of Marietta Shaginian and Vera Panova and thought—what a pity I have not kept a diary or notebook, or written memoirs' (entry dated 26 June 1973).]

Grigorovich, Yuri Nikolayevich (chief ed.), *Balet: entsiklopediya* (Sovetskaya Entsiklopediya, Moscow, 1981), 623 pp. [A large comprehensive one-volume ballet encyclopaedia, profusely illustrated with colour and monochrome photographs, sketches and diagrams. Approx. 3,400 entries and classified bibliography.]

—— and Davlekamova, Sanya, *The Golden Age: the authorized Bolshoi Ballet Book* (T.H.F. Publications, Inc., Neptune City, New Jersey, 1989), 128 pp., 72 photographs. History and synopsis of the 1982 ballet illustrated with nine black and white photographs, poster, and 62 captioned live-action colour photographs. English version by Tim Coey.]

Grum-Grzhimailo, Tamara Nikoloyevna, *Soviet Music* (Novosti Press, Moscow, 1985), 84 pp. [An informative and well-illustrated paperback booklet in the English language.]

—— *O Shostakoviche* (Zhanie, Moscow, 1990), 56 pp., 16 photographs, [No. 12 in the 1990 series of monthly art booklets published since 1967.]

Gukovsky, M., *et al.*, 'Katerina Izmailova', *Iskusstvo kino* (Moscow) No. 1, 15–24. [Op. 114—six reviews of the new film; seven stills.]

Gulyants, Sostavitel Yevgeniya (ed.), *Andrei Eshpai: becedy, stati, materialy, ocherki* (Sovetskii Kompozitor, Moscow, 1988), 172–85. [An article by M. Lobanova, with 8 music examples, on Eshpai's Fifth (Memorial) Symphony.]

Gutman, David, 'Shostakovich's Symphony No. 8', *Gramophone*, Vol. 72, No. 860 (Jan. 1995), 36–8. [A survey of the recorded history of one of his most powerful works. Twenty-three performances between 1944 and 1993 reviewed. Two photographs.]

Hall, David, *Records: 1950 Edition* (Alfred A. Knopf, New York, 1952), 438–40.

Headington, Christopher, *The Dictionary of Composers*, ed. Charles Osborne (Bodley Head, London, 1977), 309–12.

Herbage, Julian, 'Shostakovitch's Eighth Symphony', *The Musical Times*, Vol. 85, No. 1229 (July 1944), 201–3.

―――― 'The Symphonies of Shostakovich', *The Listener*, 34 (19 Sept. 1945), 305 [Mentions Nos. 1 to 8.]

Heyworth, Peter, 'Shostakovich Without Ideology', *The Music Lover's Companion* (ed. Gervase Hughes and Herbert van Thal) (Eyre & Spottiswoode, London, 1971), 198–206. [An article from *High Fidelity Magazine*, Oct. 1964.]

Hibbins, Nina, *Screen Series—Eastern Europe* (A. Zwemmer, London, 1969), 132–69 [Details of the USSR film industry; its directors, script-writers, and actors.]

Hitotsuyanagi, Fumiko, *Novii lik dvenadtsatoy*. [The hidden meanings concealed in the 'unfairly low-rated Twelfth Symphony'.] *Muzikalnaya Akademiya* 4 (1997), 87. An English translation appears in *DSCH Journal* No. 13, pp. 59–63 with six music examples.

Ho, Allan B. and Feofanov, Dmitry, *Shostakovich Reconsidered* (Toccata Press, London, 1998), 787 pp. ["In spite of 'unjust critism' that it is a forgery, it [*Testimony*] remains one of the most important and influential books in the history of music, a unique historical document of life in Stalin's Russia" (p. 15). A well-researched study, liberally peppered with footnotes. Foreword by Vladimir Ashkenazy; in defence of *Testimony* (pp. 33–311); 'Variations on a Theme' including contributions from Solomon Volkov, Mstislav Rostropovich, five considerable articles by Ian MacDonald, and report of the Shostakovich Symposium held in the Russel Sage College, Troy, New York (pp. 315–723). A 31-page bibliography and full index.]

Hinson, Maurice, *Guide to the Pianist's Repertoire* (ed. Irwin Freundlich) (Indiana University Press, Bloomington and London, 1973).

―――― *The Piano in Chamber Ensemble* (Harvester Press, Hassocks, 1978).

Hoberman, J. 'When Communism Was in Flower', *The Village Voice*, New York, Vol. 28, No. 40 (4 Oct. 1983), 66 (+ advertisement on p. 65). [A preview article for the American première of *New Babylon*, Op. 18.]

Hofmann, Michel R., *Dmitri Chostakovitch: L'homme et son œuvre* (Edition Seghers, 1963), 192 pp., 12 photographs. [This French-language book has a catalogue of works to Opus 113 and a discography.]

Holmes, John L., *Conductors on Record* (Victor Gollancz, London, 1982), 735 plus xv pp. [A major reference work on conductors and conducting; with biographical and critical assessments of past and present conductors, listing works they have recorded to 1977.]

Honegger, Marc, and Massenkeil, Günther (*Das Grosse Lexicon der Musik*: Vol. 7, Ram-Ste (Herder, Freiburg, 1982), 276–8. [Shostakovich entry.]

Hopkins, George William (Bill), 'Shostakovich's Ninth String Quartet', *Tempo*, No. 75 (Winter 1965–6), 23–5.

Hughes, Spike (Patrick Cairns), *The Toscanini Legacy* (Dover Constable, London, 1969), 371–5. [Refers to the First and Seventh Symphonies. NB. Not included in the original hardback published by Putman, London, 1959.]

Hulme, Derek Crawshaw, 'Symphonies Nos: 6 and 11' (EMI Records, London, 1980), 3 pp. [Clarifies the sources of the musical themes used in Symphony No. 11.]

International Who's Who. Their 1999 Millennium list of the 100 most influential giants of the 20th century includes Shostakovich, Sibelius, and Stravinsky; also Louis Armstrong, John Lennon, and Frank Sinatra but omits Duke Ellington.

Istoriya muzyki narodov SSSR, ed. Yuri Keldysh (Sovetskii Kompozitor, Moscow) ['The History of the Music of the People of the USSR' in six volumes: Vol. i covering 1917–32 published in 1966; Vol. ii, 1932–41 in 1970; Vol. iii, 1941–5 in 1972; Vol. iv, 1946–56 in 1973; vol. v in two books, 1956–67 in 1974. Numerous music examples and illustrations of composers, musicians, concerts, and scenes from stage productions.]

Istoriya sovetskogo kino (Iskusstvo, Moscow). ['The History of the Soviet Cinema' in four volumes: Vol. i covering 1917–31 published in 1959; ii, 1931–41 in 1973; iii, 1941–52 in 1975; iv ?]

Ivashkin, Aleksandr Vasilievich, 'Dmitri Shostakovich', *Mastera muzyki i baleta*, ed. Lev Grigorievich Ginzburg and Yakov Moiseyevich Platek (Sovetskii Kompozitor, Moscow, 1978), 260–81. ['Masters of music and ballet-heroes of Socialist Labour'. An essay on the composer with list of honours and compositions, and a brief bibliography. The volume includes articles on Gustav Ernesaks, Emil Gilels, Yevgeni Mravinsky, Svyatoslav Richter, and thirteen others.]

—— *Alfred Schnittke* (Phaidon Press, London, 1996), 240 pp. [A paperback in the series '20th-Century Composers' with many references to Shostakovich and illustrations pertaining to Soviet musical history. 'Schnittke's works are strongly original but also reveal the influence of Shostakovich among others'.]

Jackson, Stephen, *Dmitri Shostakovich: an essential guide to his life and works* (Classic FM Lifelines / Pavilion, London, 1997), 107 pp. [A paperback with brief 75-page biography, bibliography of 13 books, discography of 59 recommended compact discs, and a dated list of works.]

Jacobs, Arthur (ed.), *British Music Yearbooks 1975–80* (Bowker and latterly A. & C. Black, London).

Janczyn, Larissa, *Dictionary of Twentieth-Century Music*, ed. John Vinton (Thames and Hudson, London, 1974), 679–80 *et passim*.

Johnson, Stephen, 'Original Intentions', *Gramophone* (Nov. 1990), 953–4. [A talk with Claudio Abbado about his changes to Shostakovich's instrumentation for the recording of *Khovanshchina*.]

Jusefovich, Viktor: see under Yuzefovich.

Kandinsky, Aleksei Ivanovich (ed.), *Iz istorii russkoi i sovetskoi muzyki* (Muzyka, Moscow, 1971). [A 336-page book of musical essays including 'Compositions of D. Shostakovich's conservatory years 1919–25' by Alla Bogdanova (pp. 64–93, with thirty-one music examples) and 'On the genre nature of Shostakovich's Eleventh Symphony' by T. Leie (pp. 94–109, with eighteen music examples). Bogdanova's article concentrates on Sans op. B, Opp. 4, 6. and 8.]

Katonova, Svetlana Vladimirovna, *Muzyka sovetskogo baleta* (Sovetskil Kompozitor, Leningrad, 2nd rev. edn., 1990), 374–96. [Chapter VI deals with the 1982 revival of *The Golden Age* ballet.]

Kats, Boris Aronovich, *O muzyke Borisa Tishchenko* (Sovetskii Kompozitor, Leningrad, 1986), 168 pp. [Tishchenko's Cello Concerto No. 1 in its original orchestration reviewed on pp. 50–4 and the Symphony No. 5, dedicated to Shostakovich, analysed on pp. 149–55 of this paperback.]

Kay, Norman, 'Shostakovich's Second Violin Concerto', *Tempo*, No. 83 (Winter 1967–8), 21–3.

——, 'Shostakovich's Fourteenth Symphony', *Tempo*, No. 92 (Spring 1970), 20–1.

—— *Shostakovich* (Oxford University Press, London, 1971), 80 pp. [Oxford Studies of Composers (8). A scholarly survey of key works with numerous music examples.]

—— 'Shostakovich's 15th Symphony', *Tempo*, No. 100 (Spring 1972), 36–40.

Keldysh, Georgi (Yuri) Vsevolodovich, 'Soviet Music Today', *Tempo*, No. 32 (Summer 1954), 23–8.

—— 'An Autobiographical Quartet', trans. Alan Lumsden, *The Musical Times*, Vol. 102, No. 1418 (Apr. 1961), 226–8. [Refers to Eighth Quartet.]

—— (general ed.), *Muzykalnyi entsiklopedicheskii slovar* (Sovetskii Kompozitor, Moscow, 1990). 672 pp. [A completely rewritten music dictionary begun in 1981, with 8000 entries on all aspects of music including composers, performers, organisations, and festivals; numerous line drawings and music examples in the text.]

Keller, Hans, 'Shostakovich discovers Schoenberg', *The Listener*, 84 (8 Oct. 1970), 494. [Concerns the Twelfth Quartet.]

—— 'Shostakovich's Twelfth Quartet', *Tempo*, No. 94 (Autumn 1970), 6–15.

Kennedy, Michael, *The Concise Oxford Dictionary of Music* (Oxford University Press, London, 3rd edn., 1980), 592–5. [An excellent brief summary of the composer's achievements with a detailed classified list of works.]

Khentova, Sofya Mikhailovna, *Shostakovich—pianist* (Muzyka, Leningrad, 1964), 92pp, 12 photographs. [The appendix lists recitals and concerts given by Shostakovich, 1923–58.]

—— *Molodye gody Shostakovicha*, Book 1 (Sovetskii Kompozitor, Leningrad, 1975), 334 pp., 8 plates: Book 2 (Sovetskii Kompozitor, Leningrad, 1980), 318 pp, 12 plates. ['The Youthful Years': numerous early photographs, facsimiles, and music examples in the text. Calendar of events 1831 to 17 July 1941, bibliography of 162 books and 167 articles, and index of names for both volumes appended to Book 2.]

―――― *Shostakovich v Petrograde—Leningrade* (Lenizdat, Leningrad, 1979), 272 pp. ['Shostakovich in Leningrad': a well-informed biography, 65 photographs, list of Leningrad addresses associated with the composer, and extensive bibliography including articles written by Shostakovich.]

―――― *D. D. Shostakovich—v gody Velikoi Otechestvennoi voiny* (Muzyka, Leningrad, 1979), 280 pp. [Book 3: a detailed account of Shostakovich's life and work in cities during the Great Patriotic War, with emphasis on the Seventh and Eighth Symphonies; 55 illustrations in the text, 6 music examples, copious footnote references; diary of events from June 1941 to 10 May 1945 and a bibliography of 64 books and 119 articles appended.]

―――― *Shostakovich—tridtsatiletie 1945–1975* (Sovetskii Kompozitor, Leningrad, 1982), 415 pp, 32 plates. [Book 4: this writer's concluding biographical volume covering 'Thirty years 1945–75'; 8 music examples, diary of events from 9 March 1945 to 14 August 1975, bibliography of 63 books and 262 articles, an index of names for Books 3 and 4.]

―――― *Podvig, voploshchennyi v muzyke* (Lower Volga Book Publishers, Volgograd, 1984), 80 pp. ['A feat of Heroism in Music': facts connected with the writing of the Eighth 'Stalingrad' Symphony and information on 'Battle by the Volga', Op. 66, and *Funeral-Triumphal Prelude*, Op. 130. Originally announced by VAAP as a 324-page volume.]

―――― *Shostakovich: zhizn i tvorchestvo*, Book 1 (Sovetskii Kompozitor, Leningrad, 1985), 544 pp., 64 plates plus portraits in the text: Book 2 (Sovetskii Kompozitor, Leningrad, 1986), 624 pp., 32 plates plus portraits in the text. [A revised monograph of the composer, profusely illustrated with many photographs published for the first time, facsimiles of early compositions and birth certificates, 26 and 12 music examples in the text. In Book 1 a calendar of events from 1808 to 17 June 1941 and, in Book 2, from 22 June 1941 to 14 August 1975. Numerous references quoted in footnotes but Book 2 does not include a bibliography or index of names for these two volumes.]

―――― *Shostakovich na Ukraine* (Muzichna Ukraina, Kiev, 1986), 183 pp., 34 photographs. ['Shostakovich in the Ukraine': details of the composer's visits to cities and Crimean sanatoria, works composed there, and concert performances.]

―――― *Shostakovich v Moskve* (Moskovskii Rabochii, Moscow, 1986), 209 pp., 34 photographs. ['Shostakovich in Moscow': a paperback with information on the composer's 32-year association with the capital.]

―――― *Lyubimaya muzyka* (Muzichna Ukraina, Kiev, 1989), 174–204. ['Favourite Music': popular essays on composers and performers, including Dunayevsky, Soloviev-Sedoi, Gilels, and Richter. A thirty-page chapter on Shostakovich. Frontispiece photograph of the author.]

—— *V mire Shostakovicha* (Kompozitor, Moscow, 1996). ['In the World of Shostakovich'—the author met and talked with the composer, his family and friends—including his doctor and personal chauffeur and the family's domestic help—academics, and musicians who performed his works. The third part 'Shostakovich in the Mirror of his Letters' publishes correspondence addressed to certain pupils and Soviet musicians. The book lacks photographs, musical examples, and an index of names.]

—— *Pushkin v muzyke Shostakovicha* (Variant, St Petersburg, 1996), 88 pp. [Information on his juvenile opera *The Gipsies*, the cartoon film *The Tale of a Priest and His Servant Balda* Opus 36, *Four Romances* Opus 46, the revision of Musorgsky's *Boris Godunov* Opus 58, and the *Four Monologues* Opus 91.]

—— Also books on the composer's 'Relations with Women' and connections in 'Soccer', both published by Variant, St Petersburg, 1993.

Kholopova, Valentina Nikolayevna, and Chigaryova, Yevgeniya Ivanovna, *Alfred Shnitke—ocherk zhizni i tvorchesta* (Sovetskii Kompozitor, Moscow, 1990), 351 pp., 12 plates. ['A study of the life and works of Alfred Schnittke', with notes relating to Shostakovich in the text; seven appendices including 70 music examples, 161 bibliographical references, and a classified list of compositions 1957–89; and index of names.]

Khubov, Georgi Nikitich, *Muzykalnaya publitsistika raznykh let* (Sovetskii Kompozitor, Moscow, 1976), 432 pp. [A selection of musical essays from various Russian sources, 1936–74, with information on Opp. 10, 43, 106 *et al.*]

Koball, Michael, *Pathos und Groteske—Die deutsche Tradition im symphonischen Schaffen von Dmitri Shostakowitsch* (Ernst Kuhn, Berlin, 1997), 284 pp. ['Pathos and Grotesque—the German Tradition in the Symphonic Works of Shostakovich': illustrating the composer's connection with the pathos of Beethoven and the grotesque music of Mahler, in the German language.]

Kompaneyets, Zinovi Lvovich, *Novyi yevreiskie pesni* (Sovetskii Kompozitor, Moscow, 1970). [A compilation of new Jewish songs with Shostakovich as Editor-in-Chief.]

Kovnatskaya, Lyudmila Grigorievna (compiler), *D. D. Shostakovich—sbornik statei k 90-letiyu so dnya rozhdeniya* (Kompozitor, St Petersburg, 1996), 392 pp., 14 photographs. [Twenty-four articles for the 90th anniversary of the composer's birth, including contributions from Laurel E. Fay (on the Leningrad Association of Contemporary Music and Boris Asafiev), David Fanning (on leitmotive in *Lady Macbeth*), Nelly Kravets (a new look at Symphony No. 12), Eric Roseberry (on Britten and Shostakovich), and Rosamund Bartlet ('Shostakovich and Chekhov'). Music examples, facsimilies of letters, sketches, and cartoons in the text.]

Kozintsev, Grigori Mikhailovich, *King Lear: the Space of Tragedy*, trans. Mary A. Mackintosh (Heinemann Educational. Books, London, 1977), 260 pp. [An English translation of *Prostrantsvo tragedii*—Kozintsev's diary kept during the shooting of the film—first published by Iskusstvo, 1973. Ten stills from the film and revelatory comments on Shostakovich's collaboration, Op. 137.]

Krafft, Nathalie (ed.), *Le Monde de la Musique*, No. 244 (Paris, June 2000), pp. 28–47. [Special issue on 25th anniversary of Shostakovich's death with five illustrated articles in French.]

Kratkaya literaturnaya entsiklopediya (Sovetskaya Entsiklopediya, Moscow, 1962–75). [The brief literary encylopaedia in 8 volumes, lavishly illustrated. Useful for biographical details of Russian writers associated with Shostakovich.]

Krebs, Stanley Dale, *Soviet Composers and the Development of Soviet Music* (George Allen and Unwin, London, 1970), 185–204.

Kröplin, Eckart, *Frühe Sowjetische Oper: Schostakowitsch, Prokofjew* (Honschelverlag, Berlin, 1985), 148–294 *et passim*. [A German review of *The Nose* and *Lady Macbeth* with music examples, a list of sources, bibliography, and index of persons.]

Krŭstev, Venelin Georgiev, *Dmitri Shostakovich: biografichen ocherk* (National Committee for Defence of Peace, Sofia, Bulgaria, 1954), 69 pp. [A biographical essay in Bulgarian.]

Kryukov, Vadim Konstantinovich, *et al.*, *Katalog gramplastinok* (Ministry of Culture, Moscow, 1963), 347 pp. [Catalogue of 78 rpm recordings.]

——— *et al.*, *Katalog dolgoigrayushchikh gramplastinok* (Ministry of Culture, Moscow, 1963), 312 pp. [Catalogue of 33⅓ and 45 rpm recordings.]

——— (compiler), and Ilinskaya, S. E. (ed.), *Katalog dolgoigrayushchikh gramplastinok* (All-Union Studio of Gramophone Recording, Moscow, 1968), 722 pp. [Catalogue of 33⅓ mono and stereo recordings.]

——— *Katalog dolgoigrayushchikh gramplastinok* (All-Union Studio of Gramophone Recording, Moscow, 1972), Vol. i: 444 pp.; Vol. ii: 508 pp. [Catalogue of 33⅓ mono and stereo recordings to the end of 1970. Supplements published annually.]

Kuhn, Ernst, (ed.), *Volksfeind Dmitri Shostakowitsch—Eine Dokumentation der öffentlichen Angriffe gegen den Komponisten in der Sowjetunion* (Ernst Kuhn, Berlin, 1997), 287 pp. ['Dmitri Shostakovich—Enemy of the People: a documentary of the public attacks against the composer in the Soviet Union'. Essays dealing with the serious attacks of 1936, 1948, and 1954 and including a compilation of Soviet reactions of Solomon Volkov's *Testimony*. Bibliography.]

Kukharsky, Vasili Fyodosievich, *O muzyke i muzykantakh nashikh dnei* (Sovetskii Kompozitor, Moscow, 1979), 184–8, 212–15. [A review of *Moscow, Cheryomushki* from *Pravda* (1 Mar. 1959), and an obituary.]

Lander, Margaret, 'Music and Makebelieve', *The Gramophone* (Dec. 1946), 108. [A fanciful story set to Piano Concerto No. 1, Op. 35.]

Lawson, Peter, 'Shostakovich's Second Symphony', *Tempo*, No. 91 (Winter 1969–70), 14–17.

Layton, Robert, 'Dmitri Shostakovich', *The Symphony 2: Elgar to the Present Day*, ed. Robert Simpson (Penguin Books, Harmondsworth, 1967), 197–217. [A critical study with music examples of Symphonies Nos. 1 to 11.

Also the same pagination in hardback: David & Charles, Newton Abbott, 1972.]

—— 'Shostakovich's new symphony', *The Listener*, 83 (11 June 1970), 802–3. [Symphony No. 14.]

Lebedinsky, Lev Nikolayevich, 'The Origin of Shostakovich's 'Rayok'', *Tempo*, No. 173 (June 1990), 31–2.

Lemaire, Frans C., *La musique du xxᵉ siècle en Russie et dans les anciennes Républiques soviétiques* (Librairie Arthème Fayard, Paris, 1994), 521 pg. [A history of music in Russia and the USSR from 1905 to 1992 in the French language. Nineteen chapters (No. 9 entitled 'The posthumous dissidence of Shostakovich'), a 125-page section of biographies, a single page bibliography, and index.]

Leonard, Richard Anthony, *A History of Russian Music* (Jarrolds, London, 1956); 291–3, 322–40.

Leskov, Nikolai Semyonovich, *The Enchanted Wanderer and Other Stories*, trans. George H. Hanna (Progress Publishers, Moscow, 2nd printing 1974), 17–83. [The original short story *Lady Macbeth of Mtsensk* in English.]

Levando, Pyotr Petrovich, *Khorovaya faktura* (Muzyka, Leningrad, 1984), 124 pp. ['Choral Texture': a paperback monograph giving detailed descriptions of *Ten Poems, Op. 88* (with 25 music examples including the vocal range of the four parts for each poem), Shostakovich's choral sections of *Boris Godunov, Op. 58*, and *Two Choruses by Davidenko, Op. 124*.]

Levashev, Yevgeni M. (compiler), *Hasledie M. P. Musorgskogo* (Muzyka, Moscow, 1989), 256 pp. ['Modest Musorgsky's Heritage' introducing the publication of the complete works in thirty-two volumes. A collection of four articles in Russian with abridged English and German translations. Shostakovich's editions of *Boris Godunov* and *Khovanshchina* will appear in Volumes 23–4 and 28–9 respectively.]

Levaya, Tamara Nikolayevna, 'Taina velikogo iskusstva', *Muzyka Rossii*, Issue 2 (Sovetskii Kompozitor, Moscow, 1978), 291–328 ['The secret of a great art': a review of the late chamber-vocal cycles, Opp. 127, 143, 145, and 146, with 6 music examples.]

Library of Congress Catalogs—*Music and Phonorecords, 1953–57*, Vol. 27 (Rowman and Littlefield, Totowa, NJ, 1961), 793–5.

—— *Music and phonorecords/Music, Books on Music and Phonorecords, 1958–62*, Vol. 51 (Rowman and Littlefield, Totowa, NJ, 1963), 907–11.

—— *Music, Books on Music, and Sound Recordings, 1963–72* (J. D. Edwards, Mich., USA, 1969–73).

—— *Music, Books on Music, and Sound Recordings, 1973–88* (Library of Congress, Washington, 1974–89).

Lipovsky, Aleksandr (compiler), *Lenin Prize Winners: Soviet Stars in the World of Music*, trans. Olga Shartse (Progress Publishers, Moscow, *c.*1967), 42–79. [An article 'A rare talent' by Boris Asafiev from *Sovetskaya Muzyka*, 1959, No. 1 and excerpts from Martynov's 1962 monograph; also brief appreciatory notes on Prokofiev and Khachaturyan by Shostakovich.]

Long, Maureen W., *Music in British Libraries* (The Library Association, London, 1971).

Longman, Richard M., *Expression and Structure: Processes of Integration in the Large-Scale Instrumental Music of Dmitri Shostakovich* (Garland, New York, 1989) 2 vols, 700 pp. [Univerity of Birmingham thesis, 1984 in the series Outstanding Dissertations in Music from British Universities'.]

Lopukhov, Fyodor Vasilievich, *Shestdesyat let v balete* (Iskusstvo, Moscow, 1966), 368 pp. ['Sixty years in ballet': information on *The Bolt* and *The Limpid Stream.*]

Lourié, Arthur, 'On Shostakovich: About his Seventh Symphony', *Novyi zhurnal* [New Review, Vol. vi] (New York, 1943), 367–72.

Lukyanova, Nataliya Valerievna, *Dmitri Dmitrievich Shostakovich* (Muzyka, Moscow, 1980), 176 pp., 100 photographs (15 in colour). [A pocket-sized anthology of articles and other archive material regarding the life and compositions of the composer: lavishly illustrated, with additional facsimiles of posters, sketches, diplomas, and holograph scores in the text.]

——— *Dmitri Dmitri jewitsch Schostakowitsch*, trans. Nina Sohr, Beate Petras (Verlag Neue Musik, Berlin, 1982), 202 pp., 80 illustrations. [German translation of above.]

——— *Shostakovich*, trans. Yuri Shirokov (Paganiniana Publications, Neptune City, NJ, 1984), 175 pp., 59 photographs. [A larger format English-language edition of the former with a differing selection of photographs (poorly reproduced on non-art paper and none in colour) and lacking the in-the-text illustrations but graced with a helpful index of names and compositions.)

Lushina, Stanielava Aleksandrovicha (ed.), *Bolshoi teatr SSSR—Istoriya—Opera—Balet* (Planeta, Moscow, 1986), 248 pp. [A glossy large-format photographic album featuring fifteen each of Bolshoi Theatre opera and ballet productions, including *Boris Godunov* and *Khovanshchina* (non-Shostakovich editions) and *The Golden Age* (1982 revival; back-cloth design sketch and 24 photographs, pp. 238–47).]

McAllister, Rita, *The International Cyclopedia of Music and Musicians*, ed. Bruce Bohle (Dodd, Mead & Co., New York/J. M. Dent, London, 10th edn. 1975), 2050–7. [A good review of Shostakovich's life and music with near complete catalogue of works numbered to Op. 134.]

——— *The New Grove Dictionary of Music and Musicians*, ed. Stanley Sadie, Vol. 19, Tiomkin-Virdung (Macmillan, London, 1980), 384–8. [Russian SFSR entry: (i–iv) The political background to the Soviet period and (v) Soviet music with general and special studies bibliographies.]

McBurney, Gerard, 'Hypothetically Murdered Op. 31', City of Birmingham Symphony Orchestra Programme, 20 Nov. 1991 (CBSO Society Ltd.). [Details of the suite reconstructed and orchestrated from the composer's loose piano score.]

——— 'Not a cherry tree in sight!', *Tempo*, No. 190 (Sept. 1994), 19–22. [An 'open letter' to Dmitri Dmitrievich apologizing for the reorchestration of

Moscow, Cheryomushki, Opus 105, to suit a British pit band.] Also published in première programme booklets and *BBC Music,* Apr. 1995, 9–10.

MacDonald, Ian, 'Russian Realist: What is the use of Shostakovich?', *The Face,* No. 74 (June 1986), 74–7. ['The use to us in the West of Shostakovich's music is that it provides a detailed emotional record of what it's been like to live in Russia since the Revolution, in this respect forming a sort of high-art sound-track to Solzhenitsyn's definitive indictment of Soviet Marxism, The Gulag Archipelago.' Special emphasis on the Eleventh Symphony.]

——— *The New Shostakovich* (Fourth Estate, London, 1990), 339 pp., 37 photographs. [The 'New' of this biography's title refers to post-*Testimony* argument, relating the life of the composer to the experiences of his Soviet contemporaries. Chronology (38 pp.) and a select bibliography.] Also published by Northeastern University Press, Boston, 1990 and Oxford University Press paperback, 1911.

——— 'Fay Versus Shostakovich: Whose Stupidity?', *East European Jewish Affairs,* Vol. 26, No. 2 (1996), 5–26. [A critical reply to Laurel Fay's article, entitled 'The composer was courageous but not as much as in myth' regarding the timing of the composition of *From Jewish Folk Poetry* Opus 79, in *The New York Times,* 14 April 1996.

MacDonald, Malcolm (Calum), *Dmitri Shostakovich—a complete catalogue* (Boosey & Hawkes, London, 1977), 47 pp. (2nd edn., 1985), 56 pp. [A chronological listing of works, giving details of instrumentation, duration, and première performances.]

——— *Dimitri Chostakovitch—Catalogue Général* (Le Chant du Monde, Paris, 1988), 73 pp. (A French translation of the 2nd edn. by André Lischke.]

——— 'The Anti-Formalist 'Rayok'—Learners Start Here!', *Tempo,* No. 173 (June 1990), 23–30.

McKee, Aleksander, *Dresden 1945: The Devil's Tinderbox* (Souvenir Press, London, 1982). [Revealing examination of the bomber raids—'an act of wilful mass murder committed on a helpless civilian population'—for an appreciation of *Five Days, Five Nights* (subtitled 'Dresden Art Gallery'), Op. 111.]

McNaught, William, 'Gramophone Notes', *The Musical Times,* Vol. 83, No. 1196 (Oct. 1942), 307–8. [An early review of Fifth Symphony.]

Malko, Nikolai Andreyevich, *A Certain Art* (Morrow, New York, 1966). [The opening of *Tahiti Trot,* Op. 16, reproduced on p. 213.]

Marshak, Samuil Yakovlevich, *Detyam* (Detskaya Literatura, Moscow, 1973). [A book of verses for children including the original story 'The Tale of the Stupid Little Mouse'. See Opus 56.]

Martynov, Ivan Ivanovich, *D. D. Shostakovich* (Muzgiz, Moscow, 1946), 111 pp. [Also published in French—Paris, 1946—and German language edition trans. Ina Tinzmann-Berlin, 1947, 171 pp.]

——— *Dmitri Shostakovich: the Man and his Work,* trans. T. Guralsky (Philosophical Library, New York, 1947 and Greenwood Press, New York, 1969), 197 pp. [Valuable for biographical information and covers Opp. 1 and 70.]

—— *D. Shostakovich: tvorcheskii portret* (Sovetskaya Rossiya, Moscow, 1962). [An updated 'portrait' of the composer. Excerpts in English appear in Lipovsky, pp. 52–79.]

—— 'Soviet Chamber Music', *Corbett's Cyclopedic Survey of Chamber Music*, Vol. iii, ed. Walter Willson Corbett and Colin Mason (Oxford University Press, London, 2nd edn. 1963), 142–7.

—— *O muzyke i yeyo tvortsakh* (Sovetskii Kompozitor, Moscov, 1980), 27–53. [Articles on the Second Piano Trio and Second Quartet, Ninth and Tenth Quartets, and Fourteenth Symphony; bibliography—17 Shostakovich references.]

Mason, Colin, 'Shostakovich and the string quartet', *The Listener*, 62 (23 July 1959), 152.

—— 'Form in Shostakovich's Quartets', *The Musical Times*, Vol. 103, No. 1434 (Aug. 1962), 531–3.

—— 'Soviet Chamber Music', *Corbett's Cyclopedic Survey of Chamber Music*, Vol. iii (Oxford University Press, London, 2nd edn. 1963), 148–9. [Refers to Seventh and Eighth Quartets.]

Matthew-Walker, Robert, 'Dmitri Shostakovich—The Film Music', *Music and Musicians*, 332 (Apr. 1980), 34–9, 3 photographs. [A thorough review of the composer's important contribution in this field.]

—— 'Shostakovitch's Serial Procedures', *Music and Musicians*, 380 (Apr. 1984), 14–15. [Illustrated examples of serial thematicism running through the composer's work from the First Symphony to the Fifteenth Quartet.]

—— 'Shostakovich as populist composer', *Music and Musicians*, 402 (Feb. 1986), 7–9, 2 photographs. [A clarification of the origins of the Ballet Suites Nos. 1, 2, and 3; cross-referencing Shostakovich's original movements with the published versions assembled by Lev Atovmyan.)

Matthews, David, 'Shostakovich's Eleventh Symphony', *The Listener*, 75 (24 Mar. 1966) 488.

Mazel, Leo (Lev) Abramovich, *Simfonii D. D. Shostakovicha—putevoditel* (Sovetskii Kompozitor, Moscow, 1960), 152 pp.; 2nd rev. and enlarged edn., 1981. [The 1st edn. covers Nos. 1 to 11; the 2nd, all 15 symphonies. Numerous music examples.]

—— *Etyudy o Shostakovich: stati i zametki o tvorchestve* (Sovetskii Kompozitor, Moscow, 1986), 176 pp. ['Studies on Shostakovich; articles and notes on works'. A paperback comprising 13 articles on the composer's musical language, sonata form in the larger symphonies, the main themes of the Fifth Symphony, the production of the opera *The Nose*, the fugue of the Piano Quintet, 12-note system in his music, etc.; 84 music examples, including complete piano scores of 'Song of the Lantern' and 'Song of the Counterplan'.]

Meskhishvili, Erna Petrovna. *Dmitri Shostakovich—Notograficheskii spravochnik* (Moscow, 1996), 556 pp. [An updated and greatly extended version of Sadovnikov's 1965 catalogue with additional chapters in Part II on transcriptions,

All-Union Radio and Central Television performances recorded up to 1988, world-wide discography of selected LPs, a chronological chart, Russian documentaries and films of concerts; fully cross-referenced and indexed. Especially important for information on autograph and manuscript scores.]

Meyer, Krzysztof, *Dymitr Szostakowicz* (Kraków, 1973). [Original edition in Polish of the following biography (Meyer 1980).]

—— *Dymitr Szostakowicz — z pism i wypowiedzi* (Polskie Wydawnictwo Muzyczne, Kraków, 1975, 262 pp., 18 photographs. [Collection of articles and letters, year-by-year biography, and index of works and people mentioned in text. In Polish.]

—— *Dmitri Schostakowitsch*, trans. Ilona Reinhold (Philipp Reclam junior, Leipzig, 1980), 340 pp., 35 photographs. [A thorough biography in German, No. 809 in the Reclam paperback series, with music examples, detailed calendar of events, classified catalogue of works (19 pp.), a useful discography (32 pp) compiled by Jan Weber noting world-wide record numbers up to 1973, bibliographic references, booklist, and index of names.]

—— and Hellmundt, Christoph, *Dmitri Schostakowitsch — Erfahrungen*, trans. by Gabriele Bock (Philipp Reclam junior, Leipzig, 1983), 360 pp. [An expanded edition of Meyer 1980 in German. No. 947 in the Reclam paperback series.]

—— *Dimitri Chostakovitch* (Librairie Arthème Fayard, Paris, 1994), 605 pp., 20 photographs. [A rewritten and uncensored French version of Meyer's previous books, presented In chronological chapters, the 28th entitled 'Some personal recollections of the man who was Shostakovich'. Synopses of *Lady Macbeth* and *The Nose*, 26 music examples, list of prizes and decorations, catalogue of works arranged by genre, bibliography, indices of names and works.]

Milshtein, Yakov Isaakovich (compiler), *Aleksandr Vasilievich Gauk* (Sovetskii Kompozitor, Moscow, 1975), 123–30, 171–2, 223 *et passim*. [Memoirs of the conductor, selected articles and recollections by contemporaries (including Shostakovich); list of works in the conductor's repertoire and a discography; 5 photographs relating to Shostakovich.]

Mitchell, Donald, 'Shostakovich and his Symphonies', *Aldeburgh Anthology*, ed. Ronald Blythe (Snape Maltings Foundations/Faber Music, London, 1972), 215–18.

—— and Evans, John, *Benjamin Britten, Pictures from a Life, 1913–1976* (Faber and Faber, London and Boston, 1978), photographs nos. 363, 366–8.

Moisenko, Rena, *Twenty Soviet Composers* (Workers' Music Association, London, 1942), 56–9.

—— *Realist Music: 25 Soviet Composers* (Meridan Books, London, 1949), 200–14.

Moldon, David, *Bibliography of Russian Composers* (White Lion, London, 1976), 119–214. [Over 150 entries for Shostakovich of articles and books in the English language published up to 1974.]

Nardone, Thomas, with Nye, James H., and Resnick, Mark, *Choral Music in Print*, Vol. ii: *Secular* (Musicdata, Philadelphia, 1974).

National Union Catalog, *Pre-1956 Imprints* (Mansell Information, Salem, Mass., 1977), Vol. 544, pp. 490–500

—— *1973–77* (Rowman and Littlefield, Totowa, NJ, 1978), Prag-Staz, Vol. v, pp. 466–74.

Neuhaus, Heinrich, *The Art of Piano Playing*, trans. K. A. Leibovitch (Barrie Jenkins, London, 1973) (reissued 1983), xiii plus 240 pp.

Nesterenko, Yevgeni Yevgenevich, 'Poslednie vstrechi', *Musyka Rossii*, Issue 2 (Sovetskii Kompozitor, Moscow, 1978), 329–36. ['The last meeting': the bass singer's view of the *Suite on Verses of Michelangelo*, Op, 145.]

Nikelberg, S., *Muzyka D. Shostakovicha k kinofilmu 'Gamlet'. Iz istorii Russkoi i Sovelskoi Muzyka*, Issue 3 (Muzyka, Moscow, 1978), 234–52. ['The Music of D. Shostakovich for the cinema film Hamlet': a thorough analysis with 14 music examples.]

Nikolayev, Aleksandr Aleksandrovich, and Chinayev, Vladimir Pyotrovich, *Ocherki po istorii sovetskogo fortepiannogo iskusstva* (Muzyka, Moscow, 1979), 262 pp. [Musical information on notable Soviet pianoforte teachers, pianists, and composers of keyboard works. Shostakovich's contribution covered on pp. 30–8 *et passim*.]

Norris, Christopher (ed.), *Shostakovich: The Man and his Music* (Lawrence and Wishart, London, 1982), 233 pp. [A volume of illuminating essays by performing musicians, Western composers and critics, exploring Shostakovich's principal works and discussing the historical circumstances and the political atmosphere surrounding their composition. 49 music examples.]

—— 'The String Quartets of Shostakovich', *Music and Musicians*, 24 (Dec. 1974), 27–8, 30. [Ostensibly a review of the Borodin Quartet's box set of 13 quartets but profoundly wider in scope, covering critical assessments of the symphonies and compositional techniques. 'Shostakovich's music makes up an anatomy of the Soviet body politic. The forced, 'optimistic' final movements (Symphonies Nos. 5 and 12); the appalling hack cantatas and blatant, mindless 'light' music—all these suggest æsthetic equivalents to the forced ideology of a sick society'.]

Norris, Geoffrey, 'Shostakovich's "The Nose"', *The Musical Times*, Vol. 120, No. 1634 (May 1979), 393–4.

—— 'Bitter Memories: the Shostakovich Testimony', *The Musical Times*, Vol. 121, No. 1646 (Apr. 1980), 241–3.

—— 'An Opera Restored—Rimsky-Korsakov, Shostakovich and the Khovansky Business', *The Musical Times*, Vol. 123, No. 1676 (Oct. 1982), 672–5. [An appreciation of Shostakovich's orchestration, Op. 106, as a preface to the Covent Carden revival in this edition, Oct.–Nov. 1982.]

—— *The New Oxford Companion to Music* (General ed. Denis Arnold) Vol. ii, K–Z (Oxford University Press, Oxford, 1983), 1681–4. [Shostakovich entry: a perceptive review of the composer's career; also numerous related

articles and definitions cross- referenced throughout the two-volume encyclopaedia.]

—— 'Lady Macbeth of the Mtsensk District', *The Daily Telegraph* (28 Aug.
1999). [No. 35 in a weekly series '50 works that shaped the century', with
photograph of the 1934 Moscow première.]

Olkhovsky, Andrey, *Music Under the Soviets—the Agony of an Art* (Frederick A.
Praeger, New York, 1955), 215–22 *et passim*. [A highly critical thesis on the
musical scene in the USSR during Stalin's rule. Useful for translations and
condensations of articles from the Soviet press, and the extensive bibliography.]

Olmsted, Elizabeth H. (ed.), *Music Library Association Catalog of Cards for
Printed Music*, 1953–1972, Vol. 2, K–Z (Rowman and Littlefield, Totowa, NJ),
405–10.

O'Loughlin, N., 'Shostakovich's String Quartets', *Tempo*, No. 87 (Winter
1968–9), 9–16. [Covers Nos. 1 to 11.]

Opperby, Preben, *Leopold Stokowski* (Midas Books, Tunbridge Wells and Hippocrene, New York, 1982), 235–6. [Full discography.]

Orlov, Genrikh Aleksandrovich, *Sinifonii D. Shostakovicha* (Muzgiz, Leningrad,
1962), 68 pp. [A paperback booklet with extended programme notes for
Symphonies Nos. 1 to 12.]

—— *Dmitri Dmitrievich Shostakovich—kratkii ocherk zhizni i tvorchestva*
(Muzyka, Leningrad, 1966), 120 pp. [A paperback essay on the life and creative work of the composer written for young people; 19 illustrations in the
text.]

Ottaway, Hugh, 'Shostakovich's Tenth Symphony', *The Musical Times*, Vol. 97,
No. 1361 (July 1956), 350–2.

—— 'Shostakovich: Some Later Works', *Tempo*, No. 50 (Winter 1958–9),
2–14. [Analyses of Opp. 77, 93, and 103.]

—— 'Shostakovich and the string quartet', *The Listener*, 76 (17 Nov. 1966), 746.

—— 'Shostakovich's "Fascist" Theme', *The Musical Times*, Vol. 111, No. 1525
(Mar. 1970), 274. [Op. 60.]

—— 'Beyond Babi Yar', *Tempo*, No. 105 (June 1973), 26–30. [A review of
Op. 113.]

—— 'Shostakovich's String Quartets 1–13', EMI Records (London, 1974),
8 pp.

—— 'Shostakovich's string quartets', *The Listener*, 91 (6 June 1974), 731–2.

—— 'The Symphonies of Shostakovich 1–15' (EMI Records, London, 1975),
20 pp.

—— 'Looking again at Shostakovich 4', *Tempo*, No. 115 (Dec. 1975), 14–24.
[A detailed study of Op. 43.]

—— 'Symphonies Nos. 5 and 10' (EMI Records, London, 1976), 8 pp.

—— *Shostakovich Symphonies* (BBC Publications, London, 1978), 68 pp. [A
paperback in the BBC Music Guides series with essays on the 15 symphonies illustrated by 30 music examples.]

Paisov, Yuri, 'Pyatnadtsataya simfoniya D. D. Shostakovicha', *Muzykalnyi Sovremennik,* Vol. 3 (Sovetskii Kompozitor, Moscow, 1979), 5–38. [An analysis of Fifteenth Symphony with 9 music examples.]

Parsons, Denys, *The Directory of Tunes and Musical Themes* (Spencer Brown, Cambridge, 1975). [Examples from Shostakovich's works defined by an original code of * for starting note, R for repeated note, U for up, and D for down.]

Penney, Barbara, *Music in British Libraries — A Directory of Resources* (Library Association, London, 3rd edn. 1981).

Perényi, Eleanor, *Great Men of Music: Shostakovich* (Time-Life Records, Alexandria, Virginia, 1979), 23 pp. (An illustrated book to accompany a four-record set of RCA recordings with a listener's guide written by Jack Diether.]

Piston, Walter, *Orchestration* (Victor Gollancz, London, 1965). [Music examples from Fifth and Seventh Symphonies.]

Plaistow, Stephen (ed.); Grimley, Myra, and Wiegold, Mary, *Catalogue of Music Broadcast on Rado 3 and Radio 4 in 1974* (BBC Publications, London, 1977), 236–7. [Gives the performing times of 35 Shostakovich works.]

—— (ed.); Wiegold, Mary, and Wilkinson, Caroline, *Catalogue of Music Broadcast on Radio 3 in 1975* (BBC Publications, London, 1978), 227–8. [Performance times of 32 Shostakovich works.]

Polyakova, Lyudmila Viktorovna, *Soviet Music,* trans. Xenia Danko (Foreign Languages Publishing House, Moscow, *c.*1960). [Covers Opp. 10 to 105; well illustrated.]

—— *Vokalnyi tsikl D. Shostakovicha: iz yevreiskoi narodnoi poezii* (Sovetskii Kompozitor, Moscow, 1957), 24 pp. ['From Jewish Folk Poetry'—an analysis of the song cycle with eighteen music examples in a slim booklet.]

Porter, Andrew, *Chamber Music,* ed. Alec Robertson (Penguin Books, Harmondsworth, 1963), 420–1.

Pound, Reginald, *Sir Henry Wood — A Biography* (Cassell, London, 1969).

Pribegina, Galina Alekseyevna, *Moskovskaya konservatoriya 1866–1991* (Muzyka, Moscow, 1991), 240 pp. [A glossy cloth-bound, large format album dedicated to the 125th anniversary of the Moscow Conservatory, profusely illustrated in monochrome and colour, with Russian text and captions in English.]

Prieberg, Fred K., *Musik in der Sowjetunion* (Verlag Wissenschaft und Politik, Cologne, 1965). [Many references to Shostakovich and details of jazz music in the USSR; in German language.]

Prokhorova, Irina Adeksandrovna, and Skudina, Henrietta Semyonovna, *Sovetskaya muzykalnaya literatura* for 7th class of children's musical schools (Muzyka, Moscow, 1978), 62–92. [Essay on Shostakovich by H. S. Skudina; biography analyses of Seventh Symphony and Prelude and Fugue, Op. 87 No. 5; 16 music examples and 7 photographs.]

Rabinovich, David Abramovich, *Dmitry Shostakovich — Composer,* trans. George H. Hanna (Lawrence & Wishart, London, 1959), 166 pp., 30 photographs. [A sympathetic survey especially valuable for biographical information. Covers Opp. 1 to 103.]

Radamsky, Sergei, 'Lady Macbeth Put On for Stalin—but Shostakovich waited in vain for a call', *The Times* (18 Nov. 1963). [An article written by a guest of the composer at the performance attended by Stalin, Zhdanov, and Mikoyan.]

Reid, Charles, *Malcolm Sargent—A Biography* (Hamish Hamilton, London, 1968).

Reid, Robert H. (ed.), *The Gramophone Shop Encyclopedia of Recorded Music* (Brown Publishers, New York, 3rd edn. 1948), 482–3.

Rienäcker, Gerd, and Reising, Vera, *Die 11 und 12 Sinfonie von Dmitri Schostakowitsch* (Einführungsmaterial für Kulturfunktionäire) (Gesellschaft für deutsch-sowjetische Freundschaft, Kulturpolitik, Berlin, 1970), 55 pp. [A review of the Symphonies Nos. 11 and 12 in German with music examples.]

Rijen, Onno van, *Dmitri Shostakovich Small Catalogue* (1988), 35 pp. [Annotated list of works, premières, renumbered Sans opp., and classified index. A privately published database catalogue for DSCH Society members.]

―――― Dmitri Shostakovich Compact Discography (1994), 178 pp, [An A4-size discography of compact discs by opus and label with full reviews from *Gramophone, BBC Music Magazine,* and *DSCH Newsletter.*]

Robinson, David, *Cinema in Revolution: the Heroic Era of the Soviet Film* (Secker and Warburg, London, 1973). [A collection of essays compiled by Luda and Jean Schnitzer, and Marcel Martin, originally published in a 1966 French edition, translated and with additional material by D. Robinson. Shostakovich mentioned in two paragraphs only though the text presents background information on several films he scored and their directors.]

―――― *World Cinema—A Short History* (Eyre Methuen, London, 1973).

Roseberry, Eric, *Shostakovich: His Life and Times* (Midas Books, Tunbridge Wells and Hippocrene, New York, 1982), 191 pp. Also available as an Omnibus paperback, 1987. [With 110 photographs and drawings; reproductions of posters, newspaper articles, autograph scores, and music examples, this is a laudably well-illustrated account of the composer's life and times; expertly compiled from a wide variety of sources, placing Shostakovich's unique 'achievement in its social, political and cultural context'. A bibliography of 24 books in the English language and a discography of recommended recordings.]

―――― *Sjostakovitj* (J. H. Gottmer, Haarlem, 1987), 224 pp., 100 illustrations. [A Dutch translation of the above by Gerard Grasman, with additional catalogue of works and supplementary material by Jos van Leeuwen (ed.).]

―――― *Ideology, Style, Content, and Thematic Process in the Symphonies, Cello Concertos, and String Quartets of Shostakovich* (Garland: New York, 1989), 584 pp. [An epic thesis—University of Bristol, 1982—in the series of 'Outstanding Dissertations in Music from British Universities' in three parts: I—Ideology and creative practice, II—Studies in style, content, and thematic process, III—Individual studies (1. The first movement of the Fourth Symphony, 2. The two Cello Concertos, and 3. Aspects of the late string quartets). Numerous music examples and a seven-page bibliography.]

Roslavleva, Nataliya Petrovna, *Era of the Russian Ballet 1770–1965* (Victor Gollancz, London, 1966), chs. 10 and 12.

Rotbaum, Lii, 'V poiskakh stsenicheskogo resheniya "Kateriny lzmailovoi"', *Muzyka Rossii*, Issue 2 (Sovetskii Kompozitor Moscow, 1978), 337–51. ['The search for the theatrical solution to *Katerina Izmailova'*: an extract from a Polish producer's book.]

Rozhdestvensky, Gennadi Nikolayevich, *Preambuly* (Sovetskii Kompozitor, Moscow, 1989), 303 pp., illustrations in the text. [A compilation by Galina Sergeyevna Alfeyevskaya of forty-six articles written by the conductor: No. 5 on the *New Babylon* Suite; No. 17 including a reference to Schnittke's *In Memorian Stravinsky, Prokofiev, and Shostakovich;* No. 24, notes for the performance of *Rothschild's Violin* on 24 November 1982; and No. 33/2 on a violin and cello duet tribute to Shostakovich by Evzhen Zamechnik. Rozhdestvensky's extensive repertoire of 1950–87 is appended.]

Russcol, Herbert, *Guide to Low-priced Classical Records* (Hart, New York, 1969), 626–31.

Sabinina, Marina Dmitrievna, *Dmitri Shostakovich* (Sovetskii Kompozitor, Moscow, 1959), 53 pp.

―――― *Simfonizm Shostakovicha — put k zrelosti* (Nauka, Moscow, 1965), 176 pp., 5 photographs. ['The symphonism of Shostakovich—the path towards maturity': a paperback discussing the first six symphonies; illustrated with numerous music examples.]

―――― *Shostakovich — simfonist: dramaturgiya, estetika, stil* (Muzyka, Moscow, 1976), 480 pp. 22 photographs. ['Shostakovich—Symphonist: Dramaturgy, aesthetics, style'. Minutely detailed analyses in Russian of the first 14 symphonies and Op. 119; 164 music examples and a bibliography of 130 references.]

―――― *Muzykalnaya Entsiklopediya,* ed. Yuri Keldysh, Vol. 6, Kheintse—Yashugin (Sovetskaya Entsiklopediya, Moscow, 1982), 380–96. [Shostakovich entry: autographs of the opening of the Tenth Symphony and first page of the Eighth Quartet; appendices of the principal dates in the composer's life, classified list of works, and bibliography compiled by Leonid Borlsovich Rimsky.]

―――― *Simfonizm D. Shostakovicha v gody voiny. Muzyka v borbe s fashizmom* (Sovetskii Kompozitor, Moscow, 1985), 9–29. [An article on Symphonies Nos. 7 and 8 in a paperback dealing with the music scene on the continent during the war against Fascism.]

Sadovnikov, Yefim Lvovich (ed.), *D. D. Shostakovich — Notograficheskii spravochnik* (Sovetskii Kompozitor, Moscow, 1961), 64 pp. [A small catalogue.]

―――― (ed.), *D. D. Shostakovich — Notograficheskii i bibliograficheskii spravochnik* (Muzyka, Moscow, 2nd edn. 1965), 280 pp. [An oblong paperback catalogue with detailed lists of compositions, Opp. 1–119; 8-page discography of Melodiya recordings; alphabetical list of authors of subjects and texts; dedicatees; and a copious classified bibliography, chronologically listed under 17 headings commencing with 286 articles written by the composer, 1928–64.]

Sagayev, Lyubomir Konstantinov, *Kniga za operata* (Muzika, Sofia, Bulgaria, 4th enlarged edn. 1983), 670–84. [A review of 132 representative operas, arranged alphabetically by composer, including Shostakovich's *The Nose* and *Katerina Izmailova*. List of characters, history of the work, synopsis of the plot, and discussion on the music for all the operas, in Bulgarian.]

Sahlberg-Vachnadze, Margarita Aleksevna, *Chostakovich* (Editions Romance, Paris, 1945), 31 pp.

Salehieh, Vahid (ed.), *Melos*, No. 4–5 (Stockholm, Summer 1993), 102 pp. ['Special Issue on Dmitri Shostakovich': Swedish magazine wholly in English, including articles by Levon Hakopian (on *The Nose*); Eric Roseberry, Malcolm H. Brown, Christopher Norris, and Ian MacDonald (on *Testimony* and *The New Shostakovich*), and Krzysztof Meyer ('The recollection of a Man'). Three chapters on recommended recordings.]

Salter, Lionel, *The Gramophone Guide to Classical Composers and Recordings* (Salamander Books, London, 1978), 172–3.

Sandved, K. B., *The World of Music, Volume 2, L–Z* (Waverley, London, 2nd edn. 1957), 1903–6.

Schonberg, Harold C., *The Lives of the Great Composers* (Davis-Poynter, London, 1977), 511–21. [Chapter 34: 'Under the Soviets, Prokofiev and Shostakovich'.]

Schwann Record & Tape Guides (formerly Schwann Long Playing Record Catalog) (W. Schwann, Boston, Mass.). [Guide 1 monthly from 1949 and Guide 2 semi-annual supplement.]

Schwarz, Boris., 'Soviet Music Since the Second World War', Contemporary Music in Europe (ed. Paul Henry Lang and Nathan Broder), *The Musical Quarterly*, Vol. 51 (1965), 259–81.

—— 'The Vicissitudes of Soviet Music', *Problems of Communism*, United States Information Agency, vol. xiv, No. 6 (Nov. 1965), 67–82.

—— *Music and Musical Life in Soviet Russia, 1917–1970* (Barrie & Jenkins, London, 1972), xi plus 550 pp. [A profoundly scholarly survey—indispensable.]

—— Enlarged Edition, *1917–1981* (Indiana University Press, Bloomington, 1983), xiii plus 722 pp. [Two new chapters: 'From the Lenin Centennial to the Death of Shostakovich' and 'Dissatisfactions, Directives, and Defections (including a conversation with Maksim Shostakovich)' chronicle the period from 1970 to 1981.]

—— *The New Grove Dictionary of Music and Musicians*, ed. Stanley Sadie: Vol. 17, Schütze-Spinto (Macmillan, London, 1980), 264–75. [Shostakovich entry: a balanced assessment of the composer's achievement with his creative career divided into three periods—early 1924–36, mature 1937–66, and late 1967–75; classified list of works; bibliography of 81 references, 1928–80; 3 photographs and facsimile of the 1st page of Symphony No. 7.]

—— and Fay, Laurel E., *The New Grove, Russian Masters 2*, in the composer biography series (Macmillan and Papermac, London, 1986), 175–240. [Shostakovich section: revised dictionary article with new work-list and extended bibliography of 324 references provided by L. E. Fay.]

Seckerson, Edward, 'Ashkenazy's Shostakovich', *Gramophone*, Vol. 67, No. 798 (Dec. 1989), 1115–16. [An in-car interview with the Royal Philharmonic Orchestra's music director on interpreting the symphonies.]

Seehaus, Lothar, *Dmitrij Schostakowitsch: Leben und Werk* (Florian Noetzel Verlag, Wilhelmshaven, 1986), 224 pp., 15 illustrations. [A German monograph split into six periods of the composer's life, with list of sources, brief bibliography, and discography.]

Seroff, Viktor Ilyich, *Dmitri Shostakovich: The Life and Background of a Soviet Composer* (Alfred A. Knopf, New York, 1943), 260 pp. plus xx, 13 photographs. [In collaboration with Nadezhda Galli-Shohat, aunt of the composer. Useful for particulars of the composer's family and early life. Appends a translation of Shostakovich's article on his opera *Lady Macbeth* and Slonimsky's list of works to Symphony No. 7.]

Shaginyan, Marietta Sergeyevna, *O Shostakoviche: stati* (Muzyka, Moscow, 1979), 46 pp., 14 photographs. [A collection of ten brief articles published 1940–73, including reviews and programme notes on Symphonies Nos. 5, 11, and 14, Piano Quintet, and *Moscow, Cheryomushki*.]

Shebalina, Alisa Maksimovna, *V. Ya. Shebalin: gody zhizn i tvorchestva* (Sovetskii Kompozitor, Moscow, 1990), 304 pp., 40 photographs. [Many references to Shostakovich, including his tribute 'In memory of a friend', in this diary compiled by Shebalin's wife.]

Sheinberg, Esti, *Irony, Satire, Parody and the Grotesque in the Music of Shostakovich — A Theory of Musical Incongruities* (Ashgate, Abingdon, 2001), 390 pp., 27 plates. [A scholarly dissertation, with 106 music examples, previewed by the author at the Glasgow Symposium *Shostakovich 25 Years On*, 2 October 2000.]

Shirinsky, Aleksandr Aleksandrovich, *Skripichnye proizvedeniya D. Shostakovicha: Problemy interpretatsii* (Muzyka, Moscow, 1988), 111 pp. [A paperback on 'Problems in the interpretation of Shostakovich's violin works'. Analyses of the two Violin Concertos and the Sonata, with discussions on the recorded performances of David Oistrakh (Opp. 77—1956 and 1973; 129, and 134), Leonid Kogan (Op. 77—1962 and broadcast 26 November 1980), and Viktor Tretyakov (Op. 129—broadcast 28 December 1979). Twenty-nine single line music examples.]

Shneyerson, Grigori Mikhailovich (compiler), *D. Shostakovich: stati i materialy* (Sovetskii Kompozitor, Moscow, 1976), 336 pp., 72 photographs. [A commemorative volume planned for his 70th birthday with articles by fellow composers, musicians, and friends—living and deceased. Includes a complete list of compositions and 13 musical tributes on DSCH.]

——— (compiler), *Dmitri Shostakovich Speaks* (Melodiya, Moscow, 1979), 20 pp., 41 photographs. [A valuable booklet in record box set with foreword by Tikhon Khrennikov and full texts in English (Russian summaries) of fifteen talks given by the composer, 1941–75.]

Shostakovich, Dmitri, 'My Opera Lady Macbeth of Mtsensk', *Modern Music,* New York, xii (1934), 23–30. [Translation in Seroff, pp. 249–55.]

――――― 'Message to America from Dmitri Shostakovich, 4 January 1942', San Francisco. *The American Russian Institute,* 1942.

――――― 'My Seventh Symphony—Symphony of Struggle and Victory', *VOKS Bulletin,* Nos. 1–2 (Moscow, 1942), 55–60. [In English.]

――――― 'Soviet Music Today', *Saturday Review of Literature,* New York, Vol. xxx, No. 4 (25 Jan. 1947), p. 25.

――――― 'Po puti navodnosti i realizma', *Sovetskaya Muzyka* (Nov. 1952), 6–11. ['Along the path of nationality and realism'.]

――――― 'Radost tvorcheskikh iskanii', *Sovetskaya Muzyka* (Jan. 1954), 40–2. ['The joy of creative searching', trans. in Olkhovsky, pp. 312–14.]

――――― *The Power of Music* (*Music Journal* publication, New York, 1968), 56 pp. [A collection of essays by the composer in English language.]

Sidelnikov, Leonid Sergeyevich, *Bolshoi Simfonichesky Orkestr—Tsentralnogo televideniya i Vsesoytiznogo radio* (Muzyka, Moscow, 1981), 208 pp. [The history of the Large Symphony Orchestra of the Central Television and All-Union Radio, profusely illustrated with portraits of its chief conductors, Aleksandr Orlov, Nikolai Golovanov, Aleksandr Gauk, Gennadi Rozhdestvensky, and Vladimir Fedoseyev.]

――――― *Gosudarstvennyi akademicheskii simfonicheskii orkestr Soyuza SSR* (Muzyka, Moscow, 1986), 288 pp. [A glossy though incomplete 50-year history of the USSR (State) Symphony Orchestra, illustrated in monochrome and colour. Accent on a 'quartet of conductors': Gauk, Rakhlin, Ivanov, and Svetlanov.]

Slonim, Marc, *Russian Theater: from the Empire to the Soviets* (Methuen, London, 1963).

Slonimsky, Nicolas, 'Dmitri Dmitrievich Shostakovich', *The Musical Quarterly,* Vol. xxviii (Oct. 1942), 415–44. [Interesting overall appraisal with music examples, photographs, and list of Opp. 1 to 60 compiled by Shostakovich for the author.]

――――― *The New Book of Modern Composers,* ed. David Ewen (Alfred A. Knopf, New York, 1961), 362–72.

――――― *The International Cyclopedia of Music and Musicians,* ed. Oscar Thompson (Dent, London, 9th edn. 1964), 2011–14. [Covers Opp. 1 to 73.]

――――― *Lexicon of Musical Invective—Critical Assaults on Composers since Beethoven's Time* (University of Washington Press, Seattle, 1965), 175–7.

――――― *Music Since 1900* (Cassell, London, 4th edn. 1972). [A monumental volume in diary form, especially valuable for reviews of première performances and his correspondence with Ivan Sollertinsky.]

――――― *Baker's Biographical Dictionary of Musicians* (Oxford University Press/ Schirmer Books, 7th edn. 1984), 2118–21; (8th edn. 1991), 1701–4; (Schirmer Books, New York, Concise 8th edn. 1994), 935–7. [The authoritative single-volume musical biography reference work. The Concise 8th edn. updates the earlier editions but omits bibliographic references.]

Soblev, Romil Pavlovich, *Aleksandr Dovzhenko* (Iskusstvo, Moscow), 306 pp. plus 44 plates. [The life and work of the great Ukrainian film-director. Information (pp. 230–45), sketches, and stills on *Michurin*, Opus 78.]

Sokhor, Arnold Naumovich (ed.), *Slavini pobedu oktyabrya! 1917–1967.* Book 1: 1917–1932 (Muzyka, Moscow, 1967). [Patriotic songs including 'Song of the Counterplan', pp. 135–8 and 156–7.]

Sokolsky, Matias Markovich, *Slushaya vremya . . .* (Muzyka, Moscow, 1964), 95–143, [Selected articles about music in two parts: 'Five classical composers (Glinka, Tchaikovsky, Musorgsky, Shostakovich, and Prokofiev)' and 'From the writing-pad of a critic'. The five Shostakovich articles include reviews of Symphony No. 10, the 1962 revival of *Katerina Izmailova*, and *Satires*.]

———— 'Shostakovich's Satirical Tale', *Soviet Literature*, No. 332 (Nov. 1975), 181–3. [A Soviet critic's review of *The Nose* following its 1975 Moscow revival.]

Sollertinsky, Dmitri and L(y)udmilla, *Pages from the Life of Dmitri Shostakovich*, trans. Graham Hobbs and Charles Midgley (Robert Hale, London, 1981), 246 pp., 14 photographs. [A sketchy portrait arranged chronologically under year/period chapter headings, helpful for fresh information on the composer's extensive travels and crippling illnesses and his correspondence with Ivan Sollertinsky. Graced with a general index but lacking music references, sources of the many quotes, and a bibliography.]

Souster, Tim, 'Shostakovich at the Crossroads', *Tempo*, lxxviii (Autumn 1966), 2–9. [Refers to Fourth and Fifth Symphonies.]

Spektor, N., *'Sonet 66' V. Shekspira v tvorchestve D. Shostakovicha. Iz istorii russkoi i sovetskoi muzyka*, Issue 3 (Muzyka, Moscow, 1978), 210–17. ['Shakespeare's Sonnet 66 in the works of D. Shostakovich'.]

Stevenson, Ronald, *Western Music: an introduction* (Stanmore, London, 1971).

Streller, Friedbert, *Dmitri Schostakowitsch für Sie porträtiert* (VEB Deutscher Verlag für Musik, Leipzig, 1982), 84 pp., 33 photographs. [An East German paperback with biographical notes and list of compositions.]

Tarakanov, Mikhail Yevgenievich, *Simfoniya i instrumentalnyi kontsert v russkoi sovetskoi muzyke* (Sovetskii Konipozitor, Moscow, 1988), 272 pp. [Chapter on Symphony No. 15 and Cello Concerto No. 2 in the work of Shostakovich, pp. 41–92, and many references elsewhere with emphasis on the 1960s and 1970s; an analysis of Boris Tishchenko's Fifth Symphony dedicated to Shostakovich, pp. 108–18: appendix of music examples (see Nos. 1–15, 16–32, and 39–42), brief bibliography and index.]

Taylor, Richard, and Christie, Ian, *The Film Factory: Russian and Soviet Cinema in Documents 1896–1939* (Routledge & Kegan Paul, London, 1988), 457 pp. [The aesthetic and political development of the Russian cinema with documentary history of the classic films of the 1920s and 1930s, including ten for which Shostakovich provided the music. Stills from *New Babylon*, *Counterplan*, *The Youth of Maxim*, *The Vyborg Side*, and *The Great Citizen*.]

Tigranov, Georgi Grigorievich; Dmitriev, Anatoli Nikodimovich and Frumky, V. *55 sovetskikh simfonii* (Sovetskii Kompozitor, Leningrad, 1967), 305–412. [Detailed analyses, with music examples, of Symphonies Nos. 1 and 5–11.]

—— (ed.), *Sovetskaya simfoniya za 50 let* (Muzyka, Leningrad, 1967), 495–92. [Detailed analyses, rich in music examples, of Symphonies Nos. 1, 5, 7, and 10–13.]

—— (ed.), *Leningradskaya konservatoriya v vospominaniyakh* (Muzyka, Leningrad, 1988), 281 pp., 15 plates. [Recollections of Leningrad Conservatory by musicologists and performers.]

Tretyakova, Liliya Sergeyevna, *Dmitri Shostakovich* (Sovetskaya Rossiya, Moscow, 1976), 240 pp, 17 plates. [25 biographical essays with musical achievements considered in detail.]

Troitskaya, G., 'Muzyka Shostakovicha v kino', *Tskusstvo kino* (Moscow), 1981 No. 12, 54–67.

Tsuker, A., 'Traditsii muzykalnogo teatra Musorgskogo b simfonicheskom tvorchestvo Shostakovicha', *Muzykalnyi Sovremennik*, Vol. 3 (Sovetskii Kompozitor, Moscow, 1979), 39–74. ['The traditions of Musorgsky's musical theatre in the symphonic works of Shostakovich'. Music examples from Opp. 79, 87, 93, 113, 117, and 119.]

Unger-Hamilton, Clive, and Spek, Peter van der (eds.), *The Great Symphonies, the Great Orchestras, the Great Conductors* (Sidgwick & Jackson, London, 2nd edn., 1988), 141–3, 146, 235. [A rather grudging recognition of Shostakovich's achievement in Jan Taat's chapter on the twentieth-century symphonists. The Third Symphony is not analysed in detail as announced on the dust jacket. Select discography.]

VAAP (The Copyright Agency of the USSR), *Dmitry Shostakovich: Complete Catalogue of Works* (VAAP, Moscow, 1977), 45 pp. [A booklet listing numbered and unnumbered compositions, with instrumentation and duration, in English.]

Vanslow, Viktor Vladimirovich, *Tvorchestvo Shostakovicha* (Znanie, Moscow, 1966), 31 pp. [The works of Shostakovich.]

Vasina-Grossman, Vera Andreyevna, *Mastera sovetskogo romansa* (Muzyka, Moscow, 2nd edn. 1980), 218–54. ['Masters of Soviet Song': a detailed review of Shostakovich's song cycles with 19 music examples. The volume includes chapters on Myaskovsky, Prokofiev, Shaporin, Shebalin, and Sviridov.]

Vishnevskaya, Galina Pavlovna, *Galina: A Russian Story*, trans. Guy Daniels (Hodder & Stoughton, London, 1985), 519 pp. [This deeply moving document throws new light on several of Shostakovich's compositions (in Chapter 11 and on pp. 274–9 for the Thirteenth Syrnphony and pp. 349–61 for the film of *Katerina Izmailova*). The horrors of Stalinist Russia, the Leningrad Blockade, and KGB harassment are vividly described.]

Vladimirov, Vladimir Nikolayevich, and Lagutin, Aleksandr Ivanovich, *Muzykalnaya literatura* for 4th class of children's musical schools (Muzyka, Moscow, 1978), 40–1. ['The Homeland Hears' from Opus 86.]

Volkov, Solomon Moiseyevich, 'Dmitri Shostakovich and "Tea for Two"', *The Musical Quarterly*, Vol. lxiv, No. 2 (Apr. 1978), 223–8.

——— and Ottaway, Hugh (uncredited), *Lady Macbeth of Mtsensk* (EMI Records, London, 1979), 44 pp. [A model of all an opera booklet should be; with full cast list, historical notes, synopsis of the action, biographical details of the leading performers with portraits, information on the translit-eration system, and full libretto in three parallel columns—Russian text, English translation, and transliterated Russian.]

——— *Testimony—The Memoirs of Dmitri Shostakovich*, trans. Antonina W. Bouis (Hamish Harnilton, London, 1979), 270 pp., 16 plates. Reprinted in the Faber Paperback series in 1981. [Reminiscences of musicians, artists, and writers whom the composer knew and a record of conversations with Stalin, as related to Volkov. NB. The half-page editorial and open letter from former pupils of Shostakovich, headed 'Pitiful Forgery—about the so-called *Memoirs* of D. D. Shostakovich', that appeared in the *Moscow Literary Gazette*, No. 46, dated 14 Nov. 1979, Laurel E. Fay (1980), MacDonald (1990). Ho and Feofanov (1998), and the voluminous articles and letters in the *DSCH Journal* should be read in conjunction with Volkov's controversial book.

——— 'Dmitri Shostakovich's "Jewish Motif": A Creative Enigma', 1985, 2 pp. [Interesting notes included with the programme for the USA première of Opus 79a. According to a member of the audience Volkov and Maksim Sho-stakovich 'greeted each other warmly after the concert'.]

——— 'Preface to the Facsimile Edition of Shostakovich's Seventh Symphony ("Leningrad")', trans. Laurel E. Fay (Zen-On, Tokyo, 1992), 7–10.

Voynich, Ethel Lilian, *The Gadfly* (Mayflower, St Albans, 1973), 256 pp. [The original novel on which the Russian film was based. See Opus 97.]

Vronskaya, Jeanne, *Young Soviet Film Makers* (George Allen & Unwin, London, 1972).

Walsh, Stephen, 'Shostakovich's "Seven Romances"', *Tempo*, No. 85 (Summer 1968), 27–8. [Op. 127.]

Wang, Dajue, 'Shostakovich: Music on the Brain?', *The Musical Times*, Vol. cxxiv, No. 1684, 347–8. [An extraordinary account telling of a fragment of a wartime shell lodged in a cavity in the composer's brain.]

Werth, Alexander, *Musical Uproar in Moscow* (Turnstile Press, London, 1949), 103 pp. [A revealing account of the 1948 Zhdanov Decree.]

——— *The Khrushchev Phase* (Robert Hale, London, 1961), 218–24. [Chapter 23: 'Shostakovich and Dodecaphonic Music'.]

——— *Russia at War, 1941–1945* (Barrie and Rockcliff, London 1964).

Wilson, Elizabeth, *Shostakovich: A Life Remembered* (Faber and Faber, London, 1994), xxiv + 550 pp., 40 photographs. [A revelatory portrait, using much previously unpublished material in the form of recorded interviews, mem-oirs, and specially commissioned articles from fellow composers and musi-cians, relatives and friends, and contemporary writers. Informative biographical notes, an annotated list of sources, and a general index. Review G Oct. 1994. Also available in paperback (Princeton University Press, 1996).]

Wolter, Günter, *Dmitri Schostakowitsch—Eine sowjetische Tragödie* (Peter Lang, Frankfurt am Main, 1991), 197 pp., frontispiece portrait. ['A Soviet Tragedy': volume 27 in a series of paperback music studies, dealing with important works of three periods (up to 1936, 1936–66, and 1967–75) and including German translations of the article 'Muddle instead of music' and the text of Symphony No. 13; a fifteen-page bibliography of books mainly in the German language, and a selective list of 38 recordings.]

Yakovlev, Mikhail Mikhailovich (compiler), *D. Shostakovich o vremeni i o sebe 1926–1975* (Sovetskii Kompozitor, Moscow, 1980), 376 pp., 50 photographic illustrations in the text. [An important collection of 330 articles written by Shostakovich on himself and his times, arranged in chronological order after each year's summary of noteworthy events in the composer's life. Index of sources appended.]

Yakubov, Manashir Abramovich, *Dmitry Shostakovich—for the 75th Birth Anniversary* (VAAP-Inform, Moscow, 1981), 43 pp. [A booklet of book reviews in English, covering monographs, analytical guides and collections of articles recently published in the Soviet Union.]

―――― *Lirika i grotesk. Muzykalnaya Zhizn* (Moscow, 1986), No. 18, pp. 15–16. [The history of the Two Pieces for String Quartet.]

―――― *Shostakovich 1906–1975—Mstisiav Rostropovich* (London Symphony Orchestra, 1998), 87 pp., 58 photographs / cartoons / paintings. [Programme book for the 19 February–8 March and 10–28 October Barbican Centre concerts of the complete cycle of symphonies. Notes on all the works performed with articles by M. Yakubov, artists' biographies, and translations of letters.]

Yarustovsky, Boris Mikhailovich, *Simfonii o voine i mire* (Nauka, Moscow, 1966), 368 pp. ['Symphonies of War and Peace'. A survey of Eastern and Western symphonies, composed under the impact of the Second World War, including Shostakovich's Seventh and Eighth detailed with music examples in chapter one, pp. 27–94.]

Yutkevich, Sergei Iosifovich, *O kino iskusstve* (Publishing House of Academic Science, Moscow, 1962). ['On cinematic art': information on films mentioned under Opp. 30, 33, and 53.]

Yuzefovich, Viktor, *David Oistrakh: besedy s Igorem Oistrakhom* (Muzyka, Moscow, 1978). ['David Oistrakh: Conversations with Igor Oistrakh'. An English translation from the German edition was published by Cassell, London, 1979, 248 pp. See especially pp. 168–79. Author's name transliterated as Jusefovich.]

Zaderatsky, Vsevolod Vsevolodovich, *Polifoniya v instrumentalnykh proizvedeniyakh D. Shostakovicha* (Muzyka, Moscow, 1969), 272 pp. ['Polophony in the instrumental works of D. Shostakovich'.]

———— *et al.*, *Dmitri Schostakowitsch: Documente Interpretationen* (Herausgeber Stadt Duisburg, Dezernat für Bildung und Kultur & Westdeutscher Rundfunk Köln, 1984), 204 pp. [Programme book for the Duisburg International Shostakovich Festival, 16 Sept. 1984 to 15 Mar. 1985, with articles, concert and seminar schedule, and discography (label information given but not record numbers).]

Zakharov, Rostislav Vladimirovich, *Zapiski baletmeistera* (Iskusstvo, Moscow, 1976). [Recollections of a distinguished balletmaster.]

Zaporozhets-Ishlinskaya, Nataliya Vladimirovna, *Opery M. P. Musorgskogo — putevodite* (Muzyka, Moscow, 1980). [A paperback guide to the operas of Musorgsky with details of the Shostakovich versions of *Boris Godunov* and *Khovanshchina*.]

Zhelezny, Anatoli Ivanovich, *Nash drug—gramplastinka. Muzychna Ukrania* (Kiev, 1989), 280 pp. ['Our friend—the gramophone record'. A comprehensive history of sound recording in the USSR, with 12 pages of plates, and 79 photographs of record labels, equipment, and personalities in the text.]

Ziv, Sofya Samoilovna (compiler), *Muzykalnyi sovremennik* (Sovetskii Kompozitor, Moscow, 5th issue 1984), 75–89. [This collection of articles on contemporary music includes a review, with 5 music examples, on 'certain peculiarities of the style of Shostakovich's opera *The Gamblers*' by Alla Bogdanova.]

BBC Broadcasts

Abraham, Gerald, 'The String Quartets of Shostakovich', 15 Jan. 1977 and repeated 3 Feb. 1979. [Talk based on a lecture given at the 1976 Cheltenham Festival as an introduction to the complete cycle played by the Fitzwilliam Quartet. The quartets considered as mainly autobiographical documents in a profoundly perceptive survey, illustrated with music examples from Quartets Nos. 1, 3, 4, 5, 8, 10, 12, and 13; the Second Piano Trio, First Cello Concerto, *Lady Macbeth*, and Symphonies Nos. 1, 8, and 10.]

Amis, John, 'Shostakovich: Music in the Shadow of Stalin', BBC Transcription Service tape *c*.1988. [Interviews by John Amis; spoken contributions from Edward Downes, Solomon Volkov, Maksim Shostakovich, Galina Vishnevskaya, Mstislav Rostropovich, Luba Yedlina, Peter Pears, Rostislav Dubinsky, and the composer; illustrations from Opp. 114, 10, 16, 47, 60, 73, 79*a*, 93, 102, 110, and 135; excerpts read from *Testimony* and *Galina* by Ian Holm and Eleanor Bron respectively. Several views on the accuracy of the *Memoirs* expressed. 'My father never spoke harshly of his colleagues and other musicians and in that book there are several judgements which are extremely harsh—this was not characteristic of him at all'.]

Aronowitz, Cecil, 'The Viola Sonata', 20 June 1976. [An interview with Michael Oliver following Aronowitz's UK première of Shostakovich's last work and prior to the first broadcast performance.]

Barshai, Rudolf, 'Rudolf Barshai remembers Shostakovich', 29 and 30 Jan. 1984. [The conductor regards the controversial *Testimony* as 'true—the authentic voice of Shostakovich but not the whole story'. Music examples: the Jewish dance theme in the Finale of the Fourth Quartet and the coda of the Fifth Symphony (Barshai considered the latter 'a rejoicing sound under the stick. The axe, the guillotine is above you but you must rejoice and you must sing').]

Bell, Colin, *Northern Lights*, 20 Aug. 1997. [A recollection of the excitement surrounding Shostakovich's visit to the Edinburgh Festival in 1962 with the performance of 24 works over three weeks. Rozhdestvensky was allowed to perform the newly-released Fourth Symphony on condition that the Twelfth was also played. David Oistrakh was insistent on an extra rehearsal of the First Violin Concerto as it was to be performed in the presence of the composer. Shostakovich displeased with the rehearsal of *From Jewish Folk-Poetry*. Contributions from Lord Harewood, Andrew Porter, and conductors Rozhdestvensky and Mackerras. Excerpts from Opp. 110, 43, 112, and 70.]

Berkeley, Sir Lennox, and Layton, Robert, 'Tributes', 10 Aug. 1975. [Sir Lennox played parts of the slow movement of the Fifth Symphony, the start of the First Cello Concerto (the organic growth of which he admired), and the opening bars of the Thirteenth Quartet. Robert Layton gave an outline of Shostakovich's career as a composer, followed by analyses of the Piano Quintet and Tenth Symphony which were broadcast complete (Yedlina/ Borodin Quartet and Svetlanov respectively).]

Berkeley, Michael, 'From Lady Macbeth to Katerina and Back Again', 8 Nov. 1987. [An interval talk with translator David Pountney and conductors Mark Elder and Edward Downes about the chequered history of the opera. A simultaneous broadcast and television presentation of the English National Opera's production.]

———— 'The Leningrad Symphony', 3 Aug. 1991. [An interval talk on BBC Radio, shown simultaneously on BBC2 TV, preceding a Proms performance of the Seventh Symphony by the National Youth Orchestra of Great Britain under David Atherton. Interviews with Maksim Shostakovich, Galina Vishnevskaya (recalling the siege of Leningrad), Valeri Gergiev, and Semyon Bychov. Film clips shown on television: the composer playing the finale of the Piano Concerto No. 1, Leningrad under siege, and three conductors— Sir Henry Wood, Toscanini, and Stokowski—performing the Seventh Symphony.]

Fanning, David, 'The Breath of the Symphonist', 20 Aug. 1988 and repeated on 2 Aug. 1990. [An illustrated Proms interval talk on the Tenth Symphony.]

———— 'The Quotation Game', 11 Dec. 1991 and repeated on 12 Aug. 1992. [An interval talk before performances of the Fifteenth Symphony, discussing the secret and not-so-secret messages of musical quotation. *Tristan* quotations and cryptic allusions illustrated from the works of Wagner, R. Strauss, Berg, Ives, Tippett, and Pärt, ending with reflections on Shostakovich's Fifteenth (passing over the *William Tell* quotation as 'probably a bit of fun'). The start of the fourth movement and the Glinka song 'Do not tempt me needlessly' played.]

———— *Building a Library*, 'Shostakovich's Symphony No. 4', 24 and 28 Apr. 1993. [One music example from the deleted Kondrashin LP and eighteen from the eight recordings currently available on CD: one from Inbal, Slatkin, and Judd; two from Haitink ('a balanced integrated view on a Decca benchmark recording'), Rozhdestvensky (flawed by 'bizarre balancing acts from the recording engineers'), and Ashkenazy ('easily discarded on account of making heavy weather of the swarm-of-killer-bees first movement fugue'); four from Rostropovich ('becomes steadily more impressive and spoilt only by the last movement's rather slow dance medley and nasty aftertaste of the trumpets in the colossal apotheosis'); and five from the recommended version by the Scottish National Orchestra under Neeme Järvi ('surpassed only by Kondrashin').]

———— 'Russia in the 30s', 5 Mar. 1994. [The survival tactics of Russian composers during the age of terror. A two-hour programme of excerpts from the music of Shebalin, Knipper, Prokofiev, and Shostakovich (Op. 21—'Hopeless Love' and 'Death', Op. 27—'The Bureaucrat', Op. 32—'Night Watch' and 'Actors' Pantomine', Op. 34—four Preludes, Op. 39—Polka and Galop, and Op. 29—Passacaglia).]

——— *Symphonic Steppes*—1. 'A Breath Held Too Long', 2. 'Memorials of Our Great Epoch', and 3. 'The Tip of the Iceberg', 9–11 Nov. 1994. [Three twenty-minute talks on the surprising history of the Soviet Symphony. A listing of the musical excerpts gives an inkling of the scope of this epic series: Shostakovich No. 1, Myaskovsky No. 6 ('the first true Soviet symphony'—the finale quotes the two French revolutionary songs that Shostakovich was to use five years later in *New Babylon*), Roslavets and Popov Chamber Symphonies, Knipper No. 4 ('Meadowland' or 'Cavalry of the Steppes'), Shostakovich Nos. 4 and 5, Muradeli No. 1, Shostakovich No. 6, Prokofiev Nos. 5–7, Shostakovich Nos. 10 and 13, Boris Chaikovsky No. 2, Pärt No. 2, Kancheli No. 4, Silvestrov No. 5, and Schnittke No. 5.]

——— *Building a Library*, Shostakovich's Fifteenth Symphony, 4 and 8 Mar. 1995. [Ten CD versions appraised of the symphony Fanning likens to a Concerto for Orchestra, in order of examples: Ashkenazy, Kondrashin, Haitink, Serov, Dutoit, Järvi, Rostropovich, Sanderling, M. Shostakovich, and Slovák. The four short-listed all conducted by Russians: Rostropovich ('provides insight which no other version has to offer though with serious orchestral deficiencies'), Kondrashin ('a hard-driven performance with panache'), with the composer's son ('the only conductor who dares to let the music ebb and flow expressively') leading by a narrow margin.]

——— *Discovering Music*, Shostakovich's Eighth String Quartet, 21 Oct. 2001. (Two stories are told by means of a series of musical quotations and allusions, crafting this ready-made material into a new work of art. After three movements of quotes in chronological order, 'the fourth movement moves to a more universal level and shifts from identifying with the generality of the victims of fascism and war towards the terror in his own country'. The final movement pure fugue 'goes beyond self-absorption and self-pity, even beyond outrage and compassion, and transmutes them into high art'. Obviously with 11 September in mind, David Fanning summed up: 'It is times like this that we need music like this (Tippett), when the world seems to turn on its dark side. This music remains one of the most overwhelming, powerful memorials to humanity's victims'.]

George, Alan, 'An Interview with John Amis', 9 July 1976. [The Fitzwilliam Quartet violist's personal account of meetings with Shostakovich and the quartet's rehearsals in York in the presence of the composer.]

——— 'The Late Shostakovich Quartets', recorded on 21 July 1977, broadcast 12 Nov. 1978. [A detailed survey of Quartets Nos. 12 to 15 with music examples.]

——— 'An Autobiographical Quartet', 4 and 5 Mar. 1984. [An explanation of the motives behind the Eighth Quartet in the *Music Weekly* programme.]

Goldschmidt, Berthold, *Interpretations on Record*, 'Shostakovich's Fifth Symphony', 15 Apr. 1968. [Comparison of the versions by Ančerl, Bernstein, Horenstein, Kertész, Mravinsky, Previn, Rodzinski, Rowicki, and Silvestri. Overall preference: Mravinsky.]

Headington, Christopher, 'Fifth Symphony', 19 Oct. 1973. [Comparison of the recorded performances by Bernstein, Kertész, Previn (1965). Maksim Shostakovich, and Stokowski. Final choice: Previn.]

Hewett, Ivan, *Music Matters*, 15 and 16 Oct. 1994. [Gerard McBurney and David Pountney join in a discussion on the Pimlico Opera presentation of *Cheryomushki*. Excerpts from the original Melodiya recording and McBurney's re-orchestration.]

Hogwood, Christopher, *Comparing Notes*, 14 Dec. 1974 and 10 Aug. 1979. [An illustrated examination of some alphabetical devices used in music, including those on DSCH.]

Holm, Ian, *'Testimony*—readings from the memoirs of Shostakovich concerning the original version of *Lady Macbeth'*, 19 Nov. 1979.

Hopkins, Antony, *Talking about Music*, 29 and 30 Oct. 1978. [*Preludes and Fugues*, Opus 87.]

Johnson, Stephen, *Building a Library*, 'Shostakovich's Symphony No. 6', 24 Oct. 1987. [The Berglund, Bernstein, Chung, Haitink, Järvi, Kondrashin, Mravinsky, Previn, and Rozhdestvensky recordings compared; with Järvi's version emerging resoundingly as the library choice and a modern successor to Mravinsky's authoritative live performance of 1946.]

—— *Interpretations on Record*, 'Shostakovich's Fifth Symphony', 2 and 6 July 1988. [An hour-long review with 28 excerpts from twelve recorded versions dating from 1938 to 1986, revealing a disturbing trend towards an anti-Soviet slant following the publication of *Testimony*. 'One of the fascinating things about this great symphony is that it can lend itself to so many different kinds of interpretation. That, I think, is one of its strengths. It would be a tragedy if interpretation were to be tied to a one-sided political view.' Finest interpreters considered to be Mravinsky, Ančerl and, for all their faults, Previn and Bernstein.]

—— 'The Roots of *Testimony*', 1 and 2 Oct. 1989. [A *Music Weekly* talk exploring doubts on the authenticity of Volkov's book, with its several appropriations from the composer's own published writings, though some parts—including those dealing with Glazunov, Zoshchenko, and Meyerhold—are undoubtedly true. 'With telling, if unconscious irony, *Testimony* reproduces an old Soviet joke. Question: what's a walking stick? Answer: a well-edited Christmas tree. Is this what we have got here? Until we find out for certain, we will have to take *Testimony* with a good deal more than a pinch of salt.']

—— *Building a Library*, 'Shostakovich's Cello Sonata', 3 and 7 Feb. 1990. [Fifteen illustrations from the Rostropovich/composer 1957 recording of this 'many faceted work' ('scandalous that it has been out of the catalogue for so long') and 7 of the 10 currently available versions: Baillie, Harrell, Ma, Lloyd Webber, Turovsky, Thedeén, and Fujiwara. 'Yo-Yo Ma/Emanuel Ax offer the most deeply felt, confessional performance, with the intensity rising as it progresses, though the more classical Harrell/Ashkenazy version also has strength, vitality, and unity of vision'.]

——— *Record Review,* 'Two new versions of Shostakovich's Preludes and Fugues', 13 and 17 Apr. 1991. [Comparisons of new CD sets by Nikolayeva and Papadopoulos with music examples of the fugues of Nos. 12, 5, and 24 from the former and the prelude of No. 1 from both performers. Followed by complete recordings of Nikolayeva's Nos. 15 and 16.]

——— *Building a Library,* 'Shostakovich's String Quartet No. 8', 22 and 26 June 1991. [Seventeen currently available versions examined, six of them of the Chamber Symphony, Opus 110*a*. Examples played from the quartet performances of the Borodin (EMI and Virgin), Kronos, Manhattan, Moyzes, Duke ('tremendous playing' in the 'torrent of rage' second movement and with the finale 'heavy with personal sorrow'), Coull, Fitzwilliam, and Brodsky Quartets. Of Barshai's Chamber Symphony, Johnson sermonized 'It is an abomination. If there are gains they are heavily outweighed by the losses', though he considered the Kreisler String Orchestra's performance 'quite convincing on the whole'. Final choice: the EMI Borodin Quartet was 'the most moving interpretation. Their's is also the most complete—the one in which Shostakovich's Stations of the Cross seem to follow one another with the strongest sense of inevitability'. The Duke Quartet came a close second.]

——— 'The relationship between Britten and Shostakovich', 5 Nov. 1992. [An interval conversation with Malcolm MacDonald and John Evans, preceding a Royal Festival Hall performance of Shostakovich's Fourth Symphony, mentioning the parallels between the careers and the music of the two composers, the impression the 1936 concert version of *Lady Macbeth* made on Britten and its similarity with *Peter Grimes,* their experimentation with atonality, and the puzzling omission of Britten from *Testimony.* Music examples from Britten's *Our Hunting Fathers* (Funeral March epilogue) and Shostakovich's Fourteenth Symphony (2nd movement).]

——— 'Moscow and Leningrad in the 1920s', 23 Feb. 1993. [A cross-section of music, including Mosolov's *Iron Foundry,* Roslavet's Piano Sonata No. 5, Glière's *Red Poppy,* Leonid Utyosov's 1932 example of *Tea-Jazz* 'Wherever I might of wandered'; the two-hour programme concluding with Rozhdestvensky's recording of Shostakovich's Symphony No. 2.]

——— 'The Case of the Disappearing Symphony', 9 Mar. 1994 and repeated on 19 July 1994. [Interval talk before a concert performance of the Fourth Symphony under Simon Rattle. An investigation into the reason for its withdrawal in December 1936, with contributions from Gerard McBurney and Zinovi Zinik. From letters to Isaak Glikman, it is now believed Shostakovich wrote the Fourth as an act of defiance following mounting criticism and the jealousy of lesser composers culminating in the Pravda 'Muddle instead of music' (English translation of the article read by Gareth Armstrong). After one of many rehearsals the composer was asked to withdraw the symphony at the urgent request of the Leningrad Philharmonic's director, Isai Renzin.]

—— 'Brave Words, Brave Music', 16 Aug. 1998. [A 45-minute Proms Feature with fourteen brief music examples, starting and ending with excerpts from the Fourth Symphony—respectively, the opening pages and the frightening coda depicting the years of terror and mass treachery. David Fanning, Elizabeth Wilson, Solomon Volkov, Allan Ho, Dmitry Feofanov, and Gerard McBurney discussed with Stephen Johnson the Eighth Quartet and Symphonies Nos. 7, 10, 5, and 4. Volkov though told by the composer of a Tenth Symphony theme's connection with an Azerbaidzhan girl admitted he could not find any reference to her in the score and regretted he 'did not have the courage to press on this private matter at his next meeting'. McBurney stressed the importance to Russians of the words associated with songs quoted as themes in Shostakovich's works. The several quotations from *Testimony* were read by Christopher Scott.]

—— *Discovering Music*, 'Shostakovich's Symphony No. 6', 14 May 2000. [Unlocking the secrets of Opus 54 with the help of specially recorded examples from the BBC National Orchestra of Wales under conductor Brad Cohen.]

Kay, Norman, 'Sixth Symphony', 13 Apr. 1972. [An outline of Shostakovich's early career as a symphonist.]

—— 'Fifteenth Symphony', 20 Nov. 1972. [A detailed analysis with music examples, broadcast in the interval before the UK première.]

—— 'Thoughts on the Symphony', 10 Mar. 1974. ['Shostakovich's continuing faith in the symphony' with examples from Nos. 5 and 10.]

—— 'Shostakovich and the String Quartet', 3 Nov. 1974. [Nos. 1, 2, 3, 8, 9, and 12 discussed chronologically with music examples.]

Keeffe, Bernard, 'Russian Orchestral Style', 11 and 14 June 1989. [A historical analysis of the distinctive qualities of Soviet orchestras; illustrated by recordings of (i) Glinka's astonishing orchestral scoring, (ii) the Scherzo of Shostakovich's Tenth Symphony played at phenomenal speed by Mravinsky—'the shrill woodwind, the vibrant brass, and the tough sound of the side drum characteristic', (iii) the slow movement of Tchaikovsky's Fifth showing horn, oboe, and bassoon played with vibrato in the French style whereas the clarinet without, (iv) braying trumpets in Hindemith and, (v) Mravinsky's refined string ensemble in Stravinsky's *Apollo Musagetes*.]

Klier, John, 'Babi Yar', 18 Aug. 1992. [An interval talk before a Proms performance of Symphony No. 13, detailing the history of the massacre site at Kiev, Yevtushenko's controversial poem, and the subsequent erection of the memorials in 1976 and 1991.]

Layton, Robert, 'Shostakovich and his Eleventh Symphony', 9 Apr. 1967.

—— 'Shostakovich's Fourteenth Symphony', 14 June 1970. [An introductory talk preceding the English première from Aldeburgh.)
—— 'Shostakovich and his Thirteenth Symphony', 26 Sept. 1971.
—— 'Shostakovich as symphonist', 21 Mar. 1979 and repeated on 18 Apr. 1979.
McBurney, Gerard, 'Marking the Graves', 25 Feb. 1993. [The personal and political significance of the poems set in the Fourteenth Symphony; the subtle way one poem follows another and the often striking differences between the original eleven poems and the Russian translations that Shostakovich used. The subject of the text is death caused by oppression as opposed to the death in Musorgsky's *Songs and Dances of Death* who comes in the form of disease, snowstorm, and battle. A talk preceding a performance of the symphony at the 1993 'Festival of Britten'.]
—— 'A Hidden Agenda', 26 Feb. 1993, repeated on Aug. 1991 and 26 July 1996. [After the violence of the Fifth Symphony's finale opening march, Shostakovich as chronicler—introduces a coded message of resistance to Stalinist brutality in the lamenting central section; which opens with a haunting rocking string figure in octaves suggesting a reference to the beginning of the Monastery Scene in Musorgsky's *Boris Godunov* (where Pimen, the Scribe sets down the truth of the crimes of tyrants and the sufferings of the people in his time) and ends with a serene quotation from the composer's own setting of Pushkin's 'Renaissance' (op. 46 No. 1). Interval talk with seven music examples.]
—— *Voices*, 'The Songs of Shostakovich', 13/14 Apr., 10/11 May, 31 May/1 June, and 21/22 June 1995. [Four programmes exploring settings for voice and piano: 1. 'The Russian Classics' (Lermontov, Dostoyevsky, and Pushkin), 2. 'Shostakovich and Other Cultures' (British, Op. 62; Spanish, Op. 100; and Jewish, Op. 79), 3. 'Shostakovich and the Soviet World' ('Dundee's Romance' from *The Shot*, Mashenka's two songs from Op. 31, 'Song of the Counterplan', and the song cycles Opp. 109 and 143), and 4. 'Through Laughter and Tears' (song cycles Opp. 121 and 145). Performances specially recorded by Marina Shaguch (soprano), Mariana Tarassova, (mezzo-soprano), Konstantin Pluznikov (tenor), Mikhail Kit (baritone), Gyorgy Selezniev (bass), and Larissa Gergieva (piano) of the Mariinsky Theatre, St Petersburg.]
—— *The Fifties*, 'Music in the Soviet Union', 19 Mar. 1996; [Recollections of the transition from Stalin's final years of terror to the first euphoria of Khrushchev's reforms from Soviet musicians including Rostropovich, Tishchenko, Barshai, and Falich. Music examples from Prokofiev's Sinfonia Concertante, Ustvolskaya's Children's Suite, Khachaturyan's *Spartacus,* Shebalin's *The Taming of the Shrew,* Shostakovich's *Moscow, Cheryomushki,* Shchedrin's *Little Hump-backed Horse,* and Schnittke's Violin Concerto No. 1. The two-hour programme started and ended, respectively, with Shostakovich's *Four Monologues on Verses by Pushkin* (complete) and the Eleventh

Symphony (3rd and 4th movements from Mravinsky's 1967 Prague concert).]

———— *What's in a Name?*, 8 Aug. 1996 and repeated on 29 July 1997. [An interval talk with seven music examples, before Proms performances of Symphony No. 10, investigating its web of ciphers, initials, and allusions. The connection of the 3rd movement's 'Elmira' horn motive with the opening phrase of Mahler's *Das Lied von der Erde* and the allusions to Shostakovich's own setting of the second of the *Four Monologues on Verses by Pushkin*, Opus 91, 'What does my name mean to you?']

———— *Shostakovich's Leningrad*, 24 and 31 Oct. 1997. [McBurney wanders around the Leningrad that the composer knew during the (Nikolai Ivanovich) Yezkov Terror, with quotes from Anna Andreyevna Akhmatova's poem *Requiem*.]

———— 'A Work Withdrawn', 26 Feb. 1998. [The bizarre circumstances surrounding the cancellation of the Fourth Symphony as revealed in Isaak Glikman's letters. An interval talk recorded in St Petersburg with music examples from the choral portion of the Second Symphony and the notorious love scene from *Lady Macbeth;* followed by a synopsis of the Fourth by David Fanning and its original opening pages introduced by Mstislav Rostropovich before a complete performance broadcast from the Barbican Centre.]

———— 'Whose Shostakovich', 30 July 2000. [A BBC Proms lecture live from the Victoria and Albert Museum, London arguing that recent contradictory views on Shostakovich's life and work should not obscure his achievement as the composer of some of the most memorable music of the 20th century, with emphasis on three masterpieces *Lady Macbeth* and the 4th and 5th Symphonies.]

———— *Discovering Music*, 6 Aug. 2000. [A detailed 40-minute exploration of the Eighth Symphony with numerous recorded examples from the full and sections of the BBC National Orchestra of Wales under Philip Ellis and at-the-piano illustrations by the speaker.]

———— *Discovering Music*, 26 Aug. 2001. [An in-depth analysis of 'the formidable musical structure' of the Fifth Symphony: 'an echo chamber, a theatre of memories of Bach, Mahler, and Russian Orthodox Chant music respectively in the first three movements leading us towards that pivotal quotation in the middle section of the last movement, the Pushkin Rebirth song'. Music examples from the BBC National Orchestra of Wales under Grant Lewellyn.]

MacDonald, Calum, 'Late Shostakovich: an examination, of the last period of his career', 23 Apr. 1978. [The Fourteenth Symphony analysed in detail with music examples—found excessively depressing. Only glimmers of optimism noted in Fourteenth Quartet, Fifteenth Symphony, Viola Sonata, and Michelangelo Suite of his late works.]

———— '*Testimony:* the Shostakovich memoirs', 18 Nov. 1979. [A review in *Music Weekly* with music examples from Symphonies Nos. 10, 13, and 14.]

—— *Four Verses of Captain Lebyadkin,* 26 Jan. 1981. [An introductory talk to the first UK performance of Nesterenko's recording.]

—— 'Shostakovich's "48"', 11 Oct. 1981 and repeated three days later. [An appreciation in the *Music Weekly* series with recorded examples from the Op. 34 Preludes Nos. 1, 12, and 14 (Stokowski's transcription of the last) and the Op. 87 Prelude No. 10 (compared with Bach's 7th Prelude from *The Well-tempered Clavier,* Book 1), Fugue No. 16 (compared with Balakirev's B flat minor Piano Sonata, first movement), and the No. 24 Prelude and Fugue. The talk was followed by performances of Opp. 34 and 87 shared by Leslie Howard, John Bingham, Peter Wild, Kathryn Stott, and Martin Roscoe on five evenings.]

—— 'Shostakovich's Eighth Symphony—The Height of Tragedy', 29 and 30 Sept. 1985. [A *Music Weekly* item.]

—— 'Rothschild's Violin', 8 and 9 Dec 1985. Michael Oliver introduced the speaker's illustrated explanation of 'the opera Shostakovich completed but never started' in *Music Weekly.* 'It proves to be a score of real quality not quite like anything else in the Soviet repertory'.]

—— 'Britten and Shostakovich Compared', 3 and 4 May 1987. [A *Music Weekly* presentation with alternating music quotations from Shostakovich and Britten compositions: Interludes from *Lady Macbeth* and *Peter Grimes,* Scherzo from the Octet and a *Frank Bridge Variation,* DSCH epigram in *Preface to the Complete Collection* and *Rejoice in the Lamb,* Quartets Nos. 8 (DDS) and 3 (BB), 'O Delvig' from Symphony No. 14 and *A Time There Was.*]

—— 'Reading between the Lines', 1 Sept. 1987. [A Prom interval talk preceding a performance of the 'Leningrad Symphony'. Some of the hidden meanings in that work and other symphonies of the Stalin era explored. Four music examples: the 'ironic' Scherzo of the Seventh, the 'tragic' coda of the Fifth, and the 'Soviet Rossini' of *New Babylon* reappearing in the Ninth Symphony.]

Milner-Gulland, Professor Robin and McBurney, Gerard, 'Poet as Witness', 21 Aug. 1998. [An interval discussion, on the significance of the collaboration between the composer and the radical young poet Yevtushenko, before a Proms performance of Symphony No. 13. Including extracts from Ferlinghetti and Yevtushenko's 1972 readings of the poem 'Babi Yar' (from CBS 65052).]

Mival, William, *Building a Library,* 'Shostakovich's Piano Quintet', 20 and 21 Jan. 1996. [Nineteen music examples from the twelve currently available versions of 'simply the greatest piano quintet since Brahms'. 'Both the augmented Borodin and Beaux Arts Trios are acutely judged and sensitive performances. If you are looking for Slavic passion and melancholy perhaps the Borodin have the edge' but the very disciplined performance from the augmented Beaux Arts Trio is Mival's top recommendation.]

Morgan, Nick, *Building a Library,* 'Shostakovich's Symphony No. 4', 17 Mar. 2001. [Twenty-one excerpts from the first and third movements of fourteen

versions dating from 1962 to 1994 with the final choice falling to Simon
Rattle's performance at full price and Bernard Haitink's at mid-price.]

Nash, Peter Paul, *Building a Library*, 'Shostakovich's String Quartet No. 9', 7
Oct. 2000. [Nineteen music examples from eight recordings made between
the 1964 première and 1998. Of the Beethoven, Fitzwilliam, Eleonora,
Borodin (1981), Shostakovich, Éder, and Emerson, the first choice for their
'subtle sensitivity' was the Eleonora Quartet with the best budget CDs from
the Éder and Fitzwilliam Quartets.]

Nice, David, *Building a Library*, 'Shostakovich's Symphony No. 8', 7 and 11 Oct
1989. [The six available recordings discussed, generously illustrated with 19
music examples: Kondrashin, Mravinsky (1982), Rozhdestvensky, Solti,
Haitink, and Barshai. Library choice, despite its editing faults, Rozhdestvensky (CD only) or superbly recorded Haitink (if LP desired).]

—— *Record Review*, 9 and 13 Dec. 1989. [Reviews of *Rayok* (Rostropovich)
and *Katerina Izmailova* (Turchak) released on compact discs.]

Nicholson, Mairi, 'Solti and the BBC Philharmonic', 28 Dec. 1997. [An interval
talk with Sir Georg Solti during his only Bridgewater Hall, Manchester concert, 1 Mar. 1997, which included Musorgsky's *Khovanshchina* Prelude and
Songs and Dances of Death (both orch. Shostakovich) and the Fifteenth Symphony.]

Noble, Jeremy, 'Fifteenth Symphony', 16 Apr. 1972. [An introductory talk
prior to the first broadcast performance, with music examples from Symphonies Nos. 2, 4, 13, and 15.]

Norris, Geoffrey, 'DSCH—a musical monogram', 27 June 1976. [Musical illustrations from the Tenth and Fifteenth Symphonies, Eighth Quartet, First
Cello and First Violin Concertos.]

—— 'Tenth Symphony on Records', 18 Mar. 1978. [Comparison of the
Davis, Haitink, Karajan, and Svetlanov performances. Final choice: Haitink.]

—— *Building a Library*, 'Shostakovich's Symphony No. 10', 22 Mar. 1980.
[An illustrated review of the recorded performances of Berglund, Davis,
Haitink, Karajan, and Svetlanov. John Lade introduced the complete recom-
mended recording, Haitink's, four days later.]

—— *Building a Library*, 'Shostakovich's Piano Concerto No. 2', 14 June 1980.
[Four recordings evaluated: List/Maksim Shostakovich, Dmitri Shostako-
vich/Cluytens, Bernstein/Bernstein, and Ortiz/Berglund. John Lade introduced the recommended version, Eugene List's, five days later.]

—— 'The Suppressed Russian Avant-Garde', 15 and 16 Jan. 1984. [The
1920s—'years of trial and error'. Recorded examples from Mosolov's *Iron
Foundry* and the song *Newspaper Announcements*, Shostakovich's *The Nose*,
etc.]

Norris, Geoffrey, *Building a Library*, 'Shostakovich's Fifth Symphony', 28 Apr.
1984. [Excerpts from recorded performances of Berglund, Bernstein (1979),
Haitink, Kertész, Previn (1965 and 1978), Rostropovich, and Maksim Shostakovich.] 'I come down finally in favour of the Haitink version which for

me offers the most rewarding listening for its strength of idea, utterly convincing execution and consistent high quality of the playing.']

—— *Building a Library*, 'Shostakovich's Piano Quintet', 15 Dec. 1984. [Five
recordings discussed: Langer/Tálich Quartet, Music Group of London,
Benson/Alberni Quartet, Borodin Trio/Zweig/Horner, and Yedlina/
Borodin Quartet. While all have their fine points, the final preference was
for the Benson/Alberni Quartet.]

—— *Record Review*, 'Shostakovich's Cello Concerto No. 1', 27 Apr. 1985.
[The five recordings currently available in the West reviewed: Rostropovich, Tortelier, Wallfisch, Sádlo, and Yo-Yo Ma. Favoured performer
judged to be Rostropovich.]

—— *'Rothschild's Violin'*, 9 Dec. 1985. [An introductory talk with a synopsis
of the opera for the first UK broadcast of Rozhdestvensky's recording.]

—— *Building a Library*, 'Shostakovich's two piano concertos', 5 Apr. 1986.
[Examples played from recordings by Joyce, Ogdon, Rosenberger, Alekseyev, Previn, and Ortiz of Opus 35 and Dmitri Shostakovich junior, Bernstein, Alekseyev, and Ortiz of Opus 102. First choice for both concertos
falling to Alekseyev with an enthusiastic recommendation for Eileen
Joyce's 1941 recordings of the First which 'has much more than historical
interest'.]

Oliver, Michael, 'A conversation with the Borodin Piano Trio', 18 and 19 Nov.
1984. [The Piano Trio No. 2 'one of the greatest works of the twentieth century not only musically but as many other things are involved—the whole
life of the country, the situation in the country, years and years of pressure
from the regime—a musical protest against the violence. In the future a
study of this music will say more than a thousand pages of one's memoirs.'
And saying much for a long pause of pure silence following a performance
of the Quartet No. 8.]

—— *'D.S.C.H.'*, 6 and 7 Nov. 1988. [A *Music Weekly* examination of the
musical personality of Shostakovich. Michael Oliver talks to people who
knew him, performers and scholars: Yuli Turovsky, Mstislav Rostropovich,
Jeremy Noble, Solomon Volkov, Rudolf Barshai, Maksim Shostakovich,
Geoffrey Norris, Malcolm MacDonald, David Fanning, and Edward
Downes. Shostakovich's music is 'a mirror of his time' (Rostropovich), the
Soviet Rossini or Beethoven?, Volkov on coded messages, Barshai believing
the Ninth Symphony to be a mocking portrait of Stalin, and other topics
illustrated with recorded extracts from the key work, the Eighth Quartet
and Opp. 123, 93, 47, 70, 107, 60, and 29.]

—— *Building a Library*, 'Shostakovich's Fifth Symphony', 18 and 19 Jan.
1997. [Twenty-one music examples from sixteen performances aired and
twenty-six versions passed over (though 'remarkably few of them are actually bad but some are fairly poorly recorded'). Mackerras with the Royal
Philharmonic, Previn with the London Symphony, and Järvi with the Scottish National Orchestra on the short list; but Haitink, Bernstein, and the

1984 Mravinsky removed with regret. Previn's pre-*Testimony* recording of
1965 the library recommendation proving 'what a towering, tragic master-
piece this symphony is'.]

Ottaway, Hugh, 'Tenth Symphony', in two parts on 6 and 13 June 1961. [Nos.
36 and 37 in a series on *The Symphony*.]

—— 'Cello Concerto No. 1', 15 May 1962. [No. 31 in a series on *The Concerto*.]

—— 'Fifth Symphony', in two parts on 23 Feb. and 2 Mar. 1966. [Nos. 21 and
22 in 'Studies in Form'—a detailed analysis movement by movement.] Also
interval talks on 10 May 1970 ['Shostakovich's Fifth Symphony prompts
Hugh Ottaway to some deliberately provocative observations about the
present state of music'] and 22 Jan. 1971 (repeated on 6 Nov. 1972).

—— 'Shostakovich at 60', 4 Oct. 1966 and repeated on 11 Mar. 1967.

—— 'Eighth Symphony', 8 Mar. 1970. [Interval talk.]

—— 'The Three Wartime Symphonies', 19 May 1971 and repeated on 5 Oct.
1972. [An illustrated interval talk on Nos. 7, 8, and 9, with particular reference to the Ninth.]

—— 'Shostakovich's Symphonies', 25 Jan. 1976. [A review in *Music Weekly*.]

—— *Interpretations on Record*, 'Shostakovich's Tenth Symphony', 23 Sept.
1979. [Comparison of the versions by Ančerl, Berglund, Haitink, Karajan,
Mitropoulos, Mravinsky, Svetlanov, and Tjeknavorian. No overall preference.]

Parrott, Sir Cecil, 'Sketches of Musical Life in Moscow, 1954–7', 25 Feb. 1978.
[Illuminating recollections of meetings with Soviet composers and musicians during the time Sir Cecil was attached to the British Embassy.]

Reynolds, Peggy, Sound Stories, 2 Mar. 1999. [In the second of the week's
'Family Affairs' talks the life of Shostakovich was sketched with recorded
illustrations from the *Festive Overture*, Bach's Book 1 Prelude and Fugue in
C (Richter), Fantastic Dance from Opus 6 (Gräsbeck and Zelyakov), Sym-
phony No. 5 scherzo (Maksim Shostakovich), Suite for Jazz Orchestra No. 1,
'Babi Yar', and Piano Concerto No. 2 (Dmitri Shostakovich jr.).]

Rigby, Cormac, 'Royal Repertoire—Kenneth MacMillan's *Concerto* and *Sym-
phony*', 24 Mar. 1976. [Ballets to the music of Opp. 102 and 10 described.
Complete recordings of the Second Piano Concerto (Ortiz/Berglund) and
First Symphony (Kondrashin).]

Roseberry, Eric, 'The Humanity of Shostakovich', 13 Aug. 1979 (repeat).
[Music examples from Seventh Symphony and Second Cello Concerto.]

—— 'Shostakovich and His War Symphonies', 14 Nov. 1990. [An interval
talk, without music examples, analysing the Eighth Symphony and examining its contemporary significance.]

—— 'The Protective Mask of Buffoonery', 5 Mar. and 1 Sept. 1991.
['Sollertinsky was able to provide support for ideas embodied in Shostakovich's opera, *The Nose* . . . and open his mind to musical experience he had
hardly begun to confront . . . the complex autobiographical or programmatic symphonies of Gustav Mahler, with their idioms of Jewish music, the

mocking funeral marches, the lyric darkened by the grotesque'. Three music examples: the Jewish dance finale of the Second Piano Trio, the third movement of Mahler's Second Symphony, and the shrill woodwind cries from Shostakovich's First Cello Concerto.]

Seckerson, Edward, *Building a Library*, 'Shostakovich's Seventh Symphony, the "Leningrad"', 7 and 11 Jan. 1989. [*Record Review*, introduced by Jeremy Siepmann. Six recordings in contention: Järvi, Rozhdestvensky, Haitink, Nanut, Berglund, and Yansons. The reviewer welcomed the change of heart in universal acceptance of the symphony, once sneered at on account of the 'steam-rolling ostinato of the 1st movement . . . one of the most maligned, and I think, misunderstood passages in the whole of symphonic literature—all 280 bars of it'. Nanut considered 'dispiritingly routine' and Yansons 'cool and rather bloodless'. First choice: Järvi and the Scottish National Orchestra (in spite of the rather pressed opening) with Haitink a close second (tough the Decca CD given a black mark for the nine-second pause between the third and fourth movements).]

———— *Building a Library*, 'Shostakovich's Symphony No. 1', 4 and 8 May 1991. [*Record Review* presented by Richard Osborne. Eight recordings considered with single excerpts from the Haitink, Levine, Leighton Smith, Ashkenazy, and Kondrashin (1972) versions, three from Bernstein, and four each from Rozhdestvensky and Järvi—the powerful performance of the last-named being pronounced the library choice with Bernstein a close second.]

Smith, Professor Jerry, 'Hits of the 20s', 25 Feb. 1993. [The history of the popular post-revolutionary marching song, 'Thro' the dales and o'er the hills', utilised for Opp. 48 and 74.]

Strauss, Eva, 'Leningrad Speaks', 30 Nov. 1973. [A dramatized account of the 880-day siege of Leningrad, based on the diaries of Vera Inber, Olga Berggolts, and Vera Panova, movingly punctuated by extracts from the 'Leningrad Symphony'.]

Walsh, Stephen, *Record Review*, 'A new set of the complete quartets of Shostakovich', 16 and 20 Feb. 1991. [A review of the Brodsky Quartet's performances, with examples from the Allegretto furioso of the Tenth, the first movement of the Fifth, the Serenade of the Fifteenth, and the final bars of the Eighth. 'A fine set as a whole and an impressive conspectus of one of the most moving quartet cycles of our time'.]

Warrack, John *Building a Library*, 'Shostakovich's Tenth Symphony', 25 and 29 Man 1989. [*Record Review* introduced by Richard Osborne. Six of the nine currently available versions considered: Järvi, Karajan, Haitink, Rozhdestvensky, Rattle, and the latest, Andrew Litton. Järvi, Rattle, and Haitink proclaimed strong performances but overtaking all, Rozhdestvensky (with 6 of the 16 recorded extracts), 'The symphony's ferocity, its bleakness, its impassiveness at times: finally, its sense of suffering overcome at a terrible price: all this is understood as if in personal sympathy by Gennadi Rozhdestvensky'.]

West, Ewan, 'The Octets of Mendelssohn and Shostakovich', 15 Sept. 1988. [A Proms interval talk preceding the performance of both works by the combined Cleveland and Melos Quartets.]

This Week's Composer, 'Shostakovich', 16–22 Nov.1974. Quartets Nos. 7, 8, 11, and 12 (played by the Borodin Quartet); Prelude and Fugue No. 1 (Shostakovich), and vocal works: *The Execution of Stepan Razin* (Kondrashin), *The Song of the Forests* (Yurlov), *The Sun Shines over our Motherland* (Kondrashin), *Loyalty* (Ernesaks), and *Seven Romances on Poems of Aleksandr Blok* (Pracht).

This Week's Composer, 'Shostakovich plays Shostakovich', 30 Oct.–3 Nov. 1978. Prelude and Fugues Nos. 3, 5, 7, 16, 20 and 23; Piano Quintet, Cello Sonata, the two Piano Concertos, Concertino, *From Jewish Folk Poetry*, Piano Trio No. 2, and four Preludes from Op. 34 arranged for violin and piano.

This Week's Composer, 'Dmitri Shostakovich', 23–27 June 1980. *Lady Macbeth of Mtsensk District*—Finale of Act 1 (Rostropovich), Symphonies Nos. 4 (Previn) and 13 (Kondrashin), 'Songs of the Fool' from *King Lear* and *Preface to the Complete Collection* (Nesterenko), Third Quartet (Beethoven Quartet), *From Jewish Folk Poetry*—Nos. 1 to 8 (composer at piano), First Viol¹ ¹ Concerto (Oistrakh/Mravinsky), and *The Sun Shines over our Motherland* (Kondrashin).

This Weeks Composer, Shostakovich 'The Early Years'. 8–12 Mar. 1982. *Three Fantastic Dances* (composer), Piano Trio No. 1 (Oslo Trio), Prelude of Op. 11 (Borodin and Prokofiev Quartets), Scenes 2–4 of *The Nose* (Rozhdestvensky), *Tahiti Trot* (Svetlanov), *New Babylon* excerpts and *Columbus* Overture (Rozhdestvensky), *The Bolt* (Maksim Shostakovich), Act 1 Finale of *Lady Macbeth* (Rostropovich), Preludes Nos. 15, 16, and 19 (Berman), First Piano Concerto (Krainev), Cello Sonata (Shafran/Pecherskaya), *Five Fragments* (Blazhkov), and Symphonies Nos. 1, 2, and 3 (Kondrashin).

This Week's Composer, Shostakovich 'The Final Years'. 4–8 Mar. 1985. *Preface to the Complete Collection* (Nesterenko), Quartet No. 11 (Beethoven Quartet), Cello Concerto No. 2 (Rostropovich/Ozawa), *Seven Romances on Poems of Aleksandr Blok* (Vishnevskaya), Violin Concerto No. 2 (Oistrakh), Symphonies Nos. 14 (Rostropovich) and 15 (M. Shostakovich), *Suite on Verses of Michelangelo* Nos. 10 and 11 (Nesterenko/Shostakovich), *Four Verses of Captain Lebyadkin* (Nesterenko), and Viola Sonata (Druzhinin).

Composers of the Week, 'Shostakovich: Early Works' (coupled initially with Brahms). 4–8 July and repeated 11–15 July 1988. *Three Fantastic Dances* (composer), *Scherzo in E flat major* (Rozhdestvensky), Piano Sonata No. 1 (Postnikova), Symphonies Nos. 1 (Järvi), 2 and 3 (Haitink), Act 1 of *The Nose* (Rozhdestvensky); Preludes Nos. 1, 4, 10, and 12; *The Age of Gold* (Haitink), *Tahiti Trot* (Järvi), *The Bolt* (Maksim Shostakovich), Piano Concerto No. 1 (Alekseyev), *The Human Comedy* excerpts, *Lady Macbeth* Suite (Järvi), Cello Sonata (Turovsky/Yedlina), and Scherzo of Symphony No. 4 (Previn).

Composers of the Week, 'Shostakovich: Propagandist!' (coupled initially with Haydn). 12–16 Feb. and repeated 19–23 Feb. 1990. *The Bedbug* (Rozhdestvensky), *The Golden Age* and Symphony No. 2 (Haitink), 'The Assault on Beautiful Gorky' (Alekseyev), *Ten Poems* (Minin), *A Year as Long as a Lifetime* (Shostakovich), *Five Days, Five Nights* (Serebrier), *The Execution of Stepan Razin* (Gromadsky), *October* (Järvi), Solemn March (Sergeyev), 'Battle by the Volga' (Silantiev), Symphony No. 12 (Rozhdestvensky), *Song of the Forests* (Yurlov), and *Rayok* (Rostropovich).

Composer of the Week, 'Dmitri Shostakovich: The War Years'. 11–15 Oct. 1993, presented by David Fanning. Quartet No. 1 (Borodin Quartet), Symphony No. 6 (Mravinsky), *Rothschild's Violin* excerpts and *The Adventures of Korzinkina* (Rozhdestvensky), Piano Sonata No. 2 (Gilels), *King Lear* Op. 58*a* excerpts (Rozhdestvensky), Symphony No. 8 (Kondrashin), *Zoya* Finale (M. Shostakovich), Piano Trio No. 2 (composer), *Six Romances on Verses by British Poets* (Safiulin), *The Young Guard* Overture (Gamburg), Quartet No. 3 (Borodin Quartet), and Symphony No. 9 (Kondrashin).

Composer of the Week, 'Dmitri Shostakovich'. 14–18 Aug. 1995, presented by William Mival. *Scherzo in F sharp minor* (Rozhdestvensky), Cello Sonata (specially recorded by Ioan Davies and Jana Frenklova), Adagio from *The Limpid Stream* (Webber/M. Shostakovich), Ballet Suite No. 1 (Järvi), *Overture on Russian and Kirghiz Folksongs* (Järvi), Piano Quintet (Drucker/Dutton/Beaux Arts Trio), *Age of Gold* Suite (Järvi), *Scherzo in E flat major* (Rozhdestvensky), Piano Trio No. 2 (Beaux Arts Trio), *The Fall of Berlin* Suite Nos. 1 and 5–8 (Serebrier), Two Pieces Op. 11 (Academy of St Martin), String Quartet No. 5 (Borodin Quartet), 'The Assault on Beautiful Gorky' (Alekseyev), *Six Romances on Verses by British Poets* (Leiferkus/Järvi), *October* (Järvi), *Four Verses of Captain Lebyadkin* (Fischer-Dieskau/Ashkenazy), and *The Bolt* Suite Nos. 1–8 (Järvi).

Composer of the Week, 'Dmitri Shostakovich: The Early Years'. 16–20 Feb. and repeated 23–7 Feb. 1998, presented from St Petersburg by Gerard McBurney. 1. The Impertinent Student—*Scherzo in E flat major* (Rozhdestvensky), *Aphorisms* (Varvarova), *New Babylon* excerpts (Judd), Symphony No. 2 (Kondrashin), *The Dragonfly and the Ant* (Dyadkova/Järvi); 2. Thumbing His Nose—*The Bedbug* Suite Nos. 1, 5–7 (Rozhdestvensky), *Six Romances on Japanese Poems* Nos. 1–3 (Levinsky/Järvi), *Alone* Reel 3 No. 1 (Yurovsky), *The Nose* Scenes 3–7 (Rozhdestvensky), *Tahiti Trot* (Chailly); 3. The Professional Theatre Composer—*Columbus Overture* (Rozhdestvensky), *The Golden Mountains* Fugue (Serebrier), *The Shot* Dundee's Romance (Pluzhnikov), *Hypothetically Murdered* Galop orch. McBurney (Elder), *The Golden Age* Scene 6 (Rozhdestvensky), *Three Fantastic Dances* (composer); 4. The Irrepressible Performer—'United Nations March' arr. Stokowski (Bambert), *The Tale of the Priest and His Servant Balda* start of Act 1 (Kozhin), *The Bolt* 'The Bureaucrat' and 'The Blacksmith' (Rozhdestvensky), *Hamlet* Op. 32 score Nos. 35–8 and 44 (Elder), *The Big Lightning* Matofel's Song (Myasoyedev), Preludes Op. 34 Nos. 13–24 (Nikolayeva), *Jazz Suite No. 1* Foxtrot (Elder); 5. Gathering Clouds—*The Human Comedy* 'Police March', Gavotte and 'Bank of the Seine' (Serov), *The Limpid Stream* Adagio (Rozhdestven-sky), *The Girl Friends* Three Preludes (Postnikova *et al.*), *Five Fragments* Nos. 3–5 (Elder), *Lady Macbeth* Scene 3 complete (Rostropovich), and *Four Romances on Poems* by Pushkin No. 1 (Kharitonov/Elder).

Composer of the Week, 'Shostakovich'. 7–11 August 2000, presented by Donald Macleod. Symphony No. 1 first movement (Haitink), Two Pieces Op. 11 (Academy of St Martin), *Lady Macbeth* excerpt (Vishnevskaya/Rostro-povich), Cello Sonata (Isserlis/Mustonen), Symphony No. 5 first move-ment (Jansons), *Song of the Forests* 'When the War was Over' (Temirkanov), Quartet No. 4 first movement (Brodsky Quartet), Violin Concerto No. 1 Nocturne (Sitkovetsky/Davis), Symphony No. 10 last movement (Karajan 1981), *Four Romances on Poems by Pushkin* 'Presentiment' Op. 46*a* (Leifer-kus/Järvi), Symphony No. 7 first movement (Järvi), Quartet No. 2 second movement (Borodin Quartet), Symphony No. 8 second movement (Haitink), *From Jewish Folk Poetry* 'Lullaby' (Järvi), Piano Concerto No. 1 first movement (Ogdon), Piano Quintet Prelude and Fugue (Brown/Nash Ensemble), Fugue in C major (Nikolayeva), Piano Trio No. 2 (Mustonen), Symphony No. 15 first movement (M. Shostakovich), Quartet No. 12 first movement (Fitzwilliam Quartet), *Three Fantastic Dances* (Vazaronov), and Viola Sonata (Druzhinin).

Appendix I

Collections of Shostakovich's Music and Addresses of Music Publishers

Several collections of Shostakovich's music have been published. These include the album *Waltzes from Film Music* by Sovetskii Kompozitor in 1959, comprising full scores of eight waltzes from Opp. 45, 30, 78, 76, 97, 99, 95, and 37. A three-volume Soviet edition *Compositions for fortepiano* appeared separately in 1966, 1968, and 1969. The volume entitled *Vocal Compositions* has been published with recent additions from time to time by Muzyka; the 1974 issue containing the song cycles Opp. 46, 62, 79, 91, 98, 100, 109, and 143. The string quartet Nos. 1 to 8 were published in two volumes by Muzyka, Nos. 30858–9 (size 21 cm.) in 1964; by Edwin F. Kalmus, Nos. 429 and 430 (18 cm.), and in the Edition Peters, Nos. 5728*a* and *b* (19 cm.) in the 1970s. Hans Sikorski issued study scores (21 cm.) of the fifteen quartets in five volumes between 1978 and 1981 (No. 2265 covers 1–4; 2266, 5–8; 2267, 9 and 10; 2268, 11 and 12; 2209, 13–15). Excerpts from Symphonies Nos. 1, 5, and 7, transcribed for piano solo by Ludwig Flato, were published by Leeds Music in 1946. Lev Atovmyan compiled a volume of 24 songs from film scores, arranged for voice(s) and chorus with piano accompaniment, published by Sovetskii Kompozitor—No. 519, 1958, 29 cm. and several collections of 'not difficult pieces' for pianoforte being simplified reductions of film and ballet numbers—including a ballet suite *Choreographic Miniatures*; 21 pieces arranged as *Events of a Day* first appearing in 1962 with a second edition published by Sovetskii Kompozitor in 1973 (No. 2618, 29 cm.) and in the Edition Sikorski also in 1973 (No. 2202, 31.5 cm.); and 25 pieces entitled *Roundabout of Dances*, incorporating *Dances of the Dolls* Nos. 1–5 and 7, published by Edition Sikorski in 1970 (No. 2201, 31.5 cm.) and G. Schirmer in 1972 (No. 1887, with two piano duets added by editor Joseph Prostakoff, 31 cm.). Atovmyan accomplished sterling work in assembling suites from Shostakovich's film scores, reorchestrating numbers, extending and rounding off fragments where necessary for concert performance, with the full approval of the composer. These suites are fully detailed under the original opus numbers. Frederick Block arranged and edited various pre-1938 items for a *Contemporary Masterpieces: Album No. 19* and 1947. This collection was reissued as *Shostakovich: Nine Pieces for Piano* and published by Edward B. Marks, New York (No. 11668–8 *et al.*, 1951–7, 30 cm.). The pieces are the first movement from the First Symphony; Russian Dance and Polka from *The Golden Age;* Prelude, Opus 34 No. 4; the Scherzo of the Fifth Symphony; three extracts from *Lady Macbeth of Mtsensk District*—Dance (commencing at fig. 384), Interlude (fig. 113), and Grotesque Scene (fig. 434); and Marche Sarcastique from *Hamlet,* Opus 32. A selection of eight pieces from ballet, operetta, and film scores, arranged by Dénes Agay under the title *Melodic Moments,* was published in 1969. *Orchestral studies for flute* (excerpts from Symphonies Nos. 1–3 and 5–9), edited by John Wummer, was published by Leeds Music in 1949 (31 cm). *Orchestral studies for clarinet,* edited by H. Roscher, was published by Friedrich Hofmeister of Leipzig; and another compilation by A. A. Aleksandrov was published by Muzyka in 1964 (29 cm.). Trumpet studies compiled by H. Krumpfer from Shostakovich compositions appear in Hofmeister, Volume 10.

An enterprising subscription edition of the *Collected Works* in 42 volumes, announced by Muzyka in 1977, was published between 1979 and 1987. Many compositions appeared in print for the first time. All works were collated with the composer's manuscript. Each cloth-bound volume contains a portrait and a facsimile page of one composition's autograph. The distinguished editorial committee included Tikhon Khrennikov, Rodion Shchedrin, Vasili Kukharsky, Yevgeni Svetlanov, Leonid Sidelnikov, Konstantin Titarenko, Konstantin Fortunatov, Boris Chaikovsky, Grigori Shneyerson (d. February 1982), and Maksim Shostakovich (dropped from the panel in 1981). Manashir Yakubov compiled much of the editorial material and though his name appeared on proof pages in 1978 his considerable contribution was not credited in the published volumes. Volumes 1 to 9 cover the symphonies; 10 and 11, overtures and other orchestral works; 12 to 17, the concertos in full score and piano reduction; 18 to 25, the operas in full and vocal score; 26, the ballet suites; 27 and 28, theatre music; 29 and 30, the cantatas in full and vocal score; 31 to 33, the vocal compositions; 34, choral works; 35 to 38, chamber music; 39 and 40, the pianoforte works; and 41 and 42, suites and items for film scores. DSCH Publishers of Moscow announced a *New Collected Works* in mid-1999. This edition of 150 volumes will include over 80 works published for the first time.

Music publishers

The addresses of the main publishers and distributors of Shostakovich's music are listed below. Some refer to early publications and may be obsolete.

Anglo-Russian Music: formerly of 16 Manette Street, London W1.

Anglo-Soviet Music Press: subsidiary company of Boosey & Hawkes founded in the Second World War.

Belwin Mills Music: 250 Purley Way, Croydon, Surrey CR9 4QD.

Boosey & Hawkes: Boosey & Hawkes Music Publishers Ltd., 295 Regent Street, London W1R 8JH.

Breitkopf & Härtel: VEB Breitkopf & Härtel, Musikverlag Leipzig, 701 Leipzig C1, Karlstrasse 10, Deutsche Democratische Republik.
20 Earlham Street, London WC2H 9LN.
Le Chant du Monde: 31/33 rue Vandrezanne, 75013 Paris. France
Collets: Collets Holdings Ltd., Denington Estate, Wellingborough, Northamptonshire NN8 2QT. Ceased trading in July 1993.
Deutscher Verlag für Musik: see Breitkopf & Härtel.
DSCH Publishers: Olsufrievski Pereulok 8, No. 5, Moscow 119 021, Russia.
Edition Eulenberg: Ernst Eulenberg Ltd., 8134 Adlisivil 2 H, Grutstrasse 28, Zurich, Switzerland.
48 Great Marlborough Street, London W1V 2BN.
International Music: International Music Co., New York. Alfred A. Kalmus Ltd., 2–3 Fareharm Street, Dean Street, London W1V 4DU.
Edwin F. Kalmus: Belwin Mills Music, 250 Purley Way, Croydon, Surrey CR9 4QD.
Leeds Music: Leeds Music Corporation, New York.
138 Piccadilly, London W1V 9FH.
Leeds Music (Canada): 2540 Victoria Park Evenue, Willowdale 425, Ontario, Canada.
215 Victoria Street, Toronto 2, Ontario, Canada.
MCA: Musical Corporation of America Inc., 543 West 43rd Street, New York 10036, USA.
Musica Rara: Le Traversier, Chemin de la Buire, 84170 Monteux, France. Formerly of 2 Great Marlborough Street, London W1V 2EE.
Edition Musicus: 333 West 32nd Street, New York 10019, USA.
Muzichna Ukraina: 32 Pushkinska, Kiev, USSR.
Muzgiz: abbreviation for the Music Sector of the State Publishing House, Moscow and Leningrad. Prior to 1921 it bore the name of the Music Section of the Gosizdat of the RSFSR.
Muzyka: State Music Publishing establishment founded in 1964.
14 Neglinnaya Street, Moscow, USSR.
9 Inzhenernaya Street, Leningrad, USSR.
Edition Peters: 746 Postschliessfach, Talstrasse 10, 701 Leipzig, Deutsche Democratische Republik.
Peters Edition Ltd. formerly of Wardour Street, London.
Peters Edition Ltd., 10—12 Baches Street, London N1 6DN.
Ricordi: G. Ricordi & Co., 20121 Milano, Via Berchet 2, Italy.
1808 The Bury, Church Street, Chesham, Buckinghamshire.
Novello became the sole British selling agent in January 1979.
8 Lower James Street, London W1.
Schirmer: G. Schirmer Inc, 257 Park Avenue South, 20th floor, New York, USA.
140 Strand, London WC2R 1HG.
Hans Sikorski: Internationale Musikverlag Hans Sikorski, Postfach 13 08 48, Johnsallee 23, 20148 Hamburg, Germany.

Sovetskii Kompozitor: this off-shoot of the State Music Publishers for contemporary Soviet music was established in 1956, with the head office in Moscow and a branch in Leningrad. It was merged with Muzgiz in 1964 to form Muzyka and reinstated in mid-1967.

24 Yuzhnoportovaya Street, Moscow 109088, USSR.

Triton: Leningrad publishing house for modern music in the 1920s.

Universal Edition: Vienna, Mainz, and Zurich.

Alfred A. Kalmus, 2–3 Fareham Street, Dean Street, London W1V 4DU.

VAAP: Copyright Agency of the USSR, 6a Bolshaya Bronnaya Street, Moscow 103104, USSR.

It should be noted that, owing to copyright restrictions, many editions of the music listed are not available for sale in the United Kingdom. This applies to the rich G. Schirmer/Associated Collection of Russian-Soviet Music catalogue of VAAP authorized editions which is confined to use in the USA. For all UK enquiries regarding Soviet music contact the firm of Boosey & Hawkes. Information on the Shostakovich *New Collected Works* edition and scores and parts for hire can be obtained from DSCH Publishers, Moscow.

With the disintegration of the Soviet Union, State Music organisations have been discontinued or reorganised. Their former names and addresses are listed above for reference purposes.

Appendix II

Television and Theatre Productions

A Soviet film *Dmitri Shostakovich*, subtitled 'Études towards a portrait of the composer', directed by Albert Gendelshtein was shown in Moscow on 3 April 1967. Four further films were released between 1977 and 1982: *The Composer Shostakovich* (Yuri Belyankin), *Shostakovich—the composer and his times* (B. Goldenblank), and see under Opus 145 for the 1977 film *Recollections of Shostakovich* and Opus 147 for the 1981 film *Sonata for Viola*.

Belyankin's 60-minute film *The Composer Shostakovich* (1975) documentary includes extracts from rehearsals and première performances, in the presence of the composer, of *The Nose* (Rozhdestvensky), Quartet No. 15 (Taneyev Quartet, accompanied by wintry cityscapes of Leningrad), *Michelangelo Suite* (Nesterenko and Shenderovich, illustrated with examples of the poet's paintings and sculptures), and the finale of Symphony No. 15 (his son conducting), interspersed with an interview in the composer's Moscow flat. Screened with French subtitles on the Muzak cable television channel on 25 January 1999 and presented by its scenario author Oksana Dvornichenko, under the title 'Three Premières', at the Glasgow '25 Years On' Symposium on 27 October 2000.

Two 45-minute documentaries shown on East Germany TV (DDR 1): *Seine Musik Lebt Weiter* (His Music Lives On). A Soviet production dubbed into German includes interviews with Shostakovich and Rozhdestvensky, with film clips from several historic performances and scenes of the composer's funeral shown to the music of the Piano Trio No. 2. *Memories of Shostakovich*. Fragments from four compositions, here with the funeral scenes accompanied by Quartet No. 8, and including a complete Symphony No. 1 played by the Gewandhaus Orchestra under Kurt Masur.

Fragments from twenty-one compositions, interviews with Shostakovich and extracts from historic films were presented in the BBC Television *Omnibus* documentary 'Music from the Flames'. The hour-long film, with script by Norman Kay, was produced by Ian Engelmann and screened on BBC TV1 on 10 November 1974. It was repeated as a tribute to the composer on 10 August 1975, the day following his death. Works were featured in the following order:

Op. 93, Tenth Symphony (parts of the second movement)
Op. 5, *Fantastic Dances* (film clip of Nos. 1 and 2 played by the composer)

Op. 10, First Symphony (film clip of the first movement conducted by Maksim Shostakovich)

Op. 27, *The Bolt* (The Bureaucrat)

Op. 114, *Katerina Izmailova* (Act 3, the arrival of the police and Act 2, the flogging of Sergei—from the film starring Galina Vishnevskaya)

Op. 43, Fourth Symphony (fragments from the first and second movements rehearsed by Gennadi Rozhdestvensky)

Op. 47, Fifth Symphony (portions of the first and third movements conducted by Maksim Shostakovich)

Op. 67, Second Piano Trio (opening of the fourth movement)

Op. 60, Seventh Symphony (parts of the 1st movement march and coda conducted by Arvid Yansons at a Leningrad concert to mark the thirtieth anniversary of the siege)

Op. 110, Eighth Quartet (opening of the fourth movement and the DSCH motto)

Op. 142, Fourteenth Quartet (a fragment of the third movement played by the Beethoven Quartet)

Op. 35, First Piano Concerto (a clip of the conclusion of the work, with the composer as soloist, filmed at a 1941 concert)

Op. 57, Piano Quintet (concluding bars of the Intermezzo)

Op. 87, Preludes and Fugues (Prelude of No. 1 and Fugue of No. 15 played by Tatyana Nikolayeva)

Op. 134, Violin Sonata (film clip of the opening played by David Oistrakh and Svyatoslav Richter)

Op. 77, First Violin Concerto (the Burlesque with Igor Oistrakh as soloist)

Op. 103, Eleventh Symphony (a film of Igor Belsky's ballet danced to the second movement)

Op. 119, *The Execution of Stepan Razin* (a rehearsal under Maksim Shostakovich)

Op. 135, Fourteenth Symphony (eighth movement sung by Yevgeni Nesterenko and accompanied by the Moscow Chamber Orchestra under Rudolf Barshai)

Op. 140, *Six Romances on Verses by British Poets* (Jenny sung by Nesterenko)

Op. 141, Fifth Symphony (the coda of the fourth movement)

Op. 47, Fifth Symphony (the code of the fourth movement).

The music feature in *Saturday Review,* shown on BBC2 TV on 27 September 1986, discussed the hotly contested authenticity of Solomon Volkov's *Testimony.* Irina Shostakovich remarked that Volkov visited them but rarely. Michael Berkeley interviewed the author and Maksim Shostakovich. Volkov, 'a fanatical devotee', stated he had had regular contact with the composer over ten years and 'he happened to be the right person at the right time'. Maksim, since his defection, has more or less endorsed the controversial 'memoirs': 'It has opened a big interest [in Shostakovich] in the Western World. Sometimes too much rumour but the basis of the book is true . . . accurate.'

A music-theatre piece *Black Sea Follies* centred on the stark conflict between Stalin and Shostakovich—the struggle between tyrant and artist—conceived, directed, and music arranged by Stanley Silverman and written by Paul Schmidt, was first staged on 6 August 1986 at the Lenox Arts Center, Stockbridge, Massachusetts and brought to Playwrights Horizons, New York on 16 December 1986. The piece is for three male actors and musicians—a piano quintet on stage, mezzo-soprano, tenor, and bass-baritone. The 60 minutes of music of the piece's 90 minutes includes extracts from Quartets Nos. 1, 3, 7, 8, and 13 and the Piano Quintet; *Tahiti Trot;* prison camp scene and Katerina's aria from *Lady Macbeth of Mtsensk District;* a duet from *Moscow, Cheryomushki* and songs Op. 62 Nos. 4 and 6; Op. 121 No. 2; Op. 127 No. 3, and 'United Nations on the March'.

In the third semi-final of the BBC TV1 *Mastermind,* from Leicester University, televised on 17 May 1987, an Oxfam district organizer, Paul Henderson, correctly answered ('with no passes') all but one of Magnus Magnusson's twenty questions (set by Michael Kennedy) on the speciality subject 'The Life and Works of Shostakovich'.

The first of five programmes in BBC TV2's festival, *Shostakovich: A Career,* subtitled 'The Public and Private Voice of Dmitri Shostakovich', was screened on 7 November 1987. In this 75-minute documentary, produced by Peter Maniura, the public achievement and private struggle of the composer are retold by his third wife Irina, son Maksim, and daughter Galina; poet Yevgeni Yevtushenko, film-director Leonid Trauberg, singers Galina Vishnevskaya and Yevgeni Nesterenko, conductors Gennadi Rozhdestvensky and Rudolf Barshai, biographer Solomon Volkov, stage-director Yuri Lyubimov, and composers Karen Khachaturyan and Tikhon Khrennikov. Liberally illustrated with archive film of events and concerts including the propaganda newsreel of blockaded Leningrad, the 1949 visit to America, the First International Tchaikovsky Competition, and the funerals of Stalin and Shostakovich. Music examples from Opp. 123, 4, 1, 14, 18, 43, 46, 47, 60, 62, 70, 79, 35, 90, 109, 113, 145, and 135 with Dimiter Petkov (bass), Kathryn Harries (soprano), and Graham Johnson (piano) performing excerpts from the song cycles.

The British Television Channel Four film *Testimony,* directed by Tony Palmer, had its première at the London Film Festival, Empire Cinema, Leicester Square on 15 November 1987. It was first screened on television on 13 January 1990. David Rudkin's script was based on Solomon Volkov's book of the same title. Filmed entirely on location in the North of England (Wigan, Liverpool, Lake Windermere) with the principal parts of Shostakovich and Stalin played by Ben Kingsley and Terence Rigby respectively, and the score played by the London Philharmonic Orchestra conducted by Rudolf Barshai. A selection of the music from the film is included on the AVM Classic Movie Music LP, cassette and CD 1006 issued in September 1988. The film is available on videocassette Connoisseur CR 174.

The American award-winning television film *The War Symphonies: Shostakovich Against Stalin*, directed by Larry Weinstein and produced by Rhombus Media Inc. of Toronto in 1997, includes excerpts from six symphonies played by the Netherlands Radio Philharmonic and Orchestra of Mariinsky Theatre under Valeri Gergiev, rare newsreel footage, and statements from Shostakovich's family, friends, and colleagues. Videotape, with limited availability, from Bulldog Films, Olean, Pennsylvania.

Oksana Dvornichenko's 52-minute film of 1999 *Family Album* shows moving interviews with son Maksim, daughter Galina, and third wife Irina recollecting on the life of the composer, with Galina at the family dacha leafing through an album of personal photographs. This film was premièred in the UK at the Glasgow '25 Years On' Symposium on 27 October 2000.

Appendix III

Information on the History of Recording, Four Special
USSR Recordings, the Composer on Records,
and Samplers of Shostakovich's Music

In 1925 electrical recording came into general use and the 78 rpm turntable speed was standardized. A short-lived series of 10- and 12-inch 33⅓ rpm records was launched in the USA by RCA in September 1931.

Monophonic long-playing records were introduced in June 1948 by American Columbia. Decca issued the first LPs on the UK market in June 1950. Stereo discs were launched in April 1958. After this date an increasing number of performances were recorded simultaneously in mono and stereo modes. From July 1967 the EMI group issued stereo versions only and other companies soon followed their example. Mono record numbers are quoted first if a stereo take of the same performance is available.

The quadraphonic recordings of Shostakovich works issued between February 1973 and March 1978 number six only. See under Opp. 43, 47 (two), 93, Sans op. V, and Op. 141. All are SQ four channel system except for Op. 141 which is to CD4 standard.

Digital master tape recording was the next development in improved reproduction by increasing the dynamic range and eliminating tape hiss. Instead of recording complex sounds as a continuous, or analogue, electrical signal on tape, the music waveforms picked up by microphone are translated into a series of encoded number values. These are then expressed as a series of uniform electrical pulses that are magnetically recorded on to the master tape. A digital black disc recording of the Festive Overture issued in late 1979, was followed by Haitink's double album of the 'Leningrad Symphony'/ *The Age of Gold* Suite, Bernstein's live performance of the Fifth Symphony and others.

The technique of Direct Metal Mastering (DMM), developed by Teldec of West Germany in the early 1980s, has the stylus cutting direct into copper so that the 'mother' matrix, from which 'stampers' can be manufactured by electro-forming, is produced in a single operation.

The 12 cm (4.7 inch) diameter compact digital audio disc was launched on 1 March 1983 in the UK. Bernstein's 1979 concert performance of the Fifth Symphony was among the initial 200 laser disc releases. This new medium was quickly accepted and sales of CD players and discs increased beyond all expectations. From August 1985 the recording firm Nimbus released their own label of classical issues on compact disc only; Deutsche Grammophon following suit at the end of 1988.

Shostakovich was not represented in the initial batch of 300 mm. (12') Compact Disc Videos (or CDV, marketed as 'CD with pictures') in October 1988.

As far as known to the compiler, no tape or cassette version of a Shostakovich work was issued in Britain prior to 1985 without the performance being first made available in disc format. Details of the works currently obtainable on prerecorded tape can be found in the *Gramophone Classical Catalogue*. A selection of cassettes is listed in the second edition.

The first releases on Digital Compact Cassette appeared in September 1992, though a Shostakovich work did not materialize until March 1993 (Solti's recording of the First Symphony).

In the USSR mono LPs were first issued by the Ministry of Culture in November 1951, beginning with the record number D 01-2. Regular stereo releases commenced in 1961 with the record number C 101-2. Early LP issues sported a variety of labels though as all carried the words Министерство культуры (Ministry of Culture USSR) and export issues displayed the initial letter abbreviation for международная книга (International Book) the convenient prefix MK has been utilized to denote pre-Melodiya releases. The MK trading logo depicted a globe sliced by an open book. The Melodiya label with the design of a capital Cyrillic letter M resting on a spiral disc appeared in 1964. Up to the end of 1974 mono records were released with a D prefix (or HD[1] for restorations of historic performances): a single zero denoting a size of 300 mm. (12'); '00', 200 mm. (8'): '000', 175 mm. (7'), and without an initial nought, 250 mm. (10'). Compatible stereo/mono discs prefixed CM were issued between 1969 and 1974, ceasing at number CM 04475-6. From early 1975 these categories were replaced by a new simplified system using the letter M for mono, C for stereo, and G for flexible and a seven-figure number. The first digit indicates the genre of the material record: 0-documentary and political; 1—symphonic, opera, chamber, choral, and band music; 2—Russian folk music; 3—folk music of the Soviet republics; 4—spoken word; 5—for children; 6—variety, songs by Soviet composers and operetta; 7—educational; 8—foreign music, and 9—miscellaneous. The second digit shows the size: 0—300 mm., 1—250 mm., and 2—175 mm. These three indicators are followed by an individual five-figure number. All Soviet records up to the end of 1981 used one number per side and in the period 1975–81 most records mentioned in this book have the configuration C10 12345-6 (stereo, symphonic, and 12'). From January 1982 Melodiya records took a single eight-number figure per disc, e.g. C10 16329008 or M52 43443002. The last three digits were detached from the main record number after the second quarter of 1983. The first Soviet digital recordings were released in the first quarter of 1984. Their first batch of 65

---

[1]Melodiya prefixes HD, CM, and C transliterated ND, SM, and S respectively.

compact discs, issued in the spring of 1990, included Tatyana Nikolayeva's three-disc cycle of Shostakovich's Opus 87 Preludes and Fugues. The label name 'Melodiya' was replaced by 'Russian Disc'[2] in late 1991, with a new logo of three Kremlin wall merlons topped by the English initials 'RD'.

Through the Soviet Ministry of Trade, EMI made generally available to British collectors many Russian performances from the Melodiya catalogue in the period October 1968 to summer 1982. Olympia Compact Discs, specializing in Russian interpretations from the Melodiya catalogue and manufactured in Britain by Disctec, and later, Disctronic, released the first of their Shostakovich discs in June 1987.

In September 1989 seventy years of Russian recordings on 400,000 musical tapes, most of them suppressed by Communism, were discovered in the Archive of Gosteleradio. Releases on the Revelation label, launched in October 1996, include banned Shostakovich concert performances.

A complete world-wide listing of Shostakovich recordings is beyond the scope of this book though the majority of British releases from 78 rpm days to summer 2001 and nearly all Russian LPs are covered. Exceptions are some concert and recital collections (e.g. those including a small selection of Preludes from Opus 34, one or two Preludes and Fugues from Opus 87, and, unless of particular interest, popular single items such as the Polka from *The Golden Age* and the Romance from Opus 97[3]). Selected European and American imports are noticed if they were advertised as being available on special order, mentioned or reviewed in British catalogues and magazines though space does not permit the inclusion of but a fraction of the prolific Japanese compact disc releases in the Nineties or several important multiple issues, e.g. Kondrashin's cycle of the symphonies issued in France (fourteen-record box set with individual numbers LDX 78621-34), Germany, and Switzerland; the series of fifteen quartets by the (New) Borodin Quartet on the French label Le Chant du Monde (set of seven compact discs LDX 78025) and the Shostakovich Quartet's second complete cycle—differently coupled—recorded at the Documentary Film Studio, Moscow between 1996 and 28 April 1997 on the Japanese ATCO label Nos. 1007, 1009, 3011, 1015, 1018, and 1019. Gennadi Rozhdestvensky's complete cycle of digital recordings of the symphonies was reissued, under their original numbers, in three six-record Melodiya boxes in 1989. In the autumn of 2000 Le Chant du Monde issued a 25th Anniversary Edition of fifteen bargain-priced compact discs, including 21 reissues of Melodiya LPs incorrectly stated to be Czech Radio broadcast performances from between 1955 and 1985. The complete symphonies recorded by the Czecho-Slovak Radio Symphony Orchestra under Ladislav Slovák were reissued in a Naxos White Box set 8.501102 of eleven CDs in October 2001.

---

[2]Russian Disc prefix is an English 'R' not the Cyrillic 'Р'.
[3]Popular, that is, in the USSR and barely heard in the UK until its adoption as a signature tune for the serial *Reilly — Ace of Spies* shown on Independent TV in 1983.

Additional early recordings, issued within the period 1925–55, are listed in Clough and Cumings' *The World's Encylopaedia of Recorded Music* (abbreviated *WERM*). For performances not first issued in the United States, American readers are advised to consult their dealer's catalogues for label and number information. Equivalent American, Russian, and continental numbers up to the year 1973 are listed in Krzysztof Meyer's biography of the composer (the copious discography mentions 51 performances, mainly East European and American, not included in the present work. Of this number 7 are of Preludes from Opus 34; 7, the *Three Fantastic Dances,* and 14, the Polka from *The Golden Age*).

Only a small number of the discs mentioned are currently available from dealers. Deleted records are listed, however, as withdrawn performances are often reissued on different labels, usually at lower price levels and frequently with differing couplings. Elderly issues can occasionally be obtained from firms specializing in deletions, by browsing in second-hand shops or by advertising in the 'Records Wanted' columns of record journals.

Four Special USSR Recordings

(1) In 1967 Melodiya issued a 54-minute mono 12' record numbered D 020515-6, entitled *Dmitri Shostakovich—Monograph,* with biographical details by Lev Danilevich, read by Pavel Massalsky. This contains uncredited excerpts from the following eleven works:

Op. 10, First Symphony (first movement to fig. 12 + 3 bars)
Op. 33, *Counterplan* ('Song of the Counterplan', for chorus and orchestra)
Op. 114, *Katerina Izmailova* ('In the very depths of the forest there is a lake' from Act 4, sung by Eleonora Andreyeva)
Op. 88 No. 6, 'The Ninth of January' (the theme used in the following work)
Op. 103, Eleventh Symphony (second movement from fig. 28 to 44)
Op. 47, Fifth Symphony (fourth movement coda from fig. 128)
Op. 57, Piano Quintet (fourth movement complete played by the composer and the Beethoven Quartet)
Op. 60, Seventh Symphony (fourth movement coda from fig. 202 and first movement fig. 33 to 36 + 9 bars)
Op. 65, Eighth Symphony (third movement from fig. 86 to bar 3 of the Largo)
     Op. 80, *Meeting of the Elbe* ('Song of Peace', for male chorus and orchestra)
Op. 93, Tenth Symphony (second movement complete).

(2) A sixteen-minute telephone conversation between David Oistrakh and the composer, taped by the violinist on 15 October 1967, concerning rehearsal of the Second Violin Concerto, Opus 129, was released in 1976 on Melodiya C10 06907-8. The conversation is coupled with a reissue of Oistrakh's performance of the concerto.

(3) Melodiya issued a Shostakovich commemorative collection of 56 records in ten boxes over the four-year period 1977–80. Twenty-seven records cover

the symphonic, choral, and film music, and the ballet suites; seventeen are devoted to the chamber and instrumental compositions, and twelve to the two operas and the song cycles. These are mostly reissues, many of them long-deleted recordings, though following the defection to the West of certain conductors and performers, several records were promptly withdrawn from the boxes and subsequently replaced by new performances. The compiler was disinclined to note all these substitutions and catalogues only those records contained in the box sets in his own collection.

(4) In October 1979 Melodiya issued a box, *Dmitri Shostakovich Speaks*, containing four records numbered M40 41705-12 (announced in the 1980 first quarter catalogue). The first and third records are devoted to Items 1 and 12 respectively. The playing time of the set totals 3 hrs 4 min. This collection includes fifteen talks here listed in chronological order:

2. Excerpt from a radio address, Leningrad, 16 September 1941.
3. Speech at the International Peace Gathering, 4 September 1954.
1. A talk delivered to the Young Composers' Section of the Union of Soviet Composers, May 1955.
14. Interview with Witold Rudzinsky about the Warsaw Autumn Festival, Warsaw, September 1959.
6. Some words on the Twelfth Symphony, 10 January 1962.
7. Speech at the opening ceremony of the Second International Tchaikovsky Competition, 1 April 1962.
13. Account of the Edinburgh Festival to the Union of Soviet Composers, 15 October 1962.
4. Interview about the creative plans of the composer, 2 September 1963.
9. On the 125th anniversary of Tchaikovsky's birth, Bolshoi Theatre, 7 May 1965.
7. Some words on the Fourteenth Symphony, 21 June 1969.
10. My work in the cinema, radio interview, 1971
15. Interview with Royal S. Brown, New York, 13 June 1973.
12. Radio interview in Chicago, 15 June 1973.
8. Opening address of the Fifth Congress of the Union of Soviet Composers, Kremlin Palace of Congresses, 2 April 1974.
11. Conversation with his son, Maksim (examining old photographs) for a television film, Moscow, January 1975.

The Composer on Records

For details of recordings of Dmitri Shostakovich playing his own compositions see under the following opus numbers:

Op. 5, *Three Fantastic Dances* (piano solo)
Op. 22, *The Golden Age*—Polka (reduction for piano solo)
Op. 34, *Twenty-four Preludes*—Nos. 8, 14–19, and 22–4 (piano solo); Nos. 10, 15, 16, and 24 (transcription for violin and piano)

Op. 35, First Piano Concerto (piano, trumpet and string orchestra)
Op. 40, Cello Sonata (cello and piano)
Op. 57, Piano Quintet (piano and string quartet)
Op. 67, Second Piano Trio (violin, cello, and piano)
Op. 69, *A Child's Exercise Book* (piano solo, introduced by the composer)
Op. 79, *From Jewish Folk Poetry* (voices with piano accompaniment)
Op. 87, *Preludes and Fugues*—Nos. 1–8, 12–14, 16–18, 20, and 22–4 (piano solo)
Op. 93, Tenth Symphony (with Moisei Vainberg in piano four hands reduction)
Op. 94, *Concertino* (piano duet with Maksim Shostakovich)
Op. 97, *The Gadfly*—No. 15 Guitars (piano solo)
Op. 102, Second Piano Concerto (piano with orchestra)
Op. 134, Violin Sonata (violin and piano)

The composer's voice can be heard in speeches, talks, and interviews on the set of documentary records *Dmitri Shostakovich Speaks* and also in telephone conversation concerning the rehearsal of Op. 129, Second Violin Concerto.

On the mono cassette Regent Records MG 5020, Shostakovich can be heard as second soloist (deputizing at short notice for Mariya Yudina, who had injured a finger) in Bach's Concerto in D minor for Three Pianos, BVW 1063, with Tatyana Nikolayeva and Pavel Serebryakov, and the Berlin Radio Symphony Orchestra under Kirill Kondrashin, recorded in Leipzig, July 1950.

Shostakovich's Music on Cassettes

A substantial number of Shostakovich's orchestral compositions have been transferred to tape though chamber, instrumental, and vocal works are not so fully represented in this medium. In the 1960s the World Record Club offered the majority of their releases on mono open-reel tape and these included performances of Symphonies Nos. 6 (Boult) and 9 (Sargent). The music of Shostakovich has appeared minimally in eight-track cartridge form in the United Kingdom (Ančerl's recording of Symphony No. 6 and, again, Sargent's No. 9 being representative) though a more extensive selection is available in America. Philips and EMI introduced Musicassettes in the UK in October 1966. In the 1970s the sound quality of the four-track compact cassette improved appreciably and the wide-ranging dynamics of Shostakovich's symphonic writing proved acceptable on this convenient miniature tape format. The production of classical cassettes was greatly reduced in the 1990s. A list of cassettes released up to 1991 is printed on pages 388–92 of the second edition.

Samplers

Compared with other major composers , there have been few compilations of Shostakovich's works on compact disc; to date only seven:

Trax Classique TRXCD 131, titled '*Testimony*—Shostakovich's Greatest Hits' and issued in 1988, includes the complete Chamber Symphony Opus 110*a* and extracts from Symphonies Nos. 5 and 7, Piano Concerto No. 2, and Piano Trio No. 2, with a piano arrangement of the Romance from *The Gadfly*. The artists include the Phoenix Chamber Orchestra, Trio Zingara, and Martin Jones. The performers of the Opp. 47 and 102 excerpts are given pseudonymously as Vienna Symphony Orchestra conducted by Edouard von Lindenberg, with pianist Daniel Petrov in the concerto.

A more representative selection (though with no chamber music), originating from Melodiya, appeared on 'The Shostakovich CD' Olympia OCD 008 in 1989. The 22 tracks include a complete Opus 46 (*Four Romances on Poems by Pushkin*); movements from Symphonies Nos. 1, 9, 10, 13, 14, and 15; items from stage productions; the finale from Piano Concerto No. 1; and the *Three Fantastic Dances* played by the composer.

A Decca sampler, 'Simply Shostakovich' (448 185-2DM issued in June 1995), contains seventeen tracks from Symphonies Nos. 5, 9, 10, and 15; Piano Concerto No. 2; Chamber Symphony Opus 110*a;* and examples of ballet, film, and light music conducted by Riccardo Chailly, Vladimir Ashkenazy, Bernard Hermann, and Owain Arwel Hughes.

The Naxos sampler, 'The Best of Shostakovich' (8-556684 issued in September 1997) includes the Festive Overture Opus 96, selections from *The Gadfly* Opus 97 and *The Golden Age* Opus 22, and movements from Symphonies Nos. 1, 5, 9, and 10; Piano Concerto No. 2, String Quartet No. 4. and Piano Trio No. 2.

A German Compact Disc, Capriccio 10 822 titled 'Movie Madness', features sixteen tracks from nine film scores (Opp. 26, 30, 41 (i), 50*a*, 64, 82, 97, 111, and 116) and one stage production (Op. 58*a*) reissued from recordings conducted by Leonid Grin, James Judd, and Mikhail Yurovsky. Issued in the UK, October 1997. *Reissued:* USA: Laserlight Compact Discs 14 841 (two-disc set). ['Best of Motion Picture Scores'—as Capriccio CD plus Op. 18 'War'.] I 2000.

Revelation issued a two-disc set in 1997 comprising, on the first CD, the third movement from Third Quartet (from RV 10016), Prelude and Fugue No. 7 (RV 70001), second movement from Eighth Symphony (RV 10061), and 'Spring awakening' from *Satires* (RV 10087); and on the second CD, second movement from Fifth Symphony (RV 10025), fourth movement from Cello Sonata (RV 10017), and first movement from Cello Concerto No. 1 (RV 10087).

An American Compact Disc, Delos DE 3257, titled 'Waltzes' comprises 21 tracks of which thirteen are waltzes from film scores recorded at Moscow Conservatory on 12–14 July 1999 by the Moscow Chamber Orchestra conducted by Constantin Orbelian. The waltes are from Opp. 30, 37, 45, 76, 78, 95, 97, 99, 105, and with extra dances from Sans op. P (Ballet Suites Nos. 1–3). Also included are *Tahiti Trot,* Op. 16, *The Golden Age* Polka, Op. 22, and *The Gadfly* Folk Festival Op. 97. Recording reviewed G Dec. 1999.

Digital Versatile Discs

A major development in home entertainment was the introduction of the new digital audio technology demonstrated at the Bristol Sound & Vision Show in February 2000. For the first DVDs of Shostakovich see the Film section under *Lady Macbeth of Mtsensk District*, Opus 29 and recording for Original Jazz Suite No. 2, Sans op. G (ii).

A Shostakovich CD-ROM has been produced by Oksana Dvornichenko that includes 87 fragments of music performed by the composer and others, snatches of 33 documentaries, letters, over 800 photographs, interviews with Shostakovich, and a discography of over 2000 recordings. This is available in the English, French, and German languages. A DVD version has an extra set of video material. Both were issued by Chandos in February 2001, with the numbers CHAN 50001 CD-ROM and CHAN 55001 DVD-ROM*

---

*. Reviewed in *Gramophone* December 2001.

Appendix IV

Chronological Chart of Main Works and Historical Events

Year	Age	Main compositions	Personal events	Historical pointers
1905	—			(9) 22 Jan.: 'Bloody Sunday'— *c*.1,000 killed in Palace Square, St Petersburg. (7–13) 20–6 Dec.: abortive revolution.
1906	0		(12) 25 Sept.: born in St Petersburg.	25 Feb.: death of Arensky. 18 Apr.: San Francisco earthquake. 10 May: First Duma meets.
1907	0–1			Triple Entente (France / Russia / Britain) formed
1908	1–2		8 Aug.: sister Zoya born.	21 June: death of Rimsky-Korsakov
1909	2–3			25 July: Blériot flew across the English Channel.
1910	3–4			29 May: death of Balakirev.
1911	4–5			18 May: death of Mahler. 14 Dec.: Amundsen reached the South Pole.
1912	5–6			First issue of *Pravda*. 15 Apr.: loss of the *Titanic*.
1913	6–7			29 May: riot at *The Rite of Spring* première in Paris.
1914	7–8			31 July: full mobilization in Russia. 4 Aug.: Britain declared war on Germany.
1915	8–9		Summer: started piano lessons with mother and commenced composing.	22 Apr.: German gas attack at Ypres. 22 Apr.: death of Skryabin.
1916	9–10		Entered Glyasser's School of Music, Petrograd.	Battles of Verdun and the Somme. 17 Dec.: Rasputin murdered.
1917	10–11		Could play the whole of Bach's *Well-tempered Clavier*. Spring: performed before Petrograd Conservatory professor, Aleksandra Rozanova.	Petrograd workers' strike and army mutinies lead to Tsar Nicholas II's abdication. (25 Oct.) 7 Nov.: the October Revolution.

Year	Age	Main compositions	Personal events	Historical pointers
1918	11–12		28 Apr.: played Beethoven's Fifth Sonata at class concert.	10 Feb.: Trotsky announced war with Germany over. Summer 1918–20: Civil War in Russia 11 Nov.: Armistice Day.
1919	12–13	Op. 1, Scherzo in F sharp minor	Spring–summer: improvisation lessons with Georgi Bruni. Aug.: pupil of Aleksei Petrov for theory and solfeggio. Autumn: passed entrance examination at Petrograd Conservatory. Studying pianoforte under Professor Rozanova.	17 May: Red Army victory in Crimea. 28 June: Versailles Treaty.
1920	13–14	Op. 5, *Three Fantastic Dances*	Studying composition under Maksimilian Shteinberg. Autumn: transferred to Professor Leonid Nikolayev's piano class.	Communist victory. 14 Dec.: League of Nations 1st assembly opened.
1921	14–15		27 Sept.: first published opinion of Shostakovich (in Petrograd *Art Life*).	16 Mar.: Anglo-Russian trade agreement signed in London. Famine in Russia.
1922	15–16	Op. 3, *Theme and Variations* Op. 4, *Two Fables by Krylov* Op. 6, Suite for Two Pianos.	24 Feb.: father died.	Lenin suffered a stroke. Oct.: Fascists came to power in Italy.
1923	16–17	Op. 8, Piano Trio No. 1	Spring: completed piano course and gave concerts of Bach, Beethoven, Chopin, Liszt, Mozart *et al.* Summer: ill—sent to sanatorium in the Crimea. Oct./Nov.: played piano in Petrograd cinemas 'Harlequinade' and 'Bright Ribbon'.	11 Jan.: French and Belgian troops entered the Ruhr. 6 July: Constitution of USSR adopted.
1924	17–18		Oct.: played piano in Leningrad cinema 'Splendid Palace'.	21 Jan.: death of Lenin. 1 Feb.: Britain recognized the Soviet Government.
1925	18–19	Op. 10, Symphony No. 1 Op. 11, *Prelude and Scherzo*	Feb.: played piano in Leningrad cinema 'Piccadilly'. 20 Mar.: shared a concert with Shebalin at Moscow Conservatory performing Opp. 8, 5, and 6.	16 Oct.: Treaties of Locarno.

Year	Age	Main compositions	Personal events	Historical pointers
1926	19–20	Op. 12, Piano Sonata No. 1	12 May: première of Symphony No. 1 12 July: soloist in Tchaikovsky's Piano Concerto in Kharkov.	8 Sept.: Germany admitted to the League of Nations.
1927	20–1	Op. 13, *Aphorisms* Op. 14, Symphony No. 2	30 Jan.: won certificate of merit at 1st Chopin Pianoforte Contest, Warsaw, though ill with appendicitis.	24 May: diplomatic relations between Britain and Soviet Union severed.
1928	21–2	Op. 15, *The Nose*	8 Jan.: accepted Meyerhold's offer of post of musical director at his Moscow theatre. 2 Nov.: Stokowski conducted Symphony No. 1 in Philadelphia. 25 Nov.: Malko's Moscow concert of Opp. 15*a*, 16, and 17.	1 Oct.: first of Stalin's Five-Year Plans—collective farming intensified.
1929	22–3	Op. 18, *New Babylon* Op. 20, Symphony No. 3	Composed first film score. 3 Feb.: soloist in Prokofiev's Piano Concerto No. 1 in Leningrad.	Liquidation of the Ukrainian kulaks. Oct.: 'Wall Street Crash'.
1930	23–4	Op. 22, *The Golden Age*	18 Jan.: première of *The Nose*. 30 Mar.: offer to write opera for Bolshoi Theatre. Performed Tchaikovsky's Piano Concerto No. 1 for the last time in Rostov-on-Don.	Depression in Britain and Germany. Amy Johnson flew solo from London to Australia.
1931	24–5	Op. 27, *The Bolt*	Composing music for several stage productions and early sound films.	Statute of Westminster— British Empire in decline.
1932	25–6	Op. 29, *Lady Macbeth of Mtsensk District* Op. 32, *Hamlet*	13 May: married Nina Varzar.	23 Apr.: Union of Soviet Composers formed.
1933	26–7	Op. 34, *Twenty-four Preludes* Op. 35, Piano Concerto No. 1	Nov.: elected Deputy to the Oktyabrsky district of Leningrad.	Jan.: Hitler became Chancellor of Germany.
1934	27–8	Op. 40, Cello Sonata	22 Jan: première of *Lady Macbeth of Mtsensk District*.	23 Feb.: death of Elgar. 18 Sept.: USSR entered the League of Nations. 1 Dec.: Kirov assassinated in his Leningrad office.
1935	28–9	Op. 39, *The Limpid Stream*	1935–47: film scores mainly for Lenfilm.	Expansion of Soviet economy under 2nd Five-Year Plan.
1936	29–30	Op. 43, Symphony No. 4 (withdrawn until 1961)	28 Jan.: and 6 Feb.: *Pravda* attacks on *Lady Macbeth* and *The Limpid Stream*. 30 May: daughter Galina born.	21 Mar.: death of Glazunov in Paris. Spanish Civil War started. Aug.: trials of prominent Russian revolutionaries.

Year	Age	Main compositions	Personal events	Historical pointers
1937	30–1	Op. 47, Symphony No. 5	Spring 1937–41: teacher of Instrumentation and Composition, Leningrad Conservatory.	Jan.: political elimination of 'Old Bolsheviks'. June: Red Army Marshal Tukhachevsky and seven generals shot.
1938	31–2	Op. 49, Quartet No. 1	10 May: son Maksim born.	Mar.: Stalin's purges continue. Sept.: Munich Pact.
1939	32–3	Op. 54, Symphony No. 6	Mar.: elected Deputy to the Leningrad city council. 23 May: confirmed as professor—pupils included Veniamin Fleishman, Kara Karayev, Karen Khachaturyan, Yuri Sviridov, and Orest Yevlakhov.	23 Aug.: Stalin and Hitler signed a pact of non-aggression. 3 Sept.: outbreak of Second World War. 17 Sept.: Soviet troops crossed Polish frontier. 30 Nov.: USSR attacked Finland.
1940	33–4	Op. 57, Piano Quintet	20 May: Order of the Red Banner of Labour.	12 Mar.: USSR signed peace treaty with Finland. Late May / June: evacuation of Dunkirk and fall of France.
1941	34–5	Op. 60, Symphony No. 7	Attempted to join the People's Volunteer Corps. 1 Oct.: left Leningrad for Kuibyshev. State Prize for Piano Quintet.	22 June: Germany attacked USSR— start of Great Patriotic War. 30 Aug.: Leningrad siege began. 7 Dec.: Pearl Harbour attacked.
1942	35–6	*The Gamblers* (abandoned) Op. 62, *Six Romances*	State Prize for Symphony No. 7. Honoured Artist of the RSFSR.	Feb.: Singapore overrun. 12 Sept.: start of Battle of Stalingrad.
1943	36–7	Op. 61, Piano Sonata No. 2 Op. 65, Symphony No. 8	Moved to Moscow—post of Professor of Composition. Honorary member of American Institute of Art and Literature.	15 Jan.: Leningrad blockade ended. 7 Feb.: German troops surrendered at Stalingrad. 28 Mar.: death of Rakhmaninov. 13 Oct.: Italy declared war on Germany.
1944	37–8	Op. 67, Piano Trio No. 2 Op. 68, Quartet No. 2	11 Feb.: closest friend, Ivan Sollertinsky, died of starvation.	26 Jan.: Leningrad siege ended after 880 days. 6 June: D Day—'Operation Overlord'.
1945	38–9	Op. 70, Symphony No. 9	Celebrated victory with a 'merry, light-hearted scherzo-symphony'.	Feb.: Yalta Conference and bombing of Dresden. 2 May: Berlin surrendered to Soviet troops. 8 May: VE Day. 6 Aug.: Hiroshima. 1945–8: Zhdanov Era.
1946	39–40	Op. 73, Quartet No. 3	First Soviet monograph published to mark the composer's 40th birthday. Order of Lenin. State Prize for Piano Trio No. 2.	United Nations took over from the League of Nations.

Year	Age	Main compositions	Personal events	Historical pointers
1947	40–1		9 Feb.: Deputy of Supreme Soviet RSFSR. May: took part in Prague Spring International Festival.	1946–7 winter: severe weather in Europe—food and fuel shortages.
1948	41–2	Op. 77, Violin Concerto No. 1 Op. 79, *From Jewish Folk Poetry* (both withheld until 1955)	People's Artist of RSFSR.	10 Feb.: Central Committee's vicious attack on Soviet composers. 23 June–May 1949: Berlin blockade. 31 Aug.: death of Zhdanov.
1949	42–3	Op. 81, *The Song of the Forests* Op. 83, Quartet No. 4	25–8 Mar.: visit to New York for Congress of Peace.	4 Apr.: NATO came into being. Autumn: Stalin's purges restart, beginning with persecution of Jews.
1950	43–4		July: attended the Bach bicentenary celebrations— performed as one of the three soloists in a Bach concerto. Nov.: Second World Peace Congress in Warsaw. State Prize for *The Song of the Forests*.	June: North Korea attacked South Korea. 8 Aug.: death of Myaskovsky.
1951	44–5	Op. 87, *Twenty-four Preludes and Fugues* Op. 88, *Ten Poems on Texts by Revolutionary Poets*	Continued composing safe 'realistic' works.	May–Oct.: Festival of Britain. 13 July: death of Schoenberg.
1952	45–6	Op. 90, *The Sun Shines over our Motherland* Op. 92, Quartet No. 5	Mar.–Apr.: attended East German Beethoven Festival. Dec.: Congress in Defence of Peace in Vienna. State Prize for *Ten Poems*.	6 Feb.: death of King George VI.
1953	46–7	Op. 93, Symphony No. 10 Op. 94, *Concertino*	Resumed role as a symphonic composer.	5 Mar.: deaths of Stalin and Prokofiev. 29 May: conquest of Everest. 2 June: Queen Elizabeth II crowned.
1954	47–8	Op. 96, *Festive Overture*	27 Mar.: People's Artist of USSR. 4 Sept.: awarded International Peace Prize. 4 Dec.: wife Nina died after volvulus operation in Yerevan. 9 Dec.: honoured by Swedish Royal Musical Academy.	6 May: Bannister's under four-minute mile.
1955	48–9	Op. 97, *The Gadfly*	Nov.: attended opening of rebuilt Vienna Opera House. 9 Nov.: mother died aged 67.	Restoration of friendly relations with the West—'The Thaw'.
1956	49–50	Op. 101, Quartet No. 6	15 Jan.: Diploma of St Cecilia, Rome. Remarried—to Margarita Andreyevna Kainova. Lenin Prize on 50th birthday.	14–25 Feb.: Stalin denounced by Khrushchev at 20th Party Congress. Oct.–Nov.: Hungarian uprising and Suez crisis.

Year	Age	Main compositions	Personal events	Historical pointers
1957	50–1	Op. 102, Piano Concerto No. 2 Op. 103, Symphony No. 11	1957–75: Secretary of Union of Soviet Composers. Guest of Prague Spring International Festival.	20 Sept.: death of Sibelius. 4 Oct.: first Sputnik launched.
1958	51–2	Op. 105, *Moscow, Cheryomushki*	22 Apr.: Lenin Prize for Symphony No. 11. 9–12 May: visit to Italy. Late May: French Commander Order of Art and Literature. 25 June: honorary doctorate Oxford. Sept.–Nov.: hospital treatment for right arm. 9 Oct.: Sibelius Prize.	28 May: Central Committee adopted a resolution 'On rectifying errors of 1948 decisions'. 26 Aug.: death of Vaughan Williams.
1959	52–3	Op. 107, Cello Concerto No. 1	Sept.: attended Warsaw Festival of Contemporary Music. Late Oct.: visit to USA. Honoured by American Academy of Sciences and Mexican Conservatory. Divorced Margarita Kainova.	Beginning of Sino-Soviet conflict. Fidel Castro became premier of Cuba.
1960	53–4	Op. 108, Quartet No. 7 Op. 110, Quartet No. 8 Op. 111, *Five Days, Five Nights*	9 Apr.: First Secretary of Union of Composers of RSFSR. Hospital treatment for painful right hand in Feb. and broken left leg in Oct. Sept.–Oct.: visited Britain, Belgium, France, Italy, Switzerland, and Austria.	May: U-2 spy plane incident.
1961	54–5	Op. 112, Symphony No. 12	Sept.: accepted as full member of the Communist Party. Mid-Oct.: attended Budapest Liszt and Bartók Festival. 30 Dec.: première of Symphony No. 4.	12 Apr.: Yuri Gagarin the first man in space. 13 Aug.: construction of Berlin Wall. Oct.: Stalin's body removed from the Lenin Mausoleum.
1962	55–6	Op. 113, Symphony No. 13	20 June: hospital treatment for right hand. 15 Aug.: flew to Scotland for the 19th Edinburgh Festival where 22 of his works played. 1 Oct.: meeting with Stravinsky. 1962–75: Delegate of Supreme Soviet USSR. Nov.: remarried—to Irina Antonovna Supinskaya. 12 Nov.: conducted *Festive Overture* and Cello Concerto No. 1 (soloist Rostropovich) at Gorky concert.	11 Feb.: U-2 pilot Powers returned to USA in exchange for Soviet spy. Oct.: Cuban missile crisis.

Year	Age	Main compositions	Personal events	Historical pointers
1963	56–7	Op. 115, *Overture on Russian and Kirghiz Folksongs*	8 Jan.: opera *Katerina Izmailova* performed. 1963–7: Honorary member of International Music Committee UNESCO.	16 June: Valentina Tereshkova the first woman cosmonaut. 22 Nov.: President Kennedy assassinated.
1964	57–8	Op. 116, *Hamlet* (film) Op. 117, Quartet No. 9 Op. 118, Quartet No. 10 Op. 119, *The Execution of Stepan Razin*	15–23 Feb.: the Second Contemporary Music Festival, held in Gorky, devoted entirely to his compositions. Apr.: planted oak saplings in Tashkent's Victory Square.	15 Oct.: fall of Khrushchev— succeeded by Brezhnev.
1965	58–9	Op. 121, *Five Romances on Texts from 'Krokodil'*	Jan.: 20 days in Moscow hospital neurological unit. Nov.: honoured by Serbian Academy of Art.	Feb.: deterioration in USA / USSR relations over bombing of North Vietnam.
1966	59–60	Op. 122, Quartet No. 11 Op. 126, Cello Concerto No. 2	20 Apr.: entered Crimean sanatorium, with severe respiratory complaint. 28 May: heart attack. Aug.: Royal Philharmonic Gold Medal. 5 Oct.: Order of Lenin and Hero of Socialist Labour.	Worsening of Sino-Soviet relations.
1967	60–1	Op. 127, *Seven Romances on Poems by Aleksandr Blok* Op. 129, Violin Concerto No. 2	15 Mar.: honoured by Austrian Republic. Sept.: right leg broken in Moscow car accident. Film of *Katerina Izmailova* shown in Aldeburgh Festival.	6 Mar.: death of Kodály. 50th anniversary of the October Revolution.
1968	61–2	Op. 133, Quartet No. 12 Op. 134, Violin Sonata	15 July: honoured by Bavarian Academy of Fine Arts. 5 Nov.: Glinka State Prize for *The Execution of Stepan Razin*. 1968–75: Member of International Committee in Defence of Peace.	20–1 Aug.: invasion of Czechoslovakia.
1969	62–3	Op. 135, Symphony No. 14	Son Maksim's conducting début in USA. 1–23 Aug.: at Lake Baikal sanatorium.	16 Jan.: docking of Soyuz 4 and 5 manned space vehicles. 20 July: astronauts Armstrong and Aldrin's moonwalk.
1970	63–4	Op. 136, *Loyalty* Op. 138, Quartet No. 13	Feb.: Mozart Society of Vienna medal. Over 170 days spent at Kurgan hospital complex. Honorary member of Finnish Society of Composers.	Break up of The Beatles group.

Year	Age	Main compositions	Personal events	Historical pointers
1970 (*continued*)			10 Nov.: awarded 1st prize at All-Union Literature and Art Contest for march *Soviet Militia*.	
1971	64–5	Op. 141, Symphony No. 15	17 Sept.: second heart attack. Order of the October Revolution.	4 Feb.: Rolls-Royce collapse. 6 Apr.: death of Stravinsky. 11 Sept.: death of Khrushchev.
1972	65–6		May: Golden Order 'Friends of the People', GDR. Italian Prize: 'Golden Lira 1972'. 6 July: Doctor of Music, College of Dublin.	5 Sept.: terrorist outrage in Munich Olympic Village.
1973	66–7	Op. 142, Quartet No. 14 Op. 143, *Six Songs on Poems of Marina Tsvetayeva*	Honoured in Denmark (26 May) and at the Northwestern University, Evanstone, USA (16 June). 6 Oct.: death of sister Mariya.	27 Jan: Vietnam peace agreement signed in Paris.
1974	67–8	Op. 144, Quartet No. 15 Op. 145, *Suite on Verses of Michelangelo*	Nov.: Glinka State Prize for Quartet No. 14 and *Loyalty*.	13 Feb.: Solshenitsyn expelled from USSR. 8 Aug.: President Nixon resigned after Watergate scandal.
1975	68	Op. 147, Viola Sonata	Honoured by French Academy of Fine Arts. 3 Aug.: entered hospital for the last time. 9 Aug.: died in Moscow at 18.30 14 Aug.: buried in Moscow's Novodevichy Cemetery to strains of Schubert's Symphony No. 8.	5 June: Suez Canal reopened. 17 July: link-up of Apollo and Soyuz spacecrafts.
1976	—	———	25 Sept.: commemorative stamp issued in USSR.	4 Dec.: death of Benjamin Britten.

Appendix V

Abandoned Projects and Obscure and Doubtful Works

Further information is awaited on the following compositions and productions:

Piano Sonata in B flat minor: this composition of late 1923 destroyed by the composer.

Two Fragments for Orchestra: an 'Intermezzo' and 'Allegro' were composed in 1927. The manuscript was lost but the work was reconstructed from memory through Yuri Nikolsky in 1946.

Battleship Potemkin: on 30 March 1930 Shostakovich declined an offer to write an opera on this subject for the Bolshoi Theatre. [Oles Chishko wrote the opera in 1937.]

The Carp: in the spring of 1930 an opera on the piscine subject of an underwater society, after a short verse by Nikolai Oleinikov, was seriously considered.

The Concrete Sets: in 1931 the composer wrote that he had signed a contract for a film of this title to be produced by Aleksandr Macheret for the Moscow Film Studios.

The Negro: an operetta of this name, with lyrics by B. Gusman and Anatoli Mariengof, was also mentioned in 1931 as a signed contract.

New Year Madrigal: a humorous madrigal composed in December 1933 for New Year celebrations. Volume 93 of *New Collected Works* will contain *Two Madrigals* for tenor soloist and piano.

Mother: Mikhail Bulgaov prepared a libretto, based on Maksim Gorky's novel, for Shostakovich in the 1930s. [Tikhon Khrennikov filled the breach in 1957.]

Ankara—Heart of Turkey: a documentary film, with scenario by Leo Arnshtam and directed by Sergei Yutkevich, was made by the Lenfilm Studio in 1934. The background music was from works by Shostakovich.

Twelve Preludes for String Quartet: a suite for Bassoon and String Orchestra, a String Quartet, a Violin Concerto, various vocal works, and a 'Dance Suite for Jazz' were planned in 1934 though apparently only the last-named materialized. However, *Twelve Preludes for String Quartet* were composed while writing the film score for *The Girl Friends,* Opus 41 (ii) in late 1934 or during 1935 but these are believed to have been lost with several other works in the bombing of the Leningrad Film Studio in 1941.

Liluli: plans were made in April 1936 to compose incidental music for Romain Rolland's drama.

Volochayevka Days: many fragments and episodes written in 1937 for an opera to a libretto by N. Ya. Bersenev. See also Opus 48.

Lenin Symphony: on 15 April 1938 Shostakovich started work on a monumental choral symphony dedicated to Lenin. This symphony, scored for soloists, chorus, and orchestra, was inspired by Vladimir Mayakovsky's poem *Vladimir Ilyich Lenin* and was to have included verses from folk poets Suleiman Stalsky and Dzhambul Dzhabayev. Progress reports were published on 20 September and 20 November 1938 but the manuscript was laid aside and the Sixth Symphony, Opus 54, commenced on 15 April 1939.

The Twelve Chairs: Rena Moisenko (1949) and Gerald Abraham (1943) mentioned that Shostakovich had written an operetta in 1937 and 1940 respectively, based on the comedy by Ilya Ilf and Yevgeni Petrov. The rough draft of this three-act operetta, with libretto by Petrov and the poet, V. Vladimirov, was abandoned in 1938.

Lermontov: a contract was drawn up on 3 June 1938 to compose music for a ballet on the poet's life for Leningrad's Kirov Ballet.

A Hero of Our Time: Vsevolod Meyerhold prepared an opera libretto, based on Mikhail Lermontov's short story, for Shostakovich in June 1938.

Masquerade: Shostakovich wrote on 20 November 1938 that he intended to compose an opera on Lermontov's drama after he had completed his 'Lenin Symphony'. [Aram Khachaturyan provided incidental music in 1941.]

Romance: a song for voice and piano, with lyric by Heinrich Heine, written in 1938 or 1941 but not found in the composer's papers.

The People's Poet: another projected opera, based on a Turkmenian story.

Second Symphony: Fridrikh Ermler invited Shostakovich to write music for his film in 1940.

The Heroic Defenders of Moscow: an oratorio apparently abandoned in mid-1943 when the composer commenced work on the Eighth Symphony.

Katyushka Maslova: on 17 March 1979 *Pravda* reported that several rough music sheets of a projected opera, based on Leo Tolstoy's novel *Resurrection* and drafted in Shostakovich's thirties, were discovered by Sofya Khentova in the archives of the Glinka Museum, Moscow. Anatoli Mariengof provided the libretto and a contract was concluded on 14 October 1940.

Sonata for Violin and Piano: this instrumental work of 1945 will be published in Volume 107 of *New Collected Works.*

Three Pieces for Orchestra: this work was written in 1947–8 and originally given the opus number 77. It exists in manuscript form.

War and Peace: Shostakovich prepared the full score of Prokofiev's opera music for publication. This volume and the vocal score (by Lev Atovmyan) were published in 1958.

Fifty Russian Folksongs: in 1959 the composer selected fifty songs from Count Vladimir Odoyevsky's collection of Russian folksongs with the intention of arranging them in the manner of his *Ten Russian Folksongs,* Sans op. Q.

Blossoms: a one-act ballet performed at the Leningrad Malyi Opera Theatre on 20 October 1961, directed by Vladimir Varkovitsky, was based on existing waltzes and speciality numbers of Shostakovich. The ballet was repeated the following year at the Gorky Theatre of Opera and Ballet by Lyubov Serebrovskaya-Gryuntal and in Sverdlovsk by E. Dorofeyev.

Children's Quartet: in January 1962 Shostakovich wrote that he expected to finish his 'Ninth Quartet, a children's quartet, about toys and playing' in two weeks. However, in a letter to Isaak Glikman dated 18 November 1961, he stated that he had already burnt this manuscript. His Opus 117 Ninth Quartet was composed in May 1964.

Directive Little Bow: Konstantin Boyarsky's one-act ballet included in the Leningrad Malyi Theatre of Opera and Ballet 1962 season, with *The Young Lady and the Hooligan*.

And Quiet Flows the Don: in August 1964 the composer wrote that he was about to embark upon an opera based on the third and fourth books of Mikhail Sholokhov's *And Quiet Flows the Don* while resting at a home by Lake Balaton, Hungary. The libretto was completed by late May 1965 and a start made on composing the music. He expected to devote 'the whole of 1966 and even some of 1967' to the opera.

The Zhdanov Decree: Solomon Volkov mentions an unpublished satirical vocal work mocking the anti-formalism campaign of 1948 (*Testimony*, 1979, pp. 111 and 223). The implications of this infamous conference was the inspiration of David Pownall's play *Master Class*, premièred at the Haymarket, Leicester, on 24 January 1983. David Bamber played Shostakovich; Peter Kelly, Prokofiev; Timothy West, Stalin, and Jonathan Adams, Zhdanov. Décor was by Martin John and the producer, Justin Greene. See also *Rayok*, Sans op. X.

Yevgeni Onegin: Music for a spectacle written in 1964 and produced by Nikolai Akimov, premièred at the Leningrad Theatre of Drama and Comedy in January 1965. The piano score and orchestral parts preserved at the Leningrad (Kirov) Theatre of Opera and Ballet.

The Black Monk: Volkov states that an opera based on Anton Chekhov's story of 1893 was considered in the 1970s. Shostakovich intended to incorporate Gaetano Braga's once popular song, 'A Maiden's Prayer', which plays an important part in the story. This song, with lyric by M. Marcello (originally *Leggenda valacca* for voice with cello or violin obbligato) was also arranged as an instrumental salon piece under the name *La Serenata* or, in English, 'Angel's Serenade'. See under Sans op. X.

Envoys of Eternity: Boris Schwarz mentions a film score, *Poslanniky vechnosty,* written in 1970, under the catalogue of works in Volume 17 of *The New Grove*. This film, directed by Todor Vulfovich for Mosfilm, was released on 29 March 1971. The score was compiled from various works of Shostakovich.

Yelabuga Nail. A setting for bass and piano of Yevtushenko's poem about the suicide of Marina Tsvetayeva in 1941 composed, according to Isaak Glikman, in the spring of 1971.

Crossroads: M. Mnatsakanyan, Petrozavod Musical-Dramatic Theatre, 1971. A one-act ballet, *Perekryostok,* using music of Shostakovich, Handel, Bartók, and others.

St Petersburg Days: score commenced for Grigori Kozintsev's film, based on Nikolai Gogol's stories, left unfinished on the director's death in 1973.

Three Aphorisms: a ballet performed in 1974.

Torments of Conscience: Yevgeni Yevtushenko wrote the first poem for a pro-jected vocal symphony following his collaboration on the Thirteenth Symphony.

Sixteenth Symphony: two movements reported to have been composed in 1974–5. See the orchestrated version of Opus 145.

The Portrait: an opera on Gogol's story started in May 1975 was completed by Moishe Vainberg. The première took place in the Janáček Opera House, Brno on 20 May 1983. The libretto was written for Shostakovich by Alek-sandr Medvedev.

Wedding Procession: a ballet prepared for the Leningrad Ballet Troupe 'Choreo-graphic Miniatures' by Leonid Yakobson in 1975, based on paintings by Marc Chagall. Restaged in 1990 by a modern dance company, the Malyi Bal-let of the Yirov Theatre.

In the Name of Life: a ballet performed to the music of Andrei Shtogarenko, Boris Lyatoshinsky, and Shostakovich choreographed by Anatoli Shikero for the Ukrainian Theatre of Opera and Ballet, Kiev in 1975.

Choreographic Novella: a ballet set to the music of Shostakovich, Prokofiev, Poulenc, Tchaikovsky, Rossini, and Purcell, choreographed by Dmitri Bryantsev and performed at the Leningrad Kirov Theatre in 1977.

The Idiot: a ballet by Valeri Panov, based on Fyodor Dostoyevsky's novel *The Idiot* of 1868–9 and staged on 15 June 1979 by the Deutsche Oper Ballet, West Berlin, used music of Shostakovich (not specified in *The Guinness Guide to Ballet* by Oleg Kerensky, Guinness Superlatives Ltd., 1981). This three-and-a-half-hour ballet used extracts from the symphonies; *Hamlet* film score, Opus 116, and several other works.

Strictly Business: choreographed by Philip Taylor for Nederlands Dans Theater 2, under the guidance of Jiří Kylián, and performed at Glasgow's Theatre Royal, July 1988. This lively 'satire on yuppi efficiency and office sex' uses a medley of music from Pink Floyd and Boys Town groups, and Shostakovich.

In addition to the above there are several minor works that are preserved at the Glinka Museum and mentioned in Meskhishbili's 1996 Catalogue but not fully indexed in this present volume. These include an undated 'Galop and Lullaby' for orchestra (piano score and unfinished full score); an undated piece for piano entitled 'Chik-achi' (rough draft autograph); the famous Rus-sian folk song collected by Mili Balakirev in 1860 'Song of the Volga Boatman' (*Ei, ukhnem!* translated in *New Collected Works* Catalogue as 'Hey, Let's Bang!') arranged—probably in 1929—for bass voice and large symphony orchestra (a manuscript copy); and an undated reduction for piano four hands of the second movement, marked 'Andante in F sharp major' of Gustav Mahler's Symphony No. 10 (two examples—one unfinished).

In the early 1920s Shostakovich orchestrated Franz Schubert's Funeral March in F major and two movements from Ludwig van Beethoven's Piano Sonatas: the Adagio cantabile of No. 8 'Pathétique' Opus 13 and the first movement of No. 32 Opus 111. The autographs of these three scores are preserved at the CIS Archives of Literature and Art.

For the film *The Warmonger* (*Pogzhigateli boiny*) Shostakovich composed a 'German March' scored unusually for 2 piccolos, 2 flutes, a clarinet, and percussion (tambourine, 6 small and 4 large drums). An undated manuscript copy preserved at the Music Library of the USSR Cinematograph Symphony Orchestra.

Doubtful works

The following doubtful or erroneously attributed compositions are not indexed:

Lead Soldiers: a ballet staged by Yevgeni Vakhtangov (1883–1922) for the Bat public cabaret, Moscow, was stated by Marc Slonim (1963) to be set to specially composed music of Shostakovich. The ballet was performed around the year 1920 when the composer was only twelve years old.

Genu in Pilae: Malcolm MacDonald in the second edition of his catalogue mentions a film score of this title composed in 1932: 'The ascription of this to Shostakovich is not certain, though circumstantially strong. The music survives in a copyist's score. The original print of the film was destroyed on Stalin's orders, though it has recently been restored from fragments (which include some sound-track).' The movements are Prelude, Fanfare, Scene, two Dances, Intermezzo, Fugal Dance, and Postlude. The small orchestra includes harp, celesta, piano, and balalaika. In the 1990s Malcolm MacDonald learned that he was the victim of a practical joke (not meant for him) in Boosey & Hawkes Hire Library, where someone constructed a spoof work card that subsequently appeared in the Shostakovich card index. The title means 'A Knee in the Balls'.

Lenin in October: The Oxford Companion to Film by Liz-Anne Bawden lists this film of 1937 (not 1934) as having a film score by Shostakovich. The music was composed by Anatoli Nikolayevich Aleksandrov.

The Wayfarer: the second supplement of *WERM* incorrectly lists 'The Song of the Wayfarer' from this film (score by Isaak Dunayevsky) under Shostakovich's name. This item is also listed as a Shostakovich work in Meyer (1980).

March of the Red Army: Andrey Olkhovsky (1955) states that a march of this title was written in collaboration with Aram Khachaturyan. This is most probably the joint composition submitted as a new Soviet national anthem in 1944.

Don Quixote: this ballet, attributed to Shostakovich in *Ballet Music—an Introduction* by Humphrey Searle (Cassell, London, 1958), has music by Nikolas
Nabokov.

War and Peace: the score for this epic film of 1967 is quoted as being by Shostakovich in *The Filmgoer's Companion* by Leslie Halliwell (MacGibbon & Kee,
London, 1970), whereas it was composed by Vyacheslav Ovchinnikov. Still
not corrected in Halliwell's *Who's Who in the Movies* (HarperCollins, London, 13th edn. 1999).

Othello and *The Golden Key. Everyman's Dictionary of Music,* ed. Sir Jack Westrup
(Dent, London, 5th edn. 1977), mentions incidental music to Shakespeare's
Othello and a ballet *The Golden Key.*

Appendix VI

DSCH—the Composer's Monogram, Compositions
Based on DSCH by Other Hands, and Tributes

Shostakovich's full name in Russian Дмитрий Дмитриевич Шостакович
and this usually appears in English transliteration as Dmitri Dmitrievich Shostakovich. His first name is sometimes written as Dmitrii, Dmitry or Dimitri
and his surname, Shostakovitch [EMI, alone among the major recording companies, persisted in this surname spelling until February 1979]. The composer,
when he printed his name, used the form 'D. Schostakovich'. When the compiler first encountered the composer's name in print in 1942, on the album
and records of Stokowski's recording of the Fifth Symphony, it was spelt
Szostakowicz—in Polish! In the Italian language the spelling is Dimitri
Sciostakovic; in French, Chostakovitch and in German, Schostakowitsch. The
last-named spelling comes in useful in providing the composer with a musical
signature.

   In English musical notation we have the letters A to G (in the treble clef,
EGBDF on the lines and FACE in the spaces) and from these a limited number
of words can be concocted. The German language is more accommodating for
here we have the two additional letters 'H' and 'S'. The note B flat is written 'B'
while B natural is 'H' and E flat is called 'Es' and pronounced like the letter 'S'.
Hence the motif BACH is possible, and was used by the composer himself,
and by Brahms and Liszt (amongst others). For Shostakovich's epigram, the
composer took his initial 'D' and the first three letters of his surname in a
hybrid German/English spelling (see Example).

   Like BACH the DSCH motto does not belong to any key but is probably
more fruitful than its famous precursor. Shostakovich introduces his plaintive
motto at its original pitch in the third and fourth movements of the Tenth
Symphony and it is omnipresent in his Eighth Quartet. He first openly spot-
lighted it in 1953, though it occurs earlier and possibly unwittingly in *Lady
Macbeth of Mtsensk District* pitched a perfect fourth higher with a 'near miss' in
the Scherzo of the First Violin Concerto of 1947.

   In the Seventh Quartet his initials 'DS' are introduced in the very first bar and
are featured throughout this work, with DSCH occurring in bars 5 and 6 after
fig. 22 at the end of the *Lento*, albeit disguised in the unfamiliar rhythm
of ♪♩♩.♪ The opening viola phrase of the Fifth Quartet is an anagram of the

motto. Inexplicably, the composer introduced a slurred parody of his epigram in the third movement of the Fifteenth Symphony and humorously sets his name, occupation, and nationality to the motto in the brief work with a long title, Opus 123.

The composer's printed name from an envelope; motto, a valediction ('With best wishes') and signature in his own hand, 7 Dec. 1974.

There is a semitone between the first and second notes and the third and fourth, a minor third between the second and third notes, while the complete motto spans a diminished fourth. A number of Shostakovich's compositions—the First Cello and Second Violin Concertos, Twelfth and Thirteenth Quartets among them—do not feature the monogram but they are saturated with its intervals.

After Shostakovich was in trouble with the authorities in 1936, his fellow composer Benjamin Britten, composed a Festival Cantata, Opus 30, *Rejoice in the Lamb*. This setting of words written in a madhouse by the eighteenth-century poet, Christopher Smart, is available on Hyperion A 66126 in a performance directed by Matthew Best. The words which concern us are: 'For the officers of the peace are at variance with me and the watchman strikes me with his staff. For silly fellow, silly fellow is against me.' The Shostakovich motto is featured prominently and the chorus takes up those four notes for the words 'silly fellow'. It is surely more than coincidental that when Shostakovich was in disgrace in Russia with 'officers of the peace', Britten should introduce this secret message of sympathy. Did, then, Benjamin Britten discover and initiate the use of the DSCH motto in 1943? Later, in 1968, he was to dedicate the church parable, *The Prodigal Son*, Opus 81, to Shostakovich.

Compositions based on DSCH by Other Hands and Tributes

Witold Lutoslawski, whose music had been banned in Poland as politically undesirable, supportively quotes the DSCH monogram in the Toccata section of the third movement of his *Concerto for Orchestra* completed in 1954.

The Scottish composer Ronald Stevenson (born in Blackburn but likes to be known as a Scottish composer), greatly moved by Shostakovich's Eighth Quartet, Tenth Symphony and First Violin Concerto, composed a monumental *Passacaglia on DSCH*. Stevenson presented a copy of his 85-minute composition to Shostakovich on 6 September during the 1962 Edinburgh Festival. The première was given by the thirty-five-year-old composer in Cape Town on 10 December 1963. At the 1966 Aldeburgh and Cheltenham Festivals it was performed by John Ogdon, who later recorded the work on HMV ASD 2321-2 (three sides—reviewed G Sept. 1967). The title page of the score, published by Oxford University Press in 1967, is inscribed 'For Dmitri Shostakovich'. The composer's own 1987 recording appears on the double alburm Altarus AIR 2-9090 (G Oct. 1968) and a performance by Raymond Clarke was issued on Marco Polo Compact Disc 8.223545 in August 1994 (reviewed G Sept. 1995). In his Second Piano Concerto (*The Continents*) Stevenson includes a fugue on the combined motmi of BACH and DSCH, conflicting with Bulgarian rhythms. In 1974 the Union of Soviet Composers commissioned Stevenson to contribute an essay and a short piano piece (again based on DSCH by request) to the Shostakovich Festschrift to be published in 1976 in honour of the Soviet master's expected seventieth birthday. The title of this short work of Stevenson's is *Recitative and Air for Shostakovich*. The composer gave its first broadcast on 25 July 1976 on BBC Radio 3. The piece appears, with twelve others, at the end of the Sovetskii Kompozitor's commemorative volume compiled by Grigori Shneyerson.

Although on an altogether different plane to the tributes listed in this section, it is worth mentioning Goddard Lieberson's amusingly derivative study entitled *Shostakovich's Vacation on a Collective Farm*, from his collection of 'Piano Pieces for Advanced Children or Retarded Adults', written in 1963. André Previn included this item in a piano recital recorded on American Columbia CMS 6586.

One of Malcolm Arnold's favourite composers is Shostakovich and he quotes the DSCH signature in the second movement funeral march of his Sixth Symphony of 1967, preceded prophetically by the long-note crescendo shrieks that feature in Shostakovich's Fifteenth Quartet of 1974.

Edison Denisov, the Soviet avant-garde composer, wrote a quartet entitled *D-S-C-H* in 1969. This work for clarinet, trombone, cello, and piano was played by the Warsaw Music Workshop in their concert tour of the south of England, 15–29 October 1978. The score is published by Universal Edition.

John Rose composed a ten-minute contrapuntal *Essay on DSCH* for solo piano in 1970. He has added three further works based on the DSCH motif: the prelude of *Prelude and Fugue,* Opus 8 and *Scherzo-Intermezzo-Toccata*—both for organ—and a String Quartet. His organ works (recorded on Cathedral Classic Compact Disc CC 003) are published by Bardic Edition, Aylesbury; others by Eden Music, Glasgow.

In 1973 the Glasgow Orchestra Society commissioned a composition for full orchestra from John McLeod, the Aberdeen-born composer, clarinettist, and conductor. The work, with the title *The Shostakovich Connection,* incorporates a fanfare based on the opening theme of Shostakovich's Twelfth Quartet, variations on a theme from the Largo of the Fifth Symphony and closes with eight horns whooping glissandi as the rest of the brass blast out the Russian master's motif. The première, conducted by the composer, was given by the Society in the City Hall, Glasgow, on 12 December 1974 and has been broadcast on Radio Scotland and Radio 3. A professional orchestra—the BBC Scottish Symphony under guest conductor Janos Furst—gave the first public performance in the same hall on 11 January 1977. Shostakovich, in a personal letter to John McLeod, accepted the dedication of the work just before his death.

There is frequent reference to the DSCH motto in the first of the two movements of *Contrasts,* a work written in 1974 by David Morgan. This twenty-two-minute study in duality, premièred in London on 2 January 1975, by the Royal Philharmonic Orchestra under Vernon Handley, is available on Lyrita SRCS 97, coupled with Morgan's Violin Concerto (G May 1978).

The distinguished Soviet composer Alfred Garrievich Schnittke composed a *Prelude in Memory of Shostakovich* at Mark Lubotsky's request shortly after Shostakovich's death. The latter half of this six-minute work involves a part for a second violin, which the composer directs can either be prerecorded by the soloist on tape or played off-stage behind a screen. At the point where the second violin enters the cipher BACH is introduced and worked with the all-pervasive DSCH. Hans Sikorski published this work in their Edition No. 2255. The piece was first recorded on Melodiya C10 08753-4 (reissued on HMV Melodiya ASD 3547, G Aug. 1978), coupled with Shostakovich's Violin Sonata, by Gidon Kremer. This artist gave the British première at the Queen Elizabeth Hall on 5 March 1978. The first British broadcast was given the following day in a live performance by Mark Lubotsky, direct from St John's, Smith Square, London (see Kholopova and Chigaryova, pp. 99–101). Schnittke's pianoforte work for six hands, *Dedication to I. Stravinsky, S. Prokofiev and D. Shostakovich,* composed in 1978, is based on three themes: the 'Chinese March' from Stravinsky's opera *The Nightingale;* the Humoresque Scherzo for four bassoons, Op. 12 *bis* of Prokofiev; and the Polka from *The Golden Age.* The work is recorded on Melodiya C10 15261-2 (reissued on BMG Melodiya Musica Non Grata Compact Disc 74321 56264-2 in 1998). His 20-minute Third Quartet of 1983, in three linked movements, is built on an opening juxtaposition of a double cadence from Roland de Lassus' Stabat Mater, phrases from Beethoven's Grosse Fugue, and the DSCH motif. It is available, played by the Britten Quartet, on Gamut LDR Compact Disc 1008.

Valentin Bibik's Chamber Symphony *In Memory of D. D. Shostakovich,* Opus 29, written in 1976, opens with the DSCH motto and features two themes from Shostakovich's Fourteenth Symphony in the fourth movement *Commodo. Limpido.* The 28-minute symphony is scored for 29 instruments, including an electric organ, with an important part for solo viola in the third movement.

Igor Blazhkov conducts a performance of this moving tribute on Melodiya C10 10727-8.

The Fifth Symphony of Boris Tishchenko, composed in 1976 and awarded that year's Glinka Prize, is an impressive memorial to his teacher. The forty-three-minute continuous work is in five sections—Prelude, Dedication, Scherzo, Intermezzo, and Rondo—with the motif DSCH used as a basis of thematic material. Several of Shostakovich's themes are quoted, notably from the Eighth and Tenth Symphonies in the Scherzo. A Soviet Radio recording, conducted by Maksim Shostakovich, was broadcast on BBC Radio 3 on 24 July 1980 and a live performance by the USSR Ministry of Culture Symphony Orchestra under Gennadi Rozhdestvensky, recorded on 22 February 1985, appears on Melodiya C10 25287 005 and Olympia Compact Disc OCD 213. The symphony is analysed in a Soviet paperback by Boris Katz and the full score (No. 766, 29 cm.) published by Sovetskii Kompozitor, Leningrad, in 1980. The record is reviewed in G Dec. 1988.

The Georgian composer Revaz Gabichvadze's Fourth Symphony for string orchestra, also composed in 1976, quotes DSCH in the first movement. The movements (Prologue, Romantic Outburst, Funeral Music, Interlude, Recitative, Pathetic Monologue, and Epilogue) of this twenty-four-minute work are played continuously and, as their titles suggest, encapsulate the life of Shostakovich, with the final pages movingly introducing a metronome beating away his dying heartbeats. It has been recorded by the Chamber Orchestra of Georgia Linder conductor Shavleg Shilakadze on Melodiya C10 13235-6.

Another work of 1976 utilizing the DSCH motto in its fabric, the three-movement String Quartet of the Turkmen composer Nury Khalmamedov, was published by Muzyka in 1978.

Other compositions entitled *In Memory of D. D. Shostakovich,* recorded in the USSR, are Tigran Mansuryan's Concerto for Cello and Orchestra composed in 1976 and Martin Vartazaryan's Concerto for Cello, both performed by Karine Georgian with the Armenian State Symphony Orchestra, conducted by David Khandzhyan, on Melodiya C10 11259-60 and C10 11381-2 respectively; the Ukrainian composer Miroslav Skorik's Prelude, performed by Nikolai Suk (piano) on C10 11429-30; and Lev Abeliovich's *Vocalise,* performed by T. Pechinskaya (mezzo-soprano) and P. Nodel (violin) on C10 12705-6. The Georgian composer Sulkan Tsintsadze's Ninth Quartet of 1977, also dedicated to the memory of Shostakovich, is performed by the Georgian State Quartet on C10 13645-6. The score was published by Sovetskii Kompozitor in 1984 (No. 6809, 29.5 cm).The first movement entitled 'DSCH' opens with the motto and is in six continuous 'episodes' with the second movement, 'Epilogue', marked 'Largo' following after a pause. Yuri Falik's three-movement Fourth Quartet (1976) and Gennadi Banshchikov's Flute Sonata in four continuous movements (1977) were both recorded in 1981, respectively by the Taneyev Quartet and Valentin Cherenkov with the composer, and available on C10 16409-10. Though neither of these tributes quote Shostakovich themes, both are composed in the spirit of his style and some phrases are near quotes, e.g. the flute toys with the *sul ponticello* tremolando of the Violin Sonata, Opus 134.

Moisei Vainberg's Twelfth Symphony, Opus 114, was recorded at a live concert in the Moscow Conservatory Bolshoi Hall by the Central Television and All-Union Radio Symphony Orchestra under Vladimir Fedoseyev on 12 June 1982 and released on C10 18771 002 (reissued on Russian Disc Compact Disc RDCD 11 010 in 1994). An earlier recording of 1979, performed by the USSR TV and Radio Symphony Orchestra under Maksim Shostakovich, appeared on Olympia Compact Disc OCD 472 in 1994 (reviewed G Nov. 1994). Vainberg's masterly portrait of Shostakovich, just short of an hour's duration, is on the whole a lyrical four-movement symphony with many pages of intensely deeply felt music and, though it does not quote directly from his hero's compositions, several themes, their timbre and treatment are characteristic: e.g. (*a*) the first Sonata-Allegro movement commences with an aggressive three-note motif reinforced by timpani DD^A and ^AAD strokes punctuating passages approximating to *The Execution of Stepan Razin* and closing in an eloquent requiem: (*b*) its themes are transformed for the brilliant Scherzo; (*c*) the allusion is strengthened in the beautiful Adagio, where the haunting melody on high strings is intoned against a low bass-line; and (*d*) continuing without a pause into the Rondo Finale's initial childlike marimba tune, reminiscent of the 'Immortality' movement of Shostakovich's *Michelangelo Suite*. The full score published by Muzyka (No. 12107, 1983, 29 cm.) requires an orchestra with celesta, harp, and marimba though the percussion is reduced to prominently featured timpani and but two cymbal clashes.

Numerous memorial compositions written immediately following Shostakovich's death reflected the grief of Soviet composers. Among these must be noted an *Adagio*, Opus 25 No. 1, for string orchestra by the young woman composer, Tatyana Smirnova (written purposefully on 25 September 1975 in Moscow) and published by Sovetskii Kompozitor in *Pieces for String Quartet*, Vol. 3 (No. 4643, 1978, score, 28 cm.); the monumental Second Symphony (1976) of Voronezh composer Mikhail Nosyrev; a cantata *Sun and Stone* by Lucian Prigozhin; former pupil Yuri Levitin's Twenty-four Preludes for violin solo (first performed by Boris Gutnikov on 26 September 1976 in the Glinka Malyi Hall, Leningrad); an *Epitaph* for symphony orchestra by the Odessa composer Yan Freidlin; three pieces for flute, cello, and piano entitled *Music in Memory of Shostakovich* by the Armenian composer Ruben Sarkisyan (performed in Yerevan in November 1975); Third String Quartet by Arno Babadzhanyan, also an Armenian, composed in 1975 at the Dilizhan Composers' Retreat where Shostakovich wrote his Eleventh Quartet, and published by Sovetskii Kompozitor in 1979 (throughout there are effects reminiscent of Shostakovich, such as the ending with its striking on the back of the cello with a finger nail, pizzicato glissandi, and closing in double-stopped unison Ds on the violin and viola, finally giving way to a solitary viola D *morendo*); *Poem* of Aleksandr Fridlender, who in his time had conducted premières of Symphonies Nos. 5, 6, 8, 10, and 14 in the Urals (*Poem* performed in Sverdlovsk in

December 1976 under conductor Valentin Kozhin); *The Dowry* by Mikhail Bronner, a dramatic legend on Dmitri Kedrin's long poern and scored for soprano, tenor, baritone, and chamber ensemble (recording C10 13247-8 released in late 1980); and *Postludium DSCH* by the Kiev composer Valentin Silvestrov, was first performed in Britain by Jane Manning (soprano) and the Bedelian/Wilson/Immelman Piano Trio at the Almeida Theatre Fourth Festival of Contemporary Music and Performances, Islington, on 29 June 1984.

A separate paragraph is warranted for Yuri Levitin's *Epitaph on Words of Anna Akhmatova*, Opus 89. This thirteen-minute composition for soprano, clarinet, and string quartet is in four continuous movements: 'Prelude' (opening with a fragment from the first movement of Shostakovich's Tenth Symphony), 'Music' (quoting from the Eighth Symphony toccata and the clarinet theme of the second movement of the Ninth), 'Fugue' (an instrumental section again using the Tenth Symphony theme), and 'Death of a Poet' (closing quietly with the clarinet melismata from the Largo of the Eighth Symphony). This moving tribute, along with two others of his—the Twenty-four Preludes, Opus 84, already mentioned and the four-minute *Prelude D Es C H* for organ, Opus 105, written in 1984—appears on C10 21425 005, performed by Lyudmila Belobragina, Ivan Mozgovenko (clarinet), and the Borodin Quartet.

The Czech composer Evzhen Zamechnik's Duet for Violin and Cello (1975), in three movements—Moderato, Allegretto scherzando, and Lento moderato—was performed at the second of Rozhdestventsky's Martinů cycle concerts on 26 April 1985.

The New Zealander Robert Burch composed a nine-minute piece *Essay to the Memory of Dmitri Shostakovich,* for cello and piano, in 1975.

The news of Shostakovich's death gave the original impulse to the composition of Finnish composer Einar Englund's Fourth Symphony for Strings and Percussion (1976) though the four-movement work is based not on DSCH but the motif FEGF and the third movement entitled 'Nostalgia' quotes from Jean Sibelius's *Tapiola*. The 23-minute symphony, recorded a few days either side of New Year's Day 1981 by the youthful Espoo Chamber Orchestra under Paavo Pohjola, is available on Finlandia FA 329.

The Czech-born Vladimir Tichý's Cello Concerto, dedicated to the memory of Shostakovich, was written in 1976–7 and recorded at a Prague concert in 1980 on Panton 8110 0145 by Miroslav Petráš (cello) and the Czech Philharmonic Orchestra under Tomáš Koutník. This twenty-five-minute work, cast in two movements (Largo and Presto), is a most impressive and worthy tribute; saturated with Shostakovichian rhythmic patterns, melodic phrases, and instrumental devices. The coupling work, Štěpán Lucký's Concerto for Orchestra (1976)—conducted on the record by Václav Neumann—makes extensive use of the DSCH motto.

The third movement of the Second String Quartet of the South African composer John Joubert is subtitled 'In Memoriam DSCH' and the motif appears at the close. The première of this quartet was given by the Allegri Quartet in Birmingham on 18 February 1978. The motif appears also in his Third Quartet.

The young Dutch composer Ed de Boer's first orchestral piece *Homage à Dimitri Shostakovich,* Opus 4, written in 1978 has been published by Donemus of Amsterdam. This dichotomous piece (a haunting slow-moving first part, based on the end of 'Fantastic Dance No. 1', followed by a lively scherzo with prominent piano role) was originally scored for a student orchestra that contained three horns but no bassoons. A Netherlands broadcast played by the Amsterdam Philharmonic Orchestra under Rudolf van Dristen, timed 9' 35". The work was featured in the 1990 'Prom' season and broadcast on 29 August and 24 December, in a slightly revised form, by the Rotterdam Philharmonic Orchestra conducted by James Colon.

A ten-movement suite *Colours,* commissioned from a number of composers including David Morgan, Robert Farnon, and Malcolm Williamson, has a second movement by Vic Lewis subtitled 'Tribute to Shostakovich'. This fine piece (4' 27"), representing the colour 'Red', is based on the side drum bolero rhythm of the 'Leningrad Symphony's' first movement with the theme quoting Shostakovich's initials 'DS' and an added B natural. The entire suite, recorded by the Royal Philharmonic Orchestra under Vic Lewis, was released on RCA PL 25123 in 1978.

Karl Frederick Miller's seventeen-minute composition *Variations on a Theme by Shostakovich* was written as his doctoral dissertation in music at the North Texas State University and completed on 30 July 1977. The theme is from the fourth movement (after fig. 120) of the Fifteenth Symphony and scored for 3 flutes, 3 oboes, 2 bassoons, contrabassoon, 4 horns, 3 C trumpets, 3 trombones, harp, harpsichord, piano, percussion, and strings. The work, 'intended to be something of an orchestral requiem', has many allusions to Shostakovich in terms of gesture, orchestration, and harmonic structure.

Another important work, though not resorting to quotations from Shostakovich compositions, should be mentioned on account of the circumstances of its creation. The Finnish composer Pehr Henrik Nordgren was so shocked and moved on reading the tragic events of Shostakovich's life in the *Memoirs,* that he concluded his two-movement Second Viola Concerto of 1979 with a lamenting slow movement dedicated to Shostakovich's memory and entitled *Testimony.*

The young Australian clarinettist/composer Antony Wheeler wrote a slow-moving piece entitled *Movement for String Orchestra: In Memoriam Dmitri Shostakovich* in 1981.

Sofya Khentova mentions further compositions dedicated to Shostakovich in the fourth part of her monograph (pp. 348–54). To these may be added Moscow-born Aleksei Nikolayev's Third Quartet written in 1981. The miniature score of this work in five typically Shostakovichian-named movements (Prelude, Scherzo, Fugue, Pastorale, and Finale) was published by Muzyka In 1986 (No. 13189). The Finale movingly quotes the cello/flute passage (figs. 116–18) from the third movement of the 'Leningrad Symphony', the Kuibyshev première of which Nikolayev heard as an eleven-year-old evacuee. The work was recorded in 1982 by the Union of Soviet Composers' Quartet on Melodiya C10 20789 004.

A quote from the Tenth Symphony appears in the North Carolina composer Claude Baker's *The Glass Bead Game* of 1982–3, premièred by the Louisville Orchestra under Robert Bernhardt on 11 February 1983 and recorded by the same forces on 29 September M3 (First Edition Records LS 789). The large symphony orchestra employs a vast and varied percussion battery including exotic crotales, temple blocks, claves, guiro, bamboo wood chimes, and mandoline. In the third movement, 'Fantasia', the work of six composers (Dallapiccola, Schoenberg, Vaughan Williams, Shostakovich, Penderecki, and Liszt) combine in an involved collage relating to the famous B-A-C-H motif.

The American composer, Christopher Rouse's Symphony No. 1 of 1983—an extended single-movement Adagio—makes use of the DSCH motive. It is recorded by the Baltimore Symphony Orchestra under David Zinman on Electra/Nonesuch 9 79230-2.

Andrei Eshpai's Symphony No. 5, composed in 1985 and dedicated to Yevgeni Svetlanov, was recorded at a concert at Moscow Conservatory on 1 April 1986. This impressive and intensely-moving 28-minute continuous composition quotes DSCH after a war episode based on a boisterous German march. The performance appears on Melodiya C10 28541 006.

Nebojša Živkovč's composition entitled *Ctrax-Strah,* written in 1987, is a solo for percussion with three tape-recorded interruptions of speeches by Shostakovich and six Russian words declaimed by the performer. The instruments used are vibraphone, various drums, cymbals, temple blocks, and alpine bells. The speeches are the radio announcement from besieged Leningrad on 16 September 1941 and two excerpts from the Association of Soviet Composers meeting held in the Kremlin on 2 April 1974. The six words are 'Fear', 'Death', 'Life', 'Fatherland', 'People', and 'Party'. The eleven-minute work has been published (Edition Moeck No. 5362) and recorded by the composer on German Compact Disc Cadenza CAD D 878-8

An unusual tribute by Vladislav Uspensky entitled *Dedication to Courage*—a poem for orchestra subtitled 'In memory of the first performance of Shostakovich's Seventh Symphony in besieged Leningrad'—is recorded by the Leningrad Orchestra of Old and Modern Music under Eduard Serov on Melodiya C10 24485 007 (I 1987*c*).

The Opus 122 of the English composer Wilfred Josephs is a four-minute organ piece *Testimony: Toccata on DSCH* (in Memory of a Great Man) and appears as the final item on a 1988 record of 'Shostakovich's Greatest Hits', Trax Classique TRXLP and CD 131, performed by Robert Munns, on the organ of Bath Abbey.

This chapter was becoming, in the words of a second edition reviewer, likened to train-spotting, and as the DSCH phrase continues—and will continue in the 21st century—to be incorporated in musical compositions as a tribute to the great Russian composer, 1988 seems a convenient year to close the listing.

Appendix VII

Index of Russian Titles

«Незабываемый 1919-й» (Nezabyvayemyi 1919):
  The Unforgettable year 1919 — Op. 89
«Новороссийские куранты» (Novorossiiskie kuranty):
  Novorossiisk Chimes — Sans op. U
«Новый Вавилон» (Novyi Vavilon): *New Babylon* — Op. 18
«Нос» (Nos): *The Nose* — Op. 15
«Овод» (Ovod): *The Gadfly* — Op. 97
«Одна» (Odna): *Alone* — Op. 26
«Падение Берлина» (Padenie Berlina): *The Fall of Berlin* — Op. 82
«Первый эшелон» (Pervyi eshelon): *The First Echelon* — Op. 99
«Песнь о лесах» (Pesn o lesakh): *The Song of the Forests* — Op. 81
«Песня великих рек» (Pesnya velikikh rek): *Song of the Great Rivers* — Op. 95
«Пирогов» (Pirogov): *Pirogov* — Op. 76
«Подруги» (Podrugi): *The Girl Friends* — Op. 41 (ii)
«Позма о Родине» (Poema o Rodine): *Poem of the Motherland* — Op. 74
«Правь, Британия!» (Prav, Britaniya!): *Rule, Britannia!* — Op. 28
«Приключение Корзинкинои» (Priklyuchenie Korzinkinoi):
  The Adventures of Korzinkina — Op. 59
«Простые люди» (Prostye lyudi): *Simple Folk* — Op. 71
«Пять дней, пять ночей» (Pyat dnei, pyat nochei): *Five Days, Five Nights* — Op. 111
«Раиок» (Rayok): *Little Paradise* — Sans op. X
«Родной Ленинград» (Rodnoi Leningrad): *Native Leningrad* — Op. 63
«Русская река» (Russkaya reka): *Russian River* — Op. 66
«Салют, Испания» (Salyut, Ispaniya): *Salute to Spain* — Op. 44
«Светлый ручей» (Svetlyi ruchei): *The Limpid Stream* — Op. 39
«Сказка о попе и работнике его Балде» (Skazka o pope i
  rabotnike yego Balde): *The Tale of a Priest and his Servant Balda* — Op. 36
«Скрипка Ротшильда» (Skripka Roshilda): *Rothschild's Violin* — Sans op. K
«Софья Перовска» (Sofya Perovskaya): *Sofya Perovskaya* — Op. 132
«Условно убитый» (Uslovno ubityi): *Conditionally Killed* — Op. 31
«Целина» (Tselina): *Virgin Land* — Op. 25
«Человек с ружьем» (Chelovek s ruzhyom): *The Man with a Gun* — Op. 53
«Человеческая комедия» (Chelovecheskaya komediya): *The Human
  Comedy* — Op. 37
«Юность Максима» (Yunost Maksima): *The Youth of Maxim* — Op. 41 (i)

The Russian Alphabet

Letter		Transliteration		Pronunciation
1	А а	a		'a' as in 'clarinet'
2	Б б	b		'b' as in 'band'
3	В в	v		'v' as in 'valse'
4	Г г	g		'g' as in 'gong'
5	Д д	d		'd' as in 'drum'
6	Е е	e	(ye[1])	'ye' as in 'yell'
	Ё ё	yo	(o[2])	'yo' as in 'yodel' (always stressed)
7	Ж ж	zh		'zh' as the 's' in 'measure'
8	З з	z		'z' as in 'jazz'
9	И и	i		'ee' as in 'reed'
10	Й й	i		short 'i' as in 'unison'
11	К к	k		'k' as in 'key'
12	Л л	l		'l' as in 'lute'
13	М м	m		'm' as in 'mute'
14	Н н	n		'n' as in 'note'
15	О о	o		'o' as in 'orgran'
16	П п	p		'p' as in 'piano'
17	Р р	r		rolled 'r' as in 'rondo'
18	С с	s		's' as in 'sonata'
19	Т т	t		't' as in 'tenor'
20	У у	u		'u' as in 'flute'
21	Ф ф	f		'f' as in 'fugue'
22	Х х	kh		Scottish 'ch' as in 'pibroch' (not 'eks')
23	Ц ц	ts		'ts' as the 'zz' in 'intermezzo'
24	Ч ч	ch		'ch' as the 'c' in 'cello'
25	Ш ш	sh		'sh' as in 'sharp'
26	Щ щ	shch		'shch' as in 'Khovanshchina'
27	Ъ ъ	—		(hard sign)
28	Ы ы	y		'i' as in 'trill'
29	Ь ь	—[3]	[']	(soft sign)
30	Э э	e		'ay' as the first 'e' in 'étude'
31	Ю ю	yu	[iu]	'yoo' as in 'ukelele'
32	Я я	ya	[ia]	'ya' as in 'bayan'

[1]Transliterated thus after the vowels 'a' and 'e', e.g. Дунаевский and Сергеевич—Dunayevsky and Sergeyevich respectively; and at the beginning of words, e.g. Евгений—Yevgeni.

[2]Transliterated thus after 'ж', 'ч', 'ш', or 'щ', e.g. Чёрный = Chorny.

[3]Appears as 'i' before a vowel, e.g. Прокофьев—Prokofiev.

The dipthong ending 'ий' in personal first names appears as 'i' [ii] and in surnames, as 'y' [ii], e.g. Геннадий Рождественский = Gennadi Rozhdestvensky.

American Library of Congress deviations are given in square brackets.

Postscript

Writing a Shostakovich catalogue is much like painting the Forth Rail Bridge—a never-ending job with the flood of historic and recent compact discs, new books and films, novel arrangements of his music, and even discoveries of previously unknown works.

Since October 1991 Peter Bromley has, with the help of his many worldwide contacts in the recording industry, provided the compiler with regular—almost monthly—detailed information on releases of Shostakovich recordings. This generous on-going assistance is greatly appreciated.

In late 2001 Yosuke Kudo compiled a comprehensive online Shostakovich discography. Recordings are listed with artists arranged alphabetically under classified headings and opus numbers. The Sans op. letters of the second edition of this catalogue are adopted. For details and updating refer to the website http:homepage2.nifty.com/shostakovich/

Of the eighty plus recordings issued in the six months since the summer of 2001, a brief mention must be made of the following important performances.

A super-budget box of eleven compact discs of the fifteen symphonies, performed by the WDR Symphony Orchestra of Cologne under Rudolf Barshai between the Septembers of 1992 and 2000, was issued in the Netherlands on Brilliant Classics 6275 in December 2001.

The Debussy and Rubio Quartets are continuing their complete cycles of quartets with Nos. 1, 5, 12 and 7, 9, 12 respectively.

The Nederlands Blazers Ensemble have recorded Dmitri Smirnov's wind arrangements of *Alone* Suite, Opus 26 and Quartet No. 8, Opus 110 on Dutch Meladina MRCD 0021.

Ilya Grubert and Vladimir Tropp have added the missing Opus 34 standard Tsyganov transcriptions of the Preludes with Aleksandr Blok's Nos. 4, 7, 9, 14, and 23 to make a complete cycle of violin and piano arrangements on Channel Classics CCS 16398.

Two historic recordings have been made available: the Fifth Symphony, played by the New York Philharmonic Orchestra in 1952, under Dimitri Mitropoulos on Greek Sony S2K 89658 and his Ninth Symphony, played by the Berlin Radio Symphony Orchestra two years later, conducted by Ferenc Friscay on EMI's 'Great Conductors of the 20th Century' series on CDZ 7243 575109-2.

Mariss Jansons February 2001 recording of the Eighth Symphony with the Pittsburgh Symphony Orchestra on EMI CDC5 57176-2, including rehearsal tracks, was reviewed in *Gramophone* December 2001.

A film of Gogol's short story *The Overcoat* mimed to Shostakovich's music, though to a different selection from that of the ballet listed under Opus 32, was recorded at the Orpheum Theatre, Vancouver on 20–1 June 2001. The soundtrack comprises Piano Concertos Nos. 1 and 2, Opp. 35 and 102; excerpts from Ballet Suites Nos. 1, 2, and 3, Sans op. P and Jazz Suites Nos. 1 and 2, Sans opp. E and G (i); and the second movement of Symphony No. 10, Op. 93. The performers on the Canadian Broadcasting Company compact disc SMCD 5216 are Angela Chang (piano) and Jens Lindemann (trumpet) with the CBC Radio Orchestra conducted by Mario Bernardi.

The four-part Peter Maniura *Masterworks* BBC2 television series, exploring landmark 20th-century orchestral works, concluded with Shostakovich's Fifth Symphony on 9 and 16 February 2002. Michael Berkeley presented the 85-minute programme which included interviews with conductors Valeri Gergiev and Maksim Shostakovich and musicologist Abram Gozenpud introduced between movements of a performance of the symphony by the BBC Symphony Orchestra under Gergiev.

The *DSCH Journal* continues to publish important information; No. 16 containing a revelatory interview with Daniel Sternberg on his meetings with Fritz Stiedry, Yevgeni Mravinsky, Ivan Sollertinsky, and Dmitri Shostakovich; and articles on Symphonies Nos. 9 and 15.

A note on the artist Konstantin Vasiliev. He was born in 1942 in Nazi-occupied Maikop but when peace returned to the USSR the family moved to the Volga-bank village of Vasilyevo. He studied painting in the Repin School, Moscow, then near home at the Kazan Art School. He has painted an impressive cycle of Russian heroes and striking drawings of the composers Chopin, Mozart, Bach, Liszt, Skryabin, Rimsky-Korsakov, and—Shostakovich.

Stephen Johnson gave a thorough analysis of Shostakovich's Tenth Symphony in the BBC Radio 3 series *Discovering Music* on 4 November 2001. No less than 35 music examples were played by the BBC Philharmonic under Rumon Gamba. Johnson notes the second movement quote from Musorgsky's *Boris Godunov* and the linking of DSCH and his setting of Pushkin's poem 'What does my name mean to you?' (Opus 91) with the Elmira cipher in the third movement. After the violent disagreements among Shostakovich scholars and the furious denunciation in the old Stalinist Press Stephen Johnson 'can't help wondering if Shostakovich is sitting somewhere watching it all, chuckling wickedly!'

NB. The above late Postscript entries are not indexed

Index of Names

Numbers and capital letters refer to opus number entries
unless preceded by the abbreviation 'p' for page.

Phoenix Chamber Orchestra   110, 118
Pianka, Uri (Trio Yuval—violinist)   67
Piatigorsky, Grigori (Gregor) Pavlovich (cellist / arranger, 1903–76)   40
Piazzini, Carmen (pianist)   97
Picardie, Les Sinfonietta Orchestre Régional de   107, 110
Picavet, Bernard and Geneviève (piano duo)   94
Pidoux, Roland (cellist)   67
Pierce, Joshua (pianist)   102
Pietikäinen, Mauri (Voces Intimæ Quartet—violist)   110, 117
Pigerre, Jean-Pierre (Pro Arte Quintet—violist)   57
Pihtipudas Quintet (Jaako Untamala—pianist; Götz Bernau, Antti Meurman,
    Ulla Kekko, and Juhu Malmivaara)   57
Pilafian, J. Samuel (Empire Brass—tuba player / arranger)   96
Pimlico Opera Company   105
Pini, Anthony (cellist, b. 1902)   67
Pini, Carl (London String Quartet—1st violinist)   122
Pintavalle, John (New Amsterdam Trio—violinist)   67, 127
Pinter, Margo (pianist)   35
Piotrovsky, Adrian Ivanovich (playwright / librettist, 1898–1938)   28, 39
Pirino, Antonio (tenor)   15
Pirogov, Nikolai Ivanovich (Russian surgeon, 1810–81—subject of film)   76
Pirumov, Aleksandr Ivanovich (arranger, b. 1930)   48, 85
Pisarenko, Galina Alekseyevna (soprano, b. 1934)   79, 127
Pishchugin, Sergei (Shostakovich and Glinka Quartets—
    2nd violinist)   D, 49, 57, 68, 73, 83, 92, 101, 108, 110, 117, 118,
    122, 133, 138, 142, 144
Pittsburg Symphony Orchestra   10, 54
Pizarro, Artur (pianist)   34
Plagge, Wolfgang (Duo 'Reine Elisabeth'—pianist / solo pianist,
    b. 1960)   61, 94
Planquette, Jean-Robert (composer, 1848–1903)   X
Platt, Alexander (conductor)   M
Platt, Ian (baritone)   105
Pleeth, William (Allegri Quartet—cellist, 1916–99)   68
Pleshakov, Vladimir (pianist, b. 1934)   B, 5, 12, 13
Pletnev, Mikhail Vasilievich (pianist / conductor, b. 1957)   87, 96
Plishka, Paul (also known as Peter; bass, b. 1941)   100, 106
Plocek, Aleksandr (Czech Trio—violinist)   67
Plovdiv State Philharmonic Orchestra   54, 96
Pluzhnikov, Konstantin Ilyich (tenor)   24, K, 79, 106
Pochapski, Vyatcheslav (bass)   K
Pogodin, Nikolai Fyodorovich (alias of N. Stukalov;
    biographer, 1900–62)   53, 99
Pokorný, Jiří (pianist)   46, 91

Index of Compositions

Entry numbers in this index refer to page numbers